HANDBOOK OF LABOR ECONOMICS
VOLUME 3B

HANDBOOKS
IN
ECONOMICS

5

Series Editors

KENNETH J. ARROW
MICHAEL D. INTRILIGATOR

ELSEVIER

AMSTERDAM · LAUSANNE · NEW YORK · OXFORD · SHANNON · SINGAPORE · TOKYO

HANDBOOK OF LABOR ECONOMICS

VOLUME 3B

Edited by

ORLEY ASHENFELTER

Princeton University

and

DAVID CARD

University of California at Berkeley

1999

ELSEVIER

AMSTERDAM · LAUSANNE · NEW YORK · OXFORD · SHANNON · SINGAPORE · TOKYO

ELSEVIER SCIENCE B.V.
Sara Burgerhartstraat 25
P.O. Box 211, 1000 AE Amsterdam, The Netherlands

First edition 1999

ISBN: 0 444 82289 5 (set, comprising vols. 3A+3B+3C)
ISBN: 0 444 50187 8 (vol. 3A)
ISBN: 0 444 50188 6 (vol. 3B)
ISBN: 0 444 50189 4 (vol. 3C)

INTRODUCTION TO THE SERIES

The aim of the *Handbooks in Economics* series is to produce Handbooks for various branches of economics, each of which is a definitive source, reference, and teaching supplement for use by professional researchers and advanced graduate students. Each Handbook provides self-contained surveys of the current state of a branch of economics in the form of chapters prepared by leading specialists on various aspects of this branch of economics. These surveys summarize not only received results but also newer developments, from recent journal articles and discussion papers. Some original material is also included, but the main goal is to provide comprehensive and accessible surveys. The Handbooks are intended to provide not only useful reference volumes for professional collections but also possible supplementary readings for advanced courses for graduate students in economics.

CONTENTS OF THE HANDBOOK

PREFACE TO THE HANDBOOK

Modern labor economics has continued to grow and develop since the first Volumes of this Handbook were published. The subject matter of labor economics continues to have at its core an attempt to systematically find empirical analyses that are consistent with a systematic and parsimonious theoretical understanding of the diverse phenomenon that make up the labor market. As before, many of these analyses are provocative and controversial because they are so directly relevant to both public policy and private decision making. In many ways the modern development in the field of labor economics continues to set the standards for the best work in applied economics.

But there has been change since the first two volumes of this Handbook were published. First and foremost, what was once a subject heavily dominated by American and, to a lesser extent British, writers is now also a growth field throughout the rest of the world. The European Association of Labour Economists, formed well before its American rival, has become the largest and most active organization of its kind. These volumes of the Handbook have a notable representation of authors – and topics of importance – from throughout the world. It seems likely that the explosive growth in the development and study of modern labor economics throughout the world will be a major development that will continue throughout the next decade.

Second, whereas the earlier volumes contained careful descriptions of the conceptual apparatus for analysis of a topic, these new volumes contain a wealth of detailed empirical analyses. The chapters in the new volumes tend to be correspondingly longer, with far more detail in the empirical analysis than was possible in the earlier volumes. In some cases, the topics covered could not have even been entertained for consideration a decade ago.

The authors of the chapters in these volumes have been very responsive in the face of some strict deadlines, and we are grateful to them for their good humor. We are also deeply indebted to Barbara Radvany and Joyce Howell for their gracious assistance in helping to manage the massive task of coordinating authors and the delivery of manuscripts. We appreciate the efforts of everyone involved in the creation of these volumes, and we hope that their readers will too.

Orley Ashenfelter and David Card

CONTENTS OF VOLUME 3B

Chapter 41

Gross Job Flows

STEVEN J. DAVIS and JOHN HALTIWANGER

PART 11: EMERGENT LABOR MARKETS

Chapter 42
Labor Markets in the Transitional Central and East European Economies

Chapter 43

Labor Markets in Developing Countries

JERE R. BEHRMAN

PART 8

THE DEMAND SIDE

Chapter 32

MINIMUM WAGES, EMPLOYMENT, AND THE DISTRIBUTION OF INCOME

CHARLES BROWN*

University of Michigan and NBER

Contents

* I am grateful to Orley Ashenfelter, John Bound, David Card, George Johnson, Alan Krueger, David Neumark, Gary Solon, and Finis Welch for conversations that have influenced my views in important ways and warded off some mistakes. Thanks also to Alan Moss (for help with the coverage data), to Arthur van Soest (for help with the European literature), to Dale Mortensen (search models) and to participants at the conference organized by Ashenfelter and Card that discussed preliminary versions of the papers in this volume.

Handbook of Labor Economics, Volume 3, Edited by O. Ashenfelter and D. Card

Abstract

After nearly a decade of relative quiet, the increases in the US minimum wage that began in 1990 have coincided with a renewed interest in its effects. Recent work suggests that a relative consensus on the effects of the minimum wage on employment came undone; on balance, however, the recent estimates seem if anything smaller than those suggested by the earlier literature, and the puzzle of why they are relatively small remains. Effects of the minimum wage on the wage distribution became clearer with the declining real minimum wage in the 1980s; nevertheless, the ability of minimum wages to equalize the distribution of family incomes remains quite limited. © 1999 Elsevier Science B.V. All rights reserved.

JEL codes: J38; J23; D31; D33

1. Introduction

The effects of the minimum wage on employment and the distribution of income have been hotly debated policy questions for over 50 years. By the early 1980s, research on the effects of the minimum wage in the US began to show signs of consensus (Eccles and Freeman, 1982) – relatively modest effects of the minimum wage on employment (of teenagers who were most likely to be directly affected), and on the distribution of income (because many minimum wage workers were members of middle-income families). It was tempting to conclude, to borrow Henry Kissinger's analysis of academic politics, that the minimum wage debate was so spirited because the stakes were so low. Recent research has suggested the employment effects might be larger, or non-existent, at least for increases over the observed range. Other research has asked whether the growing inequality in the distribution of adult wages has strengthened the link between minimum wages and distributional objectives. The purpose of this chapter is to evaluate the evidence, old and especially new, on these topics. The main focus is on the US experience; minimum wages elsewhere are often intertwined with other institutions, such as unemployment transfers and collective bargaining (Dolado et al., 1997) and this complicates both the analysis of such laws and a proper evaluation of those analyses.

The next section reviews the theory that links minimum wage increases to employment; Section 3 describes historical patterns in the level of the minimum wage and of expanding coverage; the next five sections discuss empirical research on the effects of the minimum wage on employment and other employment-related outcomes. Next, we turn to the literature on the minimum wage and the distribution of wages and of income. Finally, we offer some tentative conclusions and attempt to identify themes for future work.

2. Theory

2.1. Basics

The simplest model of the effects of the minimum wage is one with complete coverage, homogeneous labor, and a competitive labor market. Instead of the familiar equilibrium where the demand for labor $D(w)$ is equal to the supply of labor $S(w)$ at equilibrium wage w^* and employment E^*, a binding minimum wage ($w_m > w^*$) leads to demand-determined employment $E_m = D(w_m)$ and an excess supply of labor $S(w_m) - D(w_m)$ (Fig. 1). Since we are simply moving back along the demand curve, the employment loss $\ln(E_m) - \ln(E^*)$ depends only on the elasticity of demand for labor and the gap between the minimum wage and the competitive wage, $\ln(w_m) - \ln(w^*)$.

Whether this excess supply of workers is counted as unemployed or as "discouraged" workers depends on whether they report searching (unsuccessfully) for work, so one needs further assumptions about labor force participation (in the presence of unemployment) to say much about the effects on unemployment. One plausible assumption is that workers decide whether to participate in the labor force based on the probability of being employed ($D(w_m)/S(w_m)$) and the wage if successful (w_m), perhaps on their product, the expected wage.[1]

The increase in measured unemployment seems a poor indicator of the costs of the minimum wage; the effect on unemployment will be small if workers are easily discouraged and withdraw from the labor force. In fact, Mincer (1976) and Wessels (1980) model labor force participation as a function of the expected reward from participating; declining labor force participation (which would minimize "unemployment effects") signals that the minimum wage has made participation less attractive.

Fig. 1 serves as a general guide to both the short- and longterm effects of a minimum wage, but the presumption is that demand is more elastic in the long run, as substitution of other factors for the more expensive labor becomes possible.

---

[1] Both Gramlich (1976) and Mincer (1976) make this sort of assumption, although in the context of more complicated two-sector models.

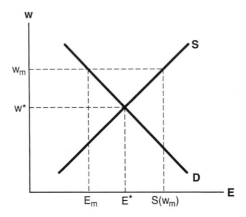

Fig. 1. Minimum wage with complete coverage.

2.2. Two-sector models

Historically, minimum wage laws in the US have not applied to all employers, with exemptions based on industry and size. As discussed in more detail in Section 3, coverage of the law has expanded gradually. Compliance with the law is not perfect; Ashenfelter and Smith (1979) argue non-compliance is important, and this increases the de facto size of the uncovered sector. Given that time series analyses have used data from periods with different levels of coverage, it is helpful to ask how our conclusions change under partial coverage. It will turn out that an uncovered sector may dilute but not eliminate the negative effects of the minimum wage on employment.

Demand for labor in the covered sector $D^c(w_m)$ depends on the minimum wage; demand for labor in the uncovered sector $D^u(w_u)$ depends on the (market-determined) wage in that sector. In the absence of a minimum wage, workers earn w^* in both sectors, and

$$S(w^*) = D^c(w^*) + D^u(w^*).$$

For simplicity, normalize employment so that $E^* = 1$, and wages so that $w^* = 1$. Then $D^c(w^*)$ is equal to c, the fraction of the market employed by covered employers prior to the minimum wage, and $D^u(w^*) = 1 - c$.

Modeling supply is more difficult once the minimum wage is introduced, however, since there are two different wages that might influence supply, and not all those willing to work at the higher of these wages will be able to find work.

Welch (1976) assumes that the $D^c(w_m)$ available positions in the covered sector are allocated randomly among the $S(w_m)$ workers willing to work at the minimum wage; $f = D^c(w_m)/S(w_m)$ is the probability that each will succeed. Because $w_m > w^*$, $f < c$. The uncovered-sector wage w_u then equates the supply of workers willing to work at that wage who have not already been hired in the covered sector with uncovered-sector demand; i.e.,

$$(1 - f)S(w_u) = D^u(w_u).$$

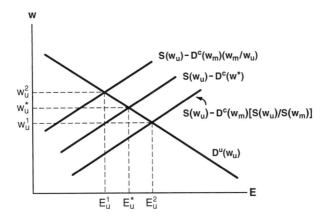

Fig. 2. Minimum wage with an uncovered sector.

This can be rewritten as

$$D^{u}(w_{u}) = S(w_{u}) - D^{c}(W_{m})[S(w_{u})/S(w_{m})].$$

Notice (Fig. 2) that at $w_{u} = w^{*}$, there is excess supply (since $D^{c}(w_{m}) < D^{c}(w^{*})$ and $S(w^{*})/S(w_{m}) < 1$), and so the wage in the uncovered sector must fall (to w_{u}^{1}). Total employment is less than employment in the absence of the minimum wage: the increase in uncovered-sector employment only partially offsets the loss in the covered sector.[2]

Gramlich (1976) and Mincer (1976) assume that workers *choose* one sector or the other, and in equilibrium expected wages must be the same in both. In the simplest versions of their models[3], this means that $w_{u} = Pw_{m}$, where P, the probability of finding work in the covered sector, is $D^{c}(w_{m})/[D^{c}(w_{m}) + U]$, and U is the number of unemployed. Since returns to participation in each sector are the same, supply is a function of just w_{u} (or, equivalently, of Pw_{m}). It is then easy to show that

$$U = D^{c}(w_{m})[(w_{m}/w_{u}) - 1].$$

The uncovered wage must then clear the market:

$$D^{u}(w_{u}) = S(w_{u}) - D^{c}(w_{m}) - U = S(w_{u}) - D^{c}(w_{m})[w_{m}/w_{u}].$$

In this model, the wage in the uncovered sector may either rise or fall (although if it falls, it does so by less than on Welch's assumptions, because the term that multiplies D^{c} is less

[2] To see this, note that the horizontal distance between the two supply curves at w^{*} is less than the loss of employment in the covered sector (since some have reservation wages above w^{*}), and the increase in employment in the uncovered sector is less than the horizontal distance between the two supply curves at w^{*}.

[3] Gramlich allows those who choose the covered sector but do not find a job to receive unemployment benefits; Mincer considers the possibility that new entrants to the covered sector are less likely to be employed next period than those already employed (so that job-finding chances depend on turnover). In the simple version of the model discussed here, unemployment benefits are ignored and there is complete turnover of jobs each period.

than one for Welch, greater than one for Gramlich–Mincer). In Fig. 2, w_u rises to w_u^2. Total employment falls in either case, and by more than in Welch's model.[4]

The Welch model assumes workers can work in the uncovered sector if they search unsuccessfully for work at w_m, while the Mincer and Gramlich models assume the worker chooses one sector or the other. The idea that workers much choose one sector or the other seems less plausible in the US than in a developing country (where the covered sector is urban, and the uncovered sector rural, as in Todaro (1969)). Brown, Gilroy and Kohen (BGK) (Brown et al., 1982, p. 492) suggest a modification of the Gramlich–Mincer model that allows those working in the uncovered sector to search for covered employment, but with lower probability of finding covered employment than those who search for such work full time. As the relative efficiency of search while employed in the uncovered sector increases, both the employment loss and the increase in unemployment due to the minimum wage are reduced.

The preceding analysis assumes that the wage in the uncovered sector is flexible, and so free to adjust to a minimum wage in the covered sector. If, on the other hand, w_m is the federal minimum wage in a state with its own lower minimum wage for small employers not covered by the federal law, it might be more appropriate to think of the "uncovered" sector as those employers subject to the state minimum. In this case, w_u would not adjust to the imbalance between demand and supply in the uncovered sector.

The Welch and Gramlich–Mincer models present uncluttered analyses of the uncovered sector; they abstract from capital reallocation across sectors and changes in relative prices of covered- and uncovered-sector output. With uncovered-sector employment held fixed, the proportional change in employment due to a change in the minimum wage is simple and intuitive, $c\eta\Delta\ln(w_m)$. But once changes in uncovered-sector employment are taken into account, neither model leads to particularly tractable functional forms for the change in total employment (Brown et al., 1982, pp. 491–492). As a result, the empirical literature is only loosely related to these formal models (for an exception, see Abowd and Killingsworth, 1981).

2.3. Heterogeneous labor

We expect minimum wages to affect the employment of relatively unskilled workers, and potentially to have indirect effects on those who are better paid. But even if we are not interested in the better-paid group directly, there is no observable skill indicator that neatly divides workers into those whose wage depends directly on the minimum wage and those

---

[4] If $w_u > w^*$, employment falls because wages in both covered and uncovered sectors have increased, and so less labor is demanded in each. If $w_u < w^*$, the labor force is smaller ($S(w_u) < S(w^*)$) than before the minimum wage, and some workers are unemployed, so that employment $S(w_u) - U$ is less than in the absence of the minimum wage $S(w^*)$.

[5] We cannot use the worker's wage directly, of course, because that wage may change when the minimum wage does. Even without a change in w_m, wages of those paid the minimum wage in one year may be very different one year later (Smith and Vavrichek, 1992).

who earn more.[5] Hence in any "low-wage" group such as teenagers, high school dropouts, or fast-food workers, there will be a mixture of directly affected and better-paid workers. In a sense, the better-paid workers are an uncovered sector, but those displaced by the minimum wage do not have the opportunity of moving there.

An increase in the minimum wage raises the price of relatively unskilled workers, and makes inputs that are good substitutes for such workers more attractive. Workers in low-wage groups who earn a bit more than the minimum wage often do the same tasks as their less-skilled co-workers, and are likely to be very good substitutes for minimum wage workers. Changes in employment for the group as a whole reflect the balance of these losses and gains. As long as less-skilled labor is also a substitute for the composite non-labor input, total employment will fall in response to an increase in the minimum wage.[6] But small overall employment impacts may reflect an unattractive balancing of gains by relatively advantaged workers and losses by those directly affected (Abowd and Killings-worth, 1981, p. 144; Deere et al., 1996, p. 35; Freeman, 1996, p. 642).

As long as the minimum wage is set low enough that it affects only a small share of employment, the effect of the minimum wage on total employment is likely to be small and in any case swamped by other factors. Thus, it makes sense to focus on the analysis of low-wage groups, where the proportion directly affected is larger and so the anticipated effect on group employment is likely to be larger. This explains the dominance of teen-agers as the group most studied in the empirical work. The same line of argument leads us to expect larger (proportionate) effects on teenagers than on young adults, and larger proportionate effects on employment of black and female teenagers than on employment of white male teens.

While recognizing that not all workers are directly affected by the minimum wage is a step in the right direction, a more satisfactory model would allow for a continuous distri-bution of worker skill. The simplest model of this type has one type of worker skill, and each worker's wage is equal to the price of skill times the worker's endowment of skill. Thus, in the absence of the minimum wage, the wage distribution reflects the distribution of skill. Once a minimum wage is introduced, those whose value of marginal product is less than w_m are no longer employed (Kosters and Welch, 1972). As fewer workers are employed the price of skill rises, and those whose wage was just below w_m are once again employable. As we shall see in Section 8, however, observed wage distributions are not simply truncated at the minimum wage; while relatively few workers are paid less than w_m, there is a pronounced spike in the wage distribution at w_m. Heckman and Sedlacek (1981) and Pettengill (1981, 1984) provide more detailed models with continuous distributions of worker ability that take account of the effect of reduction in low-skill employment on the rest of the wage distribution. Grossman (1983) suggests that relative-wage comparisons by workers may also lead employers to raise wages of workers already paid more than the minimum.

---

[6] Even if more- and less-skilled workers are perfect substitutes, overall employment falls since it takes less than one skilled worker to replace each minimum-wage worker.

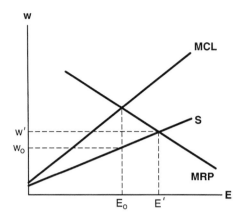

Fig. 3. Minimum wage under monopsony.

2.4. Monopsony

Although they are not, in the end, intended to believe it, undergraduate students are exposed to the possibility that a "skillfully set" minimum wage increases employment under monopsony.

The monopsonist faces an upward-sloping supply curve for labor, and so seeks to maximize π, the difference between revenue R and labor cost:

$$\pi = R(L) - w(L)L.$$

Choosing the profit maximizing level of employment yields

$$R'(L) - w(L) - w'(L)L = 0,$$

which implies the marginal revenue product of labor, R', is equal to $w(1 + 1/\varepsilon)$, where ε is the elasticity of labor supply.

A minimum wage makes the supply of labor perfectly elastic up to $S(w_m)$, and as long as $w_0 < w_m < w'$, raising the minimum wage moves the equilibrium rightward along the supply curve, increasing employment (Fig. 3). Further increases in w_m beyond w' move the equilibrium along the marginal revenue product curve. Note, however, that even a clumsily set minimum wage can leave employment higher than in the monopsonistic equilibrium, as long as $(w_m/w_0) < 1 + (1/\varepsilon)$.

How much the wage can be raised under monopsony before employment starts to fall thus depends on the elasticity of labor supply. The consensus view has been that the typical minimum-wage employer is not a mining company in an isolated company town but a retail trade or service employer in a labor market with many such employers. The elasticity of labor supply to any one such employer should therefore be "close to" infinite, and the opening for skillfully set minimum wage negligible.[7] Moreover, as Stigler (1946) argued, the fact that w' varies among employers while w_m is uniform makes it less likely that most employers affected by the law will be in the employment-enhancing range.

2.5. Search models

Card and Krueger (1995, pp. 373–379) suggest another interpretation of the monopsony model to re-establish its relevance for actual minimum-wage markets. They present a model that focuses on turnover behavior, implicitly linked to search behavior by workers and firms. In any relatively short period, the quit rate q depends on the wage, as does the number of workers who apply to and are hired by the firm H. Equilibrium requires that quits ($= q(w)L$) per period equal new hires, $H(w)$. This means that equilibrium employment is equal to $L = H(w)/q(w)$; since $H' > 0$ and $q' < 0$, if the firm wishes to increase employment it must raise the wage. In effect, $H(w)/q(w)$ is the labor supply function facing the firm. The elasticity of labor supply is then $\theta_H - \theta_q$, where θ_H and θ_q the elasticities of H and q with respect to w. Empirically plausible values of these θs yields an elasticity of labor supply of 5–10, which suggests the range of wages over which minimum wage increases could increase employment is not negligible. I see two problems with this way of rescuing the monopsony model.

First, H is surely a function of L as well as of w; a large retail outlet must get more applicants at any given wage than a mom and pop store in the same area. If we assume new hires are equal to $h(w)L$, equilibrium requires that $h(w) = q(w)$, and the firm can have any level of employment it wants at this wage. If $H = L^\lambda h(w)$, the elasticity of labor supply to the firm is now $(\theta_h - \theta_q)/(1 - \lambda)$.

Second, H (or h) and q depend on alternative wages as well as the wage offered by the firm. The elasticity derived in the previous paragraphs shows how supply changes if the firm increases its wage, alternative wages constant. An increase in the minimum wage, however, increases wages elsewhere. With complete coverage, an increase in the minimum wage increases wages at a covered firm and elsewhere (= other covered firms) in the same proportion, and so does little or nothing to increase hires or reduce quits.

Burdett and Mortensen (1998) offer a more formal search model in which search frictions generate a monopsony-like equilibrium, and a minimum wage can increase employment. In their model, employment at any one firm depends explicitly on the wage distribution as well as the wage offered by that firm. However, if many employers are paying w_m, an individual employer has an incentive to pay a slightly higher wage (profit per worker is slightly lower but equilibrium employment significantly higher). Hence, the spike in the observed wage distribution we observe at the minimum wage (Section 8) is not

---

[7] Rebitzer and Taylor (1995) present an efficiency-wage model in which the wage each firm must pay to deter shirking is an increasing function of firm size. This creates an upward-sloping wage–employment relationship that functions like the upward sloping marginal labor cost function of a traditional monopsony model, but "works" with a large number of employers.

consistent with the model.[8] And, with heterogeneous workers and employers, Stigler's doubts about the ability of a uniform minimum wage to raise employment carry over to search models as well.[9]

2.6. Offsets

Thus far, we have implicitly assumed that if the minimum wage increases by 10%, both compensation per hour to minimum-wage workers and cost per hour of minimum-wage labor to the employer increase by 10% as well. However, this need not be the case. Just as mandated improvements in non-wage aspects of a job (health insurance, safety, layoff notification) may lead to lower wages, mandated improvements in the wage give employers an incentive to cut other aspects of the job package. A number of such margins have been suggested–fringe benefits, employer-provided training, and required levels of effort (Wessels, 1980; Mincer, 1984).

To fix ideas, imagine that employers pay $5 per hour and provide "free" food that costs $0.50 (per hour worked) to provide and is valued by workers at $0.50 per hour as well. Then a $5.50 minimum wage would lead employers to end the free meals, leaving their cost of labor, the compensation received by workers, and employment unaffected. Alternatively, if the $0.50 of food is valued by workers at $1.00, eliminating the free food would reduce compensation, and so make it impossible for the employer to maintain the old level of employment; in this case, the free food would be curtailed but not eliminated. With higher labor costs, employers would employ fewer workers; with compensation as seen by workers reduced, less labor would be supplied.

From this perspective, the availability of offsets reduces the attractiveness of minimum wage increases to the workers who are directly affected, but limits the employment loss as well. If, however, employers respond by raising the effort standard they require on the job, employment effects may be *magnified* rather than mitigated. Suppose, for example, a 10% increase in the minimum wage is offset by a 10% increase in enforced effort. Then employment in efficiency units is not changed, but employment in bodies or in hours worked would be reduced by 10%.

More generally, the algebra of effort is discouraging. Suppose that we measure labor in efficiency units, defined as number of workers (or hours) L times effort e. Demand for such efficiency units will depend on the cost per unit of effort; a constant-elasticity relationship would be

---

[8] Joseph Altonji has noted that the ability of a tiny wage increase to lead to a large increase in employment depends on all employers being equally attractive to workers. If workers care about some non-wage attribute that differs for each worker-employer pair (e.g., commuting costs), tiny wage increases would not bring large increases in employment, and so would not undo the mass point at the minimum wage. I have not found a paper that explicitly models this intuition.

[9] Koning et al. (1995) model both the wage distribution and unemployment durations in an explicit equilibrium search framework. They find small reductions in search unemployment but large increases in structural unemployment due to minimum wage increases for Dutch youth. They do not discuss the spike at the minimum wage, although it appears from their wage histograms that it is not very important in their data.

$\ln L + \ln e = \eta(\ln w_m - \ln e)$,

which implies

$\ln L = \eta(\ln w_m) - (\eta + 1)(\ln e)$.

If the elasticity of e with respect to w is α, then

$d\ln L/d\ln w_m = \eta - (\eta + 1)\alpha = (1 - \alpha)\eta - \alpha$.

Larger values of α make the employment response larger unless demand is elastic; if demand is elastic, the minimum-wage elasticity of employment is less than 1 in absolute value only if α is sufficiently larger than 1.[10]

3. Evolution of minimum wage legislation in the US

In 1938, the Fair Labor Standards Act mandated a minimum wage of 25 cents per hour, or about 40% of the average hourly earnings of production workers in manufacturing. Only about half of production workers were covered, and low-wage sectors (agriculture, retail trade, and services) were largely excluded.

Since then, the nominal minimum wage has been increased at irregular intervals. When a new minimum wage becomes effective, it is typically equal to roughly 50% of average hourly earnings of private workers (closer to 55% in the 1950s and 1960s, 40% in the 1990s) (see Table 1). Moreover, since 1961 the increases have been staggered, with about half of the increase in the year the law was changed, and half in the following year. Between increases in the minimum wage, inflation and real-wage growth increase average hourly earnings by as much as 30–40%, and so reduce the ratio of the (fixed) minimum wage to (rising) average hourly earnings. As a result, the relative minimum wage follows a saw-toothed pattern (Fig. 4).

Coverage expansions have been more discrete, and usually permanent. Coverage remained essentially unchanged from 1938 until extended in 1961, 1967, and 1974 primarily in agriculture, retail trade, and services. Not only was the fraction of workers covered expanded, but the expansions were in relatively low-wage sectors where the law was likely to be a binding constraint. Within industries, coverage was extended based on firm or establishment sales, with each extension sweeping in smaller and therefore lower-wage employers in these industries. For example, at the time the $2.00 minimum wage became effective in May 1974, only 3.7% of workers covered prior to the 1966 amendments were earning less than $2.00; 13.4% of those first covered in 1967 and 18.0% of those first

---

[10] In Rebitzer and Taylor's (1995) efficiency wage model, workers either shirk or they do not, and in equilibrium none shirk. In a version of their model with continuously variable effort, one might expect effort to increase in response to the minimum wage.

Table 1
Minimum wage levels and coverage[a]

Effective date	New w_m ($)	w_m/ahe	Since last increase		Fraction covered	
			$\Delta\ln w_m$	$\Delta\ln(\text{ahe})$	Private	Government
Oct. 1938	0.25	0.37			~0.50	0
Oct. 1939	0.30	0.43	0.18	0.03	~0.55	0
Oct. 1945	0.40	0.36	0.29	0.48	~0.55	0
Jan. 1950	0.75	0.57	0.63	0.45	~0.55	0
Mar. 1956	1.00	0.56	0.29	0.30	0.55	0
Sept. 1961	1.15	0.53	0.14	0.20	0.63	0
Sept. 1963	1.25	0.54	0.08	0.06	0.63	0
Feb. 1967	1.40	0.53	0.11	0.13	0.77	0.40
Feb. 1968	1.60	0.58	0.13	0.06	0.77	0.40
May 1974	2.00	0.48	0.22	0.41	0.83	1.00
Jan. 1975	2.10	0.48	0.05	0.05	0.83	1.00
Jan. 1976	2.30	0.49	0.09	0.07	0.84	0.28
Jan. 1978	2.65	0.48	0.14	0.15	0.85	0.27
Jan. 1979	2.90	0.49	0.09	0.09	0.86	0.27
Jan. 1980	3.10	0.48	0.07	0.07	0.86	0.27
Jan. 1981	3.35	0.48	0.08	0.09	0.86	0.27
Apr. 1990	3.80	0.39	0.13	0.34	0.87	1.00
Apr. 1991	4.25	0.42	0.11	0.04	0.86	1.00
Oct. 1996	4.75	0.41	0.11	0.14		
Sept. 1997	5.15	0.43	0.08	0.03		

[a] Notes: w_m/ahe, ahe is average hourly earnings, private economy. For years prior to 1947, average hourly earnings were available only for manufacturing. Private economy ahe is estimated as 0.93 times manufacturing ahe, based on the relationship between the two series in 1947–1956. October data interpolated from annual averages. Coverage of private workers: first available coverage ratios are for 1953; 1956, 1961, and 1963 ratios are from 1957, 1962, and 1964 respectively; 1967 and 1968 ratios reflect minor coverage expansion in 1969 as well. Coverage of government workers was reduced by a Supreme Court decision in 1976, which was later reversed.

covered in 1974 were earning less than the new minimum (US Department of Labor, 1975, Table 1).[11]

Coverage of government-sector workers was introduced by the 1966 Amendments and increased to complete coverage in 1975. Coverage fell in 1976, and rebounded in 1985, due to changing Supreme Court decisions.

These patterns have a number of important implications. First, while the minimum wage relative to average hourly earnings varies significantly over the period, the saw-toothed pattern suggests that such variation is short-lived, and a rational forecast of the minimum

[11] Because the minimum wage for most of the workers first covered in 1966 or 1974 was initially set at $1.90 rather than $2.00, this calculation slightly understates the extent to which recently and newly covered workers were the most affected. For similar evidence in other years, see Peterson (1981, Tables 16 and 17).

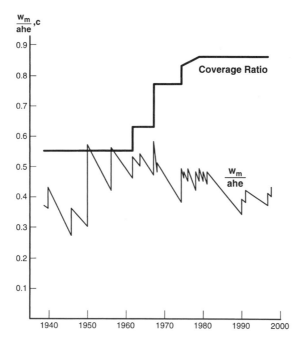

Fig. 4. Minimum wage relative to average hourly earnings and private-sector coverage ratio.

wage over a 5- or 10-year horizon would have much less variation. Second, newly covered establishments face a near-permanent change (with the only escape being to shrink below the coverage threshold).

4. Time series evidence

4.1. Overview

Given that federal law imposes the same minimum wage on high- and low-wage states, and that state minimum wage laws have historically been relatively unimportant, it is not surprising that time series variation in minimum wages and employment have been an important source of evidence on the employment effects of the minimum wage. Perhaps more surprising is that while the general trend in labor economics has been away from time-series data to cross-sectional or panel-data studies (Stafford, 1986), the time series evidence has, until quite recently, retained its primacy in the minimum wage debates.

The basic statistical model in the time series literature is

$$E_t = \alpha X_t + \beta MW_t + \varepsilon_t,$$

where E is the employment/population ratio, X is a cyclical indicator, often a time trend, plus other relevant control variables, and *MW* is the level of the minimum wage, usually relative to average wage (usually multiplied by the fraction of employment covered by the minimum, the so-called Kaitz index, following Kaitz, 1970).[12]

Most studies focus on teenagers because a sizeable minority of teenagers' wages are directly affected by the minimum wage; for older groups plausible variation in employment due to the minimum wage is swamped by other factors. Given this focus on young workers, the "other" control variables have tended to have a youth-oriented focus as well: the relative share of teenagers in the labor-force age population, the fraction of teenagers in the armed forces (and so unavailable for civilian employment, the traditional employment measure), the fraction of teenagers (16–19 year olds) who are 16–17, etc.

E and *MW* are often replaced by their logarithms, in which case β is an elasticity. But it is not a "demand elasticity" of the usual sort. With a double-log specification, we have

$$\beta = (\Delta \ln E)/(\Delta \ln w_m).$$

If we define E^* as the employment of those directly affected by the minimum wage increase and w^* as the average wage of those directly affected, then a natural measure of the elasticity of demand for low-wage labor would be

$$\eta = (\Delta \ln E^*)/(\Delta \ln w^*).$$

As noted above, only a subset of teenagers (or members of any other low-wage group) are directly affected; if employment of those not directly affected does not change (or increases, because they are substitutes for those in E^*), $\Delta \ln E$ will be significantly smaller (in absolute value) than $\Delta \ln E^*$ (Gramlich, 1976, p. 260).

Moreover, when the minimum wage is increased by 10%, many teenagers receive no increase at all. Card and Krueger (1995, p. 117) report that in 1989 two-thirds of all employed teenagers were already earning more than $3.80 (the level to which the minimum wage was raised in April of 1990), and half were already earning more than $4.25, the 1991 minimum. Some of those already earning more than the new minimum received small increases, but some of those below the minimum wage work in uncovered jobs (or for non-compliant employers). On balance, between 1989 and 1992 (when the minimum wage increased by 27%), the average wage of teenagers increased only 9% (Card and Krueger, 1995, p. 121); Deere et al. (1996, p. 31) estimate that in March 1990 the increase required to bring teenagers up to the $4.25 minimum of April 1991 was only 4%.[13] Thus, $\Delta \ln w^*$ is significantly smaller in absolute value than $\Delta \ln w_m$.

---

[12] Often when coverage was extended, the minimum wage for newly covered employers was lower than the "regular" minimum wage, and Kaitz's index took account of that difference. His index was equal to $\sum_i c_i(w_m/w_i) + c'_i(w'_m/w_i))$, where c_i is the fraction of employment in industry i covered previously, c'_i is the fraction of employment that is newly covered, w_i is the average wage in industry i, and w_m and w'_m are the minimum wage applicable to previously and newly covered employers.

[13] Difference in base period and Card and Krueger's inclusion of 1992 wage growth account for part of the difference. I suspect most of the rest is due to "spillovers" – wage increases to teens already earning more than $4.25 are included in Card and Krueger's measure, but not in Deere et al.'s.

Because the numerator of β is smaller (in absolute value) than the numerator of η, while the denominator of β is larger, $|\eta| > |\beta|$. Neumark and Wascher (1997) estimate that among those 16–24 in 1995, 21.3% earned at least the $4.25 minimum wage in force at the time but less than the September 1997 minimum wage of $5.15; because many of them were already earning more than $4.25, w^* increased by only 10.8%, even though w_m was increasing by 21.2%. If only the employment of those initially earning between $4.25 and $5.15 was affected by the 1996–1997 increases that brought w_m to $5.15, we have

$$\eta = \beta(0.212/0.108)/0.213 = 9.2\beta.$$

Implicitly, Neumark and Wascher take the 4.3% of youth whose reported wage was below $4.25 as unaffected by the law. Given that their wage data come from CPS data reports which have some random reporting error and appear to have many responses rounded to even-dollar amounts, it is not clear that someone reported to earn $4.00 is unaffected by the law. Even if they really represent employment at establishments that are uncovered by or not compliant with the law, their wages may be affected.[14]

Most studies of young workers focus on teenagers. For them, the share directly affected is larger, and the fraction of those directly affected who were at or below the old minimum (and so receiving the full increase in the minimum) is probably larger as well. A rough calculation based on Card and Krueger's tabulations of teenage wages surrounding the 1990–1991 increase suggests – assuming those below the old minimum wage are unaffected – that $\eta \approx 5\beta$.[15] The time series evidence is mostly drawn from the 1960s and 1970s, when the minimum wage had more bite on the wage distribution, so the appropriate multiplier for time series studies of teenagers is probably less than 5.

Estimates of β re-scaled as the proportional change in employment from a 10% increase in the minimum wage (coverage constant) are presented in Table 2.

Brown et al. (1982) summarized the studies available at that time, either published or in draft. We noted that the estimated reductions in teen employment from a 10% minimum wage increase ranged from 1 to 3%, and the estimates were generally "significant" statistically.[16] We did not have much luck in finding one or two key choices that would explain why some studies' estimates were higher than others. Studies which included "more recent" (i.e., 1970s) data, included more control variables (some early studies

---

[14] See Section 8 for evidence that uncovered-sector employers often pay exactly the minimum wage. To gauge the importance of those below $4.25 for the calculation, assume that they get the same 21.2% increase as those initially earning $4.25. Then $\eta = \beta(0.212/0.126)/0.266 = 6.3\beta$.

[15] The minimum wage increased from $3.35 to $4.25, a 27% increase. Based on Card and Krueger's Fig. 4.2, roughly 40% of teens earned between $3.35 and $4.24 prior to the increase, and average wages in this interval were about $3.75, so the average wage increase of those directly affected was about half of the minimum wage increase.

[16] Many of the studies reported separate regressions by race and/or sex and the estimates in the table are weighted averages of those dis-aggregated results.

Table 2
Estimated effect of a 10% increase in the minimum wage on teenage employment and unemployment: time-series studies[a]

Study	Percent change in teenage employment	Change in teen unemployment rate (in percentage points)
Kaitz (1970)	−0.98	−0.01
Adie (1971)		2.53
Moore (1971)		3.65
Kosters and Welch (1972)	−2.96	
Lovell (1972)		−0.00
Adie (1973)		0.52
Lovell (1973)		−0.25
Kelly (1975)	−1.20	
Gramlich (1976)	−0.94	
Kelly (1976)	−0.66	
Hashimoto and Mincer (1970); Mincer (1976)	−2.31	0.45
Welch (1976)	−1.78	
Ragan (1977)	−0.65	0.75
Mattila (1978)	−0.84	0.10
Iden (1980)	−2.26	
Abowd and Killingsworth (1981)	−2.13	
Betsey and Dunson (1981)	−1.39	
Boschen and Grossman (1981)	−1.50	
Hamermesh (1981)	−1.21	
Ragan (1981)	−0.52	
Freeman (1982)	−2.46	0.00
Wachter and Kim (1982)	−2.52	0.51
Brown et al. (1983)	−1.14	0.01
Solon (1990)	−0.99	
Wellington (1991)	−0.63	
Klerman (1992)	−0.52	
Card and Krueger (1995)	−0.72	

[a] Source: Brown et al. (1982), updated by author.

did not even include time trends), and included coverage in the minimum-wage variable tended toward the low end of that range. These emerged as our preferred estimates.

More recent studies (the last three in Table 2) find point estimates of the loss of teen employment from a 10% minimum wage increase that were uniformly smaller than 1%, and in some cases not statistically significant at conventional levels. Because these studies replicated earlier specifications taking advantage of additional years of data, their clear message is that including the 1980s reduces the estimated effect of the minimum wage on employment.

While the time series literature began with a focus on teen unemployment, over time fewer studies even reported unemployment effects. The available estimates varied quite a lot, although most suggested a 10% increase in the minimum wage would raise the teen unemployment rate by less than 0.75 percentage point. Labor force participation is negatively related to the minimum wage, which helps account for (or is implied by, depending where one starts) the relatively small unemployment effects.

In principle, the effect of the minimum wage on young adults (age 20–24) is ambiguous: raising the wages of those who would otherwise earn less should reduce employment, but raising the wages of teenagers (who may be good substitutes for young adults in many jobs) should raise young-adult employment. Since a smaller proportion of young adults is directly affected, any negative effect is likely to be much smaller for young adults than for teenagers when that impact is expressed as a proportionate change in employment of all young adults. While relatively few studies even consider young adult employment, those that do tend to produce smaller estimated minimum-wage impacts (Brown et al., 1982, Table 6; Wellington, 1991, Table 3).

4.2. Hours versus bodies

Based more on data availability than unconstrained preference, the time series literature has measured employment by numbers employed, and neglected variation in hours per worker. The few studies that have addressed this issue relied on the relative short time series of published information on weekly hours. This limited evidence suggests that the minimum wage reduces hours worked by employed teen-aged workers, so that "full-time equivalent" employment falls more than number employed (Gramlich, 1976; Brown et al., 1983).[17]

At first glance, this makes sense; the reduction in employment is spread across both of the available margins. However, we know that full-time workers are paid more per hour than apparently similar part-time workers. This suggests that, over the relevant range of work-weeks, those working more hours per week produce more per hour. If so, we should expect employers to lengthen work-weeks in response to a minimum wage increase (Barzel, 1973). Perhaps firms are raising average output per hour by limiting break time (Oi, 1997, p. 9).

4.3. Differences by race and sex

The effect of the minimum wage on teenage employment is a combination of effects by

---

[17] The FTE reduction is perhaps 40% larger than the more widely estimated employment loss, although this difference is estimated with lamentable imprecision.

[18] Card and Krueger (1995, Table 4.1) show that 53% of those teenagers earning $3.35–$4.24 in 1989 (and so likely to be affected by the 1990–1991 increases in the minimum wage) were female, compared to 48% of all employed teenagers. For black teenagers, the corresponding proportions were 14 and 12%. These differentials would be larger, on average, in the period covered by the time-series studies.

race and sex that might be expected to differ. Given the lower market wages of blacks and women, we expect more workers in these groups to be directly affected, i.e., their wage increased by law, and their employment prospects reduced, and fewer at higher wage levels where substitution would increase employment.[18] This formalizes a longstanding policy concern that the negative effects of the minimum wage on employment may be particularly hard on black teens.

Empirically it turns out there is very little to learn about these demographic differences from the time series studies. Differences between groups are estimated with limited precision (particularly for blacks, who are not over-sampled in the CPS data used in all the studies in Table 2), and there is no pattern as one looks across studies. Card and Krueger (1995, Table 6.9) confirm that this imprecision persists when the data are extended into the 1990s. Their point estimates suggest somewhat larger effects for blacks than whites, but larger effects for males than females; none of the differences is statistically significant.[19]

4.4. Coverage

If the minimum wage had no effect on employment in the uncovered sector, the proportional change in total employment would equal the proportional change in covered-sector employment times the fraction of employment that is covered; i.e., $\mathrm{dln}(E) = c\mathrm{dln}(E_c) = c\eta\mathrm{dln}(w_m)$. Formal two-sector models show that employment in the covered sector is likely to change, and the reduced-form employment equations that emerge from these models combine coverage and the relative level of the minimum wage in a much more complicated expression.

The dominant empirical response to this problem has been to use the Kaitz index, which is a coverage-weighted sum of the ratio of the minimum wage to the average wage in each industry.[20] Other studies try to estimate separate "level" and coverage effects. In this specification, the effect of the level of the minimum wage tends to be larger (e.g., a 2% rather than a 1% reduction in teen employment from a 10% increase in w_m) but coverage

---

[19] The typical time-series study that explores differences by race or sex simply estimates separate equations for different groups. But the variance of the difference between, say, coefficients for blacks and whites is not the sum of the two variances, because there is likely a common component between the disturbances in the black and white employment equation. Hence one cannot tell from the published tables whether the black-white or male-female difference in coefficients is estimated with reasonable precision. Calculations reported by Brown et al. (1983, p. 22) suggest that, at least in their sample, the common error component is not large enough to significantly reduce the standard error of the black-white difference.

[20] While, as noted in Section 2, the functional form suggested by formal two-sector models is too complicated to be useful, one might at least prefer a form that "makes sense" in the absence of employment responses in the uncovered sector. That would lead to the level of coverage multiplying the logarithm of the minimum wage. In principle, w_m should be normalized by w_o; in practice, the average wage is used instead. But once we normalize the minimum wage by an average wage measure (which is greater than the minimum wage for all candidate average wage measures), the logarithm of the ratio of w_m to the average wage is negative, and so this form would force coverage and level effects to be of opposite sign.

effects are weaker or non-existent (Brown et al., 1983, Table 3). However, while we could not reject the hypothesis that coverage effects were zero, we also could not reject the "Kaitz" restriction than $\ln w_{\mathrm{m}}$ and $\ln c$ have equal effects. Wellington (1991, Table 1) and Card and Krueger (1995, Table 6.8) report similarly weak coverage effects including more recent data; Wellington finds that whether one can reject the Kaitz restriction is sensitive to specification.

4.5. Leads and lags

With very few exceptions, the time series studies of the minimum wage relate employment at time t to the minimum wage at time t. This stands in contrast to most other studies of employment demand, which find that lagged adjustment is important. Two justifications for this contemporaneous-response assumption have been offered.

First, voluntary turnover rates in low-wage labor markets are very high, so that a desired reduction in employment can be achieved quickly just by not replacing those who quit. So there is no "firing cost" or increase in unemployment insurance taxes to worry about, as there might be in reducing the numbers of more skilled workers. There are relatively few hiring costs, either; because expected tenure is brief, it does not make sense to make large investments in training or even screening minimum-wage workers. Hamermesh (1995, p. 836) notes however that lagged adjustment of other inputs such as capital will delay the adjustment of labor, even if there are no direct costs of adjusting the latter.

Second, changes in minimum wage laws become effective several months after proposed increases have become law; indeed, when a phased increase is enacted the forewarning of the second increase is over a year. For example, the increases to $4.75 in October 1996 and to $5.15 in September 1997 were both enacted in August 1996.

In any case, early studies tended to allow lagged responses to the minimum wage, and for these Table 2 reports the sum of these responses. More recent studies usually assume contemporaneous response. Hamermesh (1981) and Brown et al. (1983) report the estimates both ways and find that lags (and, in BGK, leads) do not matter much.

This does not mean that the short- and longterm effects of the minimum wage are the same. The data are not rich enough to identify longterm responses if, indeed, they are different. But it does mean that shortterm estimates are not very sensitive to allowing the relatively short lags that have been considered.

4.6. What happened?

Earlier I noted that, especially among studies with sample periods including the late 1970s, there was reasonable consensus about the effects of the minimum wage on employment. Studies that include the 1980s all report estimates below this consensus range, and increasingly we cannot reject the hypothesis that the true effect is zero.

What happened? At a mechanical level, the answer is simple: between 1981 and 1990, the nominal minimum wage remained constant, and its value relative to average wages fell accordingly. While teenage employment increased, so did employment generally, and teenage employment did not increase as fast as declining adult unemployment (and a declining minimum wage variable) would have predicted.[21]

One hypothesis is that the minimum wage had declined relative to other wages by so much that its further gradual erosion had little effect (Hamermesh, 1995, p. 837). While it is true that the mid-1980s was a period of relatively low minimum wages, its impact on teenagers was probably not very different than it had been in the early 1970s.[22]

One might instead look to the data; does a more flexible functional form (e.g., quadratic) allow one to predict how much the decline in the relative minimum wage or in the Kaitz index should have reduced the marginal impact of the minimum wage? Attempts along these lines have not been successful; more complicated functions have not been estimated with any useable precision (Wellington, 1991, p. 35; Card and Krueger, 1995, p. 203).[23] Given the difficulties of estimating even first-order effects, this should not be terribly surprising.

Another important change in the 1980s was the increase in wage inequality in general, and the declining position of relatively unskilled workers in particular. This increase in the dispersion of the distribution of hourly wages has several implications. First, the minimum wage relative to the equilibrium wage for teenagers would decline less than the minimum relative to an average wage (Deere et al., 1996, pp. 37–38). This means that the number of teenagers whose wage is directly affected by the minimum would be declining less rapidly than a relative-minimum-wage variable would predict. Second, for teenagers not directly affected by the minimum wage because they earn more, increasing wage inequality could either increase or reduce average wages (relative to trend) and lead to supply responses (relative to trend). Whether the technological or other changes that dominated the 1980s can account for the relatively slow growth of teen employment in that decade remains an open question.

Kennan (1995, p. 1955) notes that the predicted change in teenage employment from the earlier "consensus" is small relative to month to month fluctuations in teen employment from all causes. "In short, we are looking for a needle in a haystack." Given that the previous studies used "different but closely related datasets", the likelihood of important omitted variables, and other problems common to all the time series studies, the "consensus" estimate was none too reliable in the first place. Kennan supports his argument by

---

[21] Deere et al. (1996, Fig. 3-6) show significant variation in the proportion of teenagers employed relative to 20–24 year olds. This ratio was rising in 1979, declined in 1980 (when the minimum wage was increased), increased from 1983–1990, and fell in 1990–1992, before recovering. They find the ratio is closely related to the relative wages of the two groups, and interpret the increase in the 1980s as consistent with a declining relative level of the minimum wage over this period. But there is no control for general business conditions in this part of their analysis.

[22] The fraction of teenagers earning the minimum wage or less in 1987 (the year after Wellington's sample ended) was 28.7% (US Census Bureau, 1989, Table 675), while in 1973 (following 5 years of rapidly rising average wages but constant minimum wage) it was 26.3% (Gilroy, 1981, Table 22). Moreover, coverage of low-wage industries was expanded in 1974, so the fraction of those at or below the minimum who were directly affected was likely to be higher in the mid-1980s than in the early 1970s.

[23] Both add the square of the Kaitz index rather than the square of the relative minimum wage.

showing wide variation in coefficients in a set of time series estimates; but none of his look much like any of those in the literature.[24] I believe he overstates the point, but it is valid nonetheless. Even within the narrow boundaries of the traditional literature, one can see the sense of his comment–the most recent estimates which have precipitated.the crisis are all within the confidence intervals of the typical early 1980s estimate.[25]

Whatever the cause, the more agnostic message of the more recent time series estimates has stimulated a revived interest in other approaches, which make greater use of cross-sectional variation.

5. Cross-state comparisons

The basic idea behind use of cross-state comparisons is straightforward and appealing: minimum wage laws will have a larger effect on employment in low-wage than high-wage states, because the minimum wage will be a binding constraint for more workers in low-wage states. More recent studies have included much more careful attempts to control for other differences between states that would otherwise bias our estimates.

5.1. Early cross-state studies

As cross-sectional data became more widely available – and more widely used in other branches of labor economics – several studies used 1970 Census data to estimate cross-sectional versions of the employment equation used in the time series studies. Replacing the time subscript with an i subscript for state (or metropolitan area), we have

$$E_i = \alpha X_i + \beta MW_i + \varepsilon_i.$$

Despite the apparent similarity to the time-series version, there was an important difference. In the time-series context, the minimum wage index varies because of variation in coverage and the periodic re-adjustment of the level of the minimum; variation in average wages is essentially trend and (with trend separately accounted for in the typical study) does not identify β. While cross-section studies also used a Kaitz-like minimum wage index, the source of variation was different. The federal minimum wage was constant across observations, state laws mattered relatively little because federal coverage had been

---

[24] Kennan presents time series regressions using employment of young teens (16–17) with minimum wage elasticities from -0.003 to -0.037. His minimum variable is deflated by the CPI and does not include coverage. He includes two lags of the dependent variable whose coefficients are, predictably, not inconsequential (they sum to 0.92–0.96), and complicate the interpretation of the minimum wage coefficient. In some specifications, the dependent variable in the logarithm of the employment/population ratio, in others it is ln(employment); in the latter, ln(population) and its lag are included (with nearly offsetting coefficients), but not adult population. There is no discussion of why these specifications are preferable to those used in other time-series papers, or why the variation among them represents variation among a reasonable set of specifications.

[25] Wolfson (1998) makes a point similar to Kennan's that changing the specification to account for possible unit roots weakens the estimated minimum wage effect and increases its standard error.

extended to most workers (and state laws specified minimums no higher than the federal law), and federal coverage varied relatively little across states. Thus, most of the variation was due to variation in average wages across states (Welch and Cunningham, 1978, p. 144).

Some of these studies estimated minimum wage effects at the upper end of the 1–3% range of the time series studies, but others found negligible effects. In general, studies that controlled for more other factors estimated smaller effects of the minimum wage. But because the crucial variation was coming from average wages rather than variation in the minimum wage itself, this approach provided "at best a weak test of the effect of the minimum" (Freeman, 1982, p. 120).

5.2. Panel-data studies

Minimum wage studies using state-level data more or less vanished in the early 1980s, but have reappeared recently in a much more interesting form. Two unrelated developments appear to be responsible for this resurgence. First, the availability of Current Population Survey files with wage-rate data allowed researchers to tabulate their own panels of state observations over time. This not only allowed researchers to introduce state-level fixed effects in the analysis, but permitted examination of the effects of the minimum wage on wages, and on enrollment as well as employment (and on the interaction between the two). Second, as the federal minimum remained constant in nominal terms in the 1980s, states began to raise their own minimum wages *above* the federal minimum. Alaska and the District of Columbia have traditionally set their minimum wage above the federal minimum; but by 1989 13 states had done so, including California, Massachusetts, and Pennsylvania (Neumark and Wascher, 1992, Table 1).

A representative estimating equation in the literature using state data over time is

$$E_{it} = \alpha X_{it} + \beta MW_{it} + \gamma_i + \delta_t + \varepsilon_{it},$$

where γ_i and δ_t are fixed effects for state and time, respectively. The state fixed effects provide protection against the danger that the minimum wage coefficient will pick up largely regional variation (since average wages are lower in the South, MW tends to be higher there).

Neumark and Wascher (1992) provide the most detailed attempt to date to combine federal and state minimum wage laws into a single "minimum wage" variable. To simplify matters somewhat, in years when a state's minimum wage is less than the federal minimum m_f, the state minimum is irrelevant to those covered by the federal law, and so "the" minimum wage is m_f for c_f of the state's employment, and m_s for c_s of its workers. (There are exemptions from state coverage, too, which make $c_s + c_f < 1$.) In years when the state minimum is higher, it applies to both federal- and state-covered workers. Thus, in the spirit of the "Kaitz" index from the time series literature, the minimum wage variable would be

$$MW^* = [c_f \max(m_f, m_s) + c_s m_s]/w_s.$$

However, data on workers covered by state laws is available for only 3 years toward the beginning of their 1973–1989 sample period. After experimenting with a patched-together measure of state coverage, they opt instead for

$$MW = c_f \max(m_f, m_s)/w_s.$$

Based on annual data for 1973–1989[26], their estimates of β are essentially zero for teenagers if enrollment rates are not included among the control variables, but in line with the time series findings when enrollment is held constant (Table 3). Neumark and Wascher also find somewhat larger effects when both MW_{it} and $MW_{i,t-1}$ are included. Estimated effects of the minimum wage on employment of those 16–24 are much less affected by controlling for enrollment; but the implied elasticities for 20–24 year olds are (implausibly, in my view) large relative to those for teenagers alone.[27] Finally, they identify states with separate "sub-minimum" wage provisions for students or youth, and find the latter somewhat moderate the effect of the minimum wage on youth employment.

Neumark and Wascher's conclusions were challenged by Card et al. (1994). A number of issues emerge from this interchange (Neumark and Wascher, 1994, 1996a; Card and Krueger, 1995).

First, as noted above, Neumark and Wascher do not have the data on state coverage rates that are needed to construct a strict analogue to the Kaitz index. Since the difference between available and true minimum wage variables amounts to $c_s m_s/w_s$, we can write

$$E_{it} = \alpha X_{it} + \beta[c_{ft}\max(m_{ft}, m_{sit})/w_{it}] + \beta[c_{sit}m_{sit}/w_{it}] + \gamma_i + \delta_t + \varepsilon_{it},$$

where the first term in brackets is the Neumark and Wascher minimum wage variable and the second term in brackets is in effect an omitted variable. Bias on this count seems more likely to overstate β (in absolute value), although this is at best an educated guess.[28] Card et al. find that, if "the" minimum wage is defined simply as the higher of the state or

---

[26] For 1973–1976, they have data for only 22 states, because in these years the Current Population Survey public use files did not separately identify small states.

[27] Using the enrollment variable in Neumark and Wascher (1992), the elasticities are -0.19 for teens and -0.17 for 16–24 year olds, and so nearly as large for young adults as teenagers despite a far smaller fraction being directly affected. Using an alternative enrollment variable that is less mechanically linked to employment status, the elasticity is larger for 16–24 year olds than for teens, and statistically significant only for the former. See Neumark and Wascher (1994, Table 2).

[28] To think about the likely bias this could create in a model with fixed effects for state and year, we need to focus on the variation in the two variables in brackets after state and year effects in these variables have been swept out. In states with no minimum wage, or one that is never increased above the federal level, the first term in brackets will be very well predicted by year and state dummies, and the omitted variable probably has little independent variation as well. In states that raised their minimum wage above the federal level in the late 1980s, both terms will likely be above the level otherwise predicted from state and year effects. Card et al. (1994, p. 492) also note that Neumark and Wascher's coverage variable refers to all workers, not teenagers, and that measured federal coverage jumps by nine percentage points in 1985, as a result of a Supreme Court decision on the applicability of the federal minimum wage to state and local government employees (few of whom are low-wage teenagers). They do not, however, argue that these measurement issues are likely to be related to fluctuations in teenage employment.

Table 3
Estimated effect of a 10% increase in the minimum wage on teenage and young adult employment: studies using states over time

Source/table	Data	Minimum wage variable	Control variables[a]	Percent change in employment due to 10% minimum wage increase		Notes
				Age 16–19	Age 16–24	
Neumark and Wascher (1992, Table 2)	May CPS, 1973–1989, $N = 751$	$\max(m_f,m_s)^*c_f/w$	UR, pop share, state, year	0.6 (0.9)	−0.7 (0.4)	
			Same + ESR enrollment	−1.4 (0.6)	−1.0 (0.4)	
Neumark and Wascher (1992, Table 5)		$\max(m_f,m_s)^*c_f/w$ current + 1 lag	UR, pop share, state, year	−0.3 (1.0)	−1.8 (0.6)	
Card et al. (1994, Table 1)		$\ln \max(m_f,m_s)$	Same + ESR enrollment	−1.9 (0.7)	−1.7 (0.4)	b
			UR, pop share, state, year	3.7 (1.9)		b
Neumark and Wascher (1994, Table 2)		Same	Same + ESR enrollment	0.9 (1.2)		
		$\max(m_f,m_s)^*c_f/w$ current + 1 lag	UR, pop share, state, year, MA enrollment	−1.1 (0.9)	−1.6 (0.5)	
Neumark and Wascher (1994, fn. 9)		$\max(m_f,m_s)^*c_f/w$ current + 1 lag	Same	−2.2 (0.8)	−1.4 (0.5)	c
Burkhauser et al. (1997, Table 1)	SIPP monthly, Jan. 1990–May 1992, $N = 1218$	$\ln \max(m_f,m_s)$	UR, pop share, ln w-all, state, month	−8.7 (1.1)	−3.6 (0.5)	d
Burkhauser et al. (1997, Table 3)	CPS monthly, Jan. 1990–May 1992, $N = 1479$			−4.9 (0.9)	−1.9 (0.5)	d

Study	Data	Controls	Dependent variable	Estimate 1	Estimate 2	Note
Burkhauser et al. (1997, Table 5)	CPS monthly, Jan. 1979–Dec. 1992, N = 8568			−3.7 (0.5)	−1.9 (0.2)	d
Burkhauser et al. (1997, Table 1A)	CPS monthly, Jan. 1979–Dec. 1992, N = 8568	Same + year		0.2 (0.9)		d
Card (1992a, Table 3)	CPS Apr.–Dec. 1989–1990, N = 51	Fraction of teens with $3.35 < w < $3.79	E/P	−0.4 (1.1)		e
Card and Krueger (1995, Table 4.4)	CPS annual 1989–1992, N = 51	Fraction of teens with $3.35 < w < $4.24	UR E/P	0.4 (1.4) 0.5 (1.5)		e e
Card and Krueger (1995, Table 4.5)		Same	Same + lagged E/P	1.0 (1.5)		e
Deere et al. (1995, Table 4)	CPS annual 1985–1992, N = 408	Dummy vars for 1990, 1991–1992	ln E/P, state, trend	−3.5 (0.5–0.6)		f

[a] Definitions of control variables: UR, prime age male unemployment rate, unemployment rate for all workers in Card (1992); pop share, teen (or young adult) population as fraction of labor-force age population; enrollment, proportion of teen (or young adult) population (ESR is based on employment status recode, MA is based on major activity); E/P, employment/population ratio, for all workers in Card (1992) and Card and Krueger (1995), for males in Deere et al. (1995); ln w-all, ln(average hourly earnings for all workers).

[b] Adding ln(adult wage) as control does not change estimated minimum wage effect.

[c] GLS estimates that allow for first-order serial correlation and heteroskedasticity.

[d] Standard errors corrected for heteroskedasticity.

[e] Dependent and independent variables (other than minimum wage variable) are 1989–1990 or 1989–1992 changes, so in effect there are fixed state effects.

[f] Separate estimates for males and females. Only female equation has time trend. My standard error calculation assumes correlation between male and female estimates is not negative.

federal minimum (without coverage adjustment), the minimum-wage coefficient is positive (although not significant when enrollment is held constant). Neumark and Wascher (1994, p. 504) suggest that *not* adjusting for coverage produces a stronger relationship between the minimum wage and teen *wages*.

Second, Neumark and Wascher do not include the state average wage as a separate independent variable, and so any effect of average state wages (or the factors that determine it) on teenage employment may lead estimates of β to be too negative. Neumark and Wascher (1994) report regressions (with current and lagged minimum wage variables[29]) that include state average wages as a separate control variable. The estimates are negative but generally not significant; however, the restriction that it is the *ratio* of the minimum wage to the average wage which affects teen employment is usually not rejected.

Third, the evidence of negative effects on employment appears to depend on controlling for enrollment. There is a strong negative relationship between enrollment rates and the minimum wage in Neumark and Wascher's data, contrary to Mattila's (1978) time-series results. If enrollment and minimum wages happen to be negatively correlated, it is important to take account of this chance correlation; in much the same spirit that, e.g., cyclical variables are typically held constant. If minimum wages reduce employment and enrollment, reduced-form and enrollment-constant employment equations have very different interpretations, and it is not clear that the latter are to be preferred. (If the minimum wage reduces school enrollment (Neumark and Wascher, 1996b), this is important in its own right, perhaps more important than the employment loss.)

Suppose there happens to be a correlation between minimum wages and enrollment. It seems unlikely that the effect of a one-point reduction in enrollment is larger than 0.01 times the raw difference in employment rates for enrolled and non-enrolled teens. Neumark and Wascher's results for teenagers are so sensitive to enrollment because the estimated effect of enrollment on employment is implausibly large; if one constrains the effect of enrollment on employment to be no larger than the raw difference in employment probabilities, minimum-wage effects for teens are small.[30]

Burkhauser et al. (1997) also use pooled data by state over time, and rely in part on differences in state minimum wage laws relative to the federal minimum to identify the

---

[29] The relative minimum wage variable is apparently not coverage adjusted, in response to Card et al.'s reservations about the use of federal-only coverage. I cannot determine from the regressions that are reported how important the different treatment of coverage might be.

[30] The difference in employment rates between teenagers who are enrolled and those who are not is -0.22 (Neumark and Wascher, 1994, p. 499). Imposing this estimate on equations that allow for lagged minimum wage effects leads to estimated effects of a 10% increase in the minimum wage on teen employment of 0.5 and .7% depending on the enrollment variable (based on Neumark and Wascher, 1994, Table 2, where the OLS effects of enrollment on employment are -0.77 and -0.37). Neumark and Wascher also present IV estimates, but the minimum wage estimates are even larger than the OLS effects. Alternatively, one can control for exogenous determinants of school enrollment (Neumark and Wascher, 1995, Table 3). This produces an employment elasticity of -0.05 in one specification and 0.05 in another – "essentially zero" (Neumark and Wascher, 1995, p. 202).

effect of minimum wage laws on employment. They use monthly data from both the Survey of Income and Program Participation and the CPS. In response to the Card et al. critique of Neumark and Wascher's work, they define "the" minimum wage as the greater of the federal and state minimum, with *no* adjustment for either federal or state coverage. They also control separately for the log of the average adult wage in the state, along with the prime age male unemployment rate, the proportion of the working age population accounted for by teenagers, and fixed effects for state and month. Here, "month" is a seasonal variable that distinguishes January from February, but not January of one year from January of the next.

They find higher minimum wages significantly reduce teenage employment, although the estimates prove quite sensitive to the sample used for the estimation. SIPP data for January 1990 to May 1992 suggest a 10% increase in the minimum wage reduces teenage employment by 8.7%; using CPS data for the same months lead to a smaller 5.9% reduction; extending the CPS sample to (include 1979–1992) reduces it still further, to 3.7%. *T*-ratios for the minimum wage variables range from 5 to 8. Using SIPP data, they estimate a 3.6% reduction for 16–24 year olds as a group, which implies a tiny positive effect on those 20–24. Among those 16–24, effects are larger for blacks (−5.1%) than others (−3.2%) although the difference does not appear statistically significant.

Burkhauser et al. show that most of the SIPP-CPS difference is due to SIPP not separately identifying (and so they excluded) small states. As between the CPS estimates based on shorter and longer samples, there is no obvious reason to prefer the shorter sample.[31]

This leaves the sizeable difference between their smallest estimate and those of Card–Katz–Krueger using the same data. As the last line from Burkhauser et al. in Table 3 shows, the key difference is that Card–Katz–Krueger and Neumark–Wascher include year dummies, while Burkhauser et al. do not. Thus, if one uses cross-sectional variation to identify the minimum wage effect, it is negligible. If one uses variation over time as well, the estimated minimum wage effects are substantial.

However, relying primarily on time-series variation when using panels of state data over time raises the question of whether the state × year design is preferable to a simple time-series approach. The state × year design uses different patterns in the control variables in different states over time to better identify these effects, but the simple time series approach can use published data for more years than are available for state × year cells built up from public-use CPS files. The wide variation across time periods in Burkhauser et al.'s estimates is discouraging.

Card (1992a,b) and Card and Krueger (1995) offer a different strategy for taking advantage of cross-state differences in minimum wage impacts while avoiding the problems posed by lack of good data on the coverage of state minimum wage laws. They focused on

---

[31] Burkhauser et al. (1999) report that if one corrects for both heteroskedasicity and serial correlation, or allows for a 1-year lag in the effect of the minimum wage, a 10% increase in the minimum wage is estimated to reduce teenage employment by about 2% (in specifications that include controls for year effects). But the estimated effects are much weaker when the sample is extended through 1997.

increases which raised the minimum from $3.35 in 1989 to $3.80 in 1990 and to $4.25 in 1991. Based on 1989 CPS data, they calculated the fraction of teenagers whose wages were above $3.35 but below $4.25; i.e., those whose wage would have to be increased to comply with the new law. While the overall increase in teen wages needed to comply with the new law was fairly small, there is considerable state-to-state variation in the fraction of teenagers between $3.35 and 4.25, in part because some states had raised their own minimums (Card and Krueger, 1995, p. 122).

They then regressed the change in the mean ln(wage) of teens and their employment/ population ratio in each state between 1989 and 1992 on this fraction. As expected, teen wages rise more in states with a larger fraction of teens directly affected by the new law[32]; each percentage point of teenagers directly affected raising wages by 0.28%. Employment, however, grew faster in states where the minimum wage impact was greater (an extra percentage point of teens between $3.35 and $4.25 increasing the teenage employment/population ratio by 0.13 point.) Controlling for the growth of over-all employment reduced the coefficient of the minimum wage variable in the wage equation to 0.22, and in the employment equation to zero (0.01, with a standard error of 0.03, to be precise!).

Because Card and Krueger's "fraction affected" is different from the minimum wage variables used in other studies, it is worthwhile to recalibrate our expectations for what this coefficient should be. If the minimum wage law simply led employers to raise those between $3.35 and $4.25 up to $4.25, the coefficient in the wage equation would be 0.15. So the coefficient of 0.22 reflects spillovers – some of those being paid $4.25 getting raises, too – or, more worrying, economies in high impact states being healthy in ways not accounted for by the increase in overall employment to population ratios. If the 27% increase in the minimum wage had reduced teenage employment by 2.7% (as might have been predicted from the time series literature) the coefficient of the mini-mum wage variable would be -0.03.[33] Thus, while the point estimate suggests no employment loss, the confidence interval stretches to (barely) include the traditional estimate.

The change when controlling for overall employment growth reflects the fact that states most affected by the minimum wage increase were those least affected by the recession.

---

[32] States which had raised their own minimums above the federal level by 1989 are partially accounted for by this procedure. A state like California that had already raised its minimum to $4.25 had few workers below $4.25, and so low "impact"; presumably this impact is reflected in 1989 employment. For states that had made smaller increases, and so had spikes at $3.65, for example, the procedure would not show a reduced "proportion affected". This is related to the fact that Card's measure counts how many are below the new minimum, but not how far below they happen to be.

[33] Simple "topping up" by employers would raise the average wage of affected teens by 15% (since average wages of those in this range increase from the actual mean of $3.68 to $4.25). The average wage would then increase by 0.15 times the proportion whose wage was increased. If the 27% increase in the minimum wage had reduced teenage employment by 2.7% (i.e., 1.35 percentage points on a base of 49%), the coefficient of the minimum wage variable would be $-0.0135/0.414 = -0.03$. (0.414 is the fraction of teenagers with wages between $3.35 and $4.25 initially – the mean of the "minimum wage" variable.)

Capturing as much as possible of this – and any pre-existing trends in growth of different states – is therefore important. While Card cannot add observations by going back to earlier years (since, in periods when the nominal minimum wage is constant and its real value is declining, his minimum wage variable is hard to define), adding lagged employment/population ratios (for adults and teenagers) in each state is feasible. Their addition make no difference to the results (if anything, the minimum wage coefficient increases).

Card (1992b) reports that teen employment grew faster in California than in neighboring states following the 1988 increase in its minimum wage. He also checks for effects on hours worked per week, but finds none.

Many of those whose wages increase in response to minimum wage increases are not teenagers, and many teenagers earn more than the minimum. With these facts in mind, Card and Krueger repeated the analysis for those whose demographic characteristics predict they would be low-wage workers.[34] The relationship between proportion actually in the $3.35–4.25 range in each state and employment/population ratios is very similar to that found for teenagers.

Deere et al. (1995) take a seemingly similar approach and obtain quite different results. Using CPS data by state from 1985 to 1992, they estimate the equation

$$\ln(E)_{it} = \alpha_{it}\ln(E')_{it} + \beta_{90} + \beta_{91-92} + \gamma_i + \varepsilon_{it},$$

where E is the teenage employment/population ratio, E' is the employment/population ratio of all men 15–64, β_{90} and β_{91-92} are year-specific dummies to capture the effect of the minimum wage increases in 1990 and 1991, and γ_i is a state fixed effect.[35] Their estimates suggest teenage employment was 7% (males) and 11% (females) lower in 1991–1992 than it would have been had the minimum wage not been increased. For blacks, their estimate is 10%, marginally larger than the average of males and females of all races. They find similar, although smaller, differences for adult drop-outs.

Probably the most important difference[36] between the Card–Krueger and Deere–Murphy–Welch results is that the Deere–Murphy–Welch minimum wage variable does not vary according to the expected impact of the minimum wage on the state's labor market. Thus, the regressions present evidence that employment of groups likely to be affected by minimum wage increases were lower than would be forecast based on the experience of the late 1980s, but the inference that these are "minimum wage effects" is indirect. Curiously, dummy variables for earlier years are not statistically significant; the

---

[34] Using a linear probability model that predicts (among those employed) the probability of earning $3.35 to $4.25 in 1989, they identify the 10% of CPS respondents (whether employed or not) with the highest predicted probability of being in this interval.

[35] The model in the text is for males. They also estimate regressions for females and for blacks (both sexes pooled). For females, they include a time trend; for blacks, a dummy variable distinguishing males and females.

[36] Other differences beyond Deere et al.'s longer sample period are the different cyclical indicator (men 15–64 rather than population of both sexes), using the logarithm rather than the level of the employment/population ratios, and including 15 year olds in the dependent variable.

gradual erosion of the minimum wage prior to 1990 seems to have left no evidence of the expected improvement in teen employment.

On balance, studies that use states over time as the unit of observation and rely on cross-state variation in the minimum wage variable find minimum wage effects that are not consistently different from zero. Those that rely primarily on time-series variation in the minimum wage (i.e., do not control separately for year or trend) tend to be much more negative than the "pure" time series studies, but the variation associated with sample period and specification is troubling.

From a methodological viewpoint, the return of "degree of impact" measures that focus on proportion of workers directly affected or wage increases needed to comply with a new minimum, rather than the "relative minimum wage" variable that dominates the time-series literature, is significant. The degree of impact measures are conceptually cleaner, and remind us that an increase in the minimum wage does not raise average wages of teenagers as a group by anything close to the legislated increase. But these measures are not well-suited for studying periods when the minimum wage is constant, and so its impact should be declining. While there is more to be learned from a year in which the minimum wage increases by 10 or 15% more than average wages than from a year of modest decline, the periods between increases should together contain about as much information as the periods of increase.

6. Studies of low-wage industries

6.1. A traditional method of studying minimum wages

Observing changes in employment in low-wage industries following an increase in the minimum wage or extension of its coverage to a new industry has a very long history in the study of minimum laws in the US.

Kennan (1995, pp. 1952–1954) noted that as early as 1915, a Bureau of Labor Statistics study by Obenauer and Nienburg compared employment before and after a minimum wage for women was introduced in Oregon retail stores. They found that women's employment fell absolutely and relative to men's, but attributed much of the decline to a recession that occurred about the same time. Later studies compared employment in power laundries in New York (which also adopted a minimum wage for women) to employment in Pennsylvania (which did not), and of dry cleaners in Ohio to those of Indiana.

Peterson (1957) and Lester (1960) studied changes in employment in low-wage manu-facturing industries as the minimum wage was increased from 40 to 75 cents per hour in 1950. They compared plants already paying 75 cents an hour to plants initially paying less, but reached different conclusions. Kennan (1995, p. 1954) notes that both recognized that the growth of high- and low-wage plants could have been affected by factors other than the minimum wage; e.g., in hosiery the high wage plants were further along in deploying new technology.

Studies of the impact of the 1959 increase in the minimum wage on low-wage manufacturing were undertaken by the US Labor Department. Establishments were classified by degree of "impact"; i.e., the proportional increase in average wages needed to bring all those below the new minimum wage up to that standard. There was general agreement in this instance that employment at high impact plants declined relative to low-impact ones, although the results were somewhat sensitive to the period over which the impact was measured. The tabular data presented by the Labor Department includes employment before and after the increase in both high- and low-impact parts of each industry; pooling these data we found each 10% increase in average wages needed to meet the requirements of the new law was associated with a 2–3% loss of employment (Brown et al., 1982, p. 521).

Similar studies were done when coverage of the minimum wage was extended to some employers in retail trade in the early 1960s. Here several comparisons are possible; different lines of business within retail trade differed in their degree of impact, and data on uncovered stores was also collected. Analysts at the time reached different conclusions as to whether the extension reduced employment (Brown et al., 1982, p. 517). Similar analyses were done in newly covered service establishments. Overall, our reanalysis of the published data finds negative but quite imprecisely estimated effects.

As this brief summary[37] indicates, these early studies implicitly identified at least four different ways of defining "treatment" and "control" groups, so that differences in employment change between treatments and controls could be calculated. The early Oregon retail trade study includes only covered establishments, but allows a comparison between adult women (whose wages were raised by the law) and adult men. This in effect identifies the elasticity of substitution between men and women, rather than the elasticity of labor demand. The early studies of power laundries and dry cleaning use states which did not implement minimum wage coverage as controls. In the later studies of the Federal minimum wage in manufacturing, high-impact establishments are the treatment group, and low-impact (i.e., high wage) units are the controls. In retail trade, the uncovered sector serves as the control for the newly covered treatments.

Reviewing this literature 30 or more years later, one is struck both by the ingenuity used in finding "control" groups and by the absence of persuasive argument in favor of the validity of the control group chosen or consideration of whether differences reported could be due to chance alone.

6.2. Methodological issues

From these variously defined treatment and control groups, an estimate of the treatment is obtained. If Y is employment, T and C stand for treatment and controls, and 1 and 2 stand

---

[37] I have emphasized studies that have the most in common with the more modern studies discussed below. A more complete survey is presented in Brown et al. (1982, pp. 514–522).

for the period before and after treatment, then the simple "difference in difference" estimate of the impact of treatment is

$$(Y_{T2} - Y_{C2}) - (Y_{T1} - Y_{C1}),$$

or, equivalently,

$$(Y_{T2} - Y_{T1}) - (Y_{C2} - Y_{C1}).$$

Given that "assignment" to treatment or controls is not random, there is always concern about the validity of the implicit assumption that the observed change for the controls, $(Y_{C2} - Y_{C1})$, tells us what would have happened to the establishments faced with raising wages to comply with the law, had the minimum wage change not taken place.

The control groups in early studies of the minimum wage are vulnerable on this account. The Oregon retail trade minimum wage was implemented in a recession, which might be expected to influence men's and women's employment differently. Dry cleaning employment in Indiana may have been growing at a different rate than that in Ohio prior to the Ohio minimum wage; or Ohio may have been subject to a different idiosyncratic shock in that year. High-wage hosiery plants were recognized to be using more advanced technology. High-wage plants may be located in different areas than low-wage plants, a particular concern if the product is sold in regional rather than national markets. The Labor Department was, however, careful to select both treatments and controls from the same broad region, typically the South, or report data separately by region. Newly covered retail trade businesses were larger than their uncovered neighbors. Assuming that small and large retail firms would have grown at the same rate is risky. And, if the minimum wage leads covered stores to raise prices and lose business, uncovered stores are a likely beneficiary.

In my reading of these early studies and later critiques of them, I find less discussion of two other concerns that have been raised about more recent studies (Hamermesh, 1995, p. 835): Y_{T1} must not be affected by the treatment, and period 2 must be sufficiently after the minimum wage becomes effective for the impact to be felt. This is, in effect, the same lags and leads issue that came up in the discussion of the time series results. But the issue of Y_{T1} being contaminated is likely to apply with greater force here. In a time series context, one has many quarters or months prior to the minimum wage increase, and the regression in effect averages these. In the studies under review here employment is typically measured only once prior to the change. If one or two quarters' employment is somewhat contaminated by anticipatory employment reductions (or increases, if the employer tries to beat the price hike) the effect will be more severe where averaging with earlier uncontaminated periods is absent.

Concern that period 2 is "long enough" after the minimum wage increase is more a matter of interpretation than a condition for unbiased estimates of the treatment effect. If T2 is a few months after the increase, the data will give us an estimate of shortterm effects; if the gap is several years we will get longer-run estimates.

In general, economists tend to be more interested in longer-run effects. However, the longer the interval between the periods 1 and 2 the greater the likely error induced by any non-comparability of the control group (e.g., if treatment and control groups a~~r~~ different underlying trend growth rates in employment, the bias is proportiona~~i~~ ~~to~~ difference between T1 and T2).

6.3. Recent studies of a low-wage industry: retail trade

In an analysis of the effects of the 1988 California minimum-wage increase on wages and employment in retail trade, Card (1992b) finds that wages grew about 5% faster in California retail trade than in the retail trade industries of a group of neighboring states without minimum-wage increases. Depending on the choice of base year and comparison group, employment increased one percentage point faster or slower than elsewhere following the increase. Given the small effect of the California minimum-wage increase on average wages in retail trade (roughly half the size of the effect on teenagers' wages) it is not surprising that employment effects are difficult to detect.[38]

Kim and Taylor (1995) use within-state variation to re-analyze Card's conclusions. They compare wage and employment growth in different sub-industries in retail trade, and in different counties, using County Business Pattern (CBP) data. They find little consistent relationship between wage growth and employment growth in the years prior to the 1988 increase (as might be expected given that both demand and supply shifts are at work), but a significant negative relationship (with estimated demand elasticities of -0.9 based on industry and -0.7 based on county contrasts) in 1988–1989, the year following the minimum-wage increase. By itself, a 5% wage increase and a demand elasticity of -0.8 would produce a 4% employment decline; Kim and Taylor argue that robust demand in 1988–1989 obscured this loss.

Ordinary least squares estimates suffer from two problems. First, the CBP "wage" is quarterly payroll divided by employment in one specified pay period. Random fluctuations in employment in this pay period relative to the quarter as a whole (or simple measurement error in reporting employment) will induce a negative correlation between measured wages and employment. Second, there is the standard simultaneous-equations bias. Kim and Taylor's instrumental variable estimates are nearly identical to those using OLS for 1988–1989, and essentially patternless in earlier years.[39]

Kim and Taylor use the lagged value of the average wage (low average wages mean a larger wage increase in response to the minimum) and average firm size (which they argue is positively related to the wage increase because of greater compliance by large firms). They note that both are significantly related to wage growth, and easily pass an over-identification test. Card and Krueger (1995) note, however, that the demand elasticities

---

[38] Machin and Manning (1994) find significant effects of minimum wages on wages, but if anything positive effects on employment, using data from industries in the UK that are covered by Wages Councils.

[39] The bias that arises from the calculation of the wage measure would bias the estimate toward -1. The simultaneous equation bias would bias it toward zero. The latter might be smaller in 1988–1989, when more of the wage variation is presumably coming from the exogenous minimum wage increase. Weak instruments would bias the IV estimates toward the OLS estimate.

one gets from using the two instruments separately are substantively different, and much rides on the use of firm size as an instrument. They also note that the results for 1989–1990 (which, without a minimum wage increase, should have reverted to the patternless of the earlier years) are in fact quite similar to those for 1988–1989; evidence of a negative demand elasticity vanishes if one looks at 1987–1989 changes; i.e., using 1987 as the base year.[40] Thus, there are uncomfortable concerns surrounding Kim and Taylor's otherwise robust elasticity estimate.

6.4. Recent studies of a low-wage industry: fast food

Several recent studies have used the difference-in-difference methodology to study the impact of minimum wage increases on employment in the fast food industry. Fast food restaurants are an important employer of minimum-wage workers, and the larger chains have sometimes taken public positions against minimum wage increases. Absence of tips make it relatively easy to measure the hourly wage and hence who is a minimum wage worker.

Katz and Krueger (1992) studied employment responses of major fast-food chains in Texas (a relatively low-wage state, and hence a sensible place to look for minimum-wage impacts) between December 1990 and August 1991, a period which brackets the April 1991 increase in the Federal minimum wage from $3.80 to $4.25. On average, restaurants in their sample needed to raise wages 8% above 1990 levels to reach $4.25, although of course this ranged from zero to 12%.

Katz and Krueger divided their sample according to the starting wage paid in December of 1990. Those paying $3.80 would face the largest wage increases the following April, while those already paying $4.25 would not need to raise wages in order to comply with the law. Restaurants with starting wages between $3.80 and $4.25 made up a third, medium-impact group.

A simple summary of their findings is that restaurants initially paying $3.80 increased the log of full-time employment by 0.168, while those initially paying $4.25 or more reduced mean log of employment by 0.168. Employment at restaurants whose wage initially fell between these extremes was essentially unchanged. A regression of the change in log employment on the proportional wage increase needed to comply with the new law (equal to max(0, ln($4.25/1990 starting wage)), and so equal to zero, by definition, for the high-wage group), yields a coefficient of 1.85 (SE = 1.00) for employment measured in bodies and 2.64 (SE = 1.06) for employment in full-time equivalents (FTEs).[41] The least absolute deviation estimate of the latter coefficient was 1.16 (0.55).

---

[40] Given the tangled history of the California minimum-wage increase (it was announced by a state commission in December 1987, effective July 1988, after a May 1987 legislative attempt at repeal was vetoed by the Governor), I would have thought the 1988 data might be contaminated by the impending increase and so using 1987 as a base would produce a larger estimate.

[41] These regressions included dummy variables for company ownership, chain to which the restaurant belonged, and the logarithm of city population. None of these mattered.

There is no sign that restaurants forced to raise their wages to meet the new minimum wage requirement reduced employment.

Card and Krueger (1994) surveyed fast-food restaurants in Pennsylvania and New Jersey in February–March and again in November–December 1992, before and after an April 1992 increase in the New Jersey minimum wage from $4.25 to 5.05. Compared to the Texas study, the analysis of the New Jersey law had four advantages. First, it allows two ways of defining treatment and control groups (New Jersey versus Pennsylvania, and, within New Jersey, the high- versus low-impact contrast used in Texas). Second, the minimum wage increase in question was larger, and the fraction initially in the high-wage, no-impact group (>$5.05) was larger. Third, interviewers were more persistent in getting interviews, and in-person visits determined whether non-responding restaurants had closed. Fourth, the sample was more than three times as large (357 versus 104).

Card and Krueger found that full-time equivalent employment increased faster in New Jersey than in Pennsylvania (by 2.75 FTEs, SE = 1.34), and faster in the New Jersey restaurants that made the largest increases in starting pay in order to comply with the law than in those already paying $5.05 or more (by 3.36 FTEs, SE = 1.30), on a base of roughly 21 FTEs per restaurant.

Regressing the proportional change in FTE employment on the required proportional increase in starting wage (= 0 for Pennsylvania and high-wage New Jersey units) gave elasticities of about 0.34 (SE = 0.26), with small variations depending on control variables. These become statistically significant if the data are weighted by initial employment (elasticity = 0.81, SE = 0.26).

Card and Krueger note that the unemployment rate increased faster in New Jersey than in Pennsylvania during 1992. This makes it unlikely that the employment gains in New Jersey were due business-cycle differences. It is harder to rule out this explanation for the within-New Jersey results, although experiments with geographically defined dummy variables make relatively little difference for the estimates.

Having two natural comparisons – New Jersey versus Pennsylvania, and high- versus low-wage restaurants in New Jersey – provides opportunities to address the control group issue. Neither high-wage New Jersey units nor those in Pennsylvania were required to raise wages in response to the New Jersey increase; if both are valid control groups for the New Jersey restaurants who were forced to raise wages, the employment changes of the two control groups should be the same. In fact, the change in mean FTE in Pennsylvania was −2.16 (1.25) while among high-wage New Jersey restaurants it was −2.04 (1.14). So if there are problems with the control groups, they must have problems with similar impacts on both.

The unexpected results of these two studies have, not unexpectedly, generated considerable controversy. Hamermesh (1995) is particularly critical of the timing of the surveys relative to the minimum wage increases, arguing that the "before" interviews occurred after employers in Texas and New Jersey knew that minimum-wage increases were coming. (In New Jersey, there was a serious movement to stretch out the increase over 2 years, which failed just before the increase took place, so what employers knew is not clear.) Similarly, he argues that the second interview took place before serious adjustment could occur. Card and Krueger (1995) rely on the traditional argument that adjustments are likely to occur with neither leads nor lags, given high turnover rates in the industry.

One disadvantage of special-purpose surveys like those considered here is that one is unlikely to be "in the field" quickly enough that T1 precedes any possible adjustment to the increase; that would require an ongoing survey program or prescience denied those who are in the industry. While these timing issues might lead to underestimating an employment reduction by affected restaurants, it is hard to see how it could change the sign of the estimated effect.

Welch (1995) raises the possibility that the employment gains reported by Card and Krueger came at the expense of non-chain restaurants, for which the minimum wage may have been an even larger burden. Card and Krueger note that this hypothesis is less plausible as an explanation for the within-New Jersey results, since presumably the demise of mom and pop restaurants benefited high- as well as low-wage chain restaurants. Without detailed information on the location of the two groups of New Jersey restaurants, it is difficult to evaluate their reply.

Welch also criticizes the survey methods of the New Jersey study, and points to implausible employment and wage changes at individual restaurants. In particular, a majority of those with wages initially above the new (federal in Pennsylvania, state in New Jersey) minimum reduced nominal starting wages at T2; virtually all of those with the lowest (highest) employment at T1 increased (reduced) employment by T2. This sort of mean reversion would be expected if employment is measured with considerable error (uncorrelated across surveys).

Both the Texas and New Jersey studies have limited assessments of the accuracy of the survey reports in the form of correlations between the original response and a re-interview. For employment reports in Texas, this is 0.76, in New Jersey 0.70. If we assume that the reporting errors are uncorrelated both with true values and with each other, these reliabilities are equal to the ratio of the variance in true employment to the variance in measured employment. This in turn would imply that the fraction of total variance in the *change* in employment that appears to be measurement error is just under two-thirds in Texas and nearly half in New Jersey.[42] Details of the calculation below:

---

[42] Let E and E' represent the original and re-interview reports, and E^* be the true value of employment. Then $\text{corr}(E, E') = \text{cov}(E, E')/[\text{var}(E)\text{var}(E')]^{0.5} = \text{var}(E^*)/\text{var}(E)$ and $\text{var}(e)/\text{var}(E) = 1 - \text{corr}(E, E')$. So on this assumption – which is the benchmark assumption in the re-interview literature – 76 (70)% of the variance in reported employment in Texas (New Jersey and Pennsylvania) would be "true", and the remainder error. For changes in employment assume that the errors at T1 and at T2 are uncorrelated with true values and each other. Then $\text{var}(E_{T2} - E_{T1}) = \text{var}(E_{T2}^* - E_{T1}^*) + 2\text{var}(e)$.

	TX		NJ + PA	
	T1	T2	T1	T2
SE of mean employment	0.49	0.46	0.65	0.63
Sample size	398	396	104	104
Variance of employment	95.6	83.8	43.9	41.3
Reliability	0.70	0.70	0.76	76
Variance of error	28.7	25.1	10.6	9.9
SE of mean Δemployment		0.46		0.65
Sample size		384		104
Variance of Δemployment		81.3		43.9
Variance of error		53.8		20.5
Variance of true change		27.5		23.4

It is not clear, however, that these difficulties can account for Card and Krueger's results. Unless the errors in measuring employment were other than random, they would inflate standard errors but would not bias coefficients. Errors in measuring T1 starting wages would presumably lead to some misclassification of New Jersey restaurants' "degree of impact" groups; this should bias the "wage increase required" coefficient toward (but not through) zero for within-New Jersey comparisons but have no effect on the New Jersey–Pennsylvania comparison.

Neumark and Wascher (1998) collected similar data for Pennsylvania and New Jersey fast-food restaurants. Because they were concerned about measurement error in the Card–Krueger data, they relied on payroll data collected from the restaurants or their headquarters. The data differ from Card and Krueger's in a number of ways, although Neumark and Wascher go to considerable effort to show that most of these differences would not account for the differences in results between their data and Card and Krueger's.[43]

They find similar mean changes in employment, but much smaller standard deviations (9.6 versus 3.2 FTEs). The difference-in-difference estimate of the effect of the New Jersey minimum wage increase is −1.0 (SE = 0.43), versus 4.0 (2.2) in the most nearly comparable estimates from the Card and Krueger data. Various refinements do not change either Neumark and Wascher's finding or the message of the corresponding reworking of Card and Krueger's.

Neumark and Wascher do offer one clue to the explanation: of the 5-FTE difference in the

---

[43] Neumark and Wascher's data are from payroll records supplied by the fast-food outlets or their headquarters, and employment is measured in hours rather than in bodies. They convert to full-time-equivalents dividing hours by 35. Their data refer to non-management employees, but show that in Card and Krueger's data this makes little difference. Finally, their sampling is from the Chain Operators Guide, while Card and Krueger used the Yellow Pages. Neumark and Wascher sampled from the same zip codes as Card and Krueger, but in some zip codes their sample is larger and in others smaller.

two estimates, four-fifths is due to different estimates of mean employment changes in Pennsylvania -3.0 (2.14) for Card and Krueger and 1.0 (0.34) for Neumark and Wascher.[44]

Both Neumark–Wascher and Card–Krueger appeal to data collected by the BLS to resolve the controversy. Neumark and Wascher find that employment in Eating and Drinking establishments (not necessarily "fast food") increased more slowly in New Jersey than in Pennsylvania (by 0.3 percentage points), although this is reversed if one limits the sample to the "border" counties originally sampled by Card and Krueger. They note that in either case, the New Jersey–Pennsylvania difference was less in New Jersey's favor in 1992 than it was in either of the surrounding years.

In response, Card and Krueger (1998) analyze data on employment at fast-food chains from BLS "ES-202" data. Results from a longitudinal file (following the same establishments over time, including closings) show that employment grew insignificantly faster (0.2–0.5 [SE $=$ 1.0] workers per establishment, or less than 1% [SE $=$ 3%] with a proportional change specification) in New Jersey between February–March and November–December 1992. Comparing employment across all establishments in February and November (and so including units that opened in between) showed employment growing about 4 percentage points faster in New Jersey, but a time-series plot of the two states' employment shows that this result is quite sensitive to choice of end month.[45]

In principle, fast-food restaurants (or eating and drinking places more generally) are a promising place to look for minimum-wage effects. The fraction of these workers who are directly affected by the minimum wage is considerably higher than the comparable fraction for teenagers,[46] and so the difference between the elasticity of employment with respect to the minimum wage and the elasticity of demand for low-wage labor should be much smaller.

Nevertheless, my reading of the evidence on employment changes following the Texas and New Jersey increases is that it is very hard to reject the hypothesis of no effect. The Texas and New Jersey papers' reliance on special-purpose surveys meant that questions about pre-existing trends in the two states must be handled indirectly (there is no evidence on whether employment was growing faster in the treatment or control group prior to the

---

[44] One other aspect of Neumark and Wascher's data has proven controversial. The initial round of data collection was conducted by the Employment Policies Institute which "has a stake in the outcome of the minimum wage debate"; Neumark and Wascher then undertook a second round to produce a combined sample as representative as possible of the zip code areas initially considered by Card and Krueger. Evidence of negative minimum wage effects is stronger in the EPI sample than in the sample collected directly by Neumark and Wascher. Neumark and Wascher went to considerable lengths to verify the accuracy of the EPI-collected data. The possibility of non-random response (particularly in the original EPI sample) remains. Since the Card–Krueger and Neumark–Wascher data essentially agree about New Jersey, the response bias would have to be in Pennsylvania. As it happens, one franchise owner supplied all of the original EPI observations in Pennsylvania.

[45] Following the 1996 increase in the Federal minimum wage, which brought the minimum in Pennsylvania closer to the New Jersey state minimum, fast-food employment grew substantially faster in Pennsylvania, although Card and Krueger acknowledge that other factors besides the minimum wage are probably at work here.

[46] Gilroy (1981) reports that 44% of teenagers earned w_m or less. Among non-supervisory workers in eating and drinking places, the corresponding fraction was 58%.

change). In principle, ES-202-based analyses could circumvent this proble
more intensive analysis of how estimated effects depend on the choice o
"after" time periods.[47] From a broader perspective, it is important to ...
whatever happened in Texas and New Jersey are just two data points, and (again, ın
principle) ES-202 data could be exploited to pool several such state-based experiments.

7. Comparisons of low- and high-wage workers

With the availability of longitudinal data on individual workers, it became possible to
compare the employment experience of individual workers who were directly affected by
a minimum wage increase with those who were not. These studies can also be understood
as applications of the difference-in-difference methodology.

The first such study (Egge et al., 1970) used data from the National Longitudinal Survey
of Young Men (age 14–24 in 1966) to study employment transitions surrounding the 1967
increase in the minimum wage from $1.00 to $1.40. They compared those paid between
$1.00 and $1.40 on their current or last job as of the 1966 survey (treatment group) to those
paid more than $1.40 (controls). Their exact results depended on how employment is
defined (employment at survey date or weeks worked in previous year), and the age-
enrollment group considered. Overall, they concluded there is little evidence of an adverse
effect on employment.

Using higher-wage workers as controls raises three issues. First, Egge et al. note that
low-wage workers are less likely to be employed, and more likely to leave employment,
even in the absence of the minimum wage. Second, there is little reason to believe that
business-cycle effects between year 0 and year 1 will be the same for high- and low-wage
workers. Third, by construction each individual in the sample ages by one year, and age
effects on employment may well differ for low- and high-wage workers.

Linneman (1982) focuses on adult employment changes due to the 1974–1975 minimum wage increases. He begins with the individual's 1973 wage (if s/he worked in 1973)
or a predicted 1973 wage for non-workers. This wage is adjusted upward for inflation (and
for changes in experience, etc.) to form a predicted 1974 wage, $\hat{w}$. Individuals are then
classified as above- or below-minimum wage depending on whether their predicted 1974
wage $\hat{w}$ is above or below the 1974 minimum w_m; for those with $\hat{w} < w_m$, he defines
GAP $= w_m - \hat{w}$ (if $\hat{w} > w_m$, GAP $= 0$).

Among those whose predicted 1974 wage is below w_m, the proportion working at all
during the year falls from 0.64 to 0.51, while the proportion working remains constant at
0.72 for those above the minimum wage. Similarly, among those working, annual hours

---

[47] Neumark and Wascher present regressions that relate the proportional change in employment (in New Jersey
and in Pennsylvania) to the proportional change in the nominal minimum wage, controlling for changes in the
unemployment rate. They find elasticities of −0.11 to −0.16, some of which are close to statistically significant.
However, their minimum wage measure does not reflect the usual presumption that the effect of the minimum
wage is eroded by increases in nominal wages in each state as a whole.

fall by 237 (14%) for those (predicted to be) below the minimum wage, and unchanged for those above (his Table 4). Given that the logarithm of the real minimum wage increased by only 0.12 between 1973 and 1974 – less if one takes account of the fact that the minimum increased in mid-year – these are very large employment changes.

Linneman then estimates probit equations for the probability of working in 1974 or 1975, and OLS hours of work equations, as functions of GAP and the standard set of control variables. Evaluating the importance of the minimum wage once other variables are held constant is difficult, but it appears that the effect of the minimum-wage increase implied by his estimates is much smaller.[48] Among those whose predicted wage would be above the minimum wage, probability of employment falls, and hours worked if employed rise, even for those earning three times the minimum wage.

Linneman concludes by combining wage, employment, and hours-worked effects. He finds that, on average, earnings increase, with those directly affected losing about $78 per year, while those above the minimum wage gain an average of $69. Since the (predicted) wage is not held constant in any of these calculations, it is hard to know how much of these effects should be attributed to being affected by the minimum wage and how much to being a low-wage worker.

Ashenfelter and Card (1981, reported in Card and Krueger, 1995) also study the 1974–1975 minimum wage increase, but they divide their sample of those employed in 1973 into four groups according to their 1973 wage (greater or less than the 1975 minimum wage of $2.10) and coverage status (based on reported industry of employment). The motivation here is the recognition that higher-wage workers are likely to have quite different employment probabilities than low-wage workers, and so they exploit differences in coverage to construct a better control group. They find 1995 employment is lower for those initially earning less than $2.10, but that this difference is the same whether or not they were directly affected by the law.

Using coverage status to define the control group has its own problems. First, coverage status depends on industry and employer size, so that assignment based on (worker-reported industry) inevitably misclassifies workers. Second, for whatever reason, wage distributions for uncovered-sector employers also show a spike at the minimum wage (see Section 8), so the control group is, to some extent, affected by the treatment. Third, in markets with high turnover rates, it is not clear that any negative effect of the minimum wage on employment would be concentrated on those *initially* employed in the covered sector.

---

[48] Consider first a worker paid the minimum wage ($1.60) in 1973, for whom GAP in 1974 would equal 0.118 (ln 2.00 − ln (1.60 + inflation factor)). Linneman's employment probit for 1974 is −0.3433GAP + 0.0588(GAP^2) + other variables. Evaluated at GAP = 0.118, the first two terms sum to −0.04. But the change in the probability of employment is this −0.04 multiplied by the value of the standard normal density, which is always less than 0.4. So the implied change in probability is −0.016, not negligible but far smaller than the 0.13 decline in probability of working among the workers below the minimum wage. Based on a similar calculation, the change in hours worked (for those employed at all) is −60 (versus a gross change of −237). For 1975, the corresponding change in employment probability is −0.004, and in hours worked is −20.

Currie and Fallick (1996) use the National Longitudinal Study of Youth (age 14–21 in 1979) to measure the effects of the 1980 and 1981 minimum wage increases, using panel data for 1979–1987. They define a dummy variable ("BOUND") equal to one if the individual is employed in year $t - 1$ at a wage $w_{m,t-1} < w_{t-1} < w_{m,t}$, and zero otherwise. In most specifications, they also require that employment in year $t - 1$ be in a "covered" industry, although they acknowledge that their ability to infer coverage (based on industry) is limited. They also construct a "WAGEGAP" variable, equal to $w_{m,t} - w_{t-1}$ when BOUND $= 1$, and WAGEGAP $= 0$ otherwise. In 1982 and later years, BOUND and WAGEGAP $= 0$ for all observations.

They then estimate an employment equation

$$E_{i,t} = \alpha \text{WAGEGAP}_{it} + X_{it}\beta + \gamma_i + \delta_t + \varepsilon_{it},$$

where $E_{i,t} = 1$ if i was employed in year $t - 1$ and again in year t, and $E_{it} = 0$ if i was employed in year $t - 1$ but not in t. They find that α is negative and statistically significant, as is BOUND when it is used instead of WAGEGAP. The probability of remaining employed is reduced by about 0.03 for the fifth or so of the sample that is directly affected by the increases in 1980 or 1981.[49]

Currie and Fallick recognize that the control group issue is fundamental to their study. They note that their control group is in fact composed of three sub-groups: those who earn less than the old minimum wage in $t - 1$, those who earn more than the new minimum wage in $t - 1$, and those who are working in uncovered jobs in $t - 1$. Separating these groups reveals that those bound by the new minimum wage increase suffer employment reductions relative to those who initially earned more than the minimum wage, marginally relative to those who earned less than the old minimum wage, and in fact do much better than those in uncovered jobs. In effect better-paid workers are the heart of the control group.

Are better-paid workers an appropriate control group? Because we expect low-wage workers will have lower employment-retention probabilities in general, one starts with serious doubts on this score. Currie and Fallick do, however, include fixed effects; so in effect their regressions tell us that employment of those who are bound by the minimum wage increases in 1980–1981 was lower, relative to higher-wage workers, in 1980–1981 than in other years. Card and Krueger (1995, p. 228) question whether the fixed effects are really fixed–employer information about productivity, which presumably drives the re-employment probabilities, evolves rapidly for young workers. It is also possible that the 1981 recession was harder on low-wage workers than others, which would contribute to Currie and Fallick's negative coefficient.

---

[49] Abowd et al. (1997) find that French men age 25–30 who earn the minimum wage are much less likely to remain employed following an increase in the minimum, compared to men paid just above the minimum. Results are weaker for younger males (which they attribute to employment promotion programs for younger workers) and for teenage and young-adult women.

Currie and Fallick respond to these concerns by defining another dummy variable NEARMIN, equal to 1 if w_{t-1} is within 0–15 cents greater than $w_{m,t-1}$, to capture the effect of having low wages apart from being BOUND. When added to the regression it is insignificant (both practically and statistically), and the coefficient of the minimum-wage variable does not change appreciably. This is a reasonably reassuring response to some of the control-group concerns,[50] although the possibility that the recession was harder on low-wage youth is harder to reject.

While the Currie–Fallick specification appears at first glance to apply the same methodology to individual data that Card and Krueger used in analyzing state-level data, there is a subtle but perhaps important difference. Unlike Card and Krueger's analysis of the 1990–1991 minimum wage increases, Currie and Fallick include years when the nominal minimum wage was constant, and so the real minimum wage was falling. One might have expected the employment-retention probabilities of low-wage workers to *increase* in these years, as the minimum wage became less binding.[51] Nothing in Currie and Fallick's specification captures this response directly, and it is possible that the coefficient of their dummy variable for low-wage workers is biased (upward) on this account.

While Currie and Fallick devote a lot more effort to reducing any bias due to control-group problems than did Egge et al., these efforts do not change the results very much. The difference between their results and Egge et al.'s is striking. Since the fixed effects and NEARMIN do not account for the difference, what does? Low-wage workers faring well in expansions and poorly in recessions is a tempting conjecture in the absence of obvious alternatives.

8. Impacts of minimum wages on other outcomes

Thus far, we have reviewed studies that focus directly on the link between the minimum wage and employment. In this section, our focus shifts to the effect of the minimum wage on related outcomes. While a range of such outcomes have been studied, the emphasis here is on outcomes that may provide indirect clues about the effect of the minimum wage on employment.

8.1. Wage distribution spike at the minimum wage

Among those who are employed, the distribution of ln(wage) tends to look bell-shaped, with occasional spikes at round-dollar amounts (particularly if the data come from house-

---

[50] In fact, their NEARMIN variable is close to Card and Krueger's (1985, p. 239) suggestion for testing the validity of their control group.

[51] Abowd et al. (1997) find that young workers in the US who are employed at the minimum wage are much less likely to have been employed the previous year and so a falling real minimum wage facilitates their entry into employment. An alternative reading of this evidence is simply that those entering employment often do so at the minimum wage.

Table 4
Frequency of minimum-wage and near-minimum-wage employment[a]

Month	w_m ($)	w_m/ahe	Type of survey[b]	Sample[c]	Interval ($)	Frequency (%)	Interval ($)	Frequency (%)	Interval ($)	Frequency
Oct.–Dec. 1996	4.75	0.40	H	WSH	<4.75	4.3	4.75	2.8		
				WSH 16–19		14.8		11.9		
Jan.–Dec. 1992	4.25	0.40	H	WSH	<4.25	3.0	4.25	4.8		
				WSH 16–19		9.3		19.8		
Jan.–Dec. 1989	3.35	0.35	H	WSH	<3.35	2.2	3.35	2.9		
				WSH 16–19		6.1		11.7		
Jan.–Dec. 1988	3.35	0.36	H	WSH	<3.35	2.2	3.35	4.3		
				WSH 16–19		6.2		16.9		
				WS	≤3.35	5.3				
				WS 16–19		23.6				
May 1978	2.65	0.47	H	PNSWS	<2.65	11.3	2.65–2.99	11.2		
			E	PNSWS		4.3		18.2		
May 1973	1.60	0.41	H	WS	≤1.60	7.9				
				WS 16–19		26.3				
Apr. 1970	1.60	0.50	E	PNSWS	<1.60	6.8	1.60–1.64	4.0	1.75–1.79	2.8
				PNSWS-OC		0.6		2.9		2.0
	1.45			PNSWS-NC	<1.45	8.3	1.45–1.49	6.5	1.60–1.64	6.9
	NA			PNSWS-U	<1.60	30.4	1.60–1.64	7.2	1.75–1.79	5.4

[a] Sources: 1996, 1992: US Census Bureau (1997, Table 675; 1993, Table 676); 1988: Haugen and Mellor (1990, Tables 2 and 1); 1978: Gilroy (1981, Table A-3); 1973: Gilroy (1981, Table 22); 1970: Peterson (1981, Table 18).
[b] H, household; E, establishment.
[c] WS, wage and salary; H, paid by the hour; NS, non-supervisory; P, private (non-agricultural); OC, old coverage (covered prior to 1967); NC, new coverage (covered by 1967 Amendments); U, largely uncovered.

hold surveys rather than employer reports). Often there is another spike, at the minimum wage, even when the minimum is not a round-dollar amount. Spikes at the minimum wage are stronger when the minimum wage is more binding; e.g., in wage distributions for teenagers rather than for all workers, and in years when the minimum wage has been raised rather than after several years of a constant nominal and eroding real minimum wage.

The first two lines of Table 4 show that, in 1996, 26.7% of teenagers paid by the hour reported wages at or below the minimum wage, including nearly 12% who were at the minimum, while for adults the mass point at the minimum is much less pronounced.[52] A similar pattern is present in other years, with the fraction at the minimum increasing between 1989 and 1992, reflecting the 1990–1991 increases in the minimum wage. Indeed, Card and Krueger (1995, pp. 156–157) show that the fraction of teenagers receiving $3.80 per hour was much larger in 1990 (when the minimum wage was $3.80) than in 1989 (when it was $3.35), and the fraction receiving $4.25 was much larger in 1991 (when the minimum wage was $4.25) than in earlier years.

Data for 1988 show that including workers not paid by the hour (calculating their wage as usual weekly earnings divided by usual weekly hours) has relatively little effect on the fraction at or below the minimum wage, because low-wage workers tend to be paid by the hour.

For 1978, data are available from an establishment survey as well as the CPS. Employers and workers tend to report similar fractions of workers paid less than $3.00 per hour, although the fraction at or slightly above the minimum is much higher in the employer reports. Whether this represents employers hiding non-compliance or workers reporting their wages with less precision than we would prefer is unclear (Gilroy, 1981).

The data for 1970 reveal several interesting patterns. First, even among non-supervisory workers as a group, there is a noticeable jump in the wage distribution at the minimum wage that is, for example, more pronounced than at $1.75 (or, not shown, $2.00). Second, employers first covered by the 1967 Amendments, for whom the legal minimum was $1.45, often paid the basic minimum. Third, even the wage distribution of the *un*covered sector exhibits a spike at the minimum.

Wage distributions for European countries also exhibit spikes at the minimum wage, often more pronounced than those in the US (Dolado et al., 1997, Table 1). Machin and Manning (1997, p. 735) attribute this to the minimum wage being higher, relative to the average wage, in Europe than in the US.

These spikes pose a puzzle for nearly all of the models presented in Section 2. Suppose a firm employs two groups of workers, one at $5.00 and one at $4.50, in the absence of the minimum wage. Now a $5.00 minimum wage is imposed. What the data show is that at least some of the $4.50 workers are now employed at $5.00. While one might imagine that employment of low-skill workers had declined enough to raise the marginal product of those who remained by 11%, enabling the some of the $4.50 workers to remain employed,

---

[52] DiNardo et al. (1996) show that minimum wage spikes are occasionally evident in the male wage distribution, and stronger in the distribution of female wages, particularly in the late 1970s when the minimum wage was high relative to average wages.

employers should now compete actively for those initially paid $5.00, bidding up their wages and unpiling the spike at $5.00.

8.2. Offsets

In the absence of a minimum wage, non-wage job characteristics are determined by a comparison of the cost of improving such characteristics against workers' willingness to pay for improvements by accepting lower wages. Other things equal, an increase in the wage (due to minimum wage legislation) increases the number of workers willing to work while reducing employers' demand for workers. This imbalance gives employers an incentive to look for cost-saving changes in non-wage job characteristics; if successful, such offsets could reduce the predicted impact of the minimum wage on employment. Moreover, offsets can potentially account for the spike at the minimum wage; among workers receiving the minimum wage, reductions in non-wage job characteristics would be most severe for those whose wage was raised most by the law.

In an influential paper on unemployment, especially among youth, Feldstein (1973) suggested that the minimum wage discouraged employers from providing training. Ordinarily, workers pay for training (all of general training, part of specific training) by accepting lower wages than they could earn in a job without training; this wage reduction offsets the cost the employer would otherwise bear in providing the training. The minimum wage interferes with this process because reducing the wage below the required minimum is illegal (even if compensation, including value of training, is above the minimum).

It is clear that, to the extent that the minimum wage reduces employment, on-the-job training and the general human capital that one obtains just by establishing a work record are reduced. It is less clear that, among those who are employed, human-capital acquisition is impaired to any significant degree; the training content of such jobs, and the scope for reducing training (without rendering the worker useless) may be limited.

Available evidence suggests that training for low-wage workers is significant enough to be a potential offset to minimum wage increases, but only for some of these workers. In a 1980 survey of employers, "Almost half of the jobs held by low-wage workers involve formal training," averaging 12.3 days. About 70% of the jobs held by low-wage workers involve "on-the-job" training, defined as jobs in which it took 5 or more days for a worker to reach company standards. On average, 24.6 days were required to reach that standard (Converse et al., 1981, p. 260). However, employers did not report cutting training in response to the minimum wage; in fact about an eighth of all establishments with minimum wage workers said they had increased the responsibilities of low-wage workers in order to offset the minimum wage increase, and half of these reported increased training along with the increased responsibility (Converse et al., 1981, p. 280).

Several studies (Lazear and Miller, 1981; Leighton and Mincer, 1981; Hashimoto, 1982) tried to determine whether minimum wage increases were associated with flatter age-earnings profiles. They obtained mixed results. In general, there are two difficulties with such approaches. First, it is likely that on-the-job training is a complement to other forms of human capital such as schooling, so that low-wage workers would get less training even in the absence of a minimum wage. Second, an increase in the minimum wage has the immediate effect of increasing the wages of directly affected workers. If the increase has no effect on such workers' wages several years later (when they would, in any case, have earned more than the new minimum), the age-earnings profile will be "flatter", but this is an artifact of the fact that the minimum wage is less likely to be binding for older workers, not (necessarily) a sign that less training is being produced (Card and Krueger, 1995, p. 171).

On balance, there does not seem to be much evidence that reductions in training are a significant offset to the increase in labor costs due to the minimum wage.

Perhaps the simplest way of offsetting the effects of a minimum-wage increase is to reduce the fringe benefits offered to workers. However, relatively few minimum-wage workers receive health insurance or participate in pension plans, so scope for such reductions is limited. Wessels (1980) reports that, in 1972, among low-wage firms (average hourly wage of $2.00 or less), only 3% of non-office workers had pension plans and 27% had health insurance; among employers offering such benefits, each accounted for only 2% of payroll. Paid leave was more common (58% of workers) but again accounted for only 2% of payroll. Not surprisingly, therefore, only 2% of establishments surveyed said they responded to a minimum wage (in retail trade in New York state) by reducing such fringes.

Fast-food restaurants provide a more promising although atypical opportunity to search for offsetting changes in fringe benefits, because such employers often provide free or reduced-price meals to their employees. Katz and Krueger (1992) asked their sample of fast-food managers in Texas whether fringe benefits had been reduced in response to the increased minimum wage. While 91% of their sample provided some fringe benefit(s) to workers, only 4% reduced fringes following the minimum wage increase, and this proportion was no higher in those restaurants forced to raise wages in order to reach the new minimum wage. Card and Krueger (1994) similarly find no significant difference in free or reduced-price meals when comparing New Jersey and Pennsylvania outlets, or high- versus low-impact outlets within New Jersey.

Another fringe benefit reported by Card and Krueger is the bonus paid to employees who help recruit new workers–just under a quarter of the restaurants surveyed had such bonuses. While one might expect a higher minimum wage would make recruiting easier and so make such bonuses less necessary, their use declined slightly faster in Pennsylvania than in New Jersey.

Overall, then, there is little evidence that minimum wage increases are offset by cutting fringe benefits.

While many low-wage employers provide little training and few fringe benefits – and so cannot reduce these in response to a minimum wage – all employers have standards for punctuality, cooperation, and effort. If employers are required to pay above-market wages, expecting more effort, etc. from workers is a natural and potentially universal response.

Given difficulties of measuring effort, evidence on changes in required levels of effort is, predictably, thin and indirect. Wessels (1980) reports that one-sixth of the establishments in his sample of New York retailers reduced hiring of extras, and another 3% reduced meal and rest periods. Above we noted employers' claiming to increase worker responsibility, which might imply additional effort as well. With effort less directly measurable than fringe benefits or even training, such hints are all the evidence we have that effort standards might be raised in response to the minimum wage.

Unlike reductions in fringe benefits, offsetting minimum wage increases with increased effort standards is unlikely to blunt the expected negative effect on employment. A 10% increase in the minimum wage offset by a 10% increase in effort and therefore labor services per worker would lead to a 10% reduction in workers (or worker hours) employed.

8.3. Spillovers

As noted in the discussions of heterogeneous workers and of the possible unpiling of the spike at the minimum wage, it is reasonable to expect that an increase in the minimum wage from $4.50 to $5.00 will make workers initially skilled enough to earn slightly more than $5.00 more attractive to employers. When the minimum wage is $4.50, employers are indifferent between such workers and workers earning $5.40 who are 20% more productive. If (some of) these $4.50 workers now must be paid $5.00, those making $5.40 are now a significantly better bargain. Surprisingly, there is relatively little evidence on the effect of the minimum wage on the wages of those higher in the wage distribution.

Gramlich (1976) indirectly estimated the importance of spillovers by comparing his estimate of the effect of the minimum wage on average hourly earnings to the effect one gets by assuming the only effect of the minimum wage is on those whose wage initially fell between the old (w_m) and new (w'_m) minimum wages (i.e., $w_m \leq w < w'_m$). This direct effect accounted for about half of the effect on average earnings. Gramlich noted that the remaining "emulation" may include effects on those initially earning less than w_m (due to incomplete coverage or noncompliance) as well as wage increases for those initially earning more than the new minimum.[53]

Grossman (1983) estimated spillover effects for workers in nine low-wage (but not minimum-wage) occupations in non-manufacturing industries. While there is some evidence of spillover effects, they are estimated with relatively large standard errors.

---

[53] Gramlich's calculation of the effect on average wages is based on a time-series analysis of data from 1954–1975, whereas the data for directly affected workers is based on analysis of CPS data surrounding the 1974 increase. While CPS wage distributions that would let one study earlier minimum wage increases are not available, it appears from BLS calculations of "wage-bill impacts" which assume wages increase only for directly affected workers (Peterson, 1981, Table 17) that the 1974 increase had a relatively small direct effect on wages in covered establishments. On the other hand, coverage had been expanded so that covered establishments accounted for a larger fraction of total employment and wages. If the "typical" increase in Gramlich's sample period had a larger direct effect than did the 1974 increase, his estimated emulation effects would be too high. Cox and Oaxaca (1981) estimate a significantly larger effect of the minimum wage on average wages than did Gramlich. However, they assume that minimum wages increases lead to a proportionate increase in the wages of all low-wage workers (including those initially somewhat above the minimum).

Given the details of her sample, her results to not allow us to say much about the importance of spillovers of those "just above" the minimum wage, where such impacts are likely to be most important.[54]

Converse et al. (1981) asked employers whether, in response to the January 1979 increase in the minimum wage to $2.90, they increased wages of workers who had previously been earning more than the new minimum. The authors tried to verify that these increases would not have been given had the minimum wage not increased; i.e., that they were not due to generally increasing nominal wage levels. By this standard, 17% of establishments employing minimum-wage workers reported a "ripple" effect on wages. For 64% of these establishments, the increases stopped at $4.00 per hour or less. Given that the 1979 increase in the minimum wage essentially matched increases in average hourly earnings in the economy as a whole, the study was forced by timing to focus on a minimum wage "increase" that was quite small by historical standards.

Katz and Krueger (1992) provide detailed information on ripple responses following the 1990 and 1991 increases in the minimum wage. Among restaurants whose starting wage was equal to the old minimum wage, a significant minority increased the wages of those paid between the old and new minimum to a level above the new minimum (for outlets that paid the old minimum wage originally, 41% raised wages of those between w_m and w'_m to a new level above w'_m in 1990, only 16% did so in 1991). But only 9% of these restaurants increased the wage of those earning $4.50 per hour before the 1991 increase. These results are consistent with the idea that spillovers are limited to a minority of workers above the minimum wage, and die out fairly quickly as one moves up the wage distribution. However, they also find that almost no employers delay or reduce the first raise that new hires receive if they remain with the firm. Card and Krueger (1994) find no significant changes in time to first raise or amount of wage in response to New Jersey's state minimum wage increase, again suggesting a spillover from the minimum wage of starting workers to the wage of those who remain long enough to progress above that level. However, since this first raise averages 5% after 19 weeks on the job, there is again not much evidence of spillovers extending very far up the wage distribution.

Card and Krueger (1995, pp. 163–166) analyze changes in the teenage wage distribution following the 1990 and 1991 increases. They find that the fraction of teenagers earning less than $4.50 declined more rapidly in states most affected by the increase to $4.25 by 1991, but there was little difference in the fractions earning less than $5.00.[55] They conclude the

[54] Because she wanted to be sure she was not capturing the direct effect of the minimum wage on those earning less than the new minimum, she eliminated occupations with any minimum-wage workers. Among the set of occupations included in the Area Wage Survey, this left nine occupations that were low-wage but not directly affected. Five of the nine were office occupations. Moreover, her sample was dominated by relatively large and relatively Northern cities, and the Area Wage Survey includes only establishments with at least 50 workers (100 in some cities). The focus on occupations not directly affected, plus the sampling of cities and establishment sizes, led to a sample where spillovers would have to go fairly high up the wage distribution in order to be detectable. In the median occupation, average hourly earnings were about 80% above the minimum wage.

[55] Of course, this might just be a reduction in employment in the lower tail of the distribution, but recall that they do not find that employment fell faster in high-impact states.

data "provide some support for the existence of spillover effects up to $4.50 per hour, but little evidence of spillovers beyond $4.50."

The evidence on spillovers is very limited, but it suggests that increases in minimum wages lead to increases for those above the minimum as well, although these spillovers do not extend very far up the wage distribution. From one perspective, such spillovers seem broadly consistent with the goals of minimum wage legislation; if raising wages of those earning the minimum wage is a good thing, increasing the wages of those who were earning a bit more than the minimum would also be viewed favorably. From another perspective, these spillovers may be cause for concern. Recall that, in discussing the effects of the minimum wage on employment of a heterogeneous group such as teenagers, "small" overall effects might result from losses to low-wage teens partially offset by increasing employment of better-paid teens. The spillovers can be read as evidence that demand for (and therefore employment of) better-paid teens (and others) increased. However, the tentative evidence that these spillovers do not extend very far up the wage distribution[56] would suggest that the gainers and losers are not *very* different in their skills or other attributes.

8.4. Prices

The standard model of labor demand predicts that employment of unskilled workers falls in response to a minimum wage because other inputs are substituted for unskilled labor and because the increased minimum wage increases the cost of and so reduces the demand for products that use such labor intensively. While there is a sizeable literature on the effects of the minimum wages on prices in general, the effects on relative prices of industries that use low-skill labor have been studied less intensively.

Wessels (1980, pp. 67–69) summarizes Department of Labor studies comparing price increases by Southern and non-Southern firms in low-wage industries following the 1961 and 1967 increases in the minimum wage. Since wages were lower in the South, it was the "high-impact" region and one might expect prices in affected industries to increase faster there. In manufacturing, Wessels finds little consistent pattern in price increases by region; but in services relative prices do increase faster in the South.

Katz and Krueger (1992) and Card and Krueger (1995) compared the price changes by fast food restaurants that were affected to different degrees by the minimum wage. Katz and Krueger found that Texas restaurants that experienced larger increases in starting wage (due to the increased federal minimum wage) increased their prices less rapidly; this relationship was not statistically significant.[57] Card and Krueger (1995, Table 2.8)

---

[56] A recent paper by Acemoglu (1997) finds positive effects of minimum wages on the number of "good" jobs (occupations with wages significantly higher than the observable characteristics of their occupants would predict), which would suggest spillovers higher up the wage distribution.

[57] The elasticity of price with respect to starting wage was estimated as -0.089 (0.133). So one could reject the hypothesis that the elasticity was equal to low-wage labor's share of total costs, as long as (as seems likely) that cost share is greater than 0.2.

report a positive, although statistically insignificant relationship in their New Jersey–Pennsylvania sample, and a positive and sometimes significant relationship in national samples (their Table 4.10).

The limited available evidence thus suggests that minimum wage increases often lead to increases in prices by the directly affected firms, although how they compare to the simplest competitive prediction is not clear.

9. The minimum wage and the wage and income distributions

Much of the justification for minimum wage laws lies in a desire to help those at the bottom of the economic ladder. Despite warnings by George Stigler over 50 years ago (Stigler, 1946) that those who work for the lowest wages are not necessarily members of the poorest families, public discussions tended to assume that those at the bottom of the wage distribution were also likely to be at the bottom of the income distribution. The first careful studies of the effect of the minimum wage on the distribution of income suggested that the link between low wage and low income was disappointingly weak (Gramlich, 1976; Kelly, 1976). More recent work has to some extent reassessed that conclusion, but has also focused more directly on the distribution of wages as well as the distribution of income.

9.1. Effects on the wage distribution

Combining the insights of the theoretical models and the evidence in the preceding sections suggests that the minimum wage may affect the wage distribution in many ways. First, some of those who would otherwise earn less than the minimum wage may be less likely to be employed, or employed for fewer hours. The loss of low-wage jobs would tend to make the measured wage distribution more equal, although this is not the sort of equalization that proponents of the minimum wage have in mind. Reduced hours have a similar effect, if the wage distribution is hours- rather than worker-weighted. Second, some of those who would otherwise earn less are boosted up to w_m, producing the spike in the wage distribution at the minimum wage. Third, wages of low-wage workers not covered by the minimum wage may be increased or reduced. Fourth, the increase in the wages of directly affected workers will make substitutes for these workers more attractive, and this is likely to raise demand for workers just above the minimum. Wages of such workers should increase, and more may be pulled into the labor force. Fifth, minimum wages may indirectly affect those further up the wage distribution, although most work on the subject implicitly or explicitly assumes the effects on well-paid workers are small.

Meyer and Wise (1983a,b) were the first to focus on the spike at the minimum wage and the apparent thinning of the wage distribution at lower wages. Their plotted empirical wage distributions strongly suggested that both thinning below w_m and a piling up at w_m

were empirically important. They fit a wage distribution that allowed for both thinning and piling up, but otherwise looked like a standard wage distribution, with ln(wage) depending on the usual schooling, experience, etc. variables and a normally distributed error. They then assumed that this distribution would hold below w_m, too, in the absence of a minimum wage. The difference between the thinned distribution below w_m plus the spike at the minimum, and the fitted distribution at or below w_m, was taken as a measure of the employment loss at the minimum wage. Meyer and Wise find that their estimate of the effect of a given minimum wage on employment was essentially the same using 1978, when the actual minimum was low (and so the estimate was based largely on the observed wage distribution) as using 1973 when the actual minimum wage was high (and so the estimate relied more heavily on projecting the wage distribution below the actual minimum).[58]

This approach was criticized by Dickens et al. (1994), who noted that spillover effects (which thicken the distribution just above w_m, and were assumed to be negligible by Meyer and Wise) would lead them to over-predict the wage density below w_m in the absence of the minimum wage, and so over-estimate the employment loss. Using British data, they find that their estimates are sensitive to the details of fitting the wage distribution above w_m and then extrapolating it back to lower wage levels.[59]

For thinking about the wage distribution, the important point is that Meyer and Wise assumed a parametric wage distribution and then estimated the effect of the minimum wage on the distribution at or below w_m. In contrast, papers that focus on the effect of the minimum wage on the distribution of wages or income typically do the reverse; they begin with the empirical distribution of wages or income, assume that an increase in the minimum wage boosts the wages of those between the old and new minimum, make some assumption about the extent of employment loss and the effect (if any) on those initially earning sub-minimum wages, and usually assume that spillovers above the minimum wage are unimportant.

DiNardo et al. (1996) analyze the effects of changes in the minimum wage on wage inequality, focusing in particular on the 1979–1988 period when inequality increased significantly for both men and women. Their baseline estimates assume no employment loss and no spillovers; they assume that, had the real minimum wage in 1988 remained at its 1979 level, the shape of the wage distribution (conditional on schooling, experience, etc.) below the minimum would been the same as it was in 1979. Between 1979 and 1988, the logarithm of the ratio of the minimum wage to average wages fall by 0.27 for men, the standard deviation of ln(wage) increased by 0.072, and the falling real minimum wage can

---

[58] Meyer and Wise tended to emphasize the employment gain from eliminating the minimum wage, which makes comparison with other studies difficult. However, they report that, over the 4 years 1973, 1976, 1977, and 1978, keeping the minimum wage at $1.60 (a 30% cut, on average, over these years) would have increased employment by 5%. This implies an elasticity of -0.16.

[59] The Meyer–Wise approach to estimating minimum wage effects has not been used in the more recent US literature, but has been used more with European data. For a brief survey and critique, see Dolado et al. (1997, p. 332).

account for 0.018 of the increase. For women, the decline in the relative minimum wage was 0.36, the increase in the standard deviation of ln(wage) 0.090, and the increase due to the falling minimum wage 0.027.

While these calculations are based on fairly strong assumptions rather than fitting a minimum wage variable to the actual changes in inequality, DiNardo et al. report the effects of various alternatives as well. Assuming that a higher minimum wage increase in 1988 would have no effect on those below the actual 1988 minimum, or allowing a disemployment elasticity of 0.15,[60] has little effect on the estimates. The baseline simulations take anyone earning less than $3.00 in $1979 (rather than $2.90) as being directly affected by the minimum wage, and this matters a lot: the spike at $3.00 is important. As one would expect, variations in the minimum wage matter more for inequality measured by the standard deviation of ln(w) or the 90–10 differential, and less for the Gini, since the latter places less weight on the low end of the wage distribution.

Changes in the standard deviation of ln(w) of 0.018 (men) or 0.027 (women) are large if measured against the increases in inequality over the period (0.072 and 0.090, respectively), and obviously smaller if compared to the initial level of inequality (0.501 and 0.429). But given the policy interest in the 1979–1988 changes, the calculated contribution of the minimum wage is too large to be ignored. These changes are larger if spillovers are important.[61]

Card and Krueger (1995) compare changes in the wage distribution between 1989 and 1992 in states according to the fraction of their workers who were directly affected by the 1990 and 1991 minimum wage increases. They confirm the prediction of DiNardo et al. that such increases measurably reduce wage inequality. Machin and Manning (1994) use data for British industries subject to different minimum wages and also find that higher relative minimum wages reduce wage dispersion.

9.2. Effects on the distribution of income

Moving from the distribution of wages to the distribution of income is complicated by several considerations. Many families have several earners, so that a minimum-wage worker can be part of a relatively affluent family. In contrast, the poorest families in the US have little or no labor earnings, and the minimum wage is powerless to improve their status. Several simple statistics have been used to characterize the relationship between having wages at or near the minimum ($w < w^*$, where w^* is often set at w_m) and being part of a low-income family or household ($Y < Y^*$).

---

[60] Since a 32 log-point increase in the minimum wage is being discussed, this presumably means a 5% loss of employment for those at or below the new minimum. This is a different elasticity notion than is found in the literature on teenagers, where the proportionate change in employment of all teens (including those above the minimum wage) is considered.

[61] The authors note that the wage distribution for women (but not for men) was much denser just above the 1979 minimum than above the same point in the real wage distribution in 1988, which suggests – but does not prove – that spillovers might be important for women.

First, among low-wage workers, what fraction are poor (i.e., what is Prob($Y < Y^*$ | $w < w^*$)? Using 1973 data, Gramlich (1976) chose $w^* = \$2.00$ (versus $w_m = \$1.60$) and $Y^* = \$4000$ (roughly, the poverty line for a family of four). He found that 23% of adult low-wage workers were "poor", as compared to 6% of all adult workers. In contrast, only 6.6% of low-wage teenage workers were in poor families, compared with 8.2% of teenagers at all wages. Since there were more than twice as many low-wage adults as low-wage teens, overall about 18% of low-wage workers were poor. Raising wages of those in the vicinity of the minimum was not a particularly target-efficient strategy for raising low incomes. A number of other studies have found the fraction of low-wage workers who are "poor" to be about 20% (Kohen and Gilroy, 1981, Table 4; Johnson and Browning, 1983, Table 1; Smith and Vavrichek, 1987, Table 2; Card and Krueger, 1995, Table 9.1; Burkhauser et al., 1996, Table 4).[62] This fraction is roughly doubled if one sets Y^* at 1.5 times the poverty line.

Burkhauser and Finegan (1989, Table 2) show that the fraction of low-wage workers who are poor fell from 42% in 1959 to 18% in 1984, reflecting both a decline in the unconditional probability of being poor and the probability that a low-wage worker would be a family "head" whose earnings would determine its economic status. Card and Krueger (1995) argue that other forces (declining relative incomes for families with children, so that now minimum-wage teens have lower family incomes than other teens, reversing the pattern in Gramlich's data, increased wage inequality among adults) has increased the fraction of minimum wage-workers who are poor.

A second summary statistic is Prob($w < w^*$ | $Y < Y^*$): among workers who are in low-income families, what fraction earn low wages? Because the proportion of *workers* who are low-wage tends to be higher than the proportion who are poor, changing the conditioning event in this way raises the conditional probability, typical values being 0.3–0.4.

Tabulations based on the fractions of workers who are low-wage and/or poor can reveal only part of the story, however. Many families are poor because they have no workers, or because those who are employed work few hours (Kelly, 1976), others because they work full time but have large families (Bell, 1981, p. 451). What is particularly striking is that 25.7% of poor families in 1989 had no workers, and only 12.6% had a "minimum wage" worker[63] (Burkhauser et al., 1996, Table 3).

Given this relatively loose link between being a low-wage worker and being a member of a low-income family, we should perhaps expect that simulations of the effect of raising the minimum wage show relatively modest effects on poverty. Most of these simulations have begun by making assumptions that minimize indirect effects – no employment loss, no offsets to increased earnings due to increased prices or reduced transfers – and no spillovers. Earnings gains per household are roughly equal across deciles of the income

---

[62] Dolado et al. (1997) report a stronger relationship in European countries.

[63] Here "minimum wage" workers are those earning \$3.35–4.25 per hour, and so include those whose wages were raised by the 1990 and 1991 minimum wage increases.

distribution (Johnson and Browning, 1983, Table 2) or the distribution of family-size-adjusted income (Burkhauser et al., 1996, Tables 5 and 1A). Of course, even an equally distributed gain improves an initially unequal distribution, and one gets modest simulated reductions in poverty (Mincy (1990) estimates that, in 1987, raising the minimum wage from $3.35 to $4.25 would, on these assumptions, have reduced the number of poor families by 6.9%). Taking account of possible dis-employment and losses of means-tested transfers reduce these impacts (Johnson and Browning, 1983; Mincy, 1990; Horrigan and Mincy, 1993).

Given uncertainty about the size of any employment losses, particularly for adults – and about whether "disemployment" is best modeled as a proportionate reduction in annual hours of all low-wage workers or a "lightening-strikes" reduction of annual hours to zero for an unlucky subset – it is natural to ask whether recent changes in the minimum wage can be linked to observable changes in the distribution of family income or the poverty rate. Card and Krueger (1995, Table 9.7) report relatively small and statistically insignificant differences in the change in poverty rates across states with differing impacts of the 1990–1991 minimum wage increase. Neumark and Wascher (1997) relate year-to-year changes in poverty status to changes in minimum wage rates and find that higher minimum wages increase poverty, although again the effect is small and statistically insignificant. Together, these studies underline the difficulty of identifying small impacts in available data.

10. Conclusions and future directions

My reading of the new and old evidence suggests that the shortterm effect of the minimum wage on teenage employment is small. Time-series estimates that centered on an elasticity of -0.10 moved closer to zero in samples that included the 1980s. Studies that relate changes in employment/population ratios by state, as a function of the "impact" of the minimum wage on the state (measured either by the minimum wage relative to the average wage, or the fraction of the workforce whose wage must be raised to comply with a new increase) show much more varied results. A tentative pattern is that studies that control for year as well as state find much smaller minimum-wage impacts than those which do not control separately for year effects, and so treat aggregate shortfalls in teen employment in years of minimum wage increases as minimum wage impacts. It is not clear why year effects matter so much; since all studies of this genre hold constant the adult or all-age employment/population ratio in the state/year cell, "year" effects associated with business cycles should already be taken care of. Given the substantial variability in estimated minimum wage effects that do not control for year separately, I would put more weight on those that do, and this tends to reinforce the message of the time-series studies that the minimum-wage effect is small (and zero is often hard to reject). The recent studies of the fast-food industry (which estimate a quite different response) and studies that follow individual employment transitions also seem broadly consistent with this conclusion.

Even an elasticity of −0.1 would likely seem small to anyone who had not been conditioned by the evolution of the minimum wage literature to expect such a small response. As emphasized in Sections 2 and 4, this is *not* a elasticity of demand for low-wage labor; but a rough correction for the fact that most teenagers are not directly affected by the minimum wage[64] would multiply the minimum wage elasticity by about 5 to get the implied elasticity of demand. As a demand elasticity, less than 0.5 in absolute value seems surprisingly small.

10.1. Accounting for "small" employment effects

Suppose one accepts this reading of the literature. How can we account for the small response?

One possible explanation is that minimum wage coverage is incomplete, and compliance among covered employers may be imperfect. Five-sixths of all non-supervisory workers are covered by the minimum wage, but the proportion of low-wage non-supervisory workers covered is lower. While we do not have a good count, we know that establishments not required to pay the minimum wage tend to be small firms in retail trade and services, who tend to be low-wage employers. But the rough correction described above counts those who report hourly wages below the minimum as not affected by the law, and this probably overstates the importance of the uncovered or non-compliant sector. Moreover, for a relatively small uncovered sector to absorb most of the workers displaced from the covered sector by a minimum wage increase, the decline in the uncovered sector wage would have to be quite large (or demand in the uncovered sector would have to be much more elastic). We have little hard evidence on what happens to uncovered-sector wages, but declines in the uncovered-sector wage of the same order of magnitude as the minimum wage increase seem implausible. Popular press stories extolling the benefits of the minimum wage for uncovered-sector employers are not a prominent feature of the minimum wage debate! More hard evidence on the behavior of wages in the uncovered-sector is needed.

A second possibility is that small effects on teenage employment mask a perverse substitution of more- for less-skilled teenagers (Neumark and Wascher, 1996). The limited evidence of limited spillovers reported in Section 7 is consistent with such substitution; the lack of strong evidence that minimum wages reduce black teenagers' employment more than whites' is less consistent. Closer analysis of wage distribution data may provide some further clues here. Moreover, studies that look at individuals' labor force transitions following minimum wage increases (as in Section 7) have not focused on those earning a bit more than the new minimum wage, whose employment prospects should be helped if such substitution is important.

---

[64] And many of those whose wage is increased when the minimum wage rises are already earning more than the old minimum, and so their wage increase is smaller than the legislated minimum wage hike.

The limited time-series literature on minimum wages and the work weeks of those who are employed suggests that hours per week fall when the minimum wage increases, so the effect on hours worked is more pronounced than the effect on bodies employed. Surprisingly, this line of attack has not been prominent in the recent research, on either side of the debate. In principle, there is more to be learned here from extending the time series than for the traditional employment regressions, since the available time series data on hours of teenagers go back only to the mid-1960s. And since all of the studies that focus on states over time use data from years when the hours data are available, a parallel focus on hours in these studies would lead to no loss of sample at all.[65]

Another possibility is that the labor market is closer to the monopsony model than to the competitive market that nearly all studies assume. This has probably been the most controversial part of the debate stimulated by Card and Krueger's *Myth and Measurement*. Card's (1992b) study of California's increase in its state minimum wage suggested teenage employment grew faster there than in comparison states, although the difference was smaller and not significant when the set of comparison states was extended. The Katz–Krueger and Card–Krueger studies of fast food also reported faster employment growth that was often statistically significant for restaurants at which the minimum wage's impact on wages was larger; but in Card and Krueger's more recent analysis of ES202 data the difference is small and statistically insignificant. Fast-food employers often pay bonuses to employees who recruit friends as new workers, suggesting a less than infinitely elastic supply of labor at the going wage. But such bonuses did not fall faster in New Jersey than in Pennsylvania following the New Jersey minimum-wage hike. Finally, the limited price data suggest that, if anything, prices rise after a minimum wage increase. If employment is expanding, so presumably is output, and prices should fall. Admittedly, the price data are limited, and it would be very useful to know whether, in sectors most affected by the minimum wage, prices rise at roughly the rate predicted by the increases in the minimum wage and the share of minimum-wage workers in the cost structure. Based on the available evidence, the monopsony model will not replace the competitive diagram in the souls of labor economists.

A more sympathetic reading of *Myth and Measurement* would view the monopsony models – including models emphasizing search by workers and employers – as being more appropriate some of the time, and so contributing to rather small effects in the aggregate. Progress in testing this possibility will depend on far better understanding of minimum wages and prices – are price increases considerably smaller than predicted by the competitive model, too? – or perhaps on specifying contexts in which the traditional model is least appropriate.

The possibility that minimum wage increases are offset by changes in other elements of the job package is unlikely to account for relatively small employment elasticities. Fringe

---

[65] Hungerford (1997) uses panel data on states over time to investigate questions about part-time work. He finds that minimum wage increases increase involuntary part-time employment.

benefit cuts that we can observe are not nearly large or widespread enough to make a large difference for employment. And, while I find it hard to believe that employers do not respond to minimum wage increases by raising standards of effort, punctuality, etc., these are likely to lead to *larger* (more negative) effects of minimum wages on numbers or hours employed. Evidence on the scale of such adjustments is sadly lacking; but if they are important, they are likely to intensify rather than resolve puzzle of the small employment elasticities.

A final possibility is that the demand for low-wage labor is just not terribly elastic in the short term. The last four words of the preceding sentence highlight the largest and most important gap in the minimum wage literature. There is simply a stunning absence of credible evidence – indeed, of credible attempts – on the longterm effects. As noted in Section 3, minimum wages are adjusted periodically, so that there is a modest amount of variation in the minimum wage, relative to other wages, over time. But this variation is not permanent, since an increase will be followed by several years of erosion, and then at some point another increase; and it provides few clues about the longterm responses (Mincer, 1984, p. 322). Baker et al. (1999) argue that regressions in the typical time-series study estimate a mixture of short- and longterm effects. In Canada, they find the shortterm responses negligible and the longterm responses substantial.[66]

Changes in coverage have been more nearly permanent. The gradual extension of coverage to ever-smaller retail trade and service firms has not been repealed. Time series studies have been consistently unable to find coverage effects in the minority of studies that try to separate coverage from the level of the minimum wage (Brown, 1996). Looking specifically at retail trade and service employment, given substantial time series both before and after the extensions, may have some ability to detect longterm changes in the structure of these industries due to the minimum wage.[67]

10.2. Effects on the distributions of wages and of incomes

While the effects of the minimum wage on employment remain somewhat controversial, and accounting for the relatively small observed responses remain a puzzle, the effects of the minimum wage on the distribution of wages and incomes seem to be more nearly settled. The minimum wage does have a visible effect on the wage distribution, particularly for teenagers although also for adults in years when it was high relative to average wages. How much of this effect is due to low-wage workers being less represented in the wage distribution (i.e., not employed or working fewer hours) is less clear, but it clear from

---

[66] Baker et al. (1999) argue that Neumark and Wascher's (1992, 1994) findings are consistent with theirs; to my eye, this pattern is weaker when Neumark and Wascher exclude enrollment.

[67] Belman and Wolfson (1997) study a range of low-wage industries including several in retail trade. Evidence that the minimum wage raises wages is weaker than one might expect, although they argue there is little evidence of employment effects in the subset of industries with significant wage effects. Their focus, however, is on shortterm impacts and does not make direct use of changes in coverage of the minimum wage law.

the spike at the minimum wage that a significant fraction of those affected do receive wage increases up to the minimum (at least in the short term).

It is much less clear how the minimum wage affects the distribution of wages measured over several years rather than in one year or at one point in time. Suppose that, at any one point in time, the minimum wage leads to $x\%$ of those affected to not be employed, and $100 - x\%$ to have their wages boosted to w_m. One extreme possibility is that $x\%$ permanently lose their jobs, never to work again. The other extreme is a daily game of musical chairs, so that over any reasonably period the gains and losses are shared equally by those directly affected. My sense is that opponents of the minimum wage tend to see gainers and losers as different people, with those who would otherwise have earned low wages earning no wages; supporters of the minimum wage see a much more nearly equal sharing of gains and losses.[68] There is not, however, much guidance in the literature for resolving this difference.

When one moves from the distribution of wages to the distribution of income, the equalizing potential of the minimum wage is greatly diluted.

10.3. The future of research on the minimum wage

A careful reader has by now noticed that under cover of summarizing what we know about the minimum wage, I have focused instead on areas where our understanding comes up short. Filling in these gaps is not easy; if it were, they would not have remained as gaps. In some but not all cases, use of the CPS micro data public use files – a useful innovation of the most recent round of minimum wage research – provides opportunities for disaggregation and focusing on wage distributions that time series studies which are captive of published CPS tabulations could not address. Progress in filling these gaps will also improve our general knowledge of how labor markets – or at least low-wage labor markets – work, and that may well be the largest payoff to the effort.

References

Abowd, John and Mark Killingsworth (1981), "Structural models of minimum wage effects: analysis of wage and coverage policies", in: Report of the Minimum Wage Study Commission, Vol. V (US Government Printing Office, Washington, DC) pp. 143–170.

Abowd, John, Francis Kramarz, Thomas Lemieux and David Margolis (1997), "Minimum wages and youth employment in France and in the US", Working paper no. 6111 (NBER Cambridge, MA).

Acemoglu, Daron (1997), "Good jobs versus bad jobs: theory and some evidence", Unpublished paper (MIT).

Adie, Douglas (1971), "The lag in effect of minimum wages on teenage unemployment", in: Proceedings of the 24th Annual Meeting (Industrial Relations Research Association, New Orleans, LA) pp. 38–46.

Adie, Douglas (1973), "Teen-age unemployment and real federal minimum wages", Journal of Political Economy 81: 435–441.

---

[68] Freeman (1996, p. 642) argues that high rates of job turnover make sharing more likely in the US, while long unemployment durations make this less likely in Europe.

Ashenfelter, Orley and David Card (1981), "Using longitudinal data to estimate the employment effects of the minimum wage", Discussion paper no. 98 (London School of Economics).

Ashenfelter, Orley and Robert Smith (1979), "Compliance with the Minimum Wage Law", Journal of Political Economy 87: 333–350.

Baker, Michael, Dwayne Benjamin and Shuchita Stanger (1999), "The highs and lows of the minimum wage effect: a time-series cross-section study of the Canadian law", Journal of Labor Economics 17: 318–350.

Barzel, Yoram (1973), "The determinants of daily hours and wages", Quarterly Journal of Economics 87: 220–238.

Bell, Carolyn Shaw (1981), "Minimum wages and personal income", in: Simon Rottenberg, ed., The economics of legal minimum wages (American Enterprise Institute, Washington, DC) pp. 429–458.

Belman, Dale and Paul Wolfson (1997), "A time-series analysis of employment, wages and the minimum wage", Unpublished paper.

Betsey, Charles L. and Bruce H. Dunson (1981), "The federal minimum wage laws and employment of minority youth", American Economic Review, Papers and Proceedings 71: 379–384.

Boschen, John and Herschel I. Grossman (1981), "The federal minimum wage, inflation and employment", Working paper no. 652 (NBER Cambridge, MA).

Brown, Charles (1996), "The old minimum wage literature and its lessons for the new", in: Marvin Kosters, ed., The effects of the minimum wage on employment (AEI Press Washington, DC) pp. 87–98.

Brown, Charles, Curtis Gilroy and Andrew Kohen (1982), "The effect of the minimum wage on employment and unemployment", Journal of Economic Literature 20: 487–528.

Brown, Charles, Curtis Gilroy and Andrew Kohen (1983), "Time-series evidence of the effect of the minimum wage on youth employment and unemployment", Journal of Human Resources 18: 3–31.

Burdett, Kenneth and Dale T. Mortensen (1998), "Wage differentials, employer size and unemployment", International Economic Review 39: 257–273..

Burkhauser, Richard, Kenneth Couch and Andrew Glenn (1996), "Public policies for the working poor: the earned income tax credit versus minimum wage legislation", in: Research in labor economics, Vol. 15 (JAI Press, Greenwich, CT) pp. 65–109.

Burkhauser, Richard, Kenneth Couch and David Wittenberg (1997), "Who minimum wage increases bite: an analysis using monthly data from the SIPP and CPS", Unpublished paper.

Burkhauser, Richard and T. Aldrich Finegan (1989), "The minimum wage and the poor: the end of a relation-ship", Journal of Policy Analysis and Management 8: 53–71.

Burkhauser, Richard, Kenneth Couch and David Wittenburg (1999), "A reassessment of the new economics of the minimum wage literature using monthly data from the CPS", unpublished paper.

Card, David (1992a), "Using regional variation in wages to measure the effects of the federal minimum wage", Industrial and Labor Relations Review 46: 22–37.

Card, David (1992b), "Do minimum wages reduce employment? A case study of California", Industrial and Labor Relations Review 46: 38–54.

Card, David and Alan Krueger (1994), "Minimum wages and employment: a case study of the fast food industry", American Economic Review 84: 772–793.

Card, David and Alan Krueger (1995), Myth and measurement: the new economics of the minimum wage (Princeton University Press, Princeton, NJ).

Card, David and Alan Krueger (1998), "A reanalysis of the effect of the New Jersey minimum wage increase on the fast-food industry with representative payroll data", American Economic Review, in press.

Card, David, Lawrence Katz and Alan Krueger (1994), "Comment on David Neumark and William Wascher, 'Employment effects of minimum and subminimum wages: panel data on state minimum wage laws'", Industrial and Labor Relations Review 47: 487–497.

Converse, Muriel, Richard Coe, Mary Corcoran, Maureen Kallick and James Morgan (1981), "The minimum wage: an employer survey", in: Report of the Minimum Wage Study Commission, Vol. VI (US Government Printing Office, Washington, DC) pp. 241–341.

Cox, James and Ronald Oaxaca (1981), "Effects of minimum wage policy on inflation and on output prices", in:

Report of the Minimum Wage Study Commission, Vol. VI (US Government Printing Office, Washington DC) pp. 171–210.

Currie, Janet and Bruce Fallick (1996), "The minimum wage and the employment of youth", Journal of Human Resources 31: 404–428.

Deere, Donald, Kevin Murphy and Finis Welch (1995), "Employment and the 1990–1991 minimum wage hike", American Economic Review, Papers and Proceedings 85: 232–237.

Deere, Donald, Kevin Murphy and Finis Welch (1996), "Examining the evidence on minimum wages and employment", in: Marvin Kosters, ed., The effects of the minimum wage on employment (AEI Press, Washington, DC) pp. 26–54.

Dickens, Richard, Stephen Machin and Alan Manning (1994), "Estimating the effect of minimum wages on employment from the distribution of wages: a critical view", unpublished paper.

Dickens, Richard, Stephen Machin and Alan Manning (1994), "Estimating the effect of minimum wages on employment from the distribution of wages: a critical view", Unpublished paper.

DiNardo, John, Nicole Fortin and Thomas Lemieux (1996), "Labor market institutions and the distribution of wages, 1973–1992: a semiparametric approach", Econometrica 64: 1001–1044.

Dolado, Juan, Francis Kramarz, Stephen Machin, Alan Manning, David Margolis and Coen Teulings (1997), "The economic impact of minimum wages in Europe", October: 319–372.

Eccles, Mary and Richard Freeman (1982), "What! Another minimum wage study?" American Economic Review 72: 226–232.

Egge, Karl, Andrew Kohen, John Shea and Frederick Zeller (1970), "Changes in the federal minimum wage and the employment of young men, 1966–67", Youth unemployment and minimum wages, Bulletin no 1657 (US Department of Labor, Bureau of Labor Statistics, Washington, DC) pp. 55–67.

Feldstein, Martin (1973), "The economics of the new unemployment", Public Interest 33: 3–42.

Freeman, Richard (1982), "Economic determinants of geographic and individual variation in the labor market position of young persons", in: R. Freeman and D. Wise, eds., The youth labor market problem: its nature, causes and consequences (NBER and University of Chicago Press, Chicago, IL) pp. 115–148.

Freeman, Richard (1996), "The minimum wage as a redistributive tool", Economic Journal 101 (436): 639–644.

Gilroy, Curtis (1981), "A demographic profile of minimum wage workers", in: Report of the Minimum Wage Study Commission, Vol. II (US Government Printing Office, Washington, DC) pp. 153–213.

Gramlich, Edward (1976), "Impact of minimum wages on other wages, employment and family incomes", Brookings Papers on Economic Activity 7: 409–451.

Grossman, Jean Baldwin (1983), "The impact of the minimum wage on other wages", Journal of Human Resources 18: 359–377.

Hamermesh, Daniel S. (1981), "Minimum wages and the demand for labor", Working paper no. 656 (NBER, Cambridge, MA).

Hamermesh, Daniel (1995), "What a wonderful world this would be, in Review symposium on Card and Krueger's 'Myth and measurement: the new economics of the minimum wage'", Industrial and Labor Relations Review 48: 835–838.

Hashimoto, Masanori (1982), "Minimum wage effects on training on the job", American Economic Review 72: 1070–1087.

Hashimoto, Masanori and Jacob Mincer (1970), "Employment and unemployment effects of minimum wages", Working paper (NBER, Cambridge, MA).

Haugen, Steven and Earl Mellor (1990), "Estimating the number of minimum wage workers", Monthly Labor Review 113: 70–74.

Heckman, James and Guilherme Sedlacek (1981), "The impact of the minimum wage on the employment and earnings of workers in South Carolina", in: Report of the Minimum Wage Study Commission, Vol. V (US Government Printing Office, Washington, DC) pp. 225–272.

Horrigan, Michael and Ronald Mincy (1993), "The minimum wage and earnings and income inequality", in: Sheldon Danziger and Peter Gottschalk, eds., Uneven tides: rising inequality in America (Russell Sage Foundation, New York) pp. 251–275.

Hungerford, Thomas (1997), "Does increasing the minimum wage increase the incidence of involuntary part-time work?" Unpublished paper.

Iden, George (1980), "The labor force experience of black youth: a review", Monthly Labor Review 103: 10–16.

Johnson, William and Edgar Browning (1983), "The distributional and efficiency effects of increasing the minimum wage: a simulation", American Economic Review 73: 204–211.

Kaitz, Hyman (1970), "Experience of the past: the national minimum", in: Youth unemployment and minimum wages, Bulletin no. 1657 (US Department of Labor, Bureau of Labor Statistics, Washington, DC) pp. 30–54.

Katz, Lawrence and Alan Krueger (1992), "The effect of the minimum wage on the fast-food industry", Industrial and Labor Relations Review 46: 6–21.

Kelly, Terence (1975), "Youth employment opportunities and the minimum wage: an econometric model of occupational choice", Working paper no. 3608-01 (The Urban Institute, Washington, DC).

Kelly, Terence (1976), "Two policy questions regarding the minimum wage", Working paper no. 3608-05 (The Urban Institute, Washington, DC).

Kennan, John (1995), "The elusive effects of minimum wages", Journal of Economic Literature 33: 1950–1965.

Kim, Taeil and Lowell Taylor (1995), "The employment effect in retail trade of California's 1988 minimum wage increase", Journal of Business and Economic Statistics 13: 75–182.

Klerman, Jacob (1992), "Study 12: employment effect of mandated health benefits", in: US Department of Labor, Pension and Welfare Benefits Administration, Health benefits and the workforce (US Government Printing Office, Washington, DC).

Kohen, Andrew and Curtis Gilroy (1981), "The minimum wage, income distribution and poverty", in: Report of the Minimum Wage Study Commission, Vol. VII (US Government Printing Office, Washington, DC) pp. 1–25.

Koning, Pierre, Geert Ridder and Gerard J. Van den Berg (1995), "Structural and frictional unemployment in an equilibrium search model with heterogeneous agents", Journal of Applied Econometrics 10: S133–S151.

Kosters, Marvin and Finis Welch (1972), "The effects of the minimum wage by race, sex and age", in: Anthony Pascal, ed., Racial discrimination in economic life (DC Heath, Lexington, MA) pp. 103–118.

Lazear, Edward and Frederick Miller (1981), "Minimum wage versus minimum compensation", in: Report of the Minimum Wage Study Commission, Vol. V (US Government Printing Office, Washington, DC) pp. 347–381.

Leighton, Linda and Jacob Mincer (1981), "The effects of the minimum wage on human capital formation", in: Simon Rottenberg, ed., The economics of legal minimum wages (American Enterprise Institute, Washington, DC) pp. 155–173.

Lester, Richard (1960), "Employment effects of minimum wages", Industrial and Labor Relations Review 13: 254–264.

Linneman, Peter (1982), "The economic impacts of minimum wage laws: a new look at an old question", Journal of Political Economy 90: 443–469.

Lovell, Michael (1972), "The minimum wage, teenage unemployment and the business cycle", Western Economic Journal 10: 414–427.

Lovell, Michael (1973), "The minimum wage reconsidered", Western Economic Journal 11: 529–537.

Machin, Stephen and Alan Manning (1994), "The effects of minimum wages on wage dispersion and employment: evidence from UK wages councils", Industrial and Labor Relations Review 47: 319–329.

Machin, Stephen and Alan Manning (1997), "Minimum wages and economic outcomes in Europe", European Economic Review 41: 733–742.

Mattila, J. Peter (1978), "Youth labor markets, enrollments and minimum wages", in: Proceedings of the 31st Annual Meeting (Industrial Relations Research Association, Chicago, IL) pp. 134–140.

Meyer, Robert and David Wise (1983a), "The effects of the minimum wage on employment and earnings of youth", Journal of Labor Economics 1: 66–100.

Meyer, Robert and David Wise (1983b), "Discontinuous distributions and missing persons: the minimum wage and unemployed youth", Econometrica 51: 1677–1698.

Mincer, Jacob (1976), "Unemployment effects of minimum wages", Journal of Political Economy 84 (4, part 2): S87–S104.

Mincer, Jacob (1984), "The economics of wage floors", in: Ronald Ehrenberg, ed., Research in labor economics, Vol. 6 (JAI Press, Greenwich, CT), pp. 311–333.

Mincy, Ronald (1990), "Raising the minimum wage: effects on family poverty", Monthly Labor Review 113: 18–25.

Moore, Thomas (1971), "The effect of minimum wages on teenage unemployment rates", Journal of Political Economy 79: 897–903.

Neumark, David and William Wascher (1992), "Employment effects of minimum and subminimum wages: panel data on state minimum wage laws", Industrial and Labor Relations Review 46: 55–81.

Neumark, David and William Wascher (1994), "Employment effects of minimum and subminimum wages: reply to Card, Katz and Krueger", Industrial and Labor Relations Review 47: 497–512.

Neumark, David and William Wascher (1995), "Minimum wage effects on employment and school enrollment", Journal of Business and Economic Statistics 13: 199–206.

Neumark, David and William Wascher (1996a), "Reconciling the evidence on employment effects of minimum wages – a review of our research findings", in: Marvin Kosters, ed., The effect of the minimum wage on employment (AEI Press, Washington, DC) pp. 55–86.

Neumark, David and William Wascher (1996b), "The effects of minimum wages on teenage employment and enrollment: evidence from matched CPS surveys", in: Research in labor economics, Vol. 15 (JAI Press, Greenwich, CT) pp. 25–63.

Neumark, David and William Wascher (1997), "Do minimum wages fight poverty?" Working paper no. 6127 (NBER, Cambridge, MA).

Neumark, David and William Wascher (1998), "The New Jersey-Pennsylvania minimum wage experiment: a re-evaluation using payroll records", American Economic Review, in press.

Oi, Walter (1997), "The consequences of minimum wage legislation", Unpublished paper.

Peterson, John (1957), "Employment effects of minimum wages, 1938–1950", Journal of Political Economy 65: 412–430.

Peterson, John M. (1981), Minimum wages: measures and industry effects (AEI Press, Washington, DC).

Pettengill, John (1981), "The long-run impact of a minimum wage on employment and the wage structure", Report of the Minimum Wage Study Commission, Vol. VI (US Government Printing Office, Washington, DC) pp. 63–104.

Pettengill, John (1984), "Minimum wage laws with a continuum of worker qualities", Working paper no. E-84-12-03 (Virginia Polytechnic Institute and State University).

Ragan, James F. (1977), "Minimum wages and the youth labor market", Review of Economics and Statistics 59: 129–136.

Ragan, James (1981), "The effect of a legal minimum wage on pay and employment of teenage students and nonstudents", in: Simon Rottenberg, ed., The economics of legal minimum wages (American Enterprise Institute, Washington, DC) pp. 11–41.

Rebitzer, James and Lowell Taylor (1995), "The consequences of minimum wage laws: some new theoretical ideas", Journal of Public Economics 56: 245–255.

Smith, Ralph and Bruce Vavrichek (1987), "The minimum wage: its relation to incomes and poverty", Monthly Labor Review 110: 24–30.

Smith, Ralph and Bruce Vavrichek (1992), "The wage mobility of minimum wage workers", Industrial and Labor Relations Review 46: 82–88.

Solon, Gary (1990), "The minimum wage and teenage employment: a reanalysis with attention to serial correlation and seasonality", Journal of Human Resources 20: 292–297.

Stafford, Frank (1986), "Forestalling the demise of empirical economics: the role of microdata in labor economics research", in: Orley Ashenfelter and Richard Layard, eds., Handbook of labor economics, Vol. 1 (North Holland, Amsterdam).

Stigler, George (1946), "The economics of minimum wage legislation", American Economic Review 36: 358–365.

Todaro, Michael (1969), "A model of labor migration and urban unemployment in less developed countries", American Economic Review 59: 138–148.

US Census Bureau (various years), Statistical abstract of the United States (US Government Printing Office, Washington, DC).

US Department of Labor, Employment and Standards Administration (1975), Minimum wage and maximum hours under the Fair Labor Standards Act – 1975 (US Government Printing Office, Washington DC).

Wachter, Michael and Choongsoo Kim (1982), "Time series changes in youth joblessness", in: R. Freeman and D. Wise, eds., The youth labor market problem: its nature, causes and consequences (NBER and University of Chicago Press, Chicago, IL) pp. 155–185.

Welch, Finis (1976), "Minimum wage legislation in the United States", in: O. Ashenfelter and J. Blum, eds., Evaluating the labor market effects of social programs (Princeton University Press, Princeton, NJ) pp. 1–38.

Welch, Finis (1995), "Comment by Finis Welch, in Review symposium on Card and Krueger's 'Myth and measurement: the new economics of the minimum wage'", Industrial and Labor Relations Review 48: 842–848.

Welch, Finis and James Cunningham (1978), "Effects of minimum wages on the level and age composition of youth employment", Review of Economics and Statistics 60: 140–145.

Wellington, Alison (1991), "Effects of the minimum wage on the employment status of youths", Journal of Human Resources 26: 27–46.

Wessels, Walter (1980) Minimum wages, fringe benefits and working conditions (American Enterprise Institute, Washington, DC).

Wolfson, Paul (1998), "A fresh look at the time series evidence on the minimum wage and teenage employment: seasonality and unit roots", Unpublished paper.

Chapter 33

FIRM SIZE AND WAGES

WALTER Y. OI

Department of Economics, University of Rochester

TODD L. IDSON

Department of Economics, Columbia University

Contents

Handbook of Labor Economics, Volume 3, Edited by O. Ashenfelter and D. Card
© 1999 Elsevier Science B.V.

Abstract

Jobs differ along many dimensions including firm size. The wage gap due to firm size of 35% is comparable to the gender wage gap of 36% for men over women and greater than the wage gap of 14% for whites over black employees. The size-wage premium is larger for men and varies across industries. It is larger in the US than in other industrialized countries. Large firms demand a higher quality of labor defined by such observable characteristics as education, job tenure, and a higher fraction of full-time workers. Part 3 examines three behavioral explanations. (1) Productive employees are matched with able entrepreneurs to minimize the sum of wages and monitoring costs. (2) Big firms pay efficiency wages to deter shirking. (3) Big firms adopt a discretionary wage policy to share rents, or in Slichter's words, "Wages over a considerable range reflect managerial discretion. When management can easily afford to pay high wages, they tend to do so." We advance a productivity hypothesis. A large organization sets a higher performance standard that raises labor productivity but has to be supported by a compensating wage difference. In the service industries, the pace of work depends on the customer arrival rate. The economies of massed reserves generates a positive wage-size profile. The capital/labor ratio is higher in bigger firms which also are early in adopting new technologies. Both forces raise the demand for skilled labor where skill and productivity are often unobservable traits. Production organized around teams calls for conformance to common work rules which result in paying rents to infra-marginal team members. The odds of survival are higher for big firms which enable them to "produce" more durable employees who are more productive because they get more training. Firm size is a function of external market forces, technology, managerial decisions, and luck. The surplus of revenues over labor costs per employee is positively related to firm size for three reasons, lower prices for non-labor inputs, possibly greater market power, or larger overhead costs to amortize the sunk costs for capital and firm -specific work force. Rent sharing cannot be dismissed as an explanation for the wage-size premium. Taxation and regulation can also affect the size distribution of firms. The organization of work and the selection of employees (whose productive traits are not always observable) are responsible for the positive relation between wages and employer size.

JEL codes: J3

> We started out to find the relation of the concentration of industry to the changing status of the laborer, and we proposed to investigate that relation from the four points of view of (1) the rate of wages, (2) the amount of employment, (3) the continuity of employment, and (4) the length of the working day. Our investigation has yielded the definite result that, as the size of the establishment increases, the condition of the laborer improves in all directions – his wages rise, he is employed a greater number of days in a year, his employment varies less from month to month, and his hours of labor, per day, decrease. (Moore, 1911, p. 153)

A labor market in which wages depend on employer size means that jobs are different. A job is described by a vector of variables including the rate of pay, the length of the workweek, the stability of employment, health and injury risks, the nature of the tasks, opportunities for promotion, and the characteristics of the workplace. Jobs can be classified by occupation, industry, ownership (public versus private), geographic location, or employer size. This chapter is concerned with the size dimension.

Large firms with more than 500 employees are few in number, comprising less than one-third of 1% of all firms but providing jobs for nearly half of all employed persons. Because firm sizes are related to industrial affiliation, the sectoral shifts over the last half century have affected the size distribution. Differences in the output mix, production technologies, and government regulations account for much of the differences in the size distribution of firms across countries. The wage differential between small and large establishments which Moore discovered is substantial and pervasive. The wage gap due to firm size is approximately equal to the gender wage gap and larger than that associated with unionism or race. The magnitude of the size–wage gap is investigated in Section 2. The literature surveyed by Brown and Medoff (1989), Groshen (1991), and Troske (1994) offers several explanations for a positive relation between wages and employer size which we call the wage–size profile. The explanations that appeal to monitoring costs, efficiency wages to deter shirking, and rent-sharing are critically evaluated in Section 3.

In Section 4, the chapter advances the elements of a productivity hypothesis. The mandated effort levels or performance standards are usually unobservable aspects of the job package. Greater effort can raise labor productivity, but to elicit it, an employer will have to pay a higher wage. There are increasing returns to establishment and firm size due to technical economies as well as agglomeration effects. The exploitation of these economies is facilitated by organizing work around teams. Wage premiums have to be paid to attract workers who will comply with the administrative rules of large organizations. The volume production of standardized goods and services is evidently more economically achieved by demanding more durable capital goods as well as durable employees who are "produced" by investments in human capital. Training raises labor productivity, and sharing the returns to training generates the upward sloping wage–size profile. Ehrenberg and Smith (1997, p. 409) identify the relationship of wages to employer size as one of three puzzles looking for a solution. The hypotheses and evidence reviewed in this chapter will bring us a little closer to a satisfactory explanation.

1. A diversity of jobs

A wage rate is not the price of labor. Adam Smith observed that competition in the labor market does not tend to an equality of wages but rather to an equality of the net advantages of employment. Marshall listed four peculiarities that distinguish labor from other factors of production: (1) labor services were perishable; (2) conditions at the workplace mattered; (3) labor was at a disadvantage in bargaining;[1] (4) it takes time to acquire skills.

---

[1] Marshall (1920, p. 559) wrote, "It is, however, certain that manual labor as a class are at a disadvantage in bargaining... and the disadvantage is likely to be cumulative in its effect." It not only lowered his current wage, but it also reduced his efficiency in future periods.

The labor market is not a single exchange. It is a multiplicity of "markets" in which a job is defined by a worker-firm attachment. Jobs differ not only in the tasks that an employee must perform, but also in the obligations of an employer to her employees. A new entrant often takes a starter job that introduces him to the world of work, teaches him to be punctual, presentable, and responsive to instructions. It also provides him with a track record. A second type can be called transitional filler jobs that yield a cash flow in return for labor time. The people who take these jobs rarely intend to stay for long. Their employers know this and design these jobs anticipating high turnover rates. A majority of all jobs are permanent employment relations supported by implicit or explicit contracts. They correspond to what Hall (1982) called "lifetime jobs" that last for 15 or more years. Some are located in small firms, but most of the lifetime jobs are in units where work is organized around teams.

Farber (1997) identified four dimensions that differentiated jobs – task, employer, location, and individual. This grid defines too many jobs for analytic or empirical research. For his empirical analysis, Farber turned to three dimensions: (a) the wage rate; (b) full- or part-time work; and (c) presence or absence of employer provided health insurance. Farber cited a report prepared by the Council of Economic Advisors dated April 23, 1996 in which jobs were classified by 45 occupations and 22 major industries. The mean wage for each occupation/industry cell was assigned to all employees in that O/I cell. A "good" job was defined as a high-wage job paying a wage above the nation-wide average. Using this criterion, a majority of the new jobs created between February 1994 and February 1996 were "good" jobs located in a high wage labor market defined by industry and occupation.

What determines the wage of a stacker working in a sawmill? The wage rate is not the price paid by the employer, nor is it the compensation received by the employee. It is, however, a useful analytic concept to describe the equilibrium in a labor market. The workers in the same "market" are presumably close substitutes for one another. Occupation hopefully controls for training and experience. Is industrial affiliation the proxy for working conditions? In practice, the boundaries of a "market" are fuzzy. Stigler and Sherwin (1985) examined the co-movements of prices over time to define a "market". Gasoline Service Stations in Denver and Omaha are placed in the same market if prices in the two cities move together. Labor economists usually accept geographic proximity to define a local labor market. They tacitly assume that the wages of lawyers and of nurses are determined in different markets. High and low wage labor markets are evidently differentiated by the skills of the workers. Doeringer and Piore (1971) distinguished between internal and secondary labor markets based on the characteristics of the employer. The size of the employer measured by assets, sales, or employment can serve as a variable differentiating related labor markets. Jobs in large firms pay higher wages and would thus be classified as "good jobs". What is a good job for one person might not be for another. The rank ordering of jobs has to account for varying preferences for other dimensions of a job package such as the disutility of work, the effort bargain, or compliance with strict orders. Although size is not a sufficient statistic to identify distinct "labor markets", the data reveal significant differences in the nature of employment relations related to employer size. The object of this chapter is to examine these differences to explain the positive relation between firm size and wages.

2. The firm in product and labor markets

A firm assembles resources and organizes production. But what is a firm? In a high information and low transaction cost world, everyone ought to have access to the same technologies and equal opportunities to bid for inputs. Firms in a given industry ought to be alike and achieve the same optimum size and structure. This implication is clearly refuted by the data which is briefly reviewed in Section 2.1. Further, the wages and working conditions of employees are systematically related to employer size. The matching of more able workers with larger employers is examined in Sections 2.3 and 2.4. Worker characteristics and sorting, however, can explain only a part of the relation.

2.1. The size distribution of firms and establishments

At the outset, two issues have to be addressed. First, what is the appropriate unit of analysis, the firm or establishment? Theory is of little help, and the data indicate that both matter. Second, how do we measure size, by assets, sales (a proxy for output), or employment? The capital/labor, K/L, ratio varies widely across industries because of differences in the technology of production. Within each industry, the K/L ratio is higher for larger firms. As a consequence, the four or eight firm concentration ratio based on assets is always larger than that based on sales or employment. Comparisons across industries or over time are complicated when one uses a sales measure of size. Variations in labor productivity over time as well as across firms and industries make employment an imperfect measure of size, but given its ready availability, we shall adopt this measure.

In 1992, there were over 5 million firms in the private sector of the US economy. Most firms are very small; 644 thousand had no employees, and 88.2% of those with workers had fewer than 20 employees. The large firms attain their size by controlling several establishments or plants. The big manufacturing companies owned an average of 10.1 establishments, while the large retail trade firms controlled an average of 111.1 establishments. Across all industries, large firms provided nearly half, 47.0%, of the 92.8 million private sector jobs. The size distributions of firms F, establishments or plants E, and employment N in 1992 and 1982 are shown in Table 1 for all industries, Manufacturing, and Retail Trade.[2] The share of industry-wide employment residing in big firms varied from lows of 11.8% in Agriculture and 11.4% in Construction to highs of 64.5% in Transportation/Communications/Utilities and 61.8% in Manufacturing; see Table 2. The growth of the economy in the postwar years was accompanied by a rightward shift in the

---

[2] These data come from the Enterprise Statistics assembled by the Census Bureau. They may differ from the establishment surveys conducted by the Bureau of Labor Statistics. We thank Elaine Manual for providing us with these statistics.

size distributions of firms and plants, at least through 1970. The shift in the industrial structure of the economy away from goods towards services pushes the size distribution toward the left. The share of total employment located in the Distributive Trades and Personal Services rose from 33.3% in 1957 to 49.8% in 1992.

Employment, by sector

	1957	1979	1992
Employment (000)	52853	89823	108437
1. Manufacturing (%)	32.49	23.42	16.77
2. Wholesale Trade (%)	5.75	5.81	5.52
3. Retail Trade (%)	14.85	16.67	17.65
4. Personal Services (%)	12.69	19.05	26.65
5. Government (%)	14.41	17.75	17.13

In addition to these sectoral shifts, the size distribution is affected by market regulations and technology. Loveman and Sengenberger (1991) reported that bread is mass produced in Norway and Sweden, but there are over 30,000 bread bakeries in Germany. The latter is attributed in part to a World War I regulation that prohibited baking bread at night. The percentage of total employment in large firms was 46% in Germany and 17% in Italy. Davis and Henrekson (1997) estimated that Sweden led the list of OECD countries with 60.4% of all employees in firms with 500 or more workers. Part of the concentration in Sweden is due to the dominance of the public sector. Health care and social services are provided by public sector employees whose pay is determined by some process other than a competitive labor market. Loveman and Sengenberger (1991) observed that there is a re-emergence of small and medium sized firms. The time series data for the OECD countries exhibit a V-shaped pattern for the share of employment in small enterprises with fewer than a hundred employees; the trough occurs around 1969–1970. The reasons for the recent growth in the small firm share include among others, privatization and technological advances which raised the efficiency of small units. Data for the US are shown below for All Industries, Manufacturing, and Retail Trade.[3]

Percentage of total employment in small firms

Year	All Industries	Manufacturing	Retail Trade
1977	40.13	16.17	53.56
1982	45.51	17.56	51.98
1987	42.46	18.44	45.53
1992	38.66	22.08	43.53

[3] The US data come from the Enterprise Statistics where a small firm is one with less than 100 employees. Data for the OECD countries are reported in Table 3 of Loveman and Sengenberger (1991, pp. 7–8), while the size distribution for manufacturing establishments is reported in their Table 4.

Table 1

Percentage distribution by size and industry, 1992 and 1982[a]

Industry and year	Number	Percent in firms with an employment of:			
		1–19	20–99	100–499	500+
A. 1992 All Industries					
Firms F	4451	88.26	9.87	1.55	0.32
Plants E	5673	70.64	11.19	5.00	13.17
Employees N	92826	20.22	18.44	14.34	47.00
Annual Pay W	24249	20156	21551	22407	27632
M. 1992 Manufacturing					
Firms F	300	71.48	21.58	5.42	1.53
Plants E	359	51.79	19.38	7.90	12.92
Employees N	18167	7.44	14.64	16.16	61.76
Annual Pay W	21916	24992	25998	34680	30909
RT. 1992 Retail Trade					
Firms F	996	86.83	11.58	1.30	0.30
Plants E	1442	59.90	11.95	5.81	22.34
Employees N	19681	22.53	21.00	10.48	45.99
Annual Pay W	11964	17900	24549	23821	18817
A. 1982 All Industries					
Firms F	3997	90.74	8.01	1.06	0.18
Plants E	55355	79.96	8.25	3.01	8.72
Employees N	61462	25.69	19.82	13.08	41.41
Annual Pay W	10837	12001	13749	18522	14631
M. 1982 Manufacturing					
Firms F	278	71.35	22.35	5.06	1.24
Plants E	483	41.80	14.70	7.27	36.24
Employees N	22008	5.70	11.86	12.74	69.69
Annual Pay W	14370	15599	16277	22032	20099
RT. 1982 Retail Trade					
Firms F	947	89.08	9.74	1.04	0.13
Plants E	1289	68.33	11.54	4.82	15.31
Employees N	14845	28.87	23.11	9.68	38.34
Annual Pay W	7849	8767	8886	10400	9140

[a] Source: Enterprise Statistics, Census Bureau.

The upward trend in the small firm share is only observed in Manufacturing where the computer and other technical advances apparently have reduced the optimum firm size where size is measured by employment. Firm size is surely endogenous. Size depends on

Table 2
Employment and annual payroll by major industry, 1992[a]

| | In firms with an employment of: | | | |
	Total	1–19	500+	Ratio[b]
A. Employment (000)				
0. Total Private	92826	18773	43625	47.0
1. Agriculture	594	332	70	11.8
2. Mining	650	82	393	60.4
3. Construction	4502	2041	515	11.4
4. Manufacturing	18167	1351	11220	61.8
5. Trans/Communication	5521	662	3564	64.5
6. Wholesale Trade	6095	1548	2030	33.3
7. Retail Trade	19681	4435	9052	46.0
8. FIRE	6904	1203	3941	57.1
9. Services	30666	7082	12840	41.9
B. Annual payroll per employee (dollars)				
0. Total Private	24249	21297	27632	1.297
1. Agriculture	16285	16787	19390	1.155
2. Mining	39179	25901	45545	1.758
3. Construction	26567	23215	35202	1.516
4. Manufacturing	30909	23187	34680	1.496
5. Trans/Communication	31648	20443	36592	1.790
6. Wholesale Trade	31085	27449	37553	1.368
7. Retail Trade	12995	12218	13442	1.100
8. FIRE	31742	25359	35460	1.398
9. Services	22670	24208	24213	1.000

[a] Source: Enterprise Statistics, US Bureau of the Census.

[b] Ratio for (A), employment, represents percentage of industry employment located in firms with 500 or more employees. Ratio for (B), annual payroll, is the ratio of pay in big firms over pay in small firms.

the market prices for inputs and the technologies chosen by the firm. This is not the place to discuss the reasons why some firms shrink and die, while others reach gigantic size. One thing is clear, the large firms in an industry evidently occupy a different place in product and input markets than their smaller competitors.

2.2. Wages in relation to firm and establishment size

Wages are higher in larger firms. This empirical regularity was discovered by Moore (1911) who conducted a statistical study. He wanted to obtain wage data that controlled for the sex and age of the worker as well as the location of the worksite – geographic region, city versus country, and industry; see Moore (1911, p. 140). He settled for data on the daily wages of Italian working women in textile mills classified by age and establishment size. His data on daily wages are shown in Table 3. Wages at the largest plants with

Table 3
Mean daily wages and mean ages of Italian women[a]

Age group	In establishments with an employment of:			
	<20	20–99	100–499	500+
A. Daily wages in lire				
15–20	0.87	0.93	1.04	1.24
20–35	1.09	1.10	1.21	1.50
35–55	1.05	1.12	1.17	1.48
>55	0.92	0.98	0.98	1.16
Mean wage	1.002	1.030	1.130	1.385
B. Mean ages				
15–20	17.32	17.30	17.30	17.31
20–35	25.83	25.33	25.22	25.34
35–55	44.43	44.72	44.89	43.63
>55	58.20	57.53	57.58	57.49
All ages	28.23	25.63	25.14	24.32
Employment N	2166	32523	93566	23058
Establishments E	239	804	619	37
Average size N/E	9.06	40.45	151.16	623.19
C. Regression coefficients				
Original		0.039	0.141	0.392
Log		0.39	0.134	0.332

[a] Source: Tables 1, 2, 4, and 5 in Moore (1911).

500 or more employees were some 38.5% above what employees received at the smallest plants. The mean wages shown in the fifth line describe a concave relationship; the arc elasticities were 0.022, 0.081, and 0.167 across the four size categories. It is also evident that wages are related to mean age. We estimated a wage equation including indicator variables for plant size and a quadratic in experience defined as $X = (\text{Age} - 16)$.[4] The addition of X and X^2 not only improves the goodness of fit (the R^2 climbs from 0.59 to 0.97), but also increases the slope of the wage–size profile. Given work experience, workers in the largest plants earned 39.2% more than their peers in small textile mills. Are workers at large plants on a higher plane of well-being than others employed at small plants? His statistical investigations led Moore to the following conclusion (p. 163), "…as

---

[4] The wage equation was, $W_{ij} = SB + c_1 X_{ij} + c_2 X_{ij}^2 + e_{ij}$, where W_{ij} is the mean daily wage in the ith age group and the jth plant size category, S is a vector of size dummy variables, and X_{ij} is the mean years of experience of workers shown in (B). The parameters were estimated by weighted least squares using the employment weights reported in Appendix Table 3 of Moore (1911, p. 166). The coefficients of the size dummies are shown in Table 3. The quadratic in experience was for the original values, $W = 0.0288X - 0.000738X^2$. For the log equation, we had $\ln W = 0.0254X - 0.000650X^2$.

the size of the establishment increases, the condition of the laborer improves in all directions – his wages rise, he is employed a greater number of days in a year, his employment varies less from month to month, and his hours of labor, per day, decrease."

The relations discovered by Moore were not unique to Italian textile mills. They prevail in nearly every labor market. Lester (1967) reported that average hourly earnings in large establishments were 20–25% above the average hourly earnings in small establishments belonging to the same industry. Mellow (1982) analyzed the May 1979 CPS data. Hourly earnings were positively related to both firm and establishment size even after controlling for worker characteristics and industrial affiliation. Brown et al. (1990, p. 30) reported patterns from the May 1983 CPS. Hourly wages in firms with 500 or more workers were 35% above wages in firms with less than 25 employees. The size–wage premium of 35% was of similar magnitude to the 36% wage gap between men and women, and exceeded the wage gap of 29% for union over non-union workers and 14% for white over black employees.

The bivariate associations between firm size and selected variables taken from the May 1993 CPS are shown in Table 4. Hourly wages of men, defined as usual weekly earnings

Table 4
Wages and related variables by firm size and sex, 1993[a]

Variable	F1 1–24	F2 25–99	F3 100–499	F4 500–999	F5 1000+	Ratio[b]
Females						
Sample size	2120	1087	1081	442	3167	
Wage	8.203	9.052	10.114	10.525	10.683	1.302
Tenure	5.664	6.093	6.843	7.212	8.128	1.435
Education	12.698	12.807	13.109	13.239	13.137	1.035
White	91.698	88.960	88.714	87.330	85.475	0.932
Married	58.726	56.486	56.152	56.335	54.500	0.928
Part-time	39.906	24.103	21.462	19.231	23.745	595
Union[c]	1.063	4.019	7.034	11.848	13.583	12.778
Pension[d]	14.554	28.044	48.293	50.856	61.544	4.229
Males						
Sample size	2144	1302	1189	451	3698	
Wage	10.289	12.381	13.459	13.528	14.951	1.452
Tenure	6.338	7.030	8.089	9.125	11.246	1.774
Education	12.515	12.786	13.193	13.181	13.494	1.078
White	90.951	90.860	91.926	89.135	88.886	0.977
Married	55.364	61.290	63.751	66.962	66.820	1.207
Part-time	18.470	8.372	7.653	7.539	9.708	0.536
Union	5.005	10.925	13.832	18.307	24.784	4.952
Pension	12.748	38.591	56.495	61.575	73.604	5.774

[a] Source: April 1993 Current Population Survey
[b] Ratio = F5/F1.
[c] Union = 1 if either a union member or covered by a union contract.
[d] Pension = 1 if covered by a pension or retirement plan.

Table 5
Hourly wages by sex and firm size[a]

Year and firm size	Male	Female	Both	Ratio[b]
A. 1983 Wages				
F1 = 1–24	6.97	5.26	6.178	0.755
F2 = 25–99	8.54	5.95	7.384	0.697
F3 = 100–499	9.57	6.51	8.132	0.680
F4 = 500–999	9.79	6.76	8.272	0.691
F5 = 1000+	11.34	7.28	9.643	0.642
B. 1979 Wages				
F1 = 1–24	5.646	4.052	4.880	0.718
F2 = 25–99	6.689	4.239	5.643	0.634
F3 = 100–499	7.427	4.689	6.208	0.631
F4 = 500–999	7.82	4.714	6.363	0.603
F5 = 1000+	8.452	5.235	7.293	0.619
C. Percent of employment in large firms				
1993	47.2	45.7	46.5	
1983	41.2	38.1	39.8	
1979	45.9	37.4	42.3	
D. Wages in small firms				
1993	11.690	8.897	10.348	0.761
1983	7.901	5.693	6.884	0.721
1979	6.350	4.289	5.405	0.675
E. Wages in large firms				
1993	14.795	10.662	12.872	0.721
1983	11.166	7.202	9.466	0.645
1979	8.381	5.158	7.183	0.615
F. Wage ratio, large/small				
1993	1.266	1.198	1.244	
1983	1.413	1.265	1.375	
1979	1.321	1.203	1.329	

[a] Source: Tabulated from CPS tapes.
[b] Gender wage ratio of female/male wages.

divided by usual weekly hours, rise from \$10.29 in small firms with 1–24 employees, size category F1, to \$14.95 in size category F5, 1000 or more employees. The wage ratio was 1.453 compared to a ratio for female workers of 1.302. Fringes increase even faster – pension coverage climbs from 12.75 for men in small firms to 73.60% in F5. Hourly compensation including fringes is more strongly related to size than wages alone, see Brown and Medoff (1989, p. 1036). The mean duration of job tenure of those on the payroll is longer in larger firms which is consistent with a model in which larger employers

Table 6
Average hourly earnings by industry and sex (by firm size, May 1983 CPS)[a]

Industry and sex	In firms with an employment of			Ratio[b]
	Total	1–24	1000+	
A. Males, 1983				
1. Agriculture	4.677	4.388	6.436	1.467
2. Mining	12.369	8.316	13.487	1.622
3. Construction	9.380	7.995	13.679	1.711
4. Manufacturing	10.300	7.344	11.705	1.594
5. Trans/Communication	11.541	7.761	13.096	1.687
6. Trade	7.433	6.253	8.438	1.349
7. Finance	11.696	8.437	12.588	1.492
8. Services	8.677	7.526	10.020	1.331
B. Females, 1983				
1. Agriculture	4.696	4.556	5.013	1.100
2. Mining	9.606	9.917	9.706	.979
3. Construction	6.687	6.344	8.262	1.302
4. Manufacturing	6.880	6.032	7.714	1.279
5. Trans/Communication	8.697	5.722	9.787	1.710
6. Trade	4.858	4.403	5.269	1.197
7. Finance	6.902	6.193	7.538	1.217
8. Services	6.656	5.955	7.759	1.303

[a] Source: Tabulated from the May 1983 Current Population Survey.
[b] Ratio = wages in firm size 1000 + /firm size 1–24.

provide more specific training. Employees in larger firms are slightly older and have more years of schooling. The fraction on part-time schedules is inversely related to size falling from 39.9 to 23.7% for females.

Table 5(A,B) describes the wage–size profiles based on the May CPS data for 1983 and 1979. The shape of the wage–size profile obviously differs by gender and has shifted over time. The wage ratio for males in the largest and smallest size categories {F5 over F1} was 1.627 in 1983 and 1.497 in 1979. The corresponding figures for females were 1.384 and 1.292. The wage–size premium is clearly larger for males. To the extent that small employers employ less skilled workers and the dispersion of wages expands in a downturn, it is not surprising to find a larger size–wage gap in 1983, a recession year. The last column presents the gender wage ratio, $G = (W_f/W_m)$ for each size group. Notice that the gender wage gap G declines with firm size; the relative wages of females are higher in small firms.

In the last four panels of Table 5, workers are divided into two size groups, <500 versus 500+ employees. In small firms with <500 workers, the gender wage ratio climbed from 0.675 in 1979 to 0.761 in 1993; the corresponding rise in large firms, panel E, was 0.615 to 0.721. Panel F presents the size–wage ratio, $S = (W_{F5}/W_{F1})$. For both sexes, this ratio fell from 1.329 in 1979 to 1.244 in 1993.

Table 6 reveals significant industry differences. The wage—size premium in Manufacturing, described by a wage ratio was, for male workers, $(w_L/w_S) = 11.705/7.344 = 1.594$. Notice that the size–wage premiums for female employees are smaller even within the same industry. A comparison of Tables 2 and 6 which come from different surveys reveals that there is a strong correspondence in the size–wage premiums across industries. Being employed by a large firm in Transportation/Communications/Utilities or in Manufacturing is associated with a larger size–wage premium than the size premium in Retail Trade or Services. Finance, Real Estate, and Insurance falls in between leaning closer to Manufacturing.

The relation of wages to firm size is ubiquitous. Idson and Ishii (1992) assembled data for Japan and the United States for 1988 (see Table 7). The wage ratio (w_L/w_S) describing the relative premium in large over small employers is seen to be considerably larger in Japan, in the neighborhood of 1.68 compared to around 1.30 in the United States. Loveman and Sengenberger (1991, pp. 18–19) assembled wage data for several advanced countries classified by employer size. We reproduce their wage indexes for small and

Table 7
Wages, tenure, and education by sex, 1988 (by firm size for Japan and the US)[a]

| | In firms with employment of: | | | |
	10–99	100–999	1000+	Ratio[b]
Japan, women				
Wages[c]	925.80	1105.04	1553.98	1.679
Tenure	6.31	6.367	7.183	1.137
Education	11.709	12.015	12.421	1.061
US women				
Wages	7.384	8.604	9.322	1.263
Tenure	3.971	5.367	6.935	1.746
Education	12.970	13.093	13.145	1.014
Japan, men				
Wages	1493.25	1866.54	2520.73	1.688
Tenure	8.958	11.460	15.321	1.710
Education	11.830	12.746	12.898	1.090
US men				
Wages	9.929	11.638	13.038	1.313
Tenure	4.890	6.587	9.711	1.986
Education	12.781	13.255	13.460	1.053

[a] Source: Idson and Ishii (1992, p. 533).
[b] Ratio = wages in firm size 1000+/firm size 10–99.
[c] Wages are average hourly earnings in 1988; in yen for Japan and dollars for the US.

medium sized firms as a percentage of the wages in large firms with 500 or more employees.

Wage indexes by country and firm size

Country	Year	Small 10–99	Medium 100–499
France	1978	83	86
Germany	1978	90	92
Italy	1978	85	93
Japan	1982	77	83
United States	1983	53	74

The flatter profiles in Germany and France can partially be explained by stronger trade unions and training. The concave pattern observed in the United States and Japan are not replicated in the European economies. Studies of the labor markets in Peru (Schaffner, 1996), Zimbabwe (Velenchik, 1996), and Guatemala (Funkhauser, 1997) reveal an even stronger concavity than that exhibited by the US data.

Are wages related to both firm and establishment sizes? Hourly wages for male employees classified by firm and plant size are shown in Table 8. Holding plant size constant at P1, wages rose from \$7.119 to \$9.849 from the smallest F1 to largest F5 firms, a 38.3 F-size wage premium. In the largest F5 firms, the wage gain from small to big plants was 28.3%. Separate tabulations were calculated for employees in Manufacturing and in Trade. The wage ratio across firm sizes, (W_{F5}/W_{F1}) was 1.588 in Manufacturing and 1.221 in Trade. Within the Trade sector, small plants in big firms, (P1-F5 cell) are located in Eating & Drinking Places, while big plants in big firms (P5-F5 cell) are located in Department Stores and Wholesale Trade. Brown and Medoff (1989) found that the partial effect of establishment size on wages was stronger than that of firm size.[5] The factors responsible for the wage–size profiles are clearly not the same across industries and gender.

The wage–size relation extends across the skill spectrum. A janitor and a lathe operator earn higher wages if they are working for a large rather than a small sawmill. Doms et al. (1997) report that across all skill levels, the elasticity of the hourly wage with respect to establishment size was around +0.06. A tenfold increase in firm size is accompanied by a 16% higher hourly wage. This elasticity appears to be smaller for workers at higher skill levels. However, at the top of the skill hierarchy, we find a reversal of this pattern. The salary of the Chief Executive Officer Y is related to size measured by annual sales S via an exponential relation of the form, $Y = AS^{\eta}$. An elasticity of $\eta = +0.25$ means that a

---

[5] Consider the regression, $W = b_0 + b_1 F + b_2 P +$ error, where all variables, wages W, firm size F, and plant size P are in logs. Data from the May 1983 CPS showed that for females, the plant size effect is stronger than the firm size effect. Brown and Medoff combined the sexes and included a female dummy variable. The relative strengths of the two size measures fluctuates by gender and by full- versus part-time status.

Table 8
Average hourly earnings by firm and plant size (male employees by industry, May 1983 CPS)

Industry/plant size[a]	F1	F2	F3	F4	F5
All industries					
P1	7.119	8.686	9.297	9.617	9.849
P2		8.631	10.162	9.326	10.444
P3			9.616	10.161	11.085
P4				9.424	12.637
P5					12.637
Manufacturing					
P1	7.344	8.034	7.63	10.412	11.664
P2		8.425	9.44	10.398	10.8
P3			8.898	9.572	10.528
P4				9.618	11.322
P5					12.61
Trade					
P1	6.253	6.529	9.638	7.129	7.634
P2		7.636	8.152	7.046	8.19
P3			8.778	9.884	8.526
P4				7.839	11.774
P5					11.396

[a] The five firm and plant size categories correspond to employments of 1–24, 25–99, 100–499, 500–999, and 1000+ employees.

tenfold increase in firm size leads to a 78% increase in the salary of the CEO, considerably more than the 16% size–wage premium enjoyed by hourly employees.[6] We shall focus on the relation of size to the pay of wage and salaried employees and leave the analysis of executive compensation to others.

2.3. Worker characteristics and the skill mix of the workforce

Workers are different, and the more able command higher wages. Are the wages at larger firms a consequence of the fact that larger employers simply demand more able employees? Henry Moore tried to isolate the partial effect of size by holding constant the gender and age of the worker. Regression models and the micro data to implement them allow us

[6] These regression equations are regularly reported by the Conference Board. Estimates for η vary across industries and over time but fall in the range from +0.25 to +0.35; see Table 2 in Baker et al. (1988). These results were also obtained by Kostiuck (1990) for several samples including a panel dataset. In fact, the relation held for the salaries of union presidents where a tenfold increase in the size of the union was associated with a 78% increase in salary.

to introduce a larger vector of variables that hopefully serve as proxies for worker ability. A standard approach is to specify two log-linear wage equations.

$$Y = SA_1 + e_1, \tag{1}$$

$$Y = SA_2 + XB_2 + e_2, \tag{2}$$

where Y is the log of hourly earnings, S is a vector of 8 dummy variables corresponding to firm/plant sizes, and X is a vector of worker characteristics identified in Table 9.[7]

The wage premiums associated with firm and plant size were converted to percentage increments in Table 10 by taking anti-logs of the parameter estimates reported in Table 9. MF and LF stand for medium and large firms with 100–499 and 1000+ employees, while SP designates a small plant with less than 25 workers. Full-time males in a small plant of medium size firms, SP/MF, earned hourly wages that were 25.7% above the mean wage of $6.62 paid to workers in the base group, single plant firms with less than 25 employees, SP/SF. Ignoring worker characteristics, Eq. (1), workers in large plants of big firms, LP/LF, received a wage premium of 62.6%. When education, job tenure, and other worker traits are included in the wage equation, this size premium drops to 27.8% which squares with a matching model. Because big firms assemble workforces with a richer skill mix, adjusting for worker characteristics reduces the magnitude of the wage–size differential. Reference to Table 10 reveals that the premium for firm/plant size is larger for males than for females. Moreover, the relation of hourly wages to firm/plant size is observed even when the sample is restricted to full-time employees.

The estimation of size effects via dummy variables is appropriate only if the partial effects of worker characteristics on log wages are the same across size categories. If the size and worker characteristic vectors are interacted, a F-test rejects the hypothesis that the slope parameters B are the same across firm size categories. However, when separate wage equations are estimated, full-time workers in small firms with less than 100 workers earned lower wages than their counterparts in large firms with 1000 or more employees in spite of differences in mean characteristics and slope parameters.[8]

Personick and Barsky (1982) analyzed the data from the white collar pay surveys. Workers in the same narrowly defined occupations such as accountant 3, secretary 2, or computer operator 3 are likely to be more homogeneous than workers with the same years of schooling, job tenure, and industrial affiliation. These data ought therefore to be superior to the CPS to measure the impact of firm size for otherwise equally qualified employ-

---

[7] Eq. (1) is a log counterpart of Table 8, but with workers classified into fewer firm and plant size categories. The base group corresponds to small firms with less than 25 employees. The remaining eight groups are defined by the four firm size categories identified in Table 4 and two plant size categories (small plants with 1–24 employees and large plants with 25 or more employees).

[8] Oi (1991) identified sub-samples which held constant full- versus part-time status, gender, age, and firm/plant size. The exercise was not wholly satisfactory, but the results lend additional support to the positive relation between firm/plant size and wages.

Table 9
Wage equations for full-time employees by sex, 1983[a,b]

Variable	Male employees			Female employees		
	Mean	B	t	Mean	B	t
A. Firm/plant size dummies[c]						
F2SP	0.030	0.110	3.96	0.032	0.088	3.06
F3SP	0.025	0.092	3.04	0.027	0.127	4.06
F4SP	0.008	0.147	2.76	0.007	0.048	0.83
F5SP	0.051	0.117	5.17	0.040	0.131	4.96
F2LP	0.115	0.087	5.32	0.116	0.075	4.41
F3LP	0.109	0.142	8.38	0.124	0.127	7.50
F4LP	0.043	0.134	5.53	0.055	0.160	7.00
F5LP	0.353	0.245	17.90	0.316	0.232	17.00
B. Worker/job characteristics						
Education	12.915	0.063	33.45	12.684	0.064	26.77
Ten	8.205	0.020	12.09	5.537	0.028	14.17
Ten-2	145.516	$-0.040e-2$	-8.01	72.606	$-0.058e-2$	-8.05
Exp	18.452	0.025	16.02	17.772	0.012	8.22
Exp-2	496.391	$-0.043e-2$	-13.10	473.881	$-0.027e-2$	-8.35
Married	0.744	0.122	10.52	0.629	0.003	0.30
Black	0.055	-0.170	-8.14	0.078	-0.100	-5.33
SMSA	0.374	0.122	11.48	0.390	0.134	13.16
South	0.280	-0.048	-4.64	0.292	-0.047	-4.29
C. Industrial affiliation						
Agriculture	0.025	-0.351	-11.28	0.005	-0.170	-2.40
Mining	0.024	0.193	6.31	0.005	0.326	4.69
Construction	0.084	0.186	9.91	0.012	0.079	1.70
TCU (Utilities)	0.094	0.103	6.08	0.055	0.161	6.86
Trade	0.216	-0.129	-9.53	0.240	-0.190	-12.44
Finance	0.055	0.031	1.43	0.119	-0.006	-0.35
Service	0.162	-0.112	-7.49	0.350	-0.026	-1.84
Summary statistics						
ln AHE	2.155			1.777		
R-square	0.4064			0.3352		
N	7833			5973		

[a] Source: May 1983 CPS.

[b] Dependent variable is ln(average hourly earnings).

[c] F2–F5 correspond to firm size categories 25–99, 100–499, 500–999, 1000+; SP, LP correspond to small plants (1–24) and larger plants (25+), respectively.

ees. For most of the occupations identified in their Table 1 (p. 24), wages are fairly stable for firms with less than 10,000 employees but rise sharply thereafter. Computer operators 3 in firms with 50 thousand employees or more earned 24% more than those in the smallest

Table 10
Percentage wage differentials by firm and plant size, 1983[a]

Firm/plant size[b]	Full-time employees			All employees	
	(1)	(2)	(3)	(1)	(2)
Male employees: percentage wage (differential)					
MF/SP	25.7	9.6	4.0	31.7	5.5
LF/SP	36.5	12.4	4.1	39.1	3.7
MF/LP	32.8	15.3	9.2	39.8	8.4
LF/LP	62.6	27.8	17.4	73.2	16.3
Mean wage	8.62	8.63	8.63	8.02	8.02
Base wage[c]	6.62				
No. in sample	7857	7833	7833	8731	8705
R-square	0.1368	0.4064	0.4268	0.1529	0.5042
Female employees: percentage wage (differential)					
MF/SP	19.7	13.5	9.9	24.5	11.5
LF/SP	21.7	14.0	7.6	19.7	8.5
MF/LP	22.4	13.5	9.0	28.4	0.2
LF/LP	41.2	26.1	16.8	46.8	17.6
Mean wage	5.91	5.91	5.91	5.55	5.55
Base wage	5.55			4.59	
No. in sample	5998	5973	5973	7193	7164
R-square	0.0911	0.3352	0.3558	0.0978	0.3824

[a] Notes: In Eq. (1), ln AHE is regressed on 8 firm/plant size dummy variables. Eq. (2) includes education, tenure, experience and industrial affiliation. Part-time employment, union and pension are included in Eq. (3). The percentage differential is the anti-log of the regression coefficient minus one, and expressed as a percentage.

[b] MF/SP denotes a medium size firm with 100–499 employees and a small plant with 1–24 employees. LF/LP stands for a large firm with 1000 or more employees and large plants with 25 or more employees.

[c] The base wage is the anti-log of the intercept corresponding to small firms and small plants with 1–24 employees. It is reported only for Eq. (1).

firms; the wage increment for Draftsmen 4 was 16%. To sum up, large employers demand more productive employees where "productive" is described by the usual proxies, education and experience. However, even after controlling for worker characteristics, the data support the presence of a positively inclined wage–size profile.

2.4. Self-selection and the size-wage gap

Workers are not randomly distributed across the size spectrum. If unobservable differences in productivity affect the allocation, neglect of these could impart a bias in the estimate of the effect of employer size on wages. Suppose that unobserved productivity is person-specific and unrelated to the identity of the employer. A fixed-effects model in which we take first-differences will yield a consistent estimate of the size effects. Let $[W_t, X_t, \delta, \varepsilon_t]$

denote a vector of wages, exogenous variables including establishment size, person-specific productivity effects, and a random variable in year t; no t subscript appears for the person-specific productivity effects which are assumed to be constant over time and across employers.

$$W_t = X_t\beta + \delta + \varepsilon_t. \tag{3}$$

Differencing eliminates the unobserved person effects.

$$\Delta W = W_{t+1} - W_t = \Delta x\beta + \Delta\varepsilon. \tag{4}$$

Dunn (1980) applied this model to a sample of 200 blue-collar workers who changed employers. Workers who moved to larger employers enjoyed wage gains. The methodology was applied to other samples by Brown and Medoff (1989) and by Evans and Leighton (1989). The size effects in these fixed effects models continued to be significant even though differencing attenuated the magnitude of the coefficient of firm size. Differencing, pushes the coefficients of size and other explanatory variables toward zero because it magnifies the effect of measurement errors. The validity of a fixed effect model was questioned by Gibbons and Katz (1992). The value of unmeasured ability need not be the same across employers. Mobility could achieve superior job matches, so that the smaller size–wage gap found using fixed effects may understate the extent to which size–wage differentials are due to unobserved attributes.

Idson and Feaster (1990) try to adjust for a selection bias by first estimating an ordered probit model to predict the size category in which a worker will be employed. This equation yields estimates of the truncated means, λ_{ij} for the ith person in category j, which is then included in the wage equation. The methodology is described by Idson and Feaster (1990). Applying this methodology to 1979 CPS data for men indicated a significant positive selection bias in small firms and negative selection bias in large firms.[9] Unobserved traits that would raise men's wages also made it more likely that they would be located in firms in the smaller size groups. The mean wages of workers in a small size category are thus higher than the mean wages that would have prevailed if workers had been randomly allocated to size categories. At the other end of the size spectrum, the men who self-selected into big firms possessed unobserved traits that depressed wages. Adjustment for the selection bias thus magnifies the size–wage gap, i.e., a random allocation of workers between large and small firms would have increased the size–wage premium. Idson and Feaster argued that this outcome is consistent with a conjecture by Stigler (1962), namely, workers with more ambition and energy would do better in a small firm where their performance will be noticed and rewarded. The procedure used to adjust the size–wage gap for self-selection into different size categories tacitly assumes that the "value" of the unobserved drive and motivation is the same across firm sizes. Attributes such as individual initiative that are productive in small firms may actually be a hindrance

---

[9] Main and Reilly (1993) applied this methodology to data for British workers and found that the selection bias was negligible.

in large firms that organize production around structured teams. A random reallocation of workers across different size firms may thereby produce very different results than those predicted from this model.

The Idson–Feaster findings are consistent with the earlier work by Garen (1985). Given the difficulty of metering performance, large firms should hire workers with easily observed productivity attributes such as education. The reward to less readily observable traits such as IQ ought, therefore, to be greater in a small firm. Garen did indeed find that the return to education was higher in big firms, while small firms paid more for higher IQ scores.

Evans and Leighton (1989) argued that low quality, unstable workers are employed by small firms, a sorting pattern at variance with the Stigler conjecture. Using firm-level data, Mayo and Murray (1991) developed estimates of firm failure and employment risk. The inclusion of these risks in a wage equation eliminated the firm size effect. Winter-Ebmer (1995) used individual-level Austrian data to compute layoff probabilities. Controlling for layoff risks reduced the wage–size premium by a third, but size still exerted a significant effect on wages. These studies introduce the effect of job insecurity on wages, a variable that was not considered by Idson and Feaster. The compensating difference of higher risks for firm failure and layoff risks cannot, though, be inferred in advance. Senior and Smith voiced opposing views: "We believe after all, that nothing is so much disliked as steady, regular labor and that the opportunities of idleness afforded by an occupation of irregular employment are so much more than an equivalent for its anxiety as to reduce (such wages)...below the common average." (Senior, 1858, p. 208)). "What he earns while he is employed, must not only maintain him while he is idle but make him some compensation for those anxious and despondent moments which the thought of so precarious a situation must sometimes occasion". (Smith, 1997, p. 105). The development of estimates of layoff and firm failure risks will allow future researchers to incorporate these variables in a wage equation which tests for any self selection bias.

3. Some behavioral explanations

Able entrepreneurs usually control large organizations. Firms differ in their choice of worker quality partly to economize on monitoring costs. Shirking obviously reduces profits, and a common theme in many models is that it can be deterred by direct supervision or the payment of an efficiency wage. Superior managers realize higher surpluses or rents which they may elect to share with their employees. They adopt a discretionary wage policy where employee compensation is a function of the firm's performance. These models offer what we call behavioral explanations for the wage–size profile.

3.1. Monitoring costs and entrepreneurial ability

McNulty (1980) recognized that there are two human factors of production, labor and entrepreneurs. The latter is characterized by the absence of a market, but the entrepreneur is the moving force who directs the activities of labor. Neoclassical theory had to reconcile the concept of an optimum firm size with the maintained assumptions of first degree homogeneity of the production function and perfect competition in factor markets. Kaldor resolved this quandary by appealing to the fixity of at least one input.

> …it is necessary to assume that the supply of at least one of the factors figuring in the production function should be fixed in which case the "optimum size"…becomes determinate as a result of the operation of the law of non-proportional returns. Moreover it is necessary that the factor whose supply is "fixed" to the firm should at the same time have a flexible supply to the "industry". In this case, therefore, the fixity of supply must not arise from the natural limitations of the amount available but from a peculiarity of the firm's production function. That is to say, there must be a factor of which the firm cannot have "two" units because only one unit can do the job." (Kaldor, 1934, pp. 66–67)

Management in Kaldor's world involves supervision and coordination. Lucas (1978) argued that individuals with more coordinating ability become entrepreneurs, while the rest are employed by them as workers. Lucas is quite candid when he writes, "This description of management does not say anything about the nature of the tasks performed by managers other than whatever managers do, some do it better than others" (Lucas, 1978, p. 511). Alchian and Demsetz (1972) posit a model where a firm coordinates production and supervises performance. Each entrepreneur in the Oi (1983) model has a fixed endowment of calendar time that is divided between management and supervision. If each worker requires h units of time for supervision, the time available for management is simply $H = (\hat{H} - hN)$. The ability to convert non-supervisory time into efficiency units of management is determined by a parameter λ; management input $T = \lambda H = \lambda(\hat{H} - hN)$. Output is a function of labor and management inputs, $Q = f(N, T) = f[N, \lambda(\hat{H} - hN)]$.[10] In equilibrium, the marginal value product of labor is equated to its full price, the sum of the wage paid to labor W plus the implicit cost of supervision occasioned by the diversion of time from management to monitoring labor.

$$Pf_N = W + \delta, \tag{5}$$

where $\delta = P\lambda h f_T$. More able entrepreneurs with larger values of λ assemble larger work forces but confront higher implicit monitoring costs. If capital is introduced, greater entrepreneurial ability is accompanied by a higher capital to labor ratio. In an obvious extension, M workers of quality μ can be combined to obtain N efficiency units of labor services, $N = \mu M$. The firm must now maximize profits along both a numbers margin as well as a quality margin. Wages are an increasing function of quality, $W = W(\mu)$ with

---

[10] One could introduce a capital input K or could introduce labor of different efficiencies. Both extensions are examined by Oi (1983).

$W'(\mu) > 0$. Equilibrium satisfies two conditions:

$$P\mu f_N = W(\mu) + \delta. \tag{6a}$$

$$W'(\mu) = [W(\mu) + \delta]/\mu. \tag{6b}$$

Better entrepreneurs hire more productive workers who entail lower supervisory costs. A positive association between firm size M and wages $W(\mu)$ is generated in this model by matching high-λ entrepreneurs with high-μ employees. The model also implies that the wage structure is convex exhibiting increasing returns to labor quality. If A is twice as productive as B in terms of generating efficiency units of labor services, $\mu_A = 2\mu_B$, then A will earn a wage that is more than twice the wage paid to B because the implicit cost of monitoring an efficiency unit of labor services is inversely related to worker quality. Kruse (1992) found that workers who are more closely monitored are paid lower wages. The ratio of supervisors to workers was higher in large hospitals, Groshen and Krueger (1990). Brown and Medoff (1989) discount the monitoring cost explanation by appealing to the fact that workers on piece rates realize higher hourly earnings at big firms.[11] Monitoring is costly, but it is not the principal reason for the firm-size profile.

3.2. Shirking and efficiency wages

The dual labor market model of Doeringer and Piore (1971) implies a wage–size effect. Workers who secure positions in the primary sector are asked to put forth more work effort in return for higher wages, fringe benefits, and job security. A higher wage has to be paid to elicit a larger supply of work effort, $e = e(w)$ with $e'(w) > 0$. The cost of a labor input defined as effort times bodies, $N = eM$, is minimized by setting the elasticity of effort with respect to the wage equal to unity.

$$we'(w)/e = 1. \tag{7a}$$

If $w = w(e)$ is the supply price of effort, the inverse of $e(w)$, cost is at a minimum when the marginal cost of effort is equal to the average cost.

$$w'(e) = w(e)/e. \tag{7b}$$

Many models do not derive the relation of w to e.

Shapiro and Stiglitz (1984) assume that if the cat's away, opportunistic workers will shirk. Such dysfunctional behavior can be discouraged by supervision which raises the probability q of being caught or by imposing a larger penalty for shirking. The wage can be elevated so that a worker enjoys a surplus which will be lost in the event of apprehension. One can determine a "no shirk wage" $\hat{w}$ which has the property that if $w = \hat{w}$, the expected

---

[11] Large employers typically have newer and more expensive equipment which can be more efficiently utilized by hiring workers who are more productive. We amplify on this point in Section 4.3.

utility of shirking (and possibly being caught and discharged) is just equal to the certain utility of working at this efficiency wage $\hat{w}$. The "no shirk wage" will be higher, the larger is the mandated effort standard e, the discount rate r, and the exogenous separation rate b; it is inversely related to the detection rate q.[12] Instead of an efficiency wage, workers might be required to post performance bonds in advance. This latter option is dismissed by asserting that employers would surely renege. Short sighted employers will allegedly collect the performance bonds and embrace a "hire and fire" policy.[13] Nothing is said about how a firm sets the effort standard e or how much is spent on setting the surveillance level q. Shapiro and Stiglitz derive an existence theorem, namely unemployment is the penalty which coerces a worker to comply with the mandated effort standard.

A more interesting model was developed by Eaton and White (1983). A firm chooses employment M and an effort e to maximize profits. Monitoring is costly, and workers demand a higher wage premium to supply more effort. There are two equilibria, one where the employee stays on her effort supply curve, and the other where she receives a super-normal wage, the incentive to refrain from shirking.[14] The effort level is now endogenous, and the shape of the effort supply curve determines whether an employer elects to pay an efficiency wage.

The relevance of paying a super-normal wage in large firms to prevent shirking is questioned by Schaffner (1996). In Peru, workers are protected by a no dismissal law. Big employers pay significantly higher wages, but the wage–size premium cannot be attributed to efficiency wages. To the extent that larger employers set higher work effort standards, they must pay higher wages. However, the wage–size premium in this event is a compensating difference discussed in Section 4.1.

3.3. Wages and the ability to pay

Even within a narrowly defined occupation, jobs can differ in tasks, responsibilities, work pace, or location. A high quality worker may be paid a higher wage but may yield a lower "price" of labor. Slichter (1950, p. 80) cautioned that "Neither wages or hourly earnings represent the price of labor". They are, however, reasonable proxies. A survey of 85 plants in Cleveland in 1947 revealed a very wide dispersion of hourly wages for unskilled labor, from 55 cents to $1.09 which is at odds with the law of "one price". Slichter examined the Conference Board data for 20 manufacturing industries in 1939 to find the reason for this dispersion. He discovered several regularities of which at least three deserve mention.

---

[12] Shapiro and Stiglitz assumed a linear utility function, $U(w, e) = w - e$. Shirking if successful yields a utility gain because e is set equal to zero. However, if caught and discharged, the worker's wage is replaced by an unemployment stipend. The model yields an equilibrium unemployment rate which serves as a disciplinary device. The same idea is present in the Bulow and Summers (1986) model where unsuccessful shirking puts the worker in the secondary market with its lower wage rate. The limitations of the Shapiro–Stiglitz model are discussed by Oi (1990).

[13] Shapiro and Stiglitz (1984, p. 442) write, "There is no way to discipline the firm from this type of opportunism". They ignore the value of establishing and retaining a reputation.

[14] The details of this model are amplified in Oi (1990, pp. S136–S139).

First, the wages of unskilled labor were positively correlated with the wages paid to skilled and semi-skilled employees in the same establishment.[15] Katz and Summers (1989) rediscovered the same regularity. If a firm paid high wages to its skilled machinists and mechanics, it also paid above average wages to its secretaries and janitors. Second, small margins of revenues over payroll were associated with low wages for unskilled labor. Third, firms that enjoy high net income per worker adopt a liberal wage policy.[16]

Wages could vary across employers to equalize the net advantages of alternative employments. Tasks, work pace, and fringe benefits are not the same and are responsible for a dispersion of wages. Slichter (1950, p. 91) rejected this hypothesis of compensating differences and embraced a doctrine of discretionary wages. "It reinforces the view that wages within a considerable range reflect managerial discretion. That when management can easily afford to pay high wages, they tend to do so." This idea may have been responsible for what Weiss (1966) called the monopoly-wage hypothesis that workers participate in the excess profits of firms in concentrated industries. Kwoka (1980) tested and rejected this hypothesis using data for blue-collar manufacturing workers from the 1977 Quality of Employment Survey (QES). Although the 4-firm concentration ratio was insignificant, the log of hourly earnings was positively related to establishment size.[17]

Hourly earnings across a sample of 41 two-digit industries exhibited a dispersion of 28% which can be reduced to 15% by controlling for worker traits and occupations. Katz and Summers (1989) concluded that the inter-industry wage structure was stable over time.[18] They contended that the inter-industry wage differences are not compensating differences but are the results of sharing rents. Boiler makers may get premiums for their exposure to noise, but why does the employer pay a premium to the secretaries who write out their paychecks? An alternative to the rent-sharing hypothesis is that high-wage industries employ a higher quality of labor where quality is unobservable. Katz and Summers ask the rhetorical question, "If sorting does not take place on observable traits such as education, why should a firm sort on an unobservable attribute?".[19]

Katz and Summers try to save the thesis that industry wage differentials represent labor

---

[15] The rank correlation coefficient across 20 industries was +0.7098. The data were collected by the National Industrial Conference Board, The Conference Board Economic Record, Vol. II, No. 10 (March 28, 1940), pp. 120–134.

[16] The rank correlation between net income per employee and the hourly wage of unskilled labor was +0.6969. Slichter chose to compute bivariate rank correlations for some nine hypotheses. He did not estimate any multivariate relations.

[17] In his regression (c), Kwoka (1980, p. 370) obtained a significant coefficient on the 4-firm concentration ratio, but when he added a vector of industry dummies, the partial effect of concentration became statistically insignificant. Weiss (1966) also rejected the monopoly–wage hypothesis.

[18] The correlation of relative wages in 1966 and 1984 across 41 industries was +0.91. Schultze (1989, p. 281) questioned the so-called stability claimed by Katz and Summers. He noted that for the seven high wage industries (Mining, Transport Equipment, Tobacco, Petroleum, Communications, Public Utilities, and Primary Metals), the average of the raw wage premiums was 32% in 1966 and 50% in 1980.

[19] The bivariate tabulations shown in Table 4 reveal that employees in large firms are, on average, of higher quality judged by education, job tenure, and marital status of men. The evidence is less clear on sorting across two-digit industries.

rents by appealing to evidence on quit and vacancy rates. Based on data for 74 two-digit manufacturing industries, the correlation between wages and quit rates was -0.70. Additionally, there were 14.0 applicants for each job vacancy in the five high-wage industries compared to only 8.5 applicants in the five low-wage industries. These findings persuade the authors to conclude that the inter-industry wage structure is generated by labor rents. High wages incorporate labor rents which are sustained by the discretionary benevolence of wealthier employers or by the need to pay efficiency wages.[20] The surplus of revenues over labor costs varies and is probably relatively larger in bigger firms which face lower prices for non-labor inputs and may have market power. The incidence of unionism is positively related to firm size. Trade unions capture a part of these surpluses in the wage premiums which they secure for their members. Threat effects may raise wages in large non-unionized firms, though Brown and Medoff (1989) found little support for this possibility. Brown et al. (1990) document the relation between wages and per worker surpluses, but they are at a loss to rationalize why employers want to share these rents with labor.

4. The productivity hypothesis

> The investigation upon which we are about to enter as to the influence of the status of the laborer of the concentration of industry in large establishments is both of theoretical and practical importance. Its practical value lies in the answer to the question as to whether the form of selection of laborers entailed by the survival in competition of large establishments places the employees upon a better plane of living than the one occupied by their fellow workers in smaller establishments. Its theoretical interest lies in the answer to the query as to whether the productivity hypothesis will explain the results to which the investigation will lead. (Moore, 1911, p. 139)

That wages are positively related to the size of the establishment and the firm is a well-established fact. In the preceding section, attention was directed to three "behavioral" explanations: (1) matching workers and entrepreneurs to minimize the sum of wage and monitoring costs; (2) paying efficiency wages to deter shirking; and (3) sharing the surplus of revenues over labor costs with workers. A strategy followed by some is to look for the right variable or vector of variables which when included in a wage equation, reduce the partial effect of firm size to zero. The covariates of firm size are numerous, and new surveys keep washing up additional covariates. Henry Moore was guided in his search for variables that could confirm or reject a productivity hypothesis.

---

[20] They appeal to the Akerlof (1984) gift exchange. If a worker is paid a fair wage, she will put forth more effort. Raff and Summers (1987) contend that Ford paid a super-normal wage as a way of buying peace and avoiding the kind of shirking found in other industrial settings. Further, Ford wages were raised when assembly line technology was introduced to improve discipline and to cut down on absenteeism. Again, this looks like paying for more work effort, a compensating difference and not an economic rent. The estimates of labor and capital rents can be found in Table 11 of Katz and Summers (1989).

We begin with a maintained hypothesis, namely wages and productivity move together. A labor contract is almost always explicit about the rate of wages but is vague about "the effort bargain", what constitutes a fair day's work. An effort standard is an unobserved condition of work. Raising that standard results in greater productivity which can support a higher wage, a topic discussed in Section 4.1. The pace of work depends, in part, on customer arrival rates in the distributive trades and the service sector. The wages in bigger stores and hospitals are higher because workers have to work harder (Section 4.2). We turn in Section 4.3 to the complementarity of capital and skilled labor. The analysis is complicated because both capital and labor are heterogeneous. Firms try to match their most powerful machines with their "best" workers where ability is often unobservable. The volume production of standardized goods is most efficiently organized around teams. Section 4.4 examines how conformance with a common set of work rules and practices can be efficient but requires the payment of "rents" to infra-marginal team members. The closing section deals with the decision by larger firms to "produce" more productive and durable employees.

4.1. Effort, productivity, and the disutility of work

A job involves more than an exchange of money for time. Some dimensions of the job package (such as the number of paid vacation and personal leave days, health and life insurance) can be explicitly incorporated into a labor contract. Compliance with autocratic orders, exposure to an unhealthy workplace, or long commutes are some negative job attributes. Positive aspects include challenging tasks, opportunities to talk to co-workers, exercising initiative, or taking time off for personal business. Large employers typically provide cleaner and safer workplaces, better lighting and climate control, generous time-off benefits, and superior fringe benefits when compared to small employers. Working conditions, at least the observable ones, are superior at larger firms and hence cannot explain higher wages.

Employment agreements, written or implicit, rarely stipulate the effort that the employee is expected to supply.

> Central to the worktime issue is the concept of a fair day's work....The differing perspective (between employer and worker) is not resolved by the forging of an employment contract. Such an arrangement normally consists of two elements: first, an agreement on the wage per unit of time or piece; second, an agreement on the amount of work to be undertaken, that is, an effort bargain. It is normal for the wage rate to be precisely defined in the employment contract. The effort bargain, on the other hand, is generally implicit and indistinct (Nyland, 1989, p. 57) ...the formal wage contract is never precise in stipulating how much effort is expected for a given wage (and vice versa). The details of the arrangement are left to be worked out through the direct interaction between the partners of the contract. (Baldamus, 1959, p. 35)

Disagreements about the duties and responsibilities of the two parties can affect morale, absenteeism, and may even lead to a job separation. If effort bargains are so important, why are they left vague and open ended? Simon (1947) offered two reasons: (a) Nothing will be gained by the organization without the employee's acceptance of the authority. (b) The precise activities that he performs within broad limits are indifferent to him. Contracts are meant to facilitate mutually advantageous exchanges, to expedite the allocation of resources to their highest valued uses. A contract that tries to anticipate too many contingencies becomes unwieldy and raises transaction costs. Some things like effort, responsibility, and loyalty might better be left understood.

Labor productivity varies not only over the hours of a day but also over the days of the week. The weekly profile almost always follows practice-efficiency. Output is lowest on Monday, rises to a peak on Wednesday or Thursday, and falls off on Friday. Vernon (1921, pp. 27–28) wrote:

> The cessation of work between Saturday afternoon and Monday morning naturally causes a greater loss of neuro-muscular co-ordination than that observed between each week day, and consequently the output on Monday morning tends to be lower than that observed on any other morning of the week. The loss of practice-efficiency owing to the week-end rest is so considerable that the remainder of the week may be needed for recovery, but…the fatigue induced by the daily round of labor gradually accumulates…first to neutralize the improvement due to practice-efficiency and then to overpower it.[21]

The model is one in which output is positively related to a stock of practice-efficiency capital P and current effort E. At the start of a week, the stock of P-capital is especially small resulting in the Monday effect. Although P-capital is replenished by work, it depreciates with the passage of time. The accumulation of work de-energizes a worker to the point where he can supply less current effort E. The latter effect overtakes the build-up of P-capital producing the Friday dip. Finally, the supply of energy is not fixed. It can be augmented through rest and nutrition. Vernon reported that piece rate workers took spontaneous breaks averaging eight minutes an hour. Output is a function of effort, but the potential supply of effort is not fixed. Jobs differ in their effort intensity, but so also do non-market activities. Watching television requires less effort than caring for a child. Becker (1985) conjectured that women might select less effort intensive and hence lower paying jobs than men because they want to conserve more effort for non-market activities.

In addition to the rate of pay, the nature of the work surely influences the amount of time and effort supplied to a job. Sebastian de Grazia (1962, p. 58) described the situation as follows:

> We should not expect the worker normally to get real satisfaction from a job on

---

[21] He continued, "In industry, it is almost invariably accompanied by low output, which Kent has termed, the Monday effect." (Kent, 1915).

which he does a piece of the work, a task chosen and organized by others, under watchful eyes, at a pace not his own, at a time and place not his to say. This, one would venture, is the disagreeable part of the job effort or exertion or exercise, physical or mental, under orders and supervision, constrained in time and space.

Physically or mentally demanding work is one dimension of a job. Baldamus reserved the term, boredom, for professional positions and introduced the concept of tedium for dull, repetitive jobs. The disutility of the latter kind of work can be partially offset by traction, the opposite of distraction. "It is the feeling of being pulled along by the inertia inherent in a particular activity. The experience is pleasant and may therefore function as a relief from tedium." (Baldamus, 1959, p. 69). At a confectionery, wrapping can acquire a rhythm and hence traction, weighing cannot. Rhythm and traction go together to reduce the disutility of a tedious job. Putting several tasks into a job might make it more attractive, but Baldamus (p. 60) found that frequent changes from one operation to another interfered with the swing of work resulting in lower output.

Work in the primary sector is characterized by strict work rules, performance standards, and incentives to supply more effort. A higher effort level means a larger flow of labor "services" measured in efficiency units. Wages rise with firm size, but labor productivity climbs even faster resulting in lower unit labor costs. Kwoka (1980, pp. 363–366) asked if differences in the organization of work led to greater "alienation" of employees in larger firms? Using a variety of subjective measures of job satisfaction, he concluded that "worker alienation" was unrelated to establishment size.[22] The payment of higher wages evidently compensated them for the stricter work rules and effort standards. In short, the observed wage–size profile can be supported by higher effort levels that result in greater labor productivity.

4.2. Economies of massed reserves

The production function applicable to firms in the distributive trades and service industries differs from that for firms making goods in two important respects (Oi, 1992). First, the customer supplies an essential input. The number of customers/buyers B per unit time period belongs as an argument of the production function alongside labor and capital, $X = f(L, K, B)$. Second, customer arrivals are random resulting in a stochastic production function. Patient care is produced by bringing together nurses L, beds K, and most importantly, patient-buyers B. A retail store produces transactions by combining customers, clerks, inventories, and capital facilities. Without a customer, a retailer could not produce a transaction, the raison d'etre for its existence. A store assembles an inventory, hires sales clerks, and stays open even when there are no customers. A teddy bear sits on a shelf awaiting the arrival of a buyer. On the other side, a shopper travels to a store and sometimes has to wait to be served. Something or someone is almost always hanging around.

---

[22] Brown et al. (1990, p. 36) identified 42 working conditions of which 21 were marginally worse in large establishments. An adjustment for the quantifiable variables appears to magnify the size–wage premium.

Hutt (1977) is correct, idle resources are productive when they are in a state of pseudo idleness. All idleness could be eliminated, but to accomplish this, the synchronization of customers, clerks, and just-in-time inventories would be prohibitively expensive. Idleness is also observed in manufacturing. Factories are closed at night, workers get rest breaks, and inventories are held. Neglecting these considerations apparently poses no serious theoretical or empirical difficulties in analyzing the goods producing sector. This is not so for the service sector.

It is instructive to review the repairman's problem in queuing theory. A firm has M machines. The number that arrive to be repaired follows a Poisson distribution with a mean arrival rate λ. The repair time is exponentially distributed with a mean service time μ. With only one repairman, there is some probability p_0 that none of the machines needs servicing, and the repairman is idle. When two or more machines break down, a queue develops. The addition of a second repairman raises labor costs but reduces the opportunity costs of idle, broken machines yielding no output. If λ and μ are known, we can solve for an optimum ratio of machines to repairmen which minimizes the sum of costs for labor and idle machines. The problem is isomorphic to the problem facing a hospital serving a population of M potential patients who arrive at random to be treated by R "servers". With a mean patient arrival rate λ and a mean length of hospital stay μ, the sum of waiting times (empty beds R awaiting a patient and patients waiting for a bed to become available) is minimized when the ratio of the population to beds satisfies the equation, $(M/R) = [1 + (\lambda/\mu)]^{-1}$. If M and R are both doubled, the mean length of a patient queue will fall and the occupancy rate of beds will rise.[23]

A firm in the service sector confronts a production function exhibiting increasing returns which is a consequence of the economies of massed reserves. Robinson (1958) showed that these economies derive from the coordination and synchronization of activities which are related to the scale of operation and are not a result of the law of large numbers. The implications of these economies are borne out in the data. A queuing model implies that if half of the hospital bed capacity in a community is controlled by the largest hospital, that hospital will realize more than half of the occupied beds. The same principle applies to airlines. If two or more carriers serve a given route, the one supplying the largest number of available seats achieves the highest load factor defined as the seat occupancy rate. A passenger-trip, a hotel room, or an exchange of goods for money may constitute the main component of the "product" of a service establishment. An examination of selected industries reveals that the output mix varies with firm and establishment size.

The corner grocery store and the giant supermarket belong to the same three-digit industry, SIC 541. However, they differ in ways that affect the relation of outputs to inputs. We begin with the capital to labor ratio. The ratio of the book value of capital to employment is higher for larger stores, but selling area and inventories per employee are lower. Delicatessens, fresh fish markets, and bakeries use less floor space but more capital equipment. Buildings and equipment are newer in bigger stores which make more use of

---

[23] The mathematical model is nicely summarized by Mulligan (1983).

scanners.[24] The capital/labor ratio is higher in bigger stores when the data are adjusted for differences in the output mix and the age and quality of capital. Larger firms utilize capital more intensively, by operating more shifts per day in manufacturing and by staying open longer hours per week in retailing. The smallest independent supermarkets were open an average of only 91 h a week in 1994 compared to 135 h for the largest supers (see Table 11).[25] The rise in the proportion of two-earner families and the spread of car ownership rates are responsible for the changing structure of retail foodstores. Higher capital/labor ratios and longer store hours have raised labor productivity, but these have not raised the real wages of retail workers.

A second significant development is the change in the relation of customer to vendor. In 1950, one could still be served by a butcher or retail clerk. Self service, an institutional innovation started in the depression, is now the rule, even at convenience stores. National advertising and brand names have replaced trained clerks who advised customers and honored implicit warranties. They have undermined the value of store specific human capital. Transactions have become impersonal and standardized. There is little to be gained from establishing on-going relations between customers and trained clerks who know one another. Bluestone (1989) concluded that we have witnessed a *Retail Revolution* and its byproduct, a de-skilling of the retail workforce. Supermarkets have increased their demands for part-time employees. Full-time clerks outnumbered part-timers in 1975, but by 1988, full-timers made up only 41% of workers at the independent supermarkets and 36% at the chain supers. Store size and the percentage of part-time employees are positively correlated (see the last column of Table 11). This pattern emerges even though the relative wages of part-time workers are higher at the larger supermarkets. Differences in the staffing practices of large and small supermarkets can be explained by a peak load model. A part-time clerk is like a standby generator which comes on-line only at peak periods. The base demand in peak and off-peak periods is satisfied by year-round genera-tors, the counterpart of full-time employees. The ratio of standby to year-round generators will be higher, the greater the gap between peak and base demands. The giant supers stay open longer and find that fully 55% of sales take place in 3 days, Thursday to Saturday. In relation to small supers, the big markets confront higher and longer peak sales periods which are staffed with part-time workers. The de-skilling of the retail work force over the last quarter century is due in large measure to the increasing dispersion of hourly sales.

Table 12 confirms the presence of the size–wage premium. Wages of part-timers at the largest independents were 18.3% higher than at the smallest. The premium was 16.3% for full-time clerks.[26] Customer arrival rates, the size of the market basket, and sales volume are all greater at larger supers. Labor is more productive as evidenced by sales per

---

[24] In 1981, the average age of buildings occupied by the largest supers was 9.8 years versus 16.6 years for small supers; see Progressive Grocer (April 1982, p. 23). The percentage of stores using scanners is positively related to size.

[25] Only 2% of independent supers with less than 10,000 feet^2 of selling area were open 24 h, 7 days a week. The fraction climbed to 47% for the largest size group. The mean store hours and percentage staying open all of the time were higher for the chain stores.

Table 11
Selected statistics by store size, 1994 (independent supermarkets by selling area)[a]

Selling area	Weekly sales (000)	Sales per employee hour	Basket size	Employees total	Percent part-time
<10	67.0	76.46	11.36	30.1	53.8
10–15	84.5	80.32	12.66	37.3	56.8
15–20	123.3	80.11	14.19	54.3	55.3
20–25	162.1	87.61	15.79	67.1	60.1
25–30	182.8	83.97	16.33	77.5	61.3
30–44	302.6	85.86	19.88	117.8	60.0
40+	446.5	109.80	22.99	135.9	63.9
Average	127.1	83.86	14.81	52.7	57.9

[a] Source: *Progressive Grocer* (April 1995) Supplement, pp. 47–52.

employee hour shown in Table 11. An employee at a larger store has to work harder. She has less idle time, accepts more responsibility, and receives a higher wage. A firm gets larger because it can attract more customers who supply inputs into the production of the services supplied by the firm. A higher customer arrival rate leads to more efficiency which supports the higher wages of more productive workers due to the economies of massed reserves.

4.3. Capital, technology, and labor productivity

Productivity and wages depend on the amounts and kinds of cooperating inputs provided by the employer. The capital to labor ratio is positively related to firm size. Large manufacturing establishments utilize capital more intensively by operating multiple shifts, a fact documented by Foss (1981). According to Shinohara (1962), used machines and equipment account for fully 40% of the assets of small Japanese firms, while large firms turned to the used markets for only 6% of their capital acquisitions.[27] The higher relative demand for capital, especially new equipment, can be explained in part by the fact that larger and older firms confront lower "prices" for non-labor inputs.[28] Interest rates are lower, and sellers of advertising, energy, communication services, and insurance typically offer

---

[26] Wages pertain to 1985, and size is measured by sales volume. The size–wage premium for the chain stores were larger, 37.8% for part-time and 22.8% for full-time clerks.

[27] Firms in the United States behave in the same manner. A Survey of Truck Inventories and Use contains data on the age distribution of truck-tractor fleets. Eric Bond at Pennsylvania State University supplied us with tabulations dividing fleets by size into thirds. The median age of trucks in the fleet was 6.3 years for small fleets and 4.8 years in the largest fleets.

[28] Evidence for this proposition is supplied in Chapter 4, especially Table 4.8 of Brown et al. (1990).

Table 12
Hourly wages ($) of part-time and full-time clerks: 1985[a]

Sales volume (in millions of dollars)	Part-time clerks	Full-time clerks	Ratio, part-time/ full-time
Independents			
2–4	3.98	4.84	0.822
4–8	4.31	5.11	0.843
8–12	4.64	5.35	0.867
>12	4.71	5.63	0.837
Average	4.18	5.01	0.834
Chains			
2–4	4.15	5.45	0.761
4–8	5.07	6.23	0.814
8–12	5.49	6.45	0.851
>12	5.72	6.69	0.855
Average	5.10	6.23	0.819

[a] Source: *Progressive Grocer* (April, 1986).

volume discounts. Finally, the largest and most profitable firms are usually the first to adopt new product and process innovations. The task at hand is to explore how these empirical regularities affect wages.

4.3.1. A neoclassical production function

Across the size spectrum, firms embrace different technologies and factor proportions. Assume for the moment that firms use the same production function combining capital K, skilled labor A, and unskilled labor B; $X = f(K, A, B)$. Large firms face a lower price for capital which is substituted for labor. The capital to output ratio (K/X) as well as the capital to labor ratio (K/L) are higher in larger establishments. A lower input price not only expands the demand for capital K but also for its complement, skilled labor A. Hamermesh (1993) and Griliches (1969) found that capital and skilled labor are complements in production. A larger firm will demand a richer skill mix (A/B) and pay a higher average wage. But this is not what we mean by a size–wage premium. An inspector at a big bottling plant earns more than an inspector at a small brewery even though the latter could, in principle, perform the tasks of the former. What sustains the size–wage premium? The quality of the machinery and/or the work pace might differ across the two bottling plants. Hence, the "work" performed by the two inspectors is not the same.

The theory has to be embellished. At a minimum, why do large firms embrace a more capital intensive mode of production? One candidate is a non-homothetic production function that yields an output elasticity of demand for capital that exceeds unity. A second proposed by Brown et al. (1990) appeals to input price differences. An airline that orders twenty new jet aircraft enjoys a lower unit price than a competitor who demands only one or two planes. The availability and terms of credit are more favorable for larger firms. The supply price of capital has to be firm specific, a function of the firm's age and size, its credit rating, reputation, and the collateral it can put up. A lower relative price for capital can explain higher relative demands for both capital and its complement, skilled labor. But why does the large employer have to pay more for skilled workers? A competitive market paradigm implies that the wage of an inspector ought to be independent of the size of the bottling plant. Yet wages are higher in the big plant. Adam Smith told us that competition equalizes the net advantages of competing employments, not wages. There must be some other factor that differs across plants. A higher ratio of machines to workers may produce more noise. The installation of new machines might prompt management to step up the pace of the assembly line. The acquisition of capital will increase the demand for a complementary input, skilled labor, but it is often associated with a faster work pace raising labor productivity and hence wages.

4.3.2. Wage premiums for computer operators

Technological advances introduce new machines and new ways of doing things that frequently increase the demands for cooperating inputs. Many of the innovations adopted by manufacturing plants involve the use of computers. Numerically controlled machines led the way, but the major changes followed the entry of the microprocessors, the Apple-2 in 1977 and the IBM-PC in 1981. Autor et al. (1997) report that the percentage of workers using a computer rose from 25.1% in 1984 to 46.6% in 1993.[29] Krueger (1993) estimated that in 1984, a worker who used a computer was paid an hourly wage that was 0.17 log points greater than a comparable worker who did not; the gap rose to 0.20 log points in 1988. His data regrettably did not identify firm or establishment size. A 1979 survey of Canadian workers in the Maritime Provinces inquired if the employee had access to a computer. Reilly (1995) estimated a wage equation in which the coefficient of establishment size was positive and significant when computer presence was excluded. A computer raised wages by 0.13 log points, but the effect of size fell to nearly zero.[30] Reilly concluded that computer access solved the mystery of a size–wage premium but replaced it with another, namely why should computer technology lead to such a large enhancement in a worker's stock of human capital?

[29] The direct use of computers at work varied by worker characteristics. Data from the 1993 CPS supplement (reported in Autor et al., 1997, Table 4) revealed computer use rates for men 41.1, female 53.2, less than high school 10.4, high school 34.6, some college 53.1, college 70.2, white 48.0, black 36.7, blue collar 17.0, white collar 67.6, union 39.1, non-union 46.9, part-time 29.3, full-time 51.7%.

[30] Reilly's sample contained 607 workers in 60 private sector establishments in manufacturing and non-manufacturing industries. Data from the General Segmentation Survey were obtained on employment size, the ratio of supervisors to employees, capital per employee, education requirements on new hires, dummy on average age of capital, and access to a computer as well as the usual worker traits. The coefficient of size was +0.035 with no other covariates, +0.039 including establishment characteristics other than computer access, and +0.011 with all covariates. Computer presence in this sample obviously exhibited a high colinearity with establishment size.

Table 13
Technology use and education of the workforce, 1988–1990[a]

In plants with X technologies	% of all workers with a college degree	% of non-productive workers with a college degree	% of production workers with some college
$X < 4$	9.4	24.1	21.2
$X = 4$–6	12.2	31.2	24.2
$X = 7$–8	14.0	34.5	27.1
$X = 9$–10	16.2	34.9	27.7
$X = 11$–13	15.2	37.5	29.7
$X = >13$	33.1	53.9	34.9
Full sample	18.3	40.1	27.9

[a] Source: Doms et al. (1997, Table 1, p. 262).

A 1988 survey collected data on the adoption of new technologies.[31] For a sample of single product plants, Dunne and Schmitz (1995) found that the incidence of establishments adopting six or more new technologies rose from 7.9% for plants with less than 100 employees to 85.4% for those with 500 or more workers.[32] Taking the plant as the unit of analysis, Dunne and Schmitz regressed the log of the hourly wage of production workers on plant size, technology use, and other characteristics of the worksite. Wages were positively related to both size and technology use. The introduction of technology use attenuated the effect of employment size on wages, but size was still significant.

A strong correlation between technology adoption and the skill mix is evident in Table 13.[33] The percentage of employees with a college degree ranged from 9.4% in plants with fewer than 4 new technologies to 33.1% in highly technical plants. The skill upgrading for blue-collar workers, shown in the third column, is less than that for white-collar workers. Controlling for education reduces the partial effect of plant size, but size is still important.

Technical progress in the last 25 years has embodied a strong skill bias. Investments in new equipment, especially computers, were accompanied by sharp increases in the

---

[31] The Survey of Manufacturing Technologies collected data from 10,526 plants with 20 or more employees in five two-digit manufacturing industries; Fabricated Metals, Machinery, Electrical Machinery, Transportation Equipment, and Instruments. The survey collected information on if the establishment used any of 17 advanced technologies including such things as computer aided design, flexible machines using programmable controls, pick/place robots, technical data network, etc. The survey did not ask about the fraction of workers who actually used the technologies in question.

[32] The figures for the intervening size classes were 24.9% in the 100–250 size class, 63.3% in the 251–499 class and 24.0% for the entire sample of 1837 single product plants. The data were taken from Table 2 of Dunne and Schmitz (1995).

[33] The number of advanced technologies was obtained from the 1988 Survey of Manufacturing Technologies. Education and payroll data come from Troske's Worker-Establishment Characteristics Database, a matched sample of 34,034 workers and 358 plants (Troske, 1999).

demand for workers with more formal education and work experience whose wages rose relative to the wages of less skilled employees.[34] The firms adopting the new production methods happen to be larger and older because there are major overhead costs. The story is that a big firm adopts a computer based production method which calls for highly skilled workers. Doms et al. (1997) assemble some data supporting an opposing scenario wherein skilled labor is the fixed factor. Older and larger plants happened to have assembled a work force of more skilled employees and were hence better situated to adopt the new innovations. The larger dataset analyzed by Autor et al. (1997) tend to support the first story in which skilled labor is a variable input. More research is required to resolve this issue.

4.3.3. Capital and labor productivity

Capital is not an amorphous, homogenous input. Capital imbedded in an air conditioning system or better lighting is a local public good. It raises the marginal product of a collective group. Little is to be gained by trying to estimate the impact of a local public good on the productivity of any particular group of employees. Land exemplifies a capital input that can be divided and allocated to workers. If land is homogenous, and labor is not, a firm will maximize output by allocating more land to more productive individuals. Further, if land is of uneven productivity, the most productive plots will be assigned to the best workers. Given heterogeneous inputs, the capital/labor ratio will not be equalized across employees in the same establishment. Given differentiated capital goods, a firm faces an assignment problem. A new computer will be allocated to the most efficient operator who has the highest shadow price. The older and less powerful calculators and word processors are passed down to less productive employees. This assortative mating of equipment and employees results in a maximum of output. The problem is analogous to a monogamous marriage market where Becker (1973) argued that "output" is maximized through the assortative mating of above average men with superior women. Sorting and matching of equipment and employees of varying qualities take place within and across establishments. Moore (1911, p. 148) observed:

> Because of the use of large fixed capital in large establishments, the more efficient workers are more valuable to the large than to the small establishments.

Moore (p. 149) goes on to quote from Marshall:

> We have hitherto supposed that it is a matter of indifference to the employer whether he employees few or many people to do a piece of work, provided his total wages-bill for the work is the same. But that is not the case. Those workers who earn most in a week when paid at a given rate for their work are those who are cheapest to their employer.... For they use only the same amount of fixed capital as their slower fellow workers; and, since they turn out more work, each part of it has to bear a less

---

[34] These trends are discussed by, among others, Behrman et al. (1994), Dunne and Schmitz (1995), and Autor et al. (1997).

charge on this account. The prime costs are equal in the two cases; but the total cost of that done by those who are more efficient, and get the higher time-wages, is lower than the total cost of that done by those who get the lower time-wages at the same rate of piece-work payment.... But when expensive equipment is used which has to be proportioned to the number of workers, the employer would often find that the total cost of his goods lowered if he could get twenty men to turn out for a wages-bill of £50 as much work as he previously got done by thirty men for a wages-bill of £40.

Hourly wages are positively related to equipment value. The occupational compensation survey for Seattle reported the following wages for truck drivers, $9.45 for light, $11.15 for medium, $14.68 for heavy trucks, and $15.74 per hour for tractor-trailers.[35] Annual earnings rise from around $30,000 to $100,000 when a pilot moves from flying a small plane for a commuter airline to a large jet for a domestic trunk airline. Imagine an equation in which the log of hourly earnings is regressed on, among other things, a dummy variable equal to one if the driver operates a tractor-trailer and zero otherwise. The coefficient will undoubtedly be positive and might be interpreted in several ways. The acquisition of tractor-trailers increased the demand for more skilled drivers, a capital/skill labor complementarity hypothesis. The larger vehicle raises productivity of the unit and yields a larger surplus which is shared, an ability to pay or what some call a rent-sharing story. Driving a larger truck or flying a bigger jet means the acceptance of more responsibility and the assumption of more effort to protect the larger investment in equipment and cargo. This last suggests that the coefficient of a dummy variable for tractor-trailer represents a compensating difference.

Large establishments surely attract and retain more capable workers. Moore (1911, p. 163) claimed that:

> The large establishments are able to carry out the work of selection (of more capable individuals) because, in consequence of their large capital and better organization, they offer opportunities for more capable laborers to reap the reward of their differential ability.

Labor productivity can vary across individuals and firms as well as over time. Some people are inherently more productive, an unobservable person-specific trait. An employer can supply the worker with a larger quantity of a cooperating input or access to a superior technology. She can also demand more work effort or insist upon a stricter performance standard which looks like an unobservable job-specific characteristic. Larger firms are better informed and have access to more favorable credit terms to acquire new capital goods. The returns to capital and adoption of new process innovations are enhanced by raising performance standards. Advanced technologies, inherently superior employees,

---

[35] Communication from Professor Michael H. Belzer, University of Michigan, May 28, 1997. The data pertain to December, 1992.

and higher work standards go together to raise labor productivity which supports the relation of wages to size.

4.4. The organization of production

An industry is defined as a set of firms that produce the same product. A firm assembles inputs, allocates them to different activities, coordinates and supervises them, and is the residual claimant to the surplus of revenues over costs, be it positive or negative. The size of a firm depends on a host of variables. Technology clearly matters. Barber shops are small, many have no paid employees. Mobile homes are manufactured by relatively small firms because of the high costs of transporting the final product. The technical economies of scale encourage the survival of large utility companies. Even a narrowly defined industry exhibits some product differentiation. The smallest firms in "Contract Construction" make home repairs, remodel kitchens, and convert garages into family rooms. High-rise apartment and office buildings are built by large companies. Big firms in the fabricated aluminum products industry manufacture standardized goods (window frames and siding) which are produced in capital intensive assembly line factories and are marketed through a nationwide distribution network. Customized aluminum extrusions (machine tools and gutters) are usually supplied by small firms. Giant super stores and convenience grocery stores belong to the same industry, SIC 541, but offer different product lines and services. Access to capital is an important determinant of size and product type. Small firms confront a higher price for capital and usually embrace older vintages of technology. Little et al. (1987) found that small soap factories did not have sufficient wealth to purchase electricity and produced a lower quality product. A fall in the price of electricity ought to lead to larger soap factories.

Chandler (1982) observed that the success of many giant firms can be traced to the introduction of a good or service which was produced in large volume. The rate or flow of output per unit time period X is the usual metric by which firm size is measured in our received theory of price. Alchian (1959) developed a model in which the rate X and accumulated volume V are two components of an output program. Production is characterized by increasing returns in the sense that the unit cost (in present value terms) is a decreasing function of volume.[36] The economies of volume production are achieved by producing a standardized good via batch, assembly line methods. The firm incurs high overhead costs for specialized equipment that is amortized by utilizing it more intensively. Foss (1981) found that only 5% of blue-collar workers in small manufacturing plants were assigned to evening or night shifts compared to 23% in large plants. Large organizations

---

[36] An output program is described by the rate of output per period X, the accumulated volume V, and the planned interval over which the output will be produced. The several dimensions are not mutually independent. Cost is an increasing function of the output rate X holding constant the total planned volume. An increase in volume holding the output rate constant leads to a decrease in the unit cost (C/V). The Alchian model is based on the cost analysis of aircraft production by Asher (1956) and is implicit in the early article by Wright (1936). The connection to production functions and learning is discussed by Oi (1967).

are more cheaply administered by standardizing products and processes, a fact recognized by Clark (1923, p. 96) who opined, "… and the satirist of *Main Street*, Mr. Sinclair Lewis, is doing his best to convince us that business is producing standardized people".

Consider two imaginary breweries. B1 has a product that has caught on and is capturing a large national market, while B2 supplies a local market where retailers handle several brands. A disruption in output is costlier for B1 who has established a marketing network. His distributors and wholesalers depend on a steady flow of output. The customers of the local brewery B2 incur a lower cost from a breakdown in output. B1 will acquire newer equipment and invest in a safer workplace. Injury rates are a lot lower in bigger plants as shown by Oi (1974). A steadier flow and larger volume of output enable the larger brewery B1 to maintain a lower inventory to sales ratio. The inspectors in the bottling plant and the men on the loading docks work harder because there are fewer breakdowns and there is less idle time due to the economies of massed reserves. Hall (1991) offers another example. The productivity of a person making sandwiches in Manhattan is an order of magnitude greater than that of a sandwich maker in a small town. Large employers who engage in the volume production of standardized goods and services demand more reliable employees and ask them to put forth more work effort. These employees earn higher wages than their friends who work for the small brewery with its slower work pace and smaller volume.

Every evening, a hundred women leaned over a hundred fires to prepare a hundred inedible meals. Better meals at lower costs could be obtained by giving the job to a team, a chef and his two assistants.[37] Team production is efficient. A person who only straightens and points the wire in Adam Smith's pin factory can learn to do this well. Time can be lost and the rhythm of work broken if one is asked to shift from one task to another. Increasing returns often accompany cooperative effort when two or more men join together to pull a barge up a canal, assemble trucks, or mine copper. Workers are placed into teams even though it becomes harder to ascertain the productivity of individual team members.

In "The O Ring Theory of Economic Development", Kremer, 1993 assumed that output Y is a multiplicative function of capital and the labor inputs of N team members.

$$Y = AK^{\alpha}[\Pi q_j]^{\beta} = AK^{\alpha}[q_1 \times q_2 \times q_3 \times \cdots \times q_N]^{\beta}. \tag{8}$$

The input by the jth employee represents her productivity as a fraction of a perfect employee so that $0 < q_j < 1$ for all j. The social product can be raised by segregating workers, putting high-q workers on one team and low-q individuals on another. High-q secretaries are matched with high-q lawyers. Low-q persons earn lower wages but can compete with high-q workers because their respective "teams" produce differentiated products. Given team size, a firm's output is an increasing function of the mean quality of its work force and a decreasing function of the dispersion of worker qualities. Team production is more efficient when workers are alike and perform tasks in the same way. By

---

[37] This is one example of the inefficiency of the family described by the 19th century utopian, Charles Fourier whose life and works were chronicled by Beecher (1986).

Table 14
The distribution of team size by size of establishment (Quality of Employment Survey, 1973)[a]

Establishment size	1–9	10–49	50–99	100–499	500–999	1000–1999	2000+
	(131)	(172)	(69)	(120)	(49)	(31)	(61)
Team size	3.22	7.54	9.36	10.66	10.94	12.90	14.31
	(3.63)	(7.77)	(12.13)	(10.75)	(16.59)	(18.24)	(15.78)

[a] Source: Idson (1995, Table 2, p. 199). *Note*: Cell sizes are reported in parentheses below the plant size category headings. In each cell the mean team size is reported with the standard deviation in parentheses.

allowing β to depend on team size, Kremer can generate a function exhibiting increasing returns. Larger teams recruit higher quality workers who are combined with high-valued capital inputs.

How prevalent are teams? In a sample of 633 non-union workers responding to the 1973 Quality of Employment Survey, 14.4% did not belong to a team. The rest belonged to teams whose average size was 8.6 persons.[38] Table 14 confirms the anticipated correlation between establishment and team sizes. Idson (1995) found that a 1% increase in team size was associated with a 3.5–4% increase in annual earnings. Deardorf and Stafford (1976) explain this outcome from a theory of compensating differences. If team members are obliged to work in tandem, they must agree on several dimensions of the job, the length of the workweek, work pace, number of rest breaks, indoor temperature, and so on. At an hourly wage of $w_0 = \$10$, workers A and B might want to supply $H_A = 35$ and $H_B = 45$ h a week. If A is required to supply 40 h, he will require a compensating earnings difference of more than $5 \times 10 = 50$ dollars to stay on the same indifference curve. Likewise if B is forced to reduce her weekly hours from 45 to 40, she will accept a cut in earnings but by an amount less than $w_0(H_B - H^*) = 50$ dollars. The common wage-hours package, (w^*, H^*) assumes the character of a local public good. With only two workers, (w^*, H^*) can be chosen to keep both workers on their respective indifference curves, but now, w^* will exceed w_0 and the employee is not free to choose hours. Becker (1985, p. s43) noted that "Firms buy a package of time and effort from each employee with the payment tied to the package". An employee is unable to optimize along each dimension of the package. If there are three or more workers who must conform to a two-dimensional package, (w, H), at least one worker will almost surely enjoy an economic rent. The magnitude of the rents will be larger, the greater is the dispersion in tastes and the bigger is the team.[39] The added

[38] The respondent was asked, "Is there a group of people that you think of as your co-workers, people whom you see just about every day and with whom you have to work closely in order to do your job?". If yes, "About how many people are there in this group?" If there were two teams with 5 and 10 members, the mean size using team weights would be $(5 + 10)/2 = 7.5$, while the mean size using worker weights would be $(5 \times 5 + 1 \times 10)/15 = 8.33$. The mean reported here is a worker-weighted mean.

cost of compensating employees to conform to prescribed work rules is more than offset by the increasing returns to volume and to team production.

4.5. Durable jobs and human capital

A good can be produced in a variety of ways. One could build a steel and concrete warehouse that will last for years or stack the goods in a wooden shack. An investment in an irrigation network is land-specific. Its durability depends on a host of variables including the expected period of production, the transferability of the network to another firm, the cost of "built-in" durability. Bohm-Bawerk believed that roundabout methods of production were more efficient, but that conclusion surely depends on the discount rate. An employer can purchase only the services of labor by turning to the temporary help industry. Most firms, especially larger ones, allocate resources to assemble a work force and to enhance the human capital of their employees in several ways. First, they establish internal labor markets so that employees can have opportunities for career growth within the firm. Second, a higher firm survival rate enhances the returns to training and the amount invested in it. Third, prices of non-labor inputs are lower for larger firms which lead to a higher capital to labor ratio as well as a higher ratio of mobility inhibiting fringe benefits to wages. Mincer (1962) introduced the idea that human capital is produced via on-the-job training. That it is optimal to share the returns was demonstrated by Hashimoto and Yu (1980). The firm and worker are partners in the decision to "produce" human capital. This decision affects not only the amount invested in OJT but also other aspects of the employment relation, the design of the pay package, recruiting practices, job security, and promotions. The literature has mainly embraced the dual labor market paradigm which emphasizes the dichotomy of primary and secondary markets and ignores the continuous variations in firm size.

4.5.1. On-the-job training

The chances of receiving any of five different kinds of training (formal, informal, by co-workers or managers) were higher in larger establishments and in multi-plant firms (Baron et al., 1987). The available international evidence goes in the same direction. In Canada, non-apprenticeship training programs were longer in larger firms, Simpson (1984). Schaffner (1996) reports on data from Peru where the percentage of workers completing OJT climbed with establishment size.

The gap in training investments between large and small employers is larger at higher skill levels; see Haber et al. (1988, Table 8). The training at larger firms is partially

---

[39] The need to compensate employees to conform to the local public goods provided by an employer was developed by Stafford (1980). With two workers and two instruments (a wage rate and weekly hours), a firm can choose (*w,H*) so that each worker remains on his/her indifference curve. With three members, an employer can recapture part of any rent by introducing a third instrument such as a fringe benefit. Increasing firm size is accompanied by a growing complexity of the compensation package which is consistent with a rent recapture thesis, a point developed by Oi (1990) in footnote 29.

directed at molding workers into teams that can work together and to learn how to operate in a bureaucracy. Haber et al. (1988) found that the ratio of on-site to off-site training is higher in larger firms suggesting that a larger fraction of the human capital investments made by large firms is firm-specific.

4.5.2. The wage-tenure profile

On-the-job training is not easily distinguished from learning through experience. Both can contribute to a worker's stock of general or firm-specific capital. If the former, an employer has to raise the employee's wage to retain her. If the investment in firm-specific capital is shared, the employee forgoes earnings during the training period to be repaid later in his tenure with the firm. A third reason for an upward sloping wage-tenure profile is the back loading of pay, the practice of promising a prize to those who stay with the firm (Lazear, 1981). The cross-sectional data generally reveal steeper slopes at larger firms.[40] The panel data are mixed and often find flatter wage-tenure profiles in larger firms. Baron et al. (1987, p. 87) found that a 10% increase in employer size was associated with a 0.13% reduction in a wage growth ratio measured by $G = (W_2/W_0)$, where W_0 is the starting wage and W_2 is the wage 2 years later. The authors argued that large employers do more screening of job applicants, while small firms evaluate the worker on the job and discharge the poor performers. Investment in entry level training is greater in larger firms which by itself implies a faster rate of wage growth. However, Holtmann and Idson (1995) suggest that the employer share of the training costs is higher in larger firms which operates in the opposing direction. The internal labor market is not a spot market but is supported by implicit contracts. There is no reason to presume that the wage will be proportional to productivity in any short period, but productivity over the contract period must equal or exceed wages plus training costs.

4.5.3. Durable jobs

Labor turnover rates are inversely related to firm size and are lower for males. Job tenure in 1993 averaged 4.92 years for men and 2.47 years for women workers. Table 15 reveals that jobs are more durable in larger firms and establishments. Employers who incur larger overhead costs for training and hiring have an obvious incentive to reduce turnover through lower discharge and layoff rates. Workers also incur fixed costs in the search for a job. The higher ratio of applicants to job vacancies means that these search costs are higher for jobs located in larger firms. Quit rates are lower not only to amortize the fixed search costs but also because workers can substitute intra-firm for inter-firm mobility to jobs in different occupations. Wages at big firms contain post-contractual rents, especially for infra-marginal team members. This is confirmed by the responses to the question,

---

[40] Pearce (1990) found that in the US non-union wage–tenure profiles are steeper in larger establishments. However, in unionized plants where workers are earning rents, the wage–tenure profiles are flatter. Hashimoto and Raisian (1985) documented steeper wage–tenure profiles in large Japanese firms. For Canada, Reilly (1995) found greater average wage growth in larger establishments in some years, but no size differences in other years.

Table 15
Average tenure by firm and plant size, 1983 and 1993[a,b]

	SF[c]	SP/LF	LP/LF
1983			
Male	4.98	8.47	11.53
Female	4.19	4.72	7.14
Union	6.85	10.80	11.86
Not union	4.52	6.16	8.66
College	4.78	7.24	10.74
High school	4.73	7.11	8.84
1993			
Male	6.34	9.24	12.06
Female	5.67	6.34	8.87
Union	7.10	14.22	14.33
Not union	5.98	7.42	9.63
College	6.37	8.17	11.66
High school	5.92	8.35	8.95

[a] Source: Current Population Survey.

[b] Average number of years of current tenure are reported, not the duration of completed spells of employment with the firm (private sector).

[c] SF = firm size 1–24, SP/LF = plant size 1–24 and firm size 1000 or more, LP/LF = plant and firm size 1000 or more.

"About how easy would it be for you to find a job with another employer with approximately the same income and fringe benefits that you now have?". Those at small firms indicated more affirmative answers.[41] The inverse relation between turnover and firm size is more carefully documented by Idson (1996).

The flex-wage model of Pissarides (1977) appears to describe the behavior of a small employer who accepts the first job applicant and offers him a wage equal to his expected marginal value product. It is consistent with a low monitoring cost and a short horizon. Performance is easily observed. Tasks can be adjusted to fit the employee's abilities. If he is unsatisfactory, he can be dismissed, and the process repeated. If by chance, a firm lands a good worker, pay can be raised, and the workload expanded. Small firms have shorter life expectancies. A shorter payout period reduces the returns to investments in specialized equipment or in searching for qualified workers.

A large employer announces a fixed wage for a position, establishes qualification standards, and searches until a suitable candidate is found. Volume production is achieved

---

[41] The responses were coded from 1 = very easy to 3 = not at all easy. The mean and standard deviation for those in establishments with less than 50 workers were $m = 1.937$ and $s = 0.784$, compared to $m = 2.399$ and $s = 0.716$ at establishments with more than 1000 workers. (*Source*: 1977 Quality of Employment Survey).

by combining specialized equipment with trained labor. According to Idson (1996), large firms have the capacity to provide durable jobs for two reasons: (1) the ability to substitute intra-firm mobility for inter-firm mobility; and (2) lower firm failure rates. To these, we may add (3) the adoption of a wage policy to encourage low labor turnover.

To sum up, the firms that get and remain "large" organize production around teams, divisions, and profit centers. Capital is substituted for labor. The capital is newer, more durable, and more intensively utilized. A large organization also acquires a higher quality work force. The individuals who are recruited, promoted, and retained possess observable personal characteristics associated with greater productivity. Education, work experience, marital status, willingness to accept a full-time position, are proxies for "built-in" productivity which is approximated by the concept of general human capital. Some firms choose to enhance the human capital of its employees by investing in training. The amount invested in training by the firm and worker (denote this by I) is positively related to firm size. The training investment and the returns to that investment depend in an obvious way on $Q =$ the quality of the trainee ("built-in" productivity), $T =$ the expected period of employment (durability of the employment relation), and $r =$ the discount rate. The back loading of pay provides an incentive to stay with the firm and will be incorporated into the pay package where the training investment I is large. The resources devoted to training will realize a higher return by hiring higher quality trainees and reducing attrition rates. The literature is rich in supplying us with evidence on various pair-wise relations. It is clear, however, that the discount rate r is inversely related to firm size. Given r, training, "built-in" worker quality, and completed job tenure $[I,Q,T]$ are determined by a system of simultaneous equations. The returns to the increment to human capital that was "produced" by the employer-employee attachment will be shared. The wages of workers in larger firms are higher because these workers are simply more productive.

5. Why does employer size matter?

This chapter dealt with the determinants of wages for jobs that are differentiated by employer size. Moore (1911, p. 163) concluded: "Our investigation has yielded the definite result that, as the size of the establishment increases, the condition of the laborer improves in all directions". Nearly a century later, the facts have not changed. A worker who holds a job in a large firm is paid a higher wage, receives more generous fringe benefits, gets more training, is provided with a cleaner, safer, and generally more pleasant work environment. She has access to newer technologies and superior capital equipment. She is, however, obliged to produce standardized as opposed to customized goods and services, and for the most part to perform the work in tandem with other members of a larger team. The costs of finding a job with a small firm are lower. The personal relation between employee and employer may be closer, but layoff and firm failure rates are higher resulting in less job security.

The size of a firm depends on external market forces, the decisions made by the entrepreneur, and luck. A firm becomes large and retains its size by organizing production and assembling the right work force. The characteristics of jobs and of the employees who staff them are jointly determined by the employer and employees. The implicit employment contracts result in a reduced form relation in which wages are positively related to size. A monitoring cost hypothesis matches productive workers with large firms to minimize the sum of wage and monitoring costs. Efficiency wages might be paid to deter shirking. Both explanations are vague about why the frequency and virulence of shirking would have been greater in larger firms in the absence of monitoring or efficiency wages. After reviewing a number of theoretical models and the empirical evidence, Brown and Medoff (1989, pp. 1056–1057) concluded:

> Our analysis leaves us uncomfortably unable to explain it.... In lieu of a more positive conclusion, we offer two observations... First, large employers pay more for their labor but less for their other inputs because of lower interest rates on borrowed funds and quantity discounts on purchased inputs... Second, large firms are also older firms. Is it possible that the size-wage premium is really a relationship between employer age and wages?... Thus, the employer size-wage effect remains a fact in need of an empirically based theory.

The surplus of revenues over labor costs per employee is positively related to firm size if a part of the income of the owner-manager of a small firm is properly counted as a labor cost. At least three factors could produce this relation of a greater ability to pay by a larger firm: (1) lower prices for non-labor inputs; (2) greater market power; or (3) larger overhead cost to amortize sunk costs for capital and a firm-specific work force. It is important to identify the source of the surplus. If it is a true economic rent (due to monopoly power, luck, or a fortuitous location), workers could capture a portion by forming a trade union. Rent sharing may be practiced by an altruistic firm, but our received theory is silent about which firms will be altruistic. There are other instances in which a post-contractual rent represents a return to the firm for an investment in human capital. The gross returns to firms and employees could be increased by sharing the returns. A specifically trained employee thus earns a wage that exceeds her wage in an alternative employment and hence has a lower propensity to separate. One could either call this rent-sharing or label it as a means of "producing" a more productive labor input. The relation of wages to "firm age" is weaker. The merits of this argument are examined in Appendix A.

The taxation and regulation of business enterprises surely affect the size distribution of firms and hence the shape of the wage–size profile. One can ask whether an industrial policy that favors some sectors over others or a policy of subsidizing small business will be beneficial to labor. The answer will depend on the theory of wages which one accepts. If wages are the results of discretionary wage policies, intervention might well improve labor's position. This chapter advanced a productivity hypothesis which begins with the premise that labor productivity is a function of work effort. Production, especially in the distributive trades, is characterized by increasing returns. A higher arrival rate of customers, clients, and patients means that workers have less idle time and hence are more productive at larger establishments. In the goods producing sector, larger firms organize work around teams, establish higher effort standards, recruit, train, and retain more productive employees. Schultze (1989, p. 280) asks us to think about two 30-year-old college graduates, one manages a Kentucky Fried Chicken outlet, and the other works at the World Headquarters of the Ford Motor Company. The two are not interchangeable. Productivity is a function of both observable traits as well as unobservable characteristics. Jobs at large firms are different from those at small firms. The organization of work and the selection of employees are responsible for the fact that wages are positively related to employer size. This view of the labor market argues against interventions to manipulate the size distribution of firms.

Appendix A. On the relationship of wages to firm age

In the conclusion to their survey, Brown and Medoff (1997) noted that large firms are older which led them to ask, "Is the size–wage premium really a relationship between employer age and wages?". The 1987 Survey of Manufactures asked for the earliest date at which production commenced at this establishment. Dunne and Roberts (1990) could thus introduce plant age as a determinant of wages (average hourly earnings of production workers). In a wage equation which included establishment size, capital stock, industry, and region, they found that plants, 30 or more years old, paid wages which were 10% higher than wages at plants 1 to 5 years old.[42] This result might have been caused by the possibility that older plants had more experienced workers. Troske (1994) found that workers in plants less than five years old earned 20% less than workers in plants in business for fifteen or more years. However, controlling for worker characteristics in his sample of manufacturing workers reduced the partial effect of plant age on wages. A more careful analysis of this relationship was undertaken by Brown and Medoff (1997). They attached additional questions to the monthly Survey of Consumers to obtain data on age of firm, probability of layoff or plant closure, and the employer's ability to pay.[43] In a linear model, a one standard deviation increase in firm age was associated with a 7% increase in wages.[44] A plot of the data revealed that the relationship was U-shaped. Wages declined with firm age, but for firms above the median "age" of 30 years, wages were positively related to firm age. Controlling for worker/job characteristics extended the negatively sloped segment. The authors advance several reasons to rationalize the downward sloping segment of the

---

[42] Establishments that were part of a multi-plant firm paid wages 21% above wages of single plant firms. There is some evidence that wages were negatively related to the exit and entry rate of plants into the industry.

[43] This last was calculated from responses to the question, "Without going out of business, do you think that your employer could afford to increase the pay of all its workers by 10%?". The questions on firm age and layoff probability are reproduced in note 6 of Brown and Medoff (1997) who collected data on worker and job traits including firm and plant size. Of the 1410 workers in private and non-profit sectors from September 1991 to March 1992, data on firm age were provided by 1076 respondents.

[44] The mean of the "firm age" variable in their sample was 40.1 years with a standard deviation of 32.0 years. In logs, the mean was 3.29 with a standard deviation of 1.09.

age-wage profile. We shall remark on two of these. First, older firms are more likely to offer fringe benefits. We are a bit confused by the chain of reasoning in the Brown-Medoff paper. "One reason is that as noted above, they tend to pay higher wages, and such fringes have a tax advantage…". Newly established firms are uncertain of their survival and choose to postpone adopting fringe benefit plans which have a significant fixed set-up cost. An older established firm can then substitute higher fringe benefits for lower wages. The relationship to be explained is that between wages and firm age, not total hourly compensation including fringes and firm age. Second the evidence is overwhelming that older firms have higher survival rates. The Survey of Consumers respondents evidently indicated that the odds of layoffs or plant closures were lower at older firms. The authors assume that workers will accept a lower wage in return for greater job security. This assumption was challenged by Mayo and Murray (1991) and Winter-Ebmer (1995) whose studies indicated that increases in the probability of job loss were accompanied by lower wages. Finally, we question the authors who wrote, "…there is undoubtedly a positive relationship between the age of the business and the age of the capital it uses. It is possible that older firms use older capital which requires less skill and so employ less skilled employees". Dom et al. (1993) found that the adoption of advanced technologies was more likely among large and hence older manufacturing plants which also hired more skilled workers and paid them higher wages. The giant supermarkets occupied newer buildings and operated more sophisticated equipment.

The upward sloping portion of the age-wage relationship was rationalized by the greater ability to pay by very old firms over 30 years of age. "Ability" in this study is based on the workers' assessment of whether the employer could raise pay by 10% without going out of business. If one could get data on profits per worker, which is an alternative and possibly better proxy for "ability to pay", its inclusion in a wage equation should do away with the positive branch of the U-shaped profile.

The firm is at best a fuzzy entity in our received theory of price, especially when one has to cope with joint ventures, multi-product "firms", partnerships, and so on. A recurring theme in Marshall (1952) is the non-constancy of the human agent. The situation is even more fluid for a firm in a changing world. The company that produced railway signals in 1920 is still in business in Rochester, but it no longer makes railway signals. Is it still the same *firm*? If Yamaha closes all of its motorcycle factories and deals only in the production and distribution of pianos, do we measure its age from the start of the motorcycle or piano eras? Acquisitions and divestures pose a hard problem. San Michelle Wines was acquired by US Tobacco. Does an employee at the vineyard report the age at which San Michelle began bottling wine or the age at which US tobacco began to make pipe tobacco? "When a business is sold to a new owner, Dunn and Bradstreet's "years in business" variable often measures years in business under current ownership" (cited in Brown and Medoff, 1997). The cross-sectional samples examined by Dunne and Roberts (1990) and by Brown and Medoff (1997) yield conflicting relationships. A strong test of the relationship of wages to firm age would require panel data in which one could follow wages as a firm gets older. We do not have such data, and given the elusive nature of the concept of a firm, it is unclear if we want to wait for someone to collect such a panel dataset.

References

Akerlof, G.A. (1984), "Gift exchange and efficiency-wage theory: four views", American Economic Review Papers and Proceedings Papers 74: 79–83.

Alchian, A.A. (1959), "Costs and outputs" in: M. Abramovitz, ed., The allocation of economic resources (Stanford University Press, Stanford, CA).

Alchian, A.A. and H. Demsetz (1972), "Production, information cost, and economic organization", American Economic Review 62: 777–795.

Asher, H. (1956), "Cost quantity relationship in the air frame industry", Report no. R-291 (RAND, Santa Monica, CA).

Autor, D.H., L.F. Katz and A.B. Krueger (1997), "Computing inequality: have computers changed the labor market?" Working paper no. 5956 (NBER, Cambridge, MA).

Baker, G.P., M. Jensen and K.J. Murphy (1988), "Compensation and incentives: practice vs. theory", Journal of Finance 43: 593–615.

Baldamus, W. (1959), Efficiency and effort (Tavistock Publications, London).

Baron, J., D.A. Black and M.A. Loewenstein (1987), "Employer size: the implications for search, training, capital investment, starting wages, and wage growth", Journal of Labor Economics 5: 76–89.

Becker, G.S. (1973), "A theory of marriage: part I", Journal of Political Economy 81: 813–846.

Becker, G.S. (1985), "Human capital, effort, and the sexual division of labor", Journal of Labor Economics 3 (part 2): S33–S58.

Beecher, J. (1986), Charles Fourier, a visionary and his world (University of California Press, Berkeley, CA).

Bluestone, B. (1989), The retail revolution (The Auburn House, Boston, MA).

Brown, C. and J. Medoff (1989), "The employer size wage effect", Journal of Political Economy October: 1027–1059.

Brown, C. and J. Medoff (1997), "Firm age and wages", Working paper.

Brown, C., J. Hamilton and J. Medoff (1990), Employers large and small (Harvard University Press, Cambridge, MA).

Bulow, J.I. and L.H. Summers (1986), "A theory of dual labor markets with applications to industrial policy", Journal of Labor Economics 4: 376–414.

Chandler, Alfred D. Jr. (1982), The visible hand (Harvard University Press, Cambridge, MA).

Clark, J.M. (1923), Studies in the economics of overhead costs (University of Chicago Press, Chicago, IL).

Davis, S. and M. Henrekson (1997), "Explaining national differences in the size and industry distribution of employment", Working paper (August).

de Grazia, Sebastian (1962), Of time, work, and leisure (Twentieth Century Fund, New York).

Deardorf, A.V. and F.P. Stafford (1976), "Compensation of cooperating factors", Econometrica 44: 671–684.

Doeringer, P. and M. Piore (1971), Internal labor markets and manpower analysis (D.C. Heath, Lexington, MA).

Doms, M., T. Dunne and K.R. Troske (1997), "Workers, wages, and technology", Quarterly Journal of Economics 102: 253–290.

Dunn, L.F. (1980), "The effect of firm and plant size on employee well-being", in: J.J. Siegfried, ed., The economics of firm size, market structure, and social performance (US Government Printing Office, Washington, DC) pp. 348–358.

Dunne, T. and M. Roberts (1990), "Plant, firm and industrial wage variations", Working paper (Pennsylvannia State University, December 1990).

Dunne, T. and J. Schmitz Jr. (1995), "Wages, employment structure, and employer size wage premia: their relationship to advanced technology usage at U.S. manufacturing establishments", Economica 62: 89–105.

Eaton, B.C. and W.D. White (1983), "The economy of high wages: an agency problem", Economica 50: 175–181.

Ehrenberg, R.G. and R.S. Smith (1997), Modern labor economics (Addison-Wesley Educational Publishers, Redding, MA).

Evans, D. and L. Leighton (1989), "Why do smaller firms pay less?" Journal of Human Resources 24: 299–318.

Farber, H.S. (1997), "Job creation in the United States: good jobs or bad?" Working paper no. 385 (Princeton University, Princeton, NJ).

Foss, M.R. (1981), Changes in the workweek of fixed capital (American Enterprise Institute, Washington, DC).

Funkhauser, E. (1997), "The importance of firm wage differentials in explaining hourly earnings variations in a large scale sector of Guatemala", Journal of Development Economics 513: 1–17.

Garen, J. (1985), "Worker heterogeneity, job screening, and firm size", Journal of Political Economy 93: 715–739.

Gibbons, R., and L. Katz (1992), "Does unmeasured ability explain inter-industry wage differentials?" Review of Economic Studies 59: 515–535.

Griliches, Z. (1969), "Capital-skill complementarity", Review of Economics and Statistics 51: 465–468.

Groshen, E.L. (1991), "Five reasons why wages vary among employers", Industrial Relations 30: 350–381.

Groshen, E.L. and A.B. Krueger (1990), "The structure of supervision and pay in hospitals", Industrial and Labor Relations Review 43: S134–S146.

Haber, S., J. Cordes and J. Barth (1988), "Employment and training opportunities in small and large firms", Report (U.S. Small Business Administration, Office of Advocacy).

Hall, R.E. (1982), "The importance of lifetime jobs in the U.S. economy", American Economic Review 72: 716–724.

Hall, R.E. (1991), Booms and recessions in a noisy economy (Yale University Press, New Haven, CT).

Hamermesh, D. (1993), Labor demand (Princeton University Press, Princeton, NJ).

Hashimoto, M. and J. Raisian (1985), "Employer tenure and earnings profiles in Japan and the United States", American Economic Review 75: 721–735.

Hashimoto, M. and B.T. Yu (1980), "Specific capital, employment contracts, and wage rigidity", The Bell Journal of Economics 11: 536–549.

Holtmann, A.G. and T.L. Idson (1995), "Information, employer size, training, and wage growth", Eastern Economics Journal 21: 187–191.

Hutt, W.H. (1977), The theory of idle resources (Liberty Press, Indianapolis, MN).

Idson, T.L. (1995), "Team production effects on earnings", Economic Letters 49: 197–203.

Idson, T.L. (1996), "Employer size and labor turnover", in: S. Polachek, ed., Research in labor economics (JAI Press, Greenwich, CT).

Idson, T.L. and D. Feaster (1990), "A selectivity model with employer size differentials", Journal of Labor Economics 8 (part 1): 99–122.

Idson, Todd L. and Hisako Ishii (1992), "Comparison of employer size effects on wages and tenure for men and women in Japan and the United States", Industrial Relations Research Association Proceedings: 531–538.

Kaldor, N. (1934), "The equilibrium of the firm", Economic Journal 44: 60–76.

Katz, L.F. and L.H. Summers (1989), "Industry rents: evidence and implications", Brookings Papers on Economic Activity, Microeconomics: 209–275.

Kent, A.S.S. (1915), Second interim report on industrial fatigue (London).

Kostiuck, P. (1990), "Firm size and executive compensation", Journal of Human Resources 25: 90–105.

Kremer, M. (1993), "The O ring theory of economic development", Quarterly Journal of Economics 108: 551–575.

Krueger, A. (1993), "How computers changed the wage structure", Quarterly Journal of Economics 108: 33–60.

Kruse, D. (1992), "Supervision, working conditions, and the employer size effect", Industrial Relations 31: 229–249.

Kwoka, J.E. Jr.(1980), "Establishment size, wages, and job satisfaction, the trade-offs", in: J.J. Siegfried, ed., The economics of firm size, market structure, and social performance (US Government Printing Office, Washington, DC) pp. 359–379.

Lazear, E. (1981), "Agency, earnings profiles, productivity, and hours restrictions", American Economic Review 71: 606–620.

Lester, R.A. (1967), "Pay differentials by size of establishment", Industrial and Labor Relations Review 7: 57–67.

Little, I.M.D., D. Mazundar and J.M. Page Jr. (1987), Small manufacturing enterprises, a comparative analysis of India and other economies (Oxford University Press, Oxford, UK).

Loveman, G. and W. Sengenberger (1991), "The re-emergence of small scale production: an international comparison", Small Business Economics 3: 1–37.

Lucas, R.E. Jr. (1978), "On the size distribution of business firms", The Bell Journal of Economics 9: 508–523.

Main, B.G.M. and B. Reilly (1993), "The employer size-wage gap: evidence for Britain", Economica 60: 125–142.

Marshall, Alfred (1952), Principles of economics (Macmillan, New York).

Mayo, J.W. and M.N. Murray (1991), "Firm size, employment risk, and wages: further insights on a persistent puzzle" Applied Economics 23: 1351–1360.

McNulty, P.J. (1980), The origins and development of labor economics (M.I.T. Press, Cambridge, MA).

Mellow, W. (1982), "Employer size and wages", Review of Economics and Statistics 54: 495–501.

Mincer, J. (1962), "On-the-job training: costs, returns, and some implications", Journal of Political Economy 70: s50–s79.

Moore, Henry L. (1911), Laws of wages (Macmillan, New York) (reprinted 1967, Augustus M. Kelley, New York).

Mulligan, J.G. (1983), "The economies of massed reserves", American Economic Review 15: 725–734.

Nyland, C. (1989), Reduced worktime and the management of production (Cambridge University Press, New York).

Oi, W.Y. (1967), "The neoclassical foundations of production functions" Economic Journal 77: 579–594.

Oi, W.Y. (1974), "On the economics of industrial safety", Law and Contemporary Problems 38: 669–709.

Oi, W.Y. (1983), "Heterogeneous firms and the organization of production", Economic Inquiry 21: 147–171.

Oi, W.Y. (1990), "Employment relations in dual labor markets", Journal of Labor Economics 8 (part 2): s124–s149.

Oi, W.Y. (1991), "Low wages and small firms", in: R.G. Ehrenberg, ed., Research in labor economics, Vol. 12 (JAI Press, Greenwich, CT).

Oi, W.Y. (1992), "Productivity in the distributive trades", in: Z. Griliches, ed., Output measurement in the service sectors (University of Chicago Press, Chicago, IL).

Pearce, J.E. (1990), "Tenure, unions, and the relationship between employer size and wages", Journal of Labor Economics 8: 251–269.

Personick, M.E. and C.B. Barsky (1982), "White-collar pay levels linked to corporate work force size", Monthly Labor Review 105: 23–28.

Pissarides, C. (1977), Labor market adjustments (Cambridge University Press, Cambridge, MA).

Raff, D.M.G. and L.H. Summers (1987), "Did Henry Ford pay efficiency wages?" Journal of Labor Economics 5: S57–S86.

Reilly, K.T. (1995), "Human capital and information: the employer size-wage effect", Journal of Human Resources 30: 1–18.

Robinson, E.A.G. (1958), The structure of competitive industry (University of Chicago Press, Chicago, IL).

Schaffner, J.A. (1996), "Premiums to employment in larger establishments: evidence from Peru", Working paper (Stanford University, Stanford, CA).

Schultze, C.L. (1989), "Industry rents: comment", Brookings Papers on Economic Activity Microeconomics: 280–283.

Senior, N. (1858), Political economy, 4th edition (Augustus M. Kelley, Publisher).

Shapiro, C. and J.E. Stiglitz (1984), "Equilibrium unemployment as a worker discipline device", American Economic Review 74: 433–444.

Shinohara, M. (1962), Growth and cycles in the Japanese economy (Kinokuniya Bookstore Co., Tokyo).

Simon, H.A. (1947), Administrative behavior (Macmillan, New York).

Simpson, W. (1984), "An Econometric analysis of industrial training in Canada", Journal of Human Resources Fall: 435–451.

Slichter, S.H. (1950), "Notes on the structure of wages" Review of Economics and Statistics 32: 80–91.

Smith, A. (1997), The wealth of nations, Cannan edition, Vol. I.

Stafford, F.P. (1980), "Firm size, workplace public goods, and worker welfare", in: J.J. Siegfried, ed., The economics of firm size, market structure, and social performance (US Government Printing Office, Washington, DC) pp. 326–347.

Stigler, G.J. (1962), "Information in the labor market", Journal of Political Economy 70 (part 2): S94–S105.

Stigler, G.J. and R.A. Sherwin (1985), "The extent of the market", Journal of Law and Economics 28: 555–585.

Troske, K.R. (1994), Evidence on the employer size wage premium from worker establishment matched data (Center for Economic Studies, US Bureau of the Census, Washington, DC).

Troske, K.R. (1999), "The worker-establishment characteristics database", in: J. Haltiwanger and M. Manser, eds., Labor statistics measurement issues (University of Chicago Press, Chicago, IL) in press.

Velenchik, A.D. (1996), "Market power, firm performance and real wage growth in Zimbabwean manufacturing", World Development 25: 749–762.

Vernon, H.M. (1921), Industrial fatigue and efficiency (G. Routledge, London).

Weiss, L. (1966), "Concentration and labor earnings", American Economic Review 56: 96–117.

Winter-Ebmer, R. (1995), "Does layoff risk explain the firm-size wage differential?" Applied Economics Letters 2: 211–214.

Wright, T.P. (1936), "Factors affecting the cost of air frames", Journal of the Aeronautical Sciences 3: 122–128.

Chapter 34

THE LABOR MARKET IMPLICATIONS OF INTERNATIONAL TRADE

GEORGE JOHNSON AND FRANK STAFFORD*

Department of Economics, The University of Michigan

Contents

* Support from the Alfred P. Sloan Foundation, grant #B1995-22 is gratefully acknowledged as are comments from numerous colleagues, particularly Alan Deardorff and Bob Stern. The authors can be reached at the following email addresses: gjohnson@umich.edu and fstaffor@umich.edu.

Handbook of Labor Economics, Volume 3, Edited by O. Ashenfelter and D. Card

Abstract

The general equilibrium analysis of many important labor market issues is very different in an economy that is open to international trade than an economy (like the US in the 1950s) in which trade is not very important. Despite the fact that individual national economies have become increasingly interdependent over the last few decades, labor economists have generally used a closed economy framework to attack many important issues (such as the determinants of the distribution of earnings) that should, in fact, be approached very differently in an open economy setting. A major task of this paper is the exposition of the correct approach to labor market analysis for the case in which the focus economy is open rather than closed. Perhaps the most important implication of neoclassical trade theory for labor economics is that, under certain conditions, the skill distribution of wages in a particular economy is unaffected by the skill distribution of the supply of labor in that economy. Our review of the trade literature focuses on the question of the degree to which these conditions are likely to be satisfied. Our general conclusion – inspired more from the empirical than the purely theoretical branch of the trade field – is that the correct specification of the behavior of the labor market is a blend of the closed and open models. © 1999 Elsevier Science B.V. All rights reserved.

JEL codes: J30; F10

1. Introduction

This paper is concerned with the general question of how the "openness" of an economy to international trade affects the analysis of the labor market within that economy. What are the differences in the way employment and wages are determined in a closed economy (a state of autarky) versus an open economy? How will various external events (ranging from a reduction in trade barriers to improvements in foreign technology) affect the domestic labor market? How does the degree of openness affect the influence of domestic events (e.g., a change in the skill composition of the labor force) on domestic labor market outcomes (e.g., the skilled/unskilled relative wage)? How does one determine the importance of international factors empirically?

Most of the literature on this topic has, of course, been developed by specialists in international economics. Our focus, however, is on issues that are of particular interest to labor economists. This may be a somewhat hard sell. The methodologies of the two relevant fields, trade and labor, are very different. Trade economists tend to think about their problems (and the $N!$ special cases) long and hard; labor economists tend to run regressions (on occasion without thinking very much about theoretical aspects of the problem).[1] However, the opening up of national economies to international competition – a process that is virtually certain to continue – has profound implications for the way

---

[1] For a similar characterization of the labor and trade fields, see Richardson (1995). See also the extended discussion at the end of a paper by a labor and a trade economist who worked together in Blanchflower and Slaughter (1998). One can either characterize the methodological differences positively (labor specialists are careful with data while trade specialists are careful with theory) or negatively (labor economists are atheoretical and trade economists are sloppy empiricists).

labor markets operate (Klodt, 1992; Freeman, 1995). It is, accordingly, important in the attack on (and the teaching about) many labor-related questions to be aware of these implications.

Consider, for example, the labor market effects of the large influx of low skilled immigrants from third world countries to industrial countries in Western Europe and North America during the past 20 years. Using a conventional closed economy framework, a labor economist would proceed to set up a model in which (a) the immigrants earn roughly the increase in aggregate output in the destination country while (b) relatively skilled workers in the destination country gain rather substantially at the expense of native low skilled workers. The size of the transfer under (b) would depend on certain parameters of production functions discussed in various sections of Hamermesh (1993). Indeed, this prediction is so obvious that the labor economist would turn immediately to the task of regressing changes in relative wages on proxies for changes in the proportion of the population who are immigrants across cities (and then spend the next day in search of instrumental variables).

A serious problem with this approach is that its basic model assumes, as most of us are used to assuming, that the economy is closed. The relative prices of all products produced in the economy are assumed to be set within the country. If, however, a set of products that are produced in the economy are traded internationally (either exported or imported), the theoretical framework that motivated the above regression (and its modifications) is not correct. Indeed, under "classical" trade theory, one would expect that (under certain conditions) the principle slope coefficient of the regression would be zero.

The plan of this survey is as follows. In Section 2 we review various facts about trends in the volume of trade and in real and relative wages around the world. In Section 3 we explore the implications of a rather simple "Ricardian" model of a single economy in which trade plays a major role. This highlights a number of issues that are especially important to labor market analysis. In Section 4 we summarize some of the major themes of neoclassical trade theory, again with emphasis on what the degree of openness of an economy implies about labor market analysis. In Section 5 the work on various empirical issues associated with trade and wages is reviewed. Section 6 concludes.

2. Stylized facts about trade and wages

The potential for trade to shape a country's labor market will depend on the extent to which the economy is based on tradable outputs, the extent to which trade is supported as a matter of public policy and business practice, and the extent to which there are inter-country differences in the capacity to produce the tradable outputs. Trade also depends on an international financial system of exchange rates or currency 'regions' and transportation costs. In this review we will pay relatively little attention to the important role of the financial and transportation systems, yet even from the basic data on trade as a share of GDP, it is quite evident that the latter two are important in defining 'openness'.

Table 1
Ratio of merchandise exports to GDP (1913, 1950) and openness (1950–1992)[a]

Country	1913	1950	1950	1973	1987	1992
Australia	18.3	22.0	25.4	19.7	17.4	19.0
Austria	8.2	12.6	16.6	30.3	35.3	38.9
Belgium	50.9	20.3	31.0	54.5	67.8	68.5
Brazil	–	–	7.9	8.9	7.8	8.3
Canada	15.1	17.5	10.3	22.9	26.1	27.0
China	–	–	–	2.9	12.6	16.7
Denmark	26.9	21.3	28.7	29.5	30.5	33.2
Finland	25.2	16.6	18.2	16.8	25.6	26.3
France	13.9	10.6	14.1	17.1	20.6	22.4
W. Germany	17.5	8.5	9.3	20.4	26.5	30.0
Hungary	–	–	–	35.9	38.1	33.7
India	–	–	6.3	4.6	7.6	10.7
Italy	12.0	7.0	9.3	18.4	19.2	19.8
Japan	12.3	4.7	9.2	10.0	8.8	9.0
Netherlands	38.2	26.9	40.7	43.8	48.5	50.6
Norway	22.7	18.2	42.4	43.8	36.6	39.5
Sweden	20.8	17.8	21.4	25.7	31.5	27.0
Switzerland	31.4	20.0	26.0	31.5	35.1	34.2
Taiwan	–	–	7.6[b]	22.3	24.4	22.5
UK	20.9	14.4	23.3	24.9	26.0	24.5
USA	6.1	3.6	4.2	6.8	9.8	10.9

[a] Source: Maddison (1991, p. 326; World Penn Tables). (Exports + imports)/2 × GDP (at current international prices).
[b] 1951.

As can be seen from Table 1, there is, at one extreme, Belgium and the Netherlands with 68 and 51% of GDP (1992) in the form of trade and at the other end of the spectrum, Brazil (8), the US (11) and Japan (9) with much lower percents of GDP (1992) arising from international trade. Presumably these differences arise, on the one hand, from the close proximity of trading partners in the Belgium and the Netherlands, low transport costs via rail and water to these trading partners, and a supportive financial infrastructure. On the other hand, the US and Brazil have intra-country differences promoting internal trade, and Japan is geographically separated from major potential trading partners.

For many countries (Australia, Belgium, Denmark, France, Japan, Sweden, Switzerland, UK, and the US), the long term trends in trade (1913–1992) show no more than a modest, not dramatic, upward drift in trade as a share of GDP.[2] Trade as a share of GDP fell during the global recession of the 1930s and then was restored in the Post War period. Many of the advanced industrialized countries (Canada, Denmark, France, Italy, Japan,

[2] The Maddison data (1913, 1950) are for merchandise trade as a share of GDP. These data necessarily understate all trade, which includes services. For this reason, the 1913–1992 change overstates the growth of 'openness'.

The Netherlands, Sweden, Switzerland, UK and the US have experienced only a modest (or no) growth in openness from 1973 to 1992.

The Post War period has been characterized by a generally supportive public policy favoring openness, and for this reason we would expect a rising share of GDP to arise internationally. On the other hand, the 'industrialized' countries have experienced unbalanced growth: services have risen dramatically as a share of GDP. For example, Sweden as of 1950 had about 55% of GDP in the form of products that could be regarded as readily 'tradable', but by the mid-1990s this has fallen to 35%. While the world economy has experienced a higher growth rate for service trade compared to other trade in recent years, this is from a low base, and there are still major limits on the tradability of most services.

Growth of services as a limit on trade was, to our knowledge, first articulated by Keynes (1933). He argued that with rising national income there would be an income elastic shift toward housing, services and other amenities, none of which is tradable, and that the world economy could experience a transition toward self-sufficiency. This thesis of a shift to services has appeared in a somewhat different and implicit form in the modern work on unbalanced growth (Baumol et al., 1985).[3]

A fascinating prospect is the potential for increased future tradability of services via global standards for telecommunications (GATT, 1994; Branscomb and Kahin, 1995) and improved video images. This new technology could transform such products as medical diagnostic, educational, consumer financial, and other services into internationally tradable services. From the perspective of this paper, such a development could impact the character of the US or Japanese labor markets, both of which are less dependent on international trade, at least as indicted by the rather modest share of GDP arising via international trade. As will demonstrated below, such a rise in "openness" could profoundly change the nature of labor market responses to such events as domestic shifts in the relative supply of skilled labor in the individual countries.

One of the central themes in the theory of trade, indeed all of economics, is the concept of comparative advantage, the relative productivity of units exchanging different outputs. The two main forces shaping comparative advantage are relative factor endowments and the technology of the potential trading partners. For purposes of simplification, attention is directed to differential factor endowment ratios as the driving force with technology differences, along with inter-country differences in preferences playing a secondary, if any, role. From the perspective of trade and especially of labor economics, an important characterization of a country's factor inventory is the relative shares of labor with different kinds and levels of skill. Unlike natural resource endowments such as agricultural land, a country's labor-based factor endowments can and do change through time. Worldwide, skilled labor has increased at an annual rate of 3.6% over the period 1973–1993 (from 185 to 371 million) while unskilled labor has increased at an annual rate of 1.6% (from 1485 to 2065 million) (Cline, 1997, p. 183). In this process the advanced industrialized countries

---

[3] Of course, trade could be small as a share of GDP if the country and its trading partners had no clear comparative advantage yet shape wages.

Table 2
Labor factor endowments[a], selected countries, 1973 and 1993

Country, group	Skilled			Unskilled		
	1973	1993	%GR	1973	1993	%GR
E U	32.4	49.2	2.1	113.1	108.5	−0.2
Japan	24.7	30.5	1.1	30.0	32.9	0.5
Canada	2.6	6.2	4.4	6.9	7.4	0.4
U S	42.6	72.1	2.7	50.8	52.7	0.2
Other OECD	5.2	9.7	3.2	32.8	41.4	1.2
Mexico	1.3	4.4	6.4	15.2	29.0	3.3
Other Latin[b]	5.4	13.6	4.7	69.8	108.8	2.2
China	28.5	80.7	5.3	431.1	626.8	1.8
India	9.9	26.3	5.0	225.6	315.2	1.7
G4	1.8	13.7	10.6	18.6	19.5	0.2
World	184.7	371.3	3.6	1485.0	2065.0	1.7

[a] Source: Cline (1997, pp. 184–185). Millions of persons.
[b] Except Venezuela

have become a smaller share of global labor resources, and the relative growth of skilled labor has been stronger in some of the industrializing countries, notably China, India and the G4 group (Table 2).

At the level of individual countries, one source of changing factor endowments, immigration, has received a great deal of policy attention. This interest is probably motivated by concerns other than wage effects and is most evident in certain regions where the relative supply effects are greater (Fernandez and Robinson, 1994). In the US an estimated 121,000 immigrants were admitted as permanent residents in 1994. Estimates of undocumented immigrants range from 3,500,000 to 4,000,000 as of 1994 with from 1,321,000 to 1,784,000 in California and a mere 10,000–53,000 in Michigan (US Bureau of the Census, 1994).

Even if all the estimated 4,000,000 undocumented immigrants were unskilled, this would alter the relative supply of skilled workers in the US, using the endowment estimates from Cline, from 1.36 to 1.47. The impact of such a change in relative factor endowments would depend in turn on the extent to which the US is a price taker in world markets and the extent to which the economy is open, as will be discussed in more detail below.

On a global basis with a stationary technology, one would expect a decline in the relative wages of skilled labor in light of the rising world relative supply. Yet, in many countries, particularly OECD countries, and especially the US, there has been a rise in the relative earnings of skilled labor. The rising relative earnings inequality appears to be appear to be globally pervasive, raising questions about the forces shaping this development.

This can be seen in Table 3 where the sector specific ratios of skilled and unskilled labor (columns (a)–(e)) and the overall ratio of skilled to non-skilled labor (e) are portrayed.

Table 3

Proportions of college equivalent labor (*S*) and high school equivalent labor (*U*) in manufacturing (*m*) and non-manufacturing (*n*) industries and the college/high school relative wage (*rel*) in the US, 1973–1989[a]

	(a) S_m/S	(b) U_m/U	(c) S_m/U_m	(d) S_n/U_n	(e) S/U	(f) *rel*
1973	0.190	0.334	0.166	0.355	0.292	1.34
1979	0.200	0.313	0.250	0.453	0.390	1.26
1989	0.161	0.228	0.390	0.602	0.554	1.45

[a] Source: Analysis of CPS data as described in Bound and Johnson (1992).

Despite the overall rise in *S/U*, the relative wage of skilled workers (*rel*) has been rising.[4] This implies that a stable relative demand for labor in a country or worldwide setting, combined with an increase relative supply of skilled labor, is not sufficient to understand the playing out of worldwide relative wages. What are the roles of trade, technology, and changing final demand which are shaping relative wages in individual countries? How do they combine to provide an understanding of the rising wage inequality, defined as increases in *rel*, set out in Table 4? In this chapter we seek to outline a framework which can be used to organize an investigation of the importance of these potential explanations.

As a background to the discussion it is important to recognize that technology is fast-moving and is distributed unevenly across countries. Much of the discussion of changing technology position has centered on manufacturing technology, largely because productivity has been better measured in this sector and over a longer time period in numerous countries – and most manufactured goods are tradable.

There have been various theories of technology. The most simple ones involve learning by individual firms and reduced costs for those with 'better' technology. Competition winnows out the technologically backward. From a trade perspective technology is often treated as having evolved from such a process and being given and known universally at a point in time. Starting with Vernon's product cycle (Vernon, 1966) and continuing to the present (Grossman and Helpman, 1991) there has been a concept of comparative advantage applied to technology creation.

One country or group of countries with high endowments of skilled labor forms a new product-based technology in Stage I. In Stage II they export and receive returns to cover the costs of investment in the new technology. In Stage III the technology moves to other countries with lower endowments of skilled labor and leads them to then produce a more standardized version on the good or service. This is in turn exchanged for a new generation product cycle good produced in the leader countries. This felicitous product cycle is contrasted with one in which technology migrates capriciously across borders. Most discussions adopt some systematic transfer as the maintained view, but it was recognized

[4] The "college equivalent" and "high school equivalent" units of labor input are defined as in Johnson (1997).

Table 4
Annual rates of growth of earnings inequality, 1980–1988 in 11 industrialized countries[a]

		% Growth in inequality	
		1980–1988	1988–1995
Australia	Men	0.7	0.2
	Women	1.2	−0.6
Austria	Men	0.4	0.5[b]
	Women	0.4	1.4[b]
Canada	Men	1.4	−0.2[b]
	Women	1.6	−0.7[b]
Finland	Men	0.6	−0.2[b]
	Women	0.6	−1.4[b]
France	Men	0.2	0.0[b]
	Women	0.2	1.2[b]
Germany	Men	−0.3[c]	−0.8[d]
	Women	−2.4[c]	−0.8[d]
Italy	Men	−0.4[e]	2.6[f]
	Women	−2.1[e]	3.3[f]
Japan	Men	0.8	−0.1[b]
	Women	1.0	−0.7[b]
Sweden	Men	0.0	0.9[d]
	Women	1.1	1.0[d]
US	Men	2.8	0.9
	Women	2.3	1.7
UK	Men	2.9	1.9
	Women	2.3	1.2

[a] Source: OECD, The OECD Employment Outlook (1996, Table 3.1).
[b] 1988–1994.
[c] 1983–1988.
[d] 1988–1993.
[e] 1980–1987.
[f] 1987–1993.

very early on (Vernon, 1979) that the window of time in which the leaders might recoup the returns to investment in new technology could be very limited. If so the incentives to utilize skilled labor for initial development of the technology may be lacking.

One of the empirical regularities receiving a great deal of attention in the early 1990s was the tendency for those countries with an initial (1950) productivity or technology deficit to 'converge' to the initial leaders (Baumol et al., 1991, pp. 102–108), with an exodus or partial exodus of the early leader nations in manufacturing from that sector – the so-called "deindustrialization" thesis. As we will show in following discussion, in contrast to a partial exodus from an industry, a *full* exodus of a country from an industry will leave them open for real income gains from any additional improvements abroad. The factors that create new technology are only partly understood, but it is worth noting that, historically, new technology has not been introduced in a steady fashion throughout the industrialized world. From 1580 to 1820, the locus of productivity leadership was the Netherlands, from 1820 to 1890 it was the UK and from 1890 to 1989 it was the US (Maddison, 1991, p. 31).

The coincident growth of trade as countries have become more similar in technological capacity (and factor endowments) in the Postwar period has given rise to the theory of inter-industry trade and emphasis on differentiated products and country-specific industry scale economies. The practical implication of this for labor economics (combined with the declining share of world factors in a single country) is that the export demand curves facing many countries are presumed to be increasingly elastic. If so, the change in the relative supply of labor in any one country should result in ever smaller wage impacts to the extent that the country is increasingly a price taker in world export markets.

Recent technology shifts are not characterized by simple convergence. Countries can regain or widen a technological lead through new forms of technology. One of the most celebrated changes is the emergence of network-based technologies as a factor defining productivity beyond the individual firm. If such infrastructure based technology is first adopted by a set of leader countries (rather than a global network), this could lead to technology "divergence" across trading nations. As we will illustrate, technology ebbs and flows across countries, by production sector, can be important in shaping terms of trade and income of the labor inputs in those economies.

Finally, there have been changing institutional arrangements and large institutional differences across countries. Trade restrictions have fallen, yet many countries have adhered to the notion of suspending free trade (which has been allowed under the General Agreement on Tariffs and Trade) to attenuate income and profit shocks. In the US there were voluntary export restraints on autos manufactured in Japan in the 1980s. The rationale for this policy included the preservation of jobs with good wages and working conditions. In Europe the support for binding minimum wages has continued, while in The US the minimum wage is rarely binding, and the US and most of Asia is often characterized as having wage flexibility. In this setting there can be important links across trading countries which play out in dramatic fashion, and impacts of institutions which are different from those to be expected in a single country model.

3. Trade and wages in Ricardian models

It is instructive to begin our exposition of the potential effects of international factors on labor market variables by considering a very simple Ricardian model of trade.[5] The model has exportable products and non-traded services with different factor intensities for relatively skilled and relatively unskilled labor. The advantages of such a model include its tractability and the important role it assigns to technological differences between industries. To start we ignore some relatively important matters that are central to the more

---

[5] See Jones and Neary (1984, Section 2.2) for a discussion of this approach.

traditional models discussed in Section 4 issues (for example, capital as a factor of production). However, the model set out in this section contains many of neoclassical trade theory's most important conclusions with respect to the labor market as an economy moves from autarky (the absence of trade) to free trade.

3.1. Wage determination in a closed economy

It is assumed that there are two types of labor in the economy: relatively skilled (the fixed aggregate effective supply of which is S) and relatively unskilled (U). The economy is initially assumed to be closed. There are up to five industries in operation in the economy. Each of the industries utilizes only one type of labor and no other factors of production. Industries 1 and 2 are manufacturing industries that use, respectively, skilled and unskilled labor; industry 3 is a manufacturing or raw materials industry using only unskilled labor; industries 4 and 5 are service industries using, respectively, skilled and unskilled labor. Thus, in a sense, industries 1 and 4 constitute the high-tech sector and industries 2, 3, and 5 the low-tech sector. Given constant returns, the production functions for the five industries can be written as

$$Q_i = A_i S_i, \qquad i = 1, 4$$

$$Q_i = A_i U_i, \qquad i = 2, 3, 5, \tag{3.1}$$

where the A_i's are fixed technological coefficients. Given competitive price and wage determination and the complete within-country mobility of labor between the industries grouped by skill, the marginal conditions for the economy imply that the skilled wage rate satisfies

$$W_S = A_1 P_1 = A_4 P_4, \tag{3.2}$$

where P_1 and P_4 are the prices of the two high-tech goods. Similarly, for the unskilled wage rate

$$W_U = A_2 P_2 = A_3 P_3 = A_5 P_5. \tag{3.3}$$

It is assumed that the utility function for the economy is Cobb–Douglas in the consumption of the five goods, that is

$$Y = \prod_{1=1}^{5} C_i^{\nu_i}, \qquad \sum_i \nu_i = 1, \tag{3.4}$$

where C_i is the aggregate consumption of good i. Maximization of Y given the appropriate budget constraint implies that expenditure on the ith good is given by

$$P_i C_i = \nu_i \sum_i P_i Q_i. \tag{3.5}$$

In the absence of international trade, all consumption is produced domestically, or $C_i = Q_i$.

These assumptions are sufficient to derive the quantity of labor employed in each of the five industries. The amount of skilled labor employed in $i = 1$ or 4 is $S_i = \nu_i/(\nu_1 + \nu_4)S$, and the amount of unskilled labor employed in $i = 2$, 3, or 5 is $U_i = \nu_i/(\nu_2 + \nu_3 + \nu_5)U$. By Eq. (5) the price of good 1 relative to good 2 is $P_1/P_2 = (\nu_1/\nu_2)/(Q_1/Q_2)$, which is equal to $((\nu_1 + \nu_4)/(\nu_2 + \nu_3 + \nu_5))(A_2 U/A_1 S)$. It then follows from the marginal conditions that the skilled/unskilled relative wage rate is

$$rel = \frac{W_S}{W_U} = \frac{A_1 P_1}{A_2 P_2} = \frac{\nu_1 + \nu_4}{\nu_2 + \nu_3 + \nu_5}\left(\frac{S}{U}\right)^{-1}. \tag{3.6}$$

The relative wage depends negatively on the relative supply of workers by skill and positively on the relative weight of skill-intensive products in the utility function. It is important to note that, because of the special functional forms, *rel* does *not* depend on the five technological parameters, the A_i's.[6]

The value of the consumption levels of each of the five goods is equal to A_i times the solution value of the relevant labor input, $C_1 = A_1 \nu_1/(\nu_1 + \nu_4)S$, etc. It then follows that the reduced form level of aggregate utility (real output) is

$$Y = A S^{\nu_1 + \nu_4} U^{\nu_2 + \nu_3 + \nu_5}, \qquad A = (\nu_1 + \nu_4)^{-(\nu_1 + \nu_4)}(\nu_2 + \nu_3 + \nu_5)^{-(\nu_2 + \nu_3 + \nu_5)} \sum_i (\nu_i A_i)^{\nu_i}. \tag{3.7}$$

The real wage rates of each type of labor equal

$$R_S = (\nu_1 + \nu_4)\frac{Y}{S} \tag{3.8}$$

and

$$R_U = (\nu_2 + \nu_3 + \nu_4)\frac{Y}{U}. \tag{3.9}$$

A proportional change in any one of the technological parameters has the same proportional effect on both real wage rates, that is $\hat{R}_S = d(\ln R_S) = \hat{R}_U = \nu_i \hat{A}_i$. Equal proportional changes, $\hat{A}$, in each of the five technological parameters causes Y, R_S, and R_U all to rise by $\hat{A}$.

3.2. Wage determination in an open economy

Now suppose that goods 1, 2, and 3 become traded internationally with prices set in world

---

[6] If the utility function (4) had been assumed to be of the CES form with an elasticity of substitution equal to ε (which may, unlike the current form of (4), differ from unity), the value of $\partial(\ln rel)/\partial(\ln(S/U))$ would equal $-1/\varepsilon$ rather than -1. Further, a ceteris paribus increase in A_1 and/or A_4 would increase or decrease rel as ε is greater or less than one.

markets (at P_1, P_2, and $P_3 = 1$). An important assumption is that foreign and domestic versions of the tradable goods are perfect substitutes for one another both domestically and in international markets. Goods 4 and 5 are non-tradables, i.e., they can be neither imported nor exported.[7] How does the advent of international trade in manufacturing industries alter the determination of *rel*, R_S, and R_U in our illustrative small economy compared to the closed economy scenario?

It is assumed that – at least initially – both goods 1 and 2 can be produced profitably in our economy but that the international price of good 3 (arbitrarily equal to one) is too low relative to home country productivity in good 3 (A_3) to justify the existence of industry 3 in our economy. Thus, in the open economy case the marginal conditions for unskilled labor, (3.3), exclude the P_3A_3 term, for $P_2A_2 > A_3$. Since P_1 and P_2 (which are interpreted in terms of the price of good 3) are determined internationally, the prices of the two non-tradable goods depend directly on these world prices, i.e., $P_4 = (A_1/A_4)P_1$ and $P_5 = (A_2/A_5)P_2$.

The first step in the solution of the open version of the model is to check to make sure that the economy is producing both goods 1 and 2. To do this, note that, with aggregate net exports held equal to zero, expenditure on the two non-tradable goods, P_4Q_4 and P_5Q_5, are equal to, respectively, v_4 and v_5 of aggregate expenditure (in terms of the price of good 3), $I = P_1Q_1 + P_2Q_2 + P_4Q_4 + P_5Q_5$. This, along with the full employment conditions $S = S_1 + S_4$ and $U = U_2 + U_5$ and the marginal conditions permits explicit solution for S_1 and U_2:

$$S_1 = U\frac{A_2P_2}{A_1P_1}\left[(1 - v_4)\frac{A_1P_1}{A_2P_2}\frac{S}{U} - v_4\right] \tag{3.10}$$

and

$$U_2 = U\left[(1 - v_5) - v_5\frac{A_1P_1}{A_2P_2}\frac{S}{U}\right]. \tag{3.11}$$

The assumption that the economy is active in both industries 1 and 2 requires that

$$\frac{1 - v_5}{v_5} > \frac{A_1}{A_2}\frac{P_1}{P_2}\frac{S}{U} > \frac{v_4}{1 - v_4}. \tag{3.12}$$

Satisfaction of Eq. (3.12) is required for the economy to be in what is called in the trade literature the "cone of diversification."

If this condition is not satisfied, the determinants of real and relative wages are, as we will see below, very different from those if it is satisfied. A relevant example of the way in which Eq. (3.12) would cease to hold is as follows: Suppose that industry 2 includes low-tech goods such as textiles and toys. Over time the technology of low wage countries (the value of A_2 the "South") with respect to good 2 increases relative to that in our economy

---

[7] Here we ignore the transformation of services into internationally traded items, as has occurred with some electronically provided services.

such that P_2 falls. This causes U_2 and Q_2 to decline until, eventually, all unskilled labor is employed in the non-tradable service sector ($U_5 = U$), making Big Macs rather than toys.

With the economy is active in both goods 1 and 2, the skilled/unskilled relative wage is seen from the marginal conditions to equal

$$rel = \frac{W_S}{W_U} = \frac{A_1}{A_2}\frac{P_1}{P_2}. \tag{3.13}$$

The determination of rel is very different in the open economy case from that in the closed economy given by Eq. (3.6). For a closed economy, a change in tastes (a change in $\nu_1 + \nu_4$ constrained to equal the change in the opposite direction in $\nu_2 + \nu_3 + \nu_5$) causes a shift in the relative demand function and resultant changes in rel and P_1/P_2. In the open economy case P_1/P_2 is determined internationally, so changes in the ν_i's simply shift the composition of output and, in particular, of net exports. In the closed economy model, an increase in the relative supply of skilled labor, S/U, causes the relative wage and the value of P_1/P_2 to fall, but in the small open economy model a change in S/U merely causes the composition of aggregate output to change with all prices unchanged.

For subsequent purposes it is useful to calculate the value of net exports in the two tradable goods industries in which the economy is active. These values (in terms of the price of good 3) are as follows:

$$P_1(Q_1 - C_1) = (1 - \nu_1 - \nu_4)P_1A_1S - (\nu_1 + \nu_4)P_2A_2U \tag{3.14}$$

and

$$P_2(Q_2 - C_2) = -(\nu_2 + \nu_5)P_1A_1S - (1 - \nu_2 - \nu_5)P_2A_2U. \tag{3.15}$$

Since the sum of these two values equals $C_3 = \nu_5(P_1A_1S + P_2A_2U)$, which is positive if the economy consumes a good it does not produce, net exports of at least one of goods 1 and 2 must be positive.

Substituting the values of each of the five C_i's into Eq. (3.4), the value of real output in the open economy case is seen to be

$$Y = \left(\prod_i \nu_i^{\nu_i}\right) P_1^{-(\nu_1 + \nu_4)} P_2^{-(\nu_2 + \nu_5)} \left(\frac{A_4}{A_1}\right)^{\nu_4} \left(\frac{A_5}{A_2}\right)^{\nu_5} [P_1A_1S + P_2A_2U]. \tag{3.16}$$

Holding S and U constant, the proportional change in Y is equal to the proportional change in the average real wage rate in the economy (R), for $R = R_S(S/L) + R_U(U/L) = Y/L$, where $L = S + U$. This is

$$\hat{Y} = [sh - \nu_1 - \nu_4]\hat{P}_1 + [1 - sh - \nu_2 - \nu_5]\hat{P}_2, \tag{3.17}$$

where

$$sh = \frac{P_1A_1S}{P_1A_1S + P_2A_2U}$$

is skilled labor's share of aggregate income. The coefficient on $\hat{P}_1$ or $\hat{P}_2$ in Eq. (3.17) is positive or negative as the economy is a net exporter or a net importer of that good. (This can be shown using Eqs. (3.14) and (3.15).) If the prices of both tradable goods change by the same proportion, say $\hat{P}_1 = \hat{P}_2 = \hat{P}_*$, the change in the average real wage rate is $\hat{P}_*$. This means that if foreign producers become more efficient in the production of goods 1 and 2 but not in the production of good 3, the decline in the relative prices of goods 1 and 2 will lower real income in our economy (because the importation of good 3 is more expensive). Finally, if all relevant foreign industries, including those associated with good 3, become equally more productive, P_1 and P_2 will not change, and real and relative wages in our economy will not be affected.

The real wages of skilled and unskilled labor in the economy are equal to

$$R_S = sh\frac{Y}{S}, \qquad R_U = (1 - sh)\frac{Y}{U}. \qquad (3.18)$$

It is straightforward to show that an increase in A_1 or P_1 causes R_S to rise and R_U to fall and that an increase in A_2 or P_2 has the opposite qualitative effect on the two real wage levels. Increases in either A_4 or A_5 cause both R_S and R_U to rise by the same proportion.

The important difference concerning the determination of wages between the closed (autarky) and open models is summarized geometrically in Fig. 1.

The relative labor demand function in the closed case is downward-sloping with respect to the relative wage, and it is shifted by changes in product demand parameters. Thus, an exogenous increase in the relative supply of skilled labor causes the skilled/unskilled relative wage to fall. In the open economy case, on the other hand, the relative prices of the goods produced by the two types of labor are determined internationally, and, given the technology of production of the two relevant tradable goods industries, the skilled/

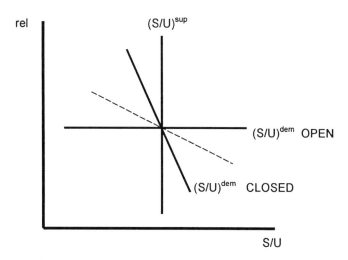

Fig. 1. Relative wage equilibrium in the open and closed models.

unskilled wage rate cannot vary. This is often called the *Factor Price Insensitivity* theorem (see Leamer and Levinsohn, 1995). Thus, the relative labor demand function is horizontal, and *rel* is unaffected by changes in S/U.

3.3. International equilibrium

Although the focus of our review is on the effects of international developments on labor market variables in a single, relatively small country, it important to understand that what is going on in one country is part of the general equilibrium of the world economy. The world economy is, after all, a closed economy. To do this we specify that there is one other very large economy on the planet,[8] the values of whose variables are denoted by the subscript r (for rest of world (ROW)). The initial factor endowments of the ROW are S_r and U_r and its technology is represented by $A_r = \{A_{1r}, A_{2r}, A_{3r}, A_{4r}, A_{5r}\}$, which is not necessarily the same as the A in our focus economy. Tastes in the ROW for consumption of each of the five goods are assumed to be identical to that in our economy, so Y_r depends on the C_{ir}'s according to Eq. (3.4) and the consumption of each good in the ROW follows Eq. (3.5).

It is assumed that the ROW is active in the production of all five goods. Since P_3 has been assumed equal to one, the marginal conditions for unskilled labor in the ROW are $W_{Ur} = A_{2r}P_2 = A_{3r} = A_{5r}P_{5r}$, which means that the world price of good 2 is $P_2 = A_{3r}/A_{2r}$. From this point, one solves the model by determining the allocation of skilled and unskilled labor between the relevant industries within each country. The world price of the skill-intensive tradable good is

$$P_1 = \frac{v_1 + v_4}{1 - v_1 - v_4} \frac{A_{3r}}{A_{2r}} \left(\frac{S_W}{U_W} \right)^{-1},$$ (3.19)

where $S_W = A_1 S + A_{1r} S_r$ is the effective world supply of skilled labor in terms of its productivity in industry 1 and $U_W = A_2 U + A_{2r} U_r$ is the effective supply of unskilled labor in terms of its productivity in industry 2. Given the assumption that our focus economy is a very small portion of the world economy, $S_W \approx A_{1r} S_r$ and $U_W \approx A_{2r} U_r$, so, holding tastes constant, the proportional change in the world price of good 1 relative to good 2 is

$$(\widehat{P_1/P_2}) \approx -(\widehat{A_{1r}/A_{2r}}) - (\widehat{S_r/U_r}).$$

The skilled/unskilled relative wage rate in our economy is, of course, still given by Eq. (3.13). Its proportional change is

$$rel \approx (\widehat{A_1/A_2}) - (\widehat{A_{1r}/A_{2r}}) - (\widehat{S_r/U_r}).$$

[8] One could easily specify any number of other countries or economic blocs. For example, Wood (1994) and Krugman (1979) usefully distinguish between the "North" and the "South" in their models. For our purposes, however, it is sufficient to look at one small (relatively skill-intensive) economy versus the aggregation of all other countries.

This means that *rel* increases when the efficiency of industry 1 relative to industry 2 in the economy rises *relative to the rest of the world* and as the relative effective *world* supply of skilled labor falls. The factor price insensitivity theorem, discussed in the case of the analysis of a single country applies only insofar as our focus country is small relative to the rest of the world. For example, the effect of a change in S on *rel* is $\partial(\ln rel)/\partial(\ln S) = -A_1 S/(A_1 S + A_r S_r)$, i.e., the negative of the focus country's share of the world supply of effective units of skilled labor. $-\partial(\ln rel)/\partial(\ln S)$ is never zero, but it is approximately zero for most country's and much less than one even for the US.

An important implication of the general equilibrium version of the simple model is that with free trade real wage rates by skill *may* tend to be equal among countries. The ratio of the skilled real wage in the focus economy to that in the ROW is

$$\frac{R_S}{R_{Sr}} = \left(\frac{A_1}{A_{1r}}\right)^{1-\nu_4} \left(\frac{A_2}{A_{2r}}\right)^{-\nu_5} \left(\frac{A_4}{A_{4r}}\right)^{\nu_4} \left(\frac{A_5}{A_{5r}}\right)^{\nu_5}. \tag{3.20}$$

Similarly, the ratio of unskilled real wage rates is

$$\frac{R_U}{R_{Ur}} = \left(\frac{A_1}{A_{1r}}\right)^{-\nu_4} \left(\frac{A_2}{A_{2r}}\right)^{1-\nu_5} \left(\frac{A_4}{A_{4r}}\right)^{\nu_4} \left(\frac{A_5}{A_{5r}}\right)^{\nu_5}. \tag{3.21}$$

In order for both skilled and unskilled real wage rates to be equal in our country and the rest of the world it is necessary that the technology parameters for each of the competitive export industries be equal, $A_i = A_{ir}$. Real wage equality between sets of countries also requires that the weighted average of the technology parameters in the non-tradable sector be equal. This means, effectively, that *Factor Price Equalization* (the tendency, under free trade, for real wages by skill in all countries to become equal regardless of initial factor endowments) requires that technology in different countries be identical. It is important to point out that even if the identical technologies assumption is not satisfied, so that we do not observe factor price equalization, the result of factor price insensitivity will still apply.

A second implication of the world general equilibrium model is the *Heckscher–Ohlin theorem*, which says that countries will tend to export goods that are relatively intensive in the factors in which they are relatively abundant.

This is seen in the context of our simple model by substituting the solution value of P_1/P_2 into Eq. (3.14), the value of net exports of good 1 by our economy:[9]

$$P_1(Q_1 - C_1) = (\nu_2 + \nu_5)P_1 A_1 S\left[1 - \frac{A_{1w}S_w/A_{2w}U_w}{A_1 S/A_2 U}\right]. \tag{3.22}$$

Given identical technologies in all economies, a relatively skilled labor abundant economy $(S/U > S_r/U_r)$ will tend to export good 1 and, with more-or-less balanced trade, import good 2. This is the strong version of the HO theorem, and, as will be discussed in Section 5.1, much of the work of empirical trade economists has been concerned with testing it. A modified version of the HO theorem, which has been used with some success in recent

---

[9] We make the additional assumption for simplicity that good 3 does not exist (i.e., $\nu_3 = 0$).

empirical work (Trefler, 1993, 1995; Davis et al., 1997), allows for differences in relative technology between the two industries engaged in tradable goods (i.e., the A_i's across countries may differ).

3.4. Wage determination outside the cone of diversification

The results of the open model depend critically on the assumption that the economy is active in both relevant tradable goods, 1 and 2. If this assumption is not correct, i.e., both the inequalities in Eq. (3.12) are not satisfied, the determination of wages in the economy more resembles the closed economy case than the open economy case.

To see this, we assume that P_2 has fallen below the point at which industry 2 is still active in our economy. (An analogous set of results follow from the assumption that industry 1 is no longer active.) In terms of Eq. (3.12), P_2 is no longer greater than $(\nu_5/(1 - \nu_5))P_1(A_1 S/A_2 U)$, and all unskilled workers are employed in industry 5. In other words, instead of some of the U's producing textiles and toys, the U's are now employed exclusively in the service sector.

The solution of the model in this "degenerate" case is quite straightforward. Since goods 2 and 3 are not produced in the economy, national income (in terms of the internationally-determined price of good 3) is $I = P_1 Q_1 + P_4 Q_4 + P_5 Q_5$. Given the assumption of unitary price and income elasticities of the demand for each good, expenditure on each of the non-tradable goods, 4 and 5, is proportional to I. Thus, the equilibrium I is a constant fraction of the value of the output is a constant multiple of the value of the output of the single remaining tradable goods industry, that is $I = ((1/(1 - \nu_4 - \nu_5))P_1 Q_1$. Further, since $P_4 Q_4 = \nu_4 I$, the fraction of all skilled workers who are employed in industry 1 is $(1 - \nu_4 - \nu_5)/(1 - \nu_5)$, the remainder of the S's being employed in the production of non-tradable good 4.

The skilled/unskilled relative wage rate in this case is

$$rel = \frac{W_S}{W_U} = \frac{A_1}{A_5} \frac{P_1}{P_5} = \frac{1 - \nu_5}{\nu_5} \left(\frac{S}{U}\right)^{-1}. \tag{3.23}$$

This is qualitatively similar to the equivalent expression for the closed economy case, Eq. (3.6). The only difference is the fact that, since both goods 2 and 3 are now purchased abroad with exports generated from industry 1, the value $\nu_2 + \nu_3$ is moved from the numerator to the denominator. The relative wage is, however, equally responsive in proportional terms to changes in the relative supply of labor by skill in the closed case and the case in which only one of the industries producing potentially tradable goods is active.

3.5. Product differentiation

A focus of a substantial chunk of the recent literature in trade theory has been on the paradox of extensive trade between countries with similar factor endowments in fairly similar products. In the model set out in Section 3.2, net exports of goods 1 and 2 were

$Q_i - C_i$. If a particular one of these was positive, exports of good i was $Q_i - C_i$ and there were no imports of that good; if $Q_i - C_i < 0$, there were imports of that good but no exports. Put differently, the absolute price elasticities of imports and exports of both goods 1 and 2 with respect to the domestic prices relative to the foreign prices of the goods, P_i/P_{if}, were assumed to be infinite.

There are several ways to justify the existence of inter-industry trade, but it seems to us that the most plausible explanation is in terms of differentiated products.[10] Some consumers strongly prefer the domestic version of the product (would drive a Buick rather than a BMW at any relative price); other consumers have the opposite preferences (their station wagon *must* be a Volvo). Further, the evidence on the magnitudes of import and export price elasticities is that they fairly large but finite.

To see what difference the assumption of product differentiation makes in the wage determination process, we modify the model to allow for finite import and export elasticities for the potentially tradable goods 2 and 3. (We continue to assume that good 3 is not produced in our economy.)

With respect to imports, it is now assumed that the utility function for the economy is given by

$$Y = \varphi^1(C_1, C_{1f})^{\nu_1} \varphi^2(C_2, C_{2f})^{\nu_2} C_3^{\nu_3} C_4^{\nu_4} C_5^{\nu_5}.$$

For goods 1 and 2, C_i is the domestic consumption of the domestically produced Q_i and C_{if} is the consumption of the foreign brand of good i. The elasticity of substitution within the composite function ϑ^i is τ_i, which is fairly large (surely greater than one) but finite. The assumption that Y is Cobb–Douglas in the five goods implies that total domestic expenditure on the domestic and foreign versions of each of the tradable goods is a constant fraction of national income, that is $P_i C_i + P_{if} C_{if} = \nu_i I$. In addition, $d(\ln(C_i/C_{if})) = -\tau_i d(\ln(P_i/P_{if}))$ with the relative tastes for the domestic versus the foreign version of the product held constant.

Holding consumer tastes constant, the resultant domestic consumption demand functions for the domestic and foreign versions of goods 1 and 2 are

$$\hat{C}_i = -(\tau_i - (\tau_i - 1)w_i)\hat{P}_i + (\tau_i - 1)(1 - w_i)\hat{P}_{if} + \hat{\imath} \tag{3.25}$$

---

[10] Goldstein and Khan (1985) distinguish between the "imperfect substitutes model" (as opposed to the "perfect substitutes model") that is central to classical trade theory) and proceed to use the model to motivate their useful review of import and export elasticities. This approach in trade theory is referred to as the Armington assumptions (Armington, 1969) that the demand for many tradable goods is distinguished by their country of origin, and such an approach to the demand side has been termed "Armington home bias" (Trefler, 1995). There is also a large literature in trade theory (some of which is reviewed in Section 5.1) about the reasons for the (puzzling from the point of view of the Hecksher–Ohlin theorem) observed pattern of trade in similar products (intra-industry trade) between nations with similar factor endowments. Most trade theorists appear to consider the Armington approach as unsatisfactorily ad hoc (although see Levey, 1997) and focus instead on monopolistic competition and/or increasing returns as the reason (see, e.g., Helpman and Krugman, 1985). Davis (1995) points to inter-country-differences in industry technology parameters (the A_i's in our notation) and resultant patterns of specialization as the reason for intra-industry trade.

and

$$\hat{C}_{if} = (\tau_i - 1)w_i\hat{P}_i - ((\tau_i - 1)w_i + 1)\hat{P}_{if} + \hat{\imath}, \tag{3.26}$$

where $w_i = P_iC_i/v_iI$ is each domestic good's share of total expenditure on good i and $\hat{\imath}$ is the proportional change in aggregate income (depending on the values of changes in P_1, P_2, Q_1, and Q_2. The coefficients on the changes in prices in Eq. (3.26) are the relevant price elasticities of imports of each of the tradable goods, and they are obviously the larger the greater is the value of the relevant τ_i. Import relative price elasticities are usually in terms of value, i.e., $-\partial\ln(P_{if}C_{if})/\partial\ln(P_{if}/P_i)$, which takes the value $(\tau_i - 1)w_i$ in Eq. (3.26).

Exports of goods 1 and 2 are the differences between Q_i and C_i. The demand for good i produced in our focus economy by the ROW is assumed to follow Eq. (3.26) with the appropriate reversal of the price changes. With the small country assumption that world consumption of our focus country's version of good i is a trivial fraction of total world consumption ($w_{ir} = 1$), this implies – foreign tastes and incomes held constant – that exports of good i are

$$(Q_i \widehat{- C_i}) = \frac{Q_i}{Q_i - C_i}\hat{Q}_i - \frac{C_i}{Q_i - C_i}\hat{C}_i = -\tau_i\hat{P}_i + (\tau_i - 1)\hat{P}_{if}. \tag{3.27}$$

In the absence of product differentiation, the model in Section 3.3, the absolute own price elasticity of exports would equal infinity, and P_i would always equal P_{if} if any of Q_i was exported. To the extent that the good produced domestically has unique features, both the import and export price elasticities will be of smaller magnitude.

The final step in the construction of the model with differentiated tradable goods is the specification of the supplies of goods 1 and 2. This is done by using the solution values of S_1 and U_2 from Eqs. (3.10) and (3.11). For example, assuming that both goods 1 and 2 can be produced profitably in the economy (i.e., that Eq. (3.12) is satisfied, the domestic supply of good 1 is $Q_1 = A_1S_1$. The proportional change in the supply of this goods is

$$\hat{Q}_1 = E_1\left(\widehat{\frac{P_1}{P_2}}\right) + (1 + E_1)(\hat{A}_1 + \hat{S}) - E_1(\hat{A}_2 + \hat{U}), \tag{3.28}$$

where the relative price elasticity of the supply of good 1 is

$$E_1 = v_4\frac{P_2}{P_1}\frac{A_2U}{Q_1}.$$

This is positive so long as there are some skilled workers employed producing non-tradables ($v_4 > 0$). The supply function for good 2 is

$$\hat{Q}_2 = -E_1\left(\widehat{\frac{P_1}{P_2}}\right) - E_2(\hat{A}_1 + \hat{S}) + (1 + E_2)(\hat{A}_2 + \hat{U}), \tag{3.29}$$

where

$$E_2 = v_5 \frac{P_1}{P_2} \frac{A_1 S}{Q_2}.$$

Combining these expressions for the proportional changes in domestic consumption, exports, and the supplies of the two tradable goods yields two equations in the proportional changes in the domestic prices of goods 1 and 2, that is

$$[Q_1 E_1 + C_1 \kappa_1 + (Q_1 - C_1)\tau_1 - shC_1]\hat{P}_1 - [Q_1 E_1 + (1 - sh)C_1]\hat{P}_2$$

$$= -[Q_1(1 + E_1) - shC_1](\hat{S} + \hat{A}_1) + [Q_1 E_1 + (1 - sh)C_1](\hat{U} + \hat{A}_2)$$

$$+ [C_1(\kappa_1 - 1) + (Q_1 - C_1)(\tau_1 - 1)]\hat{P}_{1f}, \tag{3.30}$$

$$-[Q_2 E_2 + shC_2]\hat{P}_1 + [Q_2 E_2 + C_2 \kappa_2 + (Q_2 - C_2)\tau_2 - (1 - sh)C_2]\hat{P}_2$$

$$= [Q_2 E_2 + shC_2](\hat{S} + \hat{A}_1) - [Q_2(1 + E_2) - (1 - sh)C_2](\hat{U} + \hat{A}_2)$$

$$+ [C_2(\kappa_2 - 1) + (Q_2 - C_2)(\tau_2 - 1)]\hat{P}_{2f}. \tag{3.31}$$

where $\kappa_i = (\tau_i - (\tau_i - 1)w_i)$ is the absolute elasticity of C_i with respect to P_i.

The solution of these equations yields the proportional changes in P_1 and P_2 in terms of the proportional changes in P_{1f}, P_{2f}, $A_1 S$, and $A_2 U$. Of particular interest is the effect of changes in these exogenous variables in the skilled/unskilled relative wage rate, which, in general, is

$$\widehat{rel} = \hat{P}_1 - \hat{P}_2 + \hat{A}_1 - \hat{A}_2$$

$$= m_{P_1}\hat{P}_{1f} + m_{P_2}\hat{P}_{2f} + m_S \hat{S} + m_U \hat{U} + (m_S + 1)\hat{A}_1 + (m_U - 1)\hat{A}_2. \tag{3.32}$$

Properties of these coefficients (when the τ_i's are greater than one and finite) include m_{P1} and m_U positive, m_{P2} and m_S negative, $m_{P1} = 1 - m_S$, and $m_{P2} = m_U - 1$. The solution of these equations is best viewed initially in terms of its properties in two extreme situations. At one extreme, the closed economy case in which there is no trade (i.e., $C_i = Q_i$ for $i = 1, 2$ and $v_3 = 0$), $(\widehat{P_1/P_2}) = -(\widehat{A_1/A_2}) - (\widehat{S/U})$. Since $rel = (P_1/P_2)(A_1/A_2)$, the proportionate change in the skilled/unskilled relative wage is $\widehat{rel} = -(\widehat{S/U})$. In terms of Eq. (3.32), $m_S = -1$, $m_U = 1$, and the coefficients on world prices are zero. If both τ_1 and τ_2 are equal to one, the effects on rel of changes in each of the exogenous variables are the same as in the closed model. In this case, the foreign versions of goods 1 and 2 are both as distinct from the domestic versions as they are from each other, so changes in foreign prices do not affect the relative demand for labor.

At the other extreme, that of the open economy with both products undifferentiated, the values of both τ_i's are so large that $\hat{P}_i = \hat{P}_{if}$ for both tradables and changes in factor supplies have no effect on the relative wage, i.e., $m_S = m_{P1} = 0$ and $m_U + m_{P2} = -1$

(but m_U and m_S may be of different magnitudes). Thus, only the calculated values of m_S and m_U are reported in the table.

In the intermediate case – with the existence imports and exports of both tradable goods and finite values of the τ_i's – the determination of *rel* is, needless to say, a blend of the processes associated with the closed and open economy models. The absolute values of all of the m's in Eq. (3.32) are positive but less than one. First, an increase in (S/U) causes a fall in the skilled/unskilled relative wage, but the magnitude of this effect is smaller than in the closed economy case and approaches zero as the τ_i's approach infinity. In terms of Fig. 1, therefore, the relative labor demand function in the intermediate case is the dotted line between the functions for the closed and open economies. Second, changes in the technological parameters affecting tradable goods, A_1 and A_2, have some effect on the relative price of goods 1 and 2, but the magnitude of this effect is the smaller the lower are the values of the two price elasticity parameters. This implies that in the intermediate case $1 > \partial(\ln rel)/\partial(\ln(A_1/A_2)) > 0$. Third, in the intermediate case proportional changes in the world prices of each of the two tradable goods cause the price of the domestic version to rise but by less than $\hat{P}_{if}$. This means that relative wages are only partially dependent on the world prices of exportable goods.

Given the rather extreme divergence of the implications of the closed and open economy models, it is interesting to see how different values of the degree of substitution between the domestic and foreign versions of the two tradable goods affect the values of the four coefficients in Eq. (3.32). Table 5 calculates the values of these coefficients on the assumption that $v_1 = v_2 = v_4 = v_5$; the non-produced imported good 3 is ignored without affecting the results. The results are reported for the 16 combinations of values of τ_1 and τ_2 equal to 2, 3, 5 and 10. These two values need not be equal. For example, a low value of τ_1 and a high value of τ_2 would reflect a situation in which the tradable goods produced by skilled workers are subject to a lower degree of import competition than the tradable goods produced by unskilled workers; the Q_1 goods are more differentiated than the Q_2 goods

Table 5
Hypothetical effects of proportional changes in S and U on *rel* for alternative values of the substitution parameters

τ_2		A. Trade small ($w_1 = w_2 = 0.75$) Substitution elasticity good 1 (τ_1)				B. Trade large ($w_1 = w_2 = 0.25$) Substitution elasticity good 1 (τ_1)			
		2	3	5	10	2	3	5	10
2	S	−0.82	−0.75	−0.68	−0.62	−0.68	−0.56	−0.45	−0.38
	U	0.82	0.79	0.77	0.74	0.68	0.65	0.63	0.61
3	S	−0.79	−0.70	−0.61	−0.53	−0.65	−0.52	−0.39	−0.30
	U	0.75	0.70	0.65	0.61	0.56	0.52	0.48	0.44
5	S	−0.77	−0.65	−0.53	−0.43	−0.63	−0.48	−0.35	−0.22
	U	0.68	0.61	0.53	0.47	0.45	0.39	0.35	0.29
10	S	−0.74	−0.61	−0.47	−0.34	−0.61	−0.45	−0.31	−0.16
	U	0.62	0.53	0.43	0.34	0.36	0.30	0.24	0.16

(like computer software versus textiles). In Panel A of the table, it is assumed that the value of the imports of both goods 1 and 2 are 25% of total expenditure on each of these types of goods (i.e., $w_1 = w_2 = 0.75$), so total imports are $0.25 \times 0.50 = 12.5\%$ of total expenditure in the economy. In Panel B it is assumed that imports represent 75% of expenditure on tradables ($w_i = 0.75$), which means that the aggregate import share is 37.5%. As suggested by Table 1, these are, respectively, approximately the cases of the US and a typical European economy.

Given that $m_{P1} = 1 - m_S$ and $m_{P2} = m_U - 1$, only the values of m_S and m_U are reported in the table. For example, for $\tau_1 = \tau_2 = 2$ in Panel A, a one percentage point increase in S causes a decline in *rel* of 0.82%. This means that a one percentage point in P_{1f} would increase *rel* by 0.18%. These coefficients should be contrasted with their values in the closed and open model cases, (m_S, m_U) equal to $(-1,1)$ and $(0,0)$, respectively. For the small trade case in Panel A, the assumed values have to be quite large in order for the implications of the model to be a 50–50 blend of the open and closed models. Recall from Eq. (3.26) that the absolute relative price elasticities of import demand is $(\tau_i - 1)w_i$. The consensus of estimates surveyed by Goldstein and Kahn (1985) concerning this parameter is a range from 0.5 to 1, which, at $w_i = 0.75$, suggests a range of the τ's from 1.7 to 2.3.[11] Their consensus estimates of the relative price elasticities of exports are somewhat higher than the import elasticities, suggesting a range of the τ's of from 2 to 3.

Even with both τ's equal to 3.0, the coefficients on the proportional changes in S and U suggest that the relative demand elasticity is $1/0.7 - 1 = 43\%$ greater than it would be in a closed economy setting. For the small trade case, it appears that the operation of the labor market is closer to the closed than to the classically open model.

For the large trade case, the results for which are reported in Panel B, the effects of changes in relative factor supplies on relative wages are significantly smaller than they would be if the were economy closed. In the neighborhood of the τ's equal to 3.0, the relative labor demand elasticity is about double its closed economy value. Nevertheless, relative domestic factor supplies still have a major effect in determining relative wages.

3.6. Factor immobility

The models to this point have made the assumption that both types of labor are freely mobile with the marginal revenue products of each type of labor equal in the relevant industries. Although this is a defensible assumption for the long run (after about 3 years) in certain economies (for example, the US), it is a questionable assumption for the short run and for the relatively long run in some economies (for example, many in Western Europe in which the intra-country regional mobility of labor is quite low). To see what difference the degree of internal labor mobility makes, we will modify the open model discussed in

---

[11] An interesting study by Grossman (1983) breaks down import demand for a selection of products into those from developed and those from developing nations. His reported elasticities are generally higher than the Goldstein–Kahn consensus range.

Section 3.2 by modifying the assumption that there is perfect inter-industry labor mobility of both types of labor. We could assume that fixed quantities of both factors are specific to each industry. For illustrative purposes, however, we assume that – despite any possible differences in sectoral wage rates – a constant fraction z of unskilled labor is engaged in the production of the relevant tradable good, industry 2, and that the remainder of the U's are attached to the non tradable goods industry 5. We continue to assume that skilled labor is perfectly mobile between industries 1 and 5 such that the skilled wage rates in these industries are equal.[12] We also revert back to the assumption of 3.2 that foreign and domestic versions of goods 1 and 2 are perfect substitutes and that their prices are determined internationally.

The solution of the model is similar to that of the case of perfect internal mobility of both types of labor. The only difference is that now there are two unskilled wage rates, $W_{U2} = P_2 A_2$ and $W_{U5} = P_5 A_5$, as contrasted with the single skilled wage rate, $W_S = P_1 A_1$. The price of non-tradable goods produced by unskilled workers (P_5) is determined by aggregate income, technology in that industry (A_5), and the supply of labor to that industry, zU. The average wage of unskilled workers is $W_U = W_{U2} z + W_{U5}(1 - z)$. The solution skilled/unskilled relative wage is

$$rel = \frac{W_S}{W_U} = \frac{1 - \nu_5}{(P_2 A_2 / P_1 A_1)z + \nu_5 (S/U)}. \tag{3.33}$$

In the special case in which $\nu_5 = 0$, all unskilled workers are employed in the export sector, Eq. (3.33) reduces to Eq. (3.13), the relative wage in the open economy.

If $z = 0$, all unskilled workers are employed in the non-tradable sector, Eq. (3.23) reduces to Eq. (3.23), the relative wage outside the cone of diversification.

The proportional change in the relative wage with respect to the price and technology parameters and the relative supply of labor by skill is

$$\widehat{rel} = -m\left(\widehat{\frac{S}{U}}\right) + (1 - m)\left(\widehat{\frac{P_1 A_1}{P_2 A_2}}\right), \qquad m = \frac{\nu_5 (S/U)}{(P_2 A_2 / P_1 A_1)z + \nu_5 (S/U)}. \tag{3.34}$$

For ν_5 and z both positive, the value of m is strictly between zero and one. This means that the relative labor demand function in Fig. 1 for the specific factor cases, like the case of differentiated products discussed in Section 3.5, between that for the closed and open economy models. The reason for this is that an exogenous increase in, say, P_1 causes a one-for-one proportional increase in W_S without affecting the unskilled wage rate in the tradable industry W_{U2}. The increase in P_1, however, increases national income (in terms of the price of the imports good that is not produced, P_3), which results in an increase in the demand for the non-tradable good 5 produced by unskilled workers not attached to industry 2 and an increase in W_{U3}. This means that the average nominal wage of unskilled

---

[12] The results of Bound and Holtzer (1997) suggest that the geographic mobility of relatively low skilled workers in the US is less than that of relatively high skilled workers.

workers, $W_U = W_{U2}z + W_{U5}(1 - z)$, also rises due to the increase in P_1, although by proportionally less than the increase in P_1.

3.7. Immigration and the factor content of trade

An important difference between the determination of wages in the open and closed models concerns the effect of the immigration of different types of labor on real and relative wages rates. To illustrate this, consider what happens to the skilled/unskilled relative wage, *rel*, in response to an increase in the unskilled labor force of ΔU_M effective units due to an influx of immigrants from low wage economies. What effect would this have on the level of output and the distribution of income?

Assuming that the immigrants are free to work in any of the industries that hire unskilled labor (industries 2 and 5 and, in the case of the closed economy, 3), the effects of this immigration are represented by an increase in the value of U equal to ΔU_M. In the closed economy model set out in Section 3.1, this would cause an increase in real output of approximately $R_U \Delta U_M$, which is equal to the real incomes received by the immigrants. The increase in the aggregate supply of unskilled labor also causes R_S to rise and R_U to increase. This means that the immigration also causes a transfer of income from unskilled natives to skilled labor, and the size of this transfer is approximately $(\nu_1 + \nu_4)R_u\Delta U_M$.[13]

In the open economy model in which the economy is active in the production of both goods 1 and 2, the effects of immigration are very different.

The ΔU_M increase in the supply of unskilled labor has no effect on R_U, R_S, and, of course, *rel*. Instead, the adjustment is in terms of the industry composition of output and exports – from Q_1 toward Q_2. Aggregate real output increases by (exactly) $R_U\Delta U_M$, and there is no associated redistribution from unskilled to skilled natives. If, on the other hand, the economy is outside the cone of diversification (industry 2 has disappeared), the effects of immigration on the distribution of income are qualitatively similar to the closed economy case. The results for the differentiated products version of the open economy model (with finite values of the τ_i's) or the specific factors model are between those of the open and closed models; immigration causes a smaller amount of redistribution than in the closed economy case.

Since immigration has no effect on *rel* in the fully open model,[14] it is somewhat paradoxical that the most frequently used method of discerning the effect of international trade on relative wages is based on an analogue with immigration. The factor content approach (FCA) is based on two steps. First, it is assumed (counterfactually) that relative wages are determined *as if* the economy were closed. Given, in the context of the model in this section, that there are four industries operating in the economy (all but industry 3), the relative wage is assumed to be generated by

---

[13] See Borjas (1995) and Johnson (1998) for derivation of this result in a more general context.

[14] See Bhagwati (1991) for an extensive discussion of the economics, philosophy, and politics of the relation between immigration and trade.

$$rel_f = \frac{\nu_1 + \nu_4}{\nu_2 + \nu_5}\left(\frac{S_*}{U_*}\right)^{-1}, \tag{3.35}$$

where S_* and U_* are hypothetical aggregate supplies of the two factor to be defined in the next step. Second, let the hypothetical supply of each factor equal its actual supply less the amount of labor needed to produce the net exports of the good. For skilled labor this is $S_* = S - (Q_1 - C_1)/A_1$, and for unskilled labor $U_* = U - (Q_2 - C_2)/A_2$.

Substituting Eqs. (3.14) and (3.15), the actual levels of net exports of the goods, into these expressions for hypothetical supplies and the results in Eq. (3.33), the value of rel_f reduces to $P_1 A_1/P_2 A_2$, which by Eq. (3.13) is the actual value of *rel*. Suppose that data on international prices were poor or nonexistent or were altered by overall exchange rate movements making it impossible to discern the effect of a change in P_1/P_2 (caused by changes in technology and/or factors supplies in the ROW) on *rel*. If one had data on change over a time interval in the composition of imports and exports and their current factor content (the A_i's) and *if* consumer tastes (the ν_i's) remained constant, one could use Eq. (3.35) to estimate the effect of international factors on *rel*.

An additional advantage of FCA is that Eq. (3.35) is also correct for the case of differentiated products. Now $S_* = S - (1/A_1)[(Q_1 - C_1) - (P_{1f}/P_1)C_{1f}]$, where the two terms within brackets are, respectively, the exports and the value of the imports of good 1, and U_* is defined analogously. When these are substituted into Eq. (3.33) and the results appropriately manipulated, rel_f reduces to the correct value of *rel*.[15] This is, in our view, an important attribute of FCA, for, as we will argue in Section 5, most tradable goods appear to be subject to the product differentiation phenomenon.

4. Trade and wages in neoclassical trade models

We now modify the assumption of Section 3 that each industry uses only one factor of production (the Ricardian case) and adopt the convention of neoclassical trade theory that each active industry uses some of each available factor. Initially it is assumed, as in Section 3, that skilled and unskilled labor are the only factors of production, but this is subsequently expanded to include capital.

4.1. The closed economy

We first consider the demand for labor and the determination of relative wage rates by skill in a closed economy in the case in which output in each industry depends on inputs of both skilled and unskilled labor. The production function for each industry is

$$Q_i = A_i F^i(S_i, U_i). \tag{4.1}$$

---

[15] To anticipate the discussion of Section 4.7, the FCA is only exactly correct under certain conditions, all of which are satisfied in the current simple model.

A_i is a technology parameter, changes in which are neutral with respect to skill.

Each F^i is linear homogeneous with an elasticity of intra-labor substitution σ, which is identical in all industries, and the shares of skilled and unskilled labor in each industry are, respectively, β_i and $1 - \beta_i$. The economy-wide utility function is assumed to be CES with and elasticity of substitution of ε.

To make things comparable with our initial discussion of the open economy case below, it is assumed that there are only two goods, produced in industries 1 and 2. The domestic demand for good 1 relative to good 2 is then

$$\frac{C_1}{C_2} = \Theta\left(\frac{P_1}{P_2}\right)^{-\varepsilon}, \tag{4.2}$$

where Θ is a shift parameter.[16] In the case of a closed economy (autarky), the domestic for each good is equal to domestic supply ($C_i = Q_i$). We also assume perfect labor mobility of both types of labor between industries such that wage rates by skill are equal in both industries. This implies that

$$\left(\frac{P_1 A_1}{P_2 A_2}\right) F_S^1 = F_S^2 \tag{4.3}$$

and

$$\left(\frac{P_1 A_1}{P_2 A_2}\right) F_U^1 = F_U^2, \tag{4.4}$$

where $F_S^1 = (\partial Q_1/\partial S_1)/A_1$, etc. With the addition of the full employment conditions that $S = S_1 + S_2$ and $U = U_1 + U_2$, the model can be solved for the effects of changes in S/U, A_1/A_2, and Θ on the endogenous variables. Of particular interest is the determinants of changes in the skilled/unskilled relative wage, rel.

This is found by noting that $rel = F_S^1(S_1, U_1)/F_U^1(S_1, U_1)$ and substituting the solution expressions for the proportional changes in S_1 and U_1, that is

$$\widehat{rel} = -m\left(\widehat{\frac{S}{U}}\right) + m\left(\frac{S_1}{S} - \frac{U_1}{U}\right)\hat{\Theta} + m\left(\frac{S_1}{S} - \frac{U_1}{U}\right)(\varepsilon - \sigma)\left(\widehat{\frac{A_1}{A_2}}\right), \tag{4.5}$$

$$m = \frac{1}{\sigma + (\varepsilon - \sigma)(\beta_1 - \beta_2)\left((S_1/S) - (U_1/U)\right)}.$$

Assuming that both elasticities of substitution are finite, m is positive, which means that the relation between rel and S/U in this model is the downward-sloping case in Fig. 1. Arbitrarily specifying that industry 1 is the more skill-intensive sector, i.e., $\beta_1 > \beta_2$ and $S_1/S > U_1/U$, a shift in product demand toward good 1, an increase in Θ, causes rel to rise.

[16] Θ is the ratio of the constant share parameters on C_1 and C_2 in the utility function raised to the ε. In the demand system in Section 3, ε was assumed to equal one, and, with only two goods, Θ was equal to ν_1/ν_2.

Given that industry 1 is the more skill-intensive sector, a relative increase in the technology parameter for industry 1 causes *rel* to rise or fall as ε is greater or less than σ.[17] To anticipate the discussion of the open economy model below, if ε were very large, m would be close to zero so that the absolute elasticity of relative demand would be infinite.

It is straightforward to add more industries to the model, although this adds greatly to the complexity of the algebra. Suppose, consistent with the Ricardian model discussed in Section 3, that industries 1 and 2 are manufacturing industries producing goods that would be potentially tradable if the economy were open, industry 3 is a manufacturing or raw materials industry that would not be in operation if the economy were open, and that industry 4 produces all services that would not be tradable in an open setting. (There is no point including another industry, for unskilled labor in the non-tradable sector is now accounted for.) The production functions for goods 3 and 4 are given by Eq. (4.1), and product demands would be determined by an enlarged version of Eq. (4.4) with three demand shift parameters.

For the special case in which all four industry production functions and the aggregate utility function are Cobb–Douglas ($\sigma = \varepsilon = 1$) so that the labor share parameters, the β_i's, are constant and expenditure on each of the four goods is a constant fraction, ν_i, of aggregate expenditure, it is straightforward to show that the solution skilled/unskilled relative wage rate is given by

$$rel = \frac{\bar{\beta}}{1 - \bar{\beta}}\left(\frac{S}{U}\right)^{-1}, \qquad \bar{\beta} = \sum_{i=1}^{4} \beta_i \nu_i. \tag{4.6}$$

In this case the equilibrium value of *rel* depends on the relative supply of skilled labor, the skill intensity coefficients of the four industries, and the distribution of consumer taste coefficients. For example, the sign of the effect on *rel* of a shift in consumer preferences from good 1 to good 4, $d\nu_4 = -d\nu_1 > 0$, has the same sign as $\beta_4 - \beta_1$, i.e., *rel* increases if industry 4 is more skill intensive than industry 1.

Continuing the double Cobb–Douglas assumption and holding the consumption taste parameters (the ν_i's) constant, the change in the real wage rate of skilled workers is

$$\hat{R}_S = \sum_i \nu_i \hat{A}_i - (1 - \bar{\beta})\left(\widehat{\frac{S}{U}}\right), \tag{4.7}$$

and by Eq. (4.6) the proportional rate of change of the unskilled real wage is equal to this plus $(\widehat{S/U})$. If relative factor supplies are unchanged, the proportional change in both real wage rates is equal to a weighted average of the proportional changes of the neutral technical efficiency parameters across the four industries.

It is important to point out that the classification of the aggregate labor force of a country into "skilled" and "unskilled" workers is an extreme simplification. In general, the

---

[17] Note that Eq. (4.5) reduces to the results for the Ricardian model in Section 3.1 when we set β_1, $1 - \beta_2$, ε, and σ equal to one.

production function for industry i (or, with capital and other factors added, the flow of labor services in that industry) is $Q_i = F^i(L_{1i}, L_{2i}, \ldots)$, where L_{ki} is the input of the kth type of labor in that industry. Throughout the theoretical section of this review we continue to assume for expositional purposes that there are two types of labor ($L_{1i} = S_i$ and $L_{2i} = U_i$). However, the empirical implementation of the labor aggregation issue is subject to a wide variety of treatments (see Hamermesh, 1993, Chapter 3 for detailed technical discussion), and this variety is reflected in empirical work in the trade/wages literature.

In the most general specification, the L_{ki}'s would be disaggregated by education, age (work experience), gender, and other factors such as innate or specific ability, and the cross-partial elasticities of complementarity between any two groups (the proportional change in the marginal product of one group with respect to a proportional change in the supply of the other group) would not necessarily be equal. Empirical work that requires a disaggregation of the labor force by skill, however, is constrained by data availability. Wage and employment data by industry are often only available by categories that accord only roughly with a meaningful definition of "skill". Further, differences in data availability and training institutions among countries greatly complicate the task of making international comparisons.[18]

A taxonomy of the approaches to the disaggregation of labor services that have appeared in the recent literature would break these down into four different procedures. These, with some examples from studies that involve trade/wages questions, are as follows:

(1) *Two educational groups.* In most countries estimates of the fraction of the work force who have received some or have completed secondary schooling are available, and these can be used to classify the work force into S and U, at least at the aggregate level (for example, Davis et al. (1997) and Baldwin and Cain (1997)). A modification of this approach is to calculate "equivalents" of both graduates of secondary schooling and graduates of post-secondary schooling programs, using weights estimated from wage data for those workers who did and those who did not complete the relevant programs (e.g., Katz and Murphy, 1992; Borjas et al., 1997).

(2) *More than two educational groups.* A common conceptual approach is to divide the labor force into three groups, those who have received only rudimentary education (only primary schooling), intermediate education (secondary graduates), and advanced (post-secondary graduates). This approach is taken in the influential work of Wood (1994), in which developing countries are abundant in the least skilled group whereas developed countries have very low supplies of this type of labor. A similar approach is taken in Harrigan (1997). With US data, it is common practice to distinguish between workers with less than high school, high school, some college, and college plus.

---

[18] For example, the educational system in the US is such that relatively little learning occurs until college. In Japan, it is the other way around (see Juster and Stafford, 1991), so one would expect, so comparisons of college/high school relative wages and their trends in these two countries (and the effects of "trade" thereon) would not be very informative. In Germany, on the other hand, the prevalence of apprenticeship training programs weakens the relationship between skill and education.

(3) *Several age/education/gender groups.* The most general specification of labor input allows for a large number of possible inputs. Methods 1 and 2 ignore the possibility that labor may be differentiated in production functions by other observable characteristics such as work experience and gender and implicitly assume that the elasticities of substitution between, for example, older and younger secondary school graduates and male and female secondary school graduates are infinity. Within individual countries survey data may permit a much finer breakdown of the work force by age and gender as well as education. For US data, Bound and Johnson (1992) divide the work force into 32 such cells by industry; Murphy and Welch (1992) use a still finer breakdown.

(4) *Occupational groups.* Several empirical studies on the trade/wages have used data on the occupational distribution of the labor force. For example, Trefler (1995) used the aggregate numbers of workers in six occupations in 33 countries in his tests of various predictions of trade theory.[19] A related approach is to use the dichotomy of "production" versus "non-production" workers (for example, Lawrence and Slaughter (1993) and Sachs and Shatz (1994)), data that are widely available on an international basis. The use of occupational data, although often necessitated by the lack of an alternative, has the problem of potential endogeneity.

Given the current state of knowledge about disaggregation of the labor force by skill, it is somewhat difficult to assess the implications of the many studies we will be reviewing in Section 5. There are two additional complicating factors. First, it is clear that whatever observable variables are chosen to disaggregate the labor force into distinct groups, a large component – at least half – of what labor economists call "skill" is, as stressed by Juhn et al. (1993), not observed (or proxied by available variables in even the most detailed datasets). Second, resolution of labor aggregation issues is an empirical question involving estimates of the matrix of elasticities of substitution between various sets of potentially distinct labor groups. How one would estimate these elasticities, however, depends on what assumes about the openness of the economy with respect to trade. Most of the existing estimates are based on the assumption of a closed economy, but, in theory, these estimates should be made in concert with tests of the specification of the effect of international variables.

4.2. The open economy

We now open up the economy and assume that the prices of goods 1 and 2 are determined internationally rather than solely by domestic demand/supply factors. This, as we saw in Section 3, requires that domestic and foreign goods are perfect substitutes for each other. We continue to assume that both product and labor markets are competitive, and an important assumption is that both goods 1 and 2 can be produced profitably in the economy (i.e., that the economy is within the cone of diversification).

---

[19] The six occupational categories used by Trefler were professional and technical, clerical, sales, service, agricultural, and production, transport, and unskilled workers.

Following Jones (1965), the major implications of the model for the determination of wages are seen most clearly by dealing directly with the zero profit condition for each of the industries, $P_i Q_i - W_S S_i - W_U U_i = 0$. Differentiating these totally, we have two equations determining the proportional changes in the two wage rates:

$$\hat{P}_1 + \hat{A}_1 = \beta_1 \hat{W}_S + (1 - \beta_1)\hat{W}_U \qquad (4.8)$$

and

$$\hat{P}_2 + \hat{A}_2 = \beta_2 \hat{W}_S + (1 - \beta_2)\hat{W}_U. \qquad (4.9)$$

This implies that the skilled/unskilled relative wage depends on the relative price of the two goods and the relative values of the technology parameters, that is

$$\widehat{rel} = \left(\frac{\widehat{W_S}}{W_U} \right) = \frac{1}{\beta_1 - \beta_2} \left(\frac{\widehat{P_1 A_1}}{P_2 A_2} \right). \qquad (4.10)$$

Assuming that industry 1 is the more skill intensive sector, $\beta_1 > \beta_2$, an increase in the price of good 1 relative to good 2 causes *rel* to increase more than proportionally so long as there are some skilled workers in industry 2 ($\beta_2 > 0$) and/or some unskilled workers in industry 1 ($\beta_1 < 1$). Jones (1965) calls this the *magnification effect*. Changes in the technological parameters A_1 and A_2 have the same effect as changes in the relevant prices. As with the open model in the Ricardian case discussed in Section 3.2, changes in the relative aggregate supplies of skilled and unskilled labor have no effect on *rel* (from a partial equilibrium point of view), the *factor price insensitivity* theorem.

The impact of output price changes arising from international trade on factor prices are illustrated geometrically in Fig. 2 with a representation of unit cost curves in two industries, differing in their ratios of input use. These represent the unit cost for the production of two goods with different input ratios for skilled and unskilled labor. The vertical axis represents the wage rate for skilled labor (W_S) and the horizontal axis the wage rate for unskilled labor (W_U). Each cost curve c_i, represents combinations of W_S and W_U that permit the production of one price unit's worth of the output of good i. Point E coincides with competitive equilibrium. The returns to production of each of the goods are equal. At E the economy is active in both products, but for some output price combinations the economy will specialize in the production of only one of the goods. The cone **y0z** represents the set of equilibria in which both goods are produced, given factor endowments of the economy, technology and factor prices. In this cone factor prices are locally independent of endowments.

Output price changes lead to wage changes in a magnified way. Consider an increase in the price of the output of the skill intensive good. The c_1 curve is shifted out to c_1'. In competitive equilibrium, defined by the new crossing (of c_1' and c_2), the wage of skilled workers rises while that of less skilled workers falls. If the wage increase for skilled workers were proportionate to the price increase, the new crossing would need to be on the ray **0x**. Since the new equilibrium is toward the left of **0x**, the wage increase for skilled

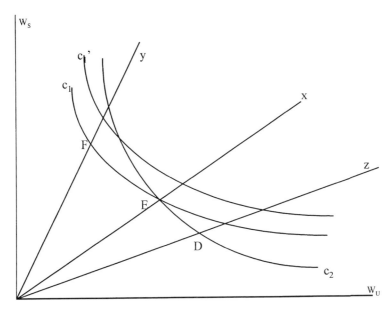

Fig. 2. The effect of price changes on wage rates in the cone of diversifiaction.

labor is in greater proportion than the price increase, a so-called magnification effect of price changes on wage changes. This disproportionate effect of output price increases on the return to one factor and the accompanying decline in the return to the other is the Stolper–Samuleson theorem (Stolper and Samuelson, 1941). For reference purposes, in our model of Section 3, c_1 and c_2 simplify to two points on the vertical and horizontal axis, respectively. The cone of diversification is the entire first quadrant, and an increase in the output price of one good simply moves the one point out in equal proportion, implying a magnification effect of one.

Suppose there is an increase in the relative supply of skilled labor. So long as output prices do not change, the factor proportions in each industry will not change, as, for example, in our small country model of Section 3, but also in a somewhat more general structure. If an increase in the relative supply of skilled labor leaves the input prices unchanged it therefore follows that the factor proportions in each industry are unchanged. The implication of this is that to absorb the added supply of skilled labor the output of the labor intensive good must have risen. It then follows that in the more general model, the share of less skilled labor employed in the production of good 2 must have fallen and the share of less-skilled labor in the skill intensive sector (good 1) must have risen. This result, that an increase in one factor induces a tandem shift in the use of the other into the industry intensive in the factor of increase, is the Rybczynski theorem.

The condition for the equilibrium of the economy to be inside the cone of diversification can be derived explicitly for the case of Cobb–Douglas production functions for both industries 1 and 2. Now the labor share parameters β_1 and β_2 are constants, and the elasticity of substitution between skilled and unskilled labor, σ, equals one. Both industries will remain active if

$$\left(\frac{\beta_2}{\beta_1}\right)^{\beta_2}\left(\frac{1-\beta_2}{1-\beta_1}\right)^{1-\beta_2}\left(\frac{S}{U}\right)^{-(\beta_1-\beta_2)} > \frac{P_1 A_1}{P_2 A_2} > \left(\frac{\beta_2}{\beta_1}\right)^{\beta_1}\left(\frac{1-\beta_2}{1-\beta_1}\right)^{1-\beta_1}\left(\frac{S}{U}\right)^{-(\beta_1-\beta_2)}.$$

$$(4.11)$$

If the left-hand side inequality is not satisfied, all resources will be devoted to industry 1, the unskilled intensive sector, and the failure of the right-hand side inequality means that all resources will be devoted to industry 1, the skill intensive sector. The left-hand side inequality is the more likely to be satisfied (industry 2 is the more likely to exist) the lower are the values of P_1/P_2, A_1/A_2, and S/U. The range of the cone is also the larger the greater is the difference between β_1 and β_2. For example, in the case in which the two industries are equally skill intensive, all resources will be devoted to the industry with the larger value of $P_i A_i$.

As long as the economy stays within the cone of diversification (both Q_1 and Q_2 are positive), the additions of a non-tradable sector (producing good 4 as in Part A of this section) and an imported good not produced in the focus economy do not upset the basic conclusions of the open model with respect to the determination of wages. The proportional changes in W_S and W_U are still determined from Eqs. (4.7) and (4.8), which make no reference to any information concerning the non-tradable sector. Since the proportional change in the price of non-tradables is $\hat{P}_4 = \beta_4 \hat{W}_S + (1-\beta_4)\hat{W}_U - \hat{A}_4$, changes in the world prices of tradable goods affect P_4 but, of course, not vice versa. The presence of a non-tradable sector, however, reduces the range within the cone of diversification (Deardorff and Courant, 1990)[20] – such that it is, for example, more likely that a given increase in P_1/P_2 will cause industry 2 to disappear.

The real wage rate of each type of labor depends on the three relevant technology parameters, A_1, A_2, and A_3, and the world prices of the two tradable goods relative to that of good 3, P_1 and P_2. These are

$$\hat{R}_S = \frac{1}{\beta_1-\beta_2}(1-\beta_2 v_3 - (1-v_3)\tilde{\beta})\hat{P}_1 - \frac{1}{\beta_1-\beta_2}(1-\beta_1 v_3 - (1-v_3)\tilde{\beta})\hat{P}_2$$

$$+ \frac{1}{\beta_1-\beta_2}((1-\beta_2 - v_4(\beta_4-\beta_2))\hat{A}_1 - \frac{1}{\beta_1-\beta_2}((1-\beta_1 + v_4(\beta_1-\beta_4))\hat{A}_2$$

$$+ v_4 \hat{A}_4$$

$$(4.12)$$

and

---

[20] This conclusion is by Eq. (3.12) obviously the same in the Ricardian case.

$$\hat{R}_U = -\frac{1}{\beta_1 - \beta_2}(\beta_2 \nu_3 + (1 - \nu_3)\tilde{\beta})\hat{P}_1 + \frac{1}{\beta_1 - \beta_2}(\beta_1 \nu_3 - (1 - \nu_3)\tilde{\beta})\hat{P}_2$$

$$-\frac{1}{\beta_1 - \beta_2}((\beta_2 + \nu_4(\beta_4 - \beta_2))\hat{A}_1 + \frac{1}{\beta_1 - \beta_2}((\beta_1 - \nu_4(\beta_1 - \beta_4))\hat{A}_2 + \nu_4\hat{A}_4,$$

$$(4.13)$$

where $\tilde{\beta} = (\beta_1 \nu_1 + \beta_2 \nu_2 + \beta_4 \nu_4)/(1 - \nu_3)$. A rise in the price of the skill intensive tradable good, P_1, causes the real wage of skilled workers to increase and the real wage of unskilled workers to fall. The effect of the increase in P_1 on the average real wage rate in the economy, $(R_S S + R_U U)/(S + U)$, is positive if the economy exports good 1;[21] otherwise it is negative. An analogous set of conclusions applies to the effects of the less skill intensive good. Suppose that a lowering of trade barriers causes the price of good 2 to fall by $X\%$. This causes R_S to rise, R_U to fall, $rel = R_S/R_U$ to rise by more than $X\%$, and the average real wage in the economy to rise if good 2 was initially imported.

Equal proportional increases in both P_1 and P_2 cause each of the real wage rates to rise by ν_3 times that proportionate increase. ν_3 is the share of goods imported but not produced in the economy, so increases in P_1 and P_2 mean that these goods have become cheaper, hence the real wage increases.

If all relevant industries in the rest of the world (including the ones producing good 3) became equally more productive, P_1 and P_2 would not change and real wage and relative wage rates in the focus country would be unaffected.

An equal proportional increase of $X\%$ in all three of the relevant technology parameters (A_1, A_2, and A_4) causes both R_S and R_U to rise by $X\%$, which is the same result as obtained in Eq. (4.7) for the closed model (with the double Cobb–Douglas assumption). If the increase in technology is confined to the non-tradable goods sector, a rise in A_4 with no change in productivity in the two tradable goods industries, both real wage rates rise by $\nu_4 X\%$. The result for the closed model is the same. Equal proportional increases in the technology parameters of the two tradable goods industries, A_1 and A_2, by $X\%$ cause both real wage rates to rise by $(1 - \nu_4)X\%$, which is, again, the same as in the closed model (with the addition of A_3 growing by $X\%$).

A change in just one of the technology parameters for the tradable goods sector causes the average real wage to change proportionally by the fraction of national income originating in that sector (ν_i plus the ratio of net exports of that good to national income) times $\hat{A}_i$, which is the same as in the closed model. However, in sharp contrast to the closed

---

[21] The proportional change in the average real wage rate is $sh\hat{R}_S + (1 - sh)\hat{R}_U$, where sh is the share of national income going to skilled workers. $sh = \beta_1(\nu_1 + x_1) + \beta_2(\nu_2 + x_2) + \beta_4 \nu_4$, where x_1 and x_2 are the ratios of the values of the ratios of net exports of each of the tradable goods to national income. With balanced trade, $x_1 + x_2 = \nu_3$. The conclusion that the effect of an increase in P_1 on the average real wage has the same sign as x_1 follows from the substitution of Eqs. (4.12) and (4.13) and the definition of sh into the expression for the change in the average real wage rate.

model, the productivity change causes a large change in relative wages. For example, $\partial(\ln R_S)/\partial(\ln A_1) > 0$ and $\partial(\ln R_U)/\partial(\ln A_1) < 0$.

The strong conclusions of the neoclassical trade model that we have discussed thus far are based on the assumption that there are two tradable goods and two (internally mobile) factors, the standard 2×2 model. In a more general setting there are m separate tradable goods and n different factors of production. The standard reference on the properties of the general case of the classical trade model is Ethier (1984). If $m = n$, there is no problem with using a set of equations like Eqs. (4.7) and (4.8) to discern the effects in a particular small country of changes in internationally determined prices on factor prices in that country. The difficulties arise when $m \neq n$. When the number of tradable goods exceeds the number of factors $(m > n)$, it is necessary to analyze the equilibrium of a particular economy in concert with the equilibrium of all other economies. However, Ethier concludes that most of the basic propositions of the 2×2 model, and, of particular interest to labor economists, the lack of a significant effect of domestic factor supplies on factor prices holds up in the $m > n$ case.[22]

When, however, the number of separate tradable goods is less than the number of factors, $m < n$, many of the implications of the model are quite different. In particular, factor supplies in a country now have an effect on factor prices. For example, suppose that the economy produces two tradable goods ((1) "high-tech" and (2) "low-tech"), both with inputs of high skilled (S), medium-skilled (M), and low-skilled (U) labor, the aggregate supplies of which are fixed. The prices of the two goods, P_1 and P_2, are determined in the world market and are (essentially) exogenous. Given the further assumption of the mobility of each of the three types of labor such that $W_{k1} = W_{k2}$ for each skill level k, wage rates are determined by the three marginal conditions, $(P_1/P_2)\partial Q_1/\partial S_1 = \partial Q_2/\partial S_2$, etc. As in the 2×2 model, the solution values of the W_k's are affected by the exogenous relative price of the two goods, P_1/P_2, and by the technology parameters A_1/A_2. However, unlike the 2×2 model, they also depend on the factor endowments of the economy. For example, an increase in S causes the high/medium relative wage, $\mathrm{rel}_{S/M} = W_S/W_M$, to decline – although by less than it would in a closed economy framework.[23]

---

[22] Leamer and Levinsohn (1995) make the point that as a practical matter economists are unsure about how to count both the number of distinct commodities (m) and the number of separate factors (n). The uncertainty with respect to the second question is reflected in our discussion in Section 4.1 concerning the appropriate way to disaggregate labor input.

[23] An example of one of N! special cases that can occur in trade models of the labor market concerns the demand for teenage labor. Suppose that there are two tradable goods industries, 1 and 2, that only use adult skilled and unskilled labor, S_i and U_i. The non-tradable goods industry in the economy, on the other hand, employs some S and U as well as the entire supply of teenage labor, say T (in the capacity of employees of the fast food industry). Assuming an equilibrium within the cone of diversification (both industries 1 and 2 are profitably operated), W_S/W_U is determined by the value of P_1/P_2 as in the standard two input model above. The market-clearing wage of teenage labor, W_T, may be affected by the aggregate supply of teenagers as in the closed model. Specifically, if teenagers and adult unskilled labor are not sufficiently perfect substitutes in the nontradable industry, $\partial W_T/\partial T < 0$. (If on the other hand, each U is perfectly substitutable for a T, the equilibrium value of W_T will be a proportional of W_U, which is determined internationally.

4.3. Modifications of the open model

The most important difference between the open and closed models from the point of view of labor market analysis is that changes in relative factor supplies, S/U, have an effect on real and relative wages in the latter but not (or, in general, very little) in the former. In Sections 3.4–3.6 it was shown in the context of a simple Ricardian framework that this conclusion is upset when any combination of three assumptions of the open model is lifted. These assumptions are as follows: (i) the economy is inside the cone of diversification (i.e., both skilled and unskilled labor are involved in the production of tradable goods); (ii) domestic and foreign versions of the two tradable goods are perfect substitutes, and (iii) both types of labor are perfectly mobile between industries.

First, suppose that the relative price of good 2 has fallen below the point at which the less skill intensive industry 2 is profitable so that only one tradable good (industry 1) and the non-tradable good (industry 4) remain active. P_1 is determined internationally, and P_4 is determined domestically. The marginal conditions are now $W_S = P_1 A_1 F_S{}^1 = P_4 A_4 F_S{}^4$ and $W_U = P_1 A_1 F_S{}^1 = P_4 A_4 F_S{}^4$. To make the point as simply as possible, we will assume that the production functions in both industries and the consumer utility function are Cobb–Douglas (so that the consumption shares, the ν_i's, are constant). This implies that the fractions of skilled and unskilled workers employed in the non-tradable sector are, respectively, $S_4/S = \beta_4 \nu_4/(\beta_4 \nu_4 + \beta_1(1 - \nu_4))$ and $U_4/U = (1 - \beta_4)\nu_4/((1 - \beta_4)\nu_4 + (1 - \beta_1)(1 - \nu_4))$. It then follows that the skilled/unskilled wage rate depends negatively on S/U, for $rel = (\beta_4/(1 - \beta_4))(S_4/U_4)$. Regardless of the skill intensity of the export industry relative to that of the industry for exclusively domestic consumption, a change in the world price of the export good has no effect on relative wages. Thus, outside the cone of diversification, the labor market of an open economy behaves essentially like that of a closed economy.

Second, it was shown in Section 3.5 that a necessary condition for the strong version of the open model to hold is that the foreign and domestic versions of tradable goods must be perfect substitutes. To the extent that the elasticities of substitution between the consumption of the domestic and foreign versions of each of the tradable goods, C_i, and C_{if}, are less than infinity, the absolute relative demand elasticity of labor will be less than infinity. We will not set out the rather tedious algebra, but the same conclusion applies to the case set out in this section in which both types of labor are used in all industries.

To see this intuitively, consider an economy that produces and consumes only goods 1 and 2, the former being more skill intensive than the latter. The relative supply of the goods depends positively on their relative price, which is represented by the upward-sloping $(Q_1/Q_2)_S$ schedule in Fig. 3. This is the flatter the more similar are the skill compositions of the two industries,[24] and (because industry 1 is more skill intensive than industry 2) it shifts to the right when the relative supply of skilled labor increases.

The relative demand curve depends on what assumes about trade. In the closed economy case, relative product demand is equal to relative consumption demand, which is downward-sloping with an absolute elasticity of ε. In the open economy model without product differentiation, each domestic price is equal to the foreign price, so the demand condition is represented as $P_1/P_2 = P_{1f}/P_{2f}$, which is, of course, horizontal. In the differentiated products version of the open model, the relative product demand curve depends on the relative domestic prices and has a finite elasticity so long as the price elasticities of imports and exports of the two tradable goods are less than infinity.[25]

A shift to the right in the relative supply curve due to an increase in S/U causes the largest decline in the relative price of the skill intensive good in the closed model and, of course, no change in the open model without perfectly substitutable products. In the differentiated products model, the shift in the relative supply curve causes some decline in P_1/P_2, the decline being the smaller the larger are the import and export elasticities. Since the change in rel is determined by Eq. (4.10) in all cases, the magnitude of the effect of an increase in S/U on rel ranges from zero in the open model to the closed economy elasticity.

Third, the strong conclusion of conventional open economy model also depends on the assumption that both skilled and unskilled labor are completely mobile across industries 1 and 2, i.e., that the *specific factors* case does not apply. This was demonstrated in the context of the Ricardian model in Section 3.6. If, as was shown for that model, one or both of the labor types cannot or does not move in response to relative wage changes, magnitudes of the effects of changes in S/U, A_1/A_2, and the internationally determined P_1/P_2 are smaller than in the model with complete labor mobility.

The same conclusion holds for the classical case in which the ouput of each tradable good depends on both factors. Assuming that unskilled labor is immobile ($U_1 = zU$ and $U_2 = (1 - z)U$) although skilled labor is still completely mobile between industries, $\hat{W}_S - \hat{W}_U$ is no longer uniquely determined from Eqs. (4.8) and (4.9), for the changes in unskilled wages in the two industries are not identical.[26] The result in this case – as was true in the Ricardian model – is that an increase in the relative world price of the relatively skill intensive good causes W_S/W_{U1} to fall and W_S/W_{U2} to rise and that the average relative wage, $rel = W_S/(zW_{U1} + (1 - z)W_{U2})$ rises by less than it would if U were mobile. Further, a given increase in S/U causes rel to fall by an amount that is less than in the closed models.

Problems associated with the analysis of the general case of many separate tradable

---

[24] The price elasticity of relative supply is

$$\frac{\partial(\ln(Q_1/Q_2))}{\partial(\ln(P_1/P_2))} = \sigma\left[\frac{1}{(\beta_1 - \beta_2)(S_1/S - U_1/U)} - 1\right].$$

The value of this elasticity ranges from to zero in the Ricardian case of $\beta_1 = 1$ and $\beta_2 = 0$ to infinity when $\beta_1 = \beta_2$.

[25] In general the magnitude of the coefficients on the proportional changes in P_1 and P_2 the proportional change in Q_1/Q_2 will not be equal. If, however, one makes the assumption that for the two tradable goods the ratios of imports to total consumption as well as the substitution.

[26] If the assumption that W_{U1} and W_{U2} can differ is replaced by the assumption instead that they move together because of union policy or governmental regulation, the model is no longer characterized by full employment.

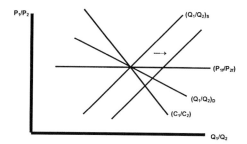

Fig. 3. Determination of relative prices and relative output in alternative models of the economy.

goods and many distinct factors of production (with m, the number of goods, either greater or less than n, the number of factors) are eased somewhat by the existence of factor immobility (see Ethier, 1984, Section 5.2) or by the assumption of differentiated products. If the latter specification is appropriate (consumers in each country treat foreign goods as (even slightly) different from domestically produced versions), the resultant equilibrium of the labor market is, once again, a blend of the closed and open models. Given that different tradable goods surely vary in the degree of differentiation (the τ_i's would not be the same), the algebra of the many goods/many factors case is sufficiently complicated that it would be necessary to move to a computable general equilibrium framework.

4.4. Capital as a factor of production

To this point we have ignored capital and other factor inputs. In part this was done to focus on the labor market; it also turns out that for many purposes the addition of capital to models does not make very much difference.

Assume that aggregate output in each industry can be represented by a two level production function of the form

$$Y_i = F^i(A_i F^i(S_i, U_i), K_i). \tag{4.14}$$

$A_i F^i(S_i, U_i)$ is the flow of labor services and is Eq. (4.1), the production function when capital was ignored. G^i is assumed to be homogeneous with respect to inputs of labor services and capital, and the output shares of the labor aggregate and capital in each industry are, respectively, α_i and $1 - \alpha_i$. The marginal products of skilled and unskilled labor in each industry are $\partial Q_i / \partial S_i = A_i G_N^i F_S^i$ and $\partial Q_i / \partial U_i = A_i G_N^i F_U^i$. The marginal product of the labor aggregate, $\partial Q_i / \partial (A_i F^i) = G_N^i$, rises as K_i rises, and the relative marginal products of skilled and unskilled labor in that industry – everything else held constant – are unaffected, for $A_i G_N^i$ is in both the numerator and denominator of the ratio.[27]

---

[27] A more general production function, $F^i(S_i, U_i, K_i, A_i)$ would allow for the two labor inputs to have different degrees of complementarity with capital, for example the Griliches (1969) hypothesis that S is more complementary with K than is U.

For simplicity, it is assumed that each G^i and each F^i is Cobb–Douglas and that both of the industries we will consider, the two tradable industries 1 and 2, are equally labor intensive (i.e., the α_i's are the same). Industry 1, however, is more skilled labor intensive than industry 2 ($\beta_1 > \beta_2$). It is also assumed that consumer preferences are generated from a Cobb–Douglas utility function, and the propensities to consume goods 1 and 2 are the constants ν_1 and $\nu_2 = 1 - \nu_1$.

In the case of a closed economy, the marginal conditions along with the relative product demand function imply, given the further assumption of mobility of both types of labor between the two industries, that the shares of unskilled and skilled labor allocated to industry 1 are $S_1/S = \beta_1 \nu_1/\bar{\beta}$ and $U_1/U = (1 - \beta_1)\nu_1/(1 - \bar{\beta}))$, where $\bar{\beta} = \beta_1 \nu_1 + \beta_2(1 - \nu_2)$ is the average value of the skill intensity parameter. There are three possible specifications concerning the aggregate stock of capital and its allocation between industries. First, in the short run (which may be up to several years) the values of K_1 and K_2 are fixed, reflecting past investment decisions. Second, in the medium run a fixed aggregate stock of capital, K, may be allocated between industries such that its marginal revenue products in each industry are equal. This implies – given the simplifying Cobb–Douglas and identical share assumptions – that the share of the aggregate capital stock allocated to industry 1 is equal to $K_1/K = \nu_1$. Third, in the long run the aggregate stock of capital adjusts in response to the rate of saving/investment. Given constant saving and depreciation rates and the assumption that investment uses the output of both industries in the same proportion as consumption (ν_1 of foods 1 and $1 - \nu_1$ of good 2), the long run K will tend toward a constant fraction of real output, $Y = Q_1^{\nu_1} Q_2^{1-\nu_1}$.

Our principal interest in this review is in the long run, so we will only consider the implications of the third specification concerning the size and the allocation of the capital stock. The aggregate value of output depends on the supplies of S, U, and K. If, however, the supply of K is proportional to Y, it follows, holding the saving rate and tastes (represented by the value of ν_1) constant, that the proportional change in aggregate real income is

$$\hat{Y} = \alpha \nu_1 \hat{A}_1 + \alpha(1 - \nu_1)\hat{A}_2 + \alpha \bar{\beta} \hat{S} + \alpha(1 - \beta)\hat{U} + (1 - \alpha)\hat{K}$$

$$= \nu_1 \hat{A}_1 + (1 - \nu_1)\hat{A}_2 + \bar{\beta} \hat{S} + (1 - \bar{\beta})\hat{U}, \tag{4.15}$$

where $\bar{\beta} = \beta_1 \nu_1 + \beta_2(1 - \nu_1)$ is the average value of the skill intensity parameter in the economy. Since the ratio of the real wages by skill is $R_S/R_U = (\nu_1/(1 - \nu_1))(S/U)^{-1}$ and the total wage bill is $R_S S + R_U U = \alpha Y$, the proportional change in the skilled real wage rate is given by Eq. (4.7), the case in which capital was ignored. In other words, under a set of quite restrictive assumptions,[28] the inclusion of capital in the closed

---

[28] Some of these assumptions are not necessary to derive Eq. (4.15). For example, the elasticity of substitution between S and U, σ, need not be unity, and approximately the same result obtains when the labor's share parameters in the two industries, the α_i's, are allowed to differ. Further, it is not necessary to confine the model to two industries, for the same basic result applies to the case in which there are any number of industries.

model does not alter the basic conclusions concerning the major determinants of real and relative wages.

The inclusion of capital in the open model presents a wide variety of possible specifications pertaining to both the allocation of an economy's aggregate stock of capital between industries and the determination and international mobility of the aggregate world capital stock. We will discuss just one specification, which is analogous to that of the above discussion of the role of capital in the model of the closed economy. The only difference is that now both goods 1 and 2 are potentially tradable at prevailing world prices P_1 and P_2. The production function for each industry is Cobb–Douglas in inputs of the two types of labor and capital. The labor's share parameter α is the same in both industries, but skill labor's share, $\alpha \beta_i$, is sufficiently greater in industry 1 than in industry 2 that the economy is within the cone of diversification.

It is assumed that in the long run each industry rents capital at a price r such that profits are maximized. The zero profit condition requires that $P_i Q_i - W_S S_1 - W_U U_i - r K_i = 0$. The total logarithmic derivative of each of these implies that $\hat{P}_i + \alpha \hat{A}_i = \alpha \beta_i \hat{W}_S + \alpha (1 - \beta_i)\hat{W}_U + (1 - \alpha)\hat{r}$. The rental price of capital is a weighted average of the prices of the two goods in the economy, P_1 and P_2. To keep the story consistent with that of the closed model, these weights are assumed to be equal to the weights in the utility function, ν_1 and $\nu_2 = 1 - \nu_1$, so $\hat{r} = \nu_1 \hat{P}_1 + (1 - \nu_1)\hat{P}_2$. Making the substitution, the two wage rates are seen to be determined in two equations as functions of the two world prices and the two productivity parameters, that is

$$[1 - (1 - \alpha)\nu_1]\hat{P}_1 - (1 - \alpha)(1 - \nu_1)\hat{P}_2 + \alpha \hat{A}_1 = \alpha \beta_1 \hat{W}_S + \alpha(1 - \beta_1)\hat{W}_U, \tag{4.16}$$

$$-(1 - \alpha)\nu_1 \hat{P}_1 + [1 - (1 - \alpha)(1 - \nu_1)]\hat{P}_2 + \alpha \hat{A}_2 = \alpha \beta_2 \hat{W}_S + \alpha(1 - \beta_2)\hat{W}_U. \tag{4.17}$$

Subtracting the second from the first of these equations yields the change in the skilled/ unskilled relative wage:

$$\widehat{rel} = \left(\widehat{\frac{W_S}{W_U}}\right) = \frac{1}{\alpha(\beta_1 - \beta_2)}\left[\left(\widehat{\frac{P_1}{P_2}}\right) + \alpha\left(\widehat{\frac{A_1}{A_2}}\right)\right]. \tag{4.18}$$

This is the same result as Eq. (4.10), the case in which capital ignored, except that the magnification effect of relative price changes on relative wages is greater (because it is one over the industry difference the *output* shares of skilled labor).

4.5. The relative wage effects of unionism

It is interesting to examine the effects of the openness of an economy in assessing the potential role of unionism in affecting the distribution of income. As we shall see in the next section, some papers have explored the hypothesis that the decline in unionism in the US has been a significant factor in the observed rise in the skilled/unskilled wage differential, and some papers have linked the decline in unionism to increases in foreign competition. Although these models are based in large part on a behavioral assumption that we will not make in the present section, it is useful to lay some of the groundwork for the subsequent discussion of this issue. The results also provide an example of the implications for labor market analysis of openness.

We assume that there are three industries, 1 and 2 that produce manufactured goods and 4 that produces services, all using the two types of labor according to the production function (4.1). It is also assumed that all unskilled workers in the two manufacturing industries are represented by unions (so that union employment is $U_1 + U_2 = tU$, where t is the proportion of the U's who are unionized) but that no unskilled workers in the service sector are organized (so $U_4 = (1 - t)U$). No skilled workers are (meaningfully) unionized.

The effect of unionism is to raise the wage of union members such that is $\gamma > 1$ times the wage of non-union unskilled workers. Thus, $W_{U_1} = W_{U1} = W_{U2} = \gamma W_{U4}$.[29] Skilled workers receive W_S in all three industries. Given that t of the unskilled work force receives the "rent" of $(\gamma - 1)W_{U4}$, the average value of the skilled/unskilled relative wage is

$$rel = \frac{W_S}{W_{U4}} \frac{1}{1 + t(\gamma - 1)}. \tag{4.19}$$

What we ask in this section concerns the effect of an increase in γ on rel, the sign and magnitude of $\partial rel/\partial\gamma$, and how these compare between the closed and open economy models.

We first consider the effect of unions in the closed economy. We assume that the underlying utility function is CES with an elasticity of substitution equal to ε. It is also assumed that the elasticity of substitution between the two types of labor is equal to σ in each industry. The solution values of the ratio of the skilled wage to the non-union unskilled wage, W_S/W_{U4}, and the fraction of unskilled workers who are employed in the unionized sector, t, depends on γ as well as the other exogenous variables we have considered above. In general the solution expressions of the model are quite messy, but, with the simplifying assumption that the two elasticities of substitution are equal, $\varepsilon = \sigma$, the messiness is avoided (because the values of the S_i's are unaffected by changes in γ). The relative demand for unionized unskilled labor in this case is $(\widehat{U_1/U_2}) = -\sigma\hat\gamma$, so the proportional change in the fraction of U's who are in the unionized sector is $\hat t = -(1 - t)\sigma\hat\gamma$. Since the relative use of skilled labor in the non-union sector is $S_4/\widehat{(1 - t)}U$, it follows that the change in the skilled/non-union unskilled relative wage is $(\widehat{W_S/W_{U4}}) = t\hat\gamma$.

In words, an increase in the union premium lowers the relative employment of unionized unskilled labor (a fall in t), and those workers "crowded out" of union jobs drive down the wage of non-union workers, thus raising W_S/W_{U1}. At the same time, the rise in γ causes, ceteris paribus, the average wage of unskilled workers to rise relative to the skilled

---

[29] In the more general (messy) version there is a similar condition involving a weighted average of σ and ε instead of $\sigma = \varepsilon$. For an approach similar to this one in the context of a closed economy, see Johnson and Mieszkowski (1969).

wage. The net effect of these three factors is

$$\widehat{rel} = \frac{t(\gamma - 1)(\sigma - 1)}{1 + t(\gamma - 1)} \hat{\gamma}. \tag{4.20}$$

Given that $\gamma > 1$, an increase in γ increases or decreases the average skilled/unskilled relative wage as $\sigma = \varepsilon$ is greater or less than one. In other words, unionism of low skilled workers increases their average relative earnings only if relative demand elasticities are fairly low.

The effect of the unionization on the relative earnings of unskilled workers is quite different in the context of an open economy (with both industries 1 and 2 active). Since $\hat{W}_{U1} = \hat{W}_{U2} = W_{U4} + \hat{\gamma}$, the total logarithmic derivatives of the three zero profit conditions are

$$\hat{P}_1 - (1 - \beta_1)\hat{\gamma} = \beta_1 \hat{W}_S + (1 - \beta_1)\hat{W}_{U4}, \tag{4.21}$$

$$\hat{P}_2 - (1 - \beta_2)\hat{\gamma} = \beta_2 \hat{W}_S + (1 - \beta_2)\hat{W}_{U4} \tag{4.22}$$

and

$$\hat{P}_4 = \beta_4 \hat{W}_S + (1 - \beta_4)\hat{W}_{U4}. \tag{4.23}$$

Since the changes in the prices of goods 1 and 2 are exogenous to the model and the change in P_4 is endogenous, the changes in W_S and W_{U4} are determined by the first two of these equations. The solution of these implies that W_S is unaffected by a change in γ and $\hat{W}_{U4} = -\hat{\gamma}$.

This means that the wage of unionized workers in terms of the price of good 3 is also unchanged. Since the average skilled/unskilled relative wage is $rel = W_S/(tW_{Ut} + (1 - t)W_{U4})$, an increase in γ unambiguously *raises* rel in an open economy setting. The increase in γ lowers W_{U4} and t without affecting either W_S or $W_{U1} = W_{U2}$. The reader will note that this conclusion is independent of the value of either of the substitution parameters, the size of which determined the sign of $\partial rel/\partial \gamma$ in the closed economy case.[30]

A rise in γ in the open economy case narrows the cone of diversification in the sense that the less skill intensive industry 2 is less likely to be profitable. If industry 2 has shut down so that all unionized workers are in industry 1, the effect of an increase in γ on *rel* is analytically similar to its effect in the closed economy case. An increase in γ causes the skilled/unskilled relative wage to rise or fall as a weighted average of σ and ε is greater or less than one.

The analysis of the effect of unionism on the skilled/unskilled relative wage can easily

---

[30] The real wage rates of skilled workers and unionized unskilled workers rise due to an increase in the union premium by $-\nu_4 \hat{P}_4 = \nu_4(1 - \beta_4)\hat{\gamma}$, for the prices of the other goods are set internationally. The average real wage rate in the economy across workers of both skills falls slightly, for there is an inefficient shift in consumption from tradable to non-tradable goods.

be extended to the case in which unskilled workers in the service sector, industry 4, are organized by unions but those in the manufacturing sector, industries 1 and 2, are not. In the closed economy case an exogenous increase in the value of W_{U4} relative to $W_{U1} = W_{U2}$ has the same qualitative effect on *rel* as in the closed model. *rel* rises or falls with γ as $\sigma = \varepsilon$ is greater or less than one.

In the open economy model, on the other hand, *rel* is always smaller when $\gamma > 1$ than when it is equal to one. This is the opposite result to that for the organization of the U's in the tradable goods sector.

4.6. Technological change

Another interesting difference between the polar closed and open models concerns their implications concerning the labor market effects of different forms of technological change (see Krugman, 1995, and especially Haskel and Slaughter, 1997). We have seen in the models in both the Ricardian and classical models discussed in Sections 3 and 4 that changes in the skill neutral technology parameters in the tradable sector, A_1 and A_2, have very different effects on relative wages in closed and open models. In the closed model, to the extent that elasticities of substitution in consumption are close to unity, *rel* is independent of the values of all the A_i's in the economy. In the closed economy, changes in the relative value of A_1/A_2 have a magnification effect on relative wages that is similar to the effect of relative international prices.

A common conclusion of the literature that attempts to explain the recent increase in the relative demand for labor in most countries is that the data suggest that there may have been a great deal of skill-biased technological change.[31] This type of technological change is modeled very differently from the neutral variety that we have considered thus far.

To explore this we will assume that there are three active industries in the economy, the two manufacturing industries producing the potentially tradable goods 1 and 2 and a non-tradable service industry 4. (Industry 3 will be ignored to facilitate comparison between the closed and open models.) The production function for each industry is assumed to be Cobb–Douglas in inputs of the two types of labor:

$$Q_i = A_i(b_i S_i)^{\beta_i} U_i^{1-\beta_i}. \tag{4.24}$$

A_i is the skill neutral technological parameter we have featured throughout. b_i refers to the quantity of efficiency units of skilled labor realized per unit input of S_i.

There are three different kinds of technological change that can affect the production function in each industry.[32] The first is a change in A_i, the skill neutral form. The second is that skilled workers can get better at the jobs they currently perform, *intensive* skill-biased technological change, which is represented by an increase in b_i. A third thing that can

---

[31] See, for example, Katz and Murphy (1992), Bound and Johnson (1992), Berman et al. (1994), Machin et al. (1996), and Autor et al. (1997).

[32] The following discussion is based on Johnson and Stafford (1998).

happen is that skilled workers can improve in their potential ability to perform some of the functions previously performed by unskilled workers. This may be termed *extensive* skill-biased technological change, and it can be represented by an increase in the value of β_i.[33] The total effect of all three forms of technological change is the proportional change in Q_i for given factor inputs in that industry, that is

$$\Omega_i = \hat{A}_i + \beta_i \hat{b}_i + \ln\left(\frac{b_i S_i}{U_i}\right) d\beta_i. \tag{4.25}$$

Barring some sort of perverse events external to firms (like an outbreak of civil disorder), the value of Ω_i has a lower bound of zero, for firms within an industry would never adopt a new technology that raised unit costs of production.

In the closed economy case with a unitary value of the elasticity of substitution in the aggregate utility function, the skilled/unskilled relative wage is determined as in Eq. (4.6) by

$$rel = \frac{\bar{\beta}}{1 - \bar{\beta}}\left(\frac{S}{U}\right)^{-1}, \qquad \bar{\beta} = \sum_{i=1,2,4} \beta_i \nu_i. \tag{4.26}$$

$\bar{\beta}$ is a weighted average of the β_i's, so the only type of technological change that affects the relative demand for labor is the extensive skill-biased variant. Increases in the A_i's and/or b_i's raise the real wage rates of both skilled and unskilled workers proportionally.[34]

In the open economy with undifferentiated products case the effects of different types of technical change on relative wage are much different from the closed economy. The logarithmic derivatives of the three zero profit conditions are

$$\hat{P}_1 + \Omega_1 = \beta_1 \hat{W}_S + (1 - \beta_1)\hat{W}_U \tag{4.27}$$

$$\hat{P}_2 + \Omega_2 = \beta_2 \hat{W}_S + (1 - \beta_2)\hat{W}_U \tag{4.28}$$

and

$$\hat{P}_4 + \Omega_4 = \beta_4 \hat{W}_S + (1 - \beta_4)\hat{W}_U. \tag{4.29}$$

Since P_1 and P_2 are exogenous and P_4 is endogenous, the solution proportional change in the relative wage rate, holding P_1/P_2 constant, is

---

[33] This is sometimes called "upskilling." There could also be downskilling – a decline in β_i as a result of the simplification of a set of jobs. See Goldin and Margo (1992) for a discussion of this in the context of manufacturing production processes in the US during the 1940s.

[34] In a more general variant of the model with ε and/or σ not equal to zero, neutral and intensive skill-biased technological change affect the relative demand for labor and hence *rel*, but, barring very large departures from unity, the magnitudes effects are not very large.

$$\widehat{rel} = \frac{\Omega_1 - \Omega_2}{\beta_1 - \beta_2} = \frac{(\hat{A}_1 - \hat{A}_2) + (\beta_1 \hat{b}_1 - \beta_2 \hat{b}_2) + \left(\ln\left(\frac{b_1 S_1}{U_1}\right) d\beta_1 - \ln\left(\frac{b_2 S_2}{U_2}\right) d\beta_2 \right)}{\beta_1 - \beta_2}.$$

(4.30)

The qualitative effect of changes in the intensive skill intensity parameters depends on whether skilled workers get better at the jobs they normally perform in the skill intensive tradable goods industry (an increase in b_1) or the unskilled intensive industry (an increase in b_2). If the b_i's rise by the same proportion in both industries, *rel* increases by that proportion. An increase in b_4 (lawyers and psychologists becoming more productive) has no effect on *rel*.

The effect of extensive skill biased technological change, increases in the β_i's, again depends on the industry in which it occurs. The qualitative effect of increases in β_1, β_2, and β_4 are, respectively, positive, negative, and zero. This is in contrast to the closed model in which increases in each of the β_i's causes an increase in *rel* roughly in proportion to the fraction of output accounted for by each industry. The most notable difference between the closed and open models, of course, is that of a ceteris paribus increase in β_2, the skill intensity parameter for the less skill intensive manufacturing industry. In the closed case, *rel* increases, but in the open case *rel* decreases.

To evaluate the relative importance of extensive skill biased technological change in the closed and open cases, let all three β_i's change by the same amount $d\beta$. Letting $v_1 = v_2 = 0.25$, $v_4 = 0.50$, $\beta_1 = 0.7$, $\beta_2 = 0.3$, $\beta_4 = 0.5$, and $rel = 1.5$, the value of $\partial(\ln R)/\partial\beta$ is 4.0 for the closed case and 1.7 for the open case.

4.7. Factor content analysis

In Section 3.7 we discussed in the context of the simple Ricardian model an empirical method for determining the effect of changes in the international prices of tradable goods on relative factor prices. Factor content analysis (FCA) treats the quantities of skilled and unskilled labor "necessary" to produce the net exports of each good like hypothetical emigration of those quantities of labor. FCA then proceeds to adjust actual aggregate labor supplies for the changes due to changes in net exports and to calculate what *rel* would be in a closed economy model. The relative wage rate implied under FCA is

$$rel_f = a_0 \left(\frac{S_*}{U_*} \right)^{-1/a_1}, \qquad S_* = S - \sum_i \left(\frac{S_i}{Q_i} \right) NX_i, \qquad U_* = U - \sum_i \left(\frac{U_i}{Q_i} \right) NX_i.$$

(4.31)

NX_i is the observed value of net exports of good i, and S_i/Q_i and U_i/S_i are the average contents of each factor used in the production of each tradable good, a_1 in Eq. (4.31) is the "elasticity of substitution" between skilled and unskilled constant, and a_0 is an arbitrary constant. Most FCA studies (e.g., Baldwin and Cain, 1997) assume that $a_1 = 1$, but a few (e.g., Borjas et al., 1997) make other assumptions.

Under certain conditions Eq. (4.31) can be used to calculate accurately the effect of changes in world relative prices (or trade policy) on relative wages over a time interval by calculating rel$_f$ with and without the observed ΔNX_i's.[35] The first set of these conditions involve the requirement that the cause of each of the ΔNX_i's must be external to the economy rather than internal to it. If, for example, there were an increase in the relative supply of skilled labor, there would be, ceteris paribus, and increase in the net exports of relatively skill intensive goods and a decrease in the net exports of unskilled intensive goods. The use of FCA in this circumstance would lead to the erroneous conclusion that the relative demand for skilled labor increased due to international factors. The same conclusion applies to increases in technological parameters across industries that are correlated with relative skill intensity.

The second set of conditions on the accuracy of FCA involve the elasticities of substitution between U and S in each production function (σ) and between commodities in the aggregate utility function (ε). Deardorff and Staiger (1988) showed that – subject to satisfaction of the first set of conditions – that FCA is accurate when the economy is characterized by the double Cobb–Douglas assumption (with the use $a_1 = 1$ in Eq. (4.31)). Deardorff (1997) has generalized this result to the requirement that production and utility functions be CES with identical substitution elasticities (with the use of a value of a_1 equal to the correct value of $\sigma = \varepsilon$). FCA obviously yields – under the best of circumstances – an approximate answer to the question it addresses. For purposes of evaluating empirical studies below, it is interesting to ask how far off this answer is given the true" combination of values of σ and ε.[36] Table 6 calculates the bias in FCA calculations for an economy producing goods 1 and 2 with CES technology (with an elasticity of substitution in both industries equal to σ) and demanding the goods on the basis of a CES utility function (with an elasticity of substitution between C_1 and C_2 of ε). All the other assumptions required for FCA to be valid are satisfied. We will distinguish three different methods that make use of three different values of a_1. Method A sets a_1 equal to the true value of σ (which is correct if the relative product demand elasticity is equal to σ).[37] Method B sets a_1 equal to one, the double Cobb–Douglas assumption. Method C set a_1 equal to 1.5, which is probably a more accurate estimate of σ than is the value under Method B. All of the simulations in Table 6 are based on the assumption that the internationally given value of P_1/P_2 increased by an amount such that *rel* increase by 16.0% above its initial value. Thus, all of the increase in

---

[35] See Leamer (1996b) for a rather strongly expressed set of objections to FCA. Labor economists who have worked in this area find FCA an intuitively appealing and practical way to proceed (sort of like running a regression with one or two of the right-hand side variables missing) – not perfection but better than simply speculating about the values of the slope coefficients of interest. See Borjas et al. (1997) for a perceptive discussion of the plusses and minuses of FCA.

[36] Baldwin and Cain (1997), who use the $a_1 = 1$ assumption in their FCA, conclude their discussion of their results with the caveat that "… it is not clear just how sensitive these conclusions are to the assumption of Cobb–Douglas production functions and tastes" (p. 59).

[37] Of course, Method A is a hypothetical rather than an actual, usable procedure. All the studies we have seen use one of the other two procedures.

Table 6
Proportional bias in estimated relative wage effects for alternative factor content methods for different values of the elasticities of substitution in production (σ) and consumption (ε)

Value of ε	Method	Value of σ						
		0.50	0.75	1.00	1.25	1.50	1.75	2.00
0.50	A	0.00	−0.08	−0.14	−0.17	−0.20	−0.22	−0.25
	B	−0.52	−0.32	−0.14	0.06	0.24	0.42	0.59
	C	−0.68	−0.56	−0.44	−0.31	−0.20	−0.08	0.02
0.75	A	0.07	0.00	−0.07	−0.11	−0.15	−0.18	−0.21
	B	−0.48	−0.26	−0.07	0.13	0.32	0.51	0.69
	C	−0.66	−0.52	−0.39	−0.27	−0.15	−0.03	0.03
1.00	A	0.15	0.08	0.00	−0.06	−0.10	−0.13	−0.17
	B	−0.45	−0.21	0.00	0.20	0.40	0.59	0.78
	C	−0.64	−0.48	−0.35	−0.22	−0.10	0.02	0.14
1.25	A	0.22	0.16	0.07	0.00	−0.05	−0.09	−0.12
	B	−0.42	−0.15	0.07	0.27	0.48	0.68	0.87
	C	−0.62	−0.44	−0.31	−0.18	−0.05	0.07	0.19
1.50	A	0.29	0.24	0.14	0.06	0.00	−0.04	−0.08
	B	−0.38	−0.09	0.14	0.35	0.56	0.76	0.97
	C	−0.59	−0.41	−0.26	−0.13	0.00	0.13	0.25
1.75	A	0.37	0.33	0.21	0.11	0.05	0.00	−0.04
	B	−0.35	−0.03	0.21	0.42	0.64	0.85	1.06
	C	−0.57	−0.37	−0.22	−0.08	0.05	0.18	0.31
2.00	A	0.44	0.41	0.28	0.17	0.10	0.04	0.00
	B	−0.31	0.03	0.28	0.49	0.72	0.94	1.16
	C	−0.55	−0.33	−0.18	−0.04	0.10	0.23	0.37

the relative wage rate is "due to trade" and none of the increase is attributable to anything that occurred domestically.

To read the table, consider the "answer" given by each of the procedures for the assumed true values $\varepsilon = \sigma = 0.5$. By method A, a_1 is set equal to 0.5, and the answer that the increase in P_1/P_2 led to a 16.0% increase in rel is correct. The bias as a proportion of the actual is 0.00. By method B, a_1 is set equal to one, and at $\sigma = \varepsilon = 0.5$, FCA attributes 7.7% of the 16.0 increase in rel to external events. The bias in the estimate as a proportion of the actual is $7.7/16.0 - 1 = -0.52$. By method C, a_1 is set equal to 1.5, and the bias as a proportion of the actual is $5.1/16.0 - 1 = -0.68$.

Our sense of the empirical literature on intrafactor elasticities of substitution is that σ is definitely greater than one, probably in the range of 1.5–2.0. It is interesting to point out that, to the extent that this sense is correct, the FCA estimates using Method B (double Cobb–Douglas) lead to an overestimate of the effect of trade in the range of ε from 0.75 to 1.25 or from 30% to 90% while FCA estimates using Method C are much closer to the true effect.

4.8. Labor markets in developing countries

Throughout this tour of the literature on the effect of openness on labor markets much attention has been focused on the effects of changes in the relative prices of tradable goods with different skill intensities (P_1/P_2) on wage rates in a typical advanced country. The reason for the focus on the effects of $\Delta(P_1/P_2)$ is the fact that perhaps the most important fact about the recent economic history of the world is the transformation of a large number of countries from quite backward (very poor, exporting only raw materials and/or fairly primitive manufactures) to major producers of unskilled intensive tradable goods. Initially these transforming countries were centered in East Asia, more recently in China and Latin America. Transformations of this sort appear to be occurring or are likely to occur in the near future in Eastern Europe and India.

Several models of the world economy have represented this transformation process by aggregating all more advanced, skill-intensive countries into "The North" and all less advanced, unskilled-intensive countries into "The South" (see, e.g., Wood (1994) and Krugman (1979)). The North produces goods the tradable goods Q_1 and Q_2 (as before, respectively the more and less skill intensive goods) as well as the non-tradable good Q_4. The South produces tradable goods 2 and 3 (the former being more skill-intensive than the latter) as well as the non-tradable good. The production function for each good is $Q_{ij} = A_{ij}F^i(S_{ij}, U_{ij})$, where $i = 1, 2, 3, 4$ denotes the good and $j = n, s$ the region. The assumption about the relative skill intensity of the three tradable goods implies that $\beta_{1j} > \beta_{2j} > \beta_{3j}$, where $\beta_{ij} = \partial(\ln Q_{ij})/\partial(\ln S_{ij})$. To use the simplest specification (Cobb–Douglas with identical preferences in all countries), the demand for each good in each of the two regions is given by $P_{ij}C_{ij} = v_i I_j$, where I_j is each region's aggregate income (in terms of the price of good 3) and $P_{ij} = P_i$ for each of the three tradable goods. The composition of the output of the two regions are determined from the relevant marginal conditions, along with the null employment conditions. For the North the marginal conditions are that

$$W_{Sn} = P_1\partial Q_{1n}/\partial S_{1n} = P_2\partial Q_{2n}/\partial S_{2n} = P_{4n}\partial Q_{4n}/\partial S_{4n} \text{ and } W_{Un} = P_1\partial Q_{1n}/\partial U_{1n}$$

$$= P_2\partial Q_{2n}/\partial U_{2n} = P_{4n}\partial Q_{4n}/\partial U_{4n}$$

,and there is a similar set of marginal conditions for the South (with $\partial Q_{3s}/\partial S_{3s}$ replacing the marginal revenue product for industry 1 and the same for unskilled labor).

The (rather large) model can be solved for changes in the equilibrium values of P_1 and P_2 in terms of the relevant technology parameters $(A_{1n}, A_{2n}, A_{2s}, A_{3s})$ and aggregate factor supplies in the two regions (S_n, U_n, S_s, U_s).[38] Of particular interest is the effect of a ceteris paribus increase in the efficiency of the production of good 2 in the South due to a diffusion

---

[38] There are in this as in previous models several possible zones in which solutions can occur. We are assuming that the latent values of A_{1s} and A_{3n} are too small relative to the values of A_{3s} to make the production of Q_1 in the South and Q_3 in the North profitable. The values of A_{2n} and A_{2s}, however, are such that good 2 is produced profitably in both regions. This is the relevant cone of diversification in the model.

of technology (A_{2s} rising toward or to the value of A_{2n}). This causes a rise in P_1/P_2, which, by Eq. (4.10), implies that the skilled/unskilled relative wage in the North, rel_n, increases. The proportional change in the skilled/unskilled relative wage in the South, everything else (including S_s/U_s) held constant, is given by

$$\widehat{rel}_s = \left(\frac{\widehat{W_{Ss}}}{W_{Us}} \right) = \frac{1}{\beta_{2s} - \beta_{3s}} \left[\hat{P}_2 + \hat{A}_2 \right]. \tag{4.32}$$

Although P_2 falls as a result of the increase in A_2, which appears to make the change in rel_s of ambiguous sign, the proportional decline in P_2 is less than the proportional increase in A_2 (because some of the world supply of good 2 comes from the North). Thus, an increase in A_2 should cause the relative wage in *both* the North and the South to rise.

4.9. Structural unemployment in the North

An important implicit assumption of the model set out in Section 4.8 is that the various countries that compose the North all have labor market institutions that permit full employment. In particular, the *rel* in each country of the North must be free to adjust so that the effective supply of unskilled labor is fully employed. If, however, political/social institutions in some countries do not permit *rel* to rise above a certain minimum value, there will be structural unemployment of unskilled labor. Further, as pointed out in an important paper by Davis (1997), the existence of labor market institutions that cause structural unemployment in part of the North dramatically changes some of the major implications of the global model. Among the major stylized facts about the trend of the world economy during the past two decades are that there has been (a) rising wage inequality in some parts of the North (particularly the US and the UK) with no increase in unemployment and (b) rising unemployment in other parts of the North (particularly Western Europe) with no significant increase in wage inequality. These facts suggest that one must treat "the North" as two distinct zones. Davis labels these "America" and "Europe."

Suppose that minimum wage institutions, where relevant, operate on the wage of unskilled workers *relative to* that of skilled workers rather than on the real *wage level* of the unskilled. This means that country j imposes a rule (either through direct legislation or encouragement of trade union activity) such that $rel_j = W_{Sj}/W_{Uj}$ cannot rise above a certain value. A minimum wage rate in real terms (the specification in Brecher (1974) and Davis (1997)) would mean that $R_{Uj} = W_{Uj}/P_j$, where P_j is the price level, cannot fall below a certain value.[39] In our opinion, the relative minimum wage specification better captures

---

[39] It is essential in this model that W_u be set relative to W_S (or to the general price level). If, following our discussion of union relative wage effects in Section 4.5, W_U in the tradable sector is set relative to W_U in the non-tradable sector, few of the interesting implications concerning interrelationships in the international economy apply.

what has happened in Western Europe during the past two decades. However, whether rel_j or R_{Uj} is assumed to be fixed does not alter the substantive implications of the model.

If Europe did not trade with America or the South, the analysis of the effect of rel_e being fixed at too high a level would be done using the closed economy model in Section 4.1. The difference would be that in Eq. (4.5), $\hat{U}_e$ is now endogenous and rel_e exogenous. This means that the level of European unskilled unemployment is affected negatively by the institutionally-fixed value of rel_e.

In the autarky case there are obviously no effects of developments in Europe on labor markets in America and the South and vice versa. In the open economy case, this is not so. Consider (for the sake of simplicity) a Ricardian model in which there are three tradable goods, the first two of which are produced both in Europe (e) and America (a) and the second two of which are produced in the South (s). The aggregate world supplies of each of the three goods are $Q_1 = A_{1e}S_e + A_{1a}S_a$, $Q_2 = A_{2e}U_e + A_{2a}U_a + A_{2s}U_{2s}$, and $Q_3 = A_{3s}U_{3s}$. The non-tradable goods 4 and 5 could be added to the model, but this only adds algebraic complexity. To simplify, none of good 1 is not produced in the South, and there are no skilled workers in that region. Given that all regions have identical Cobb–Douglas preferences, the prices of goods 1 and 2 relative to the numeraire good 3 are determined by $P_1 = (\nu_1/\nu_3)Q_3/Q_1$ and $P_2 = (\nu_2/\nu_3)Q_3/Q_2$.

There is full employment of all workers in America and the South and of skilled workers in Europe, so S_e, S_a, and U_a are given. The fixed supply of unskilled workers in the South, U_s, is allocated between the two relevant industries, U_{2s} and U_{3s}. Unskilled employment in Europe, U_e, is less than its effective labor supply, for, as above, the skilled/unskilled relative wage in Europe, rel_e, is assumed to be institutionally fixed at "too low" a value to permit full employment. Thus, U_e is an endogenous variable in the model.

The marginal conditions in the South require that $W_{Us} = P_2A_{2s} = A_{3s}$. This means that, if it is profitable to produce good 2 in the South, the value of P_2 is set there. The relative wage rate in Europe is $W_{Se}/W_{Ue} = A_{1e}P_1/A_{2e}P_2$. Since this is equal to the institutionally-fixed value rel_e, it follows that, again assuming a solution inside the relevant "cone," the world relative price of goods 1 and 2 is set in Europe and is equal to $P_1/P_2 = rel_e A_{2e}/A_{1e}$. Since the skilled/unskilled relative wage in America depends on relative prices and relative productivities, this is

$$rel_a = \frac{A_{1a}}{A_{2a}} \frac{P_1}{P_2} = \frac{A_{1a}}{A_{2a}} \frac{A_{2e}}{A_{1e}} rel_e. \tag{4.33}$$

Thus, so long as production of good 2 continues in Europe and the European relative wage continues to be fixed at rel_e, the American relative wage is, in the Davis model, "insulated" from developments in the South (notably, an increase in A_{2s}).

What drives this model is the fact that the aggregate level of European unskilled employment and the distribution of employment in the South between industries 2 and 3 are determined by the relevant exogenous variables (the factor supplies and the various technological parameters). For example, an exogenous decrease in the European relative wage $(d(\ln rel_e) = -\mu)$ and an increase in the efficiency of the production of good 2 in the

South have the following effects on unskilled employment in Europe:

$$\hat{U}_e = -\frac{1 - \nu_1}{\nu_2 b_e}\mu - \frac{\nu_3 + \nu_2 b_s}{\nu_2 b_e}\hat{A}_{2s},\tag{4.34}$$

where $b_j = Q_{2j}/Q_2$ is the fraction of the world output of good 2 accounted for by region j. The value of U_{2s} depends positively on μ and A_{2s}, but, given that wages are flexible in America, U_{2a} is independent of these parameters.[40]

The most important general implication of the Davis-type model is the following: The effects of developments in one region (changes in factor supplies and/or technology) on the labor market in another region may depend crucially on the nature of labor market institutions in each of the regions of the world.

5. Empirical studies

5.1. Tests of the Hecksher–Ohlin theorem

Much of the effort of empirical trade economists has been concerned with the fundamental prediction of the Hecksher–Ohlin (HO) model that a country should be observed exporting the goods in which it has a comparative advantage and importing the goods in which it does not.[41] This prediction was discussed in the context of the simple Ricardian model in Section 3.3 (see, in particular, Eq. (3.22)) but is fairly robust with respect to complications of the model. What motivated this empirical literature was the observation by Leontief (1953) that the US, which was at that time by far the most capital-intensive country in the world, was exporting relatively labor-intensive products. This fact became known as the "Leontief Paradox" and is referred to by virtually every paper on the subject. The early work on the subject was influenced by the Stolper–Samuelson factor price equalization theorem that showed that under certain conditions the prices of individual factors across different countries would – in the absence of tariffs or other impediments to free trade – tend to equalize. One of these assumptions is that the technology of the production of each good (usually represented above by the Hicks-neutral term A_{ij}) is identical in each country. With this assumption, the comparative advantage of a country depends only on its factor endowments relative to the rest of the world. HO predicts that a country will be a net exporter of the goods that are intensive in the factors in which it is abundant. In terms of our simple model in Section 3.3, one predicts that the net exports of good 1 by country j would depend on the value of S_j/U_j relative to the rest of the world.

---

[40] The assumption that that the long run value of rel_e is strictly exogenous is, at least, questionable on theoretical grounds. For example, one could posit a social welfare function for a country/region that depends negatively on both rel_e and the unemployment rate. Presumably rel_e would be chosen (the legal institutions of the labor market set) at a value that maximizes perceived social welfare subject to the relevant constraint (*l'inegalte contre le chomage*). Such an approach would imply that rel_e would be increased when A_{2s} increases, so that the actual effects on rel_a and U_e would be a blend of the flexible and inflexible situations.

[41] Extensive reviews of this literature are contained in Deardorff (1984) and Leamer and Levinsohn (1995).

The results of a series of papers that attempted to test this basic prediction (using, of course, much more complete models) could be characterized as, at best, weak (see, in particular, Bowen et al. (1987) and Staiger (1988)). It appears difficult to reject the null hypothesis (that patterns of trade across countries are random) against the prediction of the HO model (with the strong identical technology assumption). This was troubling to some trade economists, for there is really no alternative to the classical trade model. Further, if trade flows are determined randomly rather than on the basis of comparative advantage, the normative prescription of most trade economists ("free trade good, distortions bad") cannot be made as compellingly as they tend to do.[42]

The assumption that "technology" in individual industries is identical across countries seems (on the basis of intuition and casual empiricism) rather heroic, and it was often mentioned as an after-the-fact reason for the results with respect to HO. Some countries may – for long periods of time – simply be better than other countries in the production of particular goods (yielding relatively high values of the relevant A_{ij}'s).[43] Failure to take account of technological differences could in principle lead to serious omitted variables bias, especially if the A_{ij}'s happen to be correlated with factor endowments. Several recent papers have revisited the HO prediction with specifications that allow for estimation of inter-country differences in technology to be an additional source of comparative advantage (e.g., Trefler, 1993, 1995; Davis et al., 1997; Harrigan, 1997). The results of these studies, when technology differences are taken into account, are at least qualitatively consistent with the predictions of the HO model; countries tend to be net exporters of the services of the factors in which they are relatively abundant.

An interesting aspect of Trefler (1995) is his conclusion that observed trade flows reflect, in addition to inter-country technology differences, "Armington home bias" – the product differentiation models that are discussed in Sections 3.5 and 4.3 above. In essence, the observed volume of trade flows between economies is smaller than that consistent with a demand model in which country of origin (foreign versus domestic) made no difference. However, using Japanese regional data, Davis et al. (1997) find that the home bias demand framework is not necessary to explain the missing trade.

Another approach to testing the implications Hecksher–Ohlin theorem is to see if the pattern of net exports within an individual country conforms with what would be expected on the basis of the relative factor endowment of that country. This approach has the advantage of allowing the researcher to use the best possible data for that country – not subject to the constraint of comparability across countries. For example, using US data,

---

[42] This would be analogous in labor economics to a consistent finding that in earnings functions the coefficient on years of schooling was not statistically different from zero. Such a result would force labor economists to (a) rethink the theoretical determinants of wages and (b) avoid the standard policy prescription of encouraging more schooling.

[43] An obvious example of this is the emergence of the Japanese automobile industry in the 1970s. Another example is the US film industry, which capitalizes on the democratic nature of the national culture to produce movies of such remarkably poor taste that they are overwhelmingly popular abroad.

Cain and Baldwin (1997) report estimates of "relative comparative advantage" as a function of factor shares across industries producing tradable goods for four periods, 1967–1969, 1972–1974, 1978–1980, and 1985–1987. The dependent variable is the ratio of exports minus imports to total consumption (output plus imports minus consumption) in each industry, and the regressors include the industry shares for labor with 1–12 years of schooling and with 13+ years of schooling and a proxy for the share of capital and land.

Baldwin and Cain's estimated coefficients (with standard errors in parentheses) of (weighted) regressions of the trade ratio on the two labor share variables for all 67 traded goods and services industries for the four periods are reported in Table 7. (The estimated coefficients on the proxy for the share of capital and land's were small and statistically insignificant.) These results suggest that, ceteris paribus, the US tends to be a net exporter of goods and services that are relatively education-intensive. Further, the comparative advantage with respect to labor with relatively high levels of education increased – for whatever reason(s) – rather markedly from the 1960s to the 1980s.

5.2. Direct tests of the neoclassical model

The question of the extent to which countries are net exporters of the factor services in which they are relatively abundant is, of course, central to trade economists. Although it is comforting for labor and macro economists looking at questions involving wages and employment in a particular country to be able to assume that international trade takes place in the context of comparative advantage, the major questions relevant to labor economists involving the relevance of openness are somewhat different.

The focus of the various models of labor market equilibrium in a particular country discussed in Sections 3 and 4 was on the potential effects of domestic factor supplies, technology, and factor prices on wages and employment.

The general implication of these models for country or region j in the long run may be summarized by the implicit function

$$\Phi^j\left(rel_j, LAB_j, PR_{fj}, TECH_j, INST_j\right) = 0. \tag{5.1}$$

The average skilled/unskilled relative wage is rel_j, which was equal to W_{Sj}/W_{Uj} in most of the models discussed above. LAB_j is a vector of employment levels of different types of labor, usually equal to the exogenously fixed supplies of skilled and unskilled labor, S_j, U_j. PR_{fj} are the relative world prices of tradable goods, which, in the absence of tariffs, were

Table 7
Baldwin–Cain estimates of US/relative comparative advantage

Education level	1967–1969	1972–1974	1978–1980	1985–1987
1–12 years	−0.12 (0.07)	−0.12 (0.09)	−0.26 (0.14)	−0.35 (0.09)
13+ years	0.14 (0.11)	0.12 (0.13)	0.07 (0.19)	0.27 (0.13)

represented by the world prices of the relatively more and less skilled goods, P_{1f} and P_{2f}. $TECH_j$ is a vector of technological parameters across the relevant industries in the economy. Generally these were represented by the Hicks-neutral parameters A_{ij}, but in Section 4.6 several additional parameters representing the possibility of skill-biased technological change were introduced. Finally, $INST_j$ represents the wage-setting institutions of the economy, ranging from the most common assumption of equal wages across industries and full employment for both skills to the case discussed in Section 4.9 in which rel_j was artificially fixed in all industries at level to cause permanent structural unemployment of unskilled workers.

The form of Φ^j depends on a number of factors. Given that the $INST_j$ variable represents institutions that permit long run full employment of both types of labor, rel_j is endogenous and depends in general on the values of LAB_j, PR_{fj}, and $TECH_j$. For the case in which economy j produces two sets of tradable goods ($i = 1$ more skill intensive than $i = 2$) and a set of non-tradable goods ($i = 4$) and in which technology is fully represented by the Hicks-neutral A_i parameters, the proportional change in rel_j is given in general by

$$\widehat{rel}_j = b_{1j}\hat{S}_j + b_{2j}\hat{U}_j + b_{3j}\hat{P}_{1fj} + b_{4j}\hat{P}_{2fj} + \sum_i g_{ij}\hat{A}_{ij}. \tag{5.2}$$

For the case of a closed economy, as seen in Eq. (4.5), $-b_{1j} = b_{2j} > 0$ (and equal to one if a weighted average of the elasticities of substitution in production and consumption are equal to one) and the g_{ij}'s are of indeterminate sign (but presumably close to zero). World prices are, of course, irrelevant in the autarky case. In the polar opposite case of the classical trade model, as seen in Eq. (4.10), $b_{1j} = b_{2j} = g_{4j} = 0$ and $b_{3j} = g_{1j} = -b_{4j} = -g_{2j} = 1/(\beta_1 - \beta_2) > 1$ (the Jones magnification effect). There is a variety of intermediate cases, discussed in detail in the previous two sections, in which the predicted values of the coefficients in Eq. (5.2) are between those of the closed and classical open cases. These cases include equilibrium outside the cone of diversification (either good 1 or 2 is not profitable to produce), (2) less than perfect inter-industry mobility of labor (the specific factors model), and (3) differentiation of tradable products by country of manufacture. These modifications lead to predicted values of the coefficients in Eq. (5.2) that are between those of the two extreme models.

In the case of structural unemployment of unskilled labor ($j =$ "Europe" in Section 4.8), rel_j is exogenous and U_j is endogenous. This requires that $\hat{U}_j$ be moved to the left-hand side of Eq. (5.2) and $(\widehat{rel}_j)$ moved to the right-hand side.

In principle an equation like Eq. (5.2) could be estimated across countries and/or over time to test between alternative hypotheses concerning the openness of economies. There would be, however, many complications associated with such a procedure. First, definitions of skill should vary according to national educational practices, which makes comparisons across countries difficult. Second, changes in relative wages and employment levels should be examined over relatively long periods of time rather than on an annual basis. Otherwise, the results may be muddled due to business cycle factors and the short run importance of factor immobility. Third, skill-biased technological change, which in practice is necessarily left in the residual, may be systematically related across countries and over time to some of the included variables, specifically $\hat{U}_j$ and $\hat{S}_j$, which would bias the results (in generally unknown ways). Fourth, the possibility that some countries may be subject to the sort of structural unemployment discussed in Section 4.9 limits the possibilities for cross-sectional analysis; one would have to specify the degree of labor market flexibility of each country in advance.

An interesting attempt to test for the labor market implications of changes in the degree of openness is Slaughter (1997). The idea behind the test is that, as the US economy became more open from 1960 to 1991, the absolute elasticity of labor demand in individual industries should have become larger (in our terms, moving from the closed to the differentiated products toward the neoclassical model). The results, which are based on annual observations, suggest that labor demand elasticities for non-production workers have risen over time. In his "stage-two" regressions, Slaughter relates these estimated elasticities to a variety of trade-related variables, but the results are somewhat mixed, with time per se rather than the trade variables explaining most of the trends.

A problem with Slaughter's framework in terms of the question of the relevance of different long run models of long run equilibrium as outlined above is that it focuses on short run variation in employment and wages. This runs into subsidiary issues associated with short run factor immobility and the effects of business cycle factors on labor demand. Nevertheless, this paper comes closer than any other that we have seen in establishing a direct test of the Factor Price Insensitivity theorem.

5.3. International competitiveness

Most trade models and empirical research assume universal and stationary technology. It is evident from Eqs. (3.20) and (3.21) that differential growth of technology across trading partners can influence relative wages between skill groups within a country and between countries (Johnson and Stafford, 1993; Gomery and Baumol, 1997; Johnson and Stafford, 1997).[44] What is especially interesting from the point of view of labor economics is the possibility that *the general real wage level of a country may be affected by its productivity in certain industries relative to the productivity in those industries in the rest of the world.* In other words, it is possible that an innovation that raises the general level of real wages in one country may lower wages in other countries. Although this has received relatively little attention from trade economists (see, however, Lawrence (1996) and Cline (1997)), it is useful to look further into the issue.

To do this, we will first use a simplified version of the Ricardian model of international equilibrium discussed in Section 3.3. The simplification is that there is only one type of labor, N_i in each industry, rather than the two types in all other models to this point. Two goods are produced in the focus economy (which is small relative to the rest of the world),

---

[44] This notion was first seen in Hicks (1953), who argued that The UK's economic decline after World War II was partly attributable to competition in tradable goods from other countries, particularly the US. The application of this model to The UK is explored further in Johnson and Stafford (1995).

good 1, which is tradable, and good 4, which is produced solely for domestic consumption. The production functions of these industries is $Q_i = A_i N_i$. The rest of the world produces goods 1 and 4 as well good 3, which cannot be profitably produced in our focus economy, using production functions $Q_{ir} = A_{ir} N_{ir}$. Letting good 3 be the numeraire good ($P_3 = 1$), the wage rate (in units of good 3) is $W = P_1 A_1 = P_4 A_4$ in our focus economy and $W_r = P_1 A_{1r} = A_{3r} = P_{4r} A_{4r}$ in the rest of the world.

Consumption of the three goods, 1, 3, and 4, are assumed to be generated by the same Cobb–Douglas utility function in all countries, and the expenditure shares of the three goods are v_1, v_3, and v_4, which sum to one. It follows that the proportional change in the aggregate price level in the focus economy is $\hat{P} = v_1 \hat{P}_1 + v_4 \hat{P}_4$ and $\hat{P}_r = v_1 \hat{P}_1 + v_4 \hat{P}_{4r}$ in the rest of the world. From the marginal conditions, however, $\hat{P}_1 = \hat{A}_{3r} - \hat{A}_{1r}$, $\hat{P}_{4r} = \hat{A}_{3r} - \hat{A}_{4rr}$ and $\hat{P}_4 = \hat{A}_{3r} - \hat{A}_{1r} + \hat{A}_1 - \hat{A}_4$.

Since the real wage in country j is W_j / P_j, the ratio of the proportional change in the real wage in the focus economy to that in the rest of the world is

$$\frac{(\widehat{W/P})}{(\widehat{W_r/P_r})} = \frac{(1 - v_4)\hat{A}_1 + v_4 \hat{A}_4 + v_3 \left(\hat{A}_{3r} - \hat{A}_{1r}\right)}{v_1 \hat{A}_{1r} + v_3 \hat{A}_{3r} + v_4 \hat{A}_{4r}}. \tag{5.3}$$

This expression may be interpreted as the effect of a change in the real wage rate in the rest of the world on the real wage rate in our focus economy – depending on the source of the real wage change in the rest of the world. In the *extreme case of international competition*, all of the average productivity growth originates in industry, so $\hat{A}_{1r} > 0$ and $\hat{A}_{3r} = \hat{A}_{4r} = 0$. In this case the elasticity of the real wage in the focus country with respect to the real wage rate in the rest of the world, $\partial(\ln(W/P))/\partial(\ln(W/P)_r)$, is equal $-v_3/v_1$.

The parameter v_3 is interpreted in this model as the share of imports to GDP. Under the assumptions that trade is balanced (exports are roughly equal to imports), the value of v_3 in OECD countries 1992 (see Table 1) ranged from around 0.10 for geographically isolated countries like the US and Japan to 0.2–0.3 for the larger European economies to much higher values for the smaller European countries.

5.4. The effect of trade on relative wages

Much of the recent empirical literature on the effects of trade has focused on the role of globalization on relative wage rates by skill. Most of this literature has focused on the US, in part because of the dramatic rise in the skill differential in that country during the 1980s, but some of the papers also consider international comparisons.

The key facts motivating the literature on relative wage performance during the 1980s are that (i) the relative wage rate of skilled workers grew precipitously in the face of (ii) a large increase in its relative supply. Several papers (e.g., Bound and Johnson, 1992; Katz and Murphy, 1992; Murphy and Welch, 1992; Johnson, 1997) used a conceptual framework that can be summarized in Fig. 4. The relative supply of skilled labor shifted from L'

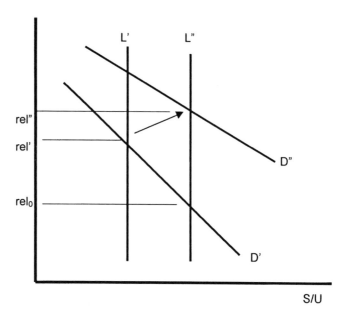

Fig. 4. The determination of relative wages by skill under conditions of shifting demand and supply.

to L'', but, instead of falling from R' to R_0, the relative wage increased to R''. Therefore, the relative demand for labor by skill had to have shifted during this period from D' to D''.

The obvious question within this framework is "what made relative demand shift?". The major candidates for explaining the demand shift include international factors ("trade"), skill-biased technological change, and a variety of institutional changes.

The traditional trade economists response to this approach, as set out in Sections 3 and 4, is that, assuming a solution within the cone of diversification, the relative product demand function is horizontal (see Fig. 1) and that relative factor prices are insensitive to relative supplies. Instead, R depends only on the relative prices of imported goods and technology across industries.

In this section we review four approaches to the question of how much of the rightward shift (or, in the case of the Neoclassical trade model, the upward shift) in the relative demand curve is attributable to trade effects. These four approaches involve (a) price equations, (b) factor content analyses, (c) changes in within-industry factor proportions, and (d) institutional changes brought about by increased foreign competition. The reader is also referred to several recent interpretative reviews of this literature, including Richardson (1995), Deardorff and Hakura (1994), Burtless (1995), Lawrence (1996), Slaughter and Swagel (1997), and Cline (1997).

5.4.1. Price equations

The approach to testing for the effect of international developments on relative factor prices that is most favored by empirical trade economists is the estimation of price equations. These, which follow from the total differentiation of the zero (or constant) profit equation (see, e.g., Eqs. (4.27) and (4.28)), suggest that over a time interval one should run a regression across tradable goods of the price change in that industry on the shares of the different factors of production.[45] Such a regression takes the form

$$\hat{P}_i = b_0 + b_1 X_{Si} + b_2 X_{Ui} + \cdots + e_i, \tag{5.4}$$

where X_{Si} and X_{Ui} are the shares of skilled and unskilled labor in industry i.

In order for international competition to be an important determinant of changes in skill differentials, the estimated value of $b_1 - b_2$ must be significantly positive.

Otherwise, "something else" is the cause of changes in *rel*. The various studies that have estimated price equations for the US along the lines of Eq. (5.4) have arrived at somewhat different conclusions. Lawrence and Slaughter (1993), using the production/non-production worker dichotomy, find insignificant coefficients for the 1980s and conclude that trade effects had a small effect on relative wages.[46] Sachs and Shatz (1994) estimate a price equation similar to Lawrence and Slaughter's, but they include a dummy variable for the computer industry – on the grounds that prices in that industry are poorly measured due to quality changes. When this dummy is included, the results are slightly more in the direction a "trade matters" conclusion.

Baldwin and Cain (1997), using labor shares by educational attainment, also find relatively small and generally insignificant coefficients for the various sub-periods, including 1979–1991, in which they estimate their price equations, leading them to the conclusion that "trade, by itself, cannot explain the increased wage inequality in favor of groups of workers with more education." However, in the price equation in which labor was decomposed into three groups (less than high school, high school, and more than high school), the coefficient on the share of the least educated group was significant less than the coefficients on the shares of the other groups, leading Baldwin and Cain to the conclusion that some of the especially poor wage performance of the least educated is attributable to international factors.

Among the problems with these studies is the fact that the output of each detailed industry is far from homogeneous (the Q_i used in Sections 3 and 4), and aggregation error may systematically bias the magnitudes of the estimated b_i's. Thus, the "price puzzle" posed by the results of the early studies may reflect measurement factors rather

---

[45] A single equation of this form follows from a model with two tradable goods and two factors within the cone of diversification, but, as Deardorff and Hakura (1994) point out, it is not so simple in the multiple good-multiple factor case.

[46] Neven and Wyposz (1996) estimate price equations along the lines of Lawrence and Slaughter for manufacturing data for the UK, Germany, France, and Italy. The results were similar to those for the US in that the estimated coefficients on the share variables were of variable sign and statistically inconsistent.

than economic reality. Using expanded industry price and share data for the 1989–1995 period, Krueger (1997) reports estimates of price equations that have much larger skill effects than was true of the earlier studies. It is tempting to suppose on the basis of Kreuger's results that, given better data for the 1980s, the estimates of price equations might have been more consistent with the Stolper–Samuelson model, suggestive of a greater effect of trade on relative wages. A difficulty with the Krueger results in this regard, however, is that during the 1989–1995 period observed skill differentials increased much more slowly than in the 1980s (see the chapter by Katz). Thus, one would not *expect* for this period b_1 would be significantly larger than b_2.

A second problem with the straightforward estimated price equations in the above studies is the possibility that changes in total factor productivity (the Ω_i term in Eqs. (4.27) and (4.28)) are systematically correlated with factor shares. In this case, estimates of the b's in Eq. (5.4) would in general be biased. Leamer (1996a,b) and Feenstra and Hanson (1997) have attempted to include estimates of the growth in total factor productivity in price equations, but it is difficult to figure out how the conclusions of these analyses are affected by this modification.

5.4.2. Factor content analyses
An alternative way to estimate the effects of international developments is to estimate the effect of observed changes in net exports across industries on implicit relative factor supply. Under certain conditions involving elasticities of substitution between products and factors, as was shown in Sections 3.7 and 4.6, the factor content (FC) procedure gives a reasonably accurate estimates of the effect of trade on relative factor prices. FC is appealing to labor economists, for it is directly applicable to the framework embodied in Fig. 4. FC estimates indicate, on the basis of industry export and import data, how much a closed economy relative demand function has shifted due to trade – even if the economy is characterized by the Neoclassical or differentiated-products model (such that the actual demand curve is much more elastic than it would be under autarky). The various FC studies for the US (e.g., Murphy and Welch, 1991; Borjas et al., 1992; Sachs and Shatz, 1994; Baldwin and Cain, 1997) conclude that trade developments during the 1980s contributed only slightly to the large widening of relative wage differentials by skill during that period.

A much-cited paper that uses FC to analyze the effects of trade is Katz and Murphy (1992). Using employment and import-export data for 21 two-digit manufacturing industries, KM calculate the implicit effects of trade on the labor of eight gender-education groups (along the lines of Eq. (4.31)). The annual rate of growth in the relative implicit labor supply of each of these eight groups due to changes in net exports for the 1970s and 1980s (calculated from KM's Table VII, the figure for the 1980s being the annual rate of growth from 1979 to 1985) is reported in under Trade$_1$ in Table 10. Because of the possibility that industries retained their administrative, developmental, and sales forces in the US and "outsourced" production to foreign countries, an alternative calculation was made on the assumption that the effect of increased imports fell entirely on production workers versus (generally more highly educated) non-production workers.[47] The relative rates of growth of implicit labor supply for the eight groups under this alternative assumption are reported under Trade$_2$.

To see how estimates of the effects of trade based on FC compare with what happened to wages during these two periods, the annual percentage growth of relative hourly average wage rates for the eight demographic groups (based on data from Bound and Johnson (1992, Table 1)) are given in Table 8. For the 1980s, the male college/high school relative wage increased at the rate of $1.00 - (-0.81) = 1.81\%$ per year.

The conventional labor economics approach to the explanation of changes in the wage structure, which has been summarized in Fig. 4, is to calculate the relative rates of growth of the supplies of the different types of labor, SShift in Table 8, and then, with an assumed value of the intra-factor elasticity of substitution, calculate the rate at which the relative demand functions must be shifting in order to yield the observed changes in the relative wage structure. This yields the annual percentage rate of growth of the position of each relative demand function, DShift in Table 8, which is based on the assumption that the intra-factor elasticity of substitution elasticity equals 1.5.[48] The calculated absolue values of DShift are very large relative to the KM estimates of the effect of trade. For example, the implied relative demand curve for males who had not completed high school shifted to the right at a rate of 5% per year during both the 1970s and 1980s, but even the higher KM estimates of the effect for the trade are a very small fraction of this total shift.

It could be argued – and we would agree – that this particular disaggregation of labor input into eight demographic groups that are equally substitutable for each other is somewhat arbitrary. It was chosen in this case because KM reported trade effects on this basis. There are, as pointed out in Section 4.1, several other plausible aggregations. The resultant values of Trade1 and Trade2 from any other aggregation assumption, however, would not substantially different implications concerning the effects of trade on either relative wages or the implied demand shift parameter.[49]

Adherents of the Neoclassical trade model would also argue that the results for the 1980s in Table 8 are quite consistent with the Factor Price Insensitivity (FPI) theorem that changes in relative factor relative supplies have no effect on relative factor prices. To this labor economists reply that the observed large increases in the relative supply of highly educated workers in the 1970s (caused in part by the demand for college enrollment by

[47] Borjas et al. (1997) go further into the issue of assigning the correct weights on different types of labor in the context of FC analysis. They discuss the argument of Wood (1994) of using input ratios used in developing countries rather than those for the home country as well as the results of Bernard and Jensen (1995) concerning the skill composition of firms within industries most impacted by trade.

[48] This specification assumes explicitly that the aggregate flow of labor services is a CES function of inputs each of these eight different groups.

[49] A common alternative aggregation alternative, used by, among many others, Katz and Murphy, is to calculate the sums "college equivalent" and "high school equivalent" labor (so that, for example, there is an infinite elasticity of substitution between dropouts and high school graduates of both genders). We have made these calculations, but, as would be expected, they do not change the conclusions with respect to the importance of trade and are not reported.

Table 8

Annualized percentage changes in US wages by education and gender in the 1970s and 1980s, demand shifts, supply shifts, and alternative Katz–Murphy estimates of the relative wage effects of trade

	Education	ΔW	DShift	SShift	Trade$_1$	Trade$_2$
1973–1979						
Men	Dropouts	0.08	−5.50	−5.65	0.02	0.02
	High school	−0.03	−0.30	−0.26	0.02	0.00
	Some college	−0.12	2.23	2.41	0.01	0.05
	College+	−0.60	2.33	3.24	0.01	0.09
Women	Dropouts	0.90	−3.06	−4.40	−0.04	−0.04
	High school	0.35	2.02	1.49	−0.02	−0.02
	Some college	−0.64	5.28	6.25	−0.02	−0.02
	College+	−0.87	3.27	4.58	−0.03	−0.02
1979–1988						
Men	Dropouts	−0.63	−5.59	−4.95	−0.08	−0.19
	High school	−0.81	−1.56	−0.35	−0.02	−0.06
	Some college	−0.36	−0.13	0.41	0.04	0.13
	College+	1.00	3.03	1.52	0.12	0.31
Women	Dropouts	−0.30	−3.94	−3.50	−0.34	−0.61
	High school	0.11	0.68	0.52	0.00	0.01
	Some college	0.81	4.61	3.40	0.04	0.07
	College+	1.53	6.69	4.39	0.24	0.31

males in the 1960s so as to avoid participation in the Vietnam War) resulted in the observed 1973–1979 decline in the relative wages of college graduates, which is inconsistent with FPI. It is, of course, possible is that the US economy became sufficiently open to international trade around 1980 such that FPI applied in the 1980s but not in the 1970s or earlier. This is the Slaughter hypothesis discussed in Section 5.2 above, but the resolution of this must await a considerable amount of further research.

The labor economists' rebuttal to the application of FPI to the 1980s would be that, even if relative labor demand functions are highly or evenly infinitely elastic, the results of FC analyses strongly suggest that the shifts in these functions that caused the relative wage structure to change were not substantially the result of changes in the volume and content of trade.

5.4.3. Changes in within-industry factor proportions

A third way of assessing the effect of trade developments on relative wages is to look at changes in factor proportions across sectors or industries. In the models of labor market equilibrium within the cone of diversification discussed in Sections 3 and 4, a decrease in the world price of the less skill-intensive tradable good (industry 2) relative to that of the more skill-intensive tradable good (industry 1) causes, ceteris paribus, the relative wage of skilled workers, *rel*, to increase. An increase in P_1/P_2 also implies that the skill intensity of the non-tradable goods sector will rise relative to that of the tradable goods sector (indus-

Table 9
Between- and within-industry decomposition of the change in the employment of college-educated labor in the US, 1960–1995[a]

	All industries		Manufacturing		Non-manufacturing	
	Between	Within	Between	Within	Between	Within
1960–1970	0.24	0.09	0.04	0.12	0.29	0.07
1970–1980	0.12	0.46	0.02	0.38	0.12	0.49
1980–1990	0.10	0.37	0.06	0.44	0.06	0.35
1990–1995	0.04	0.21	−0.14	0.27	0.05	0.19

[a] Source: Autor et al. (1997).

tries 1 and 2 combined), for the displaced unskilled workers will have to find work in service industries.

The data on relative employment levels for manufacturing (tradable) and non-manufacturing (non-tradable) sectors by skill (S = college equivalent and U = high school equivalent labor) in the US reported in Table 3 appear to be consistent with this prediction. Between 1979 and 1989, a period in which there was a large increase in the openness of the economy (see, e.g., Table 1), the annual rate of growth of S/U was 4.4% in manufacturing versus 2.8% in non-manufacturing industries. Although something else obviously occurred during this period (that shifted the relative demand function to the right in the non-tradable goods sector),[50] the larger growth of S/U in manufacturing is consistent with a conventional trade effects explanation.

Disaggregated analyses of employment shifts by skill, however, usually find that most of the changes in the skill composition of employment is accounted for changes within industries rather than between industries. Table 9 gives decomposition of changes in the fraction of college-educated labor versus other works based on 59 manufacturing and 81 non-manufacturing industries in Autor et al. (1997). This implies that, since 1960s, the source of most of observed increase in the demand for relatively skilled labor has been the results of developments – such as skill-biased technological change – within industries. Machin et al. (1966) report similar results for the UK and, using the production/non-production worker breakdown, for Denmark and Sweden.

The lack of large between-industry relative skill shifts has been taken by several authors (notably Berman et al., 1994) as evidence against a major role for trade in the explanation of increasing wage inequality, and the basic result does appear to be consistent with the results of factor content studies and the lack of strong results for price equations. There are two possible qualifications of these results. First, the theoretical models that lead to predictions about the effects of trade developments on changes in industry skill composi-

---

[50] In terms of the framework in Table 8, the calculated annual rate of shift in the implicit demand shift parameters (DShift) over the 1979–1989 interval were 4.4% in manufacturing and 2.8% in non-manufacturing. For the 1973–1979 interval, the growth rates of DShift were 6.8 and 4.1%.

tion assume implicitly that all firms within an industry are identical. It is, in fact, quite likely that there is considerable heterogeneity among firms within highly detailed industrial classifications with respect to production processes and that trade developments may accordingly affect relative skill demand within industries. In this spirit, Bernard and Jensen (1994) examine changes in skill composition based on a samples of 50,000 firms and find that there were much greater intra-firm changes in skill demand (based on the production/non-production worker distinction) than is apparent from inter-industry data. Further, Bernard and Jensen find that export shocks had a very significant effect on skill composition.

A second reason for caution with respect to the implications of the between- and within-industry skill composition change results involves the possibility that a significant amount of the observed increase in imports is of that part of the production process that would otherwise be done by production (relatively unskilled) workers domestically. To the extent that this "outsourcing" practice is a significant fraction of imports, we would observe changes in skill composition within detailed industries that are in fact caused by imports. Feenstra and Hanson (1995, 1996) examine this possibility and conclude that outsourcing and imports had a large impact on changes in the relative employment of production workers within manufacturing industries. When Autor et al. (1997) include data on the share of total investment in each industry that was for purchases of computers in a Feenstra–Hanson type of regression, the estimated outsourcing variable becomes small and statistically insignificant. Berman et al. (1997) also address the question of the plausibility of the Feenstra–Hanson estimates of the effect of outsourcing on changes in relative skill demand in manufacturing. They conclude that – although outsourcing was very important in two industries (automobiles and semi-conductors) – it "cannot account for the bulk of skill upgrading that occurred within manufacturing over the last two decades".[51]

Given the present state of the literature on the determinants of the skill composition of employment within the tradable sector, we feel confident in predicting that much additional work will be done on this topic over the next several years.

5.4.4. Endogenous institutional changes

An additional way in which trade developments can affect relative wages is through their effect on labor market institutions. There is a fairly large literature that focuses on the effect of institutions – unionism and government regulation of wages – on wage variation within individual countries,[52] and institutional change (deunionization and deregulation) has in several studies (see, e.g., DiNardo et al., 1997) been given prominence as an

---

[51] This conclusion is consistent with the Katz-Murphy "Trade2" results in Table 8. Slaughter (1997) examines the quantitative impact of outsourcing by multinational corporations on relative wages in the 1980s and finds very small effects.

[52] See, in particular, Blau and Kahn (1996) for an extremely perceptive inter-country analysis of the effects of labor market institutions on the residual variance of earnings.

independent reason (besides international competition and technological change) for the rise in income inequality in the US during the 1980s.

Of interest here is the question of the way in which increased international competition can influence labor market institutions in such a way that the relative wages of skilled labor changes. The most direct way that this can happen is, as investigated by Katz and Summers (1989), is for trade to shift unskilled employment from relative high wage industries. In other terms, the average wage rate of unskilled labor is where W_{Uc} is the unskilled wage rate in a particular "competitive" reference industry and γ_i is the unskilled wage in industry i relative to W_{Uc}. If trade makes the values of U_i/U fall in industries with high values of γ, the average unskilled wage will presumably fall relative to the average skilled wage.[53]

Although the employment of relatively low educated workers in manufacturing in the US is generally estimated to have fallen during the 1980s as a result of trade, the size of the $\Delta(U_i/U)$'s interacted with the γ_i's is not sufficiently large for this to have had more than a negligible influence on *rel* during this period. Lawrence (1996) performs the relevant calculation based on estimates of the employment impact of trade in manufacturing of Sachs and Shatz (1994) and the Katz and Summers' estimates of industry rents, and he concludes that this effect was about 0.1% of the observed 15% increase in the relative wage of college graduates.

The other way that wages may be influenced by institutional changes brought about by increased international competition is through the reductions in the rents received by unskilled workers in some industries, i.e., declines in some high values of the γ_i's in Eq. (5.5). This is the central point of the theoretical model of Borjas and Ramey (1995).[54] To show the flavor of this approach, we will set out a somewhat different model of the determination of γ_i in an individual industry that yields Borjas and Ramey's basic conclusion but which ties more closely into the trade models set out in Section 3 and 4.

We assume that some industries, including the one we are examining, in the tradable sector are monopolies rather than perfectly competitive. The product demand function for our industry (arbitrarily $i = 1$) is given by $Q_1 = B_1 P_1^{-\eta}$, where B_1 a shift parameter and η is the absolute price elasticity of product demand in this industry. Following the model of product differentiation discussed in Section 3.5, this price elasticity will be equal to

$$\eta = [\varepsilon_1 w_{1\tau 1}(1 - w_1)](1 - x_1) + \tau_1 x_1, \tag{5.6}$$

where ε_1 is the domestic price elasticity of all goods (foreign and domestic) in this

---

[53] In the model discussed in Section 4.5, W_{Uc} was the wage rate in the non-union non-tradable sector ($i = 4$) and the $W_{U1} = W_{U2} = \gamma W_{u4}$ the wage rates in the unionized tradable goods industries. $t = 1 - U_4/U$ is the fraction of unskilled workers who are represented by unions.

[54] This paper also attempts to estimate the effects of trade through rent reduction on regional data. Borjas and Ramey (1994) also test a central prediction of their model – that skilled/unskilled relative wage should depend positively on the trade deficit in durable manufactured goods – on aggregate data. Buckberg and Thomas (1996) follow up on this approach.

category, τ_1 is the elasticity of substitution between the domestic and foreign versions of the good (both at home and abroad), w_1 is the proportion of total domestic expenditure on the good that is on the domestic version ($1 - w_1$ the value of "import penetration", and x_1 is the proportion of the domestic production of the good that is exported. It is assumed explicitly that $\varepsilon_1 > 1$ and is constant and, as in Section 3.5, that $\tau_1 > \varepsilon_1$. Thus, the total labor price elasticity in this industry is a weighted average of ε_1 and τ_1 and is the greater the more open is the industry to foreign competition (the smaller is w_1 and the larger is x_1). A decline in the foreign price of the good, P_{1f}, or a shift in tastes toward the foreign version of the good would be represented by a decline in the demand shift parameter B_1.

The production function for the firm is assumed to be Cobb–Douglas with coefficients on S_1 and U_1 of, respectively, β_1 and $1 - \beta_1$. It follows that the marginal revenue product of unskilled labor is $(1 - 1/\eta)(1 - \beta_1)B_1^{-1/\eta}Q_1^{1-1/\eta}/U_1$. The firm bargains with a trade union over the wage it pays unskilled workers, W_{U1}, but it pays its skilled workers the prevailing wage W_S. The firm's profit is given by $\pi_1 = B_1^{-1/\eta}Q_1^{1-1/\eta} - W_S S_1 - W_{U1}U_1$, and the union's objective function is assumed to be the maximization of the collective wage rents of unskilled workers employed by the firm, $\text{Rent}_1 = (W_{U1} - W_{Uc})U_1$, where W_{Uc} is the alternative wage prevailing in the competitive, non-union sector.

It is also assumed that the union representing unskilled workers bargains over either both W_{U1} and U_1 (Pareto-efficient bargaining) or just W_{U1} (with management retaining the right to set the profit maximizing level of U_1).[55] The standard approach to the solution of this bargaining problem is the maximization of the expression $(\text{Rent}_1)^{\rho}(\pi_1)^{1-\rho}$, where ρ is the union's fraction of total "bargaining power". Regardless of whether or not the union and the firm bargain over employment, the solution value of the unskilled wage rate is

$$\gamma_1 = \frac{W_{U1}}{W_{Uc}} = \frac{(1 - \beta_1)(\eta - 1) + \rho}{(1 - \beta_1)(\eta - 1)}.$$

This implies that the negotiated wage in an industry will be the greater relative to the competitive wage the smaller is unskilled labor's output share ($1 - \beta_1$), the smaller (the closer to one) is the absolute price elasticity of product demand (η), and, of course, the greater is the union's bargaining power (ρ).

The process of globalization in an industry means that the import fraction rises (w_1 falls) and/or the export fraction (x_1) rises, both of which imply a rise in η and a consequent drop in γ_1. Thus, a removal of tariff barriers to the importation of a good, the development of foreign technology, or reduction in transportation costs have the ultimate effect of eroding union wage premia. In the extreme case of the neoclassical trade model ($\tau_1 = \infty$), η becomes infinitely large, and, as seen in Section 4.5, unionism in the tradable goods sector cannot do very much. Alas, unions in this sector can have no effect on relative wages, and,

---

[55] See Farber (1986) for extended discussion of both union bargaining objectives and the scope of bargaining. Most recent papers on the role of institutions in the determination of relative wages, for example DiNardo et al. (1996) and Borjas and Ramey (1994) make the assumption that bargaining is Pareto-optimal, i.e., unions and management bargain over employment levels and wage rates. However, the evidence that this assumption is appropriate is, at best, quite shaky (see Oswald, 1993).

apart from their effect on working conditions, there is little reason for them to continue in operation.

The model set out above assumes that the "threat point" of the firm is to shut down and earn zero profits. An alternative is for firms to have the possibility of moving their production processes to lower wage countries, the outsourcing practice discussed above. In this case, the threat point of the firm is $\pi_1(\text{out})$, which is presumably positive, instead of zero. This, like the effect of an increase in η, has the effect of reducing the solution value of γ_1. In other words, as firms realize the option of moving their production processes (of US firms outsourcing to Mexico, German firms to the Czech Republic, etc.), we would expect wage rents in the unionized portion of the tradable goods sector to be reduced.

Although the prediction of the model concerning the effects of increased trade on high rents in the tradable sector is quite clear, this prediction does not appear to be borne out by the data. Blanchflower (1997) reports estimates of the relative wage effects of unionism in the UK and the US – the two countries that had the largest increase in earnings dispersion – from 1983 through 1994. There is no trend in these estimates in either country over this period (remaining at about 10% in The UK and 15% in the US). Similarly, Lawrence (1996) notes that relative wages in durable goods industries in the US, the industries most likely to be subject to falling γ_i's due to trade pressures, remained at their original levels during the 1980s. MacPherson and Stewart (1990), however, find that the union wage differential fell slightly during the 1980s in trade-impacted compared to other industries.

5.5. Political economy models

It is evident from almost any formal trade model that there is a potential for rent-seeking within a country or region with respect to trade policy. Although most of the focus of the review of models of the effect of trade in Sections 3 and 4 was on the relatively long run, it is clear that the present values of the real incomes of workers with different skills in different industries (the R_{Si}'s and R_{Ui}'s) as well as the real incomes of the owners of capital in different industries can be affected by the effective prices of the foreign versions of tradable goods (the P_{if}'s). Empirical work shows that the displacement costs for workers affected by "trade shocks" are often quite substantial initially but attenuate through time, with the rate of attenuation depending on the overall condition of the local labor market (see, e.g., Jacobson et al., 1993).[56]

The political economy approach looks at how different groups behave with respect to political questions involving trade (which groups, for example, supported or opposed the passage of NAFTA). Empirical information on this kind of behavior is informative of *perceptions* of the short and medium run effects of changes in the P_{if}'s.

As a matter of trade policy there has been the "escape" clause in GATT (Article XIX) (GATT, 1994) that provides for the suspension of free trade via tariffs when increased

---

[56] With these displacement costs in mind there has been some effort to incorporate uncertainty into trade models (Cordon, 1974; Newberry and Stiglitz, 1984).

imports "cause or threaten serious injury to domestic producers." This can be interpreted as an attempt to stabilize income (see Baldwin, 1985, pp. 183–184) and raises the more general question of income insurance. Economic analysis clearly indicates that market restrictions will be a higher cost approach to stabilizing income than alternative insurance based institutions, provided that the latter does not create incentives for moral hazard (Varian, 1980) and are not derailed by costs of operating a practical insurance system.[57] With strong currency changes and resulting trade inflows, political support for trade restrictions seems to rise in support of the status quo, indicating an underlying insurance motivation or a general aversion to change. In the US the escape clause is implemented by a vote of the International Trade Commission (ITC) commissioners, who are asked to rule whether imports are a substantial cause of 'serious injury' as measured by idling of productive facilities, inability of firms to operate at reasonable profit levels, and significant unemployment or underemployment. while in the European Union there is the Commission of the European Community. It decides, subject to judicial review, whether foreign products are being dumped on the EC market. Do the decision criteria actually used by the ITC connect to items recognized in the simplest models of trade?

A decline in profits, if pervasive could reflect changing terms of trade, but since it is meant to be industry specific, the more plausible interpretation seems to run along the lines of a system intended to provide insurance, or support of the status quo to industry specific capital. Similarly, the criteria for labor, unemployment and underemployment suggests a disequilibrium, not a trade induced wage decline in the wage. Empirical studies of the ITC decisions indicate that the intent of the system is carried out: declining profits and a longer run decline in employment in the identified industry are more likely to lead to the recommendation of import relief. Measurable political factors, such as whether the president or Congress requests the investigation, size of the industry, or whether labor joins management in requesting an investigation were not important predictors (Baldwin, 1985).

Rent seeking by organized interest groups would probably occur behind closed doors, so empirical evidence on the systematic impact of coalitions would be far harder to measure and study. The voluntary export restraints (VER's) in the US auto industry during the 1980s presumably involved the specific factors in the US industry (both capital and industry-specific human capital) as well as shareholders of the Japanese producers receiving import quotas under the agreement, who saw profits and share prices rise (Reis, 1990). Outcomes of this type could be interpreted as the underlying motivation for developing what have become known as political economy models. In the case of political support for VER's, it has been shown how such a policy can gain support by both domestic and foreign producers (Hillman and Ursprung, 1988).

---

[57] In the US the Trade Adjustment Assistance program, which was designed to compensate for labor displacement costs arising from trade induced change, is regarded as having failed to deliver insurance effectively and to have discouraged reallocation of resources to new activities (Lawrence and Litan, 1986, p. 52). Further, there is the question of why labor market displacement arising from international trade should be afforded a status separate from displacements arising from other influences, such as product obsolescence or domestic competition.

Table 10
Types of political economy models of trade policy

Approach	Author(s)	Who sets tariffs?	How it works	Protection depends on
Median voter (direct democracy)	Mayer (1984)	Median voter: by selecting tariff that maximizes the voter's welfare	Population derives income from industries, possibly protected. They vote on level of tariff, which therefore maximizes the income of the median voter	+ Median voter's share of ownership + number of people in industry + size of sector elasticity of import demand
Campaign contributions (electoral competition)	Magee et al. (1989)	Politicians and lobbyists jointly; parties select tariffs to benefit their associated factor, while lobbyists contribute to their probability of election	Elections depend on contributions. Factor owners contribute to precommitted political parties to maximize their earnings	Outcome of Nash game
Tariff-formation function	Findlay and Wellisz (1983)	Industries: by spending resources on lobbying and optimizing on the given tariff-formation function	Tariff assumed to depend directly on resources spent on lobbying. All individuals maximize their incomes	+ Relative effectiveness of pro- vs. anti-protection dollars − number of people in industry + size of sector − elasticity of import demand
Political support function	Hillman (1989)	Policy makers: by selecting tariffs to maximize given political support function	"Political support" depends on industry profits and efficiency. Policy makers maximize political support	− Weight of efficiency in political support + Size of sector − elasticity of import demand
Political contributions	Grossman and Helpman (1994)	Politicians: to maximize objective function defined on contributions and welfare	Single incumbent chooses policy to maximize contributions and economic welfare. Industry (specific factor) lobbyists offer optimal contributions contingent on policies	− Number of people in industry − weight attached to welfare + size of sector − elasticity of import demand

The main ingredients in the political economy models are a demand side for trade interventions on the part of factors subject to trade and a supply side of policy makers who are willing to intervene based on some inducement, ranging from "support" for reelection to outright bribery. This process is then benchmarked against a free trade equilibrium with compensation. Of course the latter is, in principle, better since there are no deadweight inefficiencies or resources dissipated in rent seeking. In fact, the main purpose of such models is to articulate the puzzlement or reasons for sustained pressure against free trade by the political process. This inventory of models is set out in Table 10, developed from Rodrik (1995) and Helpman (1995), as summarized by Deardorff and Stern (1998).

As can be seen from the table, there is a wide range of models and often conflicting predictions. For example, in the median voter model (Mayer, 1984). the number of people in the industry increases the probability of protection, while in the Grossman–Helpman political contribution (GH-PC) approach (Grossman and Helpman, 1994) the number of people in the industry reduces the extent of protection. In the former model the prediction arises from the connection between industry employment and probability of being the median voter. In the latter model as the lobby become more encompassing of the population the limiting case predicts free trade which enhances the well-being of the society as a whole.

The setting for these models is one in which world prices are exogenous, so tariffs do not provide possible favorable terms of trade for the country, nor are there issues of technology diffusion. Lobbying by foreign producers to maintain open markets or provide trade restrictions such as the auto VER's is, logically, not considered, since there are parametric world prices. In short, the underlying trade theory is kept as simple as possible. One widely predicted pattern in political economy models is that the extent of protection will be inversely realted to the elasticity of demand for the import. An inelastic demand gives rise to rent potential for specific factors owned by domestic producers which 'fuel' the engines of distortion. On the other hand there are implicit limits, particularly in the GH-PC model. There the policy maker weights overall economic welfare, so deadweight losses do curb the willingness to provide protection beyond some level.

Empirical testing of the models to determine a role for labor in the political economy of trade has been quite limited. Recently there has been empirical testing of the GH-PC approach. The model assumes $n + 1$ inputs, labor and one specific factor per sector, except for the numeraire good, produced only with labor. The government sets tariffs and subsidies, with net revenue redistributed to each citizen in a lump sum transfer or tax. Aggregate welfare is the sum of specific factor returns, tariff revenue and indirect utility of the individuals. A lobby of specific factor owners (in the labor context, this could be industry specific capital, particularly of experienced workers who still have substantial years to retirement) is assumed to form. Their objective is to maximize their welfare net of contributions, while the government seeks to maximize overall welfare plus contributions from the lobby. Bargaining between the lobby and the government can lead to a non-zero tariff (subsidy) to the organized sector. Essentially, the lobby group purchases a tariff from the government in return for protection. The lobby's willingness to pay will depend on the level of domestic output using their specific factor(s), since a higher price will induce more specific factor rents. The government's willingness to supply protection depends on the their preference weight for overall welfare versus the bribe or contribution. Trade protection for an inelastically demanded good like basic food products is predicted to be more likely.

Structural estimation of the GH-PC model (Goldberg and Maggi, 1997) gives some support to this approach. A less structural approach to factors influencing votes on NAFTA, GATT/WTO and MFN for China indicates that elements of the protection for sale model along with other influences shape voting on US Congressional voting (Baldwin and Magee, 1997). This work shows that the lobby groups appear to be defined along factor lines (labor and business (capital, skilled labor)) and comparative advantage as indexed by net export position of the industries in the districts. Political contributions to the individual legislators by organized labor and business groups did significantly affect the voting outcome in two of the three bills in the House of Representatives (GATT/WTO and NAFTA) and two of the three bills in the Senate (NAFTA and MFN for China). General economic conditions in the district or state were found to influence voting as was the industry specific distribution of employment, giving some support to trade restrictions as derivative form an underlying insurance motivation on the part of policy makers as suggested by Cordon.

6. Conclusion

We have surveyed the field of international economics with reference to how trade among nations affects labor market analysis. As seen in several in several examples set out in Sections 3 and 4, a large class of traditional problems – the effects of minimum wages, immigration, union wage policy, skill biased technological change, etc. – are handled *very* differently if the economy is open to trade (under certain conditions) instead of our standard closed economy assumption. Most important from the point of view of labor market analysis, is the Factor Price Insensitivity theorem (the prediction that relative wages in an economy are unaffected by relative factor supplies) that flows from the conventional Neoclassical trade theory framework. We labor economists simply are not used to thinking along these lines.

However, there is ample reason for expecting that – in the absence of some unthinkably dreadful event (like the collision of the Earth with a large asteroid) – trade and global interdependence are virtually certain to continue to increase. Accordingly, we labor economists are going to have to get used to thinking in international terms.

Our reaction to the standard trade theory that yields these implications is that it may place too much emphasis on models based on the assumption that domestic and foreign versions of particular goods are particular substitutes. We have emphasized an alternative model – implicit in some of the early empirical work in the trade field – finite substitution elasticities for some traded goods. The resultant, somewhat inelegant "differentiated products" model has implications that are, not surprisingly, between those of the closed and textbook open model. Unfortunately, although the task of testing between alternative specifications has begun, the questions are as yet unresolved.

The major set of empirical issues in the intersection of labor and international economics is concerned with the effect of increased international interdependence on the general level of real wages and the distribution of wages and labor demand for different types of labor. There are, as seen in Section 5, several alternative approaches to estimation of the effects of globalization, and labor and trade economists have tended to pursue different empirical strategies.

The majority – but hardly unanimous – conclusion of these studies on US data using each of the different approaches is that the contribution of changes in trade to shifts in relative labor demand functions since the 1970s has been in the small to modest range. We have the expectation that, as global interdependence continues to increase and comparable data among different countries become more available, the majority view of future studies concerning the labor market impact of trade will shift toward the modest to fairly large range. We also have the expectation – with a much smaller forecast error – that there will be a large number of such studies.

References

Armington, Philip S. (1969), "A theory of demand for products distinguished by place of origin", IMF Staff Papers 26: 159–178.

Autor, David H., Lawrence F. Katz and Alan Krueger (1997), "Computing inequality: have computers changed the labor market?" Working paper no. 5956 (NBER, Cambridge, MA).

Baldwin, Robert (1985), The political economy of U.S. import policy (MIT Press, Cambridge, MA).

Baldwin, Robert E. and Glen C. Cain (1997), "Shifts in U.S. relative wages: the role of trade, technology and factor endowments", Working paper no. 5934 (NBER, Cambridge, MA).

Baumol, William J., Sue Anne Batey-Blackman and Edward J. Wolff (1985), "Unbalanced growth revisited; asymptotic stagnancy and evidence", American Economic Review 75 (4): 806–871.

Baumol, William J., Sue Anne Batey-Blackman and Edward J. Wolff (1991), Productivity and American leadership: the long view (MIT Press, Cambridge, MA).

Berman, Eli, John Bound and Zvi Griliches (1994), "Changes in the demand for skilled labor within U.S. manufacturing industries", Quarterly Journal of Economics 109: 367–398.

Berman, Eli, John Bound and Stephen Machin (1997), "Implications of skill-biased technological change: international evidence", Working paper no. 6166 (NBER, Cambridge, MA).

Bernard, Andrew B. and J. Bradford Jensen (1995), "Exporters, jobs and wages in U.S. manufacturing: 1976–1987", BPEA: Microeconomics: 67–119.

Bhagwati, Jagdish (1991), "Free traders and free immigrationists: strangers or friends?" Working paper no. 20 (Russel Sage Foundation).

Blanchflower, David G. (1997), "Changes over time in union relative wage effects in Great Britain and the United States", Discussion paper no. 15 (LMCTSC, Centre for Economic Performance, London School of Economics).

Blanchflower, David and Matthew Slaughter (1998), "The causes and consequences of changing income inequality: w(h)ither the debate?" Discussion paper no. 27 (LMCTSC, Centre for Economic Performance, London School of Economics).

Blau, Francine D. and Lawrence M. Kahn (1996), "International differences in male wage inequality: institutions versus market forces", Journal of Political Economy 104 (4): 791–836.

Borjas, George J. (1995), "The economic benefits from immigration", Journal of Economic Perspectives 9 (2): 3–22.

Borjas, George J. and Valerie A. Ramey (1994), "Time-series evidence on the sources of trends in wage inequality", American Economic Review 84: 10–16.

Borjas, George J. and Valerie A. Ramey (1995), "Foreign competition, market power and wage inequality", Quarterly Journal of Economics 110 (4): 246–251.

Borjas, George J., Richard B. Freeman and Lawrence F. Katz (1992), "On the labor market effects of immigration and trade", in: George J. Borjas and Richard B. Freeman, eds., Immigration and the work force (University of Chicago Press, Chicago, IL).

Borjas, George J., Richard B. Freeman and Lawrence F. Katz (1997), "How much do immigration and trade affect labor outcomes?" Brookings Papers on Economic Activity 1: 1090.

Bound, John and Harry Holtzer (1997), "Demand shifts, population adjustments and labor market outcomes during the 1980's", University of Michigan, mimeo.

Bound, John and George Johnson (1992), "Changes in the structure of wages in the 1980's: an evaluation of alternative explanations", American Economic Review 82 (3): 371–392.

Bowen, Harry P., Edward E. Leamer and Leo Sveikauskas (1987), "Multicountry, multifactor tests of the factor abundance theory", American Economic Review 77: 791–809.

Branscomb, Lewis M. and Brian Kahin (1995), "Standards, processes and objectives for the national information infrastructure", in: Brian Kahin and Janet Abbete, eds., Standards for information infrastructure (MIT Press, Cambridge, MA).

Brecher, Richard A. (1974), "Minimum wage rates and the pure theory of international trade", Quarterly Journal of Economics 88 (1): 98–116.

Buckberg, Elaine and Alun Thomas (1996), "Wage dispersion in the 1980's: resurrecting the role of trade through the effects of durable employment changes", IMF Staff Papers 43 (2): 336–354.

Burtless, Gary (1995), "International trade and the rise in earnings inequality", Journal of Economic Literature 33: 800–816.

Cline, William R. (1997), Trade and income distribution (Institute for International Economics, Washington, DC).

Cordon, W. M. (1974), Trade policy and economic welfare (Oxford University Press, Oxford, UK).

Davis, Donald R. (1995), "Intra-industry trade: a Hecksher–Ohilin–Ricardo approach", Journal of International Economics 39: 201–226.

Davis, Donald R. (1997), "Does European unemployment prop up American wages? National labor markets and global trade", American Economic Review, in press.

Davis, Donald R. (1997), "Technology, unemployment and relative wages in a global economy", European Economic Review, in press.

Davis, Donald R., David E. Weinstein, Scott C. Bradford and Kazushige Shimpo (1997), "Using international and Japanese regional data to determine when the factor abundance theory of trade works", American Economic Review 87 (3): 421–446.

Deardorff, Alan V. (1984), "Testing trade theories and predicting trade flows", in: R.W. Jones and P.B. Kenen, eds., Handbook of international trade, Vol. 1 (North-Holland, Amsterdam) pp. 467–517.

Deardorff, Alan V. (1997), "Factor prices and the factor content of trade revisited: what's the use?" Mimeo. (University of Michigan).

Deardorff, Alan V. and Paul N. Courant (1990), "On the likelihood of factor price equalization with non-traded goods", International Economic Review 31(3): 589–596.

Deardorff, Alan V. and Dalia S. Hakura (1994), "Trade and wages – what are the questions?" in: Jagdish Bhagwati and Marivin Kosters, eds., Trade and wages: leveling wages down? (AEI Press, Washington, DC).

Deardorff, Alan V. and Robert W. Staiger (1988), "An interpretation of the factor content of trade", Journal of International Economics 24 (1): 93–107.

Deardorff, Alan V. and Robert M. Stern (1998), "An overview of the modeling of the choices and consequences of U.S. trade policies", in: A. Deardorff and R. Stern, eds., Representation of constituent interests in the design and implementation of U.S. trade policies (University of Michigan Press) in press.

DiNardo, John, Nicole M. Fortin and Thomas LeMieux (1997), "Labor market institutions and the distribution of wages, 1973–1992: a semiparametric approach", Econometrica 64(5): 1001–1044.

Ethier, Wilfred J. (1984), "Higher dimesional issues in trade theory", in: R.W. Jones and P.B. Kenen, eds., Handbook of international trade (North-Holland, Amsterdam) pp. 131–184.

Farber, Henry S. (1986), "The analysis of union behavior", in: O. Ashenfelter and R. Layard, eds., Handbook of labor economics, Vol. 2 (North-Holland, Amsterdam) pp. 1039-1138.

Feenstra, Robert C. and Gordon H. Hanson (1995), "Foreign investment, globalization and relative wages", Working paper no. 5121 (NBER, Cambridge, MA).

Feenstra, Robert C. and Gordon H. Hanson (1996), "Globalization, outsourcing and wage inequality", American Economic Review 86(2): 240–245.

Feenstra, Robert C. and Gordon H. Hanson (1997), "Productivity measurement and the impact of trade and technology on wages: estimates for the U.S., 1972–1990", Working paper no. 6052 (NBER, Cambridge, MA).

Fernandez, Edward W. and J. Gregory Robinson (1994), "Illustrative ranges of the distribution of undocumented immigrants by state", Technical working paper no. 8 (US Bureau of the Census).

Findlay, Ronald and Stanislaw Wellisz (1983), "Some aspects of the political economy of trade restrictions", Kyklos 33: 469–481.

Freeman, Richard B. (1995), "Are your wages set in Beijing?" Journal of Economic Perspectives 9 (3): 15–32.

GATT (1994), Trends and statistics, international trade (GATT).

Goldberg, Pinelopi Koujianou and Giovanni Maggi (1997), "Protection for sale: an empirical investigation", Working paper no. 5942 (NBER, Cambridge, MA).

Goldstein, Morris and Mohsin S. Khan (1985), "Income and price effects in foreign trade", in: R.W. Jones and P.B. Kenen, eds., Handbook of international economy, Vol. 2, pp. 1041–1105.

Gomery, Ralph E. and William J. Baumol (1997), "Productivity differences, world market shares and conflicting national interests in linear trade models", Japan and the World Economy 9: 136–150.

Griliches, Zvi (1969), "Capital-skill complementarity", Review of Economics and Statistics 51: 465–468.

Grossman, Gene M. (1983), "Import competition from developed and developing countries", Review of Economics and Statistics: 271–281.

Grossman, Gene and Elhanan Helpman (1991), Innovation and growth in the international economy (MIT Press, Cambridge, MA).

Grossman, Gene and Elhanan Helpman (1994), "Protection for sale", American Economic Review 84: 833–850.

Hamermesh, Daniel (1993), Labor demand (Princeton University Press, Princeton, NJ).

Harrigan, James (1997), "Technology, factor supplies and international specialization: estimating the neoclassical model", American Economic Review 87 (4): 475–494.

Helpman, Elhanan (1995), "Politics and trade policy", Discussion paper no. 1269 (Centre for Economic Policy Research, London).

Haskel, Jonathan E. and Matthew J. Slaughter (1997), "Does the sector bias of skill-biased technological change explain rising wage inequality?" Mimeo. (Dartmouth College).

Hicks, J.R. (1953), "An inaugural lecture", Oxford Economic Papers 5 (2): 117–135.

Hillman, A.L. and H.W. Ursprung (1988), "Domestic politics, foreign interests and international trade policy", American Economic Review 78 (4): 729–745.

Jacobson, Louis S., Robert J. LaLonde and Daniel Sullivan (1993), "Earnings losses of displaced workers", American Economic Review 83 (4): 685–709.

Johnson, George (1997), "Changes in earnings inequality: the role of demand shifts", Journal of Economic Perspectives 11 (2): 41–54.

Johnson, George (1998a), "Estimation of the impact of immigration on the distribution of income among minorities and others", in: D. Hamermesh and F. Bean, eds., Help or hindrance: the economic implications of immigration for African Americans (Russell Sage Foundation, New York).

Johnson, George and Frank Stafford (1993), "International competition and real wages", American Economic Review 83 (2): 127–130.

Johnson, George and Frank Stafford (1995), "The Hicks hypothesis, globalization and the distribution of real wages", Paper presented at the Econometric Society Meeting, Washington, DC.

Johnson, George and Frank Stafford (1997), "Productivity differences, world market shares and conflicting national interests in linear trade models", Japan and the World Economy 9: 151–158.

Johnson, George and Frank Stafford (1998), "Technology regimes and the distribution of real earnings", in: G. Eliasson and C. Greene, eds., Microfoundations of economic growth: a Schumpeterian perspective (J.A. Schumpeter Society, Stockholm, Sweden).

Johnson, Harry and Peter Mieszkowski (1969), "The effects of unions on the distribution of income: a general equilibrium approach", Quarterly Journal of Economics 84: 539–561.

Jones, Ronald W. (1972), "Technical progress and real incomes in a Ricardian trade model", in: R. Jones, ed., International trade: essays in theory (North-Holland, Amsterdam) pp. 279–286.

Jones, Ronald W. (1965), "The structure of simple general equilibrium models", Journal of Political Economy 73: 557–572.

Jones, Ronald W. and Peter Neary (1984), "The positive theory of international trade", in: R.W. Jones and P.B. Kenen, eds., Handbook of international trade (North-Holland, Amsterdam).

Juster, Thomas and Frank Stafford (1991), "The allocation of time: empirical findings, behavioral models, and problems of measurement", Journal of Economic Literature 29: 471–522.

Katz, Lawrence F. and Kevin M. Murphy (1992), "Changes in relative wages, 1963–1987: supply-demand factors", Quarterly Journal of Economics 107 (1): 35–78.

Katz, Lawrence F. and Lawrence H. Summers (1989), "Industry rents: evidence and implications", Brookings Papers on Economic Activity 2: 209–291.

Keynes, John Maynard (1933), "National self-sufficiency", The Yale Review: 752–769.

Klodt, Henning (1992), "Technology based trade and multinational investment in Europe: structural change and competition in Schumpeterian goods", in: Michael W. Klein and Paul J.J. Welfens, eds., Multinationals in the new Europe and global trade (Springer-Verlag, Berlin).

Krueger, Alan B. (1997), "Labor market shifts and the price puzzle revisited", Working paper no. 375 (Industrial Relations Section, Princeton University).

Krugman, Paul (1979), "A model of innovation, technology transfer and the distribution of world income", Journal of Political Economy 87: 253–266.

Krugman, Paul (1995), "Growing world trade: causes and consequences", Brooking Papers on Economic Activity 1: 327–377.

Krugman, Paul (1995), "Technology, trade and factor prices", Working paper no. 5355 (NBER, Cambridge, MA).

Lawrence, Robert Z. (1996), Single world, divided nations? (Brookings and OECD, Paris).

Lawrence, Robert Z. and Robert E. Litan (1986), Saving free trade (Brookings Institution, Washington, DC).

Lawrence, Robert Z. and Matthew J. Slaughter (1993), "International trade and American wages in the 1980's: giant sucking sound or small hiccup?" Brookings Papers on Economics Activity: Microeconomics 2: 161–226.

Leamer, Edward (1996a), "In search of Stolper–Samuelson effects in US wages", Working paper no. 5427 (NBER, Cambridge, MA).

Leamer, Edward (1996b), "What's the use of factor content?" Working paper no. 5448 (NBER, Cambridge, MA).

Leamer, Edward E. and James Levinsohn (1995), "International trade theory: the evidence", in: G. Grossman and K. Rogoff, Handbook of international economics, Vol. 3 (North-Holland, Amsterdam) pp. 1139–1194.

Leontief, Wassily (1953), "Domestic production and foreign trade: the American capital position re-examined", Proceedings of the American Philosophical Society 97: 332–349.

Machin, Stephen, Annette Ryan and John Van Reenen (1996), "Technology and changes in skill structure: evidence from an international panel of industries", Discussion paper no. 4 (LMCTSC, Centre for Economic Performance, London School of Economics).

MacPherson, David A. and James B. Stewart (1990), "The effect of international competition on union and nonunion wages", Industrial and Labor Relations Review 43 (4): 434–446.

Maddison, Angus (1991), Dynamic forces in capitalist development: a long run comparative view (Oxford University Press, Oxford, UK).

Mayer, Wolfgang (1984), "Endogenous tariff protection", American Economic Review 74: 970–985.

Magee, Stephen P., William A. Brock and Leslie Young (1989), "Black hole tarrifs and endogenous policy formation", (MIT Press, Cambridge, MA).

Murphy, Kevin M. and Finis Welch (1991), "The role of international trade in wage differentials", in: M.H. Kosters, ed., Workers and their wages: changing patterns in the United States (AEI Press, Washington, DC) pp. 39–69.

Murphy, Kevin M. and Finis Welch (1992), "The structure of wages", Quarterly Journal of Economics 107 (1): 285–326.

Nevan, Damien and Charles Wyposz (1996), "Relative prices, trade and restructuring in European industry", Cahier no. 9615 (Department d'Econometrie et de d'Economie Politique, Universite de Lausanne).

Newbury, David M.G. and Joseph E. Stiglitz (1984), "Pareto inferior trade", Review of Economic Studies 51: 1–12.

Oswald, Andrew J. (1993), "Efficient contracts are on the demand curve: theory and facts", Labour Economics 1: 85–113.

Ries, John C. (1990), "Vertical integration, quotas and profits: voluntary export restraints on Japanese automobiles", unpublished doctoral dissertation, The University of Michigan.

Richardson, J. David (1995), "Income inequality and trade: how to think, what to conclude", Journal of Economic Perspectives 9 (3): 33–55.

Rodrik, Dani (1995), "Political economy of trade policy", in: G. Grossman and K. Rogoff, Handbook of international economics, Vol. 3 (North-Holland, Amsterdam).

Sachs, Jeffrey D. and Howard Shatz (1994), "Trade and jobs in US manufacturing", Brookings Papers on Economics Activity 1: 1–84.

Slaughter, Matthew J. (1995), "Multinational Corporations, outsourcing and american wage divergence", Mimeo. (Dartmouth College).

Slaughter, Matthew J. (1997), "International trade and labor-demand elasticities", Mimeo. (Dartmouth College).

Slaughter, Matthew J. and Phillip Swagel (1997), "The effect of globalization on wages in the advanced economies", IMF Staff Studies for the World Economic Outlook, in press.

Stolper, Wolfgang and Paul A. Samuelson (1941), "Protection and real wages", Review of Econimic Statistics 9 (1): 58–73.

Trefler, Daniel (1993), "International factor price differences: Leontief was right!" Journal of Political Economy 101 (6): 961–987.

Trefler, Daniel (1995), "The case of the missing trade and other mysteries", American Economic Review 85 (5): 1029–1046.

Varian, Hal (1980), "Progressive taxes as social insurance", Journal of Public Economics 14(1): 49–68.

Vernon, Raymond (1966), "International trade and international trade in the product cycle", Quarterly Journal of Economics 80 (2).

Vernon, Raymond (1979), "The product cycle hypothesis in a new international environment", Oxford Bulletin of Economics and Statistics 41: 255–267.

Williamson, Jeffrey G. (1991), "Productivity and American leadership: a review article", Journal of Economic Literature 29: 51–68.

Williamson, Jeffrey G. (1996), "Globalization and inequality then and now: the late 19th and late 20th centuries compared", Working paper no. 5491 (NBER, Cambridge, MA).

Wood, Adrian (1994), North-south trade, employment and inequality (Clarendon Press, Oxford, UK).

PART 9

LOOKING WITHIN FIRMS

Chapter 35

INDIVIDUAL EMPLOYMENT CONTRACTS

JAMES M. MALCOMSON[*]

University of Oxford

Contents

* This chapter has benefited greatly from comments by Orley Ashenfelter, David Card, Ernst Fehr, Simon Gächter, Bob Gibbons, Georg Kirschsteiger, Jens Larsen, Bentley MacLeod, Jonathan Thomas and participants in the Handbook workshop, and from data supplied by Dean Hyslop and Francis Kramarz.

Handbook of Labor Economics, Volume 3, Edited by O. Ashenfelter and D. Card

Abstract

This chapter reviews recent developments in the study of individual employment contracts. It discusses three reasons for an employer and an employee to have a contract: (1) to allocate risk in a way different from a spot market; (2) to enhance the efficiency of investment decisions by protecting the return on investments made by one party from being captured by the other; and (3) to motivate the employee by making compensation depend on performance. The main emphasis is on issues that arise from the problems of enforcing contracts in practice and from renegotiation by mutual agreement. © 1999 Elsevier Science B.V. All rights reserved.

JEL codes: J41; K31; D82

1. Introduction

There are numerous reasons for doubting that labor markets can be adequately described as spot markets. When employment is not a simultaneous transaction of work for pay, with the rights and responsibilities of employer and employee then at an end, contracts play a role because they specify what the on-going rights and responsibilities are. To be enforceable, a contract does not have to be written down – a verbal agreement can be as legally binding a contract as a written one, although for obvious reasons what was agreed may be less easy to demonstrate in court. Nor does a contract have to be explicit. This is particularly important in the case of employment where traditional custom and practice, statements of policy in company handbooks, and decisions by one party have all been used by courts as evidence of an implicit contract.

This chapter discusses three reasons for an employer and an employee to have a contract: (1) to allocate risk in a way different from a spot market; (2) to enhance the efficiency of investment decisions by protecting the return on investments made by one party from being captured by the other; and (3) to motivate the employee by making compensation depend on performance. Contracts to select those employees who best match a job arise most naturally in the context of internal labor markets and of careers within organizations – they are left to the chapter by Gibbons and Waldman. Issues specific to contracts for senior executives are left to the chapter by Murphy, those specific to retirement to the chapter by Lumsdaine and Mitchell. Contracts between trade unions and firms are also not covered here – they raise additional issues that are discussed in the chapters by Bertola, by Blau and Kahn, and by Nickell and Layard. Even so, there is inevitably some overlap with other chapters. Where this occurs, the relationship to the framework used here is explained but detailed discussion left to those chapters.

The earlier literature on contracts for reasons (1)–(3) was reviewed by Parsons (1986) in Volume 2 of this Handbook. The present chapter concentrates on more recent developments although, to keep it self-contained, there is inevitably some discussion of the earlier literature. The main emphasis here is on the issues that arise from the problems of enforcing contracts in practice and from the recognition that, at law, any contract can be renegotiated by mutual agreement.

2. Some evidence

If the economic theory of contracting is of relevance to labor markets, one would expect forms of contract that emerge from theory to be used in practice. In addition, those contracts should fit with characteristics of wages that are otherwise problematic to explain. This section briefly discusses evidence about forms of employment contracts and wage characteristics that one might hope would be explained by contracts agreed for the reasons discussed in this chapter.

There are two issues to bear in mind in this discussion. First, it would be unrealistic to expect one limited class of theories to explain all the characteristics of labor markets so, in setting out the evidence in this section, a judgement has been made about what it is reasonable to expect. Second, to evaluate individual empirical studies and provide an overall assessment of the empirical evidence would require a chapter on its own. The purpose here is not to do that. It is merely to set out some of the empirical findings that seem a reasonable basis to judge the theories.

2.1. Employment contracts

Because this chapter is not concerned with union bargaining, it is the contracts of individual employees that are of concern. Direct evidence on individual contracts is not widely available. However, the law puts restrictions on the contracts that can be used (e.g., outlawing slavery and restricting the penalties that can be used for breach of contract) and provides rules and doctrines for determining contractual obligations where these have not been specified by the parties. Contracts to explain labor market behavior clearly need to be consistent with the former. To the extent that the latter correspond to what would be sensible arrangements under typical employment conditions, it would be reassuring if they were consistent with what contract models predict.

In the US, unless there is evidence to the contrary, the presumption is that employment is *at will*, in which case either party can terminate the employment without notice for any reason, or for no reason at all (Rothstein et al., 1994, Section 1.4). With employment at will, either party can unilaterally announce modifications to the terms on which it is prepared to continue the employment. There is, however, an asymmetry between employer and employee about what constitutes acceptance of a modification proposed by the other. If the employer announces a change in conditions then, as Specter and Finkin (1989, Section 3.03) put it, "the employee's continuance in service with knowledge of the change has generally been held to constitute acceptance.... Under this rule, continuance under protest would not preclude an effective modification". In contrast, if the employee proposes a change in conditions and the employer, while stating explicitly that the change is unacceptable, nevertheless allows the employment to continue, that would not be held to constitute acceptance of the employee's demands. Legal details are discussed by Malcomson (1997).

The presumption of employment at will does not preclude employers and employees from making enforceable contracts with alternative provisions. A formal written agreement is not necessary for this. Verbal assurances to individual employees, statements of company policy contained in, for example, employee handbooks, assignment of an employee to a task that is clearly longterm in nature (e.g., developing a sales territory or supervising construction of a major building project), and even in some states longevity of service per se have all been held by courts to be reasons for employment not being at will. See Specter and Finkin (1989, chapter 2) for details. Krueger (1991a) documents the increasing numbers of these cases. That they came to court indicates that the parties themselves were not clear what courts would decide.

In European countries the position is different. Under English law, when there is no explicit contract to the contrary, the current terms of employment are a legal contract, even where not written down. As such, those terms can be varied only by mutual agreement, so they continue to apply until either there is mutual agreement to modify them or the contract is properly terminated. An important difference from the US is that an employee is not deemed to have agreed to a modification proposed by the employer merely by continuing to work. Thus, if either party proposes a change in the current wage terms, the other party makes clear that the change is not acceptable, and employment nevertheless continues, the current wage terms must continue to be honored until the contract is terminated. Seen from this perspective, wage negotiation with current employees is formally renegotiation of an existing contract. If the duration of the contract has not been stated explicitly, employment can be terminated with proper advance notice, the minimum length of which is specified by law and during which employees must be paid at the current rate, or by making appropriate payment in lieu of notice. Longer serving employees also have rights to minimum levels of redundancy payment specified in law. However, there are legal restrictions on terminating a contract in order to offer a new contract on modified terms. These can make the outcome of disputed cases difficult to predict. Again, legal details are discussed by Malcomson (1997). In other European countries, terminating a contract of employment is typically more difficult or more costly for employers than in England. Emerson (1988) and Lazear (1990) provide further information.

As in the US, the parties can agree contracts with alternative provisions as long as these satisfy the minimum legal requirements. However, courts can enforce a contract provision contingent on certain events only if they can verify whether those events have occurred. It is assumed throughout the labor contracts literature that courts can verify whether an employee did in fact work for the employer. If the employee did not work despite an agreement to do so, it may not in practice be easy to verify whether the employee chose to stay away from work or was turned away by the employer.[1] It may thus be uncertain what a court would decide and expensive in court costs to find out. If the parties can do without payments contingent on events that may not be verifiable, it makes sense for them to do so.

Also important is the remedy that courts apply if one party is held in breach of contract. Some contributions to the economic theory of contracts, for example Chung (1991) and Aghion et al. (1994), base their analyses on the remedy of *specific performance*, that is, the court requires the breaching party to carry out the contract as specified. Courts occasionally order that an employee dismissed in breach of contract be reinstated but, as Specter and Finkin (1989, Section 15.07) make clear for the US, they are reluctant to do so "except in extraordinary cases" in view of "the common-law notion that courts could not compel an employer to retain the services of an employee because of the difficulty of policing an order compelling an obnoxious personal relationship." With breach by an employee, in the US "a court cannot order specific performance, and thereby compel an employee to continue an employment relationship" (Specter and Finkin, 1989, Section 15.02). But, even where specific performance in employment is not ruled out by law, there is an obvious practical reason for the difference between employment and some other types of contract in its use. With a contract to sell property (e.g., an old master), to enforce specific performance a court need only get a bailiff to seize the property and hand it over. With a contract to provide a service, a court cannot force a recalcitrant supplier to provide it. At best, it has to induce the supplier to do so by threatening severe penalties that are in practice limited by what is socially acceptable.

Typically then, breach remedies in employment cases are restricted to monetary compensation. If the amount of compensation is specified in the contract (*liquidated damages*), these are enforceable "if they do not constitute a penalty but, rather, reflect a reasonable estimate of the actual damages anticipated to arise from the breach" (Specter and Finkin, 1989, Section 15.06). In the context of economic models, it is thus important to recognize that penalty provisions included in a contract to give the parties incentives to behave in certain ways will not be enforced by courts if they are far in excess of the actual damages incurred.

Since a contract can always be modified by mutual agreement, employers and employees can avoid a possible charge of breach if they stick to the practice of modifying terms only by mutual consent. That may be entirely rational if it avoids the possibly substantial expenses of being challenged in court. Indeed, Krueger (1991a) argues that employer groups in a number of US states have supported unjust dismissal legislation that restricts employment at will because they are prepared to give up some potential rights for the reduced litigation and damage costs that result from clarification of the legal position. Mutual agreement on modification of terms does not preclude rights to unilateral decisions

---

[1] This is different from being able to verify whether, in the event of a permanent separation, an employee quit voluntarily or was dismissed, which courts must be able to do to enforce certain notice and redundancy provisions. Even the latter is not always easy, as is evidenced by the cases brought for "constructive discharge", see Specter and Finkin (1989, Chapter 4).

by the employee to quit or by the employer to make layoffs for legitimate business reasons if not ruled out by the contract. The latter right has typically been recognized explicitly in unjust dismissal proposals. Nor does mutual agreement on modification preclude wage changes – employees may well agree to a wage cut if the alternative is being laid off.

Data on wage changes of those who stay with the same employer provide circumstantial evidence on how the parties actually behave over modification of terms. With pure employment at will, the only special status for the wage paid in the previous period of employment is that it continues to apply unless the employer has announced, or explicitly agreed to, a change. Thus, one would expect the wage to change whenever it is in the employer's interest and thus whenever market conditions change. In contrast, with rene-gotiation by mutual consent, the wage changes only if *both* parties agree to it. Thus the wage may not change when market conditions change. The formal basis for these predic-tions is discussed later. Hence, evidence on individual wage changes over time may throw light on whether behavior in the US is typically consistent with pure employment at will. The next subsection looks at some of that evidence.

2.2. Changes in pay over time

Fig. 1 (Card and Hyslop, 1997) shows the distribution of real annual wage rate changes for hourly rated employees staying with the same employer from the US Panel Study of Income Dynamics (PSID) for the relatively high inflation years 1976–1979 and the rela-tively low inflation years 1985–1988. A vertical line at minus the annual rate of inflation is drawn for each year to identify the real wage rate change associated with a zero nominal change. A significant proportion of the changes correspond to nominal wage cuts, so nominal wages are not completely rigid downwards. But particularly striking is the promi-nence of the band corresponding to a zero nominal change – around 10% of these employ-ees in the high inflation period 1976–1979, closer to 20% in the low inflation period 1985–1988. Moreover, in each year for over four-fifths of employees in that band, the nominal wage rate change was precisely zero. Kahn (1997) gives the percentages of wage and salary earning heads of household with precisely zero nominal change separately for each year 1971–1988. These are reproduced in columns (1) and (2) of Table 1, together with the inflation rate in column (4). The percentages for salary earners are lower than for wage earners but still large enough to make the band corresponding to a zero nominal change stand out (see Kahn, 1997 for details). The percentages for the whole period at the bottom of the table indicate that the zero nominal effect is more prominent for non-union employ-ees, the group with which this chapter is concerned.

Fig. 1 certainly looks more like data in which the previous wage has some special status above what it would be accorded with pure employment at will. That may be the result of something other than contracts. McLaughlin (1994) and Kahn (1997) consider the possi-bility of *menu costs* (the physical costs of changing wages) but the former notes substantial numbers of quite small nominal wage changes which one would not expect with menu costs. Card and Hyslop (1997) subject the data for hourly paid workers, and similar data

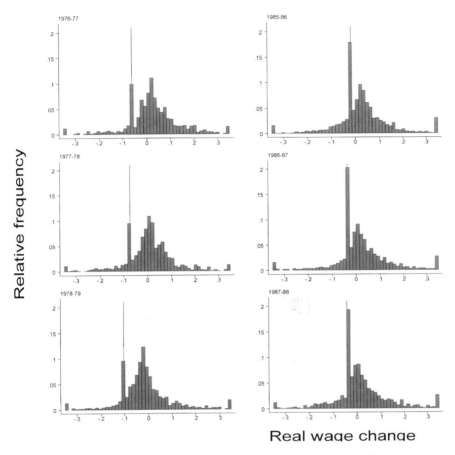

Fig. 1. Distribution of log real wage changes, PSID samples 1976–1979 and 1985–1988, hourly rated workers staying with same employer.

from the Current Population Survey (CPS), to extensive tests for menu costs by constructing a counterfactual distribution based on symmetry with the upper tail, which is assumed not to be affected by nominal rigidities. They find that the actual distribution near the spike at zero is pulled down relative to the counterfactual distribution, as one would expect with menu costs. But this happens more just below the spike at zero than just above it. Thus the effect is not symmetric and, for this reason, they conclude that it is probably not all the result of menu costs.

There is always concern with data of this type that reporting errors may bias the results if, for example, an employee paid $4.95 an hour one year and $5.05 the next reports both as $5. Card and Hyslop (1997) estimate that this could account for at most one-quarter of the observed nominal rigidities in the mid-1980s. By comparing with other studies, Akerlof et

Table 1
Percent staying with same employer with zero nominal change in pay rate over year[a]

End year	Wage earners (1)	Salary earners (2)	Managerial employees (3)	Inflation rate (4)
1971	10.42	–	8.52	4.3
1972	10.33	–	11.84	3.4
1973	7.44	–	11.95	5.1
1974	7.19	–	0.20	10.1
1975	8.07	–	10.24	10.2
1976	7.24	–	12.02	6.1
1977	6.34	7.96	15.29	6.8
1978	8.12	5.53	10.79	6.6
1979	6.34	6.49	8.53	10.4
1980	3.77	5.75	3.92	14.7
1981	7.33	3.53	3.17	10.0
1982	6.48	3.93	2.51	6.6
1983	14.68	6.75	7.23	3.9
1984	13.28	4.27	6.34	4.5
1985	10.60	4.73	8.26	3.7
1986	15.58	2.06	7.13	1.6
1987	15.50	3.19	5.51	3.8
1988	17.04	3.89	2.44	3.8
Whole period				
All	10.51	4.68	–	–
Non-union	14.22	4.75	–	–

[a] Columns (1) and (2): PSID data for US. Source: Kahn (1997). Column (3): Unspecified US service industry firm. Source: Baker et al. (1994b). Column (4): Percent change in CPI March to March. Source: Kahn (1997).

al. (1996) conclude that reporting errors in PSID data actually reduce measured nominal rigidities. As a further check, column (3) of Table 1 gives corresponding figures for managerial employees from Baker et al. (1994b) that were taken from the personnel tapes of a firm and thus should have a high degree of reliability. Because these are for just one firm, the percentages differ from those in column (2) but they give no reason to doubt that the importance of precisely zero nominal changes is genuine.

2.3. Wages and business cycle shocks

A related issue is how wages respond to business cycle shocks. A major concern in the empirical literature on cyclical behavior is that average wages appear more damped in response to shocks than a spot market model would predict. The basic observation has been around at least since Keynes and has been documented by Hall (1975) and Gordon (1983). It is one of the properties that real business cycle models find hard to explain, at least for plausible assumptions about labor supply. Boldrin and Horvath (1995) have a recent discussion of this. Blanchard and Diamond (1990) ran into the same problem with the matching model that they calibrate to US data. The staggered contract models of Gray (1976) and Taylor (1979), in which wages are fixed for several periods and negotiated for different groups in different periods, were designed to replicate the damped response but they do so by making the timing of wage negotiations exogenous. Some authors attribute the persistent high unemployment in Europe since the oil price shocks of the 1970s to the inflexibility of wages. See Bean (1994) for a discussion of this issue.

Reviewing the evidence from a number of studies, Abraham and Haltiwanger (1995) conclude that some of the damped response may be simply the result of aggregation. In response to an adverse shock, a higher proportion of lower paid than of higher paid employees lose their jobs. As a result, the average wage fluctuates less than individual wages because of this composition effect. But the damped response still seems to exist, see Blanchflower and Oswald (1994). Moreover, Bils (1985) and Solon et al. (1994) find the wages of new hires more flexible cyclically than those of existing employees, which is at least suggestive of a contract or menu cost effect.

Beaudry and DiNardo (1991) investigate whether slow adjustment can be attributed to contract effects by relating current wages to labor market conditions (principally the unemployment rate) in the past. They find that the lowest unemployment rate since the start of a job has a strongly significant upward effect on the current wage, whereas the current unemployment rate, and the unemployment rate at the start of the job, have a smaller impact. Boldrin and Horvath (1995) and Gomme and Greenwood (1995) argue that real business cycle models with labor contracts fit the data better than those without. Because the authors of all these studies consider contracts to share risk, they investigate only wages in real terms and so it is not clear whether the effect is best described as a real, or as a nominal, contract effect.

2.4. Cross-section earnings functions

There is a widespread view that a significant amount of wage dispersion is not easily reconciled with a spot market model given the available data on human capital and demographic variables, even with allowance for mobility frictions that slow down adjustment to shocks. Regressions of wages on the variables in the data typically leave substantial unexplained inter-industry or inter-firm wage differentials. For examples, see Dickens and Katz (1987) and Krueger and Summers (1988). Helwege (1992) shows that those differentials are not highly positively correlated with subsequent employment growth as one would expect if they resulted from mobility frictions. Because datasets are limited, one can never rule out the possibility that additional data would provide a reconciliation, though studies such as Gibbons and Katz (1992) that investigate the possibility that differentials are explained by unmeasured ability differences are not encouraging. It would thus certainly be convenient if contract models were consistent with the observations.

In theoretical discussions of earnings functions, specific investments have traditionally been associated with wages that increase with tenure for reasons originally explained by

Becker (1975). The significant positive tenure effects found by Becker (1975) and Mincer (1962) were taken as an indication of the importance of specific investments for employment. Brown (1989) argues that there is certainly a tenure effect during initial training periods and Jacobson et al. (1993) show that high tenure employees typically suffer substantial longterm wage reductions when separating from distressed firms. However, some of the more recent literature, for example Abraham and Farber (1987), Altonji and Shakotko (1987), Altonji and Williams (1997) and Topel (1991), finds an effect that is smaller than the earlier estimates. A natural question for contract models is what these estimates imply about the importance of specific investments for labor markets.

2.5. Summary of "stylized facts"

The empirical evidence discussed in this section can be loosely summarized in terms of the following "stylized facts":

1. Nominal wages are somewhat rigid in the short term and are certainly not all adjusted instantaneously to labor market changes.
2. Wage levels do not appear to fluctuate as much over the business cycle as a spot market model would predict, especially for longterm continuing employees.
3. Individual wages seem to depend on the past, for example the sequence of unemployment rates over the history of the job.
4. At least some wages include firm or job specific premia, although there is debate about the extent of wage growth with tenure.

These "stylized facts" are not easily reconciled with spot market models of labor markets. There certainly seems plenty here for other theories, such as those based on contracts, to explain.

3. Contracts to allocate risk

Contracts to allocate risk have an obvious attraction for explaining wages that, in response to shocks, fluctuate proportionately less relative to employment than in a spot market. Risk averse employees would like insurance against fluctuations in consumption without, at least in a formulation with no income effects on leisure, changing employment fluctuations. If financial markets cannot be used to provide that insurance, employers may provide it instead. That is efficient if the employer observes something relevant that an independent insurer cannot. The theoretical literature on employment contracts to allocate risk was reviewed by Parsons (1986) and surveyed in detail by Rosen (1985) and Hart and Holmström (1987). Some results discussed there are summarized here briefly to provide the background for theoretical developments concerned with enforceability and renegotiation and for more recent empirical evidence.

3.1. The basic model

The basic model stemming from the original work of Azariadis (1975), Baily (1974) and Gordon (1974) has a risk averse employee hired by a firm. The employee has von Neumann–Morgenstern utility function $u(w,h)$, where w is real income consisting only of earnings from the firm that are all spent on consumption, h is hours of work, and $u(\cdot)$ is strictly increasing in w, decreasing in h, and strictly concave. The firm makes profit $\pi(w,h,s) = R(h,s) - w$, where $R(h,s)$ is its revenue that is strictly increasing and concave in h, and s is a state of nature describing everything exogenous that is relevant to the firm's owners and that is revealed only after the employment contract is agreed. To allow the firm to be risk averse, its utility of profits is written $v[\pi(w,h,s),s]$, where s appears as a separate argument to allow for the possibility that the value of profits to the firm's owners may depend on other variables (e.g., how well their shares in other companies are performing on the stock market), and $v(\cdot)$ is concave and strictly increasing in profit. An efficient employment contract consists of a real wage $w^*(s)$ and hours $h^*(s)$ for each possible state s that maximize the employee's expected utility subject to the firm's owners receiving a given expected utility level denoted $\underline{v}$. That is, $[w^*(s),h^*(s)]$ for all s solves

$$\max_{w(s),h(s)} Eu[w(s), h(s)] \quad \text{subject to} \quad Ev[R(h(s), s) - w(s), s] \geq \underline{v}, \tag{1}$$

where E denotes the expectation taken over the states of nature s. (An efficient contract can equally well be specified as maximizing the firm's utility subject to an expected utility constraint for the employee – the implications for what follows are the same.) Let λ denote the multiplier attached to the constraint in Eq. (1). Then $[w^*(s),h^*(s)]$ must satisfy the first order condition with respect to $w(s)$

$$u_w[w^*(s), h^*(s)] = \lambda v_\pi[R(h^*(s), s) - w^*(s), s] \quad \text{for all } s, \tag{2}$$

where a subscript indicates the derivative of a function with respect to that argument.

Suppose the firm is risk neutral so that $v_\pi(\cdot)$ is a constant independent of profit and the state s. Then Eq. (2) implies the standard fair insurance condition that the marginal utility of the employee's income is the same in every state. If also hours of work are fixed ($h^*(s) = \bar{h}$ for all s, so the only employment decision is whether or not the employee works), this in turn implies that employee income is the same in every state in which employment occurs. The contract wage is set to yield the firm expected profit $\underline{v}$ and thus may be different for employees with identical characteristics hired by the firm at different starting dates when market conditions are different. These basic conclusions extend directly to a multiperiod model with utility additively separable over time. If firm and employee discount future payoffs at the same rate, the real income paid to an employee never changes once a contract has been signed. Real income increases (decreases) steadily over time, but remains constant across states at each date, if the employee has a lower (higher) rate of time preference than the firm – the firm in effect acts as a banker to the employee for borrowing and lending that is not state contingent.

Under these conditions, insurance certainly reduces variations in earnings but it is clearly counterfactual that real earnings of those staying in the same job do not change – see for example the data for salaried employees discussed in Section 2.2. To have the employee's real earnings depend on the state requires at least one of the following: (a) the marginal utility of income $u_w(\cdot)$ varies with the state for constant w; (b) the marginal utility of profits $v_\pi(\cdot)$ varies with the state for constant w; or (c) enforcement difficulties make a contract satisfying Eq. (2) unenforceable in practice. The first two of these are discussed in the remainder of this subsection and the third in the next.

One reason the employee's marginal utility of income may vary even for a constant wage is that hours of work may change. In many jobs, hours vary with demand conditions. With variable hours, an optimal contract specifies hours that vary with the state to satisfy the first order condition with respect to hours

$$-u_h[w^*(s), h^*(s)] = \lambda R_h(h^*(s), s)v_\pi[R(h^*(s), s) - w^*(s), s] \qquad \text{for all } s. \qquad (3)$$

If hours affect the marginal utility of income then, even with a risk neutral firm, Eq. (2) requires earnings to change with the state. This mechanism is not, however, particularly plausible for explaining the evidence. As Rosen (1985) shows, Eq. (2) implies hours and real earnings negatively related when, as typically assumed, leisure is a normal good. With leisure a normal good, lower hours (more leisure) implies higher marginal utility of income for a given wage. To equate this marginal utility across states then requires higher income in states with more leisure. That is inconsistent even with a constant hourly wage rate, let alone the widespread use of premium rates for overtime hours. It certainly implies that earnings respond less than hours to a change in marginal product. In contrast, in a spot market model, because wage rates equal marginal products and earnings are the product of wage rates and hours, earnings respond more than hours to a change in marginal product. In data from the PSID and the National Longitudinal Survey of Men (NLSM), Abowd and Card (1987) find that earnings of those staying with the same employer vary less than earnings of those switching employers, which certainly suggests a contract effect. However, earnings of the former are as responsive as hours to changes in marginal product, which is not consistent with full insurance when leisure is a normal good.

Suppose next that, instead of being risk neutral, the firm is risk averse with its owners' utility depending only on profit (that is, s does not enter as a separate argument in $v(\cdot)$). Eq. (2) then implies that, for jobs in which hours of work do not depend on the state, employee income and profit always move in the same direction across states. However, the model implies more than just positive correlation. In a firm with many employees, the same marginal utility of profit $v_\pi(\cdot)$ applies to all employees, so Eq. (2) implies that the marginal utilities of different employees should differ at most because of differences in the multiplier λ. Thus even employees with different utility functions should all have their earnings move in the same direction as profits, which is not consistent with the evidence in Baker et al. (1994b) that, even with employees of the same firm, some have real increases and some real decreases. Moreover, the natural way to implement such an arrangement is via a formal profit sharing scheme so, for employees whose hours of work do not vary, one would expect to observe earnings changes tied formally to such schemes. For jobs with flexible hours, the relationship between earnings and hours depends on profit, and hence on the productivity of hours, when the firm is risk averse. However, it would be a pure fluke if either a constant real hourly wage rate, or a constant nominal hourly wage rate, two of the more frequent outcomes in the data in Card and Hyslop (1997), corresponded to the correct relationship.

The final case considered in this subsection is that in which the owners' utility of profit function $v(\cdot)$ itself depends on the state. This would be the case if some components of the state correspond to risks that are insurable (by, for example, diversification of share holdings) but others to risks that are not (because, for example, they correspond to aggregate risks that affect the economy as a whole). Rosen (1985) has emphasized the importance of this distinction. A formulation that captures the distinction is

$$v[\pi(w,h,s),s] \equiv \theta(s)\pi(w,h,s), \tag{4}$$

where two states that differ only in insurable risks result in the same value of $\theta(s)$. Then $v_\pi(\cdot) = \theta(s)$. An implication is that, across any two states differing only in insurable risks, an efficient contract has the same properties as if the firm were risk neutral. Thus, if hours of work are not variable, employees' real incomes are constant. However, real incomes differ across states that differ in non-insurable risks (and thus have different values of $\theta(s)$), as for a risk averse firm. Thus straightforward profit sharing is not appropriate in this case. For jobs with fixed hours of work, real income varies only, and inversely, with $\theta(s)$. So, even if employees of the same firm have different utility functions, their real incomes should all move in the same direction which, as already noted, is not the case for the data of Baker et al. (1994b). Moreover, to the extent that uninsurable risks are uninsurable because of aggregate fluctuations in, for example, the stock market, $\theta(s)$ should be highly correlated across firms, so the components of wage changes that are idiosyncratic to firms should be small. I know of no attempts to test the extent to which this is the case in practice. For jobs with variable hours, this formulation does not alter the characteristic that, across states that differ only in insurable risks, longer working hours should go with lower real incomes when leisure is a normal good, which is hard to square with the widespread use of premium overtime rates for above normal hours in such jobs.

Neither variable hours nor risk aversion of firms thus seems sufficient to reconcile the full insurance model with the evidence. The next subsection considers difficulties in enforcing a full insurance contract.

3.2. Enforcement problems

There is an obvious problem of enforcing contracts with payments contingent on the state s if that state is not public information that can be verified in court. This will not prevent efficient risk sharing with a risk neutral firm and fixed hours of work because in that case an efficient contract has a wage independent of the state and there is thus no need to make payments contingent on the state. If the firm is not risk neutral only because shareholders cannot diversify aggregate risks on the stock market, aggregate measures like a stock market index should be at least reasonably good substitutes on which to make payments contingent. Moreover, even if the firm is risk averse for other reasons or if hours of work are variable, there is not a problem as long as the firm's profit is public information and all relevant information about the state can be inferred from the wage, profit and hours worked. Thus the real problems with non-verifiable states arise only when the state cannot be inferred from public information and either the firm is averse to idiosyncratic risk or hours of work are variable.

Suppose the state is observed only by the firm. For fixed hours of work, the only feasible contracts have a wage independent of the state because otherwise the firm would always announce the state corresponding to the lowest wage. If efficient hours of work depend on the state and the revenue function $R(\cdot)$ is such that marginal and average products always move in the same direction across states, the firm can be induced to truthfully reveal the state, see Hart (1983), but only if higher hours are associated with higher employee income. Otherwise, the firm would always make more profit by claiming that the state was one with lower employee income and/or longer hours. Thus it is no longer the case that, as implied by Eq. (2) when leisure is a normal good, longer hours are associated with lower incomes. Moreover, the model becomes consistent with *compulsory* overtime in which the firm not only decides when overtime will be worked (that must obviously be the case if only the firm knows s) but also has the right to require employees to work overtime. The reason is that, with leisure a normal good and the firm risk neutral, an efficient contract has the employee's utility lower in states with higher productivity, see Chari (1983) and Green and Kahn (1983). More generally, the differences between hours in good states and those in bad are inefficiently large in the sense that equating marginal rates of substitution between hours and income with marginal rates of transformation between hours and output in each state would require either fewer hours in at least one high hours state or more hours in at least one low hours state than under the contract.

In these circumstances, however, the characteristics of efficient contracts are in general altered if employment continues for more than one period. If states in different periods are independently distributed, the firm cannot credibly claim that the state is one corresponding to a low wage in every period. One would then expect an efficient contract to depend on the history of states claimed by the firm despite the independence. If states are persistent, and the state that occurs is one for which the contract specifies inefficient hours, both parties can gain from renegotiating the contract so that hours are efficient once the employee has acquired information about the state. In that case, as Dewatripont (1989) shows, at least one party is worse off at the stage the contract is agreed than if the parties could commit themselves not to renegotiate. Moreover, the possibility of renegotiation may result in hours being set in such a way that information about the state is revealed to the employee only slowly over time. These kinds of considerations greatly complicate the nature of contracting and I am unaware of attempts to assess the extent to which they influence the contracts actually used in employment.

The other type of enforcement problem discussed in the literature is the effect of the parties being able to quit the contract for an alternative match. The essence of earnings insurance for employees is that employees are better off in some states than working at the spot market wage and worse off in others. The same applies to a firm that offers earnings insurance. Thus, there are generally gains to one or the other from breaking the contract if they could do so without penalty. Holmstrom (1983), Harris and Holmström (1982) and Meyer (1987) analyze the case in which the firm always sticks to a contract but it cannot be enforced on the employee if the employee is better off quitting. While that is not strictly the case at law (the US doctrine of *employment at will* only makes a presumption that the parties to employment can quit without penalty, but can be overridden by a formal contract), it may in practice not be worthwhile trying to enforce a contract on an unwilling employee. That puts a floor on how low the employee's utility can be in each state. An implication when hours of work are not variable is that, instead of being constant across states, the wage is higher in states in which the employee would otherwise quit. Harris and Holmström (1982) show how, when employees differ in ability that is unknown to both employee and firm when initially hired but revealed over time through work performance, this results in real wages that are rigid downwards but increase over time for those employees who turn out to be more able. The implications are discussed more fully in the chapter by Gibbons and Waldman. Meyer (1987) shows that, when the state is observed only by the firm, employment distortions are reduced when leisure is not an inferior good.

If there is also a possibility of the firm reneging on the contract, real earnings may fall in some states, as in the data discussed in Section 2.2. Concern for reputation ensures that the firm complies with the contract only if the value of a good reputation is worth more in the long run than the short run gains from not complying. In general, a contract that is not legally enforceable will be adhered to only if it is in the interests of both parties to do so, that is, if it is *self-enforcing*. Holmstrom (1981) and Thomas and Worrall (1988) discuss this issue. The latter analyze an infinite horizon game with the state observed by both employee and firm but not verifiable in court. Non-compliance is punished by an agent being required to trade for ever after in a spot market in which the wage is a random variable determined by the state. If the spot market wage is sufficiently high relative to the contract wage, the gain to an employee from quitting the contract exceeds the future loss of insurance from having to trade in the spot market thereafter. If the spot market wage is sufficiently low, the gain to the firm from replacing the employee with another from the spot market exceeds the future loss from having to pay a higher average wage to an employee who is uninsured. To make the insurance contract self-enforcing, therefore, the wage must be kept within appropriate bounds around the spot market wage.

To see the implications, let s_t denote the state in period t, $s^t = (s_1, s_2, \ldots, s_t)$ the history of states up to t, and $p_{t+1}(s;s^t)$ the probability that $s_{t+1} = s$ given s^t. Let $\bar{U}_t(s^t)$ and $\bar{\Pi}_t(s^t)$ denote the expected present discounted values of the employee's future utility and the firm's future profits respectively if they were to trade in the spot market from t on given the history s^t. Also, suppose firm and employee both use the same discount factor δ and the firm is risk neutral. A self-enforcing contract consists of sequences of wages $w_t(s^t)$ and hours $h_t(s^t)$ for each s^t and t such that neither prefers to trade in the spot market from t on as long as it is efficient for employment to continue. Consider the properties of an efficient self-enforcing contract with components $w_t^*(s^t)$ and $h_t^*(s^t)$ for all s^t and t. Let $\Pi_t(s^t)$ denote the expected present discounted value of the firm's future profits from such a contract from t on given the history s^t and $U_t[\Pi_t(s^t)]$ the corresponding present discounted value of the employee's utility. (Formally, the latter is a function representing the Pareto frontier.) These can be written recursively as

$$U_t[\Pi_t(s^t)] = u[w_t^*(s^t), h_t^*(s^t)] + \delta \sum_s U_{t+1}[\Pi_{t+1}(s^t, s)]p_{t+1}(s; s^t), \qquad \text{all } t; \tag{5}$$

$$\Pi_t(s^t) = R[h_t^*(s^t), s_t] - w_t^*(s^t) + \delta \sum_s \Pi_{t+1}(s^t, s)p_{t+1}(s; s^t), \qquad \text{all } t. \tag{6}$$

To be self-enforcing, the contract must satisfy the incentive compatibility constraints

$$U_{t+1}[\Pi_{t+1}(s^t, s)] \geq \bar{U}_{t+1}(s^t, s), \qquad \text{for all } s, s' \text{and } t \geq -1; \tag{7}$$

$$\Pi_{t+1}(s^t, s) \geq \bar{\Pi}_{t+1}(s^t, s), \qquad \text{for all } s, s' \text{ and } t \geq -1, \tag{8}$$

which will be called the *employee's* and the *firm's outside option constraints* respectively because they require that the parties do as well from sticking to the contract as from taking up an alternative opportunity in the market. For the contract to be efficient, it must (in the present context) be efficient from all dates t on, and thus maximize the employee's expected future utility for any given level of the firm's expected future profits at every t. Formally, it must therefore be that $w_t^*(s^t)$, $h_t^*(s^t)$ and $\Pi_{t+1}(s^t, s)$ maximize the right-hand side of Eq. (5) subject to the constraints Eqs. (6)–(8) for each possible s for given $\Pi_t(s^t)$. Denote the Lagrange multipliers attached to those constraints by $\lambda_t(s^t)$, $\delta p_{t+1}(s; s^t)\phi_{t+1}(s^t, s)$, and $\delta p_{t+1}(s; s^t)\psi_{t+1}(s^t, s)$ respectively. Then the first order conditions that must be satisfied can be written

$$u_w[w_t^*(s^t), h_t^*(s^t)] - \lambda_t(s^t) = 0, \qquad \text{all } s^t \text{ and } t, \tag{9}$$

$$u_h[w_t^*(s^t), h_t^*(s^t)] + \lambda_t(s^t)R_h[h_t^*(s^t), s_t] = 0, \qquad \text{all } s^t \text{ and } t, \tag{10}$$

$$U_{t+1}'[\Pi_{t+1}(s^t, s)][1 + \phi_{t+1}(s^t, s)] + \psi_{t+1}(s^t, s) + \lambda_t(s^t) = 0, \qquad \text{all } s, s^t \text{ and } t, \tag{11}$$

together with complementary slackness conditions on the inequality constraints. From Eq. (5), we also have the envelope condition

$$U_t'[\Pi_t(s^t)] = -u_w[w_t^*(s^t), h_t^*(s^t)], \qquad \text{all } s^t \text{ and } t. \tag{12}$$

Use of this and Eq. (9) allows Eq. (11) to be written

$$u_w[w_t^*(s'), h_t^*(s')] = u_w[w_{t+1}^*(s', s), h_{t+1}^*(s', s)][1 + \phi_{t+1}(s', s)] - \psi_{t+1}(s', s),$$

all s, s' and t.   (13)

For jobs in which hours of work do not vary (and thus condition (10) does not apply), a number of conclusions follow directly. Consider how the wage at $t + 1$ relates to the wage already paid at t. If s is such that it is possible to satisfy both outside option constraints only with equality, the present values of payoffs from $t + 1$ on are given uniquely by those constraints and both parties receive what they would receive from trading on the spot market. For worse states in which it is not possible to satisfy both outside option constraints, it is inefficient for the employment to continue because at least one party would be better off, and the other no worse off, if they took their outside options. Thus a separation occurs. In such a state, the firm will pay layoff pay only if concerned about its reputation with other employees or possible new hires in the future. For better states, one of the two outside option constraints is not binding and the corresponding multiplier is therefore zero. In this case, the relationship between the wage at t and the wage at $t + 1$ is given by Eq. (13). In particular, since the multipliers $\phi_{t+1}(s', s)$ and $\psi_{t+1}(s', s)$ are necessarily non-negative, $w_{t+1}^*(s', s) > w_t^*(s')$ only for s such that $\phi_{t+1}(s', s) > 0$, so the employee's outside option constraint binds at $t + 1$. Thus the wage is increased from its level at t by just enough to ensure that, given the consequential changes in future wages from continuing efficient insurance, the employee does not quit. In contrast, $w_{t+1}^*(s', s) < w_t^*(s')$ only for s such that $\psi_{t+1}(s', s) > 0$, so the firm's outside option constraint binds at $t + 1$. Thus the wage is reduced from its level at t by just enough to ensure that, again given the consequential changes in future wages from continuing efficient insurance, the firm does not lay the employee off. For other values of s, the wage remains unchanged. How wide the gap is between the outside option constraints (and thus how close a self-enforcing contract can get to the first best of a constant wage) depends on the discount rate and the penalties from breaking an agreement.

The conclusion is thus that the firm provides insurance to the employee in the form of a constant real wage until such time as the wage is either too low to prevent the employee quitting (in which case it is increased by just enough to ensure the employee stays) or it is too high to prevent the firm laying off the employee (in which case it is reduced by just enough to avoid layoff). This is equivalent to a contract specifying a constant real wage that is renegotiated by just enough for employment to continue when one of the parties would otherwise quit. The implications for the dynamics of real wages are illustrated in Fig. 2. Beaudry and DiNardo (1991) investigate some of these implications empirically for the US on both PSID and CPS data. With a fully binding contract that neither party could quit, the wage is set at the start of the contract and remains unchanged. Its level thus depends only on labor market conditions at the start of the contract. If the contract is not binding on the employee, the wage is bid up whenever outside labor market conditions are sufficiently favorable. Beaudry and DiNardo (1991) use the unemployment rate as a measure of labor market tightness and regress the log of the wage on three unemployment

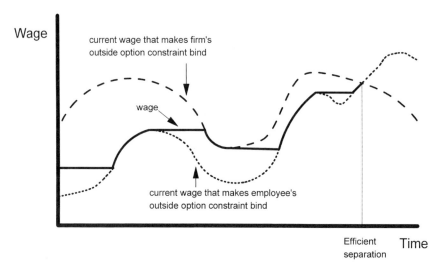

Fig. 2. Dynamics of wages.

rates, the contemporaneous rate, the rate at the start of the job, and the lowest rate since the start of the job, plus a standard set of control variables. In a spot market, only the first should be significant; with a fully binding contract, only the second. With a contract not binding on the employee, only the third should be significant. If, however, there is a penalty from breaking the contract in the form of less good offers for given labor market tightness, the employee's alternative opportunities may not be as good when the labor market is only slightly tighter than at the start of the contract, so both the second and third may play a role. In each case, the coefficient should be negative. (Beaudry and DiNardo (1991) do not include the highest unemployment rate since the start of the job, which would be appropriate if the contract was not binding on the firm.) Over a variety of specifications in both datasets, and both in aggregate and at the industry level, they find that, consistent with the contract not being binding on employees and inconsistent with a spot market model, the lowest unemployment rate since the start of the job has a significant negative coefficient in almost all cases, though in some specifications the other unemployment rates are significant, sometimes even with a positive sign. A further implication is that anything reducing the probability that continuing the job will be efficient at some time in the future narrows the gap between the upper and lower bounds in Fig. 2. It should thus on average increase the sensitivity of wages to the contemporaneous unemployment rate and reduce sensitivity to the unemployment rate at the time of hiring. Bertrand (1999) finds effects of increased competition (measured by import penetration in the employing indus-
ry, instrumented by the exchange rate) and of increased financial constraints (measured by
ploying industry average return) consistent with this in both CPS and PSID data.
s with insurance models discussed previously, this model has the consequence that

different firms may pay different wages to employees with the same outside option values if they were hired at different times and thus naturally generates inter-firm wage differentials that are not simply the result of differences in the characteristics of employees. But in the present case the differentials between two firms disappear at any time at which the outside option constraints of their employees are both binding. Thus the model is a less plausible explanation of differentials that persist over long periods of time.

Fig. 2 refers to the wage of somebody already employed. With new hires, there is no existing contract so, as in the insurance models already discussed, in a perfectly competitive hiring market the wage for them adjusts to equate supply and demand. The wages for new hires are thus more flexible than those for existing employees, consistent with the evidence from Bils (1985) and Solon et al. (1994) discussed in Section 2.3. There is a contrast with the menu cost approach to wage stickiness. With menu costs, when wage changes occur they will be substantial relative to the menu cost.[2] In contrast, in Fig. 2 the wage changes that occur may be large or small – they are just enough to give either the firm or the employee exactly the same payoff as the outside option.

In the case just discussed, with a risk neutral firm and fixed hours of work, full insurance consists of earnings independent of the state and there is no obvious reason why the parties could not write a legally enforceable contract to achieve that even if the state is not verifiable in court. That would not apply in any of the circumstances discussed above in which full insurance involves state contingent earnings. One such case is that of jobs with variable hours. For such jobs, Eq. (13) implies exactly the same relationship between changes in wages and hours between t and $t + 1$ as with a fully binding contract for states at $t + 1$ in which neither of the constraints (7) and (8) binds at that date and thus $\phi_{t+1}(s^t,s)$ and $\psi_{t+1}(s^t,s)$ are both zero. When leisure is a normal good, hours and earnings then vary inversely independent of changes in anything else, such as productivity. That is what one would expect because, when neither of the outside option constraints binds, the firm effectively provides full insurance. As noted above, this conclusion is inconsistent with the use of overtime premiums for above normal hours of work when leisure is a normal good. However, the argument is not so simple for states at $t + 1$ in which either of the constraints (7) and (8) binds at that date. Consider s such that $\phi_{t+1}(s^t, s) > 0$. Then Eq. (13) implies $u_w[w_t^*(s^t), h_t^*(s^t)] > u_w[w_{t+1}^*(s^t, s), h_{t+1}^*(s^t, s)]$. Thus either $w_{t+1}^*(s^t,s)$ is higher than it would otherwise have been or $h_{t+1}^*(s^t,s)$ is higher. This attenuates the negative relationship between earnings and hours. Alternatively, consider s such that $\psi_{t+1}(s^t, s) > 0$. Then Eq. (13) implies $u_w[w_t^*(s^t), h_t^*(s^t)] < u_w[w_{t+1}^*(s^t, s), h_{t+1}^*(s^t, s)]$. Thus either $w_{t+1}^*(s^t,s)$ is lower than it would otherwise have been or $h_{t+1}^*(s^t,s)$ is lower. Again, this attenuates the negative relationship between earnings and hours.

If there were changes in wages that arose independently of changes in the state, then hours changes and wage changes would still be negatively related when leisure is a normal good. (This can be seen by using Eqs. (9) and (10) to eliminate $\lambda_t(s^t)$ and totally differ-

---

[2] As shown by Caplin and Spulber (1987) and Caballero and Engel (1993), wage changes may be smoothed in macroeconomic data as the result of aggregation but that does not affect the implications for the individual data discussed here.

entiating the resulting expression with respect to h, w and s.) For any given employee, of course, wages and hours change only when the state changes. However, otherwise identical employees who start contracts at dates with different labor market conditions will have different levels of expected utility from their contracts. Beaudry and DiNardo (1995) identify two effects that result from this. First, for contracts for which neither outside option constraint has yet been binding, these differences in expected utility persist and are reflected in different hours as well as different wages – with leisure a normal good, hours are negatively correlated with hourly wages. Second, when one of the outside option constraints (say the employee's) binds, wages and hours must adjust more for some employees than for others. Suppose the outside option constraint binds for two employees with contracts that previously provided different expected utility. To satisfy the constraint, both must end up with the same expected future utility. Thus the employee whose expected utility was previously lower has larger adjustments in wages and hours. Beaudry and DiNardo (1995) use these properties to investigate whether the behavior of wages and hours in PSID data is consistent with the model and conclude that hours are indeed negatively correlated with hourly wages when productivity is held constant, as would be implied by leisure a normal good. That unemployment rates are likely to be inversely correlated with marginal productivity might also be the reason for a significant coefficient on the contemporaneous unemployment rate in Beaudry and DiNardo (1991).

3.3. Conclusions on contracts to allocate risk

Contracts to insure employees' earnings have a number of characteristics that are promising for understanding the empirical evidence. Obviously, with such contracts, earnings, hours and employment do not correspond to points on conventional labor supply curves. In particular, such contracts are consistent with earnings that fluctuate less than spot market earnings of employees with identical characteristics. Employees hired at different dates under different labor market conditions also have different earnings, though that will generate systematic inter-industry differentials only to the extent that different industries have different hiring patterns at given stages of the business cycle. When account is taken of the difficulties of enforcing state contingent contracts, earnings may rise and fall over time even when hours of work are not variable without responding to every change in labor market conditions and layoff pay may no longer be part of an enforceable contract. When hours are variable, enforcement problems can get away from the unpalatable conclusion from the simpler cases that earnings and hours should be inversely correlated when leisure is a normal good.

There are, however, reasons to doubt that such contracts are the whole story. In response to a question to 19 personnel managers in New Jersey and eastern Pennsylvania in 1988 about providing earnings insurance to employees, Blinder and Choi (1990, p. 1005) report only "ten of the 19 managers (53%) indicated that they found the idea somewhat 'plausible or relevant'." Hall (1993) found more support among 39 personnel managers interviewed in Northeast England in 1993; 77% thought the idea very, or fairly, plausible and

46% of these indicated that they experienced higher rates of staff turnover in boom years as a result of providing wage stability. Campbell and Kamlani (1997) also found reasonably strong support among their sample of 111 Business Week 1000 firms and 32 smaller firms contacted via university alumni. However, contracts to provide insurance are necessarily concerned with insurance of *real* earnings, whereas the data discussed in Section 2.2 provide at least some indication of *nominal* contract effects. Of course, as Wright (1988) emphasizes, in a world with many different types of transactions, it is the net effect of all transactions contingent on a state that is important and there may be many different sets of contracts that have the same net effect. But even with a risk averse firm concerned with a different price index from employees, it is not obvious why insurance motives would result in contracts in nominal terms – contracts should be indexed to *some* price index as long as there is an index correlated with the relevant price levels of both agents. Such index linking could, of course, be implicit. But if the idea of insurance seems relevant to half of the managers interviewed by Blinder and Choi (1990), their practical implementation of it would seem to be undermined by half of them viewing (and more than half of them regarding their employees as viewing) real wage cuts that result from nominal wage cuts as very different from real wage cuts that result from inflation. It certainly seems that, to fully understand wage behavior, we need to consider contracts that arise for reasons other than insurance of employee earnings.

4. Contracts to protect investments

This section explores the implications for labor markets of an alternative approach to contracts, contracts to protect investments from what is termed *hold-up*. Most employment makes use of investments of one sort or another. These may be *general investments* that are equally valuable in any employee-firm match or *specific investments* that are valuable only for a particular match. In many cases, matches involve *turnover costs* of hiring new employees (e.g., costs of advertising, interviewing, appointing, and providing essential basic training) and of firing an employee who is to be replaced by another. The hold-up literature is concerned with economic relationships with the following characteristics: (1) because of turnover costs or specific investments, there are rents to continuing a relationship once started that are, in principle, available for the parties to bargain over; (2) there are problems in writing contracts contingent on all the future events that are important for the relationship; and (3) any contract that is made between the parties can be renegotiated by mutual consent. The first two of these have been widely discussed in the literature on specific investments in labor markets that stems from Becker (1975) and is surveyed in Parsons (1986). It is the third, renegotiation, that distinguishes the recent literature reviewed in this section. This review is an abbreviated version of Malcomson (1997).

With turnover costs and specific investments, demand and supply conditions do not determine a unique equilibrium wage. Instead, they determine the lowest wage for which an employee will work and the highest wage the employer will pay. In the absence of a contract, bargaining determines where between those two the wage lies and thus how the rents to continued employment are divided. If the size or division of the rents depends on the return to an investment undertaken by a firm, bargaining may result in the employee capturing some of that return. That is hold-up. As Grout (1984) showed formally, the firm may then invest less than would be efficient. This inefficiency is a transactions cost in the sense of Williamson (1985).

A contract governs the allocation of rents and may, as a result, be able to reduce transactions costs. Because of characteristic (2), however, any contract is incomplete in the sense that it cannot be conditioned on all the events that affect the payoffs to the parties. Tirole (1994), Hart (1995) and MacLeod (1996) discuss the foundations for incomplete contracts in depth. Two reasons for incompleteness are emphasized in the literature discussed here. First, investments may be too complex or too multidimensional for a court to verify whether they have been carried out as specified in a contract. Although it may, for example, be feasible to specify the number of hours of specific training unambiguously, specifying the quality of training during those hours is more problematic. Second, efficient choices (e.g., whether to continue employment) may depend on exogenous events that occur after a relationship has started but these events are not themselves verifiable. Renegotiation of contract terms may then be required to enable an efficient outcome if, for example, one party would not continue the employment on the current terms even though continuation is efficient. But renegotiation may itself affect the distribution of rents and hence the incentives of the parties to make investments at the start of a relationship. Thus, although renegotiation can reduce transactions costs by allowing the contract to be adapted to changing circumstances, it may adversely affect investment decisions.

In hold-up theories, hold-up is an issue because turnover costs and specific investments generate rents to continued employment. Table 2 reproduces estimates of turnover costs from the literature, expressed as a percentage of first year earnings. Where possible, a

Table 2
Average recruitment, exit, and training costs[a]

Source	Sample	Recruitment (%)	Recruitment + exit (%)	Training (%)	Recruitment + exit + training (%)
Oi (1962)	International Harvester Co., US 1951	–	0.7	7.2	7.9
Campbell (1993)	Unspecified US, 1980	–	–	–	33
Hart and Kawasaki (1999)	Japan, all industries, 1991	10.5	–	–	–
Abowd and Kramarz (1997)	France, most industries, 1992	5.9	107.8*	–	–

[a] All figures are % of first year earnings. –, figure not available; *, terminations for all reasons except retirements.

distinction is drawn between recruitment, exit, and training costs because the extent to which they give rise to rents from continued employment may differ. Such rents are generated by costs incurred or avoided that yield a return only if the employment continues. Recruitment costs almost certainly fall into that category. Exit costs do so only when they are not transfers between employer and employee, so severance payments need to be excluded from measures of rents. Training costs create rents only when they are specific to the employer. With the latter two, therefore, not all the costs listed in the table may result in rents. Of the figures in Table 2, only those from Hart and Kawasaki (1999) and Abowd and Kramarz (1997) are at all comprehensive. Incomplete as they are, the figures certainly indicate the existence of turnover costs and, hence, the potential relevance of hold-up.

4.1. Hold-up in the absence of a contract

It is useful to formalize the basic issue of hold-up in the simple context of a purely bilateral relationship in which there are no other potential employees for the firm, no alternative jobs for the employee, and information is entirely symmetric so that both firm and employee know as much as the other knows. Suppose the firm's net revenue from the employee is $R(I,s)$ where I is the money it invests in capital equipment, specific training, etc., and s is a state of nature describing everything relevant to the relationship (e.g., the prices of outputs and of non-labor inputs) that is revealed only ex post (that is, *after* the investments are made). Investment increases the productivity of the employee, so $R'(I, s) > 0$, but with decreasing marginal returns, so $R''(I, s) < 0$. (Primes denote derivatives with respect to the amount of the investment.) The firm's profit ex post is

$$\pi(w, I, s) = R(I, s) - w - I, \tag{14}$$

where w is the wage it pays the employee. The employee's utility depends only on the wage. Both are risk neutral. The total payoff to the firm and the employee (the sum of wages and profits) is then just $R(I, s) - I$, so the efficient level of investment that maximizes the total return is $\hat{I}$ defined by

$$E\{R'(\hat{I}, s)\} = 1. \tag{15}$$

Because investment must be made before the state is known, the efficient level equates the expected marginal return on investment to the marginal cost of investment. Because the investment is measured in money terms, the latter is 1.

If the firm invests before fixing the wage with the employee, the employee may be able to bargain for a higher wage as a result of the investment. In the simplest bargaining framework, the only additional ingredients are the *default payoffs* the parties receive while they continue to bargain. In the absence of other potential employees or jobs, these are the payoffs when no employment takes place. Since these default payoffs may depend on the state of nature s, denote them by $w^0(s)$ and $\pi^0(I,s)$ for the employee and the firm respectively. (The latter may well be negative. It is unaffected by I when the default payoff corresponds to no employment but may be affected by I with alternative interpretations discussed later.) The gain from reaching agreement once the investment has been made and the state is known is $R(I, s) - w^0(s) - \pi^0(I, s)$ because the cost of the investment has already been incurred and is thus a bygone. (For the present, this gain is taken to be positive. If it is negative, continued employment is inefficient and the parties simply go their separate ways.) Suppose bargaining enables the employee to capture a share α $(0 \leq \alpha \leq 1)$ of this gain. That will be the case for some α if bargaining takes the form of, for example, a Rubinstein (1982) alternating offers bargaining model. Then the bargained wage is

$$w^*(I, s) = w^0(s) + \alpha[R(I, s) - w^0(s) - \pi^0(I, s)]. \tag{16}$$

With $\pi^0(I,s)$ independent of the amount of the investment, the bargained wage increases with the amount of investment. The employee thus captures part of the return on the firm's investment. This is hold-up. Anticipation of hold-up affects the firm's choice of investment because the firm anticipates expected profit $E\{R(I, s) - w^*(I, s) - I\}$ from investment of I and so its profit maximizing level of investment is I^* defined by

$$E\{R'(I^*, s)\} = \frac{1}{1 - \alpha}.$$

Thus, as observed by Grout (1984), hold-up affects investment like an increase in the cost of investment by a factor of $1/(1 - \alpha)$. With decreasing marginal return on investment $(R''(I, s) < 0)$, $I^* < \hat{I}$ for any $\alpha > 0$ so, if the employee has any bargaining power at all, the firm will *under-invest*.

What drives this result is that the payoffs while bargaining, $w^0(s)$ and $\pi^0(I,s)$, do not increase as the result of the investment. Consequently, the gain from reaching agreement, $R(I, s) - w^0(s) - \pi^0(I, s)$, increases with the amount of investment. Since this gain is shared between firm and employee, the expected wage increases with the firm's investment, so the firm does not receive all the return on its investment and thus does not invest the efficient amount. Under-investment occurs even when investment increases the payoff $\pi^0(I,s)$ if it does so by less than it increases the revenue $R(I,s)$. This follows from Eq. (16) because $w^*(I,s)$ is then still increasing in I, so the employee still captures some of the return on the investment. An example is when the employee works less effectively (by, for example, "working to rule") during bargaining so that, although there is some return on the investment while bargaining continues, the full return is not reaped.

Now consider the effect of markets. Markets have a role in hold-up because, as Becker (1975) observed, whether investments are general or specific depends on how valuable they are in trade with other parties. For the discussion here, the firm's general investments are taken to be in physical capital that can be transferred to another employee, not in human capital that is retained by the employee in the event of separation.

One way in which market opportunities may enter is by increasing the payoffs $w^0(s)$ and $\pi^0(I,s)$ that the employee and the firm receive while continuing to bargain. Formally, market opportunities operate in that way under two sets of circumstances. The first is if the employee takes another job temporarily, and the firm hires another employee temporarily, during the process of negotiation, but with less good matches so that there are potential gains to continuing negotiation. For obvious reasons, such opportunities serve simply to increase what the parties can get individually if they have not yet reached agreement. The second is if, every time an agreement is delayed, there is some probability that negotiations break down irrevocably and the parties then have no choice but to take alternative market opportunities. The reasoning in this case is that the risk of breakdown reduces the expected payoff each party gets from refusing an offer made by the other because the resulting delay in reaching agreement may mean having to settle for the next best alternative. The better the market alternative, the less cost to that party in delaying agreement. Thus a better market alternative acts to reduce the cost of delay in the same way as an increase in the payoff while continuing to negotiate. For a fuller discussion, see Sutton (1986). These two interpretations have the same implications for the present analysis. I refer to this as the *no friction* case because, with the first interpretation, it applies only if temporary alternatives are readily available. Edlin and Reichelstein (1996) and Stole and Zwiebel (1996) analyze hold-up issues when market opportunities increase the payoffs from delaying agreement.

For market opportunities of this kind, hold-up is a problem only for specific investments. A fully specific investment by the firm is valuable only if the employee to whom it is specific works for the firm. It does not therefore affect $\pi^0(I,s)$ even if $\pi^0(I,s)$ is the profit from employing an alternative employee. That corresponds precisely to the analysis in the preceding section. A fully general investment, on the other hand, is just as valuable with an alternative employee. It thus increases $\pi^0(I,s)$ by just as much as it increases $R(I,s)$. (Formally, $\partial \pi^0(I,s)/\partial I = R'(I,s)$, for all I and s.) In this case it follows from Eq. (16) that $w^*(I,s)$ is in fact independent of I because a change in I does not affect the gain $[R(I,s) - w^0(s) - \pi^0(I,s)]$ that is shared between the firm and employee. Thus, even without a contract, the wage is independent of the amount of general investment and the firm invests efficiently. A partially specific investment by the firm is one that increases $\pi^0(I,s)$ but by less than $R(I,s)$. In this case, it follows from Eq. (16) that, without a contract, the wage is affected by the amount of investment, though by less than for a fully specific investment.[3]

But not all market opportunities take this first form. To replace an employee with somebody equally good, a firm will often have to incur substantial hiring costs. For an employee to move to another equally good job often involves substantial search and relocation costs. If these turnover costs are sufficiently large, it is not worth incurring them for a short period of negotiation. The firm will incur them only if it decides to replace the employee permanently, the employee only to get another job permanently. Thus,

---

[3] General investments made by the *employee* (in, for example, general training) are also not subject to hold-up in the no friction case. Because they increase $w^0(s)$ by just as much as $R(I,s)$, the wage in Eq. (16) ensures the employee receives the return from the investment.

taking up such a market opportunity effectively ends the current employment for good. I refer to this as the *turnover cost* case.[4]

Market opportunities of this kind are *outside options* in the game theory terminology. There are two formulations of outside options in the literature. In that of Shaked and Sutton (1984), one party is always able to make a final offer before the other quits for an outside option. In that of Shaked (1994), one party can make an offer to the other and, if it is turned down, quit for an outside option without waiting for a counteroffer. In the former, for reasons to be explained shortly, a party receives a payoff strictly better than its outside option only if it would have received that payoff in the absence of the outside option. In the latter, that is not necessarily the case. Thus, in a labor market context, the first formulation implies that an outside offer better than what would otherwise have been paid is at best matched by the current employer. In the second formulation, it may be more than matched. Thus there is, in principle, a way in which these two formulations may be distinguished empirically, though in practice that is complicated by the possibility of multiple equilibria in the Shaked (1994) formulation that makes it hard to come up with a tightly specified empirical test. The assumption behind the first formulation, however, seems plausible for many labor markets. In face to face negotiations, as Shaked (1994) notes, one party can typically respond with an offer before the other walks out of the door. That formulation is, in fact, implicit in most of the labor contracts literature, for example, Hall and Lazear (1984) and Harris and Holmström (1982). It has been used in the analysis of hold-up by Che and Hausch (1999), MacLeod and Malcomson (1993a) and Ramey and Watson (1996). It also provides a natural framework for the results in Hart and Moore (1988). The second formulation has not, as far as I am aware, been applied either to labor markets or to hold-up. The discussion that follows, therefore, uses the first formulation.

This type of market opportunity cannot be captured through $w^0(s)$ and $\pi^0(I,s)$ because those represent the payoffs if negotiations continue. Instead, denote the values of the outside options by $\underline{w}(s)$ for the employee and $\underline{\pi}(I,s)$ for the firm. Both may depend on s because they may be uncertain at the time investment decisions are made. The latter will depend on I if the investment is general and so generates returns even with a replacement employee. In this case, $w^0(s)$ may be the employee's utility from staying at home unpaid and working for nobody, $\pi^0(I,s)$ the firm's profit from employing nobody but still keeping the job available in case it reaches agreement with the employee. Alternatively, these payoffs may correspond to having a temporary job or employee that can be obtained without incurring the turnover cost. Whichever applies, it is assumed that $\partial \pi^0(I,s)/\partial I < R'(I,s)$ for all I and s in the turnover cost case. To ensure that incurring the turnover cost always provides better market opportunities, it is also assumed throughout discussion of the turnover cost case that $\underline{w}(s) > w^0(s)$ and $\underline{\pi}(I,s) > \pi^0(I,s)$, for all I and s.

In the turnover cost case, outside options affect the bargaining outcome as follows. The

---

[4] The turnover cost worth incurring for a temporary alternative becomes smaller as the time between successive offers in negotiation becomes shorter. In the limit, as the time between offers goes to zero, no turnover cost is worth incurring and the labels *no friction* and *turnover cost* applied to the two cases become precise descriptions.

highest wage the firm would be prepared to pay the current employee given the alternative market opportunities is $\overline{w}(I, s) = R(I, s) - \pi(I, s)$. For employment to continue, the wage has to lie between $\underline{w}(s)$ and $\overline{w}(I,s)$. Shaked and Sutton (1984) show that, if the wage would lie between $\underline{w}(s)$ and $\overline{w}(I,s)$ without the outside options, the existence of those options makes no difference. If it would otherwise be less than $\underline{w}(s)$, it is renegotiated to $\underline{w}(s)$ but no higher. If it would otherwise be greater than $\overline{w}(I,s)$, it is renegotiated to $\overline{w}(I,s)$ but no lower. If s is such that $\underline{w}(s) > \overline{w}(I, s)$, there is no wage that is acceptable to both firm and employee, so they separate. Thus $\underline{w}(s)$ and $\overline{w}(I,s)$ act as *constraints* on the wage and, for this reason, are referred to as *outside option constraints*.

The intuition behind the result is as follows. Suppose the employee is considering quitting for an outside option. Before the employee quits, the current employer can make an offer. As long as that offer is preferred by the employee to the outside option, the employee will stay. If the bargaining outcome in the absence of an outside option would have been better than the outside option, an offer of that outcome is enough to stop the employee quitting. If it would not have been, the employer need only raise the offer to match the value of the outside offer. There is no need to raise it further.

In the turnover cost case, a fully specific investment does not affect $\pi(I,s)$ because it has no value with an alternative employee. A fully general investment, on the other hand increases $\pi(I,s)$ by just as much as it increases $R(I,s)$ because it is just as valuable with an alternative employee. (Formally, for a general investment $\partial\pi(I, s)/\partial I = R'(I, s)$ for all I and s.) With a general investment $\overline{w}(I,s)$, which by definition equals $[R(I, s) - \pi(I, s)]$, is thus independent of I. A partially specific investment by the firm is one that increases $\pi(I,s)$ but by less than $R(I,s)$.

In the turnover cost case, there can be hold-up of general, as well as specific, investments. In the absence of outside options, the bilaterally bargained wage when there is no initial contract is given by $w^*(I,s)$ in Eq. (16). With outside options, that is still the wage provided it is greater than $\underline{w}(s)$ and less than $\overline{w}(I,s)$. Thus when $\pi^0(I,s)$ is unaffected by the investment (as when there is no employment during negotiations), the expected wage depends on the investment, so the firm does not invest efficiently. The essential point is that the gap between $\underline{w}(s)$ and $\overline{w}(I,s)$ gives scope for bargaining that allows general investments to affect the wage. All a firm's investments in buildings, plant and equipment except those specific to a particular match are general investments. Estimates of turnover costs were given in Table 2. Taken together these indicate the scope for hold-up of general investments.

4.2. Hold-up and employment at will

Grossman and Hart (1986) recognized that hold-up will be avoided if the parties make an arrangement that gives the investing party all the bargaining power in any negotiations that occur after the investment has been made. The reason is that if the employee has no bargaining power, α in Eq. (16) is zero. The bargained wage is then equal to $w^0(s)$ (or

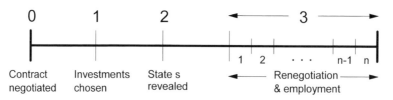

Fig. 3. Timing of events for hold-up models.

$\underline{w}(s)$ in the turnover cost case) and is thus independent of the firm's investment, so the firm invests efficiently.

That can be achieved by a contract that gives the firm the right to set the wage after making the investment and observing s but allows the employee to quit without penalty. Hall and Lazear (1984) call this a "firm sets wage" contract. It is a special case of what Hermalin and Katz (1993) call a "fill in the price" contract. Obviously, the firm then sets the lowest wage for which the employee will work ($w^0(s)$ or $\underline{w}(s)$, as the case may be). At issue is whether the employee can renegotiate the wage upwards and so capture part of the return on the firm's investment.

To analyze that issue, consider the renegotiation framework illustrated in Fig. 3. As before, both firm and employee are assumed to know everything the other knows. At stage 0, they negotiate a contract. At stage 1, investments are chosen.[5] At stage 2, all the relevant information is revealed to both parties – in particular, the employee learns how much the firm has invested and both learn the realized state s. Stage 3 consists of n days on which employment can take place and on any of which the contract may, in principle, be renegotiated.[6] Suppose a "firm sets wage" contract is agreed at stage 0 and the firm sets the wage w marginally above $w^0(s)$ (or $\underline{w}(s)$ in the turnover cost case) at the beginning of stage 3. Suppose also that this wage has not been renegotiated on the first $n - 1$ days of stage 3 and the employee tries to get a pay rise for day n by refusing to work without one. Even if employment would still be profitable at the higher wage, the firm will refuse a pay rise. It knows that the employee prefers employment at w to the alternatives for day n itself, that there can be no adverse future consequences from the employee working for w on day n because day n is the last day of employment, and thus that the employee will in fact turn up for work on day n even without a pay rise.

Suppose next the employee tries to get a pay rise at day $n - 1$. By the argument just given, both parties know that, if the wage is not renegotiated for day $n - 1$, employment

---

[5] Ramey and Watson (1996, 1997) analyze hold-up in a model in which a contract is agreed only after the investments have been made because they are concerned with the implications of hold-up that actually occurs, not with contracts to prevent it occurring.

[6] Much of the hold-up literature uses models in which trade occurs only once. Here, I use a framework that reflects the on-going nature of most employment. This difference is not important for the analytical issues discussed. It also makes no important difference if the employee works during the period the investments are being made.

will take place on day n at the wage w, whether or not employment actually takes place on day $n - 1$. Given this, the firm knows that, even if it refuses to increase the wage, the employee is better off turning up for work at wage w for day $n - 1$ than not doing so because turning up for work has no adverse consequences for the future. Thus, the firm refuses to increase the wage for day $n - 1$ too. This argument can be repeated for each day back to day 1 to establish that the wage set by the firm is not renegotiated. Because $w^0(s)$ (or $\underline{w}(s)$ in the turnover cost case) is independent of the amount the firm invests, the employee captures none of the return on the firm's investment and the firm invests efficiently. The firm may also need to offer a signing payment at stage 0 to induce the employee to accept the contract if utility of more than $Ew^0(s)$, or $E\underline{w}(s)$ in the turnover cost case, can be obtained from some other job taken at stage 0. While it is important for the formal argument that the firm sets the wage marginally above the employee's reservation wage because an indifferent employee might decide not to turn up for work on day n and thus deprive the firm of the profits from that day's employment, such marginal differences will be glossed over for simplicity in the discussion that follows.[7]

This argument assumes that $R(I, s) > w^0(s) + \pi^0(I, s)$ (or $R(I, s) > \underline{w}(s) + \underline{\pi}(I, s)$ in the turnover cost case) so that it is efficient for employment to take place at stage 3. If the state s is such that continued employment is not efficient, the parties simply separate. Since the contract imposes no severance payment, it does not matter whether the separation is a quit or a layoff. Indeed, the only enforcement required from a court is to ensure the firm pays the wage once the employee has worked.

Widely quoted in the specific investment literature is the argument in Becker (1975) that, to avoid inefficient separations destroying the value of specific investments, the costs and returns to such investments should be shared between the firm and the employee. Since specific investments in on-the-job training are assumed to increase with tenure, wages also increase with tenure. As noted in Section 2.4, the recent literature examining the effect of wages on tenure using panel data finds that the measured effect of tenure on wages is much smaller than earlier measures in the pioneering work of Becker (1975) and Mincer (1962). Ransom (1993) even finds a strongly negative tenure effect for research academics. A common interpretation is that specific investments are less important than had earlier been thought.

Becker's original insight was formalized by Hashimoto (1981) and Carmichael (1983). A crucial assumption in these models is that there is no renegotiation of the wage in response to an outside offer. Thus if there is an outside offer better than the contract wage, a separation occurs even if it is inefficient. A "firm sets wage" contract, however, ensures that separation occurs if and only if it is efficient given the specific investments already made. (This is provided the values of the alternative opportunities are known to both parties. The case in which the values of alternative opportunities are not known to both parties is discussed in Section 4.7.) It also ensures that the firm invests efficiently in both the no friction and turnover cost cases. But such a contract does not imply a positive

---

[7] See footnote 11 for discussion of the case in which n is not known in advance.

tenure effect. Indeed, it is consistent with a negative tenure effect in a cross-section of employees. To see why, suppose a number of employees, all with the same productivity to the firm, are hired at the same time but that, because they have different match qualities with outside firms, they have different values for their market alternatives, with stochastic components unobserved by the econometrician. Efficient employment implies that employees quit only if their market alternative is better than the highest wage the firm is prepared to pay. Thus those who quit (and so have zero tenure in their new job) will be those with higher positive unobserved stochastic components in their market alternatives. But since, with firms setting wages, employees are all paid wages equal to the values of their market alternatives, the measured cross-section effect of tenure on wages is negative. This result is formalized in MacLeod and Malcomson (1993b). The conclusion applies to both no friction and turnover cost cases.[8]

Contracts in which the firm is explicitly given the right to set the wage are not standard in employment. However, employment at will as interpreted by US courts has exactly the same effect. The reason is the asymmetry between employer and employee about what constitutes acceptance of a modification of terms proposed by the other. As long as the proposed modification is not retroactive and the employee is made clearly aware of its implications, an employee continuing in service is deemed to have accepted a modification proposed by the employer. In contrast, an employer who allows an employee to continue working after clearly rejecting a modification proposed by the employee is not deemed to have accepted the proposal. Thus, in negotiations for day n, whatever the wage up to that day, the firm always proposes a wage w marginally above $w^0(s)$ (or $\underline{w}(s)$ in the turnover cost case), rejects any higher counterproposal by the employee and, since the employee is better off working for the firm at w than not, the employee continues to work and so is deemed to have accepted the modification of the wage to w. In contrast, any proposal by the employee for a higher wage is rejected by the firm and, even if the firm prefers the employment to continue at the higher wage than not at all, allowing it to continue does not constitute acceptance of the employee's offer. Thus the employee's proposal does not affect the wage. Application of this argument to previous days establishes that the firm proposes a wage marginally above $w^0(s)$ (or $\underline{w}(s)$ in the turnover cost case) at the first opportunity no matter what the wage agreed at stage 0 and the employee continues to work, thus being deemed to have accepted the modified wage. The outcome is then the same as with a "firm sets wage" contract. This argument applies whether the labor market that determines $w^0(s)$ (or $\underline{w}(s)$ in the turnover cost case) is perfectly competitive, imperfectly competitive, or involves search and matching.[9]

On the US interpretation then, employment at will has the implication that the wage is always equal to the employee's reservation wage and is thus subject to the same influences

---

[8] Felli and Harris (1996) consider the case in which specific capital takes the form of acquired knowledge about an employee's aptitude for the job.

[9] Under employment at will, the employer may have to pay for a short time at the wage originally agreed. This wage can incorporate any signing payment required to induce the employee to take the job and has no effect on the argument about the efficiency of investment.

as if it were determined in a spot market. This conclusion is consistent with the legal view expressed by Rothstein et al. (1994, Section 1.4) that employment at will is "a legal device for guaranteeing to management the unilateral power to make rules and exercise discretion,... (a) prerogative contract." It thus protects the firm's investments whether market opportunities affect the default payoff $w^0(s)$ (the no friction case) or the outside option $\underline{w}(s)$ (the turnover cost case). Employment at will is thus a robust arrangement for protecting a firm's investments from hold-up under a variety of market conditions. As such, it is a sensible default rule for courts to adopt where the parties have not specified an alternative.

Even so, there are several reasons for studying other forms of contract. First, the evidence in Section 2 indicates that employment at will is by no means universal even in the US. Second, as explained in Section 2.1, employment at will does not apply in most European countries. And third, there are reasons discussed later why it may not be efficient to adopt employment at will. The next subsection analyzes a different employment arrangement, a formal *fixed wage contract* specifying a wage at the start of employment that can be renegotiated only by mutual consent.

4.3. Fixed wage contracts and renegotiation

As already shown, a contract that ensures a wage independent of the amount the firm invests ensures those investments are efficient. But it may not be enough to make a contract at stage 0 that specifies the wage in advance because, once the investment has been made and the state revealed, that wage may be renegotiated in such a way that it is no longer independent of the firm's investment.[10] With a formal employment contract, the renegotiation process is different from employment at will. As Specter and Finkin (1989, Section 3.02) put it: "An offer to modify the terms... does not constitute a repudiation of the contract. Thus a rejection of the offer merely leaves the existing terms in place". In this case then, refusal of an offer of modification by either party followed by continued employment leaves the contract unchanged. The same applies if the parties are unsure whether a court would deem the employment to be *at will* and, to avoid the possibly substantial expenses of being challenged in court, make changes only by mutual consent. Even so, renegotiation may occur. The framework illustrated in Fig. 3 can be used to show when this happens.

To start with the simplest case, return to the assumption of a purely bilateral relationship with no other potential employees for the firm and no alternative jobs for the employee. At

---

[10] A wage independent of the amount of investment is a *sufficient*, but not a *necessary*, condition for efficient investment. Edlin and Reichelstein (1996) show that, for the no friction case when the quantity traded is a continuous variable (e.g., variable hours) and not (as here) a simple choice of trading or not trading, a fixed price contract can be designed so that, even when renegotiation results in the price depending on the level of investment, the incentive to under-invest that arises when renegotiation results in hold-up is exactly counterbalanced by an incentive to over-invest resulting from legal compensation when breach occurs. By balancing these, the contract induces efficient investment. Their result holds under both specific performance and expectation damages for breach (monetary compensation that leaves the non-breaching party as well off as if the contract had been fulfilled).

stage 0 the firm and the employee make a contract specifying a wage w^c that can be renegotiated only by mutual consent. The contract specifies no penalties if either party decides to terminate the employment at any time. (Formally, the contract specifies that, if employment takes place, the wage will be w^c but leaves it up to each party to decide whether employment in fact takes place.) As long as this contract is not renegotiated at stage 3, the wage is independent of how much the firm invests, so the firm chooses the efficient level of investment.

Suppose the firm invests I and the state s that occurs is such that

$$w^0(s) < w^c < R(I, s) - \pi^0(I, s). \tag{18}$$

The left-hand inequality implies that the employee prefers employment at w^c to no employment, the right hand inequality that the firm does too. Then the wage w^c is not renegotiated as long as renegotiation requires mutual consent. The argument is essentially the same as for a contract in which the firm sets the wage except that now refusal by either party to accept an offer of modification means that the previously agreed wage still holds. Consider day n. Both parties know that the other prefers employment to continue for day n at w^c than not to continue. Thus any increase in the wage proposed by the employee for day n is rejected by the firm and any decrease in the wage proposed by the firm is rejected by the employee, in both cases in the knowledge that the other will continue the employment. Backwards repetition of this argument establishes that the wage is not renegotiated for any day.[11]

It is worth emphasizing why, if bargaining without a contract would result in a wage $w^*(I, s) < w^c$, the firm cannot simply terminate the employment unilaterally (as it is entitled to do under the contract) and start bargaining afresh for a lower wage. The formal reason is that the contract specifies a wage conditional on employment – the right to terminate employment unilaterally is not a right to terminate the contract unilaterally if the employment actually continues. This distinction between unequivocal termination of employment and use of termination as a bargaining ploy to change the terms of employment is clearly recognized under English law, as explained in Section 2.1. Under US law, if the employment is deemed not to be *at will* for any reason (such as those listed in Section 2.1), a firm that tried to change the wage in this way would be liable to a charge of breach of contract, the expense of defending itself in court, and possibly substantial damages.

The crucial difference from having no contract is that Eq. (18) ensures employment

---

[11] Formally, this is the unique subgame perfect equilibrium of the renegotiation game, see MacLeod and Malcomson (1995). The argument continues to hold if n is uncertain as long as it is known not to be infinite. There may be multiple subgame perfect equilibria if the parties think it possible that employment may last for ever, see Holden (1999). In that case, however, not all subgame perfect equilibria seem equally reasonable. MacLeod and Malcomson (1995) argue that, in the present context, it is reasonable to impose the additional criterion of *strong renegotiation proofness* due to Farrell and Maskin (1989) and show that the only subgame perfect equilibrium that satisfies this additional criterion is that identified in the text. (That equilibrium also satisfies the additional criterion when n is known to be finite.) The same applies to renegotiation of any wage that satisfies Eq. (18) with the "firm sets wage" contract discussed in Section 4.2.

takes place even if there is no renegotiation. Under the mutual consent rule, not having a contract is equivalent to having a contract that specifies $w^c = 0$. As long as $w^0(s) > 0$ (that is, the employee prefers not working to working at a zero wage), the employee is worse off with employment at $w^c = 0$ than without employment, so employment will not occur unless the "wage" is renegotiated. By enabling employment to take place, renegotiation can benefit both parties. In particular, both prefer employment at the wage $w^*(I,s)$ in Eq. (16) to no employment. Thus neither blocks renegotiation to that wage. The same applies to any contract wage w^c that lies outside the range $w^0(s)$ to $R(I, s) - \pi^0(I, s)$. In this case too, the wage is renegotiated to the level $w^*(I,s)$, so the employee captures some of the return on the firm's investment in any state in which renegotiation occurs.[12]

Now consider the effect of alternative market opportunities. In the no friction case, market opportunities merely affect the default payoffs $w^0(s)$ and $\pi^0(I,s)$, so the argument is unchanged. In the turnover cost case, market opportunities correspond to outside options $\underline{w}(s) > w^0(s)$ for the employee and $\overline{w}(I, s) < R(I, s) - \pi^0(I, s)$ for the firm. By the outside option argument of Shaked and Sutton (1984), a contract wage w^c satisfying Eq. (18) is still not renegotiated if it lies between the outside option values, that is, if $\underline{w}(s) \leq w^c \leq \overline{w}(I, s)$ for the state s that actually occurs. With $\underline{w}(s) > w^0(s)$, it might however be that $w^c < \underline{w}(s)$ in some state s even though Eq. (18) is satisfied, in which case the employee will quit unless the wage is renegotiated to at least $\underline{w}(s)$. The wage is then renegotiated to exactly $\underline{w}(s)$ and employment continues at that wage (provided it is no more than $\overline{w}(I,s)$, the maximum the firm will pay). Similarly, it may be that $w^c > \overline{w}(I, s)$ for some s even though Eq. (18) is satisfied, in which case the firm will replace the employee unless the wage is renegotiated downwards to no more than $\overline{w}(I,s)$. The wage is then renegotiated downwards to exactly $\overline{w}(I,s)$ and employment continues at that wage (provided it is no less than $\underline{w}(s)$, the minimum for which the employee will work). If s is such that $\underline{w}(s) > \overline{w}(I,s)$, there is no wage acceptable to both firm and employee, so they separate.

It follows that, if there exists a fixed wage w^c independent of the shock s that satisfies

$$w^0(s) < w^c < R(0, s) - \pi(0, s), \qquad \text{for all states } s, \tag{19}$$

and the firm and the employee specify this wage in their initial contract, condition (18) will be satisfied whatever state s occurs and however much the firm invests. Then the wage w^c

---

[12] As modeled here, whenever the wage is renegotiated because Eq. (18) is not satisfied, it is renegotiated to the level $w^*(I,s)$ in Eq. (16) which is independent of the contract wage. In their analyses of contract data for Canadian unions, Card (1990a,b) and Abowd and Lemieux (1993) suggest that this characteristic does not hold because wage settlements depend on the previous contract wage, though it should be emphasized that this is for union, not individual, wage negotiations. That characteristic, however, applies in the present framework if the default payoffs in the absence of agreement, $w^0(s)$ and $\pi^0(I,s)$, depend on the current wage. An example is when, as in Moene (1988), Cramton and Tracy (1992) and Holden (1994), employees use some form of "go slow", "hold-out" or "work to rule" (during which they are paid something) as an alternative bargaining ploy to not working at all because then the last agreed wage affects their payoff while negotiating a new wage. To incorporate this formally requires the framework to be extended so that working is not just an all or nothing decision but has a variable dimension (hours of work or effort on the job). To incorporate union bargaining requires addition of an employment dimension to negotiation.

is never renegotiated in the no friction case and is only ever renegotiated to the values of the outside options in the turnover cost case. In the former, the wage is then clearly independent of the amount the firm invests, hold-up does not occur and the firm invests efficiently. Thus, provided there exists a wage w^c that satisfies Eq. (19), a fixed wage contract can overcome the hold-up problem in the no friction case.

For Eq. (19) to hold in the no friction case, it must always be more efficient for the parties to continue the employment than to separate. Moreover, there must be a wage at which both parties would individually want to continue the employment whatever state occurs. As a result, the wage would never change. That is not a particularly plausible scenario in practice. Thus, in the no friction case, a fixed wage contract is unlikely to do much to protect specific investments and is unnecessary to protect general investments, which are always chosen efficiently.

It is different in the turnover cost case. Then the left hand inequality in Eq. (19) requires only that the employee would always work at wage w^c if no other job were available. The right hand inequality likewise requires only that the firm would always retain the employee at w^c if there were no other potential employees. In a multiperiod context with repeated shocks, the states for which the condition is required to hold are only those that may occur in the next period, not those that might occur at some date far in the future. That this is the case for many everyday shocks seems plausible enough. It is consistent with separations occurring as the result of a match no longer being efficient – in the turnover cost case, separation is efficient when $R(I,s) < \underline{w}(s) + \underline{\pi}(I,s)$ which is not inconsistent with Eq. (19). Moreover, renegotiation of the wage to the values of the outside options may still occur, though the actual negotiation required is minimal – the firm simply offers a pay rise when it knows the employee would otherwise quit and presents the employee with the offer of a pay cut when the alternative is being laid off. The rest of the time, both parties know that negotiations would change nothing, so there is no point in actually negotiating. How such renegotiation affects the efficiency of investments is the subject of the next subsection.

A fixed wage contract is no more difficult for courts to enforce than a "firm sets wage" contract. Each party has the right to terminate the employment straightaway so specific performance is not an issue and there are no liquidated damages to be enforced. All courts are required to do is to ensure the firm pays the agreed wage once the employee has worked.

4.4. Fixed wage contracts, turnover costs and hold-up

4.4.1. General investments

General investments can be protected by a contract that gives the firm the right to set the wage. They can also be protected by a fixed wage contract that satisfies Eq. (19). However, as noted above, Eq. (19) is likely to be at best rarely satisfied in the no friction case, so the explanation here is concerned the turnover cost case. Recall that the highest wage the firm would pay to keep the employee, $\overline{w}(I,s)$, is independent of the amount of general investments and can thus be written $\overline{w}(s)$. The essential point is that, because the investment is just as valuable with another employee, the amount of investment does not affect the highest wage the firm would pay its current employee before switching to another. Suppose the parties make a contract at stage 0 specifying a fixed wage w^c that satisfies Eq. (19). The analysis in Section 4.3 has shown that this wage will not be renegotiated if $\underline{w}(s) \leq w^c \leq \overline{w}(s)$. In that case the wage is clearly independent of the firm's investment. If $w^c < \underline{w}(s)$, the contract wage is renegotiated upwards to $\underline{w}(s)$ and employment continues at this wage provided that is efficient. But, since $\underline{w}(s)$ is independent of the investment, such a renegotiation will not result in the actual wage being affected by the level of investment. Similarly, if $w^c > \overline{w}(s)$, the contract wage is renegotiated downwards to $\overline{w}(s)$ and employment continues at this wage provided that is efficient. But, since $\overline{w}(s)$ is independent of the investment, such a renegotiation will also not result in the actual wage being affected by the level of investment. Thus the wage stays at w^c or is renegotiated to either $\underline{w}(s)$ or $\overline{w}(s)$. In each case, the wage is independent of the level of general investment, so the firm chooses the efficient level. Even if Eq. (19) is not satisfied for every state s, the inefficiency from hold-up may not be large. The effect of hold-up on investment depends on the *probability* that Eq. (19) will not be satisfied, as anticipated when the investment is made. Thus the loss will be small if that probability is sufficiently small.

The use of fixed wage contracts to induce efficient general investments has implications for the dynamics of wages. For a multiperiod extension of the model with new investments and a new shock s each period, MacLeod and Malcomson (1993a) show that it is in many cases sufficient for the contract wage w^c to be the wage actually paid in the previous period. This can be seen intuitively from Eq. (19). The wage w_{t-1} actually paid at $t-1$ must satisfy Eq. (19) for the s realized at $t-1$ and the cumulative investment to that date because otherwise it would have been renegotiated. Thus, as long as the terms in Eq. (19) are not too sensitive to changes in s from one period to the next, much of the time w_{t-1} will satisfy Eq. (19) at t. (In the multiperiod context, "zero investment" should be interpreted as "no investment in this period".) Then not only does the originally agreed wage remain unchanged until renegotiated but, once renegotiated, the new wage also remains in force until it is, in turn, renegotiated.

The properties of wages with such a contract are then identical to those illustrated in Fig. 2 for contracts to insure employees with fixed hours of work that are not legally enforceable. The wage remains unchanged unless one of the parties can get a better deal elsewhere. If one of them can, the wage is renegotiated by just enough to prevent separation occurring, until such time as it is efficient to separate. As a result, the wage demonstrates some, but not complete, rigidity in the face of shocks that affect wages elsewhere in the market, as well as in the face of firm specific shocks that affect productivity. This model thus fits with the evidence from Beaudry and DiNardo (1991) discussed in Section 2.3 that the best labor market conditions since the start of the job have a strongly significant effect on a person's current wage, whereas current labor market conditions and those prevailing at the start of the job have a smaller impact, just as well as the insurance model. It also has the same implications that different firms may pay different wages even when their employees have the same outside option values if these employees were hired at different dates. It thus naturally generates inter-firm wage differentials. But, as with risk sharing contracts that are not legally enforceable, the differentials between two firms disappear at any time at which the outside option constraints of their employees are both binding. A further similarity with insurance contracts is that, in a perfectly competitive hiring market, the wage for new hires adjusts to equate supply and demand and is thus more flexible than wages of existing employees, consistent with the evidence from Bils (1985) and Solon et al. (1994) discussed above. Again, in contrast with the menu cost approach to wage stickiness, in Fig. 2 the wage changes that occur may be large or small – they are just enough to give either the firm or the employee exactly the same payoff as the outside option.

There are, however, implications different from those of contracts to insure employees. First, there may be times at which the employee's outside option constraint is binding at t but the wage the firm would have to pay to induce the employee to stay is too high to satisfy Eq. (19) for $t + 1$. This might occur if the lowest anticipated value of $R(0,s)$ is substantially below the current value. One response to this situation is for the firm to pay part of the remuneration for period t in the form of a bonus that does not become incorporated into the contract wage. It would thus be natural to expect bonuses to be paid at some times, particularly in firms with highly volatile revenues. When employees are not risk averse, there is no efficiency loss from the resulting fluctuations in wages.

Second, a wage fixed in money terms is just as good at protecting general investments as one fixed in real terms. Thus, if there is any cost or inconvenience (however small) to writing a contract that indexes the wage, contracting will be in nominal terms and the wage in Fig. 2 will be the nominal wage.[13] Then the nominal wage stays unchanged until renegotiation is triggered by one of the outside option constraints binding, which is consistent with the spike at zero in the distribution of nominal wage increases discussed in Section 2.2. This also suggests a way to make sense of the statements by employers reported in Blinder and Choi (1990) that nominal wage cuts are different from real wage cuts that arise because the wage is not adjusted for inflation. A nominal wage cut involves renegotiating an existing agreement. To do that, *both* parties must agree to it. A real wage cut arising because the wage is not adjusted for inflation merely involves not agreeing to renegotiate to a new contract that maintains the real wage. To use the terminology of Blinder and Choi (1990), "not giving" *is* (legally at least) different from "taking away" because the latter involves *re*negotiating an existing agreement.

With nominal contracting, the model is also consistent with the finding of Card and Hyslop (1997) that nominal rigidities reduce the distribution of nominal wage changes more just below the spike at zero than just above it. With money wages in the hiring market rising most of the time, the wages of those hired previously will (as in Fig. 2) most of the time be closer to the employee's outside option than to the firm's. Thus a downward

---

[13] As noted in Section 4.3, renegotiation costs are trivial when both parties know the values of both outside options. Private information about those values is discussed later in Section 4.7.

shock of a given magnitude to money wages for new hires that reduces the upper boundary in Fig. 2 (because it reduces the cost of a replacement employee) reduces the wages of fewer employees on average than are increased by an upward shock of the same magnitude that raises the lower boundary.

If the value of an employee's outside option increases steadily with inflation, a contract with a fixed nominal wage will eventually result in the employee's outside option constraint binding no matter what the original wage. Thereafter, the wage will be negotiated up steadily with inflation. The outside option value, however, reflects not only inflation, particularly for jobs in which the quality of the match is important, because it will go up when suitable vacancies arise elsewhere and down when they are filled, thus following a spiky path over time. The wage will be bid up when a good alternative opportunity comes along (the employer matching the value of the outside offer), but once that offer has been declined, another good opportunity may not occur for some time.[14] Thus, even with continuing inflation, there may be substantial periods when no upward renegotiation occurs.

In the market as a whole, of course, the high rate of job creation documented for the US by Davis et al. (1996) (see the chapter by Davis and Haltiwanger) implies a substantial proportion of employees in the early stages of a contract and thus for whom the outside option value may not have caught up with their contract wage. Moreover, with contracts started at different dates, a small increase in demand increases the outside option value for employees but results in renegotiation only of contracts for which the employees' outside option constraints were previously (close to) binding. In aggregate this will appear as a partial adjustment to a new equilibrium following a shock. With a sequence of such shocks, contract renegotiations are staggered as in Gray (1976) and Taylor (1979), though with the time between renegotiations for any match determined not exogenously, but endogenously by an outside option constraint becoming binding. Thus the framework has the potential for providing a micro-theoretic basis for staggered contract models and for the apparent slow adjustment of average wages to aggregate shocks.

The discussion so far in this section applies to general investments when there are turnover costs. General investments are clearly widespread. All a firm's investments in buildings, plant and equipment that are not specific to a particular match come into this category. Figures for firms' turnover costs were presented in Table 2. (As already noted, training costs are turnover costs in the sense used here only when they are essential. Otherwise the subsequent analysis of specific investments applies.) The implications of these figures for the gap between the upper and lower bounds on the wage in Fig. 2 depend on how long it is before a replacement employee would earn as much as the current employee, that is, how long it is before a binding outside option enables the replacement employee to obtain as high a wage as the current employee. To illustrate, suppose the replacement's wage remained unchanged for one year and then jumped to the wage that

---

[14] In such circumstances, employees may actively search for alternative jobs to raise their outside option values. If search involves effort that detracts from productivity, as in Mortensen (1978), the firm may increase pay above the current value of the outside option to deter search.

the current employee would have earned. Then, ignoring discounting, the figures in Table 2 for turnover costs as a percentage of first year earnings correspond to the maximum percentage wage differential that could result from those costs. If this illustration is at all a useful guide, the figures in Table 2 are not inconsistent with quite substantial wage differentials. Moreover, that table lists only turnover costs incurred by firms. For a complete picture, those incurred by employees in obtaining new jobs must be added. The use of fixed wage contracts to protect general investments thus seems a potentially promising way to explain many of the empirical features of wages discussed in Section 2.

4.4.2. Specific investments

With specific investments and turnover costs, investment may be inefficient for two reasons. One is renegotiation that results in the wage being renegotiated as in Eq. (16) to share the gains from employment. That is the same as with general investments. The other was identified by Hart and Moore (1988). Although separation occurs only when efficient, renegotiation to prevent an inefficient separation when an outside option constraint binds may allow one party to capture part of the returns to specific investments made by the other. Anticipation of that means that the original investment may not be efficient. Put more formally, with a fully specific investment, the profit $\underline{\pi}(I,s)$ the firm receives if it takes up an alternative market opportunity does not depend on the level of investment. Suppose renegotiation of a contract wage were to occur because, although continuing the employment is efficient in the state s that occurs, the contract wage is so high that paying it would result in profit less than $\underline{\pi}(I,s)$. Then the renegotiation would lead to a reduction in the wage to $\overline{w}(I, s) = R(I, s) - \underline{\pi}(I, s)$. But, with $\underline{\pi}(I,s)$ independent of the amount of investment, $\overline{w}(I,s)$ increases with the investment. Thus the wage paid if this state occurs is not independent of the amount of investment and the firm does not in general choose the efficient level.[15]

This inefficiency arises only with renegotiation that occurs when the firm's outside option is better than employment at the contract wage. In contrast, if renegotiation occurs only because the employee's outside option is better than the contract wage, there is no inefficiency. The reason is that then the wage is renegotiated to the value of the employee's outside option $\underline{w}(s)$ and, because the investment is specific (and thus, even if in training for the employee, not valuable in any alternative employment), $\underline{w}(s)$ is independent of the amount of investment the firm undertakes.

A fixed wage contract that satisfies Eq. (19) is renegotiated only when one of the outside

---

[15] The same argument applies to investments that are *partially specific* in the sense that, although they increase $\underline{\pi}(I,s)$, they do so by less than they increase $R(I,s)$. In this case $\overline{w}(I,s)$ still increases as investment increases. An investment is partially specific in this sense even if it is general by Becker's definition but there is a turnover cost in the form of the time it takes for the firm to hire a replacement employee, as in the matching models of Blanchard and Diamond (1989), Pissarides (1985, 1987), and Mortensen and Pissarides (1994). The reason is that during the time the job is vacant the firm does not earn a return on its investment, so the investment increases the profit from an outside opportunity less than from continuing the current match. Acemoglu (1996) and Acemoglu and Shimer (1997) study the impact of matching frictions on hold-up.

option constraints is not satisfied, so it avoids the first type of hold-up. If in addition the contract wage is sufficiently low that the firm's outside option constraint never binds, the wage is not renegotiated downwards, so it also avoids the second type of hold-up and the firm invests efficiently. The practical implication is that the wage is only renegotiated upwards and never downwards. If there is inflation, that is more likely if the contract wage is specified in nominal terms than in real terms, which provides a positive reason for not indexing the wage. If inflation is not significant, rising real wages in the economy as a whole may be sufficient. But even if not, the extent of the inefficiency depends on the *probability* of downward renegotiation anticipated by the firm at the time the investment is made. The loss is therefore small if downward renegotiation is sufficiently unlikely. With fixed wage contracts, all the characteristics of wages discussed in connection with general investments and illustrated in Fig. 2 carry over to the case of specific investments, though one would then expect downward renegotiation of nominal wages to be relatively rare. This would not be inconsistent with the pattern of nominal wage changes in Fig. 1 if those employees receiving nominal wage reductions are primarily those in jobs without specific investments. For a discussion of other types of contracts that can protect a firm's specific investments when downward renegotiation cannot be largely avoided, see Malcomson (1997).

4.4.3. Employment

What are the implications of fixed wage contracts for employment? In the current framework, renegotiation ensures that, whatever the form of contract, employment continues if and only if it is privately efficient in the sense that the sum of the payoffs to the parties exceeds the sum of their outside option values. McLaughlin (1991) investigates the efficiency of quits and layoffs for the US. He finds that the natural interpretation under fixed wage contracts of quits as efficient separations that occur when the employee's outside option rises above the current wage, and of layoffs as efficient separations that occur when the highest wage the firm is prepared to pay falls below the current wage, is consistent with many of the empirical regularities that distinguish quits from layoffs. He also tests for the efficiency of separations. Efficient separations occur only when the highest wage the firm is prepared to pay falls below the lowest wage the employee is prepared to accept and so are independent of the current wage. He finds this is not the case but argues that the result is not robust to model specification.

Renegotiation continues to ensure efficient separations even where, as in many European countries, firms are required to make redundancy payments, seek approval from government agencies, etc., before they can lay off employees. The reason is that, when the employee and firm can jointly do better by ending the employment than by continuing it, there is always some deal that makes separation mutually beneficial. This is most apparent in the case of redundancy payments. Such payments are pure transfers between firm and employee and so cannot affect the conditions under which separation is efficient for the two parties. If the firm must make a redundancy payment, the wage at which it is better for it to end the employment is higher than if no redundancy payment is required. But if the wage is not high enough to make it worth the firm paying the redundancy payment and yet it is still efficient to separate, the employee will be prepared to accept voluntary severance for a payment that is smaller than the full redundancy payment and that the firm *is* prepared to pay. This conclusion contrasts with those of Bentolila and Bertola (1990) and Bertola (1990) because they are concerned with wage-setting institutions (e.g., trade unions) that do not allow individual wage bargaining. See the chapter by Bertola for further discussion of that case.

Provided a contract ensures efficient investments, hold-up provides no reason for inefficiency in the market for new hires. The analysis of redundancy provisions in Lazear (1990) also applies: provided potential employees are free to negotiate starting wages, government imposed redundancy payments or delays on severance can be compensated for perfectly by a lower initial wage and thus make no difference to hiring as long as employees and firms have the same effective discount rates. (*Effective* in this context means after taking account of any borrowing and saving the parties make in financial markets.) Inefficiencies may result from an imperfect hiring market, from search externalities, and so on but that is not related to hold-up.

A point to be emphasized in hold-up models is that, as with insurance models, it is not in general appropriate to think of employment being determined by the wage negotiation process and the labor demand curve. When firm and employee are equally well informed, wage renegotiation ensures that employment continues whenever it is efficient, no matter what the contract may say about the wage. The role of the contract is to ensure efficient investments and thus increase productivity and employment. Where wage stickiness is observed as the result of fixed wage contracts, it is only because no wage change is required to ensure efficient employment. The situation is, of course, more complicated if the firm does not know the value of the employee's outside option or the employee does not know the value of the firm's. The issues to which that gives rise are taken up in Section 4.7.

4.5. Investments by employees

Employees, as well as firms, make investments that enhance the productivity of employment. General investments by the employee are fully reflected in the value of the employee's alternative market opportunities. They are thus not subject to hold-up in the no friction case. They are protected from hold-up even in the turnover cost case by either employment at will (because the wage is then always equal to the employee's next best alternative) or, for essentially the same reasons as with the firm's general investments, a fixed wage contract that satisfies Eq. (19).

With specific investments by only the employee, the roles of the firm and employee in the discussion of specific investments above are reversed – investments are efficient if the firm is not able to increase its expected profits as a result of the employee's investment. The employee's reservation wage does not reflect the return on a specific investment, so renegotiation to that in some state results in the firm capturing the return on the investment in that state. If, therefore, employee specific investments are valuable, it is important to move away from employment at will. The inappropriateness of employment at will in these circumstances has been implicitly recognized by US courts in accepting as grounds for employment not to be *at will* that, with the employer's knowledge, the employee has taken some action (*additional consideration* in legal terminology) that would be insufficiently rewarded if employment were for only a short term, see Specter and Finkin (1989, Section 2.11).

Efficient specific investment by the employee can be achieved by reversing the roles in a contract that generates efficient specific investments by the firm. An example is a contract that gives the employee the right to set the wage (which will not be renegotiated by an argument similar to that in Section 4.2). But this may require an up-front payment from the employee to induce the firm to accept the contract because the employee always chooses the highest wage the firm is prepared to pay *ex post*. If employees have limited access to capital, such payments may be problematic. An alternative explored by Kahn and Huberman (1988) and by Waldman (1990) is an *up-or-out* contract of the type used in US law firms to govern promotion to partnerships and in US universities to govern tenure decisions. With an up-or-out contract, the firm commits to either promote the employee (to, for example, full partner or tenured professor) or terminate the employment after a fixed period of time. The prospect of promotion provides the incentive for the employee to invest but the wage for promoted employees must be set so that it is more profitable for the firm to promote than to terminate the employee if and only if the employee makes the specific investment. This requirement may prevent the parties achieving fully efficient investments.[16] Moreover, terminating employment is inefficient if some employees turn out to be of too low ability to be profitably employed at the promoted wage despite having made the specific investment. Then both parties would like to renegotiate to avoid the termination. An alternative mechanism suggested by Prendergast (1993) has these employees work in a less demanding job at a lower wage. The firm can be induced to promote employees who invest and turn out to be of high ability because they have a comparative advantage in the more demanding job. These types of contract are discussed more fully in the chapter by Gibbons and Waldman.

Such mechanisms avoid the problems of contracts that require employees to make payments to firms. They also give rise to positive tenure effects. However, with none of these contracts is there an obvious reason for wages to display the damped response to shocks or the nominal rigidities discussed in Section 2.

4.6. Investments by both firms and employees

Employment at will ensures efficient general investments by both firm and employee. When, however, both firm and employee make specific investments, achieving efficient levels of those investments typically requires a more complicated contract. For reasons

---

[16] Kahn and Huberman (1988) assume the employee's investment is not observed by the firm and productivity not observed by the employee, but what is crucial for their conclusion is that neither is verifiable in court.

just explained, a contract that gives the firm the right to set the wage results in no specific investments by the employee, although the firm's investment will be efficient. Conversely, a contract in which the employee sets the wage results in no specific investments by the firm, though the employee's investment will be efficient. A fixed wage contract with an appropriately chosen wage that satisfies Eq. (19) can typically induce both to make some specific investment because each captures the return on their investments until the wage is renegotiated. However, neither invests efficiently if there is a positive probability that their outside option will bind. A fixed wage contract is, nevertheless, an improvement over either of the preceding contracts if there are diminishing returns to the investments such that it is more efficient to have both invest a little than for one to invest efficiently and the other not at all. It is also an improvement over having no contract at all if the absence of renegotiation in some states allows both parties a higher proportion of the expected returns on their own investments than if they share the gains from employment with the wage in Eq. (16).

The contracts discussed in the literature that induce efficient specific investments by both parties rely on at least one of: (1) no renegotiation; (2) payments conditioned on more than just the employee working for the firm; and (3) the specific performance breach remedy. In the first category is the adaptation of the Crémer and Riordan (1985) mechanism by Rogerson (1992). The problem here is that it is hard to see what can stop renegotiation in labor markets when both parties gain from it. Certainly courts will not. In the second category are contracts that have payments contingent on which party refuses to trade if trade does not occur and thus rely on courts being able to verify this. Hermalin and Katz (1993) use a contract in which one party (say the seller) sets the price and the buyer's payment depends both on the price set and on whether the buyer accepts delivery. Nöldeke and Schmidt (1995) use a contract that gives the seller the right to decide whether to trade at a contracted price and makes the amount the buyer must pay contingent on the seller's decision. The problem with applying such contracts to employment is that, as noted in Section 2.1, it may not in practice be easy to verify whether an employee chose to stay away from work or was turned away by the employer. Also in the second category are contracts for the turnover cost case conditioned on the values of the outside options (by, for example, indexing to prices or to wages paid by other firms). Hashimoto and Yu (1980) investigate contracts with the wage conditioned on proxy indicators correlated with productivity and the employee's outside option that are designed to minimize the loss from binding outside options but do not analyze the impact of renegotiation. MacLeod and Malcomson (1993a) give conditions under which an indexed contract can avoid renegotiation, and thus achieve efficient specific investments by both parties, without the need either for breach penalties or for courts to observe which party refused to trade if no trade occurs. This case seems to fit the longterm coal contracts studied by Joskow (1990) but the explicit use of such indicators in employment seems rare.

In the third category (namely, contracts that rely on the specific performance breach remedy), Chung (1991) and Aghion et al. (1994) show that, even if courts cannot observe which party refused to trade, a contract that structures renegotiation so that all the bargaining power is assigned to one party can achieve efficient investments by both if courts will, when requested by either party, enforce specific performance of a default outcome specified in the contract. Edlin and Reichelstein (1996) show a similar result using a fixed price contract under specific performance. But, as explained in Section 2.1, there are good reasons why specific performance is rarely used in the employment context.

None of the contracts discussed here for inducing efficient specific investments by both parties thus seems unproblematic when applied to labor markets. This suggests a powerful case for, wherever possible, *all* the specific investments to be carried out by either the firm or the employee, which may explain why firms make specific investments that one might otherwise expect employees to make (e.g., paying the relocation costs involved in switching jobs). Failing that, a fixed wage contract that induces at least some investment by both parties may be better than a contract that results in one party not investing at all.

4.7. Private information

This discussion of contracts to protect investments has so far assumed firm and employee both have the same information. However, in some cases at least, a firm will not know the value of the employee's outside option $\underline{w}(s)$, if only because it does not know how much the employee enjoys this job relative to others. Similarly, an employee may not know the value of the firm's outside option $\underline{\pi}(I,s)$. Little is known about hold-up and renegotiation under these circumstances.[17] However, it seems likely that, if the firm does not know exactly how low the wage can go before the employee quits, and the employee how high it can go before the firm hires a replacement, renegotiation can no longer guarantee that separations occur only when efficient. Thus the effect of contract choice on the efficiency of separation discussed in Carmichael (1983) and in Hall and Lazear (1984) must be considered alongside its effect on the efficiency of investments.

For the case with turnover costs (but investment levels exogenous) and no renegotiation, Hall and Lazear (1984) consider the impact on separations of three types of contract: (1) a "firm sets wage" contract (equivalent, as argued above, to employment at will); (2) an "employee sets wage" contract; and (3) a fixed wage contract. Consider the first of these when the firm knows enough about s to know everything at stage 3 except $\underline{w}(s)$. Let $Q(w)$ denote the firm's assessment of the probability the employee will quit if offered w. (This probability depends on what the firm knows about the state s but, for notational simplicity, that is not made explicit.) It is reasonable to suppose $Q'(w) \leq 0$. Given what the firm knows about s, its expected profit for given w is

$$[R(I, s) - w][1 - Q(w)] + \underline{\pi}(I, s)Q(w), \tag{20}$$

since profit if the employee stays is $R(I, s) - w$, an event the firm believes will happen with

---

[17] Tirole (1986) considers private information about the amount of investment in the context of government procurement, Hermalin and Katz (1993) private information about the amount of investments and the value of the current match. The latter relies on specific performance which, as explained above, is rarely used in employment cases.

probability $1 - Q(w)$, and profit if the employee quits is $\pi(I,s)$, an event it believes will happen with probability $Q(w)$. The firm chooses the contract wage to maximize this expected profit, provided that wage gives expected profit no lower than its own outside option. Differentiation of Eq. (20) with respect to w establishes that the profit maximizing wage $\underline{w}^*(I,s)$ must satisfy the first order condition

$$[R(I, s) - \underline{w}^*(I, s) - \pi(I, s)]Q'[\underline{w}^*(I, s)] + \{1 - Q[\underline{w}^*(I, s)]\} = 0. \tag{21}$$

For the discussion that follows, I assume $\underline{w}^*(I,s)$ is sufficiently high that $Q(\cdot) < 1$ and $Q'(\cdot) < 0$. Then Eq. (21) implies $R(I, s) - \underline{w}^*(I, s) > \pi(I, s)$, so $\underline{w}^*(I,s)$ is less than $\overline{w}(I, s) \equiv R(I, s) - \pi(I, s)$, the highest wage the firm is prepared to pay to continue the employment. Thus, if the employee were to quit for an outside offer $\underline{w}(s)$ between $\underline{w}^*(I,s)$ and $\overline{w}(I,s)$, the separation would be inefficient. There is, therefore, always some probability of an inefficient quit by the employee. This is illustrated in Fig. 4, which plots values of $\overline{w}(I,s)$, the highest wage the firm is prepared to pay to continue employment, on the horizontal axis and values of $\underline{w}(s)$, the lowest wage the employee is prepared to accept, on the vertical. For points above the 45 degree line, $\underline{w}(s) > \overline{w}(I, s)$ so separation is efficient. For any realized value of $\overline{w}(I,s)$ such as that illustrated, the firm sets a wage $\underline{w}^*(I, s) < \overline{w}(I, s)$ and the employee quits if $\underline{w}^*(I, s) < \underline{w}(s)$. This is efficient if $\underline{w}(s) > \overline{w}(I, s)$ but inefficient if $\underline{w}(s) < \overline{w}(I, s)$.

For a contract in which the employee sets the wage, one can derive in a corresponding way the wage $\overline{w}^*(I, s)$ the employee would set and show that $\overline{w}^*(I, s) > \underline{w}(s)$. Then, if the value of the firm's outside option is between $\underline{w}(s)$ and $\overline{w}^*(I, s)$, the firm lays off the

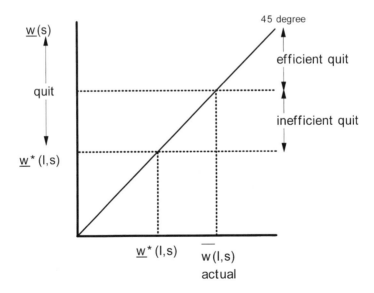

Fig. 4. Inefficient quits with employment at will.

employee even though a layoff is inefficient. A fixed wage contract with the wage fixed between $\underline{w}^*(I,s)$ and $\overline{w}^*(I, s)$ has a lower probability of an inefficient quit than a "firm sets wage" contract, but typically at the expense of some probability of inefficient layoff, and a lower probability of an inefficient layoff than an "employee sets wage" contract, but typically at the expense of some probability of an inefficient quit. The relative efficiency of the three types of contract depends on the expected losses from these inefficient separations. In particular, employment at will may not be the best choice.

Now consider the case with the level of investment chosen by the firm but still without renegotiation. A straightforward argument suggests that it chooses general investments efficiently under all three types of contract. In the fixed wage case, the argument is simply that the wage is independent of the amount of investment, so the firm captures all the return on a general investment when no separation takes place and, by definition, it also captures the return on a general investment when a separation occurs. Consider next the "firm sets wage" case. With general investments, $R(I, s) - \pi(I, s)$ is independent of I and it then follows from Eq. (21) that $\underline{w}^*(I,s)$ is also independent of I, so the same argument applies as in the fixed wage case. A corresponding argument applies in the "employee sets wage" case. The conclusion is that general investments are chosen efficiently by the firm under all three contracts and the choice between them depends, as in Hall and Lazear (1984), only on how well the contracts avoid the losses from inefficient separations. The same does not apply to specific investments. With a specific investment, $\pi(I,s)$ is independent of I and thus, from Eq. (21), $\underline{w}^*(I,s)$ depends on I. When the employee's outside option is private information, therefore, a "firm sets wage" contract (or US style employment at will), as well as resulting in inefficient separations, can no longer be guaranteed to generate efficient specific investments by the firm. A corresponding argument applies when the employee sets the wage.

The analysis in Malcomson (1997) indicates that these conclusions survive certain limited renegotiation. They concern, however, only three types of contract. What happens with a richer set of contracts and more extensive renegotiation has yet to be investigated.

4.8. Conclusions on contracts to protect investments

This section has assessed the implications of the recent hold-up literature for labor markets. That literature is concerned with contracts to protect the return from investments when there are turnover costs or specific investments and when contracts are both incomplete and renegotiable. There is direct evidence that turnover costs are significant in labor markets. Renegotiation is always possible if both parties agree to it and is a standard feature of labor markets – wage changes for those hired on other than fixed term and union contracts are formally modifications of an existing agreement.

An important conclusion for labor markets is that, in the presence of turnover costs, there can be hold-up of general, as well as specific, investments. Since general investments include all a firm's investments in buildings, plant and equipment not specific to a particular employee, that greatly widens the range of circumstances in which hold-up is potentially important. A firm's investments, both general and specific, can be protected by a contract that gives it the right to set the wage after the investment has been made and the employee the right to quit without penalty. *Employment at will* has the same effect under the interpretation of US courts that an employee's continuing to work by itself constitutes acceptance of a modification of terms proposed by the employer. Thus this long-established principle of employment in the US is an effective way to protect a firm's investments. However, it need not result in a positive measured tenure effect on wages, so one cannot in general conclude anything about the extent of specific investments from observations on the wage tenure profile.

Other jurisdictions do not interpret an employee's continuing at work as acceptance of a modification of terms if it is done "under protest". Moreover, even for the US there is substantial evidence, both from legal cases and from data on wage changes, that employment at will is by no means universal. In such circumstances, both parties must agree to changes in terms of employment. It then turns out that, under appropriate conditions, fixed nominal wage contracts that are renegotiated by mutual consent can do a good job of protecting general investments and ensuring efficient employment provided both firm and employee have a reasonably good idea of the value of the alternative opportunities available to the other. No breach penalties or severance payments are required for this – either party can terminate the employment without penalty at any time. Such contracts are consistent with nominal wage stickiness and the damped response of wages to shocks that has been discussed extensively in the business cycle literature. In view of the extent of general investments, it is a striking conclusion that contracts consistent with these characteristics of wages serve to protect those investments when there are turnover costs.

Fixed wage contracts may even do a reasonable job of protecting specific investments by the firm if nominal wage cuts are unlikely to occur and they have the advantage over employment at will that they can induce employees, as well as firms, to make specific investments. But they cannot typically induce both firms and employees to make specific investments at the efficient level – that would require the wage never to be renegotiated either upwards or downwards. However, the contracts discussed in the literature that achieve efficient investments by both parties require either no renegotiation, or payments conditional on additional information, or courts to require specific performance in the event of breach. Since there are problems with each of these in labor markets, there are good reasons to avoid having both parties make specific investments. But if that is not possible, a fixed wage contract that induces at least some specific investment by both parties may be better than a contract that results in one party making no specific investment or than no contract at all.

The existing literature on hold-up has focussed mainly on cases in which the firm knows how low the wage can go before the employee quits and the employee how high it can go before the firm hires a replacement. Initial investigations indicate that, when that is not the case, fixed wage contracts, contracts in which the firm sets the wage, and contracts in which the employee sets the wage all result in efficient general investments but, for the reasons discussed by Hall and Lazear (1984), all generally result in inefficient separations.

Thus the choice between these types of contract rests on how well they can reduce the losses from inefficient separation. With specific investments, there is in some cases a conflict between contracts that result in more efficient investments and contracts that result in more efficient separations but no robust general conclusions have been found.

There are obviously many aspects of wages and employment not covered in the models discussed in this section (variable hours of work, for example). But, given the importance of investments, turnover costs and renegotiation, models of hold-up look promising candidates for providing rigorous theoretical foundations for at least some of the observed behavior of wages. These models are, however, too new for the empirical studies drawn on in the discussion to have been designed with them in mind and so those empirical studies have not tested their predictions at all rigorously.

5. Contracts to motivate employees

The design of contracts to motivate employees to take appropriate actions has been central to the contracting literature. Hart and Holmström (1987) have surveyed the theoretical literature on principal-agent contracts. Gibbons (1997) reviews the applicability of this literature to labor markets, the chapter by Murphy its applicability to executive pay. A major focus recently has been with an issue long recognized in the management literature on performance pay, namely that the objective measures of performance available are often such poor measures of the performance firms really care about that use of formal performance related pay schemes can be counterproductive. Baker (1992, p. 608), for example, quotes from Lawler (1990) that:

> the literature on incentive plans is full of vivid descriptions of the counterproductive behaviors that... incentive plans produce. One of the first books I read in compensation provided story after story about how employees were outsmarting and defeating piece-rate systems (White, 1955). Indeed, as I read this classic book, I marvelled at the ingenuity of the worker.... It was clear that the systems were motivating behavior – but unfortunately they were motivating the *wrong* behavior.

Modelling such behavior requires moving away from an approach in which there are verifiable measures of performance (e.g., profit from the employment) that capture all aspects of performance with which the firm is concerned, even if they are only noisy signals of the effort of the employee to achieve that performance. Lazear (1995, Chapter 8) discusses the many problems associated with evaluating performance. In the *multitask agency* approach of Holmstrom and Milgrom (1991), the employee's job consists of a complex of different tasks, performance in some of which is more easily verifiable than in others. For example, quantity of output may be easily measured but quality not. Giving incentives for quantity can then have an adverse effect on quality. In Baker (1992), verifiable performance is a biased measure of actual performance with the degree of bias observed by the employee but not the firm. The implications of such measurement problems for formal incentive pay schemes are discussed in the chapter by Gibbons and Waldman. However, in some cases there simply are no verifiable measures of performance. Even when there are, basing formal performance pay on them may be too counterproductive to be worthwhile – Holmstrom and Milgrom (1991) give examples in which the adverse effect on the non-measured aspects outweigh the beneficial effects on the measured ones. Yet in such circumstances, a manager or supervisor often has additional subjective information about performance that is not readily verifiable. The issue of concern in this section is how that information can be used to motivate performance.

5.1. Motivation with unverifiable performance: framework

I start with the case in which no measures of an employee's performance are verifiable. To focus on the implications of non-verifiability, rather than inaccuracy of observation or risk sharing, consider a risk neutral employee whose performance can be observed perfectly by the firm but cannot be verified in court. The employee's utility in period t from earning W_t with effort e_t is $W_t - c(e_t)$, where $c(e_t)$ is the cost of effort (the monetary value of its disutility). The minimum level of effort consistent with, for example, turning up for work is $e_t = 0$. Disutility increases with effort at an increasing rate ($c'(\cdot) > 0$ and $c''(\cdot) > 0$) and is normalized so that $c(0) = 0$. The firm's profit in period t from this employment is $e_t - W_t$. The firm monitors the employee's performance in each period with probability p. If it does so, it observes performance perfectly but is unable to document that, or the output e_t, in court. Both employee and firm discount the future with the same discount factor δ. In the spirit of the substantial turnover of jobs in the economy (see the chapter by Davis and Haltiwanger), jobs become unprofitable at the rate $1 - \alpha$ per period for reasons exogenous to the relationship between firm and employee. Unemployment provides utility of $u_t > 0$ for period t. Since zero effort produces zero output, employment would not be worthwhile unless $e_t > 0$.

Bull (1987) and MacLeod and Malcomson (1989) observed that, in addition to a basic wage w_t independent of performance, the employee's earnings at t can in principle include a bonus element b_t conditional on the employee not being caught shirking. Thus $W_t = w_t + b_t$. Because performance is unverifiable, this bonus payment cannot be enforced at law but it may still be in the firm's interest to pay it as promised. Bonus payments of this type are widely used in practice. For example, in the 1990 Workplace Industrial Relations Survey for the UK, 34% of employees were recorded as receiving some form of *merit pay*, defined as payments "which depended on a subjective judgement by a supervisor or manager of the individual's performance" (Millward et al., 1992). Eccles and Crane (1988) describe the use of subjectively determined bonuses for traders in investment banks.

The timing of events for period t is indicated in Fig. 5. At the beginning of each period, matching occurs between unmatched firms and employees. Employees then decide the level of effort and, after any monitoring, the firm decides whether to pay the agreed bonus.

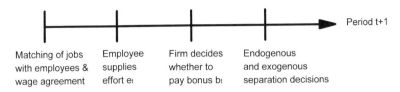

Fig. 5. Timing of events for motivation models.

Finally in the period, separations may occur either because jobs become unprofitable for exogenous reasons or because one or other party decides to end the match.

If the employee and the firm agree on effort e_t and bonus b_t for period t and each sticks to their side of the agreement, the employee's lifetime utility from t on for a match started at τ is

$$U_t = w_t + b_t - c(e_t) + \delta EU_{t+1} \qquad \text{for all } t \geq \tau, \tag{22}$$

where

$$EU_{t+1} = \alpha U_{t+1} + (1 - \alpha)\bar{U}_{t+1} \tag{23}$$

is the expected utility from $t + 1$ on given that the match finishes at the end of period t with probability $1 - \alpha$ because the job has becomes unprofitable and $\bar{U}_{t+1}$ denotes the expected future utility if a separation occurs for this reason. If, on the other hand, the employee shirks (that is, performs below the agreed effort), this is undetected with probability $(1 - p)$ and everything continues as if no shirking had occurred with the employee receiving subsequent expected utility $b_t + \delta EU_{t+1}$. Shirking is detected with probability p, but the worst that can happen is that the employee is fired for shirking (or quits if the firm would otherwise impose a worse penalty) without payment of the bonus. Let U_{t+1}^0 denote the employee's expected future utility from $t + 1$ on if fired for shirking at the end of period t. Then the employee will certainly shirk by setting $e_t = 0$ unless

$$U_t \geq w_t + (1 - p)(b_t + \delta EU_{t+1}) + p\delta U_{t+1}^0, \qquad \text{for all } t \geq \tau. \tag{24}$$

If other potential employers do not know the reason why an applicant's previous job came to an end, then $U_{t+1}^0 = \bar{U}_{t+1}$ but that may not always be the case. Substitution for U_t from Eq. (22) and re-arrangement allows Eq. (24) to be written as the *no shirking condition*

$$E\{\text{future gains to employee} \mid t\} \equiv \delta(EU_{t+1} - U_{t+1}^0) \geq \frac{c(e_t)}{p} - b_t, \qquad \text{for all } t \geq \tau. \tag{25}$$

For the employee to be prepared to continue in the job, the participation condition

$$U_t \geq \bar{U}_t, \qquad \text{for all } t \geq \tau, \tag{26}$$

must also be satisfied. The analysis thus far follows the spirit of Becker and Stigler (1974).

5.2. The Shapiro–Stiglitz model

The best known model within this framework is that of Shapiro and Stiglitz (1984). That model uses the following additional assumptions (the *Shapiro–Stiglitz assumptions*):

1. no bonuses: $b_t = 0$, for all t;
2. effort choices restricted to working, $e_t = 1$, and shirking, $e_t = 0$ (with, for simplicity, $c(1)$ denoted by $c > 0$);
3. anonymous market: $U_t^0 = \bar{U}_t$, for all t;
4. stationarity: $U_t = U$, $\bar{U}_t = \bar{U}$ and constant numbers of employees and jobs for all t.

The anonymous market assumption is plausible where differences between employees that are important for the job are readily apparent and acquiring information about past employment history is costly. Even where employers would like to find out information, it may not be easy for them to do so. In his interviews with (mostly) Connecticut firms, Bewley (1997, Chapter 17, p. 36) found that 69% of the 48 employers with whom the issue was discussed reported that it was difficult to get information from former employers. Reasons given included legal problems arising from saying something negative.

Under the Shapiro–Stiglitz assumptions, the no shirking condition (25) with (23) used to substitute for EU_{t+1} simplifies to

$$\delta\alpha(U - \bar{U}) \geq \frac{c}{p}. \tag{27}$$

Since $c > 0$, this can hold only if $U > \bar{U}$.[18] The implication is that the utility U of those whose jobs continue is strictly greater than the utility $\bar{U}$ of those whose jobs come to an end. Since firms offer newly hired employees the same lifetime utility as continuing ones, that can be the case only if some of those whose jobs come to an end are unable to obtain another straightaway. Thus, there has to be some unemployment and firms pay newly hired employees an efficiency wage above the market clearing level.

The equilibrium employment level is determined as follows. Let L denote the (fixed) number of workers and J the (endogenous) number of jobs. In a stationary equilibrium, $(1 - \alpha)J$ jobs are created each period to replace those that become unprofitable for exogenous reasons. The workers seeking these jobs consist of $L - J$ who were unemployed in the previous period plus $(1 - \alpha)J$ who have just lost their jobs because these have become unprofitable, a total of $L - J + (1 - \alpha)J = L - \alpha J$. Thus the matching probability m of obtaining a job in any one period is

$$m = \frac{(1 - \alpha)J}{L - \alpha J} = \frac{1 - \alpha}{(L/J) - \alpha} \tag{28}$$

and the expected future utility of a worker looking for a job is

$$\bar{U} = mU + (1 - m)(u + \delta\bar{U}), \tag{29}$$

---

[18] In a discrete time model with $\delta\alpha < 1$, this conclusion applies even if $p = 1$.

where $u > 0$ is utility from one period of unemployment. Use of Eqs. (28), (29) and the expression for U in Eq. (22) allows the no shirking condition (27) to be written

$$w \geq u + \frac{c}{p\delta\alpha}\left[1 - \delta\alpha(1 - p) + \frac{1 - \alpha}{(L/J) - 1}\right].\tag{30}$$

This is illustrated in Fig. 6, together with a zero profit condition derived from $\bar{\Pi} = k$, where k is the once-off capital cost of creating a job. Following Shapiro and Stiglitz (1984), the zero profit condition is shown as downward sloping because of aggregate diminishing returns (s is a decreasing function of total employment). The no shirking condition is asymptotic to $J/L = 1$ because employees always shirk if they can get another equally good job straightaway and cuts the vertical axis above $u + c$. Shapiro and Stiglitz (1984) assume firms pay the lowest wage consistent with this condition, so in equilibrium it holds with equality and the unique such equilibrium is at point A in Fig. 6.

Clearly firms would make greater profits if they could motivate employees without paying a wage above the market clearing level. Since, as is clear from the form of the no shirking condition (25), the incentive not to shirk depends only on future earnings, firms could lower the first period basic wage w_τ for employees hired at τ below that paid subsequently to reduce the utility from acquiring a job to the market clearing level. Combined with a bonus, this can still be consistent with stationary utility U and a stationary wage w. For p sufficiently small, however, it may require $w_\tau < 0$, which is equivalent to requiring employees to post a performance bond. If employees do not have access to capital to make such payments, an alternative is to use delayed payments of the type

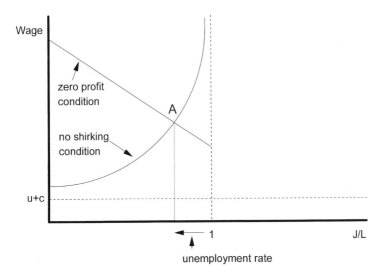

Fig. 6. Efficiency wage equilibrium.

discussed by Lazear (1979, 1981) so that $w_\tau < w_{\tau+1} < w_{\tau+2}$, and so on. However, as Akerlof and Katz (1989) show, this may not be sufficient to reduce the utility of acquiring a job to the market clearing level without $w_\tau < 0$ if p is sufficiently small.

There are, however, several reasons for doubting whether employees' difficulty in raising money to pay bonds is actually a reason for paying efficiency wages. First, as Baker et al. (1988, p. 613) note, it is "inconsistent with commonly observed franchise fees that can run into hundreds of thousands of dollars for jobs such as managing a hamburger stand." Rebitzer and Taylor (1995) argue that associates in law firms receive substantial rents on hiring despite posting performance bonds that seem unlikely to exhaust their capacity to pay. Second, if limits on feasibility of bonds were indeed a reason for paying efficiency wages, the starting wage w_τ for matches started at τ would be set at the lowest possible level, that is, at subsistence. (The same applies to any alternative job with no monitoring problem in which an employee might be hired initially at a wage less than marginal product in order to build up an implicit bond, as suggested by Murphy and Topel (1990).) But the folklore about high paying jobs is that they offer attractive wages and fringe benefits right from the start, not just for older employees and this view is supported by the findings of Krueger and Summers (1988) that the wage premiums across industries for younger and older employees are highly positively correlated, as are wage premiums for employees with one year or less of job tenure and those with more than 10 years.

Difficulties employees may have raising funds for performance bonds are not, however, the only concern with schemes of this sort. In all of them, expected future wages for an employee must at some point exceed expected future marginal productivity, so the firm can make a short term gain by replacing the employee by a newly hired one. It may not, of course, do that if it is concerned for its reputation. But a firm's reputation is worth only as much as the additional profits it generates in the future. A full analysis must, as in Bull (1987) and MacLeod and Malcomson (1989), take account of that.

5.3. Self-enforcing agreements

If the employee puts in agreed effort e_t and the firm pays the agreed bonus b_t, the firm's expected future profit from t on for a match started at τ is

$$\Pi_t = se_t - w_t - b_t + \delta E\Pi_{t+1}, \qquad \text{for all } t \geq \tau, \tag{31}$$

where $E\Pi_{t+1} = \alpha\Pi_{t+1}$ is its expected profit from $t + 1$ on because the job remains profitable with probability α and closes down (with no future profits) with probability $1 - \alpha$. If the firm cheats on a promised bonus or future wage payment, the worst that can happen is that there is a separation – if an employee kept on was expected to exact even more in the way of retribution, the firm would always dismiss that employee first. Let Π_{t+1}^0 denote the firm's expected future profits if that happens. Then the firm would certainly cheat on a promised bonus unless the expected future profit from paying and having the match continue, Π_t, is at least as great as that from not paying (having already received the product se_t and being unable to escape paying the wage w_t) and having the match end (which results in expected future profit $\delta\alpha\Pi_{t+1}^0$). The firm's profit must therefore satisfy

$$\Pi_t \geq se_t - w_t + \delta\alpha\Pi_{t+1}^0, \qquad \text{for all } t \geq \tau. \tag{32}$$

Substitution for Π_t from Eq. (31) and re-arrangement allows this to be written as the *incentive compatibility condition for the firm*

$$E\{\text{future gains to firm} \mid t\} \equiv \delta(E\Pi_{t+1} - \alpha\Pi_{t+1}^0) \geq b_t, \qquad \text{for all } t \geq \tau. \tag{33}$$

For the firm to be prepared to continue the job, the participation condition

$$\Pi_t \geq \bar{\Pi}_t, \qquad \text{for all } t \geq \tau, \tag{34}$$

must also be satisfied. Addition of the *no shirking condition* for the employee (25) to the incentive compatibility condition for the firm (33) gives the following necessary condition for overall incentive compatibility:

$$E\{\text{future gains to match} \mid t\} \equiv \delta(EU_{t+1} - U_{t+1}^0 + E\Pi_{t+1} - \alpha\Pi_{t+1}^0) \geq \frac{c(e_t)}{p},$$

$$\text{for all } t \geq \tau. \tag{35}$$

It follows directly from their derivations that (35), (26) and (34) are necessary conditions for payoffs to be supported by a self-enforcing agreement. MacLeod and Malcomson (1989) show that they are also jointly sufficient for payoffs to be supported as subgame perfect equilibria. The formal argument is a standard game-theoretic one. Its essence is as follows. When (35) is satisfied, it is clearly possible to find a value of the bonus b_t that satisfies both (25) and (33). If there were only one period, employment would be a one-shot game with a Prisoners' Dilemma type structure. The firm would not pay a bonus even if the employee did not shirk because a bonus would be costly and have no influence on the future. In view of that, the employee would always choose zero effort. But with zero effort, employment cannot be mutually beneficial and so it would not take place even though both parties would be better off with the employee working and the firm compensating the employee for the disutility of effort. When the game is repeated indefinitely, a "Folk Theorem" result applies. As the discount factor δ increases, the condition (35) becomes less stringent. Provided there is some value of δ at which it is satisfied, any payoffs that satisfy the participation conditions (26) and (34) can be supported for any higher δ by a self-enforcing agreement with the following strategies. If either side deviates from the agreement, the employee puts in zero effort thereafter, or quits if that is better, while the firm never again pays a bonus, or fires the employee if that is better. As already noted, with zero effort employment cannot be mutually beneficial. Thus, it is always better for one side to end the employment than let it continue with zero effort in the future. Hence, if either cheats at t, the continuation equilibrium has the match end and the payoffs to the employee and the firm from that point on are U_{t+1}^0 and Π_{t+1}^0 respectively. But if these are to be the payoffs if either cheats, it is clear from (25) and (33) that both do better by not cheating for an appropriately chosen bonus b_t.[19],[20]

Equality in condition (35) defines the lowest value of δ for which all feasible individually rational payoffs are subgame perfect equilibria for given effort. In the case in which effort is either 0 or 1, for any lower δ the only subgame perfect equilibrium is for a match not to be formed. Note that this condition is independent of the wage and bonus payments for the match – since both firm and employee are risk neutral, these payments cancel from the sum $EU_{t+1} + E\Pi_{t+1}$. Thus whether or not it is satisfied for given δ depends only on the agreed effort and things that are exogenous to the individual firm and employee, specifically the productivity s, the disutility of effort $c(\cdot)$, the probability shirking is detected p, and the payoffs in the event of separation as the result of one party cheating U_{t+1}^0 and Π_{t+1}^0. The result is not restricted to stationary contracts or payoffs. Deferred payment profiles of the type discussed by Lazear (1979) and by Akerlof and Katz (1989) are all covered by the formulation.[21]

Evidence on whether firms and employees actually behave in ways consistent with the argument are discussed in Section 5.6. Here I concentrate on the implications if they do. Consider the case of an anonymous market, which implies $U_t^0 = \bar{U}_t$ and $\Pi_t^0 = \bar{\Pi}_t$ for all t. Note that $EU_t < U_t$ and $E\Pi_t < \Pi_t$ for all t because of the probability that a match will come to an end for exogenous reasons. Since $c(e_t) > 0$ for any effort level at which employment is mutually beneficial, Eq. (35) implies that it is not possible for both employee and firm to be indifferent between their current agreement and what they would receive if they were to seek alternative matches in the spot market. Then, as with insurance, turnover costs and specific investments, there is a gap between the lowest pay the employee will accept and the highest the firm is prepared to offer to continue the employment, a gap just like that illustrated in Fig. 2. However, in the present case, the model has no prediction about the path of pay within that gap – as long as Eq. (35) is satisfied, pay can move anywhere within the outside option constraints. In particular, there is no necessity for the employee to be paid a wage such that $U_t > \bar{U}_t$ as in the Shapiro–Stiglitz case (though employees' utility may not be able to fall as low as $\bar{U}_t$ if p is

---

[19] MacLeod and Malcomson (1993c) show that similar conditions apply to the continuous time case used originally in Shapiro and Stiglitz (1984).

[20] As written, Eq. (35) can be satisfied only if there is some probability that the match will continue at $t + 1$, so there cannot be a date t known with certainty to be the last (because, for example, the employee is to retire). Empirically, however, it is a robust finding in experiments with games of this type that players behave in the earlier stages as if the game will continue for ever even though it is in fact finite, see Roth (1995, Section III.A.1). Moreover, Crémer (1986) and Kandori (1992) show that, even in theory, incentive compatibility conditions of this type can be satisfied with finitely-lived agents if successive generations overlap and acquire information about the play of the preceding generation (as when younger employees in a firm observe the performance and reward of those about to retire).

[21] The probability p that shirking is detected is exogenous in the above formulation. If reducing p saves costs, it is obviously efficient to reduce it until the incentive compatibility condition (35) holds with equality. However, unlike in the formulation of Dickens et al. (1989) in which firms are assumed never to cheat, it is not possible to reduce it further without violating that condition.

sufficiently low that this would require $w_t < 0$ and if employees are unable to finance performance bonds). However, if $U_t = \bar{U}_t$, then Eq. (35) implies that $\Pi_t > \bar{\Pi}_t$, so firms are receiving supernormal profits. Thus either the firm or the employee must receive a rent from continued employment. Similar conclusions apply to non-anonymous markets whenever satisfying Eq. (35) requires $U_t + \Pi_t > \bar{U}_t + \bar{\Pi}_t$.

Although condition (35) requires that there is a gain to continuing a match only once started, it can also have implications for the start of the match. As already noted, that condition depends only on the agreed effort and things exogenous to the match. Thus, if there is a strictly positive gain at t to *continuing* a match started before t, there may also be an effort level at which there is a strictly positive gain to *forming* a match at t over what the parties would receive if they did not form the match. That is, there may be a gap between the lowest pay the employee is prepared to accept and the highest the firm is prepared to offer in order to get the match started. The above result implies that any such gain can go to the firm or to the employee, or be divided between them in any proportions, so it may be that $\Pi_t > \bar{\Pi}_t$, $U_t > \bar{U}_t$, or both. Of course, with variable effort, the parties could reduce any such gain by choosing a lower effort for the initial period without affecting the left-hand side of Eq. (35), which depends on payoffs only in the future. However, they can do strictly better if they can reach agreement on dividing the gains from higher effort.

In the Shapiro–Stiglitz case, the gain to continued employment required to satisfy Eq. (35) is generated by involuntary unemployment – employees are better off keeping their current job than losing it simply because they may not find another straightaway. But there are alternative ways to generate this rent. First, it could equally well be generated by unfilled vacancies, with firms better off keeping than losing their current employee because they may not find another straightaway and hence $\Pi_t > \bar{\Pi}_t$. Second, if there are turnover costs, specific investments or matching frictions, as in Ramey and Watson (1997) who use a condition similar to Eq. (35) to study cyclical effects, it will automatically be the case that $EU_t > \bar{U}_t$ and $E\Pi_t > \bar{\Pi}_t$ and if those are sufficiently large they may by themselves be enough to provide the necessary gains. Third, if being fired for shirking results in a loss of reputation with other potential employers, then $\bar{U}_t > U_t^0$. Similarly, if having an employee quit because a promised bonus has not been paid results in loss of reputation for the firm, then $\bar{\Pi}_t > \Pi_t^0$. If these reputation effects are sufficiently strong, Eq. (35) may be satisfied even with $U_t = \bar{U}_t$ and $\Pi_t = \bar{\Pi}_t$ for all t. Finally, it may be possible for firms or employees to commit themselves in ways that relax the condition Eq. (35).

If turnover costs, specific investments and matching frictions are sufficient to ensure that Eq. (35) is satisfied, providing motivation need impose no additional constraints on the outcomes discussed earlier except for choosing a contract such that both Eqs. (25) and (33) are satisfied. In particular, it is not inconsistent with starting wages being set to clear a competitive hiring market. Here I discuss the other possibilities. I start with the possibility of unfilled vacancies substituting for involuntary unemployment in anonymous markets.

5.4. Equilibrium in anonymous markets

Consider, following MacLeod and Malcomson (1998), the Shapiro–Stiglitz assumptions except for allowing payment of bonuses. In an anonymous market, $U^0 = \bar{U}$ and $\Pi^0 = \bar{\Pi}$. The incentive compatibility conditions (25), (33) and (35) then reduce to

$$E\{\text{future gains to employee}\} \equiv \delta\alpha(U - \bar{U}) \geq \frac{c}{p} - b, \tag{36}$$

$$E\{\text{future gains to firm}\} \equiv \delta\alpha(\Pi - \bar{\Pi}) \geq b, \tag{37}$$

$$E\{\text{future gains to match}\} \equiv \delta\alpha(U - \bar{U} + \Pi - \bar{\Pi}) \geq \frac{c}{p}, \tag{38}$$

Employment N is the lesser of the number of jobs and the number of workers, that is $N = \min\{J, L\}$. If all workers are employed ($N = L$), an employee whose job ends can find another straightaway. Thus

$$N = L \text{ implies } \bar{U} = U. \tag{39}$$

Similarly, if all jobs are filled ($N = J$), a vacant job can always be filled straightaway. Thus

$$N = J \text{ implies } \bar{\Pi} = \Pi. \tag{40}$$

Free entry for new jobs implies $\bar{\Pi} = k$, where k is the once-off capital cost of creating a new job. It follows immediately from these conditions that it is not possible to have an equilibrium with $J = L$ because that would require $\bar{U} = U$, $\bar{\Pi} = \Pi$ which is inconsistent with Eq. (38).

Consider therefore the possibility of equilibrium with fewer jobs than workers ($N = J < L$). Condition (40) then implies $\bar{\Pi} = \Pi$. Condition (38) in turn implies $\delta\alpha(U - \bar{U}) \geq c/p$, exactly the no shirking condition (27) for the Shapiro–Stiglitz case. This results in an efficiency wage outcome just like in the Shapiro–Stiglitz case except for one thing. Since the no shirking condition is an inequality and we know that all outcomes satisfying both it and the participation constraints are equilibria, all points on the zero profit line above the no shirking line in Fig. 6 are equilibria. Once one analyses formally the reason why wages are not reduced despite excess supply of labor in an efficiency wage equilibrium, it turns out that there is a whole set of equilibria, not a unique equilibrium. Among these equilibria, employment will be highest at that identified by Shapiro and Stiglitz (point A in Fig. 6). The other equilibria have higher wages. However, sustaining any efficiency wage equilibrium (including that corresponding to point A) requires a mechanism to prevent wages falling. The mechanism discussed here can also prevent wages falling to the efficiency wage equilibrium with the highest level of employment.

It is worth emphasizing that these efficiency wage equilibria are not simply the result of the assumption of stationary payoffs. If firms were able to pay newly hired employees a lower wage than previously hired employees, they would make more profits by dismissing current employees and replacing them with new hires. If current employees anticipate this, they will shirk in the previous period and, anticipating that, firms would not hire them in the first place. To sustain employment, it is essential that there is some mechanism to prevent wages of new hires falling despite excess supply of labor. A notion of a "fair" wage below which employees do not trust a firm to stick to its side of any agreement would suffice for this, see MacLeod and Malcomson (1998).

We need also to consider the possibility of equilibrium with fewer workers than jobs ($N = L < J$). Condition (39) then implies $\bar{U} = U$. Condition (36) thus implies $b \geq c/p$, so there must be some form of bonus or performance pay. Moreover, Eq. (38) implies $\delta\alpha(\bar{\Pi} - \Pi) \geq c/p$, so firms with filled jobs get strictly positive profits even though there are unfilled vacancies. For given total pay, the value of $\bar{\Pi}$ is determined by the probability of filling a vacancy that depends on the ratio of vacancies to jobs in a way similar to the determination of $\bar{U}$ in Eq. (28) for the Shapiro–Stiglitz model. The resulting incentive compatibility condition for the firm is represented by the *no cheating condition* in Fig. 7. The left-hand side of that figure simply reproduces Fig. 6. The no cheating condition is asymptotic to the vertical line $J/L = 1$ because a firm will always cheat on a bonus if it can get another worker straightaway. It is asymptotic to the horizontal line at which pay becomes so large it is worth cheating on a bonus even if there are so many vacant jobs that the probability of hiring another employee is zero. Pay must lie below this line to ensure future profits sufficiently high to prevent firms cheating on the bonus. The zero profit condition continues to the right of $J/L = 1$ (though, because employment is constant at L and there are thus no further diminishing returns, it need no longer slope downwards if there is no cost to creating vacancies). Equilibrium must lie on this line for

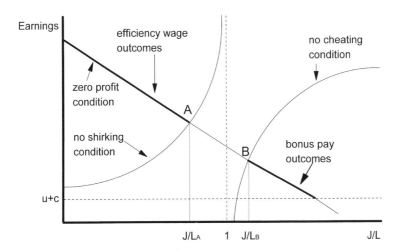

Fig. 7. Efficiency wages and performance pay.

firms exactly to replace those jobs that become unprofitable. Thus, there exist bonus pay equilibria provided the zero profit line does not slope downwards so steeply that the point B corresponds to earnings below $u + c$, the lowest that satisfies the employee's participation condition. Moreover, if such equilibria exist there are typically a multiplicity of them, as in Fig. 7, because any point on the zero profit line and below the no cheating condition is an equilibrium. If there is a cost to creating vacancies, then the equilibrium at point B Pareto dominates the other bonus pay equilibria because wages are higher and equilibrium profits are always zero. However, there is no mechanism within the model that ensures the market settles at point B.

Equilibria with bonus or performance pay thus mirror efficiency wage equilibria. Efficiency wage equilibria have employees receiving wages above the market clearing level that are sustained by involuntary unemployment. Performance pay equilibria have jobs receiving above market clearing profits that are sustained by unfilled vacancies. In an anonymous market, it is simply not possible to have equilibria in which employees do not receive efficiency wages and firms do not receive supernormal profits, or in which there are neither unemployed workers nor unfilled vacancies. Note that performance pay equilibria require a mechanism to prevent wages being bid up despite excess demand for employees in a way precisely analogous to efficiency wage equilibria requiring a mechanism to prevent wages being bid down despite excess supply of employees.

The main conclusions from this discussion are as follows. Once one models the process that prevents wages being bid down despite excess supply of labor in an efficiency wage equilibrium, there turn out to be multiple efficiency wage equilibria. Moreover, provided diminishing returns are not too strong and the capital cost of creating jobs not too high, there also exist performance pay equilibria in which all workers are employed, there are unfilled vacancies, and filled jobs receive supernormal profits. Obviously, employment is higher in performance pay equilibria and, if diminishing returns are not too strong, so also is output. Whether output net of capital costs is higher depends on the capital cost k of creating new jobs.

It is, however, important to remember that these conclusions have been derived for anonymous markets in which turnover costs, specific investments and matching frictions are not by themselves sufficient to ensure that condition Eq. (35) is automatically satisfied. In the next subsection, I consider the power of reputations when markets are not anonymous. I also consider the possibility of firms and employees making commitments that reduce the need for strictly positive gains to continuing a match to ensure incentive compatibility.

5.5. Reputations and commitment

If agents learn the past employment histories of potential partners, it may be that losing one's job as the result of insufficient effort, or losing one's employee as the result of not paying a promised bonus, results in future opportunities worse than when a match terminates for other reasons. Then $U_t^0 < \bar{U}_t$ and $\Pi_t^0 < \bar{\Pi}_t$. The most extreme case is that in which no potential partner ever trusts such an agent again, so employees fired for shirking remain unemployed for ever and jobs made vacant because an employee was cheated of a bonus remain unfilled for ever. In this case, with u denoting (as before) the utility from one period of unemployment, $U_t^0 = u/(1 - \delta)$ and $\Pi_t^0 = 0$. Then the incentive compatibility condition with continuously variable effort Eq. (35) becomes

$$\delta\left(EU_{t+1} + E\Pi_{t+1} - \frac{u}{1 - \delta}\right) \geq \frac{c(e_t)}{p}, \qquad \text{for all } t \geq \tau. \tag{41}$$

By the result given above, any effort e_t satisfying this condition, and for which the participation conditions (26) and (34) can be satisfied, can be sustained as part of a self-enforcing agreement. Since in equilibrium neither party cheats on such an agreement, there is no need for actual unemployment or unfilled vacancies.

It may, however, be implausible that an employee once fired for shirking is never employed again, particularly when employees are in fact all equally productive. If there is some probability of getting another job at date $t + \tau$ in the future, then U_t^0 depends on $U_{t+\tau}$. The position of firms losing employees because of cheating may be similar, so that Π_t^0 depends on $\Pi_{t+\tau}$. This has two consequences. First, it is no longer possible to sustain all the effort levels satisfied by Eq. (41) and consistent with the participation conditions. Second, there may, as in the previous section, need to be unemployment or unfilled vacancies to maintain incentive compatibility. It is perhaps more plausible that longterm loss is sustained in markets in which the employment histories of prospective employees and employers provide valuable information about employee characteristics or match quality. Then losing a job may be taken as a signal that the person is not well suited to that level or type of job and losing an employee be taken as a signal that the job is not well suited to that type of employee as in Strand (1987) and Flinn (1997), with implications for promotion discussed in MacLeod and Malcomson (1988). This issue is taken up in the chapter by Gibbons and Waldman. In interpreting the empirical evidence discussed later, it is important to remember that the consequences of shirking for an employee may be felt via the impact on the assessment of the employee's type, with adverse implications for promotions and layoffs in the future.

Even in their strongest form represented in Eq. (41), reputations may not be able to achieve efficient effort in every period. Efficient effort maximizes $se - c(e)$ and so is given by $\hat{e}$ that satisfies

$$s = c'(\hat{e}), \tag{42}$$

which is the same in every period. Suppose for simplicity that $p = \alpha = 1$. (This is not crucial for the conclusions that follow but simplifies the algebraic representation.) Then use of Eqs. (22) and (31) in Eq. (41) with the same effort in every period allows that expression to be written

$$\frac{1}{1-\delta}[se - c(e) - u] \geq \frac{c(e)}{\delta} \qquad (43)$$

or

$$se - \frac{c(e)}{\delta} \geq u. \qquad (44)$$

Efficient effort $\hat{e}$ can be sustained only if it satisfies Eq. (44). Where it does not, employment may still be able to take place at lower levels of effort since the effort that maximizes the left-hand side of Eq. (44) is given by $e*$ that satisfies $s = c'(e*)/\delta$, which is less than $\hat{e}$.

If the parties can credibly commit themselves to certain types of payment, they may be able to improve on an inefficient outcome. A possibility discussed in Lazear and Rosen (1981) and Malcomson (1984, 1986) is a tournament in which a firm with multiple employees commits itself to total prize money of b_t per employee, to be distributed according to subjectively assessed performance. Since the firm then has to pay b_t per employee to somebody regardless of individual performance, the condition (33) for the firm not to cheat is replaced by

$$\delta\left(E\Pi_{t+1} - \alpha\Pi_{t+1}^0\right) \geq 0, \qquad \text{for all } t \geq \tau, \qquad (45)$$

and thus the overall incentive compatibility condition Eq. (35) is replaced by

$$\delta\left(EU_{t+1} + E\Pi_{t+1} - U_{t+1}^0 - \alpha\Pi_{t+1}^0\right) \geq \frac{c(e_t)}{p} - b_t, \qquad \text{for all } t \geq \tau. \qquad (46)$$

A prize per employee of $b_t \geq c(e_t)/p$ for all t is then sufficient to ensure incentive compatibility of effort level e_t even with $U_t = \bar{U}_t = U_t^0$ and $\Pi_t = \bar{\Pi}_t = \Pi_t^0$ for all t as long as there are gains from employment. In principle, there is no need for the reward to go to another employee if one employee shirks – any third party would do. However, although commitment to a tournament prevents the firm escaping from paying bonuses to somebody, it leaves it open to collusion by employees to exert low effort and raises issues of industrial politics discussed in Lazear (1995, Chapter 3). Tournaments are also open to influence activities on the part of employees of the type discussed by Milgrom (1988). Once employees have put in effort, it makes no difference to this period's incentives how the firm allocates the prizes, so there is a temptation to allocate them to employees who offer favors or bribes, see Fairburn and Malcomson (1994). This is an example of the general problem analyzed in Eswaran and Kotwal (1984) of using third parties to break budget balance in contracts. A firm's concern for its long run reputation may stop the firm's owners succumbing to influence activities but a manager who has to implement its personnel policies may not have the same concern for that reputation as the firm's owners and thus indulge in favoritism or accept favors. Some of the consequences are explored in Fairburn and Malcomson (1995) and Prendergast and Topel (1996). See also, Manove (1997). Tournaments are discussed more fully in the chapter by Gibbons and Waldman.

Another possibility for improving on an inefficient outcome is to supplement the non-enforceable bonus with enforceable performance pay based on any verifiable, even though potentially biased, measures of performance that are available. Suppose, following Baker (1992), there is a verifiable measure $x_t = \mu_t e_t$, with $\mu_t > 0$ the realization of a random variable that is unverifiable but observed by the employee before choosing e_t. Basing performance pay on this measure alone distorts incentives – with a legally enforceable piece rate element of βx_t (with $\beta > 0$) added to the basic wage, actual effort depends on μ_t even though efficient effort does not. Suppose however, along the lines of Baker et al. (1994a), the firm commits itself to paying the enforceable piece rate βx_t in addition to the non-enforceable bonus b_t.[22] (I ignore the possibility that b_t could now depend on x_t.) Since the firm then has to pay βx_t in any case, the condition (33) for the firm not to cheat on the bonus is unaffected. However, even a cheating employee will now put in effort $\tilde{e}(\beta\mu_t)$ defined by $c'[\tilde{e}(\beta\mu_t)] = \beta\mu_t$. Then the incentive compatibility condition for the employee corresponding to Eq. (25) is

$$\delta\left(EU_{t+1} - U_{t+1}^0\right) \geq \frac{c(e_t) - c[\tilde{e}(\beta\mu_t)] - \beta\mu_t[e_t - \tilde{e}(\beta\mu_t)]}{p} - b_t, \qquad \text{for all } t \geq \tau, \quad (47)$$

and the overall incentive compatibility condition corresponding to Eq. (35)

$$\delta\left(EU_{t+1} + E\Pi_{t+1} - U_{t+1}^0 - \alpha\Pi_{t+1}^0\right) \geq \frac{c(e_t) - c[\tilde{e}(\beta\mu_t)] - \beta\mu_t[e_t - \tilde{e}(\beta\mu_t)]}{p},$$

$$\text{for all } t \geq \tau. \quad (48)$$

For any $e_t > \tilde{e}(\beta\mu_t)$, the right-hand side of Eq. (48) is smaller than that of Eq. (35), so a higher effort can be sustained for any given future rent and this makes it feasible to sustain effort closer to the efficient level $\hat{e}$ when that is not possible without the piece rate. But β high enough to achieve efficient effort $\hat{e}$ when μ_t is low may result in $\tilde{e}(\beta\mu_t) > \hat{e}$ when μ_t is high. Effort can still be kept to the efficient level, provided that level satisfies Eq. (48), by the firm not paying the bonus if effort is too high as well as if it is too low, but it may not be possible to choose β to sustain efficient effort for both high and low realizations μ_t. Even so, appropriate choice of β enables the firm and employee, at least on average, to get closer to the efficient level. The existence of such imperfect verifiable measures is not, however, necessarily an unmixed blessing. It may increase the payoffs U_{t+1}^0 and Π_{t+1}^0 the employee and the firm receive after cheating because it may enable them to guarantee to other potential partners that an alternative match will be productive even if they are no longer trusted. Baker et al. (1994a) show that, for certain configurations, it may even destroy incentive compatibility of incentives based on subjective measures of performance. A combination of a formal performance related pay scheme with an informal bonus scheme may also help in the framework of Holmstrom and Milgrom (1991) in

---

[22] Baker et al. (1994a) consider only the case in which the firm receives all the future gains but the insight applies more generally.

which the employee carries out more than one task (formally, e_t and s are vectors) but verifiable measures of performance are not available for all tasks.

5.6. Managers' views

Assessing the empirical significance of the motivation framework outlined here is not straightforward because, at least in the general form set out in Section 5.3, it does not have as tight predictions as, for example, the risk allocation models discussed in Section 3. There are three main reasons for this. First, if reputation effects or the ability to commit are sufficiently strong that the incentive compatibility condition Eq. (35) is satisfied for the efficient level of effort with $U_t = \bar{U}_t$ and $\Pi_t = \bar{\Pi}_t$ for all t, motivating employees need have no implications for levels of wages and profits. Second, even where satisfying Eq. (35) requires either $U_t > \bar{U}_t$ or $\Pi_t > \bar{\Pi}_t$, the need to motivate employees by itself implies only that at least one party gains from a match, it does not determine *which* party gains. Third, sufficiently large turnover costs, specific investments and matching frictions can ensure $U_t > \bar{U}_t$ or $\Pi_t > \bar{\Pi}_t$ for continuing matches at t by enough to satisfy Eq. (35) without implying rents to forming new matches. Thus, although much of the empirical literature on motivation models has focused on whether employees receive rents as implied by the Shapiro–Stiglitz model, that is not necessary for motivation with unverifiable performance to be an important issue in practice. Nor is it sufficient because there are other reasons why employees may receive rents.

For these reasons, it is helpful to consider empirical evidence in two categories. The first category concerns the basic building blocks, evidence for the basic elements that are central to the framework – whether adequate verifiable measures of performance are available, whether the basic mechanisms required to sustain employment occur in practice, and so on. The second concerns the economic consequences, especially the extent to which motivation issues actually affect earnings. In the first category is most of the evidence based on interview and questionnaire studies of managers' opinions: Blinder and Choi (1990) of 19 managers in the New Jersey and eastern Pennsylvania area in 1988; Bewley (1997) (summarized by Bewley, 1995) of some 250 managers (as well as some others) in the Connecticut area in 1992–1993; Campbell and Kamlani (1997) of 184 US firms in 1993–1994; Kaufman (1984) of 26 firms in Wales, the West Midlands and Greater London in Britain in 1982; Hall (1993) of 39 personnel managers in Northeast England in 1993; and Agell and Lundborg (1993) (summarized in Agell and Lundborg, 1995) of 179 firms in Sweden in 1991–1992. This subsection is concern with that evidence. Subsequent subsections discuss evidence from experimental and econometric studies.

A first building block of the theory is that employees have sufficient scope to vary performance that motivation and morale matter. The evidence that managers think this the case is strong. Management books on pay, for example Lawler (1990), devote considerable attention to the issue. Even though the numbers involved in the studies of managers' opinions are not large, it seems clear that the managers perceived employee performance as something not simply controlled by supervision and formal performance related pay. In the interviews of Blinder and Choi (1990, p. 1007) and of Hall (1993), 100% of firms believed that workers sometimes shirk on the job. Bewley (1995, p. 252) comments on the managers' views "that workers have so many opportunities to take advantage of employers". As Kaufman (1984, p. 107) puts it: "Because many of the smaller employers did not have foremen or supervisors and often had to leave the 'shop', they relied heavily on the goodwill of their employees." Agell and Lundborg (1993) specifically asked "How common is it for your employees to provide less effort than expected?" and, while the answers reveal that most firms did not regard it as very common, the responses certainly indicate that it is an issue.

A second main building block of the theory is that firms believe employees would respond disadvantageously, and employees that firms would respond disadvantageously, if they do not behave in a way regarded as appropriate. The framework outlined above is not specific about what those responses are because, to characterize the set of equilibria in models of this sort, it is sufficient to consider the most detrimental credible responses, see Abreu (1988), and these are unnecessarily harsh to prevent some types of cheating. Moreover, the specification in the model that the probability of being caught shirking is independent of the extent of shirking means that there is no point in employees shirking a little – though that might well be a sensible alternative if, as may well be the case in practice, minor infringements are less likely to be detected than major ones. There must, however, be some adverse response to inappropriate behavior for employment to occur in the theory. Start with employees' responses to inappropriate behavior by firms. In response to the question "If your wage policy is generally considered to be unfair, how will this affect: the work effort of your current workers? the number of workers who quit?", Blinder and Choi (1990) report 95% of managers as saying that work effort would fall, 85% that more workers would quit. The corresponding responses in Hall (1993) were 74% to both questions. Without knowing what respondents mean by "fair", we do not, of course, know whether the additional quits would simply be because wages would fall below those available elsewhere but the response on work effort seems unambiguous. In Campbell and Kamlani (1997), a decrease in effort was given reasonably strong support as a reason for not cutting wages (more so for blue-collar and less skilled, than for white collar, employees but always with a mean elasticity greater than 1), disadvantageous quits very strong support. In response to a similar question, Agell and Lundborg (1993) also report a difference between white collar and blue collar workers, quitting dominating for the former, both quitting and lower effort occurring for the latter, though they do not provide percentage responses. Kaufman (1984) writes: "employers often feared that wage reductions would impair X-efficiency". The views summarized in Bewley (1995) indicate that pay affects morale which affects profitability in the longterm, though not necessarily in the short term. An example of employee retaliation is described in Stewart (1993), who reports an episode at First Boston Bank in which a group of highly paid traders quit because they were paid bonuses smaller than they believed they had been promised and as a result no longer trusted promises for the future.

On how firms respond to shirking by workers, Blinder and Choi (1990), Campbell and

Kamlani (1997), and Kaufman (1984) do not report responses. Hall (1993) reports that 90% of respondents would *always* terminate the contracts of workers who persistently shirked. (British employment law requires employees to be warned before being dismissed for offences of this sort, so dismissal can be used only for persistent offenders and many firms recognize that unsatisfactory performance can occur for temporary reasons or because an employee does not fully understand what is expected.) In response to a question about the most common measures taken against employees caught shirking repeatedly, Agell and Lundborg (1993) report that 70% of firms regarded firing as very uncommon, a wage reduction as slightly less uncommon and the only common response as a reprimand but recognize that this may be the result of the difficulty of dismissing employees under Swedish law. Bewley (1995) summarizes the views expressed to him as follows: "Good management practice uses punishment largely as a way to weed out bad characters and incompetents and to protect the group from malefactors. Many managers stress that punishment should rarely be used as a way to obtain cooperation." The interpretation to be placed on this is not obvious, however. In the motivation framework outlined here, all workers are equally productive and no actual firing occurs in equilibrium. In practice, some workers are better than others and, if persistent shirking results in classification as incompetent, firing of incompetents is a potential penalty for shirking. Moreover, Bewley (1997, Chapter 15, p. 28) reports that every company with which the issue was discussed used performance as the criterion for selecting office personnel for layoffs and 72% of those not unionized used performance as a criterion (sometimes along with inverse seniority) for selecting hourly paid employees for layoffs. Thus, even if shirking does not result directly in firing, it can have adverse consequences when layoffs next occur. Moreover, the respondents obviously thought employees would recognize this because they thought that: "Layoffs according to the performance criterion stimulated those remaining to work harder so as to avoid dismissal" (Bewley, 1997, Chapter 15, p. 49). And, even for Sweden where legal restrictions make dismissal problematic, Agell and Lundborg (1993) found that 90% of the managers thought an increase in local unemployment, and 59% a reduction in unemployment benefits, would increase work effort at least some. Penalties for shirking can also come in the form of withdrawal of bonuses and of reduced prospects for pay rises and promotions in the future. Hall (1993) reports that 69% of respondents would withdraw promotion opportunities from workers who persistently shirked. The other studies do not report explicitly on this issue because their questions about shirking were directed towards the Shapiro–Stiglitz model.

  A final building block for any version of the theory that involves either party receiving a rent over the return from quitting is some mechanism that prevents wages being bid up if there are unfilled vacancies and bid down if there is involuntary unemployment. The surveys provide no information about the former. On the latter, most of the surveys asked directly why firms do not cut wages. Blinder and Choi (1990, p. 1009) report that 95% of respondents thought cutting nominal wages to take advantage simply of labor market slack would be regarded as unfair by their employees (with consequences of being perceived to behave unfairly already mentioned). Kaufman (1984) comes to a similar conclusion for Britain, even for non-unionized firms. Bewley (1995) and Campbell and Kamlani (1997) report effects that work through morale. However, in all these studies it is explicit that wage cuts may be regarded differently in one or more of the following circumstances: to save the firm from failure, when accompanied with credible information about a financial crisis, or to avoid a large number of layoffs. See also Bewley (1997, Chapter 13, p. 20) and Kahneman et al. (1986). Thus the implication is not that nominal wages are never reduced (which would be clearly counterfactual on the basis of the evidence in Section 2.2) but that labor market slack is not in itself a sufficient condition for wage cuts to be acceptable. Of course, for there to be efficiency wages as in Shapiro and Stiglitz (1984), the wages of new recruits would also have not to be reduced to the market clearing level. Both Kaufman (1984, p. 109) and Bewley (1995, p. 252) are explicit that employers resist this because it would result in new hires becoming resentful or disgruntled, thus affecting their morale.

An interpretation of this evidence in line with the framework set out here is as follows. The incentive compatibility condition (35) and the participation conditions (26) and (34) impose bounds on payoffs. If these conditions enable at least one party to receive a rent over what that party would get from quitting the match (that is, $U_t > \bar{U}_t$ or $\Pi_t > \bar{\Pi}_t$ or both), then some notion of fairness or norm determines how hard employees should work and how the rent should be divided. If fairness requires that employees receive some of the rent, any attempt by the firm to capture their share results in less work effort, either directly or in the long run through morale, that makes the attempt not worthwhile. There would have to be a corresponding response if employees try to capture rent that fairness would give to the firm but the studies are silent on that issue. A unilateral offer of more pay may not, however, result in more effort, an issue raised by respondents to Blinder and Choi (1990) and emphasized strongly by both Bewley (1997) and Campbell and Kamlani (1997), unless that has become part of the accepted notion of fairness. Around 95% of managers interviewed by Hall (1993) thought that a worker's decision on how hard to work is affected by *group* customs or norms of what constitutes a fair day's work, which may give an indication of why it may be difficult to affect individual behavior. Firms do not discriminate against new hires because they too regard that as unfair and consequently perform less well. In a formal sense, fairness is a convention that enables the parties to coordinate on one of the multiple equilibria. It plays an important role because, if an employee and a firm behave in ways appropriate for different equilibria, breakdown of the employment relationship occurs, which is detrimental to all. This is not so far from the views expressed by Akerlof (1982) and Solow (1990) except for the addition of formal constraints that describe the set of feasible outcomes. In practice, of course, things may be less clear cut. Some employees may shirk (in the eyes of the firm) because the notion of fairness may not be unambiguous and some employees may want to see whether less effort is consistent with the firm's understanding of fairness (or they might be trying to see if it can be changed), in which case a reprimand may be sufficient to make clear what the firm regards as acceptable.[23]

None of the surveys asked managers explicitly about this interpretation, however, so there is no direct evidence about how far it accords with their perceptions. Moreover, it leaves a large hole concerning the determination of what is regarded as fair. The surveys reveal that managers' thought such issues as equity and relativities important. The discussion by Levine (1993) of surveys of compensation executives reveals similar responses. However, that still leaves open the question of what is meant by equity and how appropriate relativities get set. That the responses of managers to questions about why they did not cut pay were not simply that employees would quit implies that they thought fairness enables employees to earn wages above the market clearing level, at least at some times, but give little idea of the magnitudes involved. MacLeod and Malcomson (1998) explore some of the implications of fairness corresponding to what is required to sustain an efficient equilibrium (point A or point B in Fig. 7 depending on the extent of diminishing returns and the capital cost of creating jobs) but do not provide any formal reason for the market to converge to such outcomes. Thus what fundamentals might determine which of the feasible outcomes emerges is very much an open question. How rents available at the start of a match are divided is an issue that has been addressed by experimental studies. The evidence from these is discussed in the next subsection.

5.7. Experimental evidence

Fehr et al. (1996) report experiments in which firms offered contracts consisting of a wage and a specified effort. Employees then chose actual effort and were considered to be shirking if effort was below the level specified in the contract. Employment lasted only one period but employees who shirked had a penalty p, set by the firm up to some maximum level equal to the wage minus a constant $\kappa > 0$, deducted from their wage with probability one-half.[24] Thus the no shirking condition (25) is replaced by

$$U = w - c(e) \geq (1 - p)w + p(w - \rho). \tag{49}$$

Experimental subjects in the firm role typically set the penalty at the maximum level $(w - \kappa)$, consistent with providing maximum incentive not to shirk, and received higher effort on average with a higher wage offer, consistent with Eq. (49) holding with equality. On average they also set lower wages than would be optimal given risk neutrality, and workers shirked more than consistent with risk neutrality. However, since the actual risk aversion of the experimental subjects should, in theory, affect their responses and were in

---

[23] Bewley (1997, Chapter 10, p. 11) concludes that: "Business people believed that the shirking theory did not apply to them". Campbell and Kamlani (1997) reach a similar conclusion. These views are, however, based on responses to questions directed specifically at the Shapiro–Stiglitz model in which there is a mechanical relationship between wages, unemployment and effort represented by the no shirking condition. They might more appropriately be taken as indicating that firms are not operating at wage and effort levels at which the no shirking condition is a binding constraint.

[24] Formally, this is not consistent with effort being unverifiable by third parties since the experimenter observes it and enforces a penalty for shirking but the restriction on the penalty is a way of capturing the limited punishment that results from non-verifiability.

practice unknown to their partners, this might be the result of risk aversion inducing firms to set lower contract wage offers.

Other experiments, however, suggest that employees can be induced to provide higher effort than a pure contract model of motivation would imply. Fehr et al. (1997) report experiments using the same basic structure as Fehr et al. (1996) except that the maximum penalty, $\bar{\kappa}$, was independent of the wage and employees knew their firm's value of s, thus enabling them to calculate the firm's payoff, as well as their own, from any contract. Then the maximum effort that satisfies Eq. (49) is attained by setting $\rho = \bar{\kappa}$ and is given by $\tilde{e}$ defined by

$$c(\tilde{e}) = p\bar{\kappa}. \tag{50}$$

In the experiments, employees on average provided effort above this maximum when offered a sufficiently high wage, though not by a large amount. The authors interpret this additional effort as a reciprocity effect or gift exchange as in Akerlof (1982). When firms were also allowed to offer non-enforceable bonuses after observing effort to employees who performed above the specified level, they did so even though there was nothing to compel them. Employee effort was substantially increased as a result.

These studies suggest that effort higher than implied by pure self-interest models of motivation can be sustained. Falk et al. (1997) report experiments with repeated periods of employment in which repetition increased average employee effort above the reciprocity effects found in earlier studies with little change in the wage. But the additional effort largely disappeared in the final period of employment, as one might expect with a repetition effect. This suggests that additional feasible outcomes arise from repetition, as in a pure self-interest model, even in the presence of reciprocity. Finally, it is interesting to note that Fehr et al. (1998) found that firms offered substantially lower wages when employees had no choice of effort, and hence no way to reciprocate the generosity of firms in offering high wages.

There are several comments about these studies. First, they are, of course, all carried out on experimental subjects, not on real firms and real employees in actual employment situations. Second, one of the responses given to Bewley (1997, Chapter 10, p. 7) suggests that the manager concerned thought reciprocity effects likely to be short-lived: "All employees, no matter how well paid, feel they are underpaid. A few weeks after every increase, people want more." Any such effects may not be picked up in experiments lasting only a few hours. Third, where reputations are important and additional commitments feasible, it is perfectly possible that Eq. (35) can be satisfied with $U_t = \bar{U}_t$ and $\Pi_t = \bar{\Pi}_t$ for all t. In that case, all these issues become irrelevant in interpreting observed wages because wages are simply driven by what is available in the outside market and the disutility of working at the efficient level of effort. In that case, there is no role for reciprocity to affect actual wages. If, alternatively, turnover costs and specific investments are sufficiently large to ensure that Eq. (35) is always satisfied, starting wages can be determined simply by traditional market forces and only subsequent wages affected by the need to ensure that both (25) and (33) are satisfied. In that case, reciprocity and the processes described in the surveys of managers' opinions are concerned only with how the rents from continuing employment are divided. The next subsection therefore turns to the econometric evidence for the extent to which motivational issues actually affect market outcomes.

5.8. Econometric evidence

One issue raised in the literature on wage differentials for employees with the same measured characteristics is whether, if such differentials correspond to rents, those rents can be attributed to motivation effects rather than to such alternatives as turnover costs, specific investments, costly search for the best quality of match between job and employee, and firms' concerns to avoid unionization that may result from paying low wages. A second is whether any rents accrue to newly hired recruits or only to continuing employees.

One piece of evidence that differentials correspond to rents is the finding of Krueger and Summers (1988) that quit rates are inversely correlated with industry wage premiums – rents make it less attractive for employees to quit. However, quit rates inversely related to wages can arise for a number of reason unrelated to motivation. An example is the model in Section 4.7 in which firms are not fully informed about the value of the employees' outside options. In that model, the higher are turnover costs or specific investments the higher the wage it is worth the firm offering to reduce turnover. A second piece of evidence in favor of rents is the finding of Lazear and Moore (1984) that the lifetime wage profiles of employees are steeper than those of the self-employed. However, those too can arise for reasons unrelated to motivation. Moreover, both these findings are consistent with the same present discounted value of earnings (and thus no rents) for new recruits if they are associated with lower starting wages. To investigate whether new recruits receive rents, Krueger and Summers (1988) consider inter-industry wage differentials for employees with less than one year of tenure. They find these significant and highly positively corre-lated with differentials for employees with more than ten years of tenure, which they interpret as evidence that newly hired employees receive rents too. Manning and Thomas (1996) adopt the more direct approach of comparing reported reservation wages and subsequent starting wages of unemployed UK workers who become employed. Their finding of positive but insignificant rents, however, relies on a particular interpretation of reported reservation wages, many of which are actually above the wages subsequently earned. Although any such rents would not arise from turnover costs or specific invest-ments alone, they do not, of course, differentiate between motivation and other reasons for efficiency wages.

An alternative approach to testing for efficiency wages is to investigate whether higher wages are associated with higher productivity by including in the labor input in a produc-tion function an efficiency of labor effect that depends on the wage paid, alternative wages, and/or the local unemployment rate. Both Green and Weisskopf (1990), for US 3-digit industries, and Wadhwani and Wall (1991), for UK manufacturing companies, find significant effects of unemployment on productivity. Both Wadhwani and Wall (1991) and Levine (1992), for large North American manufacturers, find significant relative wage effects on productivity. But estimates of production function parameters derived in this way do not identify whether the reason for a positive wage-productivity relationship is motivation, compensating differentials that arise from unobserved ability differences between employees, efficiency wages paid to attract better employees as in Weiss (1980), or rent sharing arising from union bargaining. Moreover, a positive unemployment-productivity relationship could arise because firms hire a higher proportion of better workers when unemployment is high. Two studies that try to differentiate between at least some of these possibilities using data at the company level are Machin and Manning (1992) and Konings and Walsh (1994). The latter use a duopoly model in which two firms compete in both product and labor markets to distinguish between rent sharing and efficiency wages but their method does not discriminate between motivation and other reasons for paying efficiency wages. Machin and Manning (1992) exploit the dynamic nature of the motivation model as a way to discriminate between motivation and other possibilities. The no shirking condition (25) is a present value condition in which current sustainable effort depends positively on future wages, negatively on future effort, and negatively on future alternative utility. In contrast, with compensating differentials in a spot market setting, future values should be irrelevant. Moreover, in the particular form of rent sharing Machin and Manning (1992) investigate that increases the present discounted value of employee utility by a fixed markup on market utility, a higher future wage decreases, and a higher future market utility increases, current effort. Using the same data as Wadhwani and Wall (1991), they separate the sample into firms in high and firms in low union density industries and estimate a coefficient on the future wage that is positive for low union density firms (consistent with the motivation model) and negative for high union density firms (consistent with the rent sharing model).

Investigations based on wage-productivity and unemployment-productivity relationships are, at best, rather weak tests of the motivation model because they do not make use of direct measures of variables that enter that model. A number of papers have looked at variables more directly related to the model, though primarily in the Shapiro and Stiglitz (1984) version. Three such variables have been used, the extent of supervision (which relates to the probability p that shirking is detected), disciplinary dismissals, and direct measures of effort.

Studies that investigate the effect of supervision include Leonard (1987), Groshen and Krueger (1990), Rebitzer and Robinson (1991), Krueger (1991b), and Rebitzer (1995). Leonard (1987) finds little evidence for a negative tradeoff between wage premiums and the number of supervisors per employee across firms for specific occupations (though some evidence for a positive tradeoff for production assemblers and machinists), which is inconsistent with Eq. (30) holding with equality when p is exogenous and varies across firms. However, it is not clear that such a negative relationship is robust to minor variants in the model. If, for example, work effort differs across firms, which amounts to the disutility of work c varying across firms, and intensity of supervision can be increased at increasing cost, firms requiring higher effort would have both more supervisors *and* higher wages. Groshen and Krueger (1990) point out that the same applies if there is a possibility of substitution between staff and supervisors because higher staff wages lead firms to substitute supervisors for staff for given supervisor wages. They investigate the wage-supervision relationship for registered nurses in the US, for whom they argue supervision can be taken as predetermined because minimum standards are set by states. For nurses, they find a significant negative relationship, though not for other hospital staff for whom they argue state regulated supervision appears more limited. They note, however, that their method does not distinguish between more supervision reducing shirking for a given wage and more supervision resulting in firms substituting low quality/low pay nurses for high quality/high pay ones. Rebitzer and Robinson (1991) treat plant size as the predetermined variable that affects the ability to monitor those workers that their switching regression model selects as being in primary sector jobs, with monitoring assumed to be more difficult in large plants than in small, and thus interpret the positive effect of plant size on wages as resulting from monitoring intensity. The weakness here is that they have no direct evidence on the amount of monitoring. Krueger (1991b) uses whether or not a fast-food restaurant is company owned or a franchise as the predetermined variable that affects ability to monitor. Contract arrangements give managers of company-owned outlets less incentive to monitor and supervise, which is supported by survey evidence from employees about the adequacy of supervision in the two types of outlet. Company-owned restaurants appear to pay assistant and shift managers significantly more (around 9%), though the difference for crew workers is small (2% for full-time, insignificant for part-time). All these studies of supervision use cross-section data and so are not in a position to test for employee fixed effects. Rebitzer (1995) uses data on workers employed by contractors to plants in the petrochemical industry. He argues that supervision by the host plant (as opposed to that by the contractor) is decided without clear knowledge of the contractor's practices, so the relationship between the wage and host plant supervision is less likely to be affected by omitted variables than where the employer makes both decisions. This relationship has a significant negative slope, as predicted by the theory.

Cappelli and Chauvin (1991) and Campbell (1994) investigate disciplinary dismissals. The former use data on production workers from a large multi-plant manufacturing firm in which all plants have the same wages and conditions of employment, negotiated with a union on a firm-wide basis, and virtually identical production jobs within categories of plants (assembly versus component plants). The one difference across plants is geographical location, and hence the wages available in other jobs in the local labor market. Thus, in terms of the no shirking condition in its form (27), plants differ only in $\bar{U}$. In the Shapiro–Stiglitz model there are no dismissals in equilibrium but these can be introduced by having heterogeneous workers. Cappelli and Chauvin (1991) assume heterogeneity in the discount factor δ, though heterogeneity in the disutility of work c would do equally well. Then a higher value of $\bar{U}$ means that the no shirking condition is satisfied for only a smaller proportion of employees, so a higher proportion shirk and are dismissed. In the data, the average disciplinary dismissal rate (dismissals per employee in the year studied) was approximately 10%. They find that a higher wage premium does indeed have a significant negative effect on the disciplinary dismissal rate, though the effect of local unemployment rates and unemployment benefits (which one would expect also to affect $\bar{U}$, see Eq. (29)) are insignificant. They conclude that this is not a selection effect that results from higher wage premia enabling the firm to hire employees less likely to shirk because the wage premium at an earlier date (12 years earlier) is not significant in explaining dismissals. Campbell (1994) looks at disciplinary dismissals rates using Employment Opportunity Pilot Project (EOPP) data and, in this case, finds that they are significantly reduced by higher local unemployment. The interpretation in this case is, however, more complex because the wage may not be exogenous to the production unit. Consider Eq. (30). Heterogeneity among workers is introduced by differences in c and, for any given wage, those with c too high for this condition to be satisfied shirk and are dismissed as a result. But when the wage w is endogenous, the production unit chooses the wage optimally given the proportion of workers who shirk. While a higher value of L/J would presumably make it optimal to offer a lower wage, it is not clear that it is optimal to set the wage such that a higher proportion of workers shirk.

Two studies, Drago and Heywood (1992) for the US and Ackum Agell (1994) for Sweden, investigate motivation effects by using direct measures of employee effort derived from surveys of employees. The former measures effort by a binary variable that takes the value 1 if the employee responds that the job requires working hard. The latter uses the employee's report of the proportion of time at work spent actually working. The results are very different. The former find that both the hourly wage and a supervisor's reported "insistence" on hard work have significant positive effects on work effort and a shortage of comparable jobs in the local area a significantly negative effect. The latter finds no significant wage effect, though some effect from unemployment, but comments that smaller effects may be expected in Sweden because of the difficulty of dismissing employees. In both cases, however, the authors recognize the limitations of their measures of work effort.

Brandt and Hosios (1996) consider explicitly the possibility that motivation need not result in employees receiving rents. They have an exceptionally complete dataset providing detailed information about the timing of wage payments and other characteristics of employment contracts, and about the characteristics of both parties to those contracts, for 21 villages in rural Northeast China in 1935. Limited access to credit by workers favors front-loading of wage payments, as does concern about whether an employer will renege by, for example, changing working conditions. Limited access to credit by employers favors back-loading of wage payments, as does concern about employee shirking. By estimating a hedonic equation for the present discounted value of contracts in terms of their characteristics, and both a demand equation by workers and a supply equation by firms for the degree of front-loading, they conclude that both sides were credit constrained. Moreover, by using variables related to reputation effects (whether parties to the contract are from the same village and the involvement of third parties), they conclude that the primary incentive concern was with employee shirking and that this was dealt with primarily by reputation effects. It thus seems that in markets that are not anonymous, reputation effects are an effective response to motivation issues.

In summary, there is considerable evidence from these econometric studies that employees receive rents from continuing employment but that, in itself, is consistent with many explanations other than motivation with unverifiable performance. There is some, though rather less, evidence of employees receiving rents at the time of hiring. Several studies have found significant effects of wages and unemployment on productivity, though it is hard to be sure that these are genuine efficiency wage effects. Of the studies more directly focused on variables relating to the motivation model, the evidence on supervision is conflicting, though it is not clear that all the studies actually identify relationships appropriate for testing the model. The direct measures of effort that have been used to estimate wage-effort relationships have serious limitations. That higher wages reduce disciplinary dismissals seems to be rather more securely established. Taken together, these econometric studies provide sufficient evidence not to reject out of hand that motivational issues have an impact on wages, but the evidence they provide is not overwhelmingly convincing on this.

In interpreting this evidence, it should be remembered that motivational issues may be important in the minds of managers and employees because of the need to make sure the incentive compatibility constraints are satisfied without preventing market clearing at the start of matches if reputation, turnover costs, specific investments, or commitments to performance bonuses or promotions are important in practice. In looking for motivational effects on wages, it makes sense to look at jobs, for example those in fast-food restaurants studied by Krueger (1991b), in which these other elements are less likely to play an important role.

5.9. Conclusions on contracts to motivate employees

A central point from the theory of motivation with unverifiable performance is that, for employment to take place, there must be sufficient gain in the future from sticking to an agreement over what the parties would individually receive if the match ended because one or the other cheated. If, however, reputation effects are sufficiently strong, that does not necessarily require either party to make a gain over what they would get by simply quitting the match. Even if reputation effects are not sufficiently strong, the need to motivate employees by itself implies only that at least one party gains from a match, it does not determine *which* party gains. A high basic wage without a bonus can, for example, ensure the employee receives a gain, a lower basic wage with a bonus that the firm does. Or they can divide the gain between them. Or, if turnover costs or specific investments are sufficiently large, who gains from continuing an existing match can be determined by the contracts used to protect investments, without any need for there to be a gain from forming a new match. And, if there is a gain to one party from forming a new match, it can as well go to firms in a market with unfilled vacancies as to employees in the form of efficiency wages in a market with unemployment.

Faced with so many possibilities, a natural way to start investigating the model empirically is to look for evidence of the basic building blocks that are fundamental to it. There seems ample evidence that managers regard motivation as a serious issue, that appropriate performance cannot simply be guaranteed by formal performance incentives, monitoring, and supervision alone. There also seems evidence that managers think that, if they cut wages below what employees regard as fair, employees will respond in a way that will hurt the firm, not just by immediately quitting. A weak labor market is not thought sufficient reason for cutting wages to be regarded as fair. Experimental evidence indicates that some of these views are actually practiced by experimental subjects in the laboratory, though other effects such as gift exchange seem to be present there as well. However, econometric evidence has not provided a very convincing answer as to how much impact the underlying mechanisms have on wages and profits in practice. A sensible conclusion would thus seem to be that, while the basic issue of motivating employees when performance is unverifiable seems real enough in practice, there is not yet a clear picture about the quantitative significance of its overall effect on wages, profits, and employment.

If it were to have a significant effect, could it account for the evidence on wage behavior discussed in Section 2? Clearly, it could account for similar employees earning different wages in different firms if monitoring costs, exogenous turnover rates, effort requirements, or divisions of rents are different. The business cycle properties are less immediately apparent from what has been said above. For efficiency wage equilibria as in Shapiro and Stiglitz (1984), differences in productivity levels that result in different zero profit lines in Fig. 6 trace out wage-employment combinations along the no shirking condition, which is more elastic than the labor supply curve. (The latter is vertical in this case.) Kimball (1994) and MacLeod et al. (1994) show that this property applies also to (different) dynamic versions of the model in which productivity *shocks* shift the zero profit condition though, for yet another different dynamic specification, Strand (1992) argues that the effect is likely to be smaller than indicated by the elasticity of the no shirking condition itself. Nevertheless, MacLeod et al. (1994) show that, calibrated to standard deviations in GNP and real wages for the US economy over the period 1954–1989, the model does a good job of accounting for standard deviations in unemployment, though less so for standard deviation in employment.

These analyses all presume that the market outcome is always a point on the no shirking condition, so all the rents from continued employment go to employees. Ramey and Watson (1997) consider the case in which rents are shared in exogenous proportions unless renegotiated to avoid inefficient separation. With specific investments and matching frictions added, they show that the effect of a productivity shock on output is both magnified and highly persistent. At present, however, there is no well developed theory of rent division in this context and, unless supplemented by such a theory, the underlying framework implies only that the wage lies within the bounds of the participation conditions illustrated in Fig. 2. To generate the nominal wage effects illustrated in Fig. 1, what determines the division of rents in any such theory (e.g., the concept of fairness) would have to be sensitive to nominal, as well as real, aspects of the economic environment.

6. Concluding remarks

This chapter has reviewed recent developments in three types of individual employment contracts, contracts to allocate risk, contracts to protect investments, and contracts to motivate employees when performance is not verifiable in court. Other reasons for contracts between employers and employees are discussed in other chapters of this Handbook.

The extent to which each of these three types of contract generates patterns resembling those in actual labor markets has been discussed extensively above. A recurring theme is that they are better able to generate those patterns when the practical issues of enforcement and the possibilities for renegotiation are recognized. Once those practical issues are taken into account, all three types of contract can generate wage changes that are more damped relative to employment changes than in a spot market with the same labor supply and marginal product curves without resulting in a complete rigidity of wages for continuing employees that would be clearly counterfactual. They can also generate wages that differ for equally productive employees depending on how tight the labor market in which they were initially hired, the extent of turnover costs, the type of investments they work with, and the arrangements adopted for motivating them. The literature on contracts to protect investments provides an interesting link with the legal presumptions about conditions for modification of contracts in the absence of specific agreement to the contrary. That on contracts to motivate employees provides a framework within which one may possibly interpret employers' views about the roles of fairness and morale.

A serious weakness in generating patterns in the data concerns the nominal effects that appear in wage changes. Insurance models have an inherent problem here since their whole purpose is to insure real variables and the literature on motivation has contributed little on this issue. With contracts to protect investments, contracts in nominal terms are efficient in some circumstances and differ from menu cost explanations of nominal effects in having no bias against very small nominal wage changes. However, contracts in real terms are also efficient under many of these circumstances and then the positive case for nominal contracts depends on there being some cost, however small, to indexing.

In common with other contracting models, the equilibrium wage-employment combinations in the models reviewed here do not typically correspond to intersections of demand and supply curves. Indeed, they may not correspond to points on either of those curves. As a result, it is not appropriate to view employment as determined by a wage negotiation process given a labor demand curve. When renegotiation ensures efficient employment, a more appropriate view is that employment is determined at the efficient level and wages are the outcome of a contracting process to allocate risk or protect investments given that the parties recognize that renegotiation may occur. The wage-employment relationship may then look very different from either a supply or a demand curve. With turnover costs and fixed wages, for example, sticky wages and wages that respond asymmetrically to upward and downward shocks are an efficient response to a well defined contracting problem and do not, by themselves, indicate inefficiencies in labor markets. This does not, of course, mean that the forces of supply and demand are absent. By determining the values of alternative opportunities (the outside options), these forces constrain the set of possible wage outcomes. The scope for contracts to have significant effects on wage levels depends on how tightly constrained those possible outcomes are.

References

Abowd, J.A. and T. Lemieux (1993), "The effects of product market competition on collective bargaining agreements: the case of foreign competition in Canada", Quarterly Journal of Economics 108 (4): 983–1014.

Abowd, J.M. and D. Card (1987), "Intertemporal labor supply and long-term employment contracts", American Economic Review 77 (1): 50–68.

Abowd, J.M. and F. Kramarz (1997), "The costs of hiring and separations", Working paper no. 6110 (NBER Cambridge, MA).

Abraham, K.G. and H.S. Farber (1987), "Job duration, seniority, and earnings", American Economic Review 77 (3): 278–297.

Abraham, K.G. and J.C. Haltiwanger (1995), "Real wages and the business cycle", Journal of Economic Literature 33 (3): 1215–1264.

Abreu, D. (1988), "On the theory of infinitely repeated games with discounting", Econometrica 56 (2): 383–396.

Acemoglu, D. (1996), "A microfoundation for social increasing returns in human capital accumulation", Quarterly Journal of Economics 111 (3): 780–804.

Acemoglu, D. and R. Shimer (1997), Holdups and efficiency with search frictions (Department of Economics, Massachusetts Institute of Technology).

Ackum Agell, S. (1994), "Swedish evidence on the efficiency wage hypothesis", Labour Economics 1 (2): 129–150.

Agell, J. and P. Lundborg (1993), "Theories of pay and unemployment: survey evidence from Swedish manufacturing firms", Working paper no. 1993:8 (Department of Economics, Uppsala University).

Agell, J. and P. Lundborg (1995), "Theories of pay and unemployment: survey evidence from Swedish manufacturing firms", Scandinavian Journal of Economics 97 (2): 295–307.

Aghion, P., M. Dewatripont and P. Rey (1994), "Renegotiation design with unverifiable information", Econometrica 62 (2): 257–282.

Akerlof, G.A. (1982), "Labor contracts as partial gift exchange", Quarterly Journal of Economics 97 (4): 543–569.

Akerlof, G.A. and L.F. Katz (1989), "Workers' trust funds and the logic of wage profiles", Quarterly Journal of Economics 104 (3): 525–536.

Akerlof, G., W.T. Dickens and G. Perry (1996), "The macroeconomics of low inflation", Brookings Papers on Economic Activity 1: 1–59.

Altonji, J.G. and R.A. Shakotko (1987), "Do wages rise with job seniority?" Review of Economic Studies 54 (3): 437–459.

Altonji, J.G. and N. Williams (1997), "Do wages rise with job seniority? A reassessment", Working paper no. 6010 (NBER Cambridge, MA).

Azariadis, C. (1975), "Implicit contracts and underemployment equilibria", Journal of Political Economy 83 (6): 1183–1202.

Baily, M.N. (1974), "Wages and employment under uncertain demand", Review of Economic Studies 41 (1): 37–50.

Baker, G. (1992), "Incentive contracts and performance measurement", Journal of Political Economy 100 (3): 598–614.

Baker, G., M.C. Jensen and K.J. Murphy (1988), "Compensation and incentives: practice vs. theory", Journal of Finance 43 (3): 593–616.

Baker, G., R. Gibbons and K.J. Murphy (1994a), "Subjective performance measures in optimal incentive contracts", Quarterly Journal of Economics 109 (4): 1125–1156.

Baker, G., M. Gibbs and B. Holmstrom (1994b), "The wage policy of a firm", Quarterly Journal of Economics 109 (4): 921–955.

Bean, C.R. (1994), "European unemployment: a survey", Journal of Economic Literature 32 (2): 573–619.

Beaudry, P. and J. DiNardo (1991), "The effect of implicit contracts on the movement of wages over the business cycle: evidence from micro data", Journal of Political Economy 99 (4): 665–688.

Beaudry, P. and J. DiNardo (1995), "Is the behavior of hours worked consistent with implicit contract theory?" Quarterly Journal of Economics 110 (3): 743–768.

Becker, G.S. (1975) Human capital: a theoretical and empirical analysis, with special reference to education, 2nd edition (Columbia University Press, New York).

Becker, G.S. and G.J. Stigler (1974), "Law enforcement, malfeasance, and compensation of enforcers", Journal of Legal Studies 3 (1): 1–18.

Bentolila, S. and G. Bertola (1990), "Firing costs and labour demand: how bad is eurosclerosis?" Review of Economic Studies 57 (3): 381–402.

Bertola, G. (1990), "Job security, employment and wages", European Economic Review 34 (4): 851–886.

Bertrand, M. (1999), "From the invisible handshake to the invisible hand? How import competition changes the employment relationship", Working paper no. 6900 (NBER, Cambridge, MA).

Bewley, T.F. (1995), "A depressed labor market as explained by participants", American Economic Review 85 (2): 250–254.

Bewley, T.F. (1997), "A depressed labor market as explained by participants" Unpublished (Yale University).

Bils, M.J. (1985), "Real wages over the business cycle: evidence from panel data", Journal of Political Economy 93 (4): 666–689.

Blanchard, O.J. and P. Diamond (1989), "The Beveridge curve", Brookings Papers on Economic Activity 1: 1–60.

Blanchard, O.J. and P. Diamond (1990), "The aggregate matching function", in: P. Diamond, ed., Growth/productivity/unemployment (MIT Press, Cambridge, MA) pp. 159–201.

Blanchflower, D.G. and A.J. Oswald (1994), The wage curve (MIT Press, Cambridge, MA).

Blinder, A.S. and D.H. Choi (1990), "A shred of evidence on theories of wage stickiness", Quarterly Journal of Economics 105 (4): 1003–1015.

Boldrin, M. and M. Horvath (1995), "Labor contracts and business cycles", Journal of Political Economy 103 (5): 972–1004.

Brandt, L. and A.J. Hosios (1996), "Credit, incentives and reputation: a hedonic analysis of contractual wage profiles", Journal of Political Economy 104 (6): 1172–1226.

Brown, J.N. (1989), "Why do wages increase with tenure? On-the-job training and life-cycle wage growth observed within firms", American Economic Review 79 (5): 971–991.

Bull, C. (1987), "The existence of self-enforcing implicit contracts", Quarterly Journal of Economics 102 (1): 147–159.

Caballero, R.J. and E.M.R.A. Engel (1993), "Heterogeneity and output fluctuations in a dynamic menu-cost economy", Review of Economic Studies 60 (1): 95–119.

Campbell, C.M. III (1993), "Do firms pay efficiency wages? Evidence with data at the firm level", Journal of Labor Economics 11 (3): 442–470.

Campbell, C.M. III (1994), "The determinants of dismissals: tests of the shirking model with individual data", Economics Letters 46 (1): 89–95.

Campbell, C.M. III and K.S. Kamlani (1997), "The reasons for wage rigidity: evidence from a survey of firms", Quarterly Journal of Economics 112 (3): 759–789.

Caplin, A.S. and D.F. Spulber (1987), "Menu costs and the neutrality of money", Quarterly Journal of Economics 102 (4): 703–725.

Cappelli, P. and K. Chauvin (1991), "An interplant test of the efficiency wage hypothesis", Quarterly Journal of Economics 106 (3): 769–787.

Card, D. (1990a), "Strikes and wages: a test of an asymmetric information model", Quarterly Journal of Economics 105 (3): 625–659.

Card, D. (1990b), "Unexpected inflation, real wages and employment determination in union contracts", American Economic Review 80 (4): 669–688.

Card, D. and D. Hyslop (1997), "Does inflation 'grease the wheels of the labor market'?" in: C.D. Romer and D.H. Romer, eds., Reducing inflation: motivation and strategy (University of Chicago Press, Chicago, IL) pp. 71–114.

Carmichael, H.L. (1983), "Firm-specific human capital and promotion ladders", Bell Journal of Economics 14 (1): 251–258.

Chari, V.V. (1983), "Involuntary unemployment and implicit contracts", Quarterly Journal of Economics 98 (3): 107–122.

Che, Y.-K. and D.B. Hausch (1999), "Cooperative investments and the value of contracting", American Economic Review 89(1), 125–147.

Chung, T.-Y. (1991), "Incomplete contracts, specific investments and risk sharing", Review of Economic Studies 58 (5): 1031–1042.

Cramton, P.C. and J.S. Tracy (1992), "Strikes and holdouts in wage bargaining: theory and data", American Economic Review 82 (1): 100–121.

Crémer, J. (1986), "Cooperation in ongoing organizations", Quarterly Journal of Economics 101 (1): 33–49.

Crémer, J. and M.H. Riordan (1985), "A sequential solution to the public goods problem", Econometrica 53 (1): 77–84.

Davis, S.J., J.C. Haltiwanger and S. Schuh (1996), Job creation and destruction (MIT Press, Cambridge, MA).

Dewatripont, M. (1989), "Renegotiation and information revelation over time: the case of optimal labor contracts", Quarterly Journal of Economics 104 (3): 589–619.

Dickens, W.T. and L.F. Katz (1987), "Inter-industry wage differences and industry characteristics", in: K. Lang and J.S. Leonard, eds., Unemployment and the structure of labor markets (Basil Blackwell, New York) pp. 48–89.

Dickens, W.T., L.F. Katz, K. Lang and L.H. Summers (1989), "Employee crime and the monitoring puzzle", Journal of Labor Economics 7 (3): 331–347.

Drago, R. and J.S. Heywood (1992), "Is worker behaviour consistent with efficiency wages?" Scottish Journal of Political Economy 39 (2): 141–153.

Eccles, R. and D. Crane (1988) Doing deals: investment banks at work (Harvard Business School Press, Boston, MA).

Edlin, A.S. and S. Reichelstein (1996), "Holdups, standard breach remedies, and optimal investment", American Economic Review 86 (3): 478–501.

Emerson, M. (1988), "Regulation or deregulation of the labour market: policy regimes for the recruitment and dismissal of employees in the industrialised countries", European Economic Review 32 (4): 775–817.

Eswaran, M. and A. Kotwal (1984), "The moral hazard of budget-breaking", RAND Journal of Economics 15 (4): 578–581.

Fairburn, J.A. and J.M. Malcomson (1994), "Rewarding performance by promotion to a different job", European Economic Review 38 (3,4): 683–690.

Fairburn, J.A. and J.M. Malcomson (1995), "Performance, promotion and the Peter principle, Discussion papers W.P. 304.95 (IAE, Universitat Autònoma de Barcelona).

Falk, A., S. Gächter and J. Kovacs (1997), Reputation or reciprocity (Institute for Empirical Economic Research, University of Zurich).

Farrell, J. and E. Maskin (1989), "Renegotiation in repeated games", Games and Economic Behavior 1 (4): 327–360.

Fehr, E., S. Gächter and G. Kirchsteiger (1997), "Reciprocity as a contract enforcement device: experimental evidence", Econometrica 65 (4): 833–860.

Fehr, E., E. Kirchler, A. Weichbold and S. Gächter (1998), "When social norms overpower competition: gift exchange in experimental labor markets", Journal of Labor Economics 16 (2): 324–351.

Fehr, E., G. Kirchsteiger and A. Riedl (1996), "Involuntary unemployment and non-compensating wage differentials in an experimental labour market", Economic Journal 106 (434): 106–121.

Felli, L. and C. Harris (1996), "Learning, wage dynamics, and firm-specific human capital", Journal of Political Economy 104 (4): 838–868.

Flinn, C.J. (1997), "Equilibrium wage and dismissal processes", Journal of Business and Economic Statistics 15 (2): 221–236.

Gibbons, R. (1997), "Incentives and careers in organizations", in: D.M. Kreps and K.F. Wallis, eds., Advances in economics and econometrics: theory and applications, Vol. 2 (Cambridge University Press, Cambridge, UK) pp.1–37.

Gibbons, R. and L.F. Katz (1992), "Does unmeasured ability explain inter-industry wage differentials?" Review of Economic Studies 59 (3): 515–535.

Gomme, P. and J. Greenwood (1995), "On the cyclical allocation of risk", Journal of Economic Dynamics and Control 19 (1/2): 91–124.

Gordon, D.F. (1974), "A neo-classical theory of Keynesian unemployment", Economic Inquiry 12 (4): 431–459.

Gordon, R.J. (1983), "A century of evidence on wage and price stickiness in the United States, the United Kingdom and Japan", in: J. Tobin, ed., Macro-economics, prices, and quantities (Brookings Institution, Washington, DC) pp. 85–121.

Gray, J.A. (1976), "Wage indexation: a macroeconomic approach", Journal of Monetary Economics 2 (2): 221–235.

Green, F. and T.E. Weisskopf (1990), "The worker discipline effect: a disaggregative analysis", Review of Economics and Statistics 72: 241–249.

Green, J. and C.M. Kahn (1983), "Wage employment contracts", Quarterly Journal of Economics 98 (3): 173–187.

Groshen, E.L. and A.B. Krueger (1990), "The structure of supervision and pay in hospitals", Industrial and Labor Relations Review 43 (3, Special Issue): 134S–146S.

Grossman, S.J. and O.D. Hart (1986), "The costs and benefits of ownership: a theory of vertical and lateral integration", Journal of Political Economy 94 (4): 691–719.

Grout, P. (1984), "Investment and wages in the absence of binding contracts: a Nash bargaining approach", Econometrica 52 (2): 449–460.

Hall, J.D. (1993), "The wage setters guide to wage rigidity", Master's thesis (University of Southampton).

Hall, R.E. (1975), "The rigidity of wages and the persistence of unemployment", Brookings Papers on Economic Activity 2: 301–335.

Hall, R.E. and E.P. Lazear (1984), "The excess sensitivity of layoffs and quits to demand", Journal of Labor Economics 2 (2): 233–257.

Harris, M. and B. Holmström (1982), "A theory of wage dynamics", Review of Economic Studies 49 (3): 315–333.

Hart, O. (1983), "Optimal labour contracts under asymmetric information: an introduction", Review of Economic Studies 50 (1): 3–35.

Hart, O. (1995) Firms, contracts, and financial structure (Clarendon Press, Oxford, UK).

Hart, O. and B. Holmström (1987), "The theory of contracts", in: T.F. Bewley, ed., Advances in economic theory: fifth world congress (Cambridge University Press, Cambridge, UK) pp. 71–155.

Hart, O. and J. Moore (1988), "Incomplete contracts and renegotiation", Econometrica 56 (4): 755–785.

Hart, R.A. and S. Kawasaki (1999), Work and play in Japan (Cambridge University Press, Cambridge, UK).

Hashimoto, M. (1981), "Firm-specific capital as a shared investment", American Economic Review 71 (3): 475–482.

Hashimoto, M. and B.T. Yu (1980), "Specific capital, employment contracts, and wage rigidity", Bell Journal of Economics 11 (2): 536–549.

Helwege, J. (1992), "Sectoral shifts and interindustry wage differentials", Journal of Labor Economics 10 (1): 55–84.

Hermalin, B.E. and M.L. Katz (1993), "Judicial modification of contracts between sophisticated parties: a more complete view of incomplete contracts and their breach", Journal of Law, Economics, and Organization 9 (2): 230–255.

Holden, S. (1994), "Wage bargaining and nominal rigidities", European Economic Review 38 (5): 1021–1039.

Holden, S. (1999), "Renegotiation and the efficiency of investments", RAND Journal of Economics 30(1), 106–119.

Holmstrom, B. (1981), "Contractual models of the labor market", American Economic Review 71 (2): 308–313.

Holmstrom, B. (1983), "Equilibrium long-term labor contracts", Quarterly Journal of Economics 98 (3): 23–54.

Holmstrom, B. and P. Milgrom (1991), "Multitask principal-agent analyses: incentive contracts, asset ownership and job design", Journal of Law, Economics, and Organization 7: 24–52.

Jacobson, L.S., R.J. LaLonde and D.G. Sullivan (1993), "Earnings losses of displaced workers", American Economic Review 83 (4): 685–709.

Joskow, P.L. (1990), "The performance of long-term contracts: further evidence from coal markets", RAND Journal of Economics 21 (2): 251–274.

Kahn, C. and G. Huberman (1988), "Two-sided uncertainty and 'up-or-out' contracts", Journal of Labor Economics 6 (4): 423–444.

Kahn, S. (1997), "Evidence of nominal wage stickiness from microdata", American Economic Review 87 (5): 993–1008.

Kahneman, D., J.L. Knetsch and R. Thaler (1986), "Fairness as a constraint on profit seeking: entitlements in the market", American Economic Review 76 (4): 728–741.

Kandori, M. (1992), "Repeated games played by overlapping generations of players", Review of Economic Studies 59 (1): 81–92.

Kaufman, R.T. (1984), "On wage stickiness in Britain's competitive sector", British Journal of Industrial Relations 22: 101–112.

Kimball, M.S. (1994), "Labor-market dynamics when unemployment is a worker discipline device", American Economic Review 84 (4): 1045–1059.

Konings, J. and P.P. Walsh (1994), "Evidence of efficiency wage payments in UK firm level panel data", Economic Journal 104 (424): 542–555.

Krueger, A.B. (1991a), "The evolution of unjust-dismissal legislation in the United States", Industrial and Labor Relations Review 44 (4): 644–660.

Krueger, A.B. (1991b), "Ownership, agency, and wages: an examination of franchising in the fast food industry", Quarterly Journal of Economics 106 (1): 75–101.

Krueger, A.B. and L.H. Summers (1988), "Efficiency wages and the inter-industry wage structure", Econometrica 56 (2): 259–293.

Lawler, E.E. III (1990) Strategic pay: aligning organizational strategies and pay systems (Jossey-Bass, San Francisco, CA).

Lazear, E.P. (1979), "Why is there mandatory retirement?" Journal of Political Economy 87 (6): 1261–1284.

Lazear, E.P. (1981), "Agency, earnings profiles, productivity, and hours restrictions", American Economic Review 71 (4): 606–620.

Lazear, E.P. (1990), "Job security provisions and employment", Quarterly Journal of Economics 105 (3): 699–726.

Lazear, E.P. (1995), Personnel economics (The Wicksell Lectures, MIT Press, Cambridge, MA).

Lazear, E.P. and R.L. Moore (1984), "Incentives, productivity, and labor contracts", Quarterly Journal of Economics 99: 275–296.

Lazear, E.P. and S. Rosen (1981), "Rank-order tournaments as optimum labor contracts", Journal of Political Economy 89 (5): 841–864.

Leonard, J.S. (1987), "Carrots and sticks: pay, supervision, and turnover", Journal of Labor Economics 5 (4, part 2): S136–S152.

Levine, D.I. (1992), "Can wage increases pay for themselves? Tests with a production function", Economic Journal 102 (414): 1102–1115.

Levine, D.I. (1993), "Fairness, markets, and ability to pay: evidence from compensation executives", American Economic Review 83 (5): 1241–1259.

Machin, S. and A. Manning (1992), "Testing dynamic models of worker effort", Journal of Labor Economics 10 (3): 288–305.

MacLeod, W.B. (1996), "Decision, contract, and emotion: some economics for a complex and confusing world", Canadian Journal of Economics 29 (4): 788–810.

MacLeod, W.B. and J.M. Malcomson (1988), "Reputation and hierarchy in dynamic models of employment", Journal of Political Economy 96 (4): 832–854.

MacLeod, W.B. and J.M. Malcomson (1989), "Implicit contracts, incentive compatibility, and involuntary unemployment", Econometrica 57 (2): 447–480.

MacLeod, W.B. and J.M. Malcomson (1993a), "Investments, holdup, and the form of market contracts", American Economic Review 83 (4): 811–837.

MacLeod, W.B. and J.M. Malcomson (1993b), "Specific investment and wage profiles in labour markets", European Economic Review 37 (2,3): 343–354.

MacLeod, W.B. and J.M. Malcomson (1993c), "Wage premiums and profit maximization in efficiency wage models", European Economic Review 37 (6): 1223–1249.

MacLeod, W.B. and J.M. Malcomson (1995), "Contract bargaining with symmetric information", Canadian Journal of Economics 28 (2): 336–367.

MacLeod, W.B. and J.M. Malcomson (1998), "Motivation and markets", American Economic Review 88(3): 388–411.

MacLeod, W.B., J.M. Malcomson and P. Gomme (1994), "Labor turnover and the natural rate of unemployment: efficiency wage versus frictional unemployment", Journal of Labor Economics 12 (2): 276–315.

Malcomson, J.M. (1984), "Work incentives, hierarchy, and internal labor markets", Journal of Political Economy 92 (3): 486–507.

Malcomson, J.M. (1986), "Rank-order contracts for a principal with many agents", Review of Economic Studies 53 (5): 807–817.

Malcomson, J.M. (1997), "Contracts, hold-up, and labor markets", Journal of Economic Literature 35 (4): 1916–1957.

Manning, A. and J. Thomas (1996), A simple test of the shirking model (Department of Economics, London School of Economics).

Manove, M. (1997), "Job responsibility, pay and promotion", Economic Journal 107 (440): 85–103.

McLaughlin, K.J. (1991), "A theory of quits and layoffs with efficient turnover", Journal of Political Economy 99 (1): 1–29.

McLaughlin, K.J. (1994), "Rigid wages?" Journal of Monetary Economics 34 (3): 383–414.

Meyer, M.A. (1987), "Labor contracts under asymmetric information when workers are free to quit", Quarterly Journal of Economics 102 (3): 527–551.

Milgrom, P.R. (1988), "Employment contracts, influence actitivities, and efficient organization design", Journal of Political Economy 96 (1): 42–60.

Millward, N., M. Stevens, D. Smart and W.R. Hawes (1992), Workplace industrial relations in transition (The ED/ESRC/PSI/ACAS Surveys, Dartmouth, Aldershot, UK).

Mincer, J. (1962), "On-the-job training: costs, returns, and some implications", Journal of Political Economy 70 (5, pt. 2, suppl.): S50–S79.

Moene, K.O. (1988), "Union threats and wage determination", Economic Journal 98 (391): 471–483.

Mortensen, D.T. (1978), "Specific capital and labor turnover", Bell Journal of Economics 9 (2): 572–586.

Mortensen, D.T. and C.A. Pissarides (1994), "Job creation and job destruction in the theory of unemployment", Review of Economic Studies 61 (3): 397–415.

Murphy, K.M. and R.H. Topel (1990), "Efficiency wages reconsidered: theory and evidence", in: Y. Weiss and G. Fishelson, eds., Advances in the theory and measurement of unemployment (Macmillan, London).

Nöldeke, G. and K.M. Schmidt (1995), "Option contracts and renegotiation: a solution to the hold-up problem", RAND Journal of Economics 26 (2): 163–179.

Oi, W.Y. (1962), "Labor as a quasi-fixed factor", Journal of Political Economy 70 (6): 538–555.

Parsons, D.O. (1986), "The employment relationship: job attachment, work effort, and the nature of contracts", in: O. Ashenfelter and R. Layard, eds., Handbook of labor economics, Vol. 2 (North-Holland, Amsterdam) pp. 789–848.

Pissarides, C.A. (1985), "Short-run equilibrium dynamics of unemployment, vacancies and real wages", American Economic Review 75 (4): 676–690.

Pissarides, C.A. (1987), "Search, wage bargains and cycles", Review of Economic Studies 54 (3): 473–483.

Prendergast, C. (1993), "The role of promotion in inducing specific human capital acquisition", Quarterly Journal of Economics 108 (2): 523–534.

Prendergast, C. and R.H. Topel (1996), "Favoritism in organizations", Journal of Political Economy 104 (5): 958–978.

Ramey, G. and J. Watson (1996), "Bilateral trade and opportunism in a matching market", Discussion paper no. 96-08 (Department of Economics, University of California, San Diego, CA).

Ramey, G. and J. Watson (1997), "Contractual fragility, job destruction, and business cycles", Quarterly Journal of Economics 112 (3): 873–911.

Ransom, M.R. (1993), "Seniority and monopsony in the academic labor market", American Economic Review 83 (1): 221–233.

Rebitzer, J.B. (1995), "Is there a trade-off between supervision and wages? An empirical test of efficiency wage models of wage determination", Journal of Economic Behavior and Organization 28 (1): 107–129.

Rebitzer, J.B. and M.D. Robinson (1991), "Employer size and dual labor markets", Review of Economics and Statistics 73 (4): 710–715.

Rebitzer, J.B. and L.J. Taylor (1995), "Efficiency wages and employment rents: the employer-size wage effect in the job market for lawyers", Journal of Labor Economics 13 (4): 678–708.

Rogerson, W.P. (1992), "Contractual solutions to the hold-up problem", Review of Economic Studies 59 (4): 777–793.

Rosen, S. (1985), "Implicit contracts: a survey", Journal of Economic Literature 23 (3): 1144–1175.

Roth, A.E. (1995), "Introduction to experimental economics", in: J.H. Kagel and A.E. Roth, eds., Handbook of experimental economics (Princeton University Press, Princeton, NJ) pp. 3–109.

Rothstein, M.A., C.B. Craver, E.P. Schroeder, E.W. Shoben and L.S. VanderVelde (1994), "Employment law", in: Practioner treatise (West Publishing Co., St Paul, MN).

Rubinstein, A. (1982), "Perfect equilibrium in a bargaining model", Econometrica 50 (1): 97–109.

Shaked, A. (1994), "Opting out: bazaars versus 'high tech' markets", Investigaciones Económicas 18 (3): 421–432.

Shaked, A. and J. Sutton (1984), "Involuntary unemployment as a perfect equilibrium in a bargaining model", Econometrica 52 (6): 1351–1364.

Shapiro, C. and J.E. Stiglitz (1984), "Equilibrium unemployment as a worker discipline device", American Economic Review 74 (3): 433–444.

Solon, G., R. Barsky and J.A. Parker (1994), "Measuring the cyclicality of real wages: how important is composition bias?" Quarterly Journal of Economics 109 (1): 1–25.

Solow, R.M. (1990), The labour market as a social institution (Basil Blackwell, Oxford, UK).

Specter, H.A. and M.W. Finkin (1989), Individual employment law and litigation, Vols. 1 and 2 (Michie, Charlottesville, VA).

Stewart, J.B. (1993), "Taking the dare", The New Yorker, July 26, pp. 34–39.

Stole, L.A. and Zwiebel, J. (1996), "Organizational design and technology choice under intrafirm bargaining", American Economic Review 86 (1): 195–222.

Strand, J. (1987), "Unemployment as a discipline device with heterogeneous labor", American Economic Review 77 (3): 489–493.

Strand, J. (1992), "Business cycles with worker moral hazard", European Economic Review 36 (6): 1291–1303.

Sutton, J. (1986), "Non-cooperative bargaining theory: an introduction", Review of Economic Studies 53 (4): 709–724.

Taylor, J. (1979), "Staggered wage setting in a macro model", American Economic Review 69 (2): 108–113.

Thomas, J. and T. Worrall (1988), "Self-enforcing wage contracts", Review of Economic Studies 55 (4): 541–554.

Tirole, J. (1986), "Procurement and renegotiation", Journal of Political Economy 94 (2): 235–259.

Tirole, J. (1994), Incomplete contracts: where do we stand? (Walras-Bowley Lecture, Summer Meetings of the Econometric Society).

Topel, R. (1991), "Specific capital, mobility and wages: wages rise with job seniority", Journal of Political Economy 99 (1): 145–176.

Wadhwani, S.B. and M. Wall (1991), "A direct test of the efficiency wage model using UK micro-data", Oxford Economic Papers 43: 529–548.

Waldman, M. (1990), "Up-or-out contracts: a signaling perspective", Journal of Labor Economics 8 (2): 230–250.

Weiss, A. (1980), "Job queues and layoffs in labor markets with flexible wages", Journal of Political Economy 88 (3): 526–538.

Williamson, O.E. (1985), The economic institutions of capitalism: firms, markets, relational contracting (The Free Press, New York).

Wright, R.D. (1988), "The observational implications of labor contracts in a dynamic general equilibrium model", Journal of Labor Economics 6 (4): 530–551.

Chapter 36

CAREERS IN ORGANIZATIONS: THEORY AND EVIDE

ROBERT GIBBONS

Sloan School of Management, Massachusetts Institute of Technology

MICHAEL WALDMAN

Johnson Graduate School of Management, Cornell

Contents

  * We thank George Baker, Bengt Holmstrom, Ed Lazear, Bentley MacLeod, Jim Malcomson, Kevin J. Murphy, and Canice Prendergast for conversations that helped develop our thinking on these issues. Both authors thank Cornell's Johnson Graduate School of Management for financial support. Gibbons also thanks MIT's Sloan School of Management for financial support. Waldman also thanks the University of Chicago's Graduate School of Business and George J. Stigler Center for the Study of the Economy and the State for financial support.

Handbook of Labor Economics, Volume 3, Edited by O. Ashenfelter and D. Card

Abstract

We survey the theoretical literature on careers in organizations, focusing on models that address detailed evidence or stylized facts. We begin with what we call building-block models: human-capital acquisition, job assignment, incentive contracting, efficiency wages, and tournaments. We then show how these building blocks can be combined and enriched to address various aspects of careers. We first focus on applied models aimed at outcomes familiar from labor economics: wage growth in the absence of promotions, promotions used for job assignment, promotions used to provide incentives, and separation. We then consider topics more often discussed in human resource management and organization theory than in labor economics: politics, social relations, and work practices. We end by reviewing three models that address broad patterns of detailed evidence rather than a few stylized facts. © 1999 Elsevier Science B.V. All rights reserved.

JEL codes: J24; J31; J33; J41; M12

1. Introduction

Sociologists have long argued that we live in an organizational society: "all important social processes either have their origin in formal organizations or are strongly mediated by them" (Perrow, 1986, vii). In particular, classic accounts such as Whyte's (1956) *The Organization Man* and Kanter's (1977) *Men and Women of the Corporation* strongly suggest that pay, promotions, occupational choice, skill development, mobility, and a host of other employment outcomes are not determined in an institution-free labor market but instead are deeply affected by organizational structures and processes.

Economists, for their part, have produced substantial evidence that long-term attachments between workers and firms are important. For example, Hall (1982) found that over 25% of all workers were in jobs that would last 20 years or more and over 60% were in jobs that would last 5 years or more. More recently, Farber (1997) found that long-term attachments declined somewhat between 1979 and 1996 but still characterize a substantial fraction of current jobs. Beyond this kind of evidence, however, modern labor economics has relatively little to say about employment relationships. Several research areas in labor economics (such as unemployment duration and labor-force participation) end precisely when an employment relationship begins; others (such as on-the-job search and human-capital models of earnings) reduce the employment relationship to a wage, or at most a wage profile.

One could argue that economics is about markets, so labor economics should focus on the labor market, leaving the study of employment relationships to scholars in human resource management, industrial relations, organizational psychology, and organizational sociology. In this chapter we attempt to jump-start the opposite approach: we survey the emerging labor-economics literature on careers in organizations, focusing on theoretical models that can be (or, better still, have been) tested, and we suggest how future models promise to explain detailed patterns of evidence about employment relationships.

Most of the early labor-economics literature on careers in organizations was either theoretical or empirical. The theoretical side was dominated by analyses of labor- and product-market structures (monopsony, monopoly, and so on) and the prediction in the competitive case that a worker's wage should be equal to his marginal product. In these theories, the firm was a black box: predictions concerning wages and hours worked were derived by considering aggregate labor- and product-market conditions, and predictions concerning career development and job design were essentially non-existent. In contrast, the empirical side was dominated by descriptive analyses of how work is actually organized inside firms. Much of the empirical work, such as the landmark treatise by Doeringer and Piore (1971), suggested that the existing theoretical analyses were either incomplete or wrong.

Beginning with work by Becker, Holmstrom, Lazear, and Rosen, a new literature has begun to reduce this dichotomy between theory and evidence. These and subsequent authors have taken descriptive and econometric analyses of careers in organizations more seriously, and have modeled what goes on inside the black box in ways that help us understand this evidence. Rather than the old state of affairs, where the theoretical and empirical perspectives were often either unrelated or contradictory, we now see the beginnings of a symbiotic relationship between the two.

The chapter is divided into three parts. In part one (Section 2), we discuss building-block models. In part two (Sections 3 and 4), we discuss applied models that attempt to explain various pieces of evidence, often by extending or combining building-block models. Section 3 covers applied models in labor economics, Section 4 human resource management and organization theory. Finally, in part three (Section 5) we discuss an emerging literature that considers integrative models – that is, models built to explain broad patterns of detailed evidence rather than a few stylized facts.

The building-block models we consider in Section 2 are human-capital acquisition, job assignment, incentive contracting, efficiency wages, and tournaments. The human-capital discussion begins with the seminal work of Becker (1962, 1964). We then discuss the limitations of the Beckerian framework, focusing on issues such as observability, contractibility, and ex post bargaining. In the job-assignment discussion we begin with models of full information and clarify the circumstances under which efficient assignment is determined by comparative advantage. We then consider models of how a worker's job assignment may vary during her career due to learning. Finally, we consider three ways in which incentives are provided within firms: contracts, efficiency wages, and tournaments. The discussion of incentive contracts begins with the classic agency perspective developed in Holmstrom (1979, 1982a) and then considers what happens when performance measures do not perfectly capture the worker's contribution to the firm. The discussion of efficiency wages begins with a simple repeated-game model and then considers how bonding affects the analysis. The discussion of tournaments begins with Lazear and Rosen (1981) and then considers the differences between a single contest and a sequence of contests.

The second part of the survey shows how the building-block models discussed in Section 2 can be extended and combined to address various aspects of careers in organizations. This part of the survey is divided into two sections. Section 3 focuses on applied models aimed at outcomes familiar from labor economics: wage growth in the absence of promotions, promotions used for job assignment, promotions used to provide incentives, and separation. In the discussion of wage growth we consider how monitoring, self-selection, and learning can all lead to substantial wage growth during a worker's career, even in the absence of human-capital acquisition and promotion possibilities. In the discussion of promotions as assignments, we consider how both learning and human-capital acquisition can explain why workers move up a job ladder as they age, while the discussion of promotions as incentive devices considers incentives for effort and incentives for skill acquisition. Finally, the discussion of separations considers issues such as why quits are associated with higher average wage changes than are layoffs, and how the information structure in the labor market affects separation decisions.

Section 4 again considers applied models, but this time focused on topics more often discussed in human resource management and organization theory than in labor economics: politics, social relations, and work practices. By politics we mean interactions across levels of a hierarchy, in cases where the subordinate would like to influence a (non-contractible) decision to be taken by the superior. As aspects of politics we discuss influence activities and side contracting. By social relations we mean interactions within a level of a hierarchy rather than across. We discuss how peer pressure and mutual monitoring affect equilibrium effort levels. Finally, by work practices we mean innovative human-resource practices such as teams and empowerment that many argue are associated with high levels of firm performance. Here we consider whether theories of complementarities in the workplace can explain this evidence.

The third part of the survey, which appears in Section 5, reviews papers from an emerging literature in which integrative models address a broad pattern of evidence rather than one or a few facts. The advantage of this approach is that any single fact may be consistent with multiple theoretical models, so one way of choosing among theories is by evaluating the extent to which a theory is consistent with a broad pattern of evidence. We review three papers from this literature. The first is an early paper in this vein, Harris and Holmstrom (1982), in which firms learn about workers' abilities and provide insurance to risk-averse workers through the compensation scheme. Harris and Holmstrom show that their model can explain a number of empirical findings, including that wages grow with labor-market experience even if productivity does not (Medoff and Abraham, 1980, 1981), that the variance of wages grows with labor-market experience (Mincer, 1974), and that the wage distribution exhibits positive skewness (Mincer, 1974).

The more recent papers we review are Demougin and Siow (1994) and Gibbons and Waldman (1999). Demougin and Siow construct a model in which some young unskilled workers undergo training, in the hope that they will become qualified to be a manager. A key assumption of their model is that a firm incurs a hiring cost when the managerial position is filled with an outsider. Demougin and Siow show that their model can generate various familiar practices, such as fast-track promotions, up-or-out rules, and promotion from within. Gibbons and Waldman consider a model that combines job assignment, on-the-job human-capital acquisition, and learning. They show that their model explains many of the findings in the recent empirical study by Baker et al. (1994a,b), as well as a number of the earlier empirical results of Medoff and Abraham (1980, 1981).

Throughout the chapter we attempt to assess the extent to which the theoretical models surveyed match the available evidence concerning careers in organizations. Gibbons (1997) summarizes much of the evidence available through 1995. Even though Gibbons largely focuses on white-collar, salaried workers in large, contemporary US firms, the evidence he summarizes comes from a variety of sources, including human resource management, industrial relations, organizational psychology, organizational sociology, as well as labor economics. The evidence also comes in a variety of styles: longitudinal microdata on individuals of the kind commonly used in labor economics, such as Abowd and Card (1989); longitudinal personnel files from single firms, such as Baker et al. (1994a,b); and static case studies, such as Murphy (1991). Some of the latest evidence comes in an exciting new form: longitudinal data on individuals and firms (Abowd et al., 1999), allowing one to distinguish between unmeasured aspects of workers (such as ability) and unmeasured policies of firms (such as efficiency wages and wage-tenure profiles).

Because of these varieties of data sources and styles, it is important to know which findings hold in which environments. Gibbons therefore suggests ten core questions that future empirical papers could usefully address before focusing on their particular concerns. (In fact, it would be helpful if authors of existing papers could return to their datasets to answer any of the questions they did not answer in their original papers.) Some of these questions are: Is there a fast track? Are nominal wage cuts rare? Are changes in wage residuals serially correlated? Do wage increases forecast promotions? Do wages increase and are promotions more likely for those with higher performance evaluations? And is the effect of seniority on wages independent of controls for performance evaluation? The three theoretical papers we summarize in Section 5 show that models can speak to collections of questions of this kind, and more importantly that some models match broad patterns of evidence rather well.

In spite of our discussions of building-block models, applied models, and integrative models, we are unable to offer a comprehensive survey of all the work related to careers in organizations. For example, there has been significant recent progress in understanding the nature of contracts in the labor market; our survey only touches on some of these recent developments, but see Malcomson (1999) in this Handbook. Similarly, the nature of careers in organizations is clearly affected by decisions about the boundaries of the firm (i.e., which tasks and production processes are housed within a firm and which are in other firms); our survey scarcely mentions this boundaries issue, but it is the main subject of the theory of the firm, on which see Holmstrom and Tirole (1989) and Holmstrom and Roberts (1998).

2. Building-block models

This section surveys models and concepts that are frequently employed as building blocks in more complex models of careers in organizations. The five topics we cover are human-capital acquisition, job assignment, incentive contracting, efficiency wages, and tournaments.

2.1. Human-capital acquisition

The modern theory of human-capital acquisition within the firm begins with the seminal contribution of Becker (1962, 1964); other early work includes Mincer (1962) and Schultz (1963). Becker's analysis focused on two distinct cases: general and firm-specific human capital. General human capital refers to training that is valued equally by many firms, while specific human capital refers to training that has value at the firm providing the training but no value elsewhere. Becker's analysis of general human capital is straightforward: a worker's wage after training simply equals the value of the worker at both the initial employer and elsewhere, so the worker must finance the training through a lower wage during the training period. That is, since the return to training is completely captured by the worker rather than the firm, the firm will be willing to provide training only if the worker (ultimately) bears the cost.

In contrast, the cost of and the return to specific human capital are shared by the worker and the firm. The logic here is as follows. Since specific training is not valued by alternative employers, the firm is not forced by outside offers to have the post-training wage reflect the increased productivity from training. But if the firm captures all the returns from the worker's increased productivity then the worker may have an incentive to quit (e.g., to follow a spouse), and this possibility decreases the firm's expected return from training. As a result, the firm chooses to pay a post-training wage that includes at least part of the increased productivity from training, which in turn means that the worker will again be willing to finance part of the cost of training through a lower wage during the training period.

One literature that grew out of Becker's work focuses on general human capital and optimal investment decisions; see Weiss (1986) for a survey. For example, Ben-Porath (1967) considers a setting where at each instant a worker must decide how to allocate his time between producing output and investing in the accumulation of general human capital (i.e., there is no specific capital or leisure). Other important assumptions are that an individual's capital stock depreciates at a constant rate, that there is unlimited borrowing and lending, and that the human-capital production function exhibits diminishing marginal returns. Ben-Porath shows that this simple model captures a number of characteristics of observed life-cycle earnings such as an initial period of no earnings (e.g., during schooling), a subsequent period where earnings rise at a decreasing rate, and a final period in which earnings decline.

This life-cycle approach has been extended to incorporate leisure (Weiss, 1972; Killingsworth, 1982), borrowing constraints (Wallace and Inhen, 1975), and uncertainty (Levhari and Weiss, 1974; Williams, 1979). These extensions have shown that the approach can capture further empirical regularities. For example, incorporating leisure allows the framework to capture the findings of Mincer (1974) and Ghez and Becker

(1975) that hours of work first rise and then decline with age, and that hours peak prior to the peak in earnings.

Another literature that grew out of Becker's work focuses on specific human capital. In Becker's analysis of specific human capital, the determination and consequences of the quit decision are not formally derived. Hashimoto (1981) formalizes Becker's argument; see also Parsons (1972). In Hashimoto's analysis, there is uncertainty concerning the worker's post-training productivity at both the current employer and other potential employers, and the post-training wage is decided prior to the realization of these productivities. Hashimoto shows that, if the post-training wage cannot be made a function of these productivity realizations and there is no renegotiation, then it is efficient for the cost of training and the return to training to be shared by the worker and the firm. Similar to the logic from Becker, the rationale is that sharing minimizes the losses associated with inefficient quit and dismissal decisions.[1]

Hall and Lazear (1984) also consider quit and dismissal decisions in the presence of specific human capital, but their analysis moves away from a focus on Becker's sharing hypothesis. They begin by considering three simple ways that the post-training wage can be determined: (i) the wage is fixed prior to training, as in the Becker and Hashimoto analyses; (ii) the firm sets the wage after observing the realization of the worker's post-training productivity with the current employer; and (iii) the worker sets the wage after observing the realization of her post-training productivity with potential employers. Hall and Lazear show that none of these wage-determination schemes leads to first-best quit and dismissal decisions, and that any of the three can be superior to the other two. They then consider a variety of other wage-determination schemes such as piece rates, severance payments, and offer matching (where each party matches the alternative offers of the other) and argue that, although each may theoretically result in efficient separation, each is typically infeasible because of information limitations.[2]

Becker's analysis of human-capital investment is clearly an important contribution to our understanding of earnings and skill development, but in some ways the analysis is

---

[1] Other studies that consider Becker's sharing hypothesis are Mortensen (1978) and Carmichael (1983). Mortensen argues that sharing does not lead to a first-best outcome because each party does not take into account the effects of its quit/dismissal decision on the welfare of the other. In the context of a job-matching model, he then explores the efficiency properties of severance payments and offer matching. Carmichael considers a two-period model where a worker's second-period productivity and second-period job satisfaction are stochastic, and focuses on the efficiency properties of a compensation scheme characterized by a fixed number of high-wage jobs into which workers are promoted at the end of their careers. He shows that the optimal compensation scheme of this type results in smaller efficiency losses than the sharing arrangement considered by Becker and Hashimoto.

[2] Meyerson and Satterthwaite (1983) provide a formal analysis of a more general problem that supports Hall and Lazear's conclusion. Meyerson and Satterthwaite consider the most efficient trading mechanism when there is a buyer and a seller of a single object, and each party's valuation for the object is privately known. Consistent with Hall and Lazear's conclusion, Meyerson and Satterthwaite show that it is impossible to have a trading mechanism that satisfies incentive compatibility, individual rationality, and ex post efficiency. In other words, in the setting considered by Hall and Lazear, there exists no feasible wage-determination scheme that achieves separation efficiency.

quite limited. His analysis implicitly assumes that a worker and firm can sign a court-enforceable contract that specifies pre- and post-training wages and investment levels in general and specific human capital. But it is not at all clear that such an approach is realistic. Human-capital investment levels are typically not specified in contracts, and it is not clear that such investment levels are even contractible variables. Furthermore, post-training wages are not typically specified in a contract, and can often be renegotiated after training has taken place.

Our feeling is that an equally useful approach to human-capital investment would assume that investment levels are not contractible and that post-training wages are determined by bargaining. Malcomson (1997) surveys recent models in this spirit. As one simple base case, imagine a two-period setting where a worker acquires general and/or specific human capital during the first period, leading to increased productivity during the second period. Rather than having the investment levels being enforced by contract, both the worker and the firm choose human-capital investments non-cooperatively. Further, whether separation occurs and the second-period wage if it does not are determined by Nash bargaining between the worker and the firm after second-period productivities have been revealed.

This approach to human-capital investment introduces a number of issues that do not arise in Becker's formulation. For example, the hold-up problem originally analyzed by Williamson (1975, 1979) and Klein et al. (1978) suggests that both parties will underinvest in specific human capital; see Grout (1984) and Hart and Moore (1988) for formal analyses related to this argument. The logic is as follows. Consider the worker's choice of an investment level in specific human capital. Given that the post-training wage is determined by Nash bargaining, an increase in second-period productivity due to an increase in this investment level will be partially, but not fully, captured by the worker through a higher second-period wage. In turn, since the increase in the second-period wage does not fully reflect the increase in productivity, the worker has an incentive to underinvest. A similar argument suggests the firm will also underinvest in specific human capital.[3]

Other interesting issues arise in this framework when asymmetric learning is introduced. Asymmetric learning means that a worker's current employer learns more about the worker's productivity than do other potential employers. For example, Chang and Wang (1996) consider a model with some of the features described above, but also assume asymmetric learning; see also Katz and Ziderman (1990). Specifically, in Chang and Wang's model, investment in human capital is not contractible and the post-training wage for a worker who remains with the first-period employer is determined by Nash bargaining between the worker and the first-period employer. The authors introduce asymmetric learning by assuming that the investment choice of the first-period employer is not observed by other potential employers.

---

[3] Williamson (1985, chapter 10) analyzes hold-up in the labor context and develops arguments concerning unions, grievance procedures, and seniority rules. Zabojnik (1998) argues that, in response to workers' incentive to underinvest in specific capital, firms may provide managers with an incentive to maximize sales in addition to profits. The logic is that this makes managers less aggressive in post-investment bargaining over wages, which in turn increases workers' incentive to invest.

Chang and Wang derive two major results. First, there is underinvestment in human capital, where the severity of the underinvestment is negatively related to the specificity of the capital. This result contrasts with Williamson's perspective described above, where underinvestment is more severe when human capital is more specific. Second, investment in human capital is positively related to the probability that the worker remains with the first-period employer in the second period, even when human capital is purely general. This result contrasts with the standard argument in which investments in general human capital are independent of the probability that the worker remains with the pre-training employer. Both of Chang and Wang's results follow from the non-contractibility of the investment in combination with asymmetric learning. Because potential employers cannot observe the firm's investment, the market wage is independent of the investment the firm chooses. Because the investment is not contractible, the firm cannot offer a trade-off between the pre-training wage and the investment level. As a result, the firm's incentive to invest is determined solely by the amount of the increased productivity that the firm is able to capture in second-period profits. The two results described above then follow because Nash bargaining determines the post-training wage.

Acemoglu and Pischke (1998) develop an alternative model of asymmetric learning about human-capital acquisition.[4] They incorporate asymmetric learning into a Beckerian framework (i.e., both the training level and the post-training wage are specified in the initial employment contract). Their information asymmetry was initially explored by Greenwald (1986): a worker's first-period employer observes the worker's ability but potential employers do not; as a result, workers who change employers are drawn disproportionately from the low end of the ability distribution. (See Section 3.4 for more on Greenwald's analysis.) Because of adverse selection, the firm earns monopsony-type rents on the workers that are retained. Thus, in contrast to the standard Beckerian story, firms have an incentive to finance the acquisition of purely general human capital.[5] In addition to developing the theory, the authors provide evidence concerning German apprentices that supports their theoretical analysis.[6]

2.2. Job assignment

An important feature of careers in organizations is the assignment of workers to jobs within the firm; see Sattinger (1993) for a survey. Sattinger (1975) and Rosen (1978)

---

[4] Scoones and Bernhardt (1998) also consider a model of human-capital acquisition involving asymmetric information. In their model human-capital investment is not contractible, and the worker must decide whether to invest in general or specific capital. Scoones and Bernhardt show that, if workers can commit to the nature of their human-capital investment, then they will choose to invest in specific capital. The logic of their argument is that, by committing to invest in specific human capital, the worker creates a return for the initial employer in later periods, and so increases the willingness for firms to bid for the worker up front.

[5] Acemoglu and Pischke (1996) generalize the argument by showing that asymmetric learning is not necessary to find this result; several labor-market imperfections that create monopsony-type rents can yield this conclusion.

[6] For other evidence that firms share some of the costs and returns to general training see Barron et al. (1989), Bishop (1991), and Loewenstein and Spletzer (1998).

show that comparative advantage determines the assignment of workers to jobs in many settings. But there are other settings in which comparative advantage is not the determining factor. We begin by describing a simple environment where comparative advantage does determine assignments.[7]

Suppose each firm consists of two jobs, denoted 1 and 2. Let a_{ij} denote worker i's productivity in job j, and let a representative firm's output be

$$Y = f(\Sigma a_{i1}, \Sigma a_{i2}), \tag{1}$$

where Σa_{ij} is the sum of the a_{ij}'s for all the workers that the firm assigns to job j (if a worker splits his time between jobs then his ability is multiplied by the proportion of the time he spends in job j). In this setting, assignments will typically be determined by comparative advantage.[8] For example, suppose that an individual of type 1 has a comparative advantage at job 1 (and thus an individual of type 2 has a comparative advantage at job 2):

$$a_{11}/a_{21} > a_{12}/a_{22}. \tag{2}$$

Then it cannot be the case that an individual of type 1 will be assigned to job 2 and an individual of type 2 will be assigned to job 1. To see this, note that in staffing job j, a firm will prefer a worker of type i over a worker of type i' if the wage per unit of productivity is lower for worker i: $w_i/a_{ij} < w_{i'}/a_{i'j}$ or $a_{ij}/a_{i'j} > w_i/w_{i'}$, where w_i is the wage for a worker of type i. Eq. (2) tells us that it cannot simultaneously be the case that $a_{12}/a_{22} > w_1/w_2$ and $a_{21}/a_{11} > w_2/w_1$. Thus, a worker of type 1 cannot be assigned to job 2 while a type 2 worker is assigned to job 1.

In contrast to the setting above, there are many environments in which comparative advantage is not the deciding factor; for examples, see Rosen (1982), Waldman (1984a), and MacDonald and Markusen (1985). As a simple example, suppose again that each firm consists of two jobs, but now suppose each job can be filled by at most one worker and a worker cannot split his time between jobs. To see that assignment is not always consistent with comparative advantage in this setting, suppose that output is $a_{i1} + a_{i2}$ if both jobs are filled but is zero if one or both jobs is left vacant, and that there are two worker types of equal numbers in the economy, where $a_{11} = 10$, $a_{12} = 5$, $a_{21} = 25$, and $a_{22} = 15$. Eq. (2) tells us that workers of type 1 have a comparative advantage in job 1, while workers of type 2 have a comparative advantage in job 2. But a firm that hires a type 1 worker for job 1 and a type 2 worker for job 2 produces an output of 25, while reversing the assignments keeps the wage bill the same and increases output to 30. Thus,

---

[7] Our discussion assumes that workers are heterogeneous. Rosen (1983) shows how human-capital accumulation can create comparative advantage starting from a situation where workers are identical. The logic is that in equilibrium workers have an incentive to specialize in the skills that they acquire.

[8] We are assuming that workers do not inherently prefer one job over another (i.e., a worker simply takes the job that offers the highest wage). See Friedman and Kuznets (1954) for an early analysis in which workers have inherent preferences for one job over another and Rosen (1986a) for a survey on the resulting "equalizing differences."

the equilibrium assignment is that type 2 workers are assigned to job 1 while type 1 workers are assigned to job 2.

A key difference between our two examples concerns whether assigning multiple workers to a job is identical to assigning a single worker whose productivity is the sum of the productivities of the multiple workers. In settings where these options are identical, comparative advantage will typically determine the equilibrium assignments. But when there are jobs in the firm that must be staffed by a single worker, equilibrium assignments will frequently not be consistent with comparative advantage.[9] In many of the papers that develop this point, jobs vary in terms of the value that is placed on ability, with the result that high-ability workers are assigned to the jobs that value ability more highly.[10]

Neither of the examples above assumes (or derives) that jobs are ordered in a job ladder, but both have been extended in this direction. Sattinger (1975) considers a model where output on each job is a function of the sum of the productivities of the (potentially) multiple workers assigned to the job, and thus comparative advantage determines assignment in his setting. Rosen (1982) and Waldman (1984a) consider models in which at least some jobs must be staffed by a single worker, with the result that high-ability workers are assigned to jobs that value ability more highly. In all three models, for some parameterizations, higher-ability workers are assigned to higher levels of the firm's job ladder. Geanakoplos and Milgrom (1991) develop a more detailed model of workers' decision-making limitations, and also derive conditions under which higher-ability workers are assigned to higher levels of the firm's job ladder.

So far, we have considered job assignment under full information: all firms know each worker's ability exactly. A number of authors have considered symmetric learning: all firms gradually learn workers' abilities, but at any point in time all firms are equally well informed about each worker's ability. For example, MacDonald (1982a) considers a setting in which assignments would be determined by comparative advantage under full information; related analyses appear in Ross et al. (1981) and MacDonald (1982b). MacDonald (1982a) finds that equilibrium assignments are still determined by comparative advantage, although this is now determined by expected worker types rather than actual worker types. Another finding is that expected productivity and expected wage are both positively related to labor-market experience. This occurs because, as a worker ages, firms become more certain of the worker's ability, so assignments become more efficient and expected output rises. This result is of interest because it provides a rationale other

---

[9] There are many settings in which assigning multiple workers to a job is not identical to assigning a single worker whose productivity is the sum of the productivities of the multiple workers. For example, this arises when a job is associated with the use of a machine that can only be used by one person at a time, so any additional workers would be idle.

[10] This last point is sometimes referred to as the "scale of operations effect," because high-ability workers are assigned to jobs that have control over more resources, since it is these jobs which value ability more highly; see Mayer (1960) and Spurr (1987). A related idea is the assignment of workers to jobs in "winner-take-all" markets; see Rosen (1981) and Frank and Cook (1995).

than the standard human-capital explanation for why wages grow over a career. In Section 3.1 we discuss still other explanations for this evidence.

Murphy (1986) also considers a setting in which firms are imperfectly informed about a worker's ability at the beginning of the worker's career and gradually learn about the worker's ability as the career progresses. Murphy assumes that ability is single-dimensional, but a worker's output depends on both the worker's ability and the amount of capital that she is assigned. He also assumes that ability and capital are complements: output is the product of the two. From these assumptions, Murphy derives three results. First, because ability and capital are complements, the amount of capital assigned to a worker in any period is an increasing function of the worker's expected ability at that date. Second, because beliefs about ability become more precise as a worker ages, the assignment of capital to workers becomes more efficient, so expected productivity and expected wage are positively related to labor-market experience. Third, because the rate of learning decreases with age, the rate of increase in expected output eventually declines with age, so expected productivity and expected wage are both concave in labor-market experience.

2.3. Incentive contracting

Another important issue concerning careers in organizations is the manner in which firms provide workers with incentives to exert effort. This subsection briefly introduces the contracting approach to this problem.[11] The following two subsections consider the efficiency-wage and tournament approaches to incentives.

The classic approach to incentive contracting is the agency perspective developed by Mirrlees (1974, 1976), Holmstrom (1979), and Shavell (1979), which focuses on the trade-off between risk and incentives. In this approach, an agent chooses an effort level e, but incurs a cost of effort $c(e)$, where $c' > 0$ and $c'' > 0$. There is noise in the production process, in the sense that the output produced by the agent's effort is uncertain, but higher effort levels lead to higher expected output. The agent's output, y, is owned by an individual called the principal. A contract between the principal and the agent specifies a wage for the agent, $w(y)$, that is contingent on the realized value of output. Finally, the agent is risk-averse and has a reservation utility level U_0. To provide full insurance to the risk-averse agent, the principal should pay the agent a constant wage, but that provides no incentive for effort. To provide first-best incentives, the principal should pay the worker $w(y) = y - F$ (equivalent to selling the firm to the agent for a fixed fee of F), but that provides no insurance. The efficient contract trades off these goals of full insurance and first-best incentives.

To develop intuition, consider the linear-normal-exponential case. Let the production function be linear: $y = e + \varepsilon$, where ε is a normally distributed noise term with mean zero and variance σ^2. Assume that the contract is also linear: $w(y) = s + by$, where s is the

---

[11] See Malcomson (1999) and Prendergast (1999) for surveys that emphasize theoretical perspectives, and Rosen (1992) and Murphy (1999) for surveys that focus on executive compensation.

worker's salary and b is the proportion of output that the worker receives as a bonus or commission. The agent's utility function is $U(x) = -e^{-rx}$, where $r > 0$ is the agent's coefficient of absolute risk aversion and $x = w - c(e)$ is the agent's net payoff (i.e., the realized wage minus the cost of effort). For simplicity, assume the principal is risk neutral and so seeks to maximize the expected value of profit, $y - w$.

To maximize expected utility, the agent should choose the effort level that equates the marginal cost of effort with its marginal benefit: $c'(e) = b$. Knowing that this is how the agent will behave, the principal chooses s and b to maximize the expected value of profit, namely $(1 - b)e*(b) - s$, where $e*(b)$ solves $c'(e) = b$. Analysis of the principal's maximization problem yields that the efficient bonus rate, $b*$, is

$$b* = 1/(1 + r\sigma^2 c'').\tag{3}$$

This result is intuitive. Since r, σ^2, and c'' are all positive, the optimal bonus rate is strictly between zero (full insurance) and one (first-best incentives, where $c'(e) = 1$). Further, Eq. (3) also tells us that the optimal bonus rate is negatively related to the agent's risk aversion, to the uncertainty in the production process, and to the rate at which marginal cost of effort increases.[12,13]

A natural extension of the basic analysis concerns relative performance evaluation. That is, if a single principal is contracting with multiple agents, to what extent should the contract between the principal and any single agent depend on the realized outputs of the other agents?[14] This issue is considered in Holmstrom (1982a). Suppose there are n agents, where $y_i = e_i + \theta_i + \varepsilon_i$. Both θ_i and ε_i are noise terms; the ε_i's are independent across agents but the θ_i's may not be. Holmstrom showed that if the θ_i's are also independent of each other then it is optimal to have each agent's pay depend on only the realization of his own output, but that if the θ_i's are correlated then it is optimal for each agent's pay to depend on the realized outputs of the other agents. The basic idea underlying these results is that, for any agent i, relative performance evaluation is useful only to the extent that other agents' outputs provide information about agent i's noise terms. When the θ_i's are independent, no information is provided and relative performance evaluation is not used. When the θ_i's are correlated, other outputs provide information about θ_i and some form of relative performance evaluation is optimal.

---

[12] Garen (1994) and Aggarwal and Samwick (1999) find evidence from executive compensation that the optimal bonus rate is negatively related to the uncertainty in the firm's stock price.

[13] In most cases the efficient linear contract derived here is inferior to various non-linear contracts. This was first shown by Mirrlees (1974). See Holmstrom and Milgrom (1987) for a setting in which the best linear contract is the optimal contract overall.

[14] A similar analysis arises when there are multiple principal–agent relationships in the economy, each consisting of a single principal and a single agent. The issue then is whether the agent's pay in any specific principal–agent relationship should depend on the performance of other agents in the economy. A real-world example here is whether a CEO's pay should depend only on the performance of the CEO's own firm, or whether performance should be compared with the performances of competing firms. This issue has been studied by Antle and Smith (1986), Gibbons and Murphy (1990), and Janakiraman et al. (1992). Antle and Smith find weak support for the use of relative-performance evaluation in CEO pay; the others find stronger support.

To see how relative-performance evaluation might work when the θ_i's are correlated, consider the following example. Suppose that $\theta_i = \theta$ for all i, so that $y_i = e_i + \theta + \varepsilon_i$, where $(\theta, \varepsilon_1, ..., \varepsilon_n)$ are independent normal noise terms. Let z_i denote the average of the $n - 1$ other agents' outputs: $z_i = (y_1 + \cdots + y_{i-1} + y_{i+1} + \cdots + y_n)/(n - 1)$. In this case, the pure own-performance contract, $w_i = s + by_i$, subjects agent i to two noise terms, θ and ε_i, while the pure relative-performance contract, $w_i = s + b(y_i - z_i)$, eliminates the risk due to θ but subjects the agent to risk from ε_i and from the average of the realizations of the $n - 1$ values for $\varepsilon_j, j \neq i$. In this example the efficient contract is neither the own-performance contract nor the relative-performance contract, but instead is a contract of the form $w_i = s + by_i - dz_i$, where $b^* > d^* > 0$. This contract reflects a trade-off between eliminating the risk from θ and avoiding the risk from the average of the realizations of the $n - 1$ values for ε_j. In particular, as the variance of θ increases, eliminating the risk from θ becomes more important and d^* approaches b^* (i.e., the optimal contract approaches pure relative performance).

This classic agency analysis is clear and compelling, but also has two important short-comings. First, similar to our discussion of Becker's human-capital analysis, most workers do not work under contracts of the sort assumed in the classic agency model. Instead, incentives are often provided through bonuses, wage increases, and promotions, but these payments or decisions are not formally tied to one's own performance or the performance of others. Second, the trade-off between incentives and insurance is only one of the important aspects of real-world attempts to tie pay to performance. In many cases, tying pay to performance had consequences that are not captured by classic agency analysis. For example, at Bausch and Lomb the hurdle for a bonus often entailed double-digit earnings growth. Managers often met their targets in ways that were not obviously in the best long-run interest of the firm (e.g., over half a million pairs of "sold" sunglasses were discovered in a warehouse in Hong Kong (Maremont, 1995).[15]

In the remainder of this subsection we consider two alternative approaches to incentive contracting, each of which addresses one or both of the concerns just raised about the classic agency analysis. The first approach follows Holmstrom and Milgrom (1991) and Baker (1992) to offer an explanation for why incentive contracting sometimes leads to undesired consequences. Their explanation focuses on the distinction between a worker's total contribution to firm value, denoted by y, and the worker's measured performance, denoted by p. In classic agency analysis, y and p are identical, but in many real-world settings the two are very different. A worker's total contribution to firm value frequently includes components such as the contemporaneous effects of the worker's actions on co-workers and the long-run effects of the worker's current actions that are not captured in contemporaneous measures of the worker's performance.

In Baker's model the worker's contribution to firm value is given by $y = \theta e + \varepsilon$, but

---

[15] See Brown et al. (1996), Chevalier and Ellison (1997), Cragg (1997), and Oyer (1998) for systematic empirical evidence in this spirit. On the other hand, see Lazear (1997) for systematic evidence that in some environments piece-rate pay plans can function precisely as intended, with regard to both incentives and selec-tion, as predicted in Lazear (1986a).

measured performance is $p = \mu e + \gamma$. The variables ε and γ are noise terms, but θ and μ are features of the environment that are privately observed by the worker before choosing an effort level. The worker's wage is a linear function of measured performance: $w = s + bp$. In this setting, the worker has an incentive to work hard when doing so will increase measured performance (i.e., when $dp/de = \mu$ is large) but the firm wants the worker to supply high effort when doing so will increase the worker's contribution to firm value (i.e., when $dy/de = \theta$ is large). Hence, Baker finds that p is a good performance measure when there is a high correlation between dp/de and dy/de. When this correlation is high, it is optimal for the firm to provide strong incentives by making b large. In contrast, when this correlation is low, it is optimal for the firm to offer weak incentives by making b small. The reason is that, related to the Bausch and Lomb example discussed above, when measured performance is not closely related to the firm's goals, then strong incentives can be dysfunctional, making weak incentives optimal.

The second alternative approach to incentive contracting considers "relational" contracts used to provide incentives in ongoing relationships.[16] In many cases it is impossible to measure a worker's total contribution to firm value in a manner that could be verified by a court, yet well informed insiders may agree on the worker's contribution (or at least on an estimate of that contribution). When this is the case, the worker and firm may decide to use a relational contract that is based on their mutual assessment of the worker's total contribution y rather than a formal contract based on an objective but distortionary performance measure p. The potential drawback is that relational contracts are backed only by the parties' reputations rather than the courts, which means that when the contract calls for the firm to pay a large wage the firm may be tempted to renege.

The idea of a relational incentive contract has been formalized in a repeated-game model by Bull (1987); see MacLeod and Malcomson (1989, 1998) for related analyses and Carmichael (1989) and Malcomson (1999) for surveys. As a simple example of these ideas, consider an infinitely lived firm that faces a sequence of workers, each of whom is in the labor market for one period. Let each worker's contribution to firm value be either high or low ($y = H$ or L). Suppose that the firm pays a salary of S at the beginning of each period and promises that it will pay a bonus B at the end of a period if $y = H$. If the worker believes the promise, then the bonus induces an effort level $e^*(B)$ from the worker, and this determines the firm's expected profit per period from keeping its promise, $E\Pi(S,B)$. Whether the firm has an incentive to keep its promise depends on two things: the behavior of future workers if the firm reneges today and the discount rate of the firm. If reneging today causes future workers to punish the firm (say, by choosing to supply no effort) and the discount rate is sufficiently low (so that the present value of being punished outweighs the current return to reneging), then there is a relational contract that results in first-best effort.

---

[16] Contracts we call "relational" are sometimes called "self-enforcing" (Klein, 1996), "implicit" (MacLeod and Malcomson, 1989), or both (Bull, 1987). Our use of relational follows the legal literature such as Macneil (1978). Authors who use the term implicit naturally call formal contracts explicit. The problem with this usage is that implicit can connote vague, when in practice it is frequently important that relational contracts be clearly understood.

In real-world settings, it is clear that firms frequently employ a mix of formal and relational contracts. For example, Lincoln Electric is well known for its use of piece rates, but half of compensation at that firm is delivered through subjectively determined bonuses (Fast and Berg, 1975). Baker et al. (1994) developed a model that combines these two alternative approaches to incentive contracting: formal contracts based on a distortionary performance measure (as in Baker's model), and relational contracts based on total contribution to firm value (as in Bull's model). They find that employing both formal and relational contracts allows the firm to do better than using only one type or the other. One role of the relational contract is to reduce the distortionary incentives associated with the formal contract; one role of the formal contract is to reduce the size of the relational-contract bonus that the firm could save by reneging.

Hayes and Schaefer (1999) test the idea that compensation is frequently determined by a mix of formal and relational contracts. They begin by deriving two predictions from this perspective. First, the variation in current compensation that is not explained by current measured performance should be positively correlated with future measured performance. Second, this relationship should be stronger when performance measures are noisier and thus less useful for contracting. Hayes and Schaefer test these predictions using CEO compensation data, and find evidence that supports both predictions.

2.4. Efficiency wages

This subsection considers the efficiency-wage approach to incentives. In the contracting approach just discussed the firm makes the wage an increasing function of output, and this elicits effort as the worker attempts to increase her realized wage. In the efficiency-wage approach, in contrast, the wage does not depend on output, but the firm elicits effort by paying a single wage that is above the market-clearing level and threatening to fire the worker if performance is too low.[17]

A classic model in this vein is Shapiro and Stiglitz (1984); other early models of this type include Calvo (1979, 1985) and Bulow and Summers (1986). Shapiro and Stiglitz focus on the implications for unemployment. In order to focus on effort incentives, we present a simplified model that abstracts from unemployment. Consider a single risk-neutral worker and single risk-neutral firm. In each period, the firm offers a wage w and the worker either accepts or rejects the offer. If the worker rejects, then she becomes self-employed at wage w_a. If the worker accepts, then she chooses either high effort (which entails disutility c) or low effort (which entails no disutility). The worker's output is either high or low ($y = H$ or L). Output is certain to be high if the worker chooses high effort, but if the worker chooses low effort then output is high with probability p and low with

---

[17] An efficiency wage refers to an above-market-clearing wage that is paid because of the resulting increase in worker productivity. Sources of the increase in productivity include but are not restricted to increased effort. Other sources include reductions in turnover (Salop, 1979; Stiglitz, 1985) and the selection of high-ability workers (Weiss, 1980). Our focus is on efficiency wages that increase effort incentives; see Katz (1986) and Weiss (1990) for surveys.

probability $1 - p$. Suppose that $H - c > w_a > pH + (1 - p)L$, so it is efficient for the worker to be employed by the firm and to choose high effort. Finally, suppose the firm does not observe the worker's effort choice but does observe output. The firm therefore knows with certainty that the worker chose low effort when it observes low output.

In the one-shot version of this game, the outcome is bleak. Because the firm pays w in advance, the worker has no incentive to choose high effort, so the firm offers $w = pH + (1 - p)L$ (or any other $w < w_a$) and the worker chooses self-employment. In the infinitely repeated version of the game, however, the firm can induce effort by promising a wage $w^* > w_a$ for every period and threatening to fire the worker if output is ever low. To be precise, suppose behavior switches to the equilibrium of the one-shot-game if the firm ever fails to offer w^* or if output is ever low, and let r be the players' common discount rate. If $w^* \geq w_a + c + rc/(1 - p)$ and the worker believes the firm's promise concerning future wages, then the worker will choose high effort. The key point here is that the firm must pay not only $w_a + c$ (to compensate the worker for the foregone opportunity of self-employment and for the disutility of high effort) but also the wage premium $rc/(1 - p)$. Absent the wage premium, the worker will accept the firm's offer (because $w_a + c > w_a$) but choose low effort and hope not to get caught. The firm is prepared to pay this wage premium as long as $H - w^* \geq 0$. That is, the discount rate must be sufficiently small and/or the probability of detecting low effort sufficiently high that the wage premium is not too high.

The result that workers are paid a wage premium naturally suggests the issue of bonding and entrance fees; see Carmichael (1985) and Dickens et al. (1989) for discussions. That is, if a firm pays a wage that is above workers' alternatives, then a worker should be willing either to post a bond that is forfeited if shirking is detected or to pay an entrance fee to acquire the job. Bonding and entrance fees have different implications for the existence of a wage premium. Bonding is a substitute for the wage premium in the creation of effort incentives, so the introduction of bonding should cause the wage premium to disappear. An entrance fee eliminates the rents associated with the job, but is not a substitute for the wage premium in creating effort incentives. Hence, the introduction of an entrance fee would not eliminate the wage premium. Real-world examples of bonding and/or entrance fees are rare. One possible explanation is that workers face capital-market constraints that make bonding and entrance fees infeasible. Another possible explanation is that firms may be tempted to abscond with bonds or fees.

Capelli and Chauvin (1991) provide a test of this efficiency-wage argument.[18] They use

---

[18] Other tests include Leonard (1987), Krueger (1991), Machin and Manning (1992), and Rebitzer and Taylor (1995). Leonard employs survey data from the high-technology sector in one state, and finds little evidence for the efficiency-wage prediction that more supervision should lead to lower wage premia. Krueger considers outlets in the fast-food industry, and finds consistent with efficiency-wage theory that wages are higher at outlets where monitoring is more difficult (i.e., company-owned outlets as opposed to franchises). Machin and Manning employ panel data from 486 UK firms to test whether short-run dynamics are better explained by a shirking-efficiency-wage model, a compensating-differentials model, or a union-firm bargaining model. They find that the shirking model is supported in firms with low levels of unionization, while the bargaining model is best for highly unionized firms. Rebitzer and Taylor employ law-firm data to test the efficiency-wage prediction that bonding should eliminate wage premia. They find the evidence does not support the prediction.

data from a single firm that has multiple plants. A single union agreement specifies a common wage at all the plants, but the wage in the local labor market varies across plants. Capelli and Chauvin test the prediction that larger wage premia (measured by the union wage minus the local wage) should result in less shirking (measured by the rate of disciplinary dismissals). They find evidence that supports the prediction. They also find evidence that supports the related prediction that there should be less shirking when labor-market conditions make it harder to find alternative employment. For example, they find that the rate of disciplinary dismissals is negatively related to the level of unemployment in the local labor market.

There is a close similarity between Bull's (1987) analysis discussed in the previous subsection and the efficiency-wage argument described above. In Bull's argument the firm promises a bonus at the end of each period in order to induce high effort, but because the bonus is paid at the end of the period the firm may be tempted to renege on its promise. The result is that the promise of a bonus will induce a high-effort equilibrium only if the firm faces a future punishment associated with reneging. In the efficiency-wage argument, in contrast, the worker can be seen as promising to supply high effort if the firm offers an above-market-clearing wage, but because the wage is paid at the beginning of the period (or is independent of the worker's output that period) the worker may be tempted to renege on his promise. The result is that the firm will pay an above-market-clearing wage in equilibrium only if the worker faces a future punishment associated with reneging.

MacLeod and Malcomson (1998) provide an analysis of relational contracting in which firms offer incentives for effort through either performance bonuses or efficiency wages or both (see also MacLeod and Malcomson, 1989). In their analysis the punishment associated with either side reneging is that the relationship is terminated at the end of the period. MacLeod and Malcomson show that equilibrium entails either performance bonuses or efficiency wages (not both), and which arises depends on whether there is an excess supply of workers or an excess demand. Their results can be understood in terms of the above discussion. When there is excess supply of workers, terminating the relationship does not punish the firm (because a new worker is easy to find) but does punish the worker (because a new job is hard to find). Thus, under excess supply, equilibrium entails efficiency wages. In contrast, when there is excess demand for workers, terminating the relationship punishes the firm but not the worker, so equilibrium entails bonuses.

MacLeod and Parent (1998) provide a test of this theory (and others). They employ a variety of data sources to explore the relationship between job characteristics (such as whether the tasks associated with a job are repetitive) and the form of compensation (such as whether the worker receives a piece rate or an hourly wage). MacLeod and Parent find that the likelihood that a bonus is paid is negatively related to the local unemployment rate. This finding is consistent with the theory above, because low unemployment can be interpreted as an excess demand for workers.[19] They also find that the use of objective performance measures is negatively related to the number of tasks that a job entails; see also Brown (1990) for this result. This finding is consistent with the theories of Holmstrom and Milgrom (1991) and Baker (1992) concerning the distinction between a worker's contribution to firm value and measured performance (see the discussion in the previous subsection), under the assumption jobs with more tasks are harder to measure.

2.5. Tournaments

Tournaments are another way to provide incentives inside organizations. In this approach there need not be formal contracts between the firm and its workers, provided that incentives are created through a prize structure that is rank-order in nature. That is, the firm establishes a fixed set of prizes and then awards the largest prize to the worker who produces the highest output, the second-largest prize to the worker who produces the second-highest output, and so on. Most of the papers in this literature are not explicit about whether these prizes should be thought of as promotions or as bonuses, although a few recent papers are cast explicitly in terms of the promotion process. In this subsection we focus mostly on papers in which the prizes can be thought of either as promotions or bonuses, while Section 3.3 discusses a number of the papers that are explicitly about the promotion process.

The seminal paper on tournaments is Lazear and Rosen (1981). There are two workers. The output of worker i is given by $y_i = e_i + \varepsilon_i$, where e_i again denotes the effort level of worker i and ε_1 and ε_2 are noise terms independently drawn from a density function $f(\varepsilon)$ with zero mean. Each worker incurs a cost of effort $c(e_i)$, $c' > 0$ and $c'' > 0$, and each has a reservation utility level U_0. For purposes of exposition, assume the workers and the firm are all risk neutral. The compensation scheme is very simple: the firm specifies a high wage and a low wage, w_H and w_L; the worker who produces more output (the winner) receives w_H and the worker who produces less output (the loser) receives w_L. Notice that because it is a rank-order tournament it is not necessary to assume that the firm perfectly observes each of the outputs. All that is required is that the firm observes which of the two workers produced more output.

As in the classic agency analysis, a worker maximizes expected utility by choosing the effort level that equates the marginal cost of effort with its marginal benefit. Let e_j^* denote the equilibrium effort choice of worker j. Worker i's optimal effort choice is then defined by

$$(w_H - w_L)(\partial \mathrm{Prob}\{y_i(e_i) > y_j(e_j^*)\}/\partial e_i) = c'(e_i), \tag{4}$$

where $\mathrm{Prob}\{y_i(e_i) > y_j(e_j^*)\}$ is the probability worker i's output exceeds worker j's when worker i chooses e_i and worker j chooses e_j^*. In a symmetric Nash equilibrium (i.e., $e_1^* = e_2^* = e^*$), the first-order condition (4) reduces to

---

[19] An alternative explanation for this finding follows from supply/demand analysis. If low unemployment indicates a temporary increase in the demand for labor, then supply/demand analysis would suggest a temporary increase in the wage. If firms are hesitant to respond by increasing the wage because future nominal wage decreases are not feasible, there may be an increased use of bonuses because bonuses can be discontinued once the demand for labor returns to its normal level.

$$(w_H - w_L) \int_{\varepsilon_j} f(\varepsilon_j)^2 d\varepsilon_j = c'(e^*). \tag{5}$$

It follows that larger wage gaps, $w_H - w_L$, induce more effort. In particular, there exists a wage gap that will induce the first-best level of effort, $c'(e) = 1$. For risk-neutral workers there is no demand for insurance so the equilibrium wage gap is the one that induces first-best effort. If the workers were risk averse, the firm would provide some insurance by reducing the wage gap (and hence the induced effort), just as the efficient contract slope b^* is less than one in the classic agency analysis when $r > 0$.[20]

In addition to deriving the optimal tournament for risk-neutral and risk-averse workers, Lazear and Rosen compare the optimal tournament to the optimal piece-rate (i.e., linear) compensation contract. They find that in the risk-neutral case the two are equally efficient: both yield the first-best outcome. Under risk aversion they show that either can be superior. This comparison is misleading, however, because under risk aversion the optimal compensation contract is typically not linear. In fact, Mookherjee (1984) shows that under risk aversion the optimal tournament is typically inferior to the optimal (non-linear) contract.[21] Mookherjee's result raises the question of why tournaments are used at all. Malcomson (1984) gave a simple response: in some instances individual performance is not verifiable, so individual incentive contracts cannot be enforced, yet tournaments can still be used to provide incentives. We discuss this further in Section 3.3.

One downside of tournaments is that they discourage cooperation among co-workers. Lazear (1989) explores this issue in a model where a worker can exert two kinds of effort: effort that increases the worker's own output and effort that "sabotages" (i.e., reduces) other workers' outputs. Lazear shows that conducting a tournament in such a setting induces both productive and sabotage efforts from workers. He then demonstrates that the optimal prize in such a setting is smaller than it would be in the absence of the possibility of sabotage. This result offers one explanation for the wage compression frequently described by personnel managers. A complementary perspective, however, is that when sabotage activity is important firms should not employ tournaments or other types of relative-performance evaluation.[22]

[20] Empirical tests of tournament theory include Ehrenberg and Bognanno (1990a,b) and Knoeber and Thurman (1994). Ehrenberg and Bognanno use data from professional golf tournaments and find evidence consistent with tournament theory's prediction that larger prize gaps induce higher effort, but an alternative explanation of their findings is that the level of the prizes as opposed to the size of the gaps induces higher effort. Knoeber and Thurman use data from the broiler chicken industry and find that effort is positively related to the size of prize gaps but independent of the level of prizes. Becker and Huselid (1992) study auto racing. They too find that performance improves when prize gaps are larger, but they also find that safety falls, consistent with the single-agent models of Holmstrom and Milgrom (1991) and Baker (1992) discussed above.

[21] Green and Stokey (1983) and Nalebuff and Stiglitz (1983) are other early papers in this literature that consider comparisons between tournaments and contracting. As with Lazear and Rosen, however, because those comparisons are not relative to optimal contracting, those papers are more positive concerning the optimality of tournaments than the correct comparison warrants.

[22] Garvey and Swan (1992) and Drago and Garvey (1998) extend Lazear's theory, and the latter provides supporting evidence.

Most of the papers in the tournament literature analyze one-period models. But tournaments in real organizations frequently consist of several rounds or contests, where the winners in one round face each other in the next. Rosen (1986b) analyzes such a single-elimination tournament. In each round, workers are divided into pairs and each worker competes against the other worker in the pair. The winners in one round then proceed to the next round, where they are again divided into pairs. The tournament ends (and all wages are then paid) when only one winner remains. Rosen assumes that workers are risk neutral and homogeneous in ability. He does not attempt to derive the optimal prize structure, but rather derives the prize structure that induces all surviving workers to exert the same level of effort in each round.

Suppose there are initially 2^n workers, so that the tournament consists of n rounds. Let w_k be the wage received at the end of the tournament by workers who won through round k but lost in round $k + 1$. In this notation, w_0 is the wage received by workers who lost in the first round and w_n is the wage received by the winner remaining at the end of the tournament. Rosen shows that for incentives to be constant throughout all the rounds of the tournament, the wage increase for winning a round of the tournament is constant for the first $n - 1$ rounds but larger for winning the last round. Formally, $w_k = z + kx$ for $0 \leq k \leq n - 1$, but $w_n > w_{n-1} + x$, where z and x are constants. This result follows from the fact that, for any round before the last, the prize for winning the round consists of two components: a guaranteed wage increase (even if the worker loses the next round) and the expected value of further wage increases from participating in the subsequent round(s) of the tournament. For the two workers who compete in the final round, however, the second component equals zero. The result is that to induce these two workers to provide as much effort as in earlier rounds requires the final wage increase to be larger than the wage increases associated with earlier rounds. The analysis thus provides a potential explanation for why wage increases from promotions seem to be larger at the top ranks of firms; see Murphy (1985) and Baker et al. (1994a) for supporting evidence.

Meyer (1992) also studies tournaments as a sequence of contests, but without elimination: two identical risk-averse workers participate in two consecutive rank-order contests. The firm has the option of setting up the second contest with a bias. That is, the firm can choose a worker and an amount Δ such that the chosen worker wins the second contest unless the other worker's output is larger by at least Δ. Meyer shows that the firm has an incentive to bias the second contest in favor of the first contest's winner. The reason is that a small amount of bias causes a second-order decrease in second-period effort levels, but a first-order increase in first-period effort levels. The analysis thus provides a rationale for a fast track (i.e., a setting in which workers who earn large bonuses or quick promotions early are also unusually successful later).[23]

---

[23] Meyer (1991) derives a similar result in a model where there is no effort choice but workers vary in terms of ability. The firm receives a noisy signal about the workers' relative abilities by observing who wins each round. After two rounds the firm wishes to assign the more able worker to a new job. As before, the firm biases the second round in favor of the first-round winner. This bias is optimal because under no bias (or the opposite bias) the firm learns nothing useful if the first-round loser wins the second round.

3. Applied models: labor economics

The previous section focused on building-block models. In Sections 3 and 4 we show how such models can be extended and combined to explain various aspects of careers in organizations. This section focuses on models aimed at outcomes familiar from labor economics; the following section considers models aimed at issues familiar from human resource management and organization theory. The first two subsections below concern theories of wage growth during careers. We therefore begin by summarizing the evidence about the extent to which wage growth over the career is due to firm-specific seniority in addition to general labor-market experience. This topic has received considerable attention in the empirical literature over the last 15 years. Early influential papers include Abraham and Farber (1987) and Altonji and Shakotko (1987), both of which conclude that firm-specific seniority has a minor effect on wage growth. Topel (1991), however, shows that the estimates in those papers are biased downwards, and then derives new estimates consistent with a large effect of seniority. For example, Topel finds that 10 years of seniority increase the wage of the average male worker by over 25%. More recently, Altonji and Williams (1997) argue that Topel's estimate is biased upwards and that the actual effect of firm-specific seniority is somewhere between the low numbers found in the early papers and Topel's higher estimate. But even Altonji and Williams's estimates indicate that firm-specific seniority has a significant effect on wage growth.

3.1. Wage growth without promotions

Both human-capital acquisition and job assignment provide rationales for wage growth during careers. This subsection discusses three other models that predict wage growth but that do not involve the promotion process. The two subsequent subsections discuss models of the promotion process.

Becker and Stigler (1974) develop an argument related to the efficiency-wage argument described in Section 2.4. As in the efficiency-wage argument, the firm elicits effort by paying an above-market wage and threatening to fire the worker if the performance is too low. In the Becker–Stigler model, however, workers have finite careers so the model predicts wage growth over the career. Consider a model where workers are in the labor market for n periods. Workers have the opportunity to shirk, but the firm detects shirking with probability p. A worker receives utility from shirking equal to b, r is the discount rate, and w_a is the alternative wage. Let w_t be the wage paid by the firm to a worker of age t. Becker and Stigler show that an optimal policy for the firm is to fire a worker detected shirking (who then receives the alternative wage in the period he is fired) and to offer the wage schedule

$$w_t = w_a + (1-p)\frac{b}{p}\frac{r}{1+r}, \qquad \text{for } t = 1, \ldots, n-1, \tag{6}$$

and

$$w_n = w_a + (1 - p)\frac{b}{p}. \tag{7}$$

Further, because the wages described in (6) and (7) are higher than a worker could earn elsewhere, the firm should charge an entrance fee equal to $(1 - p)b/p$.

Eqs. (6) and (7) tell us that the firm pays a constant premium for ages 1 to $n - 1$, and then a higher premium for a worker of age n. The result and logic are similar to Rosen's (1986b) sequential-tournament model discussed above. At any age, a worker's incentive not to shirk consists of two components: the wage premium for that period and the present discounted value of future wage premia. For a worker of age n the second component equals zero, so shirking can be stopped at age n only by having the premium for age n distinctly larger than the earlier wage premia.

The Becker–Stigler analysis has been extended by Lazear (1979, 1981), who shows two results.[24] First, the specific wage schedule derived by Becker and Stigler is just one of many wage schedules that prevent shirking over a worker's career. The common feature of these wage schedules is that wages are an increasing function of firm-specific seniority: the worker's wage is below his marginal product at low levels of seniority and above the marginal product at high levels.[25] Second, Lazear's perspective provides an explanation for the use of mandatory retirement, which was a common practice prior to being outlawed in the US in the 1980s. The logic is as follows. The efficient age of retirement is the age at which the value of the best alternative use of the worker's time first exceeds the worker's marginal product. But to prevent shirking, the worker's wage at the end of his career exceeds his marginal product. Thus, workers will not voluntarily retire at the efficient age. Mandatory retirement is used to achieve retirement at the efficient age, and the efficiency gain is then shared between the worker and the firm.[26]

Another rationale for wage growth over the career is the self-selection argument of Salop and Salop (1976) in which firms use a sloped wage schedule to sort workers.[27] Consider a world populated by two types of workers: one with a high probability of quitting after each period and the other with a low probability. Suppose that every work-

---

[24] Akerlof and Katz (1989) also extend the Becker–Stigler argument. They consider a continuous-time setting and show that an upward-sloping age–earnings profile is not a perfect substitute for an up-front bond or entrance fee. The reason is that, if time is continuous, when the worker is young the accrued bond associated with any upward-sloping age–earnings profile must be very small. The result is that, if up-front bonds or entrance fees are not feasible (say, because of capital-market constraints), the total compensation paid the worker is above the market-clearing level.

[25] This is consistent with the Becker–Stigler analysis if one interprets the entrance fee in their analysis as a wage that is below the worker's marginal product (equal to zero) at the entrance date.

[26] Hutchens (1986, 1987) presents tests of the Becker–Stigler–Lazear theory for wage growth during careers. One test involves characteristics of jobs that employ older workers but do not hire older workers; the other involves characteristics of jobs that consist of repetitive tasks. Both tests support the Becker–Stigler–Lazear theory.

[27] An alternative approach to sorting workers involves hiring standards; see Guasch and Weiss (1980, 1982). An important finding in those papers is that individuals who are above the standard are paid more than their marginal products, while those below are paid less. But those papers have no implications for wage growth.

er's contribution to firm value is y per period, but that a firm incurs a cost T from specific training given to the worker the first period she is at the firm. Other than the training cost, a worker's productivity does not vary with the worker's seniority at the firm. All workers and firms live forever. Finally, suppose that a worker's probability of quitting is privately known by the worker but not observable by firms. Because of the training cost, firms have an incentive to induce workers to self-select. That is, starting from a situation where all firms hire random samples of workers, any single firm could increase its profit by designing a compensation scheme that attracts only workers with a low probability of quitting.

Salop and Salop assume that each firm can contractually commit to a wage schedule: the firm will pay the wage w_t to all workers in their tth period at the firm. They derive an equilibrium in which firms offer wage schedules that induce workers to self-select: those with high quit probabilities choose firms offering a flat wage schedule ($w_t = w_0$ for all t, where w_0 earns the firm zero expected profits on the high-turnover workers), while those with low quit probabilities choose firms offering a two-step wage schedule ($w_1 = w_L$ and $w_t = w_H$ for all $t \geq 2$, where $w_H > w_L$). If $w_H - w_L > T$ then firms would have an incentive to hire workers and then fire them after one period of employment. But if $w_H = y$ and $w_L = y - T$ then workers self-select and firms never fire. In contrast to Becker's human-capital analysis, where the costs and returns to specific capital either all accrue to the firm (in the no-turnover case) or are shared by the firm and the worker (in the case where turnover is possible), here all the costs and returns to specific training accrue to the worker (for low-turnover workers).

The final rationale for wage growth we consider in this subsection is Freeman's (1977) learning/insurance argument. (Harris and Holmstrom's (1982) model discussed in Section 5 builds on Freeman's model.) In Freeman's analysis both firms and workers are uncertain about a worker's ability at the beginning of the worker's career, but the worker's ability becomes publicly known after his first period in the labor market. Workers are risk-averse but firms are risk neutral, so there is a possibility for insurance. That is, at the beginning of a worker's career the worker faces risk concerning the realization of his ability, and it would be efficient for firms to insure workers against this risk.

Similar to the Salop and Salop approach, Freeman assumes that firms can contractually commit to a wage policy. Workers on the other hand cannot commit to their future actions. In particular, a worker cannot be prevented from quitting to accept a better offer. In a two-period model, Freeman shows that the equilibrium has two features. First, real wages are downward rigid (i.e., a worker's real wage never falls). This follows from the attempt to insure each worker against the risk associated with the realization of his own ability. Second, a worker's wage rises if the worker is revealed to be of high ability. Workers face risk concerning a positive movement in the wage because workers cannot commit to staying with the current employer when other potential employers offer higher wages. These two results imply that, on average, wages rise with labor-market experience even though each worker's true productivity is independent of experience.

We end this subsection by considering how the three models just described relate to the empirical literature concerning wage growth. One important branch of this literature is the set of papers summarized above that measure the extent to which wage growth over the career is due to firm-specific seniority. Although the exact size of the return to seniority is still being debated, the emerging consensus seems to be that firm-specific seniority has a significant positive effect on wage growth.

An obvious explanation for seniority-related wage growth is that workers accumulate specific human capital during their careers and the increased productivity is shared between the worker and the firm. But wage increases with seniority can also be explained by two of the theories discussed above. The Becker–Stigler–Lazear argument tells us that, even if productivity is independent of seniority, firms may have an incentive to have wages depend positively on seniority in order to induce worker effort. And Salop and Salop's argument also results in wages depending positively on seniority. (Their argument is similar to Becker's in that it relies on firm-specific human capital, but in Becker's argument the wage increase serves to decrease the probability the worker will quit, while in Salop and Salop's argument each worker's quit probability is taken as fixed and wages depend positively on seniority in order to induce self-selection.) Finally, because there need not be any turnover in Freeman's analysis, his model explains why wages are positively related to labor-market experience, but not why wages are positively related to firm-specific seniority.

In addition to the evidence on wage growth with seniority, there is also evidence involving performance evaluations. The seminal papers are Medoff and Abraham (1980, 1981). In their 1980 paper, Medoff and Abraham find that within-job wages are positively related to labor-market experience and firm-specific seniority, but that performance evaluations are either unrelated or slightly negatively related to experience and seniority. Medoff and Abraham argue that if performance evaluations are unbiased measures of productivity then their pair of findings is inconsistent with Becker's human-capital explanation for wage growth. The same argument implies that Medoff and Abraham's findings are inconsistent with the Salop and Salop argument, provided that a newly employed worker's performance evaluation reflects the first-period training cost; but see the discussion of Gibbons and Waldman (1999) in Section 5 for a different view of the Medoff–Abraham evidence and the Becker and Salop–Salop theories. On the other hand, the Medoff–Abraham evidence is consistent with the Becker–Stigler–Lazear argument for seniority-related wage growth, and with Freeman's prediction that wages are positively related to labor-market experience, because neither of these arguments relies on worker productivity being positively related to experience or seniority.

3.2. Promotions as assignment mechanisms

In this subsection and the next we discuss models of the promotion process. We begin by assessing the evidence concerning the importance of promotion-related wage growth versus non-promotion-related wage growth. Not surprisingly, promotions are associated with large wage increases; see Gerhart and Milkovich (1989), Lazear (1992), and McCue (1996). However, while these wage increases are large relative to those associated with not being promoted, they are small relative to the difference between average wages across levels of a job ladder; see Murphy (1985), Main et al. (1993), and Baker et al. (1994a). One interpretation of the latter result is that wages are not (completely) attached to jobs: workers typically receive some wage increase even when a promotion does not occur. In other words, a realistic model of the promotion process should exhibit large wage increases upon promotion, and smaller but positive wage increases in other periods.

In Section 2.2 we discussed models of job assignment, and some of the papers cited, such as Sattinger (1975), Rosen (1982), and Waldman (1984a), consider how workers are assigned to different levels of a job ladder. Those papers develop single-period models, however, and thus do not address how workers move up a job ladder as they age. This subsection considers models of the promotion process that focus on movement across levels of a job ladder.

Two standard ways of adding dynamics to a job-assignment model are learning and human-capital acquisition. To illustrate these two ideas, consider the following simple example of the job-assignment/promotion process. Let η_i be worker i's ability, and let each firm have two jobs, denoted 1 and 2, where the output of worker i assigned to job j is given by $b_j + c_j \eta_i$. Assume that $b_1 > b_2$ and $c_1 < c_2$ and let η' solve $b_1 + c_1 \eta' = b_2 + c_2 \eta'$, so that workers with ability $\eta_i < \eta'$ are more productive in job 1 and workers with ability $\eta_i > \eta'$ are more productive in job 2.

The first way to generate movement within this job ladder is through learning about ability, which is closely related to Murphy's (1986) model discussed in Section 2.2; a related analysis appears in Gibbons and Katz (1992).[28] Specific parameterizations produce movement up the ladder. For example, suppose a proportion p of the workforce has ability η_H while a proportion $(1 - p)$ has ability η_L, where $\eta_H > \eta' > \eta_L$ and $E(\eta) = p\eta_H + (1 - p)\eta_L < \eta'$. Assume that when a worker enters the labor force no one knows the worker's true ability, but all firms learn gradually about the worker's ability from noisy productivity observations over time. Then all young workers will be assigned to job 1, and over time some of the workers will be promoted to job 2, whenever learning causes beliefs about expected ability to rise above η'. Further learning may then cause demotions and other career paths.

The second way to generate movement up this job ladder as workers age is through human-capital acquisition. For example, suppose worker i has innate ability θ_i but "effective" ability in period t given by $\eta_{it} = \theta_i f(x_{it})$, where x_{it} is the worker's labor-market experience in period t and $f(x_{it})$ reflects human-capital acquisition (so $f' > 0$). Assume that

---

[28] Other papers that employ the learning approach to movement up a job ladder include Prescott and Visscher (1980) and O'Flaherty and Siow (1992, 1995). In O'Flaherty and Siow's model a firm consists of multiple production units, each of which is composed of a senior worker and a junior worker. All new workers are placed in junior positions, and if the firm learns the worker is likely to be of high ability then she is promoted to a senior position at a new production unit. O'Flaherty and Siow show that for some parameterizations workers are either promoted or released by some finite date. The analysis thus provides a rationale for the use of up-or-out promotion rules. Up-or-out refers to situations in which workers who do not earn a promotion by a fixed date are released; it is observed in a variety of settings such as academia and professional partnerships.

innate ability is publicly known and that each worker enters the labor force with an effective ability below η'. Then all young workers will again be assigned to job 1, and now as workers age there will be promotions to job 2 whenever human-capital acquisition results in effective ability exceeding η'.[29] In this case there will not be demotions or other complications.

A number of papers have combined the learning and human-capital approaches to the job-assignment/promotion problem.[30] An early paper of this kind is Waldman (1984b), which focuses on the importance of asymmetric learning. In Waldman's analysis, workers are in the labor market for two periods and there are two jobs, one of which values ability more highly than the other (such as job 2 in the example above). A firm that employs a young worker observes the worker's ability after the first period of production, while other firms observe only the job the worker is offered at the beginning of the worker's second period in the labor market. The other important assumption is that workers accumulate firm-specific human capital during their first period in the labor market.

The central result in Waldman's analysis is that promoting a worker serves as a positive signal of the worker's ability, so potential employers are willing to bid more for the services of a worker who has been offered a promotion. The initial employer thus must offer a large wage increase upon promotion to keep the worker from leaving. Waldman also finds that an inefficiently small number of workers are promoted, because the large wage increase required at promotion means that the firm does not have an incentive to promote workers who are only slightly more productive in the new job. In the limit, as the amount of firm-specific human capital goes to zero, the proportion of workers promoted goes to zero.

Bernhardt (1995) extends Waldman's analysis by allowing workers to be in the labor market for more than two periods and to accumulate general as well as specific human capital.[31] After showing that the basic findings from Waldman's analysis still hold, Bernhardt derives a number of additional results. For example, he considers what happens when there are three job levels and derives the existence of a fast track: a worker who earns her first promotion quickly is more likely than others to be promoted again. This holds for two reasons. First, workers who earn an early promotion are those with the highest productivity in the lowest level job, and in Bernhardt's setting these are the workers for

---

[29] We are not familiar with any early paper that develops a simple version of the human-capital-acquisition approach to movement up the job ladder. Simple versions of this approach do appear, however, in a recent paper such as Jovanovic and Nyarko (1997) and Gibbons and Waldman (1999).

[30] A recent paper that considers both approaches is Jovanovik and Nyarko (1997), but their emphasis is not on combining the two approaches. Jovanovik and Nyarko refer to the learning approach as the Bandit model and the human-capital approach as the Stepping Stone model.

[31] Other papers that explore the signaling aspects of promotion include Ricart i Costa (1988) and Bernhardt and Scoones (1993). Ricart i Costa allows firms to offer output-contingent contracts to older workers, and shows that wages are then mostly determined by assignment but vary to a small degree within jobs as a function of ability. Bernhardt and Scoones consider a setting in which upon promotion other firms can learn the worker's ability exactly but at a cost. Their main result is that firms may offer particularly large wage increases upon promotion in order to stop other firms from investing in information acquisition.

whom the efficient job assignment by the end of their careers is most likely to be job 3. The second reason for the fast track is similar to Waldman's analysis: because promotion to job 3 sends a positive signal about ability to the market, firms have an incentive to promote too few workers to job 3. But given that the market already has very positive beliefs about the abilities of those who earn their first promotions very quickly, the cost to a firm from sending the positive signal associated with promotion to job 3 is smaller.

Milgrom and Oster (1987) also consider a model where a promotion affects other firms' beliefs about a worker's ability, but their focus is labor-market discrimination. The model is similar to the two papers just discussed in that firms have two jobs, one of which values ability more highly than the other, and a worker's wage at a firm is influenced by the wage that other firms are willing to offer. The main difference is in the information assumptions. Milgrom and Oster assume there are two groups of workers – visible workers and invisible workers. A visible worker's ability is publicly known from the date the individual enters the labor market. When an invisible worker enters the labor market, however, all that is known is the distribution of ability for the worker's group. After one period of employment, the initial employer learns an invisible worker's ability, and all firms learn it if the invisible worker is promoted.

Milgrom and Oster provide a number of reasons why those in minority groups are more likely to suffer from invisibility. They then show that in their model invisibility leads to a type of labor-market discrimination, including the following three results. First, average wages are lower for invisible workers, even though their ability distribution is the same as that of visible workers. Second, a smaller proportion of the invisible group earns a promotion. In particular, only those with high but not very high ability are promoted. Third, the return to investing in human capital is smaller for invisible workers, and thus on average this group invests less.[32] The logic behind these results is familiar: promotion of an invisible worker allows other firms to observe the worker's ability, so a firm is hesitant to promote invisible workers of very high ability because of the effect on the wage offers from other firms.

As in the previous subsection, we again conclude by considering how these models relate to empirical findings concerning wage growth. We begin by discussing the learning approach to the job-assignment problem. The learning approach explains a positive return to experience because assignments will become more efficient as workers age. (See MacDonald (1982a) and Murphy (1986) discussed in Section 2.2 for earlier discussions of this point.) But the learning approach makes no obvious prediction concerning returns to seniority because the models do not incorporate turnover. Learning does result in large wage increases upon promotion, and these wage increases are especially large if learning is asymmetric. In the symmetric-learning case, promoted workers are, on average, those for whom learning caused large improvements in the market's belief about the worker's

---

[32] This result is similar to Lundberg and Startz's (1983) finding that statistical discrimination can reduce human-capital investments for those workers for whom information about productivity is less precise. In both the Milgrom–Oster and Lundberg–Startz arguments, the lack of full information about productivity reduces the return to investing in human capital and consequently the investment level.

ability, while in the asymmetric-learning case there is the additional factor that promotion serves as a positive signal of ability. Finally, the learning approach predicts little or no wage growth in periods in which promotion does not occur.

Now consider the human-capital approach to the job-assignment problem. This approach explains a positive return to experience if the human capital is general, as in most of the discussion above. Further, if one were to instead assume that some of the human capital is specific, then Becker's sharing argument predicts that there would also be a positive return to seniority with the firm. The human-capital approach also explains why there would be wage growth in periods in which promotion does not occur, but does not explain large wage increases upon promotion.

In summary, the main drawback of the learning approach is that it does not explain wage growth in the absence of promotion, while the main drawback of the human-capital approach is that it does not explain why wage increases at promotion are particularly large. One solution is a model that incorporates both learning and human-capital acquisition. Gibbons and Waldman (1999) do precisely this; see Section 5.

3.3. Promotions as incentive mechanisms

This subsection focuses on the role of promotions in providing incentives for effort or skill acquisition. Even casual observation suggests that promotions are associated with large wage increases, so it is not mysterious why promotions create incentives. The tougher question, posed by Baker et al. (1988) is why promotions seem more important than bonuses as a source of incentives in many firms. That is, since promotions unavoidably serve to assign workers to jobs (as in the models of the previous subsection), why do firms not use bonuses to provide incentives, rather than using promotions for both purposes? Using promotions to achieve both goals forces the firm to trade-off incentives and assignment, presumably doing neither perfectly. In this subsection we present a number of potential answers to this puzzle.

As noted in Section 2.5, Malcomson (1984) generalizes the Lazear and Rosen rank-order tournament model by considering an overlapping-generations setting in which workers are in the labor market for two periods and a firm can hire as many young workers as it wishes in any period. All workers are identical, except for belonging to different generations. A worker's output is the sum of the worker's effort level and a stochastic term. Because Malcomson assumes that an individual's output is not verifiable (but is privately observed by the firm), incentive contracts of the sort discussed in Section 2.3 are not effective. Rather, the firm establishes a tournament where the prize is a higher wage associated with promotion. In particular, the compensation scheme consists of three wages and a number: the wage paid to young workers, w_0; the wage paid to old workers who are not promoted, w_1; the wage paid to old workers who are promoted, w_2; and the number of young workers who will be promoted, n. To maximize the incentive for effort among young workers, the firm promises to promote the n workers who produced the most during their first period in the firm.

Because an individual's output is not verifiable, the firm cannot create incentives via a contract that depends only on individual performance. But a tournament (i.e., $0 < n < N$ and $w_2 > w_1$, where N is the number of young workers in the firm) does create incentives and so is superior to contracts that depend only on individual performance. The key feature of a tournament is that it allows the firm to commit to a fixed set of prizes; for example, the firm could put the aggregate second-period wage bill in escrow before the tournament begins. In brief, Malcomson's paper offers one possible answer to the Baker–Jensen–Murphy puzzle: promotions are used because there is no alternative.[33]

Another interesting analysis of promotion as incentive for effort is Fairburn and Malcomson (1997). Their analysis directly addresses the Baker–Jensen–Murphy puzzle by allowing both bonuses and promotions as sources of incentives and then deriving the optimal way for the firm to use these two instruments. Fairburn and Malcomson first consider a model where workers are in the labor market for two periods and a firm has only a single type of job. There are both high- and low- ability workers, but a worker's type is not known when he enters the labor market. In this first part of their analysis, only the manager observes the worker's output, so a worker's compensation depends on the manager's evaluation of the worker's performance. The problem with basing the worker's compensation on the manager's evaluation is that the worker has an incentive to bribe the manager, effectively sharing the compensation increase created by an improved evalua-tion. Fairburn and Malcomson show that if such bribes are possible then in equilibrium the worker applies the minimum effort level. (See Section 4.1 for further discussion of such side contracts.) That is, if only the manager observes the worker's output, and if the worker can use bribes to influence the manager's performance evaluation, then neither the stan-dard contracting approach in Section 2.3 *nor* the tournament approach in Section 2.4 can create incentives for effort.

Fairburn and Malcomson then add a second job. High-ability workers are more produc-tive in one job, and low-ability workers in the other (as in the learning model discussed in the previous subsection). They show that using promotion for incentives in addition to assign-ment allows the firm to avoid the minimum-effort outcome discussed above, even though the worker can bribe the manager to influence both bonus and promotion recommendations. The key assumption behind this result is that the manager's compensation depends on the profits of the firm. This gives the manager an incentive to promote the high-output workers instead of low-output workers, even when bribery is possible. In other words, promotions may be used to provide incentives because the assignment aspect of promotion gives the firm better control over the agency problem between the firm and its managers.

---

[33] MacLeod and Malcomson (1988) develop a model of promotions that applies to even a single worker. In their model, effort is induced by the promise of a promotion whenever the worker's output exceeds some specified standard. They analyze a dynamic model in which workers are promoted through a set of standards until each worker reaches his efficient one. In their analysis, a worker's pay in any period depends on the current standard for promotion; the worker is fired if current performance is too low and is promoted to a higher standard if performance is sufficiently high. MacLeod and Malcomson's model is thus consistent with a type of job ladder in which a worker's pay increases as he moves up the ladder.

Another argument related to the Baker–Jensen–Murphy puzzle follows from Wald-man's (1984b) analysis discussed above: promotion serves as a positive signal of ability, so a promoted worker receives a large wage increase. If one were to add an effort choice to Waldman's model, the wage increase from promotion would serve as an incentive for workers to provide effort; see Gibbs (1995) and Zabojnik (1997a) for analyses based on this idea. Thus, one reason a firm might use promotion for both assignment and incentives is that the two are inherently intertwined: the signalling aspect of assignment means that assignment and incentives go hand in hand.[34]

In the papers discussed so far, promotion serves as an incentive for effort. In another strand of the literature, promotion serves as an incentive for skill acquisition. Prendergast (1993a) considers the issue of how firms provide incentives for workers to acquire specific capital when such an investment cannot be verified (and so cannot be enforced by contract, as in Becker's framework). As discussed in Section 2.1, when contracting is not possible the logic of the hold-up problem suggests there will be underinvestment in specific human capital. Prendergast considers this issue in a setting in which firms have two jobs. As in the models above, a worker's skill is more valuable in one of the jobs. Prendergast assumes that workers make the investment decisions and that firms can commit to a wage for each job (in the spirit of an internal labor market in which wages are attached to jobs).

Prendergast finds that under certain conditions, the firm can induce workers to acquire specific human capital by assigning a higher wage to the job that values human capital more and promising to promote those who develop appropriate skills. Part of the logic is familiar: by investing in skill a worker can increase her probability of being promoted to the higher-paying job. The new issue is whether the firm's promise to promote a high-skill worker is credible. Prendergast finds that the firm's promise is credible if the two jobs are significantly different in the value they place on human capital, but not if the two jobs place similar or identical values on human capital. In the latter case, the firm cannot be trusted to promote a high-skill worker to the high-wage job, since she is almost as produc-tive in the low-wage job. Of course, if the firm will not promote the worker then the worker has no incentive to invest. Prendergast's argument provides another potential explanation to the Baker–Jensen–Murphy puzzle: promotions are used for both assignment and incen-tives because this allows the firm to ameliorate underinvestment in specific human capital that would otherwise be caused by the hold-up problem.

Prendergast's model raises a question: in firms that do not have multiple jobs, or where all the jobs place similar values on specific capital, can the firm provide incentives for investment in specific capital? Kahn and Huberman (1988) address this question in a

---

[34] Other papers that focus on promotion as an incentive for effort include Landers et al. (1996) and Waldman (1997). Building on Akerlof's (1976) model of the rat race, Landers, Rebitzer, and Taylor show that in an adverse-selection setting the prospect of promotion can create inefficiently strong incentives for effort. Their empirical analysis of law firms supports their theoretical argument. Waldman considers a time-inconsistency problem that arises because promotions are used for both assignment and incentives. He shows that internal promotion and mandatory retirement can both be understood as practices utilized by firms to avoid problems due to time inconsistency.

setting similar to Prendergast's: workers decide whether to invest in specific capital and investment levels are not verifiable; unlike Prendergast's analysis, however, the firm has only one job.

Kahn and Huberman show that in such a setting an up-or-out promotion rule can provide incentives for investment in specific capital. Under such a rule, a worker is paid a high wage if promoted, but if the worker is not promoted then he must be dismissed. As before, part of the logic is familiar: because high-productivity workers are promoted and receive a higher wage, a worker has an incentive to invest. As in Prendergast's model, the other issue is whether the firm's promise to promote a high-skill worker is credible. Because the worker must be dismissed if he is not promoted, the firm has an incentive to promote high-productivity workers.[35]

An interesting aspect of the Prendergast and Kahn–Huberman analyses is that together they make a clear prediction concerning when up-or-out is more likely to be observed. Prendergast's simple promotion mechanism creates investment incentives at firms where higher levels of the job ladder place higher values on human capital. Furthermore, in richer settings, an up-or-out rule has some costs. For example, if a worker's investment in specific capital results in only a modest improvement in the worker's skills then the firm may choose not to promote the worker (because doing so would require a large wage increase), thereby wasting the worker's modest new specific skills through dismissal. A similar cost arises if a worker has cleared one up-or-out hurdle but fails the next. Thus, the prediction is that up-or-out should be more common at firms or organizations where different levels of the job ladder value human capital in essentially the same way. This prediction corresponds reasonably well with the situations in which we actually see up-or-out practiced, such as academia and professional partnerships.

As in the two previous subsections, one might ask how the models described above relate to empirical findings concerning wage growth. The answer is that, in contrast to the models analyzed in those previous subsections, the models here have much less to say about detailed empirical evidence. Instead, these models were constructed to explore the sources and consequences of promotions being associated with large wage increases. The models also offer some potential resolutions of the Baker–Jensen–Murphy puzzle, and shed some light on observed practices such as up-or-out rules.

3.4. Separations

There are a number of empirical findings concerning separations that have been addressed in the theoretical literature. One set of findings concerns the factors that affect the prob-

---

[35] Waldman (1990) extends Kahn and Huberman's analysis by considering what happens when human capital is general and there is asymmetric learning. He shows that, when the current employer learns the worker's ability but prospective employers do not, there is an incentive for workers to underinvest in general human capital, but the up-or-out promotion arrangement can be used to solve this underinvestment problem. He also derives a result that parallels some evidence from academic careers: the wage increase upon promotion is small but promotion frequently results in a bidding process that significantly drives up the wage.

ability of separation. Two firmly established findings are that the probability of separation declines with both labor-market experience and firm-specific seniority (Parsons, 1977; Mincer and Jovanovic, 1981).

These two facts are explained by two of the classic models of labor-market search and matching: Burdett (1978) and Jovanovic (1979). (See Mortensen and Pissarides (1999) for a survey of classic and recent search models.) Burdett provides an explanation for why the probability of separation declines with labor-market experience. In his model, jobs are inspection goods: when an offer arrives, it specifies a constant wage the worker will be paid until he chooses to leave the job. These wage offers are drawn from a fixed, known distribution. If there are no moving costs, workers simply accept better wage offers whenever they arrive. Thus, at any moment, the worker's wage is the highest of all the offers received so far. With more experience, the worker has received more offers, so the expected value of the current wage is higher. Furthermore, the probability that the next offer is high enough to induce the worker to switch firms falls as the current wage rises, and hence falls with the worker's experience.

Jovanovic (1979) provides an explanation for why the probability of separation declines with firm-specific seniority. In his model, worker-firm matches are experience goods: the quality of a given match is unknown ex ante and information is gradually revealed as production takes place. At each point in time a worker is paid the expected value of her marginal product at the current employer. The worker stays at the current employer if productivity is revealed to be sufficiently high but leaves otherwise. Jovanovic shows that the separation probability first increases and then decreases with seniority. The logic for the latter result is that at high values for seniority little learning takes place, so there is a small probability that the expected marginal product will decline sufficiently to cause the worker to move to a new firm.

Topel and Ward (1992) present empirical tests concerning the Burdett and Jovanovic explanations for why the probability of separation is negatively related to labor-market experience and (ultimately) to firm-specific seniority. In Burdett's model the probability of separation is negatively related to experience because there is a positive relationship between a worker's age and his current wage. Thus, according to Burdett, holding the wage constant there should be no relationship between the probability of separation and experience. In Jovanovic's model the probability of separation is negatively related to seniority because a higher level of seniority implies that there is less left to learn, which in turn implies that as seniority increases the current wage is less likely to fall below the value that would cause the worker to leave. This logic implies that, holding the wage constant, there should be a positive relationship between the probability of separation and seniority.[36] Topel and Ward examine how the probability of separation depends on experience and seniority after controlling for the wage, and find results that partially support an amended version of Burdett's model.[37]

[36] MacDonald (1988) develops a model of job mobility based on MacDonald (1982a) discussed in Section 2.2. He derives that, holding the wage constant, the probability of separation should be independent of both experience and seniority; see also Galizzi and Lang (1998).

A third important model of separation is the heterogeneous-worker model developed by Blumen et al. (1955). Each worker is characterized by a fixed probability of separation, which varies across workers. Farber (1994) has recently investigated the evidence for this perspective. He finds that worker heterogeneity is important for understanding the probability of separation. For example, the probability of separation at a new position is positively related to the frequency of prior moves. But his analysis indicates that time-invariant heterogeneity does not fully explain the evidence concerning the probability of separation. Instead, he finds that the probability of separation first increases with firm-specific seniority and then decreases, consistent with Jovanovic's model of the separation process.

Another well documented finding concerning separations is that wage changes at separation are higher on average for separations labeled as quits than for those labeled as layoffs (Bartel and Borjas, 1981; Antel, 1985; Mincer, 1986). There are two theoretical approaches that address this evidence. One approach assumes that renegotiation is infeasible (due to information asymmetries or other types of transactions costs); the other takes the Coasian perspective of costless renegotiation. The former approach is developed in Antel (1985), which builds on the analysis of Hashimoto (1981) discussed in Section 2.1. As in Hashimoto's analysis, there is uncertainty concerning a worker's productivity at both the current employer and other potential employers, and the worker's wage is fixed prior to the realization of these productivities. Antel notes that if renegotiation of this wage is infeasible then the pattern of wage changes upon separation is consistent with the empirical evidence discussed above, as follows. A worker quits when the alternative offer is higher than the pre-specified contractual wage, and thus quits are typically associated with wage increases. Similarly, a worker is laid off when the worker's productivity at the current employer is below the pre-specified contractual wage, and thus layoffs are typically associated with wage decreases.[38]

McLaughlin (1991) shows how the costless-renegotiation approach can also explain the evidence concerning wage changes upon separation. As in Hashimoto's and Antel's analyses, McLaughlin assumes there is uncertainty concerning a worker's productivity at the current employer and other potential employers. What differs is the wage-determination process. Let w_{t-1} be the wage received by the worker in period $t-1$, r_t be the highest wage offered in period t by an alternative employer, and y_t be the worker's marginal product in period t at the current employer. McLaughlin assumes that r_t is initially privately observed by the worker and y_t is initially privately observed by the firm. He also assumes that each party's private information can be credibly revealed to

---

[37] More specifically, Topel and Ward find that after controlling for the wage there is a positive relationship between the probability of separation and experience. Burdett's framework exhibits this property once general human capital is incorporated. But they also find that after controlling for the wage there is a negative relationship between the probability of separation and seniority. None of the models discussed above captures this finding.

[38] There is some question about how to label the case when a worker wants to quit and a firm wants to fire. If this case is labeled a quit then all layoffs will be associated with wage decreases. However, if this case is sometimes labeled as a layoff, then some layoffs will be associated with wage increases.

the other party. This latter assumption is strong and unusual, but McLaughlin shows that this assumption produces empirically appealing results.

Rather than assuming that w_t is fixed ex ante, McLaughlin assumes costless renegotiation of the following sort. If $r_t \leq w_{t-1}$ and $y_t \geq w_{t-1}$, then $w_t = w_{t-1}$. If $r_t > w_{t-1}$ and $y_t \geq w_{t-1}$ then the worker reveals the outside option and the firm has the opportunity to match it. If $y_t > r_t$ then the firm matches and the worker stays and receives r_t, while if $y_t < r_t$ then the firm does not match and the worker leaves and receives r_t from the alternative employer. The latter is labeled a quit, and since $r_t > w_{t-1}$ we have that quits are associated with wage increases. Similarly, if $y_t < w_{t-1}$ and $r_t \leq w_{t-1}$, then the firm reveals the worker's productivity and the worker has the opportunity to accept a wage equal to that productivity. If $r_t < y_t$ then the worker accepts the wage reduction and receives y_t, while if $r_t > y_t$ then the worker leaves and receives r_t from the alternative employer. The latter is labeled a layoff, and since $r_t \leq w_{t-1}$ we have that layoffs are associated with wage decreases.[39]

Another way of modeling worker-firm separations is the asymmetric-learning approach developed in Greenwald (1986), who applies Akerlof's (1970) "lemons" model to the issue of labor mobility. In Greenwald's model, all firms are uncertain about a worker's ability at the beginning of the worker's career. After the worker's first period of employment, the worker's first-period employer learns the worker's ability, but other firms receive no information about the worker's ability. The worker's wage each period is determined by spot-market contracting. Finally, there is a positive probability that the worker moves at the beginning of the second period (say, to follow a spouse) even if the worker's best second-period wage offer comes from the first-period employer.[40]

Greenwald's analysis yields two closely related findings. First, the workers who switch firms at the beginning of the second period are disproportionately drawn from the low end of the ability distribution. Second, the wage paid to these workers is very low. The intuition for these results is almost identical to the logic in Akerlof's used-car example: because the wage received by a secondhand worker reflects the average ability of such workers, most high-ability workers stay out of the secondhand market, so workers who do switch firms receive a very low wage.[41]

Gibbons and Katz (1991) construct a model that extends Greenwald's analysis to include both layoffs and plant closings, and then empirically test a number of predictions of the model.[42] The basic logic of their theoretical analysis is that the layoff case is similar

---

[39] There is again the question of how to label the case of $r_t > w_{t-1}$ and $y_t < w_{t-1}$. See the previous footnote for the implications of this choice.

[40] Lazear (1986b) develops an alternative asymmetric-learning model of the separation decision. There is a positive probability that the first-period employer learns the worker's ability after the worker's first period in the labor market, but also a positive probability that the single other potential employer learns the worker's ability after this period. Thus, at the beginning of the worker's second period in the labor market there is a positive probability that the other firm is informed but the first-period employer is uninformed. The main result is that there is a stigma associated with failing to receive an outside offer at the beginning of the worker's second period in the labor market. This stigma results in a lower second-period wage for those who do not receive offers.

to Greenwald's analysis (in that it is mostly low-ability workers who separate), while in a plant closing workers across the whole ability distribution are forced to seek new employment. The three testable implications they develop are: (i) predisplacement wages should be uncorrelated with the cause of the displacement; (ii) postdisplacement wages should be lower for workers who lost their jobs in a layoff rather than a plant closing; and (iii) postdisplacement unemployment durations should be higher for workers who lost their jobs in a layoff rather than a plant closing. Gibbons and Katz find evidence consistent with all three predictions.

The Gibbons–Katz argument could easily be extended to provide a third explanation for the empirical finding that wage changes at separation are higher, on average, for quits than for layoffs. The logic is the same as that behind the distinction between layoffs and plant closings in their original argument. Firms decide whom to layoff, so adverse selection applies in that case: those laid off are mostly low-ability workers, so those laid off earn low postdisplacement wages on average. For quits, on the other hand, workers make the decision and so adverse selection does not apply in that case: quits are not disproportionately drawn from the low end of the ability distribution, so quits earn at least average postdisplacement wages.

Another interesting extension of Greenwald's analysis concerns the issue of employee referrals (i.e., the idea that many workers find new employment through friends and relatives).[43] The argument is that, if asymmetric learning and the resulting adverse-selection problem cause insufficient movement of workers across firms (see footnote 41), then much of the movement that does occur will be due to personal knowledge of individuals at one firm concerning the abilities of those who are currently elsewhere. Montgomery (1991) develops a simple version of this story concerning the recruitment of workers who are new to the labor force. His main results are that those who are better connected (i.e., "known" by a larger number of other individuals in the economy) earn higher wages, and firms hire through referral when the opportunity arises.

---

[41] One difference between Akerlof's analysis and Greenwald's is that in Akerlof's analysis the presence of asymmetric information causes trade on the secondhand market to be below the socially-optimal level, while in Greenwald's the presence of asymmetric information does not result in trade on the secondhand market being different than the socially-optimal level, because in Greenwald's model there is no efficiency rationale for why any worker should either switch or not switch firms between periods (ignoring workers who switch firms for exogenous reasons). Novos (1992, 1995) extends Greenwald's analysis to settings where there are efficiency reasons for workers to switch firms between periods, and shows that in these settings adverse selection can reduce trade below the socially-optimal level. Novos argues that this is one perspective for understanding the allocation of jobs within firms versus across firms.

[42] To be precise, the Gibbons–Katz model allows both for the adverse-selection effect analyzed by Greenwald and for layoffs to serve as a signal of ability in a fashion similar to the promotion-as-signal argument of Waldman (1984b) discussed in Section 3.2.

[43] There is substantial empirical evidence that employee referrals are an important component of how workers find new employment (Myers and Shultz, 1951; Rees and Shultz, 1970; Granovetter, 1973, 1995; Corcoran et al., 1980).

4. Applied models: human resource management and organization theor

Section 3 focused on issues familiar from labor economics, such as wage ~~growth and~~ separations. This section focuses on issues familiar from human resource management and organization theory, including politics, social relations, and work practices.

4.1. Politics

In this subsection we consider theoretical models of what we call politics. In our usage, political models are slightly different from agency models. Both describe interactions between individuals at different levels of a hierarchy, but in agency models the superior's action (such as paying a wage that depends on output) is determined by a contract, whereas in political models the supervisor's action cannot be governed by a contract, because the action cannot be verified by a court.[44,45] We consider models of persuasion or influence, and then turn to collusion or side contracting. In our view, politics is of clear importance in real organizations, and thus a topic that justifies the theoretical attention it has received. Unfortunately, it is also a topic that lacks systematic empirical evidence.

In models of persuasion or influence, some actions during an individual's career are motivated by a desire to change others' beliefs about (say) the individual's ability. The earliest such paper is Holmstrom (1982b), which formally models Fama's (1980) informal claim that concerns about reputation will cause managers to choose efficient effort levels. In Holmstrom's model, all firms are uncertain about a manager's ability at the beginning of the manager's career. In each period, the manager's contribution to firm value is the sum of her ability, her effort level, and the realization of a noise term. Further, in each period firms cannot observe the manager's effort choice, but all firms observe her output. These output over time observations cause the firms' belief about the manager's ability to become more precise. Finally, both managers and firms are risk neutral.

Holmstrom assumes that the manager's contribution is too nuanced and subtle to allow contracts to be contingent on output. Therefore, wages are paid in advance of production at the beginning of each period. Thus, in a one-period setting, the manager would provide no effort. In a two-period career, however, the manager would provide positive effort in the first period, in an attempt to increase the second-period wage, but no effort in the second period once that wage is set. Holmstrom investigates equilibrium effort levels when managers live forever. He shows that a manager provides positive effort each period, in an attempt to increase future wages by improving firms' subsequent beliefs about the manager's ability. But Holmstrom also shows that rather than the manager's equilibrium effort choices being efficient, as conjectured by Fama, they decline with age and converge

---

[44] In some political models, the supervisor's action can be governed by a contract but the supervisor's action rule cannot. That is, the state variable on which the action depends cannot be verified by a court.

[45] The issue of internal politics has recently received substantial theoretical attention. Our focus is on papers that have direct implications for careers, but interesting papers have been developed on other topics. See, for example, Rotemberg and Saloner (1995), Rajan and Zingales (1996, 1998), and Stole and Zwiebel (1996a,b).

to zero in the limit.[46] The logic here is that managerial effort is higher when firms have more uncertainty about the manager's ability, because the manager's performance then has more impact on the firms' belief. Because the firms' uncertainty decreases to zero as the manager's performance observations accumulate, the manager's effort goes to zero as the manager ages.[47]

In Holmstrom's model, individuals provide positive effort because performance observations influence firms' beliefs about the individual's ability. Milgrom and Roberts (1988) present a related model in which an individual's current actions are again motivated by a desire to change subsequent beliefs about the individual's attributes.[48] In particular, young workers allocate their effort between two activities: a first activity that increases the probability of a high-profit outcome in the worker's current job, and a second activity that causes the worker to *appear* more suited for a "key" job in the subsequent period (i.e., there is no actual change in her ability to perform the job). Milgrom and Roberts also assume that the firm incurs a high cost if the worker assigned to the key job quits.

We will focus on the case where the cost of a quit from the key job is sufficiently high that the firm assigns a high wage to the key job to reduce the probability of quitting. The first major result is that, in this case, young workers will not allocate their efforts in accord with first-best efficiency. Rather, because they want to increase the probability of being assigned to the key job in the subsequent period, young workers devote more effort to the second activity than is efficient from the firm's standpoint. The second major result is that, in order to reduce this inefficiency, the firm may choose a promotion rule that is ex post inefficient. Milgrom and Roberts assume that a young worker's performance on the current job is uncorrelated with expected productivity on the key job. Nevertheless, for some parameters, the firm finds it optimal to commit to promoting the young worker who was most productive on the current job, ignoring the information concerning who appears most productive on the key job. By ignoring this information, the firm eliminates the incentive for young workers to exert too much effort trying to manipulate those beliefs.

Another interesting paper related to influence is Carmichael's (1988) model of tenure in academia. In contrast to the Holmstrom and Milgrom-Roberts models, in which workers

---

[46] Holmstrom also considers what happens when managerial ability is not fixed over time, but rather evolves as a random walk. In this case the effort choice converges to a positive level instead of to zero, but only under restrictive conditions will this limiting value be the efficient level.

[47] Gibbons and Murphy (1992) use the idea of effort declining with age to test Holmstrom's career-concerns theory. They argue that, in the absence of contracts, effort will decline to below the efficient effort level as a manager nears retirement, and thus explicit incentives provided through contracts should become more important for managers near retirement. They find support for this prediction in an analysis of CEO compensation. A related result appears in Brandt and Hosios (1996). They develop a hedonic analysis of labor contracting, and apply their framework to contract data from rural China in 1935. Consistent with the Fama/Holmstrom perspective, Brandt and Hosios find that worker effort is significantly affected by reputation considerations.

[48] Other related analyses include Milgrom (1988) and Meyer et al. (1992). Milgrom shows how similar results can be derived in a model where jobs differ in terms of the speed with which a worker in the job increases his stock of human capital. Meyer, Milgrom, and Roberts show how the influence-cost approach can explain the tendency of firms to sell off poorly performing units.

take actions to change beliefs concerning their own abilities, here workers take actions that affect beliefs concerning the abilities of job applicants. In Carmichael's setting, the University decides in each period which young workers to hire from a pool of applicants. The University is imperfectly informed about the abilities of the workers in the pool, and the current faculty are the best sources for information concerning each applicant's ability. The problem the University faces is that, if hiring a high-ability applicant today increases the probability that a current faculty member will be fired tomorrow then the current faculty will not truthfully report their information concerning applicants. The role of tenure is to induce truthful reporting: if current faculty cannot be fired tomorrow then they have no incentive to hinder the University's effort to hire high-ability faculty today.

Influence models have a variety of potential applications. For example, we believe this modeling approach provides a potential explanation for the phenomenon that Prendergast (1993b) refers to as "Yes Men," where workers bias their stated opinions away from their true beliefs towards the expected opinions of managers. Prendergast explains the phenomenon using an optimal-contracting argument.[49] An alternative explanation parallels the models discussed above. When a worker makes a report to a manager concerning the potential profitability of a project, the manager will typically use that report both to decide the fate of the project and to update the manager's belief concerning the worker's ability to collect and process information. Of course, for a variety of reasons a worker will typically prefer that the manager have a more positive view of the worker's ability. We conjecture that, under plausible assumptions concerning the private signals received by the worker and manager, this preference will cause the worker to bias her report towards what she believes is the manager's opinion.[50]

We now turn to collusion or side contracting. The seminal paper in this area is Tirole's (1986) model of a principal/supervisor/agent hierarchy.[51] The principal can write contracts with the supervisor and with the agent, but the latter two parties can also agree to a separate "side contract." (Fairburn and Malcomson's (1997) model discussed in Section 3.3 also employs this approach.) In Tirole's model the supervisor first monitors the value of a

---

[49] In Prendergast's model, in order to provide the worker with an incentive to improve the quality of her information, the worker is given a bonus if the worker's report concerning the profitability of a project is sufficiently close to the manager's private signal concerning profitability. The result is that the worker biases her report concerning the project's profitability towards the worker's belief about the value of the manager's signal.

[50] Our argument is related to Bernheim's (1994) model of conformity in social interactions, where an individual conforms because of positive effects on the individual's status. In both cases, an individual conforms in order to alter others' beliefs concerning the individual's type. One difference is that in our proposed model the subsequent payoffs are monetary while in Bernheim's they are non-monetary.

[51] Tirole (1992) surveys and extends the theory of collusion and side contracting. He discusses the distinction between "enforceable side contracts" and "self-enforcing side contracts." This distinction is analogous to the distinction between formal contracting and relational contracting discussed in Section 2.3: an enforceable side contract is similar to a formal contract with third-party enforcement, whereas a self-enforcing side contract is similar to a relational contract sustained by repeated interaction. Tirole points out that most of the literature models side contracts as being enforceable, although self-enforcement seems more important in practice.

productivity parameter that affects the agent's output and then makes a report to the principal concerning the value of the parameter. There are two important assumptions. First, the supervisor may observe the value of the productivity parameter but may instead observe nothing, and only the supervisor knows which of these cases occurred. Second, the supervisor can make the report in a verifiable fashion (i.e., when the supervisor observes the value of the productivity parameter, she can report it in a way that convinces the principal), but in this case the supervisor also has the option of lying and reporting that she observed nothing.

Tirole begins by showing that, in the absence of side contracts, this problem is equivalent to a standard agency model. The supervisor is paid a constant wage in all states of nature, and honestly reports her observation of the productivity parameter if she observes it. As a result, the contract between the principal and the agent is as if the supervisor did not exist. Tirole then considers the possibility of side contracting. That is, after having agreed to contracts with the principal, the supervisor and the agent agree to a side contract (unobserved by the principal) that specifies a payment from the agent to the supervisor that depends on the supervisor's report. In effect, the agent offers a bribe to the supervisor not to reveal information that reduces the agent's payment. Tirole shows that, even if the principal anticipates this type of side contracting and adjusts the original contracts accordingly, the possibility of such side contracting will typically reduce the principal's expected payoff.[52] The reason is that, because the agent is willing to bribe the supervisor not to reveal information that is damaging to the agent, it is more costly for the principal to obtain the supervisor's information.[53]

Prendergast and Topel (1996) explore a different issue in a principal/supervisor/agent framework. In Tirole's analysis the supervisor's report is not perfectly reliable because of bribes the agent offers the supervisor. In Prendergast and Topel's model the supervisor's report is similarly unreliable, but now because of favoritism. That is, the supervisor's utility depends (either positively or negatively) on the agent's pay, and the value of this utility parameter is privately known by the supervisor. The result is that the supervisor biases her report of the agent's performance, with the sign of the supervisor's reporting bias being consistent with the sign of the effect of the agent's pay on the supervisor's utility. In contrast to Tirole's analysis, where side contracting unambiguously hurts the principal, Prendergast and Topel find that favoritism can either help or hurt. It can help because supervisors value the ability to affect the agent's pay, and thus in a world of favoritism supervisors require lower expected compensation. It can hurt because biased reports both increase the agent's risk and cause inefficient job-assignment decisions.

---

[52] If the supervisor is risk neutral, then there is no reduction in the principal's expected payoff because in that case the principal simply sells the firm to the supervisor, who becomes the principal in a standard two-party relationship with the agent.

[53] In an interesting recent paper, Olsen and Torsvik (1998) consider a two-period principal/supervisor/agent setting and show that the possibility of side contracting can actually improve the principal's expected payoff. Their argument is that, in the absence of long-term commitments, side contracting can reduce the time-inconsistency problem faced by the principal when the ratchet effect is an issue.

4.2. Social relations

This subsection considers theoretical models of what we call social relations. Whereas politics referred to interactions across levels of a hierarchy, by "social relations" we will mean interactions within a level of a hierarchy. As in Prendergast and Topel's model of favoritism, some of the models of social relations involve new arguments in the parties' utility functions. The subsection includes discussions of peer pressure, mutual monitoring with side contracting, and organizational demography.

Alchian and Demsetz (1972) argued that compensating workers at a large firm using an aggregate variable such as firm profits makes little sense, because of the free-rider or $1/n$ problem: if the return to an individual's effort is divided among the n workers in the organization, then having compensation depend on profits will have little effect on effort. But a growing body of evidence indicates that this argument is not completely correct. For example, recent studies by Kruse (1992) and Jones and Kato (1995) find that profit-sharing plans and employee stock-ownership plans (ESOPs) have significant positive effects on productivity of about 5%; see Weitzman and Kruse (1990) for a survey of earlier studies.[54]

This evidence concerning profit-sharing plans and ESOPs suggests that the free-rider problem may not be as severe as in Alchian and Demsetz's original argument, but other evidence indicates that some free riding does occur when compensation depends on an aggregate variable such as profits. For example, Newhouse (1973) and Gaynor and Pauly (1990) find that for medical practices performance measures such as hours worked fall with the proportion of a physician's revenue that is shared with the group. In a similar vein, Leibowitz and Tollison (1980) find that larger law partnerships are less effective at controlling costs.

One reason that effort levels may be higher than the standard free-rider argument predicts involves peer pressure. Kandel and Lazear (1992) introduce a peer-pressure function into the representative worker's utility function. The amount of peer pressure depends on the worker's effort level, the effort levels of the other workers, and actions of other workers that increase the level of peer pressure within the organization. Kandel and Lazear assume that, if the compensation scheme ties an individual's compensation to the profits of the firm, then the worker's disutility from peer pressure is negatively related to the worker's effort level. The logic is that, because other workers benefit when the worker

---

[54] Because profit-sharing plans and ESOPs create a type of public-goods problem, another set of studies that casts some doubt on the validity of the standard free-rider argument is the experimental research on public goods; see Ledyard (1995) for a survey. Results from this literature indicate that contributions to the public good are typically higher than suggested by the standard argument, that these contributions fall with repetition (which suggests low effort levels in organizational settings), and that these contributions rise with communication (which suggests high effort levels in organizational settings). In a recent paper, Nalbantian and Schotter (1997) conduct an experimental study that more closely matches the problem of effort provision in an organizational setting. Consistent with the findings of experiments on public goods, Nalbantian and Schotter find that effort levels are above the level predicted by the standard argument, and that these effort levels fall with repetition (although even at the end of the game these levels remain above the prediction of the standard argument). They do not test the effects of communication.

exerts more effort, other workers will penalize the worker less if his effort is higher. Kandel and Lazear show that such peer pressure increases equilibrium effort levels, because peer pressure is like a reduction in the marginal cost of effort. After developing the basic argument, Kandel and Lazear discuss a variety of sources of peer pressure, including guilt and shame, group norms, and mutual monitoring.[55]

Rotemberg (1994a) develops a model of altruism rather than peer pressure: a worker's utility depends positively on the incomes of the other workers. Naturally, if compensation depends on an aggregate variable like profits and workers are altruistic toward each other, then equilibrium effort will be higher than predicted by the standard free-rider argument. Rotemberg considers a prior period when each worker can choose how altruistic she will subsequently feel toward co-workers. This altruism choice is then credibly revealed to co-workers before effort is chosen. Rotemberg shows that if workers' efforts are complementary (i.e., the marginal product of a worker's effort is positively related to the efforts of co-workers) then workers choose positive levels of altruism and corresponding high levels of effort. The logic is that if one worker chooses a positive level of altruism then that worker's effort will be higher, which in turn induces higher effort from co-workers (because of complementarity), so choosing to be somewhat altruistic maximizes the original worker's income.

An alternative approach to understanding why effort levels induced by profit sharing are often higher than predicted by the free-rider argument involves the idea of side contracting introduced in the previous subsection. Tirole (1986) allowed side contracting between a supervisor and an agent in a principal/supervisor/agent setting, and showed that the possibility of side contracting typically reduces the principal's expected payoff. We turn next to side contracting between agents in principal/agent/agent settings. In contrast to Tirole's conclusion, in this setting the introduction of side contracting frequently helps rather than hurts the principal.

Itoh (1993) considers a model with one principal and two agents and allows for both side contracting and mutual monitoring. Mutual monitoring means that each agent observes the other agent's effort level, so side contracts can depend on effort levels as well as outputs. Itoh considers both individual production and team production, but we focus solely on team production.[56] Team production in his analysis means that the principal cannot observe each agent's individual output, but aggregate output is both observable and contractible, so the problem is similar to the profit-sharing models discussed above. Itoh shows that under team production, side contracting helps the principal. In particular,

---

[55] Barron and Gjerde (1997) extend Kandel and Lazear's analysis by explicitly incorporating the firm's choice of a compensation scheme. They argue that using profit sharing to induce peer pressure can be advantageous to the firm, but should be done in moderation. The logic is that too much peer pressure can be bad from the firm's perspective, because the firm must compensate workers for the corresponding disutility from peer pressure (as well as high effort) and this decreases the firm's profits.

[56] Holmstrom and Milgrom (1990) and Varian (1990) also consider side contracting in principal/agent/agent settings, but they do not consider team production. One result in both papers is that if agents have no private information then the principal cannot be helped by side contracting.

any symmetric effort pair can be implemented at lower cost to the principal with side contracting than without. The logic is that, because side contracts can be made contingent on individual effort levels, they increase the penalty for shirking and thus enable agents to achieve higher equilibrium effort levels than in the absence of side contracts.[57]

So far we have discussed how various social interactions can help solve the free-rider problem. There is some evidence, however, that some social interactions result in decreased rather than increased levels of effort. Miller (1992) revisits Homans' (1950) description of the bank-wiring room from the Hawthorne plant of Western Electric.[58] In the bank-wiring room there were two inspectors, nine wiremen, and three solderers, whose job was to connect wires in telephone-switching systems. The compensation scheme was a group piece rate. The group received a fixed amount for each piece of equipment produced. The resulting pool of money was first used to pay each worker his wage times the number of hours he worked. Any remaining money was then split across the workers in proportion to their respective wages. There was also an individual component to the compensation: the firm collected productivity measures for each worker (e.g., the number of connections made per hour) and wage rates were occasionally adjusted to reflect productivity differences.

Consistent with earlier parts of this subsection, some of Miller's discussion concerns how interactions among the workers served to avoid the free-rider problem. Another part of Miller's discussion, however, concerns how social interactions were used to reduce rather than increase some workers' outputs. For example, the workers had a game they called "binging," where a worker would hit another very hard on the upper arm and the worker who had been hit would have a chance to hit back. By having a large number of workers choose to play the binging game with the same high-productivity worker, the game could be used as a form of punishment and thus a way of reducing that worker's output. One question that arises here is, given that the compensation scheme was a group piece rate, why did workers seek to stop individuals from producing too much? One possibility is that there was a potential ratchet effect associated with the group piece rate: producing too much could cause the firm to reduce the future payment received by the group for a unit of output.[59] This reduction in the group piece rate would be bad for

---

[57] Borek (1997) considers mutual monitoring in a model of self-enforcing side contacts. That is, side contracts cannot be enforced by third parties, so enforcement must occur through the threat of future punishments associated with repeated interaction (see footnote 51 for a related discussion). An interesting result concerns imperfect mutual monitoring (i.e., each worker observes the effort levels of only some of the other workers). Borek holds fixed the number of other workers that each worker is able to monitor and yet shows that the effectiveness of mutual monitoring falls very slowly as the size of the firm increases. The reason is that, if a worker shirks then only a small number of others respond to the shirking immediately, but through a contagion process, even in a very large firm it does not take long before almost everyone in the firm has changed his behavior in response to the initial shirker.

[58] The Hawthorne plant is also famous for two other studies. The most famous, involving changes in lighting, suggests that workers work harder when they know they are being observed. We describe another study, based on the relay-assembly-testing room in footnote 60.

high-productivity workers, but they are also rewarded for their individual productivity (through the payment scheme described above) and they do not internalize the effect of the reduction in the group piece rate on the other workers. Thus, the group as a whole would have an incentive to stop any particular worker from producing too much as well as from producing too little.[60]

Frank (1984, 1985) develops another argument concerning social relations, relating to wage distributions rather than effort levels. Frank argues that workers derive utility both from their absolute level of income and from their relative income. That is, holding her own income fixed a worker gets additional utility (disutility) if her income is higher (lower) than the incomes of co-workers. Given these preferences, Frank shows that a firm's wage distribution will be compressed relative to the workers' marginal products. The reason is that a worker is willing to give up income to be at the top of a firm's wage distribution, but a worker must be compensated to be at the bottom of the wage distribution. Frank provides now familiar evidence that piece-rate contracts are less sensitive to performance than predicted by standard agency analysis and then argues that his relative-income perspective explains this evidence; see Baker (1992) discussed in Section 2.3 for an alternative explanation.

Other interesting perspectives on the effects of social relations exist in the sociology literature. One such perspective involves networks. In a classic study, Granovetter (1973, 1995) investigated the effects of friends and relatives as sources of information for individuals seeking employment; Montgomery's (1991) paper discussed in Section 3.4 offers an economic model along these lines. Inspired by Granovetter, Burt (1992), Fernandez and Weinberg (1997), Podolny and Baron (1997), and others have investigated the effects of social networks within the firm. An important finding is that the structure and density of an individual's network can increase the individual's probability of promotion. For example, Burt argues that an individual benefits most when he brokers a structural hole (i.e., worker A knows several workers of type B and several of type C, but no B worker knows a C worker). Podolny and Baron find that such network structures accelerate promotion (of worker A) when the network is used for acquiring information or resources but not when the network is used for performance evaluation or buy-in. The existing sociology literature on this subject largely treats an individual's network as given. It would be interesting to consider endogenous network formation.

Another interesting perspective from the sociology literature is the idea of organiza-

---

[59] For a detailed description of the ratchet effect see Roy (1952). Theoretical analyses appear in Lazear (1986a), Gibbons (1987), and Carmichael and MacLeod (1998).

[60] Recently, Jones (1990) reevaluated the data from another part of the Hawthorne experiments, the relay-assembly-testing room. As with the bank-wiring room, the compensation scheme employed in the relay-assembly-testing room was a group piece rate. Jones finds strong evidence of worker interdependence: for some pairs of workers the outputs were positively correlated; in other cases the correlation was either negative or zero. Jones interprets these correlations as evidence of social interactions, and shows how the estimated correlations in output for different worker pairs match the detailed evidence on workers' demographic similarities and interactions off the job.

tional demography originally suggested by Pfeffer (1983). Researchers in this area investigate the extent to which the distribution of individual attributes (such as age, tenure, race, or gender) within a work group affects outcomes such as innovation, productivity, satisfaction, and turnover. A large literature has developed that studies these relationships. In a prominent early paper, Wagner et al. (1984) study turnover in the top-management groups of a sample of Fortune 500 firms. They find that after controlling for an individual's age and the firm's performance, the extent to which the individual is similar to other group members decreases the probability of turnover. In another important paper, O'Reilly et al. (1989) probe this relationship between group heterogeneity and turnover by suggesting that homogeneous groups achieve higher levels of social integration.

4.3. Work practices

The traditional organization of work in large US firms involves features such as narrow job definitions, hourly pay with close supervision, and decision-making responsibilities in the hands of management. Doeringer and Piore (1971) describe these and related practices as an internal labor market; Baron et al. (1986) provide evidence that the diffusion of such practices in the US was greatly accelerated by the federal government's procurement policies in World War II. During the 1980s, however, many firms began to move away from this traditional system towards innovative work practices such as flexible job assignments, increased use of teamwork, increased use of incentive pay, and increased employment security (Kochan et al., 1986; Osterman, 1994). Substantial evidence suggests that these innovative work practices have significant positive effects on firm-wide productivity. In this subsection we first briefly discuss some of the evidence and then consider recent theoretical models.

Several kinds of studies suggest that innovative work practices can have positive effects on productivity, including case studies, industry studies, and cross-industry studies; see Levine (1995) and Ichniowski et al. (1996) for overviews of the literature. For example, Ichniowski et al. (1997) study a sample of steel-production lines. They find that innovative work practices have a positive effect on productivity, but this positive effect is almost entirely confined to firms that employ several such practices in combination. For example, they find that a full bundle of innovative work practices increases productivity by more than 6%, but varying any specific work practice by itself has no measurable effect on productivity. They also find that the incidences of these practices are positively correlated: in their study, over 90% of the possible bivariate correlations across practices are positive.

From a theoretical perspective, this evidence raises the question of why such work practices might matter only when they are bundled together. A good answer to this question seems likely also to explain why the observed bivariate correlations are positive. One obvious answer to these questions is that activities pay off (and hence are observed) in bundles because they are complementary; doing more of one increases the return to doing another. In such a setting, a change in the environment that increases the return to one of the activities will cause the firm to increase both that activity and the others. Further, given such a change in the environment, the return to the firm from increasing all the activities together would be larger than the sum of the returns associated with increasing each activity by itself. Recent theoretical work, such as Milgrom and Roberts (1990) and Holmstrom and Milgrom (1994), has begun to examine what else follows from the assumption that activities are complementary besides these intuitive results that activities will be adopted in bundles and will pay off more as a bundle than the sum of the independent effects.

The theoretical literature on complementarities provides a rather abstract explanation for the evidence concerning innovative work practices and increased productivity. A more satisfying explanation would explain why certain work practices are complementary, rather than simply assuming this to be so. Milgrom and Roberts (1995) provide a discussion along these lines. They consider some of the work practices employed by the Lincoln Electric Company, which is well known for its high levels of productivity. Part of their discussion concerns the following three practices employed by Lincoln. First, Lincoln is widely known for its reliance on piece rates. All production workers and many nonproduction workers have their compensation determined in part by a piece rate. Second, a large proportion of Lincoln's shares is held by the firm's workers. This was accomplished originally by direct stock purchases, and more recently by an ESOP. Third, there is a high degree of employment security due to a no-layoff policy.

Milgrom and Roberts argue that these three work practices are complementary. First, piece rates increase incentives, but there is a potential ratchet effect. That is, as discussed in Section 4.2, workers may provide low effort because they fear that high effort will cause the firm to lower the piece rate in the future. But the ratchet effect stems from the idea that, if the owners of the firm learn that the current rate is "too high," they lower the rate and in this way transfer rents from the workers to themselves. By having a large proportion of the shares held by the workers, Lincoln greatly reduces the incentive for the owners to transfer rents away from the workers. But a quick way to turn worker-owners into simply owners is through layoffs. That is, in the absence of a no-layoff policy, the firm could fire workers and either force them to sell their shares back to the firm or even allow them to hold their shares. The result would be a lower proportion of stock held by workers, which could lead to lower piece rates.[61]

A number of the work practices discussed in the empirical literature (such as empowerment and self-managed teams) have the effect of decentralizing decision-making within the firm. Aghion and Tirole (1997) consider empowerment in a principal–agent model

[61] As discussed in Section 2.3, Baker et al. (1994) emphasize another complementarity in Lincoln's practices: the interaction of the piece rate and the bonus in Lincoln's pay plan. Burton et al. (1998) describe five other bundles of employment practices they observed in 75 young, hi-tech Silicon Valley firms, such as the "engineering" model (involving attachment through challenging work, control by the peer group, and selection based on specific task abilities) and the "autocracy" model (involving attachment through monetary motivations, control through close oversight, and selection of employees to perform pre-specified tasks). Burton, Hannan, and Baron discuss the internal consistency of these bundles of employment practices; more importantly, their data suggest how economists might push past the analysis of case studies such as Lincoln Electric.

concerning which, if any, of a set of new projects to undertake. The authors distinguish between formal authority and real authority: an individual with formal authority over a decision has the right to make the decision, but the decision may in fact be made by another individual (in which case the latter individual has the real authority). Aghion and Tirole impose two key assumptions. First, both the principal and the agent can invest resources in information acquisition, where a larger investment increases the probability that the individual obtains full information about the returns associated with the various projects. Second, payoffs are not perfectly aligned. That is, the project that yields the highest private benefit to the principal need not be the project that yields the highest private benefit to the agent.

Aghion and Tirole's main result is that the decentralization of decision rights can be viewed as a trade-off between incentives and agency costs. Giving the agent formal authority over project choice increases the agent's incentive to acquire information, but there is a corresponding cost because the principal's and agent's incentives concerning project choice are not perfectly aligned.[62] In addition to deriving this basic trade-off, Aghion and Tirole derive a number of other results, including one consistent with the idea of complementary work practices. As indicated at the beginning of this subsection, one of the recent trends in work practices is increased use of incentive pay. Aghion and Tirole show that, when formal authority is left in the hands of the principal, incentive pay and decentralization (i.e., giving the agent more real authority) are complementary work practices. That is, the higher the agent's monetary payment for choosing a project that benefits the principal, the more real authority the agent is given in deciding which project to undertake. One reason this is the case is that the monetary payment serves to align incentives, so the higher the monetary payment the less need the principal has to overrule the agent.

Rotemberg (1994b) also analyzes issues related to empowerment and decentralized decision-making. In particular, Rotemberg considers who should have "power" (i.e., the right to make decisions according to his wishes) within a profit-maximizing firm. There is substantial evidence in the sociology literature that power is not given to those with the highest willingness to pay to determine the decision, as might be suggested by a simple economic model. Rather, this evidence indicates that power is given either to those who control important flows of resources from outside the firm (Pfeffer and Salancik, 1978; Tushman and Romanelli, 1983) or to those who help the firm cope with uncertainty (Crozier, 1964; Hinings et al., 1974).

Rotemberg considers a two-period setting where a firm cannot observe a worker's best alternative wage offer in the second period, and also cannot commit in the first period to the wages it will pay workers in the second period. He shows that in this setting it is typically not optimal to give power to the individual who has the highest willingness to pay to determine the decision. Rather, because giving an individual power increases the

---

[62] Jensen and Meckling (1992) gave a closely related informal argument. In their view, decentralized decision-making allows the firm to take advantage of the superior information held by those lower in the hierarchy, but there is a resulting cost because incentives are not perfectly aligned.

probability that the worker will remain with the firm in the second period, the firm gives power to those it most wants to keep. That is, the firm gives power to workers whose value to the firm is much higher than the worker's expected alternative offer, such as might be the case for those who control important flows of resources or help the firm cope with uncertainty.

Several recent papers consider related issues. First, Rotemberg and Saloner (1993) consider how a firm's optimal management style varies with the nature of the firm's environment. They find that a participatory style is optimal in environments that are potentially rich in innovative ideas, while an autocratic style is optimal in environments lacking such potential. Second, Prendergast (1995) considers a setting in which a manager must decide how to divide tasks between the manager and a subordinate. In equilibrium, the manager retains too many tasks because she receives a private return from on-the-job learning. Thus, Prendergast's model suggests why empowerment runs counter to the interests of middle managers. Finally, Zabojnik (1997b) considers centralized versus decentralized decision-making in a setting where workers have an effort choice, and shows that it is sometimes optimal to let the worker make the decision even when the manager has superior information. There is an element of complementarity in Zabojnik's analysis in that decentralized decision-making is more beneficial when the worker has a high degree of employment security (although in his model the degree of employment security is an exogenous variable rather than a choice variable for the firm).

5. Integrative models

In Sections 3 and 4 we considered models that address one or a few aspects of careers in organizations. In this section we survey papers from a small but expanding literature that addresses patterns of evidence. As noted in the Introduction, the advantage of this approach is that any single fact may be consistent with a variety of theories, so one way to choose among theories is by evaluating the extent to which each is consistent with a broad pattern of evidence.

5.1. Harris and Holmstrom (1982)

Perhaps the first attempt to explain a broad pattern of evidence is Harris and Holmstrom's (1982) analysis of symmetric learning and insurance. This paper builds on Freeman's (1977) two-period model discussed in Section 3.1.[63] In Harris and Holmstrom's analysis,

---

[63] Other papers that build on Freeman's (1977) analysis include Weiss (1984) and Haltiwanger and Waldman (1986). Weiss considers a setting in which workers are homogeneous at the beginning of their careers, but heterogeneity is introduced over time as productivity grows in a stochastic fashion. Haltiwanger and Waldman consider a setting in which workers vary in terms of ability as in Freeman's analysis, but they focus on the implications of workers having imperfect access to capital markets.

all firms are uncertain about a worker's ability at the beginning of the worker's career, and all firms gradually learn about the worker's ability as they observe the worker's output over time. The learning is gradual because output is a noisy function of the worker's true ability. Ability does not vary with the worker's age or firm-specific seniority. Workers are risk averse and are in the labor market for T periods, whereas firms are risk neutral and are infinitely lived. As in Freeman's analysis, because workers are risk averse and firms are risk neutral, it would be efficient for a firm to insure each of its workers against the uncertainty about how the market's belief about the worker's ability will evolve over time.

Harris and Holmstrom assume that firms can contractually commit to a wage policy that specifies each period's wage as a function of that period's output and past outputs. Workers, on the other hand, cannot commit to their future actions; in particular, a worker always has the option of leaving the current employer and taking an alternative offer. Given these contracting assumptions, equilibrium wages have three properties. First, the desire for insurance causes the current period's wage to be independent of that period's output. Second, the desire for insurance also causes real wages to be downward rigid. That is, the firm guarantees that the worker's real wage in period $t + 1$ will be no lower than in period t. Finally, a worker's wage rises when the market's belief about her ability changes in a sufficiently positive fashion. More specifically, the wage in any such period equals the worker's expected productivity (based on the history of prior outputs) minus an insurance premium that falls to zero over the worker's T-period career. The first two results extend Freeman's conclusions to T-period careers; the third is new. The basic logic of the Harris–Holmstrom model is that, because workers cannot commit to staying with the current employer when other potential employers offer higher wages, workers cannot receive full insurance (i.e., they bear the risk of wage increases) and they must pay an insurance premium (even though there is competition among risk-neutral firms).

After deriving the results described above, Harris and Holmstrom show that their model offers an explanation for five empirical findings concerning careers. First, as found by Mincer (1974) and others, the wage is an increasing concave function of labor-market experience. In the Harris–Holmstrom model, there are two reasons why the wage is a positive function of experience. First, older workers have had more opportunities to have had their wages bid up. Second, as workers age, the size of the required insurance premium falls (both because there is less uncertainty about ability and because an older worker has fewer periods remaining in her career). The reason that the wage is concave in experience is that the incremental amount of learning goes to zero as the worker ages, so the insurance premium falls more rapidly earlier in a worker's career.

Second, like Freeman's analysis, the Harris–Holmstrom model provides an explanation for Medoff and Abraham's (1980, 1981) finding that wages increase with labor-market experience even though performance evaluations do not. Assuming that performance evaluations are an unbiased measure of productivity, this result follows in the Harris–Holmstrom model because worker productivity is independent of experience yet the average wage rises with experience. Harris and Holmstrom also show the stronger result that, in a continuous-time version of their model, the wage is a positive function of experience even after controlling for the market's current belief about the worker's productivity. This result holds because the required insurance premium falls with age.[64]

The three remaining empirical findings captured by the Harris–Holmstrom model are all found in Mincer (1974). The third is that the variance of earnings increases with labor-market experience (because of learning about workers' abilities). Fourth, assuming that a worker's expected productivity is positively related to her education level, the expected wage is a positive function of the worker's education level. Fifth, the wage distribution is positively skewed (because the insurance aspect of the wage policy truncates the lower tail of the wage distribution).

Despite providing an explanation for a variety of facts, the Harris–Holmstrom model does have some drawbacks. The most important is their prediction of real-wage rigidity. That is, because the analysis is based on an insurance argument, it predicts downward rigidity of real not nominal wages. But much evidence indicates that real wages frequently fall (Baker et al., 1994b; McLaughlin, 1994; Card and Hyslop, 1997), although nominal wages show some downward rigidity. The other drawback of the Harris–Holmstrom model is one of omission. Many of the empirical findings regarding careers in organizations concern assignment to jobs and the resulting promotion process (e.g., large wage increases upon promotion and serial correlation in promotion rates). Because firms in the Harris–Holmstrom model have only a single job, their analysis cannot address these and related findings.

5.2. Demougin and Siow (1994)

A second paper that attempts to explain a pattern of evidence is Demougin and Siow (1994). The key feature of this model is that each firm trains (some) young unskilled workers in the hope of developing the next period's manager. Demougin and Siow consider an overlapping-generations structure where firms are infinitely lived and each cohort of workers is in the labor market for two periods. In any period, a firm employs a single manager and an endogenously determined number of unskilled workers. The firm can train any or all of its young unskilled workers. If a worker is trained there is a reduction of output during the training period but there is also a positive probability that the training will be successful, in which case the worker will be qualified to be a manager in the following period (at this or any other firm). If a worker is not trained then there is no

---

[64] Harris and Holmstrom argue that their framework is also consistent with seniority-related wage growth. Their argument is as follows. Assume that turnover occurs only when the evolution of beliefs concerning a worker's ability is sufficiently positive that the worker's wage is bid up (otherwise the market wage offer is less than that of the current employer). They argue that since a worker who switches firms is earning the market wage while many others already at the new firm are earning an above-market wage, the return to seniority must be positive. This argument is incorrect. Since a worker who switches firms has just had her wage bid up, on average, such a worker will be earning more than others with the same amount of labor-market experience. This, in turn, suggests a return to seniority that is negative not positive.

chance that he will be qualified to be a manager next period. The final key assumption is that a firm incurs a training cost if the managerial position is filled with an outsider.

Demougin and Siow show that equilibrium in this setting takes one of two forms. If the probability that training will be successful is low and the productivity of unskilled workers is low then the firm hires few young workers but trains them all. For other parameters, the firm hires more young workers than it trains. Demougin and Siow show that each of these regimes has several interesting features, as follows.

Consider first what Demougin and Siow call the fast-track regime. These are the parameterizations such that the firm chooses to train some but not all of its young workers. This regime has the following features. First, as suggested by the name, there is a kind of fast track. Because the firm chooses to train only some of its young workers, some young workers have a higher probability of promotion than other young workers (specifically, some young workers have a positive probability of promotion while others have zero probability). Second, firms prefer to promote from within. That is, if at least one young worker's training succeeds then the firm fills the managerial position with such a worker. Only if no young worker's training is successful does the firm fill the position with an old worker who was successfully trained at a different firm in the previous period. Third, the span of control is larger than one (i.e., there are more unskilled workers than managers). This result follows largely from the assumption that the probability that training is successful is less than one.[65]

Consider next what Demougin and Siow call the up-or-out regime. These are the parameterizations such that the firm chooses to train all its young workers. This regime has some features in common with the fast-track regime but other features that differ. First, firms again prefer to promote from within. Second, the span of control is again larger than

---

[65] Demougin and Siow also claim that this regime provides an explanation for the Medoff and Abraham (1980, 1981) finding that wages are positively related to seniority while performance evaluations are not. Their argument is as follows. For young unskilled workers who receive training, there is a positive probability the training will be successful, in which case the individual will receive the higher managerial wage in the subsequent period. As a result, young unskilled workers who receive training are paid less than both young workers who do not receive training and old workers who are employed as unskilled workers (both of whom receive the same wage). Thus, on average, old unskilled workers are paid more than young unskilled workers. That is, wages rise with experience. Demougin and Siow's claim that the above result explains the Medoff–Abraham puzzle concerning seniority is incorrect. The reason is that old unskilled workers are paid the same whether they remain with their first-period employer or move elsewhere. Thus, controlling for experience, the seniority wage premium in Demougin–Siow's fast-track regime equals zero. There remains the issue, however, of whether the above result is an explanation for the Medoff–Abraham finding that wages are positively related to labor-market experience while performance evaluations are not. The answer here is as follows. Since there is a cost of providing training to a young worker, the above result is not an explanation for the Medoff–Abraham finding concerning labor-market experience if performance evaluations are unbiased measures of productivity. That is, the performance evaluation of young unskilled workers receiving training will be lower because there is a reduction in productivity during training. To generate the Medoff–Abraham result, one would have to assume that the performance evaluation of a young worker receiving training does not reflect this fall in productivity. Then young and old unskilled workers would receive the same performance evaluation but old unskilled workers would receive a higher wage. See the discussion of Gibbons and Waldman (1999) later in this section for a related argument.

one. Third, rather than there being a fast track, firms now employ an up-or-out promotion rule. As discussed in Section 3.3, up-or-out means that every old worker who is not promoted is forced to leave the firm. The logic here is that the firm needs all of its unskilled slots as training slots, so there is no room for an old worker to take an unskilled slot.

There are a few drawbacks of the Demougin–Siow analysis. First, they find that firms employ either a fast track or up-or-out, but not both. We know of no evidence that the two are not employed together. To the contrary, the academic labor market employs the up-or-out rule, and seems also to exhibit a fast track: our casual impression is that individuals who are promoted to associate professor more quickly typically spend less time as associate professors before promotion to full (although this is a different type of fast track than in the Demougin–Siow analysis).

The other main drawback is one of omission. Because there are only two jobs and because there is little heterogeneity across workers (the only heterogeneity is that some old workers are qualified to be managers because they previously received training and the training was successful), the analysis does not address many of the detailed empirical findings concerning careers in organizations. For example, Demougin and Siow do not address findings such as that wage increases at one level of a job ladder forecast speed of promotion to the next or that demotions are rare while real-wage decreases are not.

5.3. Gibbons and Waldman (1999)

The last paper we discuss is Gibbons and Waldman (1999). This paper integrates the two standard ways of modeling the promotion process as job-assignment mechanism discussed in Section 3.2: learning and human-capital acquisition. (Like Harris–Holmstrom and Demougin–Siow, Gibbons–Waldman abstracts from incentive issues.) Let θ_i be worker i's innate ability, which can equal either θ_H or θ_L, $\theta_H > \theta_L$. A worker's effective ability in period t is given by $\eta_{it} = \theta_i f(x_{it})$, where x_{it} is the worker's labor-market experience in period t and $f(x_{it})$ is an increasing and concave function representing general human-capital accumulation. Each firm consists of three jobs, denoted 1, 2, and 3. The output of worker i assigned to job j in period t is given by $b_j + c_j(\eta_{it} + \varepsilon_{it})$, where ε_{it} is a noise term. Let η' be the level of effective ability at which a worker is equally productive in jobs 1 and 2; that is η' solves $b_1 + c_1\eta' = b_2 + c_2\eta'$. Similarly, let η'' solve $b_2 + c_2\eta'' = b_3 + c_3\eta''$. The production-function parameters are such that the efficient assignment rule is $\eta_{it} < \eta'$ to job 1, $\eta' < \eta_{it} < \eta''$ to job 2, and $\eta_{it} > \eta''$ to job 3. Furthermore, the innate-ability and skill-acquisition parameters are such that all workers start their careers in job 1 and end their careers in job 3. Finally, both workers and firms are risk neutral and there are no hiring or mobility costs so wages and job assignments can be determined by spot-market contracting.

In this model, higher ability is more valuable in higher-level jobs, with the result that workers move up the job ladder as they age because human-capital acquisition causes effective ability to increase. Gibbons and Waldman consider this model under both full information and symmetric learning. In the latter case all workers look identical when they enter the labor market and firms update their beliefs concerning a worker's innate and effective abilities as they observe realizations of the worker's output. Our discussion will focus on the symmetric-learning case.

Gibbons and Waldman analyze the extent to which their model can explain the detailed empirical findings in Baker et al.'s (1994a,b) investigation of managerial careers inside a single firm in the financial services industry. Most of the Baker–Gibbs–Holmstrom (BGH) findings are either fully or partly supported by other empirical investigations but Gibbons and Waldman focus on the BGH findings because they all hold in one environment. Gibbons and Waldman show that their model captures a number of the BGH findings, including the following four. First, real-wage decreases are a minority of the observations, but are not rare, while demotions can be very rare. The logic here is that if a worker's output is sufficiently low then the market will reduce its belief about the worker's effective ability, causing the worker's real wage to fall, but this learning will not result in a demotion unless the worker's expected effective ability falls from above η' to below (or from above η'' to below). Second, there is serial correlation in wage increases. This occurs because innate ability and human capital interact in the production function: workers with high expected innate ability typically experience faster growth in expected effective ability, and this results in serial correlation in wage increases.

The other two BGH findings we discuss here concern the manner in which wages and wage changes are related to the promotion process. The third is that promotions are associated with larger-than-average wage increases, but these wage increases are small relative to the difference in the average wages between the relevant levels of the job ladder. In the Gibbons–Waldman model, promotions are associated with larger-than-average wage increases because of learning and sample-selection: workers whose outputs are worse than expected typically are not promoted; those who are promoted are a selected sample whose outputs are typically better than expected. The reason these wage increases at promotion are small relative to the difference in the average wages between the relevant levels of the job ladder is human-capital acquisition: some of the workers in the higher-level job are paid more because they have acquired more human capital, but the wage increase at promotion captures only one year's worth of human-capital accumulation.

The fourth BGH finding we discuss here is that workers who receive large wage increases early in their stay at one level of a job ladder are typically promoted more quickly to the next level. In the Gibbons–Waldman model, a large wage increase suggests a high value for expected innate ability, which in turn suggests that expected effective ability will increase quickly in the future. Thus, workers with large wage increases early on will typically take less time to achieve the critical value of expected effective ability needed for promotion.

In addition to exploring the extent to which their model captures these and other findings from the BGH environment, Gibbons and Waldman also consider the extent to which their model is consistent with findings in Medoff and Abraham (1980, 1981), such as within a job level wages are positively related to labor-market experience while performance evaluations fall with experience. (Unfortunately, Baker, Gibbs, and Holmstrom do not report whether their data are consistent with the Medoff–Abraham findings.) Gibbons and Waldman argue that a potential explanation for the Medoff–Abraham findings is that human-capital theory is the correct explanation for wage growth, but performance evaluations are a biased measure of productivity (see footnote 65 for a related discussion), as follows.

In the Gibbons–Waldman model, the wage is an increasing function of expected effective ability, which increases with experience because of human-capital acquisition. Now suppose that supervisors evaluate individuals relative to other individuals with the same labor-market experience (i.e., performance evaluations measure expected innate ability rather than expected effective ability). Then performance evaluations within a job level fall with experience, because workers with high expected innate ability will be promoted out of this job level as they age (and those with low expected innate ability will be promoted into this job level as they age). Thus, with this interpretation of performance evaluations, wages rise but evaluations fall with experience in the Gibbons–Waldman model. This result is perhaps modest when taken alone, but may be reassuring because it falls so easily out of a model designed to address the BGH findings.

As with the Harris–Holmstrom and Demougin–Siow models, we see a few drawbacks of the Gibbons–Waldman analysis. The most important concerns turnover. In this model there is neither specific human capital nor asymmetric learning, both of which would tie workers to firms. Gibbons and Waldman assume that there is an infinitesimal moving cost so no turnover actually occurs, but one could as easily assume that there is no moving cost, so workers could switch firms randomly from period to period. This indeterminacy means the model cannot address issues such as whether there is a positive return to seniority, what are the factors that affect separation probabilities, and whether firms prefer to promote from within.

The other drawback we see is that, even restricting the focus to the BGH firm, there are a few findings that Gibbons and Waldman do not capture. These include: (i) cohort effects (i.e., a cohort's average entry-level wage is an important determinant of the cohort's average wage years after entry); (ii) nominal wage rigidity; and (iii) a strong green-card effect (i.e., within a job level, the expected wage increase is a decreasing function of the initial wage). Of these three findings, we feel the cohort finding is the most troubling. In the Gibbons–Waldman model, wages are determined by competitive bidding, so the state of the labor market in past years has no effect on current wages. In contrast, the cohort finding suggests that workers are somewhat insulated from the market, and thus that competitive bids have a minor effect on earnings.

6. Conclusion

We have surveyed the labor-economics literature on careers in organizations, focusing on theoretical models that address detailed evidence or stylized facts. When possible we have tried to assess the extent to which the various theoretical approaches fit the data. For example, in discussing the two standard ways of modeling the promotion process as a job-assignment mechanism (learning and human-capital acquisition), we argued that the learning approach does not fit the evidence concerning wage growth in the absence of promotions, but the human-capital-acquisition approach does not fit the evidence concerning larger-than-average wage increases at promotion. Our conclusion is that the evidence favors models that combine learning and human-capital acquisition, because such models exhibit both large wage increases at promotion and significant wage increases in the absence of promotion.

We have not identified a single theoretical framework that captures most of the existing evidence. Developing such a framework should be an important goal for future contributors to the theoretical literature on careers in organizations. The integrative models summarized in Section 5 give us some hope that such a framework can be developed. Given the building-block models described in Section 2, it is now relatively easy to build theoretical models that capture a single empirical finding or stylized fact; it is much more difficult but also much more useful to construct models that match a pattern of evidence.

On the other hand, several of the existing findings come from a small set of studies such as Medoff and Abraham (1980, 1981) and Baker et al. (1994a,b), and these studies typically focus on a very small number of firms. Before much more effort is expended developing integrative theoretical models that explain these and other findings, it is crucial to know which findings are specific to the particular firms studied and which are representative of careers in a range of occupations, industries, countries, and time periods. To resolve this uncertainty, future contributors to the empirical literature on careers in organizations should address a core set of questions, such as those suggested by Gibbons (1997) before analyzing their particular concerns.

Finally, we believe more attention should be paid to the sociology literature concerning careers in organizations, such as the work discussed in Section 4. There are substantial bodies of evidence in this literature that could be combined with the empirical studies in the economics literature to develop a clearer picture of careers. There are also a number of theoretical approaches in the sociology literature that merit economists' attention, either as complements to or substitutes for the theoretical approaches in the economics literature. This paper has shown that labor economists have begun to theorize about events inside organizations, and that some of the resulting models match the available evidence fairly well, but organizational sociologists might argue that these models still describe labor markets, not life in organizations. For example, in Gibbons and Waldman (1999), workers could turn over every period or not at all; firm affiliation is simply not relevant. In this sense, labor economists (ourselves included) seem far from understanding the sociologists' claim that employment outcomes are deeply affected by organizational structures and processes, rather than being determined in an institution-free labor market.

References

Abowd, J. and D. Card (1989), "On the covariance structure of earnings and hours changes", Econometrica 57: 411–445.

Abowd, J., F. Kramarz and D. Margolis (1999), "High-wage workers and high-wage firms", Econometrica 67: 251–333.

Abraham, K.G. and H.S. Farber (1987), "Job duration, seniority, and earnings", American Economic Review 77: 278–297.

Acemoglu, D. and J. Pischke (1996), "The structure of wages and investment in general training", Mimeo. (Massachusetts Institute of Technology).

Acemoglu, D. and J. Pischke (1998), "Why do firms train? Theory and evidence", Quarterly Journal of Economics 113: 79–119.

Aggarwal, R. and A.A. Samwick (1999), "The other side of the tradeoff: the impact of risk on executive compensation", Journal of Political Economy 107: 65–105.

Aghion, P. and J. Tirole (1997), "Formal and real authority in organizations", Journal of Political Economy 105: 1–29.

Akerlof, G.A. (1970), "The market for 'lemons': quality uncertainty and the market mechanism", Quarterly Journal of Economics 84: 288–300.

Akerlof, G.A. (1976), "The economics of caste and of the rat race and other woeful tales", Quarterly Journal of Economics 90: 599–617.

Akerlof, G.A. and L. Katz (1989), "Workers' trust funds and the logic of wage profiles", Quarterly Journal of Economics 104: 525–536.

Alchian, A.A. and H. Demsetz (1972), "Production, information costs, and economic organization", American Economic Review 62: 777–795.

Altonji, J.G. and R.A. Shakotko (1987), "Do wages rise with job seniority?" Review of Economic Studies 54: 437–459.

Altonji, J.G. and N. Williams (1997), "Do wages rise with job seniority? A reassessment", Mimeo. (Northwestern).

Antel, J.J. (1985), "Costly employment contract renegotiation and the labor mobility of young men", American Economic Review 75: 976–991.

Antle, R. and A. Smith (1986), "An empirical investigation of the relative performance evaluation of corporate executives", Journal of Accounting Research 24: 1–39.

Baker, G.P. (1992), "Incentive contracts and performance measurement", Journal of Political Economy 100: 598–614.

Baker, G.P., R. Gibbons and K.J. Murphy (1994), "Subjective performance measures in optimal incentive contracts", Quarterly Journal of Economics 109: 1125–1156.

Baker, G.P., M. Gibbs and B. Holmstrom (1994a), "The internal economics of the firm: evidence from personnel data", Quarterly Journal of Economics 109: 881–919.

Baker, G.P., M. Gibbs and B. Holmstrom (1994b), "The wage policy of a firm", Quarterly Journal of Economics 109: 921–955.

Baker, G.P., M.C. Jensen and K.J. Murphy (1988), "Compensation and incentives: practice vs. theory", Journal of Finance 43: 593–616.

Baron, J.N., F. Dobbin and P. Jennings (1986), "War and peace: the evolution of modern personnel administration in U.S. industry", American Journal of Sociology 92: 350–383.

Barron, J.M. and K.P. Gjerde (1997), "Peer pressure in an agency relationship", Journal of Labor Economics 15: 234–254.

Barron, J.M., D.A. Black and M.A. Loewenstein (1989), "Job matching and on-the-job training", Journal of Labor Economics 7: 1–19.

Bartel, A. and G.J. Borjas (1981), "Wage growth and job turnover: an empirical analysis", in: S. Rosen, ed., Studies in labor markets (University of Chicago Press, Chicago, IL) pp. 65–84.

Becker, B. and M. Huselid (1992), "The incentive effects of tournament compensation systems", Administrative Science Quarterly 37: 336–350.

Becker, G.S. (1962), "Investment in human capital: a theoretical analysis", Journal of Political Economy 70: 9–49.

Becker, G.S. (1964), Human capital (NBER, New York).

Becker, G.S. and G. Stigler (1974), "Law enforcement, malfeasance and compensation of enforcers", Journal of Legal Studies 3: 1–18.

Ben-Porath, Y. (1967), "The production of human capital and the life cycle of earnings", Journal of Political Economy 75: 352–365.

Bernhardt, D. (1995), "Strategic promotion and compensation", Review of Economic Studies 62: 315–339.

Bernhardt, D. and D. Scoones (1993), "Promotion, turnover, and preemptive wage offers", American Economic Review 84: 771–791.

Bernheim, B.D. (1994), "A theory of conformity", Journal of Political Economy 102: 841–877.

Bishop, J. (1991), "On-the-job training of new hires", in: D. Stern and J.M. Rizen, eds., Market failure in training? New economic analysis and evidence on training of adult employees (Springer-Verlag, New York) pp. 61–96.

Blumen, I., M. Kogen and P. McCarthy (1955), The industrial mobility of labor as a probability process (Cornell University Press, Ithaca, NY).

Borek, T.C. (1997), "Group incentives in large firms", Mimeo. (Cornell).

Brandt, L. and A.J. Hosios (1996), "Credit, incentives, and reputation: a hedonic analysis of contractual wage profiles", Journal of Political Economy 104: 1172–1226.

Brown, C. (1990), "Firms' choice of method of pay", Industrial and Labor Relations Review 43: 165–183.

Brown, K.C., W.V. Harlow and L.T. Starks (1996), "Of tournaments and temptations: an analysis of managerial incentives in the mutual fund industry", Journal of Finance 51: 85–110.

Bull, C. (1987), "The existence of self-enforcing implicit contracts", Quarterly Journal of Economics 102: 147–159.

Bulow, J.I. and L.H. Summers (1986), "A theory of dual labor markets with application to industrial policy, discrimination and Keynesian unemployment", Journal of Labor Economics 4: 376–414.

Burdett, K. (1978), "A theory of employee job search and quit rates", American Economic Review 68: 212–220.

Burt, R. (1992), Structural holes: the social structure of competition (Harvard University Press, Cambridge, MA).

Burton, D., M. Hannan and J.N. Baron (1998), "Employment models in entrepreneurial companies", Mimeo. (Harvard).

Calvo, G. (1979), "Quasi-Walrasian theories of unemployment", American Economic Review 69: 102–107.

Calvo, G. (1985), "The inefficiency of unemployment: the supervision perspective", Quarterly Journal of Economics 100: 373–387.

Capelli, P. and K. Chauvin (1991), "An interplant test of the efficiency wage hypothesis", Quarterly Journal of Economics 106: 769–787.

Card, D. and D. Hyslop (1997), "Does inflation 'grease the wheels of the labor market'?", in: C. Romer and D. Romer, eds., Reducing inflation: motivation and strategy (University of Chicago Press, Chicago, IL) pp. 71–114.

Carmichael, H.L. (1983), "Firm specific human capital and promotion ladders", Bell Journal of Economics 14: 251–258.

Carmichael, H.L. (1985), "Can unemployment be involuntary? Comment", American Economic Review 75: 1213–1214.

Carmichael, H.L. (1988), "Incentives in academics: why is there tenure", Journal of Political Economy 96: 453–472.

Carmichael, H.L. (1989), "Self-enforcing contracts, shirking and life cycle incentives", Journal of Economic Perspectives 3: 65–83.

Carmichael, H.L. and W.B. MacLeod (1998), "Worker cooperation and the ratchet effect", Journal of Labor Economics, in press.

Chang, C. and Y. Wang (1996), "Human capital investment under asymmetric information: the Pigovian conjecture revisited", Journal of Labor Economics 14: 505–519.

Chevalier, J. and G. Ellison (1997), "Risk taking by mutual funds as a response to incentives", Journal of Political Economy 105: 1167–1200.

Corcoran, M., L. Datcher and G. Duncan (1980), "Information and influence networks in labor markets", in: G. Duncan and J. Morgan, eds., Five thousand American families: patterns of economic progress, Vol. 7 (Institute for Social Research, Ann Arbor, MI) pp. 1–37.

Cragg, M. (1997), "Performance incentives in the public sector: evidence from the Job Training Partnership Act", Journal of Law, Economics, and Organization 13: 147–168.

Crozier, M. (1964), The bureaucratic phenomenon (University of Chicago Press, Chicago, IL).

Demougin, D. and A. Siow (1994), "Careers in ongoing hierarchies", American Economic Review 84: 1261–1277.

Dickens, W.T., L.F. Katz, K. Lang and L.H. Summers (1989), "Employee crime and the monitoring puzzle", Journal of Labor Economics 7: 331–347.

Doeringer, P. and M. Piore (1971), Internal labor markets and manpower analysis (Heath Lexington Books, Lexington, MA).

Drago, R. and G.T. Garvey (1998), "Incentives for helping on the job: theory and evidence", Journal of Labor Economics 16: 1–25.

Ehrenberg, R.G. and M.L. Bognanno (1990a), "Do tournaments have incentive effects?" Journal of Political Economy 98: 1307–1324.

Ehrenberg, R.G. and M.L. Bognanno (1990b), "The incentive effects of tournaments revisited: evidence from the European PGA Tour", Industrial and Labor Relations Review 43: 74S–88S.

Fairburn, J.A. and J.M. Malcomson (1997), "Performance, promotion, and the Peter principal", Mimeo. (University of Sussex).

Fama, E.F. (1980), "Agency problems and the theory of the firm", Journal of Political Economy 88: 288–307.

Farber, H.S. (1994), "The analysis of interfirm worker mobility", Journal of Labor Economics 12: 554–593.

Farber, H.S. (1997), "Trends in long term employment in the United States 1979–96", Working paper no. 384 (Industrial Relations Section, Princeton University, Princeton NJ).

Fast, N. and N. Berg (1975), "The Lincoln Electric Company", Harvard Business School case no. 376–028.

Fernandez, R. and N. Weinberg (1997), "Sifting and sorting: personal contacts and hiring in a retail bank", American Sociological Review 62: 883–902.

Frank, R.H. (1984), "Are workers paid their marginal products?" American Economic Review 74: 549–571.

Frank, R.H. (1985), Choosing the right pond (Oxford University Press, New York).

Frank, R.H. and P.J. Cook (1995), The winner-take-all society (Free Press, New York).

Freeman, S. (1977), "Wage trends as performance displays productive potential: a model and application to academic early retirement", Bell Journal of Economics 8: 419–443.

Friedman, M. and S. Kuznets (1954), Income from independent professional practice (NBER, New York).

Galizzi, M. and K. Lang (1998), "Relative wages, wage growth, and quit behavior", Journal of Labor Economics 16: 367–391.

Garen, J.E. (1994), "Executive compensation and principal-agent theory", Journal of Political Economy 102: 1175–1199.

Garvey, G.T. and P.L. Swan (1992), "Managerial objectives, capital structure, and the provision of worker incentives", Journal of Labor Economics 10: 357–379.

Gaynor, M. and M. Pauly (1990), "Compensation and productive efficiency in partnerships: evidence from medical group practice", Journal of Political Economy 98: 544–574.

Geanakoplos, J. and P. Milgrom (1991), "A theory of hierarchies based on limited managerial attention", Journal of the Japanese and International Economies 5: 205–225.

Gerhart, B. and G. Milkovich (1989), "Salaries, salary growth, and promotions of men and women in a large private firm", in: R. Michael, H. Hartmann and B. O'Farrell, eds., Pay equity: empirical inquiries (National Academy Press, Washington, DC) pp. 23–43.

Ghez, G. and G.S. Becker (1975), The allocation of time and goods over the life cycle (NBER, New York).

Gibbons, R. (1987), "Piece-rate incentive schemes", Journal of Labor Economics 5: 413–429.

Gibbons, R. (1997), "Incentives and careers in organizations", in: D. Kreps and K. Wallis, eds., Advances in economic theory and econometrics (Cambridge University Press, New York) pp. 1–37.

Gibbons, R. and L. Katz (1991), "Layoffs and lemons", Journal of Labor Economics 9: 351–380.

Gibbons, R. and L. Katz (1992), "Does unmeasured ability explain inter-industry wage differentials?" Review of Economic Studies 59: 515–535.

Gibbons, R. and K.J. Murphy (1990), "Relative performance evaluation for chief executive officers", Industrial and Labor Relations Review 43: 30S–51S.

Gibbons, R. and K.J. Murphy (1992), "Optimal incentive contracts in the presence of career concerns: theory and evidence", Journal of Political Economy 100: 468–505.

Gibbons, R. and M. Waldman (1999), "A theory of wage and promotion dynamics inside firms", Quarterly Journal of Economics, in press.

Gibbs, M. (1995), "Incentive compensation in a corporate hierarchy", Journal of Accounting and Economics 19: 247–277.

Granovetter, M.S. (1973), Getting a job: a study of contacts and careers (Harvard University Press, Cambridge, MA).

Granovetter, M.S. (1995), Getting a job: a study of contacts and careers, 2nd edition (University of Chicago Press, Chicago, IL).

Green, J.R. and N.L. Stokey (1983), "A comparison of tournaments and contracts", Journal of Political Economy 91: 349–364.

Greenwald, B. (1986), "Adverse selection in the labour market", Review of Economic Studies 53: 325–347.

Grout, P.A. (1984), "Investment and wages in the absence of binding contracts: a Nash bargaining approach", Econometrica 52: 449–460.

Guasch, J.L. and A. Weiss (1980), "Wages and sorting mechanisms in competitive markets with asymmetric information: a theory of testing", Review of Economic Studies 47: 149–165.

Guasch, J.L. and A. Weiss (1982), "An equilibrium analysis of wage-productivity gaps", Review of Economic Studies 49: 485–497.

Hall, R.E. (1982), "The importance of lifetime jobs in the U.S. economy", American Economic Review 72: 716–724.

Hall, R.E. and E.P. Lazear (1984), "The excess sensitivity of layoffs and quits to demand", Journal of Labor Economics 2: 233–257.

Haltiwanger, J. and M. Waldman (1986), "Insurance and labor market contracting: an analysis of the capital market assumption", Journal of Labor Economics 4: 355–375.

Harris, M. and B. Holmstrom (1982), "A theory of wage dynamics", Review of Economic Studies 49: 315–333.

Hart, O. and J. Moore (1988), "Incomplete contracts and renegotiation", Econometrica 56: 755–785.

Hashimoto, M. (1981), "Firm-specific human capital as a shared investment", American Economic Review 71: 475–482.

Hayes, R.M. and S. Schaefer (1999), "Implicit contracts and the explanatory power of top executive compensation for future performance", Mimeo. (Northwestern).

Hinings, C.R., D.J. Hickson, J.M. Pennings and R.E. Schneck (1974), "Structural conditions and intraorganizational power", Administrative Science Quarterly 19: 22–44.

Holmstrom, B. (1979), "Moral hazard and observability", Bell Journal of Economics 9: 74–91.

Holmstrom, B. (1982a), "Moral hazard in teams", Bell Journal of Economics 13: 324–340.

Holmstrom, B. (1982b), "Managerial incentive schemes – a dynamic perspective", in: Essays in economics and management in honour of Lars Wahlbeck (Swenska Handelshogkolan, Helsinki, Finland).

Holmstrom, B. and P. Milgrom (1987), "Aggregation and linearity in the provision of intertemporal incentives", Econometrica 55: 303–328.

Holmstrom, B. and P. Milgrom (1990), "Regulating trade among agents", Journal of Institutional and Theoretical Economics 146: 85–105.

Holmstrom, B. and P. Milgrom (1991), "Multitask principal-agent analyses: incentive contracts, asset ownership, and job design", Journal of Law, Economics, and Organization 7: 24–52.

Holmstrom, B. and P. Milgrom (1994), "The firm as an incentive system", American Economic Review 84: 972–991.

Holmstrom, B. and J. Roberts (1998), "The boundaries of the firm revisited", Journal of Economic Perspectives 12: 73–94.

Holmstrom, B. and J. Tirole (1989), "The theory of the firm", in: R. Schmalensee and R. Willig, eds., Handbook of industrial organization, Vol. 1 (North–Holland, Amsterdam) pp. 60–133.

Homans, G. (1950), The human group (Harcourt Brace Jovanovich, San Diego, CA).

Hutchens, R.M. (1986), "Delayed payment contracts and a firm's propensity to hire older workers", Journal of Labor Economics 4: 439–457.

Hutchens, R.M. (1987), "A test of Lazear's theory of delayed payment contracts", Journal of Labor Economics 5: S153–S170.

Ichniowski, C., T.A. Kochan, D. Levine, C. Olson and G. Strauss (1996), "What works at work: overview and assessment", Industrial Relations 35: 299–333.

Ichniowski, C., K. Shaw and G. Prennushi (1997), "The effects of human resource management practices on productivity: a study of steel finishing lines", American Economic Review 87: 291–313.

Itoh, H. (1993), "Coalitions, incentives, and risk sharing", Journal of Economic Theory 60: 410–427.

Janakiraman, S., R. Lambert and D. Larcker (1992), "An empirical investigation of the relative performance evaluation hypothesis", Journal of Accounting Research 30: 53–69.

Jensen, M.C. and W.H. Meckling (1992), "Specific and general knowledge and organizational structure", in: L. Werin and H. Wijkander, eds., Contract economics (Basil Blackwell, Oxford, UK) pp. 251–274.

Jones, D.C. and T. Kato (1995), "The productivity effects of employee stock–ownership plans and bonuses: evidence from Japanese panel data", American Economic Review 85: 391–414.

Jones, S.R.G. (1990), "Worker interdependence and output: the Hawthorne studies reevaluated", American Sociological Review 55: 176–190.

Jovanovic, B. (1979), "Job matching and the theory of turnover", Journal of Political Economy 87: 972–990.

Jovanovic, B. and Y. Nyarko (1997), "Stepping stone mobility", Carnegie-Rochester Series for Public Policy 46: 289–337.

Kahn, C. and G. Huberman (1988), "Two-sided uncertainty and 'up-or-out' contracts", Journal of Labor Economics 6: 423–444.

Kandel, E. and E.P. Lazear (1992), "Peer pressure and partnership", Journal of Political Economy 100: 801–817.

Kanter, R.M. (1977), Men and women of the corporation (Basic Books, New York).

Katz, E. and A. Ziderman (1990), "Investment in general training: the role of information and labor mobility", Economic Journal 100: 1147–1158.

Katz, L. (1986), "Efficiency wage theories: a partial evaluation", NBER Macroeconomics Annual 1: 235–276.

Killingsworth, M.R. (1982), "'Learning by doing' and 'investment in training': a synthesis of two 'rival' models of the life cycle", Review of Economic Studies 49: 263–271.

Klein, B. (1996), "Why hold-ups occur: the self-enforcing range of contractual relationships", Economic Inquiry 34: 444–463.

Klein, B., R.G. Crawford and A.A. Alchian (1978), "Vertical integration, appropriable rents, and the competitive contracting process", Journal of Law and Economics 21: 297–326.

Knoeber, C.R. and W.N. Thurman (1994), "Testing the theory of tournaments: an empirical analysis of broiler production", Journal of Labor Economics 12: 155–179.

Kochan, T.A., H.C. Katz and R.B. McKersie (1986), The transformation of American industrial relations (Basic Books, New York).

Krueger, A.B. (1991), "Ownership, agency, and wages: an examination of franchising in the fast food industry", Quarterly Journal of Economics 106: 75–101.

Kruse, D.L. (1992), "Profit sharing and productivity: microeconomic evidence from the United States", Economic Journal 102: 24–36.

Landers, R.M., J.B. Rebitzer and L.J. Taylor (1996), "Rat race redux: adverse selection in the determination of work hours in law firms", American Economic Review 86: 329–348.

Lazear, E.P. (1979), "Why is there mandatory retirement?" Journal of Political Economy 87: 1261–1284.

Lazear, E.P. (1981), "Agency, earnings profiles, productivity, and hours restrictions", American Economic Review 71: 606–620.

Lazear, E.P. (1986a), "Salaries and piece rates", Journal of Business 59: 405–431.

Lazear, E.P. (1986b), "Raids and offer matching", in: R.G. Ehrenberg, ed., Research in labor economics, Vol. 8 (JAI Press, Greenwich, CT) pp. 141–165.

Lazear, E.P. (1989), "Pay equality and industrial politics", Journal of Political Economy 97: 561–580.

Lazear, E.P. (1992), "The job as a concept", in: W. Bruns, ed., Performance measurement, evaluations, and incentives (Harvard University Press, Boston, MA) pp. 183–215.

Lazear, E.P. (1997), "Performance pay and productivity", Mimeo. (Stanford).

Lazear, E.P. and S. Rosen (1981), "Rank-order tournaments as optimum labor contracts", Journal of Political Economy 89: 841–864.

Ledyard, J.O. (1995), "Public goods: a survey of experimental research", in: J.H. Kagel and A.E. Roth, eds., Handbook of experimental economics (Princeton University Press, Princeton, NJ).

Leibowitz, A. and R. Tollison (1980), "Free riding, shirking and team production in legal partnerships", Economic Inquiry 18: 380–394.

Leonard, J.S. (1987), "Carrots and sticks: pay, supervision, and turnover", Journal of Labor Economics 5: S136–S152.

Levhari, D. and Y. Weiss (1974), "The effect of risk on the investment in human capital", American Economic Review 64: 950–963.

Levine, D.I. (1995), Reinventing the workplace (The Brookings Institution, Washington, DC).

Loewenstein, M.A. and J.R. Spletzer (1998), "Dividing the costs and returns to general training", Journal of Labor Economics 16: 142–171.

Lundberg, S.J. and R. Startz (1983), "Private discrimination and social intervention in competitive labor markets", American Economic Review 73: 340–347.

MacDonald, G.M. (1982a), "A market equilibrium theory of job assignment and sequential accumulation of information", American Economic Review 72: 1038–1055.

MacDonald, G.M. (1982b), "Information in production", Econometrica 50: 1143–1162.

MacDonald, G.M. (1988), "Job mobility in market equilibrium", Review of Economic Studies 55: 153–168.

MacDonald, G.M. and J.R. Markusen (1985), "A rehabilitation of absolute advantage", Journal of Political Economy 93: 277–297.

Machin, S. and A. Manning (1992), "Testing dynamic models of worker effort", Journal of Labor Economics 10: 288–305.

MacLeod, W.B. and J.M. Malcomson (1988), "Reputation and hierarchy in dynamic models of employment", Journal of Political Economy 96: 832–854.

MacLeod, W.B. and J.M. Malcomson (1989), "Implicit contracts, incentive compatibility, and involuntary unemployment", Econometrica 57: 447–480.

MacLeod, W.B. and J.M. Malcomson (1998), "Motivation and markets", American Economic Review 88: 388–411.

MacLeod, W.B. and D. Parent (1998), "Job characteristics and the form of compensation", Mimeo. (University of Southern California).

Macneil, I. (1978), "Contracts: adjustments of long-term economic relations under classical, neoclassical and relational contract law", Northwestern University Law Review 72: 854–906.

Main, B.G.M., C.A. O'Reilly III and J. Wade (1993), "Top executive pay: tournaments or teamwork?" Journal of Labor Economics 11: 606–628.

Malcomson, J.M. (1984), "Work incentives, hierarchy, and internal labor markets", Journal of Political Economy 92: 486–507.

Malcomson, J.M. (1997), "Contracts, hold-up, and labor markets", Journal of Economic Literature 35: 1916–1957.

Malcomson, J.M. (1999), "New developments in the study of contracts in labor markets", in: O. Ashenfelter and D. Card, eds., Handbook of labor economics, Vol. 3 (North-Holland, Amsterdam).

Maremont, M. (1995), "Blind ambition: how the pursuit of results got out of hand at Bausch & Lomb", Business Week, October 23.

Mayer, T. (1960), "The distribution of ability and earnings", Review of Economics and Statistics 42: 189–195.

McCue, K. (1996), "Promotions and wage growth", Journal of Labor Economics 14: 175–209.

McLaughlin, K.J. (1991), "A theory of quits and layoffs with efficient turnover", Journal of Political Econonomy 99: 1–29.

McLaughlin, K.J. (1994), "Rigid wages?" Journal of Monetary Economics 34: 383–414.

Medoff, J. and K. Abraham (1980), "Experience, performance, and earnings", Quarterly Journal of Economics 95: 703–736.

Medoff, J. and K. Abraham (1981), "Are those paid more really more productive?" Journal of Human Resources 16: 186–216.

Meyer, M.A. (1991), "Learning from coarse information: biased contests and career profiles", Review of Economic Studies 58: 15–41.

Meyer, M.A. (1992), "Biased contests and moral hazard: implications for career profiles", Annales d'Economie et de Statistique, 25/26: 165–187.

Meyer, M.A., P. Milgrom and J. Roberts (1992), "Organizational prospects, influence costs, and ownership changes", Journal of Economics & Management Strategy 1: 9–35.

Meyerson, R.B. and M.A. Satterthwaite (1983), "Efficient mechanisms for bilateral trading", Journal of Economic Theory 29: 265–281.

Milgrom, P. (1988), "Employment contracts, influence activities and efficient organization design", Journal of Political Economy 96: 42–60.

Milgrom, P. and S. Oster (1987), "Job discrimination, market forces, and the invisibility hypothesis", Quarterly Journal of Economics 102: 453–476.

Milgrom, P. and J. Roberts (1988), "An economic approach to influence activities in organizations", American Journal of Sociology 94: S154–S179.

Milgrom, P. and J. Roberts (1990), "The economics of modern manufacturing: technology, strategy, and organization", American Economic Review 80: 511–528.

Milgrom, P. and J. Roberts (1995), "Complementarities and fit: strategy, structure, and organizational change in manufacturing", Journal of Accounting and Economics 19: 179–208.

Miller, G.J. (1992), Managerial dilemmas: the political economy of hierarchy (Cambridge University Press, New York).

Mincer, J. (1962), "On-the-job training: costs, returns, and some implications", Journal of Political Economy 70: S50–S79.

Mincer, J. (1974), Schooling, experience, and earnings (NBER, New York).

Mincer, J. (1986), "Wage changes in job changes", in: R.G. Ehrenberg, ed., Research in labor economics, Vol. 8 (JAI Press, Greenwich, CT) pp. 171–197.

Mincer, J. and B. Jovanovic (1981), "Labor mobility and wages", in: S. Rosen, ed., Studies in labor markets (University of Chicago Press, Chicago, IL) pp. 21–63.

Mirrlees, J. (1974), "Notes on welfare economics, information, and uncertainty", in: M. Balch, D. McFadden and S. Wu, eds., Essays on economic behavior under uncertainty (North-Holland, Amsterdam) pp. 243–258.

Mirrlees, J. (1976), "The optimal structure of incentives and authority within an organization", Bell Journal of Economics 7: 105–131.

Montgomery, J.D. (1991), "Social networks and labor-market outcomes: toward an economic analysis", American Economic Review 81: 1408–1418.

Mookherjee, D. (1984), "Optimal incentive schemes with many agents", Review of Economic Studies 51: 433–446.

Mortensen, D.T. (1978), "Specific capital and labor turnover", Bell Journal of Economics 9: 572–586.

Mortensen, D. and C. Pissarides (1999), "New developments in models of search in the labor market", in: O. Ashenfelter and D. Card, eds., Handbook of labor economics, Vol. 3 (North-Holland, Amsterdam).

Murphy, K.J. (1985), "Corporate performance and managerial remuneration: an empirical analysis", Journal of Accounting and Economics 7: 11–42.

Murphy, K.J. (1986), "Incentives, learning, and compensation: a theoretical and empirical investigation of managerial labor contracts", Rand Journal of Economics 17: 59–76.

Murphy, K.J. (1991), "Merck & Co. Inc. (A)", Case no. 9-491-005 (Harvard Business School).

Murphy, K.J. (1999), "Executive compensation", in: O. Ashenfelter and D. Card, eds., Handbook of labor economics, Vol. 3 (North-Holland, Amsterdam).

Myers, C.A. and G.P. Shultz (1951), The dynamics of a labor market (Prentice-Hall, New York).

Nalbantian, H.R. and A. Schotter (1997), "Productivity under group incentives: an experimental study", American Economic Review 87: 314–341.

Nalebuff, B.J. and J.E. Stiglitz (1983), "Prizes and incentives: towards a general theory of compensation and competition", Bell Journal of Economics 14: 21–43.

Newhouse, J. (1973), "The economics of group practice", Journal of Human Resources 8: 37–56.

Novos, I.E. (1992), "Learning by doing, adverse selection and firm structure", Journal of Economic Behavior and Organization 19: 17–39.

Novos, I.E. (1995), "Imperfections in labor markets and the scope of the firm", International Journal of Industrial Organization 13: 387–410.

O'Flaherty, B. and A. Siow (1992), "On the job screening, up or out rules, and firm growth", Canadian Journal of Economics 25: 346–368.

O'Flaherty, B. and A. Siow (1995), "Up-or-out rules in the market for lawyers", Journal of Labor Economics 13: 709–733.

Olsen, T.E. and G. Torsvik (1998), "Collusion and renegotiation in hierarchies: a case of beneficial corruption", International Economic Review 39: 413–438.

O'Reilly, C., D. Caldwell and W. Barnett (1989), "Work group demography, social integration, and turnover", Administrative Science Quarterly 34: 21–37.

Osterman, P. (1994), "How common is workplace transformation and who adopts it?" Industrial and Labor Relations Review 47: 173–188.

Oyer, P. (1998), "Fiscal year ends and nonlinear incentive contracts: the effect on business seasonality", Quarterly Journal of Economics 113: 149–185.

Parsons, D.O. (1972), "Specific human capital: an application to quit and layoff rates", Journal of Political Economy 80: 1120–1143.

Parsons, D.O. (1977), "Models of labor market turnover: a theoretical and empirical survey", in: R.G. Ehrenberg, ed., Research in labor economics, Vol. 1 (JAI Press, Greenwich, CT) pp. 185–223.

Perrow, C. (1986), Complex organizations: a critical essay, 3rd edition (McGraw-Hill, New York).

Pfeffer, J. (1983), "Organizational demography", in: L.L. Cummings and B.M. Staw, eds., Research in organizational behavior, Vol. 5 (JAI Press, Greenwich, CT) pp. 299–357.

Pfeffer, J. and G. Salancik (1978), The external control of organizations: a resource dependence perspective (Harper and Row, New York).

Podolny, J.M. and J.N. Baron (1997), "Resources and relationships: social networks and mobility in the workplace", American Sociological Review 62: 673–693.

Prendergast, C. (1993a), "The role of promotion in inducing specific human capital acquisition", Quarterly Journal of Economics 108: 523–534.

Prendergast, C. (1993b), "A theory of 'yes men'", American Economic Review 83: 757–770.

Prendergast, C. (1995), "A theory of responsibility in organizations", Journal of Labor Economics 13: 387–400.

Prendergast, C. (1999), "The provision of incentives in firms", Journal of Economic Literature 37: 7–63.

Prendergast, C. and R.H. Topel (1996), "Favoritism in organizations", Journal of Political Economy 104: 958–978.

Prescott, E.C. and M. Visscher (1980), "Organization capital", Journal of Political Economy 88: 446–461.

Rajan, R. and L. Zingales (1996), "The tyranny of the inefficient: an enquiry into the adverse consequences of power struggles", Mimeo. (University of Chicago).

Rajan, R. and L. Zingales (1998), "Power in a theory of the firm", Quarterly Journal of Economics 113: 387–432.

Rebitzer, J.B. and L.J. Taylor (1995), "Efficiency wages and employment rents: the employer - size wage effect in the job market for lawyers", Journal of Labor Economics 13: 678–708.

Rees, A. and G.P. Shultz (1970), Workers in an urban labor market (University of Chicago Press, Chicago, IL).

Ricart i Costa, J. (1988), "Managerial task assignments and promotion", Econometrica 56: 449–466.

Rosen, S. (1978), "Substitution and division of labour", Economica 45: 235–250.

Rosen, S. (1981), "The economics of superstars", American Economic Review 71: 845–858.

Rosen, S. (1982), "Authority, control, and the distribution of earnings", Bell Journal of Economics 13: 311–323.

Rosen, S. (1983), "Specialization and human capital", Journal of Labor Economics 1: 43–49.

Rosen, S. (1986a), "The theory of equalizing differences", in: O. Ashenfelter and R. Layard, eds., Handbook of labor economics, Vol. 1 (North-Holland, Amsterdam) pp. 641–692.

Rosen, S. (1986b), "Prizes and incentives in elimination tournaments", American Economic Review 76: 701–715.

Rosen, S. (1992), "Contracts and the market for executives", in: L. Werin and H. Wijkander, eds., Contract economics (Basil Blackwell, Oxford, UK) pp. 181–211.

Ross, S., P. Taubman and M. Wachter (1981), "Learning by observing and the distribution of wages", in: S. Rosen, ed., Studies in labor markets (University of Chicago Press, Chicago, IL) pp. 359–371.

Rotemberg, J.J. (1994a), "Human relations in the workplace", Journal of Political Economy 102: 684–717.

Rotemberg, J.J. (1994b), "Power in profit-maximizing organizations", Journal of Economics and Management Strategy 2: 165–198.

Rotemberg, J.J. and G. Saloner (1993), "Leadership style and incentives", Management Science 39: 1299–1318.

Rotemberg, J.J. and G. Saloner (1995), "Overt interfunctional conflict (and its reduction through business strategy)", Rand Journal of Economics 26: 630–653.

Roy, D. (1952), "Quota restriction and goldbricking in a machine shop", American Journal of Sociology 57: 427–442.

Salop, S. (1979), "A model of the natural rate of unemployment", American Economic Review 74: 433–444.

Salop, J. and S. Salop (1976), "Self-selection and turnover in the labor market", Quarterly Journal of Economics 90: 619–627.

Sattinger, M. (1975), "Comparative advantage and the distributions of earnings and abilities", Econometrica 43: 455–468.

Sattinger, M. (1993), "Assignment models and the distribution of earnings", Journal of Economic Literature 31: 831–880.

Schultz, T.W. (1963), The economic value of education (Columbia University Press, New York).

Scoones, D. and D. Bernhardt (1998), "Promotion, turnover and discretionary human capital acquisition", Journal of Labor Economics 16: 122–141.

Shapiro, C. and J.E. Stiglitz (1984), "Equilibrium unemployment as a worker discipline device", American Economic Review 74: 433–444.

Shavell, S. (1979), "Risk sharing and incentives in the principal and agent relationship", Bell Journal of Economics 10: 55–73.

Spurr, S.J. (1987), "How the market solves an assignment problem: the matching of lawyers with legal claims", Journal of Labor Economics 5: 502–532.

Stiglitz, J.E. (1985), "Equilibrium wage distributions", Economic Journal 95: 595–618.

Stole, L.A. and J. Zwiebel (1996a), "Organizational design and technology choice under intrafirm bargaining", American Economic Review 86: 195–222.

Stole, L.A. and J. Zwiebel (1996b), "Intra-firm bargaining under non-binding contracts", Review of Economic Studies 63: 375–410.

Tirole, J. (1986), "Hierarchies and bureaucracies: on the role of collusion in organizations", Journal of Law, Economics and Organization 2: 181–214.

Tirole, J. (1992), "Collusion and the theory of organizations", in: J.J. Laffont, ed., Advances in economic theory - sixth world congress, Vol. 2 (Cambridge University Press, Cambridge, UK) pp. 151–206.

Topel, R.H. (1991), "Specific capital, mobility, and wages: wages rise with job seniority", Journal of Political Economy 99: 145–176.

Topel, R.H. and M.P. Ward (1992), "Job mobility and the careers of young men", Quarterly Journal of Economics 107: 439–479.

Tushman, M.L. and E. Romanelli (1983), "Uncertainty, social location and influence in decision making: a sociometric analysis", Management Science 29: 12–23.

Varian, H.R. (1990), "Monitoring agents with other agents", Journal of Institutional and Theoretical Economics 146: 153–179.

Wagner, W.G., J. Pfeffer and C.A. O'Reilly III (1984), "Organizational demography and turnover in top-management groups", Administrative Science Quarterly 29: 74–92.

Waldman, M. (1984a), "Worker allocation, hierarchies and the wage distribution", Review of Economic Studies 51: 95–109.

Waldman, M. (1984b), "Job assignments, signalling, and efficiency", Rand Journal of Economics 15: 255–267.

Waldman, M. (1990), "Up-or-out contracts: a signaling perspective", Journal of Labor Economics 8: 230–250.

Waldman, M. (1997), "Ex ante vs. ex post optimal promotion rules", Mimeo. (Cornell).

Wallace, T. and L. Inhen (1975), "The theory of human capital accumulations with alternative loan markets", Journal of Political Economy 83: 157–184.

Weiss, A. (1980), "Job queues and layoffs in labor markets with flexible wages", Journal of Political Economy 88: 526–538.

Weiss, A. (1990), Efficiency wages (Princeton University Press, Princeton, NJ).

Weiss, Y. (1972), "On the optimal lifetime pattern of labor supply", Economic Journal 82: 1293–1315.

Weiss, Y. (1984), "Wage contracts when output grows stochastically: the roles of mobility costs and capital market imperfections", Journal of Labor Economics 2: 155–173.

Weiss, Y. (1986), "The determination of life cycle earnings: a survey", in: O. Ashenfelter and R. Layard, eds., Handbook of labor economics, Vol. 1 (North-Holland, Amsterdam) pp. 603–640.

Weitzman, M. and D.L. Kruse (1990), "Profit sharing and productivity", in: A. Blinder, ed., Paying for productivity: a look at the evidence (The Brookings Institution, Washington, DC) pp. 95–114.

Whyte, W.H. (1956), The organization man (Simon & Schuster, New York).

Williams, J.T. (1979), "Uncertainty and the accumulation of human capital over the life cycle", Journal of Business 52: 521–548.

Williamson, O.E. (1975), Markets and hierarchies: analysis and antitrust implications (The Free Press, New York).

Williamson, O.E. (1979), "Transaction-cost economics: the governance of contractual relations", Journal of Law and Economics 22: 3–61.

Williamson, O.E. (1985), Economic institutions of capitalism (The Free Press, New York).

Zabojnik J. (1997a), "Corporate tournaments, general human capital acquisition, and wage dispersion", Mimeo. (Queen's University).

Zabojnik, J. (1997b), "Centralized and decentralized decision-making in organizations", Mimeo. (Queen's University).

Zabojnik, J. (1998), "Sales maximization and specific human capital", Rand Journal of Economics 29: 790–802.

Chapter 37

MOBILITY AND STABILITY: THE DYNAMICS OF JOB CHANGE IN LABOR MARKETS

HENRY S. FARBER*

Princeton University

Contents

* I thank David Card and Joanne Gowa for comments on an earlier draft.

Handbook of Labor Economics, Volume 3, Edited by O. Ashenfelter and D. Card

Abstract

Three central facts describe inter-firm worker mobility in modern labor markets: (1) long-term employment relationships are common; (2) most new jobs end early; and (3) the probability of a job ending declines with tenure. Models based on firm-specific capital provide a parsimonious explanation for these facts, but it also appears that worker heterogeneity in mobility rates can account for much of what we observe in these data. I investigate tests of the specific capital model and consider whether these tests are successful in distinguishing the specific capital model from a model based on heterogeneity. One approach uses longitudinal data with detailed mobility histories of workers. These analyses suggest that both heterogeneity and specific capital (implying true duration dependence in the hazard of job ending) appear to be significant factors in accounting for mobility patterns. A second approach is through estimation of the return to tenure in earnings functions. This is found to have several weaknesses including the endogeneity of tenure and the lack of tight theoretical links between tenure and accumulated specific capital and between productivity and wages. A third approach is to use data on the earnings experience of displaced workers. Several tests are derived based on these data, but there is generally an alternative heterogeneity-based explanation that makes interpretation difficult. Nonetheless, firms appear willing to pay to encourage long-term employment relationships, and they may do so because it is efficient to invest in their workforce. On this basis, I conclude that, while deriving convincing direct evidence for the specific capital model of mobility is difficult, it appears that specific capital is a useful construct for understanding worker mobility and wage dynamics. © 1999 Elsevier Science B.V. All rights reserved.

JEL codes: J41; J63

1. Introduction

It is evident to even the casual observer that the labor market in the United States and other developed countries is not primarily a spot market characterized by short-term employment relationships between workers and firms. There is not high frequency movement by workers from firm to firm or, put another way, high frequency movement by firms from worker to worker. For example, in February 1996, 35.4% of workers aged 35–64 in the United States had been with their current employer for at least 10 years, and 20.9% of workers aged 45–64 had been with their current employer for at least 20 years.[1] On the other hand, neither is the labor market static in the sense that workers and firms are irrevocably bound to each other. For example, at the same date, 19.1% of American workers 20–64 had been with their current employer for less than 1 year.[2] Given a civilian employment level of 125.7 million workers in the United States, this suggests that about 24 million new employment relationships existed in March 1997 that did not exist in February 1996.[3] And the number of new

---

[1] These statistics are based on tabulations of data from the mobility supplement to the February 1996 Current Population Survey (CPS). See Farber (1997b) for details.

[2] These statistics are based on tabulations of data from the mobility supplement to the February 1996 Current Population Survey (CPS). See Farber (1997c) for details.

employment relationships that started between March 1995 and February 1996 is almost surely much larger than 24 million because many new employment relationships started during this time period did not survive until February 1996.[4] Since overall employment in the United States increased by only 700,000 jobs over the same period, virtually all of these new employment relationships involve job change.

Both the high incidence of long-term employment relationships and the high level of job change, defined here as change of employer, are important features of modern labor markets. In this chapter I attempt to place these facts in perspective highlighting the potential role of firm-specific capital and heterogeneity across workers. The next section contains a description of various sources of data on job mobility. This discussion focuses on the United States because of the availability there of consistent data on tenure and mobility over a fairly substantial period of time. In Section 3, I outline a set of important facts on job change that a theory of worker mobility needs to explain. These facts are that (1) long-term employment relationships are common, (2) most new jobs end early, and (3) the probability of a job ending declines with tenure. I present evidence mainly for the United States but also for other countries that establishes the basis for these facts. I also review some recent literature investigating whether job stability has been declining in the United States. Section 4 contains a discussion of models based on firm-specific capital, including match quality, as an explanation for the stylized facts. In Section 5, I establish that worker and job heterogeneity in mobility rates can largely account for the facts, without resort to the existence of specific capital.

In Section 6, I discuss some tests of the relative importance of heterogeneity and specific capital in explaining mobility rates based on the relationship of mobility rates with experience, tenure, and more detailed mobility histories. Section 7 contains a discussion of testing the specific capital model through estimation of the return to tenure in earnings functions. I also discuss the weaknesses of this approach, including endogeneity of tenure and the lack of tight theoretical links between tenure and accumulated specific capital and between productivity and wages are discussed. The recent literature on estimating the return to tenure is reviewed in some detail. In Section 8, I discuss the use of data on the earnings experience of displaced workers to test the specific capital model. Several tests are derived, but there is generally an alternative heterogeneity-based explanation that makes testing difficult. Section 9 contains some final remarks.

2. Sources of data on job mobility

The discussion in this section focuses on the United States because, in contrast to most other countries, data on worker mobility are available over a substantial period of time. As a

---

[3] The employment statistics are taken from US Bureau of Labor Statistics Series ID LFS11000000. This is the seasonally adjusted civilian employment level derived from the Current Population Survey for workers aged 16 and older.

[4] I present evidence below on the high hazard of jobs ending during the first year.

result, not surprisingly, most of the literature on worker mobility, analyzes the American experience. However, the issues of data quality and needs are of more general applicability.

2.1. The current population survey data on tenure

Much of what we know about the tenure distribution in the United States comes from the Current Population Survey (CPS). At irregular intervals, the Census Bureau has appended mobility supplements to the January Current Population Survey. The years in which they did so include 1951, 1963, 1966, 1968, 1973, 1978, 1981, 1983, 1987, and 1991. Mobility supplements were also appended to the February 1996 and February 1998 CPSs. These supplements contain information that can be used to compute job tenure, defined as time with the current employer.[5] Information on job tenure is also available in pension and benefit supplements to the CPS in May of 1979, 1983, and 1988, and in April 1993. Finally, data on job tenure can be derived from the contingent and alternative employment arrangement supplements (CAEAS) to the CPS in February 1995 and February 1997.

Important problems of comparability of data over time exist because of substantial changes in the wording of the central question about job duration. The early mobility supplements (1951–1981) asked workers what year they "...started working at their present job or business." The mobility supplements in 1983, 1997, and 1991 asked workers how many years they have "...been working continuously for the *present employer...* ." The most recent mobility supplements (1996 and 1998) asked workers how long they have "...been working continuously for the *present employer... .*" and let the respondent define the time units. The pension and benefit supplements to the CPS in May of 1979, 1983, and 1988, and in April 1993 asked workers "How many years have you worked for your present employer?". The question goes on to say "If there has been an interruption of one year or more, count only the years since that interruption." The CAEASs to the CPS in February 1995 and February 1997 asked workers how long they had been working for their present employer with no reference to continuity of employment and allowed the respondents define the time units. These differences affect the comparability of the responses.

First and most obviously, the early mobility supplement question refers to time on the present job rather than time with the present employer. If workers change jobs without changing employers (e.g., promotion or reassignment), then time on the job will be shorter than time with employer. Second, different groups of supplements handle interrupted spells differently. The recent mobility supplements ask about continuous spells without elaborating on what constitutes continuity, while the pension and benefit supplements direct the respondent to ignore interruptions of less than 1 year. There is no mention of continuity in the early mobility supplement question or in the CAEASs. Assuming that the natural inclination of workers will be to ignore interruptions of "reasonable" length if no mention is made of continuity, it appears that these differences will reduce reported

---

[5] Only the mobility supplements since 1973 are available in machine-readable form.

durations in the later mobility supplements and the CAEASs relative to both the early mobility supplements and the pension and benefit supplements. Third, there is likely to be heaping of responses at round numbers that will be different for the early mobility supplements (which ask for a calendar year) than for the later mobility supplements and the pension and benefit supplements (which ask for a number of years or simply how long). In the early mobility supplements question, the spikes occur at round calendar years (1960, 1965, etc.). In the other supplements, the spikes occur at round counts of years (5, 10, 15, etc.).[6] Additionally, an inquiry about when the job started may evoke systematically different responses than a question about length of employment.

2.2. Data from the March CPS on job change

An alternative, and rarely used source of information on worker mobility in the United States is the Annual Income Supplement to the March CPS. This supplement collects information on employment and income in the previous calendar year. Since 1976, the supplement has contained a question asking how many employers the individual had during the previous year, not counting jobs held simultaneously. In other words, dual job holders are not counted as having multiple jobs. The underlying concept is to derive a measure of the number of main jobs. The response is coded as zero, one, two, or three-or-more jobs.

The response to the question on number of jobs held last year can be used in a straightforward way to derive a lower bound estimate of the fraction of individuals who changed jobs in the previous year (and hence are in new jobs). This is computed as the number of individuals reporting more than one job divided by the number of individuals reporting at least one job. This estimate is a lower bound because some individuals may have lost a job they had held all year shortly before the year in question ended and did not find a job until early the following year. They would be counted as non-changers, but, in fact, the jobs they held did end. Stewart (1997) presents the only analysis of which I am aware that has used these data to compute rates of job change. I present my own analysis of these data in the next section.

2.3. Longitudinal data from the PSID and NLS

Longitudinal data provide important obvious advantages for analyzing worker mobility. By following workers over time, the timing of job change can be observed and, in contrast to cross-sectional data, completed job durations can be observed directly. Another advantage is that successive jobs held by individuals can be observed so that more dynamic approaches to modeling mobility can be investigated. Finally, the data generally contain information on the reason for job change, and most changes can be classified as voluntary

---

[6] Ureta (1992) presents the only analysis of which I am aware that explicitly addresses the rounding and heaping problems. In the recent supplements where the respondent selects the time units, virtually all responses greater than 2 years are reported in years and there is heaping at the usual round numbers.

(quits) or involuntary (layoffs). The standard longitudinal data sets have been used to study mobility in the United States. These include the four original cohorts of the National Longitudinal Surveys (NLS), the National Longitudinal Survey of Youth (NLSY), and the Panel Study of Income Dynamics (PSID). These data are described in more detail in the chapter in this volume by Angrist and Krueger (1998).

The longitudinal data also have some weaknesses. One is the relatively small sample sizes they offer, at least in comparison with the CPS. Another is difficulty in timing job changes. This is particularly troublesome in data sets like the PSID and original NLS cohorts that are not designed for the study of employment dynamics. For example, the PSID has surveyed individuals each year, and, apart from changes in question wording over time, contains information sufficient to determine if the main job held at the survey date is the same job as the main job held at the survey date the previous year. However, simple tabulation shows that inconsistencies and ambiguities in responses are common.[7]

The NLSY has some advantages for the study of employment dynamics because it codes the starting and ending dates of all jobs held (to a maximum of five per year). This allows more precise timing of job changes as well as the observation of jobs other than the main job held at the survey date. These advantages are particularly important when studying mobility early in jobs because a substantial fraction of jobs end within the first year.[8] Thus, surveys that can only observe jobs that are in existence at a particular survey date, like the PSID and original NLS cohorts, are likely to miss much of the detailed structure of mobility.

2.4. Aggregate turnover data from employment and earnings

Prior to the availability of large-scale cross-sectional data sets from the CPS and longitudinal data sets from the PSID and NLS in the late 1960s and early 1970s, the central source of data on worker mobility was from turnover rates collected at the establishment level as part of the *Employment and Earnings* series of the US Bureau of Labor Statistics. These data were collected monthly, available aggregated to the industry level, and measured quit rates and layoff rates separately along with the total separation rate. The data also contained information on new hires and rehires along with the total hiring rate. Unfortunately, this series was discontinued in the early 1980s.

Important early studies of turnover behavior (e.g., Pencavel, 1970, 1972) relied on these data. Unfortunately, with the discontinuation of this series, no large scale survey administered at regular intervals contains information about job change by cause (voluntary versus involuntary). The Displaced Workers Surveys, conducted since 1984 as supplements to the CPS, contain information on whether workers have changed jobs involuntarily for

---

[7] Brown and Light (1992) present a detailed useful discussion of problems in using the PSID and NLS original cohorts to time job changes. Abraham and Farber (1987) discuss some of the problems in using the PSID to develop a continuous measure of job tenure over time.

[8] See, for example, Farber (1994). Evidence on the high hazard of jobs ending in the first year is presented in the next section.

certain reasons, but there is no comparable source for data on voluntary job change or on involuntary job change generally.

2.5. The Displaced Workers Surveys

The Displaced Workers Surveys (DWSs) have been administered every 2 years since 1984 as a supplement to the monthly Current Population Survey (CPS). Each Displaced Workers Survey from 1984–92 asks workers if they were displaced from a job at any time in the preceding 5-year period. The 1994 and 1996 DWSs ask workers if they were displaced from a job at any time in the preceding 3-year period. Displacement is defined in the interviewer instructions to the relevant Current Population Surveys as involuntary separation based on operating decisions of the employer. Such events as a plant closing, an employer going out of business, a layoff from which the worker was not recalled are considered displacement. Workers who are laid off from a job and rehired in a different position by the same employer are considered to have been displaced. Other events including quits and being fired for "...poor work performance, disciplinary problems, or any other reason that is specific to the individual alone..." are not considered displacement (US Department of Commerce, 1988, Section II, p. 4). Thus, the supplement is designed to focus on the loss of specific jobs that result from business decisions of firms unrelated to the performance of particular workers.

The DWS has been used extensively in recent years to measure rates of job loss. Additionally, since those individuals identified as job losers are asked a series of followup questions about the reason for their job loss, the characteristics of their lost job, and their labor market experience subsequent to job loss, the DWS has also been used to examine the consequences of job loss. I survey some of this literature below as part of an evaluation of theories of mobility.

2.6. A proposal for improved data on mobility from the CPS

While the DWSs provide information at regular intervals on the rate of job loss for a large representative cross-section, no comparable source for data on quits or job change generally exists in the United States. The February 1996 and 1998 CPSs represent an improvement over earlier CPSs with mobility supplements or DWSs in that they include mobility supplements with data on tenure on the current job as well as DWSs with data on job loss in the previous 3 years.[9] This greatly facilitates investigating the relationship between rates of job loss and tenure. However, the information is inadequate to investigate the relationships between quit rates and tenure and the rate of overall job change and tenure.[10]

---

[9] Data from the February 1998 CPS were not yet available as this was being written.

[10] Farber (1993) uses the earlier DWSs to investigate how the probability of job loss is related to tenure, but he was forced to do this indirectly by aggregating data from the job losers in the DWS into cells defined by demographic and job characteristics (including tenure) and data from mobility supplements to the CPS aggregated in the same way.

The data available to analyze voluntary job change are relatively sparse, particularly since the discontinuation of the turnover series that was part of *Employment and Earnings.*

One useful and relatively low cost proposal to improve the data available to analyze worker mobility in the United States would be to recast the mobility and displaced workers supplements (currently administered together) as a single mobility and job-change supplement. This supplement would ask for information on current job tenure as well as on job change during some time period (e.g., 2 years) prior to the survey. Job change would be defined to include voluntary job change and job loss "for cause" as well as displacement. For individuals who report a job change, information would be collected on the reason for the job change, the characteristics of the lost job, and labor market experience since the job change. This is a straightforward generalization of the current combined mobility and DWS supplements that are scheduled to be administered every 2 years, and it would greatly enrich the information available to study labor market dynamics at relatively low cost.

Similar surveys could also be carried out as supplementary parts of the household surveys in other countries. There are important institutional differences in the labor markets across countries that may have important effects on worker mobility. Having a consistent source of information on worker mobility over time is an important precondition both for understanding mobility in modern labor markets and for investigating the role of institutions in the allocation of labor.[11]

3. A set of facts on job change

In this section, I present evidence largely from US data establishing three central facts regarding job change. They are that (1) long-term employment relationships are common, (2) most new jobs end early, and (3) the probability of job change declines with tenure. These facts have strong empirical support, and they represent the core facts that theories of job change need to explain.

3.1. Long-term employment relationships are common

Other than a series of reports issued by the Bureau of Labor Statistics (BLS) summarizing the tenure data from the CPS mobility supplements, Hall (1982) seems to have been the first to use the CPS data to analyze job tenure. In an influential analysis of long-term employment that relied on published tabulations from the January 1968 and 1978 CPS mobility supplements, Hall summarized the cross-sectional distribution of job tenure. He also used these data to calculate the probability that workers with given amounts of tenure will remain in their jobs. He approached this in two ways. First, he used the 1968 and 1978

---

[11] Burgess (1998) presents an multi-country analysis of long-term employment that relies on tabulations supplied by researchers in ten countries. However, the data are not collected on a consistent basis across countries, making interpretation difficult.

CPS tenure data to compute retention rates for workers over the 10-year period. He accomplished this using artificial cohorts of workers who are age x in 1968 and age $x + 10$ in 1978. The retention rate is defined as the ratio of the number of workers who are age $x + 10$ with tenure $t + 10$ in 1978 to the number of workers who are age x with tenure t in 1968. This is an estimate of the probability that a worker age x with tenure t in 1968 retains his job until 1978. Hall also computed contemporaneous retention rates using individual CPS mobility supplements by comparing the fraction of those workers who are age x in 1978 who had tenure t with the fraction of those workers who are age $x + y$ in 1978 who had tenure $t + y$. Relying mainly on this analysis, Hall found that (1) while any particular new job is unlikely to last a long time, a job that has already lasted 5 years has a substantial probability of lasting 20 years, (2) a substantial fraction of workers will be on a "lifetime" job (defined as lasting at least 20 years) at some point in their life, and (3) men are substantially more likely than women and whites are substantially more likely than blacks to have such a lifetime job. Ureta (1992) used the January 1978, 1981, and 1983 mobility supplements to recompute retention rates using artificial cohorts rather than contemporaneous retention rates. Like Hall, she found that lifetime jobs are an important feature of the US labor market, but she finds smaller differences by sex.

There is a substantial body of recent work that has focused on whether or not the tenure distribution has shifted over time. Specifically, there is concern that a change in employer behavior, perhaps motivated by changing market conditions, has led to a decrease in job stability. I review a portion of that literature here.

A study by Swinnerton and Wial (1995), using CPS mobility data from 1979 to 1991, analyzed job retention rates computed from artificial cohorts and concluded that there has been a secular decline in job stability in the 1980s. In contrast, Diebold et al. (1994), using CPS data on tenure from 1973 to 1991 to compute retention rates for artificial cohorts, found that aggregate retention rates were fairly stable over the 1980s but that retention rates declined for high school dropouts and for high school graduates relative to college graduates over this period. A direct exchange between Diebold et al. (1996) and Swinnerton and Wial (1996) seems to support the view that the period from 1979 to 1991 is not a period of generally decreasing job stability. I have also investigated this issue (Farber, 1998a), and, using CPS data on job tenure from 1973 to 1993, I find that the prevalence of long-term employment has not declined over time but that the distribution of long jobs has shifted. I find that less-educated men are less likely to hold long jobs than they were previously but that this is offset by a substantial increase in the rate at which women hold long jobs.

In another study (Farber, 1997b), I used CPS mobility data from 1979 to 1996 to compute the fraction of workers with more than 10 and more than 20 years of tenure, and I present some of those tabulations here.[12] The first column of Table 1 contains the

---

[12] These mobility and benefit supplements are used because they contain comparable questions asking how long workers have been with their current employer. The mobility supplements prior to 1983 asked about year of starting the current job.

Table 1

Incidence of long-term employment relationships, 1979–1996 by sex and education level: fraction of employed reporting more than 10 years tenure, 1979–1996 (ages 35–64)[a]

Survey	Pooled	Male	Female	ED < 12	ED = 12	ED 13–15	ED ≥ 16
May79	0.410	0.498	0.291	0.386	0.419	0.388	0.436
	(0.005)	(0.007)	(0.007)	(0.010)	(0.008)	(0.012)	(0.011)
Jan83	0.401	0.489	0.290	0.397	0.411	0.373	0.410
	(0.003)	(0.004)	(0.004)	(0.007)	(0.005)	(0.007)	(0.007)
May83	0.414	0.497	0.311	0.393	0.427	0.372	0.440
	(0.005)	(0.006)	(0.007)	(0.011)	(0.008)	(0.011)	(0.010)
Jan87	0.380	0.451	0.294	0.361	0.387	0.361	0.394
	(0.003)	(0.004)	(0.004)	(0.007)	(0.005)	(0.006)	(0.006)
May88	0.391	0.457	0.312	0.398	0.402	0.348	0.404
	(0.004)	(0.006)	(0.006)	(0.011)	(0.007)	(0.010)	(0.008)
Jan91	0.383	0.443	0.314	0.366	0.387	0.362	0.400
	(0.003)	(0.004)	(0.004)	(0.008)	(0.005)	(0.006)	(0.005)
Apr93	0.391	0.441	0.334	0.315	0.393	0.378	0.426
	(0.004)	(0.006)	(0.006)	(0.013)	(0.007)	(0.008)	(0.008)
Feb96	0.354	0.400	0.303	0.313	0.372	0.333	0.367
	(0.003)	(0.004)	(0.004)	(0.008)	(0.005)	(0.005)	(0.005)
N	159770	85461	74309	22836	59368	34653	42913

[a] Note: These data are derived from mobility or pension and benefit supplements to the indicated Current Population Surveys. All analyses are weighted by the CPS sampling weights. Standard errors are in parentheses These tabulations are taken from Farber (1997b).

fraction of workers aged 35–64 who report more than 10 years of tenure, and the first column of Table 2 contains the fraction of workers aged 45–64 who report more than 20 years of tenure.[13] These tabulations establish that a substantial fraction of workers are in long-term employment relationships. The most recent data in the tables (February 1996) show that about 35% of workers aged 35–64 had worked for the same employer for at least 10 years and about 21% of workers aged 45–64 had worked for the same employer for at least 20 years.

There is interesting time-series movement in these data. The incidence of long-term employment as measured by these fractions fell substantially after 1993 to its lowest level since 1979. However, in my earlier work based on the DWS (Farber, 1997b), I found that the decline in the incidence of long-term employment relationships for all workers was not mirrored in an increase in the incidence of long-term employment on lost jobs (jobs from which workers were laid off). Thus, the evidence is not consistent with the view that the decline in long-term employment relationships is the result of employers targeting long-

---

[13] These age categories were selected because younger workers would be less likely to have sufficient time in the labor market to accumulate the necessary tenure.

Table 2
Incidence of long-term employment relationships, 1979–1996 by sex and education level: fraction of employed
reporting more than 20 years tenure, 1979–1996 (ages 45–64)[a]

Survey	Pooled	Male	Female	$ED < 12$	$ED = 12$	ED 13–15	$ED \geq 16$
May79	0.251	0.338	0.131	0.225	0.263	0.255	0.266
	(0.005)	(0.008)	(0.007)	(0.010)	(0.009)	(0.014)	(0.014)
Jan83	0.232	0.325	0.111	0.215	0.235	0.218	0.256
	(0.004)	(0.005)	(0.004)	(0.007)	(0.006)	(0.009)	(0.008)
May83	0.236	0.322	0.128	0.198	0.245	0.224	0.271
	(0.005)	(0.008)	(0.007)	(0.011)	(0.009)	(0.014)	(0.012)
Jan87	0.211	0.294	0.109	0.193	0.203	0.209	0.243
	(0.003)	(0.005)	(0.004)	(0.008)	(0.005)	(0.008)	(0.008)
May88	0.237	0.314	0.145	0.218	0.238	0.215	0.267
	(0.005)	(0.008)	(0.006)	(0.011)	(0.008)	(0.012)	(0.011)
Jan91	0.226	0.305	0.135	0.187	0.225	0.217	0.258
	(0.004)	(0.005)	(0.004)	(0.009)	(0.006)	(0.008)	(0.007)
Apr93	0.232	0.307	0.147	0.173	0.226	0.242	0.259
	(0.005)	(0.008)	(0.006)	(0.013)	(0.008)	(0.010)	(0.010)
Feb96	0.209	0.270	0.143	0.198	0.220	0.192	0.217
	(0.003)	(0.005)	(0.004)	(0.009)	(0.006)	(0.006)	(0.006)
N	83224	45010	38214	15326	32124	16013	19761

[a] Note: These data are derived from mobility or pension and benefit supplements to the indicated Current
Population Surveys. All analyses are weighted by the CPS sampling weights. Standard errors are in parentheses
These tabulations are taken from Farber (1997b).

term employees for layoff. In fact, the share of displaced men who are displaced from long-term employment relationships has declined since 1979.

It is possible that the decline in the fraction of workers in long-term employment relationships in the mid-1990s could be accounted for by the strong labor market and expanding employment over this period. Indeed, similar declines are in evidence in the expansion of the mid-1980s. However, Neumark et al. (1999) using CPS data from the recent mobility supplements and February 1995 CAEAS, find that retention rates at higher tenure levels have declined in the 1990s. This decline in retention rates cannot be accounted for by expanding employment, but the authors conclude that the overall pattern of evidence does not support a long-term trend decline in aggregate job stability.

Others have used data from the Panel Study of Income Dynamics (PSID) to study the incidence of long-term employment. Rose (1995) measured job stability by examining the fraction of male workers who report no job changes in a given time period, typically 10 years. Rose found that the fraction of workers who reported no job changes in given length of time was lower in the 1980s than in the 1970s. He argued that this is evidence of decreasing stability of employment. Jaeger and Stevens (1999) used data from the PSID and the CPS mobility and benefit supplements on (roughly) annual rates of job change to try to reconcile evidence from the CPS and PSID on job stability. They find little evidence in either survey of a trend in job stability though the estimates from the PSID are rather imprecise.[14] Unfortunately, due to the design of the PSID, neither of these studies examine the mobility experience of women.

The Displaced Workers Surveys have also been used to investigate changes in job stability by examining rates of job loss. I used the five Displaced Workers Surveys (DWSs) from 1984 to 1992 to examine changes in the incidence and costs of job loss over the period from 1982 to 1991 (Farber, 1993). I found that there were slightly elevated rates of job loss for older and more educated workers in the slack labor market in the latter part of the period compared with the slack labor market of the earlier part of the period. But job loss rates for younger and less educated workers were substantially higher than those for older and more educated workers throughout the period. These findings are consistent with the long-standing view that younger and less educated workers bear the brunt of recessions.

Gardner (1995) used the six DWSs from 1984 to 1994 to examine the incidence of job loss from 1981 to 1992. While she found roughly comparable overall rates of job loss in the 1981–1982 and 1991–1992 periods, she found that the industrial and occupational mix of job loss changed over this period. There was an decreased incidence of job loss among blue-collar workers and workers in manufacturing industries and an increase in job loss among white-collar workers and workers in non-manufacturing industries.

In more recent work (Farber, 1997a, 1998b), I used the seven DWSs from 1984 to 1996 to examine incidence of job loss from 1981 to 1995. I found that rates of job loss followed the expected counter-cyclical pattern through the early 1990s. Job loss rates were high during the slack labor market of the early 1980s, subsequently decreasing during the expansion later in the decade. Job loss rates than increased during the slack labor market of the late 1980s and early 1990s. However, job loss rates did not decline and probably increased in the 1990s despite the strong labor market recovery after the slackness early in the decade. Fig. 1 contains plots of adjusted 3-year job loss rates computed from each of the seven DWSs from 1984 to 1996.[15] These stacked-bar graphs provide information on not only on overall job loss rates (the total height of each bar) but also on job loss rates by reason (the shaded segments of each bar). Four classifications of reason are presented: (1) plant closing; (2) slack work; (3) position or shift abolished; and (4) other.[16]

There are some interesting patterns in these graphs. First, the rate of job loss due to plant closings seems to have been relatively constant with a smaller secular decline over time. In contrast, the rate of job loss due to slack work seems to have a larger cyclical component combined with a smaller secular increase over time. One possible interpretation of this

---

[14] Valletta (1997) presents an analysis of data from the PSID which suggests that while the probability of job change for men has not increased, the negative relationship of the probability of job change with tenure has weakened over time.

[15] This figure is taken from Farber (1997a). Details of its construction are presented there.

[16] The "other" category I use merges the "seasonal job ended", "self-employment ended", and "other" categories as coded in the DWS.

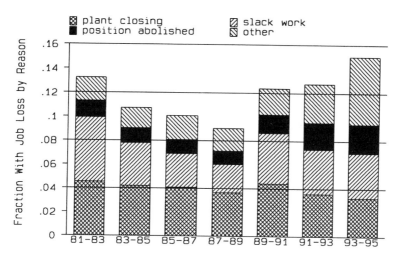

Fig. 1. Rate of job loss by reason. Based on DWS 1984–1996.

result is that plant closings are a response to secular declines in demand for specific products while job loss due to slack work is a typical response to cyclical fluctuations in demand where only marginal adjustments to output are required. Second, and more interesting from the standpoint of a secular increase in instability, is that the rates of job loss due to "position or shift abolished" and "other" were relatively constant through the 1989–1991 period but have risen substantially since then and account for all of the increase in job loss in the 1990s.

In Farber (1998b), I present an analysis of what comprises the "other" category based on debriefing questions appended to the February 1996 DWS, and it appears that much of the job loss classified as "other" is, in fact, voluntary job change. On this basis, Fig. 2 contains rates of job loss over time with a liberal discount applied to the other category in all years.[17] These adjusted rates of job loss are roughly stable since the 1989–1991 period. Given the tightening labor markets after 1991, rates of job loss would have been expected to decline. The fact that they did not do so may reflect some decrease in job stability.

Returning to the tabulations of tenure data from the CPS in Tables 1 and 2, the second and third columns of the tables contain measures of the incidence of long-term employment separately by sex. There is an important contrast between males and females in the incidence of long-term employment. Over the time period studied, the incidence of long-term employment fell substantially for men (10-year jobs by about 10 percentage points and 20-year jobs by about 7 percentage points). In contrast, the incidence of long-term

---

[17] See Farber (1998b) for details of the construction of Fig. 2. My analysis of the debriefing data yields the result that only 23.6% of the "other" job loss in the February 1996 DWS likely reflects involuntary job loss. Thus, Fig. 2 differs from Fig. 1 by discounting the "other" job loss in Fig. 1 by 76.4% in all years.

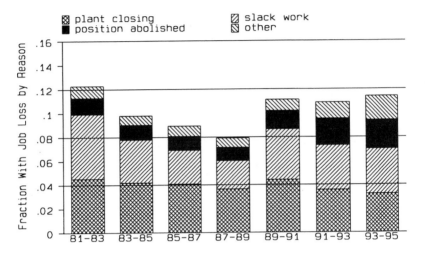

Fig. 2. Rate of job loss by reason. Based on DWS 1984–1996, discounted other job loss.

employment grew slightly for women over the same period. This difference suggests that there has been a general decline in male long-term employment that is offset by the increasing fraction of women in more recent cohorts who have continuous labor-force participation over the life-cycle. Another related interpretation is that part of the decline in long-term employment for men is due to competition from women with greater attachment to the labor force.

The last four columns of Tables 1 and 2 break down the incidence of long-term employment by educational category. Two facts are clear from these statistics. First, there has been a decline in the incidence of long-term employment in all four educational categories, and the declines are of roughly similar magnitude. As noted earlier, this may reflect nothing more than the strong labor market of the mid-1990s. Rapidly expanding employment necessarily implies and increase in the share of workers with low levels of tenure. There is not sufficient evidence to conclude that there has been a secular decline in long-term employment. A second fact evident in the tables is that the relationship between education and the likelihood of long-term employment is non-monotonic. Workers with less than 12 years of education and workers with some college (13–15 years of education) are less likely to be in long-term employment relationships than are workers with either high school (workers with 12 years of education) or college graduates (workers with at least 16 years of education).

The extensive literature surveyed here and supported by the statistics in Tables 1 and 2 establish that long-term employment relationships have been and continue to be an important feature of the US labor market. It is also the case that long-term employment relationships are an even more important feature of labor markets in other developed countries. Gregg and Wadsworth (1998) present evidence for the United Kingdom supporting this view. As in the United States, they find that the aggregate job tenure statistics have not changed very much over the past two decades but that there have been larger changes across subgroups with the incidence of long-term employment in the United Kingdom declining somewhat among men and increasing among women. Burgess (1998) presents a survey of evidence from ten countries (France, Germany, Holland, Italy, Japan, Poland, Spain, Sweden, the United Kingdom, and the United States) which shows that the fraction of workers in long-term jobs in the 1990s is higher than in the United States in virtually all of the other countries surveyed. This contrast between the United States and the other countries may be due to the relatively low level of government regulation of the employment relationship in the United States. In particular, the costs to employers of shedding workers is lower in the United States than in most other modern economies.

3.2. Most new jobs end early

While a substantial fraction of the workforce is in long-term employment relationships, most jobs last only a short time. This distinction reflects the different sampling bases when considering workers and when considering jobs. When individuals are sampled, the employment relationships of which they are part are those employment relationships that have survived, and these are disproportionately the longer jobs.[18] Longitudinal data are required in order to investigate the durations of all jobs. Mincer and Jovanovic (1981) present evidence based on the National Longitudinal Surveys (NLS) of Young Men and Older Men which shows that over half of all workers in jobs with tenure less than 1 year change jobs within 2 years. My analysis of data on job durations from the more-recent National Longitudinal Survey of Youth (NLSY), finds that about one-third of all new full-time jobs end in the first 6 months, one-half of all new full-time jobs end in the first year, and two-thirds of new full-time jobs end within 2 years (Farber, 1994).

Fig. 3 contains an updated version of my product-limit estimate of the survivor function for full-time jobs (Farber, 1994). This figure uses data from the NLSY for the period 1979–1991.[19] These estimates, because they rely on younger workers, may overstate the likelihood of new jobs ending early in the workforce as a whole. On the other hand, these data refer only to full-time jobs, and full-time jobs are of longer duration on average than are part-time jobs.

Another approach to establishing that most new jobs end early is to measure the fraction of the workforce in new jobs at any point in time. In some recent work (Farber, 1998a), I present evidence from the CPS which shows that over 28% of the workforce reports having been on their job for 1 year or less over the 1973–1993 period. Farber (1997c) presents evidence from the CPS which shows that over 18% of the workforce reports having been on their job for less than 1 year over the 1979–1996 period. More detailed

---

[18] This is the usual problem of length bias in sampling duration data at a single point in time.

[19] Farber (1994) used NLSY data covering the period from 1979 to 1988. The data underlying Fig. 3 cover the period to 1991, but they are otherwise as described in Farber (1994).

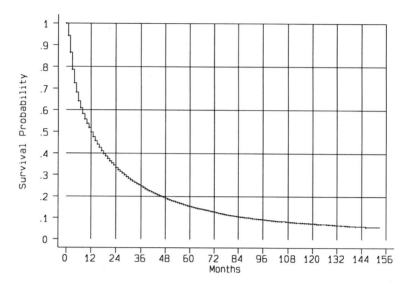

Fig. 3. Survivor function for jobs (product limit estimate). Full-time jobs, NLSY, 1979–1991.

information is in Table 3, which contains tabulations from CPS supplements between 1979 and 1996 with information on tenure of the fraction of the workforce who report having been in their job for less than 1 year.

Table 3
Fraction of workforce with less than 1 year of tenure by sex and education[a]

Year	N	Overall	Male	Female	*ED* < 12	*ED* = 12	*ED* 13–15	*ED* ≥ 16
May79	22164	0.205	0.177	0.243	0.201	0.201	0.235	0.187
Jan83	52375	0.186	0.172	0.203	0.176	0.178	0.212	0.182
May83	23417	0.172	0.157	0.191	0.179	0.169	0.199	0.150
Jan87	54778	0.190	0.173	0.210	0.202	0.184	0.211	0.173
May88	22932	0.196	0.178	0.217	0.234	0.197	0.212	0.162
Jan91	51661	0.180	0.163	0.199	0.188	0.181	0.193	0.165
Apr93	22331	0.167	0.162	0.173	0.210	0.171	0.173	0.139
Feb96	42599	0.191	0.180	0.203	0.227	0.187	0.207	0.166
All	292257	0.186	0.171	0.204	0.200	0.183	0.204	0.167

[a] Note: The numbers in the column labeled "*N*" are sample sizes. The numbers in the remaining columns are fractions of the relevent group with tenure less than 1 year based on weighted tabulations of data from the relevant supplements to the CPS. The numerator is the number of those employed who report working continuously for their current employer for less than 1 year. The denominator is the total number employed. All counts are weighted by the CPS final sampling weights. Unincorporated self-employed workers and workers with missing data on tenure are not included in the analysis. Workers 20 years of age and older are included. These tabulations are taken from Farber (1997c).

The first column of Table 3 contains the fraction of workers in new jobs in the work-force as a whole. This averages 18.6% over the period covered and moves cyclically in the sense that new-job rates are highest in tight labor markets (1979, 1987–1988, 1996).[20] This cyclicality of the new-job rate is not surprising given the fact that new hiring in an expansion implies that there will be an increase in employment at low-tenure levels. Additionally, to the extent that layoffs are concentrated among low-tenure workers and layoffs increase in slack labor markets, there will be a decrease in employment at low tenure levels (Abraham and Medoff, 1984; Farber, 1993). While it is difficult to separate secular changes from cyclical movements in a relatively short time series, there is no evidence of a systematic increase in the incidence of new jobs over the 1979–1996 period. The remaining columns of Table 3 contain the new-job rates broken down by sex and by education.

As noted in the previous section, the data from the Annual Income Supplement to the March CPS on the number of main jobs held in the prior year can also be used to derive a lower bound estimate of the fraction of individuals who changed jobs in the previous year (and hence are in new jobs). This estimate of the rate of job change is computed as the number of individuals reporting more than one job divided by the number of individuals reporting at least one job.[21]

I calculated weighted rates of job change, as described in the preceding paragraph, over the 1975–1995 period using the 1976–1996 March CPSs. These are plotted in Fig. 4. The average value over the 21-year period is 15.3%. After taking account the downward bias noted above, this corresponds well to the tabulations in Table 3 of the fraction of workers who have been in their job less than 1 year. The latter fraction averaged 18.6% over the 1979–1996 period (though without observations every year). There is no trend apparent in Fig. 4, but there does appear to be cyclical movement. The fraction of job changers is higher in the strong labor markets of the late 1970, late 1980s, and mid-1990s than in the weak labor markets of the early 1980s and early 1990s.

Burgess (1998) presents a survey of comparable statistics measuring the fraction of workers who had been in their jobs for 1 year or less in the 1990s for the ten developed countries listed earlier. This fraction is substantial in most of the countries in all age categories, but it is among the highest in the United States. For example, Burgess reports that approximately 20% of employed males in the United States ages 26–45 were on their

---

[20] Standard errors for these fractions are on the order of 0.25% so that differences of 0.7% are statistically significant at the 0.05 level.

[21] Stewart (1997) has used these data in combination with data on industry and occupation both on the main job last year and at the survey date as part of a calculation of the rate at which individuals change jobs, where job change is meant to include change of jobs within employers (e.g., promotions, new task assignments). This is a broader concept of job change than the definition of employer change I am focusing on here. Stewart defines a job change as having occurred if the individual was employed during the reference week in march and met one of three conditions: (1) had more than one employer during the previous year; (2) experienced more than one spell of unemployment; or (3) worker for only one employer in the previous year but had a change in 3-digit industry or occupation codes between the main job last year and the main job held at the survey date.

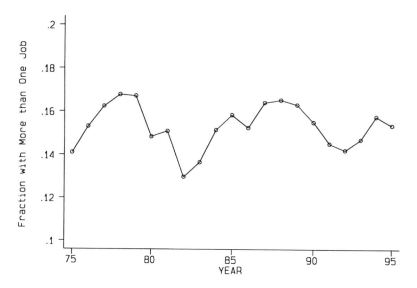

Fig. 4. Fraction of workers with more than one job, 1975–1995. Based on March CPS, 1976–1996.

jobs for 1 year or less. Comparable statistics for other countries are 20% in Holland, 11.4% in France, 16.3% in Germany, 8.2% in Italy, and 4.3% in Japan (the lowest).

Burgess's results show an interesting cross-national pattern when comparing the United States to the other nations surveyed. The United States has a relatively low (though still substantial) share of workers in long-term jobs and a relatively high share of workers in new jobs. As I noted above, this may be related to the low level of employment protection legislation in the United States compared to the other countries. The lack of institutional restrictions on hiring and firing of workers could contribute to the higher level of labor mobility in the United States implicit in these statistics.

The contrasts between the United States and other countries in worker mobility likely reflect a broader set of differences. More generally, it has been argued that the lack of institutional restrictions on hiring and firing in the United States has contributed to the relatively low unemployment rate and relatively high rate of net employment growth in the United States. This might also contribute to the relatively low level of employer and worker investment in on-the-job training in the United States relative to many European countries. Or it might be that the cross-national differences in institutions might be responses to different labor market structures. For example, the relatively high penalties for worker mobility in Germany might be a result of a labor market structure designed to encourage investment by both workers and firms in substantial amounts of on-the-job training.

The goal of this subsection was to demonstrate the fact that most jobs are short. I supplemented the direct evidence on this question from longitudinal data with indirect evidence based on the fraction of workers in new jobs that are 1 year old or less. But finding a large fraction of workers in new jobs is not sufficient to conclude that most jobs are short. New jobs start whenever (1) new entrants to the labor force take jobs, (2) workers who previously exited employment (either to unemployment or to out-of-labor-force status) are reemployed or (3) workers change jobs. First, employment growth rates in the United States have averaged about 2% per year since 1979 so that new entrants cannot have made up even close to 20% of the labor force over the last 20 years. Second, while there may be substantial gross flows of workers among employment, unemployment, and out of the labor force, the flows out of employment must be from workers who are early in their jobs in order to maintain a substantial number of workers in long jobs.[22] There cannot be enough long jobs generated on a sustained basis in the economy if they are ending at a rate sufficient to generate 15–20% new jobs. Thus, new jobs are primarily the result of job-to-job transitions, sometimes with intervening spells of non-employment, by workers in short jobs. This implies that new jobs are ending at a high rate and that most new employment relationships are short lived.

3.3. The probability of job change declines with tenure

The fact that the probability of job change declines with tenure is in important ways implied by the stylized facts that (1) long-term employment relationships are common and (2) most jobs end early. The fact that most jobs end early implies high probabilities of job change at low tenure levels. But long-term jobs can only develop if the probability of job loss moderates as tenure accumulates.

There are many studies that find a decline in the probability of job change with tenure, and I mention only a handful here. Parsons (1972) presents evidence based on industry-level data from the *Employment and Earnings* series of the BLS that both quit rates and layoff rates are strongly inversely related to tenure. Specifically, workers with less than 6 months tenure had higher quit rates and layoff rates than did workers with more than 6 months tenure. Hall (1972) presents evidence for older men using the NLS. He too finds that the probability of both quits and layoffs declines sharply with tenure. These findings are corroborated by Blau and Kahn (1981a,b) using the NLS of young men and young women and by Mincer and Jovanovic (1981) using the NLS of young men and mature men and the PSID. Abraham and Farber (1987) estimate a Weibull hazard model of the probability of job change using the PSID, and they find that the hazard declines sharply with tenure. McLaughlin (1991) also finds that job separation rates decline sharply with tenure in the PSID. My own work (Farber, 1993), using the DWS, finds that rates of job loss decline sharply with tenure.

Virtually all of the literature uses annual data on job change to investigate the relationship between tenure and the probability of job change, and, without exception, finds a

---

[22] It is unclear precisely how large are these gross flows because small amounts of measurement error in reporting labor force status can create large spurious gross flows of workers across labor force states. See Abowd and Zellner (1985) and Poterba and Summers (1986) for careful analyses of this problem.

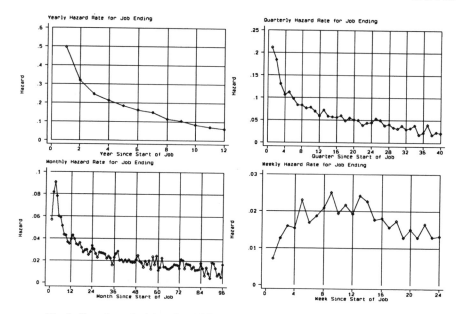

Fig. 5. Hazard rate for job ending (different frequencies). Based on NLSY, 1979–1991.

monotonic negative relationship. McCall (1990) and Farber (1994) use the fine-grained information available in the NLSY on dates of job starting and ending to investigate the relationship between tenure and job change at shorter time intervals, and the results differ importantly. Specifically, the hazard of job ending computed at higher frequencies increases with tenure early in jobs before beginning a long-term decline.

I present an updated summary of my results using NLSY data from 1979 to 1991 in Fig. 5. This figure contains empirical hazard functions for job ending at four frequencies using a sample of 19,336 full-time jobs for 4680 individuals from the NLSY. The four panels in the figure contain the hazard computed at four frequencies: annual, quarterly, monthly, and weekly. The upper-left panel contains the annual hazard function. Consistent with the earlier literature, this hazard is monotonically declining in tenure and shows the 0.5 hazard in the first year that is apparent from the survivor function in Fig. 3. The hazard falls monotonically to less than 0.1 by year 12. The upper-right panel contains the quarterly hazard function. This hazard is also monotonically declining. The decline is very sharp in the first year, with the hazard falling from greater than 0.2 in the first quarter to about 0.1 by the fourth quarter. Both the annual and quarterly hazards are monotonically declining, and it is evidence on the hazards at roughly these frequencies that has supports the fact that the probability of job change is monotonically declining with tenure.

A different picture emerges when the hazard is computed at higher frequencies. The lower-left panel of Fig. 5 contains the monthly hazard function. What is most striking about the hazard function in Fig. 5 is that the hazard is actually relatively low in the first month at 0.06, rising to a peak of almost 0.10 at 3 months and declining sharply thereafter before leveling off at less than 0.02.[23] The lower-right panel of Fig. 5 contains the weekly hazard function for the first 26 weeks on jobs. This hazard shows an increase from a low of less than 0.01 in the first week to a peak of about 0.025 in ninth week before declining to about 0.012 by week 19. These high-frequency hazards modify the standard finding about the relationship between tenure and the probability of job change. In fact, the probability of job change increases with tenure very early in jobs (less than 3 months) and declines subsequently.[24] I return to this below when discussing theories of job change.

3.4. What accounts for these facts?

The central facts regarding worker mobility in modern labor markets are clear. To recapitulate: (1) long-term employment relationships are common; (2) most new jobs end early; and (3) the probability of job change declines with tenure (perhaps after increasing during the first few months of employment). I turn now to the task of putting these facts in some theoretical perspective. I begin by discussing the implications for mobility of standard models of accumulation of specific human capital. While this model fits the facts quite well, I go on to argue that the facts could also be accounted for by unmeasured worker heterogeneity in underlying probabilities of job change. I then discuss and evaluate some tests of the specific capital model with the goal of distinguishing the role of specific capital from the role of heterogeneity in determining rates of mobility.

4. Why are there long-term employment relationships: the role of specific capital

The existence of employer-specific human capital is an obvious explanation for the existence of long-term employment relationships.[25] To the extent that there is something valuable in the particular match between the worker and the firm that has no value to either the worker or the firm outside their relationship, the worker's productivity in the firm will be both higher than the worker's productivity elsewhere and higher than the productivity of another worker if hired by the firm. This match-specific capital can be the result of investment in firm-specific skills that inhere in the worker. More generally, it could be the result of any non-recoverable expenditure in the employment relationship that has no value outside the employment relationship. Obvious examples are the fixed costs of searching for the worker and/or job and of hiring the worker. These may not enhance productivity directly, but they are costs that are borne initially, have no value elsewhere, and must be borne again in the formation of any new employment relationship. Another example is the training of the worker in particular skills that have no value elsewhere but

---

[23] McCall (1990) notes the same peak in the hazard using the NLSY data.

[24] There is some possibility that the measured increase in the hazard early in jobs results from measurement error. If survey respondents are less likely to report holding jobs that ended very early, then the hazard computed very early in jobs will be attenuated. I discuss evaluate this possible explanation in Farber (1994).

[25] See Becker (1964) for an early discussion of specific human capital.

are important to productivity within the firm. Specific capital can also take the form of information about the quality of the match between the worker and the firm (Jovanovic, 1979a).

Parsons (1972) presents a detailed model of specific capital accumulation and job change that suggests an inverse relationship between the likelihood of job change and the level of specific investment. Mortensen (1978) constructs a model of specific capital and job change that highlights both the important concepts and the inherent difficulty of generating clear testable predictions from models of specific capital. The core idea of these models is that the probability that one party or the other terminates an employment relationship depends on the value of that party's share of the specific capital inherent in the match. Jovanovic (1979b) combines specific capital and search models to analyze job separations and unemployment. I build on this work in presenting a simple illustrative model that captures the key concepts and problems in models of specific capital and turnover.

Denote the total value of the specific capital inherent in the match by Y. Consider the worker's decision first. Let W_a represent the best alternative wage available to the worker. This is the market value of the bundle of general skills that the worker brings to the labor market. The wage paid to the worker by the current firm is

$$W = W_a + \lambda Y, \tag{1}$$

where λ is the worker's share of the value of the specific capital. In the simplest world where there is complete information about worker productivity and no costs of mobility, the worker's best alternative wage will be W_a, and the worker will not quit as long as the firm pays the worker even a small amount more than W_a ($\lambda > 0$).

In order to generate quits in this model, some randomness in the alternative wage needs to be introduced. Burdett (1978) presents a model of quits relying on job search by employed workers.[26] A simplified version of this model has a wage offer, W_o, arriving each period drawn from some wage offer distribution with mean W_a. These search models are often vague regarding what generates the variation in wages that underlies the wage offer distribution, but one potential explanation is that there is ex ante observable variation in worker-firm match quality. This simple search model generates some testable implications that I discuss later.

Returning to the model of specific capital and job change, note that the wage offer can be expressed as $W_o = W_a + \theta$ where θ is a random variable with mean zero. A worker quits if the wage offer (W_o) exceeds the current wage (W), which, by the definitions of W_o and W, implies a condition for quitting of

$$W_a + \theta > W_a + \lambda Y. \tag{2}$$

Simplification implies that a worker quits if

---

[26] It is beyond the scope of this chapter to provide an adequate survey of the search literature. See Mortensen (1986) and the chapter by Mortensen in this volume for such surveys.

$$\theta > \lambda Y. \tag{3}$$

Clearly, the larger the value of the worker's share of the specific capital, the less likely it is that the wage offer will exceed the current wage and the less likely it is that the worker will quit.

An analogous model can be developed, with some relabeling of variables, regarding the firm's decision whether to replace the worker (a layoff). In the simplest case, the firm must pay the equilibrium alternative wage, W_a, to hire a replacement worker. The value to the firm of what the current worker produces is

$$V = W_a + Y, \tag{4}$$

which is the value of marginal product of an hour of this worker's labor. The marginal cost of the hour is the wage as defined in Eq. (1). The firm will lay off the worker if and only if the wage exceeds the value of marginal product. Combining Eqs. (1) and (4), the layoff condition is $\lambda > 1$. In other words, the firm will lay off the worker only if the firm has to give the worker more than the specific value of the match. The profit the firm earns is

$$\pi = V - W = (1 - \lambda)Y. \tag{5}$$

As in the model of quits, some randomness is required in order to generate layoffs. While this could be due to randomness in the wage the firm needs to pay a replacement worker, a source of randomness consistent with the macroeconomic literature on employment fluctuations is based on demand or productivity shocks. Think of these shocks as being firm or sector specific. Suppose that there is a shock to the value to the firm of the worker's output such that

$$V = W_a + Y + \phi, \tag{6}$$

where ϕ is a random variable with mean zero. The profit the firm earns is

$$\pi = V - W = (1 - \lambda)Y + \phi. \tag{7}$$

The firm will lay off the worker if profit is negative, which occurs if

$$\phi < -(1 - \lambda)Y. \tag{8}$$

In other words, the worker will be laid off only if the shock is sufficiently negative to outweigh the value the firm's share of the specific capital.[27] Obviously, the larger the value of the firm's share of the specific capital, the less likely it is that this condition will be met.

4.1. Efficient separations with specific capital

The specific capital model makes a clear statement about when separations are economically efficient and when they are not. It is efficient for an employment relationship to end if and only if the worker's opportunity wage (implicitly equal to the worker's marginal value

---

[27] This is a key insight of Oi's (1962) early work on specific capital.

product in the best alternative) is higher than the worker's marginal value product within the firm. In terms of the model, the efficient separation condition is that $W_o > V$. Using the definitions of W_o and V yields the efficient separation condition

$$\theta - \phi > Y. \tag{9}$$

In other words, an efficient separation occurs when, taken together, the random component of the draw from the distribution of wage offers (θ) is sufficiently large and the demand or productivity shock (ϕ) is sufficiently negative to offset the value of the specific capital (Y). Hall and Lazear (1984) present a clear analysis which shows that an ex ante fixed sharing rule of the type defined above will lead to excess separations. My analysis here is in the spirit of their model. In order to highlight the key points, I consider the quit and layoff decisions separately assuming that the other cannot occur. First consider quits. A worker will quit whenever $\theta > \lambda Y$, where λ is the worker's share of the value of the specific value of the match. Given some demand or productivity shock, ϕ, that does not result in layoff, the quit will be inefficient whenever $\theta < Y + \phi$. Thus, inefficient quits happen whenever $\lambda Y < \theta < Y + \phi$. This is because the worker does not consider the firm's share of the value of the specific capital ($(1 - \lambda)Y$) in making the quit decision. Similarly, there will be excess layoffs. The firm will lay off the workers whenever $\phi < -(1 - \lambda)Y$. Given some value of θ that does not result in a quit, the layoff will be inefficient whenever $\phi > \theta - Y$. Thus, there will be inefficient layoffs whenever $\theta - Y < \phi < -(1 - \lambda)Y$. This is because the firm does not consider the worker's share of the value of the specific capital (λY) in making the layoff decision.

The fixed sharing rule model implies that the quit rate will be inversely related to the value of the specific capital received by the worker and that the layoff rate will be inversely related to the value of the specific capital received by the firm. The first-best is achieved only if each side receives all of the specific value of the match, which, of course, is not possible. This is the standard problem in agency models of providing first-best incentives where there are other conflicting goals (e.g., costs of monitoring effort (Holmstrom, 1979) or the provision of insurance by a risk-neutral firm to risk-averse workers (Harris and Holmstrom, 1982).[28]

An interesting question is why contracts with fixed sharing rules (fixed wages) seem to be the norm. It must be that these contracts provide other advantages. For example, a more complicated state-contingent contract would require detailed verifiable information about the state of product demand (ϕ) or outside offers (θ). Such information might be expensive or impossible to obtain. Alternatively, risk-aversion by workers, liquidity constraints, or problems of joint production may make it infeasible to sell the firm to the worker in order to internalize the problem. Finally, paying a piece rate requires the sort of verifiable information on demand or technology shocks that may not be feasible. A piece rate also

---

[28] See Malcomson in this volume for a detailed discussion of contracting issues in the labor market that deals with agency problems and labor turnover.

has problems where output is the result of effort by groups of workers so that output cannot easily be attributed to individuals.

The specific human capital model is consistent with the major facts established in the previous section by providing an economic rationale for long-term employment relationships. To the extent that specific human capital accumulates with time on the job (tenure), the model implies that separation rates will start out high and decline with tenure. However, the simple model does not account for the initial increase in separation rates with tenure.

4.2. Match quality as specific capital

Jovanovic (1979a) presents a model of the employment relationship where the key feature is that the productivity of a particular worker-firm match varies and is not observable ex ante. The match quality is an experience good in that the quality of the match is revealed over time as tenure accumulates. More formally, think of output each period as a noisy signal of match quality. The worker's and the firm's common prior expectation about the quality of the match is updated each period based on the output signal. Each period both the worker and the firm have the option of ending the match and starting a new match (with the same ex ante expected value), but starting a new employment relationship has an explicit fixed cost attached. The model is closed by assuming that workers are paid their expected output in each period. In the notation of the model in the previous subsection, this is a fixed sharing rule where the worker receives the full value of the match-specific capital ($\lambda = 1$). In this case, firms are indifferent to whether workers stay or leave, and all relevant decisions are quit decisions rather than layoff decisions. However, assigning all of the specific value of the match to the worker is arbitrary, and the implications of this sharing rule for such outcomes as wage growth, cannot be used to test the model.[29]

The more important assumption underlying Jovanovic's model is that there is no randomness in the wage offer distribution or shocks to productivity or demand. While such considerations could be added to the model, all turnover is generated by the revelation of information about match quality. Nonetheless, the matching model generates several testable predictions regarding rates of job change.

The model yields a reservation match quality property where a worker quits if the updated expected match quality is lower than the reservation match quality. The separation rate is directly related to the reservation match quality which moves with tenure in a predictable way. Early in the match, the reservation match quality is low suggesting that separation rates start low. This is because there is option value in a new match (it might turn out to be very good). Uncertainty about the match quality is likely to be high early in the match, while quitting to take a new job is costly. Thus, a worker might stay despite some early signals of poor match quality because there remains a relatively high probability that match quality will turn out to be high. Over time, the reservation match quality

---

[29] McLaughlin (1991) presents an interesting model of efficient turnover based on matching considerations where the split of the specific value of the match affects whether separations are considered quits or layoffs.

increases as the variance of the updated beliefs about match quality falls and the option value decreases. At this point, separation rates increase. The bad matches are weeded out, and the remaining matches are high quality matches with low separation rates.

Match quality is a form of specific capital. Thus, like the specific capital model generally, the matching model accounts for the facts in general terms. However, the matching model does have some compelling features with regard to the data that the basic specific capital model lacks. First, the model accounts for the very high rate of job separation in the first year. Presumably, information about match quality is generally revealed quite early in jobs, and bad matches, therefore, will end relatively quickly once the low quality is established. In contrast, specific capital in the form of acquisition of firm-specific skills might accumulate more slowly and continuously. Second, the matching model provides an explanation for the early spike in the job-ending hazard noted in Fig. 5. The job-ending hazard in the matching model is low at the very beginning, reflecting relatively high reservation wages due to the remaining option value in the match. The hazard increases with tenure as the reservation match quality increases due to the reduction in option value in the match as the quality of the match is determined more precisely over time. The matches with a low expected quality end due to lack of a reasonable expectation that the match might, in fact, be a high-quality. The hazard subsequently declines as primarily high-quality matches remain.

5. Can heterogeneity account for the facts?

In this section, I abstract from structural variation in the probability of job change with tenure for a given worker (true duration dependence in the hazard of job ending, perhaps due to presence of specific capital) in order to focus on heterogeneity in mobility rates across workers. This is important for at least two reasons. First, heterogeneity in mobility rates across workers has the potential to provide a parsimonious alternative explanation for the stylized facts regarding mobility. Second, consistent estimates of the role of duration dependence in the probability of job change cannot be investigated without controlling for heterogeneity (e.g., Lancaster, 1979; Heckman and Singer, 1984).

In order to focus the discussion, consider a pure heterogeneity model with no duration dependence. Duration dependence as used here refers to a structural relationship between tenure and mobility of the sort implied by the specific human capital model.[30] A simple generalization of the pure mover-stayer model due to Blumen et al. (1955) where there are two types of workers (high mobility and low mobility) serves to illustrate the important points. The analysis generalizes straightforwardly to k types with an arbitrary distribution of types. The two types of workers are differentiated only by their turnover probabilities, λ_1 and λ_2. Type 1 workers are relatively more mobile so that $\lambda_1 > \lambda_2$, and these turnover probabilities are fixed over time for each worker. The proportion of the population that is of type 1 is θ. The overall turnover rate at any point in time is simply the θ-weighted

---

[30] This analysis follows that of Farber (1984).

average of the individual turnover probabilities,

$$P = \theta\lambda_1 + (1 - \theta)\lambda_2. \tag{10}$$

This very simple model of mobility can account for the fact that long-term employment relationships are common. As long as there is a reasonable percentage of low-mobility workers and the low mobility workers are reasonably immobile, there will be a substantial percentage of jobs that last a long time. As a simple example, consider a fixed population of two types of workers as described above who all start jobs at a particular date. The probability that a job lasts at least as long as some arbitrary length (t_l) is

$$P(t \geq t_l) = \theta(1 - \lambda_1)^{t_l} + (1 - \theta)(1 - \lambda_2)^{t_l}, \tag{11}$$

where t represents tenure. Clearly this probability is positively related to the share of low-mobility workers ($1 - \theta$) and negatively related to the probability of mobility of both types of workers (λ_1 and λ_2).

The fact that most new jobs end early, can be accounted for by having a sufficiently large percentage of high-mobility (type 1) workers with sufficiently large probabilities of mobility. Using the same simple example, the probability that a job lasts less than some arbitrary length (t_s) is

$$P(t \leq t_s) = 1 - \theta(1 - \lambda_1)^{t_s} - (1 - \theta)(1 - \lambda_2)^{t_s}. \tag{12}$$

This probability is positively related to the share of high-mobility workers (θ) and to the probability of mobility of the both types of workers (λ_1 and λ_2).

The fact that the probability of job change declines with tenure requires a bit more work to establish. The intuition is straightforward, however. Type 1 (high mobility) workers are relatively unlikely to have accumulated substantial tenure. Thus, the population of workers with substantial tenure is disproportionately composed of type 2 (low mobility workers). The average mobility rate among these workers will be lower as a result.

More formally, consider the subgroup of the underlying population with t years of tenure. The probability, θ_t, that a worker with t years of tenure is type 1 (high mobility) is

$$\theta_t = \frac{(1 - \lambda_1)^t \theta}{(1 - \lambda_1)^t \theta + (1 - \lambda_2)^t (1 - \theta)}. \tag{13}$$

By definition, the probability that a worker with t years of tenure changes jobs is

$$P_t = \theta_t \lambda_1 + (1 - \theta_t)\lambda_2, \tag{14}$$

It is straightforward to show that θ_t is decreasing in t so that as tenure increases the distribution of workers becomes more heavily weighted toward low mobility (type 2) workers and the probability of mobility declines.[31]

The key to understanding the heterogeneity model is that with a fixed population the

---

[31] There are three trivial cases where there is no heterogeneity ($\lambda_1 = \lambda_2$, $\theta = 0$, or $\theta = 1$). In these cases θ_t does not change with t.

overall mobility rate is constant over time. Any differences in mobility rates with tenure are due to sorting of the population into different tenure groups based on their underlying mobility. This implies that all that matters for the probabilities of turnover conditional on previous turnover history in this model is the number of prior periods with job changes (c) and the number of prior periods without job changes ($n - c$). The order in which prior turnover took place is irrelevant. The probability, θ_{nc}, that a worker with c changes in n years is type 1 (high mobility) is

$$\theta_{nc} = \frac{\lambda_1^c (1 - \lambda_1)^{n-c} \theta}{\lambda_1^c (1 - \lambda_1)^{n-c} \theta + \lambda_2 (1 - \lambda_2)^{n-c} (1 - \theta)}. \tag{15}$$

On this basis, the probability that a worker with c changes in n years changes jobs is

$$P_{nc} = \theta_{nc} \lambda_1 + (1 - \theta_{nc}) \lambda_2, \tag{16}$$

It is clear that θ_{nc}, and hence P_{nc}, is increasing in c holding n fixed and decreasing in n holding c fixed. In other words, considering workers with a given amount of experience (n), the group of workers with more changes is disproportionately composed of high mobility (type 1) workers. This implies lower turnover probability among groups of workers with fewer job changes in a given period of time. High tenure, per se, is not related to mobility beyond indicating fewer job changes. The number of job changes in the worker's job history is a sufficient statistic for the probability of job change in the next period.

6. Distinguishing heterogeneity and duration dependence: using data on mobility histories

The discussion of the heterogeneity model in the previous section provides some scope for using data on mobility rates for testing for the importance of both heterogeneity and "true" duration dependence of the sort implied by models of specific capital. The very simple heterogeneity model of mobility developed in the previous section has several clear empirical implications in addition to the core facts that are implied by the specific capital model as well.

First, the heterogeneity model with fixed worker types implies that the probability of job change for any worker is strictly a function of his or her type. Thus, the average rate of job change is constant over time for any fixed sample of workers. In other words, the fraction of workers in a fixed sample who change jobs in any period should not vary with the age or labor market experience of the sample. Second, the heterogeneity model implies that, controlling for experience, the number of prior job changes is a sufficient statistic for the probability of job change. Controlling for experience and the number of prior job changes, the probability of job change should not be related to tenure.

The existing empirical evidence suggests that simple heterogeneity in mobility rates, while important, cannot account for all of the observed relationship between the probability of job change and tenure. Fig. 6 contains the monthly probability of job ending by

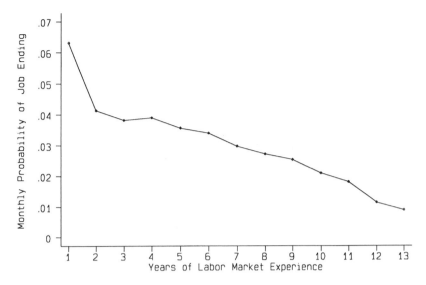

Fig. 6. Monthly probability of job ending by experience. Based on NLSY, 1979–1991.

years of labor market experience using data on 19,336 jobs for 4680 workers from the NLSY for 1979–1991.[32] It is clear that the probability of job change declines sharply with labor market experience. Note that this is not a statement about a structural relationship controlling for tenure or other characteristics. It is a statement about the unconditional bivariate relationship between rates of job change and labor market experience.

One interpretation of the decline in the overall job ending hazard that is consistent with a more general heterogeneity model is that worker types are changing over time so that workers are becoming more stable (less mobile). This could be characterized in terms of the model as θ falling over time (a larger fraction of workers of the less-mobile type as experience increases) or as decreases in λ_i with experience (workers of a given type becoming less mobile as experience increases). Of course, allowing this sort of post hoc rationalization makes it impossible to test a general (unrestricted) heterogeneity model.

Another interpretation of the negative experience-mobility relationship in Fig. 6 is that it is a result of a true negative relationship between tenure and job change. To the extent that this is the case, the simple heterogeneity model cannot explain all of the important features of the data. My earlier work (Farber, 1994), using data from 1979 to 1988 from the NLSY, presents an analysis that addresses this question. Specifically, I estimated a model of the hazard of job ending that controls for heterogeneity of the sort described above in the sense that prior turnover is controlled for directly. Separate hazard functions were estimated for each level of labor market experience (effectively controlling for n), and

---

[32] These data are an updated version of those described in detail in Farber (1994).

dummy variables for the number of prior jobs (effectively controlling for c) are included in each model along with controls for tenure and demographic characteristics. The results are clear. The probability of a job ending is strongly related to the number of prior jobs controlling for tenure on the current job. This suggests that heterogeneity is an important factor in mobility rates. At the same time, the probability of a job ending is strongly related to tenure even controlling for prior mobility. This is clear evidence that the simple heterogeneity model alone cannot account for mobility patterns and that specific capital may play an important role.

There is some evidence in the NLSY data that worker types are changing over time, leaving open the possibility that a richer model of heterogeneity may fit the data. Specifically, I found that recent prior mobility is more strongly related to the probability job ending than mobility further in the past (Farber, 1994). This is consistent with workers changing types of over time by becoming less mobile on average. This could reflect maturation of young workers as they acquire families and settle into careers.[33] Investigating this evolutionary process is an important area for further research.

7. Testing the specific capital model: using the return to tenure

There are at least two formidable obstacles to testing the specific human capital model directly. First, specific capital is not generally directly measurable or even observable. Second, only separation rates can help to distinguish the specific human capital model from plausible alternatives, and, of course, predictions for separation rates are operational only if the quantity of specific capital can be observed. A natural candidate for another outcome would be the wage rate, but the wage rate is indeterminate where there is specific capital. Essentially, the firm and the worker are in a bilateral monopoly position with respect to their specific capital, and the wage will not be market-determined without additional assumptions. In this section, I address these two issues, demonstrate how they are related, and investigate avenues for testing the specific human capital model.

The measurement issue has not yet been solved in a satisfactory way. By default, tenure has been used to index the quantity of specific capital, and the relationship between tenure and wages is used as a measure of the return to specific capital. The root of this appears to be reasoning by analogy to the use of labor market experience to index general human capital (Mincer, 1974; Willis, 1986). The idea is that if time in the labor market indexes accumulation of general skills then time with the firm indexes accumulation of firm-specific skills. There are several flaws in this analogy.

Consider the standard model of accumulation of general human capital through on the job training. A worker is willing to pay the cost of these investments because they receive the return. These investments enhance the workers productivity at all (or many firms). If any employer is not willing to pay the worker for this productivity (the return on the

---

[33] Osterman (1980) presents an interesting analysis of this process of transition.

general human capital), the worker will find an employer who will pay. Furthermore, optimal investment behavior on the part of the worker suggests an experience log-earnings profile that is increasing and concave in experience.[34] Thus, a standard "bare-bones" specification for an earnings function is

$$\ln W = \beta_0 + \beta_1 ED + \beta_2 EXP + \beta_3 EXP^2 + \varepsilon, \tag{17}$$

where ln W is the log wage rate, ED represents years of education, and EXP represents years of labor market experience. The βs are parameters to be estimated, and ϵ is a random error. The expectations are that $\beta_1 > 0$, $\beta_2 > 0$, and $\beta_3 < 0$, and these have been verified in countless empirical studies. The derivative of this function with respect to experience, $\beta_2 + 2\beta_3 EXP$, is called the return to experience, and it is commonly understood to reflect the return to the underlying quantity of general human capital acquired through post-schooling training.

Now extend this empirical model to include tenure. The resulting earnings function is

$$\ln W = \beta_0 + \beta_1 ED + \beta_2 EXP + \beta_3 EXP^2 + \beta_4 TEN + \beta_5 TEN^2 + \varepsilon, \tag{18}$$

where *TEN* represents years of tenure with the current employer. The analogous expectations with regard to the signs of the parameters are that $\beta_4 > 0$ and $\beta_5 < 0$, and, indeed, this is what empirical analyses show quite clearly. The derivative of this function with respect to tenure, $\beta_4 + 2\beta_5 TEN$, is called the return to tenure, and it is analogously interpreted as the return to the underlying quantity of specific human capital acquired through post-schooling training provided by the current employer.

There are at least three problems with this seemingly logical extension. First, it is not clear that tenure indexes accumulated specific capital in a direct way. In the standard model of investment in general human capital over the life-cycle, investment is positive and decreasing over the working life (Ben-Porath, 1967). This is what implies that the experience-earnings profile is concave. While it may be the case that an analogous optimizing model of worker and firm behavior would imply that investment in specific capital will be positive and declining throughout the employment relationship, this is not assured. Thus, it may not be that the tenure-earnings profile is concave.

The second problem is that the theoretical link between the wage and marginal product that exists in the general human capital model does not exist with respect to specific capital. Because specific capital has no value outside the employment relationship, the employer need not pay the worker for the part of productivity in excess of the workers' productivity in his/her next best employment alternative. On the other hand, if workers are not rewarded for their specific capital they will be more likely to quit (resulting in the sort of inefficiencies noted above). Additionally, it is not clear who will pay for the investment in specific capital. Consider three alternatives: (1) the firm pays for all of the specific investment and keeps all of the return; (2) the worker pays for all of the specific investment and keeps all of the return; and (3) the worker and firm share the cost of the specific

---

[34] See, for example, Ben-Porath (1967), Mincer (1974) or Rosen (1977).

investment and share the return. Using reasoning precisely analogous to the discussion of fixed-wage contracts above, all of these schemes lead to inefficiently high levels of turnover. Additionally, the tenure-earnings profile need not bear any resemblance to either the quantity of accumulated specific capital or to the productive value of any specific capital.

The third problem is that tenure is endogenous to the wage determination process. Tenure is an outcome that is simply the inverse of job change. Standard search models of labor turnover have the implication that workers with higher wages (relative to their general human capital) are less likely to quit (Mortensen, 1986; and see the chapter by Mortensen, this volume). And it has long been noted in the literature on specific capital that firms will use the wage to influence turnover behavior in the presence of specific capital (Pencavel, 1972; Parsons, 1973; Salop, 1973). Firms employing workers with substantial specific capital will devise compensation structures that discourage workers from quitting. Empirical analyses of quit behavior (e.g., Freeman, 1980) regress the probability of quitting on the wage and find a negative relationship between the probability of quits and the wage. Since tenure is the result of a series of (non)quit decisions, an earnings function with tenure as an explanatory variable can be thought of as an inverse quit function in some respects. Thus, it is a arbitrary to assign the wage as the dependent variable that is "explained" by tenure.

This discussion makes it clear that tenure, like the wage, is an outcome of optimization by firms and workers, and, as such, it cannot be used as an independent measure of accumulated specific capital in a way that can be used to test hypotheses about the role or importance of specific capital. For example, most versions of the specific human capital model predict that workers with more specific capital will change jobs with lower probability than will workers with less specific capital. It is also observed that workers with more tenure have lower probabilities of job change. By assuming that more tenure indicates more specific capital, this appears to be a test of the prediction that specific human capital implies less job change. But high tenure is the result of low probabilities of job change, whether they result from specific human capital or have some other source. Thus, the relationship between tenure and rates of job change cannot, by itself, be a test of the specific human capital model.

Still, the view that "...the volume of specific training in an individual increases along with the duration of his employment in a given job... ." (Pencavel, 1970, p. 12) is intuitively appealing. Workers with more tenure are likely to have more specific capital than workers with less tenure. And workers with substantial specific human capital may earn higher wages as they accumulate more tenure than do workers with less specific capital because the compensation structure that high specific capital firms have selected, perhaps to minimize costs of turnover, is one which has wages increase relatively rapidly. But this makes it clear that it is not appropriate to interpret the coefficients on tenure in a standard earnings function (β_4 and β_5 in Eq. (18)) as a return to tenure.

Nonetheless, the usual approach in the literature has been to ignore some of the issues of interpretation discussed here and to take the regression coefficients at face value as the return to tenure. A better interpretation is that the tenure coefficients as part of a hedonic earnings function measure how earnings vary with tenure controlling for labor market experience and other factors. This can serve as a useful summary of firm-level compensation structures and perhaps could shed some light on how compensation structures are related to turnover probabilities. I return to this question of interpretation after a review of some recent literature focused on deriving estimates of the return to tenure.

7.1. Estimating the "return" to tenure

There is a substantial literature on estimating the return to tenure in the context of a standard earnings function A typical OLS specification of Eq. (16) finds an average return to tenure of about 0.02 per year.[35] However, more recent work has focused on the interpretation of OLS estimates of the return to tenure derived in this fashion, worrying particularly about biases due to heterogeneity in workers and jobs and to the endogeneity of tenure.[36] Many of these studies find a much smaller return to tenure than do the early studies (e.g., Topel, 1986; Abraham and Farber, 1987; Altonji and Shakotko, 1987; Marshall and Zarkin, 1987; Williams, 1991; Altonji and Williams, 1997; Manning, 1997), but some continue to find a substantial return (Topel, 1991). The issues raised in this literature are central to estimation of the return to tenure and interpretation of such estimates as evidence for the evaluation of the model of accumulation of firm-specific capital.

Altonji and Shakotko (1987) argue that the estimated return to tenure is biased upward due to the fact that tenure is correlated with omitted individual, job, or match specific factors that are correlated with earnings. The basic idea is that more stable workers or workers in more stable jobs are likely to be more productive workers or on more productive jobs. On this basis, one could recast the earnings function in Eq. (18) as

$$\ln W_{ijt} = \beta_0 + \beta_1 ED_{ijt} + \beta_2 EXP_{ijt} + \beta_3 TEN_{ijt} + \gamma_i + \delta_{ij} + \varepsilon_{ijt}, \tag{19}$$

where I have omitted the second order terms in experience and tenure for expositional convenience and where i indexes individuals, j indexes jobs, and t indexes time. There are now individual specific and job specific error components (γ_i and δ_{ij} respectively), and tenure is likely to be positively correlated with both of these. The result will be an upward biased estimate of the return to tenure (β_3).

Altonji and Shakotko present an instrumental variables solution to this problem. They use data from the Panel Study of Income Dynamics (PSID) on earnings over time, which allows them to rely on within-job variation in tenure to estimate the rate of growth of wages within jobs. They find a return to tenure that are substantially smaller than those derived using OLS on the usual sort of cross-sectional data (close to 0 for the IV estimates versus 0.020 for the OLS estimates).

Abraham and Farber (1987) note the same problem with standard OLS estimates of the

---

[35] Borjas (1981) and Mincer and Jovanovic (1981) are examples of studies with OLS estimates of the return to tenure.

[36] Hutchens (1989) presents an overview of the early literature in this area.

return to tenure, but they cast it in slightly different terms and propose a different, though related, solution. They argue that the individual and job-specific error components in the earnings function are correlated with completed job duration and tenure is correlated with these error components only indirectly because tenure is correlated with completed job duration. Clearly, workers with high levels of tenure must be in long jobs while workers with low levels of tenure can be in either short jobs or long jobs. Abraham and Farber go on to argue that if completed job duration is included in the earnings function along with tenure then this new variable will eliminate the correlation of tenure with the error components and the result will be unbiased estimates of the return to tenure. They use data from the PSID to estimate the augmented earnings function,

$$\ln W_{ijt} = \beta_0 + \beta_1 ED_{ijt} + \beta_2 EXP_{ijt} + \beta_3 TEN_{ijt} + \beta_4 DUR_{ij} + \varepsilon_{ijt}, \tag{20}$$

where DUR_{ij} represents completed job duration for worker i on job j.[37] Estimation of Eq. (20) yield much smaller estimates of the return to tenure than does OLS estimation of the same equation without the completed job duration variable (0.005 for the model with completed job duration versus 0.01–0.015 for the model without completed job duration).

Abraham and Farber also present an instrumental variable approach to this problem. They note that, in a cross-section, tenure is on average half of completed job duration. On this basis, they use the residual from a regression of tenure on completed job duration as an instrument for tenure. Since, by construction, this residual is orthogonal to completed job duration, it will be orthogonal to the error components in Eq. (19) that are at the root of the bias in the OLS estimates. These IV estimates of the return to tenure are very close to those derived by including completed job duration as a regressor as in Eq. (20).[38]

While the Abraham and Farber approach to this problem is not a full structural solution since completed job duration is surely jointly determined with wages, the results are useful nonetheless. Perhaps more interesting than the reduction in the estimated return to tenure in Eq. (20) is the substantial and significant positive estimate of the coefficient of completed job duration (β_4). Their estimate for β_4 of approximately 0.02 implies that each 10 years that a job will last implies approximately 20% higher earnings throughout the job. Abraham and Farber investigate this further by modifying the specification to allow completed job duration to have different effects on earnings at different tenure levels. The results of this less restrictive specification verify that completed job duration is correlated with higher earnings at all tenure levels (including very early in jobs).

Topel (1991) takes a different approach to the problem and argues that there is, in fact, a substantial return to tenure. He rightly worries about the endogeneity of tenure and presents results from a two-stage estimation procedure that yields a lower bound estimate of the return to tenure. Topel recasts the earnings function slightly as

---

[37] Completed job durations are censored for many jobs in the sample. Abraham and Farber's solution to this problem is to use a parametric job duration model to estimate expected completed job duration for the censored jobs.

[38] Note that this IV approach and the resulting estimates of the return to tenure are very close to those of Altonji and Shakotko (1987).

$$\ln W_{ijt} = \alpha_0 + \alpha_1 ED_{ijt} + \alpha_2 EXP^0_{ijt} + \alpha_3 TEN_{ijt} + \varepsilon_{ijt}, \tag{21}$$

where α represents the parameters of the model. The key difference between Topel's specification and the earlier specification is that labor market experience (EXP_{ijt}) is replaced by labor market experience at the start of the job (EXP^0_{ijt}). Since $EXP_{ijt} = EXP^0_{ijt} + TEN_{ijt}$, the return to tenure controlling for current labor market experience is $\alpha_3 - \alpha_2$. The return to initial experience is subtracted because α_3 is an estimate of total wage growth within jobs and reflects wage growth due the accumulation of experience as well as of tenure. Topel proceeds by deriving what he argues is an unbiased estimate of α_3 and a potentially upward biased estimate of α_2. The resulting difference is then a lower bound estimate of the return to tenure.

Topel uses average within-job wage growth of workers who do not change jobs as an unbiased estimate of α_3. The underlying assumption is that the wage growth of stayers is an unbiased estimate of wage growth for all workers had they not changed jobs. This does not allow the possibility that workers change jobs for reasons related to wage growth (or the lack thereof). Topel's justification is that earnings move with a random walk after removal of trend growth so that, after allowing for trend growth, the change in earnings this period is unrelated to the change in earnings last period.[39] With this estimate of α_3 in hand Topel runs the following regression:

$$\ln W_{ijt} - \hat{\alpha}_3 TEN_{ijt} = \alpha_0 + \alpha_1 ED_{ijt} + \alpha_2 EXP^0_{ijt} + \varepsilon_{ijt}, \tag{22}$$

to derive his estimate of the return to experience (α_2). Topel argues that $\hat{\alpha}_2$ is upward biased on the basis of a very simple search model of job change over the working life (Burdett, 1978; Topel, 1986; Topel and Ward, 1992; Manning, 1997). In this model, workers face a stable wage offer distribution and offers arrive exogenously at some rate. Workers change jobs if the wage offer exceeds their current wage. Thus, wages at the start of jobs grow with experience for reasons having nothing to do with the accumulation of general human capital. On this basis, the estimate of the return to experience in a standard earnings function is an upward-biased estimate of earnings growth due to human capital accumulation. Topel's two-step procedure yields a lower bound estimate of the return to tenure that is about the same magnitude as the standard OLS estimates (about 0.025 for the two-step estimate versus 0.03 for the OLS estimates), and the conclusion is that there is a substantial return to tenure.[40]

Altonji and Williams (1997) revisit the question of the return to tenure, investigating in detail the earlier work described above, particularly with regard to issues of timing, measurement, and specification. They attempt to reconcile the earlier Altonji-Shakotko

---

[39] Topel presents evidence from the PSID that supports this assumption, but it is not clear how powerful his test or how much deviation from the random walk assumption would introduce substantial bias. Farber and Gibbons (1996) present evidence from the NLSY rejecting the hypothesis that wages evolve as a martingale (a generalization of the random walk).

[40] Topel estimates a non-linear relationship between log-earnings and tenure, and the estimates I cite here are computed at 10 years of tenure.

results with Topel's results. Their finding is that Topel's treatment of secular trends in wages and his use of lagged wages with a current measure of tenure results in upward bias in the return to tenure in his sample. Altonji and Williams also consider the role of measurement error in tenure. They conclude from their analysis that the return to tenure is relatively small (about 1% per year) and close to that estimated by Altonji and Shakotko and by Abraham and Farber.

How are these estimates of the return to tenure to be interpreted, regardless of their precise magnitude? I argue that an appropriate estimate that accounts for the sorts of biases described above measures an average rate of wage growth within jobs. This is best understood as measuring the compensation structures used by employers to achieve appropriate performance from their workforce. An important aspect of this performance is discouraging turnover where this is substantial investment in specific capital. In a well-known paper, Lazear (1979) develops a model of the compensation structure where employers who value long-term employment relationships, presumably because they want to invest in specific capital in their workers, offer a back-loaded compensation structure so that workers will want to remain with the firm.[41] In other words, these firms offer steeply-sloped compensation profiles with a high return to tenure[42]

What this discussion suggests is that the relationship between tenure and earnings is not a market-determined constant but is likely to vary across firms with different technologies and in different markets. Firms that invest heavily in workers and want stable long-term workers may use a steeply sloped earning profile as an incentive device. They may also pay higher wages throughout and offer substantial fringe benefits. Firms that are less concerned about having a stable workforce are likely to offer flatter earnings profiles. An important direction for future research will be to investigate variation in the tenure earnings profile and relate it to the underlying economic forces that cause firms to make different decisions regarding their compensation structure.[43] But there is no sense in which evidence of this sort on the tenure-earnings profile can provide direct evidence on the importance of specific human capital and its relationship with turnover.

---

[41] Lazear (1998) goes on to argue that firms then need a mechanism to end the employment relationship since workers who are highly paid at the end of the implicit long-term relationship will not want to leave voluntarily. Mandatory retirement rules can play this role, and the outlawing of mandatory retirement in the United States may have unintended negative consequences for economic efficiency.

[42] Carmichael (1989) presents a survey of the theoretical literature on life-cycle incentive issues in labor markets. Felli and Harris (1996) present a dynamic theoretical model of specific capital that incorporates issues of information, matching, and turnover and which has implications for the slope of the tenure-earnings profile.

[43] Abowd et al. (1994) report significant differences in slopes of tenure-earnings profiles across a large sample of French firms. Margolis (1995, 1996), using the same data, analyzes the return to tenure in the context of models that allow for heterogeneity in tenure slopes across firms. Margolis confirms that there is substantial heterogeneity in tenure slopes, and he concludes that accounting for self-selection of workers into firms on this basis is important in estimating the return to tenure.

8. Testing the specific capital model: evidence from displaced workers

Another approach to testing the specific capital model relies on examining the incidence of job loss and wage dynamics of workers who change jobs for reasons exogenous to their own decisions or the decisions of employers with regard to their wages or performance. The idea is that jobs are lost exogenously due to shocks to demand that cause firms to shed workers through plant closings in the extreme case and through layoffs in the less extreme case. Technology shocks can have much the same effect. Of course, the likelihood that workers will be displaced in this way is surely related to wages and productivity on the margin, but the shocks themselves can reasonably be considered exogenous.

In order to make this approach work, tenure must be accepted as being monotonically positively related to accumulated specific capital. Note that this is weaker than the relationship required to interpret the coefficient on tenure in an earnings function as a (rescaled) return to specific human capital. A second requirement is that the firm and worker share in the return to any accumulated specific capital. This seems reasonable in light of the necessary incentives to reduce labor turnover where there is specific capital.

Given these two conditions and if specific capital is an important component of employment relationships then the probability of job loss will decline with tenure. This is closely related to the stylized fact presented earlier that the probability of job change declines with tenure. Essentially, the claim is that when a firm needs to reduce employment due to a demand or technology shock, the firm will choose to lay off less senior workers because they embody less specific capital (on which the firm is enjoying some return). Using data from the 1984–1992 Displaced Workers Surveys and other CPS supplements with data on job tenure over the same period, I found support for this view (Farber, 1993).[44] The probability of job loss declines sharply with tenure. Quantitatively, my calculations yield the result that the probability of job loss in the 2 years prior to the DWS survey date declines from about 14% for workers with less than 1 year of tenure to less than 4% for workers with ten or more years of tenure.

A weakness of this approach to testing for the importance of specific capital is that a finding of a negative relationship between tenure and the probability of job loss is susceptible to an explanation based on heterogeneity. If there is persistent heterogeneity across firms in the volatility of labor demand, then firms where there is little volatility will be more likely to have high-tenure workers and less likely to have substantial lay-offs. This implies the same negative relationship between tenure and job loss without specific capital. A related argument is that firms with substantial volatility in labor of labor demand may find investment in specific capital less attractive and, hence, organize production around a high-turnover workforce.

---

[44] This is analysis is complicated by the fact that the DWSs do not contain information on tenure for workers who did not lose their jobs, and even if there was such information it will not accurately reflect job tenure during the period the worker was at risk to lose a job if the worker changed jobs for reasons other than job loss. See Farber (1993) for details.

A second test of the specific capital model is that displaced workers earn less on their post-displacement jobs than on their pre-displacement jobs. There is a substantial empirical literature that examines his issue. The bulk of the recent work on this question is based on the DWS.[45] However, there has also been research using the PSID, and administrative data from the records of state unemployment systems (Jacobson et al., 1993). There is strong consistency in this literature. Regardless of the data used, the finding is that job loss results in substantial and persistent earnings loss. This can be interpreted as evidence that specific capital is important in the labor market. It may be that specific capital represents actual skills that are useful only with the current employer or that specific capital represents the value of a good match that is sacrificed by job loss (Jovanovic, 1979a). However, these findings could be accounted for by heterogeneous job quality where the high-wage jobs are allocated in ways unrelated to ability (perhaps randomly). Agency considerations of the sort that underlay efficiency wage models could account for the finding that high-wage job losers are not able to find equivalent new jobs.

Perhaps a more focused test of the specific capital model is that the wage decline borne by displaced workers will be larger for those displaced workers with more tenure. This relies on the assumption that the workers are receiving at least some of the return to the specific capital. When a worker is displaced, the value of any specific capital is destroyed, and the worker's wage on next job will be commensurately lower by an amount equal to the worker's share of the return on the specific capital on the lost job. Since workers with more tenure are presumed to have more specific capital, the wage loss of workers with more tenure will be larger than the wage loss of workers with less tenure.

There is empirical support for this prediction. Addison and Portugal (1989) present an analysis of data from the January 1984 DWS which finds that earnings losses are larger for workers with more pre-displacement tenure. My calculations, based on the DWSs from 1984 to 1996, show that the proportional difference in weekly earnings (post-displacement minus pre-displacement) for more than 18,000 re-employed displaced workers is strongly negatively related to pre-displacement tenure. Regressing the change in log real earnings on pre-displacement tenure yields a coefficient on tenure of -0.017 (SE $= 0.0008$). Controlling additionally for survey year, education, age, sex, race, and part-time status on the old and new jobs reduces the coefficient on tenure only slightly to -0.012 (SE $= 0.0008$).

One potential criticism of this analysis is that workers who lose jobs may be selected by their employer on the basis of poor performance or relatively high pay. Gibbons and Katz (1991) argue that workers displaced due to "slack work" are subject to this sort of selection. Within the limits of human resource management policies that give preference in retention to high tenure workers, employers are likely to lay off less productive workers when demand declines. In contrast, they argue that workers who are displaced due to a

---

[45] See, for example, Flaim and Seghal (1985), Addison and Portugal (1989), and Swaim and Podgursky (1991). Hamermesh (1989) surveys some of this literature.

"plant closing" are not subject to such selection. Employers must lay off all workers in such situations. This suggests that workers who report a "plant closing" as the cause of their job loss are more likely to be exogenous job losers than are those who are displaced due to "slack work". This suggests that only a subset of displaced workers, those displaced due to "plant closing," are appropriate to use in testing models of mobility. While Gibbons and Katz present evidence from the 1984 and 1986 DWSs showing that the wage loss of job losers due to "slack work" is larger than the wage loss of job losers due to "plant closing," the differences are small. And my own analysis of data from the DWS suggests that the relationships of the wage loss with pre-displacement tenure are similar across job-loss categories.

However, there is another potential heterogeneity-based alternative explanation for the positive relationship between tenure and the wage loss of displaced workers. If jobs are heterogeneous so that some jobs pay higher wages than do others for equivalent workers, it is likely to be the case that average tenure is higher on the jobs that pay the higher wages due to a reduced probability of quits. In the extreme case where the likelihood of job losers being hired into a high-wage new job is independent of what type of job they held earlier, there will be a strong negative relationship between the wage change of job losers and tenure on the lost job. Both high- and low-tenure will receive the average wage in expectation on their new job. This implies a large decline in wages for high-tenure job losers and a smaller decline (or even an increase) in wages for low-tenure job losers controlling for observable characteristics.

There is a related prediction with regard to the relationship between tenure on the lost job and the wage *level* on the new job for job losers that can help establish the relative importance of specific capital and heterogeneity in these models. Kletzer (1989) notes that evidence that tenure on the lost job is related to the level of wages on the new job is evidence that heterogeneity is important. Clearly, if the only role of tenure on the lost job was to proxy for accumulated specific human capital, then it would have no effect on wages on the new job. But if workers are heterogeneous and more stable workers are more productive generally, then high tenure job losers (whose stable employment history is verifiable) will command higher wages in their new jobs. Kletzer, using data from the 1984 DWS, finds a positive but not statistically significant relationship between earnings on the post-displacement job and pre-displacement tenure. Addison and Portugal (1989) do find a significant positive relationship. My own calculations, based on a sample of more than 20,000 re-employed displaced workers from the 1984–1996 DWSs show a significant positive relationship. Regressing post-displacement log real earnings on pre-displacement tenure, controlling additionally for survey year, education, age, sex, race, and part-time status yields a significant coefficient on tenure of 0.0064 (SE $= 0.0009$). These estimates imply that 10 years of tenure on the lost job is associated with about 6% higher earnings on a new job. This, suggests that heterogeneity does play some role in the relationship between tenure and wages.

We can also examine the relationship between tenure on the lost job and earnings on the pre-displacement job. If job loss is exogenous, this is roughly equivalent to estimating a standard earnings function including tenure, and it is not surprising that we find a strong positive relationship.[46] My own calculations using data on a sample of more than 30,000 displaced workers from the 1984–1996 DWSs verify this strong relationship. Regressing pre-displacement log real earnings on pre-displacement tenure, controlling additionally for survey year, education, age, sex, race, and part-time status yields a significant coefficient on tenure of 0.021 (SE = 0.0006). These estimates imply that 10 years of tenure on the lost job is associated with about 21% higher earnings on the lost job.

A comparison of the magnitudes of the coefficients on tenure in these pre- and post-displacement earnings functions may shed some light on the relative importance of heterogeneity and specific capital considerations. A strong caution is that this approach is subject to the important problems, noted earlier, of interpretation of the coefficient of tenure in earnings functions as a return to specific capital. Start by interpreting the coefficient on pre-displacement tenure in the post-displacement earnings function as reflecting heterogeneity and interpreting the coefficient on tenure in the pre-displacement earnings function as reflecting the sum of heterogeneity and specific capital. Then the difference in coefficients represents the contribution of specific capital. Note that this is roughly equivalent to measuring the relationship between the change in earnings and tenure on the lost job. To the extent that this is negative, it implies that specific capital considerations are important. My estimates for the coefficients on tenure are 0.006 in the post-displacement earnings function and 0.021 in the pre-displacement earnings function.[47] Taken at face value, the difference between these estimates suggests that about 30% of the estimated return to tenure in a cross-section is due to heterogeneity with the remaining 70% being due to specific capital.

Neal (1995) presents an analysis that extends this work in an interesting way. He investigates how pre-displacement tenure is related to post-displacement earnings separately for workers who change industries and for workers who do not change industries following displacement. Using data from the DWSs from 1984 to 1990, he finds that the level of post-displacement earnings is positively related to pre-displacement tenure only for workers who are re-employed in their pre-displacement industry. There is no relationship between tenure and post-displacement earnings for industry switchers. Parent (1995), in related work using the NLSY and the PSID, finds that industry-specific experience is a more important determinant of earnings than either total labor market experience or firm-specific tenure. Perhaps most interesting is the finding that the coefficient on tenure is reduced substantially when within-industry labor market experience is included in a standard earnings function.

These findings suggest an important reinterpretation of the earlier results on the rela-

---

[46] Kletzer (1989) and Addison and Portugal (1989) carry out this analysis, and both find a strong significant positive relationship.

[47] The difference between these coefficients of −0.015 is very close to my estimated coefficient on tenure in the regression of the change in log-earnings cited above of −0.017. Addison and Portugal (1989) note this as well.

tionship between tenure and earnings. They imply that the capital that accrues with tenure has a strong industry-specific rather than firm-specific component. To the extent that this is the case, it is harder to argue that the accrual of firm-specific capital is what drives the decline in the probability of job change with tenure.

9. Final remarks

A core set of facts about worker mobility are clear: (1) long-term employment relationships are common; (2) most new jobs end early; and (3) the probability of a job ending declines with tenure. However, evidence in support of particular models that can explain these facts is relatively weak. While the specific capital model is a parsimonious explanation for these facts, it also appears that worker heterogeneity can account for much of what we observe in the mobility data.

The task of testing the specific human capital model is very difficult because specific capital is not observed directly and the wage need not reflect productivity where there is specific capital. Tenure is, at best, an imperfect proxy for accrued firm-specific capital and, at worst, another outcome jointly determined with wages.

It seems clear that high-wage workers change jobs less frequently than do low wage-workers implying that they have higher tenure. Thus, it is not surprising that tenure shows a strong positive coefficient in standard earnings functions. While this does not measure a return to specific capital, it does, when appropriately estimated to take account of heterogeneity, measure how firms structure compensation over the course of jobs. And the compensation structure may imply something interesting about the importance of specific capital.

Why is it that firms pay higher wages to some workers who will stay with the firm a long time, either as a cause or an effect of the high wages? Why is it that firms structure compensation profiles so that wages increase with tenure? It is likely because firms value and want to encourage long-term employment relationships. Since it is expensive for firms to encourage such relationships, it must be the case that these relationships are a more efficient production technology for them. The unanswered question is what attributes of long-term employment relationships make them the efficient production technology in many settings. One important advantage may be that long-term employment relationships enable firms and workers to invest in firm-specific capital. But alternative explanations remain. For example, it may be that worker quality may be difficult to observe, ex ante, so that firms that need high-quality workers want to retain workers who they learn are high quality in order to avoid the risk of hiring a series of low-quality workers before finding another high-quality worker. Or it may be that many workers prefer long-term stable employment relationships and are more willing to supply effort in such situations.

In conclusion, while deriving convincing direct evidence for the specific capital model of mobility is difficult, it appears that specific capital is a useful construct for understanding wage dynamics and worker mobility. Future progress in understanding these issues will require more and better data on mobility histories along with models that combine specific capital considerations with carefully specified models of heterogeneity and other alternatives.

References

Abowd, John M. and Arnold Zellner (1985), "Estimating gross labor force flows", Journal of Economic and Business Statistics 3: 254–283.

Abowd, John M., Francis Kramarz and David N. Margolis (1994), "High wage workers and high wage firms", Working paper no. 4187 (NBER, Cambridge, MA).

Abraham, Katharine G. and Henry S. Farber (1987), "Job duration, seniority and earnings", American Economic Review 77: 278–297.

Abraham, Katharine G. and James L. Medoff (1984), "Length of service and layoffs in union and non-union work groups", Industrial and Labor Relations Review 38: 87–97.

Addison, John T. and Pedro Portugal (1989), "Job displacement, relative wage changes and duration of unemployment", Journal of Labor Economics 7: 281–302.

Altonji, Joseph G. and Robert Shakotko (1987), "Do wages rise with job seniority?" Review of Economic Studies 54: 437–459.

Altonji, Joseph G. and Nicolas Williams (1997), "Do wages rise with job seniority: a reassessment", Working paper no. 6010 (NBER, Cambridge, MA).

Angrist, Joshua and Alan B. Krueger (1986), "Empirical strategies in labor economics" in: Orley Ashenfelter and Richard Layard, eds., Handbook of labor economics, Vol. 2 (North-Holland, Amsterdam) pp. 849–919.

Becker, Gary S. (1964), Human capital: a theoretical and empirical analysis with special reference to education (NBER, Cambridge, MA).

Ben-Porath, Yoram (1967), "The production of human capital and the life cycle of earnings", Journal of Political Economy August: 352–365.

Blau, Francine D. and Lawrence M. Kahn (1981a), "Causes and consequences of layoffs", Economic Inquiry 19: 270–296.

Blau, Francine D. and Lawrence M. Kahn (1981b), "Race and sex differences in quits by young workers", Industrial and Labor Relations Review 34: 563–577.

Blumen, Isadore, M. Kogen and Phillip McCarthy (1955), The industrial mobility of workers as a probability process, Vol. 6, Cornell studies in industrial and labor relations (Cornell University, Ithaca, NY).

Borjas, George (1981), "Job mobility and earnings over the life cycle", Industrial and Labor Relations Review 34: 365–376.

Brown, James N. and Audrey Light (1992), "Interpreting panel data on job tenure", Journal of Labor Economics 10: 219–257.

Burdett, Kenneth (1978), "A theory of employee job search and quit rates", American Economic Review 68: 212–220.

Burgess, Simon (1998), "The reallocation of labour: an international comparison using job tenure data", Mimeo (Centre for Economic Policy Research, London School of Eeconomics).

Carmichael, H. Lorne (1989), "Self-enforcing contracts, shirking and life-cycle incentives", Journal of Economic Perspectives 3: 65–84.

Diebold, Francis X., David Neumark and Daniel Polsky (1994), "Job stability in the United States", Working paper no. 4859 (NBER, Cambridge, MA).

Diebold, Francis X., David Neumark and Daniel Polsky (1996), "Comment of Kenneth A. Swinnerton and Howard Wial, 'Is job stability declining in the U.S. Economy?'" Industrial and Labor Relations Review 49: 348–352.

Farber, Henry S. (1993), "The incidence and costs of job loss: 1982–91", Brookings Papers on Economic Activity: Microeconomics: 73–119.

Farber, Henry S. (1994), "The analysis of interfirm worker mobility", Journal of Labor Economics 12: 554–593.

Farber, Henry S. (1997a), "The changing face of job loss in the United States: 1981–1995", Brookings Papers on Economic Activity: Microeconomics: 55–128.

Farber, Henry S. (1997b), "Trends in long-term employment in the United States, 1979–96", Working paper no. 384 (Industrial Relations Section, Princeton University).

Farber, Henry S. (1997c), "Job creation in the United States: good jobs or bad?" Working paper no. 385 (Industrial Relations Section, Princeton University).

Farber, Henry S. (1998a), "Are lifetime jobs disappearing: job duration in the United States, 1973–93" in: John Haltiwanger, Marilyn Manser and Robert Topel, eds., Labor statistics measurement issues (University of Chicago Press, Chicago, IL) in press.

Farber, Henry S. (1998b), "Has the rate of job loss increased in the nineties?" Working paper no. 394 (Industrial Relations Section, Princeton University).

Farber, Henry S. and Robert Gibbons (1996), "Learning and wage dynamics", Quarterly Journal of Economics November: 1007–1047.

Felli, Leonardo and Christopher Harris (1996), "Learning, wage dynamics and firm-specific human capital", Journal of Political Economy 104: 838–868.

Flaim, Paul and Ellen Seghal (1985), Displaced workers of 1979–83: how well have they fared? Bulletin no. 2240 (US Department of Labor, Bureau of Labor Statistics).

Freeman, Richard B. (1980), "The exit-voice tradeoff in the labor market: unionism, job tenure, quits and separations", Quarterly Journal of Economics 94: 643–673.

Gardner, Jennifer M. (1995), "Worker displacement: a decade of change", Monthly Labor Review 118: 45–57.

Gibbons, Robert and Lawrence F. Katz (1991), "Layoffs and lemons", Journal of Labor Economics 9: 351–380.

Gregg, Paul and Jonathan Wadsworth (1998), "Job tenure in the UK 1975–1997", Working paper no. 967 (Center for Economic Performance, London School of Economics).

Hall, Robert E. (1972), "Turnover in the labor force", Brookings Papers on Economic Activity: 709–756.

Hall, Robert E. (1982), "The importance of lifetime jobs in the U.S. economy", American Economic Review 72: 716–724.

Hall, Robert E. and Edward Lazear (1984), "The excess sensitivity of quits and layoffs to demand", Journal of Labor Economics 2: 233–257.

Hamermesh, Daniel (1989), "What do we know about worker displacement in the U.S." Industrial Relations 28: 51–59.

Harris, Milton and Bengt Holmstrom (1982), "A theory of wage dynamics", Review of Economic Studies 49: 315–333.

Heckman, James J. and Burton Singer (1984), "A method for minimizing the impact of distributional assumptions in econometric models for duration data", Econometrica 52: 271–320.

Holmstrom, Bengt (1979), "Moral hazard and observability", Bell Journal of Economics 10: 324–340.

Hutchens, Robert M. (1989), "Seniority, wages and productivity: a turbulent decade", Journal of Economic Perspectives 3: 49–64.

Jacobsen, Louis, Robert Lalonde and Daniel Sullivan (1993), "Earnings losses of displaced workers", American Economic Review 83: 685–709.

Jaeger, David A. and Ann Huff Stevens (1999), "Is job stability in the United States falling? Trends in the current population survey and panel study of income dynamics", Journal of Labor Economics, in press.

Jovanovic, Boyan (1979a), "Job matching and the theory of turnover", Journal of Political Economy 87; 972–990.

Jovanovic, Boyan (1979b), "Firm-specific capital and turnover", Journal of Political Economy 87: 1246–1260.

Kletzer, Lori G.(1989), "Returns to seniority after permanent job loss", American Economic Review 79: 536–543.

Lancaster, Tony (1979), "Econometric methods for the duration of unemployment", Econometrica 47: 939–956.

Lazear, Edward (1979), "Why is there mandatory retirement?" Journal of Political Economy 87: 1261–1284.

Malcomson, James (1999), "New developments in the study of contracts in the labor market", in: Orley Ashenfelter and David Card, eds., Handbook of labor economics (North Holland, Amsterdam).

Manning, Alan (1997), "Mighty good thing: the returns to tenure", Mimeo. (London School of Economics).

Margolis, David N. (1995), "Firm heterogeneity and worker self-selection bias estimated returns to seniority", Cahier de recherche no. 9502 (Department de Sciences Economiques, Universite de Montreal).

Margolis, David N. (1996), "Cohort effects and the return to seniority in France", Annales d'Economie et de Statistique 41–42: 443–464.

Marshall, Robert C. and Gary A. Zarkin (1987), "The effect of job tenure on wage offers", Journal of Labor Economics 5: 301–324.

McCall, Brian P. (1990), "Occupational matching: a test of sorts", Journal of Political Economy 98: 45–69.

McLaughlin, Kenneth J. (1991), "A theory of quits and layoffs with efficient turnover", Journal of Political Economy 99: 1–29.

Mincer, Jacob (1974), Schooling, experience and earnings (Columbia University Press, New York).

Mincer, Jacob and Boyan Jovanovic (1981), "Labor mobility and wages", in: Sherwin Rosen, ed., Studies in labor markets (University of Chicago Press, Chicago, IL) pp. 21–63.

Mortensen, Dale (1978), "Specific capital and labor turnover", Bell Journal of Economics 9: 572–586.

Mortensen, Dale (1986), "Job search and labor market analysis", in: Orley Ashenfelter and Richard Layard, eds., Handbook of labor economics, Vol. 2 (North-Holland, Amsterdam) pp. 849–919.

Neal, Derek (1995), "Industry-specific capital: evidence from displaced workers", Journal of Labor Economics 13: 653–677.

Neumark, David, Daniel Polsky and Daniel Hansen (1999), "Has job stability declined yet? New evidence for the 1990's", Journal of Labor Economics, in press.

Oi, Walter (1962), "Labor as a quasi-fixed factor", Journal of Political Economy 70: 538–555.

Osterman, Paul (1980), Getting started: the youth labor market (MIT Press, Cambridge, MA).

Parent, Daniel (1995), "Industry-specific capital: evidence from the NLSY and the PSID", Working paper no. 350 (Industrial Relations Section, Princeton University).

Parsons, Donald O. (1972), "Specific human capital: an application to quit rates and layoff rates", Journal of Political Economy 80: 1120–1143.

Parsons, Donald O. (1973), "Quit rates over time: a search and information approach", American Economic Review 63: 390–401.

Pencavel, John H. (1970), "An analysis of the quit rate in American manufacturing industry", Research report series no. 114 (Industrial Relations Section, Princeton University).

Pencavel, John H. (1972), "Wages, specific training and labor turnover in U.S. manufacturing industries", International Economic Review 13: 53–64.

Poterba, James M. and Lawrence H. Summers (1986), "Reporting errors and labor market dynamics", Econometrica 54: 1319–1338.

Rose, Stephen J. (1995), "Declining job security and the professionalization of opportunity", Research report no. 95–04 (National Commission for Employment Policy).

Rosen, Sherwin (1977), "Human capital: a survey of empirical research", Research in Labor Economics 1: 3–40.

Salop, Steven (1973), "Wage differentials in a dynamic theory of the firm", Journal of Economic Theory 6: 321–344.

Salop, Steven (1974), "Systematic job search and unemployment", Review of Economic Studies 40: 225–243.

Stewart, Jay (1997), "Has job mobility increased? evidence from the current population survey: 1975–1995", Mimeo. (Office of Employment Research and Program Development, US Bureau of Labor Statistics).

Swaim, Paul and Michael Podgursky (1991), "The distribution of economic losses among displaced workers: a replication", Journal of Human Resources 26: 742–755.

Swinnerton, Kenneth and Howard Wial (1995), "Is job stability declining in the U.S. economy?" Industrial and Labor Relations Review 48: 293–304.

Swinnerton, Kenneth and Howard Wial (1996), "Is job stability declining in the U.S. economy? Reply to Diebold, Neumark and Polsky", Industrial and Labor Relations Review 49: 352–355.

Topel, Robert (1986), "Job mobility, search and earnings growth: a reinterpretation of human capital earnings functions", Research in Labor Economics 8, part A: 199–233.

Topel, Robert (1991), "Specific capital, mobility and wages: wages rise with job seniority", Journal of Political Economy 99: 145–176.

Topel, Robert and Michael Ward (1992), "Job mobility and the careers of young men", Quarterly Journal of Economics 107: 439–479.

United States Department of Commerce (1988), CPS interviewer memorandum no. 88–01 (Bureau of the Census).

Ureta, Manuelita (1992), "The importance of lifetime jobs in the U.S. economy, revisited", American Economic Review 82: 322–335.

Valletta, Robert G.(1997), "Declining job security", Mimeo. (Federal Reserve Bank of San Francisco, CA).

Williams, Nicolas (1991), "Reexamining the wage, tenure and experience relationship", Review of Economics and Statistics 73: 512–517.

Willis, Robert. J. (1986), "Wage determinants: a survey and reinterpretation of human capital earnings functions", in: Orley Ashenfelter and Richard Layard, eds., Handbook of labor economics, Vol. 1 (North-Holland, Amsterdam) pp. 525–602.

Chapter 38

EXECUTIVE COMPENSATION

KEVIN J. MURPHY*

Marshall School of Business, University of Southern California

Contents

* This research has been influenced significantly by my co-authors Michael Jensen, Robert Gibbons, Jerold Zimmerman, and George Baker, and also by Sherwin Rosen, Ed Lazear, and Karen Wruck. I also thank my practitioner-colleagues from Towers Perrin, including Michael Carter, Brian Dunn, Julie Kohler, Gary Locke, Paula Todd, Peter Watson, and especially Michael Davis. In addition, I am grateful for helpful comments on an earlier draft from Rajesh Aggarwal, James Brickley, Jennifer Carpenter, Harry DeAngelo, Linda DeAngelo, Joetta Forsyth, Robert Gibbons, Kevin Hallock, Joseph Haubrich, David Hirshliefer, Bengt Holmstrom, Takao Kato, Charles O'Reilly, Paul Oyer, Darius Palia, Robert Parrino, Karen Van Nuys, David Yermack, Mark Zenner, and Jerry Zimmerman.

Handbook of Labor Economics, Volume 3, Edited by O. Ashenfelter and D. Card

Abstract

This chapter summarizes the empirical and theoretical research on executive compensation and provides a comprehensive and up-to-date description of pay practices (and trends in pay practices) for chief executive officers (CEOs). Topics discussed include the level and structure of CEO pay (including detailed analyses of annual bonus plans, executive stock options, and option valuation), international pay differences, the pay-setting process, the relation between CEO pay and firm performance ("pay–performance sensitivities"), the relation between sensitivities and subsequent firm performance, relative performance evaluation, executive turnover, and the politics of CEO pay. © 1999 Elsevier Science B.V. All rights reserved.

JEL codes: J33; J44; G3; G39; J31

1. Introduction

Few issues in the history of the modern corporation have attracted the attention garnered by executive compensation in United States companies. Once relegated to the relative obscurity of business periodicals, executive pay has become a international issue debated in Congress and routinely featured in front-page headlines, cover stories, and television news shows. Several inextricably linked factors have contributed to the widespread interest in executive pay. First is the undisputed escalation in chief executive officer (CEO) compensation: as shown in Fig. 1, the median cash compensation paid to S&P 500 CEOs has more than doubled since 1970 (in 1996-constant dollars), and median total *realized* compensation (including gains from exercising stock options) has nearly quadrupled. Second is the populist attack on wealth that followed the so-called "excesses of the 1980s," associated with the perception that high CEO salaries are coupled to layoffs, plant closings, and corporate downsizing (Murphy, 1995, 1997). Third is the bull market of the 1990s, creating windfalls for CEOs whose pay is increasingly tied to company stock-price performance.

There has also been an explosion in academic research on executive compensation. As evident in Fig. 1, CEO pay research has grown even faster than CEO paychecks, skyrocketing from 1–2 papers per year prior to 1985 to 60 papers in 1995.[1] Only a handful of studies of executive compensation were published prior to 1980, including pioneering works by Roberts (1956), Baumol (1959), and Lewellen and Huntsman (1970). Most early studies focused on whether pay was more closely tied to company size or company profits, the answer proving to be both relatively uninteresting and hopelessly lost in multicollinearity problems (Ciscel and Carroll, 1980; Rosen, 1992).

The modern history of executive compensation research began in the early 1980s and

---

[1] Data on executive compensation papers from Hallock and Murphy (1999), based initially on a search of the Social Science Citation Index database. The 1985 jump in executive pay studies can be traced directly to a 1984 University of Rochester conference on "Managerial Compensation and the Managerial Labor Market;" proceedings published the following year in the *Journal of Accounting and Economics*.

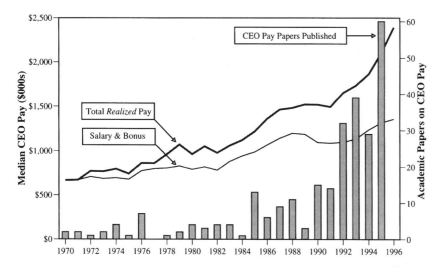

Fig. 1. Median realized cash and total compensation (including option gains) for S&P 500 CEOs, 1970–1996, and number of academic papers published on CEO pay. Sample is based on all CEOs included in the S&P 500. Compensation data, in 1996-constant dollars, are extracted from the Annual Compensation Surveys published by *Forbes* each May from 1971 to 1992; later data from Compustat's ExecuComp Database. Cash pay includes salaries, bonuses, and small amounts of other cash compensation; total realized pay includes cash pay, restricted stock, payouts from longterm pay programs, and the amounts realized from exercising stock options during the year. (Total pay prior to 1978 excludes option gains.) The number of academic papers on CEO pay was computed by Kevin Hallock and reported in Hallock and Murphy (1999).

paralleled the emergence and general acceptance of agency theory.[2] The separation of ownership and control in modern corporations is, after all, the quintessential agency problem suggested by Berle and Means (1932) and formalized by Jensen and Meckling (1976), and the executive labor market is a natural laboratory for testing its implications. Early studies in this area focused on documenting the relation between CEO pay and company performance (Coughlan and Schmidt, 1985; Murphy, 1985, 1986; Abowd, 1990; Jensen and Murphy, 1990a; Leonard, 1990). Others examined whether CEOs are terminated following poor performance (Weisbach, 1988; Warner et al., 1988) and whether CEOs are reward for performance measured relative to the market or industry (Antle and Smith, 1986; Gibbons and Murphy, 1990).

The evolving literature has been truly interdisciplinary, spanning accounting, economics, finance, industrial relations, law, organizational behavior, and strategy. Accountants, for example, have explored whether accounting-based bonuses lead managers to manipulate earnings and have compared the relative efficacy of accounting-based and stock-

---

[2] Influential papers include Jensen and Meckling (1976), Mirrlees (1974, 1976), Ross (1973), Holmstrom (1979, 1982), Fama (1980), Lazear and Rosen (1981), and Grossman and Hart (1983).

based performance measures.[3] Financial economists have studied the association between executive compensation and corporate performance, investment decisions, capital structure, dividend policies, mergers, and diversification.[4] Industrial organization economists have documented the effects of regulation and deregulation on executive compensation, and have examined the game-theoretic effects of strategic interactions on compensation policy.[5] While most research in the area has evolved as tests or applications of agency theory, sociologists and organizational behaviorists have examined non-agency-theoretic issues such as social comparisons and the behavioral effects of wage dispersion.[6]

In spite of the exploding interdisciplinary literature, executive compensation has received relatively scant attention from labor economists.[7] However, even though the managerial labor market is small and specialized, there are ample reasons to encourage labor-oriented research in the area. Executive compensation offers opportunities to analyze many concepts central to labor economics, including incentives, marginal productivity, contracts, promotions, separations, and careers. Although compensation contracts are multi-dimensional and complex, the publicly available data are relatively clean: detailed biographic and compensation data for individual executives in publicly owned corporations are widely available and easily matched to company performance data. In addition, an increasing number of researchers are gaining access to proprietary and increasingly rich data on performance measures and bonus contracts and on individual compensation far below the top executive rank.[8]

The objective of this chapter is to foster research in executive compensation by providing a rich and up-to-date description of executive incentive contracts, and by reviewing and updating much of the relevant empirical and theoretical research on executive compensation and turnover. The institutional details, summary statistics, and regression analyses are based on a variety of sources including four comprehensive databases: the Annual Compensation Surveys published in *Forbes* covering 1970–1996, Compustat's "ExecuComp" database covering CEOs in the S&P 500, the S&P Mid-Cap 400, and the S&P Small-Cap 600 from 1992 to 1996, detailed data from 1000 large companies in 1992

---

[3] The seminal article on earnings manipulation is Healy (1985); see also Pourciau (1993) and Holthausen et al. (1995). Lambert and Larcker (1988), Sloan (1993), Bushman and Indjejikian (1993), and Baiman and Verrecchia (1995) analyze accounting-based vs. stock-based performance measures.

[4] See, for example, Agrawal and Mandelker (1987) on financing decisions, John and John (1993) on capital structure, Agrawal and Walkling (1994) on takeovers, Mehran et al. (1998) on liquidation policy, and Lambert (1986), Campbell and Chan (1989), Smith and Watts (1992), Hirshleifer and Suh (1992), and Bizjak et al. (1993) on investment behavior.

[5] See, for example, Carroll and Ciscel (1982), Hubbard and Palia (1995), Joskow et al. (1996) on regulation and compensation, and Aggarwal and Samwick (1997) and Kedia (1997) on strategic interactions.

[6] See, for example, O'Reilly et al. (1988, 1998), Tosi and Gomez-Mejia (1989, 1994), Virany et al. (1992), Boeker (1992), Cowherd and Levine (1992), Hambrick and Cannella (1993), Finkelstein (1996), and Hambrick and Siegel (1998).

[7] A notable exception is the proceedings from a conference on "Do Incentives Matter" published as a supplement to the 1990 *Industrial and Labor Relations Review*.

[8] Research relying on proprietary data from compensation consulting include Abowd (1990), Leonard (1990), Holthausen et al. (1995), Bushman et al. (1996), and Murphy (1998).

based on an analysis of corporate proxy statements, and a proprietary survey of bonus plans in 177 large companies conducted by Towers Perrin in 1996. In addition, I report international comparisons of executive pay practices based on Towers Perrin's 1997 *Worldwide Total Remuneration* survey. An emerging lesson from the analyses is that it matters *where* you look and *when* you look: there is a great deal of heterogeneity in pay practices across firms, industries, and countries, and there have been dramatic shifts in pay practices across time.

Section 2 analyzes the level and structure of executive compensation packages, and serves as a primer on executive compensation. Most executive pay packages contain four basic components: a base salary, an annual bonus tied to accounting performance, stock options, and longterm incentive plans (including restricted stock plans and multi-year accounting-based performance plans). I begin this section with a descriptive analysis of how the level and composition of CEO pay in the US varies across industries and with company size, and document the substantial increases in CEO pay between 1992 and 1996. Next, I discuss the emerging international evidence on executive compensation, contrasting US pay practices with those in other countries. Then, I consider each component of pay in detail, describing how salaries are set, how annual and multi-year bonus arrangements are structured, and how stock options are awarded and valued. Particular attention is devoted to describing the performance measures, performance standards, and pay–performance structures used in annual incentive plans. Finally, I analyze the relative influence of the board of directors, the compensation committee, and managers in determining executive pay practices.

Section 3 explores the relation between CEO pay and performance. The section begins with a summary and critique of the traditional principal-agent framework as applied to executive incentive contracts. Next, I summarize the empirical evidence on the relation between pay and performance, distinguishing between *explicit* aspects (CEO pay is explicitly related to accounting returns through annual bonuses, and to stock-price appreciation through stock options and restricted stock) and *implicit* aspects (CEO pay may be implicitly tied to performance through year-to-year adjustments in salary levels, target bonuses, and option and restricted stock grant sizes). I show that total pay–performance sensitivities vary with industry and company size, and document changes in the sensitivities from 1992 to 1996 driven primarily by increases in stock-options incentives. I also analyze CEO stock ownership from 1987 to 1996, documenting that CEO stock holdings *excluding options* have increased in dollar-value but decreased when expressed as a percentage of the company's outstanding stock. I then consider the theory and evidence related to *relative performance evaluation* (RPE) for top executives: I document the explicit use of RPE in accounting-based bonus plans, and discuss the virtual absence of RPE in stock option plans. Finally, I describe the evidence on the effect of CEO pay–performance sensitivities on subsequent company performance.

Section 4 considers executive turnover and its relation to company performance. Casual empiricism, based on several recent highly publicized forced resignations, suggests that CEO firings have become more commonplace in the 1990s. However, I document that the

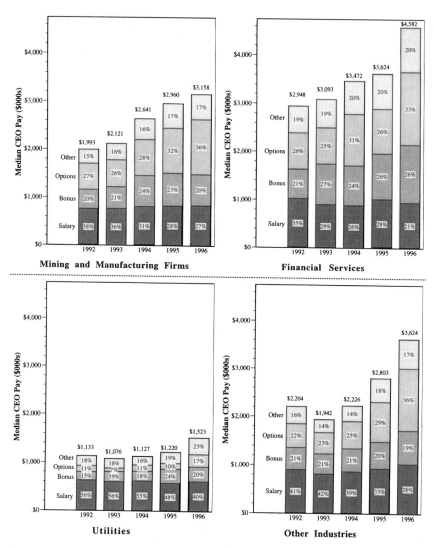

Fig. 2. Level and composition of total CEO compensation, by industry, 1992–1996. (a) Mining and manufacturing firms; (b) financial services; (c) utilities; (d) other industries. Sample includes all companies in the S&P 500, based on ExecuComp data. Pay component percentages are derived by computing the percentages for each CEO, and averaging across CEOs; the bar height depicts median compensation. Options are valued at grant date using ExecuComp's modified Black–Scholes formula. Other pay includes restricted stock (valued at face value), payouts from longterm incentive plans, and miscellaneous other compensation. Mining/manufacturing include firms with two-digit SIC codes 10–29; financial services 60–69, and utilities 49.

link between turnover and performance has declined rather than increased over the past decade. In addition, I present results suggesting that turnover is driven by executive age and not performance in the largest firms, and by performance and not (primarily) executive age in smaller firms. Finally, I document that CEOs have become less likely to depart at "normal" retirement ages, and show (following Huson et al., 1998) that companies are increasingly likely to replace CEOs through outside hires rather than through internal promotions.

Section 5 considers the politics of pay. Public disclosure of executive pay virtually guarantees that third parties such as rank-and-file employees, labor unions, consumer groups, Congress, and the media affect the type of contracts written between management and shareholders. In this section, I analyze the causes and consequences of the ongoing controversy over CEO pay, and describe the effect of politics and public perception in determining the structure and level of executive compensation.

Section 6 summarizes the emerging stylized facts, and provides some suggestions for future research in executive compensation. Although the field is fairly well-developed, researchers have just begun exploring recently available public and proprietary datasets and exploring the institutional details and the explicit features of executive contracts. The richness of the compensation and performance data offers many unexploited opportunities for research in labor economics, finance, accounting, and management.

2. The level and structure of executive compensation

2.1. Introduction

Although there is substantial heterogeneity in pay practices across firms and industries, most executive pay packages contain four basic components: a base salary, an annual bonus tied to accounting performance, stock options, and longterm incentive plans (including restricted stock plans and multi-year accounting-based performance plans). In addition, executives participate in "broad-based" employee benefit plans and also receive special benefits, including life insurance and supplemental executive retirement plans (SERPs). In contrast to mid-level management "employment at will" arrangements, top executives increasingly negotiate formal employment contracts. These formal contracts typically last five years and specify minimum base salaries, target bonus payments (with or without guarantees), and severance arrangements in the event of separation or change in corporate control.

Fig. 2 illustrates the relative importance of the various components of compensation for CEOs in the S&P 500, and also documents how the level and composition of pay varies across years for four industry groups: mining & manufacturing (two-digit SIC codes 10–29); financial services (SIC 60–69); utilities (SIC 49), and other industries (including wholesale and retail trade, and service industries). The bar height in each panel depicts median total compensation in 1996-constant dollars, including salaries, realized bonuses,

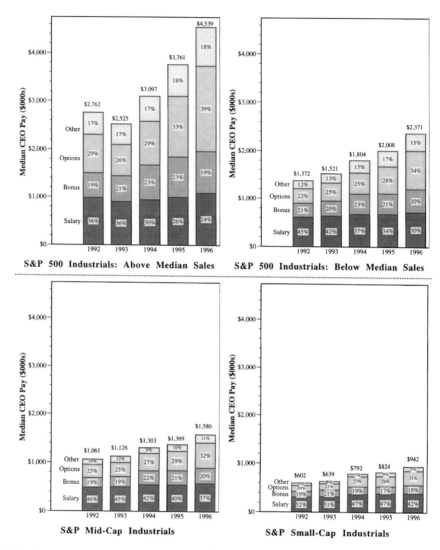

Fig. 3. Level and composition of total CEO compensation, by company size, 1992–1996. (a) S&P 500 industrials: above median sales; (b) S&P 500 industrials: below median sales; (c) S&P mid-cap industrials; (d) S&P small-cap industrials. Sample, based on ExecuComp data, excludes financial service firms and utilities. Pay component percentages are derived by computing the percentages for each CEO, and averaging across CEOs; the bar height depicts median compensation. Options are valued at grant date using ExecuComp's modified Black–Scholes formula. Other pay includes restricted stock (valued at face value), payouts from longterm incentive plans, and miscellaneous other compensation.

the grant-date value of options granted during the year (using ExecuComp's "modified" Black–Scholes formula; see the Appendix), restricted stock grants (valued at grant-date face value), payouts from accounting-based longterm incentive plans, and miscellaneous other compensation. Pay component percentages are derived from ExecuComp data by computing the percentages for each CEO, and averaging across CEOs.

Several stylized facts emerge from Fig. 2. First, pay levels vary by industry: CEOs in electric utilities earn significantly lower levels of compensation than their counterparts in other industries, while CEOs in financial services companies earn higher pay.[9] Second, the level of compensation has increased substantially between 1992 and 1996: median pay levels (in 1996 constant dollars) for manufacturing CEOs, for example, have increased 55% from $2.0 million in 1992 to almost $3.2 million in 1996. Over the same time period, median pay in financial services has increased 53% to $4.6 million, while pay in utilities has increased 34% to $1.5 million. Third, the increase in pay is largely attributable to increases in the grant-date value of stock option grants.[10] During the early 1990s, stock options replaced base salaries as the single largest component of compensation (in all sectors except utilities). Option grants in manufacturing firms swelled from 27 to 36% of total compensation, more than doubling in dollar terms.

Fig. 3 depicts the effect of company size on firm pay for industrial companies (defined as all companies except utilities and financial services). The figure shows pay trends for CEOs in four size categories: the S&P 500 industrials with above-median sales, S&P 500 industrials with below-median sales, S&P 400 Mid-Cap Industrials, and S&P 600 Small-Cap Industrials. Fig. 3 shows that the increase in option compensation and the increase in total compensation holds across size groups. Moreover, the figure illustrates the best-documented stylized fact regarding CEO pay: CEO pay is higher in larger firms.

It is not surprising that compensation increases with company size; larger firms, for example, may employ better-qualified and better-paid managers (Rosen, 1982; Kostiuk, 1990). More surprising, at least historically, has been the consistency of the relation across firms and industries. Baker et al. (1988) summarize Conference Board data on the relation between CEO cash compensation and firm sales from 1973 to 1983 and document pay-sales elasticities in the 0.25–0.35 range, implying that a firm that is 10% larger will pay its CEO about 3% more. Rosen (1992) summarizes academic research covering a variety of industries and a variety of time periods in both the US and the UK, concluding that the "relative uniformity [of estimates] across firms, industries, countries, and periods of time is notable and puzzling because the technology that sustains control and scale should vary across these disparate units of comparison."

Recent data suggest that the relation between CEO pay and company size has weakened

[9] See, for example, Carroll and Ciscel (1982), Murphy (1987), and Joskow et al. (1996) on executive compensation in electric utilities. Barro and Barro (1990), Crawford et al. (1995) and Hubbard and Palia (1995) analyze pay practices in banking; the latter two studies document increases in CEO pay in banking in the late 1980s and early 1990s (relative to pay in other industries) which the authors attribute to deregulation.

[10] Hall and Liebman (1998) show that the increase in option compensation has increased monotonically since the early 1980s.

Table 1

Estimated elasticity of CEO salary and bonus with respect to firm revenues, 1970–1996[a]

Industry	Year						
	1970–1974	1975–1979	1980–1984	1985–1989	1990–1994	1995–1996
Mining & Manufacturing	0.246 [0.37]	0.251 [0.40]	0.222 [0.30]	0.225 [0.24]	0.263 [0.30]	0.323 [0.18]
Financial Services	0.299 [0.48]	0.293 [0.48]	0.262 [0.42]	0.269 [0.28]	0.091 [0.02]	0.220 [0.08]
Utilities	0.344 [0.33]	0.341 [0.29]	0.283 [0.17]	0.234 [0.11]	0.219 [0.16]	0.211 [0.13]
Other	0.244 [0.33]	0.191 [0.23]	0.150 [0.15]	0.130 [0.06]	0.186 [0.10]	0.198 [0.11]

[a] Note: R^2 in brackets. Elasticities computed from regressions of Log(Salary & Bonus) on Log(Sales) for S&P 500 companies.

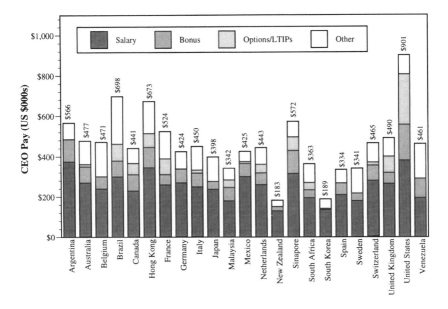

Fig. 4. International comparison of 1997 CEO pay levels and structures. Data from Towers Perrin's *1997 Worldwide Total Remuneration* report, used with permission. Data reflects Towers Perrin's estimate of competitive CEO pay as of April 1997 for industrial companies with approximately US $250 million in annual revenues. Local currency amounts are converted into US dollars using April 1997 exchange rates. Salaries are defined as base salary plus other regular payments (such as vacation pay, 13th-month pay, and regular bonuses unrelated to performance); bonuses include target performance-based cash awards. Options/LTIPs includes the grant-date expected value of option grants and annualized targets from longterm incentive plans. Other Compensation includes both voluntary and compulsory company contributions and the value of perquisites.

over time. Table 1 shows the elasticity of CEO cash compensation to company revenues for S&P 500 CEOs, by industry group, for 5-year periods beginning in 1970 and for the period 1995–1996. Pay/sales elasticities for manufacturing firms ranged between 0.22 and 0.26 until the mid-1990s, when the elasticity jumped to 0.32. Elasticities in financial services firms dropped from 0.30 in the 1970s to only 0.09 in the early 1990s (rebounding to 0.22 in 1995–1996); elasticities in utilities have similarly declined. Moreover, as suggested by the bracketed R-squares in Table 1, the "explanatory power" of firm sales has declined over time in all industries.

2.2. International comparisons

Fig. 4 shows the level and composition of CEO pay in 23 countries, based on data reported in Towers Perrin's *1997 Worldwide Total Remuneration* report. The data depict the consulting company's estimates of "typical" or "competitive" pay for a representative CEO in an industrial company with approximately US $250 million in annual revenues.[11]

This firm size corresponds roughly to US companies in the S&P Small Cap 600, and the level and structure of CEO pay for the US in Fig. 4 is nearly identical to that suggested by Fig. 3.[12] Fig. 4 supports the commonly held view that US executives are paid more than their international counterparts: the total pay for the representative CEO in the US is more than double the average total pay elsewhere. More interestingly, the data show that US executives are paid *differently* than CEOs elsewhere: US CEOs receive a larger fraction of their pay in the form of stock options, and a lower fraction in the form of salaries, than any of their global counterparts. Indeed, stock options (and other longterm incentives) are absent in nine of the 23 countries surveyed, and comprise less than 5% of total pay in 13 of the 23 countries.

There is a growing interest from researchers (as well as practitioners) on the level and structure of executive compensation outside the United States, including the United Kingdom (Cosh, 1975; Main et al., 1994; Conyon et al., 1995; Conyon, 1997; Cosh and Hughes, 1997), Japan (Kato and Rockel, 1992; Kaplan, 1994a, 1997; Kato, 1997), Germany (Kaplan, 1994b, 1997), Canada (Zhou, 1999), Spain (Angel and Fumás, 1997), Italy (Brunello et al., 1999), Denmark (Eriksson and Lausten, 1996), China (Groves et al., 1995) and Bulgaria (Jones and Kato, 1996). Although many of the country-specific studies attempt international comparisons (for example, Conyon and Schwalbach, 1997, contrast pay practices within ten European countries), such comparisons are made difficult by substantial heterogeneity in (1) available data; (2) regression specifications (including definitions of the dependent and independent variables); and (3) institutional details such as tax and exchange rates, and restrictions on insider trading.[13]

The most comprehensive international comparison to date in the academic literature is Abowd and Bognanno (1995), who use data from four international consulting firms to analyze 1984–1992 pay in 12 OECD countries (Belgium, Canada, France, Germany, Italy, Japan, the Netherlands, Spain, Sweden, Switzerland, the UK, and the US). They adjust for tax rates (on both direct pay and perquisites), purchasing power, and public benefits, and find that pay for US CEOs exceeds pay in other countries even after adjusting for these differences. Interestingly, they find that the "US premium" is limited to the CEO: there is no significant difference between US vs. international pay practices for lower-level executives and production workers.

Although our understanding of international differences in executive compensation practices is far from complete, several results emerge from the existing research. First,

---

[11] In conducting this survey, Towers Perrin asked executive pay consultants in each of the 23 countries represented in Fig. 4 to use local-market conditions to formulate competitive pay recommendations for a hypothetical CEO in a $250 million industrial company, as of April 1, 1997. Survey responses in local currencies are converted into US dollars using April 1977 exchange rates.

[12] In particular, the median CEO in the S&P Small-Cap 600 (Fig. 3) has total 1996 compensation of $898,000, comprised of salaries (44%), bonuses (18%), options (30%), and other (9%). In comparison, the representative CEO in Fig. 4 has total compensation of $901,000, comprised of salaries (42%), bonuses (20%), options (28%), and other (10%).

[13] See Hebner and Kato (1997) for US vs. Japan comparison of the insider-trading component of executive compensation.

the elasticity of cash compensation to company size is remarkably constant across countries: Zhou (1999), for example, reports pay-size elasticities for the US, Japan, the UK, and Canada of 0.282, 0.247, 0.261, and 0.247, respectively. Second, the elasticity of cash compensation to stock-price performance, and the relation between CEO turnover and performance is roughly comparable in the US, Japan, and Germany (Kang and Shivdasani, 1995; Kaplan, 1994a,b, 1997). Third, stock-based incentives from stock options and stock ownership are much higher in the US than in other countries (Abowd and Bognanno, 1995; Kaplan, 1997).

A final, but more speculative, result emerging from the existing data is that pay levels and structures are converging, reflecting an increasingly global market for managerial talent. Canadian and Mexican companies, for example, routinely now include US companies in peer groups used to determine competitive pay levels. US companies routinely export pay practices (including stock option grants) to executives of foreign subsidiaries, putting pressure on the pay policies of local competitors. And, foreign companies acquiring US subsidiaries face huge internal pay inequities, often resolved by increasing home-country executive pay. In addition, legal prohibitions on granting executive stock options in Japan were lifted in April 1997, resulting in (or from) a swell of interest in US-style compensation;[14] interest in stock options is exploding elsewhere in the Pacific Rim and in Europe and Latin America.[15]

2.3. The components of CEO pay

2.3.1. Base salaries
Base salaries for CEOs are typically determined through competitive "benchmarking," based primarily on general industry salary surveys (except for utilities and financial institutions, which utilize industry-specific surveys), and supplemented by detailed analyses of selected industry or market peers. The surveys, which report a variety of pay percentiles (e.g., 25th, 50th, 75th), typically adjust for company size either through size groupings or through simple log-linear regressions of Log(Salary) on Log(Size). Size is traditionally measured using company revenues, although market capitalization is increasingly used (especially in start-ups with low revenues but high capitalization).

The near-universal use of surveys in determining base salaries has several implications relevant to understanding levels and trends in CEO compensation. First, as suggested by Baker et al. (1988) and Rosen (1992), the size adjustments in the survey instruments both formalize and reinforce the observed relation between compensation and company size. Second, since salaries below the 50th percentile are often labeled "below market" while

---

[14] Pressures to repeal the prohibition reflected, in part, perceptions in Japan that stock-based incentives in the US have contributed to its relatively robust stock-market performance. Ironically, as recently in 1991, trade negotiations between the US and Japan dissolved into accusations that US competitiveness was hindered by its "excessive" executive compensation practices (Murphy, 1995).

[15] A notable exception is the UK, where stock option (or "share option") plans have declined in favor of performance share plans payable, in part, based on *relative* stock-market performance.

those between the 50th and 75th are considered "competitive," the surveys have contributed to a "ratchet" effect in base salary levels. Third, while the surveys adjust for company size and (less frequently) industry, they do not contain criteria many labor economists consider relevant for predicting earnings levels, including age, experience, education, and performance. Moreover, company size is at best an imperfect proxy for managerial skill requirements, job complexity, and span of control. Thus, to the extent that base salaries reflect any of these potentially important variables, they are reflected in discretionary adjustments in the target percentiles rather than incorporated as formal criteria.

Executives devote substantial attention to the salary-determination process, even though salaries comprise a declining percentage of total compensation. First, base salaries are a key component of executive employment contracts (which typically guarantee minimum increases in base salaries for the subsequent 5 years). Second, since base salaries represent the "fixed component" in executive contracts, risk-averse executives will naturally prefer a dollar increase in base salary to a dollar increase in "target" bonus or variable compensation.[16] Finally, most components of compensation are measured relative to base salary levels. Target bonuses, for example, are typically expressed as a percentage of base salary, while option grants are expressed as a multiple of base salary. Defined pension benefits and severance arrangements also depend on salary levels. Consequently, each dollar increase in base salary has positive repercussions on many other compensation components.

2.3.2. Annual bonus plans

Virtually every for-profit company offers an annual bonus plan covering its top executives and paid annually based on a single-year's performance. In spite of their prevalence and importance, however, most descriptions of executive bonus plans in the literature are anecdotal, non-representative, or gleaned from voluntary (and non-random) disclosures in company proxy statements. In this section, I offer a systematic description of bonus plans, based on what I believe to be the most comprehensive data on annual incentive plans available.

My primary data source on bonus plan design is the "Annual Incentive Plan Design Survey" conducted in 1996–1997 by Towers Perrin. The Towers Perrin survey, based on responses to an extensive questionnaire augmented by an analysis of company plan documents, contains detailed data on 264 annual incentive plans for top-level managers. Excluding private companies, foreign companies, and subsidiaries, and eliminating companies with incomplete data, results in a sample of bonus plans from 177 publicly traded US corporations.[17] The number of eligible participants in the sample plans varies

---

[16] For example, "exchange" programs in which executives accept a salary reduction in return for restricted stock or stock options typically include premiums of 20–30% for restricted stock and 100–200% for stock options, reflecting the increased riskiness of the stock-based instruments.

[17] See Murphy (1998) for a more detailed description of this database, including a list of survey participants.

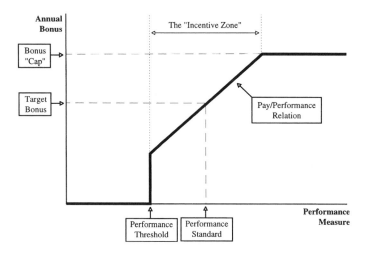

Fig. 5. Components of a "typical" annual incentive plan.

from 1 to 25,000 (the median plan has 123 participants); coverage ranges from plans covering only the CEO to plans covering all company employees.

In spite of substantial heterogeneity across companies and industries, executive bonus plans can be categorized in terms of three basic components: performance measures, performance standards, and the structure of the pay–performance relation. Fig. 5 illustrates these basic components for a "typical" bonus plan. Under the typical plan, no bonus is paid until a threshold performance (usually expressed as a percentage of the performance standard) is achieved, and a "minimum bonus" (usually expressed as a percentage of the target bonus) is paid at the threshold performance. Target bonuses are paid for achieving the performance standard, and there is typically a "cap" on bonuses paid (again expressed as a percentage or multiple of the target bonus). The range between the threshold and cap is labeled the "incentive zone," indicating the range of performance realizations where incremental improvement in performance corresponds to incremental improvement in bonuses.

One result that emerges from the descriptive analysis below is that annual bonus contracts are largely explicit, with at most a limited role for discretion. Discretion in annual bonuses shows up in a variety of possible ways. In some firms, boards can exercise discretion in allocating a fixed bonus pool among participating executives, but the discretion in this case affects only individual allocations and not the overall amount of the payouts. In addition, the CEO (and other executives) will have some portion of their bonus depend on "individual performance." Although there is a subjective flavor here, individual performance often includes performance relative to some pre-determined objectives or strategic milestones; in any case, the weight on individual performance rarely exceeds about 25% of the executive's bonus. Finally, boards can also make discretionary "adjustments" to reported earning numbers.[18] In almost all cases, board-level discretion can generate small adjustments in bonus payments, but discretion is rarely the primary determinant.

2.3.2.1. Performance measures   Table 2 describes the performance measures used in the 177 annual incentive plans for companies divided into three industry groups: utilities (SIC 4900–4999), financial companies (SIC 6000–6999), and industrials (all other SIC categories). Less than half of the companies use a single performance measure in their incentive plan; most companies use two or more measures. In most cases, the multiple measures are "additive" and can essentially be treated like separate plans.[19] In other cases, the measures are multiplicative, in which the bonus paid on one performance measure might be increased or diminished depending on the realization of another measure.[20] In still other cases, bonus payments are determined by a "matrix" of performance measures.

While companies use a variety of financial and non-financial performance measures, almost all companies rely on some measure of accounting profits. Table 2 shows that 65 of the 68 sample companies using a single performance measure use an accounting measure, including revenues, net income, pre-tax income, operating profits (EBIT), or economic value added.[21] Accounting profits also account for 189 of the 307 measures (62%) used by companies with multiple measures. In fact, 161 of the 177 sample firms (91%) explicitly use at least one measure of accounting profits in their annual bonus plans.[22] As reported in the bottom panel, although bonuses often depend on the dollar-value of profits, they also frequently depend on profits measured on a per-share basis (e.g., earnings per share, EPS) or as a margin or return (e.g., income/sales, return on assets, return on equity). In addition, performance measures are often expressed as growth rates (e.g., EPS growth).

The most common non-financial performance measure used in annual incentive plans is "Individual Performance," which includes performance measured relative to pre-established objectives as well as subjective assessments of individual performance. Other common non-financial measures include customer satisfaction, operational and/or strategic objectives (such as increasing plant capacity, bringing a new computer system on line by a particular date, reducing time-to-market, etc.) and measures of plant safety. Financial institutions are less likely to use non-financial measures than industrial firms, while utilities more often utilize non-financial performance measures.

---

[18] Dechow et al. (1994), for example, show that boards seem to take "restructuring charges" out of payouts.

[19] An example of additive measures is a plan in which 75% of the bonus is based on net income and 25% is based on sales growth, with a separate schedule relating bonus payments to each performance measure.

[20] An example here would be a bonus pool equal to 5% of income if stock-price performance exceeds a median performance in a peer group, but only 3% if stock-price performance falls short of median.

[21] The distribution of performance measures is consistent with that reported by Perry and Zenner (1997), who extracted measures from the compensation committee reports in recent proxy statements.

[22] Bonuses are largely discretionary in the other 16 firms, but may of course be implicitly tied to accounting profits through the board's subjective assessment of performance. In addition, I categorized companies using "balanced scorecards" (Kaplan and Norton, 1992) as discretionary, even though all scorecards include at least one financial performance measure.

Table 2
Performance measures used in annual incentive plans in 177 large US corporations[a]

	Industrials (n = 125)	Finance & Insurance (n = 21)	Utilities (n = 31)
Firms with a single performance measure	50	11	7

Performance measures (number of firms)

Measure	Industrials	Finance & Insurance	Utilities
Earnings[b]	(32)	(8)	(6)
EBIT[c]	(7)	(2)	
EVA[d]	(5)		(1)
Discretionary	(2)	(1)	
Individual performance	(2)		
Other financial	(2)		

	Industrials	Finance & Insurance	Utilities
Firms with two or more performance measures	75	10	24
Are measures additive?	Yes = 83%	Yes = 70%	Yes = 67%

Performance measures (number of firms)

Measure	Industrials	Finance & Insurance	Utilities
Earnings[b]	(80)	(19)	(23)
EBIT[c]	(32)		(6)
Individual performance	(25)	(3)	(2)
Sales	(21)	(1)	(3)
Customer satisfaction	(6)		(6)
Strategic Goals	(5)		(3)
Stock price	(5)		(2)
Discretionary	(4)		
Op. objective(s)	(4)	(1)	(7)
EVA[d]	(3)		(1)
Costs			(9)
Safety			(3)
Other: Financial	(11)	(1)	(3)
Other: Non-financial	(13)	(0)	(5)

Table 2 (continued)

	Industrials (n = 125)		Finance & Insurance (n = 21)		Utilities (n = 31)	
Is accounting performance measured in absolute dollars, expressed as a return (e.g., ROE),	Dollar value	44%	Dollar value	19%	Dollar value	22%
	Margin/return	20%	Margin/return	52%	Margin/return	32%
	Per share	19%	Per share	26%	Per share	34%
measured per-share (e.g., EPS), and/or measured	Growth rates		Growth rates		Growth rates	
	Dollar value	10%	Dollar value	4%	Dollar value	5%
as the growth or change	Margin/return	1%				
from prior year?	Per share	6%			Per share	5%

[a] Source: Data extracted from Towers Perrin's *Annual Incentive Plan Design Survey*, 1997.

[b] Earnings includes net income, pre-tax net income, and returns on assets, equity, and capital.

[c] Earnings before interest and taxes (EBIT) includes operating income, EBITDA, and other cash flow measures.

[d] EVA generally equals a measure of operating income less a charge for capital.

Table 3
Performance standards used in annual incentive plans in 177 large US corporations[a]

	Industrials (n = 125)		Finance & insurance (n = 21)		Utilities (n = 31)	
Performance standards based on a single criterion						
Number of earnings-based measures	164		24		23	
Performance standards (% of measures)	Budget (%)	54	Budget (%)	38	Budget (%)	35
	Prior-year	14	Prior-year	8	Prior-year	9
	Discretionary	8	Discretionary	4	Discretionary	30
	Peer group	14	Peer group	46	Peer group	26
	Timeless standard	4	Timeless standard	4	Timeless standard	0
	Cost of capital	6	Cost of capital	0	Cost of capital	0
Performance standards based on multiple criteria						
Number of earnings-based measures	76		15		23	
Performance standards (% of measures)	Budget (%)	70	Budget (%)	87	Budget (%)	70
	Prior-year	66	Prior-year	47	Prior-year	48
	Discretionary	59	Discretionary	47	Discretionary	74
	Ext. peer group	16	Ext. peer group	53	Ext. peer group	17
	Timeless standard	9	Timeless standard	0	Timeless standard	9
	Cost of capital	7	Cost of capital	0	Cost of capital	9

[a] Source: Data extracted from Towers Perrin's *Annual Incentive Plan Design Survey*, 1997. Earnings-based measures include sales, operating income, EVA, cash flow, EBIT, pre-tax income, and net income.

2.3.2.2. Performance standards Table 3 describes the how performance standards are determined for each accounting-based performance measure in Table 2. For each performance measure used in the plan, respondents were asked which of several categories best describe the performance-standard determination process. "Budget" standards include plans based on performance measured against the company's business plann or budget goals (such as a budgeted-net-earnings objective). "Prior-Year" standards include plans based on year-to-year growth or improvement (such as growth in sales or EPS, or improvement in operating profits). "Discretionary" standards include plans where the performance targets are set subjectively by the board of directors following a review of the company's business plan, prior-year performance, budgeted performance, or a subjective evaluation of the difficulty in achieving budgeted performance. "Peer Group" standards include plans based on performance measured relative to other companies in the industry or market (often a self-selected group of peer companies; see Section 3.7). "Timeless Standards" include plans measuring performance relative to a fixed standard (such as an 10% return on assets, where the "10%" is constant across years, or moves in a predetermined way independent of actual performance). Finally, "Cost of Capital" refers to performance standards based on the company's cost of capital (such as a plan based on economic value added (EVA)).

Respondents could "check" as many categories as relevant, and could also write-in additional categories (although no respondents did so). In addition to these six survey responses, I inferred performance standards in two cases. First, when the performance measure in the plan was specified as a growth measure, I define the standard as prior-year performance. Second, when the performance measure is EVA, I define the standard as the company's cost of capital.

Most performance standards for accounting-profit performance measures are based on a single criterion. For example, as reported in Table 3, the 125 industrial companies in the sample use a total of 240 accounting-based measures. The performance standards for 164 (68%) of these measures are based on a single criteria, including budgets (54%), prior-year performance (14%), board discretion (8%), peer-group comparisons (14%), timeless standards (4%), and cost of capital (6%). The performance standards for the remaining 76 measures are based on a combination of criteria, including budgets (70%), prior-year performance (66%), board discretion (59%), peer-group comparisons (16%), timeless standards (9%), and cost of capital (7%). The percentages here sum to 227%, implying that, conditional on using multiple criteria, an average of 2.3 criteria are used in setting performance standards.

2.3.2.3. Pay–performance structures Payouts from bonus plans are determined in a variety of different ways; the top panel of Table 4 documents the prevalence of various payout methods. The most common payout method (for all but financial companies) is the "80/120" plan illustrated in Fig. 5. Under a strict 80/120 plan, no bonus is paid unless performance exceeds 80% of the performance standard, and bonuses are capped once performance exceeds 120% of the performance standard. Although 80 and 120 are the modal choice for the performance threshold and performance cap, other common combinations (in descending order of frequency) include 90/110, 95/100, 50/150, 80/110, 90/120, and 80/140 plans. For lack of a better descriptor (and consistent with industry jargon), I call all these plans "80/120" plans regardless of the specific values for threshold and caps. As reported in Table 4, 42% of industrial companies and 39% of utility companies adopt 80/120-type bonus plans. Overall, 67 of the 177 (38%) sample firms report using the 80–120 approach.

The next most common type of plan, used by 55 of the 177 (31%) sample firms, is called the "Modified Sum-of-Targets" approach. Under this method, each plan participant is assigned a target bonus, and the sum of the target bonuses across individual participants defines a target bonus pool. At year-end, the actual bonus pool is determined by modifying the target pool up or down depending on whether actual performance exceeds or falls short

Table 4
Pay–performance relations in annual incentive plans in 177 large US corporations[a]

	Industrials (n = 125) (%)	Finance & insurance (n = 21) (%)	Utilities (n = 31) (%)
Type of payouts			
80/120 plans[b]	42	14	39
Formula-based pool[c]	10	14	
Modified "sum-of-targets"[d]	29	43	32
Discretionary pool[e]	5	10	3
Other	15	19	26
Shape of payouts in "incentive zone"			
Convex	27	14	13
Linear	16	38	16
Concave	15	10	23
Mixture (2 + measures)	9		3
Discretionary/other	33	38	45
Bonus paid at "threshold" performance?			
Yes	56	48	58
No	14		7
Discretionary/other	30	52	36
Bonus capped?			
Yes	87	81	90
No	13	19	10

[a] Source: Data extracted from Towers Perrin's *Annual Incentive Plan Design Survey*, 1997. Payout-shapes based on earnings-based performance measures, including sales, operating income, EVA, cash flow, EBIT, pre-tax income, and net income.

[b] Plan depicted in Fig. 5 in which threshold performance is defined in terms of some percentage (typically 80%) of target performance, and the bonus cap is reached at some higher percentage (typically 120%) of target performance.

[c] A typical formula-based pool is "5% of Net Income in excess of 12% Return on Equity." Once determined, the pool is allocated to individuals based on formula and/or discretion.

[d] The bonus pool under a "sum-of-targets" approach equals the sum of each participant's target bonus, modified up or down depending on company performance. The pool is then allocated to individuals based either on formula or discretion.

[e] Under a typical discretionary pool, top managers and the compensation committee review a variety of year-end performance measures, and subjectively determine the magnitude of the bonus.

of the performance standard. The pool is set to zero unless threshold performance is reached, and the pool is capped (typically at some multiple of the summed target bonuses). The bonus pool is typically divided among participants based on their individual target bonuses, although some portion of the pool may fund discretionary awards to recognize individual performance. Although mechanically different from 80/120 plans, the payout schedule from the sum-of-targets approach is qualitatively identical to that under the 80/120 approach and is therefore captured by the illustrative plan in Fig. 5. These two payout methods account for about 70% of the plans in the sample.

The remaining payout methods include formula-based plans (accounting for only 16 of the 177 of the sample plans) and discretionary plans (8 of 177). The typical formula-based plan determines a bonus pool which is allocated to individuals based on a combination of target bonuses and individual performance. Under the typical discretionary plan, the board meets at year-end to assess subjectively the organization's (or an individual's) performance based on a variety of financial and non-financial criteria, and determines the magnitude of the company's bonus pool.

Although the pay–performance relation depicted in Fig. 5 is linear between the threshold and cap, the second panel of Table 4 shows that the incentive zone is more often convex in industrials and concave in utilities. Table 4 also shows that 56% of the general industry sample firms pay positive bonuses at the threshold, while only 14% pay zero bonuses (the remaining firms have discretionary thresholds and indeterminate payouts at threshold). Finally, consistent with the illustration in Fig. 5, payout plans are capped in 154 of the 177 sample firms (87%). As shown in Table 4, plans in the financial sector are slightly less likely to be capped than in utilities and in industrials.

2.3.2.4. Incentive implications Although virtually all annual bonus plans provide incentives to increase company profits, plans such as that illustrated in Fig. 5 suggest a plethora of additional incentives, most conflicting with stated company objectives.

Incentive effects of performance measures. As documented in Table 2, the primary determinant of executive bonuses is accounting profits. Accounting data are verifiable and widely understood, and pass what practitioners call the "line of sight" criteria for acceptable performance measures: managers understand and can "see" how their day-to-day actions affect year-end profitability. However, it is important to note two fundamental problems with all accounting measures. First, accounting profits are inherently backward-looking and short-run, and managers focused only on accounting profits may avoid actions that reduce current profitability but increase future profitability, such as cutting R&D (Dechow and Sloan, 1991). Second, accounting profits can be manipulated, either through discretionary adjustments in "accruals" or by shifting earnings across periods (Healy, 1985).

Incentive effects of performance standards. Table 3 shows that performance standards are typically based on budgets and/or prior-year performance, and often allow for some board-level discretion. Performance standards cause problems whenever the employees measured relative to the standard have influence over the standard-setting process. Standards based on budgets and prior-year performance are particularly susceptible to this problem. Budget-based performance standards, for example, create incentives to "sandbag" the budget process and to avoid actions this year that might have an undesirable effect on next year's budget. Similarly, standards based on prior-year performance lead to the "ratchet effect" and shirking, since managers know that good current performance will be penalized in the next period through an increased performance standard. In contrast, timeless standards, standards based on the cost of capital, and standards based on the performance of an industry peer group are not as easily influenced by the participants in the bonus plan. However, even these standards are influenced to some degree, such as when the timeless standards are initially set or the external peer group initially defined. In Murphy (1998), I analyze the role of performance standards in more detail, and show that CEOs in companies using "externally determined" standards have more highly variable bonuses than CEOs in companies with "internally determined" standards. In addition, I show that income smoothing is prevalent in companies using internal standards, but not in companies using external standards.

Incentive effects of pay–performance structures. As suggested by Fig. 5 and documented in Table 4, the "incentive zone" in most annual incentive plans consists of a fairly narrow band of performance outcomes straddling the performance standard. Since bonuses are based on cumulative annual performance, and since managers can revise their daily effort and investment decisions based on assessments of year-to-date performance, the non-linearities in the typical bonus plan causes predictable incentive problems (Holmstrom and Milgrom, 1987). In particular, if year-to-date performance suggests that annual performance will exceed that required to achieve the bonus cap, managers will withhold effort and will attempt to "inventory" earnings for use in a subsequent year (Healy, 1985). Similarly, if expected performance is far *below* the incentive zone, managers will again discount the bonus opportunity, especially near the end of the year when achieving the threshold performance level seems highly unlikely. When expected performance is moderately below the incentive zone, the discontinuity in bonus payments at threshold yields strong incentives to achieve the performance threshold (through counterproductive earnings manipulation as well as through hard work), because the pay–performance slope at the threshold is effectively infinite.[23]

2.3.3. Stock options

Stock options are contracts which give the recipient the right to buy a share of stock at a pre-specified "exercise" (or "strike") price for a pre-specified term. Executive options typically become "vested" (i.e., exercisable) over time: for example, 25% might become

---

[23] Healy (1985) assumed that bonuses were continuous at the performance threshold, and hypothesized that managers would take discretionary accruals (to shift earnings to a following period) whenever performance fell short of the threshold or exceeded the cap. Later work by Gaver et al. (1995) and Holthausen et al. (1995) confirm that managers manipulate earnings downward when the cap is exceeded, but actually manipulate earnings *upwards* when below the threshold. The authors interpret these findings as rejecting the hypothesis that managers manipulate earnings in response to their bonus plans. However, given that substantial bonuses are paid for meeting the threshold (with zero bonuses paid below the threshold, as in Fig. 5), we expect that managers will manipulate earnings upward as long as there is a realistic chance of achieving the threshold.

exercisable in each of the 4 years following grant. Executive options are non-tradable, and are typically forfeited if the executive leaves the firm before vesting (although "accelerated vesting" is a commonly negotiated severance arrangement, especially following a change in control).

Conceptually, the parameters of an option contract suggest a multitude of design possibilities: for example, exercise prices could be "indexed" to the industry or market, options could be forfeited unless a performance "trigger" is reached, option terms could match the expected executive horizons, etc. In practice, however, there is little cross-sectional variation in granting practices: most options expire in 10 years and are granted with exercise prices equal to the "fair market value" on date of grant. Table 5 documents these regularities, based on the option-grant practices of 1000 large companies in 1992.[24] As reported, less than two thirds (627) of the CEOs in the 1000 sample firms received options in 1992, but many of these 627 CEOs received multiple grants (853 total grants).[25] Five companies canceled and replaced previously granted options subsequent to a large stock-price decline,[26] while 26 companies granted "reload" options (120 total grants) to replace shares used to finance the exercise of existing options.[27] Ignoring these special cases, 618 companies made 728 "regular" option grants to their CEOs during fiscal 1992.

As documented in Panel B of Table 5, the exercise price equals the grant-date fair market value in 95% of the regular option grants. About 3% of the grants were made with exercise prices below the grant-date price ("discount options") while half that many grants had exercise prices above the grant-date price ("premium options"). Out of the 1000 sample firms, only one offered "indexed options" (where the exercise price varies

---

[24] The sample covered in Table 5, described in Murphy (1993, 1996), includes the 1060 largest companies (ranked by 31 December 1992 market capitalization) filing proxy statements between January and September 1993. The sample excludes 42 companies with 1992 initial public offerings, 13 companies where the CEO is paid by another company (usually the parent of a subsidiary), and 5 companies that merged or went bankrupt after December 1992, leaving 1000 companies with fiscal closings from October 1992 through June 1993, with December 1992 market capitalization ranging from $355 million to $75.9 billion (median $1.26 billion).

[25] Of the 373 companies not granting options to the CEO in 1992, 120 made option grants to other proxy-listed executives.

[26] Although "repricing" options through cancellations and reissues has received substantial attention in both the business and academic press (see, as respective examples, Crystal and Foulkes (1988) and Saly (1994)), repricing of executive options has been extremely rare since 1988, driven both by the bull market and increased SEC repricing disclosure requirements. Companies can currently circumvent the punitive disclosure requirements by repricing options for lower-level executives (without triggering disclosure) while issuing new options for senior managers (without canceling existing options).

[27] Reload provisions issue new options to replace shares sold to pay the exercise price of exercised options. The new options are granted at fair market value with a term equal to the remaining term on the option exercised. Since executives often exercise options from several prior grants (all with different remaining terms), reload provisions often result in what appears to be several simultaneous option grants, each with the same exercise price (fair market value) but with a variety of expiration dates. See Hemmer et al. (1998) for an analysis of the valuation and optimal exercise for reload options.

Table 5
Distribution of CEO option grants for 1000 companies in fiscal 1992[a]

Type of option grant	Number of companies[b]	Number of grants
CEO received no options in fiscal 1992	373	
CEO received options in fiscal 1992	627	853
A. Type of option		
Replacement options[c]	5	5
Reload options[d]	26	120
Regular option grants	618	728
B. Exercise prices (regular grants)		
Exercise price is fair market value (FMV)	601	692
"Discount" (exercise price < FMV)	21	22
"Premium" (exercise price > FMV)	6	11
Exercise price increases over time	2	2
Exercise price indexed to market or peers	1	1
C. Term of option (regular grants)		
Term < 5 years	14	14
Term = 5 years	36	41
5 years < term < 10 years	36	41
Term = 10 years	528	602
Term > 10 years	23	27
Term depends on performance	2	2
D. Dividend protection (regular grants)		
Yes	7	8
No	611	720

[a] Data extracted from company proxy statements (see Murphy, 1993, 1995). Fiscal 1992 includes sample firms with fiscal closings from October 1992 to June 1993.

[b] Totals do not add to 1000 because some firms grant options in multiple categories.

[c] Replacement options are previously granted options that are reissued at lower exercise prices following large declines in the company's stock price.

[d] Reload options are new options granted to replace shares used to finance exercise of existing options.

with the return on a market or industry index), while another two firms had exercise prices that grew over time in a predetermined manner.

Panel C of Table 5 shows that about 83% of the grants had 10-year terms, while another 13% had terms less than 10 years and 4% had terms exceeding 10 years (including one grant with no expiration date). Two firms out of the 1000 sample firms had "performance triggered" expiration dates. In one of these, the options were forfeited unless the stock price reached a pre-determined price hurdle *and* performance exceeded the market index within a specified period of time; in the other, the options had a 5-year term unless performance exceeded a pre-determined price hurdle, in which case the term was extended to 10 years.

Stock options reward only stock-price appreciation and not total shareholder return, since the latter includes dividends. As shown in Panel D of Table 5, a handful of companies offer "dividend protection" for executive stock options. Although dividend protection can be accomplished a variety of ways (including decreasing exercise prices when paying dividends or expressing stock prices on a pre-dividend basis), the most common approach is to pay the executive accumulated dividends (plus interest) upon exercise of the underlying options.

Yermack (1995) analyzes the determinants of option grants, and concludes that cross-sectional patterns in grants are not well-explained by agency or financial contracting theory. Kole (1997) analyzes the "vesting schedule" of option grants, distinguishing between the "minimum wait" (the time from the grant-date until *any* options can be exercised) and the "average wait" (the average time until *all* options can be exercised). She finds that both the minimum and average wait times are longer in R&D-intensive firms, and are longer in chemicals, machinery, and producer firms than in metals, food and consumer firm.

2.3.3.1. Incentive implications   Stock options provide a direct link between managerial rewards and share-price appreciation, since the payout from exercising options increases dollar for dollar with increases in the stock price. The incentives from stock options do not, however, mimic the incentives from stock ownership, for several reasons. First, since options reward only stock-price appreciation and not total shareholder returns (which include dividends), executives holding options have incentives to avoid dividends and to favor share repurchases.[28] Second, since the value of options increase with stock-price volatility, executives with options have incentives to engage in riskier investments.[29] Finally, options lose incentive value once the stock price falls sufficiently below the exercise price that the executive perceives little chance of exercising: this "loss of incentives" is a common justification for option repricings following share-price declines.

2.3.3.2. Valuation issues   Most applications of executive stock options in both research and practice require placing a "value" on the options as of the grant date. In constructing such a value, it is important to distinguish between two often-confused but fundamentally

---

[28] Lambert et al. (1989) find that "expected dividends" decrease following the initial adoption of top-management stock option plans. Lewellen et al. (1987) find that dividend payout ratios are negatively (but not significantly) related to CEO stock-based compensation.

[29] DeFusco et al. (1990) find that stock-price volatility increases, and traded bond prices decrease, after the approval of executive stock option plans. Similarly, Agrawal and Mandelker (1987) find that managers of firms whose return volatility is increased by an acquisition have higher option compensation than managers whose volatility declined. Hirshleifer and Suh (1992) argue that option plans (or other plans with "convex" payouts) help mitigate the effects of executive risk aversion by giving managers incentives to adopt rather than avoid risky projects.

different valuation concepts: the cost to the company of granting the option and the value to an executive from receiving the option. In this subsection, I demonstrate that options cost more to shareholders to grant than they are worth to executive-recipients, and should therefore only be granted if the "incentive effect" (i.e., the increased performance created by improved stock-based incentives) exceeds the difference between the company's cost and the executive's value.

The company's "opportunity cost" of an option grant (ignoring, for the moment, the incentive effect) is appropriately measured as the amount an outside investor would pay for the option. The outside investor is generally free to trade or sell the option, and can also take actions (such as short-selling the underlying stock) to hedge away the risk of the option. Company executives, in contrast, cannot trade or sell their options, and are also forbidden from hedging the risks by short-selling company stock. In addition, while outside investors tend to be well-diversified (holding small amounts of stock in a large number of companies), company executives are inherently undiversified, with their physical as well as human capital invested disproportionately in their company. For these reasons, company executives will generally place a much lower value on company stock options than would outside investors.[30]

The best known and most widely utilized method for calculating the company's cost of granting an executive stock option is the Black–Scholes formula, presented and discussed in Appendix A. Black and Scholes (1973) demonstrated that, since investors can hedge, options can be valued as if investors were risk neutral and all assets appreciate at the risk-free rate. Under the risk-neutrality assumption, option values can be estimated by computing the expected value of the option upon exercise (assuming that the expected return on the stock is the risk-free rate), and discounting this expected value to the grant date using the risk-free rate. This risk-neutrality assumption forms the basis of modern option pricing theory and is central to all option pricing models and methodologies, including binomial models, arbitrage pricing models, and Monte Carlo methodologies (Hull, 1993).

In spite of its prevalence in practice, there are many drawbacks to using the Black–Scholes formula in calculating the cost of an executive stock option. First, the Black–Scholes formula assumes constant dividend yields and stock-price volatilities, assumptions which seem sensible for shortterm traded options (usually expiring in 6 months or less) but less sensible for options expiring in a decade. Second, executive stock options are subject to forfeiture if the executive leaves the firm prior to vesting; this probability of forfeiture reduces the cost of granting the option and thus implies that the Black–Scholes formula overstates option values. Finally, the Black–Scholes formula assumes that options can only be exercised at the expiration date, but executive options can be exercised immediately upon vesting, which typically occurs relatively early in the option's term. The opportunity to exercise early has ambiguous implications for the cost of granting

---

[30] However, to the extent that company executives have superior information regarding company prospects and can "time" their option grants accordingly (Yermack, 1997), executives may actually value options higher than would outside investors.

Table 6
Certainty-equivalent values of stock options to undiversified, risk-averse executives[a]

Relative risk aversion	% of wealth in firm	Restricted stock ($)	Discount option ($)	FMV option ($)	Premium option ($)
Stock price ($)		30.00	30.00	30.00	30.00
Exercise price ($)		0	15.00	30.00	60.00
Black–Scholes value ($)		30.00	22.88	17.60	11.12
1.0	50	30.00	22.88	17.60	11.12
1.0	75	27.03	17.46	13.43	6.51
1.0	90	22.90	13.38	7.88	4.43
2.0	50	19.94	12.76	7.80	3.30
2.0	75	14.31	7.42	3.57	1.17
2.0	90	10.73	4.33	1.62	0.45
3.0	50	15.67	8.63	4.28	1.27
3.0	75	10.90	4.31	1.36	0.25
3.0	90	7.84	2.04	0.39	0.05

[a] Note: The certainty equivalent is calculated as the amount of cash the executive would willingly give up to receive one option, assuming constant relative risk aversion and assuming that all stock and options are held for 10 years. Wealth invested in firm is assumed to be divided between (non-dividend-paying) stock and options; wealth invested elsewhere is assumed to grow at the risk-free rate, $r_f = 7\%$. The distribution of stock prices in 10 years is assumed to be lognormal with volatility $\sigma = 0.31$ and expected value $(r_f + \beta(r_m - r_f) - \sigma^2/2)T$, where $T = 10$, $r_m = 13\%$, and $\beta = 1$.

options. On one hand, the right to exercise early increases the amount an outside investor would pay for the option, and hence increases the option's cost. On the other hand, risk-averse undiversified executives tend to exercise much earlier than would a rational outside investor, and these early exercise decisions reduce the company's cost of granting options.[31]

There is no accepted methodology, and little research, on estimating the value of a stock option to an executive-recipient.[32] Intuitively, the valuation will depend on the executive's risk aversion, his or her wealth, the fraction of that wealth invested in company stock, and the likelihood that the executive will remain with the company until the option is vested. Table 6 estimates the "certainty equivalent" value of stock options, calculated as the amount of cash the executive would willingly give up to receive one option, assuming constant relative risk aversion and assuming the option and the rest of his portfolio is held for 10 years. Three options are considered: a discount option with an exercise price of 50% of the grant-date market value, a fair market value (FMV) option, and a premium option with an exercise price of 200% of the grant-date value. In addition, the table estimates the value of a grant of restricted stock, which (ignoring dividends) is equivalent to a stock option with an exercise price of zero.

Table 6 shows how an option's value to the executive-recipient depends on the executive's risk aversion and diversification and on the riskiness of the option. For example, the table shows that a FMV 10-year option on a $30 non-dividend-paying stock has a Black–Scholes value of $17.60. Assuming that the executive holds 50% of his wealth in company securities (equally divided between stock and options), he would be willing to pay the full Black–Scholes value if his risk aversion was low (RRA = 1.0), but would only pay $7.80 and $4.28 for relative risk aversion of 2.0 and 3.0, respectively. Similarly, assuming relative risk aversion of 2.0, the value of a FMV option falls from $7.80 to $3.57 as his stock holdings (as a fraction of his wealth) increase from 50% to 75%, and falls to $1.62 when his stock holdings account for 90% of his wealth.

The risk premium demanded for accepting options in lieu of cash increases with the riskiness of the option, which in turn reflects (in part) the probability that the option will expire unexercised. Suppose, for example, that the executive has relative risk aversion of 2.0 and holds 50% of his wealth in company securities. As reported in Table 6, the executive would only be willing to give up $19.94 to receive a share of restricted stock worth $30, suggesting a risk premium of 50%. The similarly calculated risk premium for discount options, FMV options, and premium options is 79%, 125%, and 237%, respectively: the lower the probability of exercise, the higher the risk premium.

---

[31] See, for example, Huddart (1998). In essence, the appropriate valuation methodology is the usual binomial valuation (which allows for early exercise) but with a catch: the exercise decision is not made by the investor but rather by a "third party" (in this case, an executive who for a variety of reasons is not expected to make the same exercise decisions as an unrestricted outside investor). Carpenter (1998) argues that option valuation incorporating executive exercise patterns can be approximately replicated by adding exogenous "departure rates" to a conventional binomial analysis.

[32] One important exception is Lambert et al. (1991).

2.3.3.3. Tax and accounting issues   Stock options seem a natural way to tie executive pay to company stock-price performance. However, in spite of the obvious incentive implications, the popularity of stock options reflects in large part their favorable tax and accounting treatment. In particular, stock options offer an attractive way to defer taxable income, and are largely invisible from corporate accounting statements.

Stock options represent a relatively unique form of deferred compensation in which the recipient has substantial discretion in determining when to realize taxable income. The granting of a stock option does not constitute a taxable event for either the company or the executive-recipient. What happens later depends on whether the stock options are "qualified" (called "Incentive Stock Options" or ISOs) or "non-qualified." For non-qualified options, the spread between the market price upon exercise and the original exercise price constitutes taxable personal income to the executive, and a compensation-expense deduction for the company. For qualified options, the executive pays nothing upon exercise (provided that he continues to hold the stock), and pays capital gains taxes when he eventually sells the stock; the corporation, however, cannot deduct the gain on a qualified option as a compensation expense. Most option grants are non-qualified, although recent tax law changes (reducing the capital gains tax rate from 28% to 20% or less) have made granting qualified options relatively more attractive.[33]

As long as stock options have a pre-specified exercise price and expiration date, companies incur an accounting charge equal to the grant-date "spread" between the market price and the exercise price (amortized over the life of the option).[34] This "quirk" in the US financial accounting rules – which implies no accounting charge for fair-market-value and premium options – creates a gap between the economic and accounting costs of options. As demonstrated in the preceding subsection, options are an expensive way to convey compensation because risk-averse managers will demand large premiums for accepting risky options rather than safer cash. But, stock option compensation is essentially "free" from an accounting perspective, explaining (I believe) the popularity of "broad-based" company-wide option programs that are difficult to rationalize from an incentive standpoint.[35] In addition, the accounting rules apply only to options with fixed exercise prices and expiration terms, and not to indexed options, performance-triggered options, or

---

[33] Prior to the recent reduction in capital gains rates, non-qualified options were jointly tax advantageous, since the loss in deductibility for the corporation more than offset the difference between personal income tax and capital gains rates. The recent reduction has narrowed the advantages somewhat, but not reversed them because (1) most executives sell the shares immediately following exercise of qualified options and do not meet the holding requirements for capital gains; (2) many executives exercising qualified options are subject to the "alternative minimum tax," and (3) there are restrictions on the granting and exercisability of qualified options which continue to be unattractive.

[34] The current accounting rules for stock and options issued to employees are defined by APB Opinion No. 25, issued in October 1972. In the early 1990s, the Financial Accounting Standard Board (FASB) considered explicit accounting charges for options, but adopted instead enhanced footnote disclosure.

[35] Although there is currently no accounting charge associated with granting options, outstanding options will lower a company's earnings per share when measured on a fully diluted basis.

options with variable terms. Thus, the accounting treatment explains in large part the tendency documented in Table 5 of granting only "regular" options, even when more exotic options would be beneficial from both an incentive and economic-cost perspective. Explaining why managers remain fixated on accounting rather than economic profit (apart from the obvious link to their bonus payments) is, however, beyond the scope of this chapter.

2.3.3.4. Why have options increased over time? The most pronounced trend in executive compensation in the 1980s and 1990s has been the explosion in stock option grants, which on a Black–Scholes basis now constitute the single largest component of CEO pay. Although the forces underlying this trend have not been documented or established in the literature, I believe that political, economic, mechanical, and behavioral factors have all contributed to the trend.

The controversy over CEO pay in the early 1990s was caused by a combination of political and economic forces (Murphy, 1995, 1997). The political forces (described in more detail in Section 5) reflected an attack on wealth that followed the so-called "excesses of the 1980s," while the economic forces reflected that traditional executive pay practices established in the 1960s and 1970s were ill-suited for the 1980s and 1990s economies where creating shareholder value involves innovation and entrepreneurism in some sectors, and downsizing, layoffs, obtaining concessions from unions, and in extreme cases even exit in other sectors. Most shareholder and academic criticisms of CEO pay at the time focused on the lack of meaningful rewards for superior performance and meaningful penalties for failure. Similarly, although the populist attack was implicitly focused on reducing pay levels, it was couched in terms of increasing the relation between pay and performance. Both of these forces combined to facilitate more pay for performance, predominately in the form of stock options.

The mechanical explanation for the explosion in stock options is rooted in institutional details on granting practices and exacerbated by the recent bull market. According to a 1997 Towers Perrin survey, 40% of large companies grant options on a "fixed value" basis, 40% on a "fixed share" basis, and the remaining 20% use a variety of other methods. Under fixed-value grants, the number of options granted is determined by dividing a dollar-value target award (typically determined using compensation surveys that express grant targets as a multiple of base salary) by the Black–Scholes option value.[36] Under fixed-share grants, the number of shares is determined at one date (using the same surveys), and fixed for several years. Thus, in periods of escalating stock prices, the Black–Scholes value of shares granted under fixed-share programs will also escalate. Moreover, since the companies with fixed-share programs participate in compensation surveys, the survey multiples will increase, which in turn will increase grants in companies

---

[36] For example, if the target award was $200,000 and the Black–Scholes value was $20, the CEO would receive options on 10,000 shares of stock. But, if the Black–Scholes value was $10, the CEO would receive options on 20,000 shares of stock.

with fixed-value programs. The net result is a ratcheting of option grants that corresponds to an escalating stock market.

The behavioral explanation for the stock option trend – which, by definition, will be unsatisfactory to economists – reflects an increased executive acceptance of stock options caused by nearly two decades of a sustained bull market. The current cohort of executives has not experienced a major market downturn: even the October 1987 crash was, in retrospect, a minor event for an executive holding long-lived stock options. The overwhelming majority of stock options issued since 1980 have been exercised well in-the-money, creating substantial fortunes for many CEOs. Newly appointed CEOs were not around in the early 1970s during the last sustained decline in stock prices. During this earlier period, companies systematically discontinued their "underwater" option programs and replaced them with accounting-based performance plans with higher likelihoods of payouts. Therefore, during prolonged market upturns it is not surprising that companies systematically scale back their accounting-based performance plans in favor of seemingly more-lucrative option programs.

2.3.4. Other forms of compensation

2.3.4.1. Restricted stock   Approximately 28% of the S&P 500 firms granted restricted stock to their CEOs in 1996; these grants account for an average of 6.1% of total compensation (and 22% of compensation for CEOs receiving grants). The grants are "restricted" in the sense that shares are forfeited under certain conditions (usually related to employee longevity). The forfeiture possibility allows favorable tax treatment (executives do not pay taxes on the shares until the restrictions lapse) and accounting treatment (the "cost" is amortized over the vesting period, and recorded as the grant-date stock price even if prices have increased since the grant).

Kole (1997) shows that restricted stock plans are more common in chemicals, machinery, and producer firms than in metals, food and consumer firms, and are more common in R&D-intensive firms than in non-R&D firms. Moreover, the average vesting period for restricted stock grants (i.e., the average time until the restrictions are lifted) is longer in chemicals, machinery, and producer firms (averaging 50 months) than in metals, food and consumer firm (averaging 20 months).

2.3.4.2. Longterm incentive plan   In addition to bonus plans based on annual performance, many companies offer "longterm incentive plans" (LTIPs), typically based on rolling-average 3- or 5-year cumulative performance. Approximately 27% of the S&P 500 CEOs received LTIP payouts in 1996; these payouts for 5.5% of 1996 total compensation (and 20% of compensation for those CEOs receiving payouts). The structure of the typical longterm incentive plans is similar to the structure of annual bonus plans illustrated in Fig. 5.

2.3.4.3. Retirement plans   In addition to participating in company-wide retirement programs, top executives routinely participate in supplemental executive retirement plans (SERPs). SERPs are non-qualified for tax purposes and can take a variety of different forms, including defined benefits based on "credited" years of service (which can deviate substantially from "actual" years of service) or variable benefits based on inflation or company performance. The compensation data in Figs. 1–3 ignore retirement-related compensation because (1) it is difficult or ultimately arbitrary to convert the future payments into current annual compensation; (2) payouts from SERPs are not disclosed, because the retired recipients are no longer company executives, and (3) the discussion of retirement plans in publicly available proxy statements is insufficient to calculate the actual value of these plans. Indeed, the vagueness of disclosure, coupled with anecdotes of high payouts in a few publicized cases, have led some observers to call SERPs the ultimate form of "stealth compensation."

2.4. Who sets CEO pay?

Part of the controversy over CEO compensation reflects a perception that CEOs effectively set their own pay levels. In fact, in most companies, ultimate decisions over executive pay are made by outside members of the board of directors who are keenly aware of the conflicts of interest between managers and shareholders over the level of pay. There is no doubt, however, that CEOs and other top managers exert at least some influence on both the level and structure of their pay.

Most large US corporations have a compensation committee consisting of two or more "outside" directors.[37] Although all major decisions related to top-level pay are passed through this committee, the committee rarely conducts market studies of competitive pay levels or initiates or proposes new incentive plans, and only seldom retains its own compensation experts. Rather, initial recommendations for pay levels and new incentive plans typically emanate from the company's human resource department, often working in conjunction with outside accountants and compensation consultants.[38] These recommendations are usually sent to top managers for approval and revision before being delivered to the compensation committee for consideration. The CEO typically participates in all committee deliberations, except for discussions specifically dealing with the level of the CEO's pay. The committee either accepts the recommendations or sends them back for

---

[37] "Outsiders" are typically defined as directors who are neither current nor past employees, and who have no strong business ties to the corporation. In fact, companies need such a committee to qualify for exemption under IRS §162(m), which places a $1 million limit on the deductibility of compensation for the CEO and other "proxy-named" executives.

[38] Executive compensation responsibility naturally varies with company size and complexity. Very large companies often have a fully staffed "Office of Executive Compensation," headed by a vice president who reports to either the Senior VP of Human Resources or to a VP of Compensation and Benefits (who, in turn, reports to the SVP of HR). In smaller companies, executive compensation responsibility typically rests with the executive responsible for human resources.

revision. If accepted, the committee passes its recommendations for the approval of the full board of directors.

The fact that initial recommendations are made by company management and not by the compensation committee does not necessarily imply corruption or a failure of corporate governance systems. Compensation committees, which typically meet only six to eight times a year, lack both the time and expertise to be involved in the minutia of pay design. Optimally, the role of the committee is not to set pay levels and programs, but rather to define and enforce the company's compensation strategy, and to monitor the process while being mindful that executives (like other individuals) prefer more to less. The committee must also be prepared to thwart clear violations of shareholder interests, which in most cases means "pushing back" on seemingly excessive pay recommendations.

The empirical evidence on CEO influence over the compensation committee is somewhat mixed. In a sample of 105 firms from 1984, O'Reilly et al. (1988) analyze compensation-committee members who are themselves executives in other firms, and find that CEO pay is positively related to executive pay at the committee members' firms. Main et al. (1995) investigate how CEOs "manage" their compensation committees in ways that result in higher pay, and conclude that outside board members act not as independent evaluators of CEO performance, but rather as partners in an effort to make the firm more successful. In a sample of 161 firms in 1993, Newman and Mozes (1997) finds that the level of CEO pay is significantly higher, and the pay–performance relation significantly lower, when the compensation committee contains at least one "insider." Anderson (1997) focuses on 50 CEOs who sit on their compensation committees (and are subsequently removed), and compares pay of these firms to a control sample. Based on 1985–1994 proxy data, he finds that CEOs who sit on their own committees receive lower levels of pay and tend to have very high stock ownership, acting much more like manager/owners than self-serving agents.

Based on my own observation and extensive discussions with executives, board members, and compensation consultants, I tend to dismiss the cynical scenario of entrenched compensation committees rubber-stamping increasingly lucrative pay programs with a wink and a nod. Although there are undoubtedly exceptions, outside board members approach their jobs with diligence, intelligence, and integrity, regardless of whether they have social or business ties with the CEO. However, judgment calls tend systematically to favor the CEO. Faced with a range of market data on competitive pay levels, committees tend to error on the high side. Faced with a choice between a sensible compensation plan and a slightly inferior plan favored by the CEO, the committee will defer to management. Similarly, faced with a discretionary choice on bonus-pool funding, the committee will tend to over- rather than under-fund. The amounts at stake in any particular case are typically trivial from a shareholder's perspective, but the overall impact of the bias has likely contributed to the ratcheting of pay levels evident in Figs. 1–3.

3. The relation between pay and performance

3.1. Introduction

Most research on the relation between executive compensation and company performance has been firmly (if not always explicitly) rooted in agency theory: compensation plans are designed to align the interests of risk-averse self-interested executives with those of shareholders. I begin this section by summarizing the traditional principal-agent framework based on unidimensional managerial actions, critique its limitations, and sketch intuitively the implications from a more general framework that acknowledges the complexity and unlimited scope of managerial actions. Next, I summarize the empirical evidence on the relation between pay and performance, distinguishing between *explicit* aspects (CEO pay is explicitly related to accounting returns through annual bonuses, and to stock-price appreciation through stock options and restricted stock) and *implicit* aspects (CEO pay may be implicitly tied to performance through year-to-year adjustments in salary levels, target bonuses, and option and restricted stock grant sizes). I then analyze the relation between CEO pay and *relative* performance. The section concludes with a summary of the evidence on whether increases in CEO pay–performance sensitivities affect subsequent company performance.

3.2. Principal-agent theory and executive compensation

Providing a comprehensive survey of the optimal contracting literature is beyond the scope of this chapter.[39] It is useful, however, to outline the framework and the insights emerging from the pioneering work by Mirrlees (1974, 1976), Holmstrom (1979), Grossman and Hart (1983), and others. In a typical "hidden action" model, the CEO is assumed to take actions, a, to produce stochastic shareholder value, $x(a)$, receiving compensation $w(x,z)$ and utility $u(w,a)$, where z is a vector of other observable measures in the contract. The CEO's utility function and the production function linking the CEO's actions to output are common knowledge to both shareholders and the CEO, but only the CEO observes the actions taken. That is, the shareholders know precisely what actions they want the CEO to take but cannot directly observe the CEO's actions. The optimal contract, $w(x,z)$, maximizes the risk-neutral shareholders' objective, $x - w$, subject to an incentive compatibility constraint (the CEO chooses actions to maximize $u(w,a)$), and a participation constraint (the expected utility of the contract must exceed the CEO's reservation utility).

The fundamental insight emerging from the traditional principal-agent models is that the optimal contract mimics a statistical inference problem: the payouts depend on the likelihood that the desired actions were in fact taken. This "informativeness principle" introduced by Holmstrom (1979) suggests that payouts are based on stock-based measures, x, not because shareholders desire higher stock prices but rather because reali-

---

[39] See Hart and Holmstrom (1987) for an excellent early survey on the contracting literature.

zations of x provide information useful in determining which actions the CEO took. This formulation also makes clear the role for additional performance measures (such as accounting returns) in the CEO's incentive contract: non-stock-based measures will be used to the extent that they provide information relevant in assessing whether the CEO indeed took the desired action. In fact, if these other measures constitute a "sufficient statistic" for the CEO's actions, stock-based measures need not be used at all.

Taken literally, it is difficult to use the informativeness principle to construct empirically refutable hypotheses regarding the structure or shape of actual executive incentive contracts. While Section 2 shows that actual contracts are typically linear in stock prices (above an exercise price for stock options), the relation between pay and stock-price performance predicted by the informativeness principle can be convex, linear, concave, and need not be positive through its entire range.[40] In addition, while actual contracts are non-linearly related to a variety of non-stock-based measures (see Fig. 5 and Table 2), the principle offers little guidance in determining which of these measures are "incrementally informative" about CEO actions.[41]

Taken less literally, the traditional principal-agent model yields several important and practical insights useful in understanding existing contracts (and, normatively, in designing better ones). In particular, the models highlight the trade-off between risk and incentives, as illustrated by the simple agency model.[42] Suppose that firm value is given by $x = e + \varepsilon$, where e is executive effort, and ε is (normally distributed) uncontrollable noise, $\varepsilon \approx N(0, \sigma^2)$. Moreover, suppose that managerial contracts take the simple linear form $w(x) = s + bx$, where s is a fixed salary and b is the sharing rate (or "pay–performance sensitivity"). Assuming that the executive has exponential utility, $U(x) = \exp[r(Wc(e))]$, where r is the executive's absolute risk aversion and $c(e)$ is the convex disutility of effort, the optimal sharing rate is given by[43]

$$b = \frac{1}{1 + r\sigma^2 c''}. \tag{1}$$

[40] For example, suppose that unusually high realizations of stock prices could only come from sub-optimal actions (such as gambling all corporate assets in a Las Vegas casino). Then, the optimal contract would punish these high realizations while rewarding lower realizations.

[41] The major empirical prediction of the informativeness principle has been to establish a role for relative performance evaluation (RPE) in incentive contracts; see the discussion in Section 3.7. In addition, Banker and Datar (1989) use the informativeness principle to develop predictions regarding the trade-off between stock-based and accounting-based performance measures based on signal-to-noise ratios; see Lambert and Larcker (1988), Bushman and Indjejikian (1993), and Baiman and Verrecchia (1995) for empirical applications of the Banker and Datar approach.

[42] Gibbons (1997) persuasively argues that existing contractual arrangements must reflect more than the trade-off between risk and incentives. But, this trade-off lies at the heart of the publicly traded corporation: the comparative advantage of the corporate form of organization is precisely that well-diversified atomistic shareholders are better able than managers to bear risk.

[43] For similar derivations of the optimal pay–performance sharing rate, see Lazear and Rosen (1981), Holmstrom and Milgrom (1991), Gibbons and Murphy (1992a), Milgrom and Roberts (1992), and Gibbons and Waldman (this volume).

Eq. (1) implies that the optimal pay–performance sensitivity will equal $b = 1$ when output is certain ($\sigma^2 = 0$) or executives are risk-neutral ($r = 0$). Incentives will be weaker for more risk-averse executives ($\partial b/\partial r < 0$), and will also be weaker the greater the uncontrollable noise in firm value ($\partial b/\partial\sigma^2 < 0$).

There are legitimate reasons not to take the informativeness principle literally. First, the traditional model assumes that the shareholders know which CEO actions maximize firm value: if actions were observable then a zero-risk forcing contract could be designed that induces the CEO to take the first-best actions. But the reason shareholders entrust their money to self-interested CEOs is based on shareholder beliefs that CEOs have superior skill or information in making investment decisions. Unobservable actions cannot be the driving force underlying executive contracts: even if shareholders (or boards of directors) could directly monitor CEO actions, they could not tell whether the actions were appropriate given the circumstances. Shareholder uncertainty about the production function linking CEO actions to firm value leads naturally to contracts based on the principle's objective (e.g., increasing shareholder wealth) rather than on measures that are incrementally informative of CEO actions (e.g., accounting returns or direct monitoring of CEO actions).

Second, as stressed by Holmstrom (1992), CEOs can choose from a much richer set of actions than contemplated under the original principal-agent framework. Although the CEO's "action space" is typically defined as unidimensional effort, it is widely acknowledged that the fundamental shareholder-manager agency problem is not getting the CEO to work harder, but rather getting him to choose actions that increase rather than decrease shareholder value. In general, increasing shareholder wealth involves investing in positive net present value projects, increasing profits on existing capital, and diverting resources from negative net present value projects. There is a wide array of actions that affect shareholder value, including defining the business strategy, choosing between debt and equity financing, making dividend and repurchase decisions, identifying acquisition and divestiture targets, selecting industries and markets to enter or exit, allocating capital across business units, setting budgets for developing new products and businesses, hiring productive (and firing unproductive) subordinates, and designing, implementing, and maintaining the nexus of implicit and explicit contracts that defines the organization. Expanding the set of potential actions that affect shareholder value diminishes the role for "informativeness" and increases the benefit of tying pay to the principle's objective rather than to measures of inputs.

Allowing managers to choose from an unlimited action space also has implications for the use of other performance measures and standards, z, in the contract. Payments based on incrementally informative z's can distort incentives when managers allocate their efforts across a variety of different tasks.[44] They can sandbag the budget process to achieve performance targets.[45] They can attenuate the benefits of relative performance evaluation

---

[44] Holmstrom and Milgrom (1991) and Baker (1992).

[45] Murphy (1998).

by taking unproductive actions that lower the performance of the peer group.[46] They can shift accounting returns across periods by accelerating or delaying revenues and costs.[47] They can monitor year-to-date performance and adjust actions daily to maximize bonuses based on cumulative annual performance.[48] They can make accounting choices that artificially inflate or deflate reported earnings.[49] They can make investment choices (such as cuts in R&D) that increase short-run profits at the expense of long-run profitability.[50] These unintended but predictable side effects of manipulable measures and standards are a cost that must be weighed against "informativeness" when determining the components and structure of the incentive contract.

Expanding the managerial action set has two primary implications for optimal incentive contracts. First, the payouts are predicted to be positively related to the principle's objective (increasing shareholder value) and to other "less noisy" measures that provide imperfect incentives to take actions generally consistent with value maximization. Accounting measures, for example, should be used most strongly when (i) accounting returns contain less noise than stock prices (Banker and Datar, 1989), and (ii) the actions that affect accounting returns are closely correlated with the actions that affect stock prices (Baker, 1992). Second, expanded managerial actions lead naturally to incentive structures that are linear rather than convex or concave (Hart and Holmstrom, 1987; Holmstrom and Milgrom, 1987). For example, when contracts are linear and constant across periods, managers have fewer incentives to adjust effort based on year-to-date performance or to shift earnings across periods to maximize current bonuses, because decisions that increase current earnings at the expense of future earnings will have a symmetric consequence for executive bonuses.

3.3. The implicit relation between pay and shareholder wealth

An executive's wealth is *explicitly* (and mechanically) tied to the principle's objective (creating shareholder wealth) through his holdings of stock, restricted stock, and stock options. In addition, CEO wealth is *implicitly* tied to stock-price performance through accounting-based bonuses (reflecting the correlation between accounting returns and stock-price performance) and through year-to-year adjustments in salary levels, target bonuses, and option and restricted stock grant sizes.

The CEO pay literature has yet to reach a consensus on the appropriate methodologies and metrics to use in evaluating the implicit relation between CEO pay and company stock-price performance. However, following Jensen and Murphy (1990b), Murphy

---

[46] Gibbons and Murphy (1990). See also Lazear (1989) on sabotaging the peer group, Dye (1984a,b) and Mookherjee (1984) on unproductive collusion, Carmichael (1988), Dye (1992) and Lewellen et al. (1996) on the choice of a reference group.

[47] Oyer (1998) and Murphy (1998).

[48] Holmstrom and Milgrom (1987).

[49] Healy (1985), Gaver et al. (1995) and Holthausen et al. (1995).

[50] Dechow and Sloan (1991) and Gibbons and Murphy (1992b).

(1993), and Hall and Liebman (1998), the analysis below shows that virtually all of the sensitivity of pay to corporate performance for the typical CEO is attributable to the explicit rather than the implicit part of the CEO's contract. Consequently, the methodological dispute related to measuring CEO pay–performance relations is largely second-order, and I will describe only briefly the different approaches and issues involved.

Year-to-year performance-related changes in total compensation are typically modeled as

$$(\text{CEO Pay})_{it} = \gamma_i + \alpha_i t + \beta_i(\text{Performance}), \tag{2}$$

where γ_i is a CEO or firm-specific effect that varies across CEOs but does not vary over time for a given CEO, α_i is a CEO or firm-specific time trend, "Performance" is a vector of contemporaneous and lagged performance measures, and β_i is the corresponding vector of coefficients.

Conceptually, (2) could be estimated directly for each executive, though doing so requires a prohibitively long time series in most cases.[51] Instead, most researchers assume that time trends and pay–performance relations are constant across executives ($\alpha_i = \alpha$ and $\beta_i = \beta$), and estimate (2) using fixed-effect methodologies or first-differences:

$$\Delta(\text{CEO Pay})_{it} = \alpha + \beta\Delta(\text{Performance})_{it}. \tag{3}$$

The methodological issues in estimating (3) involve choosing which components of compensation to include, and choosing the performance measures and lag structures. In addition, researchers must choose whether to measure pay in dollars or logarithms, and whether to measure performance in dollars or in rates of return. These latter choices determine whether the regression coefficients are interpreted as "pay–performance sensitivities" or "pay–performance elasticities." For example, the specification used by Jensen and Murphy (1990a) to analyze pay–performance sensitivities for cash compensation is

$$\Delta(\text{Cash Compensation})_{it} = a + b\Delta(\text{Shareholder Value})_{it}, \tag{4}$$

where $\Delta(\text{Shareholder Value})_t$ is defined as the rate of return realized by shareholders, r_t, multiplied by the beginning-or-period market value, V_{t-1}. In contrast, the specification used by Coughlan and Schmidt (1985) and Murphy (1986) is

$$\Delta\ln(\text{Cash Compensation})_{it} = \alpha + \beta\Delta\ln(\text{Shareholder Value})_{it}, \tag{5}$$

where $\Delta\ln(\text{Shareholder Value})_t$ ignores share issues or repurchases and therefore equals the continuously accrued rate of return on common stock, r_t. The estimated coefficient β is the elasticity of cash compensation with respect to shareholder value (or, following Rosen, 1992, the "semi-elasticity" of pay with respect to the rate of return).

Neither the sensitivity nor elasticity approach strictly dominates the other. The primary advantage of the elasticity approach is that it produces a better "fit" in the sense that rates

---

[51] Lambert and Larcker (1988), Janakiraman et al. (1992), and Jensen and Murphy (1990b) estimate separate regressions, by executive.

Table 7
CEO pay–performance elasticities and sensitivities for cash compensation, by industry[a]

Independent variable	Dependent variable: Δln(Cash Compensation)			Dependent variable: Δ(Cash Compensation)		
	1970s (1)	1980s (2)	1990–1996 (3)	1970s (4)	1980s (5)	1990–1996 (6)
A. S&P 500 industrials						
Intercept	0.0476 (11.8)	0.0423 (8.1)	0.0593 (6.2)	35.47 (9.5)	63.08 (6.8)	76.70 (4.1)
Ln(1 + Return)	0.0940 (7.8)	0.2143 (11.8)	0.2625 (8.1)	–	–	–
Δ(Shareholder Wealth)	–	–	–	.0042 (3.1)	.0173 (5.7)	.0138 (4.1)
R^2	0.0273	0.0558	0.0281	0.0042	0.0136	0.0078
Sample size	2192	2353	2263	2192	2341	2103
B. S&P 500 finance						
Intercept	0.0478 (5.7)	0.0620 (5.3)	0.0312 (1.9)	26.47 (4.4)	30.19 (1.4)	296.6 (1.3)
Ln(1 + Return)	0.1072 (4.0)	0.2889 (6.6)	0.4918 (9.7)	–	–	–
Δ(Shareholder Wealth)	–	–	–	0.0164 (3.6)	0.1406 (7.6)	0.0875 (1.1)
R^2	0.0556	0.1135	0.1921	0.0450	0.1476	0.0034
Sample size	270	339	399	270	339	372
C. S&P 500 utilities						
Intercept	0.0252 (4.4)	0.0736 (7.3)	0.0677 (5.1)	9.888 (3.2)	47.28 (5.6)	47.37 (3.3)
Ln(1 + Return)	0.0732 (3.3)	0.0880 (2.1)	0.3983 (6.4)	–	–	–
Δ(Shareholder Wealth)	–	–	–	0.0165 (3.0)	0.0108 (1.4)	0.0507 (4.3)
R^2	0.0410	0.0160	0.1389	0.0347	0.0072	0.0731
Sample size	252	285	256	252	285	232

[a] Note: t-statistics in parentheses. Sample is based on all CEOs included in the S&P 500. Data prior to 1992 extracted from *Forbes* Annual Compensation Surveys; data in 1992 and later from Compustat's ExecuComp database. Compensation in thousands of 1996-constant dollars; shareholder wealth measured in $millions. Cash pay includes salaries, bonuses, and small amounts of other cash compensation.

of return explain more of the cross-sectional variation of $\Delta\ln(\text{CEO Pay})$ than changes in shareholder value explain of $\Delta(\text{CEO Pay})$. In addition, while pay–performance sensitivities vary monotonically with firm size (larger firms having smaller b's), the elasticity is relatively invariant to firm size (Gibbons and Murphy, 1992a).

The primary advantage of the sensitivity approach is that sensitivities have a more natural economic interpretation. The pay–performance sensitivity represents the executive's "share" of value creation. Since agency costs arise when agents receive less than 100% of the value of output, the "sharing rate" seems a natural measure of the severity of the agency problem; elasticities have no corresponding agency-theoretic interpretation. Moreover, sensitivities are directly analogous to the executive's fractional stockholdings and, indeed, sensitivities and fractional holdings can be added together to form a more comprehensive measure of how the CEO's wealth varies with company performance. The elasticity counterpart to "full" pay–performance sensitivity (including stock and option holdings) – the elasticity of the CEO's wealth with respect to firm value – require unavailable data on non-firm-related CEO wealth.

Table 7 shows the estimated pay–performance sensitivities and elasticities for S&P 500 CEOs grouped by industry and by decade, based on pooled cross-sectional time-series regressions of (4) and (5). All data are adjusted for inflation; cash compensation (including salaries, bonuses, and small amounts of other cash pay) is in thousands of 1996-constant dollars, while the change in shareholder wealth is in millions of 1996-constant dollars. Panel A, based on S&P 500 Industrials, shows that pay–performance elasticities have nearly tripled from $\beta = 0.09$ in the 1970s to $\beta = 0.26$ during the first 7 years of the 1990s. Over the same time period, pay–performance sensitivities have more than tripled from $b = 0.004$ (representing a 0.4¢ change in CEO salary and bonus for each $1000 change in shareholder wealth) to $b = 0.014$ (1.4¢ per $1000). Panels B and C, based respectively on financial services firms and utilities, shows equally dramatic increases in pay–performance sensitivities and elasticities for cash compensation.

Fig. 6 shows graphically the estimated pay–performance sensitivities and elasticities for S&P 500 CEOs based on annual regressions of (4) and (5) from 1971 to 1996. Two facts emerge. First, replicating the result from Table 7, there has been a general increase in the relation between cash compensation and company stock-price performance over the past 25 years, measured either by sensitivities or elasticities. Second, there appears to be more year-to-year variation in pay–performance sensitivities and than elasticities, and the variance in both appears to have increased in the 1990s.

The definition of CEO pay in (4) and (5) includes realized bonuses, which (recalling Table 2) are explicitly related to accounting profitability but only implicitly related to stock-price performance. Recognizing the explicit nature of bonuses provides insights into existing empirical results on the relation between cash compensation and stock-price performance. For example, several researchers, including Jensen and Murphy (1990a), Joskow and Rose (1994) and Boschen and Smith (1995), have explored the relation between $\Delta(\text{CEO Pay})$ and lagged shareholder return and concluded that the coefficient on contemporaneous return is large and significant, the coefficient on lagged performance

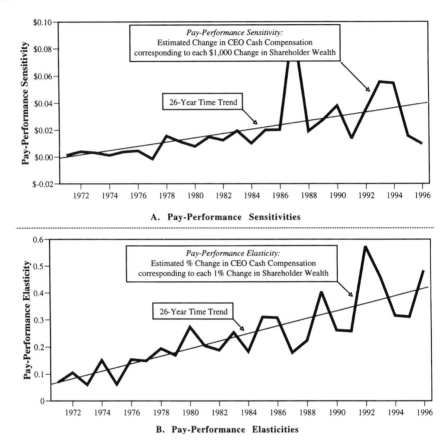

Fig. 6. Estimated pay–performance relations for cash compensation, 1970–1996. (A) Pay–performance sensitivities; (B) pay–performance elasticities. Sample is based on all CEOs included in the S&P 500. Data prior to 1992 extracted from *Forbes* Annual Compensation Surveys; data in 1992 and later from Compustat's ExecuComp database. Panel A is based on annual regressions of Δ(Cash Compensation) on Δ(Shareholder Wealth), where the latter is expressed in $1000s and where "cash compensation" includes salaries, bonuses, and small amounts of other cash compensation. Panel B is based on annual regressions of Δln(Cash Compensation) on ln(1 + Shareholder Return).

smaller but still significant, with mixed (but generally insignificant) results for prior lags. Since bonuses are based on accounting returns and not stock prices, the results in the literature are likely explained by the time-series correlations between accounting and stock returns. Since stock returns are forward-looking, in the sense that current announcements of events that affect future profitability will be immediately impounded into stock prices, it is not surprising that contemporaneous accounting returns are correlated with contemporaneous and lagged shareholder returns, with the correlation decreasing with additional lags. Ultimately, the (as-of-yet unwritten) definitive study of the lag structure of CEO pay and performance must acknowledge the explicit nature of bonuses and therefore begin with a careful analysis of the time-series properties and correlations of shareholder and accounting returns.

3.4. The explicit relation between pay and shareholder wealth

Executive wealth is explicitly related to stock-price performance through performance-related changes in the value of the executives' holdings of stock, restricted stock, and stock options. As noted in the preceding subsection, pay–performance sensitivities represent the CEO's "share" of value creation. When shareholder wealth increases by one dollar, the value of the CEO's restricted and unrestricted stockholdings increase by the CEO's fractional ownership of company shares. For example, if the CEO holds 5% of the company's stock, his wealth from stock will increase by 5¢ for every $1 increase in shareholder value, and his pay–performance sensitivity will equal his fractional ownership, $b^{\text{stock}} = 0.05$.

Calculating pay–performance sensitivities for the CEO's option holdings is slightly more difficult than for stock holdings, because option values do not change dollar-for-dollar with changes in the stock price. If the CEO holds options on 5% of the company's stock, each $1 increase in shareholder wealth will increase the CEO's wealth from options by $b^{\text{options}} = 0.05 \partial V / \partial P$, where $\partial V / \partial P < 1$ is the change in the Black–Scholes value of the

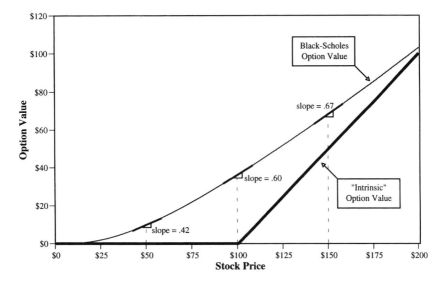

Fig. 7. Option values and pay–performance sensitivities. Options values based on an option with an exercise price of $100, dividend yield of 3%, stock-price volatility of 30%, and risk-free rate of 7%. The pay–performance sensitivity is defined as the change in option value associated with each $1 change in stock price, and is represented as the slope of the Black–Scholes valuation.

option with respect to changes in the stock price.[52] Fig. 7 illustrates how $\partial V/\partial P$ (called the option's "delta;" see Appendix A) varies with the stock price and exercise price. As shown in the figure, the slope of the Black–Scholes value is approximately $\partial V/\partial P = 0.60$ when the stock price is close to the exercise price (assuming a 3% dividend yield), suggesting that an at-the-money option increases in value by about 60¢ whenever stock prices increase by $1.00. The slope is substantially lower than.60 for out-of-the-money options, and (ignoring dividends) approaches $\partial V/\partial P = 1.00$ for deep in-the-money options.

Calculating pay–performance sensitivities for options requires exercise price and expiration-term information for each outstanding option grant. As a practical matter, the sensitivity for current grants can be computed precisely for US CEOs (because the required data are publicly disclosed), but the sensitivity for prior grants must be approximated. In particular, in the following sensitivity calculations I treat options granted in prior years as a single grant with 5 years remaining and an exercise price equal to the year-end stock price less the "intrinsic value" (i.e., the current "spread" between the stock price and exercise price) per share of the unexercised options.[53] Pay–performance sensitivities for both current and prior grants are then calculated as (Options Granted)/(Shares Outstanding)) $\times \partial$(Option Val)/∂P, using the actual exercise price and term for current grants, and the approximate price and term for prior grants. Apart from the approximation for prior grants, the calculation can be made at a point in time based on data from a single-year's proxy statement.

3.5. Total pay–performance sensitivities

Fig. 8 shows median pay–performance sensitivities for S&P 500 CEOs, by industry, from 1992 to 1996. Sensitivities are scaled to reflect changes in CEO wealth per $1000 change in shareholder wealth. The explicit sensitivities for stock, restricted stock, and stock options are calculated as described in the preceding subsection. Implicit sensitivities for cash compensation are determined by first estimating pay–performance elasticities for each year and for each of the four major industry groups in Fig. 8. This industry-level elasticity is converted into a company-specific pay–performance sensitivity by multiplying by the CEO's salary and bonus, and dividing by the market value of the company's

[52] More formally, suppose that the CEO holds N stock options, and suppose that shareholder wealth increases by $1. If there are S total shares outstanding, the stock price P will increase by $\Delta P = \$1/S$, and the value of the CEO's options will increase by $N\Delta P(\partial V/\partial P)$, where V is the Black–Scholes value of each option. Substituting for ΔP, the pay–performance sensitivity for stock options is given by $(N/S)(\partial V/\partial P)$, or the CEO's options held as a fraction of total shares outstanding multiplied by the "slope" of the Black–Scholes valuation. For examples of this approach, see Jensen and Murphy (1990b), Murphy (1993), and Yermack (1995).

[53] US proxy statements provide information on the number and intrinsic value of options held at the end of the fiscal year (based on the fiscal year-end stock price, P). The number (N) and intrinsic value (Y) of previously granted options is calculated by subtracting new grants from total outstanding options, and adjusting the year-end intrinsic value of the new grants from the total intrinsic value. I treat the previously granted options as a single prior grant with exercise price X, where $N(P - X) = Y$, or $X = P - (Y/N)$.

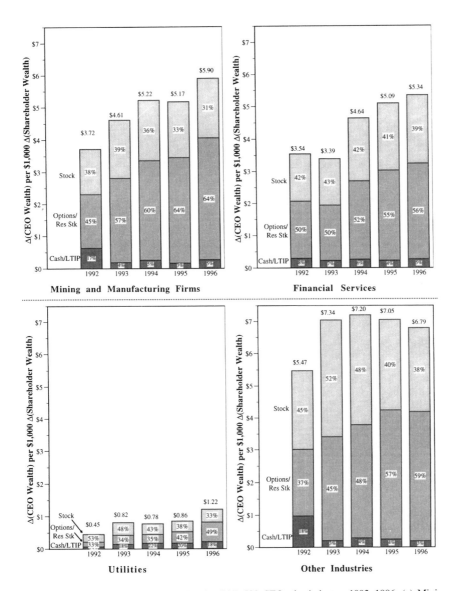

Fig. 8. Median pay–performance sensitivities for S&P 500 CEOs, by industry, 1992–1996. (a) Mining and manufacturing firms; (b) financial services; (c) utilities; (d) other industries. Sample includes all companies in the S&P 500. Pay component percentages are derived by computing the percentages for each CEO, and averaging across CEOs; the bar height depicts median pay–performance sensitivity. Manufacturing include firms with 2-digit SIC codes 10–29; financial services 60–69, and utilities 49.

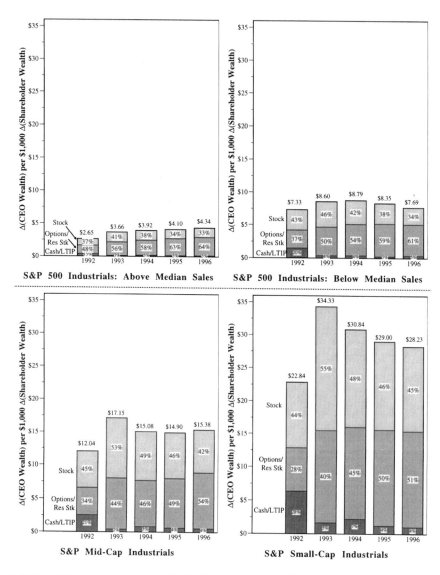

Fig. 9. Median CEO pay–performance sensitivities, by company size, 1992–1996. (a) S&P 500 industrials: above median sales; (b) S&P 500 industrials: below median sales; (c) S&P mid-cap industrials; (d) S&P small-cap industrials. Sample includes all companies in the S&P 500. Pay component percentages are derived by computing the percentages for each CEO, and averaging across CEOs; the bar height depicts median pay–performance sensitivity.

common stock (in $1000s). The pay–performance sensitivity for accounting-based long-term incentive plans is determined by dividing the LTIP payment received by the CEO in each year by the change in shareholder wealth over the period covered by the plan.[54]

Several stylized facts emerge from Fig. 8. First, pay–performance sensitivities are driven primary by stock options and stock ownership, and not through other forms of compensation (see also Jensen and Murphy, 1990b; Murphy 1993; Hall and Liebman 1998). For example, 95% of the estimated 1996 pay–performance sensitivity for CEOs in manufacturing companies reflects stock options (64%) and stock (31%). This result is not sensitive to the methodology for estimating pay–performance relations for cash compensation and LTIPs, since the magnitude of these compensation components are small relative to year-to-year variance in the dollar value of options and stock. Second, pay–performance sensitivities vary across industries, and are particularly lower in regulated utilities. Third, pay–performance sensitivities have become larger from 1992 to 1996. Finally, the increase in pay–performance sensitivities has been driven almost exclusively by stock option grants.

Fig. 9 depicts the effect of company size on firm pay–performance sensitivities for industrial companies, and illustrates another stylized fact: pay–performance sensitivities are smaller in larger firms. The 1996 median pay–performance sensitivity for the largest half of the S&P 500 is $4.36 per $1000 (reflecting an effective ownership share of about $b = .44\%$), compared to $7.69 per $1000 ($b = 0.77\%$) for the smaller S&P 500 firms. The median pay–performance sensitivities for S&P Mid-Cap and Small-Cap firms are $15.38 per $1000 ($b = 1.54\%$) and $28.23 per $1000 ($b = 2.82\%$), respectively. Moreover, Fig. 9 suggests that the increase in pay–performance sensitivities documented in Fig. 8 is largely a phenomenon associated with large S&P 500 companies, and not with mid-size and smaller companies.

The inverse relation between company size and pay–performance sensitivities is not surprising, since risk-averse and wealth-constrained CEOs of large firms can feasibly "own" only a tiny fraction of the company cash flows through their stock, options, and incentive compensation. Nor does the inverse relation invalidate pay–performance sensitivities as a meaningful metric for measuring CEO incentives; rather, the result merely underscores that increased agency problems are a cost of company size that must be weighed against the benefits of expanded scale and scope. The inverse relation does suggest, however, the importance of allowing for size-related heterogeneity when making comparisons across industry groups, time periods, or countries.

Company size is the most important but not the only source of heterogeneity in calculated pay–performance sensitivities. The distributions of both stock and option ownership are highly skewed, and *average* sensitivities are much higher than the *median* sensitivities depicted in Figs. 8 and 9. Indeed, an important advantage of analyzing explicit incentives

---

[54] For example, the LTIP sensitivity for companies using 3-year performance is determined by dividing the payout in year t by the change in shareholder wealth in t, $t-1$, and $t-2$. To avoid negative sensitivities and to mitigate the effects of large LTIP awards paid for poor stock-price performance, the LTIP sensitivity is assumed to be zero whenever shareholder returns failed to exceed 5% annually over the performance period.

(based on actual contracts) rather than implicit incentives (based on pooled cross-sectional time-series data) is that the explicit approach better identifies the heterogeneity. The next step, of course, is *explaining* the cross-sectional heterogeneity in pay–performance sensitivities.[55]

Jensen and Murphy (1990a) conclude that CEO pay–performance sensitivities are "low" in the sense that they correspond to a median sharing rate of only about 0.325% for their sample of *Forbes* executives from 1970 to 1988. The analysis in Fig. 8, although based on the S&P 500 rather than the *Forbes* 800, shows that pay–performance sensitivities have nearly doubled to 0.6% by 1996. In spite of the sensitivity increase, however, there remains a large gap between the interests of managers and shareholders. For example, each $10 million of perquisite consumption (e.g., a new headquarters building, or pet acquisition, or a corporate jet) costs the CEO only about $60,000 (or, based on the median annual compensation in Fig. 2 of $3.2 million, 1 week's compensation). Similarly, resisting a hostile takeover attempt promising a $500 million premium to shareholders will personally "cost" the typical CEO about a year's compensation, which is substantial, but likely small compared to the lost power and prestige of running a large corporation.

Several researchers have disputed the Jensen–Murphy estimates on econometric and theoretic grounds. The econometric criticisms are easily dismissed, since there are no econometric issues involved in determining the performance measure or estimating the explicit relation between performance and the value of an executive's stock and option holdings. The theoretic criticisms, however, clearly have merit. Haubrich (1994), for example, correctly points out that the Jensen–Murphy estimates, however low, may well be consistent with the predictions of agency theory for sufficiently risk-averse executives. Moreover, as emphasized by Hall and Liebman (1998) and others, modest movements in shareholder returns can lead to large swings in executive wealth even when the pay–performance sensitivity is small: $b\Delta V$ can be large even when b is small, for sufficiently large ΔV. For example, a 10% shareholder return for a $10 billion company will increase the median CEO's wealth by $6 million (assuming $b = .6\%$). However, while factors such as executive risk aversion and company size and volatility can "explain" low pay–performance sensitivities, these factors exacerbate rather than mitigate the large conflict of interest between managers and shareholders.

3.6. Trends in CEO stock ownership

Stock ownership provides the most direct link between shareholder and CEO wealth. Fig. 10 describes CEO stock ownership *ignoring stock options* from 1987 to 1996 and documents a curious result of the prolonged bull market: the *value of stock* held by S&P 500 CEOs has increased substantially over the past decade, while the *percentage of shares* held

---

[55] Garen's (1994) analysis of agency-theoretic heterogeneity is a promising start; see also Aggarwal and Samwick (1999). However, much of the variation in sensitivities is driven by CEO stockholdings, outside of the control of shareholders and therefore outside the scope of the traditional principal-agent framework. See Himmelberg et al. (1998) for an analysis of the determinants of managerial ownership.

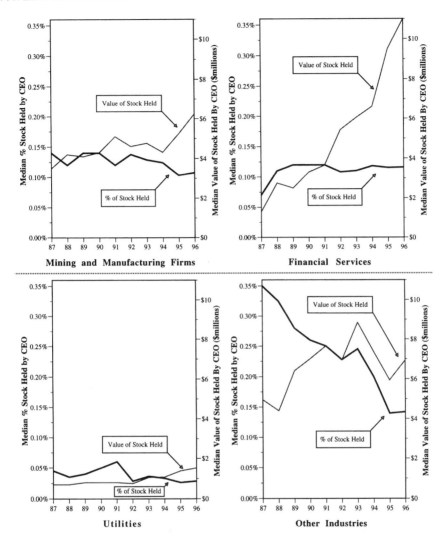

Fig. 10. Trends in stock ownership for S&P 500 CEOs, by industry, 1987–1996. (a) Mining and manufacturing firms; (b) financial services; (c) utilities; (d) other industries. Sample includes all companies in the S&P 500. Stock ownership includes shares held directly and by family members, but excludes all stock options.

by the CEO has been declining. For example, among S&P 500 manufacturing firms, median CEO ownership has increased from $3.5 million to over $6 million, while median percentage ownership has fallen from 0.14% to 0.11%.[56] Similarly, the median percentage

---

[56] The average ownership has increased from $19 million to $74 million over this same time period, while the average percentage ownership has fallen from over 1.1% to 0.8%.

ownership in financial services companies increased from 0.07% to 0.12% between 1987 and 1989, and fallen slightly since 1989. In contrast, the dollar value of median stock ownership in financial firms has increased tenfold from $1.3 million to over $11 million from 1987 to 1996.[57] Median ownership in utilities has nearly doubled from $0.7 million to $1.5 million from 1987 to 1996, while median percentage ownership has fallen from 0.05% to 0.03%. Finally, median ownership in "all other S&P 500 industries" has increase from $5.0 million to $6.9 million, while median percentage ownership has fallen from 0.35% to 0.14%. In part, these trends reflect the increasing prevalence of "stock ownership guidelines" (i.e., board-level mandates stipulating ownership targets expressed in dollars, or as a multiple of base salary). When stock prices are increasing, executives can sell stock and still achieve the guideline.

Researchers as well as practitioners would likely be split on whether the evidence in Fig. 10 implies that incentives from stock ownership have increased or decreased over the past decade. The only meaningful measure of CEO incentives and the severity of the agency problem is, however, the percentage ownership (that is, the pay–performance sensitivity) and *not* the dollar value of ownership. As an example to illustrate the distinction, suppose that a CEO is considering perquisites (headquarters, pet acquisitions, corporate jets) that he personally values at $1 million but costs shareholders $100 million. The CEO's decision will depend solely on his percentage ownership and not his dollar ownership.[58] Alternatively, suppose that a risk-averse CEO is considering a risky project that has a small but positive net present value. The CEO will be less likely to adopt the project when his dollar ownership is higher, since dollar holdings essentially measures the extent to which the CEO is undiversified. Therefore, in terms of the conflicts of interest between managers and shareholders, increases in percentage ownership holding dollar ownership constant reduces agency problems related to perquisite consumption, while increasing dollar ownership holding percentage ownership constant increases agency problems related to risk taking.[59]

In interpreting the results of Fig. 10, it is important to note that the definition of stock ownership ignores outstanding options. As suggested by Figs. 8 and 9, the "fully diluted" percentage of stock owned by executives has increased substantially over the past decade, even though direct stock ownership has declined. Consistent with Ofek and Yermack (1997), the results in Fig. 10 suggest that executives with large stock option holdings rationally reduce their unrestricted stock holdings, likely reflecting both a desire to diversify and to consume. Moreover, the fact that declines in ownership have been more than

---

[57] Average ownership in financial firms has increased from $8 million to $110 million over the same period.

[58] In particular, he will adopt the project if he owns less than 1% of the company's stock, and reject it if he owns more, independent of the dollar value of his holdings. Of course, to the extent that perquisites such as corporate jets and pet projects have income elasticities exceeding unity, we expect that *wealthier* managers will be more likely to pursue perquisites, *ceteris paribus*.

[59] Note that management-led leveraged buyouts, in which existing managers buy the company from shareholders using debt and proceeds from selling their old shares, are an example of how managers can substantially increase percentage ownership while holding dollar ownership constant.

offset by increases in option grants underscores the importance of recognizing options in studies of the relation between management ownership and corporate performance (e.g., Morck et al., 1988; McConnell and Servaes, 1990; Himmelberg et al., 1998).

3.7. Relative performance evaluation

A major empirical prediction of agency theory concerns the use of relative performance evaluation (RPE) in incentive contracts (Holmstrom, 1982). RPE is a direct implication of the informativeness principle with unidimensional executive actions: if the stochastic component of company performance contains an industry or market effect as well as an idiosyncratic effect, then "taking out the noise" through RPE is incrementally informative in assessing the actions taken by the CEO. Relative performance evaluation remains a strong prediction of the model after expanding the managerial action set, since paying based on relative performance provides essentially the same incentives as paying based on absolute performance, while insulating risk-averse managers from the common shocks.

3.7.1. Implicit relative performance evaluation
Existing studies of RPE have focused on the implicit relation between CEO cash compensation, company performance, and market and/or industry performance.[60] Gibbons and Murphy (1990) document the strongest support for the RPE hypothesis, finding that changes in CEO pay are positively and significantly related to firm performance, but negatively and significantly related to industry and market performance, ceteris paribus. In addition, Gibbons and Murphy find that CEO performance is more likely to be evaluated relative to aggregate market movements than relative to industry movements. Table 8 replicates and updates their analysis based on the following pooled cross-sectional time-series regression for companies grouped according to major industry and decade:

$$\Delta \ln(\text{CEO Pay}) = \alpha + \beta(\text{Shareholder Return}) + \gamma(\text{Industry and/or Market Return}).$$

Panel A of Table 8 shows that CEO pay in S&P 500 industrials is positively and significantly related to firm performance but negatively related to two-digit SIC industry performance (columns (1), (4), and (7)) and market performance (columns (2), (5), and (8)). Columns (3), (6), and (9) include both industry and market performance as explanatory variables. The market-return coefficient is negative and significant in all three regressions, suggesting that market risks are partially filtered out of executive compensation after controlling for industry returns. Holding market returns constant, however, CEO pay growth is negatively and significantly related to two-digit industry returns only in the 1980s, and insignificantly related to industry performance over earlier and later time periods. These results support the Gibbons–Murphy conclusion that performance is more likely to be evaluated relative to aggregate market movements than relative to

---

[60] See, for example, Coughlan and Schmidt (1985), Murphy (1985), Antle and Smith (1986), Gibbons and Murphy (1990), Janakiraman et al. (1992), and Sloan (1993).

Table 8

Coefficients of ordinary least squares regressions of Δln(CEO cash compensation) on firm, industry, and market rates of return on common stock, 1970–1996[a]

Independent variable	1970s			1980s			1990–1996		
Dependent Variable: Δln(Cash Compensation)	(1)	(2)	(3)	(4)	(5)	(6)	(7)	(8)	(9)
A. S&P 500 industrials									
Ln(1 + Return)	0.1112	0.1147	0.1129	0.2740	0.2581	0.2774	0.3158	0.3392	0.3504
	(6.7)	(7.7)	(6.8)	(12.8)	(13.4)	(13.0)	(10.8)	(12.5)	(9.6)
Ln(1 + Industry Return)	−0.0360	—	0.0088	−0.1894	—	−0.0918	−0.1756	—	−0.0621
	(−1.5)		(0.3)	(−5.2)		(−2.1)	(−3.5)		(−1.2)
Ln(1 + Market Return)	—	−0.0601	−0.0671	—	−0.3196	−0.2494	—	−0.4928	−0.4436
		(−2.3)	(−1.8)		(−6.3)	(−4.1)		(−5.6)	(−4.5)
R^2	0.0283	0.0297	0.0297	0.0665	0.0714	0.0732	0.0333	0.0415	0.0420
Sample size	2192	2192	2192	2354	2354	2354	2264	2264	2264
B. S&P 500 finance									
Ln(1 + Return)	0.0778	0.1173	0.0946	0.2687	0.2845	0.2691	0.6988	0.6993	0.7070
	(1.8)	(2.7)	(2.1)	(5.0)	(7.6)	(5.0)	(9.4)	(9.9)	(9.5)
Ln(1 + Industry Return)	0.0473	—	0.1349	0.0667	—	0.0602	−0.4669	—	−0.0861
	(0.8)		(1.6)	(0.7)		(0.5)	(−3.7)		(−0.4)
Ln(1 + Market Return)	—	−0.0202	−0.1430	—	0.0480	0.0165	—	−0.7310	−0.6234
		(−0.3)	(−1.4)		(0.4)	(0.1)		(−4.1)	(−1.7)
R^2	0.0581	0.0559	0.0650	0.1147	0.1140	0.1147	0.2196	0.2250	0.2252
Sample size	270	270	270	339	339	339	399	399	399
C. S&P 500 utilities									
Ln(1 + Return)	0.0771	0.0667	0.0773	0.1016	0.0967	0.1012	0.4305	0.4238	0.4292
	(2.2)	(2.2)	(2.2)	(2.3)	(2.3)	(2.3)	(5.8)	(5.8)	(5.7)
Ln(1 + Industry Return)	−0.0056	—	−0.0481	−0.0868	—	−0.0444	−0.1115	—	−0.1826
	(−0.1)		(−0.7)	(−0.8)		(−0.3)	(−0.8)		(−0.5)
Ln(1 + Market Return)	—	0.0130	0.0496	—	−0.0790	−0.0566	—	−0.0881	0.0751
		(0.3)	(0.7)		(−0.9)	(−0.5)		(−0.7)	(0.2)
R^2	0.0410	0.0414	0.0431	0.0182	0.0187	0.0191	0.1411	0.1404	0.1413
Sample size	252	252	252	285	285	285	256	256	256

[a] Note: *t*-statistics in parentheses. Regressions include (suppressed) intercepts. Sample is based on all CEOs included in the S&P 500. Data prior to 1992 extracted from *Forbes* Annual Compensation Surveys; data in 1992 and later from Compustat's ExecuComp database. Cash pay, in 1996-constant dollars, includes salaries, bonuses, and small amounts of other cash compensation. Industry return equals the value-weighted total shareholder return of all Compustat companies in the same two-digit industry; market return equals the value-weighted return of all Compustat companies.

industry movements. The results also suggest that RPE among S&P 500 industrials was less important in the 1970s than in the 1980s and 1990s.

Panel B of Table 8 finds little evidence of RPE among S&P 500 financial services companies in the 1970s or 1980s. The results for the 1990s is similar to the results from industrial companies: CEO pay in financial services is more likely to be evaluated relative to aggregate market movements than industry movements. Finally, Panel C of Table 8 finds no evidence for RPE among S&P 500 utilities in any time period.

3.7.2. Explicit relative performance evaluation

The descriptive analysis of CEO pay contracts in Section 2 suggests that the scope for RPE in actual explicit contracts is rather limited. Although stock options could theoretically be indexed to industry or market movements, indexed options are virtually nonexistent in practice. Similarly, the payouts from restricted stock (as well as stock directly held without restriction) are based solely on absolute returns and not relative returns. Payouts from annual bonus plans could be based on relative returns, but, as documented in Table 3, only a minority of industrial companies utilize external peer-groups in determining performance standards.

Table 9 describes the use of relative performance evaluation in annual bonus plans, based on the Towers Perrin survey of 177 large US companies described in detail in Section 2.3.2. Just over one-fifth of the 125 surveyed industrials companies use some form of RPE in annual bonus plans. However, while agency theory predicts measuring performance relative to the mean or median of the peer group, companies using RPE tend to use it somewhat differently. In particular, among the industrial companies using RPE, only five (19%) evaluate performance relative to the mean or median of the industry or market. More frequently, bonuses are based on a percentile ranking of performance (e.g., a schedule indicating the bonuses paid for achieving 25th, 50th, and 75th percentile performance relative to a peer group). Ten respondents (representing 38% of industrial companies using RPE) indicated that peer-group performance was considered in the standard-determination process, but did not specify how it was used. In most cases, RPE is based on the performance of specific industry peers identified and selected by the company; this peer group may or may not correspond to the peer group used in the company proxy statements.[61]

Table 9 shows that explicit RPE is used more extensively in financial-services firms and utilities than in industrial companies: 57% of the financial-services firms, and 42% of the utilities report using RPE in their annual bonuses, compared to only 21% of the industrials. Similar to the results for industrials, RPE is based on the performance of specific industry peers, and RPE-based bonuses typically depend on percentile performance (rather than performance measured relative to the peer-group mean or median).

---

[61] As part of the enhanced SEC proxy disclosure requirements introduced in October 1992, companies must provide a chart showing their 5-year stock-price performance measured relative to the market and to an "industry peer group" which may be either self-selected or a published industry index.

Table 9
Relative performance evaluation (RPE) in annual incentive plans in 177 large US corporations[a]

	Industrials ($n = 125$) (%)	Finance & insurance ($n = 21$) (%)	Utilities ($n = 31$) (%)
Number of firms using RPE (%)	26 (21)	12 (57)	13 (42)
How RPE is used[b]			
Determining threshold performance	0	0	30
Defining performance	100	100	70
How RPE is measured			
Perform. percentile or ranking[c]	42	50	77
Perform. vs. peer group mean/median	19	0	0
Subjective assessment of performance vs. peers	15	8	0
Unknown/other	23	42	23
How peer groups are defined			
Peer group used in proxy statement[d]	20	25	0
Self-selected industry peer group	58	75	85
Published industry index	8	0	8
Broad-based peer group	15	0	8

[a] Source: Data extracted from Towers Perrin's *Annual Incentive Plan Design Survey*, 1997.

[b] Threshold performance must be attained before any bonuses are paid. The threshold performance measure is often different from the performance measure that determines the magnitude of bonuses. For example, bonuses equal to 2% of net income might be paid *only if* company return on equity exceeds the peer group return on equity: the performance measure is net income but the threshold major is relative return on equity.

[c] A typical formula might pay "75th percentile bonuses for 75th percentile performance.".

[d] Proxy statements include a chart showing the companies 5-year stock-price performance measured relative to the market and to an "industry peer group" which may be either self-selected or a published industry index.

The results on explicit RPE in Table 9 seem at odds with the results on implicit RPE in Table 8. In particular, while Table 8 suggests that relative performance is an important determinant of year-to-year changes in cash compensation, Table 9 suggests that few industrial companies explicitly tie pay to relative performance. In addition, while Table 8 shows that implicit RPE is most likely based on the market rather than the industry, Table 9 shows than companies using RPE seldom use broad-based market peer groups. Finally, while Table 8 provides stronger support for the RPE hypothesis for industrials than for utilities and financial services companies, Table 9 shows that the prevalence of explicit RPE contracts is actually higher in utilities and financial services than in industrials.

The differences in Tables 8 and 9 may be explained by differences in sample composition and time periods analyzed. More important, I believe, is the fact that the implicit RPE relations in Table 9 are based on relative stock-market performance, and yet annual bonuses are directly tied to accounting profits and not stock-market returns. Sloan (1993) shows that accounting profits are more closely correlated with "market-adjusted returns" than with raw returns. Thus, the market effect documented by Gibbons and Murphy (1990) and replicated in Table 8 may simply reflect the correlation between accounting profits and market-adjusted stock returns.

As discussed in Section 2.3.3, the absence of indexed stock option plans reflects, in part, both unfavorable accounting consequences and the fact that fully indexed options expire worthless half of the time. Still, the paucity of RPE in options and other components of executive compensation remains a puzzle worth understanding. One potential explanation concerns the costs of obtaining performance data for industry peers: relative accounting data are only available at annual (or at best quarterly) intervals, and only then with a substantial lag. However, while their are problems in measuring relative accounting performance, relative stock-price data are available instantaneously at trivial cost. Another explanation for the paucity of RPE is that executives can construct RPE on their own account, by "selling short" industry or market portfolios commensurate with their stock and option holdings. However, there is to my knowledge no evidence (including anecdotal accounts) supporting this investment behavior, and it seems unlikely that executives have the financial resources available to offset fully their holding in company stock and options. Similarly, although companies might avoid RPE in anticipation of executives "undoing" RPE through long positions in industry or market portfolios, it is unclear why executives would want to undo RPE. Finally, there may be strategic reasons (such as covert collusion) why companies avoid RPE (Aggarwal and Samwick, 1997).

3.8. Do incentives matter?

Over the past decade, academics, institutional shareholders, and shareholder-activist groups have called for tying CEO pay more directly to changes in shareholder wealth. These pressures have played at least some role in the increasing prevalence of stock ownership guidelines and the recent explosion in stock option grants. Underlying the push towards increasing the sensitivity of CEO pay to stock-price performance is the belief that such policies will improve management incentives and subsequent company performance. Unfortunately, although there is a plethora of evidence on dysfunctional consequences of poorly designed pay programs, there is surprisingly little direct evidence that higher pay–performance sensitivities lead to higher stock-price performance.[62] In this subsection, I comment on the difficulty of conducting this seemingly straightforward

---

[62] Exceptions include Masson (1971) and Abowd (1990), who offer evidence suggesting that stock-based incentives improve subsequent stock-price performance.

experiment, and then describe some of the approaches taken by researchers to address this important question.

3.8.1. Experimental difficulty: efficient capital markets

The scarcity of empirical evidence linking stock-based compensation to shareholder returns reflects financial economists' belief in efficient capital markets: the current stock price reflects all publicly available (and some privately available) information. Information on managements' pay–performance sensitivities is publicly available and thus already incorporated into stock prices. For example, suppose there are two firms, Firm A with high pay–performance sensitivities and Firm B with low sensitivities. Investors, realizing that Firm A has better managerial incentives, will bid up the price of Firm A until the expected risk-adjusted returns from investing in Firm A are exactly equal to the expected risk-adjusted returns from Firm B. An experiment that measures pay–performance sensitivities at a point in time, and examines shareholder returns over subsequent years will, therefore, find no difference in the average returns based on initial stockholdings.

The result that current incentives have no effect on expected subsequent returns does not mean incentives are unimportant. In fact, managers in Firm A are predicted to be working harder, smarter, and more in the interest of shareholders than managers of Firm B. In addition, the scenario described assumes that markets are completely efficient and incorporate all relevant information regarding managerial incentives. Subsequent stock returns can clearly be affected when relevant information is non-public (such as the details of annual bonus plans, or unannounced commitments for future option grants) or when shareholders misestimate or misinterpret compensation's impact on managerial behavior.

Another experimental difficulty is that aggressive and innovative incentive plans are often introduced as a "last resort" by troubled companies. Gilson and Vetsuypens (1993), for example, document significant increases in stock-option compensation for companies in financial distress. Dial and Murphy (1995) document significant increases in stock-based compensation at General Dynamics and other defense firms forced into decline and financial jeopardy following the end of the Cold War. In contrast, many historically successful companies (e.g., General Electric) adopt mundane and traditional compensation plans characterized by large base salaries with modest bonus and option opportunities. One hypothesis is that aggressive pay plans are not needed in rapidly growing and successful organizations, because growth provides ample promotion opportunities and because pay tends to rise with company size. In any case, cross-sectional comparisons of pay structures and company performance will lead to misleading conclusions about the impact of managerial incentives.

3.8.2. Event-study analyses

Under the efficient-markets hypothesis, the effect of increased managerial incentives – through increased stock ownership or introduction of new stock-based compensation plans – will be incorporated into the stock price upon announcement. Therefore, the natural test for analyzing the effect of managerial incentives is to analyze the stock-price reaction to announcements of stock-based plans and increased managerial shareholdings. The general problem in identifying this effect is that the announcement "dates" are often ambiguous. The appropriate date for increased shareholdings, for example, might be the date the transaction was anticipated, or actually made, or disclosed in insider-transaction filings with the SEC. Similarly, the appropriate "announcement date" for new compensation plans might be the date management passed the proposal to the board for approval, the date the board agreed on the plan, the date the plan was printed in the proxy statement, the release date for the proxy, the SEC-stamp date for the proxy, or the date the proxy was actually delivered to shareholders and the media.

An relevant early study is Brickley et al. (1985) who document a 2.4% abnormal return (that is, return after factoring out all market effects) for firms adopting stock-based compensation plans. The authors carefully screen for other announcements made in the proxy, and consider a variety of possible announcement dates. More recently, Yermack (1997) finds that stock prices increase after (non-publicly announced) grants of executive stock options. In both cases, the results are consistent with reduced agency costs but are also consistent with a more sinister hypothesis: executives push to adopt options programs, and time option grants, in anticipation of announcements likely to boost stock prices.[63]

3.8.3. Evidence on managerial stockholdings and Q-ratios

Several researchers have attempted to circumvent the implications of efficient capital markets by examining the relation between management stockholdings and company performance as measured by Tobin's Q-Ratio, defined as the market value of the firm divided by the replacement costs of the assets. The earliest and best-known study of management holdings and Q-Ratios is Morck et al. (1988). They find that firm performance increases with managerial holdings when managers hold between 0 and 5% of the outstanding stock. They document a negative (but weak) relationship between management holdings and performance when managers hold between 5 and 25% of the stock (which they attribute to an "entrenchment effect"), and a renewed positive relation for holdings exceeding 25%. McConnell and Servaes (1990) re-examine the evidence on managerial stockholdings and firm value, and find that Q's increase as share ownership becomes concentrated in the hands of the managers and board members until insider ownership exceeds 40 or 50% of the outstanding shares. More recently, Mehran (1995) finds that firm performance (measured by Tobin's Q and return on assets) is positively

---

[63] Yermack (1997) assumes that executives control the timing of option grants, and receive grants just prior to the release of favorable information. I believe a more sensible interpretation of Yermack's data is that option grants are largely exogenous, and executives "time" the release of the favorable information until after the exogenous option grant. This interpretation is based on the facts that (1) most large corporations make option grants at a fixed time each year (*e.g.*, following the March compensation committee meeting), and (2) Yermack finds no evidence that executives receive larger quantities of options prior to favorable announcements. Option exercises may also be unrelated to timing: Carpenter and Remmers (1998) find no evidence that options are exercised in advance of unfavorable announcements (or adverse stock-price performance).

related to the percentage of executive compensation that is stock-based, and the percentage of equity held by management. However, Himmelberg et al. (1998) control for the endogeneity of ownership, and find little evidence that changes in managerial ownership affect performance.

3.8.4. Evidence from LBOs and management buyouts

Leveraged management buyouts are a natural testing ground for stock-based incentives, since (for the most part) the same managers are managing the same assets and employees before and after the restructuring, and the primary differences are changes in the incentives (derived from increased equity holdings, increased stock-based compensation, the discipline of debt, and the increased monitoring from the LBO-association). Kaplan (1989, 1991) finds that, subsequent to LBO transactions, CEO holdings increase from about 1% of the firm to 6.4%, while the holdings for the top-management team increase to over 20%. He also finds that operating income increases by more than 20% by the third post-buyout year (relative to the pre-buyout period) and that cash flows increase by 80%. Pre-buyout public shareholders earn an average 38% market-adjusted return at the buyout. For LBO companies making the "round trip" back to public ownership, Kaplan estimates an additional market-adjusted return of 42% for the investors in the post-buyout capital.

In addition to Kaplan's large-scale data analysis, there have been numerous case studies that describe the effects of incentives in highly leveraged organizations. For example, an LBO at Cain Chemical produced a 100% return in 9 months (Jensen and Barry, 1991) and O.M. Scott's LBO produced similar results (Baker and Wruck, 1989). Leveraged recapitalizations at Sealed Air and other firms have produced spectacular increases in shareholder value (Wruck, 1994). In all of these studies and cases, the authors document systematic changes in managerial behavior consistent with the changes in stock-based managerial incentives.

Overall, the evidence is consistent with the hypothesis that stock-based incentives are important drivers of managerial actions and corporate performance. There remains little direct evidence, however, on the returns a company can expect from introducing aggressive performance-based compensation plans. The evidence is, at best, suggestive, and I believe that fully analyzing and documenting the effect of executive incentives on subsequent performance is a fruitful, if not critical, direction for future research in executive compensation.

4. Executive turnover and company performance

Closely related to research on executive compensation is the growing body of research on company financial performance surrounding CEO turnover (Murphy and Zimmerman, 1993). Several stylized facts regarding CEO turnover emerge from the literature. First, as documented in the pioneering studies by Coughlan and Schmidt (1985) and Warner et al. (1988), there is an inverse relation between net-of-market performance and the probability of management turnover.[64] Second, the magnitude of the turnover-performance relation is strongest in companies dominated by independent outside directors (Weisbach, 1988). Third, companies performing poorly relative to their industry are most likely to hire a replacement CEO from outside the firm (Parrino, 1997). Fourth, following management changes there are greater frequencies of asset write-offs (Strong and Meyer, 1987; Elliott and Shaw, 1988), income-reducing accounting method changes (Moore, 1973), income-reducing accounting accruals (Pourciau, 1993), and divestitures of previous acquisitions (Weisbach, 1993).[65]

The negative relation between stock-price performance and subsequent turnover has generally been interpreted as evidence that boards fire poorly performing CEOs. However, until very recently, managers were rarely openly fired from their positions. Warner et al. (1988), for example, analyzed 272 firms from 1963 to 1978 and found only a single case of an outright firing and only 10 cases in which poor performance was cited as one of the reasons for the separation. Weisbach (1988) examined 286 management changes for 1974–1983 and found only nine cases in which boards mention performance as a reason why the CEO was replaced. These data seem at odds with the highly publicized recent management changes at companies such as American Express, Apple Computer, Digital, Eastman Kodak, IBM and Westinghouse, suggesting that forced resignations have become more commonplace, and indicating a potential "regime shift" in disciplinary management turnover in the 1990s.

Two recent studies, Mikkelson and Partch (1997) and Huson et al. (1998), have analyzed secular changes in turnover-performance relations. Mikkelson and Partch compare the relation between CEO turnover and company performance for approximately 200 firms during two periods: an "active takeover market" from 1984 to 1988 and an "inactive takeover market" from 1989 to 1993. They document a slight decrease in "CEO departure rates" across the two 5-year periods: 39% of their sample CEOs left their firms in the earlier period, compared to 34% in the later period.[66] Moreover, for their 1984–1988 sample they find that CEOs performing in the lowest quartile of performance (measured by industry-relative operating performance) are significantly more likely to depart than CEOs performing in the top quartile. However, they find no relation between CEO departure rates and quartile performance over the 1989–1993 period. They conclude that disciplin-

---

[64] See also Weisbach (1988), Gilson (1989), Jensen and Murphy (1990), Gibbons and Murphy (1990), Murphy and Zimmerman (1993), Kaplan (1994a,b), Denis and Denis (1995), Hadlock and Lumar (1997), Parrino (1997), Mikkelson and Partch (1997), and Huson et al. (1998). International comparisons of executive turnover include Kang and Shivdasani (1995), Kaplan (1994a,b, 1997).

[65] The post-turnover behavior has generally been interpreted as incoming managers boosting future earnings at the expense of transition-year earnings by writing off unwanted operations and unprofitable divisions (that is, by taking an earnings "bath" that can be blamed on their predecessors). Murphy and Zimmerman (1993), however, control for the endogeneity of CEO turnover and show that post-turnover behavior is driven primarily by pre-turnover deteriorating performance rather than by managerial discretion.

[66] This difference is not statistically significant. However, when the authors analyze "complete management changes," defined as changes in three job titles (often held by the same individual) – CEO, President, and Chairman – they find a significant secular decline in management departures.

ary management turnover has declined, and suggest that this decline is associated with the decline in takeover activity.

Huson et al. (1998) analyze 1316 CEO successions from 1971 to 1994. They divide their sample into four 6-year periods, 1971–1976, 1977–1982, 1983–1988, and 1989–1994. In addition to analyzing the performance-determinants of period-by-period departure rates, the authors distinguish between "forced" and "voluntary" departures and examine whether the replacement CEO is promoted from within the company or appointed from outside the company.[67] In contrast to the Mikkelson–Partch results, Huson, Parrino, and Starks document that frequencies of forced turnover and outside succession have increased over time, and conclude that internal monitoring by boards of directors has become more effective in recent years, in spite of the decline in takeover activity. Resolving the differences between the results in these two studies is beyond the scope of this chapter.[68] However, in the remainder of this section, I will describe some basic facts and trends in CEO departure and turnover-performance sensitivities to help reconcile these results and to encourage future research in this important area.

Fig. 11 shows year-by-year departure rates for S&P 500 CEOs grouped according to whether company performance over the prior 2 years fell below or above the bottom quartile of performance for S&P 500 companies. For purposes of this analysis, departure rates are defined as the percentage of CEOs serving in their last fiscal year, and performance is defined as the 2-year return to shareholders minus the value-weighted 2-year return of all Compustat companies in the same two-digit SIC industry. Departure rates for poorly performing CEOs range from 22.5% in 1971 to 7.7% in 1976 (averaging 15.0%) while departure rates for better-performing CEOs range from 15.6% in 1970 to 8.0% in 1986 (averaging 10.8%). Departure rates for poorly performing CEOs exceeded those for better-performing CEOs in all but three of the 26 years in the sample, suggesting that the probability of CEO departure is higher following bad performance than following good.

Most studies of CEO turnover have attempted to distinguish between "normal" retirements and abnormal separations driven by poor performance. The natural proxy for normal retirement is the executive's age, since older CEOs are likely to leave their positions for reasons having nothing to do with performance. Fig. 12 describes the distribution of CEO age-at-departure, for S&P 500 CEOs grouped by decade and by whether their net-of-industry stock performance is below or above the bottom quartile. The figure is based on 1,089 CEO departures from 1970 to 1995, and illustrates the well-documented result that CEOs are most likely to leave their firm at ages 64 or 65. In fact, across the 26-year

---

[67] The authors define forced departures as (1) public firings reported in the *Wall Street Journal* and (2) departures in which the incumbent CEO is younger than 60 and does not leave for health reasons or for other employment. Outside replacements are defined as executives serving in the firm less than 1 year prior to being appointed CEO.

[68] Huson, Parrino, and Starks conclude that the differences may reflect secular changes in the measures used by boards to evaluate CEO performance. In particular, while Mikkelson and Partch find a decline in the relation between turnover and industry-relative accounting profits, Huson, Parrino, and Starks replicate this finding in their data, but find an increased relation between turnover and the *change* in industry-relative accounting profits.

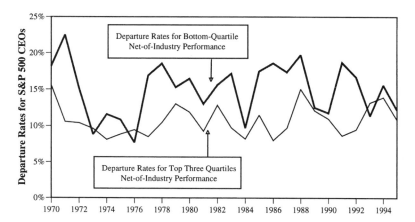

Fig. 11. Departure rates for CEOs S&P 500 CEOs, by 2-year net-of-industry stock price performance, 1970–1995. Departure rates reflect the percentage of CEOs in serving in their last full fiscal year. Sample is based on all CEOs included in the S&P 500. Data prior to 1992 extracted from *Forbes* Annual Compensation Surveys; data in 1992 and later from Compustat's ExecuComp database. Net-of-industry stock price performance defined as total shareholder return minus the value-weighted return of all Compustat companies in the same two-digit industry. "Bottom Quartile Performance" based on the cumulative net-of-market return realized during the CEO's last full fiscal year, and in the preceding year.

sample, 32.8% of the CEOs left their firms at ages 64 or 65, and 62% of the CEOs left the firm between the ages of 60–66. However, the figure shows that the prevalence of departing upon "normal retirement" has diminished over time. In particular, the percentage of good performers retiring at age 64 or 65 (i.e., the right-hand column of Fig. 12) fell from 39% in the 1970s to 35% in the 1980s to only 29% in the 1990s.

Fig. 12 also shows that the prevalence of normal retirement varies with company performance. In particular, 35% of the 780 CEOs performing above the bottom quartile retired at ages 64 or 65, compared to only 28% of the 309 poor performing CEOs. Executives in poor-performing companies tend to depart at younger ages: 34% of the poor-performing CEOs left before age 60, compared to only 24% of the CEOs from better-performing companies. Prior research on management turnover has generally interpreted these results as reflecting CEOs who were implicitly (but rarely publicly) fired for poor performance before reaching normal retirement ages.

Table 10 reports coefficients from ordinary least-squares regressions predicting the annual probability of CEO turnover as a function of firm performance and a dummy variable for retirement-aged CEOs.[69] In order to test whether performance-related dismissals have increased in recent years, I estimate the following regression for the 1970s, 1980s, and for 1990–1995:

---

[69] I also estimated turnover probabilities using logistic methodologies and obtained qualitatively identical results; I focus on the OLS results because of efficiencies in interpretation and exposition.

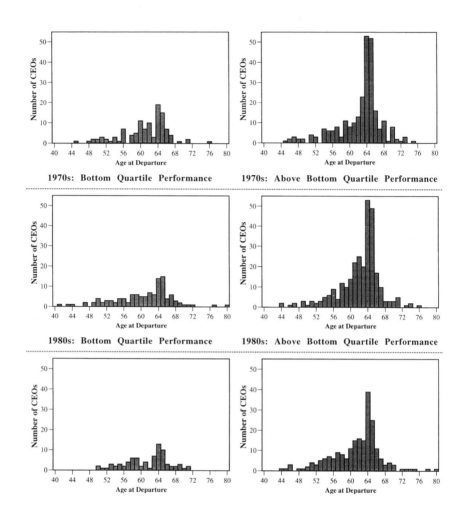

Fig. 12. Age at departure for S&P 500 CEOs, by 2-year net-of-industry stock price performance, 1970–1996. (a) 1970s: bottom quartile performance; (b) 1970s: above bottom quartile performance; (c) 1980s: bottom quartile performance; (d) 1980s: above bottom quartile performance; (e) 1990–1996: bottom quartile performance; (f) 1990–1996: above bottom quartile performance. Sample is based on all CEOs included in the S&P 500. Data prior to 1992 extracted from *Forbes* Annual Compensation Surveys; data in 1992 and later from Compustat's Execu-Comp database. Data reflect CEO age as of the end of the CEO's final full fiscal year. Net-of-industry stock price performance defined as total shareholder return minus the value-weighted return of all Compustat companies in the same two-digit industry. "Bottom Quartile Performance" based on the cumulative net-of-market return realized during the CEO's last full fiscal year, and in the preceding year. The charts ignore one CEO departing below age 40, and six CEOs departing after age 80.

$$\text{Prob(Turnover)} = a + b(\text{Dummy} = 1 \text{ if age } \geq 64 + c_2(\text{net -of-industry return})$$

$$+ c_2(\text{lagged net-of-industry return}). \quad (6)$$

The dependent variable is equal to 1 if the CEO is serving in his last full fiscal year and 0 otherwise. Column (1) reports "pooled" 1970–1995 results for S&P 500 Industrials (which exclude utilities and financial services). The regression intercept of 0.0784 implies that a young executive in an average-performing firm (i.e., realizing zero net-of-industry returns) has a departure probability of about 7.9%. The positive and significant coefficient on the retirement-age dummy of 0.2849 implies that an average-performing old CEO (i.e., over 63 years old) has an annual departure probability of about 36.3% (i.e., 0.0784 + 0.2849). The negative and significant coefficient on contemporaneous net-of-industry performance of -0.0188 implies that a young executive realizing returns 30% below the industry average (roughly corresponding to the bottom quartile) has a departure probability of 8.5%. Thus, consistent with prior research, column (1) shows that poor performance increases departure probabilities, although the *economic significance* of the turnover-performance relation (measured by the increased departure probability associated with poor performance) is fairly small (Jensen and Murphy, 1990a).

Columns (2), (3), and (4) of Table 10 compare the results from turnover-performance regressions for S&P 500 CEOs in the 1970s, 1980s, and 1990–1995, respectively. The coefficient on the retirement-age dummy remains positive and significant in all three regressions, but diminishes over time (consistent with Fig. 12). The coefficient on contemporaneous net-of-industry performance increases (in absolute value) from -0.0514 in the 1970s to -0.0769 in the 1980s, but then falls to an insignificant -0.0042 in the 1990s. The coefficient on lagged performance falls monotonically (in absolute value), but is statistically insignificant in all three regressions. Therefore, consistent with the Mikkelson–Partch results, I find that the relation between management turnover and stock-price performance has declined since the 1980s. Moreover, even when statistically significant, the effect is economically small: it is difficult to conclude that the "threat of termination" provided meaningful CEO incentives in the 1970s and 1980s; this conclusion is even more difficult to reach based on 1990s data.

Columns (5) to (8) of Table 10 show how the relation between performance and turnover varies with company size for CEOs in industrial companies in the S&P 500, the S&P Mid-Cap 400, and the S&P Small-Cap 600, based on 1992–1995 data from Compustat's ExecuComp database. The coefficient on the retirement-age dummy variable is monotonically increasing in company size: annual departure probabilities for average-performing "old" CEOs are 42.2% for large S&P 500 firms, 27.5% for small S&P 500 firms, 17.4% for Mid-Cap firms, and 15.3% for Small-Cap firms. The coefficient on current net-of-industry performance is statistically significant only for Small-Cap firms. Taken together, the results suggest that turnover is driven by executive age and not performance in the largest firms, and by performance and not (primarily) executive age in smaller firms.

Although most research on CEO turnover focuses on the characteristics of *departing*

Table 10
Linear probability models predicting CEO departures using CEO age = 64, net-of-industry return, and lagged net-of-industry return[a]

Independent variable	S&P 500 Industrials, 1970–1995				S&P Industrials, 1992–1995			
	All years (1)	1970–1979 (2)	1980–1989 (3)	1990–1995 (4)	Large S&P 500 (5)	Small S&P 500 (6)	Mid-Cap 400 (7)	Small-Cap 600 (8)
Intercept	0.0784	0.0700	0.0747	0.0898	0.0877	0.0976	0.0934	0.0948
	(21.1)	(11.6)	(11.5)	(13.1)	(8.0)	(18.4)	(10.7)	(12.7)
(Dummy) age $\geq$ 64	0.2849	0.3118	0.2885	0.2435	0.3346	0.1769	0.0805	0.0584
	(27.6)	(18.1)	(17.0)	(12.3)	(9.7)	(5.6)	(2.9)	(2.3)
Net-of-industry return	−0.0188	−0.0514	−0.0769	−0.0042	−0.0022	0.0017	−0.0043	−0.0371
	(−2.8)	(−2.6)	(−3.9)	(−0.5)	(−0.1)	(0.2)	(−0.6)	(−4.7)
Lagged net-of-industry return	−0.00275	−0.0308	−0.0265	−0.0047	0.0022	0.0069	0.0013	−0.0001
	(−0.4)	(−1.6)	(−1.4)	(−0.6)	(0.1)	(0.8)	(0.4)	(−0.4)
R^2	0.0885	0.1103	0.1042	0.0578	0.0909	0.0346	0.0066	0.0149
Sample size	7922	2733	2701	2488	957	911	1365	1832

[a] Note: t-statistics in parentheses. The dependent variable is equal to 1 if the CEO is serving in his last full fiscal year and 0 otherwise. Data prior to 1992 extracted from *Forbes* Annual Compensation Surveys; data in 1992 and later from Compustat's ExecuComp database. Net-of-industry return equals the total shareholder return less the value-weighted return of all Compustat companies in the same two-digit SIC industry. Young CEOs are defined as CEOs younger than 64 as of the fiscal year-end. Qualitative results unchanged using logistic methodologies.

CEOs, Parrino (1997) and Huson et al. (1998) analyze the relation between company performance and the characteristics of the *newly appointed* CEO. These papers find that poorly performing companies often replace CEOs through external appointments rather than internal promotions. In addition, Huson, Parrino, and Starks document that the prevalence of outside appointments has increased substantially since the late 1980s.

Fig. 13 describes the distribution of tenure-in-company for new CEOs, for S&P 500 companies grouped by decade and by whether their net-of-industry stock performance is below or above the bottom quartile. The figure is based on 1005 CEO hires among S&P 500 companies from 1971 to 1996, and replicates the Huson-Parrino-Starks finding that outside hiring is more commonplace in the 1990s. In particular, in the 1970s only 31 of 373 new hires (8.3%) came from outside of the company. During the 1980s, 36 of the 347 (10.4%) new hires came from outside the company. During the first 7 years of the 1990s, 54 of 285 new hires (18.9%) were new to the company. Over the same time period, the percentage of "seasoned executives" (defined as executives with tenure exceeding 20 years) promoted to CEOs fell from 58 to 46%.

Fig. 13 also replicates the finding that outside hires are more likely following poor performance than following good performance. In particular, across the 26-year sample, 15.8% of the new hires in poorly performing firms came from outside, compared to 10.6% for companies performing above the bottom quartile of net-of-industry stock-price performance. However, the difference in outside hiring prevalence explained by poor performance has diminished over time. For example, in the 1970s, 14% of new CEOs in poor performing firms came from outside, compared to only 6% in good performing firms. In the 1980s, the percentage of outside hires among poor performance remained at 14%, while the prevalence of outside hiring among good performers grew to 9%. By the 1990s, the percentage of outside hires in poor and good performing firms was, respectively, 21 and 18%.

The year-by-year prevalence of outside hiring is explored in Fig. 14. The figure shows outside hiring percentages for S&P 500 companies above and below the bottom performance quartile. Outside hiring for poorly performing CEOs ranges from 0% (in 6 years) to over 45% in 1996 (averaging 14.6%). Outside hiring in better-performing companies ranges from 0% (in 3 years) to 21% in 1991 and 1995 (averaging 10.1%). Outside hiring percentages for poorly performing CEOs exceeded those for better-performing CEOs in 15 of the 26 sample years.

Taken together, the results in Table 10 and Figs. 11–14 offer mixed support for the regime shift in executive turnover suggested by a few highly publicized management changes. On the one hand, performance-related turnover has diminished rather than increased in recent years, and turnover among S&P 500 CEOs in the 1990s is statistically unrelated to stock-price performance. On the other hand, there has been a dramatic increase in replacing CEOs through external hires rather than internal promotions. Although the causes and consequences of this shift is left to future research, I believe the increased prevalence of outside hiring reflects a regime shift with important implications for management incentives and organizational performance.

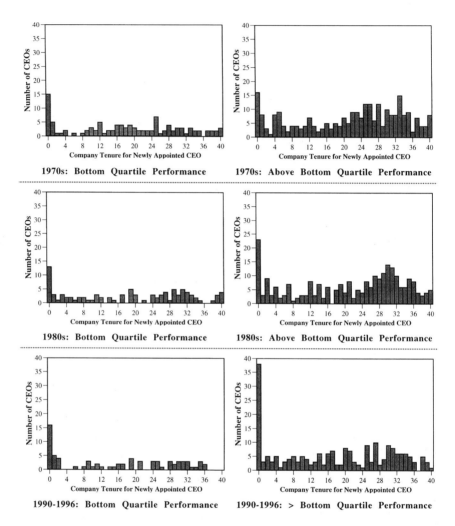

Fig. 13. Tenure in firm upon appointment for S&P 500 CEOs, by 2-year net-of-industry stock price performance, 1970–1996. (a) 1970s: bottom quartile performance; (b) 1970s: above bottom quartile performance; (c) 1980s: bottom quartile performance; (d) 1980s: above bottom quartile performance; (e) 1990–1996: bottom quartile performance; (f) 1990–1996: above bottom quartile performance. Sample is based on all CEOs included in the S&P 500. Data prior to 1992 extracted from *Forbes* Annual Compensation Surveys; data in 1992 and later from Compustat's ExecuComp database. Data reflect years employed by the firm prior to becoming CEO. Net-of-industry stock price performance defined as total shareholder return minus the value-weighted return of all Compustat companies in the same two-digit industry. "Bottom Quartile Performance" based on the cumulative net-of-market return realized during the 2 fiscal years prior to the incoming CEO's appointment.

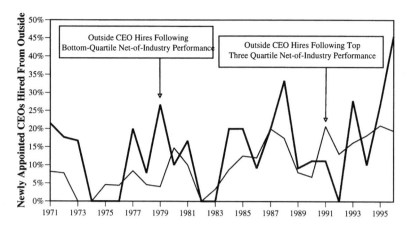

Fig. 14. Percentage of new S&P 500 CEO appointments coming from outside the firm, by 2-year net-of-industry stock price performance, 1971–1996. Chart is based on S&P 500 CEOs serving in their first year as CEO, and depicts the percentage of these newly appointed CEOs employed by their firm for less than 1 year prior to their appointment as CEO. Net-of-industry stock price performance defined as total shareholder return minus the value-weighted return of all Compustat companies in the same two-digit industry. "Bottom Quartile Performance" based on the cumulative net-of-market return realized during the 2 fiscal year's preceding the new CEO's appointment.

5. The politics of pay

No survey of US executive compensation is complete without some discussion regarding the political factors that influence the level and structure of CEO pay. As emphasized by Jensen and Murphy (1990a), CEO pay contracts are not a private matter between a principal and an agent. The public disclosure of executive pay required by the Securities and Exchange Commission (SEC) virtually guarantees that third parties such as rank-and-file employees, labor unions, consumer groups, Congress, and the media affect the type of contracts written between management and shareholders.

Although the business press had followed CEO pay for decades,[70] CEO pay did not really become a public "issue" until 1991. Feature stories on CEO pay aired on the nightly news broadcasts of the three major networks in the Spring of 1991, and CNN, *60 Minutes* and *Nightline* devoted segments to CEO pay. The controversy heightened with the November 1991 introduction of Graef Crystal's (1991) expose on CEO pay, *In Search of Excess*, and exploded following President George Bush's ill-timed pilgrimage to Japan in January 1992, accompanied by an entourage of highly paid US executives. What was meant to be a plea for Japanese trade concessions dissolved into accusations that US

---

[70] *Forbes*, for example, began its annual survey of executive compensation in 1971.

competitiveness was hindered by its excessive executive compensation practices as attention focused on the "huge pay disparities between top executives in the two countries."[71]

Consistent with *Time* magazine's labeling of CEO pay as the "populist issue that no politician can resist,"[72] CEO pay became a major political issue. High CEO salaries emerged as a bipartisan campaign issue among the leading candidates in the 1992 presidential election.[73] Legislation had been introduced in the House of Representatives disallowing deductions for compensation exceeding 25 times the lowest-paid worker, and the "Corporate Pay Responsibility Act" was introduced in the Senate to give shareholders' more rights to propose compensation-related policies.[74] The SEC preempted the pending Senate bill in February 1992 by requiring companies to include non-binding shareholder resolutions about CEO pay in company proxy statements,[75] and announced sweeping the new rules affecting the disclosure of top executive compensation in the annual proxy statement in October 1992. In 1993, the Internal Revenue Service defined non-performance-related compensation in excess of $1 million as "unreasonable" and therefore not deductible as an ordinary business expense for corporate income tax purposes, and the Financial Accounting Standards Board proposed deducting the value of stock options upon grant from corporate earnings.

By the mid-1990s, media and political attention focused on the growing disparity between CEO pay and average worker pay, and on escalating CEO pay in downsizing companies. *Newsweek* ran a February 1996 cover story on "Corporate Killers: The Hitmen," which identified CEOs both by their salaries and by how many employees had been fired in recent restructurings (Sloan, 1996). In September 1996 a national coalition of labor, religious, student, and community groups called "Jobs With Justice" held rallies and marches in 33 cities "to denounce corporations that downsized and cut wages and benefits for working people while increasing compensation for corporate executives." In 1997, the AFL-CIO launched a website focusing exclusively on "exorbitant pay schemes that have created unprecedented inequities in the American workplace" and

---

[71] "SEC to push for Data on Pay of Executives," *Wall Street Journal* (January 21, 1992). An interesting postscript to Bush's 1991 trip is that, by 1997, Japanese executives were claiming that *Japan's* competitiveness was hindered by its out-dated executive compensation practices, and pushed for government reforms to allow US-style stock options for Japanese executives.

[72] Thomas McCarroll, "The Shareholders Strike Back: Executive Pay," *Time* (May 5, 1992).

[73] "Politics and Policy – Campaign '92: From Quayle to Clinton, Politicians Are Pouncing on the Hot Issue of Top Executive's Hefty Salaries," *Wall Street Journal*, January 15, 1992. Bill Clinton promised to "end the practice of allowing companies to take unlimited tax deductions for excessive executive pay;" Dan Quayle warned that corporate boards should "curtail some of these exorbitant salaries paid to corporate executives that are unrelated to productivity;" Bob Kerry called it "unacceptable" for corporate executives to make millions of dollars while their companies are posting losses; Paul Tsonga argued that "excessive pay is hurting Americas ability to compete in the international market;" and Pat Buchanen argued "you can't have executives running around making $4 million while their workers are being laid off."

[74] "Executive Pay (A Special Report)," *Wall Street Journal*, April 22, 1992.

[75] "Shareholder Groups Cheer SEC's Moves On Disclosure of Executive Compensation," *Wall Street Journal* (February 14, 1992).

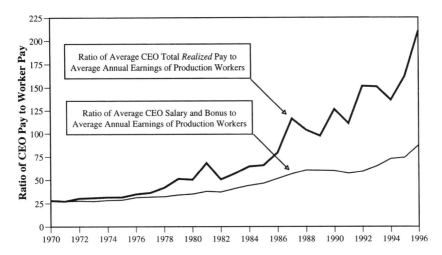

Fig. 15. Ratio of average CEO pay to average pay for production workers, 1970–1996. CEO sample is based on all CEOs included in the S&P 500, using data from Forbes and ExecuComp. CEO total realized pay includes cash pay, restricted stock, payouts from longterm pay programs, and the amounts realized from exercising stock options during the year. (Total pay prior to 1978 excludes option gains.) Worker pay represents 52 times the average weekly hours of production workers multiplied by the average hourly earnings, based on data from the Current Employment Statistics, Bureau of Labor Statistics.

described as a "working families' guide to monitoring and curtailing the excessive salaries, bonuses and perks in CEO compensation packages."[76]

Fig. 15 illustrates relative trends in CEO pay and worker compensation contributing to the ongoing controversy over CEO pay levels. In 1970, the average S&P 500 CEO made about 30 times more than the average production worker.[77] By 1996, the average S&P 500 CEO received cash compensation nearly 90 times greater than the average earnings for production workers, and total realized compensation (including gains from exercising stock options) of *210 times* the earnings for production workers. Moreover, since down-sizing increases stock prices in industries saddled with excess capacity (Jensen, 1993), layoff announcements have generally increased the value of executive stock options, further fueling resentment among disgruntled and displaced workers.

Jensen and Murphy (1990a,b) predicted that the populist attack on CEO pay would lead to both lower pay levels and lower pay–performance sensitivities. However, as documented in this chapter, both the level of CEO pay and the sensitivity of CEO wealth to stock-

---

[76] Quotes taken from the AFL-CIO website, http://aflcio.paywatch.org/ceopay. This website also discusses Teamsters publications titled *America's Least Valuable Directors* and *Runaway Executive Pay at Union Pacific and the Clubby Board of Directors Responsible for It.*

[77] Production worker pay calculated as 52 × (average weekly hours of production workers) × (average hourly earnings of production workers), based on data from the Current Employment Statistics, Bureau of Labor Statistics.

price performance have increased substantially since the pay controversy "peaked" in the early 1990s. The increase in pay levels and sensitivities, reflecting in large part the recent explosion in stock option grants, is consistent with the Jensen–Murphy normative prescriptions (that companies should increase pay sensitivities regardless of the political cost) but inconsistent with their "implicit regulation" hypothesis.

One interpretation of the recent trends in CEO pay is that a bull market is the "best defense" against political pressure. The US Congress cannot effectively regulate CEO pay without widespread shareholder consent, and shareholders in a bull market are relatively complacent. Still, there is ample evidence that politics and public perception play an important role in determining the structure and level of executive compensation, even in a bull market. DeAngelo and DeAngelo (1991), for example, study the US steel industry in the 1980s and document that CEOs receive lower cash compensation in union-negotiation years than in other years, interpreting these cuts as representing "symbolic sacrifices that encourage all stakeholders to participate in the concessions needed to salvage the firm." Joskow et al. (1996) analyze the relation between CEO pay and firm characteristics in the electric utility industry, and conclude that political pressures constrain CEO pay levels in that industry. Murphy (1996) finds that managers adopt disclosure methodologies that reduce reported or perceived compensation, interpreting this evidence as supporting the hypothesis that managers bear non-pecuniary costs from high reported levels of compensation. Dial and Murphy (1995) document the political pressures on pay at General Dynamics, leading the company to replace a controversial bonus plan with conventional stock options. Perry and Zenner (1997) and Rose and Wolfram (1997) analyze the impact of the $1 million "cap" on deductibility of non-performance-pay, finding that companies subject to the cap have reduced relative levels of base salaries, while increasing stock options and other performance-related pay.

Organizational Behaviorists have focused on the potential political costs of wage disparities among the top management group and between executives and lower level workers.[78] From an economic perspective, high pay disparity across hierarchical levels can strengthen incentives for employees in promotion tournaments (Lazear and Rosen, 1981). However, from an sociological and psychological perspective, perceived "pay inequities" lead to lower productivity and product quality, decreased employee morale, and increased turnover.[79] Understanding the effects of pay inequities in organizations, and understanding more generally the role of politics in shaping compensation practices, seems a natural direction for future research in executive compensation.

---

[78] See, for example, Cowherd and Levine (1992), Finkelstein (1996), O'Reilly et al. (1998), and Hambrick and Siegel (1998).

[79] See O'Reilly et al. (1998) for a survey of the extensive literature on social comparison theory (Festinger, 1954) as applied to employees and executives. In addition, see Lazear (1989) for an economic model incorporating the effects of such social comparisons in organizations.

6. Conclusions

The objective of this chapter is to encourage research in executive compensation by equipping potential researchers with a comprehensive description of pay practices and a representative summary of the empirical and theoretical research. The chapter is largely descriptive, and focused on the explicit rather than the implicit aspects of executive incentive contracts.

This chapter has documented and updated several cross-sectional stylized facts, and has shown how executive compensation practices vary with company size, industry, and country. For example, the analysis has shown that (1) levels of pay are higher, and pay–performance sensitivities are lower, in larger firms; (2) levels of pay and pay–performance sensitivities are lower in regulated utilities than in industrial firms; (3) levels of pay and pay–performance sensitivities are higher in the US than in other countries. The analysis has also documented that pay–performance sensitivities are driven primary by stock options and stock ownership and not through other forms of compensation.

The chapter has also documented several recent trends in executive compensation and turnover. In particular, levels of pay and pay–performance sensitivities in the US have increased substantially over the past decade, driven primarily by an explosion in stock-option compensation. In addition, although the relation between company performance and executive turnover has weakened over the past decade, CEOs in the 1990s are less likely to depart at "normal" retirement ages than in earlier years, and are more likely to be replaced through outside hires rather than through internal promotions.

Although the theoretical and empirical literature on executive compensation is fairly well developed, it is far from complete and there are many issues worthy of continued research. For example, while the recent increase in CEO pay levels is well documented, the factors underlying the trend (e.g., the bull market and a "ratchet effect" caused by compensation surveys) are not. Why have stock options become such an important part of the compensation package in recent years? Why are US executives paid more than their foreign counterparts? Are international practices converging? And, what are causes and consequences of the effects of the growing disparity between CEO and rank-and-file pay?

The parameters of the executive contract also merit additional attention. Why are executive bonus contracts inherently non-linear while stock-based pay is inherently linear? Why are performance standards in bonus plans typically based on annual budgets rather than on external measures such as the cost of capital or peer-group performance? Why is there *so little* variation in option parameters (e.g., exercise prices, expiration terms) across companies? Why are executives allowed, if not encouraged, to exercise options immediately upon vesting rather than holding them until expiration? Why is RPE scarce, and observed only for accounting returns and not stock returns?

Perhaps the most important area for future research is on the effect of CEO incentives on subsequent company performance. Although there is ample evidence that CEOs (and other employees) respond predictably to dysfunctional compensation arrangements, it is more difficult to document that the increase in stock-based incentives has led CEOs to work harder, smarter, and more in the interest of shareholders. Do executives understand how their actions affect shareholder value? Has the increase in stock-based incentives contributed to the recent bull market, or resulted from it? Do increases in broad-based stock incentives for lower-level employees lead to improved stock-price performance?

Finally, I believe our understanding of the relative importance of accounting-based bonuses and stock-based compensation is far from complete. The fact that stock-based compensation accounts for most of the variation in executive wealth (see, for example, Figs. 8 and 9) does not imply that executive incentives are driven primarily by stock rather than accounting performance. Many CEOs understand how their actions affect accounting profits, but do not understand how their actions affect shareholder value. Rational managers will naturally focus on increasing accounting bonuses and devote less attention to stock prices if they know how to affect the former but not the latter.

Labor economists have traditionally focused on markets rather than firms, not because labor inside organizations is unimportant but rather because data inside organizations are unavailable and inherently messy. The managerial labor market offers a unique and data-rich environment to analyze many concepts central to labor economics, including incentives, marginal productivity, contracts, promotions, separations, and careers. Even when results for executives cannot be easily extrapolated to other labor groups, the results are important in their own right: top managers are critical and highly visible inputs into the corporate production function, and understanding better their role can enrich our understanding of both incentives and organizations.

Appendix A. Option valuation and the Black–Scholes formula

The Black–Scholes option valuation formula, modified to incorporate continuous dividend payments, is given by

Option value $P\exp[-\ln(1 + d)T]N(z) - X\exp[-\ln(1 + r)T]N(z - \sigma\sqrt{T})$,

where P is the grant-date stock price, X is the exercise price, T is the expiration term (years), d is the annualized dividend yield, σ is the annual stock-price volatility, r is the risk-free interest rate,

$$z = \frac{\ln(P/X) + (\ln(1 + r) - \ln(1 + d) + \sigma^2/2)T}{\sigma\sqrt{T}},$$

and $N(\ )$ is the cumulative normal distribution function.

The risk-free rate (for options denominated in US dollars) is typically defined as the annualized yield US Treasury securities maturing on the option's expiration date. Conceptually, dividend yields and stock-price volatilities correspond to anticipated yields and volatilities over the option term. As a practical matter, however, these parameters are typically computed based on historical data. For example, volatilities are most often defined as $\sqrt{12}$ times the standard deviation of $\ln(1 + \text{Monthly Return})$, measured over the prior 36, 48, or 60 months. Similarly, dividend yields are typically measured as the annualized yield over the past 1, 2, or 3 years. In both cases, outliers are omitted; Execu-Comp's "modified" Black–Scholes involves adjusting volatility and yield estimates towards their historical mean.

References

Abowd, J. (1990), "Does performance–based managerial compensation affect corporate performance?" Industrial and Labor Relations Review 43 (3): S52–S73.

Abowd, J. and M. Bognanno (1995), "International differences in executive and managerial compensation", in: R. Freeman and L. Katz, eds., Differences and changes in wage structures (The University of Chicago Press, Chicago, IL) pp. 67–103.

Aggarwal, R. and A. Samwick (1997), Executive compensation, strategic competition and relative performance evaluation: theory and evidence (Dartmouth College).

Aggarwal, R. and A. Samwick (1999), "The other side of the tradeoff: the impact of risk on executive compensation", Journal of Political Economy 107 (1): 65–105.

Agrawal, A. and G. Mandelker (1987), "Managerial incentives and corporate investment and financing decision", Journal of Finance 42 (4): 823–837.

Agrawal, A. and R. Walkling (1994), "Executive careers and compensation surrounding takeover bids", Journal of Finance 49 (3): 985–1014.

Anderson, R. (1997), Compensation committees: it matters who sets pay (Washington and Lee University).

Angel, P. and V. Fumás (1997), "The compensation of Spanish executives: a test of a managerial talent allocation model", International Journal of Industrial Organization 15 (4): 511–531.

Antle, R. and A. Smith (1986), "An empirical investigation of the relative performance evaluation of corporate executives", Journal of Accounting Research 24 (1): 1–39.

Baiman, S. and R. Verrecchia (1995), "Earnings and price-based compensation contracts in the presence of discretionary trading and incomplete contracting", Journal of Accounting and Economics 20 (1): 93–121.

Baker, G. (1992), "Incentive contracts and performance measurement", Journal of Political Economy 100: 598–614.

Baker, G. and K. Wruck (1989), "Organizational changes and value creation in leveraged buyouts: the case of O.M. Scott & Sons Company", Journal of Financial Economics 25: 163–190.

Baker, G., M. Jensen and K.J. Murphy (1988), "Compensation and incentives: practice vs. theory", Journal of Finance 43 (3): 593–616.

Banker, R. and S. Datar (1989), "Sensitivity, precision and linear aggregation of accounting signals", Journal of Accounting Research 27 (1): 21–39.

Barro, R. and J. Barro (1990), "Pay, performance and turnover of bank CEOs", Journal of Labor Economics 8 (4): 448–481.

Baumol, W. (1959), Business behavior, value and growth (New York).

Berle, A.A. and G.C. Means (1932), The modern corporation and private property (New York).

Bizjak, J., J. Brickley and J. Coles (1993), "Stock-based incentive compensation and investment behavior", Journal of Accounting and Economics 16 (1–3): 349–372.

Black, F. and M. Scholes (1973), "The pricing of options and corporate liabilities", Journal of Political Economy 81: 637–659.

Boeker, W. (1992), "Power and managerial dismissal: scapegoating at the top", Administrative Science Quarterly 37: 400–421.

Boschen, J. and K. Smith (1995), "You can pay me now and you can pay me later: the dynamic response of executive compensation to firm performance", Journal of Business 68 (4): 577–608.

Brickley, J., S. Bhagat and R. Lease (1985), "The impact of long-range managerial compensation plans on shareholder wealth", Journal of Accounting and Economics 7 (1–3): 115–129.

Brunello, G., C. Graziano and B. Parigi (1999), Executive compensation and firm performance in Italy (University of Udine).

Bushman, R. and R. Indjejikian (1993), "Accounting income, stock price and managerial compensation", Journal of Accounting and Economics 16 (1–3): 3–23.

Bushman, R., R. Indjejikian and A. Smith (1996), "CEO compensation: the role of individual performance evaluation", Journal of Accounting and Economics 21 (2): 161–193.

Campbell, T., Y. Chan and Marino, A. (1989), "Incentive contracts for managers who discover and manage investment projects", Journal of Economic Behavior and Organizations 12: 353–364.

Carmichael, H.L. (1988), "Incentives in academia: why is there tenure?" Journal of Political Economy 96 (3): 453–473.

Carroll, T. and D. Ciscel (1982), "The effects of regulation on executive compensation", Review of Economics and Statistics 64 (3): 505–509.

Carpenter, J. (1998), "The exercise and valuation of executive stock options", Journal of Financial Economics 48 (2): 127–158.

Carpenter, J. and B. Remmers (1998), Stock price performance following insider option exercise (Stern School of Business, New York University).

Ciscel, D. and T. Carroll (1980), "The determinants of executive salaries: an econometric survey", Review of Economics and Statistics 62 (1): 7–13.

Conyon, M. (1997), "Corporate governance and executive compensation", International Journal of Industrial Organization 15 (4): 493–510.

Conyon, M. and J. Schwalbach (1997), European differences in executive pay and corporate governance (Warwick Business School).

Conyon, M., P. Gregg and S. Machin (1995), "Taking care of business: executive compensation in the United Kingdom", The Economic Journal 105: 704–714.

Cosh, A. (1975), "The remuneration of chief executives in the United Kingdom", Economic Journal 85: 75–94.

Cosh, A. and A. Hughes (1997), "Executive remuneration, executive dismissal and institutional shareholdings", International Journal of Industrial Organization 15 (4): 469–492.

Coughlan, A. and R. Schmidt (1985), "Executive compensation, management turnover and firm performance: an empirical investigation", Journal of Accounting and Economics 7 (1–3): 43–66.

Cowherd, D. and D. Levine (1992), "Product quality and pay equity between lower-level employees and top management: an investigation of distributive justice theory", Administrative Science Quarterly 37: 302–320.

Crawford, A., J. Ezzell and J. Miles (1995), "Bank CEO pay-performance relations and the effects of deregulation", Journal of Business 68 (2): 231–56.

Crystal, G. (1991), In search of excess: the overcompensation of American executives (W.W. Norton & Company, New York).

Crystal, G. and F. Foulkes (1988), "Don't bail out underwater options", Fortune, March 14.

DeAngelo, H. and L. DeAngelo (1991), "Union negotiations and corporate policy: a study of labor concessions in the domestic steel industry during the 1980s", Journal of Financial Economics 30 (1): 3–44.

Dechow, P. and R. Sloan (1991), "Executive incentives and the horizon problem", Journal of Accounting and Economics 14 (1): 51–89.

Dechow, P., M. Huson and R. Sloan (1994), "The effect of restructuring charges on executives' cash compensation", Accounting Review 69 (1): 138–156.

DeFusco, R., R. Johnson and T. Zorn (1990), "The effect of executive stock option plans on stockholders and bondholders", Journal of Finance 45 (2): 617–627.

Denis, D.R. and D.K. Denis (1995), "Performance changes following top management dismissals", Journal of Finance 50: 1029–1057.

Dial, J. and K.J. Murphy (1995), "Incentives, downsizing and value creation at general dynamics", Journal of Financial Economics 37 (3): 261–314.

Dye, R. (1984a), "The trouble with tournaments", Economic Inquiry 22 (1): 147–149.

Dye, R. (1984b), "Relative performance evaluation and project selection", Journal of Accounting Research 30 (1): 27–52.

Elliott, J. and W. Shaw (1988), "Write-offs as accounting procedures to manage perceptions", Journal of Accounting Research 26 (suppl.): 91–119.

Eriksson, T. and M. Lausten (1996), Managerial pay and firm performance: Danish evidence (Aarhus Business School).

Fama, E. (1980), "Agency problems and the theory of the firm", Journal of Political Economy 88 (2): 288–307.

Festinger, L. (1954), "A theory of social comparison processes", Human Relations 7: 117–140.

Finkelstein, S. (1996), Understanding pay dispersion within top management teams: a social comparison perspective (Amos Tuck School of Business, Dartmouth College).

Garen, J. (1994), "Executive compensation and principal-agent theory", Journal of Political Economy 102 (6): 1175–1199.

Gaver, J., K. Gaver and J. Austin (1995), "Additional evidence on bonus plans and income management", Journal of Accounting and Economics 19 (1): 3–28.

Gibbons, R. (1997), "Incentives and careers in organizations", in: D. Kreps and K. Wallis, eds, Advances in economic theory and econometrics (Cambridge University Press, Cambridge, UK) pp. 1–37.

Gibbons, R. and K. J. Murphy (1990), "Relative performance evaluation for chief executive officers", Industrial and Labor Relations Review 43 (3): 30s–51s.

Gibbons, R. and K.J. Murphy (1992a), "Optimal incentive contracts in the presence of career concerns: theory and evidence", Journal of Political Economy 100 (3): 468–505.

Gibbons, R. and K.J. Murphy (1992b), "Does executive compensation affect investment?" Journal of Applied Corporate Finance 5 (2).

Gilson, S. (1989), "Management turnover and financial distress", Journal of Financial Economics 25: 241–262.

Gilson, S. and M. Vetsuypens (1993), "CEO compensation in financially distressed firms: an empirical analysis", Journal of Finance 48 (2): 425–458.

Grossman, S. and O. Hart (1983), "An analysis of the principal–agent problem", Econometrica 51: 7–45.

Groves, T., Y. Hong, J. McMillan and B. Naughton (1995), "China's evolving managerial labor market", Journal of Political Economy 103 (4): 873–892.

Hadlock, C. and G. Lumar (1997), "compensation, turnover and top management incentives: historical evidence", Journal of Business 70: 153–187.

Hall, B. and Leibman, J. (1998), "Are CEOs really paid like bureaucrats?" Quarterly Journal of Economics 113 (3): 653–691.

Hallock, K. and K.J. Murphy (1999), The economics of executive compensation (Edward Elgar Publishing Ltd.).

Hambrick, D. and A. Cannella (1993), "Relative standing: a framework for understanding departures of acquired executives", Academy of Management Journal 36 (4): 733–762.

Hambrick, D. and P. Siegel (1998), Pay dispersion within top management groups: evidence of its harmful effects on performance of high-technology firms (Columbia University).

Hart, O. and B. Holmstrom (1987), "The theory of contracts", in: T. Bewley, ed., Advances in economic theory, fifth world congress (Cambridge University Press, Cambridge, UK).

Haubrich, J. (1994), "Risk aversion, performance pay and the principal-agent problem", Journal of Political Economy 102 (2): 258–276.

Healy, P. (1985), "The effect of bonus schemes on accounting decisions", Journal of Accounting and Economics 7: 85–107.

Hebner, K. and T. Kato (1997), "Insider trading and executive compensation: evidence from the US and Japan", International Review of Economics and Finance 6 (3): 223–237.

Hemmer, T., S. Matsunaga and T. Shevlin (1998), "Optimal exercise and the cost of granting employee stock options with a reload provision", Journal of Accounting Research 36 (2): 231–255.

Himmelberg, C., R.G. Hubbard and D. Palia (1998), Understanding the determinants of managerial ownership and the link between ownership and performance (Columbia University).

Hirshleifer, D. and R. Suh (1992), "Risk, managerial effort and project choice", Journal of Financial Intermediation 2: 308–345.

Holmstrom, B. (1979), "Moral hazard and observability", The Bell Journal of Economics 10: 74–91.

Holmstrom, B. (1982), "Moral hazard in teams", The Bell Journal of Economics 13 (2): 324–340.

Holmstrom, B. (1992), "Contracts and the market for executives: comment", in: Lars Wein and Hans Wijkander, eds., Contract economics (Blackwell Publishers).

Holmstrom, B. and P. Milgrom (1987), "Aggregation and linearity in the provision of intertemporal incentives", Econometrica 55: 303–328.

Holmstrom, B. and P. Milgrom (1991), "Multitask principal-agent analyses: incentive contracts, asset ownership and job design", Journal of Law, Economics and Organization 7: 24–52.

Holthausen, R., D. Larcker and R. Sloan (1995), "Annual bonus schemes and the manipulation of earnings", Journal of Accounting and Economics 19 (1): 29–74.

Holthausen, R., D. Larcker and R. Sloan (1995), "Business unit innovation and the structure of executive compensation", Journal of Accounting and Economics 19 (2,3): 279–313.

Hubbard, R. and D. Palia (1995), "Executive pay and performance: evidence from the US banking industry", Journal of Financial Economics 39 (1): 105–130.

Huddart, S. (1998), "Patterns of stock option exercise in the United States", in: J. Carpenter and D. Yermack, eds., Executive compensation and shareholder value (NYU and Kluwer Academic Publishers, Norwell, MA) pp. 113–140.

Hull, J. (1993), Options, futures and other derivative securities, 2nd edition (Prentice Hall, New Jersey).

Huson, M., R. Parrino and L. Starks (1998), The effectiveness of internal monitoring mechanisms: evidence from CEO turnover between 1971 and 1994 (University of Texas).

Janakiraman, S., R. Lambert and D. Larcker (1992), "An empirical investigation of the relative performance evaluation hypothesis", Journal of Accounting Research 30 (1): 53–69.

Jensen, M. (1993), "The modern industrial revolution, exit and the failure of internal control systems", Journal of Finance 48 (3): 831–857.

Jensen, M. and B. Barry (1991), "Gordon Cain and the Sterling Group (A)", HBS Case 9-492-021.

Jensen, M. and K.J. Murphy (1990a), "Performance pay and top-management incentives", Journal of Political Economy 98 (2): 225–264.

Jensen, M. and K.J. Murphy (1990b), "CEO incentives: it's not how much, but how", Harvard Business Review May/June.

Jensen, M. and W. Meckling (1976), "Theory of the firm: managerial behavior, agency costs and ownership structure", Journal of Financial Economics 3: 305–360.

John, T. and K. John (1993), "Top-management compensation and capital structure", Journal of Finance 48 (3): 949–974.

Jones, D. and T. Kato (1996), "The determinants of chief executive compensation in transitional economies: evidence from Bulgaria", Labour Economics 3 (3): 319–336.

Joskow, P. and N. Rose (1994), "CEO pay and firm performance: dynamics, asymmetries and alternative performance measures", Working paper no. 4976 (NBER, Cambridge, MA).

Joskow, P., N. Rose and C. Wolfram (1996), "Political constraints on executive compensation: evidence from the electric utility industry", RAND Journal of Economics 27 (1): 165–182.

Kang, J. and A. Shivdasani (1995), "Firm performance, corporate governance and top executive turnover in Japan", Journal of Financial Economics 38 (1): 29–58.

Kaplan, R. and D. Norton (1992), "The balanced scorecard: measures that drive performance", Harvard Business Review January/February: 71–79.

Kaplan, S. (1989), "The effects of management buyouts on operating performance and value", Journal of Financial Economics 24 (2): 217–254.

Kaplan, S. (1991), "The staying power of leveraged buyouts", Journal of Financial Economics 29 (2): 287–314.

Kaplan, S. (1994a), "Top executive rewards and firm performance: a comparison of Japan and the United States", Journal of Political Economy 102 (3): 510–546.

Kaplan, S. (1994b), "Top executives, turnover and firm performance in Germany", Journal of Law, Economics and Organization 10 (1): 142–159.

Kaplan, S. (1997), Top executive incentives in Germany, Japan and the US: a comparison (University of Chicago).

Kato, T. and M. Rockel (1992), "Experiences, credentials and compensation in the Japanese and US managerial labor markets: evidence from new micro data", Journal of the Japanese and International Economy 6 (1): 30–51.

Kato, T. (1997), "Chief executive compensation and corporate groups in Japan: new evidence from micro data", International Journal of Industrial Organization 15 (4): 493–510.

Kedia, S. (1997), Strategic interactions in executive compensation contracts (Harvard University).

Kole, S. (1997), "The complexity of compensation contracts", Journal of Financial Economics 43 (1): 79–104.

Kostiuk, P. (1990), "Firm size and executive compensation", Journal of Human Resources 25 (1): 90–105.

Lambert, R. (1986), "Executive effort and the selection of risky projects", RAND Journal of Economics 17 (1): 77–88.

Lambert, R., W. Lanen and D. Larcker (1989), "Executive stock option plans and corporate dividend policy", Journal of Financial and Quantitative Analysis 24 (4): 409–425.

Lambert, R. and D. Larcker (1988), "An analysis of the use of accounting and market measures of performance in executive compensation contracts", Journal of Accounting Research 25: 85–129.

Lambert, R., D. Larcker and R. Verrecchia (1991), "Portfolio considerations in valuing executive compensation", Journal of Accounting Research 29 (1): 129–149.

Lazear, E. (1989), "Pay equality and industrial politics", Journal of Political Economy 97: 561–580.

Lazear, E. and S. Rosen (1981), "Rank-order tournaments as optimum labor contracts", Journal of Political Economy 89 (5): 841–864.

Leonard, J. (1990), "Executive pay and firm performance", Industrial and Labor Relations Review 43 (3): S13–S29.

Lewellen, W. and B. Huntsman (1970), "Managerial pay and corporate performance", American Economic Review 60 (4): 710–720.

Lewellen, W., C. Loderer and K. Martin (1987), "Executive compensation and executive incentive problems: an empirical analysis", Journal of Accounting and Economics 9: 287–310.

Lewellen, W., T. Park and B. Ro (1996), "Self-serving behavior in managers' discretionary information disclosure decisions", Journal of Accounting and Economics 21 (2): 227–252.

Main, G., C. O'Reilly and J. Wade (1995), "The CEO, the board of directors and executive compensation: economic and psychological perspectives", Industrial and Corporate Change 11: 606–628.

Main, G., C. O'Reilly and G. Crystal (1994), "Over here and over there: a comparison of top executive pay in the UK and the USA", Contributions to Labour Studies 4: 115–127.

Masson, R. (1971), "Executive motivations, earnings and consequent equity performance", Journal of Political Economy 79 (6): 1278–1292.

McConnell, J. and H. Servaes (1990), "Additional evidence on equity ownership and corporate value", Journal of Financial Economics 27 (2): 595–612.

Mehran, H. (1995), "Executive compensation structure, ownership and firm performance", Journal of Financial Economics 38 (2): 163–184.

Mehran, H., G. Nogler and K. Schwartz (1998), "CEO incentive plans and corporate liquidation policy", Journal of Financial Economics, in press.

Mikkelson, W. and M. Partch (1997), "The decline of takeovers and disciplinary turnover", Journal of Financial Economics 44: 205–228.

Milgrom, P. and J. Roberts (1992), Economics, organizations and management (Prentice Hall, New Jersey).

Mirrlees, J. (1974), "Notes on welfare economics, information and uncertainty", in: M. Balch, D. McFadden and S. Wu, eds., Essays on economic behavior under uncertainty (North Holland, Amsterdam).

Mirrlees, J. (1976), "The optimal structure of incentives and authority within an organization", Bell Journal of Economics 7: 105–131.

Mookherjee, D. (1984), "Optimal incentive schemes with many agents", Review of Economic Studies 51 (3): 433–446.

Moore, M. (1973), "Management changes and discretionary accounting decisions", Journal of Accounting Research 11: 100–107.

Morck, R., A. Shleifer and R. Vishny (1988), "Management ownership and market valuation: an empirical analysis", Journal of Financial Economics 20: 293–316.

Murphy, K.J. (1985), "Corporate performance and managerial remuneration: an empirical analysis", Journal of Accounting and Economics 7 (1–3): 11–42.

Murphy, K.J. (1986), "Incentives, learning and compensation: a theoretical and empirical investigation of managerial labor contracts", RAND Journal of Economics 17 (1): 59–76.

Murphy, K.J. (1987), Executive compensation in regulated utilities (University of Rochester).

Murphy, K.J. (1993), Executive compensation in corporate America 1993 (United Shareholders Association).

Murphy, K.J. (1995), "Politics, economics and executive compensation", University of Cincinnati Law Review 63 (2).

Murphy, K.J. (1996), "Reporting choice and the 1992 proxy disclosure rules", Journal of Accounting, Auditing and Finance 11 (3): 497–515.

Murphy, K.J. (1997), "Executive compensation and the modern industrial revolution", International Journal of Industrial Organization 15 (4): 417–426.

Murphy, K.J. (1998), Performance standards in incentive contracts (University of Southern California).

Murphy, K.J. and J. Zimmerman (1993), "Financial performance surrounding CEO turnover", Journal of Accounting and Economics 16 (1–3): 273–315.

Newman, H. and H. Mozes (1997), Compensation committee composition and its influence on CEO compensation practices (Fordham University).

Ofek, E. and D. Yermack (1997), Taking stock: does equity-based compensation increase managers' ownership? (Stern School of Business, New York University).

O'Reilly, C., B. Main and G. Crystal (1988), "CEO Compensation as tournament and social comparison: a tale of two theories", Administrative Science Quarterly 33: 257–274.

O'Reilly, C., J. Wade and T. Pollock (1998), Overpaid CEOs and underpaid managers: equity and executive compensation (Stanford University).

Oyer, P. (1998), "Fiscal year ends and non-linear incentive contracts: the effect on business seasonality", Quarterly Journal of Economics 113 (1): 149–185.

Parrino, R. (1997), "CEO turnover and outside succession: a cross-sectional analysis", Journal of Financial Economics 46: 165–197.

Perry, T. and M. Zenner (1997), Pay for performance? Government regulation and the structure of compensation contracts (University of North Carolina).

Pourciau, S. (1993), "Earnings management and nonroutine executive changes", Journal of Accounting and Economics 16 (1–3): 317–336.

Roberts, D. (1956), "A general theory of executive compensation based on statistically tested propositions", Quarterly Journal of Economics 70 (2): 270–294.

Rose, N. and C. Wolfram (1997), Regulating CEO pay: assessing the impact of the tax–deductibility cap on executive compensation (MIT).

Rosen, S. (1982), "Authority, control and the distribution of earnings", The Bell Journal of Economics 13 (2): 311–323.

Rosen, S. (1992), "Contracts and the market for executives", in: Lars Wein and Hans Wijkander, eds., Contract economics (Blackwell Publishers).

Ross, S. (1973), "The economic theory of agency: the principal's problem", American Economic Review 63: 134–139.

Saly, J. (1994), "Repricing executive stock options in a down market", Journal of Accounting and Economics 18 (3): 325–356.

Sloan, A. (1996), "Corporate killers: the hitmen", Newsweek, February 26.

Sloan, R. (1993), "Accounting earnings and top executive compensation", Journal of Accounting and Economics 16 (1–3): 55–100.

Smith, C. and R. Watts (1992), "The investment opportunity set and corporate financing, dividend and compensation policies", Journal of Financial Economics 32 (3): 263–292.

Strong, J. and J. Meyer (1987), "Asset writedowns: managerial incentives and security returns", Journal of Finance 20: 643–663.

Tosi, H. and L. Gomez-Mejia (1989), "The decoupling of CEO pay and performance: an agency theory perspective", Administrative Science Quarterly 34: 169–189.

Tosi, H. and L. Gomez-Mejia (1994), "CEO compensation monitoring and firm performance", Academy of Management Journal 37 (4): 1002–1016.

Virany, B., M. Tushman and E. Romanelli (1992), "Executive succession and organization outcomes in turbulent environments: an organization learning approach", Organization Science 3 (1): 72–91.

Warner, J., R. Watts and K. Wruck (1988), "Stock prices and top management changes", Journal of Financial Economics 20: 461–492.

Weisbach, M. (1988), "Outside directors and CEO turnover", Journal of Financial Economics 20 (1,2): 431–460.

Weisbach, M. (1993), "The CEO and the firm's investment decisions", Journal of Financial Economics 37 (2): 159–188.

Wruck, K. (1994), " Financial policy, internal control and performance: sealed air corporation's leveraged special dividend", Journal of Financial Economics 36: 157–192.

Yermack, D. (1995), "Do corporations award CEO stock options effectively?" Journal of Financial Economics 39 (2,3): 237–269.

Yermack, D. (1997), "Good timing: CEO stock option awards and company news announcements", Journal of Finance 52 (2): 449–476.

Zhou, X. (1999), "CEO pay, firm size and corporate performance: evidence from Canada", Canadian Journal of Economics, in press.

PART 10

INTERACTIONS BETWEEN
DEMAND AND SUPPLY

Chapter 39

NEW DEVELOPMENTS IN MODELS OF SEARCH IN THE LABOR MARKET

DALE T. MORTENSEN

Northwestern University

CHRISTOPHER A. PISSARIDES

London School of Economics, Centre for Economic Performance and Centre for Economic Policy Research

Contents

Handbook of Labor Economics, Volume 3, Edited by O. Ashenfelter and D. Card

Abstract

Equilibrium models of labor markets characterized by search and recruiting friction and by the need to reallocate workers from time to time across alternative productive activities represent the segment of the research frontier explored in this chapter. In this literature, unemployment spell and job spell durations as well as wage offers are treated as endogenous outcomes of forward looking job creation and job destruction decisions made by the workers and employers who populate the models. The solutions studied are dynamic stochastic equilibria in the sense that time and uncertainty are explicitly modeled, expectations are rational, private gains from trade are exploited, and the actions taken by all agents are mutually consistent. We argue that the framework provides a useful setting in which to study the effects of alternative wage setting institutions and different labor market policy regimes. © 1999 Elsevier Science B.V. All rights reserved.

JEL codes: D58; E24; J31; J41; J64

1. Introduction

Equilibrium models of labor markets characterized by search and recruiting friction and by the need to reallocate workers from time to time across alternative productive activities represent the segment of the research frontier explored in this chapter. In this literature, unemployment spell and job spell durations as well as wage offers are treated as endogenous outcomes of forward looking job creation and job destruction decisions made by the workers and employers who populate the models. The solutions studied are dynamic stochastic equilibria in the sense that time and uncertainty are explicitly modeled, expectations are rational, private gains from trade are exploited, and the actions taken by all agents are mutually consistent. In contrast to the earlier literature on individual worker job search decisions, for example, much of that reviewed by Mortensen (1986), the equilibrium search approach explicitly accounts for and indeed emphasizes the role of employers on the demand side of the labor market. As a consequence, we argue, the framework provides a rich and useful setting in which to study the effects of alternative wage setting institutions and different labor market policy regimes.

The need for a richer equilibrium framework for labor market analysis then that provided by the frictionless competitive model is both empirical and conceptual. Large numbers of workers and jobs flow between inactivity and market production at the aggregate level. At the level of individual workers and employers, worker flows between labor market states and job creation and job destruction flows are reflected in activity spells found in panel data whose durations reflect the time spent searching for work, filling a vacancy, and working in a particular job. These movements are concealed in existing models of employment that focus on stocks. The emphasis on mobility makes the types of models reviewed here part of the so-called flows approach (see Blanchard and Diamond, 1992). to labor market analysis.[1]

Still another empirical reason for interest in the framework is wage dispersion across observably identical workers. These differentials have led many observers to question and some to reject perfectly competitive wage theory. Search and matching frictions inevitably generate match specific rents that the wage must divide between worker and employer. Because the precise way in which these rents might be shared is indeterminate, the framework requires some alternative to the marginal productivity theory of wages, at least in its simplest form. Although the natural and usual specification is ex post bargaining in the models reviewed, alternatives such as a monopoly union specification, an insider–outsider story, and efficiency wage theories can all be accommodated and studied within the framework. The principal alternative to the wage as a bargaining outcome, that studied most extensively in the literature, is the assumption that employers post wage offers.

What new lessons can be learned about the effects of policy using the new approach? Because unemployment has an economic role in the flows framework, welfare statements about the effects of policy on unemployment and on the cost of unemployment experienced by those who bear it are possible. Also, the total effect of a policy can be decomposed into effects on unemployment duration and on unemployment incidence. As a consequence of this fact and the two sided nature of the models, multiple channels of influence arise. For example, unemployment benefits influence both worker incentives to accept employment and the wage. Because the wage affects employer incentives to create vacancies and recruit workers, the total impact on unemployment duration is a consequence of decisions made on both sides of the labor market. As the wage impacts job destruction as well, there are a least three different channels through which unemployment insurance benefits might be expected to affect unemployment.

Consider the effects of different forms of employment subsidies as another example of fruitful policy application. In conventional static models, a subsidy is treated as a reduction in labor costs which increases the demand for labor. Whether the subsidy is paid to employers on a per employee hired basis or is proportional to the employment stock is immaterial. Because these two alternative subsidy forms have different effects on the job

---

[1] We have also written a companion paper, Mortensen and Pissarides (1998), on the macroeconomic implications of the flows approach for the forthcoming *Handbook of Macroeconomics*. For that reason, the focus of this chapter is more microeconomic.

creation and job destruction decisions that determine worker and employer flows, questions the form that subsidies should take can be analyzed within the equilibrium flows framework.

The comments above suggest that the existing literature on equilibrium search forms a unified whole. Although related, there are two quite different branches of the search equilibrium literature, each with its own primary concerns. The goal of the first is to explain worker and job flows and levels of unemployment within the rational forward looking agent paradigm. Fundamental is the idea that two-sided frictions exist in the process of matching trading partners and that agents on both sides of a market make investments in overcoming them. As a result, the job creation flow depends on the numbers of unemployed workers and vacant jobs available and on the intensities with workers search and employers recruit, a relationship which has become known as the matching function. The effects of market friction on the incentives to invest in search, recruiting, training and other forms of match specific capital which in turn determine the equilibrium level of employment are the primary concerns in the literature based on the "matching approach" to labor market analysis.

Contributors to the second literature show that wage dispersion can be an equilibrium outcome in markets with friction. By assumption, wage offers are set by employers in a non-cooperative setting while workers search for the best among them. Here, search friction is regarded as simply the time required for workers to gather information about wage offers. The outcomes of these strategic "wage posting" games are studied as explanations of wage differentials that are not associated with observed worker skill.

Although a review of recent developments in search equilibrium is a principal purpose of the chapter, it is not the exclusive one. Another goal is to show how the general approach has and can be used to study the employment effects of different wage determination mechanisms and can be applied to labor market policy analysis. We also show how the two branches of the search equilibrium literature can be reintegrated and suggest some of the rewards that such a synthesis offers.

This chapter is composed of seven sections. The tools used and the concepts applied by contributors to the literature on search equilibrium market models are briefly introduced in Section 2. Formal models of job-worker matching, labor market flows, and equilibrium unemployment are the topics of Section 3. In these models, wages are determined by a specific rent sharing rule that can viewed as the outcome of a Nash bargain between worker and employer engaged in when they meet. Section 4 reviews variations of the matching model characterized by different wage determination mechanisms. In Section 5, applications of the matching approach to the analysis of labor market policy are reviewed and illustrated. Forms of wage dispersion that arises as equilibrium outcomes of wage posting games are the principal topics of Section 6. The implications of a synthesis of the matching and wage posting approaches to modeling labor market equilibrium are sketched in Section 7. Finally, a very brief summary concludes the chapter.

2. Modeling markets with friction

Market friction, the costly delay in the process of finding trading partners and determining the terms of trade, is ignored in the standard theory of perfectly competitive markets. Friction is explicitly modeled in the work reviewed in this chapter. The central problem of the theory of markets with friction is to find a useful way to make the behavior of individual agents both individually rational and mutually consistent. In this section, we survey the concepts introduced in the recent literature on the problem.[2]

2.1. The stopping problem

The tools of dynamic optimization applied in the equilibrium search literature are introduced first. We do so in the process of reviewing the sequential job search model, the workhorse of the literature, which is based on the decision theoretic optimal stopping problem.

A distribution of payoffs characterized by a c.d.f. $F(W)$ is postulated which is known to the searcher. A sequential sample of realizations can be drawn with replacement at a constant per observation cost denoted by a. Only one of the realizations can be accepted and acceptance is a sequential decision without recall. A search strategy determines when to accept, i.e., it is a stopping rule. An *optimal stopping strategy* maximizes the expected present value of the realization accepted net of the accumulated costs of search.

Application of the model to the job search problem in which workers are not fully informed about the terms of available employment offers is simply a matter of interpretation of this structure. Think of the sampling process as that of sequentially applying for jobs selected at random and let each realization of W represent the value of an offered employment contract, either the wage or more generally the present value of a worker's future utility stream conditional on accepting the offer. In discrete time, the stopping decision is easily formulated as a dynamic programming problem. If a single sample is taken in every period until the process stops and past realizations cannot be recalled, then the value of searching in each period, U_t, is generated by the Bellman equation

$$U_t = \frac{b-a}{1+r} + \frac{1}{1+r} \int \max\{W, U_{t+1}\} dF(W), \qquad t = 1, 2, ..., \tag{1}$$

where r is the discount or risk free interest rate, b is income flow received contingent on unemployment, and a represents the cost of search per period. Namely, the optimal strategy involves comparing the observed current realization of the sampling process W_t with the value of continued search U_{t+1} in the next period. If the former exceeds the latter, then the search process stops, i.e., the optimal strategy satisfies a *reservation property*. In the infinite horizon case, the value of continued search is the stationary solution to Eq. (1),

---

[2] Some of the original papers that raised the issues discussed in this section include Diamond (1981, 1982a,b), Mortensen (1982a,b), and Pissarides (1984a,b).

i.e., $U_t = U$ for all t where

$$U = \frac{b-a}{1+r} + \frac{1}{1+r} \int \max\{W, U\} dF(W), \tag{2}$$

As the right side is a contraction map for all $0 < r < 1$,[3] call it $T(U)$, a unique finite solution $U = T(U)$ exists provided that the c.d.f. F has a first moment.

Virtually all the literature on equilibrium search is cast in continuous rather than discrete time. Although this fact is partially a historical accident, continuous time techniques can often reduce the apparent complexity of sequential search and recruiting problems. For example, allowing for a stochastic time interval between offer arrivals is one realistic extension easier to formalize in continuous time. Because arrival dates are separated in continuous time, decisions are revised only after arrivals. Hence, the analysis reduces to a dynamic programming formulation in which the time intervals between decision dates is a strictly positive random variable with a know duration distribution.

Characterize the distribution of random waiting time between offer arrivals by its generally duration dependent hazard function $\lambda(t)$, i.e., the probability that an offer will not arrive before T, the associated survivor function of the waiting time distribution, is $\exp[-\int_0^T \lambda(t)dt]$. Taking account of the waiting duration, the Bellman equation for the extended model becomes

$$U(t) = E_T\{(b-a) \int_t^T \exp(-rs)ds + \exp[-r(T-t)] \int \max\{W, U(T)\}dF(W)\}$$

$$= \int_t^\infty ((b-a) \int_t^T \exp(-rs)ds + \exp[-r(T-t)]$$

$$\times \int \max\{W, U(T)\}dF(W))\lambda(T)\exp\left[-\int_0^T \lambda(t)dt\right]dT, \tag{3}$$

where $U(t)$ is the value of search at time t and $T > t$ is the future random date at which the first offer arrives. Given an exponential waiting time distribution, a constant hazard $\lambda(t) \equiv \lambda$, the value of search is stationary and solves

$$U = \int_0^\infty \left[\frac{b-a}{r}(1 - \exp(-rT)) + \exp(-rT) \int \max\{W, U\}dF(W)\right]\lambda\exp(-\lambda T)dT$$

$$= \frac{b-a}{r+\lambda} + \frac{l}{r+\lambda} \int \max\{W, U\}dF(W), \tag{4}$$

where λ is the Poisson offer arrival rate. Note that Eq. (4) is a simple generalization of Eq. (2) that accounts for the duration of the waiting period, $1/\lambda$ in the exponential case.

The full power of the continuous time formulation is suggested by the following equivalent "asset pricing" representation of Eq. (4):

---

[3] It satisfies Blackwell sufficient conditions (see Lucas and Stokey, 1989, p. 54).

$$rU = b - a + \lambda \int [\max\{W, U\} - U] dF(w). \tag{5}$$

U represents the "asset" or "option" value of search activity. Given this interpretation, Eq. (5) simply prices the option by requiring that the opportunity cost of holding it, the left hand side, is equal to the current income flow, $b - a$, plus the expected capital gain flow, the product of the arrival frequency λ and the expected capital gain given an offer arrival.

In the general case, one can show that $U(t)$ must be a solution to the generalized asset pricing equation, the differential equation

$$rU(t) = b(t) - a(t) + \lambda(t) \int [\max\{W, U(t)\} - U(t)] dF(W) + \frac{dU(t)}{dt}, \tag{6}$$

where the duration derivative dU/dt is the pure rate of capital gain or loss attributable to waiting another instant for an offer arrival. This equation can be obtained directly by differentiating both sides of Eq. (3) with respect to t. Using the fact that

$$\frac{dU(t)}{dt} = \lim_{dt \to 0} \left\{ \frac{U(t + dt) - U(t)}{dt} \right\},$$

one can also write

$$U(t) = \frac{1}{1 + rdt} [(b(t) - a(t))dt + \lambda(t)dt \int \max\{W, U\} dF(W) + [1 - \lambda(t)dt]U(t + dt)]$$

as an approximation to Eq. (6) for all sufficiently small values of the period length $dt > 0$. Obviously, this relationship has a natural interpretation as a Bellman equation in a discrete time formulation of the problem where $\lambda(t)dt$ is the probability of an offer arrival during the period $(t, t + dt)$ and rdt is the discount rate for the specified period length dt. Of course, time paths for the value of an optimal search strategy must also satisfy the transversality condition $\lim_{t \to \infty} U(t)\exp(-rt) = 0$. The general fact that the option value of search solves a general asset pricing equation and transversality condition of this form provides a very quick and powerful characterization of optimality conditions in equilibrium search models in continuous time.[4]

Interest among empirical labor economists in search theory was generated initially by the fact that it addressed observations on unemployment spell duration lengths and subsequent accepted wage distribution in panel data. As the unemployment spell hazard is $\lambda(t)[1 - F(U(t))]$ and the conditional acceptable wage distribution conditional on duration is $F(W)/[1 - F(U(t))]$, the model can be formally applied to interpret available data and to generate testable empirical hypotheses. There is now a substantial literature that does just

---

[4] The value of continued search is not stationary if (a) the horizon is finite, (b) payoff realizations reveals information about its distribution to the searcher, or (c) the environment is non-stationary. Although all of these cases have been studied in the partial equilibrium literature, (c) is the principal source of non-stationarity considered in the equilibrium literature.

that.[5] A principal shortcoming of most of it, however, is that only generalizations of this decision theoretic formulation of the optimal stopping problem are typically applied. General equilibrium considerations that may well make primitives endogenous, the offer arrival rate and the distribution offers in particular, are not raised in much of the literature. The remainder of this review points out these equilibrium effects and reviews the existing empirical work that takes them into account.

2.2. Two-sided search and wage determination

In labor, marriage, and related markets, the central problem is the creation of cooperating coalitions composed of two or more agents of different types, e.g., worker and employer, men and women, etc. In the labor market case, a cooperating coalition is a producing unit composed of a job-worker match. The job-worker match is formed when a qualified unemployed worker and a sufficiently attractive vacancy meet.

The value of search for an unemployed worker, U, is given by Eq. (4). An employer with a vacancy faces a similar problem. Let c denote the flow cost of recruiting a worker to fill a vacancy and let η denote the frequency with which an employer encounters workers seeking employment. Clearly, the value of holding the job vacant V, the expected present value of future profit, solves the following analogue of Eq. (4).

$$V = \frac{-c}{r + \eta} + \frac{\eta}{r + \eta} \int \max\{V, J\} \mathrm{d}G(J), \tag{7}$$

where J represents the value of filling the job and G denotes its distribution across workers.

In the case of *transferable utility*,[6] the total value of the match to the pair is the sum of the shares received by its partners, i.e.,

$$W + J = X. \tag{8}$$

In market equilibrium, the value of each share will be determined by the wage outcome. To satisfy individual rationality, the share received by each partner must exceed the forgone option of continued search. Regarding these values (U, V) as the "threat point", a general solution to this problem is one that gives some fraction β of the net surplus $X - (U + V)$ to the worker and the remainder to the firm, i.e.,

$$W - U = \beta(X - U - V), \qquad \beta \in [0, 1]. \tag{9}$$

A necessary and sufficient condition for the formation of a match under individual rationality and transferable utility is that $X - (U + V) \geq 0$.

Match rents are divided between firm and worker by the wage rule. Wage determination

---

[5] See Devine and Kiefer (1991), Wolpin (1995), and Neumann (1997) for reviews of the empirical literature on unemployment and job spell duration and postspell wage rate that apply this theory.

[6] The case of non-transferable utility in a search equilibrium context, the marriage problem, is not reviewed here although there are a number of excellent recent papers available on the topic. For example, see Coles and Burdett (1997), Burdett and Wright (1998), and Smith (1997).

is a major issue in the context of search equilibrium modelling. Unlike competitive theory without friction, an existing match will always command quasi-rents ex post because it is costly in time and resources for either party in the pair to seek the next best alternative. Given the existence of these quasi-rents, the "market wage" is not unique in this environment. Any division that satisfies individual rationality is a formal possibility. However, the most common specification found in the literature is the assumption that rents are divided with the worker's share β regarded as a free parameter. Possible justifications as well as alternatives assumptions about wage determination are considered subsequently.

2.3. Matching technology

A *matching technology*, like a production technology, is a description of the relation between inputs, search and recruiting activity, and the output of the matching process, the flow rate at which unemployed worker and vacant jobs form new job-worker matches. Because an employer joins a worker when a worker joins an employer to form a match, an "adding up" condition holds that needs to be made explicit. The flow rate at which unemployed workers meet vacancies is identically equal to the flow rate at which employers with vacant jobs meet applicants. Formally, the assumption that each searching worker meets prospective employers at frequency λ implies that the expected aggregate rate at which unemployed workers meet vacant jobs is equal to λu where u denotes the measure of unemployed workers. Similarly, the assumption that each vacancy is visited by workers at frequency η implies that the aggregate rate at which vacancies meet applicants is ηv where v represent the measure of vacancies. These two flows are identically equal. Obviously, since the vacancy and unemployment pair (v,u) can be anything, the identity $\lambda u \equiv \eta v$ requires that the arrival frequencies are functions of the measures of participation, u and v.

The general solution to this problem found in the literature is to invoke a *matching function*, denoted as $m(v,u)$, which characterizes the aggregate meeting rate. Then

$$\lambda u \equiv m(v,u) \equiv \eta v \tag{10}$$

implies that the two meeting rate functions, $\lambda = m(v,u)/u$ and $\eta = m(v,u)/v$, represent the average rates at which unemployed workers and vacancies meet potential partners. The matching function summarizes all the details of the meeting process is a manner analogous to the way an aggregate production function summarizes a production process. Namely, it is the "output" of the meeting process expressed as a function of its inputs, as reflected in the measures of agents of each type participating in the process.[7]

At the micro level, different matching functions can be derived from specific specifications of the meeting process. For example, if each agent on one side of the market has all the telephone numbers of unmatched agents on the other side and each makes contact by phoning a number chosen at random from time to time, then one can show that the meeting

---

[7] Although the matching function was not stated and estimated explicitly until the early 1980s, it features in earlier search models, most notably Phelps (1968) and Bowden (1980).

function in continuous time takes the linear form $m = fu + gv$ where f represents the calling frequency of the typical unemployed worker and g is the average frequency with which employers with vacancies make calls. Formally, fu calls are made per period of length dt by the searching workers. As the expected number of calls made by workers per employer with a vacancy per period of length dt is $fudt/v$ and the actual number of calls received by any one employer is a Poisson random variable, the probability that a particular employer is not called during the interval is $\exp(-(fu/v)dt)$. Hence, the number of employers who receive one or more calls is $v(1 - \exp(-(fu/v)dt)$. Analogously, the number of workers who receive at least one call from some employer with a vacancy is $u(1 - \exp(-(gv/u)dt)$. The aggregate contact rate per unit period is the sum of these two numbers divided by the period length dt. Taking the limit as the latter tends to zero, one obtains

$$\lim_{dt \to 0} \left\{ \frac{v[1 - \exp(-(fu/v)dt)] + u[1 - \exp(-(gv/u)dt)]}{dt} \right\}$$

$$= \lim_{dt \to 0} \{fu\exp(-(fu/v)dt) + gv\exp(-(gv/u)dt)\} = fu + gv$$

provided that $(u, v) > 0$.

However, if the telephone book includes all agents on the other side of the market, matched and unmatched, then the aggregate rate at which *unmatched agents* of the two types meet is $m = fuv/k + gvu/l$, where l and k represent the total number of worker and jobs, since v/k is the probability that a randomly selected employer will have a vacancy and u/l is the probability that a randomly selected worker will be unemployed. Although in both cases the aggregate matching rate is increasing (and continuous) in its arguments, a condition any reasonable meeting process should have, the matching function is homogenous of degree one in the first case but exhibits increasing returns in the second in the sense that doubling the numbers of participates of the two types quadruples the meeting rate.[8]

The most common specification in the applied literature is the log linear or Cobb–Douglas matching function with constant returns, i.e.,

$$m(v, u) = m_0 v^{1-\alpha} u^{\alpha},$$

with $0 < \alpha < 1$. Although the nature of the specific matching process that might generate such a function is not known, Pissarides (1996) and Blanchard and Diamond (1989) provide empirical justification for this form. Indeed, their results suggest that an elasticity parameter α is in the neighborhood of one-half is consist with aggregate data.[9]

---

[8] Diamond and Maskin (1979) call the first the "linear" case and the second the "quadratic" case.

[9] However, more recent research based on micro panel data suggest important elements of increasing returns to scale. For example, see Warren (1996), Coles and Smith (1994), and Munich et al. (1997).

2.4. Search equilibrium

As participation is voluntary, a full definition of search equilibrium must specify the measures of search participants, u and v, as well as the participation values for worker and employer, U and V. The form of the matching function and the specific model of unemployment and vacancy determination have important consequences for the existence and uniqueness of search equilibrium because they characterize the ways in which the decisions to participate strategically interact. For example, suppose that search participation is "essential" in the meeting process in the usual sense of production theory, i.e., $m(0, u) = m(v, 0) = 0$. No participation by all, $(v, u) = (0, 0)$, is always an equilibrium in the non-cooperative game theoretic sense in this case. Formally, $v = 0 \Rightarrow \lambda = m(0, u)/u = 0 \Rightarrow U = (b - c)/r \le b/r$ for all $u > 0$ by Eq. (4) and $u = 0 \Rightarrow \eta = m(v, 0)/v = 0 \Rightarrow V = -c/r \le 0$ for all $v > 0$ by Eq. (7). As a worker's value of not participating is b/r and an employer's value of not participating is 0, no one on either side of the market has an incentive to participate if no one participates on the other side of the market.

With the matching technology determining the arrival rates, Eqs. (2), (7), (9), and (10) imply that the value of unemployed search U, and job vacancy V solve the system of equations

$$U = \frac{b - a + [m(v, u)/u]\beta \int \max\{X, U + V\}dF(X)}{r + [m(v, u)/u]} \tag{11}$$

and

$$V = \frac{-c + [m(v, u)/v](1 - \beta) \int \max\{X, U + V\}dF(X)}{r + [m(v, u)/v]}. \tag{12}$$

Because the matching function, $m(v, u)$, is increasing in both arguments, the unemployed workers and vacant jobs are *complements* in the sense that an increase in the measure of either increases the value of participation for agents on the other side of the market. On the same side of the market there is a *congestion effect*, i.e., greater number of either type reduce the value of their own participation. This, however, requires that the meeting rate $m(v, u)/u$ for unemployed workers and $m(v, u)/v$, decreases with that type's participation measure; a property possessed by both the "linear" and the "quadratic" forms of the function derived in the previous section and by all constant returns matching functions.

There are several alternative approaches to modelling the specifics of unemployment and vacancy determination. The simplest supposes an unlimited supply of participants of both types. In this case, worker and jobs enter until the numbers are such that each is indifferent between participating and not participating. Because workers earn b per period when not participating and there are no pure profit opportunities for employers, a *search equilibrium unemployment–vacancy pair* (u, v) is any solution to $U = b/r$ and $V = 0$. As a consequence of the properties of Eqs. (11) and (12), if there are constant returns in the matching technology, only a non-participation equilibrium or a continuum of equilibria

$(u, v) = (0, 0)$ exists since both $m(u,v)/u$ and $m(u,v)/v$ are function of the ratio u/v. Indeed, a solution pair $(u^*, v^*) > 0$ exists which is also "stable" in the sense that the value of participation diminish with the participation measures if and only if the matching technology exhibits decreasing returns to scale in some range.[10] Finally, if the matching function exhibits increasing returns for small values of u and v as well, multiple equilibria are possible.

These results follow from other strong specification assumptions. The value of a match, X, is independent of the number of matches is one. The supply of participants is unbounded for any positive value of participation is another. Partly motivated by these observation but also by the empirical fact that the aggregate labor supply does not change very much over time for endogenous reasons, much of the labor market literature has adopted the assumption that the total labor supply is constant. Given the fixed size, a natural normalization is unity, so u becomes the unemployment rate and v the vacancy rate. The assumption of unlimited entry of vacancies has, however, been retained, so the equilibrium level of vacancies v solves the no profit condition $V = 0$. A steady condition determines unemployment u. Once again, in most of the existing analyses X is independent of employment, i.e., there are no diminishing returns to scale in production. Constant returns to scale in the matching technology, in the sense that $m(v,u)$ is homogenous of degree one, is also typically assumed.

A third approach to the determination of v and u is that adopted by Diamond (1982b) and Blanchard and Diamond (1989). They fix both the labor force size and the total number of jobs. The equilibrium pair in this case is found from two steady state conditions, one for unemployment and one for vacancies.

3. Equilibrium unemployment

In this section we review the theory of equilibrium unemployment for labor markets characterized by frictions developed in Pissarides (1990). The flow of newly created jobs is the outcome of a matching process in which both workers and employers participate. Wages are determined by a generalized Nash bargain after worker and employer meet. The labor force size is constant but firms create job vacancies until any incremental profit is exhausted.

3.1. Exogenous job destruction

Consider first a simple environment characterized by identical workers and employers with no uncertainty about match product, a matching function that determines the flow of new jobs created, and a fixed job destruction rate (see Pissarides, 1990, for a detailed analysis of this case). Jobs are created at the rate $m(v,u)$, where, as before, v is the vacancy

---

[10] We leave a proof of this assertion as an excercise for the reader.

rate and u is the unemployment rate. The matching function is increasing, concave, and homogenous of degree 1. All jobs have the same productivity denoted as p. Employer and worker negotiate a wage when they meet and subsequently produce until an idiosyncratic shock arrives that destroys the job match. At separation, the firm leaves the market and the worker joins unemployment to look for another job. The arrival rate of the idiosyncratic shock is a constant δ.

The evolution of unemployment is given by

$$\dot{u} = \delta(1 - u) - m(v, u). \tag{13}$$

Under the assumption that the matching technology exhibits constant returns, this equation has a unique stable steady state solution for every vacancy rate v, i.e.,

$$u = \frac{\delta}{\delta + m(v/u, 1)} = \frac{\delta}{\delta + \lambda(\theta)}, \tag{14}$$

where the vacancy to unemployment ratio $\theta = v/u$ signals market *tightness* and $\lambda(\theta) = m(v/u, 1)$ represents the unemployment spell hazard.

When Eq. (14) is drawn in vacancy-unemployment space it generates a *Beveridge curve*, a negative relation between vacancies and unemployment. It is convex to the origin by the properties of the matching function. One can also express the relationship in terms borrowed from the empirical literature on job creation and job destruction. Divide both job creation and job separation flows by employment $1 - u$ to generate the *job creation rate* $m(v, u)/(1 - u)$ and the *job destruction rate* δ. Eq. (14) gives the unemployment rate that equates the endogenous job creation rate with the constant job destruction rate.

Equilibrium unemployment depends on the parameters of the model through the dependence of endogenous market tightness on them. Market tightness, in turn, uniquely determines the duration of unemployment, $u/m(v,u)$. Equilibrium market tightness is obtained from profit maximization given the wage bargain. The firm maintains a job vacancy by incurring a flow cost of recruiting a worker c. Applications arrive at the rate $m(v,u)/v$ which we denote by

$$\eta(\theta) = \frac{m(\theta, 1)}{\theta} = \frac{\lambda(\theta)}{\theta}. \tag{15}$$

Since $\lambda(\theta)$ is increasing and concave, $\eta'(\theta) < 0$ with elasticity $1 - \theta\lambda'(\theta)/\lambda(\theta)$ between zero and one.

When any unemployed worker and employer with a vacancy meet, wage bargaining takes place. The outcome is a wage w that divides the quasi-rents associated with a match between worker and employer. Given an arbitrary wage w, the associated value of a filled job to the employer, J, solves the asset pricing equation

$$rJ = p - w - \delta J, \tag{16}$$

where p represents the output of the match. As the value is lost in the event of destruction,

Eq. (16) is equivalent to the continuous time Bellman equation

$$J = \frac{1}{1 + rdt}((p - w)dt + (1 - \delta dt)J),$$

where δdt represents the probability of job destruction during any sufficiently small time interval of length dt. Analogously, the value of the job to the worker satisfies

$$rW = w - \delta(W - U). \tag{17}$$

The difference in the workers case is that job destruction generates unemployed search which has value U.[11]

We seek the generalized Nash bargaining wage outcome, that which solves

$$w = \mathrm{argmax}(W - U)^\beta (J - V)^{1-\beta} = \mathrm{argmax}\left(\frac{w - rU}{r + \delta}\right)^\beta \left(\frac{p - w - (r + \delta)V}{r + \delta}\right)^{1-\beta}, \tag{18}$$

where V equals the employers value of holding the job vacant and U is the value of continued search, i.e., the values of the agents outside options. The maximization implies that the worker's share of match surplus is the constant β, formally

$$W - U = \beta(W + J - U - V). \tag{19}$$

Substitution from Eqs. (16) and (17) into (19) gives the implied wage equation

$$w = rU + \beta[p - rU - (r + \delta)V]. \tag{20}$$

The wage outcome compensates the worker for the loss of his return to unemployment rU, and pays in addition a fraction β of the net flow return of the match, which is the match product p, net of the worker's and firm's reservation incomes, $r(U + V)$, and the lost value of the job site in the event of destruction, δV.

The value of unemployment U satisfies

$$rU = b + \lambda(\theta)(W - U). \tag{21}$$

where here b represents the value of leisure or home production foregone when employed, less any cost of search denoted as a above but suppressed here. Similarly, the value of a new vacancy, V, solves

$$rV = -c + \eta(\theta)(J - V), \tag{22}$$

where here c represents the flow cost of recruiting a worker expressed as a fraction of the worker's productivity once employed. Profit maximization and free entry require that all rents from new vacancy creation are exhausted, i.e., the *job creation condition*

---

[11] Alternatively, if δ were interpreted as the worker "death" rate, the employer would have a vacant job in the event of separation which has value V. The simplifying assumption here is that all separations are the consequence of job destruction rather than worker quitting behavior. One can easily generalized the value equations to account for both reasons for separation.

$$V = 0 \tag{23}$$

holds.

A steady state *search equilibrium* for this simple economy is vector (u,w,θ,V,U) that satisfies Eqs. (14), (20), (23), (22), and (21). Substitution from Eqs. (16) and (23) into (22) yields the alternative form for the job creation condition

$$\frac{c}{\eta(\theta)} = \frac{p - w}{r + \delta}. \tag{24}$$

Note that Eq. (24) is a dynamic demand for labor condition. The expected duration of the vacancy is $1/\eta(\theta)$, so with a flow recruiting cost c, the expected hiring cost for this job is $c/\eta(\theta)$. Thus, the condition requires that the expected hiring cost equal the present discounted value of the difference between the future flows of marginal product and wage payments where the discount rate is the sum of the interest and job destruction rates. Because Eqs. (22), (21), (19) and (23) imply

$$rV = -c + \frac{(1 - \beta)(rU - b)}{\beta\theta} = 0,$$

substitution into Eq. (20) for rU gives the equilibrium *wage equation*

$$w = (1 - \beta)b + \beta(p + c\theta). \tag{25}$$

The wage increases with the unemployment benefit, job productivity, and market tight-

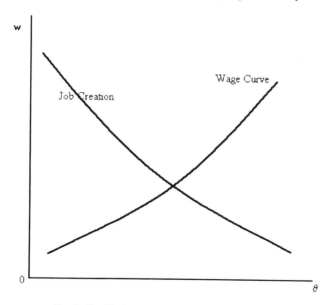

Fig. 1. Equilibrium market tightness and wage rate.

ness. Finally, the equilibrium is fully described by the wage and market tightness pair (w, θ) that satisfies Eqs. (24) and (25).

The two equilibrium conditions have useful descriptive properties shown in Fig. 1. They intersect only once, hence equilibrium is unique. An increase in the worker's unemployment income b shifts the wage curve up and so increases wages and reduces market tightness. An increase in the worker's share parameter β has similar effects. In contrast, an increase in match product p shifts the job creation condition up, increasing both wages and market tightness. More turbulence in the labor market in the sense of an increase in the arrival rate of negative reallocation shocks, δ, shifts the job creation condition down reducing both wages and tightness.

Given the solution for tightness obtained from Fig. 1, we can now draw the Beveridge diagram to derive equilibrium unemployment and vacancies as illustrated in Fig. 2. With fixed productivity, the solution for θ is independent of unemployment, so equilibrium θ in the Beveridge diagram is shown as a straight line through the origin. Call it the job creation condition. Equilibrium unemployment is at the point where the job creation condition intersects the Beveridge curve.

Following on from our previous analysis, an increase in either the worker's share parameter or unemployment income rotates the job creation line down in Fig. 2 and so increases equilibrium unemployment. A higher job productivity rotates it up and reduces unemployment. Higher arrival rate of idiosyncratic shocks shifts the Beveridge curve out and rotates the job creation line down, so it increases unemployment but has ambiguous effects on vacancies.

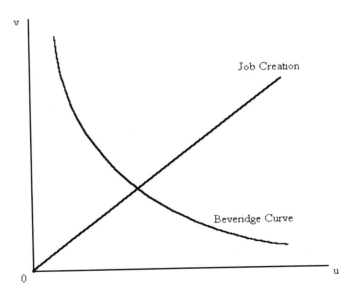

Fig. 2. Equilibrium vacancies and unemployment.

The contrasting results that we obtained for different productivity levels and different arrival rates of idiosyncratic shocks form the basis of much of the discussion about whether changes in unemployment (and hence the business cycle) are driven by aggregate shocks or reallocation shocks. Papers that have explored this contrast include Jackman et al. (1989) who find that the rise in UK unemployment in the 1970s and to some extent in the 1980s was not due to aggregate shocks and Abraham and Katz (1986) and Blanchard and Diamond (1989), who attributed cyclical shocks in the United States largely to aggregate shocks, changes in p.

Andolfatto (1996) and Merz (1996) adopt the search equilibrium approach as a characterization of the labor market in a dynamic stochastic general equilibrium macroeconomic model of capital accumulation. In these models, a household sector decides how to allocate current production between consumption and saving as well as how to divide a time endowment between work, search and leisure. See Merz (1997) for a review of the contributions of these hybrid models found in the "real business cycle" literature. These applications include studies of the tradeoff between the insurance benefits provided and the allocation distortions induced by unemployment insurance systems by Andolfatto (1996), Costain (1995), and Valdivia (1995).

3.2. Job and worker flows

Empirical evidence shows that the job destruction rate, δ in the notation of the preceding section, is not constant, especially over business cycle frequencies (see Davis et al., 1996). In this section we generalize the model to variable job destruction flow and derive the equilibrium conditions (see Mortensen and Pissarides, 1994).

The model builds on that of the preceding section by allowing future job productivity to take more than two values. We write job productivity as px where $x \in [0, 1]$ represents the relative value of a job's specific service or product. Suppose that the product or service provided by the match is a irreversible decision made at the time the job is created. An idiosyncratic shock to the productivity of a match, a new value of its relative value x, arrives at a finite constant rate δ and is distributed according to the c.d.f. $F(\cdot)$, assumed independent of previous realizations. Thus, the idiosyncratic shock process to the value of worker product has persistence but no memory. Profit maximization at the time the job is created requires that product or service be of highest relative value, $x = 1$, given that future values are determined by the first order Markov process assumed above. The model of the previous section can now be re-interpreted as one where the support of the distribution of a future idiosyncratic productivity shock is the unit interval. The value of a filled job with idiosyncratic productivity x is denoted $J(x)$ and satisfies the functional equation

$$rJ(x) = px - w(x) + \delta \left[\int \max \langle J(\tilde{x}), 0 \rangle dF(\tilde{x}) - J(x) \right], \tag{26}$$

where the expression on the right accounts for the fact that the employer will end the match if its future expected present value falls below zero. Job creation takes place as before, so condition (23) still holds but where the value of a new vacancy satisfies

$$rV = -c + \eta(\theta)[J(1) - V] = 0. \tag{27}$$

because a new job has initial relative value $x = 1$. The value of a job to the worker when idiosyncratic productivity is x solves the functional equation

$$rW(x) = w(x) + \delta[\int \max\langle W(\tilde{x}), U\rangle dx - W(x)], \tag{28}$$

where the right side reflects that fact that the worker would quit to search were the worker's value of match to fall below the value of unemployment. Finally, the value of unemployed search solves

$$rU = b + \lambda(\theta)[W(1) - U]. \tag{29}$$

The Nash wage bargain is a contingent wage contract defined by

$$w(x) = \text{argmax}[W(x) - U]^\beta[J(x) - V]^{1-\beta}.$$

Because

$$W(x) = U + \beta[J(x) + W(x) - U - V] \tag{30}$$

is implied, the wage contract is

$$w(x) = \beta px + (1 - \beta)rU. \tag{31}$$

Given the wage equation, Eq. (31), both job values, $J(x)$ and $W(x)$, are monotonically increasing in x. Furthermore, $J(x) - V$, is positive if and only if $W(x) - U$ is positive. Therefore the job destruction policy satisfies a reservation property, i.e., a job is destroyed only if its idiosyncratic productivity falls below a critical level R, which satisfies

$$W(R) - U = J(R) - V = 0. \tag{32}$$

Job separations are still equal to total job destruction. With unemployment given by u, total job destruction is given by $\delta(1 - u)F(R)$. Therefore, the job destruction rate now is $\delta F(R)$, with R satisfying Eq. (32) and, therefore, the evolution of unemployment is given as

$$\dot{u} = \delta(1 - u)F(R) - m(v, u). \tag{33}$$

In steady state, unemployment satisfies

$$u = \frac{\delta F(R)}{\delta F(R) + \lambda(\theta)}, \tag{34}$$

where as before $\theta = v/u$ is market tightness and $\lambda(\theta) = m(\theta, 1)$.

Steady-state *search equilibrium* is a tuple $(u, v, w(x), R, V, U)$ that satisfies the job creation and job destruction conditions (23) and (32), the wage equations (31), the flow equilibrium condition for unemployment, (34), and the values of vacancy and of search unemployment equations, (27) and (29). Equilibrium is again unique, a property that we illustrate with a diagram after derivations of more explicit expressions for the job creation and job destruction conditions.

The job value equation, Eq. (26), can be rewritten as

$$(r + \delta)J(x) = (1 - \beta)(px - rU) + \delta \int_R^1 J(\tilde{x})dF(\tilde{x}) \tag{35}$$

when the wage contract satisfies (31) and the reservation product solves (32). As $J'(x) = (1 - \beta)p/(r + \delta)$ by implication and $J(R) = 0$, it follows that

$$J(x) = (1 - \beta)\left(\frac{x - R}{r + \delta}\right)p, \qquad \text{for all } x. \tag{36}$$

Hence, for the case of $x = R$, Eqs. (32), (35) and (36) imply that the reservation product solves

$$\left(R + \frac{\delta}{r + \delta} \int_R^1 (x - R)dF(x)\right)p = rU. \tag{37}$$

The reservation productivity, pR, falls short of the worker's return to search, the term on the right side, by the option value of continuing the match, the second term on the left side. The option value is positive because the relative value of an existing job may increase in the future.

Eqs. (23), (27), (30) and (36) imply that the job creation condition can be written as

$$c = (1 - \beta)\eta(\theta)\left(\frac{1 - R}{r + \delta}\right)p. \tag{38}$$

The relation between the two unknowns implied by the job creation condition is negative because the vacancy hazard, $\eta(\theta)$, decrease with tightness and because at a higher reservation productivity the expected life of a new job is shorter, and so the expected profit from a new job is lower. Fewer job vacancies are created, reducing market tightness, as R, increases given the free entry condition. The negative relation between R and θ implied by Eq. (38) is indicated in Fig. 3 by the job creation curve, JC in the sequel. Finally, the flow return to unemployment search is an increasing linear function of market tightness

$$rU = b + \frac{\beta c\theta}{1 - \beta} \tag{39}$$

by virtue of Eqs. (29) and (30). These three equations, (37), (38), and (39), characterize search equilibrium in the model of job creation and job destruction flows.

For given θ, Eqs. (37) and (39) imply that the reservation productivity falls with δ and rises with r, because of the effects that each has on the option value of continuing the job-worker match. It rises with unemployment income b and falls with match product p because of their effects on the forgone relative income when the worker is unemployed. Finally, the reservation productivity increases with market tightness because the expected

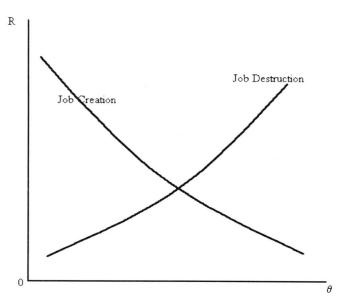

Fig. 3. Equilibrium market tightness and reservation productivity.

returns to unemployed search increases with θ. The dependence of the reservation productivity on market tightness is illustrated in Fig. 3 by the job destruction curve referred to as *JD* in the sequel. The equilibrium solution for the pair (R, θ), lies at the unique intersection of the two curves *JC* and *JD* drawn in Fig. 3.

As an illustration of the new results obtained with endogenous job destruction flow, consider the implications of two parametric shifts, higher unemployment income b and greater market "turbulence' δ. Because a higher b represents an increase in the opportunity cost of employment, the *JD* curve shifts up in Fig. 3. Equilibrium R rises and equilibrium θ falls in response. Thus, the job destruction rate, which is equal to $\delta F(R)$, unambiguously rises. At a given unemployment rate, job creation falls because the fall in θ implies a fall in vacancies. Because the job creation rate has to increase to match the higher job destruction rate, the steady state employment falls and the unemployment rate rises. We also see this in the Beveridge diagram in Fig. 2, where the fall in θ rotates the job creation line down and the rise in R shifts the Beveridge curve out, increasing steady state unemployment. Finally, wages may rise or fall in equilibrium because, on the one hand, wages rise with b but, on the other, they fall with θ. In sum, higher unemployment income implies more job destruction and less job creation.

Consider now the implication of faster arrival of idiosyncratic productivity shocks, an increase in δ. In response, the option value of continuing a match increases so that the reservation productivity must fall given θ from Eq. (37), i.e., the *JD* curve in Fig. 3 shifts down. Because higher δ reduces the expected life of a job and so leads to less vacancy

creation from Eq. (38), the *JC* curve shifts to the left. The equilibrium reservation productivity *R* falls but the diagram does not give a clear answer about the change in θ. However
by completely differentiating the equilibrium conditions, one can show that θ also falls.

The implications of an increase in δ for unemployment and for the job destruction and
job creation rates are not clear-cut. The job destruction rate, $\delta F(R)$, may rise or fall
because the direct effect from an increase in δ can in principle be offset by the fall in
the equilibrium value of *R*. Although the fall in θ initially implies less job creation, the
resulting change is unemployment is also ambiguous. In the Beveridge diagram, the fall in
θ rotates the job creation line down, but the ambiguity about the change in job destruction
introduces an ambiguity about the direction of the shift in the Beveridge curve.

Mortensen and Pissarides (1994), Mortensen (1994b) and Cole and Rogerson (1996) all
find that an extension of the model that regards *p* as a stochastic process characterizing an
aggregate shock are consistent with the time series characteristics of job creation and job
destruction series reported by Davis et al. (1996).

3.3. Social efficiency

There are two offsetting external effects of the decision to participate in any labor market
with search friction. Because the expected time required to fill a vacancy, $v/m(v, u)$, is
increasing in *v*, the marginal vacancy has a congestion effect on other competing vacancies. However, the marginal vacancy also decreases the time a worker can expect to spend
searching for a job, $u/m(v, u)$. For a class of related models, Hosios (1990) establishes that
these two externalities just offset one another in the sense that search equilibrium is
socially efficient if and only if the matching function is homogeneous of degree one
and the worker's share of surplus β is equal to the elasticity of the matching function
with respect to unemployment. This same condition is both necessary and sufficient in the
case of the Mortensen and Pissarides (1994) model as well as its extension by Merz (1995).

Hosios' efficiency condition characterize the solution to a utilitarian social planner's
problem. Namely, in the case of a linearly homogenous matching function

$$\beta = \frac{um_u(v, u)}{m(v, u)} = 1 - \frac{\theta \lambda'(\theta)}{\lambda(\theta)} \tag{40}$$

is necessary and sufficient for a search equilibrium to maximize the expected present value
of future aggregate income where $\lambda(\theta) = m(\theta, 1) = m(v, u)/u = \theta \eta(\theta)$ is the unemployment hazard rate. We provide a derivation of this result below.

Recall that new matches produce at rate *p*, subsequently productivity shocks arrive at
rate δ, the new value is *px* with *x* distributed $F(x)$, and only jobs that have realization $x \geq$
R continue. Hence, gross market output rate evolves according to

$$y' = \lambda(\theta)\text{d}tup + \delta \text{d}t(1 - u)p \int_R^1 x\text{d}F(x) + [1 - \delta \text{d}t]y, \tag{41}$$

where $y' = y(t + \text{d}t)$ is the market output rate at the end of the time interval $[t, t + \text{d}t)$ and

$y = y(t)$ is the rate at the beginning of the interval. As before, the path of unemployment solves

$$u' = \delta dt F(R)(1 - u) + [1 - \lambda(\theta)dt]u, \tag{42}$$

where $u' = u(t + dt)$ and $u = u(t)$. The aggregate net income flow during the interval is $(y + bu - cv)dt$ after account is taken of unemployment income and recruiting costs.

The utilitarian social planner's problem is to choose a future time path for the decision variables, the reservation product and tightness pair (R, θ), that maximizes the expected present value of future aggregate income, defined as market output net of recruiting costs plus unemployment income. The value function for the problem solves the Bellman equation

$$L(y, u) = \max_{r, \theta} \left\{ \left(\frac{1}{1 + rdt} \right) [(y + bu - c\theta u)dt + L(y', u')] \right\}. \tag{43}$$

As the right side is a contraction map for all $rdt > 0$, a unique solution exists for the value function $L(y, u)$. Because the right sides of Eqs. (41) and (42) are linear in y and current income is also linear in both given the decision variables, the contraction maps the set of linear functions, a compact metric space, to itself. Hence, the solution is necessarily linear by the contraction map theorem.

The first order necessary conditions required of an optimal choice of (R, θ) are

$$[L_u - L_y pR]\delta dt F'(R)(1 - u) = 0,$$

$$[(L_y p - L_u)\lambda'(\theta) - c]udt = 0,$$

where L_y and L_u are the constant partial derivatives of the value function. Note that the second order conditions are satisfied at any solution if $m(v, u)$ is concave in v and homogenous of degree one since then $\lambda''(\theta) < 0$. By the envelope theorem, the partial derivatives of the value function must satisfy

$$L_y = \left(\frac{1}{1 + rdt} \right) [dt + L_y(1 - dt\delta)],$$

$$L_u = \left(\frac{1}{1 + rdt} \right) [bdt + L_u(1 - \delta dt F(R) - \lambda(\theta)dt) + L_y(\lambda(\theta) - \delta \int_R^1 x dF(x))pdt].$$

Because the first equation in each group together imply $L_y = 1/(r + \delta)$ and $L_u = pRL_y = pR/(r + \delta)$, appropriate substitution into the remaining two equations yields the necessary and sufficient conditions characterizing the stationary optimal decision pair:

$$c = \lambda'(\theta) \frac{p(1 - R)}{r + \delta} \tag{44}$$

and

$$(R + \int_R^\infty (x - R)\mathrm{d}F(x))p = b + c\left(\frac{\lambda(\theta) - \theta\lambda'(\theta)}{\theta\lambda'(\theta)}\right)\theta. \tag{45}$$

By inspection, these necessary and sufficient conditions for social optimality are equivalent to the equilibrium conditions, Eqs. (37)–(39), given $\lambda(\theta) \equiv \theta\eta(\theta)$, if and only if the employer's share of match surplus is equal the elasticity of the matching function with respect to vacancies, i.e., the Hosios condition (41) holds.

Because the participation externalities on the two sides of the labor market are off setting, the job creation and job destruction flows can be either too high or too low when social optimality fails. To see this, consider the dependence of the decentralized equilibrium on the share parameter β. In Fig. 3, the *JC* curve shifts left and the *JD* curve shifts up in response to an increase in β. Hence, the equilibrium value of θ unambiguously falls but the effect on R is not clear-cut. A complete differentiation of the equilibrium conditions, however, establishes that R reaches a maximum when β satisfies the Hosios condition (40). Hence, job destruction is always too low when efficiency fails but market tightness is too low if β is above its efficient level and too high if it is below it.

4. Alternative models of wage determination

The search equilibrium framework is useful in the study of the unemployment effects of alternative wage determination mechanisms (see Mortensen, 1989). Although most of the literature on equilibrium unemployment incorporates the Nash bargaining assumption, many of the most salient implications of the theory are robust to the wage mechanism specifically assumed. In this section we explore the differing implications of several alternative models of wage determination. We ask how the unemployment equilibria obtained in each case compare with the efficient outcome, that chosen by a social planner. First, we study a "competitive" mechanism that ensures efficiency and subsequently consider the implications of a "monopoly union" wage model, an "insider–outsider" model and an "efficiency wage" model.

4.1. Competitive search equilibrium

Moen (1997) and Shimer (1995) construct and analyze closely related wage formation models that generate the socially optimal match surplus sharing rule characterized by the Hosios condition, Eq. (40). As demonstrated by Greenwald and Stiglitz (1988) and by Mortensen and Wright (1997), the same solution can also be viewed as the outcome of competition among third party market makers who offer unemployed workers and employers with vacant jobs a tradeoff between future income when matched and matching delay. Perfect competition among match makers in this economy generates implicit prices for expected waiting times and these prices provide the appropriate incentives for worker and employer participation in the matching process in the sense that the marginal social return is equal to the perceived private return of each agent.

Suppose that each of potentially many middleman offers a particular element (β, θ) in an available set of sharing rule and waiting time pairs, denoted as Ω. Given that each employer and worker can freely choose to participate in any one of the markets organized by these middlemen, the values of holding a vacancy and of searching for employment solve

$$rV = \max_{(\beta,\theta)\in\Omega} \left\{ (1 - \beta)\eta(\theta)\left(\frac{1-R}{r+\delta}\right)p - c \right\} \tag{46}$$

and

$$rU = \max_{(\beta,\theta)\in\Omega} \left\{ b + \beta\lambda(\theta)\left(\frac{1-R}{r+\delta}\right)p \right\} \tag{47}$$

because the surplus sharing rule requires

$$\frac{1-R}{r+\delta} = \frac{J(1)-V}{1-\beta} = \frac{W(1)-U}{\beta}.$$

Free entry, $V = 0$, implies that

$$(1 - \beta)\left(\frac{1-R}{r+\delta}\right)p = \frac{c}{\eta(\theta)} \tag{48}$$

must hold in every sub-market. Finally, the reservation product R is the submarket characterized by a given pair (β, θ) must solve

$$\left(R + \frac{\delta}{r+\delta}\int_R^1 (x-R)\mathrm{d}F(x)\right)p = rU = b + \frac{\beta c\theta}{1-\beta}. \tag{49}$$

In competitive equilibrium in this environment, no market maker earns pure profit. Out of equilibrium, however, a market maker can profit by charging an arbitrarily small fee provided that the sub-market characteristics offered $(\beta', \theta') \notin \Omega$ attract both employers and workers.[12] To do so, both of the following inequalities must hold and one holds strictly:

$$(1 - \beta')\eta(\theta')\left(\frac{1-R}{r+\delta}\right)p - c \geq rV,$$

$$b + \beta'\lambda(\theta')\left(\frac{1-R}{r+\delta}\right)p \geq rU.$$

To eliminate such pure profit potential, then, every element (β, θ) of the equilibrium set Ω must satisfy the tangency condition

[12] For simplicity, we assume that middlemen incur no costs.

$$\left.\frac{\mathrm{d}\beta}{\mathrm{d}\theta}\right|_V = -\frac{\lambda(\theta) - \theta\lambda'(\theta)}{\theta\lambda(\theta)}(1 - \beta) = -\frac{\lambda'(\theta)}{\lambda(\theta)}\beta = \left.\frac{\mathrm{d}\beta}{\mathrm{d}\theta}\right|_U \tag{50}$$

given the definition $\theta\eta(\theta) = \lambda(\theta)$. In other words, for any member of the equilibrium set of sub-markets, the rate at which an unemployed worker who participates is willing to exchange market tightness for a share of surplus once matched must equal the rate at which any participating employers with a vacant job is willing to trade the two.

Since the zero profit condition for match making, Eq. (50), is equivalent to the Hosios condition (40) for a socially efficient search equilibrium, Moen (1997) calls any pair (Ω, R) that satisfy Eqs. (49), (50), and $V = 0$ a *competitive search equilibrium*. When workers and employers are respectively identical as assumed here, Ω is a singleton pair determined by the unique solution to Eqs. (48) and (49) and the associated equilibrium worker's share of match surplus is that which solves Eq. (50).

One interpretation of the tale told in this section is that the general inefficiency of search equilibrium is due to incomplete markets. In particular, in a complete market model such as that just described, waiting times are appropriately priced, search externalities are internalized, and the overall market equilibrium is Pareto optimal. As it turns out, Pareto optimality implies social efficiency given the linear preferences assumed. Obviously, wages determined by bargaining or many other mechanisms are not likely to yield this outcome.

4.2. Monopoly union

In many labor markets, terms of employment are determined by collective bargaining agreements. The monopoly union formulation represents the standard approach to modeling wage formation in this context. In this Stackelberg game of wage and employment determination, the union first sets the wage and then employers respond by determining employment. The wage determination mechanism can be placed in a search equilibrium framework by supposing that employers create and destroy jobs given a wage contract that specifies the share β of match surplus obtained by workers.[13]

Pissarides (1990) shows that a union would set the worker's share β at its efficient value given by the Hosios condition (40) were all of its members unemployed. However, if the union acts in the interest of employed workers instead, the share exceeds the social optimum, but still the union does not fully exploit market power by appropriating the entire match surplus. Thus, an "insider–outsider" conflict between members of the union exists. Employed workers, the "insiders", want the union to choose higher wages than unemployed workers, the "outsiders".

The proof is simple. If a union were to represent unemployed workers, it would choose β to maximize the equilibrium return to search, which can be written as

[13] The worker's share of match rents is set as the parameter of a contingent wage contract rather than a fixed wage level to quarantee job destruction that is individually rational from the view of both worker and employer.

$$rU = \left(R + \frac{\delta}{r + \delta} \int_R^1 (x - R) \mathrm{d}F(x) \right) p \tag{51}$$

by Eqs. (37) and (39). As the right hand side is increasing in R, the optimal choice maximizes the reservation product. As noted above, a complete differentiation of the equation system composed of Eqs. (37)–(39) implies that the equilibrium value of R is a concave function of β which is maximized when the worker's share of match surplus satisfies the Hosios condition, Eq. (40).

In practice, unions represent employed worker. Suppose that the union is a democracy and the median voter is employed in some job with match product $\hat{x}R$. As Eqs. (23), (30), and (36) imply

$$W(\hat{x}) = U + \beta p \left(\frac{\hat{x} - R}{r + \delta} \right),$$

the share β that maximizes $W(\hat{x})$ is defined by

$$\hat{\beta} = \operatorname*{argmax}_{\beta \in \{0,1\}} \left\{ U + \beta p \left(\frac{\hat{x} - R}{r + \delta} \right) \right\}. \tag{52}$$

Eq. (51) implies

$$r \frac{\partial u}{\partial \beta} = p \left(\frac{r + \delta F(R)}{r + \delta} \right) \frac{\partial R}{\partial \beta},$$

so the first order condition for a interior solution to the optimization problem is

$$\frac{\partial W(\hat{x})}{\partial \beta} = p \left(\frac{\hat{x} - R}{r + \delta} \right) + \frac{p}{r} \left(\frac{r(1 - \beta) + \delta F(R)}{r + \delta} \right) \frac{\partial R}{\partial \beta} = 0. \tag{53}$$

Hence, if more than half of all members are employed, $\hat{x} > R$ for the median voter, then $\partial R / \partial \beta < 0$ at $\beta = \hat{\beta}$. But, we have already noted that R decreases with β only for values above the efficient share.

Because the associated reservation product is less than the social optimal, the incidence of unemployment, $\delta F(R)$, is also less than that for a competitive search equilibrium. However, the expected duration of an unemployment spell, $1/\lambda(\theta)$ is longer than in the competitive case. As these two effects of a higher worker's share on the steady state unemployment rate are offsetting, the qualitative relationship between the competitive and monopoly unemployment rates is unclear. Interestingly, unemployment duration is longer and incidence is lower in European countries than in the US. As European labor markets are also more unionized, the model may have explanatory power for these differences.

4.3. Strategic bilateral bargaining

The match surplus sharing rule characterized by the generalized Nash bargaining outcome has also been interpreted as a solution to a strategic bargaining game. For example, consider the following simple setting. Imagine that both on meeting and after a productivity shock is realized for a continuing match, worker and employer engage in a bargaining game obeying the following rules: The worker is allowed to make a wage demand with probability β. With complementary probability $1 - \beta$, the employer makes a wage offer. After either a wage offer or demand is made, the other party accepts or rejects. In the event of rejection, negotiation stops and worker and employer both search for an alternative partner.

Given the rules of this simple game played under conditions of complete information, the dominant strategy is to demand or offer a wage equal to that needed to make the other party just indifferent between accepting or not. Given that rejection implies search, a worker will demand the entire match surplus $S(x) \equiv J(x) + W(x) - U - V$ while the employer offers a future income stream equivalent to the value of unemployment, U. The expected outcome for the worker in a continuing match is

$$W(x) = \beta(U + S(x)) + (1 - \beta)U = U + \beta[J(x) + W(x) - U - V], \tag{54}$$

for all x. These bargaining outcomes yield the same wage contract as that derived for the generalized Nash bargaining model with worker bargaining power parameter equal to β.

In Rubinstein's (1982) model of strategic bargaining, the negotiation process cannot end in the event of rejection given any strictly positive match surplus, i.e., no positive surplus can be "left on the table". Furthermore, the identity of the party making the initial offer is determined by the flip of fair coin and the parties alternate roles in subsequent negotiation rounds. Rubinstein and Wolinsky (1985) show that the symmetric case, $\beta = 1/2$, approximates the unique solution to the bargaining game played by the Rubinstein rules if worker and employer can costlessly search while negotiating and either switches bargaining partners when search generates an alternative.

Binmore et al. (1986) and Wolinsky (1987), argue that other outcomes can also obtain in general. For example, in the extreme case in which the arrival rate of an outside bargaining option during the negotiation process is zero for both parties and the worker makes the wage demand with probability β in each round, the expected present value of earning prior to negotiation is

$$W(x) = \max\langle\beta[J(x) + W(x)], U\rangle. \tag{55}$$

In other words, the worker receives a fixed share of match value, if that amount exceeds the value of unemployed search, and the value of unemployment otherwise, where the share β is the worker's probability of setting the terms. This outcome is the consequence of the fact that the party who realizes the right to set terms in any round of the negotiation will demand the entire value of the match less whatever must be transferred ex ante to induce the other party to participate in the match. Although this outcome will generate the same job destruction rule, the decision to invest in job creation is distorted even if the share parameter β satisfied the Hosios condition.

4.4. Rent sharing with turnover costs

The differences in preference over wages of the unemployed and those of the employed in the monopoly union case is an example of what Linbeck and Snower (1988) have termed "insider–outsider" conflict. The conflict arises in that case because the costs of finding a job are sunk for an employed worker but not for an unemployed worker. Insider-outsider conflict also arises in hold-up problems.[14] Hiring and firing costs, which we interpret as the fixed costs of job creation and job destruction respectively, motivate hold-ups.

Assume that the legal and economic environments are such that the firm is liable for initial hiring and training costs and for subsequent firing costs in the event of job destruction but worker and employer are able to precommit to an enforceable wage contract which determines terms of employment contingent on future events when they form a match. In general, the wage structure that arises as a Nash bargaining solution has two-tiers under these conditions with the property that the worker shares the initial hiring cost and prepays expected firing cost by accepting a lower initial wage but later enjoys a higher wage.[15] The lower first tier wage reflects the fact that hiring costs are directly relevant to the decision to accept a match and that the possibility of incurring firing costs in the future affects the value the employer places on the match. The higher second tier wage applies at some later tenure when firing costs are directly relevant to continuation decision and when separation without renegotiation would otherwise violate the interests of both parties.

Because the second tier wage is generally higher than the first tier, a worker, once "inside", has an incentive to default on the original two-tier agreement by demanding to renegotiate immediately after being hired. Indeed, as Linbeck and Snower (1988) argues, evidence suggests that workers once employed do take actions designed to extract the quasi-rents created by recruiting, hiring, and firing costs, i.e., a "hold-up" problem exists. The employment effects of such behavior can be studied in the search equilibrium framework by comparing equilibrium conditions with and without the two-tiered wage structure.

We first introduce fixed hiring and firing costs and derive the two-tier wage structure that they induce. Suppose the employer is obliged to pay hiring cost C in order to begin production and firing costs T at time of job destruction. The former can be viewed as the sum of application, processing, and training costs, forms of match specific investment. Examples of the latter include the costs implicit in mandated employment protection legislation and in experience rated unemployment insurance taxes. However, a pure severance transfer, a payment to the worker by the employer, is not included in T. For reasons pointed out by Lazear (1990) and Burda (1992), the equilibrium values of the

---

[14] Caballero and Hammour (1994, 1999) and Acemoglu (1996) discuss hold-up problems in search and matching problems.

[15] Alternatively, the worker could "buy" rights to the job by making an initial transfer to the employer. This kind of side payment is ruled out here on empirical grounds. One theoretical explanation for why side payments of this form are not observed is that no employer can precommit to a future employment duration under the "employment at will" doctrine.

relevant decision variable pair (R, θ) is unaffected by a severance payment although the magnitude of the payment will effect the wages over the duration of the match.

Let the subscript $i = 0$ index the initial wage and values of a job and employment under the terms of the two-tier contract. For simplicity, we assume that the second tier of the wage contract applies to all matches once an idiosyncratic shock to match productivity occurs.[16] The value of a new job match to the employer under these assumptions and notational conventions is

$$rJ_0 = p - w_0 + \delta \left[\int_R^1 J(\tilde{x}) dF(\tilde{x}) - F(R)T - J_0 \right], \tag{56}$$

while the initial value of the match to the worker is

$$rW_0 = w_0 + \delta \left[\int_R^1 W(s) dF(s) - F(R)U - W_0 \right], \tag{57}$$

where $J(x)$ and $W(x)$ are the values of continuing the match to worker and employer under the second tier contract. These value functions solve the analogous functional equations

$$rJ(x) = px - w(x) + \delta \left[\int_R^1 J(\tilde{x}) dF(\tilde{x}) - F(R)T - J(x) \right] \tag{58}$$

and

$$rW(x) = w(x) + \delta \left[\int_R^1 W(s) dF(s) - F(R)U - W(x) \right], \tag{59}$$

where $w(x)$ represents the productivity contingent second tier wage contract.

The value of unemployment satisfies

$$rU = b + \lambda(\theta)[W_0 - U] \tag{60}$$

and, because the creation cost C is incurred when the match forms, the value of a vacant job solves

$$rV = -c + \eta(\theta)[J_0 - V - C] = 0 \tag{61}$$

given free entry. Finally, the job destruction condition requires a future expected loss greater in expected present value than the cost of termination, i.e.,

$$J(R) = -T. \tag{62}$$

The initial first tier wage rate satisfies the Nash condition

---

[16] MacLeod and Malcomson (1993) argue that the initial wage agreement will be renegotiated only if not doing so would result in an inefficient separation, i.e., the destruction of the job when the sum of both partners future income given continuation exceeds the firing cost. The contract we study has the same two-tier feature, yields the identical job creation and job destruction decision, and is much easier to characterize. None the less, our contract generates a much more "flexible" wage than theirs.

$$w_0 = \text{argmax}(W_0 - U)^\beta (J_0 - C - V)^{1-\beta}. \tag{63}$$

The employer's threat point includes hiring costs in the initial bargaining problem because they are not yet incurred when bargaining takes place and will not be incurred unless the employer can expect to cover them with future income. As the first order condition requires $\beta (J_0 - C - V) = (1 - \beta)(W_0 - U)$, the initial "outsider" wage implied by Eqs. (56) and (57) is

$$w_0 = \beta(p - (r + \delta)C - \delta T) + (1 - \beta)rU, \tag{64}$$

given $V = 0$.

In the subsequent bargaining problem, the employer's threat point does not include hiring costs, those are sunk. Instead, the threat point is the negative of the firing cost which would have to be paid were the job destroyed as reflected in the job destruction condition (62). Hence, the second tier wage contract solves

$$w_1(x) = \text{argmax}(W(x) - U)^\beta (J(x) + T)^{1-\beta}. \tag{65}$$

Here, the first order condition requires $\beta(J_0(x) + T) = (1 - \beta)(W - U)$. Equivalently, the "insider" wage paid after an idiosyncratic shock is

$$w_1(x) = \beta(px + rT) + (1 - \beta)rU \tag{66}$$

from Eqs. (58) and (59). Thus, hiring and firing costs reduce the initial wage, because they reduce the ex ante value of the match but, given the value of search U, hiring costs do not influence the insider wage because they are sunk whereas firing costs increase it, because they represent a legal commitment that employer must pay in the event of a layoff.

As this definition of R, Eq. (62), and the form of the continuing wage contract specified in Eq. (66) imply that the solution to Eq. (58) takes the form

$$J(x) = (1 - \beta)p\left(\frac{x - R}{r + \delta}\right) - T, \tag{67}$$

the reservation product solves the following generalization of Eq. (37):

$$\left(R \frac{\delta}{r\delta} \int_R^1 [x - R] dF(x)\right)p + rT = rU. \tag{68}$$

The option value of continuation is augmented by the foregone interest on the firing cost in the generalization, an implicit return attributable to continuing the match one more period.

As the job creation condition, that implied by $V = 0$, can be written

$$c = \eta(\theta)[J_0 - C],$$

the following generalization of Eq. (38) holds:

$$\frac{c}{\eta(\theta)} + (1 - \beta)(C + T) = (1 - \beta)\left(\frac{1 - R}{r + \delta}\right)p. \tag{69}$$

The employer's share of the total return on a new job-worker match now has to cover the employer's share of all three types of costs, recruiting, which is all paid by the employer and is sunk at the initial bargaining date, plus hiring and firing, both of which are shared with the worker. Finally, the return to search is

$$rU = b + \frac{\beta c}{1 - \beta} \theta \qquad (70)$$

as before.

A *rent sharing search equilibrium* is a two-tier wage contract $\{w_0, w_1(x)\}$, a tightness-reservation pair (θ, R), and a value of unemployed search U that solves Eqs. (64), (66), (68), (69) and (70). Once the pair (θ, R) is determined, unemployment equilibrium is obtained as before using the Beveridge equation, Eq. (34).

By reducing θ for given R an increase in job creation cost C shifts the JC curve to the left in Fig. 3. Equilibrium reservation productivity (and job destruction) and market tightness (job creation) both fall in response. Market tightness decreases because fewer vacancies are created when job hiring and training costs are higher. Job destruction decreases because a decrease in market tightness reduces the worker's outside options and so reducing wages. An increase in job destruction cost T shifts the JC curve to the left and in the JD curve down in Fig. 3. Job destruction falls for both reasons: Since it is now more expensive to destroy jobs, fewer are destroyed and since fewer jobs are created, wages are lower and fewer jobs are destroyed as a secondary consequence. Because jobs live longer given the reduction of R, the net effect of an increase in destruction cost on job creation is ambiguous.

4.5. Insider wage

As already noted, hold-up problems arise in the absence of a two-tier wage structure. Furthermore, new workers, outsiders, once hired have an ex post incentive to renege on the two-tier structure by demanding the higher insider wage. Indeed, some claim that the two-tier structure is infeasible as a consequence. In this section, we look at the implications of a pure insider equilibrium, that which obtains when the second tier wage contract applies initially as well as subsequent to any shock to match productivity.

Given that the initial wage is determined by the continuing wage bargaining outcome, the initial values of a match are given by the values of the match at $x = 1$, i.e.,

$$W_0 = W(1) \qquad \text{and} \qquad J_0 = J(1) \qquad (71)$$

replace Eqs. (56) and (57). In this case, the wage rate now solves Eq. (66) in all jobs. Because turnover costs are not shared with workers in the insider case, one can show that the free entry condition $V = 0$ implies

$$\frac{c}{\eta(\theta)} + C + T = (1 - \beta)\left(\frac{1 - R}{r + \delta}\right) p. \qquad (72)$$

Consequently, market tightness is less at given reservation productivity than it would be under a two-tier contract. Although the job destruction condition is the same as before

$$\left(R + \frac{\delta}{r + \delta} \int_R^1 [x - R]dF(x)\right)p + rT = rU, \tag{73}$$

now the return to search is more responsive to market tightness than it was in the two-tier case, i.e.,

$$rU = b + \frac{\beta}{1 - \beta}(c\theta + (C + T)\lambda(\theta)). \tag{74}$$

After substituting from this expression into Eq. (66), one obtains the insider equilibrium wage contract

$$w(x) = (1 - \beta)b + \beta[px + rT + c\theta + (C + T)\lambda(\theta)]. \tag{75}$$

A comparison with Eqs. (64) and (66) reveals that all workers earn more at a given level of market tightness θ when insiders impose a uniform wage. This fact is the essence of the hold-up problem, by forcing the employer to bear the whole of the job creation and job destruction costs, that firm's employed workers gain. However, in equilibrium all employers collectively have less incentive to create new jobs.

An *insider search equilibrium* is a wage function $w(x)$, a reservation-tightness pair (R, θ), and a value of unemployed search U that solves Eqs. (72)–(75). Given the results that we have already discussed, the implications of switching from the two-tier wage structure to the pure insider equilibrium is to increase R (and job destruction) at every given value of θ and to reduce θ (and job creation) at every given value of R. In Fig. 3, these effects can be represented by shifts in the *JD* curve up and the *JC* curve left, reducing equilibrium market tightness but having ambiguous effects on the reservation productivity. Because of the fall in tightness, unemployment durations are higher in the insider equilibrium but the unemployment incidence effect is unclear.

4.6. Efficiency wage

The idea that the wage is set to motivate worker effort provides the basis for an alternative theory of wage and unemployment determination. In this sub-section, a version of the Shapiro and Stiglitz (1984) efficiency wage model is incorporated into the search equilibrium framework. As pointed out by Ramey and Watson (1997), a study of this synthesis suggests that job destruction is excessive when a high wage combined with a threat of dismissal is used to motivate workers.

Workers would rather take leisure on the job than supply effort is the critical assumption. An employer fires any worker found shirking but monitoring is imperfect. To motivate effort, the employer pays an "efficiency wage", one that equates the expected loss in future worker income if caught shirking to the value of leisure enjoyed while shirking. Formally, the wage is set so that the product of the monitoring frequency, denoted as ϕ, and the difference between the value of employment and unemployment to the worker, $W - U$, is equal to the flow cost of effort, which might be regarded as equal to the value of forgone unemployment income b, i.e., the wage solves

$$\phi(W - U) = b. \tag{76}$$

Since the values of employment with effort and unemployment satisfy

$$rW = w + \delta F(R)(U - W)] \qquad \text{and} \qquad rU = b + \lambda(\theta)(W - U)$$

given the reservation product–market tightness pair (R,θ), the efficiency wage equation is

$$w = b + \frac{b}{\phi}[r + \delta F(R) + \lambda(\theta)]. \tag{77}$$

Note that the efficiency wage increases with both R and θ, because a higher wage is required to compensate for a higher layoff frequency and because a higher wage is required when an alternative job is easier to find to maintain the employment surplus needed to motivate worker effort.

As the value of a job with worker productivity x satisfied

$$rJ(x) = px - w + \delta\left[\int_R^1 J(\tilde{x})dF(\tilde{x}) - F(R)T - J(x)\right]$$

$$= px - w + \delta\int_R^1 [J(\tilde{x}) - J(x)]dF(\tilde{x}) - \delta F(R)[J(x) + T], \tag{78}$$

the solution is

$$J(x) + T = \left(\frac{x - R}{r + \delta}\right)p, \tag{79}$$

where by definition the value at the reservation product plus firing cost equal zero, i.e., $J(R) + T = 0$. By setting $x = R$ and by substituting for $J(x)$ using Eq. (79), Eq. (78) implies

$$\left(R + \frac{\delta}{r + \delta}\int_R^1 (x - R)dF(x)\right)p + rT = w = b + \frac{b}{\phi}[r + \delta F(R) + \lambda(\theta)]. \tag{80}$$

Given the free entry condition

$$rV = \eta(\theta)[J(1) - C] - c = 0,$$

Eq. (79) implies

$$\frac{c}{\eta(\theta)} + C + T = \left(\frac{1 - R}{r + \delta}\right)p. \tag{81}$$

An *efficiency wage search equilibrium* is a wage w and a reservation product and market tightness pair (R,θ) that satisfy Eqs. (77), (80), and (81). Because workers do not share job creation and job destruction costs in this case as well, the job creation condition is the same as in the insider model. Comparison of the job destruction conditions reveal the differences between the two models. Specifically, the rent obtained by worker in an equilibrium increases with market tightness and turnover costs in the insider case and with the cost of monitoring and the sum of the unemployment and employment hazards in the efficiency wage case.

The possibility of multiple equilibria is an interesting feature of the efficiency wage model. Because the right side of the job destruction condition, Eq. (80), is increasing in R but the left side is increasing in R as well, there can be multiple values of the reservation product consistent with a given value of the market tightness θ. Because the wage is also increasing in θ, one can show that the JD curve defined by the job destruction condition is upward sloping when the reservation product is outside the support of the distribution match productivity but can slope backward in its interior if the expected gain from shirking, equal to b/ϕ, is large enough. Namely, the locus of reservation product and market tightness pairs that solve Eq. (80) can be S-shaped, as represented in Fig. 4. As the job creation condition, Eq. (81), defines a negatively sloped job creation relation between R and θ represented by the curve JC in the figure, three or even more intersections of the two equilibrium relationships are possible.

The reason for the multiplicity is the positive feedback between the wage and the reservation product. Namely, a higher reservation product requires a higher wage to compensate for the increase in the layoff frequency while a higher wage induces an increase in the reservation product. The necessary and sufficient condition for JD to have a negative slope is that the marginal effect of the reservation product on the wage,

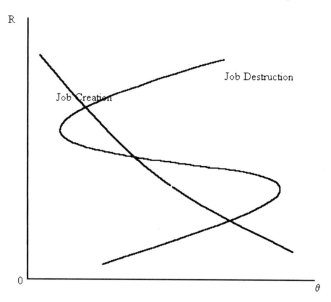

Fig. 4. Efficiency wage search equilibria.

$\delta F'(R)(b/\phi)$, exceeds the marginal effect of an increase on the left side of the job destruction condition, $(r + \delta F(R))/(r + \delta)$. On the support of F, this condition can be ruled out only in the extreme case of a very small ratio of the productivity shock to monitoring frequency.

When multiple equilibria exist, they are Pareto ranked. This fact is the immediate consequence of two observations. First, as all the equilibria lie on the negatively sloped JC curve, the equilibrium with the lowest reservation product most also be the one with the highest degree of market tightness. Second, because the equilibrium worker return to unemployment is $rU = b + \lambda(\theta)(b/\phi)$, worker value of employment is $W = U + r(b/\phi)$, and employer value is $rJ(x) = (x - R)p/(r + \delta) - T$ for all $x \geq R$, all agents prefer the equilibrium with the highest degree of market tightness and lowest reservation product. Of course, this Pareto dominant equilibrium also yields the lowest unemployment rate since both duration and incidence are minimum here on the set of equilibria.

If the equilibrium is unique, the comparative statics of the model are qualitatively similar to the rent sharing models. For example, by shifting the job destruction curve JD to the left, a higher unemployment income decrease equilibrium market tightness and the reservation product. Note, however, that the response of the middle equilibrium point is perverse. For example, unemployment falls in response to an increase in b if three equilibria exist as illustrated in Fig. 4.

5. Labor market policy analysis

The equilibrium job creation and job destruction framework reviewed above is a relatively new tool for labor market policy analysis. Still a small and growing literature exists. Millard and Mortensen (1996), Mortensen (1994, 1995), Pissarides (1996), and Coe and Snower (1996) use search equilibrium models to study the effects of payroll and employment taxes and the provision of unemployment insurance (UI) benefits on employment and some cases aggregate income. Ljungqvist and Sargent (1996) look at the interaction effects of more frequent reallocation shocks and a more generous income support policy using a related model. Millard (1995) studies the effects of employment protection policies modeled as a tax on firing and Mortensen (1996) derives the effects of active labor market policy in the form of a hiring subsidy using related versions of the Mortensen–Pissarides model. Mortensen and Pissarides (1997) use a generalization of their model to study the interaction effects of "skill biased" technology shocks and both unemployment compensation and employment protection policy.

These authors generally find that policy effects on unemployment can be large in calibrated versions of their models, indeed the effects of policy differences are sufficient to explain observed differences between US and European unemployment rates. Those who raise the issue also find that the forgone output attributable to the disincentive effects of labor market policy can be substantial. The purpose of this section is to illustrate these results in the context of the rent sharing model rather than review the specifics of each application of the approach.

5.1. Modeling labor market policy

Both passive and active labor market policies are incorporated in the extensions considered in the section. Passive policies include unemployment compensation, payroll or employment taxes, and employment protection policy. In the model, we assume that unemployment income is augmented by unemployment compensation equal to ρw, where $\overline{w}$ represents the average wage paid by all employers and ρ denotes the *replacement ratio*. Employers are assessed a tax proportional to the wage bill. Let τ represent the payroll tax rate. As *employment protection policy* inhibits the employers ability to fire workers, it can be modeled as a contribution to the firing cost, T. Finally, active labor market policy is interpreted as a *hiring subsidy*, a lump sum H paid to the employer when a new worker is hired which is equivalent to a reduction in the private cost of job creation C.

In the sequel we interpret the wage as the earnings the workers receive net of a payroll tax paid by the employer. Since $(1 + \tau)w$ replaces w when computing the value of match to an employer but not in the computation of the value of employment to a worker, the net contribution of an increase in the wage to the employer's and worker's values of a match are

$$\frac{\partial J_0}{\partial w} = \frac{\partial J(x)}{\partial w} = \frac{-(1 + \tau)}{r + \delta}$$

and

$$\frac{\partial W_0}{\partial w} = \frac{\partial W(x)}{\partial w} = \frac{1}{r + \delta},$$

respectively both initially and for any subsequent realization of x by Eqs. (56)–(59). As a consequence, the first order conditions for the bargaining problems (63) and (65) are now

$$(1 + \tau)(1 - \beta)(W_0 - U) = \beta(J_0 - V - C)$$

and

$$(1 + \tau)(1 - \beta)(W(x) - U) = \beta(J(x) + T),$$

respectively. In short, the tax affects the share of match surplus that worker and employer receive. Because $\beta/(1 + \tau)$ replaces β and $b + \rho\overline{w}$ replaced b in all the equations that characterize the efficient rent sharing equilibrium, the equilibrium conditions can be expressed as follows:

$$w_0(1 + \tau) = \beta(p - (r + \delta)C - \delta T) + (1 - \beta)rU(1 + \tau), \tag{82}$$

$$w(x)(1 + \tau) = \beta(px + rT) + (1 - \beta)rU(1 + \tau), \tag{83}$$

$$\frac{c}{\eta(\theta)} = (1 - \beta)\left[\left(\frac{1 - R}{r + \delta}\right)p - (T + C)\right], \tag{84}$$

$$p\left[R + \frac{\lambda}{r + \lambda} \int_R^1 (x - R)\mathrm{d}F(x) \right] + rT = rU(1 + \tau), \tag{85}$$

$$rU(1 + \tau) = [b + p\bar{w}](1 + \tau) + \frac{\beta c\theta}{1 - \beta}. \tag{86}$$

The imposition of a payroll tax is equivalent in effect on the equilibrium reservation product and market tightness pair to a proportional increase in the worker's private opportunity cost of employment, unemployment income as represented by $b + p\bar{w}$, where the factor of proportionality is the payroll tax rate. This outcome is a consequence of the fact that the bargaining solution is sensitive to the effects of the wage choice on the size of the match surplus that the parties share. In short, they set the wage so as to minimize the distortionary effects of the tax given relative bargaining power.[17]

To close the model, we need the following expression for the average wage paid in equilibrium

$$(1 + \tau)\bar{w} = (1 + \tau)\left(F(R)w_0 + \int_R^1 w(x)\mathrm{d}F(x) \right)$$

$$= \beta\left[(p - (r + \delta)(C + T))F(R) + p\int_R^1 x\mathrm{d}F(x) + rT \right] + (1 - \beta)rU(1 + \tau), \tag{87}$$

one implied by the fact that the steady state fraction of new matches, those for which $x = 1$, is $F(R)$ and the fact that $F(x) - F(R)$ represents the steady state fraction of matches with idiosyncratic productivity x or less given $x < 1$.

For the purpose of policy analysis, we are also interested in both the steady state unemployment rate,

$$u = \frac{\delta F(R)}{\delta F(R) + \lambda(\theta)}, \tag{88}$$

and the steady state aggregate income net of recruiting and hiring costs, which is

$$y = p\left(F(R) + \int_R^\infty x\mathrm{d}F(x) \right)(1 - u) + (b - c\theta - C\lambda(\theta))u. \tag{89}$$

The latter represents a measure of overall welfare, one that does not necessarily move in the same direction as employment.

5.2. The qualitative effects of policy

The qualitative comparative static effects of changes in policy parameters can be derived

---

[17] In the US where the UI benefit is proportional to earnings in the preceding employment spell, the division of match surplus is similarly effected by the replacement ratio. It does not appear in these equation because a common benefit is assumed which depends on the average but not the individual worker's wage.

using the two equilibrium relationships and these outcome measures. As both unemployment compensation and a payroll tax increase the effective "supply price" of labor, their effects are qualitatively the same as an increase in unemployment income b. Namely, an increase in either ρ or τ shifts the JD curve in Fig. 3 up and to the left but does not directly effect the JC curve. The equilibrium responses are a decrease in tightness and an increase in the reservation product, both of which induce a rise in unemployment. A hiring subsidy shifts the JC curve rightward by reducing the private cost of job creation C but has no effect on the JD curve. Market tightness increases but the reservation product rises reflecting the fact that jobs will have shorter lives when they are easier to create. Because unemployment duration decreases but incidence increases in response, the net impact on unemployment is ambiguous. A firing tax has the opposite effect on job creation and decreases the reservation product given tightness, i.e., the JC curve shifts left and the JD curve shifts down. Although the net effect is again unclear, an increase in T decreases unemployment when incidence falls by proportionately more than duration increases.

Because aggregate income is not generally monotone in the unemployment rate, there is no general prediction about the directions of any marginal change in a policy parameter given that all policy parameters are positive. However, if the equilibrium with no policy were the solution to the social planner's problem, as is the case when the worker's share of surplus satisfies the Hosios condition, then a small value of any policy parameters would be associated with a lower level of future income because all of the policies induce distortions.

5.3. The quantitative effects of policy

Indeterminate direction of effects on both unemployment and income reflect the multiple channels of influence on equilibrium outcomes incorporated in the model. Which effect dominates is a quantitative question. Computing responses for specific functional forms and parameter values is a feasible first step in providing quantitative answers, one pursued in several papers in the literature. To illustrate the nature of their results, we report the outcome of similar computational experiments for the rent sharing case.

A matching function of the Cobb–Douglas form is assumed, i.e., $\ln(\lambda(\theta)) = \alpha \ln(\theta)$ where α is the elasticity with respect to vacancies. The distribution of shocks is assumed to be uniform on the support $[\gamma, 1]$, i.e., $F(x) = (x - \gamma)/(1 - \gamma)$. The base line parameters used in the computations are reported in Table 1. The policy parameters are chosen to reflect values in the US case, productivity in a new job is normalized at unity, the elasticity of the matching function is consistent with the Blanchard and Diamond (1990) and Pissarides (1996) estimates, the workers' share of match surplus is set to satisfy the Hosios condition for social efficiency, and the costs of recruiting and hiring a worker are consistent with survey results reported by Hamermesh (1993). Finally, unemployment income b and the lower support of the distribution of market product γ are chosen so that the implied steady state unemployment rate is 6.5% and average duration of an unemployment spell is one quarter, numbers that reflect the average experience in the US. over the past 20 years.

Table 1
Baseline parameter values: efficient rent sharing

New job productivity	$p = 1$
Interest rate	$r = 0.02$ per quarter
Matching elasticity	$\alpha = 0.5$
Recruiting cost	$c\theta/\lambda(\theta) = 0.3$ per worker
Training cost	$C = 0.3$ per worker
Productivity shock frequency	$\delta = 0.1$
Minimum match product	$\gamma = 0.64$ per quarter
Value of leisure	$b = 0.35$ per quarter
Worker's rent share	$\beta = 1 - \alpha = 0.5$
UI benefit replacement ratio	$\rho = 0.2$
Payroll tax rate	$\tau = 0.2$

The quantitative implications of variation in the payroll tax rate and UI benefit replacement ratio on unemployment and aggregate income are illustrated in Table 2. The signs of the effects on unemployment are obviously consistent with the known qualitative implications of the model and aggregate income responds in the same direction as employment in these cases. The first panel clearly suggests that the quantitative magnitude of employment effects of these two forms of passive policy are large enough to provide an explanation for the observed cross OECD country variation in the unemployment rate. In particular, replacement ratios and payroll tax rates in the order of 35% are not uncommon in Europe. Were the US. rates both in that range, the computations imply that the US unemployment rate too would be of European magnitude.

Although the efficiency loss of an increase in either the unemployment compensation benefit replacement ratio or the payroll tax rate is not all that large in a neighborhood of the

Table 2
Effects of the payroll tax (τ) and UI benefit (ρ) given a rent sharing wage contract

	$\tau = 0.0$	$\tau = 0.1$	$\tau = 0.2$	$\tau = 0.3$	$\tau = 0.4$
(a) *Unemployment rate (%)*					
$\rho = 0.0$	4.5	4.7	4.9	5.1	5.4
$\rho = 0.1$	5.1	5.3	5.6	5.9	6.3
$\rho = 0.2$	5.8	6.1	6.5	7.0	7.5
$\rho = 0.3$	6.8	7.4	8.0	8.7	9.7
$\rho = 0.4$	8.5	9.4	10.5	12.1	14.6
(b) *Income (percent of p = 1)*					
$\rho = 0.0$	90.5	90.5	90.5	90.5	90.5
$\rho = 0.1$	90.5	90.5	90.5	90.4	90.4
$\rho = 0.2$	90.4	90.4	90.3	90.2	90.0
$\rho = 0.3$	90.2	90.1	89.9	89.6	89.2
$\rho = 0.4$	89.7	89.4	88.9	88.1	86.9

baseline values, they become very significant at higher tax and replacement rates, particularly as the two increase together. Although the US. would lose only about $1\% = 100(90.5 - 89.6)/90.3$ of its income per participant in the labor force were both the replacement ratio and the payroll tax rate raised from roughly 20% to 30%, it would lose about $4\% = 100(90.5 - 86.9)/90.3$ of income were they both raised to 40%. Indeed, these numbers imply that liberal unemployment benefit and high payroll tax policies may have a important impact on the average standard of living in Europe relative to the US under the hypothesis that the model describes difference between the performance of the two economies induced by known policy parameter differences.

The tables also suggest that the two policies have increasing and complementary effects in the sense that a larger value of either the payroll tax rate or the replacement ratio contributes positively to both its own marginal effect and to the marginal effect of the other. As emphasized by Coe and Snower (1996), this property implies that a smaller joint policy reform designed to reduce both the payroll tax and the replacement ratio may be far more effective that a large reduction in just one of the two.

The unemployment and income effect of a firing tax T and hiring subsidy H are reported in Table 3a,b. For reference, the tax or subsidy increment assumed, 0.3, is approximately equal to 1 month's average output per worker.

There are three observations of interest. First, a employment protection policy lowers unemployment in this experiment while a hiring subsidy increases unemployment. The reason is the same in both cases: The effect on unemployment duration, $1/\lambda(\theta)$, is proportionately smaller than the offsetting effect on unemployment incidence, $\delta F(R)$. Second, the marginal income effect of either a hiring subsidy or a firing tax can be of the *opposite* sign of the marginal employment effect. Finally, as the results along the diagonals of both table imply, a hiring subsidy financed by a severance tax $(H = T)$ can lower the unem-

Table 3
Effects of the firing cost (T) and hiring subsidy (H) given a rent sharing wage contract

	$H = 0.0$	$H = 0.25$	$H = 0.5$	$H = 0.75$	$H = 1.0$
(a) *Unemployment rate (%)*					
$T = 0.0$	6.5	7.0	7.9	7.9	8.3
$T = 0.25$	6.0	6.5	7.4	7.4	7.9
$T = 0.5$	5.3	5.9	6.9	6.9	7.4
$T = 0.75$	4.6	5.3	6.4	6.4	6.9
$T = 1.0$	3.9	4.6	5.8	5.8	6.4
(b) *Income (percent of p = 1)*					
$T = 0.0$	90.3	90.2	89.9	89.4	88.7
$T = 0.25$	90.2	90.3	90.2	89.9	89.4
$T = 0.5$	89.9	90.2	90.3	90.2	89.9
$T = 0.75$	89.4	89.9	90.2	90.3	90.2
$T = 1.0$	88.7	89.4	89.9	90.2	90.3

ployment rate with no loss in steady state income although admittedly the effect of such a revenue neutral policy on unemployment is quite small in this simulation.

5.4. A call for research

As stated in the introduction to the section, the computational exercise is meant to be illustrative. As an indication of results that are consistent with the general theory presented in this chapter, they demonstrate potentially important implications of the framework. However, more analysis of three kinds is needed. First, how sensitive are these quantitative results to variation in parameter values? Second, how robust are they to alternative specifications of the wage determination process? Finally, econometric research within the framework is required to generate valid information about the reasonable ranges of parameter values and about the actual wage determination process.

6. Wage posting games

The idea that employers set the terms of employment while workers choose among available offers is consistent with how many labor economists view the wage setting process. The presence of search friction in the form of incomplete information on the workers side about specific employer offers is a source of monopsony employer power in this setting. Relative to the bilateral bargaining formulation, the model's structure is asymmetric in that it gives the power to set wages to the employer. However, unlike the standard model of static employer monopsony, an employer's market power is constrained by competition with other similar employers over time. The purpose of this section is to review the results drawn from an analysis of a set of models in which employers post wage offers and workers seek the highest offer.

The wage posting approach is consistent with the idea that each employer chooses a particular wage policy, say to be either a "high" or a "low" wage firm. Those that offer high wages are more attractive to outsiders and retain insiders more readily. Facing the same trade off between wage, size and quit rate, some choose the high wage even though profit generated per worker is lower, making up the difference in higher volume. More productive firms find it profitable to acquire more workers by outbidding their less efficient competition. Although "wage policy" plays no role in formal market models with complete information, the recent work on search equilibrium in wage posting games gives formal content to these ideas.

The models reviewed in the section were also motivated by a purely theoretical question. After the adaptation of optimal stopping theory to the price search problem, Rothschild (1973) asked whether it was possible to derive the distribution of wages that motivate wage search as a market equilibrium phenomenon. In particular, does dispersion exist even when all buyers and sellers are respectively identical? Interesting, the answer is a qualified yes. As a consequence, the theory also has substantive content as an explanation for wage differences across observably identical workers and jobs.

6.1. The Diamond paradox

As is well known, non-cooperative price posting under perfect information generates a Bertrand equilibrium, one in which all charge a common competitive equilibrium price, even when the number of competitors is small. Diamond (1971) was the first to solve a fully consistent equilibrium version of the price posting game under imperfect information about offers. He finds that *only the monopoly (monopsony) price* is offered in equilibrium if the price setters are the sellers (buyers) of the good or service in question even when the number of competitors is large. Indeed, Diamond's unique solution to a wage posting game when workers and employers are identical yields the same outcome as a bargaining-matching model in which the employer has all the "bargaining power" in the sense that the worker's Nash bargaining parameter β is equal to zero. However, because employers capture all the match surplus, there is no non-trivial equilibrium in which workers are willing to participate if the cost of gathering wage information is strictly positive. This result is known as the *Diamond paradox*.

Formally, the structure of the model follows. There is a continuum of active employers represented by the unit interval and a given continuum of potential worker participants represented by $[1,n]$ where n is the measure of workers per firm. Both workers and employers are respectively identical. Each participating worker searches by drawing a sequential random wage sample at frequency λ, without recall from the wage offer c.d.f. $F(w)$. Existing job-worker matches dissolve at exogenous rate δ. Under stationary conditions, the value of employment at a job paying wage w, denoted as $W(w)$, and the value of unemployment U given that worker search employers at random solve the following continuous time Bellman equations:

$$rW(w) = w + \delta[U - W(w)] \tag{90}$$

and

$$rU = b - a + \int \max\langle W(w) - U, 0\rangle dF(w), \tag{91}$$

where b represents an unemployment income, any unemployment compensation plus the value of time which would otherwise be gone once an employment spell begins, and a is the out-of-pocket cost of search. Since the first equation implies that the value of employment increases with the wage, the optimal acceptance strategy has the reservation property and the reservation wage, the solution to $W(R) = U$, solves the standard reservation price equation

$$R = b - a + \frac{\lambda}{r + \delta} \int_R^\infty [w - R] dF(w). \tag{92}$$

As participation in the labor market while not employed requires search activity and because any out-of-pocket cost of search a is avoided when not searching, participation requires $U \geq b/r$. Assuming that this participation condition holds, the potential labor force is fixed and equal to n. Hence, the measure of the stock of searching unemployed u evolves according to

$$\dot{u} = \delta(n - u) - \lambda u S(r),$$

where

$$S(R) = \int_{x \geq R} dF(x)$$

is the probability that a randomly searched employer is offering an acceptable wage and $\delta(n - u)$ is the exogenous worker flow from employment to unemployment. Hence, the number of workers who participate in non-trivial equilibrium is

$$u = \frac{\delta n}{\delta + \lambda S(R)}. \qquad (93)$$

Again, let p, a positive constant, represent the value of a worker's marginal revenue flow once employed. Given that the set of employers is represented by the unit interval, every employer hires a flow of workers equal to λu provided that her wage offer w is acceptable and losses workers at rate δ so that the steady state employment of a firm offering wage w is $l(w) = \lambda u/\delta$ if the offer is acceptable and is 0 if not. Hence, the expected present value of the flow of profits is

$$\pi(w, R, F) = (p - w)l(w) = \begin{cases} \dfrac{\lambda(p - w)n}{\delta + \lambda S(R)} & \text{if } w \geq R, \\ 0 & \text{otherwise.} \end{cases} \qquad (94)$$

A *wage posting equilibrium* is a reservation wage R, which is optimal chosen by workers in these sense of Eq. (92) and taken as given by employers, and a offer distribution F, also taken as given by each employer, such that every wage offered is profit maximizing, i.e.,

$$w = \text{argmax}\{\pi(w, R, F)\} \qquad \text{for every } w \text{ on the support of } F. \qquad (95)$$

In short, an equilibrium is a reservation wage and wage offer distribution pair (R,F) that represents a non-cooperative solution to a game in which each worker chooses his reservation wage given the wage offers of employers and the reservation wage of other workers and each employer chooses her wage offer taking as given the reservation wages of the workers and the offers of other employers.[18]

The Diamond paradox is easily stated: there is no equilibrium in which exchange takes place if the cost of search is strictly positive. Instead, no workers participate. The proof is

---

[18] The assumption that an employer acts to maximize steady state profit is a simplification. Given that the interest rate r is small relative to the offer arrival rate λ, the wage offer strategies chosen in equilibrium approximate those chosen were one to use the more appropriate expected present value of future profit criterion in the sense that they are the limiting strategies as the ratio r/λ tends to zero.

simple. Given Eq. (94), the only solution to Eq. (95) is a wage offer equal to the reservation wage no matter what other employers offer simply because a higher wage attracts no additional worker, i.e., a unit mass on $w = R$ is the only candidate for an equilibrium offer distribution F. But given this offer distribution, $R = b - a$ from Eq. (92) which implies that the value of search unemployment is less than the value of non-participation if cost of search is positive, i.e., $U = W(R) = (b - a)/r < b/r$ given $a > 0$ from Eqs. (90) and (91). As a corollary, all workers participate and the common equilibrium wage offered by all employers is b if $a = 0$.

6.2. Wage dispersion: differential costs of search

One implication of Diamond's paradox is that market failure is the inevitable consequence of costly search and market power on one side of the market. Albrecht and Axell (1984) show that this conclusion is a consequence of the assumption that all workers have identical search and opportunity costs of employment provided that some subset of workers can search costlessly. The essence of their argument follows.

Suppose there are two groups of workers, indexed by $i = 0$ and $i = 1$, that face different search costs a_i satisfying $0 = a_0 < a_1$. Assume further, that the opportunity cost of employment, b_i, enjoyed while either searching or not participating is strictly larger for the group with zero out of pocket costs of search, i.e., $b_0 > b_1 = 0$.[19] In this case, the reservation wages of the two types solve

$$R_i = b_i - a_i + \frac{\lambda}{r + \delta} \int_{R_i}^{\infty} [w - R_i] dF(w), \qquad i = 0 \text{ and } 1, \tag{96}$$

and $rU_i = R_i \geq b_i$ is necessary and sufficient for participation by worker type i. One can easily verify, the workers with the lower search cost and higher outside option value are more selective, i.e., $R_0 > R_1$. In steady state, the measure of each type who participate as unemployed workers is determined by

$$u_i = \begin{cases} \dfrac{\delta n_i}{\delta + \lambda S(R_i)} & \text{if } U_i \geq b_i/r, \ i = 0, 1, \\ 0 & \text{otherwise.} \end{cases} \tag{97}$$

where n_i represents the measure of the total labor force of type i workers per firm.

Obviously, only Diamond's outcome is obtains if only one of the two types participate. Given that both types will search when wage offers are high enough, the possibility of an equilibrium in which both types participate needs to be investigated. Because the application flow to every employer is $\lambda(u_0 + u_1)$ per period, both types accept if the offer is R_0 or more, but only type 1 workers accept for wage offers in the interval $[R_1, R_0)$, and those that accept are employed for an average spell of length $1/\delta$, employer profit is

[19] The assumption that $a_0 = 0$ is critical but $b_1 = 0$ can be regarded as a normalization.

$$\pi(w, R_0, R_1, F) = (p - w)l(w)$$

$$= \begin{cases} \dfrac{\lambda(p - w)n_0}{\delta + \lambda S(R_0)} + \dfrac{\lambda(p - w)n_1}{\delta + \lambda S(R_1)} & \text{if } w \geq !R_0 \\[3mm] \dfrac{\lambda(p - w)n_1}{\delta + \lambda S(R_1)} & \text{if } R_0 > w \geq R_1, \\[3mm] 0 & \text{otherwise,} \end{cases} \tag{98}$$

given that cost of search and opportunity cost of employment assumptions and Eq. (96) imply $R_0 > R_1$ for any offer distribution F. Hence, a steady state equilibrium with both types participating is a triple (R_0, R_1, F) that satisfies Eq. (95) with employer payoffs defined by Eq. (98) and reservation wage rates that satisfy Eq. (96) provided profits are non-negative and workers of both types are willing to participate.

Because an employer's payoff strictly declines with the wage offered between worker reservation wage rates but jumps up as the wage offered crosses these two critical numbers, a wage offer is profit maximizing only if it is the reservation wage rate of some worker type. Hence, if there is a non-Diamond outcome, some positive fraction of employers must offer R_0 while the others offer $R_1 < R_0$. Of course, the expected profit made by these two groups of employers must be the same by virtue of Eq. (95). Because all offers are no less than R_1, i.e., $S(R_1) = 1$, the equal profit condition requires

$$\pi(R_0, R_0, R_1, F) = \frac{\lambda(p - R_0)n_0}{\delta + \lambda q} + \frac{\lambda(p - R_0)n_1}{\delta + \lambda},$$

$$\pi(R_1, R_0, R_1, F) = \frac{\lambda(p - R_1)n_1}{\delta + \lambda},$$

where $q \equiv S(R_0)$ is the fraction of employers who offer the higher wage $w = R_0$ and $1 - q$ is the fraction that offer the lower wage $w = R_1$. Finally Eq. (96) and the assumption $a_0 = b_1 = 0$ imply that the value of reservation wage rates satisfy

$$R_0 = b_0 \qquad \text{and} \qquad R_1 = \frac{\lambda q}{r + \delta}(R_0 - R_1) - a_1,$$

provided that $R_1 \geq rU_1 = b_1 = 0$ so that type 1 workers participate.

By substituting from the last two equations back into the equal profit condition, one obtains

$$\frac{(b_0 - R_1)(\delta + \lambda q)}{(b_0 + a_1)(\delta + \lambda)} = \frac{(p - b_0)n_0}{(b_0 + a_1)n_1} = \frac{(r + \delta)(\delta + \lambda q)}{(\delta + \lambda)(r + \delta + \lambda q)}$$

after manipulating terms. As positive profits are required in equilibrium to guarantee employer participation and the last term on the right is strictly increasing in q, a unique fraction of the employers pay the high wage and the remainder offer the low wage if and only if

$$\frac{\delta}{\delta + \lambda} < \frac{(p - b_0)n_0}{(b_0 + a_1)n_1} < \frac{r + \delta}{r + \delta + \lambda}.$$

Because an open set of parameters satisfies these necessary and sufficient conditions, equilibria with distinct wage offers generically exist. Finally, when the left hand inequality does not hold, then $q = 0$ which implies that all employers offer the wage $R_1 = -a_1 < 0$ and none of the workers participate. Similarly, all employers offer a single wage equal to $R_0 = b_0$ and type 1 worker participate if and only if $R_1 = (\lambda b_0 - (r + \delta)a_1)/(r + \delta + \lambda) \geq 0$, when the right inequality fails. Note in passing that a single wage equal to the reservation wage of the high reservation type is always the outcome in the limit with no friction in the sense that offer arrival rate λ is infinite.

6.3. Wage dispersion: more than one offer

Diamond's paradox is also sensitive to the assumption that search is sequential without recall. Burdett and Judd (1983) show that other equilibria also exist when workers are able to compare two or more offers simultaneously. Indeed, if every searching workers chooses among two or more randomly selected offers, then the outcome of the wage posting game is identical to Bertrand's, i.e., all employers offer $w = p$. However, if some positive strict fraction receive two or more offers and another fraction receives only one, the unique equilibrium is characterized by a non-degenerate offer distribution. Furthermore, the distribution converges to a point mass on p as the fraction that receive two or more tends to unity and to a point mass on the common reservation wage R as the fraction who receive more than one offer tends to zero. Hence, all intermediate cases lie somewhere midway between the single wage competitive (Bertrand) equilibrium and single wage monopsony (Diamond) equilibrium even though wages are disperse.

Prior to the Burdett–Judd analysis, Butters (1977) proposed and studied a model that satisfied the Burdett–Judd comparative shopping condition. In that formulation, employers "advertise" wage offers by sending messages, "help wanted ads", to workers at random. Each worker chooses among all advertised job offers received within some specified "period", say a week. Given that offers arrive continuously over the week at frequency λ, the number received is a random Poisson variable. As the fraction of searching worker's who receive one and two or more wage offer during the period satisfy $0 < \lambda \exp(-\lambda) < 1$ and $0 < 1 - \exp(-\lambda)(1 + \lambda) < 1$, respectively, the only equilibrium offer distribution is disperse. Of course, one can interpret the arrival rate here as the outcome of the recruiting activity by employers in Butters.

The Burdett–Judd comparison shopping condition is satisfied automatically when unemployed workers search sequentially but employed workers search as well because employed workers who find an alternative can compare it with the wage earned on their current job. Mortensen (1990), Burdett (1990) and Burdett and Mortensen (1989, 1998) use this fact to develop models in which wage dispersion is an equilibrium phenomenon under quite general conditions. Because the solution can be characterized in closed form, its structure can and has been estimated using data on wages and unemployment spell durations. This model and its implications are reviewed in the remainder of the section.

6.4. Search on the job

In order to incorporate on the job search, the duration of a job spell must be explicitly modeled. Let $\delta > 0$ denote the exogenous rate of job turnover. Assume that employed workers receive outside offers at arrival frequency $\lambda_1 > 0$, generally different from the arrival rate of offers conditional on unemployment denoted as $\lambda_0 > 0$. Mortensen and Neumann (1988) have shown that employed workers accept any offer greater than their current wage and the unemployed accept all wage offers in excess of a reservation wage R which in this case solves

$$R - b = (\lambda_0 - \lambda_1) \int_R^\infty \left(\frac{1 - F(x)}{r + \delta + \lambda_1[1 - F(x)]} \right) dx. \tag{99}$$

Eq. (99) is a generalization of the reservation wage equation, Eq. (92), which holds when search on the job occurs (where out of pocket search costs are ignored for simplicity). Note that when the offer arrival rate is independent of employment status (as well as out of pocket search cost), the reservation wage is simply equal to the unemployment income b. Furthermore, the effects of the interest rate, the turnover rate and the form of the wage offer distribution on the reservation wage depend critically on the difference between the two arrival rates simply because the relative desirability of search while unemployed depends on the difference between the two arrival rates. For example, given an improvement in the offer distribution is the sense of first order stochastic dominance (an increase in $1 - F(x)$ for all x), the reservation wage increases (decreases) if the offer arrival rate when unemployed exceeds (is less than) that when employed because search while unemployed (employed) is more efficient.

Since employed workers move from one job to another without an intervening unemployment spell, the equality of worker flows into, $\lambda_0[1 - F(R)]u$, and out of employment, $\delta(n - u)$, yields the steady state unemployment rate

$$u = \frac{\delta n}{\delta + \lambda_0[1 - F(R)]} \tag{100}$$

as before, where n represents the number of workers per employer and the total labor supply is fixed and normalized at unity.

By equating the flows into and out of employment at each wage offer, steady state employment at each wage can be derived for any offer distribution. The flow into employment at a wage equal to w or less is $\lambda_0[F(w) - F(R)]u$ given that only offers greater than or equal to the reservation wage are acceptable. The worker flow out of the same category is the sum of exogenous turnover plus the flow of quits to jobs offering a higher wage. The latter flow is equal to $(\delta + \lambda_1[1 - F(w)])G(w)(n - u)$ where $G(w)$ is the fraction of workers employed at wage w or less. Hence, the unique steady state distribution of workers over wage rates associated with any offer distribution is

$$G(w) = \frac{\lambda_0[F(w) - F(R)]u}{(\delta + \lambda_1[1 - F(w)])(n - u)} = \frac{\delta[F(w) - F(R)]}{(\delta + \lambda_1[1 - F(w)])(1 - F(R))}. \tag{101}$$

In the case of a differentiable wage offer distribution, the steady measure of workers employed per firm offering a particular wage w, its steady state labor force, is equal to the ratio of the measure of worker earning the wage divided by the measure of firms offering the wage, i.e.,

$$l(w \mid R, F) = \frac{G'(w)(n - u)}{F'(w)} = \frac{n\delta\lambda_0(\delta + \lambda_1[1 - F(R)])}{(\delta + \lambda_0[1 - F(R)])[\delta + \lambda_1[1 - F(w)]]^2}, \tag{102}$$

provided $F'(w) > 0$ at w. Hence, the steady state profit per firm offering any wage w in the support of F can be written

$$\pi(w \mid R, F) = (p - w)l(w \mid R, F). \tag{103}$$

A *wage posting equilibrium* is a common maximal profit earned by each employer π, a reservation wage R and a offer distribution F which satisfy Eq. (92) and

$$\pi(w \mid R, F) = \pi \qquad \text{for all } w \text{ on the support of } F,$$

$$\pi(w \mid R, F) < \pi \qquad \text{otherwise.} \tag{104}$$

As the employer offering the lowest wage loses all of her workers to competitors anyway, the profit maximizing condition implies that the lower support of the offer distribution is the common reservation wage of all the identical workers. Given Eqs. (102), (103) and $\underline{w} = R$, Eq. (104) implies a single candidate for the offer distribution function. Namely,

$$F(w) = \left(\frac{\delta + \lambda_1}{\lambda_1}\right)\left[1 - \sqrt{\frac{p - w}{p - R}}\right], \qquad \text{for all } w \in [R, \bar{w}] \tag{105}$$

with upper support

$$\bar{w} = p - \frac{\delta^2(p - R)}{(\delta + \lambda_1)^2}.$$

After substituting from Eq. (105) into Eq. (99), one finds that the equilibrium reservation wage can be represented as a weighted average of the unemployment benefit and worker productivity.

$$R = \frac{(\delta + \lambda_1)^2 b + (\lambda_0 - \lambda_1)\lambda_1 p}{(\delta + \lambda_1)^2 + (\lambda_0 - \lambda_1)\lambda_1}. \tag{106}$$

Finally, note that $R < p$ so that $\pi = \pi(R \mid R, F) = \pi(w \mid R, F) > 0$ on the support of the candidate. Because $l(w \mid R, F) = 0$ for all $w < R$ and $l(w \mid R, F) = l(\bar{w} \mid R, F)$ for all

$w > \overline{w}$, the candidate equilibrium wage offer distribution derived above satisfies the profit maximization condition (104), namely $\pi(w \mid R, F) < \pi$ for all $w \notin [R, \overline{w}]$, and, consequently, is the only equilibrium offer distribution.[20]

The Burdett–Mortensen equilibrium is in between Diamond's equilibrium and Bertrand's in the sense that both are limiting cases generated by the two extreme assumptions about the rate at which employed workers receive offers. Because $\overline{w} \to R \to b$ as $\lambda_1 \to 0$, the support of the equilibrium wage offer distribution converge to a point equal to the reservation wage as the offer arrival rate when employed tends to zero. Because $G(w) \to 0$ for all $w < \overline{w}$ and $\overline{w} \to p$ as $\lambda_1 \to \infty$, equilibrium converges to a degenerate wage distribution with unit mass concentrated on the competitive outcome, wage equal to the value of marginal product, as the friction vanishes in the sense that the offer arrival rate when employed tends to infinite.

Note that the equilibrium distributions of wages offered and earned, F and G, have increasing convex densities that are highly left skewed with mass concentrated to the right toward the competitive wage p when λ_1 is large. Specifically,

$$F'(w) = \left(\frac{\delta + \lambda_1}{\lambda_1} \right) \sqrt{\frac{1}{(p - R)(p - w)}} \tag{107}$$

and

$$G'(w) = \frac{\delta(\delta + \lambda_1) F'(w)}{(\delta + \lambda_1[1 - F(w)])^2}. \tag{108}$$

The left skew simply reflects the fact that all wage offers w are less than p but most are concentrated near the competitive wage p, at least when λ_1 is large. From an econometric point of view then, the Burdett–Mortensen model implies that competitive wage theory has a highly asymmetric "error term" with a negative expectation.

6.5. Worker and employer heterogeneity

Mortensen (1990) demonstrates that a mixture of the Burdett–Mortensen and the Albrecht–Axell outcomes is obtained when workers enjoy different unemployment benefits or search costs. In the generalization, wages other than those on the support of reservation wage distribution are offered but still the wage offer support generally is not convex. Mortensen (1990) also shows how differences in employer productivity can contribute to variance in wage offers. An important characteristic of the equilibrium in this case is that more productive employers offer higher wage rates. Burdett and Mortensen (1998) and Bontemps et al. (1997) derive closed form offer distributions in the case of continuous distribution of types for both of these cases. These results and their significance are briefly summarized below.

---

[20] The possibility of an equilibrium offer distribution with mass points is ruled out in Burdett and Mortensen (1989).

First, consider the case of a continuum of worker types described by a continuous worker supply price c.d.f. $H(b)$. Assume for simplicity that when the arrival rate is independent of employment status, i.e., $\lambda_0 = \lambda_1$ which implies $R(b) = b$ for each type from Eq. (99). All employers have the same labor productivity p. The only equilibrium wage offer distribution is of the form

$$F(w) = \left(\frac{\delta + \lambda_1}{\lambda_1}\right)\left[1 - \sqrt{\frac{(p - w)H(w)}{(p - \underline{w})H(\underline{w})}}\right],$$ (109)

where the lowest wage, $\underline{w}$, is the largest solution to

$$w = \operatorname*{argmax}_{w}\{(p - w)H(w)\},$$ (110)

the highest wage, $\bar{w}$, is the largest solution to

$$\frac{(p - \bar{w})H(\bar{w})}{(p - \underline{w})H(\underline{w})} = \left(\frac{\delta}{\delta + \lambda_1}\right)^2$$

and w is in the support of F if and only if

$$w' > w \quad \Rightarrow \quad (p - w)H(w) > (p - w')H(w') \qquad \text{for all } w \in (\underline{w}, \bar{w}).$$ (111)

As $H(w)$ is the Marshallian market supply curve in this environment, the lower support is simply the monopsony wage by Eq. (110). Note, that the equilibrium offer distribution still has an increasing density with a left skew although possibly less so in general than in the case of no dispersion in the unemployment benefit.

Next, consider the case of a continuum of employer types described by the continuous employer productivity c.d.f. $J(p)$. Without loss of generality, assume that the lower support $\underline{p}$ is no less than the common reservation wage R. The only equilibrium wage offer distribution is

$$F(\omega(p)) = J(p),$$ (112)

where the wage-productivity profile $w = \omega(p)$ is implicitly defined by the first order condition for profit maximization, which is

$$2\lambda_1 F'(w)(p - w) - [\delta + \lambda_1(1 - F(w)] = 0$$ (113)

on the support of F. It can be shown that the only solution must be

$$\omega(p) = p - \int_R^p \left(\frac{\delta + \lambda_1(1 - J(p))}{\delta + \lambda_1(1 - J(x))}\right)^2 dx.$$ (114)

Note, the lowest offer is the common reservation wage, i.e., $J(x) = 0$ for all $x \leq \underline{p}$ implies $\omega(\underline{p}) = R$, wage offers increase with productivity, i.e., $\omega'(p) > 0$, but all offers are strictly greater than the worker's reservation wage but less than the value of marginal product and $R < \omega(p) < p$ for all $p > \underline{p}$. In the case of $R > \underline{p}$, employer's with labor product $p < R$ cannot earn a positive profit and therefore don't participate. The equilibrium offer distribution takes the same form with the truncated distribution of productivity $J(p)/[1 - J(R)]$ replacing J in Eqs. (112) and (114).

Obviously, the shape of the offer distribution is influenced by the shape of the distribution of labor productivity in this case. Indeed, because Eqs. (112) and (114) imply

$$F'(w) = \frac{2\lambda_1}{\delta^2 \int_R^p \frac{(\delta + \lambda_1(1 - F(w)))}{(\delta + \lambda_1(1 - F(x)))^2} \, dx} , \qquad (114)$$

the offer density is not generally increasing. Still, as Bontemps et al. (1997) show, Eq. (107) holds in the limit as dispersion in productivity vanishes. Consequently, the theory implies restriction regarding its form, particularly on the shape of its right tail. These are characterized and used to develope an empirical test of the theory by Bontemps et al. (1997).

6.6. Structural estimation

What might be called the "first generation" empirical search literature uses the stopping problem to interpret empirical observation on unemployment spell durations and wages earned immediately after such a spell taking the offer distribution as given. This literature is reviewed in detail by Devine and Kiefer (1991), Wolpin (1995), and Neumann (1997). The papers summarized in this subsection represents on going "second generation" literature in which authors exploit the structure of equilibrium search models in the estimation procedures applied.

The literature starts with Wolpin (1987) and Eckstein and Wolpin (1990) who estimate the Albrecht and Axell (1984) model using panel data on unemployment durations and subsequent earnings. Although the model provides an acceptable fit to the duration data, the fit of the wage data is less satisfactory because each point in the support of the wage offer distribution is necessarily the reservation wage of some worker type in the model. As the complexity of the computation of the equilibrium increases rapidly with the number of types, only a small finite number of types could be considered.

The simple Burdett–Mortensen with homogenous workers and employers is consistent with a number of stylized facts: wage offers generally exceed reservation wages, workers with more experience and tenure earn a higher wage on average, larger firms offer higher wage rates, and quit rates fall with wage offers in cross-section. However, in the absence of exogenous worker or employer heterogeneity in labor productivity, the approach implies increasing densities for both the wage offer and wage earned distributions. Specifically both have left tails skewed away from the unique competitive wage for reasonable values of the offer arrival rates. This implication is at odds with wage distributions which have always have long and thick right tails. As a weaker version of the perfectly competitive implication that every worker's wage is equal to her value of marginal product, it is not a problem in principle. In either case, worker and employer heterogeneity are required to explain the observed shape of earning distributions.

Kiefer and Neumann (1993), Koning et al. (1995), and van den Berg and Ridder (1993, 1995) all estimate the simplest Burdett and Mortensen (1989) version of the model in which all workers and employers are assumed identical using unemployment and job spell durations and wage data drawn from panel data. They do so by assuming that the labor market is segmented by the usual observable indicators of worker and employer heterogeneity – education, experience, occupation and industry. All the structural parameters, e.g., the offer arrival rates and separation rate, are allowed to vary across the sub-market segments but workers and employers within each sub-market are homogenous by assumption. Although the estimated models provide an accurate fit of both unemployment duration and cross-section wage data, the implied dispersion in the sequence of wages that an individual can earn over a work life is too narrow, i.e., the implied return to experience is too small.

Bowlus et al. (1995, 1997) provide the first estimates of a version of the model in which exogenous heterogeneity in employer productivity is allowed. They assume only a finite number of employer types, each defined by a different value of labor productivity, p, in the formal model. Because the model's solution cannot be expressed in closed form in this case, their maximum likelihood estimation procedure requires the repeated computation of a candidate equilibrium offer distribution F. Consequently, the computational complexity of the approach grows rapidly with the number of employer productivity types allowed in the support of J. Still their approach fits the data with only four or five points of support and yields interesting and useful results. For example, in their second (1997) paper based on US. data drawn from the NLS, their results suggest that the earnings distribution of young whites stochastically dominates that of young blacks among those transiting from higher school to work primarily because blacks are exposed to twice the subsequent job destruction risk. The estimated offer arrival rates are essentially identical for blacks and whites with the arrival rate when unemployed roughly three times larger than when employed.

Bontemps et al. (1997) avoid problems of computational complexity by assuming a continuous distribution of employer types. Their approach permits the application of the first order profit maximization condition, Eq. (113), and the one to one association it and continuity imply between the distribution of wage offers and the distribution of employer productivity, Eq. (112). Exploiting these continuous relationships, they obtain joint estimates of the offer arrival rate and separation rate parameters, and a non-parametric estimate of the distribution of employer labor productivity using unemployment and job duration data and earnings data drawn from a French panel survey on individual worker histories. After stratifying the data by industry, the model fits well, even though workers in each industry are assumed equally productive, and the fitted wage offer and wage earned distribution satisfy the tail restrictions implied by the theory. As a further check of adequacy, the authors compare the distribution of productivity over firms implied by the wage data with an independent empirical distribution of value added per worker derived from a sample of French firms in each industry considered. They find that the shapes of these two distributions are broadly consistent with one another. Finally, their empirical results suggest that the most productive employers have significant monopoly power and use it by paying wages substantially below value of marginal product while the least productive have almost none and earn little pure profit.

The estimation methodology applied by Bontemps et al. (1997) is both simple and powerful. As such, a brief sketch is appropriate. First, the authors use a kernel estimator and the data on employed worker earnings to fit the wage distribution G. Conditional on this estimate, call it $\hat{G}$, and the parameter λ_1/δ, the inverse of Eq. (101) generates an associated consistent estimate of the offer distribution $\hat{F}$ and its density. Second, they substitute these estimates in the unemployment and job spell duration likelihood functions and maximize to obtain consistent estimates of the parameters R, λ_0, λ_1, and δ.[21] Third, they use the first order condition, Eq. (113), and $\hat{F}$ to obtain an estimate of the inverse of $\omega(p)$. After inverting and substituting the result back into $\hat{F}$, the associated estimate of the distribution of labor productivity $\hat{J}$ is obtained using Eq. (112). Note, the method avoids the repeated integration required to obtain $\omega(p)$ using the equilibrium equation, Eq. (114), which is required by a joint maximum likelihood estimation procedure.

7. Wage posting in a matching model

As suggested by the organization of this essay, the literature on search equilibrium approaches to labor market equilibrium analysis has developed along two somewhat different branches. Although the matching approach has found application primarily in the macroeconomic literature on unemployment determination while the wage posting approach has been used in empirical analysis of wage differentials, the separate lives of these two literatures are difficult to explain, especially since several authors have contributed to both. As potential fruit, a graft of the two strands promises a joint theory of wage offers and market tightness in which employers play the active role of both wage setter and job creator.

A synthesis is sketched in this section based on Mortensen (1998). As his approach is inspired by the related model of Acemoglu and Shimer (1997), the principal results presented here are similar to theirs. First, although Diamond's equilibrium generally exists in the synthesis, so does another equilibrium, one both strictly preferred by all agents and stable under competitive rent seeking job creation behavior. Second, wage dispersion can induce endogenous differentials in labor productivity rather than simply reflect exogenous differences as in the extended version of the Burdett–Mortensen model. In our formulation, this result occurs as a consequence of a standard specific human capital partial equilibrium result, an employer offering a higher wage has an greater incentive to make match specific productivity enhancing investments because the future return on the investment is subject to a less quit risk.

---

[21] Since R varies one for one with b given the other parameters from Eq. (99), the reservation wage rather than the unemployment benefit can be regarded as a structural parameter.

7.1. Search and matching

As in the matching model, firms create "job sites" and each is either vacant or filled. In equilibrium, the vacancy measure v is determined by a zero profit free entry condition. The total labor force size is fixed. Each individual worker is either employed or not and the measure of unemployed, u, evolves according to the usual law of motion. As in Burdett–Mortensen model, workers search while employed as well as unemployed and, consequently, the numbers in each category are inputs, along with the vacancy measure, in the matching technology. Specifically, let $m(v, u, 1 - u)$ represent the matching function equal in value to the total flow of offers received by workers. It is increasing and concave in the three arguments.

For simplicity, we assume that employed and unemployed workers are perfect substitutes in the matching process, i.e., only their sum matters. Because the total flow of contacts must equal the sum received by both unemployed and employed workers, the offer arrival rate is independent of employment status and an increasing concave function of vacancies, i.e., as $\lambda_0 u + \lambda_1(1 - u) = m(v, u, 1 - u) = m(v, u + 1 - u) \equiv \lambda(v)$ for all u,

$$\lambda_0 = \lambda_1 = \lambda(w), \tag{115}$$

where $\lambda(v)$ is an increasing and concave function.

Workers behave as in the Burdett–Mortensen model: unemployed workers accept the first offer no less than the reservation wage R defined by Eq. (99) and an employed work accepts any offer in excess of that currently earned. The simplifying assumption that employed and unemployed workers are perfect substittes implies that the reservation wage is exogenous, i.e., $R = b$. Consequently, the steady state unemployment rate is

$$u = \frac{\delta}{\delta + \lambda(v)[1 - F(b)]}. \tag{116}$$

Finally, the associated steady state distribution of earnings across employed worker is

$$G(w) = \frac{\delta[F(w) - F(b)]}{(\delta + \lambda(v)[1 - F(w)])(1 - F(b))} \tag{117}$$

from Eqs. (100), (101), and (115).

7.2. Wage posting

In the matching framework, it is the future expected return to the creation of a vacancy which is the critical profit concept. Wages are set to maximize this return and entry drives it down to recruiting and hiring costs. Formally, the asset value of a vacant job solves

$$rV = \max_{w \geq R} \{ \eta(v)[u + (1 - u)G(w)](J(w) - V) - c \}, \tag{118}$$

where $\eta(v) \equiv \lambda(v)/v$ is the average rate at which vacancies are filled and $c > 0$ is the recruiting cost per vacancy. The first term on the left is the expected return to vacancy creation, the product of the rate at which workers are contacted per vacancy ($\eta(v)$), the probability that the worker contacted will accept (unity if unemployed given $w \geq R$ and $G(w)$ if employed where G is the distribution of wage rates across employed workers), and the capital gain associated with converting a vacancy job to a filled one ($J(w) - V$). As employed workers quit when they are offered a higher alternative wage, the expected present value of the future flow of quasi-rents once a worker is hired, $J(w)$, solves

$$rJ(w) = p - w + (\delta + \lambda(v)[1 - F(w)])[V - J(w)], \tag{119}$$

where w is the wage offered, p is match product, δ is the exogenous separation rate and $\lambda(v)[1 - F(w)]$ is the expected rate at which an employed worker finds a job paying more than w. Finally, free entry eliminates pure profit in vacancy creation

$$V = 0. \tag{120}$$

Given the reservation wage, which is tied down by $R = b$ in the case under study, a steady state *wage posting search equilibrium* is an unemployment rate u, a vacancy rate v, a wage c.d.f. G, and a wage offer c.d.f. F which satisfies Eqs. (116), (117), and (120) given that every wage in the support of F is a solution to the profit maximization problem formulated on the right side of Eq. (118).

Because no employed worker accepts the lowest wage offer and all unemployed workers accept wages at or above the reservation wage, the lower support of the equilibrium offer distribution is $R = b$. As $F(b) = 0$, an appropriate sequence of substitutions from the other equations into Eq. (118) yields

$$\frac{c}{\eta(v)} = \delta \max_{w} \left\{ \frac{(p - w)}{(r + \delta + \lambda(v)[1 - F(w)])(\delta + \lambda(v)[1 - F(w)])} \right\}. \tag{121}$$

But note, in the limiting case of $r = 0$ considered by Burdett and Mortensen, this equation simplifies to

$$\frac{c}{\eta(v)} = \delta \max_{w} \{(p - w)l(w \mid R, F)\}, \tag{122}$$

where

$$l(w \mid R, F) = \frac{1}{(\delta + \lambda(v)[1 - F(w)])^2} \tag{123}$$

is the size of an employer's steady state labor force when offering a wage w in the Burdett and Mortensen model for the special case of offer arrival rates independent of employment status from Eq. (102).[22] Hence, the equilibrium distribution of offers here is the same as in their model, namely

---

[22] However, in the case of a matching model $\delta l(w \mid R, F)$ represents the accumulated flow of future quasi rents per worker hired in steady state.

$$F(w) = \left(\frac{\delta + \lambda(v)}{\lambda(v)} \right) \left[1 - \sqrt{\frac{p - w}{p - b}} \right]. \tag{124}$$

In addition, however, the offer arrival rate is endogenously determined as the solution to the following implication of Eqs. (122) and (124) and the fact that the lower support of F is b

$$cv = \frac{\delta \lambda(v)(p - b)}{(\delta + \lambda(v))^2}. \tag{125}$$

As $\lambda(v)$ is increasing and concave, exactly two solution exist, one at $v = 0$, and the second strictly positive under the Inada condition $\lambda(0) = 0$, $\lambda'(0) = \infty$, and $\lambda'(\infty) = 0$ in the only interesting case, that in which labor output exceed the opportunity cost of employment, i.e., $p > b$. Of course, these conditions are quite natural given the production function interpretation of the matching function.

Only the positive solution is stable in the sense that the return to vacancy creation exceeds (is less than) the cost for positive values to its (left) right. In short, a simple entry process starting with positive vacancies will find the positive equilibrium. Finally, note $c \to 0$ implies that the equilibrium vacancy rate $v \to \infty$. Hence, if the matching function $\lambda(v)$ is unbounded, then competitive equilibrium with all workers earning the common wage p is the result in the limit as recruiting costs vanish.

7.3. Endogenous productive heterogeneity

As demonstrated above, more productive employers offer higher wages in equilibrium in an extended version of the Burdett–Mortensen model characterized by an exogenous distribution of labor productivity over employers. Acemoglu and Shimer (1997) show the causality can be reversed in their model. That is, firms that offer higher wages also have an incentive to differentiate themselves by investing in their worker's. In this section we show that the same result also holds in our synthesis of the matching and wage posting approaches simply because higher wage employers enjoy lower quit rates. Hence, both models suggest a parsimonious explanation for the positive correlation between the wage and labor productivity across employers: The correlation may be the consequence of strategic wage competition.

In the extension, let k represent the cost of training a new hire and let worker productivity be an increasing concave function of this investment denoted as $p(k)$. The value equations, Eqs. (118) and (119), can be rewritten as

$$rV = \max_{(w,k)} \{ \eta(v)[u + (1 - u)G(w)](J(w, k) - k - V) - c \} \tag{126}$$

and

$$rJ(w, k) = p(k) - w + (\delta + \lambda(v)[1 - F(w)])[V - J(w, k)] \tag{127}$$

to reflect this extension where the maximization with respect to both wage and investment reflect the simultaneous choice of wage offer and training policy adopted by a particular employer. After the appropriate substitution are made from equations (116), (117), and (120), the equilibrium characterization (121) can be rewritten as

$$\frac{c}{\eta(v)} = \delta \max_{(w,k) \ge (b,0)} \left\{ \frac{p - w - k(r + \delta + \lambda(v)[1 - F(w)]}{r + \delta + \lambda(v)[1 - F(w)])(\delta + \lambda(v)[1 - F(w)])} \right\}. \tag{128}$$

In the limiting case of $r = 0$, the equilibrium wage offer distribution and training investment solve

$$\max_{k \ge 0} \left\{ \frac{p(k) - w - k(\delta + \lambda(v)[1 - F(w)])}{(\delta + \lambda(v)[1 - F(w)])^2} \right\} = \max_{k \ge 0} \left\{ \frac{p(k) - b - k(\delta + \lambda(v))}{(\delta + \lambda(v))^2} \right\} \tag{129}$$

on the support of F given that $\underline{w} = b$ where any equilibrium vacancy rate solves

$$cv = \frac{\delta \lambda(v)}{(\delta + \lambda(v))^2} \max_{k \ge 0} (p(k) - b - k(\delta + \lambda(v))). \tag{130}$$

Provided that $p(0) > b$, the Inada conditions applied to the matching technology again guarantee a unique stable positive solution for v. Furthermore, because the left side of Eq. (129) is strictly increasing in F given w and is strictly decreasing in w, there is a unique increasing function $F(w)$ which satisfied the equation. Hence, the equilibrium in the extended model is unique and wage offers are dispersed.

The only issue that remains is to characterize differences in the investment policy adopted by employers that offer different wage rates. As the investment decision criterion, implicit in the problem defined on the left side of Eq. (129), is strictly concave given the assumption that $p(k)$ is increasing and strictly concave, the investment decision has a unique solution. Assume $p'(0) = \infty$ so that investment for an employer who offers wage w, uniquely solves the first order condition

$$p'(k(w)) = \delta + \lambda(v)[1 - F(w)]. \tag{131}$$

The optimal investment policy expressed as a function of an employer's wage offer $k(w)$, that implicitly defined by the first order condition, is increasing ($k'(w) = -\lambda(v)F'(w)/p''(k) > 0$) because offering a higher wage lowers an employer's match separation rate, the effective rate of depreciation on match specific capital.

8. Summary

This chapter has a simple message. Search equilibrium approaches to modeling markets characterized by friction in the form of information gathering delay and turnover costs have matured in the past decade. They are now capable of providing a framework for understanding empirical observation on labor reallocation flows and wage dispersion and for generating important new insights into the effects of labor market policy. We look forward to future applications of the approach to many other substantive questions of interest.

References

Acemoglu, D. (1996), "A microfoundation for increasing returns in human capital formation", Quarterly Journal of Economics 111: 779–804.

Acemoglu, D. and R. Shimer (1997), "Efficient wage dispersion", Working paper (Department of Economics, MIT).

Andolfatto, D. (1996), "Business cycles and labor market search", American Economic Review 86: 112–132.

Albrecht, J.W. and B. Axell (1984), "An equilibrium model of search unemployment", Journal of Political Economy 92: 824–840.

Binmore, K.G., A. Rubinstein and A. Wolinsky (1986), "The Nash bargaining solution in economic modelling", RAND Journal of Economics 17: 176–188.

Blanchard, O.J. and P.A. Diamond (1989), "The Beveridge curve", Brookings Papers on Economic Activity 1: 1–60.

Blanchard, O.J. and P.A. Diamond (1990), "The cyclical behavior of the gross flows of U.S. workers", Papers on Economic Activity 2: 85–143.

Blanchard, O.J. and P.A. Diamond (1992), "The flows approach to labor markets", American Economic Review 82: 354–359.

Bontemps, C., J.-M. Robin and G. van den Berg (1997), "Equilibrium Search with Productivity Dispersion: Theory and Estimation", Presented at the 1997 meeting of the Society for Economic Dynamic, Oxford.

Bowden, R.J. (1980), "On the existence and secular stability of the u-v loci", Economica 47: 35–50.

Bowlus, A.J., N.M. Kiefer and G.R. Neumann (1995), "Estimation of equilibrium wage distributions with heterogeneity", Journal of Applied Econometrics 10: S119–S131.

Bowlus, A.J., N.M. Kiefer and G.R. Neumann (1997), "Equilibrium search models and the transition from school to work", Working paper (Department of Economics, University of Iowa).

Burda, M.C. (1992), "A note on firing costs and severance benefits in equilibrium unemployment", Scandinavian Journal of Economics 39, 479–489.

Burdett, K. (1990), "A New Framework for Labor Market Policy", in: J. Hartog, G. Ridder and J. Theeuwes, eds., Panel data and labor market studies (North-Holland, Amsterdam) pp. 297–312.

Burdett, K. and K. Judd (1983), "Equilibrium price distributions", Econometrica 51: 955–970.

Burdett, K. and D.T. Mortensen (1989), "Equilibrium wage differentials and employer size", Discussion paper no. 860 (Northwestern University).

Burdett, K. and D.T. Mortensen (1998), "Wage differentials, employer size and unemployment", International Economic Review 39: 257–273.

Burdett, K. and R. Wright (1998), "Two-sided search with non-transferable utility", Review of Economic Dynamics 1: 220–245.

Butters, G.R. (1977), "Equilibrium distributions of sales and advertising prices", Review of Economic Studies 44: 465–491.

Caballero, R.J. and M.L. Hammour (1994), "The cleansing effect of recession", American Economic Review 84: 1350–1368.

Caballero, R.J. and M.L. Hammour (1999), "On the timing and efficiency of creative destruction", Quarterly Journal of Economics, in press.

Coe, D.T. and D.J. Snower (1996), "Policy complementarities: the case for fundamental labor market reform", Working paper (IMF).

Cole, H. and R. Rogerson (1996), "Can the Mortensen-Pissarides matching model match the business cycle facts?" Working paper (University of Minnesota).

Coles, M.G. and K. Burdett (1997), "Marriage and class", Quarterly Journal of Economics 1: 141–168.

Coles, M.G. and E. Smith (1994), "Market places and matching", CEPR Discussion Paper No. 1048 and International Economic Review, in press.

Costain, J.S. (1995), "Unemployment insurance in a general equilibrium model of job search and precautionary savings", Working paper (University of Chicago).

Davis, S.J., J. Haltiwanger and S. Schuh (1996), Job creation and destruction (MIT Press, Cambridge, MA).

Devine, T.J. and N.M. Kiefer (1991), Empirical labor economics: a search approach (Oxford University Press, Oxford, UK).

Diamond, P. (1971), "A model of price adjustment", Journal of Economic Theory 3: 156–168.

Diamond, P.A. (1981), "Mobility costs, frictional unemployment and efficiency", Journal of Political Economy 89: 798–812.

Diamond, P.A. (1982a), "Aggregate demand management in search equilibrium", Jounrla of Political Economy 90: 881–894.

Diamond, P.A. (1982b), "Wage determination and efficiency in search equilibrium", Review of Economic Studies 49: 217–227.

Diamond, P. and E. Maskin (1979), "An equilibrium analysis of search and breach of contract. I: steady states", Bell Journal of Economics 10: 82–105.

Eckstein, Z. and K.I. Wolpin (1990), "Estimating a market equilibrium search model from panel data on individuals", Econometrica 58: 783–808.

Greenwald, B. and J.E. Stiglitz (1988), "Pareto efficiency of market economies: search and efficiency wage models", American Economic Review 78: 351–356.

Hamermesh, D.S. (1993), Labor demand (Princeton University Press, Princeton, NJ).

Hosios, A. J. (1990), "On the efficiency of matching and related models of search and unemployment", Review of Economic Studies 57: 279–298.

Jackman, R., R. Layard and C. Pissarides (1989), "On vacancies", Oxford Bulletin of Economics and Statistics 51: 377–394.

Kiefer, N.M. and G.R. Neumann (1993), "Wage dispersion with homogeneity: the empirical equilibrium search model", in: H. Bunzel et al., eds., Panel data and labor market analysis (North-Holland, Amsterdam) pp. 57–74.

Koning, P., G. Ridder and G.J. van den Berg (1995), "Structural and frictional unemployment in an equilibrium search model with heterogeneous agents", Journal of Applied Econometrics 10: S133–S151.

Lazear, E. (1990), "Job security provisions and employment", Quarterly Journal of Economics 105: 699–726.

Linbeck, A. and D.J. Snower (1988), The insider-outsider theory of employment and unemployment (MIT Press, Cambridge, MA.

Ljungqvist, L. and T.J. Sargent (1996), "The European unemployment dilemma", Working paper (Federal Research Bank of Chicago).

Lucas Jr., R.E. and N.L. Stokey (1989), Recursive methods in economic dynamics (Harvard University Press, Cambridge, MA).

MacLeod, W.B. and J. Malcomson (1993), "Investments, holdup and the form of market contracts", American Economic Review 83: 811–837.

Merz, M. (1995), "Search in the labor market and the real business cycle", Journal of Monetary Economics 36: 269–300.

Merz, M. (1996), "Search theory rediscovered: recent develpments in the macroeconomics of the labor market", Working paper (Department of Economics, Rice University).

Millard, S.P. (1995), "The effect of employment protection legislation on labour market activity: a search approach", Working paper (Bank of England).

Millard, S.P. and D.T. Mortensen (1996), "The unemployment and welfare effects of labour market policy: a comparison of the U.S. and U.K", in: D. Snower and G. de la Dehesa, eds., Unemployment policy: how should governments respond to unemployment? (Oxford University Press, Oxford, UK).

Moen, E.R. (1997), "Competitive search equilibrium", Journal of Political Economy 105: 385–411.

Mortensen, D.T. (1978), "Specific capital and labor turnover", The Bell Journal of Economics 9 (2): 572–586.

Mortensen, D.T. (1982a), "The matching process as a noncooperative/bargaining game", in: J.J. McCall, ed., The economics of information and uncertainty (University of Chicago Press, Chicago, IL) pp. 233–254.

Mortensen, D.T. (1982b), "Property rights and efficiency in mating, racing and related games", American Economic Review 72: 968–979.

Mortensen, D.T. (1986), "Job search and labor market analysis", in: O. Ashenfelter and R. Layard, eds., Handbook in labor economics (North-Holland, Amsterdam) pp. 849–919.

Mortensen, D.T. (1989), "The persistence and indeterminacy of unemployment in search equilibrium", Scandinavian Journal of Economics 91: 347–370.

Mortensen, D.T. (1990), "Equilibrium wage distributions: a synthesis", in: J. Hartog, G. Ridder and J. Theeuwes, eds., Panel data and labor market studies (North-Holland, Amsterdam).

Mortensen, D.T. (1994b), "The cyclical behavior of job and worker flows", journal of economic dynamics and control 18: 1121–1142.

Mortensen, D.T. (1994a), "Reducing supply side disincentives to job creation", in: Reducing unemployment: current issues and policy options (Federal Research Bank of Kansas City Kansas City) pp. 189–220.

Mortensen, D.T. (1996), "The unemployment and income effects of active labor market policy: the case of the U.K", in: H. von Christian Drager, P. Pissulla and A. W. von Czege, eds., More competition, more jobs - is full employment an illusion? (Nomos Verlagsgesellschaft, Baden-Baden) pp. 157–180.

Mortensen, D.T. (1998), "Equilibrium unemployment with wage posting", Working paper (Northwestern University).

Mortensen, D.T. and C.A. Pissarides (1994), "Job creation and job destruction in the theory of unemployment", Review of Economic Studies 61: 397–415.

Mortensen, D.T. and C.A. Pissarides (1997), "Unemployment responses to 'skill-biased' technology shocks: the role of labor market policy", Working paper (Northwestern University).

Mortensen, D.T. and C.A. Pissarides (1998), "Job reallocation, employment fluctuations and unemployment differences", in: M. Woodford and J. Taylor, eds., Handbook of macroeconomics (North-Holland, Amsterdam) in press.

Mortensen, D.T. and G.R. Neumann (1988), "Estimating structural models of unemployment and job duration", in: W.A. Barnett, E.R. Bernt and H. White, eds., Dynamic econometric modelling, Proceedings of the Third International Symposium in Economic Theory and Econometrica (Cambridge University Press, Cambridge, UK).

Mortensen, D.T. and R. Wright (1997), "Competitive pricing and efficiency in search equilibrium", Working paper (Northwestern University).

Munich, D., J. Svenjar and K. Terrell (1997), "The worker-firm matching in transition economies: (why) are Czechs more successful than others?" Working paper (William Davidson Institute, University of Michigan).

Neumann, G.R. (1997), "Search models and duration data", in: M.H. Pesaran and P. Schmidt, eds., Handbook of applied econometrics, Vol. II - Microeconometrics (Basil Blackwell, Oxford, UK) pp. 300–351.

Phelps, E.S. (1968), "Money-wage dynamics and labor market equilibrium", Journal of Political Economy 76: 254–281.

Pissarides, C.A. (1979), "Job matching with state employment agencies and random search", Economic Journal 89: 818–833.

Pissarides, C.A. (1984a), "Short-run equilibrium dynamics of unemployment, vacancies and real wages", American Economic Review 75: 676–690.

Pissarides, C.A. (1984b), "Efficient job rejection", Economic Journal Conference Papers 94: 97–108.

Pissarides, C.A. (1990), Equilibrium unemployment theory (Basil Blackwell, Oxford, UK).

Pissarides, C.A. (1996), "Are employment tax cuts the answer to Europe's unemployment problem", Working paper (London School of Economics).

Ramey, G. and J. Watson (1997), "Contractual fragility, job destruction and business cycles", Quarterly Journal of Economics CXII: 873–912.

Rothschild, M. (1973), "Models of market organization with imperfect information: a survey", Journal of Political Economy 81: 1283–1308.

Rubinstein, A. and A. Wolinsky (1985), "Equilibrium in a market with sequential bargaining", Econometrica 53: 1133–1150.

Shimer, Robert (1995), "Contracts in a frictional labor market", Working paper (MIT).

Shapiro, C. and J.E. Stiglitz (1984), "Equilibrium unemployment as a worker discipline device", American Economic Review 74: 433–444.

Smith, L. (1997), "The marriage model with search frictions", Working paper (MIT).

Valdivia, V. (1995), "Evaluating the welfare benefits of unemployment insurance", Working paper (Northwestern University).

van den Berg, G.J. and G. Ridder (1993), "On the estimation of equilibrium search models with panel data", in: J.C. van Ours et al., eds., Labor market demand and equilibrium wage formation (North-Holland, Amsterdam).

van den Berg, G.J. and G. Ridder (1995), "Empirical equilibrium search models", Working paper (Department of Econometrics, Free University, Amsterdam) and Econometrica, in press.

Warren, R.S. (1996), "Returns to scale in a matching model of the labor market", Economic Letters, 50: 135–142.

Wolpin, K.I. (1987), "Estimating a structural search model: the transition from school to work", Journal of Political Economy 55: 801–817.

Wolpin, K.I. (1995), Empirical methods for the study of labor force dynamics (Harwood Academic Publishers, Luxembourg).

Wolinsky, A. (1987), "Matching, search and bargaining", Journal of Economic Theory 42: 311–333.

Chapter 40

THE ANALYSIS OF LABOR MARKETS USING MATCHED EMPLOYER–EMPLOYEE DATA

JOHN M. ABOWD*

Cornell University, NBER and CREST

FRANCIS KRAMARZ

CREST-INSEE and CEPR

Contents

* Abowd acknowledges support from the National Science Foundation (SBER-9618111 to the NBER).

Handbook of Labor Economics, Volume 3, Edited by O. Ashenfelter and D. Card

Abstract

Matched employer–employee data contain information collected from households and individuals as well as information collected from businesses or establishments. Both administrative and sample survey sources are considered. Both longitudinal and cross-sectional applications are discussed. We review studies from 17 different countries using 38 different systems for creating the linked data. We provide a detailed discussion of the methods used to create the linked datasets, the statistical and economic models used to analyze these data, and a comprehensive set of results from the different countries. We consider compensation structure, wage and employment mobility, and the relation between firm outcomes and worker characteristics in detail. Matched employer–employee data provide the empirical basis for further refinements of the theory of workplace organization, compensation design, mobility and production; however, the arrival of these data has been relatively recent. © 1999 Elsevier Science B.V. All rights reserved.

JEL codes: J3; J6; C1; C8

1. Introduction

On the empirical side of these questions, the greatest potential for further progress rests in developing more suitable sources of data on the nature of selection and matching between workers and firms. Virtually no matched worker-firm records are available for empirical research, but obviously are crucial for the precise measurement of job and personal attributes required for empirical calculations. Not only will the availability of such data produce sharper estimates of the wage-job attributes equalizing differences function but also will allow more detailed investigations of the sorting and assignment aspects of the theory, which have not received sufficient attention in past work. (Rosen, 1986, p. 688).

The recent stress on the role of specific as opposed to general human capital and the development of agency theories of the employee–employer relationship may result in the modification of some of the received doctrines but these theories also serve to enrich the scope of the theory by pointing towards interesting and potentially important connections between wages, job mobility and institutional practices. Future progress in this area will hinge crucially on the development of data which links information on the individual characteristics of workers and their households with data on the firms who employ them (Willis, 1986, p. 598).

In the decade since Sherwin Rosen and Robert Willis wrote these words, economists have made enormous strides in finding and using matched employer–employee data. This chapter reviews about 100 studies from more than 15 different countries. Virtually all of these papers have been written in the last 5 years and many are still only available in working paper form. As this chapter was being prepared more than 40 new papers using matched employer–employee data appeared as a part of a conference organized specifically to investigate this issue.[1]

From the many papers that we discuss below, two broad themes emerge. The first is the relative importance of person and firm variables in the determination of compensation. The second is the relative importance of individual mobility in relation to firm-specific employment adjustments. These questions have now been addressed by dozens of researchers. In contrast to many other areas of empirical labor economics, the results we discuss on these questions have largely been estimated from European, and not American, matched employer–employee data, a situation that was foreshadowed by evident advance of the European statistical systems in providing support for the microeconometric analysis of human resource decision making.[2] It is clear from the degree of professional interest in these research efforts that the availability of the type of data Rosen and Willis called for in the original handbook has already produced many important new results.

2. The different types of matched employer–employee datasets

In order to describe the potential that matched employer–employee datasets offer for labor economists, we begin by describing the datasets that exist and some of the basic applications analyzing compensation, mobility, unemployment insurance and other aspects of the labor market. Table 1 presents a complete summary of each of the datasets we describe as well as basic references for further information and applications.

---

[1] The International Symposium on Linked Employer–Employee Data was held on May 21–22, 1998 in Washington, DC. The preliminary versions of papers from this conference are discussed in this chapter. See Lane et al. (1997a) for an earlier review.

[2] See Abowd and Kramarz (1996b).

Two important dimensions distinguish the matched employer–employee data that we present. First, some are cross-sectional datasets while others are longitudinal. Second, some sampling designs focus on the employee while others use the firm as the primary unit of analysis.[3] When considering issues of representativeness, we show that certain samples, with a longitudinal component, are representative of the target population in the cross-section without being dynamically representative. In particular, certain sampling techniques do not permit entry and exit of individuals from the labor market and/or entry and exit of firms, phenomena which cannot be ignored with matched employer–employee.

Most labor economists are not familiar with the methods used to construct matched employer–employee data. We have, therefore, taken some care to describe the technical details so that potential users of these data can use this chapter to select data sources that are appropriate for the questions they wish to investigate.

2.1. Representative cross-sections of firms with representative data on workers

We begin with the basic design of datasets in which both the sample of firms and the sample of individuals are cross-sectionally representative of the population under study. We start by describing the French program since it follows closely a structure that has been widely adopted across Europe. The Wage Structure Surveys (Enquête sur la Structure des Salaires, ESS), performed by the French National Statistical Institute (INSEE) in 1986 and 1992, were initiated in 1966 by the European Statistical Office (ESO). However, after the 1966, 1972 and 1978 surveys, the ESS was abandoned by the ESO. INSEE decided to resume this survey because of the importance of the information collected at each round and the uniqueness of the statistical design. The ESS collects data on the structure and amount of individual compensation within a sample of establishments from the manufacturing, construction and service industries.

The sampling frame has two stages: at the first stage, production units are sampled; at the second stage, individuals employed at these sampled units are sampled. The target population is all establishments with at least ten employees in general industry. In the construction and in the service industries, the first stage sampling unit is the firm. Furthermore, agriculture, transportation, telecommunication and services supplied directly to individuals are excluded from the scope of the ESS except for insurance, banks and all industries where services are also supplied directly to firms. The universe is constructed from the SIRENE system, a unified database recording all existing establishments and firms in France. The sampling rates are stratified according to the industry, the region, and the size of the unit – from unity for the establishments above 500 employees to 1/48 for establishments between 10 and 20 employees. The sampling frame for the employees at sampled units is based on the employee's year and month of birth. The sample is exhaus-

---

[3] Hildreth and Pudney (1999) provide an interesting methodological discussion of the statistical properties of many of these methods of creating matched datasets.

Table 1
Comparison of matched employer–employee data sources from different countries

Country	Name	Sampling plan	Dates	Main variables	Unique features	References
Algeria	Algiers Regional Manufacturing Establishments	42 manufacturing enterprises in the Algiers area, 1,000 employees of these firms	1992	Daily wage, employee demographics, education, seniority, other work experience; employer information is limited to detailed industry and employer ID	Data for a developing country	Chennouf et al. (1997)
Australia	Australian Workplace Industrial Relations Survey	Probability sample of workplaces with 20 + employees. Probability sample of employees at that workplace	1995, (earlier survey without the employee questionnaire: 1990)	Workplace qualitative and interval information on wages, profits, productivity, competition. Detailed employment and industrial relations data. Individual data on wages, hours, demographics and unions	Focused on industrial relations issues. Close collaboration with the British Workplace Industrial Relations Survey permits comparative analyses	Callus et al. (1991), Morehead et al. (1997), Alexander and Morehead (1999), Blanchflower and Machin (1996)
Austria	Social Security Files Sample (SSFS, Austria)	Probability sample of firms (1/50)	1975–1991	Simple individual demographic variables, detailed earnings and labor force variables; establishment and firm IDs from the SSFS	Exhaustive within establishments; no longitudinal information on individuals in the sample	Winter-Ebmer and Zweimüller (1997)

Table 1 (continued)

Country	Name	Sampling plan	Dates	Main variables	Unique features	References
Belgium	Social Security Administrative Records	Universe of private firms	1978–1985	Individual earnings histories, demographic variables, and broad occupation, firm-level accounting data for larger firms	Universe of private employees permits detailed mobility analyses	Leonard and Van Audenrode (1996, 1997), Leonard et al. (1999)
Canada	Workplace and Employee Survey (WES)	Clustered probability sample of establishments	1996 (pilot), 1997	Detailed establishment information from the human resource manager; detailed demographic, labor force, and earnings variables; establishment IDs from Statistics Canada	Designed to collect longitudinal information on establishments (including birth, death, and mergers); no longitudinal information on workers	Picot and Wannell (1996)
Canada	T-4 Supplementary Tax File	1% simple random sample of individuals ever filing a tax return	1975–1993, ongoing	Individual age, sex, taxable earnings, taxpayer ID and employer ID	Very long employment histories	Morissette and Berube (1996), Baker and Solon (1997)
Denmark	Integrated Database for Labor Market Research (IDA)	Universe of the Danish population based on the person ID used in Danish government registers	1970, 1980–1994, ongoing	Detailed demographic and labor force variables; employer reported earnings; employer IDs from the Danish establishment register	Complete census; individuals who are unemployed or not in the labor force are included	Albaek-Sorensen (1999)

Finland	Employment Register matched with manufacturing establishments in Register of Establishments	Census of employed persons and census of manufacturing establishments and plants with 5 + employees	1988–1994, ongoing but 1995 changes in industrial register present comparability problems	Earnings, other income, education, demographics, employment history for workers; Output, value added, inputs, price indices, some capital measures	Because both sides of the match are based on registers, the coverage is very good when supplemental data from other sources are added	Laaksonen et al. (1998)
France	Déclaration Annuelle de Données Sociales (DADS), formerly DAS; Bénéfices Industriels et Commerciaux (BIC); Bénéfices Réels (BRN), Echantillon Démographique Permanent (EDP); Enquête Structure des Emplois (ESE)	1/25th of private and semi-public workforce (born October, even years); supplemental individual data for 1/10th from the EDP; employer information from BIC (larger enterprises), BRN (smaller enterprises) and ESE (establishments)	1976–1995, ongoing	Individual data: earnings, days worked, payroll taxes, occupation, industry, demographic data, education, detailed individual data from EDP; longitudinal firm data from sources keyed to Siren/Siret: production, value added, operating income, assets, employment, imports, exports, prices	Based on a set of databases that permits any data coded by firm or person identifier to be added. Longitudinal for firms and individuals	Abowd et al. (1999a), Kramarz and Roux (1998), Margolis (1999)
France	Déclaration Mensuelle de Mouvements de Main d'Oeuvre (DMMO), matched to the sources cited above	All establishments with 50 + employees complete the monthly questionnaire,	1987–1990, ongoing	Individual data: demographics, type of contract, type of entry, skill-level for all entries, seniority at exit, type of exit,	Permits monthly analysis of employment flows as well as job creation and destruction	Abowd et al. (1999b)

Table 1 (continued)

Country	Name	Sampling plan	Dates	Main variables	Unique features	References
		which includes the reports on each movement for the individual employees		and skill-level for all exits; establishment data: employment, skill distribution, profit/loss		
France	Enquête Emploi (EE) and Enquête sur la Technique et l'Organisation du Travail auprès des Travailleurs Occupés (TOTTO)	Clustered probability sample of domiciles 1/300, longitudinal with 3 years in sample. Employer identifiers since 1990	1990–1996, ongoing1987 and 1993 new technologies supplement	Full complement of household-based labor force variables; periodic topical supplements; longitudinal firm data from sources keyed to Siren/Siret; new technologies supplements have a full complement of computer and computer-assisted production questions	Overlapping samples with 3-year rotation groups permit dynamic analyses; employer IDs for establishments (Siret) permit linking to establishment or firm data	Entorf and Kramarz (1997, 1999), Entorf et al. (1999), Kramarz (1997)
France	Enquête Structure des Salaires (ESS)	Probability sample of establishments with 20 or more employees; Probability sample of employees at the establishment	1967, 1978, 1986, 1992	Very detailed job and compensation descriptions, earnings; establishment level work place organization; longitudinal firm data from sources keyed to Siren/Siret	Large representative samples of employees within establishment; employer IDs for establishments (Siret)	Rotbart (1991), Kramarz et al. (1996)

Country	Name	Sample	Year	Variables	Notes	Reference
France	Enquête Formation Qualification Profession (FQP)	Clustered probability sample of domiciles 1/1,000	1993	Full complement of labor force variables; detailed education and training, apprenticeships; retrospective from 1988; longitudinal firm data from sources keyed to Siren/Siret	Employer IDs for establishments (Siret) permits addition of other information	Goux and Maurin (1997)
Germany	Beschäftigungs-stichprobe (BS) matched with the Leistungsempfänger-datei (LD)	Probability sample of the Historikdatei (HD), 1/100th sample, of the Bundesanstalt für Arbeit (BfA)	1975–1990	Simple individual demographic variables (sex, education, nationality), gross earnings; benefits for the unemployed; employer IDs from the HD	Longitudinal information on individuals even when unemployed or on training programs; plant-level statistics from the HD	Bender et al. (1996), Dustmann and Meghir (1997)
Germany	Gehalts- und Lohnstruktur-erhebung (GLS) matched to social insurance registry	Multistage probability sample of establishments, probability sample of employees. Lower Saxony.	1990, 1995	Employer supplied detailed data on the structure of compensation and conditions of employment in October. Demographic, education, occupation for employee	Two representative cross-sections, 5 years apart with very similar structure to ESS in France	Stephan (1998)

Table 1 (continued)

Country	Name	Sampling plan	Dates	Main variables	Unique features	References
Italy	Ricerche e Progetti (R&P)	Universe of private firms (industrial and service) and records of self-employed	1985–1991, ongoing	Social security earnings, wage supplements, months, weeks or days paid, occupation, employment contract type	Longitudinal information on workers and firms, transitions to self-employment can be included. Availability of universe permits different sampling schemes	Contini et al. (undated)
Japan	Establishment Census (EC) matched with Basic Survey on Wage Structure (BSWS), Census of Manufactures (CM) and Census of Commerce (CC)	EC is a census of establishments with 5 employees or more (10 + in public establishments). BSWS, see below, CC every 3 years and CM annual	1991–1994, ongoing, not all years for all sources	Wages, bonuses, seniority, occupation, employee demographics and education from BSWS, detailed business data from CM and parts of CC, varies by industry	Some longitudinal information on both workers and firms	Hayami and Abe (1998)
Japan	Basic Survey on Wage Structure (BSWS)	Probability sample of all establishments with at least 5 employees or government sector if covered by the National Enterprise Labor Relations Law or by the Local Public Labor Relations Law and at least 10 employees	1982–1994, ongoing	Simple information on the establishment; simple individual demographic and labor force variables, detailed earnings	Large sample within establishments	Abe and Sofer (1996)

Country	Source	Sampling	Years	Variables	Comments	Reference
Netherlands	Wage Survey, Production Survey, RD Survey and Survey of Manufacturing Technology	Probability sample of firms, simple random sample of employees at each firm	1979, 1985, 1989, ongoing	Detailed individual and job characteristics, gross weekly earnings, hours worked per week, firm data on inputs, outputs, value added, profits, R&D activities (larger firms), computer technologies used	Very comprehensive set of repeated cross-sections with detail on both the individual and the firm	Boon (1996)
Netherlands	Ministry of Social Affairs and Employment (AVO)	Probability sample of firms, probability sample of employees of those firms	1993, 1994	Detailed salary information, separation reasons, demographic data, seniority; firm level aggregates of these variables and employment	Two observations (successive Octobers) for each employee	Hassink (1999)
Norway	Employer–employee Register and Education Register	Universe of the Norwegian population based on the person ID used in Norwegian government registers	1986–1994, ongoing	Detailed demographic and labor force variables; employer reported earnings; employer IDs from the Norwegian Employer–employee establishment register	Not a sample; individuals who are unemployed or not in the labor force are included	Salvanes and Forre (1997)

Table 1 (*continued*)

Country	Name	Sampling plan	Dates	Main variables	Unique features	References
Portugal	Social Security Files Sample (SSFS, Portugal)	Clustered probability sample, 1/5 of all firms	1983–1992, ongoing	Simple individual demographic variables, detailed earnings and labor force variables; establishment and firm IDs from the SSFS	Exhaustive within establishments; no longitudinal information on individuals in the sample	Ministério do Emprego e da Segurança Social (1993), Cardoso (1997)
Sweden	Register of Income Verifications, Register of Jobs and Other Activities, Register of Employment, Register of Enterprises and Register of Establishments	All registers are censuses of the relevant population.	ongoing, dates depend upon specific application	Earnings and income, job characteristics, demographics, enterprise and establishment characteristics	Surveys with more detailed information can be linked to any of the component registers	Tegsjö and Andersson (1998)
Sweden	Labor Force Survey (Arbetskraft-sundersök-ningarna, AKU) matched with the Registers of Employment, Enterprises and Establishments	Probability sample of households, census of business establishments with at least one employee	1987–1993, ongoing	Detailed employment data from the AKU, other data as described above	Makes use of the register system described above	DiPrete et al. (1998)

UK	Panel Study of Manufacturing Establishments (PSME)	Probability sample of establishments, most recently hired employee and one randomly sampled production employee	1994, 1995	Detailed employer information on the personnel, financial, investment policy; detailed demographic and earnings variables on individual	Longitudinal in the establishment, employees are not followed due to legal restrictions in the UK	Hildreth and Tremlett (1994, 1995)
UK	New Earnings Survey (NES), Joint Unemployment and Vacancies Operating System (JUVOS), Annual Census of Production (ACOP)	1/100 sample of employees enrolled in the Pay As You Earn (PAYE) tax system linked to administrative universe of unemployment system and universe of firms with 100 or more employees. Probability sample of smaller firms	1994, 1995	Employee information on weekly earnings, demographic data, unemployment spells. Firm information on inputs, production, profitability	The links can be used along several dimensions to follow individuals in and out of employment and/or to follow individuals from firm to firm	Hildreth and Pudney (1999)
UK	Workplace Employee Relations Survey	Probability sample of workplaces, 25 employees per workplace	1997, earlier surveys without the employee segment: 1980, 1984, 1990, called Workplace Industrial Relations Survey	Workplace qualitative and interval information on wages, profits, productivity, competition. Detailed employment and industrial relations data	Focused on industrial relations issues. Close collaboration with the Australian Workplace Industrial Relations Survey permits comparative analyses	Cully (1998), Blanchflower and Machin (1996)
UK	British Household Panel Study	Probability sample of households, details of employer data not available	in progress	Detailed data on individuals in the household, including labor market earnings, education and demographics.	Design permits analysis of the effects of employer variables on household outcomes	Hildreth, private communication

Table 1 (*continued*)

Country	Name	Sampling plan	Dates	Main variables	Unique features	References
United States	Worker-Employer Characteristics Database (WECD) and New Worker-Employer Characteristics Database' (NWECD)	Manufacturing establishments from the Longitudinal Research Database (LRD), a probability sample; matched to 1990 Census of Population long form responses; NWECD establishments from the Standard Statistical Establishment List (manufacturing and non-manufacturing)	1990 match	WECD: longitudinal data on establishments income, balance sheet, investments; NWECD: employment and sales; Both datasets: full complement of labor force variables and household variables from the Census of Population	Very large samples within establishments	WECD, Troske (1998); NWECD, Bayard et al. (1998)
United States	State Unemployment Insurance Systems	Simple random samples from state unemployment insurance records Mexico, Pennsylvania, South Carolina, and Washington	various years, matched on the individual ID from Georgia, Idaho, Louisiana, Maryland, Missouri, New	Earnings and employment data required to calculate UI benefits; employer UI-related data (tax rates, taxable compensation); employer IDs from the federal employer ID system	Some states have labor force variables (sex, education, etc.) for a subsample who received UI benefits, other states have demographic data for representative samples, others have no demographic data	Jacobson et al. (1993), Anderson and Meyer (1994)

Country	Dataset	Sample/design	Time period	Variables	Notes	Reference
United States	Maryland Unemployment Wage Records, Current Population Survey, Standard Statistical Establishment List (SSEL)	Universe of Maryland UI records matched to CPS (probability sample); Employers matched using the SSEL	1985–1997	Individual and household data from the Current Population Survey including demographic, earnings, education; establishment data from the SSEL (employment, payroll, sales, industry)	Limited to the State of Maryland. Longitudinal information on UI earnings matched to longitudinal information on the SSEL	Lane et al. (1999)
United States	National Longitudinal Survey of Youth '79 (NLSY-79)	Clustered probability sample of individuals aged 14–21 on January 1, 1979	1986–1994	All variables from the public-use NLSY files; employer IDs from private lists, Compustat and CRSP	Unique IDs for all available employers on the NLS; employer data for publicly-held firms, some data for governments	Abowd and Finer (1998)
United States	Survey of Consumers (University of Michigan Survey Center)	Clustered probability sample	September 1991-March 1992	All variables in the Survey of Consumers; employer IDs from Dun and Bradstreet	Some employer data for 700 matches	Brown and Medoff (1996)
United States	Employment Opportunity Pilot Project (EOPP) and Multi-City Study of Urban Inequality (MCSUI)	Probability sample in metropolitan areas, data on a representative employee and the most recently hired employee	1982, 1993 (repeated the design of 1982 survey)	Detailed employer information from the human resource manager; labor force variables on individual	Heavy focus on training and training related variable	Bishop et al. (1983), Holzer and Reaser (1996).

Table 1 (*continued*)

Country	Name	Sampling plan	Dates	Main variables	Unique features	References
United States	Continuous Work History Sample (CWHS) and Longitudinal Employer–employee Database (LEED)	1/100 sample of Social Security earnings reports	1957–1972, other files continue	Social Security earnings, total employment in the firm, basic demographic variables, some schooling, hours and weeks worked information. Employer and employee identifiers	Most extensive US sample. Internal Social Security files are produced on an ongoing basis	Smith (1989), Topel and Ward (1992)
United States	Survey of Employer-Provided Training (SEPT95)	Probability sample of private establishments with 50 + employees, two employees per establishment	1995	Detailed training information at the establishment level, earnings, seniority, training and demographics for employees	Design permits analysis of both establishments and individuals for population training models	Bureau of Labor Statistics (1996)
United States	Longitudinal Research Database (LRD) and the National Labor Relations Board (NLRB) files	Probability sample of manufacturing establishments (LRD) matched with the annual NLRB election data	1977–1989	Detailed establishment data on inputs, production, costs, production and non-production employment. NLRB election data describe the proposed bargaining unit and election results	Match of union representation vote data to detailed history of the establishment permits studies of effects of new unionization on factor use and production. Establishment data available from 1963	LRD, McGuckin and Pascoe (1988); match to NLRB, Lalonde et al. (1996)

| United States | White Collar Pay Survey (WCP) supplement | Probability sample of establishments, simple random sample of employees in certain white collar occupations | 1989 (service), 1990 (goods) | Detailed earnings and components of compensation from employer survey, starting pay, demographics, education, seniority | Sample focuses exclusively on white collar occupations | Bronars and Famulari (1997) |

tive in small units and the sampling rate is 1/24 in the largest establishments (above 5000 employees).

In the 1986 version of the survey, annual and October compensation are available for each sampled employee. The October compensation for each employee includes all employee and employer-paid benefits but excludes non-wage benefits. It can be decomposed into total wage, overtime compensation and October-specific bonuses. The total annual compensation includes all benefits and bonuses, even those not paid on a monthly basis. Finally, information on the method of pay is given (time versus piece rates, for instance). In 1992, total annual compensation, decomposed as described above, is available but the October compensation is not decomposed.

In both versions of the ESS, occupation, firm-specific seniority, age, country of origin, hour schedule (number of hours and shifts), days of absence are measured for the employee. In addition to this individual-level information, the surveyed unit gives the following information: total employment, existence of shifts and night work, existence of a firm-level agreement, of a branch-level agreement. Since some questions in the 1986 and 1992 versions of the ESS were not formulated identically, the two surveys are not always comparable.

The basic research data files for the ESS contain 16,239 establishments with 678,798 interviewed employees in 1986 and 15,858 establishments with 148,976 interviewed employees in 1992. More detailed technical information on the 1986 version of the ESS is available in Rotbart (1991). The technical report on the 1992 version of the ESS is not yet available.

Salary structure surveys with the same structure as the ESS exists in most EC countries, for instance in Germany (see Stephan, 1998) and the United Kingdom. Unfortunately, the statistical offices in charge of collecting and storing these data have been generally reluctant to let researchers access them. In France, however, the policy for non-INSEE researchers has been more generous (see Arai et al., 1997, among others). Statistics Canada is now in the process of building such a dataset called the Workplace and Employee Survey. Data collection should be completed by the end of 1997. A pilot, designed to be one-fifth of the production version, was conducted in 1996 with approximately 1000 establishments and 6000 workers (see Picot and Wannell, 1996). In the United Kingdom, the Office for National Statistics now allows contracted researchers access to these confidential data.

Salary structure data also exist in Japan, based on a annual survey called the Basic Survey on Wage Structure (see Abe and Sofer, 1996). The universe of establishments sampled every year includes all establishments of the private sector with at least 5 employees and the public sector establishments if covered by the National Enterprise Labor Relations Law or by the Local Public Labor Relations Law and at least 10 employees. Each year, approximately 70,000 establishments with 1.4 million workers are sampled. The survey is conducted during the month of July, with information recorded about the month of June (apart from annual bonuses, which come from the previous fiscal year). General information about the establishment is collected: industry, size, product, enterprise to which the establishment belongs, entry wage for the youngest hires. Information on individual workers includes: sex, age, education, type of contract, number of days and hours worked, experience, job position, June earnings (before taxes), and annual bonuses.

2.2. Representative cross-sections of firms with non-representative data on workers

In this type of data, a sample is designed to be representative of the cross-section of firms (or other business units) in a given year and data on some workers are collected. Some of the surveys have longitudinal or panel components but the sampling frame was, nevertheless, constructed using a universe that was fixed at a particular date. Hence, they are not dynamically representative even though they are representative over time of the business units and employees at risk to be sampled at that date.

The best example is the European Commission-sponsored research data collected in the United Kingdom, called the Panel Study of Manufacturing Establishments (PSME). The description is based on Hildreth and Tremlett (1994, 1995). The stage of the sample is based upon an establishment universe called a business location and defined as the activities of a single employer at a single address. The sample of business locations is based on British Telecom's (BT) business line records. If an establishment has a business telephone line, it is included in the population at risk to be sampled. As seems natural given the origin of the sample, the BT sample provided a contact phone number as well as an establishment name, and address. This allowed the interview to be conducted over the telephone. BT also reported the industry classification as well as size of the establishment. The sample was restricted to manufacturing establishments only (Divisions 1–4 of the 1980 Standard Industrial Classification, SIC code). Using this information, the frame was stratified according to area, size, and industry. Details of the sampling scheme can be found in Hildreth and Tremlett (1994). The initial sample comprised 881 establishments of which nearly a quarter (23%) was found to be out-of-scope for the survey.

From the original 881 establishments, 682 were in the scope for interview. Interviews were conducted between February and April 1994 using Computer Assisted Telephone Interviewing (CATI). The average interview lasted 45 min and was conducted by interviewers at the Social and Community Planning Research (SCPR) telephone interviewing unit. The questionnaire covering a range of areas of the establishment operation: ownership and control, markets and products, innovation and investment, employment and human resources, financial performance, and, finally, detailed information on two workers – the most recent hire and a randomly selected employee. There were several respondents at each establishment – the Chief Executive or Senior Manager, the Personnel or Human Resources Manager, and the Chief Accountant or Financial Director. Of the original sample of 682 establishments within scope for the survey, 430 completed interviews, of which 398 have consistent information on the establishment. Not all establishments gave complete worker information on both of the employees. The number of observations for the worker selected at random from the list of production line employees is 339 while the number of observations for employees selected as the most recent hire is 346. Only 312 establishments have complete information for both workers.

The Employment Opportunity Pilot Projects (EOPP) employer survey for the US is based on a very similar sampling scheme as the PSME (the description is based on Bishop, 1994). The survey covers a sample of 3412 employers. It was sponsored by the National Institute on Education (NIE) and the National Center for Research in Vocational Education (NCRVE). Interviews were conducted between February and June 1982. This survey was a two-wave longitudinal survey of employers from selected geographic areas across the country. The ES-202 list of companies paying unemployment insurance taxes provided the sampling frame for the survey. Establishments in industries with a relatively high proportion of low-wage workers have been oversampled. The survey was conducted over the phone and obtained a response rate of 75%.

The second wave tried to interview all of the respondents from the first wave survey. Approximately 70% of the original respondents completed surveys for the second wave. Seventy percent of the establishments have fewer than 50 employees and 12% have more than 200 employees. In large organizations, the main respondent was most often the personnel officer in charge of hiring. Employers who received the full questionnaire were asked to select the "last new employee your company hired prior to August 1981 regardless of whether that person is still employed by your company." A total 818 employers could not provide information for a recent new hire. The employers who provided information on one new hire were also asked to provide data on a second new hire in the same job but with a different amount of vocational education. Of the 2594 employers who provided data on one new hire, 1511 had not hired anyone else in that job in the last 2 years, and 424 had not hired anyone with a different amount of vocational training for that position in the last 2 years. As a result, data are available for 659 pairs of individuals who have the same job at the same establishment. Missing data on specific questions used in the model reduce the sample to about 480. The questionnaire focused primarily on training activities on the job. See Bishop (1994) for more information on the questionnaire.

2.3. Representative cross-sections of workers matched with longitudinal data on firms

A representative cross-section of workers is often matched with longitudinal data on the employing firms. The data source for the individual workers and the source for the employing firms are not generally coordinated ex-ante, as was the case for the data described in Sections 2.1 and 2.2. In the United States, the Longitudinal Research Database (LRD) – a panel of manufacturing establishments (see McGuckin and Pascoe, 1988) – has been linked by Troske (1998) with the 1990 Decennial Census of Population. In France, the supplement to the 1987 Labor Force Survey on New Technologies contains the firm identifier and the establishment identifier number for most employed workers, which permits researchers to match with the Echantillon d'Entreprises (based on the BIC), a dynamically representative sample of French firms or the Enquête Structure des Emplois (ESE) (see Entorf and Kramarz, 1997, 1999).

We first describe the Worker-Establishment Characteristics Database (WECD) based on Troske (1998). The data for workers were extracted from the 1990 Sample Detail File (SDF), which consists of all households questionnaires from the 1990 Decennial Census of Population long form. The data for establishments come from the 1990 Standard Statistical Establishment List (SSEL), a register of all establishments active in the US in 1990. From the SSEL, a 4-digit SIC code giving the establishment primary industry and a geographic code giving location were extracted. Only manufacturing establishments were retained. Equivalent industry and location information was obtained for the individuals in the SDF through individual responses coded by the Census Bureau (using Census industry codes, however). All workers employed in manufacturing in 1990 who responded to the long form are in the sample file. The number of individual observations is 4.5 million. These individuals were at risk to be matched to an employing establishment.

The matching procedure has four steps. First, Troske standardized the geography and industry definitions across the two data sources. Second, he eliminated all establishments that are not unique in each location-industry cell. Third, he assigned a unique establishment identifier to all workers located in the same location-industry cell. Fourth, he eliminated all matches based on imputed industry or location data in the Census of Population.

To understand the first step, one must know that each Census of Population geographic code consists of a region code, a state code, and a county code. Each county code is further divided into incorporated and unincorporated areas. Each incorporated area gets a unique place code. Finally, in highly populated places, a further subdivision, blocks, is added. Since the 1990 SSEL only contains place codes, which are not the same as these Census of Population location codes, Troske used the Census Bureau's Address Reference List (ARF) to assign blocks to the 1987 SSEL which was then matched to the 1990 SSEL. In addition, the Standard Industrial Codes (4-digits) were recoded into the Census Industry Codes (3-digits).

The second step forces Troske to use only establishments that meet one of these three criteria:

- Establishments that are unique in an industry-block cell;
- Establishments in the same industry-place cell with missing block codes when all other establishments in the same industry-block cell have valid block codes;
- Establishments unique in the industry-place cell.

In the third step, Troske matched individuals using industry-block codes (first group above). Next, all remaining workers were matched to establishments with identical industry-place codes (next two groups). All matches in which the industry or the geographic code were imputed were deleted. Finally, all matches for which the total number of matched workers exceeded the establishment employment were deleted. The resulting dataset contains 200,207 workers employed in 16,197 manufacturing establishments. Troske (1998) describes various tests of the quality of the WECD. On average, 16% of an establishment's work force is included in the WECD. This match rate is correct given the sampling frame of the SDF.

Different measures of average earnings per employee result from aggregating individual data to the establishment level and calculating per employee averages directly from the LRD. These earnings measures are positively and significantly correlated. An analysis of the structure of the establishments shows that large plants and plants located in urban areas are over-represented in the WECD. This induces overrepresentation of white, male, and educated workers in comparison to the original SDF data.[4]

The techniques used to create the WECD have been extended by Bayard et al. (1999) to create a cross-sectional matched employer–employee dataset that includes both manufacturing and non-manufacturing establishments. The new dataset, which is called the New Worker-Employer Characteristic Dataset (NWECD), has not yet been as widely used in empirical analyses; however, the addition of non-manufacturing establishments greatly extends the potential of these data. The authors obtained their individual and household data from the same 1990 decennial Census of Population SDF file described above. The information on establishments was taken from the Bureau of the Census Standard Statistical Establishment List (SSEL), which provides the sampling frame for Census Bureau surveys of establishments in virtually all regions and industries. The main difference between the NWECD and the original WECD is the breadth of establishment data available. The SSEL has only limited employer information (employment, payroll, sales and industry), whereas the WECD, which permits access to all of the LRD data but for manufacturing only, contains detailed longitudinal information on establishments that appear in the LRD.

Entorf and Kramarz (1997, 1999) have constructed similar data for France by matching four different INSEE sources. The basic sources are the "Enquête Emploi," 1985–1987, a single rotation group from the French Labor Force Survey, and the"Enquête sur la Technique et l'Organisation du Travail auprès des Travailleurs Occupés" (TOTTO) from 1987, a supplement to the labor force survey, which asked questions about the diffusion of new technologies and the organization of the work place. In addition to the usual questions on labor force surveys (earnings, wage rates, tenure, age, education, etc.) the supplement contains a rich source of information on the use (e.g., intensity and experience) of microcomputers, terminals, text processing, robots and other well specified groups of "New Technologies." Likewise, questions concerning the hierarchy of labor and working-time schedules help in drawing more detailed conclusions concerning the impact of new technologies than would be possible by the analysis of usual labor force surveys.

Additional information on employing enterprises (a business unit in American terminology, not an establishment) for individuals in the EE and TOTTO was added using the standardized Siren enterprise identification number, which was coded for the first time in an INSEE survey for this particular year (1987) and survey (TOTTO). This feature of the French INSEE classification system enables the researcher to employ information from corresponding firm-level surveys (such as profits and share of sales going to exports, for instance). Entorf and Kramarz used information from the 1985–1987 period. No informa-

---

[4] Hildreth and Pudney (1998) consider likelihood corrections for these kinds of sampling problems.

tion on the employing firm in years 1985 and 1986 is available for workers who changed firms between these dates and 1987. Entorf and Kramarz use two additional sources: the "Bénéfices Industriel et Commerciaux" (BIC) and the "Enquête sur la Structure de l'Emploi" (ESE). From the first source, which collects annual information on balance sheets and employment, they use the measure of the annual average full-time employment, the total capital in the firm as the sum of debt and owners' equity (this sum is equal to total assets in the French accounting system), the annual operating income, and, finally, the export ratio computed as the ratio of the firm's exports to its sales. From the second source, which collects information on the employment structure, they compute a proportion of engineers, technicians and managers in the work force and a proportion of skilled workers in the work force, both expressed as ratios using the employment measure described above.

The survey "Enquête sur la Technique et l'Organisation du Travail auprès des Travailleurs Occupés" (TOTTO) was performed in March 1987. It covers a total of about 20 million individuals in civilian employment. The probability of being selected is 1/1000; thus the survey contains about 20,000 workers. Questions concerning the organization of the workplace were asked to wage-earners and salaried employees only, questions concerning the use of "New Technologies" were asked to all members (including civil-servants) of the civilian work force (according to the definition of the OECD). The sample used for cross-section estimation consists of 15,946 wage-earners and salaried employees, based on TOTTO. The longitudinal sample where individual workers are followed at least 2 years and at most 3 years has 35,567 observations. When merged with firm-level information, the cross-section dataset includes 3446 individuals and the longitudinal dataset reduces to 7965 observations. The firm-level data are based on a panel of firms covering the years 1978–1987. The firm-level information comes from an exhaustive sample for large firms (more than 500 employees) and an INSEE probability sample plan for smaller firms. The sample plan provides a weighting variable which is used in subsequent estimation in order to estimate the variance–covariance matrix that is representative of the population of individuals (such that the bias arising from the higher probability of large firms to be in the sample can be offset).

Starting in 1990, most individual-level surveys performed at INSEE contain the same firm-level identification number, the Siren; mentioned above. This means that matched worker-firm data are available on a regular basis. For instance, the "Formation, Qualification, Profession" 1993 survey on education and continuous training has the employing firm for more than 90% of the employed workers in the dataset (see Goux and Maurin, 1997). We will also examine later longitudinal uses of the French Labor Force Survey, a 3-year rotating panel for which the Siren is available in every year a worker is employed.

Other interesting examples of representative cross-section data for the employee matched to longitudinal data for the firm include the Portuguese file used by Cardoso (1997) and the British file created by Hildreth and Pudney (1997). Cardoso used Social Security files (see the discussion in Section 2.4), to construct a random sample of 20% of the firms, stratified by economic activity. For each such firm, information on workers employed in a given year is available–sex, age, skill, occupation, schooling, tenure, earnings split into different components (base pay, bonuses, tenure-related pay, overtime pay), and hours. The sample of firms is designed to be dynamically representative of the Portuguese economy (starting in 1982). Hence, firms were initially sampled in 1983, the first year available. Then, all sampled firms were followed until their death. All new firms are at risk of being sampled at most once. Sampling frames like the one used to construct the Portuguese data make it difficult to follow the workers from firm to firm since the plan does not ensure the presence of the same workers from year to year. The Portuguese data have been used primarily to assess firm-specific wage inequality at different dates (see Cardoso, 1997). Hildreth and Pudney (1999) use the New Earnings Survey (NES), the Joint Unemployment and Vacancies Operating System (JUVOS), and the Annual Census of Production (ACOP), all for the United Kingdom. The different data sources permit dynamic links but the ACOP rules for sampling establishments changed between 1994 and 1995, creating difficulties for longitudinal analyses.

2.4. Representative matched worker-firm panels (administrative origin)

Many matched employer–employee datasets are based on administrative files. In this section we discuss some leading examples.

Every state in the US, except New York, maintains very complete information on quarterly employment and earnings so that the State Employment Security Agency (or State Unemployment Insurance Agency, depending on the state) can manage the state unemployment benefits program. The exact details of these programs may vary from state to state. However, such UI wage records cover almost all of the employment (at least 90% of the work force but more in some states). Self-employed individuals are never covered. Other categories, such as federal and military personnel, employees of the US postal service, railroad employees, employees of religious and philanthropic organizations, those who receive only commissions, and some agricultural employees may not be covered in some states (Maryland is an example; see Burgess et al. 1999).

Starting with the base UI earnings files, the different states have constructed random samples of the eligible work force. The sampling rate varies by state: 5% in Pennsylvania, 10% in Washington State to 100% in Maryland. Eight states participated in an early attempt to coordinate such data, the Continuous Wage and Benefit History Project (Georgia, Idaho, Louisiana, Missouri, New Mexico, Pennsylvania, South Carolina, and Washington, see Anderson and Meyer, 1994, who use these datasets for the period 1978–1984). Apart from the wage amount received by workers (total wages, including tips, commissions, and bonuses, up to a ceiling of $100,000 that may depend on the state), each quarterly record includes a person identifier, a firm identifier–the federal employer identification number (FEIN), and some other firm characteristics such as the industry (4-digit SIC), average monthly employment, total wages, taxable wages and tax rate as computed by the State Agency.

Unemployment benefit claim records for any worker who filed for UI are also available in certain states (for an example, see Anderson and Meyer, 1997. These datasets contain, for each claim filed, the worker's personal identifier, the date the claim was filed, the first pay date and the exhaustion date, the total amount of benefits paid, the reason for work separation, as well as personal characteristics (age, sex, race, schooling). In addition, it is possible in some states, for some firms (mostly publicly traded firms) to merge with financial data using the FEIN. Even though this is possible for only a small fraction of firms – the largest, in general – more than half of the workers are employed in such companies. Hence, financial data, balance-sheet information may be available for a large share of the records at hand.

Lane et al. (1999) recently completed a pilot project in which the information from the State of Maryland UI wage records was matched to data from the Current Population Survey (also called the monthly household survey in the United States) and the Standard Statistical Establishment List (SSEL, Bureau of the Census). The use of data from the Current Population Survey provides demographic, educational and other individual and household data to complement the earnings history in the UI wage records. The SSEL provides longitudinal, but limited, data on the employing establishments.

Topel and Ward (1992) use the Social Security earnings reports made by employers to the Social Security administration, a Federal version of data similar to the state UI reports. The Longitudinal Employer–Employee Data (LEED) contain quarterly information for over one million individuals for the period 1957–1972. In addition to employee and employer identifiers, available individual characteristics are the age, the race, and the sex. Earnings are reported on a quarterly basis (see Smith, 1989). According to Topel and Ward (1992), top-coding problems, common with US Social Security-based data, are minimized because of the quarterly reporting. Jacobson et al. (1993) use both types of data – UI and Social Security – or a subsample of the Pennsylvanian displaced workers that they analyze.

The administrative source from which similar French data files were constructed are derived from records received by the Tax and Social Security Authorities in order to compute the wage-related taxes, to cross-check with employees' own income tax reports, to compute employers' contributions to Social Security, and to manage employees' individual accounts for entitlements to pensions and health benefits. INSEE also receives these files, called the Déclaration Annuelle de Données Sociales (DADS). As in the US, the coverage is very broad, every employer except those employing only domestic staff must report. INSEE files exclude agricultural workers as well as government employees from the statistical operations (all of whom have special social security systems). Information on the establishment consists of: Siren (firm) and Siret (establishment) identification numbers, address, 4-digit industry code (APE), work force (December 31), and total wage bill. For each individual employee, INSEE receives the name, national identity number, occupation, number of hours (since 1993), start and end dates of the employment period, employment status (full-time, part-time, home work, irregular), total compensation (before as well as after deduction of social security contributions), total benefits in kind, and total allowances for business expenses. Because of the work load that the data entry imposes, not all of this information is accessible at all dates. For instance, the employer identifier is only available starting in 1976. The start and end dates of the employment period are not on the research files that, for instance, Abowd et al. (1999a) have used (they only have its length). Starting in 1964, only those workers born in October of an even year were kept in the research files, resulting in a 1/25 sample of the private and semi-public sector employees. The file used in Abowd et al. (1999) includes more than 1.1 million individuals and 500,000 firms for the period 1976–1987. Kramarz and Roux (1998) have extended the dataset to 1995. This new dataset includes approximately two million individuals and one million firms.

Because of the centralized nature of the French statistical system, identical identifiers (firm or individual) can be found in different data sources. It is therefore very easy to match establishments from the DADS with other firm-level or establishment-level data sources such as balance-sheet information. It is possible, subject to the approval of the "Commission Nationale Informatique et Liberté" (CNIL), to match the DADS with other individual level datasets using the person identifier. However, due to the CNIL policy, this has not been done frequently in the past. The most important example is the match between the DADS and the Echantillon Démographique Permanent (EDP). The EDP collects for 1/10th of the population, information drawn from Civil Status registers on marriage, births, deaths, as well as data from the decennial Censuses of Population (in particular, completed education).

The French Déclaration Mensuelle de Mouvements de Main d'Oeuvre (DMMO), used by Abowd et al. (1999b), is another administrative data source in which all establishments with 50 or more employees register all hiring or separations every month. Information on the workers includes age, sex, type of contract, type of entry (shortterm contract (CDD), longterm contract (CDI), or transfer from another establishment of the same firm), skill-level for all entries and age, sex, seniority at exit, type of exit (end of shortterm contract, quit, retirement, firing for cause, firing for economic reasons, transfer to another establishment of the same firm), military service, death, and skill-level for all exits. These movements are usually aggregated at the monthly level by categories of entry/exit and skill-level. Notice that no wage information is available. The data source includes the establishment identifiers required to link to other information on the establishment and enterprise, including employment structure. Thus the data are dynamically representative of establishments and of mobile workers.

Danmarks Statistik has constructed a similar database with longitudinal information on workers and their establishments (IDA, see Leth-Sørensen, 1995) based on administrative registers on individuals. All persons in the population are covered, irrespective of their labor market status, and are identified by their person ID. Starting in 1980, annual information on each person's labor situation at the end of November is available. For persons born after 1960, there are also references to the person IDs of their parents. Notice also that, since the 1970 Census of Population was the first ever to include this person number, it is possible to get information back to 1970. For all employed workers, the employing establishment identifier is known. The information available at the establishment level consists of: years of operation, industry, and location. Many individual characteristics are collected: sex, age, family and marital status, education, employment experience, unemployment history, income, full-time or part-time job, hourly pay, seniority. There are, however, no other data on firms such as balance sheets, production, factor use or financial information. The same kind of data, based on individual registers, are also available in Norway (see Salvanes and Forre, 1997) and Sweden (Tegsjö and Andersson, 1998).

In Japan, an establishment register called the Establishment Census forms the basis of matched data that is dynamically representative. The information in the establishment census has been matched to wage information in the Basic Survey on Wage Structures, a probability sample of establishments with 5 or more employees. Other information on the firms is taken from periodic censuses of manufacturing and commercial establishments. See Hayami and Abe (1998) and Abe and Sofer (1996) for details.

In Germany, starting in January, 1973, in order to collect all the necessary information for unemployment insurance and health-retirement payments, employers have been required to report information regarding any employment relation subject to social security contributions (more specifically, at the beginning, at the termination, and on December 31st for any employee). The reporting form, known as the Historikdatei (HD), is collected by the Bundesantalt für Arbeit (BfA). A 1% sample of the HD has been used by the Institut für Arbeitsmarkt und Berufsforschung (IAB) to construct a research dataset called the Beschäftigungsstichprobe (BS), from January 1, 1975 to December 31, 1990. The information reported in every record includes sex, nationality, education, gross earnings over the spell (with both left- and right-censoring because of the floor and the ceiling in the base formula for the computation of contributions), reasons for interruption of the spell (maternity leave, military service). As in other countries, self-employed individuals as well as civil-servants are not covered by the data. The HD comprises 79% of the labor force in 1979 (see Dustmann and Meghir, 1997, for further references to this data file). In addition to the BS file, the IAB has added information from another administrative data source, the Leistungsempfangerdatei (LD). The LD provides information on all spells that resulted in benefits from the BfA: unemployment benefits, unemployment assistance, and payments while in training program. Individuals can be followed from employment to registered unemployment spells. The IAB dataset (i.e., the BS plus the LD datasets) also contain a plant and a firm identifier. Using the entire HD dataset, aggregate individual characteristics have been created at the establishment-level, making firm size and within-firm educational structure available.

Similar data are also available in Austria (see Winter-Ebmer and Zweimüller, 1997) and in Italy (see Contini et al., undated). For Belgium, the data used by Leonard and Van Audenrode (1996, 1997) are based on Social Security declarations for the national pension system of private sector workers and cover the period from 1977 to 1985.

2.5. Representative matched worker-firm panels (statistical surveys)

The French Labor Force Survey (Enquête Emploi, EE) is conducted every year by the

French National Statistical Institute (INSEE). Because this survey routinely includes the employer identifier (firm and establishment), it has become a standard for matched employer–employee database upon labor force surveys.

The universe of individuals sampled in EE includes all ordinary households in metropolitan France. In 1990, INSEE started a new series of March EEs, administered to the household sample every March for three consecutive years using a sampling frame based on the 1990 census. The sampling rate is 1/300. There are three rotation groups, so the sample is refreshed by one-third every year. Each year, a supplement (enquête complémentaire) is administered to the outgoing rotation group, one-third of the sample. Because the sampling technique is based on housing in tracts built in French territory with further inclusions or modifications in case of construction or reconstruction of buildings not known at the 1990 Census of Population, it is possible to have a dynamically representative survey (see INSEE, 1994 for all the technical details on the survey methodology).

The data collected in the EE include both standard and more unusual questions from labor force surveys–wage, country of origin, sex, marital status, number of children and their ages, region of residence, age, detailed education, age at the end of education period, occupation (4-digit classification), father's last occupation, mother's last occupation, employment status (employed, unemployed, inactive), usual number of hours, seniority in the employing firm, sector and size of the employing firm, nature of the contract (shortterm, longterm, program for young workers (stage)) for each of the individuals in the sample. Furthermore, each employed individual is asked the name and address of the employment location. This information is given to the INSEE regional agencies where the Siret (establishment identification number) is coded using the on-line SIRENE computerized system. This number is the unique establishment identifier that links the employer to the rest of the French statistical system. The first nine digits represent the enterprise to which the establishment belongs, based on an economic and not a financial definition. Employer Siret number can be coded in the EE for more than 90% of the workers. Hence, it becomes possible to use this type of dataset in the same fashion as the DADS was used in Abowd et al. (1999a) (see Goux and Maurin, 1999). In particular, the EE can be matched with other firm level datasets as the Echantillon d'Entreprises (based on the BIC), the Déclaration de Mouvements de Main d'Oeuvre (DMMO), a record of all entries and exits in all establishments with at least 50 employees (see Abowd et al., 1999b). Such matches have been performed by Entorf et al. (1999) to study New Technologies or Kramarz (1997) to analyze trade, wages, and unemployment.

In the United States, a longitudinally representative matched employer–employee data file has been created for the National Longitudinal Survey of Youth 1979 Cohort (NLS-Y).[5] The description is based on Abowd and Finer (1998). The creation required the resolution of two conceptual difficulties and one procedural problem. The conceptual difficulties were (1) defining an employer and (2) specifying the level of aggregation to

---

[5] As Hildreth and Pudney (1998) note, samples of this structure are representative for the target age group of the population but the resulting sample of employers is not necessarily representative of employers.

use on the employer unit. The procedural problem is to find a method for performing the analysis that is consistent with the confidentiality requirements that have been specified for NORC and the Center for Human Resource Research at Ohio State University, the two primary contractors for the survey.

The simplest and most comprehensive definition of an employer is any organization for which the respondent completed the employer questionnaire during any year of the NLS-Y. For the purposes of preparing the matched data file, this definition maximizes the number of employers for which information would be available. Employers are divided into primary employers (main job; full- and part-time employees) and secondary employers (no main job or several part-time jobs). Ultimately, all types of employers will be covered; thus, private for-profit employers (firms), public sector employers (units of government) and private not-for-profit employment (other organizations) would all be included in the file. Some summary measures about the employer (size, type) are available for all types of employers. Other measures (sales, profits, assets) are only available for some private for-profit employers. Detailed analysis of the characteristics of the employing firms, therefore, requires careful attention to the type of firm. The level of aggregation to use for the employer depends upon the purpose of the analysis and the prospects for collecting data at that level of aggregation. Three potential definitions are possible: establishment (the physical location where work occurs), business or governmental unit (the economic entity at which decisions are made concerning employment, investment, etc.) or company/governmental aggregate (the entity required to disclose information to public sources). Currently, the employer identifier file includes an ID for the company/governmental aggregate and the business/governmental unit, where possible. This level of identification permits merging information about companies and lines of business from sources like Compustat and Dun & Bradstreet. More specifically, approximately 49,000 unique employer names were checked for relevant (time period consistent) matches in a variety of public sources.

This matching process was done in several phases. First, the raw files of the NLS-Y for the years 1986–1994 were accessed to acquire the employer names for up to 5 employers per year. The first stage match attempts to match the respondent employer names with employer names in the Compustat (Standard and Poors) and CRSP header files. There were approximately 159,000 non-blank employer name fields for the years 1986–1994. Government coded employers, self-employed jobs, and employers with less than 50 workers were all eliminated. This left exactly 48,422 unique employer names eligible for match. These employer names were placed in a database with the Compustat headers and CRSP name histories. One by one, the respondents employers were checked against the Compustat headers. At the end of this process, around 8000 employer names were matched with Compustat and CRSP employers. These unique names accounted for roughly 18% of the master list of employer names. In addition to checking for matches, unmatched records were coded for additional checking, military employer, and public or non-profit. Unmatched small employers are left initially unmatched. The second stage match was used to double-check suspicious first stage matches, and further match unmatched first stage names that may be subsidiaries of publicly-traded parent companies. A total of 9000 such names were resolved using the Directory of Corporate Affiliations for several years both in printed and machine readable formats. These second-stage names were then recoded to reflect their status as private companies, subsidiaries of public parents, franchises, help-supply services. The third phase of the match procedure was to check improperly coded government, non-profit, and military employers. Approximately 2000 employer names were checked and coded as religious organizations, military, federal government, state government, local government, and educational institutions. In addition, private and non-profit health care facilities were reserved for the future processing. The fourth stage consisted of internal matching of companies with no publicly disclosed parent that appear multiple times.

2.6. Non-representative cross-sections and panels of workers and firms

Not all datasets matching workers with their firms were designed by statistical agencies with the avowed goal of representativeness of the set of workers or firms in a country, a state, or any geographic unit of some importance. This is most apparent the matched job-firm data that have been studied by Groshen (1996), who uses employer-based salary surveys in many of her papers. In this subsection, we give examples of such datasets. Our requirement for discussion herein is that multiple firms in which multiple workers or jobs are surveyed be present.

Employers have conducted salary surveys for many years in which they collect matched worker (or job) and firm information. We base our description of the American salary surveys on Groshen (1996). Salary surveys are used by large employers as a source of information on external wage opportunities of the workers they employ. These employers are very different in nature and scope. Groshen cites the following examples: "the federal government, most of the regional Federal Reserve banks, Hay Associates, Inc., the American Hospital Association, the National Association of Business Economists, and the American Association of University Professors." Access to the data is generally granted to the members of the collecting association, which may entail a large fee or to clients (in the case of Hay Associates, Inc. for instance).

These datasets contain annual information on wages, including bonuses and incentives, of all persons with a job in predefined occupations. They also have information on the participating employers themselves: industry, total employment, and firm-specific compensation policy elements. As is obvious from the list of organizations that collect Salary Surveys, the coverage largely depends on the purpose of the user. Groshen notes that "if a survey is geographically based, then the occupations covered will be those commonly found and most comparable across industry: usually clerical, administrative, maintenance, and managerial positions." Hence, occupations such as secretaries, drivers, painters, accountants are often included. She adds that "These surveys have the advantages over industry and professional wage surveys that they allow control for regional wage differences, they include many different industries, and they are longitudinal in establishments. While they do not cover all occupations, they do cover a broad mix...."

Industry-based surveys differ in their scopes. They generally cover a large fraction of those workers employed in a particular industry. This allows jobs and occupations to be very precisely defined. In particular, for blue-collar workers, information on training, on machines, and tools needed or used in the job is available.

Profession-based surveys focus on one narrowly-defined occupation and tend to be national in scope since professions have generally a national market, the characteristics of which the survey organizers want to know. In particular, information on the educational background and employment experience of the participants is often collected. In his chapter on executive pay, Murphy describes many of these surveys for CEOs.

All these different types of salary surveys have several common features. First, the description of the job is very detailed, "two to three paragraphs long, and specify the responsibilities, training requirements, how the job is done, what is produced, position in the corporate hierarchy, the occupation of direct supervisor, and number of supervisees," according to Groshen. Furthermore, the jobs may be classified into job families defined as all members of a career path. Finally, demographic information is usually not collected.

Although salary surveys are an important source of information in the private sector of the American economy, Groshen is one of the few to use these for research purposes. A number of researchers, however, have recently made use of similar Bureau of Labor Statistics surveys of occupational or industrial salaries matched to employer information. These are noted in Table 1 and discussed in the relevant sections below. Most of the design features noted by Groshen apply to these surveys as well.

Brown and Medoff (1996) describe a dataset for which individuals interviewed for the Survey of Consumers, a survey run by the Survey Research Center at the University of Michigan, between September 1991 and March 1992 were asked to complete a supplement on their employer. Supplementary questions were only asked to workers with a private-sector employer. These questions included workers' experience, seniority, occupation, and wage rate as well as information on the employer, more specifically, the collective bargaining status, the number of employees, the industry, the age of the business, fringe benefits, personnel policies, and related features of the workplace. The sample has 1410 private-sector workers of which 1168 gave information on the name and address of their employer. Brown and Medoff asked Dun & Bradstreet to locate the employer and, when located, to give the establishment and the company employment, the age of the business, and the industry. All of 863 reported matches were hand-checked, generating a set of 701 "clean matches" as described in Brown and Medoff (1996). Employers in those clean matches are larger and older (longer in business) than the employers in the original sample.

A recent study by Chennouf et al. (1997) uses matched worker-firm data for a small sample of Algerian firms in the Algiers region. This dataset comprises 42 firms from diverse manufacturing industries and 1007 employees. The available individual characteristics are the wage, the number of days worked, the education level, seniority, experience, age, sex, and the marital status. On the firms themselves, apart from the industry and private/public status, variables are mostly defined as an aggregation of the individual characteristics of workers employed at that firm (average seniority, experience, and education).

3. Statistical models for matched employer–employee datasets

3.1. The basic linear model

Virtually all of the papers that we discuss below use a variant of the linear model that can be identified with matched employer–employee data:

$$y_{it} = x_{it}\beta + \theta_i + \psi_{J(i,t)it} + \varepsilon_{it}, \tag{3.1}$$

in which y_{it} is some measured outcome (compensation, layoff event, etc.) for the individual $i = 1, ..., N$ at date $t = 1, ..., T$; x_{it} is a vector of P time-varying exogenous characteristics of individual i; θ_i is a pure person effect; $\psi_{J(i,t)it}$ is a pure firm effect for the firm at which worker i is employed at date t (denoted by $J(i,t)$), and ψ_{it} is a statistical residual. Assume that a simple random sample of N individuals is observed for T years. The firm and person effects in Eq. (3.1) can be decomposed into components relating to seniority and non-time-varying personal characteristics as follows:

$$\psi_{jit} = \phi_j + \gamma_j s_{it}, \tag{3.2}$$

where s_{it} denotes individual i's seniority in firm $j = J(i, t)$ in year t, ϕ_j denotes the firm-specific intercept, and γ_j is the firm-specific seniority coefficient; while

$$\theta_i = \alpha_i + u_i \eta, \tag{3.3}$$

where u_i is a vector of non-time-varying measurable personal characteristics, α_i is the person-specific intercept, and η is the vector of coefficients on the non-time-varying personal characteristics.

In matrix notation we have

$$y = X\beta + D\theta + F\psi + \varepsilon, \tag{3.4}$$

where X is the $N^* \times P$ matrix of observable, time-varying characteristics, D is the $N^* \times N$ matrix of indicators for individual $i = 1, ..., N$, F is the $N^* \times J$ matrix of indicators for the firm at which i works at date t (J firms total), y is the $N \times 1$ vector of outcomes, ε is the conformable vector of residuals, and $N^* = NT$. Balanced samples are not necessary but simplify the discussion of the statistical models. The firm effect can also have higher dimension, as for example in Eq. (3.2), but we use this simpler form for the discussion herein.

The parameters of Eq. (3.4) are β, the $P \times 1$ vector of coefficients on the time-varying personal characteristics; θ, the $N \times 1$ vector of individual effects; ψ, the $J \times 1$ vector of firm effects; and the error variance, σ_ε^2. The parameter θ includes both the unobservable (to the statistician) individual effect and the coefficients of the non-time-varying personal characteristics. Eqs. (3.1) and (3.4) are interpreted as the conditional expectation of individual outcomes given information on the observable characteristics, the date of observation, the identity of the individual, and the identity of the employing firm. In this section we want to make precise the interpretation of Eq. (3.4) under classical least squares when some of the effects, β, θ, and ψ are missing or are aggregated into linear combinations. The discussion draws heavily on Abowd et al. (1999a).

3.2. Aggregation and omitted variable biases

The omission or aggregation of one or more of the effects in Eq. (3.4) can change the meaning of the other effects in important and subtle ways that are not always clear from the specific equation that various authors have estimated. Variations in the set of conditioning effects, which give rise to omitted-variable biases, are one source of confusion about the interpretation of the statistical parameters. The use of different linear combinations of the effects in Eq. (3.4), which gives rise to aggregation biases, is another source of differential interpretations for the parameters. These are considered in turn.

When the estimated version of Eq. (3.4) excludes the pure firm effects (ψ), the estimated person effects, θ^*, are the sum of the pure person effects, θ, and the employment-duration weighted average of the firm effects for the firms in which the worker was employed, conditional on the individual time-varying characteristics, X:

$$\theta^* = \theta + (D'M_XD)^{-1}D'M_XF\psi, \tag{3.5}$$

where the notation $M_A \equiv I - A(A'A)^{-1}A'$ for an arbitrary matrix A. Hence, if X were orthogonal to D and F, so that $D'M_XD = D'D$ and $D'M_XF = D'F$, then the difference between θ^* and θ, which is just an omitted variable bias, would be an $N \times 1$ vector consisting, for each individual i, of the employment-duration weighted average of the firm effects ψ_j for $j \in \{J(i,1), ..., J(i,T)\}$:

$$\theta_i^* - \theta_i = \sum_{t=1}^{T} \frac{\psi_{J(i,t)}}{T}.$$

The estimated coefficients on the time-varying characteristics in the case of omitted firm effects, β^*, are the sum of the parameters of the full conditional expectation, β, and the omitted variable bias that depends upon the conditional covariance of X and F, given D:

$$\beta^* = \beta + (X'M_DX)^{-1}X'M_DF\psi.$$

Similarly, omitting the pure person effects (θ) from the estimated version of Eq. (3.4) gives estimates of the firm effects, ψ^{**}, that can be interpreted as the sum of the pure firm effects, ψ, and the employment-duration weighted average of the person effects of all of the firm's employees in the sample, conditional on the time-varying individual characteristics:

$$\psi^{**} = \psi + (F'M_XF)^{-1}F'M_XD\theta. \tag{3.6}$$

Hence, if X were orthogonal to D and F, so that $F'M_XF = F'F$ and $F'M_XD = F'D$, then the difference between ψ^{**} and ψ, again an omitted variable bias, would be a $J \times 1$ vector consisting, for each firm j, of the employment-duration weighted average of the person effects θ_i for $i \in \{J(i,t) = j \text{ for some } t\}$:

$$\psi_j^{**} - \psi_j = \sum_{i=1}^{N} \sum_{t=1}^{T} \left[\frac{\theta_i 1(J(i,t) = j)}{N_j} \right],$$

where

$$N_j = \sum_{i=1}^{N} \sum_{t=1}^{T} 1(J(i,t) = j),$$

and the function $1(A)$ takes the value 1 when A is true and 0 otherwise. The estimated coefficients on the time-varying characteristics in the case of omitted individual effects, β^{**}, are the sum of the parameters of the full conditional expectation, β, and the omitted variable bias that depends upon the covariance of X and D, given F:

$$\beta^{**} = \beta + (X'M_FX)^{-1}X'M_FD\theta. \tag{3.7}$$

Almost all existing analyses of equations like (3.4) produce estimated effects that confound pure person and pure firm effects in a manner similar to that presented above. The possibility of identifying both person and firm effects thus allows users of matched employer–employee data to reexamine many important topics in labor economics using estimates that properly allocate the statistical effects associated with persons and firms. Of course, other identification issues also arise, such as in the estimation of person effects, so that longitudinal matched data are usually required.

3.3. Identification of person and firm effects

Although Eq. (3.1) is just a classical linear regression model, the full design matrix $[X \ D \ F]$ has high column dimension. The cross-product matrix

$$\begin{bmatrix} X'X & X'D & X'F \\ D'X & D'D & D'F \\ F'X & F'D & F'F \end{bmatrix} \tag{3.8}$$

is patterned in the elements $D'D$ and $F'F$. The separate identification of the individual and firm effects requires the presence in the sample of individuals who move from firm to firm. The individual and firm effects are both identified whenever an individual that appears in the sample works for a firm that employs at least one individual, also in the sample, who moves to another firm, which, necessarily, also appears in the sample. The simplest example of the complexities of identification in this model can be seen by considering an example in which there are three individual (1, 2, and 3), two firms (*A* and *B*) and two time periods. Suppose that individual 1 is continuously employed at firm *A*, individual 2 is continuously employed at firm *B*, and individual 3 moves from firm *A* to firm *B*. Then all three individual effects are identified (subject to the usual identification restriction that they sum to zero) and both firm effects are identified (again, subject to the usual identification condition that they sum to zero). If individual 3 is not mobile (stays at firm *A*), then firm effect *B* cannot be distinguished from person effect 2 and person effects 1 and 3 are entirely within firm effect *A*.

There are many computational difficulties associated with inverting the matrix (3.8). These computational problems are directly related to the fact that the basic statistical model is neither hierarchical nor balanced. Thus, projecting onto the columns *D*, the method usually called "within persons estimation," leaves a high-dimension unpatterned, non-sparse matrix to invert for the solution for β and ψ. Similarly, projecting onto the columns of *F*, the method usually called "within firms estimation," leaves a high-dimension unpatterned, non-sparse matrix to invert to solve for β and θ. Clearly, the usual computational methods for least squares estimation of the parameter vector $[\beta' \ \theta' \ \psi']'$ are not generally feasible. Hence, one usually cannot compute the unconstrained least squares estimates for the model (3.1). Correlated random effect models, which permit the estimation of all effects without restricting the design matrix in Eq. (3.8), also require solution of the full least squares normal equations (see Scheffé, 1959; Searle et al. 1992). See Abowd et al. (1999a) for a detailed discussion of the identification and estimation issues in models using Eq. (3.1).

3.4. Aggregation and omitted variable biases for inter-industry wage differentials[6]

Define a pure inter-industry wage differential, conditional on the same information as in Eqs. (3.1) and (3.4), as κ_k for some classification $k = 1, ..., K$. By definition, pure firm effects are fully nested within pure inter-industry effects so that κ_k can be represented as an employment-duration weighted average of the firm effects within the classification *k*:

$$\kappa_k \equiv \sum_{i=1}^{N} \sum_{t=1}^{T} \left[\frac{1(K(J(i,t)) = k)\psi_{J(i,t)}}{N_k} \right],$$

where

$$N_k \equiv \sum_{j=1}^{J} 1(K(j) = k)N_j$$

and the function *K*(j) denotes the classification of firm *j*. If we insert pure inter-industry effects as the appropriate aggregate of the firm effects in Eq. (3.1), then the equation

---

[6] This subsection draws heavily on Abowd et al. (1999a).

becomes

$$y_{it} = x_{it}\beta + \theta_i + \kappa_{K(J(i,t))} + (\psi_{J(i,t)} - \kappa_{K(J(i,t))}) + \varepsilon_{it}$$

or, in matrix notation as in Eq. (3.4),

$$y = X\beta + D\theta + FA\kappa + (F\psi - FA\kappa) + \varepsilon, \tag{3.9}$$

where the matrix A, $J \times K$, classifies each of the J firms into one of the K categories; that is, $a_{jk} = 1$ if, and only if, $K(j) = k$. The parameter vector κ, $K \times 1$, may be interpreted as the following weighted average of the pure firm effects:

$$\kappa \equiv (A'F'FA)^{-1}A'F'F\psi,$$

and the effect $(F\psi - FA\kappa)$ may be re-expressed as $M_{FA}F\psi$. Thus, the aggregation of J firm effects into K inter-industry effects, weighted so as to be representative of individuals, can be accomplished directly by estimation of Eq. (3.9). Only rank$(F'M_{FA}F)$ firm effects can be separately identified; however, there is neither an omitted variable nor an aggregation bias in the classical least squares estimates of (3.9).

Estimates of inter-industry effects, κ^*, that are computed on the basis of an equation that excludes the remaining firm effects, $M_{FA}F\psi$, are equal to the pure inter-industry effect, κ, plus an omitted variable bias that can be expressed as a function of the conditional variance of the inter-industry effects, FA, given the time-varying characteristics, X, and the person effects, D:

$$\kappa^* = \kappa + \left(A'F'M_{[D|X]}FA\right)^{-1}A'F'M_{[D|X]}M_{FA}F\psi, \tag{3.10}$$

which simplifies to $\kappa^* = \kappa$ if, and only if, the inter-industry effects, FA, are orthogonal to the subspace $M_{FA}F$, given D and X, which is generally not true even though FA and $M_{FA}F$ are orthogonal by construction. Thus, it is not possible to estimate pure inter-industry wage differentials consistently, conditional on time-varying personal characteristics and unobservable non-time-varying personal characteristics, without explicit firm-identifiers unless this conditional orthogonality condition holds. A similar argument applies to the estimates of β. Industry effects as defined by Eq. (3.10) are directly comparable to those estimated by Krueger and Summers (1988) when they include person effects.

When the estimation of Eq. (3.9) excludes both person and firm effects, the estimated inter-industry effect, κ_k^{**}, equals the pure inter-industry effect, κ, plus the employment-duration weighted average residual firm effect inside the category k, given X, and the employment-duration weighted average person effect inside the category, given the time-varying personal characteristics X:

$$\kappa^{**} = \kappa + (A'F'M_XFA)^{-1}A'F'M_X(M_{FA}F\psi + D\theta),$$

which can be restated as

$$\kappa^{**} = (A'F'M_XFA)^{-1}A'F'M_XF\psi + (A'F'M_XFA)^{-1}A'F'M_XD\theta. \tag{3.11}$$

Hence, the raw inter-industry effects consist of the sum of the properly-weighted average person effect and average firm effect, conditional on X. Thus, analyses that exclude person effects confound the pure inter-industry wage differential with an average of the person effects found in the category, given the measured personal characteristics, X. The inter-industry wage differentials in Eq. (3.11) are directly comparable to those studied by Krueger and Summers (1988) when person effects are omitted.

3.5. Aggregation and omitted variable biases for inter-person wage differentials

Another line of research attempts to explain inter-personal wage differentials conditional on firm effects without explicit controls for unobservable personal heterogeneity. None of the studies in this strain of the wage-determination literature includes both pure person and pure firm effects, as defined in Eq. (3.1) or (3.4) above. In our notation, studies like Groshen (1991a) estimate ψ^{**}, from Eq. (3.6), and β^{**}, from Eq. (3.7).

3.6. Firm-size wage effects

The repeated finding of a positive relation between the size of the employing firm and wage rates, even after controlling for a wealth of individual variables (see Brown and Medoff, 1989), has also generated many alternative interpretations. Properly modeled, the firm-size wage effect can also be fully decomposed using matched employee–employer data. Using our notation, a firm-size effect, δ, can be modeled using a matrix S, $J \times R$, that maps the size of firm j into R linearly independent functions of its size. Using the same methods as above, we express the wage equation, Eq. (3.4), as

$$y = X\beta + D\theta + FS\delta + M_{FS}F\psi + \varepsilon, \tag{3.12}$$

so that the pure firm-size effects are related to the underlying pure firm effects by the equation:

$$\delta \equiv (S'F'FS)^{-1}S'F'F\psi. \tag{3.13}$$

The firm-size effect is also an aggregation of the pure firm effects and can be analyzed using the same tools that we used for the inter-industry wage differential. The raw firm-size wage differential, δ^{**} (in our notation), can be represented as

$$\delta^{**} = (S'F'M_XFS)^{-1}S'F'M_XF\psi + (S'F'M_XFS)^{-1}S'F'M_XD\theta, \tag{3.14}$$

which can be interpreted as the sum of the firm-size, employment-weighted average firm effect and the similarly-weighted average person effect, conditional on personal characteristics, X, and firm size, FS.

3.7. Other methodological issues

There are a variety of technical statistical issues surrounding the use of different sampling frames to construct matched employer–employee issues. Recently, several teams of authors have begun to examine these issues. Hildreth and Pudney (1997, 1999) examine the issues of non-random missing data, choice based sampling induced by the matching process and correlated random effects modeling of the heterogeneity. They provide full likelihoods for the hierarchical case (individual effects are fully within firm effects) and some likelihood models for non-hierarchical case (individuals move from firm to firm within the sample). Abowd et al. (1999c) address the issue of non-random missing data following the match. Dolton, Lindeboom and van den Berg (1999) address the issues of non-random missing matches (of the employer or employee), attrition and endogenous sampling. Mairesse and Greenan (1999) consider the problem of modeling employee and employer behavior when only a single employee observation is available per firm, as is common in matched training surveys.

4. From theoretical models to statistical models: potential interpretations of the descriptive models

We illustrate the relation between structural heterogeneity in the populations of workers (heterogeneous abilities or tastes) and firms (heterogeneous efficiencies or technologies) and the statistical heterogeneity in Eq. (3.1) using four economic models with very simple population structures. In each case we derive the conditional expectation of individual compensation given the identity of the employing firm and the individual. We then relate the parameters of this conditional expectation to the statistical parameterization above.

4.1. Measurement of the internal and external wage

Virtually all economic models of labor market outcomes require an estimate of the opportunity cost of the worker's time. In simple, classical equilibrium models without unmeasured person or firm heterogeneity, this generally corresponds to the measured wage rate. In models of wage determination such as quasi-rent splitting or imperfect information (efficiency wage and agency models), unmeasured statistical heterogeneity (person or firm) breaks the direct link between the observed wage rate and the opportunity cost of time. Moreover, such models usually make an explicit distinction between the compensation received and the wage rate available in the employee's next best alternative employment. The statistical model in Eq. (3.1), while not derived from an explicit labor market model, contains all the observable elements from which non-classical labor market models derive their empirical content. Indeed, the simplest definition of the components of the external and internal wage rate based a structural model leading to Eq. (3.1) is given by the following model:

$$y_{it} = x_{it}\zeta + \nu_{it},$$

where $\{x_{it}, \nu_{it}\}$ follows a general stochastic process for $i = 1, ..., N$ and $t = 1, ..., T$ with

$$\mathrm{E}[\{x_{it}, \nu_{it}\}\{x_{ns}, \nu_{ns}\} \mid i, n, s, t, J(i, t), J(n, s)] \neq 0 \qquad \text{iff } i = n \text{ or } J(i, t) = J(n, s).$$

Then,

$$\theta_i = E[x_{it}\zeta + v_{it} \mid i] - E[x_{it}\zeta + v_{it}]$$

and

$$\psi_j = E[x_{it}\zeta + v_{it} \mid J(i,t) = j] - E[x_{it}\zeta + v_{it}].$$

4.2. A matching model with endogenous turnover

This model is based on Jovanovic (1979). Suppose that workers are homogeneous. There are two types of firms, m and n, and two periods. In type m firms a worker's marginal product and wage rate are always w^*, and employment is always available in a type m firm. In type n firms there is a matching process. Worker i's productivity is $w^* + \varepsilon_{in}$ in both periods with ε_{in} drawn from a binomial distribution $B(-H, H, 1/2)$. The matching outcome, ε_{in}, unknown to both the worker and the firm at the beginning of the first period of employment, is realized at the end of the first period and becomes public information. Workers are offered contracts at the beginning of the first period of the form (w_1, w_2) and workers may leave firm n at the end of the first period. All workers are risk-neutral and earn no rents. The equilibrium contract for firms of type n is $(w^* - H/2, w^* + \varepsilon_{in})$. All workers in type n firms with a bad matching outcome $-H$ quit to type m firms.

To simplify the model, we consider a stationary situation with nine workers who live for two periods each, three born in period 0, three born in period 1, three born in period 2. Two workers in each generation enter type n firms, one worker in each generation enters a type m firm. Of the two workers who entered type n firms, let one draw a positive matching outcome and the other draw a negative matching outcome. The worker with the negative matching outcome leaves the type n firm for a type m firm when the matching parameter is made public.

The structure of the data implied by this theoretical model is shown in Table 2. This corresponds to the following parameter values in the descriptive model:

$$\mu = w^*,$$

where μ is the overall mean;

$$\alpha_i = 0, i = 1, \ldots, 9,$$

where α_i is person i person-effect;

$$(\phi_m, \gamma_m) = (0, 0),$$

for the type m firm compensation policy; and

$$(\phi_n, \gamma_n) = \left(-\frac{H}{2}, \frac{3H}{2}\right),$$

for the type n firm compensation policy.

4.3. A rent-splitting model with exogenous turnover

Suppose there are four different individuals, two types of firms, m and n, and two time periods. Each of the two firms earns quasi-rents of q_{it}, and the quasi-rents are split by negotiation so that the workers receive a share s_j of the quasi-rent in firm j. Suppose that each firm employs two workers. With probability one, exactly one worker is randomly selected to separate from the period one employer and be re-employed at the other firm in the second period. All information about the workers and firms is known to those parties but not to the statistician. All workers are included in the data sample and the typical worker has wages of the form

$$y_{it} = x_i + s_j q_{jt},$$

where x_i is the measure of wage rate heterogeneity, i.e., the worker type, q_{jt} follows a binomial distribution $B(-Q, Q, 1/2)$, $i = 1, ..., 4$, $j = m, n$, and $t = 1, 2$.

Table 3 shows the relation among the theoretical parameters, x_i, s_j, and Q, and the statistical parameters of Eq. (3.1) for each worker and each period. The model cannot be solved exactly. Thus, we use these relations to solve, by least squares, the moment equations that determine the relations between the statistical parameters and the model parameters. This yields

$$\mu = \frac{1}{4} \sum_{i=1}^{4} x_i,$$

where μ is the overall mean;

$$\alpha_1 = \frac{1}{4} \left(-3 s_m Q - s_n Q - \sum_{i=1}^{4} x_i \right) + x_1,$$

$$\alpha_2 = \frac{1}{4} \left(-s_m Q - 3 s_n Q - \sum_{i=1}^{4} x_i \right) + x_2,$$

$$\alpha_3 = \frac{1}{4} \left(s_m Q + 3 s_n Q - \sum_{i=1}^{4} x_i \right) + x_3,$$

$$\alpha_4 = \frac{1}{4} \left(3 s_m Q + s_n Q - \sum_{i=1}^{4} x_i \right) + x_4,$$

where the α_i are the four person effects;

$$(\phi_m, \gamma_m) = \left(\frac{(s_n - s_m) Q}{4}, 2 s_m Q \right)$$

and

Table 2
Matching model with homogeneous workers[a]

Individual	Wage period 1	Wage period 2
1	$y_{11} = \mu + \alpha_1 + \phi_m = w^*$	$y_{12} = \mu + \alpha_1 + \phi_m + \gamma_m = w^*$
2	$y_{21} = \mu + \alpha_2 + \phi_m = w^*$	
3	$y_{31} = \mu + \alpha_3 + \phi_m + \gamma_m = w^*$	
4		$y_{42} = \mu + \alpha_3 + \phi_m = w^*$
5	$y_{51} = \mu + \alpha_5 + \phi_n = w^* - (H/2)$	$y_{52} = \mu + \alpha_5 + \phi_n + \gamma_n = w^* + H$
6	$y_{61} = \mu + \alpha_6 + \phi_n + \gamma_n = w^* + H$	
7	$y_{71} = \mu + \alpha_7 + \phi_n = w^* - (H/2)$	$y_{72} = \mu + \alpha_7 + \phi_m = w^*$
8		$y_{82} = \mu + \alpha_8 + \phi_n = w^* - (H/2)$
9		$y_{92} = \mu + \alpha_9 + \phi_n = w^* - (H/2)$

[a] Individual 1 enters type m firm in period 1; individual 2 entered type m firm in period 0 (before period 1); individual 3 entered type n firm in period 0 (before period 1), had a negative matching outcome and left for a type m firm; individual 4 enters type m firm in period 2; individual 5 enters type n firm in period 1, has a positive matching outcome; individual 6 entered type n firm in period 0 (before period 1), had a positive matching outcome and remained in type n firm for period 1; individual 7 enters type n firm, has a negative matching outcome and leaves for a type m firm in period 2; individuals 8 and 9 enter type n firm in period 2.

$$(\phi_n, \gamma_n) = \left(\frac{(s_n - s_m)Q}{4}, -2s_n Q \right)$$

are respectively the type m and type n firms' policies.

4.4. An incentive model with unobserved individual heterogeneity

Following Kramarz and Rey (1995), consider workers who are heterogeneous with respect to a parameter $q \in [0, 1]$, which is known to them but not known to the firms. Suppose, furthermore, that there are two types of firms, m and n, that differ according to their technology, and that there are two time periods. At type m firms, workers are hired for one period and have a level of productivity y^* regardless of their q. At type n firms, workers are hired in period one, produce y regardless of their q, and choose an effort level, either 0 or E, to exert during on-the-job training. At the end of the first period, workers in firm type n take a formal, verifiable test. If worker q exerts effort E, the test is passed with probability q. Otherwise, the test is passed with probability kq, where $(0 < k < 1)$. At the beginning of the second period, the firm decides which workers to keep and the workers may leave on their own. Workers who exert effort E have a level of productivity in the second period of $y + \tau_q$ if they remain in a type n firm.

There are many type m firms and two type n firms, which compete for workers in both periods. Workers in type m firms always receive a wage w^*. Workers in type n firms are offered a wage contract $(w_1(q), w_2(q), b(q))$, where $w_1(q)$ is the first period wage, $w_2(q)$ is the second period wage, and $b(q)$ is the bonus paid to those who pass the test. In equilibrium

Table 3
Rent-splitting model[a]

Individual	Wage period 1	Wage period 2
1	$y_{11} = \mu + \alpha_1 + \phi_m = x_1 - s_m Q$	$y_{12} = \mu + \alpha_1 + \phi_m + \gamma_m = x_1 + s_m Q$
2	$y_{21} = \mu + \alpha_2 + \phi_m = x_2 - s_m Q$	$y_{22} = \mu + \alpha_2 + \phi_n = x_2 - s_n Q$
3	$y_{31} = \mu + \alpha_3 + \phi_n = x_3 + s_n Q$	$y_{32} = \mu + \alpha_3 + \phi_n + \gamma_n = x_3 - s_n Q$
4	$y_{41} = \mu + \alpha_4 + \phi_n = x_4 + s_n Q$	$y_{42} = \mu + \alpha_4 + \phi_m = x_2 + s_m Q$

[a] The quasi-rent is $-Q$ in type m firm in period 1 and q in period 2. The quasi-rent is q in type n firm in period 1 and $-Q$ in period 2. Individual 1 works in type m firm in both periods. Individual 2 works in type m firm in period 1 and in type n firm in period 2. Individual 3 works in type n firm in both periods. Individual 4 works in type n firm in period 1 and in type m firm in period 2.

all firms of both types make zero profits because of the competition to attract workers. Furthermore, if $y + \delta(y + \tau_q)$ is convex in q (δ being the rate of discount of future earnings), the equilibrium contract will be such that $w_1(q) = y - qb(q)$, $w_2(q) = y + \tau_q$, and

$$b(q) = \frac{d}{dq}(y + \delta(y + \tau_q)).$$

All workers with type q, $q \geq p$, will choose to enter one of the type n firms and will choose to exert effort E when $b(p) \geq E/(1 - k)p$.[7] To simplify the model, we suppose that $\tau_q = \pi(Q^2/2)$ and that parameters are such that $p = 1/3$. We also suppose that there are nine workers, three of whom are employed by type m firms and the remaining six work in type n firms.

Table 4 shows the wage of every individual in each firm and in each period in terms of the theoretical model, as well as in terms of the descriptive model. These equations can be solved in order to express each parameter of the descriptive model using parameters of the theoretical model. As in the rent-splitting model, the solution is not exact–we must use least squares to express the function of the theoretical parameters that is closest to the statistical parameter. To see why, consider the workers in type n firms. Individual 7 passed the test and, consequently, received a bonus. This result generates a seniority slope for individual 7. Individual 8 did not pass the test and therefore received no bonus in period 2. Thus individual 8 has a different seniority slope in the same firm. The statistical parameter γ_n measures the average seniority slope in the firm n. Thus, the resulting estimated seniority slope will be the least squares estimate of the average of the two slopes. We illustrate these solutions for all the statistical parameters below.

The overall mean, μ, is given by the following:

$$\mu = \frac{\delta\tau}{18} \sum_{i=4}^{7} q_i \left(1 - \frac{q_i}{2}\right) - \frac{\delta\tau}{18} \sum_{i=8}^{9} \frac{q_i^2}{2} + \frac{w^*}{3} + \frac{2y}{3}.$$

[7] Proofs of all these assertions can be found in Kramarz and Rey (1995).

The individual effects, α_i, $i = 4, 5, 6, 7$ are

$$\alpha_i = \frac{\delta\tau}{24}\left[\sum_{j=4,j\neq i}^{7} q_j\left(\frac{q_j}{2} - 2\right) + 5q_i(2 - q_i) + \sum_{j=8}^{9} q_j^2\right], \qquad i = 4, 5, 6, 7$$

and those for individual $i = 8, 9$ are

$$\alpha_i = \frac{\delta\tau}{24}\sum_{j=4,j\neq i}^{7} q_j(q_j - 2) + q_k^2 - 5q_i^2],$$

where $k = 8, 9$, $i \neq k$. Finally, the individual effects for $i = 1, 2, 3$ and the firm effects for m are not separately identifiable, since there are no movements between firms. We arbitrarily set

$$\alpha_i = 0, \qquad i = 1, 2, 3$$

for these individuals, implying a firm effect of

$$\phi_m = \frac{\delta\tau}{36}\left[\sum_{i=4}^{7} q_i(q_i - 2) + \sum_{i=8}^{9} q_i^2\right] + \frac{2w^*}{3} - \frac{2y}{3}.$$

For type n firms, we have

$$\phi_n = \frac{\delta\tau}{36}\left[\sum_{i=4}^{7} q_i(-5q_i - 2) - 5\sum_{i=8}^{9} q_i^2\right] - \frac{w^*}{3} + \frac{y}{3}.$$

The seniority slopes are

$$\gamma_m = 0$$

for firm m and

$$\gamma_n = \frac{\delta\tau}{12}\left[\sum_{i=4}^{7} q_i(3q_i + 2) + 3\sum_{i=8}^{9} q_i^2\right]$$

for firm n.

Notice that the α_i of the workers in the type n firm depend upon their hidden characteristics q_i as well as the characteristics of their fellow workers. Note also that the intercept in type m firms is larger than that of type n firms. Finally, as mentioned above, the seniority slope, γ_n, in type n firms is the least squares average of the career paths in the firm, depending on the success or failure of the test.

No single economic model is likely to explain a large, diverse labor markets like the ones studied in virtually all of the papers we discuss below. Nevertheless, it is important to keep in mind that it is not always possible to make a direct interpretation of the statistical parameters (for individuals or firms) in terms of simple economic parameters. In general,

Table 4
Incentive model with heterogeneous workers[a]

Individual	Wage period 1	Wage period 2
1	$y_{11} = \mu + \alpha_1 + \phi_m = w*$	$y_{12} = \mu + \alpha_1 + \phi_m + \gamma_m = w*$
2	$y_{21} = \mu + \alpha_2 + \phi_m = w*$	$y_{22} = \mu + \alpha_2 + \phi_m + \gamma_m = w*$
3	$y_{31} = \mu + \alpha_3 + \phi_m = w*$	$y_{32} = \mu + \alpha_3 + \phi_m + \gamma_m = w*$
4	$y_{41} = \mu + \alpha_4 + \phi_n = y - \delta\tau q_4^2$	$y_{42} = \mu + \alpha_4 + \phi_n + \gamma_n = y + (\delta\tau/2)q_4^2 + \delta\tau q_4$
5	$y_{51} = \mu + \alpha_5 + \phi_n = y - \delta\tau q_5^2$	$y_{52} = \mu + \alpha_5 + \phi_n + \gamma_n = y + (\delta\tau/2)q_5^2 + \delta\tau q_5$
6	$y_{61} = \mu + \alpha_6 + \phi_n = y - \delta\tau q_6^2$	$y_{62} = \mu + \alpha_6 + \phi_n + \gamma_n = y + (\delta\tau/2)q_6^2 + \delta\tau q_6$
7	$y_{71} = \mu + \alpha_7 + \phi_n = y - \delta\tau q_7^2$	$y_{72} = \mu + \alpha_7 + \phi_n + \gamma_n = y + (\delta\tau/2)q_7^2 + \delta\tau q_7$
8	$y_{81} = \mu + \alpha_8 + \phi_n = y - \delta\tau q_8^2$	$y_{82} = \mu + \alpha_8 + \phi_n + \gamma_n = y + (\delta\tau/2)q_8^2$
9	$y_{91} = \mu + \alpha_9 + \phi_n = y - \delta\tau q_9^2$	$y_{92} = \mu + \alpha_9 + \phi_n + \gamma_n = y + (\delta\tau/2)q_9^2$

[a] Individuals 1–3 belong to type m firm with q_i, $i = 1,2,3$ between 0 and 1/3, individuals 4–9 belong to type n firm with q_i, $i = 4$–9 above 1/3. Individuals 4–7 pass the test and receive the bonus; individuals 8 and 9 fail.

the interpretation of a given statistical parameter depends upon all the elements of the economic model under consideration.

5. New results with matched employer–employee datasets: compensation structure

5.1. Models with both person and firm effects

The papers we consider in this section all estimate a variant of the full model (3.1) and then use the results to consider related sets of questions about the links between individual heterogeneity, firm heterogeneity and observable wage differentials. We consider Abowd et al. (1999a,c), Bingley and Westergård-Nielsen (1996), Burgess et al. (1997), Goux and Maurin (1999), Finer (1997), Leonard and van Audenrode (1996, 1997), and Leonard et al. (1999). Belzil (1997) estimates the full model but is concerned primarily with worker mobility, see Section 7.5 for a discussion. Entorf et al. (1999) also estimate the full model, but their focus is on computer and wages, so this article is described in Section 7.4. Pacelli (1997) estimates the full model but is concerned primarily with seniority effects; see Section 5.3 for a discussion.

Abowd et al. (1999a) provide a very complete discussion of the statistical and economic issues surrounding estimation of Eq. (3.1) for log wage rates, much of which is summarized in Section 3. In their analysis of the French data from the DADS (see Table 1), they find that person effects, without controlling for non-time-varying personal characteristics, θ_i, or after such controls, α_i, account for 60–80% of the variation in log annual wage rates while the full firm effect (including a heterogeneous seniority effect discussed in Section 5.3) accounts for only 4–9%. The two effects are not highly correlated (0.09–0.26, depending on the statistical model).

Abowd et al. (1999a) use the estimated person and firm effects to address a number of other questions. They show that raw interindustrial wage differentials, as defined in Eq. (3.11), can be decomposed into a part due to the industry-average person effect and a part due to the industry-average firm effect. The decomposition is exact when there is no estimation error in the relevant industry averages and the large sample sizes from the French data essentially eliminate this estimation error. These authors find that, for France, 90% of the raw inter-industry wage differential is explained by the industry-average person effects and between 7% and 25% is explained by the industry-average firm effect (according to the method used, the average effects are correlated at the industry level). They perform the same decomposition for the firm-size wage effect in France and the results are that 90% of the firm-size wage differential is due to the firm-size-average person effect and 25–40% is due to the firm-size-average firm effect (again, according to the estimation method for the basic effects and allowing for correlation among the firm-size averages). These differentials are examined in more detail in Abowd and Kramarz (1996a, 1998a).

Abowd et al. (1999c) examine the same questions as Abowd et al. (1999a) using two American data sources (Washington State UI and NLSY '79, see Table 1). As in France, individual heterogeneity (θ_i or α_i) is the most important source of variation in log wage rates for these American data, explaining about twice as much of the variance as firm-level heterogeneity. Again, as in France and the other countries discussed below, there is only a weak correlation between person and firm effects. The results concerning inter-industry wage differentials are again similar to those for France. Industry-average person effects are very important in explaining the raw differentials. In contrast to the results for France, however, the industry-average firm effect is also important in explaining the raw differentials, although less important than person effects.

In a series of papers, Leonard and Van Audenrode (1996, 1997) and Leonard et al. (1999), consider the wage determination process using longitudinal matched Belgian data that are capable of identifying both firm and individual effects as defined in the full model (3.1). Because their focus is on wage and employment mobility and, in particular, the interaction of individual and firm wage components on the subsequent wage and mobility of individuals, they model these effects differently. These authors use log wage equations of the form

$$\ln w_{it} = x_{it}\beta_{tJ(i,t)} + \psi^{**}_{itJ(i,t)} + \varepsilon_{it}, \tag{5.1}$$

where the firm-specific component of the wage equation contains a firm-specific effect, $\psi^{*}_{tJ(i,t)}$, and a within-firm person effect $\psi^{**}_{itJ(i,t)} - \psi^{*}_{tJ(i,t)}$. In the first paper (1996), these authors fix $t = 1984$. They show that there is considerable heterogeneity in β (coefficients on functions of age, seniority and sex, education is not available in the data) and in $\psi^{**}_{i1984J(i,1984)}$. This heterogeneity is directly related to employee mobility. Higher composite firm effects, $\psi^{**}_{i1984J(i,1984)}$, are associated with lower mobility, a result interpreted as supporting the hypothesis that the component of $\psi^{**}_{i1984J(i,1984)}$ due to the average person effect within the firm, $\bar{\theta}_{J(i,1984)}$, is less important that the effect due to the firm, $\psi_{J(i,1984)}$. Steeper profiles as a function of age or seniority are associated with lower separation rates.

In the second paper (1997), these authors estimate Eq. (5.1) using samples of non-movers and movers. The resulting parameters have the interpretation

$$\psi^{**}_{ij} = \theta_i + \psi_j, \qquad \psi^*_j = \psi_j + \bar{\theta}_j \qquad\qquad (5.2)$$

$$\psi^{**}_{ij} - \psi^*_j = \theta_i - \bar{\theta}_j. \qquad\qquad (5.3)$$

They find that pay is persistent, by which they mean that the components of pay, ψ^*_j and $\psi^{**}_{ij} - \psi^*_j$ estimated on the observations prior to the move are significantly related to compensation on the next job. There are two possibilities for the persistence of the effect in Eq. (5.2). Either a substantial proportion of the effect is due to unmeasured human capital, an interpretation of $\bar{\theta}_j$, or there is non-random mobility, $\psi_{J(i,t)}$ is correlated with $\psi_{J(i,s)}$ when $J(i,t) \neq J(i,s)$ because of the mobility decisions of the firms and workers. There is only one explanation for the persistence of $\psi^{**}_{ij} - \psi^*_j$, as Eq. (5.3) shows, unmeasured human capital. Leonard and Van Audenrode conclude, after considering some additional mobility evidence, that the unmeasured general human capital hypothesis is the most reasonable explanation for their results.

In the third paper, with Leonard et al. (1999), they estimate a version of Eq. (5.1) with full heterogeneity in both the observable characteristics coefficients, β, and the combined person-firm effects, ψ^{**}_{ij}. They show that there is considerable persistence in these effects by examining autocorrelation matrices. Because they do not use the longitudinal nature of the data to distinguish person and firm effects, we discuss these results in Section 5.2. They also relate the heterogeneous coefficients to productivity measures in the firm, results which we discuss in Section 7.1.

Burgess et al. (1997) analyze data from the State of Maryland unemployment insurance system (see Table 1). These authors are primarily interested in studying the effect of reallocations of workers among firms on the resulting distribution of earnings. They present several models of mobility that depend upon detailed knowledge of the parameters in Eq. (3.1). They present two methods for estimating the model. In the first, they take a subset of 4000 of the workers with 10-quarter continuous employment histories. These individuals are used to select 2426 employers who ever employed these individuals. Then, they add all of the other employees of these 2426 firms to the analysis sample but only for the quarters in which these individuals worked for the 2426 employers originally selected. The procedure is equivalent to selecting a probability sample of employers with probabilities proportional to the distribution of long term employment at a point in time. The identification of the firm effects is with respect to this sampling frame, which is not representative of the same populations as the other articles discussed in this section. This sample is used to estimate a variant of Eq. (3.1) by full least squares. They also use the methods of Abowd et al. (1999a) for comparison. Regarding the basic structure of compensation, these authors report summary statistics on the correlation between firm and worker effects (small and negative) and on the correlation between successive firm effects for movers (essentially zero). The estimated firm and worker effects are used to study the effect of worker reallocation among firms on the distribution of earnings in the State of Maryland. The individual effects (θ_i, the person effect including permanent differences in observables like education) account for 55% of the variation in log wages. Firm effects account for 35%. The small negative correlation of the firm and worker effects is associated with relatively large changes in the distribution of earnings over the period.

Bingley and Westergard-Nielsen (1996) consider the determinants of log wages using the Danish IDA (see Table 1). They adopt the specification in Eq. (3.4) but they use a random effects, say $\theta^*_i + \phi^*_j + \psi^*_{ij}$, that permits correlation between the person and firm effects but assumes that both effects are orthogonal to all observable variables. The rationale for considering this form of model stems from the method that the authors use to sample the IDA data. They construct a 5% sample of workplaces (rather than employees) and, hence, there is no observed firm-to-firm mobility. Their person effect, θ^*_i, is, therefore, defined relative to the firm in which the worker is employed, rather than relative to the employee's entire measured work history. Their firm effect is defined in a manner that includes the average person effect within the firm ($\phi^*_j = \phi_j + \overline{\theta}_j$). Finally, their interaction measures the correlation within a firm of the random person and firm effects. Thus, the authors force a hierarchical structure on the person and firm effects (see Scheffé, 1959; Searle et al., 1992) implying that their effects relegate a part of the person effect, $\theta_i - \theta^*_i - \phi^*_j - \psi^*_{ij}$, to the model residual rather than to the person effect they estimate. Keeping these statistical qualifications in mind, they find that 38% of the variance (after controlling for x_{it}) is due to the person effect, 26% is due to the firm effect and 5.8% is due to the interaction. Their commentary indicates that the person and firm effects are of approximately equal magnitude and that the correlation between the two is not strong (due to the small contribution of the interaction term) but, because of the sample design, this conclusion is not strictly comparable to the other studies in this section.

Goux and Maurin (1999) use data from the French labor force survey (see Table 1) matched with employer information to study the influence of individual and firm factors on inter-industry wage differentials. Using Eq. (3.4), these authors estimate the underlying model, identifying about 1000 firm effects and about 10,000 individual effects (over two 3-year periods), by full least squares and by a correlated random effects method. They find that person effects are more important than firm effects as components of the variance of log wages. They also find that the correlation between firm and person effects is small and negative. Goux and Maurin use the results of their statistical analysis of the components of earnings to the decomposition of inter-industry wage differentials in Eq. (3.9), these authors find that the inter-industry differences in average person effects are the main source of inter-industry wage differences in France. The part of the inter-industry wage differential explained by the firm effects is very small. There is more firm effect variation within an industry than between industries.

Finer (1997) uses the matched employer–employee NLSY '79 data (see Table 1) to estimate Eq. (3.4) directly by least squares and by a variety of other methods proposed by Abowd et al. (1999a) and Abowd and Kramarz (1999). Their full least squares results show that the person effect θ_i, and its counterpart with observable non-time-varying effects removed, α_i, explain about 35% of the variation in log hourly wages, while the firm effect $\psi_{itJ(i,t)}$, which includes a heterogeneous seniority effect, accounts for 5% of the variation. The correlation between the two effects is -0.049.

5.2. Models with firm effects only

In this type of work, analysts estimate a variant of Eq. (3.1) in which person fixed-effects, θ, are absent. Thus, the estimated firm effect is the sum of the true firm effect, ψ, and the firm-average of the persons effects, appropriately corrected for correlation between personal characteristics and person effects. The evidence discussed in the previous section for Danish, French, and American data, suggests that the correlation between the person effects and the individual characteristics causes a large omitted variable bias and prevents a clean interpretation of the studies discussed in this section. The introduction of plant or firm effects does not help to capture a lot of the correlation between individual effects and personal characteristics because of the low correlation between person and firm effects, again, as shown in all estimated equations discussed in the subsection above.

The papers considered in this subsection use data from a variety of countries. Two of them use French data (Kramarz et al., 1996; Pelé, 1997), two use American data (Groshen, 1991a; Troske, 1999), one uses both American and French data (Abowd et al., 1998b), one uses Belgian data (Leonard et al., 1999), one uses Portuguese data (Cardoso, 1997), and one uses German data (Stephan, 1998).

The work of Groshen (1991a, in particular, and surveyed in 1996) is an important precursor to the papers that use matched employer–employee data discussed in this section. Groshen uses employer-based salary survey data to study the role of employer effects on wages. Employer-based salary surveys contain information about the participating firms. Generally, however, the only characteristic of the employer used in the statistical analysis is the identity. Estimating Eq. (3.1) with the person effects replaced by occupation gives Groshen's primary result, which is that establishment effects are a very significant component of compensation. The papers discussed in this section try to link this finding to basic characteristics of the establishment or firm.

Kramarz et al. (1996) first document the increasing inequality in France between 1986 and 1992, the dates at which the ESS was performed. A large part of this increasing dispersion is due to firm-specific compensation policies as measured by the firm effects. Indeed, the standard deviation of this firm effect increased by almost 30% between the two dates. On the other hand, the observable characteristics explain a smaller fraction of the variance in 1992 than in 1986. Furthermore, the authors compute a specialization index proposed by Kremer and Maskin (1996) to examine whether workers with the same observed characteristics are employed increasingly in the same firms. These indices grow strongly between 1986 and 1992, implying that workers are increasingly employed in firms with other similar workers. Another important feature, also found in Cardoso (1997), is the decreasing importance of returns to seniority: the wage-setting rules rely more on experience and less on seniority.

For each firm, the authors estimate the fixed firm effects. These estimates are then used in a second set of regressions that tries to explain the level and the growth of firm-effects for all firms that are present in 1986 or 1992. In all these regressions, the establishment or firm-level variables used as independent variables are the size, the existence of a firm-level collective agreement, existence of an industry-level collective bargaining agreement, the proportion of workers employed at different skill-levels, the existence and number of shifts (in level at each date for the first two regressions and in difference (1992 minus 1986) for the growth regression). Indeed, most variables matter both in 1986 and 1992, with the size of the establishment, the proportion of highly skilled workers, and the existence of 4 or 5 shifts being the most important. Interestingly, these same variables are also best (positively) correlated the growth of the fixed-effects between 1986 and 1992. Finally, in order to investigate the firm by firm compensation policies, the authors concentrate on a subsample of 132 establishments or firms for which they have a sufficient number of observations both in 1986 and 1992 and perform firm by firm wage equations for both dates. They use the estimated coefficients (on experience, measured as the experience prior to entry in the firm, and seniority) to examine how they relate one to the other as well as their correlation with mean experience and seniority at the firm. They show that the firm-specific intercept is negatively correlated to the seniority coefficient, a feature also found in Abowd et al. (1999a). They also find that the seniority coefficient is also negatively related to the mean seniority; high-seniority firms do not reward seniority very highly. Finally, the authors show that the evolution of the mean seniority at the firm (which increased by 3 years between 1986 and 1992) is negatively correlated to evolution in the mean experience (which only slightly increased) which shows that firms reduced drastically their hiring of young workers and separated mostly from workers with little seniority.

Cardoso (1997) used a very similar dataset (described above) to examine related issues. More specifically, she tried to understand the origin of the increase in wage inequality in Portugal, an increase that started between 1983 and 1986, a timing that is identical to what was observed for France (Kramarz et al., 1996). In addition, she showed that most of this increasing inequality occurred within firms rather than between firms. Therefore, she tried to identify the dimensions along which this within-firm inequality developed. First, she computed a specialization index as in Kramarz et al. but, in contrast with what was found for France, specialization decreased in Portugal between 1983 and 1992, i.e., workers with different attributes have been working more and more together. Then, the author estimate a hierarchical model of the following form:

$$y_j = X_j \beta_j + e_j,$$

where y_j is a $(n_j \times 1)$ vector with n_j being the size of the employing firm, where X_j is a $(n_j \times K)$ matrix of workers observables, β_j is the $(K \times 1)$ vector of coefficients, and e_j is the $(n_j \times 1)$ statistical residual vector which is assumed to be distributed $N(0, \sigma^2 I_{n_j})$ with I_k being the identity matrix of size k. Furthermore, each coefficient β_j is modelled as the sum of a fixed component, β_0, and a random component, α_j, normally distributed with zero mean, Γ variance matrix, and independent of e_j.

The author estimated this model both in 1983 and in 1992. She displayed the distribution of these coefficients at both dates for the following variables: experience, tenure, tenure smaller than 1 year, sex, and schooling. She also tested the equality of the two distributions (using a Kolmogorov–Smirnov test). The main features that emerge from this statistical analysis are the following. Apart from experience, all other returns changed between 1983 and 1992. In particular, the gender gap increased, returns to schooling increased very strongly, while returns to tenure decreased. Such conclusions are directly related to the process of modernization that was taking place during this period, and still is, in the Portuguese economy.

Troske (1999) examines the employer size-wage premium using the WECD (see Table 1). As in most earnings function, the author starts by estimating the following equation

$$\ln w_i = X_i \beta + Z_{j(i)} \gamma + u_i,$$

where X_i is a vector of individual i's characteristics, $Z_{j(i)}$ is a vector of the employer j of individual i's characteristics, and u_i is a residual term. Among those employer characteristics, Troske uses the logarithm of the establishment employment as well as the logarithm of the firm employment. First, he shows that all results obtained using the WECD, without employers characteristics, are identical to those obtained using the 1990 SDF (Sample Detail File, from the Census, used to construct the WECD). Then, Troske shows that the size of the employing establishment or firm generates large returns (for instance, workers in plants with log employment one standard deviation above mean log employment receive 13% higher wages than workers in plants with log employment one standard deviation below mean log employment, the equivalent number for firms is 11%). After having established these basic facts, the author tries to find potential explanations for these large returns. First, to check if these returns come from the fact that large firms hire more skilled labor than other firms, he introduces measures of skills of the work force in the above regression. More specifically, the added variables are the mean years of potential experience of workers in the plant, the percentage of workers who are scientists, engineers, or technical workers, the percentage of workers who have some post-secondary education (but no college degree), and the percentage of workers with at least a college degree. The returns to size of the establishment fall from 13% (see above) to 11%, and from 11% to 9%. Second, the author examines the capital-skill complementarity hypothesis by introducing the capital–labor ratio of the plant. Once the skills of the work force variables are in the equation, the introduction of the capital–labor ratio reduces the coefficient of the firm-size variable (yielding a 6% premium). But, the introduction of this capital–labor ratio does not reduce the establishment size-wage premium. Then, the plant age is shown to be uncorrelated to the wage, once workers' characteristics are controlled for. To assess the rent-sharing hypothesis as an explanation of the firm-size wage premium, Troske uses the proportion of the total value of a seven-digit product produced by the plant and an Herfindahl index of concentration computed at the primary five-digit product of the plant. None of these variables affect the firm-size wage premium. The same diagnostic applies to measures of the managerial skills at the plant, the proportion of supervisors at the plant (as a measure of the cost of monitoring). Finally, the inclusion of the logarithm of total new investment in computers (in 1987) per employee adds no information as soon as the size and the labor–capital ratio are present in the regression.

Troske's conclusion is consistent with the results reported by Abowd et al. (1998b). Large employers appear to employ better workers. Most establishment or firm-level variables do not explain a large fraction of the firm-size wage premium.

Stephan (1998) uses a German dataset to examine similar questions to those we just analyzed. This dataset, the GLS (see Table 1), has matched employer–employee information for two cross-sections (1990 and 1995) of firms active in Lower Saxony, one of the largest German Länder. Each wave contains approximately 65,000 employees and 1500 firms. The sampling frame is such that for small firms all employees are included in the data while less than 10% of employees are in firms with 1000 employees or more. In addition to sex, tenure, age, contractual and effective working hours, shift or night work, and wages (with information on overtime, taxes and social security contributions) reported directly by the firm, schooling and occupation come from social insurance data, matched to this survey by the German statistical office. Indeed, the structure of the dataset is very similar to the French ESS. Stephan uses the hourly wage rate excluding overtime pay as the dependent variable. For blue-collar workers, between-plant dispersion accounts for a large fraction of the variance in wages (80% for females but less so for males) while this is the reverse for white-collar workers (60% for males and 40% for females). Then, Stephan notes that the inclusion of fixed-effects modifies the estimated coefficients in wage regressions. For firms with more than one sampled worker, the author computes establishment fixed-effects from the first-stage regressions for the above four groups of workers. Stephan finds that the dispersion of these fixed-effects is not different from those observed in other countries and that the standard deviation of these fixed-effects has increased between 1990 and 1995. Since Stephan estimates at most four effects per firm, it becomes possible to look at their correlation. He finds positive correlation between these effects. Finally, Stephan also performs firm by firm regressions and analyzes correlations between various estimated coefficients. His results show that returns to age and returns to tenure are negatively correlated. The author's results give the impression that pay determination in Germany does not differ widely from what is observed in other countries including the United States.

Leonard et al. (1999) use a Belgian dataset (see Table 1) to examine productivity in relation to firm compensation policy. To do that, they start their analysis by performing the same kind of regressions as done by Kramarz et al. (1996) and Stephan (1998)-firm by firm regressions of individual wages on observed characteristics in each year of their sample period. This results in 695 (number of firms) times 8 (years) of firm-specific estimates of a constant, age profiles, sex differentials, and white-collar/blue-collar differentials. They find that, as in all other countries, pay dispersion between and within-firms has increased over the period. By examining correlations across time of the estimated coefficients, as in Kramarz et al., they find evidence of large persistence of pay policies (see Section 5.2). These pay policies differ widely from firm to firm.

Chennouf et al. (1997) estimate the same type of equation using matched worker-firm data for a sample of establishments of the Algiers region (see Table 1). As in Cardoso (1997), the authors try to control for the group effects when estimating Mincer's model that includes both years of education and potential experience. Their results show that returns to education decrease when firm-effects are introduced.

Abowd et al. (1998b) compare the relative importance of employer and employee effects in compensation in France and in the United-States. For the US, they use the 1990 WECD while, for France, they use the ESS for 1986 and 1992. The basic statistical model used throughout the paper is identical to the one described in the statistical section in which the wage is regressed on worker's characteristics and a firm (or establishment) specific constant as follows:

$$\ln w_{it} = X_{it}\beta + \phi_{j(i,t)} + \varepsilon_{it}.$$

Then, the authors use the estimates to decompose the average wage at the firm into a part due to the average observed characteristics of the workers employed at the firm and a part due to the firm-effects, $\phi_{j(i,t)}$, to analyze the impact of compensation structure on firm's productivity and profitability.

The wage equations give the following results. First, coefficients are not very dissimilar across countries. A first noticeable difference is the shape of returns to experience which are steeper and never turn down in the US whereas the French profile peaks at 34 years of potential experience. A second interesting difference are the respective R^2 which are larger in France (around 0.80) than in the US (around 0.60). Therefore, firm fixed-effects obviously explain a larger fraction of wages in France than in the US.

Then, the authors present a table of correlation among the components of individual compensation. Strikingly, the correlation structure is very similar in the two countries. In particular, individual characteristics and firm fixed-effects are comparable in terms of their contribution to the variation of annual wages (approximately from 0.6 to 0.7) with an inter-correlation of 0.25 in the two countries. None of the above results are inconsistent with those of Abowd et al. (1999a,c) since the firm fixed-effect as estimated by Abowd et al. (1998b) are a mixture of individual and firm fixed-effects (see Eqs. (3.4) and (3.7)).

Finally, the authors estimate the impact of the compensation structure on firm's productivity and profits. They show that firms who employ workers with higher predicted wage rates (based on observed characteristics) are more productive (both in terms of log value-added per employee and of log sales per employee) in the two countries. The same is true for firms with higher fixed-effects. However, none of these two components have an impact on profitability.

This study confirms the above findings: the structure of compensation is very similar across countries. In addition, the effects of the compensation structure on firm outcomes appear roughly identical in two apparently different countries, France and the US.

Pelé (1997) also uses the French ESS to examine the effect on compensation of the coexistence of different methods of pay in the same firm for the same detailed occupation. This type of dataset, by matching firm and workers, enables him to compare within a firm and within an occupation (in a 4-digit classification) workers paid under time-rates or piece-rate (measured under different rules). There has been a great body of literature dealing with the choice of method of pay and the wage differentials due to various ways of payment. For example, Seiler (1984) showed that incentive workers receive more disperse and higher earnings than time workers. Brown (1992) found that piece-rate workers receive higher earnings than time-rate workers but when compensation is linked to merit (an evaluation by supervisors), it is lower than time-rate.

The data come from the Wage Structure Survey (Enquête Structure des Salaires) carried out by INSEE in 1986 (see above). For each worker, the age, seniority in the firm, sex, method of pay, conditions of work (especially work in shifts), occupation are used as control variables in the wage equation. Besides, for each firm or establishment, a the identification number is used to identify workers employed at the same establishment or firm. Four methods of pay are possible. The first one is time-rate, which consists in a salary. The three other ones are bonus payments. The bonus is based either on individual output, or on collective output or on both kinds of output. A worker can receive a bonus of exclusively one of those three types. Pelé used the total wage in October 1986, the amount and the type of the bonus (if it is the case) and the payment for overtime. He corrected for differences in hours worked in order to compare wages for a same duration (which is equivalent to use an hourly wage). To estimate the wage equation, he added indicator variables for each bonus method. To control for the exact occupation in the firm, Pelé introduced an indicator for each 4-digit occupation within each firm or establishment. Only those couples (occupation-establishment) with two workers employed in the same occupation within the same establishment under different methods of pay contribute to the identification of the coefficients of the bonus methods variables. Therefore, the occupa-tion-establishment fixed-effects are nested within the pure establishment fixed-effects.

The results are the following. First, he found that bonus payments lead to higher compensation, result which is consistent with a selection of workers among the different payment schemes. It is profitable to give incentives through a bonus payment only to the best workers. But beyond this first conclusion, Pelé also showed that workers who get a bonus also receive a higher base wage, when comparing within homogeneous groups of workers of the same occupation in the same firm. High French minimum wages may partly explain such an observation, by preventing firms to set a low value to the base wage.

Other recent papers that include employer effects in wage equations and use matched data to study the resulting estimates include Bronars et al. (1999) and Vainiomäki (1999).

5.3. Models of the wage-seniority relation

How large are returns to seniority? This question has generated many important articles in the last 20 years. Some authors argue that returns to seniority are large and pervasive (on the order of 5% a year) while others find these returns to be small.

Although Topel and Ward's data were based on a matched employee–employer dataset, the LEED file constructed from the Social Security reports by employers, these authors did not use this aspect of their file. Indeed, they restricted their initial sample of over one million individuals to a final sample of 872 persons. Therefore, they lost the potential of looking at the inter-firm variability in the returns to seniority.

The possibility that returns to seniority might vary between firms has only been examined recently. Abowd et al. (1999a) allow for such variation in an exogenous mobility framework using French data. Margolis (1996) reexamines Topel's two stage estimator on the same French dataset. At least five other papers examine this issue of firm-specific compensation policies, two on US data (Bronars and Famulari, 1997; Finer, 1997), two on Norwegian data (Barth, 1997; Barth and Dale-Olsen, 1999), one on Italian data (Pacelli, 1997), and one on Portuguese data (Cardoso, 1997). Another paper (Dustmann and Meghir, 1997), based on German data, allows for the possibility of firm-specific returns to tenure even though the authors do not introduce firm fixed effects.

Abowd et al. (1999a) provide different estimation techniques for firm-specific returns to seniority. These different estimation methods (see above for brief description) provide estimates that differ in their levels but which are largely correlated across methods.

The consistent methodology, which uses first differences for workers who do not move between two consecutive years, gives the largest estimates and, indeed, the closest to the OLS results. Notice however that this methodology assumes that mobility is exogenous. All other techniques examined in this paper give returns to seniority that are close to zero. But all methodologies show that there is considerable between-firm variation in these returns. And, furthermore, all of these estimated firm-specific returns are strongly correlated across estimation techniques. Unfortunately, these authors do not examine the same question when mobility is endogenous.

Margolis (1996) tries to address this issue by allowing firm-specific compensation policies to vary by entry-cohort (the cohort of entry refers to entry in the firm). The data he uses are identical to Abowd et al. (1999a). Margolis compares OLS estimates other techniques. First, he examines on French data the results using Topel's two-stage techniques. He shows that based on French data, the returns to tenure are much lower than those estimated by Topel, 2% against 5% using US data. But, Margolis also notes that unobserved heterogeneity may well bias these results. Hence, he goes one step ahead of Abowd et al. (1999a) by introducing within-firm cohort-effects. Although the value of the mean value of the estimated seniority slopes is close to zero, Margolis (1996) finds even more variance in the returns to seniority than previously found in Abowd et al. (1999b).

Bronars and Famulari (1997) examine similar questions use a US dataset, the WCP (see Table 1), matching roughly 1700 workers and 241 firms. In addition, for 736 workers employed in 130 establishments, retrospective information on the starting pay is available. That allows the authors, first, to estimate returns to seniority based on a cross-section equation that includes firm or establishment fixed-effects. Then, they look at within-firm wage growth with, once more, establishment fixed-effects. Hence, the first estimates are directly comparable to the OLS with firm fixed-effects given in Abowd et al. (1999a) while the second are also directly comparable to the consistent estimates from the same authors.

At least for men, the authors find that estimated returns to tenure are roughly equal to 1% a year and approximately invariant across estimation techniques. This result does not hold for women. In addition, women's wage growth is larger than man's wage growth. This result, consistent with Abowd et al.'s (1999a) findings, demonstrates that exogenous mobility is not a very reasonable assumption and that all these estimated returns to seniority are likely to be biased upwards. Finally, Bronars and Famulari find important variation across firms in returns to tenure; standard deviation of the estimated firm-specific slopes is equal to 0.022, consistent with the French estimates giving a larger number based on a much greater number of firms.

Barth (1997) estimates related coefficients for Norway. He uses a cross-section of 2321 workers employed in 549 firms. His base equation is identical to the one estimated by Bronars and Famulari (1997). As found by Abowd et al. as well as Bronars and Famulari, the estimated coefficients are identical across estimation techniques, i.e., OLS, firm random effects, and firm fixed-effects. One additional year of seniority adds approximately 0.3–0.4% to the individual's wage, a much lower number than the one found in the US or in France. Interestingly, Barth finds no evidence of correlation between seniority and firm fixed-effects while there is a positive correlation between education or age and these fixed-effects. These final results are consistent with those given in Kramarz et al. (1996) (see Section 5.2). Barth and Dale-Olsen (1999) examine the relation between wage-seniority profiles and worker turnover using a heterogeneous firm effect model as in Eq. (3.2). They show that employee lower turnover is associated with having higher initial wages (ϕ_j) and higher slopes (γ_j).

Cardoso (1997) examines identical issues with the same type of dataset, i.e., cross-sections of matched employer–employee data (see Section 5.2 for other results using the same dataset). Using a multilevel model with the associated estimation method, the author confirms the heterogeneity of the returns to seniority across firms. Most estimated returns are inferior to 1%. She also estimates the distribution of firm-specific starting wages (hence, the firm-specific component of wage is either this latter part for the entrants or the former part for those with 1 year or more seniority), negative indeed for most of the distribution. Notice once more that these results are not widely different from those estimated in all other European countries.

The technique used in Dustmann and Meghir (1997) for Germany is completely different. Even though their data is based on Social Security reports of firms, these authors do not have full access to the matched employer–employee component of their data source. But, the principle of their technique – instrumental variables – is directly applicable and conceived for matched employer–employee data.[8] Their instruments are firm closure and information on the job held two jobs ago (available only for workers with at least three jobs in their dataset). Indeed, allowing for heterogeneous returns across firms yield surprisingly high estimates (which jump from 4.5% to 9%), casting some doubt on these exact

---

[8] That they should eventually obtain.

values based on approximate data, for instance sector-specific firm closures instead of firm-specific firm closure, on a selected sample of young apprentices, but showing the fruitfulness of the general approach.

Finer (1997) uses the same models as Abowd et al. (1999a). He finds that the average return to 1 year of additional seniority is 5% for the first 5 years and zero thereafter in the NLSY '79 data. The standard deviation of the estimated seniority coefficient is of the same order of magnitude, which indicates that in this younger sample there is still considerable heterogeneity in the return to seniority.

Pacelli (1997) examines identical issues using a longitudinal sample of 1737 young Italian workers under a period of 5 years with information on the employing firm constructed from the R&P dataset (see Table 1). The methodology adopted resembles Topel and Ward's. All estimates show that returns to seniority are, once more, smaller in Europe than in the US, even when controlling for firm-specific variables in a wage growth equation (see also Entorf and Kramarz, 1999, for similar results), but still significant.

6. New results with matched employer–employee datasets: wage and employment mobility

In this section we consider models of the changes in wage rates and employment that have been estimated using matched employer–employee data. All of the papers make use of large longitudinal administrative data sources that are dynamically representative of the target populations.

Jacobson et al. (1993) study the earnings losses of displaced workers in the State of Pennsylvania. A 5% random sample of the quarterly earnings reports from the State's unemployment insurance tax records for the period from 1974 to 1986 were matched to employer data from the State's ES-202 files, which are also administrative data from the unemployment insurance system. These authors define large involuntary worker displacements using the matched data. In particular, using the matched information about the employer, these authors are able to define a mass-layoff displacement, where there is a large reduction in the employment of the firm surrounding the displacement, and a non-mass-layoff displacement. They find that the earnings losses for mass-layoff displacements are very large: initially 25% of predisplacement earnings, rapid recovery during the first two post-displacement years to losses of around 15% of predisplacement earnings, followed by many years of stable earnings with no further recovery. The non-mass-layoff displacement sample has an initial loss of about 15% followed by a rapid recovery during the 2 years following displacement in which the full earnings loss is recovered. For all of the comparisons it is possible to use the earnings histories of workers who do not suffer displacements as the comparison group, including the possibility of comparing workers who were not displaced during the mass layoff, but who worked for the firm that incurred the mass layoff, with those who were displaced. Using this information, these authors find that individuals who are going to suffer a mass layoff also experience an earnings decline in the 3 years prior to the mass-layoff displacement. Workers who are going to be displaced in a non-mass-layoff displacements do not experience a predisplacement earnings decline.

Topel and Ward (1992) use the quarterly LEED data for 1957 to 1972 (see Table 1) to study the early career wage and employment mobility of young male workers. Although these authors use the employer identifying information only to identify the within-job wage growth, they are among the very few researchers to have used the LEED data in this manner. They find that the typical young male worker holds seven full-time job during his first 10 years in the labor force. Within job wage growth is one-third of total wage growth over this period and between job wage growth accounts for the remainder. Wages grow at an annual rate of 11%. Although the authors do not directly implement Eq. (3.1), their basic model is consistent with this formulation and their method for identifying within and between job wage growth.

Burgess et al. (1997, 1999) examine earnings dispersion using a decomposition similar to those described previously. They first decompose wages into a person fixed-effect, a firm fixed effect, a time trend, an unemployment effect, and a residual. Then, they examine the share of earnings dispersion that can be attributed to the different components. In particular, they focus on the share attributed to individual fixed-effects, the share attributed to establishment fixed-effects, the share due to the correlation between individual and firm fixed-effects, and, finally, the residual unexplained variance. Using a sample and a technique described above, they estimate individual and establishment fixed-effects for 2000 individuals and their 1432 employers based on a dataset with more than 2,700,000 quarterly observations. Their estimates show that 55% of the variance in log wages can be attributed to individual heterogeneity while firm-effects account for 35% and the correlation between person and firm effects is virtually nil. Then, they try to assess the share in the increased earnings dispersion over the 1980s that can be attributed to reshuffling of jobs between and within employers. Their first estimates seem to support the idea that, indeed, reallocation of jobs across firms was an important source of increase in the dispersion of wages under the sample period.

Abowd et al. (1998a) examine job and wage mobility in France and in the US using comparable matched employee–employer panel datasets for both countries. Most of their analysis focuses on employment durations and wage changes both between and within firms. The employment spells can be constructed because of the matched nature of the data; the employer identifier is a crucial component when constructing the individual careers across time and firms. Even though the analysis is still preliminary, the authors findings show that, in contrast with the usual view that the French labor market is inflexible i.e., little employment mobility and considerable real wage stability, in France there is substantial employment mobility, although the most mobile groups in France are not the same as those in the United States, and there is substantial real wage mobility on changes of employers.

Margolis (1998) uses several sources of matched employer–employee data (the DADS, BIC and BRN) to consider the effect of firm closure on workers in France. He find that a st 60%) of workers displaced by firm closure find new jobs without interruption in their employment histories. In addition, falling into none-s to be a relatively transitory phenomenon for displaced workers, with finding a new job within the year following displacement and essen-tially all of them being reemployed 6 years after displacement. Workers who separate for reasons other than firm closure, on the other hand, have a much harder time, with 25% still without a job 6 years after separation. Wage changes for displaced workers in France reflect a major difference between those who find new jobs quickly and those who do not, with a wage penalty of over 20 percentage points for displaced workers who do not find new jobs in the year following their separation. The pre-separation pattern of wages shows a drop in the year preceding separation. Controlling for seniority differences causes wages for displaced workers to be consistently below those of continuously employed workers, even in the pre-separation period, and the penalty for finding a job slowly drops to under 10%.

7. New results with matched employer–employee datasets: firm outcomes and worker characteristics

7.1. Productivity

In this subsection we consider studies that relate individual characteristics of the employ-ees and of their compensation to the productivity of the enterprise or establishment. The employer-level measures of productivity come either from direct measures of production or value-added per worker or from full production function specifications.

Hellerstein et al. (1996) use the WECD (see Table 1) to study the relative productivity of employee characteristics, estimated directly from a production function, that they compare to the relative pay earned by these different characteristics, estimated directly from a wage equation. They use a variety of production function specifications to capture the marginal productivity associated with employee characteristics like sex, race, marital status, age, and education. They use standard cross-sectional wage equations (estimated for the US census year 1990, which is the only year of individual data available in the WECD) to capture the market compensation associated with these factors. The find that workers who have ever been married are paid more than never-married workers and that there is a corresponding productivity difference of the same magnitude. On the other hand, prime-age workers (35–54) are as productive as younger workers but earn a wage premium. Wage premia for older workers (55–64) exceed all estimated productivity premia for this group. The same technique is used to conclude that wage differentials unfavorable to blacks are also associated with productivity differentials of the same magnitude. Wage differentials favoring men are not associated with productivity differ-entials of the same magnitude. Bayard et al. (1999) extend the analysis of Hellerstein et al.

(1996, 1997) to include non-manufacturing establishments using the NWECD (see Table 1). Their results are discussed below under sex segregation in the workplace.

Haegeland and Klette (1999) estimate similar productivity and wage models using Norwegian data. They find that education, except those with the lowest education, premia are directly and appropriately related to productivity differentials. Workers with highest experience have wage premia that exceed their productivity while the opposite is true for those in lower experience categories. The lower wages of females correspond to productivity differences of equal size.

Hayami and Abe (1998) use the Japanese matched data to estimate a full set of labor demand equations for age and sex categories for retail trade to study the deregulation of this labor market and the resulting effects on wages, employment and productivity.

Abowd et al. (1999a) develop a method for relating the firm effect, ψ_j, and the average value of the person effects (θ_j and its components $\bar{\alpha}_j$ and $\bar{u}_j\eta$) to firm-level productivity, profitability and factor use. The profitability results are discussed in Section 7.1. To measure productivity, they use firm-level value-added and sales per worker, averaged over the period 1978–1988. They find that all firm-level compensation components related to personal and enterprise heterogeneity are positively related to both productivity measures.

Abowd et al. (1998b), also take the firm effects from their analysis of compensation (see Section 5.2) and relate these to value-added and sales per worker for both the US and France firm effects inclusive of the average value of person effects within the firm, $\psi_j + \bar{\alpha}_j$, are positively related to the productivity measures.

Finer (1997) estimates an equation relating productivity, measured as ln(sales/employee), to the components of compensation structure. He finds that all compensation structure components are strongly related to sales/employee.

Using the estimated coefficients of firm by firm regressions across time, Leonard et al. (1999) examine the relation between firm-specific compensation policies and productivity (measured by value-added per worker). Since they have multiple estimates of the same coefficient for the same firm but different years, these authors are able to estimate this relation with fixed firm effects. They find that firms with high wage levels (i.e., the firm-specific constant of the firm by firm regression), returns to age, white-collar pay premium, or male pay premium also have high productivity.

7.2. Productivity and seniority

Kramarz and Roux (1998) use the DADS for the period 1976–1995 to examine the relationship between within-firm seniority structure and firm performance. Hence, these authors provide one of the first analysis of the impact of hiring and separations decisions on firm-specific outcomes such as productivity or profitability as well as employment or capital structures.

They first measure the seniority at the end of all job spells (either censored or non-censored). Then, these seniorities are aggregated at the firm-level for three subperiods

(1977–1982, 1983–1988, 1989–1994) in order to compute firm-specific descriptive statistics of the seniority structure. Using the Echantillon d'Entreprises (see Table 1) that gives information on balance-sheet, skill structure, and employment, Kramarz and Roux estimate various equations relating tenure structure and firm performance. The use of three subperiods allows these authors to perform instrumental variable techniques, in particular, they estimate their coefficients with equations in first difference (subperiod 3 minus subperiod 2) instrumented by the levels of subperiod 1. Their results show that a low turnover rate is associated with higher productivity but a high turnover rate slightly favors profitability. In addition, an increase in the within-firm variance of the seniority of the stayers (i.e., those workers who stay employed at the firm until the end of the subperiod, and, therefore, have censored spells) boosts profitability. Finally, capital, firm size, and the capital–labor ratio are all positively related to low turnover rates.

7.3. Profits

Four papers consider the relation between profits and firm-specific compensation or hiring and separation policies using matched employer–employee data. In all cases, the profit measure is operating income divided by total assets. Two papers focus on France (Kramarz and Roux, 1998; Abowd et al., 1999a), one uses American data (Finer, 1997), and one compares the French and the American case (Abowd et al., 1998b). The equation relating firm level profits, π_j, to firm level compensation policies, ψ_j and $\bar{\theta}_j$, and other firm level measures, z_j, is given by

$$\pi_j = z_j \gamma + \alpha \psi_j + \beta \bar{\theta}_j + \varepsilon_j. \tag{7.1}$$

This equation is estimated directly in Abowd et al. (1999a) and Finer (1997) while Abowd et al. (1998b) cannot separate person from firm-effects since they use cross-sections (WECD and ESS for the US and France, respectively). Kramarz and Roux replace ψ_j and θ_j by the within-firm seniority structure (see Section 5.3).

Abowd et al. find that those firms with higher wages because of observed characteristics, $\bar{x}_j \beta$ (in z_j), or with a larger firm effect, ψ_j, (thus, high-wage firms) are more profitable, while those employing high-wage workers (large values of $\bar{\theta}_j$) are not. Finer finds no effects on profits, although his data are from a sample representative of younger workers. Interestingly, Abowd et al. (1998b) find no effect for the same equation as soon as ψ_j and θ_j are confounded, a result which is fully consistent with the previous one. Finally, Kramarz and Roux find that a higher turnover rate as well as a larger variance of within-firm seniority tend to induce a larger profitability.

7.4. New technologies

We know that changes in the structure of wages were dramatic along the 1980s in the US while unemployment increased in Western Europe. Many analysts have blamed the same technical shocks that affected differentially the two continents. The role of computers has been central in the indictment, in particular after Krueger's seminal work (Krueger, 1993) that showed that computer users were better paid than non-users. On both sides of the Atlantic, researchers have tried to understand the nature of the computer wage premium. Two sets of studies, one for the US and one for France, are of particular interest for us since they use matched employee–employer datasets. They both demonstrate that new technology (NT) workers were better paid than non-users even before using NT (Entorf and Kramarz, 1997, 1999; Entorf et al., 1999) or that NT firms employed high-wage workers even before implementing NT (Doms et al., 1997).

Doms et al. (1997) use the WECD (see Table 1) in conjunction with the 1988 Survey of Manufacturing Technologies (SMT) among many data sources. The 1988 SMT contains plant-level information on NT use in American manufacturing plants. The techniques surveyed are production technologies such as robots, computer-aided design (CAD), lasers, networks, automatic systems, or computers used on the factory floor. To assess the technical development of the plant, the authors use the count of different techniques used at the plant. The SMT is matched to the WECD. This allows Doms et al. to examine the relation between the spread of techniques and education or the occupational mix of the work force. To perform this analysis, since they do not know if individual workers use a given technique, they create various plant-level measures of the educational or occupational structures. Results demonstrate that plants that use more advanced technologies employ a more educated or a more skilled work force. Using the same framework, they examine the relation between wages, once more averaged at the plant-level, and NT. The analysis is performed for different subgroups (production workers, managers and professionals, other non-production workers) and include average characteristics of the group under consideration together with plant-level employment and capital–labor ratio. These results show that, as in Krueger (1993), technology use is associated with a premium even after inclusion of workers characteristics. Then, using the LRD and the 1993 SMT, a longitudinal analysis demonstrates that the most technology advanced plants paid their workers higher wages prior to adoption of NT.

The same pattern emerges from the three studies performed on French matched employee–employer data. However, since the datasets used in these studies are built from the supplements on NT of the1987 and the 1993 waves of the French Labor Force Survey (LFS) in which workers can be followed at most three times (from 1985 to 1987 and from 1991 to 1993, respectively), it is possible to perform an individual-level longitudinal analysis while controlling for the employing firm.

The data used in Entorf and Kramarz (1997, 1999) come from four different INSEE sources. The basic sources are the French LFS, 1985–1987, a 3 year rotating panel, and the "Enquête sur la Technique et l'Organisation du Travail auprès des Travailleurs Occupés" (TOTTO) from 1987, an appendix to the labor force survey that asked questions about the diffusion of new technologies and the organization of the work place. Besides usual questions from labor force surveys (salary, tenure, age, education, etc.) the appendix contains information on the use (e.g., intensity, experience) of microcomputers, terminals, text processing, robots and other well specified groups of "New Technology" labor. The use of computers is described in more detail than in other surveys (see Krueger, 1993, for instance). The questionnaire provides explicit categories for using microcomputer for text processing only, data entry and use of listings. "Terminal" even covers a distinction between "reception only," "emission only" and both reception and emission while information on production techniques are also present.

In the first version of the TOTTO survey, only the 1987 employing firm is known (using the standardized Siren enterprise identification number). This feature of the French INSEE classification system enables the authors to employ information from corresponding firm-level surveys (BIC, which collects annual information on balance sheets and employment and ESE, which collects information on the employment structure).

In the cross-section, the approach is identical to Krueger's (1993). Entorf and Kramarz regressed the log of monthly wage on a vector of characteristics of the individual X_i and a vector of indicator variables for workers using one (or more) of the various NT groups. These variables were supplemented with firm-level characteristics $Z_{j(i)}$ (where $j(i)$ denotes the firm at which i is employed), some of which are available from the complement to the labor force survey (working time schedules, sector, size) and the others from the firm-level panel dataset (size, assets, profits, skill structure, export ratio). In all regressions, they control for the usual observable variables. Their results show that, in 1987, a worker receives a 16% bonus for using modern computer-related NT. This premium can be decomposed into two parts: for a worker with no NT-experience, a NT worker receives a premium of approximately 6%. Returns from experience with NT add 10% to the above premium (when estimated at the average level of experience in the population of modern computer-related NT users). When firm-level variables are introduced, some of the above results seem to be attenuated: the coefficient of the modern computer-related NT dummy is smaller (5%) and the standard error is larger. However, the role of experience with modern computer-related NT is increased. The firm-level variables that are used, even if they do not seem to be correlated with the individual NT variables, are important and increase significantly the explanatory power of the regression. Most important is the skill structure : the more skilled the structure is, in terms of larger shares of skilled workers and of managers, professionals and technicians, the larger is the influence on the wage. This effect is particularly strong for the latter category: a 1% increase in this share entails a 0.27% increase in the individual wage. The profits (profits/assets) also have a positive impact on wages. Finally, total employment has no significant influence on earnings. Finally, if firm fixed-effects are introduced, results are unchanged.

In the longitudinal dimension, all the above effects of NT almost completely disappear. The coefficients on the NT indicator variables are never significantly different from zero. However, even though NT use per se does not yield an immediate wage gain, coefficients of the experience with modern computer-related NT variables are significantly different from zero. In Entorf and Kramarz (1997), another version of the same equation in which a dummy for each year of experience (1,2,...,9 and more) is included is estimated and results are quite similar: returns increase until workers have 5–6 years of experience and then slightly decrease. The introduction of the firm-level variables do not change these results.[9]

In addition, these firm-level variables that represent the firm-specific policy have little impact on the individual wage once individual fixed effects are introduced. Coefficients are either not significantly different from zero or small (assets).

Most of the results that we have described for the 1985–1987 period also hold between 1991 and 1993. Most datasets are identical. A new feature of the LFS is the inclusion of the employing firm identifier in every year while only the 1987 employing firm was known previously (see above). In addition, the authors use a newly available dataset, the "Déclarations de Mouvements de Main d'Oeuvre (DMMO)," an establishment-based survey on hiring and separations. Entorf et al. are therefore able to follow the workers across firms in the 3 years of the panel.

Entorf et al. (1999) estimate wage equations with NT indicator variables without and with individual fixed-effects as well as without or with firm fixed-effects. Returns to computer use in 1993 are not different from those observed in 1987. The introduction of individual fixed-effects has the same impact as obtained in Entorf and Kramarz (1997, 1999). Returns are maximal, 2%, after 2 or 3 years experience with NT. The introduction of firm fixed-effects has no impact on the estimated coefficients, both in the cross-section dimension and in the longitudinal dimension.[10] This is consistent with the Abowd et al. (1999a) findings for France as well as those of Abowd et al. (1999c) for the US-firm compensation policies (as captured by the firm fixed-effects) are not highly correlated with individual observables and individual fixed-effects. To test other explanations of the results (in particular, to control for firm-level idiosyncratic shocks), the authors use the matched worker–establishment information on hiring, quits, and terminations coming from the DMMO. Results are identical to those described above. Finally, Entorf et al. use the quarterly LFS where workers are followed for three quarters after the TOTTO survey to test whether NT workers are protected from unemployment. Indeed, they find that in the short-run, NT users are protected from job losses. This result is stable, even when using the DMMO information on quits and terminations to measure the business conditions at the firm-level.

7.5. Creation and destruction of jobs

In this part, we do not intend to describe the whole "creation-destruction" vision of the labor market. Davis and Haltiwanger's chapter in this Handbook is fully devoted to this task. In this subsection we concentrate on the new types of results that matched worker-firm data have helped to bring to researchers' attention. Many of the papers that are discussed below use the basic definitions and analysis techniques that initiated by Leonard

---

[9] Since only the 1987 employing firm is known, the 1985 and 1986 firm is unknown for workers who changed firm at one of these dates. Entorf and Kramarz (1999) use the 1987 firm also for the movers.

[10] As indicated in Abowd et al. (1999a), in the longitudinal dimension, firm fixed-effects can only be separately identified from worker fixed-effects when at least one worker in the firm quits for another firm in the sample. Here, the authors are able to identify 494 of the 1045 firm dummies.

(1987) and Davis and Haltiwanger (1992, 1996), neither of whom used matched employee–employer data.

The analysis of worker flows, in contrast to the study of job flows, has been made possible by the use of matched worker-firm data. The researchers who started this vein, which is flourishing now, were Anderson and Meyer (1994). Using the CWBH dataset for the years 1978–1984 (see Table 1), they compare worker turnover defined as the sum of total accessions – recalls plus new hires – and total separations – temporary layoffs plus permanent separations – to job creation and job destruction measures as promoted by Davis and Haltiwanger. In addition, they use firm-level measures computed from their individual-level data in relation with their measures of job turnover. They compute firm-size, quarterly payroll per worker, and tenure at the firm to create categories such as high- or low-paying firm, high- or low-tenure firm. Then, they present a tabulation of job creation, destruction, and turnover statistics for every of the above firm-level categories (Table 2, p. 191).[11] For instance, Anderson and Meyer (1994) show that high and low-tenure firms do not differ in their temporary separation rates but widely differ in their permanent separation rates. Indeed, the same pattern is exhibited for high and low-paying firms. The same type of analysis is pursued on the number of earnings weeks lost after separations followed by reemployment (Table 9, p. 212). They are able to show that the distribution of weeks lost is extremely skewed (the mean is roughly 13 weeks as the median is equal to 2 for total separations). In addition, they show that mean weeks lost after a temporary separation are a decreasing function of firm size while mean weeks lost after a permanent separation are an increasing function of firm size. Similar computations are provided for high- and low-paying firms. These statistics being computed from individual-level data, the authors also regress the above separations variables onto the (time-varying) firm-level variables and individual fixed-effects taking advantage of the structure of the dataset in which workers can be followed from firm to firm (Table 10, p. 214).

The main disadvantage of the CWBH dataset lies in the absence of individual characteristics of the employed workers. Even though the states may have collected such information for the beneficiaries of unemployment insurance, these complementary datasets are inaccessible to the researchers. Of course, for each individual, it is always possible to compute a date of appearance and a firm-specific tenure, which is left-censored for all observations in the first-quarter of 1978. But no information on age, sex, education is used.

The same problem affects the recent analyses of Lane et al. (1997b) and Burgess et al. (1999). These articles have mostly focused on churning, the hires and separations in excess of total job reallocation using the Maryland quarterly employment and earnings information from the unemployment insurance dataset (see above). The period of analysis, 1985–1994, is the only difference between the data used in these papers and those used in Anderson and Meyer (1994). Lane et al. (1997b) provide an description of hiring and exit flows. The individual data on the characteristics of the movers have been aggregated

---

[11] Hamermesh et al. (1996) also document the importance of worker flows as compared to job creation and destruction for data from the Netherlands, although they do not use matched employer–employee data.

to the establishment-level and used as explanatory variables in the churning regression (Eq. (1) in their paper). The longitudinal component of the dataset allows the authors to include firm fixed-effects in this regression. One striking result, also found in Abowd et al. (1999b) for France, is that most of the changes in employment are accommodated through changes in the hiring rate.

Abowd et al. (1999b), who use an administrative dataset of all entries and exits in French establishments (see Table 1), perform most of their flow analysis at the establishment-level. Their empirical analyses distinguished between flows of workers, directly measured, and job creation and destruction, again, directly measured, using a representative sample of all French establishments for 1987–1990 (with more than 50 employees). The most important findings were that (a) annual job creation can be characterized as hiring three persons and separating two for each job created in a given year; (b) annual job destruction can be characterized as hiring one person and separating two for each job destroyed in a given year; (c) when an establishment is changing employment, the adjustment is made primarily by reducing entry and not by changing the separation rates; (d) for the highest skill groups, 10% of months with firm-initiated exits also have new hiring in the same skill group and, for the lowest skill groups, 25% of the months with firm-initiated separations also have new hiring in that skill group; (e) the rate of internal promotion into higher skilled positions is about three times the size of net employment changes inside the job category; (f) two-thirds of all hiring is on short term contracts and more than half of all separations are due to the end of these short term contracts; (g) approximately one-third of all short term employment contracts are converted to longterm contracts at their termination; (h) controlling for between-establishment heterogeneity and common trends, entry and exit of workers are both countercyclical.

Other studies that use matched employer–employee data to analyze these issues of job creation and job destruction are Norwegian (Salvanes and Forre, 1997), Austrian (Winter-Ebmer and Zweimüller, 1997), Danish (Belzil, 1997; Bingley and Westergård-Nielsen, 1998, Vejrup-Hansen, 1998; Albaek and Sørensen, 1999), Swedish (Persson, 1998), and Finnish (Laaksonen et al., 1998).

Albaek and Sørensen (1999) examine the relation between worker flows and job flows using the Danish IDA (see Table 1). In that respect, the type of analysis they perform is close to Hamermesh et al. (1996) and even closer to Abowd et al. (1998). These authors find that annual rates of hires and separations are much higher than the job creation or job destruction rates–28% and 12% respectively for Danish manufacturing. They also find that separations from existing jobs are dominated by quits. Another issue studied at length by these authors is cyclicality of the flows. They show that worker flows are strongly asymmetric over the business cycle.

Bingley and Westergård-Nielsen (1998) use the Danish IDA to show that the Danish labor market is dynamic and flexible. Among growing establishments two hires and one separation are required for each net job creation. Among shrinking establishments they find that one hire and two separations are required for each net job destroyed. Vejrup-

Hansen (1998) finds that workers separated from establishments with job destructions have unemployment incidence that is comparable to the general Danish population.

Salvanes and Forre (1997) use the individual information on the education-level of the employed workers from their registers (see above) to examine creation, destruction, entry, exit, and churning for three groups of education. They find an asymmetric and inverse U-shaped churning curve (the churning rate, i.e., the entries and exits in excess of job creation or job destruction, is larger for medium-education workers).

Winter-Ebmer and Zweimüller (1997) examine the relationship between firm-level measures of earnings dispersion and employment growth. To examine this issue they use a firm-based random sample of the Social Security files for the period 1975–1991 (see Table 1). With the resulting 130 firms, for which they have all employed workers (with their earnings – top-coded for 9% of them – and most other individual characteristics but education), they compute within firm measures of earnings dispersion as follows. Because of top-coding, they run a Tobit regression for each year and each firm. The resulting standard error of the residual of this regression is used as a first measure of dispersion due to all unobserved factors. They also perform the same regression using only male workers (they do not have hours worked, hence working with males reduces the part-time probability). Then, they use these variables in their firm-level employment growth regressions (1236 observations). These regressions are estimated without and with firm fixed-effects. While there is some evidence with OLS that an increased earnings variance reduces employment growth, the introduction of fixed-effects wipes out any such effects.

Interestingly, Belzil (1997) and Burgess et al. (1997) do the same type of analysis, but in the reverse direction. They both use measures of employment growth (creation, destruction, reallocation, or churning) as additional regressors for explaining wage structure of wage changes.[12] Belzil (1997) use a subsample of the IDA dataset to perform individual-level wage regressions. Since the dataset is longitudinal and contains both employee and employer identifier, it is possible to control for person fixed-effects as well as firm fixed-effects. Even though none of the reported regressions include firm fixed-effects, the author states that the introduction of these effects does not affect the coefficients of interest, a feature consistently found in France (Abowd et al., 1999a; Entorf et al., 1999), in the US (Abowd et al., 1999c), or in Denmark (Bingley and Westergard-Nielsen, 1996). Belzil also finds that employment creation, destruction, or reallocation affects wages, even though no systematic pattern seems to emerge across the different subsamples that he analyzes.

DiPrete et al. (1998) use matched employee–employer longitudinal data from France (LFS matched with firm-level information using the SIREN number, see Table 1) and Sweden (LFS matched with establishment registers, see Table 1) to examine the relation between the dynamics of employment of the employing establishment and job mobility. They model simultaneously unemployment, exit from an establishment, job mobility within an establishment, and entry into an establishment and estimate jointly five probit

---

[12] Other studies use employment growth as a regressor in their analysis of earnings (Kramarz et al., 1996; Entorf and Kramarz, 1997). But, they do not focus on the resulting estimates of employment growth coefficients.

equations. In particular, they try to examine the age of the mobile workers and how the selection process of such age category is determined in each country by the specific labor market institutions that prevail. Even though their results are only preliminary, the estimation methodology and the way the different datasets are matched constitute an excellent example of the potentialities of the use of matched employee–employer longitudinal data.

Hassink (1999) uses longitudinal matched Dutch data (see Table 1) to examine the effects of firm and employee characteristics on the probability of layoffs. He conducts parallel analyses using the firm's lay off rate and the individual's layoff event as the two dependent variables. Using a specification that includes firm effects, firm characteristics and individual characteristics. The effect of seniority is negative and essentially linear in both equations. The minimum layoff probability occurs at age 32, a result that is interpreted as supporting Lazear-style compensation models.

7.6. Training

The potential of matched employer–employee data to address issues surrounding training is enormous. Indeed, we believe that questions such as the identification of general versus specific knowledge can only be addressed with such longitudinal datasets. And movements of workers between firms, workers for which we measure most individual characteristics would help isolate those firms which provide firm-specific training on one side and those firms which provide general training on the other. Unfortunately, there are few datasets that provide information on training of individuals together with employer information. Even though some are being built now.

Bishop (1994) uses the EOPP which provides retrospective longitudinal data on training and productivity of two new hires at 659 firms. Using this pair, Bishop is able to estimate all equations of interest by doing within-firm difference, therefore eliminating all firm-specific unobserved heterogeneity. The dependent variables are respectively the logarithm of training time, the productivity at the end of first week, the starting wage, the current productivity, the current wage, and the profit in the first months. The results can be summarized as follows. New hires with relevant previous work experience, relevant employer-sponsored formal training, and relevant vocational education tend to require less training, to be more productive, and to receive higher starting wages and higher wages after 1 year of seniority.

Similar questions are examined in a group of papers based on a newly available dataset, the Multi-City Study of Urban Inequality for Holzer and Reaser (1996), the 1995 Survey of Employer-Provided Training for Frazis et al. (1997) (see Table 1). Unfortunately, the first of these two datasets only has one observation per person or per firm, while the paper which uses the second dataset does not use the full potentiality of matched employer–employee data which makes most estimated coefficients difficult to interpret since they are likely to be biased due to unobserved person or worker heterogeneity. Frazis et al. (1998) extend this analysis to show that those establishments that encourage long term relationships, using pension plans and other employee benefits, also provide more training.

Finally, Goux and Maurin (1997) use the French FQP dataset (see Table 1) to examine the impact of training on wages and mobility. Interestingly, they show that having been trained in the past years is associated with a higher wage (approximately 6%) in a simple OLS regression. However, the introduction of firm fixed-effects reduces this effect to less than 3%. Furthermore, when a correction for the selection bias induced by participation in a training program is introduced, all effects of training on wages disappear. Hence, they conclude that the higher wage associated to training is partly due to firm-specific compensation policies and partly due to unobserved worker heterogeneity.

7.7. Unions and collective bargaining

This section discusses the use of matched employer–employee data to study the behavior of unionized firms and negotiated wage rates. We consider, in sequence, Abowd and Allain (1996), Cahuc and Kramarz (1997), Lalonde et al. (1996), Hildreth (1996), Hildreth and Pudney (1997) and Margolis (1993).

Abowd and Allain (1996) use data from the French DADS and BIC (see Table 1) to model the division of the quasi-rent per worker in collectively bargained French wage rate.[13] They fit an equation of the form

$$w_j = x_j + \gamma_j q_j + \varepsilon_j, \tag{7.2}$$

where w_j is the negotiated wage rate, x_j is the opportunity cost of the worker's time, γ_j is the bargaining power of the union, and q_j is the expected quasi-rent per worker. The heterogeneity in γ_j is modeled using q_j and other variables z_j. Using the decomposition in Eq. (3.1), the opportunity cost of the workers is modeled as

$$x_j = \bar{\theta}_j + \psi_{10},$$

where ψ_{10} is the firm effect at the 10th percentile of the French labor force.[14] The quasi-rent per worker has two components: an expected part, which is related to international competition using export prices (from France or from the United States), and a measurement error, which is eliminated by the instrumental variable procedure (see Abowd and Lemieux, 1993). Two empirical measures of the quasi-rent per worker were used—one which eliminated only the opportunity cost of the workers' time and the other which also eliminated an estimate of the opportunity cost of capital. The interpretation of the coefficient on the quasi-rent per worker is, therefore, the average part of the expected quasi-rent per worker that goes to the workers. Abowd and Allain estimate that this coefficient is 0.4 in the French economy.

Hildreth (1996) investigates the same question as Abowd and Allain using the British PSME, a panel of manufacturing establishments (see Table 1) and the British Household

---

[13] In an earlier effort, Abowd and Kramarz (1993) use the firm data from the BIC combined with occupation data from the ESE and aggregated wage data from the DADS to fit models similar to those in Abowd and Allain. This earlier paper does not make direct use of matched employer–employee data.

[14] Approximately 90% of French jobs are covered by collective bargaining agreements.

Panel Study (BHPS). The basic wage equation is essentially the same as Eq. (7.2), except that Hildreth specifies the relation using log wage as the dependent variable, which means that the coefficient on q_j cannot be interpreted as the bargaining power of the union. The method of calculating the quasi-rent per worker is also different. Hildreth defines the opportunity cost of the worker's time using a table of the usual weekly earnings cross-classified by education, age and sex, with further refinements for the location and industry of the establishment. The appropriate value from this table was subtracted from the value-added per worker to get the quasi-rent per worker. There was no correction for the opportunity cost of capital. Hildreth gets estimates that are much smaller than those of Abowd and Allain, but of the same order of magnitude as those found in other studies using British data (e.g., Hildreth and Oswald, 1993). The main difference appears to be the interpretation of the bargaining power parameter. Abowd and Allain (following Abowd and Lemieux) interpret this parameter as applying to the expected quasi-rent per worker, that is, the part related to the price instruments, and not to the realized profit per worker, which is much more variable.

Cahuc and Kramarz (1997) use the French ESS of 1986 and 1992 (see Table 1) to examine the impact of the signature of a firm-level agreement on the stability of the work force. In some sense, they try to find an exchange of voice, as approximated by the existence of an agreement, against stability. Their analysis uses both the cross-sectional dimension of the ESS, i.e., individual information on multiple employees in each estab-lishment, and the longitudinal dimension, i.e., the same establishments can be found in 1986 and 1992. Cahuc and Kramarz start by examining the probability of signature of an agreement at the firm-level. They show that this probability is positively affected by most variables that increase the cost of turnover, more particularly by training expenses and by the presence of workers with intermediary skills. Then, they examine the relation between workers' seniority and the impact of the signature of an agreement between 1986 and 1992. The relevant regressions have approximately 50,000 observations and more than 250 firm fixed-effects. Results show that the signature of an agreement induces an increase in the average seniority of the work force of roughly one month for every additional year of the agreement.

LaLonde et al. (1996) use an unusually well-conceived matched dataset containing longitudinal information on American manufacturing establishments and employee infor-mation on the conduct and results of union representation elections. The establishment data come from the Longitudinal Research Database while the union election data come from the National Labor Relations Board (see Table 1). A union representation election is necessary in the United States before the employees of an ongoing business can negotiated collectively over wages and working conditions. By following establishments over a period of 4 years prior and 9 years after the election, these authors were able to measure the effects of the newly formed union on total output, employment, other factor utilization, wage rates, and productivity. LaLonde et al. present both short and long term evidence comparing the profiles of establishments where the representation election was successful (union wins) with those which had an unsuccessful (union losses) representation election.

Following a successful representation election, establishments reduce their output, material purchases and employment levels permanently (an effect that lasts at least 9 years). The establishments do not, however, experience higher wage rates.

Margolis (1993) uses data from the French Enquête Structure des Salaires (see Table 1) matched with detailed information on the collective bargaining agreements supplied by the Ministry of Labor to study the consequences of mandatory extension of the collective agreements to firms and workers who did not participate in the negotiations, a common practice in France. He finds that the willingness of employers to join the negotiation is strongly affected by the probability that the agreement will be extended. He also finds that the possibility of non-compliance with the collective bargaining agreement influences the behavior of the firms during the negotiations.[15]

Hildreth and Pudney (1997) use the British Panel Study of Manufacturing Establishments (PSME, see Table 1), which includes information on two workers: the most recently hired and one randomly selected, cooperating, individual, to study the effects of union recognition on firm outcomes. In the United Kingdom, there is no statutory requirement that an employer recognize and bargain with a union. Employees can choose whether or not to join a union independent of the employers negotiating stance towards that union. Any collective agreement applies to all workers in the covered jobs regardless of the employees' union status. Hildreth and Pudney model the two-sided decision process that determines the union status of the employee and of the job using the matched data. Their statistical models correct for a variety of sampling and self-selection problems. They find that firms that recognize unions have lower quit rates and higher wage rates. Interestingly, the union wage premium is higher for individuals who are covered by the collective agreement but who do not join the union. The results also suggest that applicant workers do not find the jobs covered by a collective agreement more attractive than non-covered jobs, so there are not increased applicant rates for these jobs. These statistical results generally allow for firm effects in all equations.

7.8. Other firm outcomes

The new data sources matching workers and their firms have allowed American researchers to re-examine classical issues of American labor economics: race discrimination and sex segregation. All these new analyses have been based on the WECD (see Table 1 and Section 2.3). The matched data using state unemployment insurance records have also permitted the examination of the effects of changes in the tax system on layoffs and other employment decisions. We discuss these applications, as well as those that do not have an obvious place in other sections, in this subsection.

---

[15] Non-compliance with collective bargaining agreements in France is accomplished by reclassifying jobs into lower pay categories and gambling that the labor inspector will not force a higher classification.

7.8.1. Segregation of the work force

Carrington and Troske (1998b) examine the extent to which blacks and whites are integrated at work. In addition to the WECD (see Table 1), the authors use the Characteristics of Business Owners (CBO) database which give demographic information on owners, employees, and customers of small businesses (hence complementing the WECD which is particularly strong on large businesses). Then, the authors propose different measures of segregation and assess their adequacy in a multifirm context. First, they define the Gini coefficient as follows:

$$G = 1 - \sum_{i-1}^{T} s_{bi} \left(s_{wi} + 2 \sum_{j=i+1}^{T} s_{wj} \right),$$

where T is the number of firms, s_{bi} and s_{wi} are firm i's share of the black and white sample populations, respectively, and where firms are sorted in ascending order of s_{bi}/s_{wi}. Then, they define the Gini coefficient of random segregation in order to take into account the fact that random allocation of black and white workers will never generate a zero Gini coefficient. Based on the comparison of the two Gini indices, they create a Gini coefficient of systematic segregation.

Their results suggest that the national distribution of black and white employees across employers is far from even, as some employers have mostly white employees while others have mostly black. They also show that this segregation is due to black-white differences in MSA residence. Most of the remaining interfirm segregation come from racial differences in occupation, industry, or by simple random allocation which can almost never be rejected. Then, using more classical tools, they regress the black share of non-supervisory employment in the establishment on the share of black supervisors, the black sample share within each MSA, the log of establishment employment, the average age and education of non-supervisory employees, and indicator variables for industry and region. They show in particular that, using the WECD, black workers tend to be supervised by black managers (and vice-versa for whites). While, using the CBO, they show that black workers are more likely to work for firms with black owners and customers.

Finally, they decompose the black-white wage gap into a between and a within-plant component. In particular, they use the same type of techniques already described at many places in the preceding subsections, i.e., they introduce establishment fixed-effects. Carrington and Troske' s results demonstrate that the wage gap is mostly a within-plant phenomenon. Very little of the black-white wage gap comes from the allocation of black and white workers into firms that pay systematically different wages. Moreover, a large fraction of the within-plant gap is explained by the observable characteristics of the workers even though a significant fraction cannot be explained. In addition, when wages are regressed on the racial structure of the employing firm, it appears that black-majority plants pay their black employees less than black-minority plants. But these black-majority plants also pay their white employees more than their black employees.

The same authors use the same database, the WECD, and the same techniques to examine sex segregation (Carrington and Troske, 1998a). They find that the distribution of men and women across plants is far from even. But, they also find that much of this apparent segregation appears to be due to random allocation. Similarly to the race analysis, they examine the plant female share of non-supervisory employees and regress it on variables similar to those described above. Of interest are the following results that female managers tend to supervise female employees and that women have higher employment shares in large establishments. The analysis of the male-female wage gap proceeds along the same lines as those presented for the black-white wage gap. The authors show that there is an important, even dominant in the case of blue-collar workers, role played by between-plant segregation in explaining this wage gap. Therefore, men work in relatively high paying plants while women work in relatively low paying plants even after controlling for observable characteristics of the workers. In addition, they demonstrate that workers, either men or women, are paid less if they work in largely female plants.

Hellerstein et al. (1997) continue the analysis of sex discrimination. They match the WECD with information from the Longitudinal Research Database (LRD) to get information on the employing establishment or firm. They find that large firms or large establishments make more profits if they employ more women. No such relation exist for small firms. In the present version of the paper at least, the authors are not able to provide a definitive explanation of this phenomenon. Bayard et al. (1999) also study sex segregation and male-female wage differentials. In the current version of the paper, they find that a substantial portion of the male-female wage gap takes the form of wage differentials within narrowly-defined occupations within establishments, results that stand in marked contrast to Groshen (1991b), who found that sex-segregation into occupations within establishments explained most of the gap.

7.8.2. Unemployment insurance and layoffs

In Anderson and Meyer (1994), these authors begin a long series of papers that used state-level unemployment insurance system matched employer–employee data to study the effects of the unemployment insurance tax and benefit system on a variety of outcomes: layoffs, employment, wages, and UI benefit takeup. The 1994 paper is discussed in section 7.5. The data structure in the other papers is very similar and is not discussed again. Anderson and Meyer (1996a,b, 1997) use the state unemployment insurance data and the establishment employment information to establish a number of basic features of the UI system and its effects on labor market outcomes.

Anderson and Meyer (1996a) studies the effects of firm-level experience rating on layoff probabilities. Experience rating is the system of UI financing that increases a firm's UI tax payments as the firm imposes benefit liabilities on the system. The effect of such financing systems on a the firm's propensity to use layoffs and on its wage structure is an old an important question in the labor economics literature. They use the same States as the 1994 paper. They use a form of Eq. (3.1) in which the dependent variable is the event that a worker is laid off during the quarter. Both person and firm effects are included. The firm's UI tax rate is included in the model and instrumental variables are used to correct for the endogeneity that experience-rating induces. They find that the elasticity of the layoff rate with respect to the firm-specific tax cost is -0.3 and the corresponding fraction of temporary layoff unemployment that can be attributed to incomplete experience-rating is 20%.

Anderson and Meyer (1996b) studies the adoption of experience rating in the State of Washington UI system. Because the State of Washington adopted experience rating in 1985 to avoid a massive surplus in the system, these authors, who have data from 1979 to 1993 are able to provide direct evidence on the changes surrounding the adoption. They examine in detail the changes between the last half of 1984 (third and fourth quarters) and the last half of 1985 (again, third and fourth quarters). The change in the in the UI tax rates that was induced by the adoption of experience ratings was based on layoff rates over the period 1980:3–1984:2; however, the firm's only learned of the adoption of experience rating in 1984:3. Thus, this period represents an essentially exogenous change in the UI tax rates. The authors report that the full amount of the market-level change in tax rates is passed on to the workers in the form of lower earnings but that the firm-specific component is borne completely by the firm. They report mixed results of the effects of the experience rating on layoffs.

Anderson and Meyer (1997) use the CWBH data discussed in conjunction with their 1994 paper to study the effect of UI benefit levels and benefit tax treatment on the take-up rate for UI. They explain the late 1980s–early 1990s decline in UI receipts. According to these authors there is a strong positive relation between benefit levels and take-up rates. There are smaller, but still important effects arising from the tax treatment and potential duration of benefits. The inclusion of UI income in the US income tax base, therefore, accounts for most of the recent decline in UI receipts.

Abowd and Allain (1997) use the State of Washington UI data (see Table 1) to study the role played by workers and firms observable characteristics, as well as unobserved heterogeneity, in the probability that an individual participates in a short-time UI compensation (STC) program. Short-time compensation programs allow firms to pay UI benefits to workers whose hours have been reduced to avoid layoffs. These authors show that both types of unobserved heterogeneity are strongly correlated with this probability, with the individual effect having stronger correlation than the firm effect. In the context of Eq. (3.1), the dependent variable is the incidence of short-time compensation. A person-effect means that the individual has experienced short-time UI compensation and a firm effect means that the firm has used short-time compensation. Thus, the results are interpreted as meaning that some individuals have a greater propensity to be employed in short-time compensation jobs than others and some firms have a greater propensity to use this form of UI compensation. Firms with higher experience ratings were more likely to use short-time compensation.

Needels and Nicholson (1998) also study short time compensation systems using UI data from the states of California, Florida, Kansas, New York and Washington for the period 1991–1993 for 3300 establishments. They use a statistical matching algorithm to pair establishments with short-time compensation programs to those without. The statistical analyses are all conducted by differencing the paired establishments. Establishments with STC programs have higher layoff levels than those without, which they interpret as evidence of unmeasured heterogeneity among the establishments.

7.8.3. International trade and other topics

Kramarz (1997) examines the impact of international trade on wages and mobility of French workers using the matching of the French labor force survey with a unique dataset on all imports (to France) and exports (from France) of goods during the period 1986–1990. Origins of the imports and destination of the exports are known at the firm-level and are disaggregated into eight groups of countries. It comprises all movements of goods since it is an administrative data source from the customs administration. Matching is performed using the Siren number present in both files. This import-export dataset is also matched to the Echantillon d'Entreprises to measure total sales and total purchases. Hence, the independent variables on trade in the regressions are the ratio of imports to total purchases – a way to measure the reorientation of purchases from local markets to outside suppliers – and the ratio of exports to total sales. Then, Kramarz computes the change in these ratios between 1986 and 1990 for firm j and relates them to the probability of being unemployed at date $t + 1$ conditional on being employed in the same firm j at date t (t going from 1990 to 1993). He also examines the impact on the level of wage at date t in firm j. All these regressions include individual characteristics from the LFS that one expects to find in this type of analysis. In addition, to assess the impact of the competitive pressure, he also includes the change of the ratio of imports to purchases of all firms in the same 4-digit sector as well as in firms from the trade (retail or wholesale) industries. Results are the following. The unemployment probability is positively affected by increasing imports from the 4-digit competitors of the firm; a best response for the firm being to increase its imports. Hence, importing protects workers from unemployment when most other firms in the same sector increase their imports. The impact of imports and exports on wages have a similar structure. An increase of the share of firm-level purchases coming from outside France between 1986 and 1990 negatively affect the level of future wages while the opposite is true both for exports and imports from the firms of the same 4-digit sector. Origins of the imports appear to matter. For instance if these imports come from Germany, the impact on wage is positive, while if they come from developing countries or from the UK, the impact is large and negative. Similarly, workers employed at date t in firms that increase their share of exports to Japan have higher wages. Of course, these results could be seen as evidence of the impact of international trade on prices or, on the contrary, as showing nothing on international trade but capturing worker unobserved heterogeneity.

Abowd and Kramarz (1998b) analyze the costs of separating from French workers using the 1992 ESS (see Table 1). In this study, the authors used the individual-level variables: total annual compensation inclusive of all employee- and employer-paid benefits and bonuses but exclusive of non-wage-benefits, firm seniority, type of contract (permanent, CDI, or temporary, CDD), number of days of employment in the establishment in 1992, sex, age, nationality (French or non-French), skill-level (in 4 groups), bonuses for retirement and severance payments for workers that retired or were fired in 1992. They present estimates of the structure of retirement, termination, and hiring costs using, representative establishment-level data matched with individual-level information. These costs are directly reported by the sampled establishments. Both retirement and termination costs are increasing and mildly concave in the number of retired or terminated workers. The fixed costs are very large. Hence, these costs act as fixed adjustment costs, giving the firm an incentive to group exits instead of adjusting gradually. Termination costs are largest for collective terminations as opposed to individual ones. These costs are largest for highly skilled employees. Hiring costs also exhibit the same structure; concave adjustment costs with a strong fixed component. But these hiring costs do not have the same structure for all skill levels. Only hires of managers on longterm contracts (CDI) have an increasing and concave impact on the cost. For all other skill levels and types of contract, hiring costs do not depend upon the number of entries. Thus, for hiring costs, the firms have an incentive to group the managerial hiring but no adjustment costs for other hiring. The costs of hiring are much less important in France than the costs of separations (retirements and terminations).

Abowd et al. (1996) consider the following question: Are high-quality products produced by high-quality workers? To do this they use the decomposition of wages from Abowd et al. (1999a) and price measures of product quality. To measure the quality of a product, they use prices for very detailed products (8-digit classification) collected at the firm-level. Each basic product is allocated to a 6-digit basic commodity group. Therefore, quality can be measured as either the relative price of a 8-digit elementary product within a 6-digit basic commodity group or as the price change of each elementary product within the basic commodity group. Abowd et al. find little relation between worker quality and product quality within basic products. Hence, technological differences among firms, given basic products, seem very small. They conclude that, if worker quality and product quality are positively related, the effect is apparently more important for sorting workers among diverse and non-substitutable products than for explaining variation within groups of imperfectly substitutable detailed products.

7.9. Specialized applications

There are a variety of specialized uses of matched employer–employee data that we have not discussed in detail in this chapter because they figure prominently in other surveys. Pension data collected from the employers have been matched to several nationally representative cross-sectional and longitudinal databases in the United States including the Health and Retirement Survey, Mature Cohorts from the National Longitudinal Surveys, and the Survey of Consumer Finances. See the chapter on retirement issues by Mitchell and Lumsdaine for a discussion of these applications. Health researchers have also used administrative matched data to study productivity issues in the health service industry (see Dunn et al., 1998, and the chapter on health issues by Currie).

8. Conclusion

As the beginning of our chapter makes clear, new economic and statistical problems will emerge as new types of labor market questions are investigated with detailed data concerning both the worker and the firm. Even though the analysis of matched employer–employee data is relatively new, we are already confronted with some puzzling new results: the lack of correlation between person and firm effects in wage determination and the enormous employment flows associated with job creation and destruction, among others. To model such new facts, standard models of the allocation of workers among firms must be modified.

New statistical problems have also emerged: the analysis of duration models with correlated person and firm effects and the design of statistical models for non-random matches, for example. To estimate such statistical models, some solutions already exist, based on simulations, but they are extremely computer-intensive. Some simpler ones will surely be implemented in the near future. These statistical models could also be useful in other areas, such as health economics (doctors and hospitals–on one side–and their clients–on the other) or education economics (schools and professors–on one side–and their students–on the other) to resolve the same type of identification questions that the analysis of matched employer–employee data have helped resolve.

An area that will be even more demanding is the formulation and estimation of structural economic models. As we show in our discussion of the relation between different theoretical models and the simplest wage equation with correlated person and firm effects and firm-specific returns to seniority, an enormous amount of detail is required to assign the statistical effects to an economic model. Recovering the deep structural parameters from statistical models that include such effects will surely be difficult. In addition, one can argue that it is very unlikely that all firms follow the same model. Hence, the estimation of structural models will force the researcher to address structural heterogeneity problems, for instance, is rent-sharing more important than agency problems for a particular firm?.

Matched longitudinal employer–employee datasets should constitute the basis for further refinements of the theory of production and of the theory of the workplace organization. The possibility of evaluating the various combination of workers, jobs, and machines within a firm should allow labor economists to delve deeper into the internal organization of the firm. Indeed, data collected in the future should give information on each job in conjunction with each individual job holder in each individual firm. We are back to the "get more data" conclusion, so that we can play the role of Rosen and Willis for this volume of the *Handbook*.

References

Abe, Masahiro and Catherine Sofer (1996), "Effets de l'ancienneté sur le salaire: une comparaison France/Japon", Comparaisons internationales de salaires (INSEE-DARES, Paris) pp. 198–222.

Abowd, John M. and Laurence Allain (1996), "Compensation structure and product market competition", Annales d'économie et de statistique 41–42: 207–217.

Abowd, John M. and Laurence Allain (1997), "The Washington State short-time compensation program and its implication for European work share programs", Working paper (Cornell University).

Abowd, John M and Hampton Finer (1998), "Incorporating employer data into the National Longitudinal Survey Of Youth 1979 cohort: methods and results", Working paper (Cornell University).

Abowd, John M. and Francis Kramarz. (1993), "A test of negotiation and incentive compensation models using longitudinal French enterprise data", in: J.C. van Ours, G.A. Pfann and G. Ridder, eds., Labour demand and equilibrium wage formation (North Holland, Amsterdam) pp. 111–146.

Abowd, John M. and Francis Kramarz (1996a), "Les politiques salariales: individus et entreprises", Revue Economique 47: 611–622.

Abowd, John M. and Francis Kramarz (1996b), "The microeconometrics of human resource management: international studies of firm practices, introduction and overview", Annales d'économie et de statistique 41–42: 11–19.

Abowd, John M. and Francis Kramarz (1998a), "Internal and external labor markets: an analysis of matched employer-employee data", in: J. Haltiwanger, M. Manser and R. Topel, eds., Labor statistics measurement issues (University of Chicago Press, Chicago, IL).

Abowd, John M. and Francis Kramarz (1998b), "The cost of hiring and separations", Working paper no. 6110, revised (NBER, Cambridge, MA).

Abowd, John M. and Francis Kramarz (1999), "Econometric analysis of linked employer-employee data", Labour Economics 6: 53–74.

Abowd, John M. and Thomas Lemieux (1993), "The effects of product market competition on collective bargaining agreements: the case of foreign competition in Canada", Quarterly Journal of Economics 108: 983–1014.

Abowd, John M., Francis Kramarz and Antoine Moreau (1996), "Product quality and worker quality", Annales d'économie et de statistique 41–42: 299–322.

Abowd, John M., Hampton Finer, Francis Kramarz and Sébastien Roux (1998a), "Job and wage mobility: an analysis of the dynamics of employment durations using matched employee and employer data from the U.S. and France", Working paper (Cornell University and INSEE-CREST).

Abowd, John M., Francis Kramarz, David N. Margolis and Kenneth R. Troske (1998b), "The relative importance of employer and employee effects on compensation: a comparison of France and the United States", Mimeo.

Abowd, John M., Francis Kramarz and David N. Margolis (1999a), "High wage workers and high wage firms", Econometrica 67: 251–333.

Abowd, John M., Patrick Corbel and Francis Kramarz (1999b), "The entry and exit of workers and the growth of employment: an analysis of French establishments", Review of Economics and Statistics 81: in press.

Abowd, John M., Hampton Finer and Francis Kramarz (1999c), "Individual and firm heterogeneity in compensation: an analysis of matched longitudinal employer-employee data for the State of Washington", in: J. Haltiwanger et al., eds., The creation and analysis of employer-employee matched data (North-Holland, Amsterdam) pp. 3–24.

Albaek, Karsten and Bent E. Sørensen (1999), "Worker flows and job flows in Danish manufacturing, 1980–91", Economic Journal, in press.

Alexander, Michael and Alison Morehead (1999), "The 1995 Australian Workplace Industrial Relations Survey – a discussion of the methodology used to create linked employer-employee data", in: J. Haltiwanger et al., eds., The creation and analysis of employer-employee matched data (North-Holland, Amsterdam) pp. 535–552.

Anderson, Patricia M. and Bruce D. Meyer (1994), "The extent and consequences of job turnover", Brookings Papers Microeconomics: 177–248.

Anderson, Patricia M. and Bruce D. Meyer (1996a), "The effects of unemployment insurance taxes and benefits on layoffs using firm and individual data", Working paper (Dartmouth College).

Anderson, Patricia M. and Bruce D. Meyer (1996b), "Using a natural experiment to estimate the effects of the unemployment payroll tax on layoffs, employment and wages", Working paper (Dartmouth College).

Anderson, Patricia M. and Bruce D. Meyer (1997), "Unemployment insurance takeup rates and the after-tax value of benefits", Quarterly Journal of Economics 112: 913–937.

Arai, Mahmood, Gérard Ballot and Ali Skalli (1997), "Différentiels intersectoriels de salaire et caractéristiques des employeurs en France", Economie et Statistique 299.

Baker, Michael and Gary Solon (1997), "Earnings dynamics and inequality among Canadian men, 1976–1992: evidence from longitudinal income tax records", Mimeo.

Barth, Erling (1997), "Firm-specific seniority and wages", Journal of Labor Economics 15 (3 part 1): 495–506.

Barth, Erling and Harald Dale-Olsen (1999), "The employer's wage policy and worker turnover", in: J. Haltiwanger et al., eds., The creation and analysis of employer-employee matched data (North-Holland, Amsterdam) pp. 285–312.

Bayard, Kimberly, Judith Hellerstein, David Neumark and Kenneth Troske (1999), "Why are racial and ethnic wage gaps larger for men than for women? Exploring the role of segregation using the new worker-establishment characteristics database", in: J. Haltiwanger et al., eds., The creation and analysis of employer-employee matched data (North-Holland, Amsterdam) pp. 175–204.

Belzil, Christian (1997), "Job creation and destruction, worker reallocation and wages", Working paper (Department of Economics, Concordia University).

Bender, S., J. Hilzendegen, G. Rohwer and H. Rudolph (1996), "Die IAB Beschaeftigungsstichprobe 1975–1990", Beitraege zur Arbeitsmarkt- und Berufsforschung (BeitrAB 197, Nuernberg).

Bingley, Paul and Niels Westergård-Nielsen (1996), "Individual wages within and between establishments", Working paper (University of Århus).

Bingley, Paul and Niels Westergård-Nielsen (1998), "Establishment tenure and worker turnover", Working paper (University of Århus).

Bishop, John (1994), "The impact of previous training on productivity and wages", in: Lisa Lynch, ed., Training and the private sector (University of Chicago Press for NBER, Chicago, IL).

Blanchflower, David and Stephen Machin (1996), "Product market competition, wages and productivity: international evidence from establishment-level data", Annales d'économie et de statistique 41–42: 219–254.

Boon, Martin (1996), "Effects of firm performance and technology on wages: evidence from cross-sectional matched worker-firm data", Working paper no. 4692-96-RSM (Department of Statistical Methods, Statistics Netherland).

Bronars, Stephen G. and Melissa Famulari (1997), "Wage, tenure and wage growth variation within and across establishments", Journal of Labor Economics 15 (2): 285–317.

Bronars, Stephen G., Paul Bingley, Melissa Famulari and Niels Westergård-Nielsen (1999), "Employer wage differentials in the United States and Denmark", in: J. Haltiwanger et al., eds., The creation and analysis of employer-employee matched data (North-Holland, Amsterdam) pp. 205–230.

Brown, Charles and James L. Medoff (1989), "The employer size-wage effect", Journal of Political Economy 97: 1027–1059.

Brown, Charles and James L. Medoff (1996), "Employer characteristics and work environment", Annales d'économie et de statistique 41–42: 275–298.

Bureau of Labor Statistics (1996), "BLS reports on the amount of formal and informal training received by employees", Press release (December 19) pp. 1–21.

Burgess, Simon, Julia Lane and David Stevens (1997), "Jobs, workers and changes in earnings dispersion", Discussion paper no. 1714 (CEPR).

Burgess, Simon, Julia Lane and David Stevens (1999), "Job flows, worker flows and churning", Journal of Labor Economics 17, in press.

Cahuc, Pierre and Francis Kramarz (1997), "Voice and loyalty as a delegation of authority: a model and a test on a matched worker-firm panel", Journal of Labor Economics 15: 658–688.

Callus, R., A. Morehead, M. Cully and J. Buchanan (1991), Industrial relations at work. The Austrialian workplace industrial relations survey (Australian Government Publishing Service, Canberra, Australia).

Cardoso, Ana Rute (1997), "Company wage policies: do employer wage effects account for the rise in labor market inequality?" Working paper (European University Instititute, Italy).

Carrington, William J. and Kenneth R. Troske (1998a), "Sex segregation in U.S. manufacturing", Industrial and Labor Relations Review 51: 445–464.

Carrington, William J. and Kenneth R. Troske (1998b), "Interfirm segregation and the black-white wage gap", Journal of Labor Economics 16 (2): 231–260.

Chennouf, S., L. Lévy-Garboua and C. Montmarquette (1997), "Les effets de l'appartenance à un groupe de travail sur les salaires individuels", Working paper (LAMIA, University of Paris-I).

Contini, Bruno, Riccardo Revelli et al. (undated), "The R&P longitudinal sample of workers and firms based on the Social Security archives", Working document (Ricerche e Progetti, Turin, Italy).

Cully, Mark (1998), "Guvnors, employees and brothers: triangulation and noise in workplace surveys", Working paper (UK Department of Trade and Industry).

Davis, Steven J. and John Haltiwanger (1992), "Gross job creation, gross job destruction and employment reallocation", Quarterly Journal of Economics 107: 819–863.

Davis, Steven J. and John Haltiwanger (1996), "Employer size and the wage structure in the United States", Annales d'économie et de statistique 41–42: 323–368.

DiPrete,Thomas A., Dominique Goux, Eric Maurin and Michael Tåhlin (1998), "Establishment dynamics and job mobility: a comparative analysis of the age-mobility relationship in France and Sweden using linked employer-employee data", Working paper (Duke University, CREST, Stockholm University).

Dolton, Peter, Maarten Lindeboom and Gerard J. van den Berg (1999), "A taxonomy of survey nonresponse and its relation to labor market behavior", in: J. Haltiwanger et al., eds., The creation and analysis of employer-employee matched data (North-Holland, Amsterdam) pp. 439–460.

Doms, M., T. Dunne and K.R. Troske (1997), "Workers, wages and technology", Quarterly Journal of Economics CXII: 253–290.

Dunn, Rodney L., Ronald J. Ozminkowski, Ron Z. Goetzel and Teresa B. Gibson (1998), "Issues and challenges when merging health and productivity management (HPM) and insurance claims data", Working paper (MEDSTAT Group).

Dustmann, Christian and Costas Meghir (1997), "Seniority and wage growth", Working paper (IFS and University College London).

Entorf, Horst and Francis Kramarz (1997), "Does unmeasured ability explain the higher wage of new technology workers", European Economic Review 41: 1489–1510.

Entorf, Horst and Francis Kramarz (1999), "The impact of new technologies on wages: lessons from matching panels on employees and on their firms", Economics of Innovation and New Technology, in press.

Entorf, Horst, Michel Gollac and Francis Kramarz (1999), "New technologies, wages and worker selection", Journal of Labor Economics 17: in press.

Finer, Hampton (1997), "Firm and individual wage components in the national longitudinal survey of youth", Working paper (Department of Labor Economics, Cornell University).

Frazis, Harley, Maury Gittleman, Michael Horrigan and Mary Joyce (1997), "Formal and informal training: evidence from a matched employee-employer survey", in: G.D. Libecap, ed., Advances in the study of entrepreneurship, innovation and economic growth, Vol. 9 (JAI Press, Greenwich, CT) pp. 9–46.

Frazis, Harley, Maury Gittleman and Mary Joyce (1998), "Determinants of training: an analysis uing both employer and employee characteristics", Working paper (Bureau of Labor Statistics).

Goux, Dominique and Eric Maurin (1997), "Train or pay: does it reduce inequalities to encourage firms to train their workers", Working paper no. G9703 bis (INSEE, Direction des Études et Synthèses Économique).

Goux, Dominique and Eric Maurin (1999), "Inter-industry wage differentials: the role of employers", Journal of Labor Economics 17: in press.

Groshen, Erica (1991a), "Sources of intra-industry wage dispersion: how much do employers matter?" Quarterly Journal of Economics 106: 869–884.

Groshen, Erica (1991b), "The structure of the female/male wage differential: is it who you are, what you do, or where you work?" Journal of Human Resources 26: 457–472.

Groshen, Erica (1996), "American employer salary surveys and labor economics research: issues and contributions", Annales d'économie et de statistique 41–42: 413–442.

Haegeland, Torbjörn and Tor Jakob Klette (1999), "Do higher wages reflect higher productivity? Education, gender and experience premia in a matched plant-worker data set", in: J. Haltiwanger et al., eds., The creation and analysis of employer-employee matched data (North-Holland, Amsterdam) pp. 231–260.

Hamermesh, Daniel, Wolter Hassink and Jan Van Ours (1996), "Job turnover and labor turnover: a taxonomy of employment dynamics", Annales d'économie et de statistique 41–42: 21–40.

Hassink, Wolter (1999), "On the incidence of layoffs", in J. Haltiwanger et al., eds., The creation and analysis of employer-employee matched data (North-Holland, Amsterdam) pp. 329–344.

Hayami, Hitoshi and Masahiro Abe (1998), "Labor demand by age and gender: evidence from linked micro data", Working paper (Keio University).

Hellerstein, Judith K., David Neumark and Kenneth R. Troske (1996), "Wages, productivity and worker characteristics: evidence from plant-level production functions and wage equations", Working paper no. 5626 (NBER, Cambridge, MA).

Hellerstein, Judith K., David Neumark and Kenneth R. Troske (1997), "Market forces and sex discrimination", Working paper no. 6321 (NBER, Cambridge, MA).

Hildreth, Andrew K. (1996), "Rent-sharing and wages: product demand or technology driven premia?" Working paper (University of Essex).

Hildreth, Andrew K. and Andrew J. Oswald (1993), "Rent-sharing and wages: evidence form company and establishment panels", Working paper no. 154 (Institute of Economics and Statistics, Oxford University).

Hildreth, Andrew K. and Stephen E. Pudney (1997), "Employers, workers and unions: an analysis of a firm-worker panel with endogenous sampling, attrition and missing data",Working paper (University of Essex).

Hildreth, Andrew K. and Stephen Pudney (1999), "Econometric issues in the analysis of linked cross-section employer-worker surveys", in: J. Haltiwanger et al., eds., The creation and analysis of employer-employee matched data (North-Holland, Amsterdam) pp. 461–488.

Hildreth, Andrew K. and N. Tremlett (1994), "Panel study of manufacturing establishments - first stage", Technical paper no. 8 (ESRC Research Centre on Micro-Social Change, University of Essex).

Hildreth, Andrew K. and N. Tremlett (1995), "Panel study of manufacturing establishments - second stage", Technical paper no. 10 (ESRC Research Centre on Micro-Social Change, University of Essex).

Holzer, Harry J. and Jess Reaser (1996), "Firm-level training for newly hired workers: its determinants and effects", Working paper (Michigan State University).

Jacobson, Louis S., Robert J. LaLonde and Daniel G. Sullivan (1993), "Earnings losses of displaced workers", American Economic Review 83: 685–709.

INSEE (1994), Enquêete sur l'emploi de 1993: résultats détaillés, no. 59-60 (INSEE, Paris).

Jovanovic, Bojan (1979), "Job matching and the theory of turnover", Journal of Political Economy 87: 972–990.

Kramarz, Francis (1997), "International competition, employment and wages: the microeconometrics of international trade", Working paper (CREST-INSEE).

Kramarz, Francis and Patrick Rey (1995), "The dynamics of wages", Working paper (CREST-INSEE).

Kramarz, Francis and Sébastien Roux (1998), "Within-firm seniority structure and firm performance", Working paper (CREST-INSEE).

Kramarz, F., S. Lollivier and L.P. Pelé (1996), "Wage inequalities and firm–specific compensation policies in France", Annales d'economie et de statistique 41–42: 369–386.

Kremer, Michael and Eric Maskin (1996), "Specialization by skill and the rise in inequality", Working paper (MIT).

Krueger, Alan B. (1993), "How computers have changed the wage structure: evidence from microdata, 1984–1989", Quarterly Journal of Economics 108: 33–60.

Krueger, Alan B. and Lawrence H. Summers (1988), "Efficiency wages and the inter-industry wage structure", Econometrica 56: 259–293.

Laaksonen, Seppo, Mika Maliranta, Hannu Piekkola, Jarl Vainiomäki, Pertti Haaparanta and Pekka Ilmakunnas (1998), "Linking of employee and plant characteristics for the analysis of Finnish manufacturing", Working paper (Statistics Finland).

Lalonde, Robert, J. Gérard Marschke and Kenneth Troske (1996), "Using longitudinal data on establishments to analyze the effects of union organizing campaigns in the United States", Annales d'économie et de statistique 41–42: 155–186.

Lane, Julia, Simon Burgess and Jules Theeuwes (1997a), "The uses of longitudinal matched worker/employer data in labor market analysis", American Statistical Association Papers and Proceedings 249–254.

Lane, Julia, D. Stevens and Simon Burgess (1997b), "Churning dynamics: an analysis of hires and separations at the employer level", Mimeo.

Lane, Julia, Javier Miranda, James Spletzer and Simon Burgess (1999), "The effect of worker reallocation on the earnings distribution: longitudinal evidence from linked data", in: J. Haltiwanger et al., eds., The creation and analysis of employer-employee matched data (North-Holland, Amsterdam) pp. 345–374.

Leonard, Jonathan (1987), "In the wrong place at the wrong time: the extent of structural and frictional unemployment", in: K. Lang and J. Leonard, eds., Unemployment and the structure of labor markets (Basil Blackwell, Oxford, UK), pp. 141–163.

Leonard, Jonathan S. and Marc Van Audenrode (1996), "Worker's limited liability, turnover and employment contracts", Annales d'économie et de statistique 41–42: 41–78.

Leonard, Jonathan S. and Marc Van Audenrode (1997), "The persistence of pay", Working paper (University of California at Berkeley).

Leonard, Jonathan S., Benoit Mulkay and Marc Van Audenrode (1999), "Compensation policies and firm productivity", in: J. Haltiwanger et al., eds., The creation and analysis of employer-employee matched data (North-Holland, Amsterdam) pp. 79–114.

Leth-Sørensen, Søren (1995), The IDA database - a longitudinal database of establishments and their employees (Statistics Denmark, IDA Project).

Mairesse, Jacques and Nathalie Greenan (1999), "Using employee-level data in a firm-level econometric study", in: J. Haltiwanger et al., eds., The creation and analysis of employer-employee matched data (North-Holland, Amsterdam) pp. 489–514.

Margolis, David N. (1993), "Compensation practices and government policies in western European labor markets", PhD dissertation (Cornell University).

Margolis, David N. (1996), "Cohort effects and returns to seniority in France", Annales d'économie et de statistique 41–42: 443–464.

Margolis, David (1999), "Past-year employment, slow reemployment and earnings losses: the case of worker displacement in France", in: J. Haltiwanger et al., eds., The creation and analysis of employer-employee matched data (North-Holland, Amsterdam) pp. 375–418.

McGuckin, Robert and George Pascoe (1988), "The longitudinal research database (LRD), status and research possibilities", Survey of Current Business: 30–37.

Ministério do Emprego e da Segurança Social (1993), Quadros de Pessoal, 1992, Colecçao Relatórios e Análises, Série estatísticas, 32 (Departamento de Estatística, Lisbon, Portugal).

Morehead, Alison, Mairi Steele, Michael Alexander, Kerry Stephen and Linton Duffin (1997), Changes at work: the 1995 Australian Workplace Industrial Relations Survey (Addison Wesley Longman, Melbourne, Australia).

Morissette, Rene and Charles Berube (1996), "Longitudinal aspects of earnings inequality in Canada", Working paper (Statistics Canada).

Needels, Karen and Walter Nicholson (1998), "The value of employer-based, linked UI data sets", Working paper (Mathematica Policy Research).

Pacelli, Lia (1997), "Wage growth of young Italian workers: does the firm matter?" Working paper (Ricerche e Progetti and University College London).

Pelé, Louis-Paul (1997), "Method of pay, worker selection and minimum wages", Working paper no. 9721 (CREST).

Persson, Helena (1998), "Job and worker flows in Sweden 1990—1995: who gets the new jobs and who loses the old jobs?" Working paper (Stockholm University).

Picot, Garnett and Ted Wannell (1996), "An experimental Canadian survey that links workplace practices and employee outcomes: why it is needed and how it works", in: Comparaisons internationales de salaires (Ministère du travail et des affaires sociales and INSEE, France) pp. 17–34.

Rosen, Sherwin (1986), "The theory of equalizing differences", in: Orley Ashenfelter and Richard Layard, eds., Handbook of labor economics (North Holland, Amsterdam), pp. 641–692.

Rotbart, Gilbert (1991), Enquête sur la structure des salaires (INSEE-Méthodes, Paris).

Salvanes, Kjell G. and Svein E. Forre (1997), "Employment policies at the plant-level: job and worker flows for heterogeneous labor in Norway", Mimeo.

Scheffé, H. (1959), The analysis of variance (Wiley, New York).

Searle, Shayle R., George Casella and Charles E. McCulloch (1992), Variance components (Wiley, New York).

Seiler, Eric (1984), "Piece rate vs. time rate: the effect of incentives on earnings", Review of Economics and Statistics 66 (August) 363–376.

Smith, Creston M. (1989), "The social security administration's continuous work history sample", Social Security Bulletin 52: 20–27.

Stephan, Gesine (1998), "Establishment effects on wages in West Germany", Working paper (University of Hanover).

Tegsjö, Björn and Jan Andersson (1998), "Labor satistics based on administrative registers: the Swedish system linking individual data with enterprise information", Working paper (Statistics Sweden).

Topel, Robert and Michael Ward (1992), "Job mobility and the careers of young men", Quarterly Journal of Economics 107: 441–479.

Troske, Kenneth R. (1998), "The worker-establishment characteristics database", in: J. Haltiwanger, M. Manser and R. Topel, eds., Labor statistics measurement issues (University of Chicago Press for the NBER, Chicago, IL).

Troske, Kenneth R. (1999), "Evidence on the employer size-wage premium from worker-establishment matched data", Review of Economics and Statistics, in press.

Vainiomäki, Jari (1999), "Technology and skill upgrading: results from linked worker-plant data for Finnish manufacturing", in: J. Haltiwanger et al., eds., The creation and analysis of employer-employee matched data (North-Holland, Amsterdam) pp. 115–146.

Vejrup-Hansen, Per (1998), "The effect of job destruction on worker mobility and unemployment", Working paper (Copenhagen Business School).

Willis, Robert (1986), "Wage determinants: a survey", in: Orley Ashenfelter and Richard Layard, eds., Handbook of labor economics (North Holland, Amsterdam), pp. 525–602.

Winter-Ebmer, R. and J. Zweimüller (1997), "Intra-firm wage dispersion and firm performance", Working paper no. 9708 (Universität Linz).

Chapter 41

GROSS JOB FLOWS

STEVEN J. DAVIS*

University of Chicago and NBER

JOHN HALTIWANGER*

University of Maryland, NBER and US Bureau of the Census

Contents

* We thank John Baldwin, Michael Kiley, Kjell Salvanes and Bent Sorensen for kindly supplying data. Tomas Dvorak and Andrew Figura provided extremely helpful research assistance. We gratefully acknowledge research support from the US National Science Foundation.

Handbook of Labor Economics, Volume 3, Edited by O. Ashenfelter and D. Card

Abstract

Market economies experience high rates of job creation and job destruction in almost every time period and sector. Each year, many businesses expand and many others contract. New businesses constantly enter, while others abruptly exit or gradually disappear. Amidst the turbulence of business growth and decline, jobs, workers and capital are continually reallocated among competing activities, organizations and locations. We synthesize the growing body of research on this process, especially as it pertains to the creation and destruction of jobs. We summarize and analyze empirical regularities related to cross-sectional, cross-country and cyclical variation in job flows. We also relate theories of heterogeneity, growth and fluctuations to the large magnitude of job flows and to systematic patterns of cross-sectional and time variation. Other major themes include the connection between job flows and worker flows, creative destruction and the productivity-improving role of factor reallocation, reallocation behavior and consequences in transition economies, and the productivity and welfare effects of policies that impede or encourage job flows. © 1999 Elsevier Science B.V. All rights reserved.

JEL codes: J21; J23; J63; D21; E24; E32

1. Introduction

Market economies experience high rates of job creation and job destruction in almost every time period and sector. Each year, many businesses expand and many others contract. New businesses constantly enter, while others abruptly exit or gradually disappear. Amidst the turbulence of business growth and decline, jobs, workers and capital are continually reallocated among competing activities, organizations and locations. We synthesize the growing body of research on this process, especially as it pertains to the creation and destruction of jobs.

Changes in the number and mix of jobs at individual firms and production sites reflect many forces: the diffusion of new products and technologies, the success or failure of research and marketing efforts, negotiations with employees and labor organizations, learning by doing on the part of managers and workers, the costs of hiring, training and firing workers, the costs of adjusting co-operating factors of production, changes in the availability of inputs, competition from rivals, access to financial backing, ownership changes and corporate restructurings, regulatory and tax law changes, and the growth and decline of particular markets. As this list suggests, job creation and destruction are part of a larger process of adjustment, reallocation and growth.

Much of the reallocation process, and much of our interest in it, centers on the labor market. The creation and destruction of jobs require workers to switch employers and to shuffle between employment and joblessness. Along the way, some workers suffer long unemployment spells or sharp declines in earnings; some retire early or temporarily leave the labor force to work at home or upgrade skills; some switch occupation or industry; some change residence to secure a new job, migrating short or long distances, often with considerable disruption to the lives and jobs of family members.

The workers who participate in this process differ greatly in the bundle of skills, capabilities and career goals that they bring to the labor market; likewise, jobs differ greatly in the skill requirements, effort and diligence that they demand from workers. The diversity of workers and jobs, and their large flows, underscore the truly breathtaking scale and complexity of the search, assignment and reallocation processes carried out by the labor market and supporting institutions. Research in this general area has mushroomed in the past twenty years and is now the subject of several excellent surveys and book-length treatments.[1] The matching process and the prospect of match termination also influence the nature of ongoing employment relationships and the patterns of investment by both workers and firms, as emphasized in another strand of the literature.[2]

On the macroeconomic level, the extent to which the reallocation and matching process operates smoothly determines, in large measure, the difference between successful and unsuccessful economic performance. The persistently high unemployment rates in France, Spain and several other Western European countries over the past two decades point to the enormous costs of a partial breakdown in the reallocation and matching process.[3] The recent and ongoing transition to market-oriented economies in Eastern Europe and the

---

[1] See Mortensen (1986), Pissarides (1990), Devine and Kiefer (1991) and Mortensen and Pissarides (1999) on the search approach to labor market analysis. Sattinger (1993) surveys assignment models of the labor market.

[2] Parsons (1986, Section 4) and Section 4 in Malcomson (this volume) review work in this area.

[3] Recent work on this topic includes Caballero and Hammour (1998b), Cabrales and Hopenhayn (1997), Ljungqvist and Sargent (1996), Millard and Mortensen (1997), and chapters by Machin and Manning, and Nickell and Layard in this volume.

former Soviet Union brought tremendous shifts in the industrial structure of employment and in the ownership and operation of business enterprises. Large differences in output movements, unemployment rates, private-sector expansion and other performance indicators in formerly statist economies suggest that the efficiency of the restructuring and reallocation process varies greatly. A different line of empirical research focused on the US economy suggests that job reallocation from less to more productive plants plays a major role in longer term productivity gains. On another related front, much of the initial and continuing impetus behind research on gross job flows reflects a desire to better understand cyclical fluctuations in employment, output and productivity.

These introductory remarks suggest that job flows are closely connected to worker flows, unemployment behavior, individual wage dynamics, the evolution of firms and industries, economic restructuring, and aggregate productivity growth. Naturally enough, then, much research on job flows stands at the intersection of labor economics, macro-economics and industrial organization. New data on job flows and related theoretical developments have helped build new bridges and solidify old links between labor economics, on the one hand, and macroeconomics and industrial organization on the other. Some specific examples give content to this claim.

- *Employer lifecycle dynamics:* Cross-sectional evidence on gross job flows sheds light on the lifecycle dynamics of establishments and firms. Dunne et al. (1989b) and Davis and Haltiwanger (1992) report a strong, pervasive pattern of larger gross job flow rates at younger US manufacturing plants, with detailed controls for size and industry in the latter study.[4] The same pattern shows up repeatedly in empirical studies of firm-level and plant-level growth behavior (Evans, 1987a,b; Dunne et al., 1989a; Troske, 1996). This ubiquitous pattern highlights the connection between employer lifecycle dynamics and the gross flows of workers and jobs, and it points to the importance of selection effects in the evolution of plants and industries (Jovanovic, 1982).

- *Reallocation and productivity growth*: Recent studies by Baily et al. (1992, 1996), Olley and Pakes (1996) and others find that the reallocation of jobs and factor inputs from less efficient to more efficient plants accounts for a large fraction of industry-level productivity gains. In related work, Basu and Fernald (1995) quantify the implications of cyclical variation in factor reallocation activity for Solow-type measures of aggregate technology shocks.

- *Reallocation and business cycles*: Time-series data on gross flows shed new light on the nature of business cycles and the connection between recessions and the reallocation of workers and jobs. Empirical regularities in job flow behavior have helped stimulate a renewed interest in labor market dynamics and a new generation of equilibrium business cycle models that emphasize frictions in the reallocation of workers and jobs (e.g., Mortensen, 1994; Ramey and Watson, 1997).

---

[4] Similar findings hold in data on the Maryland private sector (Lane et al., 1996), the French private sector (Nocke, 1994) and the Norwegian manufacturing sector (Klette and Mathiassen, 1996).

- *Lumpiness, heterogeneity and aggregation*: The pervasiveness and magnitude of large-scale gross job flows underscore the dangers of reasoning about aggregate and industry-level dynamics from representative-employer models. Large-scale heterogeneity among employers implies considerable scope for aggregation to smooth away even pronounced non-linearities and asymmetries in firm-level and establishment-level employment dynamics (e.g., Caballero, 1992). Gross job flow data also point to considerable lumpiness in establishment-level employment changes. Taken together, lumpiness and heterogeneity imply that aggregate employment dynamics are closely intertwined with the evolution of the cross-sectional distribution of establishment-level employment changes.

Research on job flows also addresses important topics that lie squarely within the domain of labor economics:

- *Reasons for worker mobility*: Many prominent and insightful theories of worker mobility dynamics stress match quality and supply-side concerns such as job-shopping, human capital acquisition, career progression and events that affect preferences regarding work (e.g., children). Without downplaying the importance of these considerations, recent research on job flows highlights the major role of demand-side disturbances that induce shifts in the distribution of job opportunities across locations. It is now apparent, as perhaps it was not a decade ago, that a satisfactory account of worker mobility dynamics in market economies requires a major role for demand-side disturbances as well as for supply-side and match-quality effects.
- *Worker sorting and job assignment*: Many economic theories deal with assignment problems that arise when workers are imperfect substitutes in production, or when they differ in their ability or desire to work with cooperating factors. Assignment models underlie the analysis of several important topics in labor economics including dual labor markets, equalizing differences in wage payments, labor market sorting based on comparative and absolute advantage, and the organization of workers into teams and hierarchies (Sattinger, 1993). Worker and job flows across locations are among the most important mechanisms by which the economy continually adjusts the assignment of workers to each other and to cooperating factors of production.

The chapter proceeds as follows. Section 2 introduces basic definitions and important measurement issues. Section 3 synthesizes several of the main empirical regularities to emerge from research on job creation and destruction behavior. Section 4 provides an in-depth characterization of how job flows vary with employer characteristics such as size, age, wages and capital intensity. Section 5 reviews theories and empirical studies that help to explain the large magnitude of gross job flows and their systematic variation with employer and industry characteristics. Section 6 takes up the relationship between job flows and worker flows. Section 7 considers the connection between job flows and creative destruction, drawing on two largely distinct lines of research: theoretical studies of real-location and growth and empirical studies that quantify the role of between-plant factor reallocation in productivity growth. Section 8 considers the reallocation process in transition economies. Section 9 focuses on the cyclical dynamics of job creation and destruction. Section 10 develops a theoretical model of costly factor reallocation and uses it to investigate the productivity and welfare effects of job flows. Section 11 concludes.

2. Concepts and measurement

2.1. Job flow concepts

The concept of a job is a familiar one, but meaningful measurement and interpretation of job creation and destruction statistics require careful definitions and assumptions. A job, in our terminology, means an employment position filled by a worker. With this in mind, we define gross job creation and destruction as follows:

Definition 1. (Gross) job creation at time t equals employment gains summed over all business units that expand or start up between $t - 1$ and t.

Definition 2. (Gross) job destruction at time t equals employment losses summed over all business units that contract or shut down between $t - 1$ and t.

Under these definitions, the net employment change is simply the difference between gross job creation and destruction.

Some studies measure job creation and destruction using establishment-level employment changes, where an establishment (or plant) is a specific physical location at which production of goods or services takes place. Other studies use firm-level employment changes, where a firm (or company) is an economic and legal entity that encompasses one or more establishments. For our purposes, establishment-level data are preferred on both conceptual and measurement grounds. Firm-level data mask the job flows between establishments of the same firm. In addition, accurate longitudinal linkages are more difficult to achieve with firm-level data because of sometimes complicated changes in ownership and organization (mergers, acquisitions and divestitures).

Most studies fail to capture job flows within establishments. Suppose, for example, that an establishment replaces several secretaries with an equal number of computer programmers. Employment at the establishment is unchanged, so that calculations based on establishment-level data record no job creation or destruction associated with the replacement of secretaries by programmers. A few studies summarized in Section 3.1 seek to measure job flows within establishments or firms. Section 4.3 suggests an indirect approach to estimating job flows within establishments using only establishment-level data.

We interpret measured increases and decreases in employment at a business unit as changes in desired employment levels rather than as changes in the stock of unfilled positions. When a vacancy arises as the result of a quit, for example, the position can likely be refilled within three or twelve months, if desired. Since the highest sampling frequency we examine is quarterly, we are reasonably confident in this interpretation. The interpretation is buttressed by the fact, reported below, that measured job creation and destruction occur primarily at business units that undergo substantial contraction or expansion during the sampling interval.[5]

A useful way to summarize the heterogeneity of employment changes across business units is to count the number of jobs that either disappear from shrinking units or newly appear at expanding units. We refer to this job destruction and creation activity as job reallocation, because it entails the reshuffling of job opportunities across locations.

Definition 3. (Gross) job reallocation at time t is the sum of all business unit employment gains and losses that occur between $t - 1$ and t.

Job reallocation equals the sum of job creation and job destruction.

Another measure derived from establishment- or firm-level employment changes will prove useful for understanding the sources of job reallocation and, in particular, the role played by shifts in the sectoral composition of employment demand.

Definition 4. Excess job reallocation equals (gross) job reallocation minus the absolute value of the net employment change.

Excess job reallocation represents that part of job reallocation over and above the amount required to accommodate net employment changes. It is an index of simultaneous job creation and destruction.[6] As we show below, excess job reallocation admits an exact decomposition into two components: one that captures between-sector employment shifts, and one that captures excess job reallocation within sectors.

As employment opportunities shift across locations, workers undertake conformable shifts. Job-losing workers find employment at different establishments, become unemployed and search for a new job, or leave the labor force. Newly available jobs become filled by jobless or already employed workers. Of course, workers often switch employers or change employment status for reasons largely unrelated to the reallocation of jobs. Thus, job reallocation should be distinguished from worker reallocation, which we define as follows:

Definition 5. (Gross) worker reallocation at time t equals the number of persons who change place of employment or employment status between $t - 1$ and t.

---

[5] Blanchard and Diamond (1990) measure job creation as the sum of employment gains at new and expanding establishments plus an estimate of the change in outstanding vacancies. The resulting job creation time series for the US manufacturing sector differs little from the one defined in the text and plotted in Fig. 4.

[6] Gross job reallocation rises with simultaneous job creation and destruction, but – unlike excess job reallocation – it also rises with the absolute value of net employment change. For this reason, excess job reallocation is a more appropriate index of simultaneous creation and destruction than gross job reallocation.

We elaborate on the connection between job and worker reallocation and consider other measures of labor market flows in Section 6.

2.2. Measurement issues and comparisons across studies

Several measurement problems and conceptual differences hamper easy comparisons of gross job flows across studies and countries.[7] First, as noted above, the definition of business units differs among datasets. As a related point, the procedures for defining the boundaries of firms and establishments, even if applied carefully and consistently over time, differ among data sources and especially countries. Second, the integrity of longitudinal linkages for establishments and firms varies greatly across datasets and, in some cases, over time for the same dataset. Failures to adequately track changes in organizational structure, ownership and administrative identifiers in longitudinal business data can yield spuriously large gross job flows, especially in the form of spurious entry and exit. Third, the concept of a job differs across studies. Most studies calculate gross job flows from point-in-time changes for all workers, but some studies use changes in time-averaged employment measures or restrict attention to full-time or permanent workers. Fourth, the sampling interval differs across studies, which influences the share of transitory employment movements captured in measured job flows. Fifth, sectoral coverage and sampling frames vary markedly across datasets. Some datasets are drawn from the universe of all business units in a sector, while others are restricted to units above a certain size (e.g., 20 employees). Many datasets are restricted to particular industries or regions or omit the public sector.

Another measurement difference across studies involves the growth rate concept. Some studies use a traditional growth rate measure, namely the employment change from period $t-1$ to t divided by employment in period $t-1$. This measure has two unattractive features: it is asymmetric about zero, and it cannot accommodate births and deaths in an integrated manner. An obvious alternative is the log difference, which has the advantage of symmetry about zero. However, the log difference is unbounded above and below and hence does not easily afford an integrated treatment of births, deaths and continuing employers. For these reasons, we prefer a non-traditional growth rate measure that has become the standard approach to measurement in recent studies of gross job flow behavior. Our preferred growth rate measure equals the change in employment between period $t-1$ and t, divided by the simple average of employment in $t-1$ and t. This growth rate measure is symmetric about zero, lies in the closed interval $[-2,2]$, facilitates an integrated treatment of births and deaths, and is identical to the log difference up to a second-order Taylor series expansion.

Differences in datasets and measurement procedures call for the exercise of sound judgment and some caution in comparing gross job flows across studies and countries. When making cross-country comparisons, in particular, we emphasize within-country

---

[7] Our discussion here of measurement-related issues is brief. Davis and Haltiwanger (1998) discuss measurement in several US datasets at length, and Davis et al. (1990, 1996) extensively treat issues that arise in measuring gross job flows in the Longitudinal Research Datafile for the US manufacturing sector.

patterns that are less susceptible to distortions caused by differences in data quality and measurement procedures.

2.3. Notation and formulas

Some notation helps to clarify the concepts introduced above and to spell out the relationships among them. Let EMP_{est} denote the number of workers at employer e in sector s at time t. S_t denotes the set of employers with positive employment in t or $t-1$. S_t^+ denotes the subset of employers that expand or enter between $t-1$ and t, and S_t^- denotes the subset that contract or exit.

Gross job creation (Definition 1) in sector s at time t is

$$C_{st} = \sum_{e \in S^+} \Delta EMP_{est}, \tag{1}$$

where $\Delta Y_t = Y_t - Y_{t-1}$, and gross job destruction (Definition 2) is

$$D_{st} = \sum_{e \in S^-} |\Delta EMP_{est}|. \tag{2}$$

The net sectoral employment change is $NET_{st} = C_{st} - D_{st}$. Gross job reallocation (Definition 3) can be expressed as

$$R_{st} = \sum_{e \in S} |\Delta EMP_{est}| = C_{st} + D_{st}. \tag{3}$$

Excess job reallocation (Definition 4) in sector s equals $R_{st} - |NET_{st}|$. Given a particular classification of sectors indexed by s, the aggregate excess reallocation of jobs satisfies the decomposition,

$$R_t - |NET_t| = \left(\sum_s |NET_{st}| - |NET_t| \right) + \sum_s (R_{st} - |NET_{st}|). \tag{4}$$

The first term on the right-hand side captures between-sector employment shifts, and the second summation captures excess job reallocation within sectors. Note that the first term equals zero if all sectors change in the same direction.

To express the job flow measures as rates, we divide by a measure of size. We measure the time-t size of a business unit as the simple average of its employment in $t-1$ and t: $Z_{est} = 0.5(EMP_{est} + EMP_{es,t-1})$. Summing Z_{est} over units within sector s yields Z_{st}, the size of the sector at t. In terms of this notation, the time-t growth rates can be written $g_{est} = \Delta EMP_{est}/Z_{est}$ for unit e, and $g_{st} = \Delta EMP_{st}/Z_{st}$ for sector s. As mentioned above, these growth rate measures lie in the closed interval $[-2,2]$, with endpoints corresponding to exit and entry.

Using lower-case letters for rates, the sectoral creation, destruction and reallocation rates can be written

$$c_{st} = \frac{C_{st}}{Z_{st}} = \sum_{e \in S^+} \left(\frac{Z_{est}}{Z_{st}} \right) g_{est}, \tag{5}$$

$$d_{st} = \frac{D_{st}}{Z_{st}} = \sum_{e \in S^-} \left(\frac{Z_{est}}{Z_{st}} \right) |g_{est}|, \tag{6}$$

$$r_{st} = \frac{R_{st}}{Z_{st}} = \sum_{e \in S} \left(\frac{Z_{est}}{Z_{st}} \right) |g_{est}| = c_{st} + d_{st}. \tag{7}$$

Eqs. (5)–(7) express the job flow rates in terms of the size-weighted frequency distribution of employment growth rate outcomes. Eq. (7), in particular, states that the job reallocation rate is equivalent to the size-weighted mean of absolute growth rates among business units. The decomposition for the excess job reallocation rate can be written

$$x_t = r_t - |g_t| = \left[\sum_s \left(\frac{Z_{st}}{Z_t} \right) |g_{st}| - |g_t| \right] + \left[\sum_s \left(\frac{Z_{st}}{Z_t} \right) (r_{st} - |g_{st}|) \right]. \tag{8}$$

3. Key facts about gross job flows

3.1. Large magnitude

We begin our characterization of the facts by reviewing findings about the magnitude of job flows. Table 1 presents average job flow rates from various studies on US data. The studies differ in time period, sampling interval, sectoral coverage and definition of business unit, but some clear patterns emerge. First, and most important, the pace of job creation and destruction is rapid. Using annual figures, roughly 1 in 10 jobs are created and another 1 in 10 are destroyed each year. Second, rates of job creation and destruction are somewhat lower for manufacturing than private-sector non-manufacturing. Third, there is a large transitory component in the higher frequency job flows, especially the quarterly flows, as the quarterly (annual) rates do not simply cumulate to the annual (5-year) rates. Fourth, rates for between-firm job reallocation are typically lower than corresponding rates for between-establishment reallocation. This pattern reflects employment shifts between establishments of the same firm.

Table 2 presents average annual job flow rates for 18 countries. Rather strikingly, high rates of job creation and destruction are pervasive. The constant churning of job opportunities that characterizes the US labor market represents the normal state of affairs for both developed and developing economies. Differences in sectoral coverage, data quality, and business unit definitions hamper fine cross-country comparisons, but Table 2 also indicates that, within countries, gross job flow rates for non-manufacturing tend to be higher than those for manufacturing.

The measures reported in Tables 1 and 2 do not capture employment shifts within business units. A few studies, summarized in Table 3, provide some analysis of within-

Table 1
Average gross job flow rates: US studies

Geographical coverage	Period	Industry coverage	Sampling unit	Job creation	Job destruction	Net growth	Job reallocation	Source
5-Year changes								
United States	1967–1982	Manufacturing	Establishments	29.6	30.9	-1.3	60.5	Dunne et al. (1989b, Table 1)
Annual changes								
United States	1973–1993	Manufacturing	Establishments	8.8	10.2	-1.3	19.0	Baldwin (1996, Table 1)
Selected states[a]	1979–1983	Private sector	Reporting units[b]	11.4	9.9	1.4	21.3	Anderson and Meyer (1994, Table 11)
Selected states[a]	1979–1983	Manufacturing	Reporting units	10.2	11.5	-1.3	21.6	Anderson and Meyer (1994, Table 11)
Wisconsin[a]	1978–1982	Manufacturing	Reporting units	12.1	9.1	3.0	21.2	Leonard (1987, Table 6.6)
Wisconsin[a]	1978–1982	Non-manufacturing	Reporting units	14.8	12.3	2.5	27.1	Leonard (1987, Table 6.6)
Michigan[a]	1978–1988	Manufacturing	Firms	6.2	8.5	-2.3	14.7	Foote (1997, Table 1)
Michigan[a]	1978–1988	Private sector	Firms	10.0	9.6	0.4	19.6	Foote (1997, Table 1)
Pennsylvania[a]	1976–1985	Private sector	Reporting units	13.3	12.5	0.8	25.8	OECD (1987, Table 4.1)
Quarterly changes								
United States	1947–1993	Manufacturing	Establishments	5.8	6.0	-0.2	11.8	Davis and Haltiwanger (1998)
United States	1930–1940	Manufacturing	Establishments	11.5	10.3	1.2	21.8	Davis and Haltiwanger (1998)
Maryland[a]	1985–1993	Manufacturing	Reporting units	7.5	8.8	-1.3	16.3	Lane et al. (1996, Table 1)
Maryland[a]	1985–1993	Private sector[c]	Reporting units	8.7	8.9	-0.2	17.6	Lane et al. (1996, Table 1)
West Virginia[a]	1990–1994	Manufacturing	Establishments	4.9	5.8	-0.9	10.7	Spletzer (1997)
West Virginia[a]	1990–1994	Total	Establishments	8.4	8.0	-0.4	16.4	Spletzer (1997)

[a] Based on data for employers covered by the Unemployment Insurance (UI) system. The UI system covers all private sector employment except self-employed persons, domestic workers, some railroad workers, and certain non-profit organizations.
[b] Reporting units are a mixture of establishments, firms and tax-paying units.
[c] The agriculture, mining and contract construction, and the government sector are not included. The reported numbers are unweighted averages across sectors.

Table 2
International comparison of annual gross job flow rates (annual averages as percentages of employment)

Country	Period	Coverage	Employer unit	Job creation	Job destruction	Net growth	Job reallocation	Source
Australia	1984–1985	Manufacturing	Establishments	16.1	13.2	3.9	29.3	Borland and Home (1994)
Canada	1974–1992	Manufacturing	Establishments	10.9	11.1	-0.2	21.9	Baldwin et al. (1998, Table 2)
Canada	1983–1991	All employees	Firms	14.5	11.9	2.6	26.3	OECD (1996, Table 2)
Chile	1976–1986	Manufacturing	Establishments	13.0	13.9	-1.0	26.8	Roberts (1996, Table 2.1)
Colombia	1977–1991	Manufacturing	Establishments	12.5	12.2	0.3	24.6	Roberts (1996, Table 2.1)
Denmark	1983–1989	Private sector	Establishments	16.0	13.8	2.2	29.8	OECD (1996, Table 2)
Denmark	1981–1991	Manufacturing	Establishments	12.0	11.5	0.5	23.5	Albaek and Sorensen (1996, Table 2)
Estonia	1992–1994	All employees	Firms	9.7	12.9	-2.2	22.6	Haltiwanger and Vodopivec (1997)
Finland	1986–1991	All employees	Establishments	10.4	12.0	-1.6	22.4	OECD (1996, Table 2)
France	1984–1992	Private sector	Establishments	13.9	13.2	0.6	27.1	OECD (1996, Table 2)
France	1985–1991	Manufacturing	Firms	10.2	11.0	-0.8	21.2	Nocke (1994, Table3)
France[a]	1985–1991	Non-manufacturing	Firms	14.3	11.8	2.4	26.1	Nocke (1994, Table3)
Germany	1983–1990	All employees	Establishments	9.0	7.5	1.5	16.5	OECD (1996, Table 2)
Germany (Lower Saxony)	1979–1993	Manufacturing	Establishments	4.5	5.2	-0.7	9.7	Wagner (1995, Table A2.1)
Italy[b]	1984–1993	Private sector	Firms	11.9	11.1	0.8	23.0	Contini et al. (1995, Table 3.1)
Israel	1971–1972	Manufacturing	Establishments	9.7	8.2	1.5	17.9	Gronau and Regev (1997)
Morocco	1984–1989	Manufacturing	Firms	18.6	12.1	6.5	30.7	Roberts (1996, Table 2.1)
Netherlands	1979–1993	Manufacturing	Firms	7.3	8.3	-1.0	15.6	Gautier (1997, Table 3.3)
New Zealand	1987–1992	Private sector	Establishments	15.7	19.8	-4.1	35.5	OECD (1996, Table 2)
Norway	1976–1986	Manufacturing	Establishments	7.1	8.4	-1.2	15.5	Klette and Mathiassen (1996, Table 1)
Sweden	1985–1992	All employees	Establishments	14.5	14.6	-0.1	29.1	OECD (1996, Table 2)
USA	1973–1993	Manufacturing	Establishments	8.8	10.2	-1.3	19.0	Baldwin et al. (1998, Table 1)
USA[c]	1979–1983	Private sector	Establishments	11.4	9.9	1.4	21.3	Anderson and Meyer (1994, Table 11)
USA[c]	1979–1983	Manufacturing	Establishments	10.2	11.5	-1.3	21.6	Anderson and Meyer (1994, Table 11)
United Kingdom	1985–1991	All employees	Firms	8.7	6.6	2.1	15.3	OECD (1996, Table 2)

[a] Non-manufacturing includes commerce, transport and communications, services, insurance, banking and financial institutions.
[b] Contini and Pacelli (1995, p. 33) report that efforts to purge the data of spurious births and deaths reduce the Italian gross job flow rates by about one-fifth.
[c] Selected states. Based on data for employers covered by the Unemployment Insurance (UI) system. The UI system covers all private sector employment except self-employed persons, domestic workers, some railroad workers, and certain non-profit organizations.

unit job reallocation. The Hamermesh et al. (1996) study for the Netherlands relies on survey responses to questions about whether hires were to new or existing positions. Based upon the survey responses, about 11% (0.8/(6.2 + 0.8)) of total measured job reallocation arises from within-firm reallocation. Dunne et al. (1997) rely on a classification into production and non-production workers to measure within-establishment reallocation. They find that about 12% of total measured job reallocation reflects within-plant reallocation. Lagarde et al. (1994) exploit detailed information on job classifications to study within-establishment flows. Measurement difficulties presented by worker movements between job classifications cloud the interpretation of their results, but taken at face value, Lagarde et al. find that within-establishment job shifts between skill categories account for almost half of total job reallocation.

3.2. Predominance of idiosyncratic factors

A second basic fact is the dominant role of plant-specific and firm-specific factors in accounting for the large observed magnitudes of gross job flows.

Table 4 illustrates the pervasiveness of high job reallocation rates across manufacturing industries. Virtually every 2-digit industry in each country exhibits an annual rate of job reallocation that exceeds 10%. Interestingly, Table 4 also suggests that the industry pattern of job reallocation intensity is quite similar across countries. A simple regression of industry-level reallocation rates on country and industry fixed effects for the United States, Canada and the Netherlands yields the following. The R-squared on country effects alone is 0.08, the R-squared on industry effects alone is 0.48, and the R-squared on country and industry effects together is 0.56. Further, the F-tests for the specification with both effects yield P-values of 0.06 for country effects and 0.03 for industry effects. In short, even this small sample of three countries provides clear evidence of systematic industry-level patterns in the pace of job reallocation.[8]

The high pace of job reallocation in every industry suggests that a large fraction of gross job flows reflects within-sector reallocation activity rather than between-sector employment shifts. We evaluate this hypothesis in Table 5 by reporting the decomposition (8) for several countries and sectoral classification schemes.

A remarkable aspect of Table 5 is the inability of between-sector shifts to account for excess job reallocation. For example, employment shifts among the approximately 450 four-digit industries in the US manufacturing sector account for a mere 13% of excess job reallocation.[9] Simultaneously cutting the US manufacturing data by state and two-digit

---

[8] Rank correlations of the industry reallocation rates make the same point. The pairwise rank correlation of industry reallocation rates is 0.56 between the United States and Canada, 0.28 between the United States and the Netherlands and 0.60 between the United States and Norway. Similarly, Roberts (1996) reports positive rank correlations of industry-level reallocation rates among Chile, Colombia and Morocco. The correlations reported in his Table 2.6 are higher for excess reallocation rates than for gross job reallocation rates.

[9] The average four-digit manufacturing industry has about 39,000 employees and accounts for about 0.04% of aggregate US employment.

Table 3
Job reallocation rates between and within employers[a]

Study	Coverage	Employer unit	Between reallocation rate	Within reallocation rate	Notes
Hamermesh et al. (1996, Table 2)	Netherlands, all sectors, 1988–1990	Firms	6.2	0.8	Changes in number of jobs within the firm are identified by respondents of the survey. Respondents report whether a hire occurred to a new or to an existing job
Lagarde et al. (1994, Table 1)	France, all sectors, 1984–1991	Establishments	7.9	6.7	Changes in number of jobs within the plant are identified by observing changes in six skill categories of workers
Dunne et al. (1997, Table 5)	USA, manufacturing 1972–1988	Establishments	19.2	2.7	Changes in number of jobs within the plant are identified by observing changes in two categories of workers: production and non-production

[a] Within reallocation equals jobs created plus jobs destroyed within the establishment's (firm's) net employment change. Summing this quantity over all establishments (firms) and dividing by aggregate employment yields the within reallocation rate. The between reallocation rate is the job reallocation rate in Definition 3.

Table 4
Average annual job reallocation rates by country and industry[a]

	USA 1974–1992	Canada 1974–1992	Netherlands 1979–1993	Norway 1976–1986
Food	17.9	19.5	18.4	15.3
Tobacco	12.7	12.3		
Textiles	16.9	21.3	19.1	18.3
Apparel	25.2	27.8	23.4	
Lumber	25.8	26.2	20.8	15.7
Furniture	20.7	27.7		
Paper	12.5	11.1	14.6	12.6
Printing	17.1	22.0	16.3	
Chemicals	14.0	18.7	12.1	12.7
Petroleum	14.2	15.6	10.1	13.2
Rubber	20.3	21.5	12.1	
Leather	22.4	24.2	17.5	
Stone, clay, glass	20.4	23.0	15.6	
Primary metals	16.0	13.3	5.2	6.3
Fabricated metals	20.0	27.7	18.8	18.7
Non-electric machinery	20.5	27.8	16.4	
Electric machinery	19.5	24.6	11.3	
Transportation	18.4	20.6	14.6	
Instruments	10.5	28.1	19.7	
Miscellaneous	14.4		28.5	18.3
Total manufacturing	19.0	21.9	15.6	15.5

[a] Sources: USA, Baldwin et al. (1998, Table 2) except the data for instruments and miscellaneous, which are from 1973–1988 data in Davis et al. (1996); Canada, Baldwin et al. (1998, Table 2); Norway, Klette and Mathiassen (1996, Table 6); Netherlands, Gautier (1997, Table 3.7).

industry yields a contribution of only 14% for between-sector shifts. Davis and Haltiwanger (1992) report that even when sectors are defined by simultaneously crossing 2-digit industry, region, size class, plant age class and ownership type (14,400 sectors), between-sector shifts account for only 39% of excess job reallocation.[10] The same finding holds up in studies for other countries. For example, using detailed industry classifications (600 industries), Nocke (1994) finds that only 17% of excess job reallocation in France is accounted for by between-sector employment shifts.

These results provide little support for the view that high rates of job reallocation arise primarily because of sectoral disturbances or economy-wide disturbances with differential sectoral effects – at least when sectors are defined in terms of industry, region, size and age. Instead, the results in Table 5 imply that job flows are largely driven by plant-level and firm-level heterogeneity in labor demand changes.

[10] To appreciate the level of detail captured by this sectoral classification scheme, we remark that the average nonempty "sector" contains only about five sampled plants.

Table 5
Fraction of excess job reallocation accounted for by employment shifts between sectors

Country	Period	Classification scheme	Unit of analysis	Number of sectors	Average number of workers per sector (in 000's)	Fraction resulting from shifts between sectors	Source
USA	1972–1988	4-Digit SIC manufacturing	Plant	448/456	39.1[a]	0.13	Davis and Haltiwanger (1992, Table 3.8)
USA	1972–1988	2-Digit SIC manufacturing by state	Plant	980	17.9	0.14	Davis and Haltiwanger (1992, Table 3.8)
Denmark	1983–1989	1-Digit ISIC private sector	Plant	8	196.1	0.00	OECD (1994a, Table 3.5)
Finland	1986–1991	2-Digit ISIC	Plant	27	48.9	0.06	OECD (1994a, Table 3.5)
Germany	1983–1990	2-Digit ISIC	Plant	24	1171.2	0.03	OECD (1994a, Table 3.5)
Italy	1986–1991	2-Digit ISIC private sector	Firm	28	321.5	0.02	OECD (1994a, Table 3.5)
Netherlands	1979–1993	2-Digit SIC	Firm	18	10.0	0.20	Gautier (1997, Table 3.12 (and calculations))
Sweden	1985–1991	2-Digit ISIC	Plant	28	112.4	0.03	OECD (1994a, Table 3.5)
Norway	1976–1986	5-Digit ISIC manufacturing	Plant	142	2.4	0.06	Klette and Mathiassen (1996, Table 8 (and calculations))
France	1984–1988	NAP private sector	Plant	15	883.3	0.06	OECD (1994a, Table 3.5)
France	1985–1991	Detailed industry	Firm	600	36.6	0.17	Nocke (1994, Table 6)
France	1984–1991	NAP	Plant	100	27.5	0.12	Lagarde et al. (1994, Table 2)
New Zealand	1987–1992	2-Digit ISIC	Plant	28	3.7	0.01	OECD (1994a, Table 3.5)
Chile	1979–1986	4-Digit manufacturing	Plant	69		0.12	Roberts (1996)
Colombia	1977–1991	4-Digit manufacturing	Plant	73	6.31	0.13	Roberts (1996)
Morocco	1984–1989	4-Digit manufacturing	Plant	61	4.0	0.17	Roberts (1996)

[a] The US numbers are based on a sample of establishments with the reported number of workers per sector equal to the sample weighted totals. The unweighted averages for the US are 29.3 and 13.5 thousand for the 4-digit and 2-digit, state excercises, respectively.

3.3. Persistence of underlying employment movements

How persistent are the employment changes that underlie the job creation and destruction figures? An answer to this question helps to understand business-level employment dynamics and the character of the worker reallocation associated with job reallocation. To the extent that measured job creation and destruction represent short-lived employment changes, the changes can be implemented largely through temporary layoffs and recalls. To the extent that plant-level employment changes are persistent, they must be associated with longterm joblessness or worker reallocation across plants.

In thinking about how to measure persistence, we stress that our focus is on the persistence of the typical newly created or newly destroyed job. This focus is distinct from a focus on the persistence of the typical existing job or the persistence of establishment size. In line with our focus, we measure persistence according to the following definitions:

Definition 6. The *N*-period persistence of job creation is the percentage of newly created jobs at time *t* that remain filled at each subsequent sampling date through time *t* + *N*.

Definition 7. The *N*-period persistence of job destruction is the percentage of newly destroyed jobs at time *t* that do not reappear at any subsequent sampling date through time *t* + *N*.

These persistence measures lie between 0 and 100% and are non-increasing in *N* for any given set of jobs destroyed or created at *t*.

Table 6 summarizes the persistence properties of job creation and destruction over 1 and 2 year horizons for several countries. Roughly 7 in 10 newly created jobs survive for at least 1 year, and roughly 8 in 10 newly destroyed jobs fail to reappear 1 year later. At 2 years, the persistence of annual job creation and destruction is somewhat lower. The most important aspect of these results is the implication that annual job creation and destruction figures largely reflect persistent plant-level employment changes.[11]

3.4. Concentration and lumpiness of underlying employment movements

Many studies find that births and deaths account for large fractions of job creation and destruction. But, more so than most other gross job flow statistics, the measured roles of births and deaths are influenced by sample design, the sampling interval, the unit of observation (firm or establishment), and the quality of longitudinal links. Since available

---

[11] It may be helpful to reconcile the high persistence of annual job creation and destruction with some well-known facts about the importance of temporary layoffs in the US manufacturing sector. For example, Lilien (1980, Table III) estimates that 60–78% of all manufacturing layoffs ended in recall during the years 1965–1976, which might seem difficult to square with the results in Table 6. But Lilien also reports that 92% of manufacturing unemployment spells ending in recall last three months or less. Hence, most of the short-duration temporary layoffs are not captured by the annual job creation and destruction numbers, which are based upon point-in-time to point-in-time changes from one year to the next.

Table 6
Average persistence rates for annual job flows

	USA 1973–1988		Denmark 1980–1991		Netherlands 1979–1993		Norway 1977–1986		France 1985–1990	
	1 year	2 years	1 year	2 years	1 year	2 years	1 year	2 years	1 year	2 years
Job creation	70.2	54.4	71.0	58.0	77.9	58.8	72.7	65.1	73.4	51.5
Job destruction	82.3	73.6	71.0	58.0	92.5	87.3	84.2	79.8	82.1	68.2
Sources	Davis et al. (1996, Table 2.3)		Albaek and Sorensen (1996, Table 3)		Gautier (1997, Tables 3.16 and 3.19)		Klette and Mathiassen (1996, Table 5 and 4)		Nocke (1994, Table 4)	

datasets often differ greatly along these dimensions, it is difficult to directly compare the prominence of births and deaths across countries and studies.

On a conceptual level, births and deaths are simply the extremes of an underlying growth-rate distribution. It is more informative to characterize how creation and destruction are distributed over the entire distribution rather than just reporting the mass at the endpoints.

These considerations prompt us to characterize the distribution of job creation and destruction over the underlying growth-rate distributions for studies that meet the following criteria: annual sampling frequency, comprehensive or nearly comprehensive sample frame for a major sector, clearly defined observational unit, high quality longitudinal links, and availability of the data (to us). Two studies fully meet these criteria: Davis et al. (1996), who study the US manufacturing sector, and Albaek and Sorensen, 1996, who study the Danish manufacturing sector. For these two countries, Fig. 1 displays the distributions of job creation (to the right of zero) and job destruction (to the left of zero) over intervals of the symmetric growth rate measure defined in Section 2.3. The intervals have width 0.10 and are centered on the reported midpoints. Two additional mass points at $+2$ and -2 correspond to births and deaths.

Fig. 1 shows that gross job flows in manufacturing are concentrated in a relatively small number of plants that experience high rates of expansion or contraction. Table 7 makes the same point, adding Canada and Israel to the data displayed in Fig. 1. All four countries show high concentration of job creation and destruction at relatively few plants, and equivalently, considerable lumpiness in plant-level employment adjustments.

This concentration, or lumpiness, carries some important implications that merit a few remarks here. First, the lumpiness of plant-level employment movements points to a major role for fixed costs in the adjustment of labor or cooperating factors of production. Put differently, such lumpiness is difficult to reconcile with traditional models of convex adjustment costs that long dominated work on dynamic labor demand issues (see Nickell, 1986; Hamermesh and Pfann, 1996). Some recent empirical work on employment dynamics accommodates a much richer specification of adjustment costs (e.g., Caballero and Engel, 1993; Caballero et al., 1997). In addition to characterizing microeconomic adjustment patterns, this work shows how the cross-sectional distribution of outcomes for individual employers influences the behavior of aggregate employment. Parallel work on consumer durables and business investment, surveyed in Attanasio (1998) and Caballero (1998), also highlights the interaction between the cross-sectional distribution of microeconomic outcomes and the behavior of aggregates.

Second, Fig. 1 and Table 7 contain an important message about the connection between job flows and worker flows. As we discuss in Section 6, many firms experience worker attrition rates of 10–20% per year. This high attrition rate suggests that most job destruction is easily and painlessly accommodated by workers who are nearly indifferent about separation in any event. But Table 7 tells us that over two-thirds of job destruction in the manufacturing sector takes place at establishments that shrink by more than 20% over the span of a year. In other words, the bulk of the job destruction measured in annual data

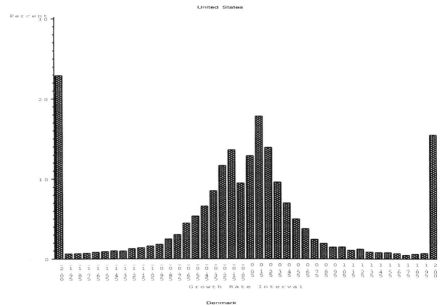

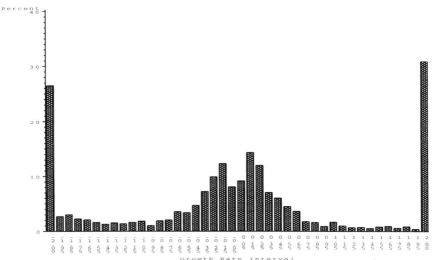

Fig. 1. Distribution of plant-level job creation and destruction. Creation (destruction) percentages are depicted for positive (negative) growth rate intervals. Source: US, Davis et al. (1996); Denmark, Albaek and Sorensen (1996).

represents job loss from the point of view of workers.[12] The "job loss" component of measured job destruction is even higher during recessions, when job destruction rates rise and quit rates fall.

Table 7
The concentration of job creation and job destruction[a]

Country	Sector	Percent of job creation or destruction accounted for by plants with growth rates in the indicated interval					
		[−2,−1)	[−1,−0.2)	[−0.2,0)	(0,0.2]	(0.2,1]	(1,2]
United States	Manufacturing	32.9	44.0	23.1	30.7	45.1	24.2
Canada	Manufacturing		77.7	22.3	24.8	75.2	
Denmark	Manufacturing	45.9	33.7	20.4	23.4	37.4	39.1
Israel	Manufacturing		84.7	15.3	21.8	78.2	

[a] Sources: United States, Davis et al. (1996); Canada, Baldwin et al. (1998); Denmark, Albaek and Sorensen (1996); Israel, Gronau and Regev (1997).

Third, the high concentration of job creation and destruction may accentuate effects on workers and local economies. A sharp employment reduction at a single large plant can flood the local labor market, which increases the hardship that falls on each job loser. Conversely, a sharp employment increase at a single plant can induce an in-migration of workers and their families that strains the capacity of the local community to provide schooling, housing, roads and sewers. The local economy effects of job creation and destruction events are probably most important for manufacturing and a few other industries dominated by large establishments.[13] We are not aware of much research at this intersection point between labor and spatial economics, but the growing availability of matched longitudinal employer–worker datasets suggests that it may become an important topic in future work.

3.5. Systematic differences across sectors: magnitude

Table 4 points to systematic differences in the pace of job reallocation across industries. It turns out that there are many strong cross-sectional patterns in the intensity of job reallocation. We defer a detailed examination of these cross-sectional patterns to Section 4, but Fig. 2 displays two of the most consistent and powerful relationships. These figures show how the excess job reallocation rate varies with employer size and age in the US manufacturing sector. They also show the relationship of size and age to the net job growth rate, a topic of independent interest. These figures are based on size-weighted plant-level regressions of the employment growth rate and the absolute growth rate on a quartic in employer size interacted with dummy variables for the indicated employer age categories.

[12] This inference is less secure for non-manufacturing sectors for two reasons. First, worker attrition rates tend to be higher outside the manufacturing sector. Second, we know of no studies that examine whether non-manufacturing job flows are more or less concentrated than shown in Fig. 1 and Table 7.

[13] Davis and Haltiwanger (1991, Fig. 4.B) report that in 1986, for example, the average manufacturing employee worked at a facility with nearly 1600 workers.

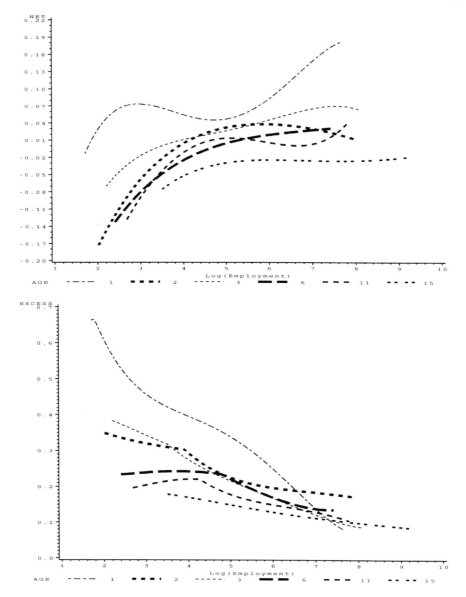

Fig. 2. (a) Net growth rate for age classes, by employer size; (b) excess job reallocation for age classes, by employer size. Source: authors' calculations for the US manufacturing sector.

Age refers to the number of years since the establishment first had positive employment. We use pooled data for the US manufacturing sector in 1978, 1983 and 1988, three years that allow us to construct detailed age measures. The regression specifications include year effects.

Using the estimated regression functions, we calculated the fitted relationships of the net growth rate and the excess reallocation rate to employer size and age.[14] Fig. 2 displays the fitted relationships from the 5th to the 95th percentile of the employment-weighted distribution of plant size.

Some clear and very strong patterns emerge. Holding size constant, net growth declines sharply with age; excess job reallocation also declines with age, except for the largest plants. Holding age constant, net growth increases with size, and excess reallocation declines sharply with size.

Nocke's (1994) study allows for a crude investigation of size and age relationships in data on French job flows. His Table 10 presents employment-weighted net and gross job reallocation rates cross-tabulated by detailed employer size and age classes. Using the information in his table, we generated Fig. 3. The Nocke tabulations are equivalent to a cell-based regression of net growth and job reallocation on detailed employer size and age classes and are roughly comparable to the ones presented in Fig. 2. Although the patterns are somewhat less dramatic, they are basically the same as in the US manufacturing sector.

These results highlight the important role of employer characteristics in accounting for the magnitude of job flows, and they provide clues about the reasons for large job flows. They also suggest that systematic differences in the size and age structure of employment partly account for the industry differences in job reallocation rates in Table 4 and the country differences in Table 2. The strong relationship of employer age to both net growth and excess reallocation points to a major role for employer lifecycle effects. We return to these and related themes in Section 4.

3.6. Distinct cyclical dynamics of creation and destruction

This section addresses two straightforward questions about time variation in gross job flows. First, does the magnitude of gross job flows vary much over time? Second, is there an asymmetry in the respective roles of job creation and destruction in accounting for the dynamic adjustment of employment?

Fig. 4 presents quarterly job creation, job destruction and net growth rates for the US Manufacturing sector from 1947:1 to 1993:4.[15] It is apparent that gross job flow rates vary considerably over time. The job destruction rate ranges from 2.9% to 10.8% of employment per quarter, while the job creation rate ranges from 3.8 to 10.2%. Job creation and destruction covary negatively, but the correlation of -0.17 is small. A noteworthy feature of the data is the relatively volatile nature of job destruction. As measured by the time-series variance, destruction varies 50% more than creation in the quarterly data.

---

[14] We fit the excess reallocation rate as the difference between the fitted absolute growth rate and the absolute value of the fitted net growth rate for each value of size and age.

[15] We constructed these time series by splicing BLS data on worker separations and accessions to LRD data on job flows using the method described in Davis and Haltiwanger (1996, Appendix A).

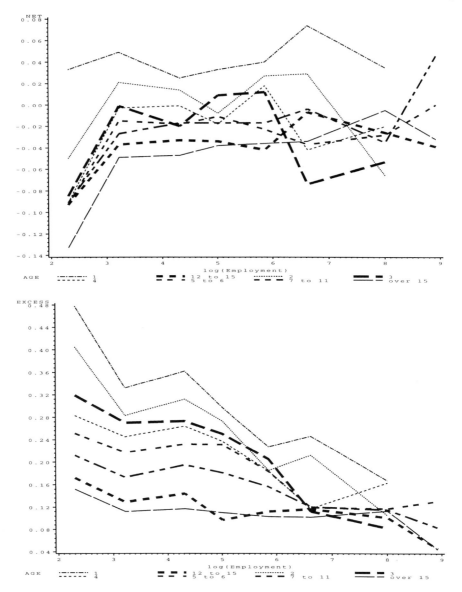

Fig. 3. (a) Net growth rate for age classes, by employer size; (b) excess reallocation for age classes, by employer size. Source: authors' calculationsa based upon French data reported by Nocke (1994, Table 10).

Fig. 4 points to distinctly different cyclical dynamics in job creation and destruction. As expected, creation tends to fall and destruction tends to rise during recessions, but the

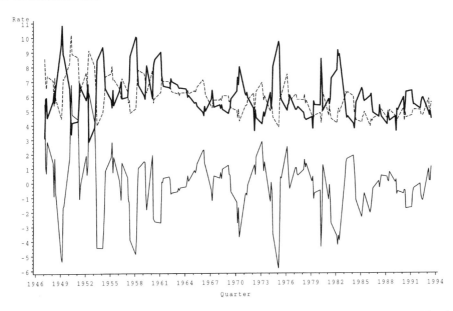

Fig. 4. Job creation and job destruction in US manufacturing. Dashed line, job creation; heavy solid line, job destruction; light solid line, net growth.

cyclical behavior of the two series is not symmetrical. Job destruction rises dramatically during recessions, whereas job creation initially declines by a relatively modest amount. There is some tendency for an upturn in job creation one or two quarters after a spike in destruction.

Fig. 5 presents annual job creation and destruction rates in the manufacturing sector for eight countries. Unfortunately, the available sample period for most countries other than the United States is quite short, and there are some important differences in the nature of the samples across countries. The US and Canadian series are the most comparable, as Baldwin et al. (1998) harmonized the measurement of the gross job flow series from establishment-level data in these two countries. The series for Denmark, Norway and Colombia are establishment-based and have been tabulated using procedures similar to the US data. The German series are also establishment-based but less comparable, because they reflect somewhat different measurement procedures. The series for the Netherlands and the United Kingdom are firm-based, and the UK sample is restricted to continuing firms with more than 20 employees.

It is apparent that job flow rates exhibit considerable volatility in all countries. Except in Denmark and Colombia, job destruction is more volatile than job creation. The variance of destruction divided by the variance of creation is 2.04 for the United States, 1.49 for Canada, 1.48 for Norway, 1.0 for Denmark, 2.68 for the Netherlands, 1.69 for Germany, 0.68 in Colombia, and 18.19 for the UK. The especially high relative volatility of job

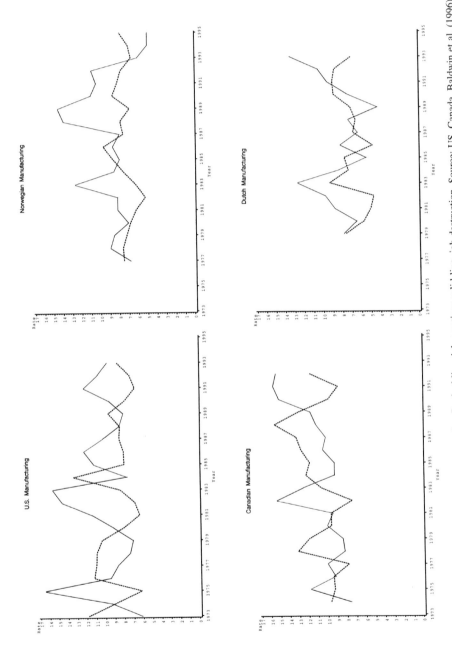

Fig. 5. Job creation and job destruction across countries. Dashed line, job creation; solid line, job destruction. Source: US, Canada, Baldwin et al. (1996); Norway, Salvanes (1997); Netherlands, Gautier (1997); Germany, Wagner (1995); Denmark, Albaek and Sorensen (1996); UK, Konings (1995); Colombia, Roberts (1996).

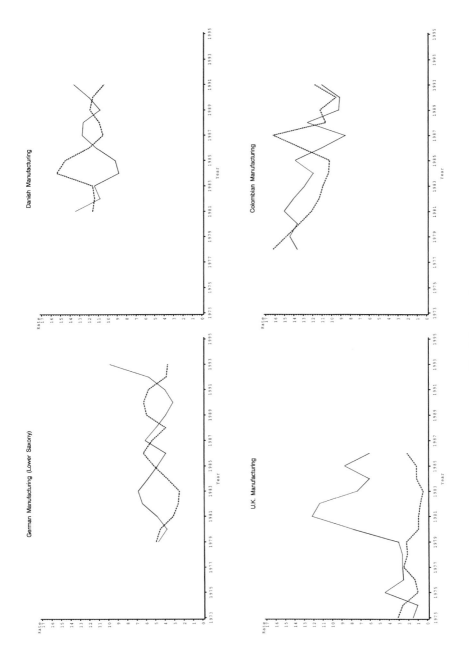

Fig. 5. (*continued*)

destruction in the UK probably reflects the restricted sample underlying the study. We show below, using US data, that the relative volatility of job destruction is systematically lower for younger and smaller businesses.

3.7. Systematic differences across sectors: cyclical dynamics

The asymmetric cyclical behavior of job creation and destruction in the manufacturing sector has attracted much attention in recent work. A natural question is whether this cyclical asymmetry extends to non-manufacturing industries. Information about non-manufacturing industries is limited to fewer studies, shorter sample periods and, on the whole, lower quality data, but the available evidence points to important between-industry differences in cyclical dynamics.

Foote (1997, 1998) shows that the relative variance of job destruction declines sharply with an industry's trend employment growth rate. He finds this relationship in annual data on a broad set of Michigan industries from 1978 to 1988 and in annual data on 4-digit US manufacturing industries from 1972 to 1988. Most industries in his Michigan sample exhibit positive trend growth and show at least as much volatility in creation as in destruction. Foote also proposes an explanation for this relationship based on a mechanical (S,s) model with a fixed set of employers. The basic idea is that a negative (positive) employment trend leads the cross-sectional density of deviations from desired employment to bunch near the destruction (creation) boundary, so that job destruction (creation) is more responsive to common shocks. Foote's simple (S,s) model also yields quantitative predictions, and on this score the model deviates from the empirical evidence in two respects. First, the relative standard deviation of job creation rises more rapidly with trend growth than predicted by the model. Second, conditional on trend growth, the standard deviation of destruction exceeds that of creation, in contrast to the model's prediction of equal variability.

Boeri (1996) presents evidence on the cyclical behavior of gross job flows using annual data for 8 countries (US, Canada, Denmark, France, Germany, Italy, Norway and Sweden). The data for most countries are based on administrative records that cover most or all of the private sector. Boeri finds that the variance of job creation tends to be larger than the variance of job destruction in most of these countries.[16] However, the time series for most countries are quite short and, in many cases, limited to rather quiescent periods that lack sharp variation in employment growth rates. For example, Boeri's Chart 1 shows relatively little cyclical variation in Italy, approximately zero or positive employ-

---

[16] Boeri argues that the US manufacturing pattern is an outlier, but the evidence presented in Fig. 5 indicates otherwise. Boeri also argues that the measured volatility of creation and destruction in the US manufacturing sector is distorted by the exclusion of (most) establishments with fewer than 5 employees. However, the very small plants omitted from the LRD sampling frame comprise only 4% of manufacturing employment, too little to account for the greater measured volatility of job destruction. Foote notes that the cyclical behavior of manufacturing job flows in the Michigan data is unaffected by the exclusion of establishments with fewer than 5 employees.

ment growth in all years in Denmark, a slow secular decline in employment growth that eventually became negative but no apparent cycle in Sweden, and modest contraction (less than 5%) in the early 1980s but no sharp cycles in France. In contrast, US manufacturing employment contracted by almost 10% per year in the middle 1970s and again in the early 1980s but grew modestly in other years. These observations suggest the limited cyclical variation in Boeri's sample may account for his failure to find sharp differences in the relative volatility of creation and destruction.[17]

Despite short sample periods and other data problems, the evidence amassed in Boeri (1996), Foote (1997, 1998) and Fig. 5 clearly suggests that manufacturing and non-manufacturing sectors exhibit systematically different job flow dynamics. Another way to shed light on this issue is to focus on the relationship between employer characteristics and cyclical dynamics within manufacturing. In particular, the US manufacturing data are rich enough to examine a variety of employer characteristics like size, age, capital intensity, product market concentration and trend growth. The effects of these industry characteristics are interesting in their own right, but their study also enables us to explore what might be special about manufacturing.

To pursue this approach, we conducted the following exercise. Using 4-digit quarterly job creation and destruction rates for US manufacturing industries from 1972:2 to 1993:4, we constructed the ratio of the time-series standard deviation of destruction to the standard deviation of creation for each industry. Fig. 6 presents scatter plots of the log standard deviation ratios against the trend employment growth rate, a measure of the employment-weighted firm size distribution, a measure of the employment-weighted establishment age distribution, and the inventory-sales ratio in the industry. Table 8 shows related bivariate and multivariate regression results.

The scatter plots show that the relative volatility of destruction falls with trend growth and rises with firm size, plant age and the inventory-sales ratio. Table 8 shows that the relative volatility of destruction also rises with capital intensity in a bivariate regression. The size and age patterns confirm results in Davis and Haltiwanger (1992) and Davis et al. (1996), while the trend growth rate pattern reproduces results in Foote (1997, 1998). The capital intensity relationship is in line with the theoretical model of Caballero and Hammour (1994), and the inventory relationship is in line with the theoretical model of Hall (1997b).

---

[17] The administrative data underlying the job flow measures in Boeri's study are another concern. He provides little information about data quality and longitudinal linkage procedures. While administrative (tax) data hold great promise for longitudinal analyses, there are pitfalls in their use given the inherent difficulties in maintaining longitudinal identifiers. In the United States, for example, multi-establishment firms may have one or several taxpayer identification numbers (EINs). EINs for establishments and firms may change for a variety of reasons related to administrative convenience, organizational change and ownership change. These problems with taxpayer identification numbers present serious difficulties in measuring job flows accurately. Ongoing analysis at the US Bureau of the Census suggests that the identification number and associated longitudinal linkage problems are more severe for small establishments, especially in retail trade and the service sectors. See Davis and Haltiwanger (1998) for further discussion of longitudinal linkage problems in US datasets.

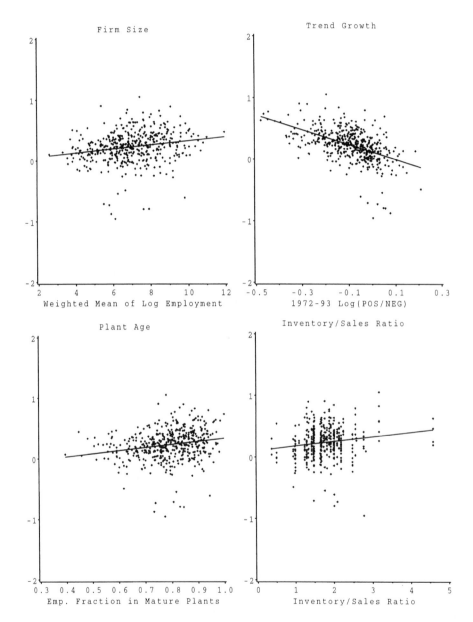

Fig. 6. The relative volaltility of destruction and industry characteristics. The scale on the vertical axes shows the log of the job destruction standard deviation divided by the log of the job creation standard deviation.

Table 8
Job flow standard deviation ratio regressions, four-digit US manufacturing industries, 1972:2 to 1993:4 (dependent variable, log [(job destruction rate standard deviation)/(job creation rate standard deviation)])[a]

Variable	Mean (SD)	Coefficient (standard error)							
		(1)	(2)	(3)	(4)	(5)	(6)	(7)	(8)
Log standard deviation ratio	0.23 (0.26)								
Trend growth[b]	−0.094 (0.11)	−1.19 (0.09)						−1.14 (0.10)	−1.51 (0.17)
Trend squared	0.021 (0.033)								−1.48 (0.56)
Firm size[c]	8.78 (1.59)				0.035 (0.008)			0.035 (0.009)	0.036 (0.008)
Plant age[d]	0.79 (0.11)					0.51 (0.11)			
4-Firm concentration[e]	0.38 (0.21)						0.06 (0.12)	−0.22 (0.07)	−0.22 (0.07)
Capital intensity[f]	4.14 (0.89)		0.032 (0.014)						
Inventories/sales[g]	1.76 (0.55)			0.074 (0.022)					
R^2		0.264	0.012	0.027	0.047	0.044	0.002	0.289	0.300

[a] After dropping two industries with missing data on TFP growth, there are 425 observations. Each industry receives equal weight in the calculation of descriptive statistics and regression coefficients. All regressions include an intercept. The following variables are statistically insignificant when added to the multivariate specification (8): (i) plant age, (ii) capital intensity, (iii) 1972–1993 TFP growth rate, (iv) mean hourly wage for production workers, and (v) the inventory-sales ratio (smaller sample). Including these variables has little effect on the coefficient estimates and standard errors reported in (8).

[b] Trend growth equals the log of the 1972–1993 mean creation rate minus the log of the 1972–1993 destruction rate.

[c] Firm size equals the weighted mean of log firm employment in 1972, 1977, 1982 and 1987. Results with an analogous establishment-based size measure are very similar.

[d] Plant age equals the fraction of industry employment at mature plants in the years from 1973 to 1986, where "mature" means at least 9-13 years old. See Section 7.3.2 in the Appendix to Davis et al. (1996) for details.

[e] 4-Firm concentration equals the fraction of 1987 shipments accounted for by the four leading firms in the industry. These data were kindly supplied by Michael Kiley.

[f] Capital intensity equals the log of capital per production worker (thousands of 1982 dollars).

[g] The inventory-sales ratio equals the average ratio of monthly nominal inventories to sales from the M3 data for the 1972–1993 period.

The multivariate regression results in Table 8 indicate that several independent effects underlie cross-sectional differences in the cyclical dynamics of creation and destruction. In this regard, recall Foote's (1997, 1998) proposed explanation for the relative volatility of creation and destruction. As Foote notes, trend growth does not help explain differences in the relative volatility of creation and destruction among two-digit manufacturing industries. Even in the 4-digit industry data, much of the systematic variation in the standard deviation ratios is unexplained by trend growth differences. This point can be seen in Fig. 6 by observing that the predicted standard deviation ratio at a zero trend growth rate is substantially greater than zero. Foote's theory predicts that the ratio should be greater or less than zero as the trend growth rate is negative or positive. Most importantly, the relative volatility of destruction rises with firm size and declines with industry concentration after controlling for trend growth effects.

These results provide clear evidence that the cyclical dynamics of job creation and destruction vary sharply and systematically with observable industry-level characteristics. The pattern of results helps explain the somewhat different nature of job flow dynamics in the manufacturing and non-manufacturing sectors of the economy. Except for product market concentration, every statistically significant variable in the bivariate and multivariate regressions of Table 8 reinforces a tendency towards greater relative volatility of destruction in manufacturing industries. Manufacturing industries exhibit slower employment growth, greater capital intensity, higher inventories, older establishments, and larger firms and establishments in comparison to most other industries. Each of these characteristics is associated with a positive effect on the relative volatility of destruction.

4. Employer characteristics and the magnitude of job flows

4.1. Sectoral differences

Section 3.5 highlights important differences in net and gross job flow rates by industrial sector and employer characteristics. This section expands upon Section 3.5 by summarizing the main empirical regularities found in previous work on sectoral differences in job flows.

The most heavily studied characteristics in this regard are employer size and age. According to Figs. 2 and 3, excess job reallocation rates decline sharply in employer size and age, a pattern that stands out clearly in other studies. Fig. 7 depicts the relationship between job reallocation and employer size for 8 studies spanning 7 different countries. Some of the studies rely on firm-level data, others use establishment-level data. The message is clear: job reallocation rates decline with employer size. A similar figure (not shown) reveals that job reallocation also consistently declines with employer age. These robust patterns with respect to employer size and age are quite striking in light of the major differences among studies in measurement, country and sectoral coverage, and data.

The results in Fig. 2 on the relationship between net job growth and employer age are

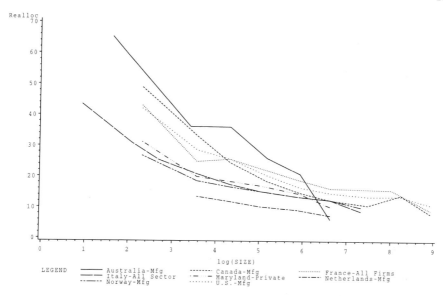

Fig. 7. Annual job reallocation rates by employer size. Source: Norway, Klette and Mathiassen (1996, Table 4); US, Davis et al. (1996, Table 4.1); Canada, Baldwin and Picot (1994, Table 7); Netherlands, Gautier (1997, Table 3.8); Australia, Borland and Home (1994, Table 3); France, Nocke (1994, Table 9); Maryland, Lane et al. (1996, Table 4); Italy, Contini et al. (1995, Table 3.7).

also typical of many studies. For example, Hall (1987), Evans (1987a,b), and Dunne et al. (1989a,b) all find that net growth declines with employer age, even after controlling for employer size.

In contrast, previous work presents sharply different characterizations of the relationship between employer size and net job growth. A common finding that seemingly contradicts Fig. 2 is that net growth tends to decline with employer size, even after controlling for employer age. This finding appears in Evans (1987a,b) and Hall (1987), among others. Controlling for age, Dunne et al. (1989a,b) find that net growth declines with size for single-unit establishments and is U-shaped in size for multi-unit establishments.

Several factors potentially contribute to the sensitivity of the size-net growth relationship, but the most important consideration is probably regression-to-the mean effects.[18] Evans et al. investigate the relationship between the growth rate of employment from period $t - 1$ to t and employer size in period $t - 1$. In contrast, Fig. 2 depicts the relationship between the employment growth rate and the average of employer size in periods $t -$

---

[18] Other considerations include the use of firm-level data in Hall and Evans, the use of different growth rate concepts, and the weighting of employer-level observations. Hall and Evans measure growth as the log first difference and use standard econometric selection techniques to adjust for omitted births and deaths. Dunne et al. use the traditional growth rate measure, which allows them to include deaths but not births in their cell-based regressions. Finally, these studies are carried out on an unweighted basis, whereas our analysis is employment weighted.

1 and t. As explained in Leonard (1987) and Davis et al. (1996, Chapter 3), regression-to-the-mean effects overstate the relative growth performance of smaller employers when there is an important transitory component in (measured) employment. Davis et al. demonstrate that the employer size measure used in Fig. 2 (based upon the average of employment in period $t - 1$ and t) substantially mitigates these effects.[19]

Beyond size and age effects, previous work documents several other sectoral patterns in the magnitude of job flows. Davis et al. (1996) find that excess job reallocation rates decline in average plant-wages, decline in capital intensity, increase in plant-level product specialization, decrease in energy intensity, and increase with industry-level total factor productivity growth. Chow et al. (1996), Konings et al. (1996) and Leonard and Zax (1995) report strikingly smaller job flow rates in the public sector as compared to the private sector.

4.2. Plant-level regressions

Previous work on sectoral differences in job flow magnitudes is limited to one-way and two-way tabulations by employer characteristics. To shed light on how job flow magnitudes vary with employer characteristics in a multivariate setting, we extend the analysis in Fig. 2 to encompass a wide range of employer characteristics. We pool plant-level data from the LRD for 1978, 1983 and 1988,[20] and we then fit employment-weighted regressions of net employment growth and the absolute value of net growth to a variety of controls and plant-level regressors. We report results for the predicted variation in the net employment growth rate and for the difference between the predicted absolute growth rate and the absolute value of the predicted net growth rate. This difference yields the predicted excess reallocation rate as a function of employer characteristics.

Control variables in the regression specification include year effects, 4-digit industry effects, ownership-type effects and state effects. The other regressors are a quartic in log employment interacted with detailed age (as in Fig. 2), a quartic in plant-level energy intensity, a quartic in wages per worker, percentiles of the capital-per-worker distribution, and a measure of plant-level product specialization.[21] To characterize the marginal influence of each employer characteristic on the net growth and excess reallocaton rates, we evaluate the predicted variation associated with that characteristic while holding other characteristics fixed at their medians. Figs. 8 and 9 display the results.

According to Fig. 8, the age and size related patterns exhibited in Fig. 2 continue to hold after controlling for many additional characteristics. Holding age and other employer

---

[19] Other work on this point includes Borland and Home (1994), Baldwin and Picot (1995), Huigen et al. (1991) and Wagner (1995).

[20] As noted above, these sample years allow us to construct the most detailed plant age measures.

[21] Wages per worker are measured as the ratio of total salary and wages to total employment; energy intensity is measured as the ratio of energy expenditures to the total value of shipments; product market specialization is measured as the share of the plant's shipments value accounted for by its chief five-digit product class – the seven categories include complete specialization and then six remaining classes; and capital intensity is measured as the adjusted book value of capital per worker. The adjusted book value makes use of a capital goods price deflator as described in Haltiwanger (1997).

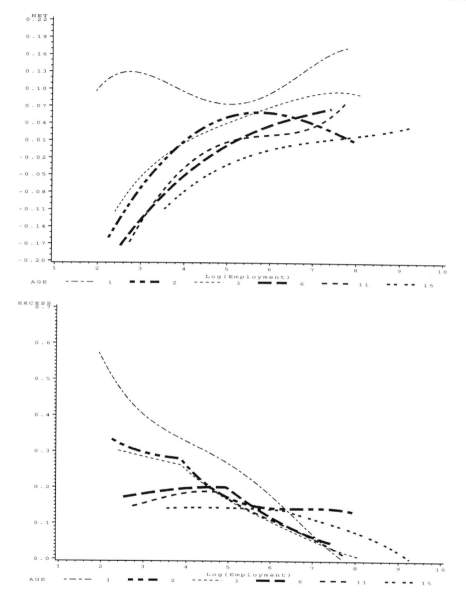

Fig. 8. (a) Net growth rate for age classes, by employer size; (b) excess job reallocation for age classes, by employer size. In contrast to Fig. 2, the relationships plotted in this figure control for a large collection of employer characteristics as described in the text.

characteristics constant, the net employment growth rate rises sharply and the excess reallocation rate falls sharply with employer size. Holding size and other characteristics

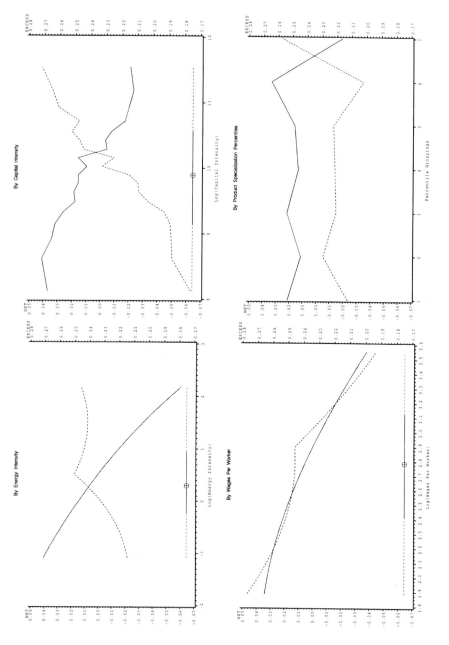

Fig. 9. Growth rate and excess reallocation by employer characteristics. The solid line is net; the dashed line is excess. The horizontal lines above the horizontal axes for energy intensity, wages and capital intensity depict the 5th, 25th, 50th (circle), 75th and 95th percentiles.

constant, the net growth and excess reallocation rates tend to fall with employer age. The age effects on excess reallocation are more pronounced among smaller plants.

Net job growth and excess reallocation also show strong and systematic relationships to several other employer characteristics. Net employment growth decreases in energy intensity, wages per worker and capital intensity. Excess job reallocation rises with energy and capital intensity and falls with wages per worker. These fitted relationships are very strong, and they highlight large predictable variation in the level and volatility of plant-level employment growth rates. For example, conditional on other regressors, the 90–10 differential in the predicted net growth rate is about 10 percentage points for energy intensity, 6 percentage points for capital intensity, and 7 percentage points for the wage variable. The predicted variation in excess job reallocation rates are similarly large.

4.3. Employer size and job reallocation

The evidence presented in Sections 3.5, 4.1 and 4.2 shows that excess job reallocation rates decline sharply with employer size. This strong empirical regularity holds in every industry, country and time period studied, and it survives the introduction of an extensive set of controls for age, capital intensity, worker skill and other observable employer characteristics. The same empirical regularity turns up in the industrial organization literature as a negative relationship between firm size and the variance of growth rates in employment, sales or other measures of economic activity (Caves, 1998).

A natural question is whether, and to what extent, this empirical regularity can be accounted for by a simple statistical model that interprets each large unit as a collection of independent smaller units. An affirmative answer suggests that the observed relationship between size and job reallocation is merely an artifact of how we draw the boundaries of the firm or establishment. Thus, a simple statistical model can provide a useful benchmark for gauging whether there is an economic phenomenon to be explained and, if so, the strength of the size-reallocation relationship.

We address this question as follows. For establishments of size z, we fit LRD data to a grid of 203 annual growth rate outcomes on $[-2,2]$, with outcome probabilities denoted by the vector p. The outcomes are birth, death, no change and 200 subintervals of length 0.02 on $(-2,0)$ and $(0,2)$. We set the grid point for each subinterval to its mean observed growth rate outcome in the data.

Now consider a large establishment that consists of n independent subunits of size z, each of which has outcome probabilities p. Independence implies that the joint distribution of growth rate outcomes for the subunits is multinomial with parameters n and p. Specifically, let x be a vector with elements corresponding to the 203 outcomes on $[-2,2]$, and let each x_i be a nonnegative integer that denotes the number of subunits that experience the ith growth rate outcome, for $i = 1, 2, ..., k = 203$. The probability of each possible outcome vector for the aggregate of the n subunits is given by

$$f(x|n,p) = \left(\frac{n!}{x_1! \cdots x_k!} \right) p_1^{x_1} \cdots p_k^{x_k}. \tag{9}$$

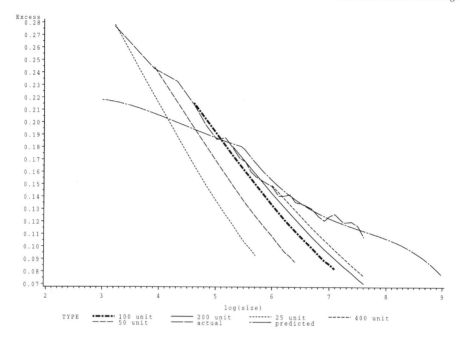

Fig. 10. Actual, predicted and theoretical excess reallocation rates as a function of log plant size.

Using this fact, we can calculate the rates of job creation, job destruction and excess reallocation implied by the statistical model for establishments of size zn for various values of z, thereby tracing out the predicted relationship between size and gross job flows. We carry out these calculations for five alternative definitions of a subunit or "small" establishment: $z_1 = 25$, $z_2 = 50$, $z_3 = 100$, $z_4 = 200$, and $z_5 = 400$. For each value of z, we use all observations in the symmetric (in logs) interval $[0.9z, 1.11z]$ to fit p and select grid points. We select grid points separately for each value of z.[22]

Fig. 10 plots the predicted relationship between (log) size and excess reallocation for each value of z under the assumption of independent, equal-size subunits.[23] The actual relationship is overlaid against the relationships predicted by the model of independent subunits. The results show clearly that the predicted relationships are approximately linear in logs and more steeply sloped than the actual relationship. Evidently, large establishments are not random collections of smaller establishments.

In fact, the visual test provided by Fig. 10 understates the failure of the independent subunits model, because it ignores powerful correlates of size that also affect job realloca-

---

[22] The LRD contains over one million annual plant-level growth rate observations in the 1973–1993 period, so that the data afford ample leverage for estimating p on narrow intervals about each z.

[23] We generated the predicted relationships by Monte Carlo simulation.

tion intensity. The two most important correlates in this respect are plant age and the level of plant wages. In particular, plant age and mean worker wages rise sharply with plant size, but job reallocation intensity declines with wages and plant age. To account for these correlates of plant size, Fig. 10 also plots the fitted relationship between excess reallocation and size based on a regression model that controls for plant-level age and average wage. The regression-based relationship shows essentially the same degree of departure from the independent subunits model for larger plants but a much stronger departure for smaller plants.

While the model of independent equal-size subunits fails to account for the observed relationship between size and excess reallocation, it remains an open question as to whether a slightly richer model fits the data. In particular, consider a slight generalization of Eq. (9) that replaces the parameter n by a smooth function of size, say $n(\text{size})$, with $0 < n'(\cdot) < 1$. According to this model, a large plant is a random collection of subunits that have the same growth rate distribution as small plants, but subunit size grows with plant size. We plan to explore the performance of this simple model and its implications in future work.

Our analysis of the relationship between size and job reallocation is also relevant to the earlier discussion of within-plant and within-firm job reallocation in Section 3.1. In particular, statistical models of the sort set forth above could be used to estimate the "missing" intra-plant (intra-firm) job flows in studies based on plant-level (firm-level) data. While the specific model (9) is overly simple for this purpose, it is easily modified to specify n and p as smooth functions of size and possibly other employer characteristics. Such models, if successfully fit to data on job flows between employers, generate implied measures of job flows within employers.

5. Theories of heterogeneity

This section draws together theories and evidence related to the reasons for cross-sectional heterogeneity in plant-level and firm-level employment adjustments. We focus on how the theories and evidence relate to the magnitude of gross job flows and cross-sectional patterns in the magnitudes.

5.1. Explaining the magnitude of gross job flows

Sectoral shocks with differential effects among industries, regions, plant birth cohorts and employer size categories are natural suspects as driving forces behind job creation and destruction. As it turns out, however, the empirical evidence accumulated over the past several years (summarized in Table 5) shows quite clearly that such sectoral shocks account for a very small fraction of gross job flows. To the best of our knowledge, the only favorable evidence for this type of sectoral shock interpretation of gross job flows appears in Konings et al. (1996), who find that sharp employment contractions at state-owned manufacturing enterprises account for a large fraction of gross job flows in the manufacturing sector during Poland's transition to a market-oriented economy. More generally, the Konings et al. study favors the view that in the early years of transition from statist to market-oriented economies the huge employment shifts between industries and from state-controlled to private enterprises account for a large fraction of overall job flows. Other than such dramatic episodes of wrenching change, the magnitude of gross job flows is not explained by sectoral shocks at the level of industries, regions and other easily measured sectoral groupings.

The magnitude of within-sector heterogeneity implies that idiosyncratic factors dominate the determination of which plants create and destroy jobs, which plants achieve rapid productivity growth or suffer productivity declines. One likely reason for such heterogeneity in plant-level outcomes is the considerable uncertainty that surrounds the development, adoption, distribution, marketing and regulation of new products and production techniques. Uncertainty about the demand for new products or the cost-effectiveness of alternative technologies encourages firms to experiment with different technologies, goods and production facilities (Roberts and Weitzman, 1981). Experimentation, in turn, generates differences in outcomes (Jovanovic, 1982; Ericson and Pakes, 1995). Even when motives for experimentation are absent, uncertainty about future cost or demand conditions encourages firms to differentiate their choice of current products and technology so as to optimally position themselves for possible future circumstances (Lambson, 1991).

Another likely reason for heterogeneity is that differences in entrepreneurial and managerial ability lead to differences in job and productivity growth rates among firms and plants. These differences include the abilities to identify and develop new products, to organize production activity, to motivate workers and to adapt to changing circumstances. There seems little doubt that these and other ability differences among managers generate much of the observed heterogeneity in plant-level outcomes. Business magazines, newspapers and case studies (e.g., Dial and Murphy, 1995) routinely portray the decisions and actions of particular management teams or individuals as crucial determinants of success or failure. High levels of compensation, often heavily skewed toward various forms of incentive pay (see Murphy's chapter in this volume), also suggest that senior managers play key roles in business performance, including productivity and job growth outcomes.[24]

Another important source of heterogeneity involves the selection process whereby new businesses learn over time about initial conditions relevant to success and business survival (Jovanovic, 1982). As learning about initial conditions diminishes with age, its contribution to job flows among plants in the same birth cohort eventually diminishes. This type of theory provides an appealing interpretation of the strong and pervasive negative relationship between employer age and the magnitude of gross job flows shown in Figs. 2 and 8. However, it provides a seriously incomplete explanation for the overall magnitude of job flows, because it fails to explain the large gross flows among mature plants. Based on

---

[24] Many economic analyses attribute a key role to managerial ability in the organization of firms and production units. Lucas (1978) provides an early and influential formal treatment.

some simple identifying assumptions, Davis and Haltiwanger (1992) conclude that learning about initial conditions in the sense of Jovanovic (1982) accounts for only about 10% of gross job flows in the US manufacturing sector. The underlying reasons for this result are straightforward: the fraction of employment in young establishments is small, and the pace of job reallocation among mature plants is rapid.

Other factors that drive heterogeneity in plant-level productivity and job growth outcomes involve plant- and firm-specific circumstances and disturbances. For example, energy costs and labor costs vary across locations, and so do the timing of changes in factor costs.[25] Cost differences induce different employment and investment decisions among otherwise similar plants and firms. These decisions, in turn, influence the size and type of labor force and capital stock that a business carries into the future. Thus, current differences in cost and demand conditions induce contemporaneous heterogeneity in plant-level job and productivity growth, and they also cause businesses to differentiate themselves in ways that lead to heterogeneous responses to common shocks in the future. The role of plant-specific shocks to technology, factor costs and product demand in accounting for the pace of job reallocation has been explored in Hopenhayn (1992), Hopenhayn and Rogerson (1993), Bergin and Bernhardt (1996), Campbell and Fisher (1996), Campbell (1997) and Gouge and King (1997).

Slow diffusion of information about technology, distribution channels, marketing strategies, and consumer tastes is another important source of plant-level heterogeneity in productivity and job growth. Griliches (1957) finds a gradual diffusion of hybrid corn technology among US farmers. Nasbeth and Ray (1974) and Rogers (1983) document multi-year lags in the diffusion of knowledge about new technologies among firms producing related products. Mansfield et al. (1981) and Pakes and Schankerman (1984) provide evidence of long imitation and product development lags. Rhee et al. (1984) report that foreign buyers and sellers were important transmitters of technical information in the Korean industrialization process. The remarkable proliferation of differentiated computerware suggests an important role for information diffusion in the production and use of computer products.[26]

Between-plant heterogeneity in employment outcomes also arises from capital vintage effects.[27] As an extreme example, suppose that new technology can only be adopted by constructing new plants. In this case, technologically sophisticated plants enter to displace older, out-moded plants, and gross job flows reflect a productivity-enhancing process of creative destruction. While holding some appeal, this interpretation of gross job flows runs

---

[25] On large spatial variation in energy prices and in the timing of major energy price changes, see King and Cuc (1996) and Woo et al. (1997).

[26] Knowledge diffusion plays a key role in many theories of firm-level dynamics, industrial evolution, economic growth and international trade. See, for example, Grossman and Helpman (1991), Jovanovic and Rob (1989), and Jovanovic and MacDonald (1994).

[27] See Aghion and Howitt (1992, 1994), Caballero and Hammour (1994, 1996a), Campbell (1996), Stein (1997), Cooley et al. (1996), and Chari and Hopenhayn (1991).

counter to the prevalent findings that failure rates decrease sharply with plant and firm age (e.g., Dunne et al., 1989a,b), and that productivity rises with plant age (e.g., Baily et al., 1992; Bahk and Gort, 1993). As discussed above, empirical regularities related to plant age and capital vintage are likely to reflect important selection effects. Depending on precisely how one slices the data and the quality of measures for capital vintage, vintage effects may be obscured by selection effects. Vintage and selection effects may also interact in important ways. For example, although new plants may more readily adopt technological advances embodied in new capital goods, the probability of successful adoption may vary with managerial ability. Regardless of these barriers to clean identification of capital vintage effects in empirical work, the basic point remains that the vintage of installed capital (properly measured) is probably an important source of heterogeneity in plant-level behavior. Similarly, the vintage of the manager or the organizational structure may also induce plant-level heterogeneity (Nelson and Winter, 1982) and interact with other factors that contribute to differences in behavior among seemingly similar plants.

5.2. Explaining cross-sectional variation in the magnitude of job flows

As shown in Sections 3.5 and 4, there is substantial variation in the pace of job reallocation across sectors defined by industry and other employer characteristics. Important employer characteristics include employer size, employer age, factor intensities and wages. Many of the explanations for the overall magnitude of reallocation also have the potential to account for cross-sectional patterns in job flow magnitudes. An obvious case in point is learning about initial conditions as an explanation for sharply higher job reallocation rates at younger plants. Empirical evidence is highly favorable to this view. Relevant empirical studies include Dunne et al. (1989a,b), Davis and Haltiwanger (1992), Lane et al. (1996), Nocke (1994), Klette and Mathiassen (1996), Evans (1987a,b) and Troske (1996) as well as the evidence presented in Figs. 2 and 8.

Learning about initial conditions and differences in the plant-age structure of employment also help explain industry and sectoral differences in the pace of reallocation. Davis and Haltiwanger (1992) find that differences in the plant-age structure of employment account for about one-third to one-half of the variation in job reallocation rates across industries, regions and employer size classes in the US manufacturing sector. A major role for employer age in this regard, even conditional on employer size, is unsurprising in light of Figs. 2 and 8.

Evidence for the US manufacturing sector indicates that the magnitude of gross job flows declines sharply with plant-level wages. For example, Davis et al. (1996, Table 3.4.) report that the excess job reallocation rate in the bottom quintile of the plant-wage distribution is nearly double the corresponding rate in the top quintile. The plant-level regression results in Fig. 9 confirm this empirical regularity after conditioning on a large set of other employer characteristics.

Human capital theory offers a simple interpretation for this wage-related pattern in gross job flows.[28] Under a human capital interpretation of wage differentials, high-wage plants operate with workers who have high average levels of human capital. Differences in average wages across plants partly reflect differences in plant- and firm-specific components of human capital. Because specific human capital strengthens the durability of the employment relationship in the face of changes and disturbances that alter the match continuation value, the magnitude of gross job flows declines with average plant wages.[29]

Simple statistical models like the one developed in Section 4.3 also have the potential to account for much of the between-sector and between-size class variation in job reallocation. The basic idea is that large employers have lower rates of job reallocation, because they smooth out the idiosyncratic disturbances that hit smaller units.

A related idea is that differences in the degree of product specialization lead to differences in job reallocation intensity. According to this hypothesis, diversified plants are able to provide a more stable employment environment by diversifying the idiosyncratic component of product-specific shocks. Davis et al. (1996, Table 3.6) provide some supportive evidence in that the pace of job reallocation is substantially higher among completely specialized plants than more diversified plants. This phenomenon may contribute to between-industry differences in job flow magnitudes, given Gollop and Monahan's (1991) evidence that plant-level product specialization varies among industries. Another related hypothesis is that the degree of product differentiation influences between-industry variation in job reallocation rates. Boeri (1994, Table IV) contains a bit of supportive evidence for this hypothesis.

Yet another hypothesis emphasizes that the intensity of the shocks that drive reallocation varies across industries. A potentially important driving force is the pace of technological change and any associated process of creative destruction. In this regard, Davis et al. (1996, Table 3.7) report that industries with more rapid productivity growth exhibit greater rates of within-industry reallocation. This finding supports the view that industry differences in the pace of technological advance contribute to differences in job reallocation rates. However, we find no marginal effect of total factor productivity growth on excess job reallocation when we introduce industry-level productivity growth measures into plant-level regression specifications similar to the one considered in Section 4.2.

5.3. National differences in the magnitude of gross job flows

In our presentation of Table 2, we intentionally refrained from detailed cross-country comparisons of job flow magnitudes. There are major pitfalls in simple comparisons of this sort. Differences in sample coverage and in the definitions of business units cloud direct comparisons of magnitudes. In addition, many gross job flow measures suffer from serious longitudinal linkage problems in the underlying dataset. The ability to accurately

---

[28] Oi (1962), Becker (1975, Chapter 2), Jovanovic and Mincer (1981), and Parsons (1986) are especially pertinent to the discussion at hand.

[29] Of course, this conclusion could be overturned if the variance of shocks to the demand for labor rises sharply enough with specific human capital intensity.

identify ownership and organizational changes varies across datasets, and the frequency of such unidentified changes probably varies greatly across datasets for different countries.

In spite of measurement difficulties, some studies seek to interpret cross-country differences in broad measures of job reallocation intensity. Of particular interest is the connection between the role of institutions that impede employment adjustment and the pace of job reallocation. Cross-country analyses (e.g., Garibaldi et al., 1997) find no apparent relationship between the pace of job reallocation and mandated job security provisions, but Bertola and Rogerson (1997) contend that the failure to find a relationship reflects more than measurement problems. They argue that it is important to look at the full range of labor market institutions and, in particular, the role of wage-setting institutions. They show that policies that contribute to wage compression yield a greater pace of reallocation, holding job security provisions constant. Accordingly, they suggest that the surprisingly high rates of job reallocation in many Western European countries may reflect the impact of wage compression policies that offset the impact of job security provisions.

We do not believe that strong inferences about the effects of economic policies and institutions can be drawn from cross-country comparisons of aggregate job flow rates. Aside from measurement problems and the limited number of data points, this chapter compiles ample evidence that the magnitude of job flows vary quite sharply with industry, employer size and employer age. Hence, the large country differences in the industry, size and age structure of employment lead to major differences in aggregate job flow rates, apart from any effects of labor market policies and institutions. Careful, disaggregated studies are essential to convincingly identify the effects of policies and institutions on labor market flows in a cross-country context.

A disaggregated approach has other advantages as well. It can greatly expand the usable variation in the data, and it facilitates the study of how labor market policies regarding job and worker flows influence the structure of employment. For example, Davis and Henrekson (1997, Table 9.12) report mild evidence that, relative to a US benchmark, the distribution of Swedish employment is systematically shifted away from industries with high job reallocation rates. This finding suggests that Swedish policies that penalize job and worker flows systematically alter the structure of Swedish employment.

6. Job flows and worker flows

The preceding sections focus on the flow of jobs across production sites rather than the flow of workers. This section treats worker flows and their connection to job flows. We consider the relative magnitude of various labor market flows and other evidence on how job flows relate to worker flows.

6.1. Relative magnitudes

Davis and Haltiwanger (1998) review US-based research on the magnitude of worker and job flows. Early work in this area (e.g., Blanchard and Diamond, 1990) relies on household surveys to measure worker flows and separate data on employers to measure job flows. Drawing on several studies, our review concludes that total worker turnover (accessions plus separations) in the United States amounts to about one third of employment per month, and worker reallocation (Definition 5) amounts to about 25% of employment per quarter and 37% of employment per year.[30] Job reallocation accounts for about 35-46% of worker turnover in quarterly data.

The relative size of job and worker flows varies over time and among industries. In manufacturing, job reallocation accounts for a relatively high fraction of worker turnover, even though job flows in manufacturing are smaller than in non-manufacturing. Cyclical variation in the relative size of job and worker flows is large. Quits fall sharply in recessions (Hall, 1972) and job reallocation rises, which imparts strong countercyclic movements to the ratio of job reallocation to worker turnover (Akerlof et al., 1988; Albaek and Sorensen, 1996).

Recent work exploits matched employer–worker data to examine how worker separations and accessions covary with employer-level creation and destruction. Table 9 reports average accession, separation, creation and destruction rates from several such studies. Each study finds an important role for job creation and destruction in worker accessions and separations, but there are large differences in the creation-accession and destruction-separation ratios across studies.

Reported differences in the role of job flows reflect important differences in measurement procedures. To develop this point, we compare the Anderson and Meyer (1994) and Lane et al. (1996) studies, both of which rely on administrative records for the US unemployment insurance system. These studies rely on quarterly wage records for individual workers, but they process the records differently, and Anderson and Meyer also draw on unemployment benefit records.[31]

Both studies use quarter-to-quarter changes in employment levels and employment affiliations to measure job flows and worker flows. In addition, Anderson and Meyer include temporary layoffs spells that end in recall within the quarter in their measures of separations and accessions. They identify these within-quarter layoff-recall events from records on unemployment benefits paid, rather than from changes in the employment affiliation or status of workers. They do not count within-quarter layoff-recall events in their measures of job creation and destruction. Hence, Anderson and Meyer count short-

---

[30] Worker turnover measures the gross number of labor market transitions, whereas worker reallocation measures the number of persons who participate in transitions. Worker turnover exceeds worker reallocation for two reasons. First, job-to-job movements induce two transitions per transiting worker. Consider, for example, two workers who exchange jobs and employers. Two workers move, but there are four transitions – two separations and two accessions. Other worker mobility events induce equal-sized increments to worker turnover and worker reallocation. Second, worker turnover measures often encompass all separations and accessions that occur during an interval of time, whereas worker reallocation measures typically reflect changes in employer or employment status between discrete points in time. See Davis and Haltiwanger (1998) for an extended discussion of the relationships among the various worker flow and job flow measures that appear in the literature.

[31] The two studies also differ in that Anderson and Meyer limit attention to employers that have 50 or more employees at least once in the sample period.

Table 9
Worker and job flow rates in matched worker-employer datasets (percentage of sectoral employment)

Country/ state	Period	Coverage	Sampling frequency	Acces- sion rate	Job creation rate	Separ- ation rate	Job destruction rate	Creation/ accession (%)	Destruction/ separation (%)	Source
USA (selected states)	1979–1983	Private sector	Quarterly	22.3	7.1	21.4	6.4	31.8	29.9	Anderson and Meyer (1994, Table 13)
USA (selected states)	1979–1983	Manufacturing	Quarterly	24.7	5.8	24.6	6.2	23.5	25.2	Anderson and Meyer (1994, Table 13)
USA – Maryland	1985:3–1993:3	Private sector[a]	Quarterly	18.4	9.0	18.7	9.3	49.1	49.7	Lane et al. (1996, Table 1)
USA – Maryland	1985:3–1993:3	Manufacturing	Quarterly	12.9	7.5	14.2	8.8	58.1	62	Lane et al. (1996, Table 1)
Denmark	1980–1991	Manufacturing	Annual	28.5	12.0	28.0	11.5	42.1	41.1	Albaek and Sorenson (1996, Tables 3 and 4)
Netherlands	1979–1993	Manufacturing[b]	Annual	16.3	7.3	15.7	8.3	44.8	52.9	Gautier (1997, Tables 2.2 and 3.3)
Norway	1987–1994	Manufacturing	Annual	21.0	11.0	23.0	13.0	52.4	56.5	Salvanes (1997, Table 1)
Norway	1987–1994	Banking and insurance	Annual	21.0	12.5	22.0	14.5	59.5	65.9	Salvanes (1997, Table 1)

[a] Employment-weighted means of one-digit industry rates. 1992 employment figures from the Economic Report of the President were used as weights.
[b] Job creation and job destruction are for manufacturing for the period of 1979–1993. Accession and separation rates appear to be for the entire economy for the period of 1971–1991.

term worker flows in separations and accessions, but they do not count the corresponding shortterm job flows in creation and destruction. In this respect, the Anderson and Meyer results provide a lower bound on the true creation-accession and destruction-separation ratios.

Lane et al. (1996) examine job and worker flows that involve "full-quarter" employees and employment spells. A full-quarter employee in quarter t is one who receives compensation from the employer in quarters $t-1$, t and $t+1$. After restricting attention to full-quarter employees and employment positions, Lane et al. (1996) proceed to measure job and worker flows using quarter-to-quarter changes in employment levels and employment affiliations. Clearly, this procedure excludes the within-quarter layoff-recall events that Anderson and Meyer capture in their accession and separation measures. The "full-quarter" requirement also excludes other shortterm worker and job flows. Given the probationary nature of many new employment relationships and, consequently, the very high separation hazards in the first month or two of new matches (Hall, 1982; Anderson and Meyer, 1994), the "full-quarter" requirement probably screens out a larger portion of worker flows than job flows. In this respect, Lane et al. (1996) provide an upper bound on the true creation-accession and destruction-separation ratios.

These remarks explain why Lane et al. (1996) consistently find a much larger role for job flows than Anderson and Meyer (1994). The creation-accession ratio is 32% for the private sector and 23% in manufacturing according to Anderson and Meyer (1994), but 50% in the private sector and 58% in manufacturing according to Lane et al. (1996). Similarly, the destruction-separation ratio is 31% for the private sector and 25% in manufacturing according to Anderson and Meyer (1994), but 51% in the private sector and 62% in manufacturing according to Lane et al. (1996). The especially large differences between the two studies for the manufacturing sector reflect the high incidence of short layoff-recall events in the US manufacturing sector.

Two messages emerge from this discussion. First, matched employer–worker data do not automatically yield precise, unambiguous characterizations of the relationship between worker flows and job flows. Measurement procedures matter greatly, as highlighted by the comparison between the Anderson–Meyer and Lane et al. studies. Sampling frequency and sample coverage (industry, employer size, etc.) are also likely to have a major bearing on findings about the relative size of worker flows and job flows. Second, despite these difficulties (and related difficulties in the earlier literature), a wide range of studies find that job flows underlie a big fraction of worker flows. The broadly similar results for the United States, Denmark, the Netherlands and Norway indicate that this feature of labor markets is prevalent across countries. In this respect, the findings summarized by Table 9 confirm findings in the earlier literature that compared worker flows and job flows based on tabulations of separate worker and employer datasets.

6.2. Other evidence on the connection between job and worker flows

Some additional remarks help to flesh out the role of job flows in worker reallocation activity. First, the evidence on relative magnitudes neglects secondary waves of worker reallocation engendered by job creation and destruction. For example, a person who quits an old job in favor of a newly created job potentially creates a chain of further quits as other workers reshuffle across the new set of job openings. It follows that the direct plus indirect contribution of job flows to worker reallocation exceeds the figures reported in Table 9. Hall (1995) advances a related argument to explain the cyclical dynamics of unemployment flows. He shows that persistence in unemployment inflows can be largely accounted for by the burst of permanent job destruction that occurs at the onset of recessions. His story emphasizes that separations beget further separations because of high failure rates in new employment matches.

Second, the facts about concentration and persistence in Section 3 shed light on the connection between job flows and worker reallocation. Since more than two-thirds of job destruction reflects establishments that shrink by more than 25% over the span of a year, the bulk of annual job destruction cannot be accommodated by normal rates of worker attrition. In other words, annual job destruction largely represents job loss to workers. Since annual job creation and destruction primarily reflect persistent establishment-level employment changes, the bulk of annual job creation and destruction cannot be implemented by temporary layoff and recall policies. Hence, most of annual job destruction reflects permanent job loss that leads to a change in employer, a longterm unemployment spell, exit from the labor force, or some combination of these events.

The role of plant-level job destruction in worker displacement and unemployment depends partly on the extent to which establishments shrink by simply reducing accession rates. Perhaps employers can implement even large job destruction rates by a cutting back on new hires. Abowd et al. (1996) investigate how establishment-level accession and separation rates vary with the employment growth rate in French data. They find that employers mainly vary the hiring rate and not the separation rate to achieve net employment changes, provided that the establishment does not contract too rapidly – i.e., by more than about 15% per year. Abowd et al. conclude that "establishments shrinking in a given year reduce employment by reducing entry, not by increasing separations." Hamermesh et al. (1996) report similar results in Dutch data.

We view these results as fully consistent with the claim that most job destruction is not accommodated by normal worker attrition. Only a small percentage of employers contract by more than 15% within a year, but these employers account for most of the job destruction. Thus, while it may be that most employers achieve employment changes by altering the hiring rate, most job destruction reflects employers with high separation rates.

Putting these results together supports the view that job loss and job destruction are costly events. Firms show a strong preference for natural attrition over costly layoffs as a tool for reducing employment. Only when required employment reductions exceed normal attrition do firms initiate separations at a higher rate. The spatial concentration of job destruction at relatively few establishments adds to the costs of job loss, because it limits the role of normal worker attrition. The temporal concentration of job destruction in recessions adds to the costs of job loss for the same reason. The costs of job destruction in recessions are further compounded, because worker attrition rates (quits) are unusually low, and because spatial concentration rises.

6.3. Job destruction and worker displacement

One way to assess the impact of job destruction on job loss is to consider the connection between job destruction and unemployment flows. Davis et al. (1996, Chapter 6) and Hall (1995) present evidence of a close connection between increases in job destruction and increases in the unemployment inflow rate, especially for workers who consider themselves permanently laid off. Hall (1995) also emphasizes that the initial unemployment inflow associated with job destruction and permanent layoffs at the onset of a recession is only the beginning of the story, because the fragility of new worker-firm matches leads to higher unemployment re-entry rates in subsequent periods.

Another way to evaluate the connection between job destruction and unwelcome job loss is to consider the evidence on self-reported job displacement in the Displaced Worker Survey (DWS) supplement to the CPS. According to the DWS, a worker is displaced if he lost a job within a specified period of time because of a plant closing, an employer going out of business, a layoff without recall, or some similar reason.

To investigate this connection, we compare job loss rates tabulated by Farber (1997) using the DWS with measures of job destruction. The job loss rates from the DWS that Farber considers pertain to various 3-year horizons from the early 1980s to the mid 1990s. Job loss is defined as an involuntary separation based on the operating decisions of the employer for one of the reasons given above. Farber converts the number of displaced workers to a job loss rate by dividing through by the total number of workers at risk at the survey date. Multiple job losers are not double-counted. Using this methodology, the average job loss rate over a 3-year horizon is approximately 12%. This figures means that 12% of the workforce experiences at least one separation that is classified as a displacement over a 3-year horizon.

In contrast, the annual rate of job destruction in the US economy is approximately 10% in manufacturing industries and somewhat higher in most non-manufacturing industries (Table 1). To compare these annual rates to the 3-year job loss rates, it is not quite appropriate to simply cumulate the annual job destruction rate to generate a 3-year destruction rate, because some fraction of the annual job destruction is reversed and the affected workers recalled. From Table 6, roughly 74% of annual job destruction in US manufacturing persists for more than 2 years. The job destruction rate for US manufacturing over a 5-year horizon calculated by Baldwin et al. (1998) is approximately 26%. Putting these figures together, and taking into account that job destruction rates are higher for non-manufacturing, suggests that the 3-year job destruction rate exceeds 20% – a rate that is much greater than the corresponding 3-year job loss rate in the DWS.

Fig. 11 compares the time-series movements in the Farber job loss rates and the 3-year job destruction rates.[32] The job loss rates depicted are the overall rate and a rate for

---

[32] The destruction series terminates in 1993.

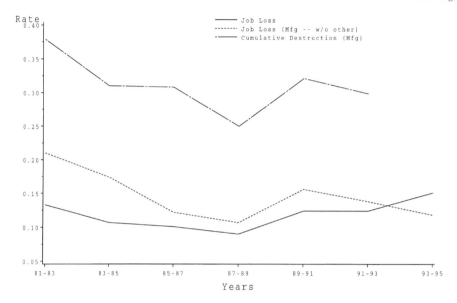

Fig. 11. Comparison of job loss rates and cumulative 3-year job destruction rate. Source: destruction tabulations from the LRD and job loss rates from the DWS supplement to the CPS.

manufacturing. Even though the industry-level job loss rates excludes the "other reason" category of job loss, the job loss rate for manufacturing typically exceeds the rate for the whole economy. The cumulative job destruction rates are much higher than the job loss rates, but the time series fluctuations in the manufacturing job destruction and job loss rates are quite similar.

Several factors probably underlie the large gap between the DWS job loss or displacement rate and the job destruction rate. First, the job loss rate counts workers only once over a 3-year horizon, even if they suffer multiple displacements. In contrast, a worker who moves from one declining establishment to another could show up several times in the cumulative job destruction figure, even if each job destruction event is permanent. Second, a major difficulty in interpreting the displacement measure is whether all workers who experience an employer-initiated separation consider themselves displaced. Third, as discussed above, establishments accomplish job destruction through a variety of means – attrition, hiring freezes and layoffs – that vary in importance over time and space.

The basic point is that many factors influence the relationship between job destruction and DWS measures of job loss. The large difference in magnitudes suggest that these factors matter greatly, but the job destruction and job loss rates nonetheless show similar patterns of time variation. Further study is required to understand the precise sources of the differences between the job destruction and job loss rates.

The effect of job destruction on workers is a central issue in welfare analyses of the reallocation process. On the one hand, the continuous reallocation of resources to their highest valued uses is a necessary component of economic growth. (In the next section, we will see that much of aggregate productivity growth is accounted for by ongoing reallocation.) On the other hand, this reallocation process produces displaced workers who often experience large and persistent earnings losses.[33] Beyond important unresolved conceptual issues, a major barrier to greater progress in understanding these issues is the availability of suitable data. Ideally, we need data that simultaneously tracks the movement of jobs and workers and their relationship to earnings, unemployment, productivity and output. The importance of the underlying issues argues for assigning a high priority to the further development of integrated employer–worker datasets.

7. Job flows and creative destruction

7.1. Theoretical models

A long-standing view holds that economic growth in a market economy invariably involves reallocation. Schumpeter (1942) coined the term, "creative destruction", which he described as follows (p. 83):

> The fundamental impulse that keeps the capitalist engine in motion comes from the new consumers' goods, the new methods of production or transportation, the new markets....[The process] incessantly revolutionizes from within, incessantly destroying the old one, incessantly creating a new one. This process of Creative Destruction is the essential fact about capitalism.

Creative destruction models of economic growth stress that the process of adopting new products and new processes requires the destruction of old products and processes.

An important paper that formalizes this Schumpeterian idea is Aghion and Howitt (1992). They develop a theoretical model in which endogenous innovations drive creative destruction and growth. The creator of a new innovation receives monopoly rents until the next innovation comes along, at which point the knowledge underlying the rents becomes obsolete. The incentives for investment in R&D and thus growth depend on this process of creative destruction. Appropriability and intertemporal spillover effects lead equilibrium growth to be slower than optimal. The appropriablity effect arises because skilled labor receives a portion of the rents generated by innovation. The intertemporal spillover effect arises because current innovators are uncompensated for the knowledge benefits that they provide to future innovators. Set against these two effects, research firms do not internalize the destruction of rents generated by their own innovative activity. By itself, this business stealing effect leads to an excessively high growth rate. Aghion and Howitt (1992) show that the business stealing effect also tends to make innovations too small. On net, growth may be more or less rapid than optimal.

---

[33] See, e.g., Anderson and Meyer (1994), Dardia and Schoeni (1996), Farber (1993), Hall (1995), Jacobson et al. (1993), Ruhm (1991) and Topel (1990) for studies of the impact of displacement on earnings.

Some vintage capital models provide an alternative conceptualization of Schumpeterian views about creative destruction. One class of vintage models (e.g., Caballero and Hammour, 1994; Campbell, 1997) emphasizes the role of entry and exit. If new technology can only be adopted by new establishments, growth occurs only via entry and exit, which requires input reallocation. Another class of vintage models (e.g., Cooper et al., 1997) emphasizes that existing plants can adopt new technology by retooling. The retooling process may generate within-plant and between-plant job reallocation. For example, retooling to adopt a skill-biased technological improvement can bring changes to both the level and skill mix of the plant's work force.[34]

In all of these models, the reallocation of outputs and inputs across producers plays a critical role in economic growth. Stifling reallocation stifles growth. For several reasons, the rate of growth and the pace of reallocation may deviate from optimal outcomes. In this regard, Aghion and Howitt emphasize that agents (firms, innovators, workers) fail to internalize the effect of their innovative activities on others. Caballero and Hammour (1996a,b) emphasize that the sunkness of investment in new capital (human or physical) leads to ex post holdup problems with many harmful side effects.

Even when reallocation is vital for growth, there are losers in the process. Losers include the owners of the outmoded businesses that fail and the job-losing displaced workers. Set against these losses to particular businesses and individuals, reallocation leads to greater efficiency in resource allocation, increases in output and, according to the Schumpeterian view, sustained economic growth. The next two subsections review empirical studies that quantify the productivity benefits of factor reallocation and present evidence on these benefits in US manufacturing. Section 10 considers some welfare and productivity aspects of reallocation in a simple theoretical model of costly worker and capital mobility.

7.2. Empirical studies of reallocation and productivity growth

The theories of heterogeneity treated in Section 5 and much theoretical work on creative destruction characterize technical change as a noisy, complex process that involves considerable experimentation (entry and retooling) and failure (contraction and exit). The large-scale, within-sector job reallocation documented in Sections 3 and 4 favors this view, but evidence on job flows alone says little about the strength of any relationship between reallocation and productivity growth.

Several recent empirical studies of plant-level and firm-level productivity behavior provide direct evidence on the role of factor reallocation in productivity growth.[35]

---

[34] See, e.g., Dunne et al. (1997) and Abel and Eberly (1997) for analysis of how changing technology affects the mix and scale of factors of production.

[35] See Baily et al. (1992), Olley and Pakes (1996), Bartelsman and Dhrymes (1994), and Foster et al. (1998), all of whom use the LRD, Aw et al. (1997) who use firm-level data from Taiwan and Liu and Tybout (1996), who use establishment-level data for Chile, Colombia and Morocco. Tybout (1996) contains a brief survey of the literature.

These studies find that the reallocation of output and inputs from less-productive to more-productive plants plays a major role in industry-level multifactor productivity growth. A closely related literature investigates the connection between employment reallocation and labor productivity growth.[36] The labor productivity studies yield a more mixed set of results and a typically smaller role for reallocation.

To see the basic approach in these empirical studies, start with the expression

$$P_{it} = \sum_{e \in I} s_{et} p_{et}, \tag{10}$$

where P_{it} denotes an index of labor or multifactor productivity for industry i, p_{et} denotes a corresponding productivity measure for plant or firm e, and s_{et} is the eth unit's share of industry activity (e.g., output share). For convenience, we henceforth refer to the individual units as plants. Now consider the following decomposition of the industry-level productivity index:

$$\Delta P_{it} = \sum_{e \in C} s_{et-1} \Delta p_{et} + \sum_{e \in C} (p_{et-1} - P_{it-1}) \Delta s_{et} + \sum_{e \in C} \Delta p_{et} \Delta s_{et} + \sum_{e \in N} s_{et}(p_{et} - P_{it-1})$$

$$- \sum_{e \in X} s_{et-1}(p_{et-1} - P_{it-1}), \tag{11}$$

where C denotes continuing plants, N denotes entering plants, and X denotes exiting plants. The first term in this decomposition reflects within-plant productivity gains weighted by initial shares. The second term is a between-plant effect that reflects changing shares of industry activity, weighted by the initial-period deviation of the plant's productivity from industry productivity. The third term is a covariance-type cross product that reflects whether activity shares shift towards plants with relatively rapid productivity growth. The last two terms capture the contribution of entering and exiting plants, respectively.

In this decomposition, the between-plant term and the entry and exit terms involve deviations of plant-level productivity from the initial industry index. For a continuing plant, an increase in its share contributes positively to the between-plant component when the plant has higher productivity than average initial productivity for the industry. Similarly, an exiting (entering) plant contributes positively when its productivity is lower (higher) than the initial average.

Several related productivity decompositions appear in the literature, and they differ from Eq. (10) in sometimes subtle but important ways. The main distinguishing features of Eq. (10) are (i) an integrated treatment of entrants, exits and continuing plants, and (ii) a separation of between-plant and within-plant effects from covariance-type cross products. Because they do not separate out covariance-type terms, some decompositions in the literature are difficult to interpret for our purposes. For example, Griliches and Regev

---

[36] See Griliches and Regev (1995) who examine Israeli data, and Baily et al. (1996) and Foster et al. (1998), who use the LRD.

(1995) measure the within effect as the productivity change weighted by the average of shares in t and $t-1$. This method yields a seemingly cleaner decomposition than Eq. (10), but the resulting within effect then partly reflects reallocation effects.

Another important issue involves the treatment of net entry. Many of the decompositions in the literature that consider net entry (e.g., Baily et al., 1992) measure its contribution as a simple difference in the weighted mean productivity for entering and exiting plants:

$$\sum_{e \in N} s_{et} p_{et} - \sum_{e \in X} s_{e,t-1} p_{e,t-1}.$$

Even if there are no productivity differences among plants, this method yields a positive (negative) contribution of net entry to industry-level productivity gains whenever the share accounted for by entrants ($\sum_e \in_N s_{et}$) exceeds the share accounted for by exiting plants ($\sum_e \in_X s_{e,t-1}$). There are corresponding (and offsetting) problems in the treatment of the contribution of continuing plants.

7.3. Evidence for the US manufacturing sector

We apply Eq. (11) to four-digit US manufacturing industries using plant-level data from the Census of Manufactures in 1977 and 1987.[37] We first decompose industry-level multi-factor productivity changes using plant-level gross output to compute the shares (s_{et}). This weighting methodology is common in recent work on multifactor productivity decompositions. Next, we decompose industry-level labor productivity changes using both plant-level gross output and labor input to compute the shares. Labor-based shares are more natural for labor productivity decompositions, but aggregation using gross output shares helps understand the relationship between multifactor and labor productivity decompositions and the role of reallocation in productivity growth.

Our index of plant-level multifactor productivity is

$$\ln MFP_{et} = \ln Q_{et} - \alpha_K \ln K_{et} - \alpha_L \ln L_{et} - \alpha_M \ln M_{et}, \tag{12}$$

where Q_{et} is real gross output, L_{et} is labor input (total hours), K_{et} is real capital and M_{et} is real materials. In practice, we separate capital inputs into structures and equipment. We measure outputs and inputs in constant (1987) dollars using industry-level price deflators, and we set factor elasticities to industry-level factor cost shares. Our index of plant-level labor productivity is the difference between log gross output and the log labor input. Applying these measurement and weighting procedures to the plant-level data yields industry-level productivity growth rates that correspond closely to the rates computed directly from industry-level data.

Table 10, Panel A reports weighted averages of the industry-level productivity decompositions. Following Baily et al. (1992), we aggregate over the nearly 450 industries using

---

[37] The measurement and analysis here follows closely Foster et al. (1998), and the results in Table 10 are drawn directly from that paper. See that paper and Haltiwanger (1997) for detailed discussion of measurement issues.

Table 10
Role of reallocation in productivity growth[a]

Panel A: Decomposition of multifactor and labor productivity growth, 1977–1987

Productivity measure	Weight	Overall growth	Within share	Between share	Cross share	Net entry share
Multifactor	Gross output	10.24	0.48	-0.08	0.34	0.26
Labor	Gross output	25.56	0.45	-0.13	0.37	0.31
Labor	Employment	23.02	0.74	0.08	-0.11	0.29

Panel B: Output shares and relative productivity, 1977–1987

Relative multifactor productivity

	Exiting plants (t−1)	Entering plants (t)	Continuing plants (t−1)	Entering plants (t)	Continuing plants (t)
Output shares	0.22	0.21			
	0.96	1.09	1.00		1.10

Relative productivity of entrants in 1987 by entry cohort

	Entry: 1978–1982	Entry: 1983–1987
	1.10	1.07

Panel C: Correlations between plant-level productivity, output and input growth, 1977–1987 (continuing plants)

	Multifactor productivity	Labor productivity	Output	Labor	Capital equipment	Capital structures	Capital intensity
Multifactor productivity	1	0.41	0.24	-0.04	-0.06	-0.07	-0.03
Labor productivity	0.41	1	0.47	-0.22	0.16	0.15	0.34

[a] Source: Foster et al. (1998).

the average of nominal gross output in the initial and terminal years. In this way, we focus on within-industry productivity dynamics and exclude any effects of shifting industry composition.

Consider first the decomposition of the industry-level multifactor productivity changes. The within-plant component accounts for nearly half of the overall within-industry growth in multifactor productivity. In contrast, the between-plant component is small and negative. The cross-product term accounts for 34% of multifactor productivity growth from 1977 to 1987 in the average industry. This finding shows that a large fraction of multifactor productivity growth reflects rising output shares at plants that also experience productivity gains. Net entry plays an important role as well, accounting for 26% of the average industry change.

Taken together, the net entry and cross-product results show that 60% of the 10-year increase in multifactor productivity for the average manufacturing industry is accounted for by effects that involve the reallocation of output across production sites. Similar findings appear in other work on the decomposition of plant-level multifactor productivity changes. While the measurement methodology, decomposition technique and sectoral coverage vary among studies, a large contribution of output reallocation across production sites to multifactor productivity growth is a recurrent finding.

Panel B of Table 10 provides information about some underlying determinants of the multifactor productivity decomposition. The productivity indexes are reported relative to the weighted average for all plants in 1977. According to Panel B, entering plants have higher productivity than the average level among exiting and continuing plants in 1977 but slightly lower productivity than the continuing plants in 1987. Exiting plants have lower productivity than continuing plants. In short, entering plants tend to displace less-productive exiting plants, but they enter with about the same productivity as continuing plants.

A simple cohort analysis, also reported in Panel B, reveals that plants that entered in 1983–1987 have lower productivity than plants that entered in 1978–1982. In other words, the older cohort of entering plants is more productive than the younger cohort. This pattern suggests that selection and learning effects play an important role in plant-level productivity dynamics, an interpretation that finds further support in the more detailed analysis of Foster et al. (1998).[38]

Combining the results on multifactor productivity with evidence in Section 3 on the magnitude of job flows suggests that job reallocation plays an important productivity enhancing role. However, the precise connection between *job* reallocation and *output* reallocation is unclear. Put differently, output reallocation reflects many possibilities – changing labor shares, changing capital shares, changing material shares and changes in productivity itself. To shed further light on the connection between job and output reallocation, we turn now to labor productivity decompositions and compare the results using labor shares and gross output shares to aggregate over plants.

---

[38] Aw et al. (1997) present similar evidence of important and distinct roles for learning and selection effects in Taiwan. Also, see Bahk and Gort (1993).

The decompositions of labor productivity appear in Panel A of Table 10. Using labor or output shares yields similar rates of average labor productivity growth over this period. The contribution of net entry to labor productivity growth is also quite similar whether we use labor or output shares. Thus, in either case, reallocation plays an important role in labor productivity growth via net entry.[39]

For continuing plants, large differences arise between results based on output weights and results based on labor weights. The labor productivity decompositions based on output weights are very similar to the multifactor productivity decompositions. In sharp contrast, the labor productivity decomposition based on labor weights shows a much larger contribution for within-plant effects and a negative contribution for the cross-product term. The between-plant contribution to labor productivity gains is small and positive using labor weights. These results suggest that most of the 1977–1987 gains in labor productivity would have taken place even if labor shares had been held constant at initial levels.

To shed some light on the differences in results, Panel C of Table 10 presents simple correlations of plant-level growth rates in multifactor productivity and labor productivity with each other and with the growth in output, labor, capital inputs and capital intensity. Multifactor productivity growth is positively correlated with output growth but nearly uncorrelated with the input growth measures. Labor productivity growth is more strongly correlated with output and input growth. Labor productivity covaries negatively with labor inputs and positively with capital inputs. These different correlation patterns for plant-level growth in multifactor and labor productivity hold despite a strong positive correlation of 0.75 between the two productivity growth measures.

These results show that it is inappropriate to infer that all or even most job reallocation reflects the movement of employment from less productive to more productive sites. Instead, employment downsizing often accompanies or precedes large productivity gains. For example, as described in Davis et al. (1996, Chapter 5), the US steel industry underwent tremendous restructuring during the 1970s and 1980s. Much of this restructuring involved a shift from large, integrated mills to more specialized mini mills. Entry and exit played a major role, but the restructuring of the industry also involved the retooling of many continuing plants. The employment-weighted mean number of workers at a US steel mill fell from 7000 in 1980 to 4000 in 1985. Baily et al. (1996) find that continuing plants in the steel industry experienced substantial productivity gains while downsizing. Moreover, the downsizing episode in the early 1980s was followed by dramatic productivity gains in the steel industry in later years (Davis et al., 1996, Fig. 5.8).

This discussion highlights the point that job destruction should not be presumed to indicate poor performance for affected plants. As the steel industry example illustrates, in some cases the job destruction is part of a within-plant restructuring process that yields large productivity gains. It is also incorrect to draw the opposite inference – i.e., to equate down-

---

[39] In contrast to the findings here, Griliches and Regev (1995) do not find much of a role for net entry in their decomposition of labor productivity. The likely reason is the short horizon, three years, over which they measure productivity changes. Similarly, Liu and Tybout (1996) and Baily et al. (1996) find little contribution of net entry to annual productivity changes.

sizing with subsequent success. The weak correlation between multifactor productivity growth and labor input growth shows that neither upsizing nor downsizing of employment is an accurate indicator of strong productivity performance (Baily et al., 1996).

More generally, this discussion points out that the relationship of productivity growth to the reallocation of inputs and outputs is quite complex. Plants often change the mix of inputs as they change the scale of production. Some technological innovations lead to large employment declines at plants that adopt the new technology. Other technological innovations take the form of cost savings or quality improvements that enable adopting plants to increase market share and input usage. Another complicating and interesting factor is policy interventions that stifle or encourage reallocation. As shown in Olley and Pakes (1996), productivity movements in the manufacture of telecommunications equipment appear closely related to the regulatory process and its effect on factor reallocation. Important deregulatory events coincided with or shortly preceded large increases in the cross-sectional covariance between plant-level market share and productivity.

The young empirical literature on reallocation and productivity growth has already uncovered some provocative results. A better understanding of how input and output reallocation are connected to industry-level and aggregate productivity growth probably requires more structure than we (or the literature) have brought to bear. Given the importance of the topic, and the limits of our knowledge, this area of research merits a high priority in future work.

8. Job and worker flows in transition economies

The transition from centrally planned to market-oriented economies in Central and Eastern Europe and in the former Soviet Union would seem to call for the reallocation of jobs and workers on a truly grand scale. Great reallocations have indeed been underway in these economies, but the reallocation process has some distinctive and surprising features. As emphasized by Blanchard (1997), Boeri (1997) and others, large net flows of workers across firms and sectors have been associated with small gross flows and a stagnant unemployment pool. On a similar note, the available evidence points to surprisingly small gross job flows in post-communist transition economies. We review this and other evidence below. We also try to place the evidence in perspective as it relates to the broader transition experience and to the behavior of job and worker flows in more settled market economies.

This section proceeds as follows. We begin with an overview of the post-communist transition experience and the role of reallocation activity.[40] Next, we summarize the evidence on broad patterns of reallocation activity in these economies. Lastly, we examine gross job and worker flows in Poland and Estonia, two transition economies for which more detailed data are available.

---

[40] The reader may wish to consult Svenjar's (1999) piece in this volume for a more detailed treatment of labor markets in post-communist transition economies.

8.1. Background and theoretical issues

The post-communist transitions have been marked by dramatic output declines and (except for Russia and the Czech Republic) sharp, sustained increases in unemployment. To convey the magnitude of the output declines, we draw on de Melo et al. (1996), who summarize outcomes for 26 countries in Central and Eastern Europe and the former Soviet Union plus Mongolia. The timing and extent of economic liberalization differs among these countries, but most initiated or greatly accelerated the transition to a market-oriented economy in the years from 1990 to 1992.

With this rough generalization about the starting point of transition in mind, consider the following numbers. Among the 20 transition economies not afflicted by regional conflicts, measured gross domestic product in 1993/1994 stood at only 70% of its 1989 level.[41] Among the six countries with regional conflicts, the corresponding figure is 45%. The top-performing transition economies in this respect are Poland (88%) and Uzbekistan (89%). While measurement problems overstate the size of the contractions, the existence of large, persistent output declines is confirmed by other evidence and widely accepted by informed observers.[42]

The demise of central planning involved several major sectoral and structural shocks: large cuts in subsidies to state-owned enterprises, the freeing of relative prices, a collapse in established patterns of domestic and international trade, the restructuring and (in some countries) large-scale privatization of state-owned enterprises, and the removal of restrictions on private ownership and labor mobility.[43] Most transition economies also experienced extreme fiscal imbalances and brief or extended bouts of high inflation (Aslund et al., 1996). Prior to economic liberalization, and relative to market economies, the transition economies had high employment rates, overly large industrial sectors, small and repressed service sectors and compressed wage structures. In short, the economic liberalizations associated with the transition process introduced several major shocks into economies that already had a pent-up demand for reallocation.

Given the costly nature of much reallocation activity and the obsolescence of information, organization and physical capital developed under a regime of central planning, it is not surprising that transition involved initially sharp output declines and slow recoveries. Job loss brings unemployment and lost earnings even in well functioning market economies. This fact suggests that substantial unemployment and lost earnings are inevitable consequences of any ambitious program to restructure state-owned enterprises.

---

[41] By way of comparison, Blanchard (1997, p. 3) notes that "US GNP stood in 1933 at 70% of its 1929 level."

[42] Fischer et al. (1996, pp. 47–49) provide a short, useful discussion of problems in the measurement of output and its growth. Kaufman and Kaliberda (1996) use electricity consumption to proxy for true GDP growth in sixteen post-communist transition economies. Their Table A.2 suggests that the true decline in GDP from 1989 to 1994 averages about 70% of the officially reported decline.

[43] See Blanchard (1997), Svenjar (1999), Commander and Tolstopiatenko (1996) and the articles in Commander and Coricelli (1995) for description and analysis of these shocks with an emphasis on labor market implications. Rodrik (1994) treats the collapse of international trade among transition economies in Eastern Europe. Brada (1996) discusses differences among countries in privatization.

Capital reallocation is also costly. In an interesting case study of the closure of a California aerospace plant, Ramey and Shapiro (1996, Table 3) find that equipment resale prices average only 35% of net-of-depreciation purchase values. They also find low and declining capital utilization rates at the plant for several years prior to closure. Both findings point to a high degree of capital specificity at a large manufacturing facility – the same type of facility that predominated in the pre-transition economies. The Ramey–Shapiro results strongly suggest that large reductions in the flow of services from the pre-existing stock of physical capital are necessary consequences of the closure and restructuring of state-owned enterprises.

A sharp reduction in the flow of services from pre-existing information and organization capital is another likely consequence of restructuring and reallocation in transition economies. The development of information and organization capital suitable for the new market-oriented regime is likely to be slow. In this spirit, Atkeson and Kehoe (1997) show how the reallocation of productive factors to new activities and organizations involves a sacrifice of current for future (measured) output as the economy accumulates a new stock of organization capital. When calibrated to US data on job flows by plant age, their model implies that it takes 5–7 years before a transition economy begins to grow rapidly. The central message of their analysis is that, even in a well functioning transition economy, it takes several years before the favorable effects of economic liberalization show up in measured output.

The evidence and interpretations related to reallocation activity in transition economies are mixed. The rapid development of small private businesses in many transition economies, especially in the service sectors, fits the image of a creative destruction process unleashed by economic liberalization. But other aspects of the transition process are more aptly characterized as "disruptive destruction" or even "destructive creation". In this regard, some potential pitfalls of economic liberalization are made clear in recent work.

Aghion and Blanchard (1994), for example, stress the negative fiscal effects of rapid reductions in subsidies to state-owned enterprises. If subsidy cuts lead to labor shedding in the state sector and large inflows into the unemployment pool, taxes on the private sector may rise to support increased government expenditures on social insurance programs; alternatively, budgetary pressures may induce the government to reduce investments in public infrastructure that facilitate private sector growth. Either way, private sector job creation and output growth are hampered. The main message is that excessively rapid restructuring and job destruction in the state sector can slow down private sector job creation.

Blanchard and Kremer (1997) stress the disruptive economic consequences of an end to central planning. In their model, transition undermines the system of bilateral relationships through which interfirm and international trade occurred under central planning. Given the demise of central planning, they show how an improvement in private opportunities for the sale of goods and services can disrupt the flow of intermediate inputs between state enterprises. The result is a collapse of output in the state sector. Asymmetric information about the value of private opportunities facing suppliers and thin markets in the supply of intermediate inputs are central to their explanation for the transition-induced output decline. Blanchard (1997, pp. 43–45) presents suggestive evidence that disruptive effects of this sort were important in certain transition economies.

Murphy et al. (1992) stress how the freeing of some prices, but not others, leads to the diversion of inputs away from highest value uses. They analyze Russia's unhappy experience with partial price reform between 1988 and 1990. During that period, the input prices offered by state enterprises were often set below market-clearing levels, which allowed private firms to bid essential inputs away from the state sector by paying (slightly) higher prices. Because more severely underpriced inputs were likely to be in shorter supply in the state sector, the incentives for private sector entry were greatest in precisely those activities that diverted inputs with a high shadow value in the state sector. Under this regime, private sector entry and job creation destroyed potential output in the state sector. The Russian experience with partial price reform is but one example of the privately profitable but socially inefficient diversion of goods and services in post-communist transition economies. Credit subsidies, tax breaks, tariff exemptions and other special privileges have contributed enormously to rent seeking and resource misallocation in these economies.[44]

Furthermore, the demise of central planning and the introduction of economic reforms do not ensure secure property rights and enforceable contracts in the post-communist regime. Uncertain property rights and unenforceable contracts discourage investment and distort the allocation of productive inputs, which in turn lowers output and slows growth (Caballero and Hammour, 1996b). So, in addition to the other potential pitfalls of liberalization remarked upon above, the legal institutions required to sustain a healthy process of creative destruction were often lacking.

Despite these concerns about excessively rapid or radical reform, the weight of the evidence for post-communist transition economies suggests that faster and deeper liberalization have been associated with smaller output declines and speedier recovery.[45] Taken at face value, this cross-country evidence is hard to fully reconcile with most theories of costly reallocation addressed to outcomes in settled market economies. It is also hard to reconcile with theories of transition that emphasize the costs of rapid liberalization. As Aslund et al. argue, the evidence instead suggests an important role for complementarities between policy reforms (e.g., price liberalization and monopoly elimination) or positive externalities in the transition process (e.g., private-sector growth promotes the diffusion of useful information). The weight of the evidence also seems to support the view that delayed privatization worsens medium-term economic performance, because it leads to

---

[44] See Aslund et al. (1996). Their footnote 50 reports a striking example of rent extraction: "The Russian Sports Foundation, run by President Yeltsin's tennis trainer, was the main importer of alcohol into Russia in 1994 and 1995, as it was exempt from import tariffs and excise taxes. For 1995, the Russian Ministry of Finance valued the tax exemptions of the Sports Foundation at no less than $6 billion, or 2% of Russia's GDP in that year."

[45] See de Melo et al. (1996), Fischer et al. (1996) and Aslund et al. (1996). Ickes (1996) sounds some cautionary notes regarding the interpretation of the evidence.

Table 11
Sectoral shifts in output at current prices, 1989–1994, post-communist transition economies, by country reform group[a]

Country reform group	Cumulative liberalization index[b]	Change in percentage of GDP		
		Industry	Agriculture	Services
Advanced reformers	3.91	−11.2	−3.7	14.9
High-intermediate reformers	2.55	−11.0	0.7	10.4
Low-intermediate reformers	1.66	−1.9	−4.9	6.8
Slow reformers	0.90	2.9	−1.4	−1.5
Affected by regional tensions	2.11	−7.9	15.3	−7.4

[a] Source: de Melo et al. (1996, Table 5). The table summarizes outcomes for 26 post-communist countries in Eastern and Central Europe, the former Soviet Union and Mongolia. Countries are grouped and ordered by a cumulative index of economic liberalization as follows: Advanced reformers (Slovenia, Poland, Hungary, Czech Republic, Slovak Republic); High-intermediate reformers (Estonia, Bulgaria, Lithuania, Latvia, Albania, Romania, Mongolia); Low-intermediate reformers (Russian Federation, Kyrgyz Republic, Moldova, Kazakstan); Slow reformers (Uzbekistan, Belarus, Ukraine, Turkmenistan); Affected by regional tensions (Croatia, Macedonia, Armenia, Georgia, Azerbaijan, Tajikistan).

[b] The cumulative liberalization index is a composite of quantitative rankings in three areas of economic liberalization: internal markets, external trade and payments, and the facilitation of private sector entry. Each country was assigned an index value between 0 and 1 in each year from 1989 to 1994. The index values were then summed over years to arrive at a cumulative liberalization index for each country. Hence, the cumulative index reflects both the depth and duration of economic liberalization. See de Melo et al. (1996) for details.

greater asset stripping in the state sector and greater appropriation of the income flows generated by state enterprises (Kaufman and Kaliberda, 1996).

On balance, it seems reasonable to maintain that the post-communist transition experience has been characterized by major unavoidable costs (e.g., loss of specific capital), much creative destruction, much socially harmful diversion of goods and services, some disruptive destruction, and the ongoing accumulation of new and socially useful forms of information and organization capital. The evidence below on reallocation activity in transition economies should be approached in this light.

8.2. Broad patterns of reallocation in transition economies

Table 11 reports enormous shifts in the sectoral composition of output for 26 post-communist transition economies. Each country is ranked by a cumulative index of economic liberalization and placed into one of five country reform groups. The two groups with the greatest reform show a tremendous reallocation of output from Industry to Services between 1989 and 1994. The low-intermediate reform group also shows a large increase in the share of GDP in Services, but little decline in the Industry share.[46] The "slow refor-

---

[46] As de Melo et al. (1996) point out, the shift to Services took place despite a precipitous decline in government services between 1990 and 1992 in the former Soviet Union.

Table 12
Industry reallocation intensity, selected transition and other economies (standard deviation of employment growth rates across one-digit industries, annual averages)

Country	Period	Standard deviation (%)	Source
Czech Republic		20.9	Boeri (1996, Table 1)
Slovakia		14.2	Boeri (1996, Table 1)
Hungary		9.0	Boeri (1996, Table 1)
Poland		20.3	Boeri (1996, Table 1)
Bulgaria		11.0	Boeri (1996, Table 1)
Estonia	1989–1991	2.7	Haltiwanger and Vodopivec (1997)
Estonia	1991–1994	8.5	Haltiwanger and Vodopivec (1997)
OECD	1990–1993	3.4	Blanchard (1997, p. 5)
United States	1939–1942	6.0	Authors' calculations
United States	1944–1947	6.4	Authors' calculations

mers" show comparatively modest changes in the sectoral composition of output. Finally, countries affected by regional tensions show a very different reallocation pattern that reflects a large-scale return to subsistence farming.

Measurement problems notwithstanding, there is little reason to doubt the basic impressions conveyed by Table 11. On the whole, the post-communist transition brought about major output shifts from Industry to Services. Greater output reallocations took place in countries with deeper and earlier reforms. The main countervailing pattern has been a return to Agriculture in countries afflicted by regional tensions.

Table 12 reports a measure of between-industry reallocation intensity for several transition economies and for several other countries. The measure, introduced by Lilien (1982) to explain cyclical fluctuations in the US unemployment rate, equals the standard deviation of the employment growth rate across one-digit industry groups. The message in Table 12 is clear: post-communist transition economies experienced enormous and rapid shifts in the industrial distribution of employment, even in comparison to the transformations associated with the US entry into World War II and the demobilization after the war's end.

Of course, the transition economies also underwent profound changes in the ownership and control structure of business enterprises. Table 13 addresses this matter, showing how the private sector share of GDP evolved in 17 post-communist transition economies. Once again, tremendous change is evident: the private sector share of GDP rose from an average of 14% prior to economic reform to 46% in 1995.

Impressive as they are, these numbers fail to convey the complexity and magnitude of transition-economy changes in the ownership and control of business enterprises. Without pretending to treat this issue in a serious way, we offer four remarks to supplement Table

Table 13
Private sector percentage of GDP in post-communist transition economies[a]

Country	Year of most intense reform	Prior level	Change in year of most intense reform	Change over next 2 years	Level in 1994	Level in 1995
Armenia	1992	24.2	12.5			45
Belarus	1993	8.1				15
Bulgaria	1991	7.2		19.3	40.2	45
Croatia	1990	8.5		16.0	44.9	45
Czech Republic	1991	12.3	5.0	17.8	56.3	70
Estonia	1992	17.7	4.3	13.0	58.0	65
Georgia	1992	27.3	12.7	19.6	60.0	30
Hungary	1990	14.9				60
Kazakhstan	1992	12.2			20.2	25
Latvia	1992	12.0	19.8	16.0	53.0	60
Lithuania	1991	11.6	3.8			55
Poland	1990	28.6	2.8	16.8	56.0	60
Romania	1990	12.8	3.6	10.0	35.0	40
Russia	1992	10.1	3.9	11.0	25.0	55
Slovenia	1990	8.1	3.3	8.1		45
Ukraine	1994	7.5				35
Uzbekistan	1990	9.8	−3.2		54.2	30
Simple average		13.7				45.9

[a] Source: Aslund et al. (1996, Table 8). Estimates are for the "pure" private sector (that is, excluding cooperatives) and, as far as possible, for 100% privately owned companies. The numbers include agriculture. The original source varies with country and column. Measurement error probably accounts for reported declines in the private sector share of GDP for some countries and time periods.

13.[47] First, the role of new private firms, as opposed to newly privatized state firms, varies widely among countries. Second, many privatized firms are effectively controlled by insiders – managers and workers – whose objectives differ greatly from those of outside equity holders. Third, with the withering of central authority, even firms that remain in the state sector operate with a very different control structure than in the pre-transition era. Finally, the line between state and private sector activity is often blurry, especially in the former Soviet Union, and many "unofficial" private activities take place alongside official state sector activities.

Tremendous industrial reallocation and private sector growth would seem to set the stage for large gross flows of workers and jobs. The available evidence says otherwise. Table 14 summarizes the most widely available form of evidence on gross flows in the post-communist transition economies – unemployment inflows and outflows. Except for the Czech Republic, the table shows a stagnant unemployment pool with very small unemployment outflow rates – especially flows from unemployment to employment. The idea of a stagnant unemployment pool emerges as a chief theme in several multi-country studies of transition economies (OECD, 1994b; Commander and Coricelli, 1995; Blanchard, 1997). The available evidence also indicates that a high fraction of open positions are filled by workers who transit directly from another job, rather than from unemployment or nonparticipation. Blanchard (1997, pp. 90–91) reports the fraction of new hires that came directly from another job: 40% in Poland and 71% in Hungary in 1992, as compared to only 20% in the United States.

8.3. Gross flows in Poland and Estonia

The two transition economies that offer the richest data on labor market flows are Poland and Estonia. We draw on evidence for these two countries in an effort to sketch a more detailed picture of labor flows in the post-communist transition. In doing so, it is helpful to note how the broader transition experience of Poland and Estonia compares to that of other countries. Both Poland and Estonia undertook more radical liberalizations than most other transition economies and with decidedly better outcomes. Poland implemented major reforms in 1990; Estonia implemented major reforms in 1992. Both stayed the course of liberalization – initial reforms remained largely intact and further reforms followed. Initial conditions were also relatively favorable. Prior to 1990, the Polish and Estonian economies were more liberalized than most other communist countries, and both countries inherited a legacy of market-oriented economies in the pre-World War II era.

Estonian policies have been especially, indeed remarkably, conducive to job realloca-tion, worker mobility and high employment. According to Noorkoiv et al. (1997), Esto-nian unemployment benefits average less than 10% of wages, and the eligibility period

---

[47] The ownership and control structure of business enterprises in transition economies is a major research topic. For studies that treat this topic in connection with labor market implications, the interested reader might wish to begin with Blanchard (1997) and Commander and Tolstopiatenko (1996).

Table 14
Summary measures of unemployment rate dynamics: selected countries[a]

	Unemployment rate	Monthly inflow rate to unemployment	Monthly hazard rate from unemployment	Monthly hazard rate from unemployment to employment	Percent longterm unemployment
Advanced economies (averages for 1989–1991)					
Canada	8.63	2.10	27.8		6.6
France	9.23	0.35	6.10		39.8
Germany	4.93	0.25	7.80		47.7
Italy	11.40	0.20	3.20		70.8
Japan	2.17	0.35	22.80		18.6
UK	6.80	0.60	13.55		38.5
US	5.8	2.05	42.8		5.9
Transition economies (averages for 1992)					
Czech Republic	3.1	0.6	25.8	18.0	28.4
Hungary	11.7	0.5	7.0	3.0	37.3
Poland	14.9	0.7	4.0	2.3	43.4
Slovakia	11.4	1.0	9.8	4.8	25.5
Romania	8.3	–	0.9	0.9	–
Bulgaria	6.0	1.8	5.5	1.1	–
Estonia	5.7	4.5	50.1	39.2	–
Russia	1.3	0.3	18.0	7.5	–

[a] Source: Tabulations for advanced economies are from OECD Employment Outlook (OECD, 1993). Tabulations for transition economies (except for Estonia) are from Blanchard et al. (1995, Table 7–8). Estonia tabulations are from Haltiwanger and Vodopivec (1997). Inflow rate to unemployment is percentage of labor force entering unemployment each month. Hazard rate from unemployment is percentage of unemployed leaving unemployment each month. Longterm unemployment is the percentage of unemployed with durations longer than 12 months.

lasts no more than nine months. Unemployment benefits are reduced or cut off for failure to report regularly to the employment office, failure to accept a suitable job when offered, and failure to accept temporary employment in public works. Subsidized job training and assisted self-employment programs dominate unemployment benefits for many workers. Furthermore, Estonia has no mandatory firing costs, very low minimum wages, no effective trade union movement, no restrictions on foreign investment, and no policy of propping up bankrupt firms to avoid layoffs. The taxes required to sustain unemployment and employment programs are less than 0.2% of GDP. Taxes to support pension benefits are also small. In short, taxes (explicit and implicit) on employment, worker flows and job flows are extremely low.

Table 15 summarizes some major changes in the distribution of Estonian employment from 1989 to 1995. Private enterprises accounted for less than 2% of employment in 1989 but 35% by January 1995. Over the same period, the share of employment in establishments with 100 or more workers fell from 75% to 46%. Employees accounted for 99% of the work force in 1989 as compared to 93% in 1995. These changes began before 1992, when Estonia implemented deep economic reforms, and accelerated thereafter. More

Table 15
Employment shares by employer characteristics for Estonia, 1989–1995[a]

Year	By enterprise type		
	Collective	Private	State
1989	20.9	1.5	77.6
1992	18.9	9.4	71.7
1995	11.1	34.8	54.0

Year	By enterprise size			
	1–19	20–99	100–499	500+
1989	7.6	17.2	34.7	40.6
1992	12.4	20.3	31.4	35.9
1995	25.8	28.0	23.4	22.7

Year	By employment status		
	Employee	Employee/owner[b]	Self-employed
1989	99.0	0.5	0.5
1992	96.9	1.2	1.9
1995	93.2	3.2	3.7

[a] Shares are based upon employment on January 1 of each year. The tabulations are from Haltiwanger and Vodopivec (1997) and are based upon a labor force survey of households.

[b] Employee/owner refers to business owners with employees.

detailed annual data in Haltiwanger and Vodopivec (1997) show slow, steady change from 1989 to 1992 and rapid change in each year from 1992 to 1995.

Worker and job flow rates for Estonia and Poland appear in Table 16. The Estonian figures cover the entire economy and are broken down by type of enterprise. The Polish figures derive from two different sources: one covers only continuing state enterprises in the manufacturing sector; the other is broken down into state and private enterprises, but the extent of coverage is unclear.

Gross job flows were extremely small in both economies prior to economic liberalization. (An exception is the Estonian private sector, which enjoyed very high creation rates before and after 1992 but on a very small base.) To the extent that this pattern of minimal job flows prevails in other centrally planned economies, it helps understand their tendency to fall ever farther behind the productivity levels of market-oriented economies with comparable factor endowments. In particular, the evidence suggests that centrally planned economies choke off the productivity-enhancing role of job reallocation (Section 7).

Worker flows were also small prior to liberalization. In Poland, state-sector hiring and separation rates were less than 20% per year. In Estonia, they were even smaller in 1989 and 1990, except for hiring rates in the small private sector. Annual quit rates (separation minus destruction) in Estonia were only 9% in 1989, 11% and in 1990 and 12% in 1991. These low worker mobility rates suggest that centrally planned economies also choke off the productivity-enhancing role of worker sorting among employers and occupations.[48]

Liberalization brought a sharp jump in the state-sector job destruction rate in both countries. While the jump is large, the post-reform destruction rates are no higher than in a typical US recession.[49] This finding is remarkable on two counts. First, even in the post-reform period, gross job flows in transition economies are relatively small. Despite tremendous shifts in the industry and ownership structure of employment, job destruction in post-reform Poland and Estonia occurs at the same rate as in the much more modest sectoral transformations that typify US recessions. Second, this finding provides an interesting perspective on the performance of more settled market economies. The United States, for example, accommodates periodic episodes of annual job destruction rates on the order of 15–17% with a 1–2% decline in aggregate employment and consumption that persists for no more than 2 years. A similar job destruction intensity in the post-reform transition economies involves much, much larger employment and consumption declines that persist for several years. One can read this comparison as a sign of dismal labor market

---

[48] Theoretical models that incorporate a social return to worker mobility include Jovanovic (1979), Miller (1984), Kremer (1993), Jovanovic and Nyarko (1997) and Davis (1997). Topel and Ward (1992) provide a detailed empirical study of the connection between job matching and wage growth among young men. Jovanovic and Moffitt (1990) estimate that the worker-job match quality improvements associated with worker mobility increase GNP by 6–9% in the United States.

[49] The annual job destruction rate in the US manufacturing sector was 16.5% in 1975, 14.5% in 1982 and 15.6% in 1983 (Davis et al., 1996, Table 2.1).

Table 16
Annual worker and job flow rates by enterprise types, Poland and Estonia[a]

	1988	1989	1990	1991	1992	1993	1994
Worker hiring rates							
Estonia, collective		9.9	12.2	11.6	12.5	14.6	16.7
Estonia, private firms		70.2	104.5	125.6	104.8	76.6	59.8
Estonia, state enterprises		8.6	11.1	11.4	12.7	14.1	13.5
Estonia, all employees		9.7	13.5	16.4	21.1	25.3	26.5
Poland, continuing state enterprises, manufacturing	17.1	17.9	12.9	9.7			
Poland, state sector	17.3	16.2	12.2		11.9		
Poland, private sector					38.8		
Job creation rates							
Estonia, collective		0.4	0.4	0.0	0.0	0.0	0.0
Estonia, private firms		64.9	93.5	113.3	89.4	60.0	39.0
Estonia, state enterprises		0.0	0.5	0.0	0.0	0.4	0.5
Estonia, all employees		0.5	2.7	4.5	6.9	11.1	10.9
Poland, continuing state enterprises, manufacturing	0.7	2.0	0.6	1.0			
Worker separation rates							
Estonia, collective		10.9	15.8	20.7	34.3	36.4	29.8
Estonia, private firms		6.4	18.4	20.4	27.3	28.7	32.4
Estonia, state enterprises		10.7	13.9	18.0	28.0	26.8	21.9
Estonia, all employees		10.7	14.3	18.4	28.7	28.2	25.5
Poland, continuing state enterprises, manufacturing	20.0	22.9	27.6	26.0			
Poland, state sector	18.0	19.8	23.0		22.4		
Poland, private sector					36.3		
Job destruction rates							
Estonia, collective		1.4	3.9	9.1	21.9	21.8	13.1
Estonia, private firms		1.1	7.8	8.1	11.9	12.3	11.5
Estonia, state enterprises		2.1	3.2	6.6	15.4	13.1	8.9
Estonia, all employees		1.5	3.5	6.5	14.5	14.1	10.0
Poland, continuing state enterprises, manufacturing	3.6	6.1	15.3	17.6			

[a] Sources: (1) The figures for Estonia are from Haltiwanger and Vodopivec (1997) and are based upon a labor force survey of households. They measure point in time to point in time flows – i.e., flows for 1989 are changes for the period from January 1, 1989 to January 1, 1990. Job creation and destruction represent lower bounds on job flows. (2) The figures for Poland (continuing state enterprises, manufacturing) are from Konings et al. (1996, Table 2). They are based on firm-level measures of full-time employment. State firms include unincorporated state-owned enterprises, joint stock companies with 100% state ownership, and majority state-owned firms. (3) The other figures for Poland are from Coricelli et al. (1995, Table 2-13). The precise coverage of these data and their relationship to the data used by Konings et al. (1996) are unclear.

performances in the transition economies or as a sign of remarkable resilience in the United States and many other market economies.

Liberalization also brought a sharp jump in worker mobility. In Estonia, the sum of annual hiring and separation rates rose from 20–33% in 1989–1991 to 50–53% in 1992–1994. Over the same period, annual quit rates rose from 9–12% to 14–15%. The evolving employment distribution plays a surprisingly minor role in this aspect of the Estonian experience. Indeed, the rise in quit rates and the sharp jump in worker turnover rates holds separately for each type of Estonian enterprise listed in Table 16.

The fragmentary Polish evidence also points to greater worker mobility as a consequence of economic reform. In the Polish case, composition effects appear to be the main story. Within the state sector, the sum of hiring and separation rates changes little during the period covered by Table 16. The quit rate at continuing state manufacturing enterprises actually falls with the onset of major reforms in 1990. But sharp differences in worker mobility rates between the Polish private and state sectors imply large increases over time in economy-wide worker mobility rates. The sum of hiring and separation rates in 1992 is 34% in the Polish state sector and 75% in the Polish private sector. Projecting these figures onto the rising share of employment in the Polish private sector (Table 13) implies an increase in the economy-wide sum of hiring and separation rates from 46% in 1989 to 59% in 1995.

In summary, the evidence indicates that Polish and Estonian labor markets are evolving from a central planning regime with sharply curtailed worker mobility and job reallocation to a regime more like that of the United States or Western Europe. The Estonian economy has already progressed a great distance toward US-style labor market flows (Tables 14 and 16). The evidence for Poland points to a less rapid evolution of the labor market and perhaps an eventual destination more like that of labor markets in many Western European countries.

9. Cyclicality in job flows

Prevailing academic theories of the business cycle stress the role of aggregate shocks that induce broadly similar outcomes among households and among workers. See, for example, the fine collection of essays in Cooley (1995). These theories abstract from mobility costs and other frictions associated with the reallocation of jobs, workers and capital. For the most part, they also abstract from heterogeneity on the household and firm sides of the economy. Because they abstract from reallocation frictions and heterogeneity, these theories of the business cycle are silent about the behavior of job and worker flows. For the same reason, they deliver rather stunted interpretations of unemployment fluctuations and related phenomena.

Recent research on labor market flows has greatly stimulated attention on the role of reallocation frictions and heterogeneity in aggregate economic fluctuations. Several facts about labor market flows contribute to this stimulus. We mention a few. First, cyclical increases in unemployment predominantly reflect an increase in the number of workers who experience permanent job separations (e.g., Davis and Haltiwanger, 1998, Table 5). Second, postwar US recessions are characterized by an increase in the number of workers who flow through the unemployment pool (e.g., Davis et al., 1996, Chapter 6). Third, recessions often coincide with sharp spikes in job destruction activity for major sectors of the economy (Section 3.7). This burst of job destruction largely reflects permanent employment declines at the affected establishments (Section 3.3). Fourth, job loss often leads to repeated spells of unemployment before the displaced worker settles into a new stable employment relationship. As a consequence, cyclical increases in job destruction lead to persistent increases in the aggregate unemployment rate (Hall, 1995). These facts, and many others, point to an intimate relationship between aggregate fluctuations and the intensity of reallocation activity, as reflected in labor market flows.

Once we build models that incorporate reallocation frictions and heterogeneity among production units, two central implications become evident: (i) aggregate shocks influence the intensity of reallocation activity, and (ii) shocks to the structure of factor demand can drive fluctuations in the economic aggregates that occupy the attention of business cycle researchers. The precise nature and strength of these influences depend on the details of the economic environment.

Models with reallocation frictions also help to address some well-recognized short-comings in prevailing theories of the business cycle. Standard equilibrium business cycle models generate little amplification of shocks for standard specifications of technology and preferences (Campbell, 1994, Table 3). Standard models also fail to explain the persistence properties of aggregate fluctuations (Cogley and Nasson, 1995; Rotemberg and Woodford, 1996). As emphasized by Hall (1997a), the introduction of labor market frictions improves the performance of standard models along both of these dimensions.

We now review recent research that investigates the relationship between labor market flows and aggregate fluctuations. We focus on broad themes and omit many important details of theoretical and empirical work in this area. As complements to our discussion here, we encourage the reader to consult Mortensen (1994), Davis et al. (1996) and Hall (1997a).

9.1. Theoretical perspectives

Most theories that incorporate job and worker flows adopt the premise that the economy is subject to a continuous stream of *allocative shocks* – shocks that cause idiosyncratic variation in profitability among job sites and worker-job matches.[50] The continuous stream of allocative shocks generates the large-scale job and worker reallocation activity

---

[50] See Aghion and Blanchard (1994), Andolfatto (1996), Blanchard and Diamond (1989, 1990), Burda and Wyplosz (1994), Caballero (1992), Caballero and Hammour (1994, 1996a), Campbell (1997), Campbell and Fisher (1997), Davis and Haltiwanger (1990), Foote (1998), Gautier and Broersma (1993), Greenwood et al. (1994), Hall (1991), Hosios (1994), Mortensen (1994), Mortensen and Pissarides (1993, 1994), Ramey and Watson (1997), Yashiv (1995), Den Haan et al. (1997), Bergin and Bernhard (1996) and Saint-Paul (1996).

observed in the data. To explicitly model the job and worker reallocation process, these theories incorporate heterogeneity among workers and firms along one or more dimensions. Various theories also emphasize search costs, moving costs, sunk investments and other frictions that impede or otherwise distort the reallocation of factor inputs. The combination of frictions and heterogeneity gives rise to potentially important roles for allocative shocks and the reallocation process in aggregate economic fluctuations.

Theories of cyclical fluctuations in job and worker flows can be classified into two broad types. One type treats fluctuations over time in the intensity of allocative shocks as an important driving force behind aggregate fluctuations and the pace of reallocation activity. A second type maintains that, while allocative shocks and reallocation frictions are important, aggregate shocks drive business cycles and fluctuations in the pace of worker and job reallocation. Although different in emphasis, the two types of theories offer complementary views of labor-market dynamics and business cycles, and both point toward a rich set of interactions between aggregate fluctuations and the reallocation process.

9.1.1. Allocative shocks as driving forces behind aggregate fluctuations

One can think of allocative shocks as events that alter the closeness of the match between the desired and actual characteristics of labor and capital inputs (Black, 1987, Chapter 13). Adverse aggregate consequences can result from such events because of the time and other costs of reallocation activity. For example, the OPEC oil price shock of 1973 increased the demand for small, fuel-efficient cars and simultaneously reduced the demand for larger cars. American automobile companies were poorly situated to respond to this shock, because their capital stock and work force were primarily directed toward the production of large cars. Consequently, capacity utilization and output fell in the wake of the oil price shock, even though a handful of plants equipped to produce small cars operated at peak capacity (Bresnahan and Ramey, 1993).

In considering this view, it is important to emphasize that allocative shocks affect tangible inputs to the production process (labor and physical capital) and intangible inputs. These intangible inputs include the information capital embodied in an efficient sorting and matching of heterogeneous workers and jobs, knowledge about how to work productively with coworkers, knowledge about suitable locations for particular business activities and about idiosyncratic attributes of those locations, the information capital embodied in longterm customer-supplier and debtor-creditor relationships, and the organization capital embodied in sales, product distribution and job-finding networks. When allocative shocks upset established patterns of production, they devalue information and organization capital specific to that pattern of production (Caplin and Leahy, 1993; Blanchard and Kremer, 1997). Recreating information and organization capital suited to the new pattern of production requires experimentation, time and expense (Atkeson and Kehoe, 1997). Meanwhile, the productive potential of the economy is reduced by the obsolescence of old information and organization capital. In addition, measured output may decline relative to true output because of a shift toward unmeasured investment activities (Section 10.3).

These remarks make clear why the economic adjustments to these shocks are often costly and time consuming. It follows that sharp time variation in the intensity of allocative shocks can cause large fluctuations in gross job flows and in conventional measures of aggregate economic activity such as the output growth rate and the unemployment rate.

9.1.2. Reallocation timing effects

For many reasons, adverse aggregate shocks can lead to a concentration of certain reallocation activities during recessions. First, an adverse aggregate shock can push many declining and dying plants over an adjustment threshold. During boom times, a firm may choose to continue operating a plant that fails to recover its long-run average cost, because short-run revenues exceed short-run costs, or because of a sufficiently large option value to retaining the plant and its work force. Adverse aggregate shocks also lead to a burst in job destruction and job search in the equilibrium search models of Mortensen and Pissarides (1993, 1994).

Second, the reallocation of specialized labor and capital inputs involves foregone production due to lost work time (e.g., unemployment or additional schooling), worker retraining, the retooling of plant and equipment, the adoption of new technology, and the organization of new patterns of production and distribution. On average across firms and workers, the value of foregone production tends to fluctuate procyclically, rising during expansions and falling during recessions. This cyclical pattern generates incentives for both workers and firms to concentrate costly reallocation activity during recessions, when the opportunity cost of the resulting foregone production is relatively low. This mechanism is highlighted in the models of Davis and Haltiwanger (1990), Hall (1991), Caballero and Hammour (1994) and Bergin and Bernhardt (1996).

Third, the curtailment of credit availability that often accompanies a recession causes investment cutbacks, employment declines and business failures among firms with imperfect access to credit markets, especially if those firms simultaneously experience declines in cash flow. To some extent, the cutbacks and failures induced by a credit crunch are likely to be concentrated among firms with weaker prospects for future profitability, but they are also concentrated among firms that – for whatever reason – face greater difficulties in overcoming informational problems that impede the flow of credit. Thus, a credit crunch induces a reallocation of capital and employment away from credit-sensitive sectors and firms toward sectors and firms that are less dependent upon outside sources of credit to fund current operations and investments. Blanchard and Diamond (1990) discuss this idea in the context of cyclical dynamics in job flows.

Fourth, adverse aggregate shocks may trigger the revelation of accumulated pieces of information that bear upon the desired allocation of jobs, workers and capital inputs. In other words, an adverse aggregate shock can lead to an increase in the intensity of allocative shocks. Schivardi (1997) develops this theme in an explicit theoretical model that builds on earlier work on information spillovers by Caplin and Leahy (1993, 1994). Davis et al. (1996, Chapter 5) and Horvath et al. (1997) provide related discussions.

9.1.3. Non-convex adjustment costs

As we pointed out in Section 3.4, the lumpiness of establishment-level employment adjustments points to a major role for fixed costs in the adjustment of labor or cooperating factors of production. Fixed costs of adjustment can strongly influence the cyclical behavior of job flows. A key point is that the cross-sectional distribution of production units, in terms of where they stand relative to their adjustment thresholds, influences the response to aggregate shocks.

Fixed cost of adjustment induce a subtle relationship between microeconomic and aggregate adjustment dynamics. Caballero (1992) considers an environment in which individual employers face asymmetric fixed costs of adding and shedding workers. In his setup, the adjustment cost asymmetry leads to greater lumpiness in destruction than creation at the plant level but equally volatile fluctuations in destruction and creation at the aggregate level. The heterogeneity among employers completely smoothes away the pronounced asymmetry in plant-level employment adjustments.

Nevertheless, non-convex adjustment costs can interact with other features of the economic environment to generate asymmetric cyclical dynamics in job creation and destruction. In Caballero's (1992) environment, destruction is more volatile than creation at the aggregate level, if aggregate shocks are positively serially correlated and negative ones tend to be less frequent and stronger than positive ones. Campbell and Fisher (1996) develop a related framework with asymmetric costs of employment changes and (S,s) adjustment behavior. They show that fixed costs of job creation can cause the optimal (S,s) bands to respond to aggregate disturbances in a manner that yields asymmetries in the cyclical dynamics of creation and destruction. Foote's (1997, 1998) explanation for the relative volatility of job creation and destruction, which we discussed in Section 3.7, plays off of the interaction between lumpy microeconomic adjustment behavior and trend growth in desired employment.

9.2. Normative issues

Caballero and Hammour (1996a, 1998a) highlight the potential for labor markets to malfunction because of appropriability or hold-up problems. These problems arise whenever investment in a new production unit or the formation of a new employment relationship involves some degree of specificity for workers or employers, and there are difficulties in writing or enforcing complete contracts. In their (1996a) model, Caballero and Hammour show that efficient restructuring involves synchronized job creation and destruction and relatively little unemployment. In contrast, the inefficient equilibrium restructuring process that emerges under incomplete contracts involves the decoupling of creation and destruction dynamics and relatively large unemployment responses to negative shocks. As discussed in Mortensen and Pissarides (1994), appropriability problems arise naturally in many search and matching models. Malcomson (1999) provides a broad discussion of hold-up problems in the labor market.

Ramey and Watson (1997) highlight the potential for inefficient separation outcomes in a dynamic environment with incentive problems in the employment relationship. They develop an equilibrium search model with the following key features: (i) employment relationships that require cooperative behavior (high effort) to achieve efficient output levels, (ii) difficulty in maintaining cooperative behavior in bad states of the world, and (ii) sunk investments made by firms prior to match formation that influence the incentives for firm and worker to sustain cooperative outcomes in the face of bad shocks. In the Ramey–Watson environment, fragile employment relationships can develop in which bad shocks bring about a collapse in the incentives to put forth effort and sustain cooperation. In this way, bad states of the world trigger inefficient separations. Larger sunk investments lead to higher match surplus and hence stronger incentives to maintain cooperative behavior in order to preserve the relationship.

Incomplete risk-sharing raises important normative questions with respect to labor market flows. The welfare consequences of job creation and destruction activity obviously depend on the availability of risk-sharing mechanisms to job-losing and job-seeking workers. Risk-sharing opportunities are also likely to influence the efficiency of job search activity, separation behavior and match-specific investment decisions. Despite the importance of incomplete risk sharing in the context of job and worker reallocation activity, the analysis of dynamic labor market models with incomplete risk sharing is in its infancy. Gomes et al. (1996) is a first attempt to grapple with this issue. They analyze a dynamic equilibrium matching model with incomplete risk sharing and aggregate shocks that influence the distribution of match productivities and consumption levels. As modeling and computation techniques continue to improve, dynamic labor market models with incomplete risk sharing are likely to receive much greater attention.

9.3. Empirical evidence on the role of allocative shocks

Many empirical studies shed light on some of the theoretical issues discussed above. One issue that has received considerable attention is whether time variation in the intensity of allocative shocks is an important driving force behind aggregate fluctuations. A provocative paper by Lilien (1982) documented a strong, positive time-series relationship between aggregate unemployment and the cross-industry dispersion of employment growth rates in postwar US data. He interpreted this relationship as supporting the view that half or more of cyclical unemployment fluctuations were driven by sectoral shifts in labor demand or, in our terminology, the intensity of allocative shocks. Abraham and Katz (1986) questioned this interpretation. They set forth empirically plausible conditions under which Lilien's empirical evidence is consistent with the view that aggregate shocks are the main driving force behind aggregate fluctuations They also documented a pattern of strong negative comovements between unemployment and vacancies over the business cycle, which they interpreted as confirming an aggregate shock view of unemployment fluctuations.[51].

---

[51] Blanchard and Diamond's (1989, 1990) conclusion that allocative shocks play little role in driving aggregate fluctuations also rests heavily on this interpretation of unemployment-vacancy comovements. On the suitability of this identifying assumption, see Hosios (1994) and Davis (1987).

The subsequent literature has tried various methods to identify the underlying contribution of allocative shocks to business cycle fluctuations. Many studies have adopted Lilien's basic approach but explored alternative and arguably better proxies for sectoral shocks. For example, Loungani et al. (1990) and Brainard and Cutler (1993) argue that the dispersion in stock returns is a better proxy for the intensity of allocative shocks. Both papers find that aggregate unemployment rises when stock return dispersion rises. Davis et al. (1997) find similar results in regional unemployment fluctuations. Shin (1997) relates unemployment fluctuations to intersectoral and intrasectoral dispersion in accounting measures of economic performance. However, like Lilien's measure, stock return and accounting measures of dispersion are outcomes and not direct measures of the intensity of allocative shocks.

An alternative approach imposes identification assumptions in structural VAR models. Blanchard and Diamond (1989, 1990), Davis and Haltiwanger (1990, 1996) and Campbell and Kuttner (1996) pursue the idea that aggregate shocks and allocative shocks generate different covariance properties for key variables like unemployment and vacancies or job creation and destruction. In terms of job flows, the basic insight is that aggregate shocks cause job creation and destruction to move in opposite directions, whereas allocative shocks cause them to move in the same direction. This insight is helpful but provides only qualitative identifying restrictions rather than exact identification. Davis and Haltiwanger (1996) and Campbell and Kuttner (1996) both conclude that these qualitative restrictions are insufficient to pin down with much precision the importance of allocative shocks as driving forces behind aggregate fluctuations.[52] However, the qualitative restrictions imply a systematic tradeoff between the contribution of aggregate shocks and the contemporaneous response of job destruction to an aggregate shock innovation. Specifically, aggregate shocks are the dominant driving force only if they are allowed to have disproportionately large contemporaneous effects on job destruction. In a related finding, Davis and Haltiwanger (1999) report that energy price and interest rate spread innovations lead to much larger short-run responses in job destruction than in job creation.

In another approach, Caballero et al. (1997) achieve identification by imposing a structure that permits the measurement of desired and actual employment at individual plants. Their structure allows for nonlinear employment dynamics of the sort that arise in models with fixed costs of factor adjustment, and it separately identifies common and idiosyncratic forces that underlie changes in desired employment.[53] Under their approach to identification, they find that aggregate shocks are the dominant driving force behind aggregate employment fluctuations. They also find a highly nonlinear plant-level employment

---

[52] These two papers also restrict contemporaneous and long run responses to aggregate shocks and allocative shocks in order to achieve exact or over identification.

[53] Unlike the structural VAR approach, the CEH approach does not require assumptions about the correlation between aggregate shocks and the intensity of allocative shocks. Empirically, CEH find a negative time series correlation between aggregate shocks and the second moment of the cross-sectional distribution of idiosyncratic shocks.

response to movements in desired employment – plants with large differences between actual and desired employment adjust relatively more.

The findings of Caballero et al. (1997) are also relevant to asymmetric cyclical dynamics in job creation and destruction. In particular, they find that the job flows generated by aggregate shocks in their framework exhibit the asymmetric cyclical patterns described in Section 3.7 for the manufacturing sector. This result implies that it is possible to account for the cyclical asymmetry in creation and destruction by allowing for sufficient non-linearity in microeconomic adjustment behavior. Finally, several studies relate direct measures of sectoral or allocative shocks to cyclical fluctuations in unemployment, employment and job flows. In light of the major oil price shocks that struck the economy in 1973–1984, 1979–1980 and 1986, most studies of this sort focus on energy price shocks. Bresnahan and Ramey (1993), Davis and Haltiwanger (1999), Davis et al. (1997), Loungani (1986) and Mork (1989) develop evidence that energy price shocks drive aggregate fluctuations by upsetting established patterns of production and triggering a costly reallocation process. Atkeson and Kehoe (1994) and Hamilton (1988) develop related theoretical interpretations.

10. Job flows, productivity and welfare: selected theoretical issues

This section provides a theoretical treatment of selected issues that arise in connection with job flows. We set forth a simple model of job flows with costly worker mobility and specific physical capital.[54] We use the model to address several topics: (i) the effects of policies that impede job flows, (ii) the productivity-enhancing role of factor reallocation, (iii) reallocation dynamics in transition economies, and (iv) the role of job flows in long-term growth.

10.1. A simple model of investment and job flows

We introduce general and specific forms of physical capital into a model of Davis and Haltiwanger (1990). The model incorporates two frictions associated with job creation and destruction: the abandonment of physical capital and a time cost of moving for workers.

Consider an economy with a unit mass of consumer-workers distributed over two types of production sites. A fraction H_t of the workers begin period t matched to high-productivity sites, and the remaining workers are matched to low-productivity sites. Each period, a fraction σ_t of the high-productivity sites suffer adverse shocks that cause them to revert to low-productivity status. As existing high-productivity sites suffer adverse shocks, an equal (or larger) number of potential high-productivity sites becomes available. These shocks to the spatial distribution of production opportunities inject a continuous stream of allocative disturbances into the economy.

When matched to a worker, low-productivity sites produce $(Q_t L_L)^{1-\alpha} K_L^{\alpha}$ units of output.

---

[54] Other dynamic equilibrium models that incorporate both costly worker reallocation and specific physical capital include Bergin and Bernhard (1996), Caballero and Hammour (1996a), and Den Haan et al. (1997).

Here, Q_t denotes the exogenously determined technology level, L_L governs labor efficiency at low-productivity plants, and K_L denotes the amount of general (i.e., mobile) physical capital allocated to low-productivity sites. *Operational* high-productivity sites produce $(Q_t L_H)^{1-\alpha} K_H^\alpha$ when matched to a worker, using analogous notation.

To make the potential new sites operational requires two forms of specific investment: site-specific physical capital, and worker mobility from a low-productivity site to the new site. These two investments capture the costly nature of job creation and match formation in a simple manner. Let γ denote the (expected) fraction of a period required for a worker to move between sites, and let θ_t denote the fraction of workers at low-productivity sites that moves in period t. The nature of the investment in site-specific physical capital is spelled out below.

We now formulate the aggregate production possibilities and laws of motion for the economy. Aggregate labor efficiency units are given by

$$Q_t l_t = Q_t \{ [H_t(1 - \sigma_t) + (1 - H_t + \sigma_t H_t)\theta_t(1 - \gamma)]L_H + (1 - H_t + \sigma_t H_t)(1 - \theta_t)L_L \},$$

(13)

which reflects the assumption that mobility occurs after the realization of shocks. The terms multiplying L_H and L_L equal employment at high-productivity and low-productivity plants, respectively.

An efficient spatial allocation of mobile capital requires equal amounts of capital per labor efficiency unit at each site. Using this spatial allocation condition and the efficiency units expression (13), we can write gross aggregate output as

$$Y_t = (Q_t l_t)^{1-\alpha} K_t^\alpha = Q_t l_t k_t^\alpha,$$

(14)

where k_t denotes capital per efficiency unit of labor in period t.

Aggregate consumption satisfies

$$C_t = Y_t - I_t - s[\theta_t(1 - H_t + \sigma_t H_t)]^\phi, \qquad s > 0, \phi > 1,$$

(15)

where I_t denotes investment in general capital, and the third term captures the output devoted to investment in specific physical capital. The quantity inside the square brackets equals the number of new sites made operational during period t through specific investment and mobility. According to Eq. (15), specific physical capital is created subject to increasing marginal costs. This assumption captures the appealing notion that rapid creation of specific assets is costly, and it facilitates the existence of a steady-state equilibrium with interior solutions for θ and H.

The two endogenous aggregate state variables in the economy satisfy

$$H_{t+1} = H_t(1 - \sigma_t) + \theta_t(1 - H_t + \sigma_t H_t)$$

(16)

and

$$K_{t+1} = I_t + (1 - \delta)K_t,$$

(17)

where δ is the depreciation rate for general physical capital.

Consumer-workers order alternative stochastic consumption streams according to the expected value of

$$\sum_{t=0}^{\infty} \beta^t A_t U(C_t)$$

where the time discount factor $\beta \in (0,1)$, A_t is an exogenous random variable that shifts the desired timing of consumption, and $U(\cdot)$ is a period utility function obeying the usual concavity and Inada conditions.

In this economy, we think of A_t and Q_t as aggregate taste and technology disturbances, and we think of σ_t as indexing the intensity of shocks to the preferred spatial allocation of factor inputs. These allocative shocks reflect location-specific disturbances to technology and the performance of installed capital goods.[55] Shocks to the size of L_H relative to L_L could be incorporated into the model to capture a different notion of allocative disturbances. Exogenously determined government consumption could be introduced through a straightforward modification to the aggregate resource constraint (15). These five categories of shocks – A, Q, σ, the ratio (L_H/L_L), and government purchases – are likely to induce different dynamics in gross job flow and investment activity.

Equilibrium outcomes in this economy hinge crucially on assumptions about market structure. One key issue involves the sharing of consumption risks implied by costly worker mobility across plants with different stochastic productivity streams. The second key issue is the bilateral monopoly problem that potentially arises in connection with the sunk investments made by workers and firms in new production sites.[56] We focus on the complete markets case with full sharing of consumption risks and competitive wage determination prior to sunk investments.

Under complete markets, and focusing on interior solutions, equilibrium dynamics satisfy the Euler equations for general investment (I) and specific investment ($\theta(1 - H + \sigma H)$):

$$AU'(C) = \beta E[(1 + \widetilde{MP}_K - \delta)\tilde{A}U'(\tilde{C})], \tag{18}$$

$$AU'(C)\{s\phi[\theta(1 - H + \sigma H)]^{\phi-1} + [L_L - (1 - \gamma)L_H]MP_L\}$$

$$= \beta E\{(1 - \tilde{\sigma})[s\phi(\tilde{\theta}(1 - \tilde{H} + \tilde{\sigma}\tilde{H}))^{\phi-1} + [\gamma L_H \widetilde{MP}_L]]\tilde{A}U'(\tilde{C})\}. \tag{19}$$

Here, a tilde denotes a next-period value, and the expectations are taken conditional on current information, which includes knowledge of A, Q and σ. The factor marginal products for general capital and labor efficiency units are given by $MP_K = \alpha k^{\alpha-1}$ and $MP_L = (1 - \alpha)Qk^{\alpha}$.

As indicated by Eq. (19), the stochastic rate of return to specific investment is influenced

---

[55] In richer formulations of the model, they might also reflect shocks to the cost of locally supplied inputs and demand for the site's output.

[56] See, for example, Gomes et al. (1996) on the first issue and Caballero and Hammour (1997) on the second.

by several current and future factors. The first term inside the braces on the left side of Eq. (19) equals current output devoted to specific investment in the marginal new site. This term depends on the current marginal product of labor and the amount of worker mobility. The second term in braces represents the current output foregone by moving one more worker, a negative quantity when the time costs of moving are sufficiently small. These two output costs are valued at $AU'(C)$. On the right-hand side of Eq. (19), the $(1 - \tilde{\sigma})$ term represents a stochastic depreciation rate on investment in specific human and physical capital. Other terms on the right side indicate that the rate of return to specific investment also depends on the future level of specific investment and the future marginal product of labor.

For suitable parameter values, this model exhibits a steady-state equilibrium with interior solutions for all variables. Table 17 displays steady-state outcomes for selected parameter settings. The outcomes look sensible, which encourages us toward further analysis of the model.

10.2. Choking off the creative destruction process

Governments often implement labor market policies that impede job flows and, as a consequence, the reallocation of workers and cooperating factors of production. These policies can hamper the efficiency of factor allocations with adverse consequences for productivity and welfare. Well-known theoretical analyses of this topic include Bentolila and Bertola (1990) and Hopenhayn and Rogerson (1993).

To address this issue, we start from a steady-state equilibrium and trace out the dynamic response to a complete shutdown of job flows in a non-stochastic version of the model. That is, we set $\theta_t = 0$ for $t \geq 0$, which we think of as an extreme version of policies that impede job reallocation. To evaluate the welfare effects of this policy intervention, we compute the equivalent consumption variation, x, as the solution to

$$\frac{\log[\bar{C}(1 - x)]}{1 - \beta} = \sum_{t=0}^{\infty} \beta^t \log(\tilde{C}_t),$$

where $\bar{C}$ denotes consumption in the initial steady-state equilibrium, and $\tilde{C}_t$ is the consumption path following the intervention.

Fixing the level of technology Q, setting $U(C) = \log C$, substituting from Eqs. (13)–(17) into Eq. (18), and imposing $\theta = 0$ yields a second-order nonlinear difference equation in K_t:

$$\frac{(Ql_{t+1})^{1-\alpha}K_{t+1}^\alpha - K_{t+2} + (1 - \delta)K_{t+1}}{(Ql_t)^{1-\alpha}K_t^\alpha - K_{t+1} + (1 - \delta)K_t} = \beta[1 - \delta + \alpha(Ql_{t+1})^{1-\alpha}K_{t+1}^{\alpha-1}, \qquad t \geq 0. \quad (20)$$

The difference equation is not autonomous, because the coefficients involving l_t and l_{t+1} evolve over time in line with Eqs. (13) and (16). The path for physical capital following the policy intervention solves Eq. (20) with boundary conditions $K_0 = \bar{K}$ (initial steady state) and $\lim_{t \to \infty} K_t = \tilde{K}$ (new steady state).

Table 17
Steady-state outcomes in theoretical model (baseline parameter settings: $\alpha = 0.3$, $\beta = 0.99$, $\delta = 0.025$, $L_L = 1$, $Q = 1$)

Row	Other parameter settings				
	L_H	σ	γ	ϕ	s
1	2.0	0.10	0.50	2.0	200
2	2.0	0.10	0.50	2.0	100
3	2.0	0.10	1.00	2.0	200
4	2.0	0.08	0.50	2.0	200
5	2.0	0.10	0.50	2.2	200
6	2.2	0.10	0.50	2.0	200

	Outcomes						
	θ	H^a	General capital share[b]	Specific capital share[c]	*SUM* $\times 100^d$	Unemployment rate $\times 100^e$	Fraction of wealth in specific forms[f]
1	0.053	0.36	0.21	0.08	7.3	1.8	0.15
2	0.203	0.72	0.21	0.12	14.9	3.6	0.22
3	0.044	0.31	0.21	0.06	6.5	3.1	0.14
4	0.092	0.56	0.21	0.11	9.2	2.2	0.23
5	0.120	0.58	0.21	0.10	11.9	2.9	0.20
6	0.071	0.43	0.21	0.10	8.9	2.2	0.19

[a] H, the fraction of workers who begin the period matched to a high-productivity site, is given by

$$H = \left(\frac{1}{\sigma}\right)\left(\frac{MP_L[(1 - \gamma)L_H + \beta(1 - \sigma)\gamma L_H - L_L]}{[1 - \beta(1 - \sigma)]s\phi}\right)^{1/(\phi - 1)},$$

where

$$MP_L = (1 - \alpha)k^\alpha \quad \text{and} \quad k = \left(\frac{1 + \beta\delta - \beta}{\beta\alpha}\right)^{1/(\alpha - 1)}.$$

[a] General capital's output share equals I/Y.

[b] Specific capital's output share equals $s[\theta(1 - H + \sigma H)]^\phi Y$.

[c] *SUM* is the job reallocation rate (the sum of job creation and destruction divided by employment), computed as $[2\theta(1 - H + \sigma H)]/(1 - \text{unemployment rate})$.

[d] The unemployment rate equals $\theta(1 - H + \sigma H)\gamma$.

[e] The fraction of wealth in specific forms equals $V_H H/(V_H H + V_K K)$.

Fig. 12 displays the pre-intervention steady-state outcomes and the post-intervention response path for a particular parameter configuration.[57] The ratio of high-to-low productivity is 2.4 for total factor productivity and 3.5 for labor productivity, which are in line

[57] To simplify the numerical solution in a more complicated experiment below, we restrict attention to the full depreciation case $\delta = 1$ for general physical capital. In this case, a simple change of variables reduces Eq. (20) to a first-order difference equation.

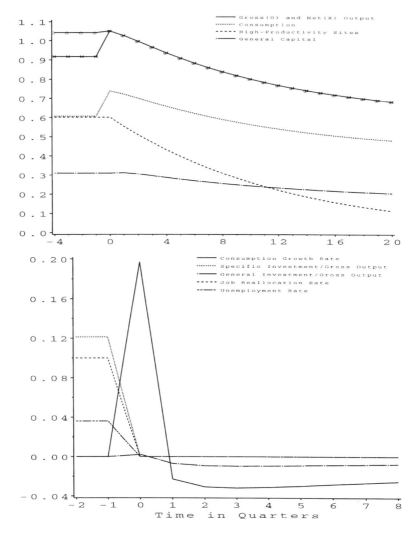

Fig. 12. Creative destruction shut down at time 0. $\sigma = 0.08$, $s = 100$, $\gamma = 0.75$, $\phi = 2.2$, $\beta = 0.99$, $\delta = 1.0$, $\alpha = 0.3$, low productivity $= 1.0$, high productivity $= 2.4$.

with empirical evidence on between-plant productivity differentials (see, e.g., Bartelsman and Doms, 1997). The value of $\gamma = 0.75$ corresponds to an unemployment spell length of slightly less than 10 weeks.

The initial steady state exhibits a job reallocation rate of 10% per quarter and a frictional unemployment rate of 3.6%. Roughly 12% of gross output is devoted to investment in site-specific physical capital. In practice, investment in specific forms of physical capital may involve foregone output rather than measured capital expenditures. For this reason, we report output gross and net of specific physical investment costs.

The shutdown of creative destruction triggers responses that look like a consumption-led business cycle boom. Consumption rises by 20% in the intervention period and remains above the pre-intervention level for 2 years. Unemployment and job reallocation decline (to zero). Investment in general physical capital rises very slightly and then declines slowly. Output rises initially, more so when calculated net of investment in specific physical capital.

The time-0 increase in gross output reflects the increase in aggregate labor efficiency units as workers shift from reallocation to production activities. The sharper, more sustained rise in net output reflects, in addition, a shift in the composition of output away from specific investment activities. In practice, certain specific investments (e.g., adjustment costs associated with changing the scale of operations) are unlikely to show up in measured output figures. In this regard, net output exceeds its pre-intervention level for one year following the shutdown of creative destruction.

These results suggest that policy barriers to job reallocation and creative destruction can have highly favorable shortterm effects on standard measures of aggregate economic performance. By enriching the model to include specific investment in information and organization capital along the lines of Prescott and Visscher (1980), Jovanovic (1982) or Atkeson and Kehoe (1997), it seems likely that the policy responses would look even more favorable (in the short term) and be more persistent. Greater substitution possibilities between specific and general forms of physical capital would presumably lead to a larger impact effect on general capital.

Despite the favorable shortterm effects, choking off the creative destruction process causes large welfare losses. For the numerical experiment in Fig. 12, the equivalent consumption variation equals 25.8% of initial steady-state consumption. In other words, the representative agent would be willing to forego one-quarter of consumption in the current and all future periods to preserve the creative destruction process. This welfare loss reflects the longer term decline in consumption and output caused by choking off productivity-enhancing factor reallocation (see Section 7).

This analysis suggests why societies might adopt policies that restrict job flows and the creative destruction process, even though such policies cause large declines in productive efficiency and welfare. In the short term, restrictions on job flows improve consumption and other standard measures of economic performance. Looking beyond the model, such policies may also function as second-best risk-sharing institutions or serve the interests of particular constituencies at the expense of the general welfare. Furthermore, when job flows and creative destruction have been suppressed for a period of time, a renewal of the process may be accompanied by highly unfavorable shortterm consequences, as we demonstrate below.

Our discussion of policies that impede job flows omits much important research on employment security laws, job destruction taxes, firing costs and related issues. Lindbeck and Snower (1988), Saint-Paul (1996), Bertola (1998), Booth (1997) and Mortensen and

Pissarides (1994) contain rich treatments of these issues and extensive references to the literature.

10.3. Unleashing the creative destruction process

We now reverse the previous experiment and trace out the dynamic response to unleashing the creative destruction process. Starting from a steady-state equilibrium with $\theta = 0$, we compute the transition path implied by Eqs. (13)–(19).[58] We think of this experiment as a crude counterpart to opening up the creative destruction process in the post-communist transition economies. While the experiment omits many important aspects of the transition experience, it captures the pent-up need for factor reallocation.

Fig. 13 displays results for the same parameters as in Fig. 12. The shortterm fallout from unleashing the creative destruction process is highly unfavorable by standard measures of economic performance. Consumption initially declines by 21% and requires six quarters to return to its initial level. Net output initially declines by 15% and requires three quarters to return to its initial level. Of course, unemployment and job destruction rise sharply. We conclude that even an optimally functioning transition economy can experience a sharp and sustained deterioration in economic performance, as conventionally measured. Recalling our discussion of Atkeson and Kehoe (1997) in Section 8.1, this conclusion is likely to be strengthened by the introduction of other mechanisms for the accumulation of specific capital.

To our surprise, the initial pace of reallocation activity undershoots rather than overshoots the new steady-state levels. The job destruction rate and the unemployment rate jump sharply at time 0 but to levels that fall well short of long-run values. (Compare the transition outcomes in Fig. 13 to the pre-intervention outcomes in Fig. 12.) Evidently, the consumption and investment smoothing incentives built into the model promote a gradual movement towards high job flow and unemployment rates. Another relevant feature of the model is the fixed relative productivity values, L_H and L_L. A richer specification in this regard might lead to a large initial burst of reallocation activity to quickly pursue the most attractive new opportunities.

Despite the shortterm pain, the longer term gains to unleashing the creative destruction process are enormous in the example of Fig. 13. Output, labor efficiency and general physical capital grow steadily following the onset of creative destruction, eventually rising more than 75% above initial values. Consumption eventually rises to 45% above its initial level, and the welfare gain (equivalent variation) amounts to nearly 35% of initial consumption.

---

[58] Substituting Eqs. (13)–(17) into (18) and (19) yields a system of two non-linear, non-autonomous, second-order difference equations in H_t and K_t. After using a change of variable to reduce Eq. (18) to a first-order equation, we numerically solve Eq. (18) and (19) one at a time, iterating back and forth between them until convergence. At each iteration, we use a shooting method to solve Eq. (19).

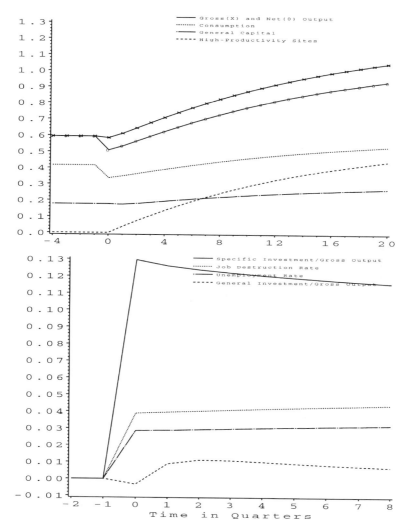

Fig. 13. Creative destruction unleashed at time 0. $\sigma = 0.08$, $s = 100$, $\gamma = 0.75$, $\phi = 2.2$, $\beta = 0.99$, $\delta = 1.0$, $\alpha = 0.3$, low productivity = 1.0, high productivity = 2.4.

10.4. Job flows and longterm growth

Suppose that Q and s grow at the steady rate Q, while A and σ remain constant over time. As before, let $U(C) = \log(C)$. Under these assumptions, the model exhibits a balanced growth path with steady growth in consumption, general capital and output at rate Q and along which the intensity of reallocation activity remains constant:

$$\text{capital per labor efficiency unit} = k = \left[\frac{1 + q + \beta\delta - \beta}{\alpha\beta} \right]^{1/(\alpha - 1)}, \tag{21}$$

$$\text{job flows} = \sigma H = \left(\frac{[(1 - \gamma)L_H + \beta(1 - \sigma)\gamma L_H - L_L](1 - \alpha)k^\alpha}{[1 - \beta(1 - \alpha)]s\phi} \right)^{1/(\phi - 1)}, \tag{22}$$

$$\text{unemployment} = \gamma\sigma H. \tag{23}$$

It follows immediately from these equations that more rapid growth corresponds to a lower stock (H) of relatively productive sites, smaller job creation and destruction rates, and a lower unemployment rate. In other words, the model delivers a negative relationship between longterm growth and the intensity of creative destruction activity.

This implication of the model runs counter to Schumpeter's "essential fact about capitalism." Moreover, choking off the creative destruction process in this model causes no permanent slowdown in economic growth. In sharp contrast, Aghion and Howitt's (1992) model incorporates Schumpeter's view by inextricably tying innovation and growth to the creative destruction process. Creative destruction is essential to growth in their model, and more rapid growth corresponds to more intense creative destruction. Similar remarks apply to the vintage models of Caballero and Hammour (1994, 1996a) that feature exogenous technological improvements embodied in new capital goods.

In comparing these models of the creative destruction process, we immediately see that theory makes no general prediction about the empirical relationship between longterm growth and the pace of factor reallocation. The comparison also highlights two very different views about the causal connection between longterm growth and factor reallocation. One view, illustrated by the numerical experiments in Figs. 12 and 13 ties creative destruction to the level of productivity and output. Another view ties creative destruction to their longterm growth rates.

The studies to date on job flows and factor reallocation provide little help in assessing the relative merits of these alternative views of the creative destruction process. The empirical work reviewed in Section 7.2 clearly points to a major role for factor reallocation in industry-level productivity gains, but it is not clear whether and how much factor reallocation contributes to the longer term growth rate of output.

11. Concluding remarks

This chapter synthesizes and adds to the growing body of research on gross job flows and related topics. Progress in this area has been rapid in recent years, but many key issues remain unresolved and some important questions have as yet received scant attention. We have pointed out some of the unresolved issues and open lines of inquiry along the way.

Our essay devotes little attention to some important topics that are closely related to the behavior of job flows or their consequences: the job search process, employer–worker matching, earnings losses among job-losing workers, inefficient separations because of asymmetric information and incentive problems, limited risk sharing and unemployment insurance, wage-setting institutions and job creation, job security provisions, and other policies that influence labor market flows and factor allocations. Fortunately, several of these topics receive careful treatment in other *Handbook* chapters. See, especially, Abowd and Kramarz, Bertola, Farber, Nickell and Layard, Machin and Manning, and Mortensen and Pissarides.

An understudied line of empirical inquiry involves questions of how and why wages vary with employer-level job growth and worker turnover. The advent of rich datasets that link workers and employers and follow each over time seems likely to bring this type of question to the forefront of future work on labor market flows. This development may eventually bring about a much closer integration of work on labor market flows with work on wage determination and other traditional topics in labor economics.

Recent work indicates that this process has begun. Belzil (1997) investigates how individual wages vary with firm-level measures of job creation and worker turnover. He exploits a remarkable dataset that links a random sample of Danish firms to their workers and follows each over a twelve-year period. The dataset contains excellent controls for standard human capital variables and is rich enough to permit worker and firm fixed effects. Conditional on firm and worker controls, Belzil finds that male wages are higher at firms with (contemporaneously) higher job creation rates. Results vary with sample and estimation method, but the effect is very large: 2–4% higher wages for each additional percentage point of (annual) net job growth. He also finds some evidence that wages are higher at firms with higher rates of worker turnover (accessions plus separations). The wage response to firm-level job creation and worker turnover is larger for new hires and for workers who have low job tenure. These results clearly point to the role of entry-level wages as an instrument for influencing the firm's job creation rate. They do not favor the view that higher wages reduce turnover costs, but instead suggest that higher wages help attract workers and compensate them for high separation risk.

References

Abel, Andrew and Janice Eberly (1997), "The mix and scale of factors with irreversibility and fixed costs of investment", Mimeo.

Abowd, John, Patrick Corbel and Francis Kramarz (1996), "The entry and exit of workers and the growth of employment: an analysis of French establishments", Working paper no. 5551 (NBER, Cambridge, MA).

Abraham, Katharine G. and Lawrence F. Katz (1986), "Cyclical unemployment: sectoral shifts or aggregate disturbances?" Journal of Political Economy 94 (3): 367–388.

Aghion, Philippe and Olivier Blanchard (1994), "On the speed of transition in central Europe", NBER Macroeconomics Annual 9: 283–319.

Aghion, Philippe and Peter Howitt (1992), "A model of growth through creative destruction", Econometrica 60 (2): 323–351.

Aghion, Philippe and Peter Howitt (1994), "Growth and unemployment", Review of Economic Studies 61 (3): 477–494.

Akerlof, George, Andrew Rose and Janet Yellen (1988), "Job switching and job satisfaction in the U.S. labor market", Brookings Papers on Economic Activity 2: 495–582.

Albaek, K. and Bent E. Sorensen (1996), "Worker flows and job flows in Danish manufacturing", Working paper (Brown University).

Anderson, Patricia M. and Bruce D. Meyer (1994), "The nature and extent of turnover", Brookings Papers on Economic Activity: Microeconomics: 177–248.

Andolfatto, David (1996), "Business cycles and labor market search", American Economic Review 86 (1): 112–132.

Aslund, Anders, Peter Boone and Simon Johnson (1996), "How to stabilize: lessons from post-communist countries", Brookings Papers on Economic Activity 1: 217–313.

Atkeson, Andrew and Patrick Kehoe (1994), "Putty clay capital and energy", Working paper no. 4833 (NBER, Cambridge, MA).

Atkeson, Andrew and Patrick Kehoe (1997), "Industry evolution and transition: a neoclassical benchmark", Working paper no. 6005 (NBER, Cambridge, MA).

Attanasio, Orazio (1998), "Consumption demand", Working paper no. 6466 (NBER, Cambridge, MA) and The handbook of macroeconomics (North-Holland, Amsterdam).

Aw, Bee-Yan, Tain-Jy Chen and Mark Roberts (1997), "Firm-level evidence on productivity differentials, turnover and exports in taiwanese manufacturing", Mimeo.

Bahk, Byong-Hyong and Michael Gort (1993), "Decomposing learning by doing in new plants", Journal of Political Economy 101 (4): 561–583.

Baily, Martin, Charles Hulten and David Campbell (1992), "Productivity dynamics in manufacturing plants", Brookings Papers on Economic Activity, Microeconomics: 187–267.

Baily, Martin, Eric Bartelsman and John Haltiwanger (1996), "Downsizing and productivity growth: myth or reality", Small Business Economics: 259–278.

Baldwin, John R. (1996), "Productivity growth, plant turnover and restructuring in the canadian manufacturing sector", in: David G. Mayes, ed., Sources of productivity growth (Cambridge University Press, Cambridge, UK).

Baldwin, John and Garnett Picot (1995), "Employment generation by small producers in the canadian manufacturing sector", Small Business Economics 7 (4): 317–331.

Baldwin, John, Timothy Dunne and John Haltiwanger (1998), "A comparison of job creation and job destruction in Canada and the United States", Review of Economics and Statistics, in press.

Bartelsman, Eric J. and Phoebus J. Dhrymes (1994), "Productivity dynamics: U.S. manufacturing plants, 1972–1986", Discussion paper no 94-1, Finance and economics discussion series (Federal Reserve Board).

Bartelsman, Eric J. and Mark Doms (1997), "Understanding productivity: lessons from longitudinal micro datasets", Working paper.

Basu, Susanto and John G. Fernald (1995), "Aggregate productivity and the productivity of aggregates", Working paper no. 5382 (NBER, Cambridge, MA).

Becker, Gary S. (1975), Human capital, 2nd edition (The University of Chicago Press, Chicago, IL).

Belzil, Christian (1997), "Job creation and destruction, worker reallocation and wages", Working paper (Department of Economics, Concordia University).

Bergin J. and D. Bernhardt (1996), "Industry dynamics over the business cycle", Working paper.

Bentolila, S. and G. Bertola (1990), "Firing costs and labor demand: how bad is eurosclerosis?" Review of Economic Studies 57: 381–402.

Bertola, Giuseppe and Richard Rogerson (1997), "Institutions and labor reallocation", European Economic Review 41: 1147–1171.

Black, Fischer (1987), "General equilibrium and business cycles", in: Business cycles and equilibrium (Basil Blackwell, New York).

Blanchard, Olivier (1997), The economics of post-communist transition (Clarendon Press, Oxford, UK).

Blanchard, Olivier and Peter Diamond (1989), "The Beveridge curve", Brookings Papers on Economic Activity 1: 1–60.

Blanchard, Olivier and Peter Diamond (1990), "The cyclical behavior of gross flows of workers in the U.S.", Brookings Papers on Economic Activity 2: 85–155.

Blanchard, Olivier and Michael Kremer (1997), "Disorganization", Quarterly Journal of Economics 112 (4): 1091–1126.

Blanchard, Olivier, Simon Commander and Fabrizio Coricelli (1995), "Unemployment and restructuring in Eastern Europe and Russia", in: Simon Commander and Fabrizio Coricelli, eds., Unemployment, restructuring and the labor market in Eastern Europe and Russia (World Bank, Washington, DC).

Boeri, Tito (1994), "Why are establishments so heterogeneous?" Small Business Economics, 6 (6): 409–420.

Boeri, Tito (1996), "Is job turnover countercyclical?" Journal of Labor Economics 14 (4): 603–625.

Boeri, Tito (1997), "Heterogeneous workers, economic transformation and the stagnancy of transitional unemployment", European Economic Review 41: 905–914.

Booth, Alison L. (1997), "An analysis of firing costs and their implications for unemployment policy", in: Dennis J. Snower and Guillermo de la Dehesa, eds., Unemployment policy: government options for the labour market (Cambridge University Press, New York).

Borland, Jeff and Richard Home (1994), "Establishment-level employment in manufacturing industry: is small really beautiful?" Working paper (University of Melbourne).

Brada, Josef C. (1996), "Privatization is transition - or is it?" Journal of Economic Perspectives 10 (2): 67–86.

Brainard, Lael and David Cutler (1993), "Sectoral shifts and cyclical unemployment reconsidered", Quarterly Journal of Economics 108 (1): 219–243.

Bresnahan, Timothy F. and Valerie A. Ramey (1993), "Segment shifts and capacity utilization in the U.S. automobile industry", American Economic Review 83 (2): 213–218.

Burda, Michael (1993), "Unemployment, labor markets and structural change in Eastern Europe", Economic Policy 16: 101–137.

Burda, Michael and Charles Wyplosz (1994), "Gross worker and job flows in Europe", European Economic Review 38: 1287–1315.

Caballero, Ricardo (1992), "A fallacy of composition", American Economic Review 82 (5): 1279–1292.

Caballero, Ricardo (1998), "Aggregate investment: a 90's view", in: John Taylor and Michael Woodford, eds., The handbook of macroeconomics (North-Holland, Amsterdam).

Caballero, Ricardo and Eduardo M.R.A. Engel (1993), "Microeconomic adjustment hazards and aggregate dynamics", Quarterly Journal of Economics 108 (2): 359–383.

Caballero, Ricardo and Mohamad Hammour (1994), "The cleansing effect of recessions", American Economic Review 84: 1350–1368.

Caballero, Ricardo and Mohamad Hammour (1996a), "On the timing and efficiency of creative destruction", Quarterly Journal of Economics 111 (3): 805–852.

Caballero, Ricardo and Mohamad Hammour (1996b), "On the ills of adjustment", Journal of Development Economics 51 (1): 161–192.

Caballero, Ricardo and Mohamad Hammour (1998a), "The macroeconomics of specificity", Journal of Political Economy 106 (4): 724–767.

Caballero, Ricardo and Mohamad Hammour (1998b), "Jobless growth: appropriability, factor substitution and unemployment", Carnegie-Rochester Conference Series on Public Policy, in press.

Caballero, Ricardo, Eduardo Engel and John Haltiwanger (1997), "Aggregate employment dynamics: building from microeconomic evidence", American Economic Review 87 (1): 115–137.

Cabrales, Antonio and Hugo A. Hopenhayn (1997), "Labor market flexibility and aggregate employment volatility", Carnegie-Rochester Conference Series on Public Policy 46: 189–228.

Campbell, Jeffrey R. (1997), "Entry, exit, embodied technology and business cycles", Working paper no. 5955 (NBER, Cambridge, MA).

Campbell, Jeffrey R. and Jonas Fisher (1996), "Aggregate employment fluctuations with microeconomic asymmetries", Discussion paper no. 112 (Institute for Empirical Macroeconomics).

Campbell, Jeffrey R. and Jonas Fisher (1997), "Understanding aggregate job flows", Economic Perspectives, Federal Reserve Bank of Chicago 21 (5): 19–37.

Campbell, Jeffrey R. and Kenneth Kuttner (1996), "Macroeconomic effects of employment reallocation", Carnegie-Rochester Conference Series on Public Policy 44: 87–116.

Campbell, John (1994), "Inspecting the mechanism: an analytical approach to the stochastic growth model", Journal of Monetary Economics 33: 563–606.

Caplin, Andrew and John Leahy (1993), "Sectoral shocks, learning and aggregate fluctuations", Review of Economic Studies 60 (4): 777–794.

Caplin, Andrew and John Leahy (1994), "Business as usual, market crashes and wisdom after the fact", American Economic Review 84 (3): 548–565.

Caves, Richard E. (1998), "Industrial organization and new findings on the turnover and mobility of firms", Journal of Economic Literature 36 (4): 1947–1982.

Chari, V.V. and Hugo Hopenhayn (1991), "Vintage human capital, growth and the diffusion of new technologygydqo;, Journal of Political Economy 99 (6): 1142–1165.

Chow, Clement K.W., Michael K.Y. Fung and Hang Y. Ngo (1996), "Job turnover in China: a case of Shanghai's manufacturing enterprises", Working paper (Chinese University of Hong Kong).

Cogley, Timothy and James M. Nasson, (1995), "Output dynamics in real business cycle models", American Economic Review 85 (3): 492–511.

Commander, Simon and Fabrizio Coricelli, eds. (1995), Unemployment, restructuring and the labor market in Eastern Europe and Russia (World Bank Washington, DC).

Commander, Simon and Andrei Tolstopiatenko (1996), "Why is unemployment low in the former Soviet Union: enterprise restructuring and the structure of compensation", Working paper no. 1617 (Policy Research, Economic Development Institute, The World Bank).

Contini, Bruno, Lia Pacelli et al. (1995), A study on job creation and destruction in Europe (Commission of the European Communities).

Cooley, Thomas, F. (1995), Frontiers of business cycle research (Princeton University Press, Princeton, NJ).

Cooley, Thomas F., Jeremy Greenwood and Mehmet Yorokoglu (1996), "The replacement problem", Working paper (University of Rochester).

Cooper, Russell, John Haltiwanger and Laura Power (1997), "Machine replacement and the business cycle: lumps and bumps", Mimeo.

Coricelli, Fabrizio, Krzysztof Hagemejer and Krzysztof Rybinsik (1995), "Poland", in: Simon Commander and Fabrizio Coricelli, eds., Unemployment, restructuring and the labor market in Eastern Europe and Russia (World Bank, Washington, DC).

Dardia, Michael and Robert Schoeni (1996), "Earnings losses of displaced workers in the 1990s", Working paper (RAND , Santa Monica, CA).

Davis, Steven J. (1987), "Fluctuations in the pace of labor reallocation", Carnegie-Rochester Conference Series on Public Policy 27: 335–402.

Davis, Steven J. (1997), "Sorting, learning and mobility when jobs have scarcity value: a comment", Carnegie-Rochester Conference Series on Public Policy 46.

Davis, Steven J. and John Haltiwanger (1990), "Gross job creation and destruction: microeconomic evidence and macroeconomic implications", NBER Macroeconomics Annual 5: 123–168.

Davis, Steven J. and John Haltiwanger (1991), "Wage dispersion between and within U.S. manufacturing plants, 1963–86", Brookings Papers on Economic Activity: Microeconomics: 115–181.

Davis, Steven J. and John Haltiwanger (1992), "Gross job creation, gross job destruction and employment reallocation", Quarterly Journal of Economics 107 (3): 819–863.

Davis, Steven J. and John Haltiwanger (1996), "Driving forces and employment fluctuations: new evidence and alternative explanations", Working paper no. 5775 (NBER, Cambridge, MA).

Davis, Steven J. and John Haltiwanger (1999), "Sectoral job creation and destruction responses to energy price changes", Working paper no. 7095 (NBER, Cambridge, MA).

Davis, Steven J. and John Haltiwanger (1998), "Measuring gross worker and job flows", in: M. Manser and R. Topel, eds., Labor statistics measurement issues (University of Chicago Press Chicago, IL) in press.

Davis, Steven J. and Magnus Henrekson (1997), "Industrial policy, employer size and economic performance in

Sweden", in: Richard B. Freeman, Robert Topel and Birgitta Swedenborg, eds., The welfare state in transition: reforming the Swedish model (The University of Chicago Press, Chicago, IL).

Davis, Steven J., John Haltiwanger and Scott Schuh (1990), "Published versus sample statistics from the ASM: implications for the LRD", Proceedings of the American Statistical Association, Business and Economics Statistics Section (American Statistical Association) pp. 52–61.

Davis, Steven J., John Haltiwanger and Scott Schuh (1996), Job creation and destruction (MIT Press, Cambridge, MA).

Davis, Steven J., Prakash Loungani and Ramamohan Mahidhara (1997), Regional labor fluctuations: oil shocks, military spending and other driving forces (University of Chicago).

Den Haan, Wouter J., Garey Ramey and Joel Watson (1997), "Job destruction and propagation of shocks", Working paper (University of California, San Diego, CA).

Devine, Theresa J. and Nicholas M. Kiefer (1991), Empirical labor economics: the search approach (Oxford University Press, New York).

Dial, Jay and Kevin J. Murphy (1995), "Incentives, downsizing and value creation at general dynamics", Journal of Financial Economics 37: 261–314.

Dunne, Timothy, Mark Roberts and Larry Samuelson (1989a), "The growth and failure of U.S. manufacturing plants", Quarterly Journal of Economics 104 (4): 671–698.

Dunne, Timothy, Mark Roberts and Larry Samuelson (1989b), "Plant turnover and gross employment flows in the U.S. manufacturing sector", Journal of Labor Economics 7 (1): 48–71.

Dunne, Timothy, John Haltiwanger and Ken Troske (1997), "Technology and jobs: secular changes and cyclical dynamics", Carnegie-Rochester Conference Series on Public Policy June: 107–178.

Ericson, Richard and Ariel Pakes (1995), "Markov perfect industry dynamics: a framework for empirical work", Review of Economic Studies 62 (1): 53–82.

Evans, David (1987a), "Tests of alternative theories of firm growth", Journal of Political Economy 95 (4): 657–674.

Evans, David (1987b), "The relationship between firm growth, size and age: estimates for 100 manufacturing industries", Journal of Industrial Economics 35 (4): 567–581.

Farber, Henry (1993), "The incidence and costs of job loss", Brookings Papers on Economic Activity: 73–119.

Farber, Henry (1997), "The changing face of job loss in the United States: 1981–1995", Brookings Papers on Economic Activity: Microeconomics: 161–166.

Fischer, Stanley, Ratna Sahay and Carlos A. Vegh (1996), "Stabilization and growth in transition economies: the early experience", Journal of Economic Perspectives 10 (2): 45–66.

Foote, Christopher L. (1997), "The surprising symmetry of gross job flows", Working paper no. 6226 (NBER, Cambridge, MA).

Foote, Christopher L. (1998), "Trend employment growth and the bunching of job creation and destruction", Quarterly Journal of Economics 113 (3): 809–834.

Foster, Lucia, John Haltiwanger and C.J. Krizan (1998), "Aggregate productivity growth: lessons from micro-economic evidence", Working paper.

Garibaldi, Pietro, Jozef Konings and Christopher Pissarides (1997), "Gross job reallocation and labour market policy", in: Dennis J. Snower and Guillermo de la Dehesa, eds., Unemployment policy: government options for the labour market (Cambridge University Press, New York).

Gautier, Pieter (1997), The flow approach to labor markets (Thesis Publishers for the Tinbergen Institute Research Series, Amsterdam).

Gautier, Pieter and Lourens Broersma (1993), "The timing of labor reallocation and business cycles", Working paper (Tinbergen Institute).

Gollop, Frank and James Monahan (1991), "A generalized index of diversification: trends in U.S. manufacturing", Review of Economics and Statistics 78 (2): 318–330.

Gomes, Joao, Jeremy Greenwood and Segio Rebelo (1996), "Equilibrium unemployment", Working paper (University of Rochester).

Gouge, Randall and Ian King (1997), "A competitive theory of employment dynamics", Review of Economic Studies 64: 1–22.

Greenwood, Jeremy, Glenn M. MacDonald and Guang-Jia Zhang (1994), "The cyclical behavior of job creation and destruction: a sectoral model", Discussion paper no. 88 (Institute for Empirical Macroeconomics, Federal Reserve Bank of Minneapolis).

Griliches, Zvi (1957), "Hybrid corn: an exploration in the economics of technological change", Econometrica 25 (4): 501–522.

Griliches, Zvi and Haim Regev (1995), "Firm productivity in Israeli industry: 1979–1988", Journal of Econometrics 5 (1): 175–203.

Gronau, Reuben and Haim Regev (1997), "The demand for labor and job turnover: Israeli manufacturing 1970–1994", Working paper no. 378 (Industrial Relations Section, Princeton University).

Grossman, Gene M. and Elhanan Helpman (1991), Innovation and growth in the global economy (MIT Press, Cambridge, MA).

Hall, Bronwyn (1987), "The relationship between firm size and firm growth in the U.S. manufacturing sector", Journal of Industrial Economics 35 (4): 583–606.

Hall, Robert E. (1972), "Turnover in the labor force", Brookings Papers on Economic Activity 3: 709–764.

Hall, Robert E. (1982), "The importance of lifetime jobs in the U.S. economy", American Economic Review 72 (4): 716–724.

Hall, Robert E. (1991), "Labor demand, labor supply and employment volatility", NBER Macroeconomics Annual 6: 17–47.

Hall, Robert E. (1995), "Lost jobs", Brookings Papers on Economic Activity 1: 221–273.

Hall, Robert E. (1997a), "The amplification and persistence of employment fluctuations through labor-market frictions", in: John Taylor and Michael Woodford, eds., The handbook of macroeconomics (North-Holland, Amsterdam).

Hall, Robert E. (1997b), "The temporal concentration of job destruction and inventory liquidation: a theory of recessions", paper presented at the NBER Economic Fluctuations and Growth Program Meeting in Chicago.

Haltiwanger, John (1997), "Measuring and analyzing aggregate fluctuations: the importance of building from microeconomic evidence", Federal Reserve Bank of St. Louis Economic Review, in press.

Haltiwanger, John and Milan Vodopivec (1997), "Gross worker and job flows in a transition economy: an analysis of Estonia", Mimeo.

Hamermesh, Daniel S. and Gerard A. Pfann (1996), "Adjustment costs in factor demand", Journal of Economic Literature 34 (3): 1264–1292.

Hamermesh, Daniel S., Wolter H.J. Hassink and Jan C. Vann Ours (1996), "Job turnover and labor turnover: a taxonomy of employment dynamics", Annales D'Economie et De Statistique 41–42: 21–40.

Hamilton, James D. (1988), "A neoclassical model of unemployment and the business cycle", Journal of Political Economy 96 (3): 593–617.

Hopenhayn, Hugo (1992), "Entry, exit and firm dynamics in long run equilibrium", Econometrica 60 (5): 1127–1150.

Hopenhayn, Hugo and Richard Rogerson (1993), "Job turnover and policy evaluation: a general equilibrium analysis", Journal of Political Economy 101 (5): 915–938.

Horvath, Michael, Fabiano Schivardi and Michael Woywode (1997), "On industry life-cycles: delay and shakeout in beer brewing", Working paper (Stanford University).

Hosios, Arthur J. (1994), "Unemployment and vacancies with sectoral shifts", American Economic Review 84 (1): 124–144.

Huigen, R.D., A.J.M. Kleijweg and G. Van Leeuwen (1991), The relationship between firm size and firm growth in Dutch manufacturing estimated on panel data (Netherlands Central Bureau of Statistics).

Ickes, Barry W. (1996), "Comment on Aslund et al.", Brookings Papers on Economic Activity 1: 298–305.

Jacobson, Louis, Robert LaLonde and Daniel Sullivan (1993), The costs of worker dislocation (W.E. Upjohn Institute for Employment Research, Kalamazoo, MI).

Jovanovic, Boyan (1979), "Job matching and the theory of turnover", Journal of Political Economy 87: 972–990.

Jovanovic, Boyan (1982), "Selection and the evolution of industry", Econometrica 50 (3): 649–670.

Jovanovic, Boyan and Jacob Mincer (1981), "Labor mobility and wages", in: Sherwin Rosen, ed., Studies in labor markets (University of Chicago Press, Chicago, IL).

Jovanovic, Boyan and Glenn M. MacDonald (1994), "Competitive diffusion", Journal of Political Economy 102 (1): 24–52.

Jovanovic, Boyan and Robert Moffitt (1990), "An estimate of a sectoral model of mobility", Journal of Political Economy 98 (4): 827–852.

Jovanovic, Boyan and Yaw Nyarko (1997), "Stepping-stone mobility", Carnegie-Rochester Conference Series on Public Policy 46: 289–325.

Jovanovic, Boyan and Rafael Rob (1989), "The growth and diffusion of knowledge", Review of Economic Studies 56: 569–582.

Kaufman, Daniel and Aleksander Kaliberda (1996), "An 'unofficial' analysis of economies in transition: an empirical framework and lessons for policy", Development discussion paper no. 558 (Harvard Institute for International Development).

King, Martin and Milan Cuc (1996), "Price convergence in North American natural gas spot markets", The Energy Journal 17 (2): 17–42.

Klette, Tor Jakob and Astrid Mathiassen (1996), "Job creation, job destruction and plant turnover in Norwegian manufacturing", Annales D'Economie et De Statistique 41–42: 97–125.

Konings, J. (1995), "Gross job creation and destruction in the U.K. manufacturing sector", Oxford Bulletin of Economics and Statistics 57 (1): 1–20.

Konings, J. H. Lehmann and M.E. Schaffer (1996), "Job creation and job destruction in a transition economy: ownership, firm size and gross job flows in Polish manufacturing 1988–91", Labour Economics 3 (3): 299–317.

Kremer, Michael (1993), "The o-ring theory of economic development", Quarterly Journal of Ecomomics 108: 551–576.

Lagarde, S., E. Maurin and C. Torelli (1994), "Job reallocation between and within plants: some evidence from French micro data on the period from 1984–1992", Unpublished working paper (INSEE).

Lambson, Val E. (1991), "Industry evolution with sunk costs and uncertain market conditions", International Journal of Industrial Organization 9 (2): 171–196.

Lane, Julia, A. Isaac and David Stevens (1996), "Firm heterogeneity and worker turnover", Review of Industrial Organization 11 (3): 275–291.

Lane, Julia, David Stevens and Simon Burgess (1996), "Worker and job flows", Economics Letters: 109–114.

Leonard, Jonathan S. (1987), "In the wrong place at the wrong time: the extent of frictional and structural unemployment", in: Kevin Lang and J. Leonard, eds., Unemployment & the structure of labor markets (Basil Blackwell, New York).

Leonard, Jonathan S. and Jeffrey S. Zax (1995), "The stability of jobs in the public sector", Working paper (University of Colorado, Boulder, CO).

Lilien, David (1980), "The cyclical pattern of temporary layoffs in United States manufacturing", Review of Economics and Statistics 62 (1): 24–31.

Lilien, David (1982), "Sectoral shifts and cyclical unemployment", Journal of Political Economy 90: 777–793.

Lindbeck, Assar and Dennis J. Snower (1988), The insider-outsider theory of employment and unemployment (MIT Press Cambridge, MA).

Liu, Lili and James R. Tybout (1996), "Productivity growth in Chile and Colombia: the role of entry, exit and learning", in: Mark J. Roberts and James R. Tybout, eds., Industrial evolution in developing countries: micro patterns of turnover, productivity and market structure (Oxford University Press for the World Bank, New York).

Loungani, Prakash (1986), "Oil price shocks and the dispersion hypothesis", Review of Economics and Statistics August: 536–539.

Loungani, Prakesh, Mark Rush and William Tave (1990), "Stock market dispersion and unemployment", Journal of Monetary Economics 25 (3): 367–388.

Ljungqvist, Lars and Thomas Sargent (1996), "The European unemployment dilemma", Working paper.

Lucas, Jr., Robert E. (1978), "On the size distribution of business firms", Bell Journal of Economics 9: 508–523.

Mansfield, Edwin, Mark Schwartz and Samuel Wagner (1981), "Imitation costs and patents", Economic Journal 91: 907–918.

Melo, Martha de, Cevdet Denizer and Alan Gelb (1996), "Patterns of transition from plan to market", The World Bank Economic Review 10 (3): 397–424.

Millard, Stephen P. and Dale T. Mortensen (1997), "The unemployment and welfare effects of labour market policy: a comparison of the USA and the UK", in: Dennis J. Snower and Guillermo de la Dehesa, eds., Unemployment policy: government options for the labour market (Cambridge University Press, New York).

Miller, Robert A. (1984), "Job matching and occupational choice", Journal of Political Economy 92: 1086–1120.

Mork, Knut A. (1989), "Oil and the macroeconomy when prices go up and down: an extension of Hamiltons results", Journal of Political Economy 97 (3): 740–744.

Mortensen, Dale T. (1986), "Job search and labor market analysis", in: Orley C. Ashenfelter and Richard Layard, eds., Handbook of labor economics, Vol. 2 (North-Holland, Amsterdam).

Mortensen, Dale T. (1994), "The cyclical behavior of job and worker flows", Journal of Economic Dynamics and Control 18: 1121–1142.

Mortensen, Dale T. and Christopher A. Pissarides (1993), "The cyclical behavior of job creation and job destruction", in: Jan C. Van Ours, Gerard A. Pfann and Geert Ridder, eds., Labor demand and equilibrium wage formation (North-Holland, Amsterdam).

Mortensen, Dale T. and Christopher Pissarides (1994), "Job creation and job destruction in the theory of unemployment", Review of Economic Studies 61: 397–415.

Murphy, Kevin M., Andrei Shleifer and Robert Vishny (1992), "The transition to a market economy: pitfalls of partial reform", Quarterly Journal of Economics 107 (3): 889–906.

Nasbeth, Lars and George Ray, eds. (1974), The diffusion of new industrial processes: an international study (Cambridge University Press, Cambridge, UK).

Nelson, Richard R. and Sidney G. Winter (1982), An evolutionary theory of economic change (Harvard University Press, Cambridge, MA).

Nickell, Stephen J. (1986), "Dynamic models of labour demand", in: Orley C. Ashenfelter and Richard Layard, eds., Handbook of labor economics, Vol. 1 (North-Holland, Amsterdam).

Nocke, Volker R. (1994), Gross job creation and gross job destruction: an empirical study with French data (Unviersity of Bonn).

Noorkoiv, Rivo, Peter F. Orazem, Allan Puur and Milan Vodopivec (1997), "Employment and wage dynamics in the Estonia transition, 1989–1995", Working paper.

Oi, Walter (1962), "Labor as a quasi-fixed factor", Journal of Political Economy 70 (6): 538–555.

Olley, G. Steven and Ariel Pakes (1996), "The dynamics of productivity in the telecommunications equipment industry", Econometrica 64 (6): 1263–1297.

OECD (1987), Employment outlook (OECD, Paris).

OECD (1993), Employment outlook (OECD, Paris).

OECD (1994a), Employment outlook, Chapter 3 (OECD, Paris).

OECD (1994b), Unemployment in transition countries: transient or persistent (OECD, Paris).

OECD (1996), Job creation and loss: analysis, policy and data development (OECD, Paris).

Pakes, Ariel and Mark Schankerman (1984), "The rate of obsolescence of patents, research gestation lags and the private rate of return to research resources", in: Zvi Griliches, ed., R & D, patents and productivity (University of Chicago Press for NBER, Chicago, IL).

Parsons, Donald O. (1986), "The employment relationship: job attachment, work effort and the nature of contracts", in: Orley C. Ashenfelter and Richard Layard, eds., Handbook of labor economics, Vol. 2 (North-Holland, Amsterdam).

Pissarides, Christopher (1990), Equilibrium unemployment theory (Basil Blackwell, Oxford, UK).

Prescott, Edward C. and Michael Visscher (1980), "Organization capital", Journal of Political Economy 88 (3): 446–461.

Ramey, Garey and Joel Watson (1997), "Contractual fragility, job destruction and business cycles", Quarterly Journal of Economics 112 (3): 873–911.

Ramey, Valerie and Matthew Shapiro (1996), "Sectoral mobility of capital: a case study of an aerospace firm", Working paper (University of California, San Diego, CA).

Rhee, Yung Whee, Bruce Ross-Larson and Garry Pursell (1984), Korea's competitive edge: managing the entry into world markets (Johns Hopkins University Press for the World Bank, Baltimore, MD).

Roberts, Kevin and Martin L. Weitzman (1981), "Funding criteria for research, development and exploration projects", Econometrica 49: 1261–1288.

Roberts, Mark J. (1996), "Employment flows and producer turnover in three developing countries", in: Mark J. Roberts and James R. Tybout, eds., Industrial evolution in developing countries: micro patterns of turnover, productivity and market structure (Oxford University Press, Oxford, UK).

Rodrik, Dani (1994), "Foreign trade in Eastern Europe's transition: early results", in: O. Blanchard, K. Froot and J. Sachs, eds., The transition in Eastern Europe, Vol. 2 (NBER and the University of Chicago Press, Chicago IL).

Rogers, Everett M. (1983), Diffusion of innovations, 3rd edition (Free Press, New York).

Rotemberg, Julio and Michael Woodford, "Forecastable movements in output, hours and consumption", Amercian Economic Review 86: 71–89.

Ruhm, Christopher (1991), "Are workers permanently scarred by job displacements?" American Economic Review 81: 319–324.

Saint-Paul, Gilles (1996), Dual labor markets: a macroeconomic perspective (MIT Press, Cambridge, MA).

Salvanes Kjell G. (1997), "Employment policies at the plant level: job and worker flows for heterogeneous labor in Norway", Working paper (Norwegian School of Business Administration).

Sattinger, Michael (1993), "Assignment models of the distribution of earnings", Journal of Economic Literature 31 (2): 831–880.

Schivardi, Fabiano (1997), "Reallocation and learning over the business cycle", Working paper (Stanford University).

Schumpeter, J.A. (1942), Capitalism, socialism and democracy (Harper and Brothers, New York).

Shin, Kwanho (1997), "Inter- and intrasectoral shocks: effects on the unemployment rate", Journal of Labor Economics 15 (2): 376–401.

Spletzer, James R. (1997), "Longitudinal establishment microdata at the Bureau of Labor Statistics: development, uses and access", Proceedings of the American Statistical Association (American Statistical Association).

Stein, Jeremy (1997), "Waves of creative destruction: firm-specific learning-by-doing and the dynamics of innovation", Review of Economics and Statistics 4 (2): 265–288.

Topel, Robert (1990), "Specific capital and unemployment: measuring the costs and consequences of job loss", Carnegie-Rochester Conference Series on Public Policy 33: 181–214.

Topel, Robert H. and Michael P. Ward (1992), "Job mobility and the careers of young men", Quarterly Journal of Economics 107 (2): 439–479.

Troske, Kenneth (1996), "The dynamic adjustment process of firm entry and exit in manufacturing and finance, insurance and real estate", Journal of Law and Economics 39 (2): 705–735.

Tybout, James R. (1996), "Heterogeneity and productivity growth: assessing the evidence", in: Mark J. Roberts and James R. Tybout, eds., Industrial evolution in developing countries: micro patterns of turnover, productivity and market structure (Oxford University Press, Oxford, UK).

Wagner, Joachim (1995), "Firm size and job creation in Germany", Small Business Economics 7 (6): 469–474.

Woo, Chi-Keung, Debra Lloyd-Zannetti and Ira Horowitz (1997), "Electricity market integration in the Pacific Northwest", The Energy Journal 18 (3): 75–101.

Yashiv, Eran (1995), "The determinants of equilibrium unemployment: structural estimation and simulation of the search and matching model", Working paper no 29/95 (Foerder Institute for Economic Research, Tel Aviv University).

PART 11

EMERGENT LABOR MARKETS

Chapter 42

LABOR MARKETS IN THE TRANSITIONAL CENTRAL AND EAST EUROPEAN ECONOMIES

JAN SVEJNAR*

The William Davidson Institute at the University of Michigan Business School and CERGE-EI, Prague

Contents

* I would like to thank Orley Ashenfelter, David Card, Katherine Terrell, and participants of the September 4–7, 1997 Handbook of Labor Economics Conference for valuable comments on an earlier draft of this chapter.

Handbook of Labor Economics, Volume 3, Edited by O. Ashenfelter and D. Card

Abstract

In this chapter, I survey principal econometric studies of several important labor market issues in Central and East European countries as they launched the transition from central planning to a market economy. The topics covered include employment, wage and fringe benefits determination in firms, individual wages and human capital, determinants of unemployment duration, and matching of the unemployed and vacancies. The studies are of interest because one can observe the functioning of nascent markets and institutions after prices and wages ceased being set by planners. Moreover, the variation in relevant variables has been tremendous, thus permitting the researchers to estimate precisely key parameters. © 1999 Elsevier Science B.V. All rights reserved.

JEL codes: J2; J3; J6; P2; P5

1. Introduction

In this chapter, I survey principal econometric studies of important labor market issues in the Central and East European (CEE) countries as they launched the transition from central planning to a market economy. As may be seen from Fig. 1, Central and Eastern Europe contains countries that were until 1989 within the Soviet bloc, as well as others that had separated themselves from it well before 1989 (former Yugoslavia and Albania). In the survey, I focus on studies dealing with Bulgaria, Czech Republic, Hungary, Poland, Romania, Slovakia, and Slovenia. Because of the size and importance of Russia, I cover some of the studies that analyze its emerging labor markets. I deal only peripherally with Albania as relatively few studies have been carried out on this CEE economy. For space limitations, I exclude the Baltic Republics.

Apart from dealing with inherently important topics, analyses of labor market phenomena in the CEE transition economies are of interest for at least four reasons. First, at a fundamental level the studies provide information about the functioning of nascent labor markets as the market system was gradually being created from a functioning or disintegrating centrally planned system. For an economist, the transition provides an interesting laboratory, with tremendous variation in key variables. For instance, unemployment rates rose from zero to double digits in all the CEE economies except for the Czech Republic. Output, employment and wages were suddenly being set by firms rather than planners and, in the first years of the transition, they registered enormous declines by western standards. Analyses of the labor market are hence able to capture the "big bang" effect of introducing a market system. From the policy standpoint, a particularly important issue is why the unemployment rate stayed in the 3–5% range in the Czech Republic and rose to double digits in all the other CEE economies. It is notable that the enormous rise in unemployment in these countries occurred despite major declines in labor force participation, competitive devaluation of the currencies, reductions in formerly generous unemployment benefits, and introduction of active labor market policies.

Second, as I discuss presently, the local political response to the first few years of the

Fig. 1. Central and Eastern Europe.

transition was unexpectedly negative. The discontent of voters reflected their anxiety that reforms require economic sacrifices without ensuring adequate social security. In this context, the former (now reformed) communists were often perceived as being better guardians of job security, living standards and social programs than the free market-oriented political parties. A major policy question that has arisen is how the transition economies can strike a balance between (i) reducing government intervention and completing the introduction of market incentives, and (ii) providing an adequate social safety net that ensures public support for the transition. Some of the studies provide answers to this question.

Third, the policy debates have increasingly moved from macro stabilization (which continues to be essential but requires standard policies), to microeconomic issues such as enterprise restructuring and privatization, the introduction and enforcement of a market-friendly legal framework, enhancing the functioning of a flexible labor market, and attracting foreign direct investment. A significant emphasis has been placed on the link between unemployment and the employment and wage behavior of privatized versus state owned firms. Labor market analyses may be particularly useful in providing policy guidance in this area.

Fourth, the economies of Central and East Europe were the first ones to enter the transition process and they differed dramatically from one another in their initial conditions, policies and outcomes. The results of studies dealing with these economies may hence provide important information for the policy makers in the numerous economies that started transition later.[1]

The chapter is organized as follows. In Section 2, I briefly review the principal features of the centrally planned system and the main statistics relating to the CEE economies during the transition. In Section 3, I describe the nature of data and principal data sources used by researchers of labor market phenomena in the CEE economies. In Section 4, I assess the findings of studies dealing with employment determination (labor demand) at the level of the firm or industry. In Section 5, I discuss studies dealing with wage setting at the firm or industry level, while in Section 6, I examine studies that analyze the provision of fringe benefits by firms during the transition. In Section 7, I review the principal studies that estimate individual wage determination in the context of a human capital framework. In Section 8, I deal with studies of unemployment, focusing on estimates of hazards of leaving unemployment and matching functions, respectively. Conclusions are drawn in Section 9.

In view of the fact that researchers have started to study virtually all aspects of labor markets in the CEE economies, I have naturally had to limit the topics that are included in the present chapter. I have therefore unfortunately excluded a number of areas, including studies of wage and employment bargaining, job creation and job destruction, labor and total factor productivity, migration, and income distribution.

---

[1] Poland and Hungary for instance entered the transition with a significant private sector in agriculture and services and limited government control over enterprises. In contrast, the Czech and Slovak economies were highly centralized and almost completely state-owned. Yet, the Czech Republic and to a lesser extent Slovakia have carried out massive privatization of state property, while others, such as Bulgaria, Poland, and Romania, have been much slower in privatizing their state sector. Some, such as the Czech Republic, have pushed through massive privatization, leaving the restructuring of firms for later. Others have stressed more the commercialization of existing state enterprises (e.g., Poland), reorientation of exports from east to west, attracting western capital (Hungary), and creating new firms.

2. Central planning, transition and labor markets

While it was functioning, the Soviet-type centrally planned system was characterized by full employment of labor (zero open unemployment) and centrally set wages, prices and output targets for state-owned enterprises. Income distribution was maintained at relatively egalitarian levels, all able-bodied individuals were required to work and enterprises were allocated funds to provide the needed jobs. Financial flows were centralized and subordinated to the fulfillment of the physical plan. Foreign trade was also centralized through state trading firms and all the Soviet bloc economies were integrated into a common trading area, the Council for Mutual Economic Assistance (CMEA), also known as COMECON. In each country, the construction of the annual and 5-year central plans was an elaborate input-output exercise. In this exercise, planners used current and past information from all parts of the economy to set ambitious but realistic targets for the firms, the economy, and through the CMEA for the Soviet bloc as a whole. With the centrally fixed prices, the system produced varying degrees of shortages and excess demand.

After World War II, the Soviet-type system was gradually imposed on all countries of Central and East Europe (CEE).[2] In the 1950s, the CEE countries grew rapidly and the system was basically maintained, although some countries, such as Czechoslovakia, implemented the system more rigorously than others, e.g., Poland.[3] Starting in the 1960s, many CEE countries experienced serious slowdowns in economic growth and, as a result of popular pressure, the system started undergoing reforms. At the economic level, full employment at centrally set (and low) wages was maintained but in many countries the requirement to work (e.g., for housewives) was not fully enforced. Rather than merely soliciting information and imposing targets, central planners increasingly engaged in bargaining with enterprise managers about plan targets, employment levels and financial allocations. Firms increasingly operated under so called soft budget constraints, being able to receive bailouts from the central authorities when producing losses. Moreover, firms could increasingly trade with one another outside of the scope of the central plan and in some countries, e.g., Poland and Hungary, workers and managers seized a significant degree of control over enterprises from the planners. By the time of the fall of the Berlin wall and other revolutions of 1989, the system was rapidly disintegrating in countries such as Poland and Hungary, but it still remained fairly intact in East Germany and Czechoslovakia.

In 1990–1991, the CEE economies started the transition to a market economy. Most of them first focused on maintaining or re-establishing macroeconomic stability, while liberalizing prices and dismantling the centrally planned system. The fall of the iron curtain was also accompanied by a major opening to world trade. Planners stopped dictating trade allocations, CMEA was officially abolished at the end of 1990 and tariffs, which had been

[2] Yugoslavia introduced the Soviet system but switched to a more decentralized system of workers self-management in the early 1950s.

[3] Poland for instance maintained private agriculture as well as some small private industry and services.

Table 1
Inflation in selected transition economies (year-on-year percent change in consumer price level)[a]

	1990	1991	1992	1993	1994	1995	1996	1997
Bulgaria	23.8	338.5	91.2	72.8	96.0	62.1	123.0	1083.0
Czech Republic	10.0	56.6	11.1	20.8	10.0	9.1	8.8	8.5
Hungary	28.9	35.0	23.0	22.5	18.8	28.2	23.6	18.3
Poland	553.6	70.3	43.0	35.3	32.2	27.8	19.9	15.3
Romania	5.1	170.2	210.4	256.1	136.8	32.3	38.8	154.8
Slovak Republic	18.0	61.2	10.0	23.2	13.4	9.9	5.8	6.1
Slovenia	549.7	117.7	201.3	32.3	19.8	12.6	9.9	8.4

[a] Source: Business Central Europe database at http://www.bcemag.com.

traditionally set at a low level (3–5% on average), provided only a limited barrier to foreign trade. As a means of macroeconomic stabilization, wages or wage bills of medium and large firms remained government-controlled in most CEE countries for several years.[4] While stabilizing, the new democratically elected governments designed and gradually implemented plans for commercializing and privatizing state-owned enterprises, stimulating growth of new private firms and creating the legal and institutional framework conducive to the functioning of a market system.

As may be seen from Table 1, within a few years the CEE economies succeeded in lowering the initial outburst of inflation that accompanied the disintegration of the centrally planned system and the initial liberalization of prices. In most of these economies inflation remained under control, but in Bulgaria and Romania there was a new outburst of inflation in the second half of the 1990s. In terms of the gross domestic product (GDP), all the CEE economies went through a major decline in the first 3–4 years of the transition, followed by varying rates of growth thereafter (see Table 2). The initially high inflation and rapidly declining output were followed with a lag by falling employment, with the fall being greater in Poland and Hungary than the Czech and Slovak republics. Real wages also fell in all the countries in the first 2–3 years of the transition as the countries devalued their currencies, freed most prices and imposed wage (bill) controls.

The most salient development has been in the area of unemployment. As may be seen from Table 3, all the CEE countries except for the Czech Republic have experienced rapidly rising and persistently high (double-digit) unemployment rates. The high unemployment rates have been accompanied by long spells of unemployment. By contrast, in the Czech Republic the unemployment rate has remained between 3 and 5% and unemployment spells have been short. The unemployment crisis in the CEE countries contributed to a political backlash as the post-revolutionary governments were soon voted out of office in all the CEE countries except for the Czech Republic.[5]

[4] See e.g., Commander et al. (1995b) for Hungary, Coricelli et al. (1995) for Poland, Ham et al. (1995) for the Czech and Slovak republics, Beleva et al. (1995) for Bulgaria, and Earle and Oprescu (1995) for Romania.
[5] In the Czech Republic, the coalition of most of the reformist parties lasted until December 1997.

Table 2
Growth in real GDP in selected transition economies (year-on-year percentage change)[a]

	1990	1991	1992	1993	1994	1995	1996	1997
Bulgaria	−9.1	−11.7	−7.3	−1.5	1.8	2.1	−10.9	−7.4
Croatia	−6.9	−20.6	−11.7	−0.9	0.6	1.7	4.2	5.0
Czech Republic	−1.2	−11.5	−3.3	0.6	2.7	4.8	3.9	1.0
Hungary	−3.5	−11.9	−3.1	−0.6	2.9	1.5	1.3	4.0
Poland	−11.6	−7.0	2.6	3.8	5.2	7.0	6.1	7.0
Romania	−5.6	−12.9	−8.7	1.5	3.9	7.1	4.1	−6.6
Slovak Republic	−2.5	−14.5	−6.5	−3.7	4.9	6.8	6.9	6.5
Slovenia	−4.7	−8.9	−5.5	2.8	5.3	4.1	3.1	2.9

[a] Source: Business Central Europe database at http://www.bcemag.com.

3. The nature of data sources

Researchers of transition phenomena have been fortunate in that the centrally planned economies collected relatively detailed data on firms as well as individuals and households. The firm-level data were of the census type, collected at various levels of detail in monthly, quarterly and annual intervals. The degree of detail was the lowest in the monthly reports and greatest in the annual data. The household and individual data were probabilistic samples carried out with varying, usually annual or multi-year, periodicity. These data collection activities have continued to the present, although in some countries the willingness of firms to furnish information has declined.

The micro data on firms and individuals have been treated by the statistical offices as confidential. Under conditions of anonymity of firms and individuals, researchers or institutions such as the World Bank have been able to obtain these micro data for research purposes from the statistical offices of the individual countries.

Table 3
Unemployment in selected transitional economies (end-of-year unemployment rate in percentage)[a]

	1990	1991	1992	1993	1994	1995	1996	1997
Bulgaria	1.7	11.1	15.2	16.4	12.8	11.1	12.5 d	13.7
Croatia	11.4	18.2	15.5	14.6	14.8	15.1	15.9	17.6
Czech Republic	0.8	4.1	2.6	3.5	3.2	2.9	3.5	5.2
Hungary	1.9	7.5	13.2	12.3	11.4	11.1	10.7	10.8
Poland	6.3	11.8	13.6	16.4	16.0	14.9	13.6	10.5
Romania	0.4	3.0	8.2	10.4	10.9	9.5	6.3	8.8
Slovak Republic	0.8	4.1	10.4	14.4	14.8	13.1	12.8	12.5
Slovenia	4.7	8.2	13.4	15.4	14.2	14.5	14.4	14.8

[a] Source: Business Central Europe database at http://www.bcemag.com.

From the early 1990s, all the CEE countries have started collecting large quarterly labor force surveys (LFSs) of large stratified random samples of individuals. The surveys are relatively similar in design and coverage. They usually rotate households into and out of the sample after four quarters, thus allowing researchers to obtain cross-sectional as well as panel data estimates of various phenomena.

As transition progressed, a number of private firms started assembling data that became commercially available for sale. Finally, a number of researchers and institutions such as The World Bank and The European Bank for Reconstruction and Development have carried out surveys of firms and households. These surveys were motivated by the occasional unwillingness of national statistical offices to release micro data or the desire of researchers to capture phenomena that were not covered by the existing databases.

4. Employment determination

There has been considerable interest in employment adjustment by firms during the transition. The interest stems in part from the fact that enterprise restructuring from a relatively inflexible (centrally planned) mode to a more flexible (market) mode of operation is a key element of the transition and employment adjustment has in turn been considered a principal measure of the ability of firms to start restructuring.[6] A number of researchers have therefore used firm- or industry-level data to analyze employment setting before and/or during the transition.

4.1. Basic estimates of employment elasticities with respect to output and wage

In estimating an employment (labor demand) equation, most authors use the following specification:

$$L = L(W/P, Q, X), \tag{1}$$

where L is the number of employees, W is the nominal wage, P is the product price index, Q is the sales or output of the firm, and X is a vector of ownership, legal structure, and industry dummy variables that may affect the firm's demand for labor. The specification in Eq. (1) corresponds to a labor demand function of an enterprise characterized by cost minimization subject to an exogenously given level of output or it may be seen as an approximation to other employment-setting relationships.

Basu et al. (1995) employ firm-level datasets covering the period both before and during the transition in order to assess how firms changed their employment setting behavior as the transition was launched. In particular, the authors use annual panels of firm-level data from the late 1980s to early 1990s to assess how Czech, Slovak, Hungarian, Polish, and Russian industrial firms adjusted their employment in response to changes in

---

[6] See e.g., Aghion et al. (1984) and Grosfeld and Roland (1995) for the use of this concept of restructuring in theoretical modeling of the transition process.

output, wages, and the ownership and legal form of the firm. Depending on the year, the datasets cover over 4181–4914 firms in Poland, 761–1451 in the Czech Republic, 311–569 in Slovakia, 326 in Hungary and 229 in Russia. In Poland, the Czech Republic and Slovakia, the datasets cover all large and medium sized industrial firms.[7] The Hungarian and Russian firms represent a smaller sample of industrial enterprises; the Russian panel comes from a dataset of 394 Russian firms that account for about 10% of Russian manufacturing output.[8]

In estimating Eq. (1), Basu et al. (1995) place considerable emphasis on the econometric issues, some of which arise because of the nature of the transition. The authors for instance treat W as endogenous and test whether the negative output shocks brought about by the dissolution of the CMEA, the collapse of the Soviet market, and the restrictive macroeconomic policies imposed exogenous output (sales) constraints on firms.[9] Basu et al. (1995) also strive to find the best compromise between two goals: (i) allowing as much as possible for dynamics and (ii) permitting the data to reveal structural changes inherent in the rapid systemic transformation. As a result, for each country the authors use consecutive 2-year panels of data and test for the stability of coefficients across the 2-year periods. Eq. (1) is specified in a log–linear form, with the left-hand side variable and all the principal right-hand side variables entering in both current and 1-year lagged form (see e.g., Hendry and Mizon (1978), Nickell (1986), and Estrin and Svejnar (1993) for other applications of this model). Formally, this first degree general distributed lag model is specified as[10]

$$logL_t = \alpha_0 + \alpha_1 log(W)_t + \alpha_2 log(W)_{t-1} + \alpha_3 logQ_t + \alpha_4 logQ_{t-1} + \alpha_5 logX_t$$

$$+ \alpha_6 logX_{t-1} + \alpha_7 logL_{t-1}. \tag{1$'$}$$

On the basis of F tests, Basu et al. (1995) also conclude that the general distributed lag model is preferred to the partial adjustment model ($\alpha_2 = \alpha_4 = \alpha_6 = 0$), a traditional static model ($\alpha_2 = \alpha_4 = \alpha_6 = \alpha_7 = 0$), and the fixed effects (first difference) model ($\alpha_2 = -\alpha_1$, $\alpha_4 = -\alpha_3$, $\alpha_6 = -\alpha_5$, and $\alpha_7 = 1$).[11]

As may be seen from Table 4(A), Basu et al.'s (1995) estimates suggest that Polish and Hungarian firms displayed significant positive short run labor demand elasticities with

---

[7] The total number of observations falls short of the total number of industrial firms as the authors had to eliminate observations with missing data and that did not meet basic consistency checks.

[8] The Russian sample was stratified by industry and region and drawn from the 1991 list of all Russian industrial firms. The firms were sampled with replacement and they were asked to furnish data covering the 1990–1994 period. For the purposes of these and other authors' estimation, the number of usable observations varies between 135 and 230, depending on the specification.

[9] W/P and Q are instrumented by regional dummy variables, (1 year) lagged capital assets of the firm interacted with industry dummy variables and output in the neighboring 2-digit industry.

[10] While the equation may be viewed as a convenient flexible form, it can also be derived from a dynamic cost minimization behavior of the firm (see e.g., Nickell, 1986).

[11] The shortterm elasticity of employment with respect to wage is given by α_1, while the corresponding longterm elasticity is $(\alpha_1 + \alpha_2)/\alpha_1 - \alpha_7)$. The short and longterm employment elasticities with respect to output and the other variables are defined analogously.

Table 4
Labor demand elasticities

Authors	Country	Elasticity pre-transition	Elasticity during transition	Data	Method
(A) With respect to output (sales)					
Firm-level studies					
Basu et al. (1995)	Poland	0.3	0.4	Large consecutive 2-year panels of annual firm-level data (all large and medium-sized industrial firms)[b]	General distributed lag model; wages and output instrumented; shortterm elasticities
	Hungary	0.4 to 0.6	0.7 to 0.8		
	Czech R.	0.0	0.5 to 0.6		
	Slovak R.	0.1	0.3		
	Russia	–	0.0		
Basu et al. (1997)	Poland	–	0.2	Two-year panel of data on 161 industrial firms	General distributed lag model; regressors assumed exogenous; shortterm elasticities
Grosfeld and Nivet (1997)	Poland	0.06	0.25	Panel of annual data on 173 large firms	First difference model; regressors assumed exogenous
Köllö (1997)	Hungary	0.2	0.2	Large panels of annual firm-level data	First difference model; 2SLS estimates jointly with a wage equation
Korosi (1997)	Hungary	0.5 to 0.6	0.5 to 0.8	Large and medium-sized exporting firms	General distributed lag model; wages and output instrumented; shortterm elasticities
Singer (1996)	Czech R.	–	0.0 to 0.1	Large panel of monthly firm-level data (all large and medium-sized industrial firms)	Dynamic labor demand model; wages and output instrumented
Industry-level studies					
Brauer et al. (1995)	Poland	–	0.4	Monthly industry-level data	Dynamic labor demand model; wages and output instrumented
	Hungary	–	0.9		
Commander and Dhar (1998)	Poland	–	0.1 to 0.9	Annual industry-level data by region	First difference model; 2SLS estimates jointly with a wage equation

(B) With respect to own wage

Firm-level studies

Study	Country			Data	Model
Basu et al. (1995)	Poland	−0.3	−0.8	Large consecutive two-year panels of annual firm-level data (all large and medium-sized industrial firms)[b]	General distributed lag model; wages and output instrumented; shortterm elasticities
	Hungary	−0.2[a]	−1.0 to −2.3		
	Czech R.	−0.4	−0.6 to −1.0		
	Slovak R.	−0.3	−0.3		
	Russia	—	0.0		
Basu et al. (1997)	Poland	—	−0.3	Two-year panel of data on 161 industrial firms	General distributed lag model; regressors assumed exogenous; shortterm elasticities
Grosfeld and Nivet (1997)	Poland	−0.03	−0.13	Panel of annual data on 173 large firms	First difference model; regressors assumed exogenous
Köllő (1997)	Hungary	−0.6	−0.3	Large panels of annual firm-level data	First difference model; 2SLS estimates jointly with a wage equation
Korosi (1997)	Hungary	−0.1 to −0.8	−0.4 to −1.4	Large and medium-sized exporting firms	General distributed lag model; wages and output instrumented; shortterm elasticities
Singer (1996)	Czech R.	—	−0.0 to −0.1	Large panel of monthly firm-level data (all large and medium-sized industrial firms)	Dynamic labor demand model; wages and output instrumented

Industry-level firms

Study	Country			Data	Model
Brauer et al. (1995)	Poland	—	−0.5	Monthly industry-level data	Dynamic labor demand model; wages and output instrumented
	Hungary	—	−1.1		
Commander and Dhar (1998)	Poland	—	−1.0 to −1.1	Annual industry-level data by region	First difference model; 2SLS estimates jointly with a wage equation

[a] Not statistically significant.
[b] The Hungarian and Russian datasets are smaller, containing 326 and 229 firms, respectively.

respect to output already in the pre-transition period of the late 1980s. In contrast, the corresponding pre-transition elasticities in the Czech and Slovak firms are either very small or statistically insignificant.[12] Thus the Polish estimates for 1988–1989, 1 year before their respective big bangs, the estimated elasticities are around 0.3 for Poland (1988–1989), 0.4–0.6 for Hungary (1987–1988), 0.1 for Slovakia (1990), around 0 for the Czech Republic (1990). With the onset of the transition, the estimated labor demand elasticities with respect to output rise to about 0.3 in Slovakia and 0.5–0.6 in the Czech Republic. They also increase to about 0.4 in Poland and 0.7–0.8 in Hungary. The findings are consistent with the perception that Polish and Hungarian firms were more market-oriented at the end of the communist regime than the Czech and Slovak ones. The results also indicate that firms in all the CEE economies covered by this study started adjusting employment to output more as the transition set in. Basu et al.'s (1995) estimate for Russia yields insignificant employment elasticity with respect to output, indicating that, as late as 1993–1994, Russian firms tended not to adjust employment with fluctuations in output. This finding is consistent with the overall observation that the Russian economy has been much slower than its CEE counterparts in transforming itself to a market economy.

Basu et al.'s (1995) estimates of the labor demand elasticities with respect to own wage are reported in Table 4(B). They suggest that these elasticities had been negative in all the CEE countries before the transition started and became more pronounced in Poland, Hungary and the Czech Republic as the transition took place. The pre-transition estimates are around -0.4 in the Czech Republic, -0.3 in Slovakia, -0.3 in Poland, and -0.2 (but statistically insignificant) in Hungary. Within 1–2 years after the transition was launched, these estimates rise to around -0.6 to -1.0 in the Czech Republic, -0.8 in Poland and -1.0 to -2.3 in Hungary. In Slovakia, the estimates stay at about -0.3. As with the labor demand elasticity with respect to output, the Russian 1993–1994 estimate of the labor demand elasticity with respect to own wage is found to be insignificant.

In a related study, Basu et al. (1997) estimate the distributed lag Eq. $(1')$ on a 2-year (1992–1993) panel of 161 Polish firms. The data come from a stratified random sample of 200 Polish firms that were surveyed in 1994 as part of a World Bank project. The sample contains state-owned enterprises, privatized firms and newly established private companies. As may be seen from Table 4(A), the shortterm elasticity of employment with respect to output is estimated to be 0.2. This estimate is lower than the 0.4 short term elasticity estimate obtained by Basu et al. (1995) for the population of all medium and large Polish industrial firms during the 1990–1991 period. The shortterm employment elasticity with respect to wage is estimated at -0.3, which is again lower than the -0.8 elasticity obtained by Basu et al. (1995) for the population of medium and large Polish firms (Table 4(B)).

Grosfeld and Nivet (1997) use panel data on 173 of the 500 largest Polish firms during the 1988–1994 period. They estimate a first difference labor demand equation corresponding to Eq. (1). Using the entire panel of data, they test for structural breaks and identify

---

[12] The big bang launch of the transition process dates to January 1, 1990 in Poland and January 1, 1991 in the Czech and Slovak republics. In Hungary, the process started earlier, dating in many respects to 1989.

1988–1990, 1990–1991 and 1991–1994 as three structurally different periods. For these three periods the authors then estimate the labor demand equation, assuming that the regressors are exogenous and using the Hausman test to select between fixed and random effects specifications. As may be seen from Table 4(A), the authors find that the estimated labor demand elasticity with respect to output is rising from 0.06 in the 1988–1990 period to 0.25 in 1991–1994.[13] Their estimates are hence lower than those obtained by Basu et al. (1995) for the population of four thousand large and medium sized Polish firms. Nevertheless, like Basu et al. (1995), Grosfeld and Nivet (1997) find that the labor demand-output elasticity was significant already before the big bang of 1990 and increased during the transition.

As may be seen from Table 4(B), Grosfeld and Nivet's (1997) estimates of the own wage elasticity of demand for Poland range from −0.03 in the 1988–1990 period to −0.13 in 1991–1994.[14] As before, these estimates are lower than those of Basu et al. (1995), but they do reflect the increase in the estimated elasticity between the late 1980 and 1990–1991.

Köllö (1997) examines employment behavior in annual panels of Hungarian firms that were continuously in existence during one of three time periods. His samples contain 3250 firms during the 1986–1989 period, 2842 firms in the 1989–1992 period and 4800 firms in the 1992–1993 period. Using first difference, log–linear employment equations, Köllö (1997) relates employment to real sales, real product wage, firm size and firm's export status. Except for the wage, the explanatory variables are considered to be exogenous and the employment equation is estimated jointly with a wage equation (reported later). As may be seen from Table 4(A), Köllö (1997) finds the annual employment elasticity with respect to sales to be 0.2 in both the 1986–1989 and 1992–1993 periods.[15] As reported in Table 4(B), Köllö (1997) estimates the labor demand elasticity with respect to own wage at −0.6 in the pre-transition period of 1986–1989 and at −0.3 during the 1992–1993 transition period. Unlike Basu et al. (1995), Köllö (1997) hence finds a significant employment elasticity with respect to own wage already before the transition. His estimates also suggest that this elasticity decreased rather than increased in the early phase of the transition.

Körosi (1997) uses the same methodology as Basu et al. (1995, 1997) to estimate labor demand equations on the population of large and medium-sized exporting firms in Hungary. His dataset contains annual data and covers the entire 1986–1995 period. As may be seen from Table 4, Körosi (1997) obtains very similar elasticity estimates to those obtained by Basu et al. (1995) with their shorter and smaller panel. The elasticity of labor demand with respect to output ranges from 0.5 to 0.6 in the pre-transition period and from 0.5 to 0.8 during the transition. The corresponding elasticity with respect to wage is in the −0.1 to −0.8 range before the transition and in the −0.4 to −1.4 range during the

---

[13] The authors also find an elasticity of 0.09 for the intermediate period of 1990–1991.

[14] The authors also find an elasticity of −0.33 for the 1990–1991 period.

[15] During the big bang period of 1989–1992, Köllö (1997) finds the elasticity to be as high as 0.35.

transition. Unlike Köllö (1997), Körosi (1997) hence finds support for the hypothesis that both elasticities increased somewhat during the transition.

Singer (1996) focuses on one of the principal disadvantages of using annual data, namely the fact that they contain aggregation over time that smoothes shortterm variation in the values of variables. He takes advantage of the fact that the Czech firm-level data used by Basu et al. (1995) contain some information on a monthly basis and, using a Nickell (1984) dynamic cost minimization framework, he estimates dynamic labor demand equations with cost of adjustment using several thousand monthly observations. Estimating equations on pooled data from 1992 and 1993 as well as 1992 and 1993 separately, Singer (1996) finds surprisingly low elasticities of labor demand, a result that is not affected by varying the set of instruments. In particular, estimates based on pooled data for 1992 and 1993 yield short and longterm labor demand elasticities with respect to output of 0.025 to 0.06, short term elasticity with respect to wage of -0.04 to -0.07 and long term elasticities with respect to wage of -0.07 to -0.11. Estimates based on 1992 data yield somewhat higher elasticities, while those based on 1993 generate somewhat lower elasticities, especially with respect to wage. It is not clear why Singer (1996) obtains such low elasticities, especially in 1993. One possible explanation is that firms set employment annually rather than at shorter (monthly) time intervals. An alternative explanation is that enterprise behavior was temporarily affected ("frozen") by the division of Czechoslovakia into separate Czech and Slovak republics in 1993. Overall, while the substantive findings are surprising, Singer's is the first study (worldwide) that uses a large dataset of monthly observations to examine dynamic labor demand.

At a more aggregate level, Brauer et al. (1997) estimate dynamic labor demand models using monthly data for the industrial sector in Poland and Hungary. The Polish data cover the period January 1990 to March 1995, while the Hungarian data cover the period January 1990 to December 1994. The labor demand equation corresponds to a CES production function with a generalized lag model to introduce dynamics. The equation is estimated jointly with a labor supply equation. The estimation method is three stage least squares, with lagged values of variables used as instruments. As may be seen from Table 4(A), Brauer et al. (1997) find the elasticity of labor demand with respect to output to be 0.36 for Poland and 0.85 in Hungary. The corresponding labor demand elasticities with respect to wages are estimated at -0.45 and -1.06, respectively (Table 4(B)). Hence, Brauer et al.'s (1997) aggregated data generate estimates that are similar in magnitude to those of Basu et al. (1995).

Commander and Dhar (1998) use Polish 2-digit level industry data disaggregated over regions and covering the 1990–1994 period. The data cover all large and a significant number of medium sized firms that existed (survived) during this entire period in Poland. Commander and Dhar (1998) estimate first difference regressions on consecutive 2-year panels of data. They relate changes in employment to changes in real sales, changes in real wage and several other variables. As may be seen from Table 4(A), the authors find a significant positive elasticity of employment with respect to sales. The elasticity fluctuates between 0.7 and 0.9 during the 1990–1993 period and surprisingly falls to 0.1 in 1993–

1994. With the exception of the estimate for 1993–1994, Commander and Dhar's (1998) estimates are higher than those obtained by Estrin and Svejnar (1998) on the population of large and medium sized Polish industrial firms and by Grosfeld and Nivet (1997) on their sample of 173 large Polish firms. Commander and Dhar's (1998) estimate of the employment elasticity with respect to wage rises from -1.0 in the 1990–1991 period to -1.1 in the 1991–1994 period. This estimate is slightly higher than the -0.8 estimate obtained by Basu et al. (1995) on the population of large and medium-sized industrial firms, somewhat larger than Brauer et al.'s (1995) -0.5 estimate based on monthly industry-level data, and substantially larger than the -0.1 to -0.3 estimates obtained on smaller samples by Grosfeld and Nivet (1997) and Basu et al. (1997).

4.2. Studies of firms with increasing versus decreasing sales

Since employment adjustment is viewed as a key indicator of early restructuring of the formerly socialist enterprises, researchers have wondered if employment behavior was affected by the negative demand shock that occurred at the start of the transition as a result of factors such as the disintegration of the CMEA and collapse of the Soviet market. In this context, Estrin and Svejnar (1998), Köllö (1997), Commander and Dhar (1998), and Körosi (1997) examine whether employment behavior was different in firms that were greatly affected by this shock (proxied by firms experiencing declining real sales) than in firms that do not appear to have been greatly affected by the shock (those with increasing real sales). The authors run separate first difference regressions on each set of firms and use as explanatory variables the change in the firm's sales, in some cases interacted with ownership and legal form dummy variables. In addition, they usually control for industry-specific effects by including a vector of industry-specific dummy variables. Except for Körosi's (1997) work, the research was part of a multi-country study employing a common methodology. In particular, the authors estimate logarithmic employment equations that correspond to Eq. (1), but exclude own wage from the right-hand side. The underlying assumption is that capital and labor are not easily substitutable within a short (e.g., 1-year) period.[16] Körosi (1997) uses the general distributed lag model. The estimates are reported in Table 5.

Estrin and Svejnar (1998) use the same data as Basu et al. (1995) and estimate the first difference equation on contiguous 2-year panels. The estimation is carried out by both OLS and instrumental variables (IVs).[17] The OLS and IV estimates are similar for all countries except for Hungary, where the IV estimates generate implausibly large elasticity coefficients (due probably to the relatively small sample). The authors find that in the Czech and Slovak Republics firms with increasing sales had insignificant employment to

---

[16] The selection of the common empirical model was guided by Olivier Blanchard.

[17] The authors used the firm's lagged capital stock, regional dummy variables, industry dummy variables, and ownership and legal form dummy variables as instruments. In Poland, they used output in the neighboring industry (measured by standard industry classification) as an additional instrument.

Table 5
Labor demand elasticities with respect to rising versus falling sales

Authors	Country	Elasticity pre-transition		Elasticity during transition		Data	Method
		↑ Sales	↓ Sales	↑ Sales	↓ Sales		
Firm-level studies							
Estrin and Svejnar (1998)	Poland	0.1	0.3 to 0.4	0.4	0.3 to 0.4	Large consecutive 2-year panels of annual firm-level data (all large and medium-sized industrial firms)[a]	First difference model; wages excluded from the set of regressors; separate regressions for firms with increasing and decreasing real sales
	Hungary	0.0	−0.0	0.0	0.7		
	Czech R.	0.0	0.04	0.4 to 0.6	0.4 to 0.5		
	Slovak R.	0.0	0.1	0.3	0.4		
Köllö (1997)	Hungary	0.0	0.2	0.0	0.3	Large annual panels of firm-level data.	Same as above
Korosi (1997)	Hungary	0.2 to 0.4	0.0 to 1.1	0.4 to 0.7	0.4 to 1.2	Large and medium-sized exporting firms	General distributed lag model; wages and output instrumented; shortterm elasticities; separate regressions for firms with increasing and decreasing real sales
Industry-level studies							
Commander and Dhar (1998)	Poland	0.2	0.15	0.3 to 0.5	0.1 to 0.2	2-digit level industry data (on large firms)	Same as Estrin and Svejnar (1998) above

[a] The Hungarian dataset is smaller, containing 326 firms.

sales elasticities in the 1989–1990 pre-transition period but that during the transition the elasticities moved to the 0.4–0.6 range in the Czech Republic (1991–1993) and 0.3 in Slovakia (1991–1992). A very similar pattern is found in both republics for firms with decreasing sales except that one observes a small (0.04–0.1) and statistically significant elasticity already in the pre-transition period. The Estrin and Svejnar (1998) results hence parallel the findings of Basu et al. (1995) in indicating that the Czech and Slovak industrial firms were unresponsive in their employment setting before the transition but quickly started adjusting during the transition. The new information is that firms with declining sales were reducing employment slightly already during the pre-transition period and that firms with rising and declining sales displayed similar employment to sales elasticities in the presence external shocks during the early transition.

With respect to Polish firms with increasing sales, Estrin and Svejnar (1998) find the estimated elasticity to increase from 0.1 in the pre-transition period to 0.35 in the year after the big bang. The corresponding elasticities for firms with decreasing sales are in the 0.3–0.4 range both before and during the transition. These findings also complement those of Basu et al. (1995) in that they show that the employment setting in Polish firms was responsive to output already before the transition and that this responsiveness came primarily from firms with decreasing sales. As in the Czech and Slovak Republics, during the early transition, when the external shocks occurred, both firms with increasing and decreasing sales display similar elasticities.

Estrin and Svejnar's (1998) estimates based on Hungarian data suggest that firms with increasing sales had an insignificant employment to sales elasticity both before and during the transition. Firms with decreasing sales generate positive but insignificant elasticities in the 1988–1989 pre-transition period and significant positive elasticities of 0.7 in the transition period of 1989–1991. The results hence suggest that Hungarian firms that suffered negative demand shocks adjusted employment while those that experienced output growth did not.

Using the data described above, Köllö (1997) estimates univariate regressions of employment on real value added. As may be seen from Table 5, Köllö (1997) finds that the elasticity from the univariate regressions is relatively high (0.2–0.3) for firms with decreasing output and insignificant for those with increasing output. The asymmetry between firms with increasing and decreasing value added parallels that found by Estrin and Svejnar (1998) in the smaller sample of Hungarian firms.

Körosi (1997) uses the aforementioned data on Hungarian exporting firms to estimate the general distributed lag model separately for firms with increasing and decreasing real sales. While Körosi's (1997) estimates vary across years, he finds positive elasticities for both types of firms before as well as during the transition, with the estimates for the transition period being generally higher than those before the transition. Unlike the studies by Estrin and Svejnar (1998) and Köllö (1997), Körosi's (1997) study hence suggests that firms with increasing real sales adjusted employment to sales already in the pre-transition period.

Commander and Dhar (1998) use the Polish 2-digit level industry data described above but covering the 1989–1990 period in addition to the 1990–1994 period. As may be seen from Table 5, in the big bang period of 1989–1990, the authors find the elasticity of employment with respect to sales to be very similar (around 0.2) in firms with increasing and decreasing sales. Surprisingly, during the 1991–1994 period of transition, the authors find the elasticity to be somewhat higher (0.3–0.5) in firms with increasing sales than in firms with decreasing sales (0.1–0.2).

4.3. Other factors affecting employment

In addition to estimating elasticities of labor demand, several studies test whether firms with different forms of ownership and legal form (type of legal registration and commercialization) display different employment patterns. With dummy variables for various ownership and legal forms entered into the labor demand equations, Basu et al. (1995) find that ownership and legal form of the firms have little systematic impact on employment. In the case of Czech and Slovak firms, the authors have enough variation in the date of the founding of firm to be able to test if firms that had existed already under Communism behaved differently during the transition than new firms (newly established firms and spin-offs from existing firms). Controlling for industry, ownership and legal form of the firm, they find that the old firms have lower elasticities than the new ones in the Czech Republic but that an opposite relationship holds in Slovakia. This suggests that managers and workers in the Czech Republic (Slovakia) who continued during the transition in firms that had operated under central planning were less (more) responsive to market stimuli than those that started or spun off new firms.

Using the aforementioned sample of 161 Polish firms, Basu et al. (1997) analyze employment effects of several variables within the framework of Eq. (1'). They find that (i) privatized firms tend to have fewer workers, ceteris paribus, than state-owned or newly established private firms, (ii) the quick ratio (liquid assets/current liabilities), which is negatively correlated with financial distress of the firm, has a positive short term effect on employment and (iii) firms with a greater share of output based on foreign design employ more workers. Age of equipment, capacity utilization, perceived market share, and the extent of unionization of the firm's labor force do not have a significant effect on employment.

Grosfeld and Nivet (1997) estimate that privatized firms increased employment 20% more and commercialized firms 11% less than other (state owned and not commercialized) firms in Poland in 1990–1991. Moreover, privatized firms continued increasing employment by about 4% a year faster than other firms during the 1991–1994 period.

Earle and Estrin (1996) use the same Russian data as Basu et al. (1995) to assess if layoffs are systematically related to certain explanatory variables. In particular, the authors regress the "rate of layoffs" (number of layoffs divided by total employment in a given year) on a number of explanatory variables that capture the firm's ownership, market structure, international competition, and hardness of the budget constraint. The authors find that the rate of layoffs is positively affected by the extent to which managers own the firm and, more generally, the extent of private ownership. In some specifications, they also find an indication that government subsidies are negatively related to layoffs. Finally, Earle and Estrin (1996) cannot reject the hypothesis that firm ownership by workers and government ownership have the same effect on layoffs and that the degree of measured competition does not affect layoffs.

Earle et al. (1995) use the same Russian dataset to examine the relationship between employment and ownership. On the basis of 337 observations they find that newly established firms are on average much smaller in terms of employment than all other types of firms. With 317 of these observations being of a panel form, the authors also run regressions with a lagged employment variable included as a regressor. In these specifications, they find no significant relationship between employment and whether the firm is principally owned by state, workers, managers or outside owners. Hence, once controlling for size in previous year, ownership does not appear to affect significantly employment behavior of these firms over time.

4.4. Summary

The labor demand studies provide several important insights. First, they suggest that the CEE countries were not homogeneous in their economic behavior under the communist regime. In particular, the studies support the popular impression that Poland and Hungary, unlike the Czech and Slovak republics, had more market-like economies already before the start of the transition. The labor demand studies indicate that, unlike the Czech and Slovak firms, Polish and Hungarian firms were adjusting employment to sales already before the end of the communist regime. Moreover, the evidence from some of the large panels of firm-level data suggests that this pre-transition adjustment was carried out primarily by firms that experienced declining sales. These firms were presumably under duress and, unlike their Czech and Slovak counterparts, faced sufficiently hard budget constraints to cut down employment.

The second important finding is that as transition unfolded, firms in all the CEE economies started adjusting employment to output changes and the estimated elasticities rapidly rose to levels that are by and large comparable to those estimated in western economies. The "inexperienced" Czech and Slovak firms hence rapidly started adjusting employment and the Polish and Hungarian firms appear to have further increased their adjustment. With the possible exception of Hungary, the adjustment of employment to sales during the transition is observed in firms with both increasing and decreasing sales. Interestingly, Russian firms appear not have been adjusting employment with output fluctuations even as late as 1993–1994, suggesting that the transition in Russia proceeded much more slowly at the micro level than in CEE.

The third finding is that labor demand elasticities with respect to own wage had been negative in all the CEE countries before the transition started and became even more pronounced in Poland, the Czech Republic and possibly Hungary as the transition unfolded. The negative relationship observed in the centrally planned Czech and Slovak

Table 6
Wage elasticities with respect to sales per worker or sales

Authors	Country	Elasticity pre-transition	Elasticity during transition	Data	Method
(A) All firms pooled					
Firm-level studies					
Basu et al. (1995)	Poland	0.3	0.3 to 0.4	Large consecutive 2-year panels of annual firm-level data (all large and medium-sized industrial firms)[a]	General distributed lag model; wages regressed on Q/L; wage equation estimated by instrumental variables jointly with the employment equation
	Hungary	0.0	0.3 to 0.4		
	Czech R.	0.0	0.3 to 0.4		
	Slovak R.	0.2	0.3 to 0.4		
Basu et al. (1997)	Poland	–	0.3	Two-year panel of data on 157 industrial firms	General distributed lag model; wages regressed on Q/L; regressors assumed exogenous; shortterm elasticities
Grosfeld and Nivet (1997)	Poland	0.2	0.1	Panel of annual data on 173 large firms	Wages regressed on Q/L

(B) Separate estimates for firms with increasing and decreasing sales

	↑ Sales	↓ Sales	↑ Sales	↓ Sales		
Estrin and Svejnar (1998)					Large consecutive 2-year panels of annual firm-level data (all large and medium-sized industrial firms)[a]	First difference; wages regressed on Q
Poland	0.1	0.4	0.4	0.0		
Hungary	0.0	−0.3	0.0	0.0		
Czech R.	0.1	0.1	0.0	0.0		
Slovak R.	0.0	0.0	0.3	0.4		
Köllö (1997)					Large annual panels of firm-level data	First difference; wages regressed on Q
Hungary	0.0 to 0.1	0.0	0.0 to 0.1	0.0		
Industry-level studies						
Commander and Dhar (1998)					2-digit level industry data (on large firms)	First difference; wages regressed on Q/L
Poland	0.3	0.8 to 0.9	0.7	0.8 to 0.9		

[a] The Hungarian dataset is smaller, containing 326 firms.

republics raises the possibility that planners controlled wage bills but allowed substitution between employment and wages within this constraint. The emphasis on wage bill was also manifest in some of the wage control regulations issued during the early transition period.

Finally, firm ownership and legal form (type of registration and hence corporate governance) are not found to have a simple and uniform effect on employment. In the large samples, covering the early transition period, there appears to be no uniform effect. In the smaller samples that extend further into the transition period, one finds some evidence that privatized firms may at first reduce employment and then increase it faster over time.

5. Wage determination by firms

In addition to estimating labor demand equations, several authors estimate wage equations using firm- or industry-level data. The estimated wage equation is usually of the form:

$$W = W(Q/L, X, Z), \tag{2}$$

where W is the average wage in the firm, Q/L is the sales (output) per employee, X is the ownership, legal structure, and industry cum regional variables discussed above and Z is a vector of structural and policy variables that may affect wages in a given firm (e.g., the firm's share of the industry output, the firm's export to sales ratio, and the local unemployment rate). Some studies use Q rather than Q/L as an explanatory variable.

The focus on the wage–sales per employee relationship is particularly interesting in the context of the transition economies. Under a strict planning system, wages are set centrally and are unrelated to enterprise performance. Similarly, in a competitive capitalist labor market, wages net of compensating differentials are expected to be equalized across comparable workers. In reality, firms under central planning were expected to fulfill output targets and the centrally set wages could be supplemented with bonus payments that depended on the extent of plan fulfillment. Since available datasets usually measure total annual earnings per employee, the authors are able to capture this potential link between output and remuneration. As the central controls were gradually lifted and the transition to a market system unfolded, average earnings started to depend on the nature and enforcement of wage controls, workers' power and the firm's ability to pay. While profit, calculated net of a reservation wage, would be an appropriate variable measuring the "pie" that workers might try to capture, the profit data are relatively unreliable in the transition economies.[18] As a result, controlling for industry differences in non-labor cost via industry dummy variables, sales per employee is used to proxy for the firm's ability to pay and hence the presence of rent sharing with workers. The Q/L variable is potentially endogenous and some authors instrument it in their regressions. The motivation for including local unemployment as a regressor in Eq. (2) is to test if local demand for and supply of labor affect wage outcomes (the "wage curve" hypothesis).[19]

[18] See e.g., Prasnikar et al. (1994).

Basu et al. (1995) instrument Q/L and estimate the wage equation jointly with the labor demand equation reported earlier, using contiguous 2-year panels of data in the general distributed lag framework. As may be seen from Table 6(A), in the immediately pre-transition period they find the estimated shortterm elasticity of the wage with respect to sales per employee to be zero in the Czech Republic and Hungary, 0.2 in Slovakia, and 0.3 in Poland. Within 1–2 years after the big bang the elasticity is estimated to be at 0.3–0.4 in all four countries. The results indicate that, except in Poland and to a lesser extent Slovakia, planners set wages relatively independently of the firm's performance, measured by sales per worker. However, during the transition wages started to vary systematically with revenues per worker, suggesting that rent sharing appeared as a phenomenon in all the transition economies. There is some indication that private firms may pay higher wages, ceteris paribus, in Poland and Slovakia, but the relationship is not robust and is absent in the Czech and Hungarian equations. The wage semi-elasticity with respect to local (district-level) unemployment rate is found to be statistically insignificant in all countries except for Poland, where a negative coefficient of -0.03 is found. Overall, the analysis based on firm-level data hence indicates that there is virtually no detectable "wage curve" effect in the CEE transition economies.

Basu et al. (1997) use panel data on 157 Polish industrial firms to estimate a first order distributed lag form of the wage Eq. (2) for the period 1992–1993.[20] Controlling for industry and region, they find the wage elasticity with respect to sales per worker to be 0.3 (Table 6(A)). This estimate is very similar to the 0.3–0.4 estimates obtained by Basu et al. (1997a) on all medium and large industrial firms. The authors find no significant association between ownership and commercialization of firms and wages, ceteris paribus.

Grosfeld and Nivet (1997) use the aforementioned dataset of 173 large Polish firms to estimate a first difference form of Eq. (2), having first established by a Chow test that the 1988–1994 period contains two structurally distinct periods, namely 1988–1991 and 1991–1994. As may be seen from Table 6(A), the authors find the wage elasticity with respect to output per worker to be declining from 0.2 to 0.1 between these two periods, but the decrease is not statistically significant. As in the case of the employment to output elasticity, their estimate is lower than that found on the population of Polish industrial firms by Basu et al. (1997). Grosfeld and Nivet (1997) also find that privatized firms increase wages about 15% faster than other firms during the 1991–1994 period.

Within the multi-country project focusing on behavioral differences between firms with increasing and decreasing real sales, Estrin and Svejnar (1998), Köllö (1997) and Commander and Dhar (1998) estimate log–linear first difference equations linking average wages to sales in the sampled firms and examining how this relationship varied across different types of firms before and during the transition.[21] Estrin and Svejnar (1998) use the same data as they did in estimating the employment equation discussed earlier. As may be

---

[19] See e.g., Blanchflower and Oswald (1994).

[20] The dataset is the same as the one containing the 161 firms used in the employment equation. However, four firms lacked all the data needed for estimating the wage equation.

seen from Table 6(B), for the Czech Republic the authors find very small (0.1) and gradually diminishing wage to sales elasticities in both the firms with increasing and decreasing sales.[22] For the transition period, these results are thus different from those obtained by Basu et al. (1995) in that the use of sales rather than sales per worker does not yield the link to wages and hence the implication that worker-insiders succeeded in appropriating enterprise revenues (profits) once central controls were lifted. On the basis of the Slovak data, Estrin and Svejnar (1998) obtain findings that parallel those of Basu et al. (1995) in that the estimated elasticities rise from 0 in the pre-transition period to 0.3 in firms with increasing sales and 0.4 in firms with decreasing sales in the early transition period (Table 6(B)). In the Slovak firms, the use of either sales per worker or sales hence leads to the conclusion that workers appear to have been able to capture some enterprise performance-related rents at the start of the transition. For Poland, Estrin and Svejnar (1998) obtain wage–sales elasticity estimates that rise from a pre-transition level of 0.1 to 0.4 during the transition in firms with increasing sales, and fall from 0.4 to 0 in firms with decreasing sales. The results suggest that in the pre-transition period workers in Polish firms experienced a relatively tight link between sales and wages in firms with decreasing sales. However, once the transition was launched, the sales-wage nexus was strengthened in firms with rising sales but it was severed in firms with declining sales. In the pre-transition period, Polish workers hence shared the firms' (mis)fortunes on the downside, while during the transition this link disappeared and they started sharing on the upside. The Hungarian elasticity estimates suggest that most firms had no significant relationship between sales and wages during the pre-transition and early transition period. The exception is firms with decreasing sales, which generated a negative elasticity estimate of −0.3 in the pre-transition (1988–1989) period. This raises the possibility that before the transition Hungarian firms actually faced softer budget constraints than firms in other CEE economies. However, as I discuss presently, Köllö's (1997) analysis of a larger dataset suggests that this finding does not hold in general.

Köllö (1997) uses the large 1986–1993 Hungarian datasets described earlier to estimate wage–sales, wage–sales per worker and wage–value added per worker elasticities. In the first difference, univariate regressions he finds continuously low (0.03–0.07) wage–sales elasticities in the firms with increasing sales and even smaller and decreasing (from 0.03 to 0) elasticities in firms with decreasing sales (Table 6(b)). The wage–sales per worker elasticities are similar, although the estimates for firms with increasing sales are somewhat higher (0.04–0.13) than in the wage–sales case. Elasticity estimates from multivariate regressions (including variables such as local unemployment and firm ownership) are similar. Köllö (1997) also reports cross-sectional estimates that yield wage-value added per worker estimates around 0.3 in 1986–1989 as well as in 1989–1992 and 1992–1993. Köllö (1997) also includes local unemployment in some of the wage regressions to check

---

[21] As mentioned earlier, these studies were constrained to use the same methodology. In this case the commonality meant that the authors used Q rather than Q/L as a regressor.

[22] The smallest value of estimates is found for firms with state and cooperative ownership.

the wage curve hypothesis. The effect of unemployment is small (0.03) and statistically insignificant in the first difference specification, but he finds a significant negative elasticity (-0.5 to -0.15) in the cross-sectional specification. Hence, the wage curve hypothesis receives little empirical support as an explanation of the annual change in wages but it seems to be consistent with cross-sectional differences.

Commander and Dhar (1998) use the Polish 2-digit industry data and estimate wage–sales per worker elasticities in a first difference log–linear regression. They obtain overall estimates of around 0.3 for firms with increasing sales and 0.8–0.9 for firms with decreasing sales. Estimates for contiguous 2-year panels indicate that the elasticity estimates remain roughly constant at 0.8–0.9 for firms with decreasing sales and that they are rising over time from 0.3 to 0.7 in firms with increasing sales. The rising elasticity estimates for firms with increasing sales are consistent with those obtained by Estrin and Svejnar (1998), but the high and constant estimates for firms with decreasing sales are at odds with the declining estimates found in the latter study.

Using the same Russian firm-level data described earlier, Earle et al. (1995) regress the average monthly wages of workers and managers, respectively, on the various ownership dummy variables. They find that newly established private firms pay higher wages to both managers and workers than do other firms, but that all ownership coefficients are statistically insignificant once the lagged dependent variable is included as a regressor. Hence, the de novo firms are on average smaller and pay higher wages, but their employment and wage behavior is not significantly different once adjusting for the level of employment or wages.

Finally, Jones and Kato (1996) use a 1989–1992 balanced panel of annual firm-level data from three Bulgarian surveys to estimate the determinants of compensation of chief executive officers (CEO) of these firms. With about 20% of the firms changing ownership from completely state-owned to at least partially non-state-owned, the authors are able to assess the effect of ownership on CEO compensation. Jones and Kato (1996) use a fixed effects model, with the regression specified with traditional as well as non-traditional explanatory variables. The authors find that in the traditional specification, including firm size and accounting measures of performance, CEO compensation is strongly linked to firm size but essentially unrelated to return on assets or profit margin of the firm. However, when labor productivity is included in the regression, the authors find a strong relationship between this variable and CEO compensation in most specifications. However, the relationship is significantly weaker in firms with complete state ownership.

5.1. Summary

The studies reviewed in this section indicate that, except for Poland, wages were set relatively independently of firms' performance under communism. During the transition, wages started to vary systematically with revenues per worker, suggesting that rent sharing appeared as a phenomenon in all the CEE economies. This relationship is not found in some studies, however, when total revenue rather than revenue per worker is used as an explanatory variable. Interestingly, evidence from Bulgaria suggests that the compensation of chief executives in not fully state-owned firms is positively related to labor productivity.

As in the case of employment, the effect of ownership and commercialization on wages is mixed. While there is some evidence that private firms tend to pay higher wages than other firms, the evidence is not robust and relates only to some countries. Finally, within the firm-level studies, there is little evidence of a detectable "wage curve" effect.

6. Fringe benefits

Several studies have examined systematically the change in fringe benefit provision during the transition. Estrin et al. (1997) use data from a sample of 200 Polish firms in the 1991–1993 period to examine the determinants of the provision of a number of benefits. Their basic finding is that benefits were found much more in state-owned and privatized firms than in newly established private firms. Most firms offered holiday subsidies, health care and a housing subsidy, while some also provided child care facilities and food subsidies. Estrin et al. (1997) first examine the determinants of the number of benefits provided by the firms. They use an ordered logit procedure estimating the probability of the number of benefits as a function of firm ownership, size of firm (proxied by employment), extent of labor force unionization, two indicators of enterprise performance (the growth of sales from 1992 to 1993 and the profit to sale ratio in 1993), the average wage in 1993, and a dummy variable for firms in which the wage control tax was binding. The authors find that state owned and privatized firms are not statistically different in their benefit provision but that *de novo* firms provide significantly fewer benefits. The effect of size is positive, while that of unionism is insignificant. The rest of the findings are somewhat surprising in that faster growing firms offer fewer benefits, the effect of profitability is insignificant, high wage firms offer more benefits (wages and benefits are complements rather than substitutes), and firms constrained by the wage tax do not offer more benefits.

Motivated by the general belief that the provision of fringe benefits would decrease during the transition, Estrin et al. (1997) also use managers' answers to questions about the increase or decrease of social benefits to assess the effect of several explanatory variables on the change in the extent of benefit provision between 1991 and 1993. With the managers' answers falling into four categories (increase, no change, small fall, and large fall), the authors use ordered logit to estimate the effects of the explanatory variables. They find that state-owned and state-owned as well as commercialized firms experienced a greater decline in benefit provision than privatized or newly established firms. The decline was positively related to the size of firm, presumably reflecting the fact that larger firms provided more benefits under the previous regime. The decline was related negatively to profitability, suggesting that the financial situation of the firm affects the size of decline in benefits. Interestingly, benefits are reduced more in enterprises where the wage control tax was binding. The estimates from these "difference" regressions based on managers' opinions are hence different from the logit regressions related to the number of provided benefits.

Earle (1997) uses data from 22 Romanian industries to test the hypotheses that (a) firms attempting to reduce costs will have an incentive to lay off workers rather than reduce hours of work since the cost of many benefits is incurred on a per worker rather than per hour basis and (b) the value of benefits to workers exceeds their cost. He finds mild support for the former but not for the latter hypothesis.

Filer et al. (1997) use 1993 data from 3500 firms in the Czech Republic grouped at the level of a two-digit industry classification. The authors regress benefits as a share of base wage on four explanatory variables (sales per worker, percentage change in the labor force between 1992 and 1993, percentage change in sales between 1992 and 1993, and percentage of privately owned firms in the industry). Benefits are measured narrowly (non-insurance benefits plus voluntary insurance) as well as more broadly (including also bonuses and profit sharing pay). The authors find that fringe benefits were more important relative to wages in industries with higher productivity and in industries with a higher proportion of non-private (primarily state-owned) firms. Moreover, there was a negative relationship between changes in the size of the firms' labor force and the broad (but not the narrow) measure of benefits. This implies that shrinking firms made greater use of bonuses and profit sharing. This finding is consistent with these firms being further along the restructuring process – shedding labor as well as relying more on incentive compensation schemes.

6.1. Summary

While data limitations prevent us from drawing strong conclusions about the provision of fringe benefits by firms in CEE countries, there appear to be some clear patterns as well as changes in the provision of these benefits. In particular, the Polish and Czech evidence suggests that benefits are more prevalent in state-owned and privatized firms than in newly established private firms. Moreover, the evidence from the Czech Republic and Romania suggests that firms that are restructuring may be exploiting the incentive aspects of fringe benefits.

7. Individual wages and human capital

A number of researchers have estimated Mincer-type earnings functions in the CEE countries. A formal analysis of the returns to education is of major interest because the Communist regime stressed equality and strove to privilege workers over the "intellectuals". A priori, one would hence expect that the rate of returns on education was low under central planning but increased as these countries moved toward a market economy. There is a competing hypothesis, however, namely that human capital and experience gained under communism may not be very useful in a market economy. If correct, this latter hypothesis would predict that the rate of return to education and experience would fall from the pre-transition to the transition period.

Flanagan (1994) provides the first set of estimates based on June 1988 and June 1991 surveys of wages in the Czech Republic. The 1988 survey covers 526,223 employees, while the 1991 survey interviewed 10,373 employees. Since individual data were not released, Flanagan uses data grouped into four schooling and 11 experience cells. For each cell he has separate data on men and women. The dependent variable is the logarithm of full-time monthly wage. As may be seen from Table 7, Flanagan's (1994) estimates indicate that already in 1988 there was a significant positive effect (0.044) of each year of schooling, with the estimated gender-specific coefficients being 0.034 for men and 0.054 for women. By 1991 the estimated overall effect is 0.049, with the coefficient for men being 0.44 and for women 0.53. The only statistically significant change is the increase in the rate of return on education for men.

Flanagan (1994) also estimates the earnings function with education entered in the form of categorical variables capturing vocational, high school and university education. In this specification he finds a decrease in the rate of return to vocational education (from 0.11 to 0.07) and an increase in the rate of return to university education (from 0.31 to 0.39) for men. Flanagan (1994) concludes that central planners provided positive returns to human capital but that these were lower than those obtained in advanced market economies. Yet, he also finds that by June 1991, the transition brought the returns to education to the level observed in some market economies with centralized wage determination. Finally, Flanagan (1994) finds that the return on experience (gained under communism) declines during the transition.

Chase (1997) uses micro data from four similar surveys to examine changes in the earnings structure between Communist and post-Communist Czech Republic and Slovakia. The micro data were collected in the two republics in 1984 and 1993 and thus span a longer pre-transition and transition period than the data used by Flanagan (1994). Chase (1997) uses the Mincer specification with a generalized Tobit model to correct for possible selection bias in the earnings function of women. As may be seen from Table 7, he finds that return to education increased for men and women, with returns to men increasing more than for women. In examining the return to different types of education, Chase's findings corroborate those of Flanagan's: the exceptional return accorded traditionally to those with secondary technical education is diminished as those with academic secondary education experienced a large earnings increase between 1984 and 1993. Returns to experience fell as private sector opportunities for younger, less experienced workers became available. Finally, earnings structures are found to have changed more in the Czech Republic than Slovakia. In particular, in the Czech lands earnings became more dispersed, returns to education increased more and returns to experience fell more.

Rutkowski (1997) uses the Polish Household Budget Survey for 1987 and 1992 to estimate the effects of education and experience before and during the transition. With data on 25,456 individuals in 1987 and 6513 individuals in 1992, he finds that the rate of return to an additional year of education rises significantly from 0.05 in 1987 to 0.07 in 1992

Table 7
Rate of return to 1 year of education

Authors	Country	Pre-transition			During transition			Data	Method
		Male	Female	M&F	Male	Female	M&F		
Flanagan (1994)	Czech R.	0.034	0.054	0.044	0.044	0.053	0.049	Grouped data from 1988 and 1991 surveys	Human capital earnings function
Chase (1997)	Czech R. Slovak R.	0.024 0.028	0.042 0.044		0.052 0.049	0.058 0.054		Micro data from 1984 and 1993 surveys	Human capital earnings function with a Tobit correction
Rukowski (1997)	Poland	–	–	0.05	–	–	0.07 to 0.08	Micro data from 1987 and 1992 household budget surveys and 1992, 1995, and 1996 labor force surveys	Human capital earnings function
Krueger and Pischke (1995)	East Germany	0.071	0.085	0.077	–	–	0.062	Micro data from 1988 and 1991 East German surveys	Human capital earnings function
Bird et al. 1994	East Germany	–	–	0.044	–	–	0.041	Micro data from 1989 and 1991 East German surveys	Human capital earnings function

(Table 7). Rutkowski (1997) also estimates the Mincerian earnings function using data from the Labor Force Surveys for 1992, 1995 and 1996. As may be seen from Table 7, these estimates yield a return to one more year of education of 0.08 in 1992, 0.07 in 1995 and 0.08 in 1996. The estimates also show that the rate of return in the private sector is almost one percentage point higher than the return in the public sector. In contrast to the increase in returns to education from pre-transition to the transition period, Rutkowski (1997) finds that the return to an additional year of experience fell from over 3% in the late 1980s to less than 2% in the early 1990s.

In two interesting studies, Krueger and Pischke (1995) and Bird et al. (1994) estimate human capital earnings functions for East Germany before and during the transition. Krueger and Pischke (1995) use the 1988 Survey on Income of Blue- and White-Collar Households in East Germany before the transition and the 1991 German Socio-Economic Panel of Households for after the transition began. The sample size ranges from 43,532 individuals in 1988 to 1795 individuals in 1991. As may be seen from Table 7, the authors find that the rate of return to education fell from 0.077 to 0.062, suggesting that education from the communist era is less valuable in the market environment, counter to the findings for the Czech Republic and Poland. Moreover, the already flat experience profiles have become even flatter during the transition. Finally, in 1988, women had higher returns to education than men.

Bird et al. (1994) use the German Socio-Economic Panel, which provides retrospective data for 1989 and current data for 1991 for East Germany. The 1989 data cover 1134 individuals and the 1991 data cover 715 persons. Bird et al. (1994) find that the point estimate of the rate of return to an additional year of education was 0.044 in 1989 and fell to 0.041 by 1991 (Table 7). The 1989–1991 decline is not statistically significant but the rate of return in East Germany in this period is significantly lower than the rate of 0.067 found in the 1989 survey in the Federal Republic of Germany. The return to overall experience did not change in East Germany between 1989 and 1991, but the return on firm-specific experience decreased from 0.002 to becoming statistically insignificant at 0.001. A comparison of the East and West German estimates for the experience coefficients indicates that the experience-earnings profile was flatter in East Germany than in West Germany.

The remaining studies use categorical variables to measure of education. Jones and Ilayperuma (1994) use subsets of 1989 and 1992 Bulgarian worker surveys, covering 2090 and 2661 workers, respectively. They estimate augmented human capital earnings functions and find that the return to higher (15+ years) education increased significantly between 1989 and 1992 for women, while for men there is no education effect found in 1989 and only a relatively small effect is found in 1991. The results are unaffected by using monthly or hourly earnings as the dependent variable. The Blinder–Oaxaca and Blau–Kahn decompositions suggest that most of the male-female gap in earnings arises because women receive a lower rate of return on their endowments. Between 1989 and 1992, the gap increased by 25% because of changes in characteristics and by 53% as a result of changes in returns to factors.

Orazem and Vodopivec (1997) use Slovene administrative data on about 15,000 individuals in 1987 and 10,000 in 1991 to estimate human capital earnings functions with education entered as a categorical variable. The authors find that average returns to education rose for all educational groups relative to those in the least educated group. Thus men with 4-year university education gained 23% relative to those with unfinished elementary education between 1987 and 1991. The relative wage gains for women are similar but less pronounced. Unlike in the other CEE economies, returns to experience are found to rise from 1987 to 1991. The effect is driven by a sharp increase in relative wages of retirement age workers, which is in turn probably brought about by large outflows of pension-age workers from the Slovene labor force.

Halpern and Körosi (1997) estimate augmented human capital earnings functions using 1986, 1989, 1992, 1993 and 1994 Hungarian labor market survey data. The number of individuals surveyed varies between 97,190 and 591,528. The authors find that the estimated return on university education relative to primary (8 years) schooling rises from 45% in 1986 to 62% in 1989 and remains in a 56 to 61% range thereafter. The relative return to those with 12 years of education rises from 14% in 1986 to 20% in 1989 and stays in a 16–20% range in the 1990s. The earnings–experience profile becomes flatter in the 1990s as compared to the 1980s, suggesting that experience from the communist period lost some of its value.

7.1. Summary

Overall, with the exception of East Germany and to some extent possibly men in Bulgaria, the various studies surveyed in this section suggest that returns to education increased during the transition as compared to the pre-transition period. This suggests that education acquired under communism has a higher payoff during the transition but that a rapid introduction of a market economy and western wage scales, as happened in East Germany with the unification, may result in a decrease in the payoff to this human capital. The studies also indicate that women enjoyed a higher rate of return on education than men under communism and that the gap narrowed as the transition started. In several countries, there is evidence that return to experience obtained under communism fell during the transition.

8. Unemployment

A fundamental systemic feature of the Soviet-type, centrally planned economies was the non-existence of open unemployment. An equally distinguishing feature of the transition to a market economy has been the rapid emergence of double-digit unemployment rates accompanied by long spells of unemployment. The rise in the unemployment rate into double digits occurred in all the rapidly transforming economies except for the Czech Republic, where the rate remained at 3–5% and spells of unemployment remained relatively short throughout the 1990s.[23]

J. Svejnar

In view of the unemployment problem, researchers have examined two important sets of issues. First, the discrepancy between the unemployment experience of the Czech Republic and the other CEE economies has posed a fundamental academic as well as policy-related puzzle. Why has the Czech Republic been exhibiting so much lower unemployment rates than its traditional counterpart republic (Slovakia) and the other transition economies? Are there policy lessons in the Czech case? Second, how can governments of the transition economies strike a balance between (a) reducing government interventions and introducing market incentives, and (b) providing an adequate social safety net that ensures popular support for the transition?

In trying to tackle the first set of issues, the researchers noted that, while all the CEE countries had similar flows into unemployment from employment at the start of the transition, the Czech Republic had a dramatically higher outflow rate of individuals from unemployment (see e.g., Boeri, 1994; Boeri and Scarpetta, 1995). This basic finding has focused the attention of researchers on the determinants of outflow from unemployment to jobs and led to a number of studies in many of the CEE economies. The studies may be divided into those using individual data to estimate unemployment duration (hazard) models and those using district or regional data to estimate the efficiency of matching of the unemployed and vacancies.

The second set of issues has been approached through analyses of the responsiveness of unemployment duration to the parameters of passive labor market policies (such as the unemployment compensation system) and active labor market policies (such as the training programs for the unemployed). The motivation for analyzing the effects of passive labor market policies is that they have provided a partial safety net (and thus mitigated the opposition to the transition) but also may have generated economic inefficiency and large government expenditures because of poor incentive effects and moral hazard. Similarly, active labor market policies tend to entail considerable government expenditures that are warranted during the austerity of the transition only if the policies result in successful re-employment of the unemployed.

8.1. Unemployment duration

Ham et al. (1998) examine both of the above issues by analyzing a) what explains the differences in the outflows to jobs in the Czech and Slovak republics and b) the extent to which the unemployment compensation system (UCS) plays a role in lengthening unemployment spells. Ham et al.'s (1998) data collection and analysis is motivated by the fact that in comparing the Czech experience to that of the other CEE countries, policy makers and researchers are hampered by the difficulty in accounting for differences in the relevant laws and institutions, and differences in the definitions of economic and demographic variables. To minimize this difficulty, the authors collected parallel micro datasets from

---

[23] The double-digit rates of unemployment emerged in all the CEE economies within 2–3 years of the launching of the transition. Economies that delayed stabilization and transformation (e.g., Ukraine) maintained low unemployment rate for a number of years.

the Czech and Slovak republics. They take the Slovak Republic as the best "comparison" country for the Czech republic, because the two republics were one country from 1918 to January 1993 (except during World War II). As a result, the two republics shared the same laws, institutions, currency and government programs both before and during the early 1990s period when unemployment rose rapidly in Slovakia and the other CEEs. Moreover, except for unemployment, aggregate economic indicators of the two countries were very similar in the early 1990s (see Tables 1–3 and Dyba and Svejnar, 1995). The Czech-Slovak comparison has a broader validity since the Slovak labor market indicators have been similar to those of the other CEE economies.

The data used by Ham et al. (1998) consist of a stratified random sample of 1262 Czech and 1292 Slovak men who registered as unemployed at the district labor offices between October 1, 1991 and March 31, 1992. The authors followed these individuals from the onset to the end of their unemployment spell or to the end of July 1993, whichever came first. The sample includes both recipients of unemployment benefits as well as non-recipients (unemployed who were not eligible for unemployment benefits), thus permitting the authors to use an additional measure of the effect of UCS on unemployment duration.[24] Ham et al. (1998) use weekly data on the duration of unemployment spells to estimate a duration model. They denote the hazard function (the probability of leaving unemployment) in week r of the spell as

$$\lambda(r|\theta) = [1 + \exp(-y(r|\theta))]^{-1}, \tag{3}$$

where

$$y(r|\theta) = h(r) + \alpha_0(B(r) + \alpha_1 W + g(E(r)) + X(r)\Pi + \theta, \tag{4}$$

θ represents an unobserved heterogeneity component, $h(r)$ is the effect of duration dependence on the hazard, $B(r)$ is unemployment benefits in week r, W is the individual's previous wage, $g(\cdot)$ equals a function of remaining entitlement $E(r)$ in week r, and $X(r)$ contains variables measuring demographic characteristics and demand conditions in week r.[25] The authors estimate the model by maximum likelihood and control for duration dependence using a high order polynomial in log duration. They follow Heckman and Singer (1984) and assume that θ is drawn from a discrete distribution with J support points and associated probabilities $P_1, ..., P_{J-1}$. The number of mass points of support J is determined by the data.

The identification of the unemployment benefit and entitlement effects is problematic in most studies since benefits and entitlement are often a function of duration and they vary little over the unemployed population. Ham et al. (1998) identify five sources of independent variation in benefit levels and two in the entitlement effects. Their methodology is

---

[24] Non-recipients are registered at the district labor offices for a number of reasons, but primarily to receive social welfare benefits.

[25] All variables are individual-specific.

instructive for other researchers of the CEE countries since the structure of the UCS is similar in these economies.

The first principal result of the Ham et al. (1998) analysis comes from their Oaxaca-type decomposition of the difference in the (non-linear) expected unemployment durations between the Czech and Slovak republics. With the average unemployment spell being four times longer in Slovakia than the Czech Republic, the authors find that nearly one-third of this difference is explained by differences in observable demand conditions (as measured by district level unemployment and vacancy rates and industrial production) and the industrial employment structure in the two republics. The remaining two-thirds are accounted for by the different behavior of firms, individuals and institutions in the labor market, as reflected by differences in the coefficients of the hazard functions. Very little of the difference in expected unemployment duration comes from differences in the demographic variables between the two republics.

The second principal finding is that in both the Czech and Slovak Republics the generosity of UCS has only a moderate negative effect on economic efficiency in terms of lengthening an unemployment spell. The elasticity of unemployment duration with respect to the level of unemployment benefits is found to be 0.6 in the Czech Republic and not significantly different from 0 in Slovakia.[26] The estimated elasticity of unemployment duration with respect to the length of remaining entitlement to benefits is 0.55 in the Czech Republic and 0.41 in Slovakia. These elasticity estimates are moderate in comparison with the corresponding western estimates. Finally, during the last week of entitlement one observes a higher exit rate among married and single men in Slovakia, as well as among married men in the Czech Republic. This raises the possibility that the UCS has a perverse incentive effect in that the unemployed delay taking jobs until they exhaust their unemployment benefits. In fact, the size of this "last week spike" effect and the proportion of unemployed that are involved are so small as to make this disincentive effect miniscule. The various UCS results hence suggest that policy makers in both the low and high unemployment transition economies have considerable latitude in providing an adequate social safety net without jeopardizing efficiency.[27]

The estimated coefficients on the demographic and demand variables indicate that the effects are qualitatively similar in the two republics. However, the effects differ in terms of the significance of some coefficients and also in that the absolute effects are greater in Slovakia than the Czech lands because of the longer unemployment spells. In particular, Ham et al. (1998) find that both Romanies (gypsies) and the handicapped have a much longer unemployment spells than others in each republic (whether or not they receive unemployment benefits). However, while in Slovakia the unemployed with only a compulsory education (8 years) have a significantly lower probability of finding a job than individuals with secondary and university education, in the Czech Republic this effect

---

[26] The Slovak point estimate of the elasticity and the associated standard error imply a upper bound for the elasticity of 0.1.

[27] For elasticity estimates in western economies, see Devine and Kiefer (1991).

holds only for non-recipients. Among the recipients of unemployment benefits, the least and most educated in the Czech Republic have similar probabilities of moving from unemployment – only individuals with vocational high school education have an easier time finding a job. Similarly, while married men have shorter unemployment spells than single men in Slovakia, in the Czech lands the effect holds only for non-recipients and in relatively restrictive specifications for recipients. Finally, one does not find a significant effect of age on the probability of exit in Slovakia but the effect is significantly negative in the Czech Republic.

In a recent analysis of the women's data from the same dataset, Ham et al. (1999) obtain broadly similar results as they do for men. Using a Oaxaca type decomposition, they find that more than two-thirds of the difference in the Slovak and Czech women's unemployment durations is accounted for by differences in the estimated coefficients of their hazard functions. The effect of the UCS (benefits and entitlement) on women's unemployment duration, estimated separately for single and married women, is insignificant for single women in both republics. While married women in both republics are somewhat sensitive to changes in entitlement, the elasticity of unemployment duration with respect to benefits is not significant. In terms of demographic variables, the findings that are different from those for men suggest that in both republics unemployment duration is unrelated to age, married women have a lower probability of leaving unemployment for a job than single women, and both the least and most educated have a lower probability of exit than those with secondary education.

Related to Ham et al. (1998, 1999) are four studies, two dealing with the Czech Republic and two with Slovakia. These studies address some of the same issues analyzed by Ham et al. (1998, 1999) but they use panel data from the recently available Labor Force Surveys (LFSs). They also use similar methodologies and it is hence useful to consider them together before turning to studies dealing with the other CEE economies.

Sorm and Terrell (1997) use micro data from the 1994, 1995 and 1996 LFS to analyze the flows of individuals across the principal labor market states in the Czech Republic using quarterly panel data for individuals in approximately 11,000 households. The authors constructed separate panels for cohorts of individuals that entered the samples in the first quarters of 1994, 1995 and 1996 and they follow them from the second through the fourth quarters of each year. The authors estimate multinomial logits for transitions out of unemployment, employment and out of the labor force. I will only report on the analysis of the unemployed. Sorm and Terrell (1997) find that no particular demographic group (in terms of age, education, marital status, and gender) is having a particularly difficult or easy time leaving unemployment for employment over the 3 years. For example, whereas in 1995 the probability of exit was positively related to the age of the unemployed, in 1994 and 1996 the effect was insignificant. In 1995 and 1996 the more educated found a job more easily than the less educated, but in 1994 education was not a determinant of flows to employment. Marital status and gender play no role except in 1996, when married men had a higher probability of finding a job than single men or women (single as well as married).

The one stable relationship is that the longer term unemployed have a more difficult time finding a job than others in all 3 years.

Using the Czech LFS data, Finta and Terrell (1997) analyze the labor force transitions of men and women separately, pooling data over 14 consecutive quarterly transitions from 1993 to 1996. They use a proportional hazard model (with a logit specification) and find that the hazard of leaving unemployment for employment falls with age for both men and women, is higher for the more educated compared to the least educated, falls for married women relative to single women but is higher for married men relative to single men, and varies across regions for both men and women. Finally, those who were registered at the district labor office (and hence more likely to be receiving unemployment or welfare benefits) tend to have longer spells and those with longer unemployment spells have a more difficult time finding a job.

In a parallel study, Lubyova and van Ours (1997a) use eight consecutive quarters of the Slovak LFS during 1994 and 1995. The Slovak and Czech LFSs have a similar design and the results may hence be compared to those of Finta and Terrell (1997) and Sorm and Terrell (1997) for the Czech Republic. Lubyova and van Ours (1997a) pool the data and estimate separate models for men and women. They use a proportional hazard model with a flexible baseline hazard and estimate the parameters by maximum likelihood. They find that the probability of exiting to a job is (a) unrelated to age, (b) lower for single than married males, (c) positively related to the level of education for men but not for women,[28] and (d) negatively related to local unemployment rate. Unemployment benefit variables and variables capturing the presence of children do not affect the hazard.

The impact of the Slovak UCS is also analyzed by Lubyova and van Ours (1997b). The authors use Slovak district-level micro data on 10,790 unemployed in 1991–1992 and 18,603 unemployed in 1994–1995 to estimate the effects of 1992 and 1995 changes in the Slovak UCS. They adopt a proportional hazard (competing risk) model with a flexible baseline hazard and find that the changes in the entitlement period increased the outflow but to destinations other than regular jobs. They suggest that the finding may mean that the unemployed may be moving into subsidized jobs.

The other studies of unemployment duration in CEE analyze the determinants of duration within individual high unemployment countries. Most of these studies use the logistic hazard model of Eq. (3) to examine the determinants of the probability that individuals move across labor market states. Relatively few studies control for unobserved heterogeneity and they differ in how they identify the unemployment benefit and entitlement effects.

Bellmann et al. (1995) use a November 1990 survey of 10,751 randomly selected individuals in East Germany. The participants were interviewed twice at 4-month intervals, enabling the authors to construct a transition database. The authors use the data to generate multinomial logit estimates of transitions from unemployment to employment at

---

[28] Women with primary and university education have the same probability of exit to job, while women with secondary education enjoy a much higher probability.

the start of the East German transition. They find that for men the outflow from unemployment is significantly lower for workers aged 50 or more, as well as for married workers. Moreover, a 1% increase in the mean monthly unemployment benefit reduces the transition probability to employment by 0.7%, a figure that is somewhat higher than but broadly comparable to the elasticity found by Ham et al. (1998) for the Czech Republic. For women, Bellman et al. (1995) find that the probability of moving from unemployment into employment rises with education but that age, marital status and other factors that mattered for men do not have a statistically significant effect.

Abraham and Vodopivec (1993) use a rich set of administrative records that contain information on labor market transitions of 46,102 individuals in Slovenia between 1986 and 1992. They estimate a hazard model of exit from unemployment to employment, treating exits to out of the labor force as censored. The authors find that older workers (aged 50 or more) and the least educated individuals had a more difficult time exiting unemployment for employment already before the transition started and that this phenomenon continued during the transition. Coefficients that were insignificant before the transition but became significant during the transition suggest that (a) the unemployed with higher education started to have a higher probability of finding a job than those with middle school education, (b) those who became unemployed because of the bankruptcy of their firm started to have an easier time finding a job than others, and (c) non-Slovenians experienced longer unemployment duration than Slovenians. The effect of non-Slovenians is interesting in comparison with the strong effect of Romanies in Ham et al.'s (1998) analysis of the Czech and Slovak data.

Micklewright and Nagy (1995) examine the effect of a major reduction in entitlement in the Hungarian unemployment compensation scheme at the end of 1992 on the speed with which individuals left the unemployment register. The authors use micro data on 80,711 unemployed, 50,411 of which were administered under the 1992 scheme and 30,270 were administered under the 1993 scheme. Using a non-parametric hazard approach, Micklewright and Nagy (1995) find little or no evidence that the introduction of the more austere 1993 entitlement scheme raised the job exit hazard, a finding which is consistent with that of Ham et al. (1998, 1999) for the Czech and Slovak Republics. Micklewright and Nagy (1995) also find very little rise in the job exit hazard near the time when unemployment benefits expire. This suggests that the UCS does not contain negative incentives that would induce claimants to put off taking a job until the unemployment benefits run out.

Micklewright and Nagy (1997) analyze the effects that the exhaustion of unemployment benefits and the probability of subsequently qualifying for means-tested social benefits have on exit of individuals from unemployment to jobs. The authors are motivated by the fact that long term unemployment has become a serious problem in Hungary, with the exhaustion of entitlement to unemployment benefits being the single most likely way of leaving the unemployment register. They use a sample of 28,600 individuals who entered the Hungarian unemployment register in March and April 1994 and had a continuous or near-continuous employment history in the preceding 4 years. This made the sampled individuals eligible for 11–12 months of unemployment benefits and almost one-half of them exhausted their entitlement. One-third of these exhaustees were surveyed at random 3–4 months after the exhaustion of unemployment benefits in order to obtain information about living standards and responses to incentives. Using non-parametric hazard analysis, the authors find that there exists a group of about 8% of unemployed who time the start of a new job to the exhaustion of unemployment benefits. They point out that this is a relatively small group and show that job search behavior around the time of exhaustion of unemployment benefits is not strongly related to the probability of entitlement to social benefits. Micklewright and Nagy (1997) go on to estimate a logistic hazard model of duration in unemployment following exhaustion of unemployment benefits. They find the elasticity of the hazard with respect to the expected social benefits to be −0.7, which is moderate by western standards and parallels the authors' (1995) estimated effect of the 1993 change in the entitlement to unemployment benefits. In terms of the demographic and other variables, Micklewright and Nagy (1997) find that age and being single has a strong negative effect on the exit hazard for men but not women, education (except for university educated men) has a positive effect on exit hazard, and the effect of local unemployment rate varies with specification.

Jones and Kato (1997) use a three-wave panel of data for a sample of 320 women and 143 men who were registered as unemployed in Bulgaria during the 1991–1992 period. They estimate multinomial and binomial logit models of unemployment transitions. The authors find that for women the probability of moving from unemployment to employment is positively related to higher education, labor force experience, union membership, and not receiving unemployment benefits, but that these factors are insignificant for men. In fact, the only variables that increase the men's probability of moving from unemployment to employment are affiliation with a political party and having participated in a retraining program. The lack of significance of most coefficients for men may in part be brought about by the small sample size.

Lenkova (1995) carried out a similar analysis on a Bulgarian micro dataset consisting of 351 randomly selected new unemployed in the last quarter of 1991, 640 new unemployed in the last quarter of 1992 and 828 new unemployed in the last quarter of 1993. Lenkova's (1995) analysis of the pooled data suggests that the hazard of leaving unemployment for a job is negatively related to age, being a woman and receiving unemployment benefits.

In assessing the impact of training programs in Albania, Dushi (1997) administered a survey to 1141 individuals from six Albanian districts. With 375 of these individuals participating and 766 not participating in a training program, Dushi (1997) estimates two hazard functions of leaving unemployment for employment with different specifications of unobserved heterogeneity (constant term vs. a discrete distribution with two points of support). She finds that the probability of leaving unemployment for employment is higher for those who participated in the training program and lower for those who never worked before. There is no statistically significant relationship of the hazard to age, gender, marital status, education local unemployment rate, number of children, and whether or not the unemployed has been receiving unemployment benefits. In terms of the paucity of significant coefficients, Dushi's (1997) results resemble those of Sorm and Terrell (1997).

Finally, Foley (1997) uses panel data from Round 1–4 (1992–1994) of the Russian Longitudinal Monitoring Survey to estimate several multinomial logit models, including those of transitions from unemployment to employment. The survey contains data on 6500 randomly selected Russian households. Foley (1997) uses a sample of 1089 unemployed, with 57% of the observations being censored. Since Russia does not have an effective system of unemployment compensation, Foley's study is unique in that it analyzes the effect of various factors on the length of unemployment spells in the absence of an unemployment compensation system. Like Ham et al. (1998), Foley (1997) controls for unobserved heterogeneity but finds that the estimated coefficients are not significantly affected by this correction. Foley (1997) finds that married women experience longer durations than married men before finding jobs, better educated individuals do not find jobs more quickly than the less-educated ones and local unemployment rate is positively related to the duration of unemployment.

8.2. Matching functions

A significant part of the western literature has approached the issues of exit from unemployment in the context of matching functions. The basic assumption in this literature is that the outflow (number of individuals flowing) from unemployment to employment O is a function of the number of unemployed U and the number of posted vacancies V, $O = f(U, V)$. The process of matching is seen as a technological process of search, with both the unemployed and employers with vacant positions striving to find the best match, given exogenous factors such as skill and spatial mismatch, as well as availability of information. Some authors (e.g., Blanchard and Diamond, 1989; Pissarides, 1990) suggest that the matching function f displays constant returns to scale, while others have identified reasons, such as externalities in the search process, heterogeneity in the unemployed and vacancies and lags between matching and hiring, why increasing returns may prevail (see e.g., Diamond, 1982; Profit, 1996). Increasing returns are conceptually important because they constitute a necessary condition for multiple equilibria and possibly a rationale for government intervention.

In specifying the matching process, the most frequently used functional form is Cobb–Douglas,

$$\log O_{i,t} = c + \beta_U \log U_{i,t-1} + \beta_V \log V_{i,t-1} + \alpha_i + \lambda_t + \varepsilon_{i,t}, \tag{5}$$

where $U_{i,t-1}$, and $V_{i,t-1}$ represent the number of unemployed and vacancies at the end of period $t - 1$, respectively, $O_{i,t}$ denotes the outflow to jobs (the number of successful matches between the currently unemployed and current vacancies) and constant c captures the efficiency of matching. The terms α_i, λ_t and $\varepsilon_{i,t}$ represent the district-specific, time-specific and overall unexplained stochastic part of the matching process.

In view of the serious unemployment problem in the CEE economies, the literature on the matching of unemployed and vacancies in these economies has grown very rapidly. It has also produced contradictory results, in part because the studies use different methodologies and data. Methodologically, the studies differ especially with respect to (a) the specification of the production function and treatment of returns to scale, (b) the extent to which Eq. (5) is augmented by other variables that might affect outflows and (c) whether or not they use static or dynamic models. In terms of data, the studies differ in whether they use annual, quarterly or monthly panels of district-level or more aggregate (regional) data and whether they cover short or long time periods.

In the first study in this area, Burda (1993) uses monthly Czech and Slovak district-level data from October 1990 to May 1992 (with considerable gaps for Slovakia) to estimate simple static matching functions, regressing the logarithm of monthly gross exits from unemployment into employment on previous month's unemployment and vacancies. His OLS estimates of Cobb–Douglas function parameters using pooled sample indicate that the coefficient on unemployment is about twice as high as that on vacancies and that the matching function displays constant or decreasing returns to scale. In Slovakia, the coefficient on vacancies is small and statistically insignificant in the cross-sectional estimates.

Boeri (1994) uses regional panel data for varying periods for the Czech Republic (1991:3–1993:5), Hungary (1991:10–1993:3), Poland (1992:9–1993:3), and Slovakia (1992:5–1993:6) to estimate a Cobb–Douglas matching function in vacancies and unemployment, with unemployment entered as a CES function of short and long term unemployment. His pooled OLS estimates also suggest that vacancies have a relatively small effect on outflow to jobs and that the impact of long term unemployed is significantly lower than the impact of short term unemployed.

Svejnar et al. (1995) estimate augmented matching functions in order to assess whether factors other than unemployment and vacancies systematically affect outflow. The authors use annual 1992 and 1993 data from the Czech and Slovak Republics and regress for each annual cross-section the logarithm of the average monthly outflows in each district on the logarithm of district-level unemployed and number of vacancies, demographic characteristics of the district, district demand variables, structural variables and the level of per capita expenditures on active labor market policies. In their seemingly unrelated regressions across the 2 years they find the coefficient on unemployment to be about 0.8 in the Czech Republic and about 0.4–0.6 in Slovakia, while the coefficient on vacancies is about 0.14–0.17 in Slovakia and insignificant in the Czech lands. In assessing the impact of active labor market policies (ALMPs), such as job subsidies, public jobs creation and training of the unemployed, the authors find that a 1% increase in per capita expenditures on ALMPs increases outflows by 0.17% in the Czech Republic but has no statistically significant effect on outflows in Slovakia in these 2 years. In addition, the analysis points to demand conditions (captured by variation in industrial production rather than just by the number of vacancies) as important determinants of the larger Czech outflow rate. In particular, decreases in industrial output in the district are found to bring about a larger decrease in the outflow rate in the Slovak Republic than in the Czech Republic. Tests of equality of coefficients across the 2 years lead to a rejection of the null hypothesis, indicating that the transition indeed changes the regime and that it is thus important to allow for changes in the structure of the underlying model over time.

Lubyova and van Ours (1994) estimate Cobb–Douglas matching functions on monthly data for the period 1990:10–1993:12 in Slovakia and 1991:11–993:12 in the Czech Republic. In order to allow for matching across districts, they estimate the matching functions on regional as opposed to the more disaggregated district-level data. The authors estimate the matching function separately on the monthly data for each region and search for structural breaks in order to allow for uneven transition process across regions. The estimated coefficients point to strongly increasing returns to scale in all eight regions of the Czech Republic and two of the four Slovak regions. The structural shift coefficients suggest that there was a negative efficiency shift in two regions of the Czech Republic, a positive shift in one Czech and two Slovak regions, and no shift in five Czech and two Slovak regions.

Boeri and Scarpetta (1995), use relatively long panels of monthly data for districts/ regions in Poland (1992:1–1993:12), Hungary (1991:1–1994:4), the Czech Republic (1991:1–1994:4), and Slovakia (1990:12–1993:12) to estimate Cobb–Douglas matching functions augmented by variables proxying for the prevalence of agricultural employment and diversification of economic activity. They find that the coefficient on the logarithm of unemployment ranges from 0.52 in Hungary to 0.78 in the Czech Republic, while the coefficient on the log of vacancies ranges from 0.05 in Hungary to 0.28 in Slovakia. Except for Slovakia, one can always reject the hypothesis of constant returns to scale in favor of decreasing returns.

Burda and Lubyova (1995) and Boeri and Burda (1996) use district-level data to estimate augmented matching functions with the aim of quantifying the effect of active labor market policies. Burda and Lubyova (1995) use a combination of monthly and quarterly Czech and Slovak data from 1992:1 to 1993:12 in augmented regressions and 1994:7 in the non-augmented runs. Boeri and Burda (1996) focus on the issue of endogeneity of ALMP measures and use Czech quarterly data over the period 1992:I–1993:IV in the instrumental variable estimation and 1992:I–1994:II in the OLS runs. Both studies control for district-specific fixed effects by estimating in differences from district means, include time dummies and allow for dynamics through a partial adjustment model. Both studies find expenditures on active labor market policies to have a significant positive effect on outflows to jobs under all specification (including in Slovakia in the Burda and Lubyova, 1995 study). The estimates again display high coefficients on unemployment and low (in Slovakia often insignificant) ones on vacancies.

Burda and Profit (1996) note that there is wide dispersion in unemployment rates across regions of the CEE countries and that standard matching functions, estimated with district level panel data, generate different coefficients across districts and regions. They present a model of non-sequential search with endogenous search intensity and show that it can provide a link between the spacial instability of the matching functions and spatial interdependence in matching. The model also induces more complex functional forms and nonconstant returns to scale in matching. In their empirical investigation, the authors use district and regional data from the Czech Republic during the period January 1992 to July 1994. They estimate augmented OLS Cobb–Douglas functions with lags in the dependent variable and various proxies for regional interactions in matching. Burda and

Profit find a statistically significant, non-uniform impact of surrounding districts on local matching within a district. However, they cannot reject the hypothesis of constant returns in matching.

Profit (1996) and Munich et al. (1997) tackle more systematically the issues of returns to scale and specification of the matching function. Profit (1996) notes that if matching does not lead to instantaneous hiring, static matching functions with autoregressive fixed effects will yield biased estimates. He estimates a Cobb–Douglas matching functions using panel data from 76 Czech districts during the period January 1992 to June 1994. In order to correct for misspecification, Profit focuses on issues of autocorrelation, hetero-scedasticity and validity of instruments and shows that constant returns to scale that are produced by simple models turn into increasing returns in more sophisticated Anderson–Hsiao Instrumental Variable and GMM models.

Munich et al.'s (1997) study is motivated by the fundamental puzzle posed by the Czech Republic's high outflow from unemployment relative to Slovakia and the other CEE economies, as well as the contradictory approaches and findings of the various other studies. The authors carry out a comparative analysis of matching in the Czech and Slovak republics with an emphasis on (a) using a translog rather than the more restrictive Cobb–Douglas specification, (b) separating the effects of new and longer term unemployed, (c) employing a dynamic specification and estimating on contiguous panels to allow for dynamic adjustment and regime change, d) testing and controlling for the endogeneity of explanatory variables, (e) controlling for heterogeneity of the unemployed searchers, and (f) accounting for the varying size of units of observation (districts). The data consist of a panel of monthly district-level data on all 76 Czech and 38 Slovak districts. The Czech data cover the period January 1991 to September 1996, while the Slovak data cover the period January 1991 to December 1994.

The usual assumptions of a Cobb–Douglas form and constant returns to scale are rejected in both countries in a number of years. The Czech estimates of the returns to scale are precisely estimated and they range from 2.5 to 3.5 without a trend. The corresponding estimates of returns to scale in Slovakia show an increasing trend with the point estimate rising from 0.5 in 1992 to 1.5 in 1993 and 2.8 in 1994. The Slovak estimates hence suggest that the matching process in Slovak districts displays a dramatic change over time, with the scale playing an increasingly important part. Vacancies and the newly unemployed play a much more important part in the matching process in the Czech Republic than in Slovakia. The Czech estimates yield vacancy elasticities that are all significantly different from 0 and range from 0.7 to 1.2. In contrast, the estimated elasti-cities in Slovakia range from 0 to 0.3. The relative part played by the newly unemployed is analogous to that played by vacancies. The estimated elasticities in the Czech Republic are all positive, significantly different from 0 and ranging from 0.4 to 0.9. In Slovakia, the estimates range from 0 to 0.2 and, with the possible exception of the 1993 estimate, they are not significantly different from 0 at conventional test levels.[29] Finally, the estimated

---

[29] The 1993 estimate is significant at the 10% test level.

elasticities of the existing unemployed are high and statistically significant in the Czech Republic, ranging from 1.0 to 1.9. The corresponding Slovak estimates rise from 0.4 in 1992 to 1.0 in 1993 and 2.5 in 1993, with the 1991 estimate not being significantly different from 0 at conventional test levels. The existing unemployed thus contribute in an important way to the outflow in the Czech Republic and increasingly so also in Slovakia.

Munich et al.'s (1997) results suggest that the demand side of the matching process, as proxied by vacancies, has been much weaker in Slovakia than the Czech Republic during the transition. Indeed, while vacancies have been an important component of the matching process in the Czech Republic, in Slovakia vacancies appear to have been an insignificant factor in the outflow of individuals from unemployment. Moreover, while the Czech matching process was relatively stable between 1992 and 1995, the Slovak process showed a major development from having virtually insignificant parameters in 1992, to becoming more structured by 1994.

8.3. Summary

In view of the high unemployment rate in all the CEE economies except for the Czech Republic, the studies of unemployment in these countries have focused on the determinants of outflow from unemployment into employment and on the efficiency of matching of the unemployed and vacancies. A particularly intriguing issue has been the difference in unemployment between the Czech Republic and the counterpart republic of Slovakia (and by implication the other CEE economies).

The estimates of the hazard models suggest that about one-third of the difference between the Czech and Slovak expected unemployment durations is brought about by differences in observable demand conditions, while the remaining two-thirds is brought about by different coefficient of the estimated hazards (proxying for different behavior of individuals, firms and labor market institutions). The second principal finding of the hazard estimates from several countries is that the generosity of the unemployment compensation scheme has only a moderate negative effect on efficiency in terms of lengthening an unemployment spell. Finally, the estimated coefficients on the demographic and demand variables indicate that minorities (e.g., Romanies in the Czech and Slovak Republics or non-Slovenians in Slovenia), handicapped, the least educated, and often also the single and the old unemployed workers have a harder time than others obtaining jobs. The estimated effects of gender and marital status vary across countries and specifications. A number of studies find that the probability of moving from unemployment to employment is negatively related to local unemployment rate.

The results of the matching function studies indicate that great care must be taken in collecting, aggregating and adjusting the data, specifying the functional form and selecting the estimating procedure. In particular, there is some evidence that the usual assumptions of a Cobb–Douglas form and constant returns to scale may be rejected when these factors are carefully taken into account. The exceptionally low unemployment rate in the Czech

Republic as compared to Slovakia and the other Central and East European economies appears to have been brought about principally by (1) a rapid increase in vacancies along with unemployment in the Czech Republic, resulting in a balanced unemployment-vacancy situation at the aggregate as well as district level, (2) a major part played by vacancies and the newly unemployed in the outflow from unemployment, (3) a matching process with strongly increasing returns to scale throughout (rather than only in parts of) the transition period, and (4) ability to keep the long term unemployed at relatively low levels. The matching function studies hence provide complementary evidence to the hazard estimates in that they identify local demand factors (vacancies) and the efficient behavior of agents and institutions (high returns to scale in matching) as being key to the low unemployment situation in the Czech Republic. Some, but not all, of the studies point to the importance of active labor market policies in increasing the efficiency of matching.

9. Concluding observations

The transition of the formerly centrally planned economies toward market economies represents one of the most fundamental economic phenomena of the twentieth century. Employment, output, wages and prices suddenly ceased being set by planners and became determined by market forces in the context of the newly emerging institutions. The process has been turbulent and in the early phases of the transition one observes major changes in the values of key economic variables. These developments, together with increasing availability of data, have attracted economic analysts to examine the underlying phenomena.

The studies surveyed in this chapter have generated a number of interesting findings. First, in terms of labor demand one finds that the transition economies started from different positions, with some of them displaying sizable and others basically zero elasticities of labor demand with respect to output. Despite this heterogeneity in initial conditions, firms in all the CEE economies have adjusted rapidly and started to display elasticity values that are close to those observed in western economies. This is important since employment adjustment is frequently viewed as a sign of successful initial transformation.

Available estimates suggest that wages were set independently of firms' performance under communism but that they started to vary systematically with performance (proxied by revenues per worker) during the transition. This suggests that rent sharing may be an important phenomenon in the transition economies.

Except for the former East Germany, the transition has generally brought about a higher rate of return on education. The market forces hence started to reward human capital and forced a greater dispersion in wages than permitted earlier by the planners. The results of several studies indicate that women enjoyed a higher rate of return on education than men under communism and that this differential has diminished during the transition. Unlike the return on formal education, the return on experience declined in a number of countries during the transition. This suggests that experience obtained under the centrally planned system is not highly rewarded in the emerging market economy.

The rapid rise of unemployment from zero to double-digit rates has been one of the main issues facing all the CEE economies except for the Czech Republic. The numerous studies reviewed in this chapter point to demand factors as well as the behavior of individuals, firms and institutions in the labor market as determinants of unemployment. This is important from the policy standpoint as governments formulate macroeconomic policies and establish local labor market institutions. An important related finding is that the generosity of unemployment benefit systems has only modest negative effect on efficiency in terms of extending unemployment spells. This provides policy makers with latitude in setting the parameters of the compensation system so as to ensure popular support for the completion of the transition process.

Finally, relatively few of the numerous labor market studies are able to identify a simple and systematic effect of changes in ownership (especially from state to private ownership) on employment or wage behavior. A systematic effect is observed in the area of fringe benefits, where state-owned and privatized firms appear to provide more than newly established private firms. Nevertheless, the lack of a strong ownership effect in general provides a warning for policy makers against relying indiscriminately on privatization as the principal tool of transition policy.

References

Abraham, K. and M. Vodopivec (1993), "Slovenia: a study of labor market transitions", Mimeo. (The World Bank, Washington, DC).

Aghion, P., O. Blanchard and R. Burgess (1994) "The behaviour of state firms in Eastern Europe, pre-privatisation", European Economic Review 38(6): 1327–1349.

Basu, Swati, Saul Estrin and Jan Svejnar (1995), "Employment and wage behavior of enterprises in transitional economies", Mimeo. (Department of Economics, University of Pittsburgh) (Revised in 1997 as working paper no. 114, The William Davidson Institute, University of Michigan Business School, Ann Arbor, MI).

Basu, Swati, Saul Estrin and Jan Svejnar (1997), "Employment and wage behavior of industrial enterprises in transition economies: the cases of Poland and Czechoslovakia", Economics of Transition 5: 271–287.

Beleva, Iskra, Richard Jackman and Mariela Nenova-Amar (1995), "Bulgaria", in: S. Commander and F. Coricelli, eds., Unemployment, restructuring and the labor market in Eastern Europe and Russia (The World Bank, Washington, DC).

Bellmann, Lutz, Saul Estrin, Hartmut Lehmann and Jonathan Wadsworth (1995), "The Eastern German labor market in transition: gross flow estimates from panel data", Journal of Comparative Economics 20, 139–170.

Bilsen, Valentijn and Jozef Konings (1998), "Job creation, job destruction and growth of newly established privatized and state-owned enterprises in transition economies: survey evidence from Bulgaria, Hungary and Romania", Journal of Comparative Economics 26 (3): 429–445.

Bird, Edward, Johannes Schwarze and Gert Wagner (1994), "Wage effects of the move toward free markets in East Germany", Industrial and Labor Relations Review 47(3): 390–400.

Blanchflower, David and Andrew Oswald (1994), The wage curve (MIT Press, Cambridge).

Boeri, T. (1994), "Labour market flows and the persistence of unemployment in Central and Eastern Europe", in: Unemployment in transition countries: transient or persistent (OECD, Paris) pp. 13–56.

Boeri, Tito (1997), "Heterogeneous workers, economic transformation and the stagnancy of transitional unemployment", in: Papers and Proceedings of the Eleventh Annual Congress of the European Economic Association. European Economic Review 41: 905–914.

Boeri, T. and M. Burda (1996), "Active labour market policies, job matching and the Czech miracle", European Economic Review Papers and Proceedings 40:805–818.

Boeri, T. and Scarpetta, S. (1995), "Emerging regional labour market dynamics in Central and Eastern Europe". in: The regional dimension of unemployment in transition countries (OECD, Paris) pp. 75–87.

Bogetic, Zeljko and Fareed M.A. Hassan (1995), "Distribution of income and the income tax burden in Bulgaria", Policy research working paper no. 1421 (The World Bank, Washington, DC).

Brada, Josef C. and Inderjit Singh (1994), "Transformation and labor productivity in Central and Eastern Europe", Paper presented at Workshop on Enterprise Adjustment in Eastern Europe, Washington, DC.

Brauer, Holger, Martin Falk and Martin Raiser (1997), "Labor markets in Poland and Hungary five years from the start of transition: evidence from monthly data", Konjunkturpolitik 43 (3): 248–274.

Brown, Annette Nicole (1996), "Issues for Economic transition in Russia: industrial structure, worker share ownership and internal migration", PhD (University of Michigan).

Burda, Michael C. (1992), "Unemployment, labor market institutions and structural change in Eastern Europe", Working papers 92/68/EP:31 (INSEAD).

Burda, M. (1993), "Unemployment, Labour markets and structural change in Eastern Europe", Economic Policy 16: 101–138.

Burda, M. and M. Lubyova (1995), "The impact of active labour market policies: a closer look at the Czech and Slovak Republics", in: D. Newbery, ed., Tax and benefit reform in Central and Eastern Europe (CEPR, London).

Burda, Michael C. and Stefan Profit (1996), "Matching across space: evidence on mobility in the Czech Republic", Labour Economics 3, 255–278.

Chase, Robert, S. (1997), "Markets for communist human capital: returns to education and experience in post-communist Czech Republic and Slovakia", Working paper no. 81 (The William Davidson Institute, University of Michigan Business School) Industrial and Labor Relations Review, in press.

Claessens, Stijn, Simeon Djankov and Gerhard Pohl (1996), "Ownership and corporate governance: evidence from the Czech Republic".

Claessens, Stijn, Simeon Djankov and Gerhard Pohl (1997), "Determinants of performance of manufacturing firms in seven European transition economies", Working paper no. 74 (The Davidson Institute, University of Michigan Business School, Ann Arbor, MI).

Commander, Simon, ed. (1998), Enterprise restructuring and unemployment in models of transition (The World Bank, Washington, DC).

Commander, Simon and Sumana Dhar (1998), "Enterprises in the Polish transition", in: S. Commander, ed., Enterprise restructuring and unemployment in models of transition (The World Bank, Washington, DC).

Commander, Simon and John McHale (1995), "Labor markets in the transition in East Europe and Russia: a review of experience", Paper prepared for the World Bank's World Development Report (The World Bank, Washington, DC).

Commander, Simon and Andrei Tolstopiatenko (1997), "Unemployment, restructuring and the pace of transition", in: Salvatore Zecchini, ed., Lessons from the economic transition: Central and Eastern Europe in the 1960s (Kluwer, Boston).

Commander, S., J. McHale and R. Yemtsov (1995a), "Russia", in: S. Commander and F. Coricelli, eds., Unemployment, restructuring and the labor market in Eastern Europe and Russia (The World Bank, Washington, DC).

Commander, S., J. Köllö, C. Ugaz and B. Vilagi (1995b), "Hungary", in: S. Commander and F. Coricelli, eds., Unemployment, restructuring and the labor market in Eastern Europe and Russia (The World Bank, Washington, DC).

Coricelli, F., K. Hagemejer and K. Rybinski (1995), "Poland", in: S. Commander and F. Coricelli, eds., Unemployment, restructuring and the labor market in Eastern Europe and Russia (The World Bank, Washington, DC).

Devine, Theresa J. and Nicholas M. Keifer (1991), Empirical labor economics (Oxford University Press, New York).

Djankov, Simeon and Gerhard Pohl (1998), "The restructuring of large firms in Slovak Republic", Economics of Transition 6 (1): 67–85.

Dushi, I. (1997), "Labor market, unemployment and the impact of training programs in the transition economies: the case of Albania", Mimeo. (CERGE-EI, Prague).

Earle, J. (1997), "Do East European enterprises provide social protection?" in: M. Rein, B.L. Friedman and A. Worgotter, eds., Enterprise and social benefits after communism (Cambridge University Press, Cambridge, UK).

Earle, John S. and Saul Estrin (1996), Privatization versus competition: changing enterprise behavior in Russia (Revised draft).

Earle, J. and G. Oprescu (1995), "Romania", in: S. Commander and F. Coricelli, eds., Unemployment, restructuring and the labor market in Eastern Europe and Russia (The World Bank, Washington, DC).

Earle, John S., Saul Estrin and Larisa L. Leshchenko (1995), "Ownership structures, patterns of control and enterprise behavior in Russia", Discussion paper 315 (London School of Economic Performance) p. 64.

Estrin, Saul and Jan Svejnar (1993), "Wage determination in labor-managed firms under market-oriented reforms: estimates of static and dynamic models", Journal of Comparative Economics 17 (3): 687–700.

Estrin, Saul and Jan Svejnar (1998), "The effects of output, ownership and legal form on employment and wages in Central European firms", in: S. Commander, ed., Enterprise restructuring and unemployment in models of transition (The World Bank, Washington, DC).

Estrin, Saul, Mark Schaffer and Inderjit Singh (1997), "The provision of social benefits in state-owned, privatized and private firms in Poland", in: M. Rein, B.L. Friedman and A. Worgotter, eds., Enterprise and social benefits after communism (Cambridge University Press, Cambridge, UK).

Finta, Jana and Katherine Terrell (1997), "Gender differences in flows across labor market states in the Czech Republic", Unpublished paper (University of Michigan, Ann Arbor, MI).

Flanagan, Robert J. (1994), "Were communists good human capitalists? The case of the Czech Republic", Mimeo, (Stanford University, Stanford, CT).

Foley, M.C. (1997), "Determinants of unemployment duration in Russia", Working paper no. 81 (The William Davidson Institute, University of Michigan Business School, Ann Arbor, MI).

Góra, Marek (1996), "Central and Eastern European labour markets in transition: selected issues", Revised version, text presented at OECD colloquium on transition, (OECD, Paris).

Góra, Marek and Fiorella Padoa Schioppa Kostoris (1994), "Mismatch unemployment and labour hoarding in Eastern Europe: the case of Poland".

Góra, Marek and Harmut Lehmann (1995), "How divergent is regional labour market adjustment in Poland?", Discussion papers no. 21 (Institute for Economic Research).

Gottvald, Jaromir, Peder J. Pedersen and Milan Simek (1995), "The Czech labour market in transition – evidence from a micro study" Bulletin of Economic Research, in press.

Grosfeld, Irena and Jean Fraincois Nivet (1997), "Firm's heterogeneity in transition: evidence from a Polish panel data set", Working paper no. 47 (The William Davidson Institute, University of Michigan Business School, Ann Arbor, MI).

Grosfeld, I. and G. Roland (1995), "Defensive and strategic restructuring in Central European enterprises", Discussion paper no. 1135 (CEPR, London).

Halpern, Làszló and Gàbor Körösi (1997), "Labour market characteristics and profitability (econometric analysis of Hungarian firms, 1986–1995)", Working paper no. 41 (The William Davidson Institute, University of Michigan Business School, Ann Arbor, MI).

Ham, J., J. Svejnar and K. Terrell (1995), "Czech Republic and Slovakia", in: S. Commander and F. Coricelli, eds., Unemployment, restructuring and the labor market in Eastern Europe and Russia (The World Bank, Washington, DC).

Ham, J., J. Svejnar and K. Terrell (1998), "Unemployment and the social safety net during transitions to a market economy: evidence from the Czech and Slovak Republics", American Economic Review 88 (5): 1117–1142.

Ham, J., J. Svejnar and K. Terrell (1999), "Women's unemployment during transistion: evidence from Czech and Slovak micro-data", Economics of Transition 7 (1): 47–78.

Heckman, James J. and Burton Singer (1984), "Econometric duration analysis", Journal of Econometrics 24 (1–2): 63–132.

Hendry, David F. and Grayham E. Mizon (1978), "Serial correlations as a convenient simplification, not a nuisance: a comment on a study of the demand for money by the Bank of England", Economic Journal 88 (351): 549–563.

Johnson, Simon, Daniel Kaufmann and Oleg Ustenko (1998), "Formal employment and survival strategies after communism", in: Joan M. Nelson, Charles Tilly and Lee Walker, eds. Transforming post-communist political economies (National Academy Press, Washington, DC).

Jones, Derek C. and Kosali Ilayperuma (1994), "Wage determination under plan and early transition evidence from Bulgaria", Working paper no. 94/7 (Department of Economics, Hamilton College, Clinton, New York).

Jones, Derek C. and Niels Mygind (1996), "The effects of employee ownership on productive efficiency: evidence from the Baltics", Preliminary draft of working paper series no. 96/6 (Department of Economics, Hamilton College, Clinton, New York).

Jones, Derek C. and Takao Kato (1996), "The determinants of chief executive compensation in transitional economies: evidence from Bulgaria", Labour Economics 3: 319–336.

Jones, Derek C. and Takao Kato (1997), "The nature and the determinants of labor market transitions in former communist economies: evidence from Bulgaria", Industrial Relations 36(2):229–254.

Jones, Derek C., Mark Klinedinst and Charles Rock (1995), "Structural adjustment and efficiency of firms in transition: evidence from a panel of data on 247 Bulgarian firms", (Draft).

Köllö, János (1997), "Three stages of Hungary's labour market transition", in: S. Commander, ed., Enterprise restructuring and unemployment in models of transition (The World Bank, Washington, DC).

Köllö, János and Gyula Nagy (1995), "Wage gains and losses from unemployment in Hungary", Paper presented at "Hungary: towards a market economy", a conference sponsored by PHARE ACE (94-0483-0), organized by the Institute of Economics.

Körosi, G. (1997), "Labor demand during transition in Hungary", Working paper no. 116 (The William Davidson Institute, University of Michigan Business School, Ann Arbor, MI).

Krueger, Alan B. and Jorn-Steffen Pischke (1995), "A comparative analysis of East and West German labor markets: before and after unification", in: Richard B. Freeman and Lawrence F. Katz, eds., Differences and changes in wage structures (The University of Chicago Press, Chicago, IL).

Lane, Julia, Harry Broadman and Inderjit Singh (1996), "Labor flexibility, ownership and firm performance in China" (Preliminary draft).

Lee, Young (1997), "Wages and employment in Chinese SOEs after reform: rent-sharing, market development and size and industry wage premium".

Lehmann, Hartmut and Jonathan Wadsworth (1997), "New jobs, worklessness and households in Poland", in: Sweder van Wijnbergen, ed., Papers and proceedings of the eleventh annual congress of the European Economic Association. European Economic Review 41: 915–923.

Lubyova, Martina and Jan van Ours (1994), " The matching process in labour markets in transition", Working paper no.13 (East European HIS, Vienna).

Lubyova, Martina and Jan van Ours (1997a), "Work incentives and the probability of leaving unemployment in the Slovak Republic", Working paper no. 82 (The William Davidson Institute at the University of Michigan Business School, Ann Arbor, MI).

Lubyova, Martina and Jan van Ours (1997b), "Unemployment dynamics and the restructuring of the Slovak unemployment benefit system", in: Sweder van Wijnbergen, ed., Papers and proceedings of the eleventh annual congress of the European Economic Association. European Economic Review 41: 925–934.

Micklewright, J. and G. Nagy (1995), "Unemployment Insurance and Incentives in Hungary", Discussion paper no. 1118 (CEPR, London) also in: D. Newbery, ed., Tax and benefit reform in Central and Eastern Europe (CEPR, London).

Micklewright, J. and G. Nagy (1997), "The implications of exhausting unemployment insurance entitlement in Hungary", Occasional papers No. 58 (Economic and Social Policy Series, United Nations Children's Fund).

Munich, D., J. Svejnar and K. Terrell (1997), " The worker-firm matching in the transition: (why) are the Czechs more successful than others?" Working paper no. 107 (The Davidson Institute, University of Michigan Business School, Ann Arbor, MI).

Nickell, Stephen J. (1986), "Dynamic models of labour demand", in: Orley Ashenfelter and Richard Layard, eds., Handbook of labor economics, vol. 1 (North-Holland, Amsterdam).

Orazem, Peter F. and Milan Vodopivec (1997), "Unemployment in Eastern Europe, value of human capital in transition to market: evidence from Slovenia", in: Papers and proceedings of the eleventh annual congress of the European Economic Association. European Economic Review 41:893–903.

Pohl, Gerhard, Simeon Djankov and Robert E. Anderson (1996), "Restructuring large industrial firms in Central and Eastern Europe: an empirical analysis", Technial paper no. 332 (World Bank, Washington, DC).

Profit, Stefan (1996), "Unemployment dynamics and returns to scale in job-matching in emerging labor markets: the case of the Czech Republic", Mimeo. (Humboldt University, Berlin).

Rutkowski, Jan (1997), "Low wage employment in transitional economies of Central and Eastern Europe", Most 7:105–130.

Singer, Miroslav (1996), "Dynamic labor demand estimation and stability of coefficients – the case of the Czech Republic", Working paper no. 99 (CERGE-EI, Prague).

Sorm, V. and K. Terrell (1997), "Employment, unemployment in transition in the Czech Republic: where have all the workers gone?" Mimeo. (The William Davidson Institute, University of Michigan Business School, Ann Arbor, MI)

Svejnar, J., K. Terrell and D. Munich (1995), " Unemployment in the Czech and Slovak Republics", in: J. Svejnar, ed., The Czech Republic and economic transition in Eastern Europe (Academic Press, San Diego, CA) pp. 285–316.

Chapter 43

LABOR MARKETS IN DEVELOPING COUNTRIES

JERE R. BEHRMAN[*]

University of Pennsylvania

Contents

* The author has benefited from comments on this chapter by the editors of this volume, Orley Ashenfelter and David Card, and from discussions of issues related to this chapter with Harold Alderman, Nancy Birdsall, Anil B. Deolalikar, Elizabeth M. King, Victor Lavy, Robert A. Pollak, Richard Sabot, John Strauss, Duncan Thomas, Kenneth Wolpin and, most substantially, Andrew Foster and Mark R. Rosenzweig. Behrman's time for writing this chapter was funded in part by NIH 5-RO1-HD30907. Behrman alone is responsible for all interpretations and any errors in this chapter.

Handbook of Labor Economics, Volume 3, Edited by O. Ashenfelter and D. Card

Abstract

This chapter covers selected topics for the 80% of the world's labor force that works in the developing countries. These topics are ones that have: (1) received relatively great attention in developing countries compared to developed economies (i.e., family enterprises, missing labor markets, geographical mobility, health/nutrition effects on productivity) because of their greater importance in developing countries; (2) been considered more extensively for developing than developed labor markets because the nature of institutions, behaviors and available data permit more extensive empirical examination of these topics (i.e., labor adjustments to shocks in the presence of imperfect markets, information problems in labor markets), and (3) been considered extensively for both developing and developed economies but with some different approaches and results for part of the developing country literature (e.g., determinants of and labor market returns to schooling). The discussion is organized around five broad topics: (1) The household enterprise model, surplus labor, disguised employment and unemployment, complete markets and separability, and labor supplies; (2) labor contracts, risks and incentives; (3) determinants of and returns to human capital investments (including health and nutrition in addition to schooling); (4) urban labor markets, labor–market regulations, international trade policies and manufacturing; and (5) distribution and mobility. © 1999 Elsevier Science B.V. All rights reserved.

JEL codes: J1; J2; J3; J4; JO

1. Introduction

This chapter is different in essence from most of the other chapters in the four volumes of the *Handbook of Labor Economics*. Almost all of the other chapters are concerned with generic and fairly narrowly focused topics in labor economics analysis, generally based on labor markets in the United States, Canada and a few Western European and very few non-European economies (e.g., Israel, Australia, Japan). This geographical concentration contrasts sharply with the distribution of the world's labor force in recent decades, and even more with the projected future distribution of the world's labor force (Table 1). The share of the world's labor force in "High-income OECD" countries (a subset of which is the focus of most of the chapters) was only 20% in 1965, 15% in 1995 and projected to be 10% in 2025. Therefore most of the *Handbook* chapters focus on a small and steadily-becoming smaller proportion of the world's labor force.

How should this narrow concentration be interpreted? One possibility is that the cover-

Table 1
The world's labor force by country income group and region[a]

Income group or region	Millions of workers[b]			Percentage of total		
	1965	1995	2025	1965	1995	2025
World	1329	2476	3656	100	100	100
Income group						
High-income	272	382	395	21	15	11
Middle-income	363	658	1020	27	27	28
Low-income	694	1436	2241	52	58	61
Region						
Sub-Saharan Africa	102	214	537	8	9	15
East Asia and Pacific	448	964	1201	34	39	33
South Asia	228	440	779	17	18	21
Europe and Central Asia	180	239	281	14	10	8
Middle East and N. Africa	29	80	204	2	3	6
Latin America and Caribbean	73	166	270	5	6	7
High-income OECD	269	373	384	20	15	10

[a] Source: World Bank (1995, Table 1.1) from International Labour Organization sources.
[b] Ages 15–64.

age in most of these chapters is indeed generic and examples just happened to be very concentrated on the same few economies because relevant information is more available for those economies. But the basic analyses hold more broadly for all economies. At a general level, I find such a possibility intellectually attractive. I think that the basic theoretical tools, empirical methods and approaches of labor economics indeed are applicable to all economies. Most of the *Handbook* chapters, however, do not explicitly argue that they are covering all economies, but using particular examples from a small subset of economies out of convenience. To the contrary they often read as if they are concerned basically with the few economies that are mentioned explicitly. Moreover, while on a general level it is attractive to say that the basic tools and methods apply to all economies, the specific application generally depends on the specific institutions being examined, which would appear in many cases to vary considerably across economies.

This chapter covers labor economics for the 80% or so of the world's labor force that lives and works in the developing countries.[1] Therefore I am almost forced to adopt a different strategy than in most of the chapters in the *Handbook on Labor Economics*. The structure of the majority of the other chapters is to develop systematically a behavioral model that addresses a fairly well-defined specific issue (e.g., women's labor supplies, the

[1] Svenjar's chapter covers about 5–6% of the world's labor force that also are included in Table 1 among the low- and middle-income developing countries (according to the World Bank (1997) Albania, Armenia, Belarus, Bulgaria, Czech Republic, Estonia, Georgia, Latvia, Lithuania, Macedonia, Poland, Romania, Russian Federation, Slovak Republic, Slovenia, and Ukraine account for 5.7% of the world's population).

impact of education on wages) that unifies the previous literature, permits a basis for evaluating empirical studies in the literature, and perhaps is tested against some (usually US or UK) data. That is an attractive prototype, one that in many areas is the most promising way for advancing our knowledge of labor market issues. But it does not seem one that I usefully can adopt in this chapter. Were I to devote the whole chapter to, say female labor supplies in Brazil or to labor mechanisms for coping with shocks in rural India, I could do so. But that would not seem to remedy much what I see as the problem of the limited coverage of 80% of the world's labor force.

The compromise that I have adopted in this chapter is to discuss selected topics related to labor markets in developing countries. By discussing several different topics I hope to be able to cover more broadly the work in labor economics in developing countries than would result if I were to concentrate on a topic that is as narrowly defined as are the topics in most of the chapters in the handbook, although of course the selective topical coverage cannot be nearly as extensive for the 80% of the world's labor force considered in this chapter as for the 15% of the world's labor force on which most of the *Handbook* chapters concentrate. An inevitable cost, I am afraid, of the effort to cover a number of topics is more superficial coverage of each topic.

That leaves the question of how to select which topics to discuss in this chapter. The decision function that I use has three criteria: (1) topics that have received relatively great attention for labor markets in developing countries compared to developed economies (i.e., family enterprises, missing labor markets, geographical mobility, health/nutrition effects on productivity) because of their greater importance in the developing country contexts; (2) topics that have been considered more extensively for developing than developed labor markets because the nature of institutions, behaviors and available data permit more extensive empirical examination of these topics (i.e., labor adjustments to shocks in the presence of imperfect markets, information problems in labor markets);[2] and (3) some topics that have been considered extensively for both developing and developed economies but with some different approaches and results for part of the developing country literature (e.g., determinants of and labor market returns to schooling).

From a broad aggregate perspective there are a number of systematic differences in the distribution and composition of labor in developing versus developed economies. Because

---

[2] Sometimes it is claimed that data are much better for developed than for developing countries, which may be part of the reason that studies have concentrated so much on the former. Certainly it would appear that labor market data often are better for developed economies because of longer-established systematic data collection procedures (although for some developing economics, such as India, public data collection procedures were established relatively early), more educated populations, and more extensive and more regulated market transactions. But there are other factors working in the opposite direction, such as lower costs of data collection and simpler institutions. The well known ICRISAT village-level data from rural India are an example. In part because of the low cost of labor, experiments could be and were performed to ascertain the extent of risk aversion with prizes on the order of magnitude of a months' wages (Binswanger, 1980) and enumerators with master degrees resided virtually full-time in the sample villages and collected detailed data over a decade, including information of certain types that is very hard to collect for developed economies (e.g., data on exogenous productivity shocks, intrahousehold food allocation).

these differences affect the choice of topics on which analysis has focused, a brief summary of these features based on aggregate data is useful for perspective before turning to the selected topics.[3]

Table 2 provides means for three country groups defined in World Bank (1997) by per capita incomes in 1995 for variables related to population and GNP per capita, labor force participation and composition, human capital, and some non-labor inputs. Some salient features of labor markets in developing (low- and middle-income) versus developed economies come through strongly even in such aggregate data. In the developing economies (in comparison with developed economies):

1. Agriculture and other rural labor activities are much more important even though average labor products in agriculture are relatively much lower than those in industry;
2. Non-wage labor (largely unpaid family workers, particularly in agriculture at lower incomes) are much more important;
3. Labor forces are growing more rapidly;
4. Labor force participation rates among 15–64 year olds are higher (particularly for low-income countries), in part because of much lower schooling enrollment rates among those who are in the youngest cohort in this age range;
5. Human capital investments are lower, with larger gender gaps favoring males; and
6. Non-labor production inputs per worker are much smaller.

These differences shape much of the difference in emphasis in labor economics for developing than for developed economies. The literature on developing countries, for example, has emphasized much more household enterprises in agriculture and rural–urban mobility than has the literature on developed country labor markets.

The remainder of this chapter is organized with reference to five broad topics, selected as indicated above, that have received considerable emphasis in the literature on labor in developing countries: (1) the household enterprise model, surplus labor, disguised employment and unemployment, complete markets and separability, and labor supplies; (2) labor contracts, risks and incentives; (3) determinants of and returns to human capital investments (including health and nutrition in addition to schooling); (4) urban labor markets, labor-market regulations, international trade policies and manufacturing; and (5) distribution and mobility.

2. The household enterprise model, surplus labor, disguised employment and unemployment, complete markets and separability, rural dualism

As illustrated in Table 2, two major features of labor markets in most developing econo-

---

[3] There are substantial limitations with aggregate data, many of which are reviewed in the symposium edited by Srinivasan (1994), with the consideration of labor and schooling in Behrman and Rosenzweig (1994) particularly relevant for this chapter. But such data of necessity shape our understanding of the broad patterns of labor markets and other aspects of economies.

Table 2

Aggregate data on population and GNP per capita, labor force participation and composition, human capital investments, and non-labor production inputs for low-, middle- and high income country groups[a]

	Low-income economies	Middle-income economies	High-income economies
Population and GNP per capita			
Population (millions) mid-1995	3180	1591	902
Population av. ann. growth (%) 1980–1990	1.9	1.7	0.7
GNP per capita US$1995	430	2390	24930
GNP per capita average annual growth rate (%) 1985–1995	3.8	−0.7	1.9
Population 15–64/total (%)			
1980	57	58	64
1995	61	62	67
Urban population % of total			
1980	21	52	63
1995	29	60	75
Urban population in cities > 1 million %			
1980	7	16	31
1995	10	20	33
Labor force and composition			
Labor force average annual growth rate (%) 1980–1995	2.0	2.0	1.1
Labor force part. rate (15–64) (%)			
1980	86	72	70
1995	81	70	71
Female/total labor force (%)			
1980	40	36	39
1995	41	38	42
Agricultural labor/total (%)			
1980	73	38	9
1990	69	32	5
Industrial labor/total (%)			
1980	13	28	35
1990	15	27	31
Agricultural value added per labor as % of industrial value added per labor			
1980	19	–	32
1990–1995	14	27	39
Non-wage labor as % of total labor 1980–1991[b]	91	41	16
Non-wage labor in agriculture as % of total labor 1980–1991[b]	59	20	3
Human capital			
Life expectancy at birth (years) 1995	63	68	77
Adult illiteracy (%) 1995 total	34	18	<5

Table 2 (continued)

	Low-income economies	Middle-income economies	High-income economies
Female	45	23	<5
Male	24	14	<5
School enrollment % of age group			
Primary			
Female 1980	81	99	103
1993	98	101	103
Male 1980	104	106	103
1993	112	105	103
Secondary			
Female 1980	26	48	–
1993	41	62	98
Male 1980	42	53	–
1993	–	64	97
Tertiary			
1980	3	21	35
1993	–	20	56
Non-labor production inputs			
Cropland/agricultural laborer (km^2)			
1980	0.0058	0.028	0.116
1994	0.0045	0.028	0.178
Oil equivalent energy use per capita (kg)			
1980	248	1537	4644
1994	369	1475	5066

[a] Source: World Bank (1997, Tables 1, 4, 7, 8, 9, 12) except as indicated in note b. Population weights used for averages.

[b] World Bank (1995, Table A-2) with population weights from World Bank (1997, Table 1)

mies are that (1) agriculture is a major (in the earlier stages of development usually the major) sector of employment and (2) family farms/enterprises are major (often the major) employers. Moreover, influential early two-sector aggregate development models of Lewis (1954) and Ranis and Fei (1961) argued that in the early stage of development, (i) workers could be shifted from traditional agriculture to modern market-oriented sectors ("industry") without any reduction in agricultural output (for which reason these models are called "surplus labor" models) and (ii) workers in traditional agriculture received their average products (i.e., their share of total household production) so that was the private opportunity costs of migrating to industry. Thus these models had assumptions about agricultural households and labor markets that are central to their implications. Further, much of the development literature on labor (and other) contracts (Section 3) and on human resources and labor markets (Section 4) focuses on rural households.

For all of these reasons, a good starting point for considering analysis of labor markets in developing countries – and how that analysis differs in some important respects from the analysis of labor markets in developed economies – is to consider models of rural households.

The standard model of labor markets used for developed economies distinguishes between labor suppliers (households) and labor demanders (firms). For a substantial proportion of both rural and urban households in developing countries, both labor supplies and labor demands are determined within the same institution – family farms or firms.

Models for family farms in traditional agriculture date back to Chayanov (1925). Singh et al. (1986) and Rosenzweig (1988a) provide summaries of the literature as of the mid-1980s. I build on the latter for my initial discussion, but I add discussion of some aspects of more recent contributions below.

2.1. Complete markets

I first consider a basic one-period model for the perfect markets case (or, more accurately, complete except for one market case – because in most of this discussion I assume that there is no land market). Assume there is a household with given size (M members), demographic composition (D dependants and N workers) and land area (A). The household welfare function depends on average consumption of the M household members (c) and average leisure of the N workers ($l = T - T_W$, where T is total time and T_W is the time worked by a worker):

$$U = U(c, l). \tag{1}$$

The farm production function gives the farm output (Q) as a function of land, labor used in agricultural production (L), and other inputs used in agricultural production (F):

$$Q = Q(A, L, F). \tag{2}$$

The household budget constraint is

$$P_Q Q - WL - P_F F + WNT + Y_O - P_Q Mc - WNl = \Pi + WNT + Y_O - P_Q Mc - WNl$$

$$= Y_F - P_Q Mc - WNl = 0, \tag{3}$$

where the P's refer to the respective prices, W is the wage rate, Y_O is other income, Π is farm/firm profits, and Y_F is full income. The profit function is

$$\Pi(P_Q, W, P_F) = P_Q Q(A, L, F,) - WL - P_F F. \tag{3A}$$

Under the assumption that the functions have the desirable properties so that there is an interior solution, constrained maximization of the welfare function subject to the production function and the budget constraint leads to optimal consumption, leisure, production, sales/purchases of outputs, time worked by household members, labor used in production and other inputs used in production.

The first-order condition for labor used in production is

$$P_Q Q_L = W. \tag{4}$$

This also is the profit-maximizing condition for use of labor, and the profit-maximizing condition for the other market input also is satisfied. So the constrained maximization of household welfare yields profit maximization for the farm. At the profit-maximizing level of labor used in farm production, the household may have positive or negative labor supplied to the labor market ($= NT_W{}^* - L^*$, where * refers to the optimum levels). Farm households with little land relative to their number of workers are positive suppliers to the labor market and farm households with a lot of land relative to their number of workers are negative suppliers (demanders).

In the case of complete markets for all but one input/product, the production-consumption decisions can be treated separately – as if in the first step the farm household maximized full income (which is equivalent to maximizing profits because the wage rate, total worker's time and other income are given) and in the second step, the farm household chooses its consumption bundle as if profits were given. This means that all prices and assets that affect the profit maximizing decision also have an impact through profits on consumption. But any prices that affect only the consumption decision do not affect the profit maximizing decision.[4] Note that it is full income (profits) and consumption that are separable, and not monetized income and consumption unless labor supply is fixed. The separability result, moreover, does not depend on the simple one-period model. If the model is extended to include S states of the world and T time periods so that all the variables have subscripts s and t, the problem is still recursive. Land and labor used in agricultural production for the sth state in the tth period appear only in the farm profit function for the sth state and the tth period so the household can maximize welfare by first maximizing profits for each state of the world in each time period and then making consumption decisions. The simplification is tremendous – reducing a possible risk-adverse household's dynamic behavior in a risky environment to a simple static profit-maximization problem.

The separability result does depend on there being no more than one missing market – the market for land is the only missing market in the above example. Separability does not exist if the labor market is not perfect, which has been the most -emphasized missing second market in the literature. But other missing second markets also may cause separability not to exist (Srinivasan, 1972; Feder, 1985; Eswaran and Kotwal, 1986; Banerjee and Newman, 1993). Consider the following simple example in Udry (1996b) in which there are two states of nature, with a probability of π of state 1 and with multiplicative production shocks θ_s. With complete labor and insurance markets (but no land market and no input F into production), the household's problem is to choose c_1, c_2, l, L to

$$\max \pi U(c_1, l) + (1 - \pi) U(c_2, l), \tag{5A}$$

---

[4] In the model discussed here there are not any such prices because the consumption good price is also the production good price and the leisure price is tied directly to the price of labor for production. But more generally households are often modeled as consuming some goods that they do not produce (often only such goods).

s.t. $P_{Q1}Mc_1 + P_{Q2}Mc_2 + WNl \le (P_{Q1}\theta_1 + P_{Q2}\theta_2)Q(A, NT - Nl)$.

Separation holds and the household maximizes farm profit. In contrast, if there is no labor market but a complete insurance market, the farm household's problem is to choose c_1, c_2, l to

$$\max \pi U(c_1, l) + (1 - \pi)U(c_2, l), \tag{5B}$$

s.t. $P_{Q1}Mc_1 + P_{Q2}Mc_2 + WNl \le (P_{Q1}\theta_1 + P_{Q2}\theta_2)Q(A, NT - Nl)$.

Separation is violated because farm output increases in the farm household's labor endowment. If the labor market is complete but there is no insurance market the household's problem is to choose c_1, c_2, l, L to

$$\max \pi U(c_1, l) + (1 - \pi)U(c_2, l), \tag{5C}$$

s.t. $P_{Q1}Mc_1 + WNl \le P_{Q1}\theta_1 Q(A, L) - WL + WNT$ and

$$P_{Q2}Mc_2 + WNl \le P_{Q2}\theta_2 Q(A, L) - WL + WNT.$$

One of the first-order conditions is

$$\lambda_1(P_{Q1}\theta_1 Q_L - W) + \lambda_2(P_{Q2}\theta_2 Q_L - W) = 0, \tag{5D}$$

where λ_s is the marginal utility of income in state s. Separation does not hold because input decisions depend on the ratio of the marginal utilities of income in the two states. An increase in the household's labor endowment affects this ratio (increasing the marginal utility of income relatively in the state in which the household has a larger production shock if the household has diminishing absolute risk aversion) and thus changes input decisions.

The first-order condition for the optimal leisure-consumption good combination is

$$U_l/U_c = -WN/M. \tag{6}$$

The shadow wage of leisure generally is less than the wage rate because consumption per family member increases less than the wage if work increases by 1 h if there are non-working household members. If the household had no land, this condition also would hold. Therefore it might appear that labor supply behavior would be identical between farm households and landless households if they faced identical prices and had identical full income.

But that is not the case. Rosenzweig (1988a) shows that the household labor supply elasticities with respect to both wages and the consumption/production good price differ depending, respectively, on whether the household is a positive or negative net supplier of labor to the wage market and on whether the household is a positive or negative net seller of the consumption/production good:

$$\eta_{Tw,w} = -\eta_{l,W^c} - W(NT_W{}^* - L^*)/Y_F \eta_{l,YF}, \tag{7A}$$

$$\eta_{Tw,P} = -\eta_{1,P^c} - W(Q^* - Mc^*)/Y_F \eta_{1,YF}. \tag{7B}$$

The first term in each expression is the negative of the compensated price elasticity (and must be positive in the first expression). The second term in both expressions is the weighted full income elasticity, with the respective weights being the share of labor market income in full income and the share of product sales in full income. The weights in both cases can be positive or negative. Thus the overall elasticities depend, for given full income, on the share of productive assets in total wealth.

Relation (7A) implies that the larger the share of land returns in full income for a given full income level, the more likely households are negative suppliers of labor to the wage market, the less are their income gains due to a wage increase, and the larger is their elasticity of household member time worked with respect to wages. Rosenzweig (1980) finds support for the model leading to this relation (see discussion of labor supplies below).

Relation (7B) implies that the larger the share of land returns in full income for a given full income level, the more likely households are positive suppliers of the production/consumption good to the market, the greater is their income gains due to a production/consumption good price increase, and the lesser is their elasticity of household member time worked with respect to the price of the production/consumption good. If a household is a net supplier of these goods, leisure is a normal good, and leisure and goods are not strong complements, the household labor supply falls with an increase in the price of goods. If a household is a net demander of these goods, household labor supply could rise with a price increase.[5]

Even though labor supplies respond differently to price and wage changes in the complete market model, depending on the composition of asset ownership, if there are constant returns to scale in production, a reallocation of land among farmers does not affect the efficiency of input use. That there is no land market, thus, does not preclude efficiency because all other production inputs (including labor) are mobile across farms.

2.2. No markets

Some of the development literature (e.g., some modeling of subsistence peasant households) assumes the other extreme of no markets, or at least no labor markets. Sen (1966) presents an autarkic model that can be viewed as a special case of relations (1)–(3), with no purchased agricultural inputs (i.e., no F) and no labor market (i.e., no W and $L = NT_W$). In this case the first-order condition for the leisure-consumption tradeoff at the optimum is

$$U_1/U_c = Q_L N/M. \tag{8}$$

This is identical to relation (6) above for the complete market case with the critical

---

[5] These, or course, are partial equilibrium results. From a general equilibrium perspective, price and wage changes may be interrelated. For instance, an upward shift in the demand for the good due to expanding urban and international markets might cause an upward shift in agricultural labor demands and, if labor supplies are not completely elastic, increase rural wages.

difference that the marginal product of labor in the household under consideration represents the relevant tradeoff rather than the market wage because the opportunity cost of increasing leisure by a small amount is foregoing the marginal product of that labor in household production. Parallel to relation (6), the shadow wage of leisure generally is less than the marginal product of labor because consumption per family member increases less than the marginal product of labor if work increases by one hour if there are non-working household members.

This model is consistent with so-called "surplus labor" if the removal of a working family member does not change the marginal product of labor so that total output is unaltered. This might occur if the remaining household members each increase their time working by $N/(N - 1)$ so total family time working is constant. Sen calls this situation one of "disguised unemployment" because the marginal product of labor is positive but workers can be removed from the household without a drop in output. In order for relation (8) to hold in the new configuration of household membership, the left side of relation (8) must adjust for the presence of one less household member and one less worker (i.e., the constant marginal product of labor is multiplied by $(N - 1)/(M - 1)$ which is not equal to the N/M that was relevant before the worker's departure except in the case in which $N = M$). That is, if a worker leaves, the marginal rate of substitution between leisure and consumption tradeoff between leisure and consumption must fall because the (in this case same) marginal product of labor has to be shared with a proportionately larger non-working share in the household. Thus the existence of surplus labor in this model depends critically on the characteristics of the family preference function.[6]

Because each household makes its decisions in isolation, these equilibrium decisions reflect directly the preference and production function parameters and the initial assets of households. This is inefficient because production could be increased with redistribution of the same assets to equalize worker/land ratios. The welfare of households in general could be improved with the introduction of a labor or a land market.

2.3. Tests of separability and of market completeness

Tests of separability have been proposed and applied to developing countries to see if the complete market assumptions hold approximately empirically. Of course a complete set of competitive markets in the strict sense does not exist in rural areas of developing countries, nor anywhere else. But a broad variety of spot markets do seem to exist and, at least in some contexts, appear to operate competitively. Moreover, informal mechanisms exist that may fill at least some of the same functions as competitive markets (e.g., insurance functions). Furthermore, most empirical studies of the farm household model have separ-

---

[6] Simpler models can yield surplus labor. For example, Rosenzweig (1988a) suggests that the simplest such model is one in which there is no labor market and the household does not value leisure so the optimizing condition is $U_C Q_L = 0$ if there are enough workers in the household both before and after the departure of a worker.

ability as a maintained assumption, so it is useful to test whether this assumption is warranted.

If there is separability, as noted above, a farm household's dynamic behavior in a risky environment leads to a recursive problem in which the first-step problem is static profit maximization. Tests of separability generally have focused on the strong exclusion restrictions that are implied by the profit function in relation (3A); input demand and output supply functions depend on prices and agricultural plot characteristics and on nothing else. A basic estimation problem is that unobserved characteristics that enter into the agricultural production function, such as soil quality, may be correlated with observed household characteristics that are excluded from such relations (e.g., wealth, assets, demographic characteristics) so that separability is wrongly rejected. A related test used by Udry (1996b) is to compare the distribution of plot-specific random shocks on output/area and on labor input/area among plots operated by the same individual versus the distribution across all plots in a village. The maintained hypothesis is that the distribution of inputs among apparently identical plots operated by the same individual is efficient, so if the distribution of random shocks among plots in a village is the same as the distribution among plots of the same individual, the distribution across village plots is efficient.

Table 3 summarizes all of the tests of separability of which I am aware. The available evidence, taken at face value is somewhat mixed, although with an increasing number of studies that reject separability and thus complete markets. Most of these studies must be qualified because of possible omitted variables that may be correlated with the included variables that are the focus of the tests (although if a linear approximation is adequate, the last of the studies discussed controls for such variables with fixed effects). Subject to this qualification, the majority of these studies reject the separability assumption necessary to consider household consumption (including leisure choices) separately from farm household production. This has important implications for modeling and estimating time allocation decisions, including those related to labor-leisure choices. This literature to date, however, is not very satisfactory in identifying the nature of critical market incompleteness, which may be important both for advancing further understanding and for considering possible policy implications. Basically it is posed in terms of the dichotomous possibilities of complete versus non-complete markets – in terms of Fig. 1, whether the complete-markets linear full income constraint or the no-markets production possibility frontier is relevant. It does not distinguish, for example, to what extent the effective budget set is kinked due to differential buying/selling prices (holding quality constant) as in the dashed lines in this figure.

2.4. Empirical studies of rural labor supplies

Given the importance of agriculture and of own-farm/firm labor in developing economies, not surprisingly much of the emphasis on labor supplies has been within this context. The better empirical studies in this literature have incorporated or tested various specific aspects of developing country contexts – distinctions between net suppliers and demanders

Table 3
Summary of tests of separability

Samples	Test	Result	Source
Indonesian farm households	Household profits affected by illness of household head	Accept	Pitt and Rosenzweig (1986)
240 Zairian farm households 1985–1986	Land cultivated per household worker affected by household size and composition	Reject	Shapiro (1990)
Indonesian rice farm households	Labor (family and hired) affected by household demographic composition	Accept	Benjamin (1992)
Burkino Fasian and Kenyan farm households	Plot agricultural supplies and inputs affected by land in other plots, household size, other income sources	Reject	Udry (1996b)
Niger farm households	Yield affected by household manpower	Reject	Gavian and Fafchamps (1996)
Pakistani farm households	Labor demand relations affected by household demographic variables	Reject	Fafchamps and Quisumbing (1997)
Pakistani rural households	Net harvest profits affected by planting season calorie consumption	Reject	Behrman et al. (1997a)
Indian rural villages	Land allocations conditional on prices affected by population	Reject	Foster et al. (1997)

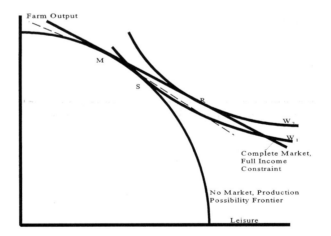

Fig. 1. No market production possibility frontier for farm output versus leisure, complete market full income constraint, dashed lines for lower selling than buying prices.

of labor; missing or incomplete labor, land, credit and insurance markets; and multi-period production processes.

Rosenzweig (1980) is an early example with static labor supply estimates that attempt to explore some of the special features of labor supplies in rural areas of developing countries. Relation (7A) above implies that the larger the share of land returns in full income for a given full income level, the more likely households are negative suppliers of labor to the wage market, the less are their income gains due to a wage increase, and the larger is their elasticity of household member time worked with respect to wages. Rosenzweig finds support for the model leading to this relation (under the added assumptions that utility functions are homothetic and leisure is a normal good) in that landless rural Indian households have lower labor supply elasticities than do rural Indian households with land.

Skoufias (1993b) is a more recent example of a static investigation similar to household labor supply studies for developed economies. He examines time allocation of all family members to the labor market, domestic production, leisure and (for children) schooling in response to market wages for different household members in rural India. Previous studies of household time allocations in such rural contexts had been few and based on cross-sectional data, which means that they had not been able to control for unobserved heterogeneity (e.g., in tastes for different time uses, in productivities) that might be correlated with right side observed variables (e.g., education) and thus lead to biases in the estimates. This study uses panel data that permit control for unobserved heterogeneity and controls for possible zero censoring in the dependent variables (i.e., many sample members do not work in the paid labor market, many children do not go to school). The estimates indicate that increases in the market wages of one household member have substantial effects on the time use of other household members.

Jacoby (1993) develops a methodology for estimating structural time-allocation models for self-employed households. The opportunity costs of time, or shadow wages, of household members are estimated from an agricultural production function that is flexible with regard to substitution among different types of family and hired workers. The household's structural labor supply parameters are recovered from variation in these shadow wages, using instrumental variables (e.g., fixed production inputs, household demographic characteristics). Because the estimation does not rely on market wages, the implications of utility theory and the hypothesis of efficient rural labor markets are not tested jointly and perfect substitutability among different types of family and hired labor is not required. Estimates are presented for peasant family labor supply behavior in the Peruvian Sierra. These estimates suggest that these households indeed allocate their members' time as if to maximize a household utility function in the sense that work effort is higher among peasants who are more productive at the margin and thus face higher opportunity costs of time. Skoufias (1994b) provides similar estimates, with control for fixed effects from panel data, for rural India.

Newman and Gertler (1994) develop an estimable structural model to deal with three aspects of farm/firm households that make empirical labor supply analysis difficult: (i) households jointly determine the consumption and the labor supplies of household members each of whom may (or may not) engage in multiple activities (i.e., own-farm production, wage labor), (ii) household members' activities are interdependent both in the utility and the enterprise production functions, and (iii) marginal returns to working in the household enterprise are not observed. The model consists of two types of structural equations and an identity: marginal return functions for each activity for each household member, the household's marginal rate of substitution of household consumption for each household member's leisure, and the household budget constraint. Conditional on the structural relations assumed, the marginal returns to work in self-employment are identified without being directly observable and without estimating the enterprise production function by using the Kuhn–Tucker conditions to infer the equilibrium values (or bounds on such values) depending on participation decisions in wage versus self-employment (or both). They present limited-information estimates of this model for household consumption and labor supply decisions of rural Peruvian land-holding households and then use these estimates to simulate the impact on consumption and on welfare (through induced leisure as well as consumption changes) of poverty alleviation programs that increase the returns to work (for females versus males) and for direct transfers. These simulations indicate, for example, that an increase in female labor market returns leads to larger changes in welfare and in consumption than does an increase in male labor market returns because of the higher estimated household evaluation of male relative to female leisure (given that in the base case prime-age males have the least leisure).

Skoufias (1996) explores intertemporal questions of substitution of labor supplies among household members in a study that basically applies the intertemporal modeling first developed for developed economies to the rural developing country context. He explicitly presents the model and the related estimation issues (e.g., unobserved heterogeneities in marginal utilities of wealth, missing wage variables) and explores carefully the sensitivity of the results to alternative assumptions and gives thoughtful discussion of why the estimates are of interest for understanding behavior and for informing policy decisions. He finds that the female intertemporal elasticity of substitution is significant but small (as in estimates for the United States), with significant differences related to land ownership and the production stage, which suggest that credit constraints limit intertemporal substitution across periods. The estimates for males are negative or zero. The low or negative elasticities suggest that there are not strong labor–leisure tradeoffs, so seasonally targeted programs such as public work programs during slack periods are likely to be effective in increasing household welfare. The sensitivity of the estimates to land ownership and production stage suggest that credit constraints are more serious for landless and small farm households in preharvest periods, so better developed credit markets would benefit relatively these relatively poor households.

Section 3 also summarizes several other recent studies that adopt a dynamic approach to labor supplies in rural areas of developing countries.

2.5. Household formation

Most of the empirical analysis of labor issues related to households in both developing and developed economies takes as given the households that are observed in the data. But households are not immutable permanent institutions. Instead they change over time due to behavioral decisions related to marriage and separations of individuals and of families in extended households and mortality.

Jacoby (1995) investigates polygyny, an institution that has been widespread in many parts of the world at different times and subject to substantial study, but not to prior modeling and empirical testing within explicit economic models that incorporate women's productivity and the effects of incomplete markets and gender divisions of labor and ownership. While there have been speculations by Becker, Boserup and others about the economic determinants of polygyny and how they would change with development, such speculations previously were not systematically modeled and tested empirically. Jacoby develops a structural model of the demand for wives from a lifecycle model of marriage and agricultural production decisions – given incomplete labor and land markets, female specialization in non-cash crops and male control of land – that permits the identification of wealth versus price (substitution) effects in a framework in which wives are explicitly recognized as an alternative to other forms of productive capital (so the latter is endogenous, not given). He then estimates this model with micro panel data from Côte d'Ivoire that permit control for measurement errors and unobserved heterogeneities across farms and in preferences by using the panel features of the data and sample-cluster-level crop shares (assumed to be independent of individual farmer preference heterogeneities) and lagged profit function residuals (with measurement errors that are independent of those in current profits) as instruments. He first estimates agricultural technology from profit functions (with control for fixed effects) and then uses the estimated farm-specific technology to estimate the demand for wives (with control for heterogenous preferences for wives, endogenous expenditures, and measurement errors in profit heterogeneity). He is sensitive in these estimates to the assumptions that he is making and how they relate to his underlying modeling, and explores how robust are the estimates to some alternative assumptions. His estimates suggest that geographical variation in cropping patterns leads to variation in female productivity, which induces demands for different numbers of wives. That is, such demands are greater where women are more productive and therefore cheaper conditional on wealth in the presence of incomplete land and labor markets. But with the process of development through expansion of "male" export crops, although the demand for wives has increased due to greater wealth, the substitution effect of higher "prices" for wives (due to their lesser productivity with the changed crop composition and maintenance of gender specialization across crops) has lessened the extent of rural polygyny.

Other recent studies explore how better earnings endowments attract more schooled-wives in rural India (Behrman et al., 1995, 1997b), how assortative mating on preferences regarding schooling causes biases in the usual estimates of the impact of parental schooling on child education (Foster, 1996) in Bangladesh, and how exogenous technological change can affect own-farm labor and human capital returns and therefore induce breakups of extended households with impact on measured income inequalities in rural India (Foster and Rosenzweig, 1999). Some of these studies are discussed in more detail below in Section 4.

3. Labor contracts, risks and incentives

Much of the development literature, as discussed in Section 2, has assumed extreme possibilities regarding labor markets. One extreme is that there are rigid, institutional determined, exogenous wages with surplus labor in rural areas. But this assumption does not seem relevant even for densely-populated South Asia, the area which inspired much of the literature on surplus labor. Rosenzweig (1984), for example, uses district level and household level data to test various hypotheses about the functioning of rural labor markets in India. Assuming that the land market is imperfect and land ownership is exogenously fixed, and that geographical mobility across districts is unimportant, he develops a competitive model of the Indian agricultural labor market with two types of labor – male and female, and three types of households – landless households, households with small plots, and households with large plots. Using district level data, Rosenzweig shows that wage rates vary systematically with variation in the factor availability, contrary to the prediction of the exogenous wage hypothesis and consistent with the competitive model.

But the other extreme assumption of complete markets also does not seem warranted, either a priori or on the basis of empirical tests of complete markets some of which are summarized in Section 2 or on the basis of other evidence. For example, Ryan and Ghodake (1984) report that in daily agricultural markets in villages in semi-arid tropical India, male laborers were not able to obtain work in about a seventh of the days that they were available. More fundamentally, the complete markets model cannot account for why the family farm is the dominant organization in rural areas of developing countries, nor for the existence of contractual arrangements such as sharecropping and the co-existence of spot labor markets and longer-run implicit or explicit contracts.

In the 1970s and 1980s there was a rapid expansion in theoretical literature concerned with how incomplete markets together with some of the special features of agricultural production shape labor and land arrangements in rural economies. There has followed an expansion of empirical tests of various aspects of these models.

These models generally emphasize one or the other of two principle themes, both of which related to the basic multistage agricultural production technology.

(1) *Risk*: agriculture is risky, particular in poor environments, because of the importance of fluctuations in weather (or other aspects of the state of nature, including disease and pest virulence), a critical input, within the multistage agricultural production process. To illustrate, the production process can be considered to have two stages, planting and

harvesting,[7] so that the production function in relation (2) becomes

$$Q_p = Q^p(A, L_p, F_p, W_p), \tag{9A}$$

$$Q_h = Q^h(A, Q_p, L_h, F_h, W_h), \tag{9B}$$

where the subscript p refers to the planting stage and the subscript h refers to the harvesting stage, W is weather, and Q_p is an intermediate output. Assume that the weather realizations occur at the start of each stage. In the planting stage, labor, land and other inputs have to be committed without knowledge of the weather that will be experienced in the harvest stage (although possibly with knowledge of the distribution of harvest weather). In the absence of insurance markets and capital investments to mitigate the impact of weather (e.g., irrigation systems, greenhouses), risk-adverse farmers might seek contractual labor arrangements that substitute in part for absent insurance markets.

(2) *Labor effort and incentive problems*: labor consists of both time and effort, so the production functions in (9A) and (9B) further become

$$Q_p = Q^p(A, L_p E_p, F_p, W_p) \tag{9C}$$

$$Q_h = Q^h(A, Q_p, L_h E_h, F_h, W_h), \tag{9D}$$

where E is the average effort of agricultural workers so LE is the labor in efficiency units. Both time and effort affect negatively the welfare of their suppliers, so the utility function in (1) for the ith period (production stage) becomes

$$U^i = U(c_i, l_i, e_i), \qquad \text{with } U_e < 0, \tag{1A}$$

where e is average effort of household workers. Effort in some important agricultural tasks (e.g., weeding and application of fertilizer and pesticides as opposed to harvesting) cannot be costlessly or cheaply monitored because of the combination of production lags, imperfect observability by farmers of the intermediate product, the spatial dispersion and heterogeneity in production conditions; there is not a distinct market for effort separate from the market for labor time; and the time–wage alone insufficiently rewards effort. Therefore contractual labor arrangements might be developed to create incentives for laborers to provide effort.[8]

3.1. Dominance of household farms in agriculture

Binswanger and Rosenzweig (1986) claim that the dominance of the household farm in developing country agriculture is due, at least in part, to household enterprises being able

---

[7] The production process may have other stages between planting and harvesting that may be important for some purposes, but the basic points for the present discussion are illustrated by collapsing all of the pre-harvest stages into the planting stage.

[8] Work effort and incentive problems also are claimed by some to be important in non-agricultural sectors of developing countries. See Section 5.1 below.

to deal relatively well with incentives for efforts in difficult-to-monitor tasks (because household members are the residual claimants on net revenues and have a long-run relation with the farm) and with risks (because of the relative effectiveness of family risk-sharing and consumption-smoothing arrangements in the market context of developing countries).[9] As the household size increases, however, monitoring becomes more difficult and the incentives for effort decline because the residual (profit) is shared among more household members. Therefore, there tends to be a limit to the size of effective agricultural households. Risk-sharing options tend to increase with numbers, but all family members do not have to be co-resident to exploit risk-sharing possibilities. In fact, to the extent that there are locally correlated shocks, having family members dispersed through migration and marriage is likely to increase the risk-sharing possibilities. Large landowners can limit their hiring of wage workers (with the accompanying incentive problems) by renting their land out to other households because tenancy arrangements can make other households residual claimants on profits with the accompanying incentive effects. For a few crops, however, (i) there are large scale economies and coordination problems in harvesting and processing and/or (ii) there is need for sustained care across crops cycles. These technological features may lead to a plantation system with large numbers of hired workers.

3.2. Day versus longer-run labor contracts

Day ("spot") and longer-run ("annual," "crop-cycle," "permanent," "attached servant") labor contracts co-exist in many rural areas of developing countries. Explanations have been proposed for this phenomenon based on both risk and monitoring effort.

Because of the uncertainty of weather in the harvest stage (even if effort is monitorable costlessly), both net buyers and sellers of labor face risks with regard to the harvest wage in the two-stage production process described above. Both net sellers and net buyers of labor, even if risk neutral, find it optimal to reduce exposure to risk by hedging with both types of contracts. The more risk adverse are households, the more attractive are the longer-run contracts. Therefore risk-adverse net labor selling households are willing to accept crop-cycle contract wage rates below the expected value of wages from the spot day market, and risk-adverse net labor buying households are willing to offer crop-cycle contract wage rates above the expected value of wages from the spot day market. Because poorer households tend to be more risk adverse (e.g., Binswanger, 1980) and net labor selling households tend to be poorer (i.e., due to less land ownership), crop-cycle wage rate contracts are likely to be below expected spot wage rates.

If planting period work effort cannot be monitored until the harvests are realized (even if there is no risk), employers have incentives to hire crop-cycle workers only for the planting period and additional spot workers if necessary for the harvest (Eswaran and Kotwal, 1985a). Crop-cycle contract workers are induced to provide the right level of effort in the

---

[9] Ben-Porath (1980) and Pollak (1985) also discuss advantages of households and families and how they relate to the completeness of various markets.

planting period because the expected worker welfare (inclusive of work effort) of the crop-cycle contract exceeds the expected worker welfare of a series of spot contracts over the crop cycle and because only if a worker is revealed to have devoted the right level of effort at harvest time will she/he be offered a crop-cycle contract for the next crop cycle. In this model, in contrast to the case discussed in the previous paragraph, crop-cycle contract workers are better off than spot contract workers and tend to continue across crop cycles in their privileged labor market positions.

Annual or crop-cycle contracts are important in some rural areas (e.g., West Bengal, see Bardhan, 1983), but not in others (Bell and Srinivasan, 1989). This may reflect differentials in risks or in labor incentives across areas, differentials in alternative mechanisms for sharing risks or for inducing efforts across areas, or differentials across areas in the correlations between harvest-stage wage rates and gross harvest incomes because, if this correlation is high, the net income risk of net labor buyers is not tied tightly to wage rate risk.

3.3. Implications of land contracts for labor

Sharecropping and other tenancy arrangements are common in many developing countries. There is a considerable literature on land tenancy arrangements in developing countries (see Bell, 1988; Binswanger et al., 1995 and the references therein), some of which has implications for the allocation of and the returns to labor. If a tenant household sharecrops land (with a marginal share s of gross output from the sharecropped land Q^s), works part-time in own production (Q^o), and works part-time in the labor market at wage W, the equilibrium condition for maximizing the household welfare in (1) subject to the production relation in (2) and the household resource constraint is to allocate labor among production on own land (L^o), production on sharecropped land (L^s), and the labor market so that

$$P_Q \partial Q^o / \partial L^o = s P_Q \partial Q^s / \partial L^s = W. \tag{10}$$

If the marginal share crop rate s is less than one and there are no other contractual stipulations, marginal returns to labor (and to all other variable inputs) are higher on the sharecropped land than in own production or wage work. Theoretical modeling of sharecropping to explain its existence in light this apparent inefficiency as compared with fixed rent contracts is concerned, again, with dealing with risk and with incentives for efforts.

If there are no insurance markets and no missing markets for effort, landlords and risk-adverse sharecropping tenants share production risks, and can share them optimally if optimal allocation of inputs on sharecropped land is enforceable. However, as Newbery (1975) noted, risk reduction to the same degree can be obtained by the tenant household by dividing household workers' time between a risky activity (own production) and a riskless alternative (crop-cycle labor contract work). Therefore the risk sharing explanation of sharecropping depends on the nature of alternative risk-reducing options.

If there is no risk but there is the double coincidence of no markets for managerial skills of landlords and for work effort of tenants, sharecropping can provide incentives for landlords to provide managerial skills and for tenants to provide work effort (Eswaran and Kotwal, 1985b). In this case, a fixed rental contract is inferior because it does not elicit managerial efforts of landlords. If tenants gain experience or new technologies appear for which the landlords do not have managerial skills, the advantage of sharecropping over fixed rents is likely to decline. If labor tasks become routinized, wage labor is likely to become more attractive relative to sharecropping.

Empirical studies have largely focused on the question of whether there is inefficiency, not what determines contract choices. Studies that compare input intensities for the same farmer on different plots with different land contracts find that observed input intensities are lower on sharecropped than on fixed rent or own plots (Bell, 1977; Shaban, 1987). Subject to the qualification that these results are not due to unobserved factors such as unobserved aspects of soil quality and water availability, they suggest that sharecropping does lead to less inputs than the two alternatives as in relation (10). Bell and Sussangkarn (1985) report that tenants with greater risk-sharing activities (e.g., receiving more transfer payments, with more non-agricultural household workers, with greater landholdings) are more likely to engage in riskier tenant contracts. But this association does not demonstrate causality because it may just reflect endogenous choices so that in riskier environments tenants choose a portfolio of means to cope with the risk. Bell and Srinivasan (1989) report that in ten villages in the Indian Punjab owners and tenants are more likely to share in allocation decisions under sharecropping than fixed-rent contracts, as in the Eswaran–Kotwal model. But there is little information on longitudinal developments in tenancy arrangements, how they are affected by experience of tenants and by changes in markets and in technology, and what are the implications for labor allocations and labor returns.

3.4. Empirical studies of rural labor supplies and risk

Fafchamps (1993) considers sequential labor decisions under uncertainty for small farmers in a developing country in order to attempt to reconcile expressed concern for possible manpower shortages with low average labor inputs. His approach is related on a general level to that used by Rust (1987) and Wolpin (1984, 1987), but explicit differences (e.g., finite horizon, non-stationarity, continuous decisions, the state space not discretized and data available only on the final, not the intermediate, state of nature). He posits a simple structural model with: three agricultural production stages (planting, weeding and harvesting with the labor demands for the third of these proportional to product); nested constant elasticity of substitution utility and production functions (with a priori equal utility effects of leisure for the planting and weeding stages and moderate risk aversion in the former and constant returns to scale in the latter) that are identical across households within a region; households differing only with regard to land assets; no labor, land or intertemporal markets; production shocks that are independent across the three stages; and rational expectations concerning production shocks. Euler equations for this stochastic control problem are invertible. The two decision variables are for planting labor and for weeding labor. He presents FIML estimates for a 3-year panel of small farmers in Burkino Faso. Vuong's non-nested model specification test indicates that the stochastic control estimates dominate those that result from considering a deterministic control problem. The estimates indicate that farmers are willing to supply considerable labor hours if there are expected returns to doing so (i.e., the intertemporal elasticity of substitution of leisure and the elasticity of substitution between consumption and leisure both are high), but that the low level of labor effort commonly observed in this area is the result of both low labor productivity in rain-fed agriculture in this environment and of farmers' awareness that, in the absence of a labor market, overly ambitious initial production plans lead to seasonal labor constraints on production. Therefore there may be considerable gains from technologies that permit farmers to have greater control (particularly over water) and greater flexibility to respond to states of nature as they develop, as well as from development of the labor market.

Rose (1995) explores the impact of risk on labor supplied to wage markets, also within a seasonal, multi-stage framework with a planting stage and a harvesting stage in the latter of which weather shocks are revealed. She distinguishes between ex ante and ex post market labor supply responses of agricultural cultivating households to deal with risky production on their own farms. The ex ante response is to the riskiness of weather distributions in a particular location and the ex post response is to the weather realization. She develops a two-stage model that incorporates both ex ante and ex post responses to wage as well as crop income risk within a stochastic dynamic programming framework. She then uses a 3-year national stratified random panel dataset for landed households in rural India that is merged with another panel dataset containing characteristics of the districts in which households live, including most importantly a 21-year series of rainfall data that is used to compute a measure of the exogenous rainfall risk faced by farmers as well as other indicators of bad weather. She specifies and estimates labor market earnings (related to supply) and profit functions. The profit function is estimated with fixed and random effects techniques, and Honore's procedure for estimating a fixed effects Tobit model is used to estimate the labor earnings equation. The results indicate that: (1) profits increase and labor supply falls in periods of good weather and high rainfall; (2) households facing greater weather risk supply more labor to the market and receive lower profits than those in less risky environments; (3) the effects of weather risk on production is reduced by irrigation and by accessibility to banks and moneylenders; and (4) the availability of non-agricultural employment increases labor income but also reduces profits by withdrawing resources from production and exacerbates the responses of profits and labor supplies to shocks and risk.

In another study Rose (1999b) examines another aspect of labor supplies related to risk, in this case the sex of a baby. She investigates the impact of a "gender shock" (i.e., birth of a girl) on time allocations in rural Indian households because of income (due to the need to pay dowries in the marriage market) and substitution effects (due to the higher returns from investing in sons than in daughters). She presents an intertemporal model that generates predictions for these effects, conditional on whether or not the household is constrained in the credit market. She presents careful empirical estimates that control for unobserved fixed effects (e.g., preferences) and endogenous sex-related infant mortality. Her empirical results indicate that the gender shock results in a decline in male leisure for poorer households, but an increase for less poor households. For all households, women work less following the birth of a son than following the birth of a daughter. These results are consistent with the model predictions if poorer, but not less poor, households are credit-constrained.

3.5. Empirical studies of imperfect information and labor markets

In addition to imperfect insurance and effort markets, there are other types of incompleteness related to rural labor markets that may affect the type of labor contracts and indeed may be illuminated if the same individuals participate in different labor contracts. Imperfect information in labor markets with heterogeneous labor is widely conjectured to be a common feature of such markets. Only recently has there been systematic empirical research investigating its importance in the developing country context in a series of studies by Foster and Rosenzweig. These studies investigate some phenomena about which there have been considerable conjectures in markets for developed country labor markets as well as for developing country labor markets, but for which the nature of institutions, behaviors and data have made possible more satisfactory empirical investigations in the developing than in more developed country contexts.

Two little researched but important issues in the study of labor markets with heterogeneous workers is how employers select workers and how worker contributions are rewarded if employers have imperfect information about work effort. Foster and Rosenzweig (1994a) present evidence that employers have imperfect information with regard to the productivity of heterogenous workers by obtaining direct measures of the completeness of employer information. Therefore they are able to consider the implications of such information asymmetries and evaluate the extent to which casual rural labor markets in developing countries exhibit these attributes using econometric tests from three large micro datasets from rural areas of Asia. They find: (1) there is considerable variance in productivity that is not associated with workers' characteristics observed by employers – from one-fifth to two-thirds of the productivity variance; (2) there is adverse selection of less productive workers into the time–wage sector of the labor market, with a 10% increase in the unobserved component of a worker's productivity increasing the share of labor market work time that the worker spends in piece-work by 6.6%; (3) employers discriminate statistically by paying time–wages that are 25–60% higher for men because the distribution of productivity is higher for men than for women, but do not have taste preferences regarding the gender of their employees (i.e., they pay the same for perceived productivity independent of gender); (4) employers exhibit learning over time by observing workers, which exacerbates wage inequalities between men and women because the latter have less labor market experience; and (5) nutrition affects productivity substantially but is not rewarded in the time–labor market presumably because of problems in monitoring productivity. This is the first paper to my knowledge to address critical labor market questions regarding how employers with imperfect information about workers' characteristics and productivities select which heterogenous workers to employ and how workers are rewarded.

The inability of employers to fully observe worker effort has a central role in many contractual models of the labor and land markets that are summarized above. While there is fairly good evidence regarding the disincentive effects of easily observed material input use associated with sharecropping (e.g., Bell, 1977; Shaban, 1987), there is no evidence regarding the impact on (much-harder-to-observe) work effort under such incentive systems prior to Foster and Rosenzweig (1994b). In this paper they develop a simple multi-stage model in which worker health is affected by effort and by calorie intakes through the energy balance condition and that permits the use of time-series information on worker health and the inputs to worker health (i.e., calories) to measure the effort effects of different labor payment schemes that award workers differentially. The Euler conditions from this model are tested empirically, with careful attention to estimation and specification issues (e.g., controlling for simultaneity and for individual worker effects using within-round data on payments received under different payment schemes). The estimates indicate that time–wage payment schemes as well as share-tenancy are associated with substantial moral hazard. Workers supply about a third more effort when working on a piece-rate scheme or on their own land than when working for time wages or under share tenancy. Thus this paper provides the first systematic empirical evidence about the importance of moral hazard in labor markets and finds that it is substantial in the particular empirical context considered.

How workers are matched with "jobs" is a fundamental issue in labor economics. A number of matching mechanisms have been posited. Foster and Rosenzweig (1996a) develop and estimate a Roy model of the allocation of heterogeneous workers to alternative productive tasks. This paper demonstrates that with data on piece rates and time rates for the same workers it is possible to distinguish among three determinants of worker-task allocations: (a) differences in the productivity of workers at different tasks; (b) preferences of workers for different tasks; and (c) preferences of employers for different types of workers. In the context of rural agriculture to which the methodology is applied, the empirical application attempts to explain the extent to which these three factors explain the over-representation of women in weeding activities relative to men. Using data from the Philippines, it is found that the greater proportion of women allocated to weeding is due their lower skill level, that women do not have a preference for weeding, and that employers do not prefer women to perform weeding tasks. The results further indicate that employers engage in statistical discrimination in the time–wage sector in that they assign women to weeding because women are on average of lower skill than are men. This paper thus provides an explanation for the ubiquitous gender specialization in tasks in agricultural societies. It shows more generally that inferences about the relative importance of worker and employer preferences as determinants of the allocation of workers to tasks cannot be made without a careful assessment of the importance of comparative advantage and information asymmetries.

4. Determinants of and returns to human capital investments

Human resource investments are hypothesized to play a major role in labor market outcomes in developing countries, as in developed economies. However, there are at least two major differences. First, while there has been considerable emphasis on schooling as for developed economies, investments in human resources in health and particularly in nutrition have received relatively much more emphasis for developing economies because such investments are thought to have relatively high productivity effects in very poor contexts. As is illustrated in Table 4, moreover, initial 1965 investments in health and nutrition (as represented in this table by life expectancies at birth relative to those predicted by per capita income in a cross-section for that year) have more predictive power for economic growth over the next quarter century than do initial schooling investments (again, in 1965 and relative to those predicted by per capita income). Second, at least some of the available studies of both the determinants and the effects of human resources in developing countries place considerable emphasis on ways in which incomplete markets, such as are discussed in Sections 2 and 3, shape such investments.

On a general level the framework for considering the determinants of human capital investments in developing countries is the same as that used for developed economies. Differences relate to the differences such as those in the completeness of markets and in the roles of households. Many of the essential features are summarized in Becker's (1967) Woytinsky Lecture.

Private maximizing behavior leads to human resource investments at the level at which the private present discounted marginal benefit of the investment equals the private present discounted marginal costs of the investment. Fig. 2A provides an illustration for one

Table 4
Estimates of the associations of initial 1965 human resources relative to the levels predicted by cross-country regressions with subsequent economic growth for the 1965–1990 quarter century[a]

Dependent variable real per capita GDP annual growth 1965–1990	Initial schooling	Initial life expectancy	Constant	R^2	F	N
Row 1	0.39 (4.0)		1.8 (9.1)	0.15	16.3	85
Row 2		0.14 (4.7)	1.7 (8.2)	0.18	23.3	96
Row 3	0.15 (1.1)	0.10 (2.6)	1.7 (8.9)	0.21	12.1	85

[a] t statistics are in parentheses to right of point estimates. The initial human resource positions are the actual values minus the values predicted by a cross-country regression on a polynomial in per capita income for 1965. Schooling is the expected schooling for a synthetic cohort. For more details see Behrman (1994b).

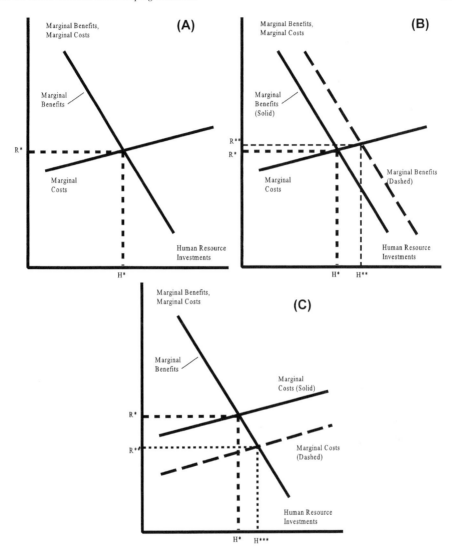

Fig. 2. (A) Private marginal benefits and private marginal costs of human resource investments. (B) Private marginal benefits and private marginal costs of human resource investments, with higher (dashed) and lower (solid) marginal benefits. (C) Private marginal benefits and private marginal costs of human resource investments, with higher (solid) and lower (dashed) marginal costs.

individual. The marginal private benefit curve depends on the expected private gains (e.g., in wages/salaries in labor markets) due to human capital investments. The marginal private benefit curve is downward-sloping because of diminishing returns to human capital investments.[10] The marginal private cost may increase with human capital investments because of the increasing opportunity costs of more time devoted to such investments (especially for schooling and training) and because of the increasing marginal private costs of borrowing on financial markets. For a human resource investment at level H^*, the private returns net of costs are maximized.

If the marginal private benefit curve is higher for every level of human capital investment as for the dashed line in Fig. 2B, all else equal, the equilibrium human capital investment (H^{**}) and the equilibrium marginal private benefit (r^{**}) both are greater. The marginal private benefit curve may be higher for one of two otherwise identical individuals except for the difference noted below because one individual (or whomever is investing in that individual, such as the parents of young children):[11] (1) has greater endowments (e.g., more ability and drive) that are rewarded in schooling and in post-schooling labor markets;[12] (2) has lower discount rates so that the future benefits of human capital investments have greater value at the time of the decision whether or not to invest; (3) has human capital investments options of higher quality (e.g., access to higher quality public schools or public health services) so that the marginal private benefits for a given level of investment are higher, and the equilibrium investments greater;[13] (4) has better health and a longer expected life due to complementary investments, so that the post-investment period in which that individual reaps the returns to the investment is greater and therefore the expected returns greater; (5) has greater marginal private benefits to a given level of such investments because of more extensive labor markets or labor market discrimination that favors that individual due to gender, race, language, family, village, or ethnic group; (6) has returns to human resources investments that are obtained more by the investor or the relevant decision maker (e.g., if traditional gender roles dictate that children of one sex, but not the other, provide old-age support for their parents, parental incentives may be greater to invest in children who are likely to provide such support unless there is an exactly compensating adjustment elsewhere such as in marriage markets); (7) has lower discount rates, given risk aversion, because of better means for coping with risks through insurance markets, public safety nets or whatever; (8) has greater marginal private benefits

---

[10] Diminishing marginal returns might be expected (at least at sufficiently high investments levels) because of fixed genetic endowments and because human capital investments take time (such as schooling and training) and greater investments imply greater lags in obtaining the returns and a shorter post-investment period in which to reap the returns from the investment.

[11] For some of these comparisons (e.g., the last three) the otherwise identical individuals would have to live in different economies.

[12] This means that to obtain an estimate of the impact of human capital investments on some outcome, one cannot just consider the association between the human capital investment and the outcome (i.e., the association between years of schooling and wage rates), but one must control for the endowments underlying the different human capital investments.

[13] If the investor (or the investor's family) must pay for greater quality, investment does not necessarily increase with a higher quality option. What happens to the equilibrium investment depends upon where the marginal private cost curve for the higher quality option is in addition to the location of the marginal private benefit curve.

to a given level of investment because of being in a more dynamic economy in which the returns to such investments are greater; (9) has greater marginal private benefits to a given level of such investments because of greater externalities from the human capital investments of others in the same labor market; or (10) lives in a more stable economy so that the discount rate for future returns is lower and thus the marginal private benefit of future returns greater.[14]

If the marginal private cost is lower for every level of human capital investment as for the dashed line in Fig. 2C, ceteris paribus, the equilibrium human capital investment (H^{***}) is greater, with the marginal private benefit (r^{***}) at the higher investment level lower. The marginal private cost might be lower for a number of possible reasons. Compare two otherwise identical individuals except that one individual: (1) has lower private cost access to educational and health services related to such investments because of closer proximity to such services or lesser user charges; (2) has less opportunity costs for time used for such investments (e.g., due to gender specialization in household and farm tasks performed by children); (3) faces lower utility costs of such investments because of cultural norms that favor some activities associated with such investments more for some individuals than for others (e.g., in some societies, it is not thought desirable that girls past puberty intermingle with males outside of the family in transit to school or in school so that the preference costs of schooling are lower for boys than for girls);[15] or (4) is from a household with greater access to credit because of greater wealth or status or better connections or better capital and insurance markets.

This simple framework systematizes four critical general points for identifying the determinants of human capital investments and what is the impact of human capital investments on outcomes of interest – in the present context labor productivity.[16] First, the determinants and the expected outcomes are interrelated, as in any investment decision. Therefore the determinants depend not only on the conditions at the time of the investment, but on expectations regarding the context in which the returns from the investment will be reaped. There also may be interactions between the various human resource investments, for example with better health and nutrition increasing the expected returns to schooling. Further, to identify the impact of human capital investments on a particular outcome, it is important to control for individual, family, and community characteristics that reflect the conditions under which the investments were made. Otherwise the estimated effect includes not only the impact of the human capital investment, but also the effects of individual, family, and community characteristics that directly affect the outcome of interest and are correlated with the human capital investment because they

---

[14] Some of these possibilities tie directly into the new economic growth models that have received a lot of attention in the past decade (e.g., the first is consistent with Stokey's, (1991) emphasis on the heterogeneity of individuals, the seventh with a product composition more conducive to learning-by-doing as in Lucas (1988) and Stokey (1991), and the eighth with the externalities broadly emphasized in this literature).

[15] For this case the marginal utilities of marginal private benefits and costs are equated.

[16] And for understanding under what conditions there may be efficiency reasons for governments or for private firms to subsidize human resource investments (Section 6.1).

partly determine that investments. Second, empirically observed returns to human capital investments are for a given macro economic, market, policy, and regulatory environment. The actual returns may change substantially with changes in that environment, such as those associated with changing from administrated to market prices, opening up an economy more to international markets, establishing greater macro balance, eliminating regulations on migration, or lessening discrimination in labor markets. Third, the marginal private benefits of human capital investments in a particular individual may differ depending upon the point of view from which they are evaluated: (i) there may be externalities such as those emphasized in the "new neoclassical growth models" or capital/insurance market imperfections so that the social returns differ from the private returns; (ii) there may be a difference between who makes the investment decision (e.g., parents) and in whom the investment is made (e.g., children) which may result in gender (or birth-order) differentials in incentives for investments in children given traditional gender (birth-order) roles in old-age care for parent; and (iii) some forms of human capital investment may have returns broadly throughout the economy and others may have returns only in specific activities or productive units. Fourth, if the marginal private benefits equal the marginal social benefits and if the marginal private costs equal the marginal social costs, optimizing investments in human capital by private investors are socially efficient.

4.1. Determinants of health and nutrition investments

There is a substantial literature on the determinants of health and nutrition by behaviors of households and other entities in developing countries (see Behrman and Deolalikar, 1988; Jimenez, 1995; Strauss and Thomas, 1995; World Bank, 1995). I limit attention here to a small subset of those studies, those that are most related to labor markets through focusing on the role of income and on expectations regarding labor market outcomes.

4.1.1. Household income

If all relevant markets were complete and the only difference between two individuals were that they came from households with different incomes, there would be no differences in human capital investments in the two individuals. However, it is widely believed that there are associations between human capital investments in individuals in developing (as well as developed) countries and income. This may reflect that such investments have some consumption components and/or that income is associated with some of the determinants of human capital investments discussed with respect to Fig. 2, such as ability, discount rates, access to capital and insurance or other markets, and access to public services.

Empirical studies of household behavior determining health and nutrition investments in developing countries generally have included income indicators among the right-side variables, usually with reference to credit market imperfections if any explicit rationale is given. In the past decade the greatest emphasis related to income in this literature has been on (1) the magnitude of income–nutrition associations and (2) whether there is complete income pooling.

The magnitude of income–nutrition associations are of interest because on the order of magnitude of a billion people in the developing world are thought to be malnourished (which is widely viewed as undesirable in itself in addition to any productivity effects) and some influential observers have argued that the most effective way to eliminate malnourishment is to increase income (e.g., World Bank, 1981). Engel curves for food purchases for poor people typically indicate income elasticities of the magnitude of 0.6–0.8, from which many observers concluded that nutrients consumed by members of poor households would increase by about 6–8% for every 10% increase in poor households' income. (Some have argued that for very poor households the nutrient elasticities with respect to income would be higher, greater than one, e.g., see Lipton, 1983.) Inferences from such empirical estimates underlay widespread optimism about reductions in malnutrition with income increases. A revisionist position emerged in the past decade, however, that questioned whether nutrient (in a particular, calorie) income elasticities were nearly this large based on claims that previous estimates had overstated calorie-income associations because of ignoring (a) the distinction between household food purchased/produced and food consumed by household members that may be strongly associated with income due to provision of food to household employees, mendicants and animals and wastage, (b) measurement error that biased the estimated associations upwards (e.g., regressing food expenditures on total expenditures), and (c) intra-food group substitution towards more expensive nutrients associated with income (see Behrman and Deolalikar, 1987; Bouis and Haddad, 1992; Alderman, 1993; Bouis, 1994; Subramanian and Deaton, 1996).

At this point the prevalent view seems to be the calorie-income associations are somewhere between those implied by the previous conventional wisdom and the revisionists, suggesting a moderate role for income increases in lessening malnutrition. But it is striking that for the most part this fairly extensive literature does not place the investigation of the determinants (and impact) of nutrients within the context of the particular market configurations faced in developing countries, nor is there much attention to timing issues regarding income receipts and food expenditures. A recent at least partial exception to this statement is Behrman et al. (1997a), who investigate calorie demands and the impact calorie consumption on farm profits in rural Pakistan. They positive a two-stage production process as in relations (9C) and (9D) above in which planting season labor markets do not reward greater efforts due to better-nourished workers because of monitoring problems and credit markets do not permit poor households to borrow for nutrition investments in the planting stage the returns from which occur at harvest time. They find that for poor agricultural households (defined by small landholdings), the income elasticity for planting-stage calories is one, in contrast to a value of about zero in the harvest stage when nutrients are much cheaper and harvest piece worker rates directly reward better current nutrition. Thus placing the nutrient investment within the particular context of incomplete markets and multi-stage agricultural production leads to different insights regarding the nature of this human resource demand and its relation to incomplete markets.

The income pooling question pertains to whether households effectively pool individual incomes or whether it matters which members of the households control income. This question originally arose in regard to bargaining models for intrahousehold allocations in developed economies (Manser and Brown, 1980; McElroy and Horney, 1981). But, as emphasized by McElroy (1990), the majority of the efforts to provide empirical tests of whether incomes are pooled by household members have been for developing countries, often with emphasis on investments in health and nutrition (e.g., Schultz, 1990b; Thomas, 1990, 1993, 1994; Strauss and Thomas, 1995; Haddad et al., 1996 and the references therein). Many commentators summarize these studies to imply that (a) income is not pooled in developing countries and (b) resources under control of women has much greater impact on human capital investments in health and nutrition than do resources under control of men. While conventional wisdom has been shaped considerably by these studies, I find them less persuasive than do many because they do not control for unobserved abilities and preferences that arguably are correlated with the indicators of individual control over resources that are used (see Behrman, 1997a for further discussion). These studies like those related to income and health/nutrition investments, moreover, generally do not place the analysis very well into the specific market and institutional contexts of developing economies.

4.1.2. Expected labor market returns

One important implication of standard models of human capital investments, as emphasized above with respect to Fig. 2, is that such investments are predicated in part on their expected returns. Most of the empirical literature on such investments in developing countries (and that on developed economies) does not directly incorporate this possibility because of the problems in representing such expectations. I now consider briefly two studies on health and nutrition in developing countries that do attempt to represent such expectations.

Rosenzweig and Schultz (1982) argue that differential child mortality rates – with mortality being the equivalent to very poor health and nourishment – by sex across India reflect differential expected labor market returns to investing in the human resources of boys versus girls. They develop a simple model consistent with this argument, and then present estimates of the model, using current adult labor force experience to represent the experience expected for current children (arguing that such a representation is good for the period that they consider because labor markets were relatively stable in that era). Their estimates suggest that differential boy-girl mortality patterns in different parts of India are consistent with the hypothesis that households invest in the children in whom the returns are greatest (i.e., reinforce endowment differentials in light of market opportunities).

Pitt et al. (1990) develop a model that incorporates linkages among nutrition, labor-market productivity, health heterogeneity, and the intrahousehold distribution of food and work activities in a subsistence economy. A household is assumed to have individuals in m classes (defined by age and sex so that within a class the health and wage production functions are the same for all members of the household). The household maximizes its consensus preference function that is defined over the health, food consumption, and work effort of each individual (with positive effects of health and food consumption and negative effects of work effort) subject to (i) a budget constraint that posits that income from labor and other sources must be greater than or equal to expenditures on food and other consumption and (ii) production functions for health and wages for each class:

$$H_j^k = h^k(N_j, E_j, G_j),$$ (11)

$$W_j^k = w^k(H_j, E_j),$$ (12)

where H_j^k is the health of the jth individual in the kth class, N_j is the nutrient or food consumption of the jth individual, E_j is the work effort of the jth individual, G_j is the health endowment of the jth individual that is observed by household members but not by social scientists, and W_j^k is the wage rate for the jth individual in the kth class.[17] Nutrients and endowments are posited to have a positive effect on health, health a positive effect on wage rates, and effort a negative effect on health and a positive effect on wage rates. Health is assumed to increase the marginal product of effort in producing wages, with all the endowments effects working through health.

The first-order conditions indicate that the marginal cost of allocating nutrients at the margin to an individual is lower the greater the extent to which that person's health improves with more nutrition and that person's wage increases with better health. If different classes of individuals participate in different work, as appears widely to be the case in developing countries with respect to gender, and the wage effects of health vary across types of work, the marginal costs of food allocated to different classes of individuals may vary substantially. Within a class the distributions of food and work effort across individuals depend on the distribution of endowments among those individuals. Compensation or reinforcement can be examined by investigating the first derivative of health with respect to endowments, which includes the partial effects on health through both work effort and nutrient intakes. In the case in which endowments enter additively in the health production relation, there is compensation (reinforcement) if the sum of these two partial effects is negative (positive). The cross effect of j's endowment on i's nutrient consumption is more negative if the household preference function is non-linear with the consumption of i and j as substitutes the stronger is the relation between health and effort productivity for j.

To explore empirically whether there is compensation or reinforcement, estimates of the endowments first must be obtained. To do so, the health production function is estimated directly and, based on the parameter estimates and the actual nutrients consumed and work effort expended by each individual, individual-specific endowments are calculated. There are two problems that must be dealt with in this "residual" endowment method. First, because endowments are not observed by social scientists and they influence household

---

[17] Work time is assumed to be the same for all individuals because there are not data on time allocations and because casual observations suggest that there is very little leisure in the sample area.

allocations, OLS estimates of the health production technology are not consistent. They therefore use as instruments "food prices, labor-market variables reflecting labor demand, and exogenous components of income" under the assumption that such variables "determine resource allocations but do not directly affect health status, given food and activity levels." (Pitt et al., 1990, p. 1145) Second, the residually-derived endowments are likely to be measured with systematic error because of random measurement error in the observed inputs into the health production function such as individual nutrients, which carry over to cause errors in the estimated endowments that in turn causes biases in the estimated impact of the endowments on allocated variables. These biases tend to make households appear more compensatory than they really are.[18] To obtain consistent estimates Pitt et al. (1990) use instrumental variables in the form of estimated health endowments for weight-for-height, mid-arm circumference, and skinfold thickness from other survey rounds than the one for which the allocation estimate is being made under the assumption that the period-specific measurement errors are not correlated across time periods.

The data requirements for this study are considerable: individual specific observations on nutrient intakes, health outcomes, and work effort; sufficient cross-sectional variation in exogenous instruments needed for consistent estimation of the health production function; and repeated observations on individuals to purge estimated endowments of measurement errors. They use data from the 1981–1982 Bangladesh Rural Nutrition Survey of 385 households in 15 villages and Food and Agricultural Organization/World Health Organization (FAO/WHO) classifications of the 14 occupations provided in the data as "very active" and "exceptionally active" to characterize higher than normal work effort and control for whether women were lactating or pregnant in the sample period to control for non-work nutrient use. Estimates of the health production function for weight-for-height suggest that the impact of calories is understated and the signs of the coefficients of the work effort variables wrong if OLS is used instead of simultaneous estimators. Then the residual endowments obtained from the consistently-estimated health production technology were used for the households with longitudinal data to obtain consistent estimates of the impact of individual endowments on individual nutrients. These estimates suggest reinforcement in the sense that individuals with better endowments receive more nutrients once there is control for the measurement error problem noted above (which, if not controlled, leads to estimates that are opposite in sign, suggesting compensation); these effects are about ten times larger for males than for females, which is consistent with their model, given that their data indicate that women do not participate in energy-intensive activities. Within-household estimates by gender with age-specific endowment effects suggest that reinforcement is significant for males 12 years of age or older and for both males and females in the 6–12 year age range, but that compensation may occur for those

---

[18] Pitt et al. (1990) show that, if the true impact of such endowments on nutrients is positive, the estimated impact will be downward biased. But if the true impact is negative, the classical measurement error bias is towards zero (and therefore positive) while the bias due to the correlation of the estimated endowment with the measurement error in nutrients is negative, so the overall effect is indeterminate.

under 6 years of age of both sexes (although the standard errors are large); for females 12 years of age or older the sign of the coefficient is positive but the magnitude is very small and the standard error very large. Next, they explore what the impact of (instrumented) endowments is on household income and on participating in an exceptionally active occupation (in the absence of data on individual wage rates or earnings). Their estimates suggest that there is a pecuniary return to health and effort, that adult males with higher endowments are more likely to undertake exceptionally energy-intensive work, and that adult female health endowments are relatively unimportant (in comparison with those for adult males) in determining activity choices or household income. Finally, the net effect of a change in own endowments on own health are calculated from the estimated health production functions and the estimated endowment effects on the nutrient and work effort variables in those production functions; the elasticities of own health with respect to own endowments are 0.88 for adult males and 0.97 for adult females. Thus, on net Bangladeshi households exhibit compensatory behavior with respect to adult health endowments so that these elasticities are less than one, with adult males being "taxed" to the benefit of other household members more than females. Therefore, by incorporating the expected impact of nutrient investments in an integrated manner with the estimates of that impact, not only do they come to fuller understanding of how nutrient investments work but also to a different understanding of the nature of intrahousehold allocations of nutrients, a question on which there has been considerable debate.[19]

4.2. Productivity impact of health and nutrition

In poor countries many people, including workers and students, have poor health or nutrition. There have been many conjectures that such poor health and nutrition has negative effects on productivities in the labor force and in forming human capital to be used subsequently in the labor force (e.g., in schooling success).

4.2.1. Nutrition-based efficiency model
The nutrition-based efficiency model of Leibenstein (1957), Mazumdar (1959), Mirrlees (1975) and Stiglitz (1976) systematizes the possible impact of nutrition on productivity as

---

[19] Limitations in the data mean that some qualifications are appropriate. The use of the instruments for the health production function to obtain consistent estimates of the production function coefficients and of the residual endowments depends upon the assumption that there are no allocated inputs into the production of health that are not observed, a strong assumption. If women's time in household production (not observed), for example, has an effect on health, instrumented nutrients and work effort may be representing in part the impact of women's time allocations since such allocations presumably respond to the same set of exogenous instruments. The assumption that measurement errors in nutrient intakes are not correlated across periods may be strong if the intrahousehold allocation of food was altered to favor certain groups identified by age or sex because of the presence of outside dietary investigators. The measure of work effort based on 14 occupational categories, finally, is quite crude, ignores what probably are substantially variations within such categories, and may impart a gender bias since some have claimed that the FAO/WHO estimates understate energy used in various household activities performed primarily by females.

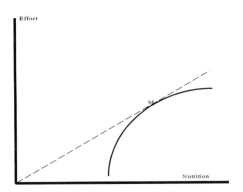

Fig. 3. Effort nutrition locus with optimal work effort at M.

a possible explanation of downward rigidity of rural wages in poor labor markets that may be associated with surplus labor. This, thus, is an alternative theoretical explanation for surplus labor to the household models discussed in Section 2.

Central to the nutrition-based efficiency model is a modified agricultural production function that is identical to that in relation (2) except the labor time is multiplied by efficiency per unit time (E) as in relations (9C,D) which in turn depends on nutrients consumed and therefore consumption (c):

$$Q = Q(A, LE(c), F). \tag{13}$$

The efficiency per unit time as a function of c is zero until some minimum consumption level and then increasing in c at a declining rate over the relevant range as in Fig. 3.[20] Under the assumptions that there is an infinitely elastic supply of workers at the wage W, that employers can appropriate all the additional product that workers with better nutrition produce, that c depends only on W so that $E(c) = E(W)$ and that the farm's land area is fixed, profit maximization implies that employers select what wage they pay and how much labor time they hire to maximize $P_Q Q(A, LE(W), F) - WL - P_F F$. The first-order conditions for this maximization imply

$$W^*/E = 1/E_W, \tag{14}$$

where * indicates the maximizing choice. Thus the efficiency wage, which minimizes the

---

[20] There is some difference in the literature regarding what this functional form is at very low levels of c. Mirrlees (1975) and Stiglitz (1976) posit a non-convexity with initially increasing marginal effects of c (i.e., with $E_{cc} > 0$) and then declining marginal effects (with $E_{cc} < 0$). Bliss and Stern (1978) and Dasgupta and Ray (1986a,b) posit a discontinuity at some minimum consumption level from no effect to decreasing marginal effects (with $E_{cc} < 0$). The non-convexity in the former case leads to some peculiarities, such as unequal distribution among household members may be optimal even if the family welfare function is additive in individual family member's utilities. With both forms the convex region is what is relevant for the basic possible explanation of downwardly-rigid wages and unemployment.

cost per level of effort, is chosen so that the average cost per unit of effort just equals the marginal cost per unit effort.

In the simplest form of this model in which workers have no alternative income sources, there would be no savings, no dependants, and no unemployed workers. If workers have alternative sources of consumption (i.e., full income in relation 3 includes not only full earnings but also positive net profits from own farming or positive other income) and if employers are informed about workers' other income sources and their family composition, time wages vary depending on workers' alternative income sources and family composition. Bliss and Stern (1978) show that if the employer is a monopolist, the employer pays out time wages so that consumption of workers is equalized, which implies lower time wages for landed than for landless workers (so that the former are hired before the latter). Dasgupta and Ray (1986, 1987) show that if there is perfect competition, each worker receives the same payment per unit of work effort, so those with higher levels of alternative consumption sources who supply more effort per time unit receive higher wages per time unit. Thus workers with more land (or other alternative consumption sources) and fewer dependants receive higher time wages and workers with limited enough alternative consumption sources and numerous enough dependants so that the time wage is at or below the efficiency wage may be unemployed (in which case redistribution of assets towards these workers may increase output). Thus, predictions about patterns of time wages and employment among potential workers with differing alternative income sources and number of dependants depends on the labor market structure.

4.2.2. Empirical estimates of health/nutrition effects on labor productivity

Rosenzweig (1988a) reviews the evidence then available regarding the predictions of (a) coexistence of high unemployment rates and downwardly-rigid wages, (b) wage diversity and (c) direct productivity effects of nutrition in rural areas of developing countries. He concludes that there is no support for (a) and (b) and that, prior to Strauss's (1986) study (see below) there was no persuasive evidence on (c) because it was not clear from such studies whether higher nutrient consumption caused higher productivity or higher income associated with higher productivity caused greater food and nutrient consumption. More recent studies are consistent with his summary regarding (a) and (b) (e.g., Richards, 1994 on Egypt).

Strauss (1986) is the first study of which I am aware that investigates the impact of nutrition on productivity with control for their possible simultaneous determination. He estimates the effect of a family's average intake of calories per adult consumer-equivalent on the productivity of on-farm family labor in Sierra Leonean agriculture. One of his production function inputs is "effective family labor," which is a non-linear function of actual on-farm family labor hours and the average availability of calories per consumer-equivalent in the household. Effective family labor has a statistically significant coefficient estimate in the agricultural production function, and effective family labor increases significantly, at a diminishing rate, with available calories, calculated on a per consumer-equivalent basis. Strauss estimates the output elasticity of available calories on a per consumer-equivalent basis to be 0.33 at the sample mean, 0.49 at 1500 calories a day, and 0.12 at 4500 calories a day. His estimates imply that an increase in caloric intake results in a substantial increase in the efficiency of an hour of labor (e.g., a laborer who consumes 4500 calories a day is 20% more productive than one who consumes 3000 calories a day). These findings are robust to several alternative specifications and to changes in the instruments used for his first-stage calorie estimates. Strauss also notes that labor market wages are not significantly related to caloric consumption, which is consistent with markets being incomplete because nutrient-related productivity is difficult to observe.

Subsequent to Strauss's study, there have been a number of other empirical investigations that attempt to investigate the impact of nutrition and health on output/income/profits or wages primarily in rural areas of developing countries [21] with some effort to control for the endogenous choices that led to the observed nutrition and health states (Table 5). These studies use some combination of nutrient and health indicators that refer to different time periods: (i) calories, which refer to recent food consumption and energy availability, (ii) weight for height or BMI (body mass index, weight/height^2), each of which is a common measure of short-run nutrition and health status, and (iii) height, which is a common measure of long-run nutrition and health status. All of these studies attempt to control for the possible endogeneity or omitted variable bias for the first two indicators through using instrumental variable and/or fixed effects estimators. Most of the studies assume that height can be treated as independent in such estimates – i.e., that height is independent of any unobserved characteristics in the disturbance term that affect labor productivity – although a few studies control for such possibilities.[22] The studies vary in their coverage of the three groups of nutrition and health indicators. If the true specification includes all three of these indicators, if all three depend on some common characteristics (e.g., genetic health endowments) or if one is an input into the production of another[23] or if the same anthropometric indicator is used to construct more than one of these three groups of indicators (i.e., height is used for both b and c), and if all three are not included (or controlled for) in the specification, the estimates of the included indicators may be biased (despite the use of instruments) because they are representing in part the incorrectly excluded nutrition/health indicators.

Though the estimates are somewhat mixed, for most part they suggest significant effects of nutrition/health on agricultural production, net profits or wages and some variations by gender with effects if anything more likely to be significant or larger for males than for

---

[21] Thomas and Strauss (1997) is the only study in this table with estimates on urban areas. Sahn and Alderman (1988) report that estimates that they made for urban areas were not very robust and therefore they do not give these estimates, but only those for rural areas.

[22] Alderman et al. (1996b) use instrumented height with instruments from parental household characteristics. Deolalikar (1988) presents household and individual fixed effects estimates that control for height, but do not permit estimation of the effect of height. Some of Haddad and Bouis' (1991) alternative estimates also use individual fixed effects.

[23] For example, BMI production functions with calories included among the inputs are presented in Pitt et al. (1990) and in Foster and Rosenzweig (1994b), both of which are discussed above.

Table 5
Summary of estimates of impact of nutrition on output/income/profits and on market wages[a]

Location, dependent variable, time, and subsamples	Elasticity with respect to			Source
	Calories	Weight/height or BMI***	Height	
Output/income/profits				
Sierra Leone (farm output) 1974–1975[b]	0.33*			Strauss (1986)
India (Semi-arid tropics farm output) 1976–1978[c]	0.07	1.90*	r	Deolalikar (1988)
Brazil (urban self-employed income) 1974–195[d]				Thomas and Strauss (1997)
Male	–	5.18*	3.58*	
Female	+	–3.92	–1.00	
Pakistan (Rabi season net farm profits) 1986–1989[e]				Behrman et al. (1997a)
<1.5 acres	0.16*			
>1.5 acres	0.06*			
Pakistan (farm crop income) 1986–1989[f]				Fafchamps and Quisumbing (1997)
Kharif season				
Male		0.08	1.84	
Female		–0.63	0.46	
Rabi season				
Male		0.73	–1.34	
Female		–0.25	–2.13	
Market wages				
India (rural semi-arid tropics) 1976–1978[g]	–0.01	0.66*	r	Deolalikar (1988)
Sri Lanka (rural) 1980–1981[h]				Sahn and Alderman (1988)
Male	0.20*			
Female	0.05			
India (rural Semi-arid tropics) 1976–1978[i]				Behrman and Deolalikar (1989b)
Slack labor demand	–0.05	0.67*		
Peak labor demand	0.27*	0.35*		
Philippines (rural Bukidnon) 1984–1985[l]				Haddad and Bouis (1991)
Adults	0.04	0.02	1.36*	
Adolescents	–0.08	0.23	Dropped	

Table 5 (*continued*)

Location, dependent variable, time, and subsamples	Elasticity with respect to			Source
	Calories	Weight/height or BMI***	Height	
Philippines (rural Bukidnon) 1984–1985[m]				Foster and Rosenzweig (1993a,b)
Piece rate wage	1.06*		0.69	
Time wage	−0.04		0.06	
Piece rate–time wage	0.76*		2.96*	
Philippines (rural Bukidnon) 1984–1985[n]				Foster and Rosenzweig (1994b)
Piece rate–time wage	0.75*	−0.41**	2.14**	
Pakistan (rural) 1989[o]		0.77	0.38	Alderman et al. (1996b)
Brazil (urban) 1974–1975[p]				Thomas and Strauss (1997)
Male	−*	4.74*	3.92*	
Female	−*	−0.41	2.46*	
Pakistan (rural) 1986–1989[q]				Fafchamps and Quisumbing (1997)
Male		0.31*	−0.00	
Female		0.34*	−0.61	

[a] *Underlying point estimates significantly non-zero at 0.05 level. **Underlying point estimates significantly non-zero at 0.10 level. ***BMI is "body mass index" defined to be weight divided by height squared (usually measured in kg/m^2). Weight/height is used unless BMI is explicitly noted to be used.

[b] At sample mean (2435 calories per day). For mean of lower tercile in terms of calorie consumption (1500 calories per day), 0.49. For mean of upper tercile in terms of calorie consumption (4500 calories per day), 0.12. Non-linear calorie effect jointly significant at 0.01 level. IV estimates of agricultural production function with average household calorie availability.

[c] Household fixed effects estimates (Hausman test rejects random effects) of log-linear agricultural production function using average adult nutrient intakes based on individual nutrient data.

[d] IV estimates for earnings (net of business expenses, but may include returns to capital) of self-employed urban workers, with BMI used instead of weight for height. The calorie effects are more positive at low calorie intake levels, but become negative above 1835 calories per day for males and 2430 calories per day for females (the former of which probably is below the sample means although they are not reported because it is reported that the mean for the bottom quartile is "around 1700 per day" on p. 173).

[e] IV fixed effects estimates of generalized Leontieff harvest stage production function with per capita calorie consumption in planting stage of production.

[f] Village fixed effects estimates for Kharif season (64% of total crop income) and Rabi season (36% of total crop income) using BMI instead of weight/ height and using average adult male and female human capital indicators (in alternative estimates with only husband's and wife's human capital only husband's height in Kharif season is significant with an elasticity of 7.03).

[g] Individual fixed effects estimates (Hausman test rejects random effects) of semilog wage function using individual nutrient intakes.

[h] IV estimates of semilog wage function (but with household per capita calories having constant elasticity) that are robust to use of different instruments. Parallel estimates for urban areas indicate positive and significant signs, but are not robust to changes in instruments or in sample size (and are not reported in the article).

[i] IV estimates of semilog wage functions, evaluated at sample mean, using individual nutrient intakes. "Peak" and "slack" refer to labor demands (high or "peak" during harvesting, threshing, clearing and plowing). These estimates combine data on 193 men and 275 women, but disaggregated estimates by sex indicate that most of the nutrition effects appear to be for the men.

[j] Hausman and Taylor random effects estimates (preferred by authors) for adults (at least 20 years of age) and adolescents (less than 20 years of age). The calorie estimates do not change much with within estimates, but appear significant with an elasticity of 0.08 for adults in OLS estimates. Weight for height is insignificant for different estimation techniques and specifications, as is BMI if it is used instead. The estimated effects of height for adults are significant and do not vary much in magnitude across estimation techniques and alternative specifications.

[k] Weighted 2SLS estimates of semilog wage functions for harvest period using individual nutrients with piece rates, time rates and within-round piece rates-time rate wage. Elasticities based on per capita daily calorie consumption of 2400 and average height of about 1.55 m (which are about the averages reported in Foster and Rosenzweig (1994) for the same dataset).

[l] Weighted 2SLS within round estimates of semilog wage functions for harvest period using individual nutrients and BMI with harvest piece rates minus harvest time rates that are robust to alternative controls for selectivity. Elasticities based on per capita daily calorie consumption of 2400, BMI of 20.4 and height of 1.55 m, which are about the averages reported for the larger sample for which a subset (47%) worked under different contracts in the same round and are used in these estimates.

[m] IV estimates for all human capital variables and control for selectivity regarding earning wages with BMI instead of weight for height. BMI (but not height) appears significant at the 10% level if cognitive achievement, years of schooling, ability and height are excluded from OLS specifications.

[n] IV estimates that appear robust with respect to control for selectivity, cluster effects, and choice of instruments, with BMI used instead of weight for height. The calorie effects are much more positive at low calorie intake levels, but become negative above 1760 calories per day for males and 1841 calories per day for females (which are probably below the sample means although they are not reported because it is reported that the mean for the bottom quartile is "around 1700 per day" on p. 173).

[o] District fixed effects estimates for off-farm net earned income with average human capital for all adult males and all adult females.

[p] Fixed effects control for health, although estimates of impact of health not obtained.

females presumably because of gender divisions of labor with males more concentrated in tasks in which strength and bursts of energy are important.

These estimates also shed some light on possible information questions relating to nutrition and health that tie in to the basic multistage agricultural production technology that is discussed in Section 3. If the production process can be considered to have two stages, planting and harvesting,[24] the production functions are (9C) and (9D). Assume that the weather realizations occur at the start of each stage. In the planting stage labor, land and other inputs have to be committed without knowledge of the weather that will be experienced in the harvest stage (although probably with knowledge of the distribution of harvest weather). As discussed in Section 3, effort in some important agricultural tasks (e.g., weeding and application of fertilizer and pesticides as opposed to harvesting) cannot be costlessly or cheaply monitored because of the combination of production lags, imperfect observability by farmers of the intermediate product, and the spatial dispersion and heterogeneity in production conditions even on one farm; there is not a distinct market for effort separate from the market for labor time; and the time–wage alone insufficiently rewards effort.

The studies that are summarized in Table 5 are generally consistent with nutrition having short term effects on labor effort and productivity that are not easily observed during the agricultural planting season.[25] For five of the six agricultural production function/net profit estimates and explicit piece-rate wage estimates, there are significant positive effects of calories. Foster and Rosenzweig (1994b) further suggest that in one of the two other cases in which there is a significant positive effect – that for peak season rural Indian labor in Behrman and Deolalikar (1989b) – harvest piece rate wages dominate so, even though the piece rate wages are not separated out explicitly, this estimate reflects the same phenomenon. For only one of the other seven estimates of rural market wage effects, in contrast, are the estimates of calories significantly positive.

In some of the studies in the top part of Table 5, moreover, the multistage nature of production is central to the analysis. For example the piece rate wages are for the harvest stage during which monitoring of harvesting productivity is relatively costless and the estimated significant impact of calories on net profits in Pakistan is for *planting stage* calories on *harvest* profits, with no significant impact of harvest calories on harvest profits,

---

[24] The production process may have other important stages between planting and harvesting, but the basic points are illustrated by collapsing all of the pre-harvest stages into the planting stage.

[25] Thomas and Strauss (1997, pp. 177–180) find significant effects of calories for wage work but not for self-employment in urban Brazil and claim, in explicit contrast to the interpretation of Foster and Rosenzweig (1994b), that "employers can observe the outputs (of better nutrition), such as better general health, improved pallor and higher levels of energy and effort, and those indicators may be used in setting wages of their workers." But, as noted in Table 5, for most the sample that Thomas and Strauss use, the significant estimates that they report imply negative effects of calories on wage rates received, which seems puzzling if employers can observe indicators of greater calories consumed and such calories affect labor productivity. Therefore, although they may be correct that their results suggest strong positive wage effects of calories for those who consume very low levels of calories even though the self-employment selected by such workers does not have such returns, the estimates of the negative wage effects of calories for most of the sample raise questions about their interpretation.

which is consistent with the monitoring problem being particularly severe for planting stage activities. The two studies of which I am aware that explicitly compare nutrient demand elasticities for small farmers between the planting and harvest seasons, moreover, report much larger elasticities in the planting season than in the harvest season in India and Pakistan (Behrman and Deolalikar, 1989a; Behrman et al., 1997a).[26] This pattern of elasticities is consistent with limited capacities for transferring resources across production stages for small farmers and relatively high returns from using any extra resources to increase own-farm productivity through consuming more calories in the planting stage because of the absence of labor market rewards for such productivity in that stage due to the monitoring problem, but the relative absence of such observability problems in the harvest stage.

Thus these estimates, although based on a few samples, suggest that information problems on work effort are significant for low-income agriculture in developing countries – particularly in planting and other pre-harvest production stages. If poor households had better means of transferring resources over times or if there were better means of monitoring work efforts, such problems would be lessened.[27] The extent of efficiency gains that could be obtained, however, are not well-quantified.

Swamy (1997), finally, also provides a simple test of the nutrition-efficiency wage model. He uses the estimates of calorie effects on productivity in rural India from Behrman and Deolalikar (1989b) that are most favorable to this model (i.e., indicating the largest response), and shows that, contrary to the claims of these models, a wage cut would lower the cost per efficiency unit of labor.

4.3. Determinants of schooling

Conventional wisdom is that, while the returns to health/nutrition investments may be relatively high in poor and stagnant societies, schooling is the human resource with the highest return in labor markets and elsewhere at somewhat higher levels of income and in dynamic economies. Most of the empirical studies of the determinants of schooling in developing countries have focused on household income and parental income, with a few

---

[26] There are many studies of the responsiveness of nutrition to income and some controversy over the magnitude of these responses that is discussed in Section 4.1, but most studies do not consider the possibility of differential responses depending on the stage of production in agricultural economies.

[27] It is useful to note that the rural employment schemes that often are advocated to address rural seasonal income problems do not fully address this problem caused by the unobservability of effort because any household member who is working on such a scheme cannot be working simultaneously on own-farm production in which the greater effort is rewarded. Such schemes may improve the capacity of poor households to exploit the greater productivity with better nutrition in own-farm production if they help provide additional planting-stage income through the use of some of the household's labor on such employment schemes so that the rest of the household's labor can be better nourished and therefore more productive in own-farm work. But the increased productivity of household own-farm labor must offset the reduction in such labor in order for there to be incentives to participate in the employment scheme.

studies on other determinants such as opportunity costs, health and nutrition, risks and expected returns.

4.3.1. Household income

As for health and nutrition investments, the implications of the standard human capital investment model are that household income in itself should not affect schooling investment unless there are incomplete markets. Most empirical studies of schooling include household income, apparently usually because of the perception (sometimes explicit) that household income facilitates schooling investments because of imperfect capital and insurance markets.

A recent survey in the Appendix of Behrman and Knowles (1999) of associations between schooling investments with household income for 42 studies for 21 (mostly developing) countries reports that estimates for about three-fifths of the schooling indicators used in these studies yield significant associations between household income and schooling. Among the cases in which income elasticities can be estimated from the information provided in the studies, the median is 0.07, with the estimated income elasticities tending to be a little higher for poorer samples and with small inverse associations of the estimates with income reported in a number of studies.[28] Such low values for most of these elasticities present a puzzle for those who perceive that there are high intergenerational correlations in income and that the income returns from income-associated schooling investments are a major mechanism through which intergenerational income correlations are generated. This survey suggests that one reason that the estimated income elasticities in many studies are low is the use of income indicators that may be contaminated by relatively large measurement errors as a representation of the true longer-run income constraint and possibly endogeneity. To illustrate, explorations with Vietnamese data suggest that using predicted income/expenditures yields estimates on the order of magnitude of 50–60% higher than using current annual income measures. This survey also suggests that another reason that most studies might underestimate income-schooling investment associations is that indicators of schooling investments generally are limited to schooling attainment or enrollments. But cognitive achievement (or other school outcomes) may differ significantly with income for a given level of schooling attainment and the age of completing a given schooling level also may be inversely associated with income (leaving more post-schooling time to reap the returns from schooling). Illustrative estimates for Vietnam in Behrman and Knowles (1999) suggest that such considerations add significantly to the income-schooling investment associations, as does selectivity regarding who continues in school (i.e., only high-ability children from poor families, but almost all children from better-off families). Thus, this survey suggests that most of the

---

[28] The largest estimates – those over 0.20 – are for low-income countries, areas or time periods: Côte d'Ivoire, Ghana, Nepal, Taiwan for the 1940–1949 birth cohort, Northeastern Brazil, and rural Pakistan. But these are the only cases in which the estimates surveyed exceed 0.20. In several cases beyond these six the specifications used allow non-linear income associations and find diminishing marginal income relations, although the changes in the elasticities implied by these inverse associations are small.

empirical literature on schooling investments probably underestimates the importance of household income, in part because of measurement issues and in part because systematic conceptual frameworks are not used for the investigations.

One recent study of schooling in developing countries that lays out much more systematically than most of the literature how income and schooling investments might be related in the presence of incomplete financial markets is Jacoby and Skoufias (1997). They note that there had been considerable prior emphasis on both financial markets and human capital as major factors in development, but not on their interaction. They also note that there have been a number of recent studies to test the implications of incomplete financial markets in both developing and developed economies, but that most of these studies shed little light on the mechanisms by which consumption smoothing is attained. They investigate how child school attendance responds to seasonal income fluctuations in agrarian Indian households using panel data. They study responses to aggregate and household idiosyncratic and anticipated and unanticipated income shocks. They posit a dynamic model of school attendance with different degrees of financial market completeness and note that with incomplete markets consumption and schooling investment decisions are not separable. Their estimation strategy is to relax successively restrictions on the relationships between school attendance and income shocks implied by successively more incomplete financial markets, all with control for unobserved household heterogeneity. Their results indicate that seasonal variations in school attendance are a form of self-insurance that significantly reduces the schooling of children in households that are vulnerable to risk, which is likely to be a costly form of insurance, particularly for poorer households. The results have a number of potentially important policy implications, such that expanding schools without understanding the nature of financial risks and market constraints may have more limited effects on education than expected, effective compulsory schooling laws or restrictions against child labor may have substantial negative effects on household welfare, and improved shortterm credit and insurance markets may have important long-term benefits in the form of greater human capital investments.

4.3.2. Parental schooling

Conventional wisdom is that: (1) mother's schooling has widespread positive substantial effects on child education; (2) these effects tend to be much larger than those of father's schooling; and (3) therefore, ceteris paribus, there is a stronger efficiency case (given education externalities) for subsidies for female than for male schooling. Behrman (1997b) first discusses a general framework for thinking about the impact of mother's schooling on child education and then surveys what is known on the basis of all 237 estimates on 22 (mostly developing) countries that were located. Examination of available estimates in light of this general framework suggests that knowledge on the impact of women's schooling on child education generally could be improved with more clarity about what model is estimated, roles of possibly important unobserved variables such as preferences and abilities, distinctions between particular and more-general total effects, and use of broader indicators of both mother's and child's education that capture outcomes rather than primarily time-in-school inputs. Taken at their face value the central tendency of current estimates is consistent with the "widespread" and "positive" part of point 1 of the conventional wisdom, but not with the "substantial" part of point 1, or for the claim that the effects of mother's schooling tend to be much greater than those of father's schooling – and therefore not with a efficiency argument for large subsidies for female schooling, or for larger subsidies for female than for male schooling.

Most studies, however, include among right-side variables some that possibly are determined partially by mother's schooling. On the basis of a priori considerations, a few studies that explore the effects of such procedures, and new estimates that characterize all estimates that have been located, the usual specifications lead to a substantial under-estimate of the total effect of mother's schooling and a smaller upward bias in the esti-mated relative impact of mother's versus father's schooling, with control for income and less so school characteristics biasing the estimated effects towards mother's schooling and control for number of children and community characteristics biasing the estimates some-what less towards father's schooling.

Most existing studies do not control for possible biases in the estimated effects of mother's schooling due to unobserved (by analysts) abilities and preferences that directly affect child education and that are correlated with mother's schooling. A few studies suggest that unobserved preference and ability endowments may affect importantly the estimated impact of mother's schooling on child education, with estimates generally (although not always) biased upwards by the failure to control for these endowments. They also suggest that marriage market considerations may be critical for analyzing the impact of mother's schooling on child education, and that such considerations at least in some contexts increase the estimated impact of mother's relative to father's schooling. But these studies also point to the sensitivity of the results to how such endowments are controlled, including the limitations of partial controls through observed indicators. There-fore it is critical for interpretation that the underlying model be spelled out explicitly and used directly as a guide to the estimation method because estimates using behavioral data are necessarily conditional on particular assumptions about the underlying model and explicit modeling makes it clear on what the interpretation is based.

I now review two recent studies of the role of parental schooling in child education in developing countries that deal with some of the problems noted in this survey.

Behrman et al. (1999) examine the role of parents' schooling in child education in the Green Revolution period in rural India. While the Green Revolution increased the rates of return to men's schooling, given the gender division of labor there is not evidence of an impact on the direct economic returns to women's schooling. Yet men in areas that benefited from the Green Revolution married more-schooled women. This is somewhat of a puzzle because, within household bargaining models, such women obtain a larger share of the economic pie without contributing directly to the size of the pie. Among the possible explanations are that men have pure consumption demands for more-schooled wives and that more-schooled women contribute indirectly to the household by raising more-educated children, a public good within the household.

This study examines the latter possibility. It presents household fixed effect estimates, controlling for unobserved characteristics of the father's household,[29] for Indian farm household children's daily school and study hours with and without instrumenting mother's schooling (literacy). In this case the instruments are local technological shocks when the father was of marriage age that the authors argue are independent of the disturbance term in the within-household estimates for time that children spend studying or in school.[30] The instrumented estimates indicate an impact of mother's literacy that is more than double the uninstrumented estimates. Also of interest is the impact of the control for the father's family endowments by using within-household estimates in a context in which extended households make possible such estimation. OLS estimates of the determination of children's school and study hours yield significant effects of mother being literate and of father having primary schooling. But within-household estimates, while still yielding estimates that imply that mother being literate has a significantly positive effect of about the same magnitude (with the exact magnitude depending on the instrumenting discussed above), yield estimates of the effect of father's primary schooling that are less than a fifth of the OLS estimate and that are very imprecisely estimated (and would not be judged non-zero even at the 50% level of significance). That is, in this case, the apparent direct effect of father's schooling of more-or-less the same magnitude as of mother's schooling in standard OLS estimates evaporates in within-household estimates while the estimated effect of mother's schooling is robust to the estimation alternatives considered. Thus in the OLS estimates the estimated direct impact of father's schooling on child educational time use is strongly contaminated and biased upwards by proxying for household preferences regarding time use and possibly household resources. To the extent that the within-household estimates of the effect of father's schooling differ from the OLS ones because of the control for household resources, of course, father's schooling still may have an important indirect effect. However, the authors downplay this possibility because, if there were such an effect, it also would seem to be reflected in subhousehold allocations of household resources so that father's schooling would still seem to be important even in the within-household estimates.

[29] Another of the studies that is included surveyed in the survey summarized above also controls for childhood family effects, in this case for the mothers, by using data on adult sisters and half-sisters in Nicaragua (Behrman and Wolfe, 1984). For completed schooling for females the within-estimates of mother's schooling are 30% of OLS estimates and the within estimates of father's schooling are 40% of the OLS estimates. For household income the within estimates of mother's schooling are significantly negative in contrast to insignificant negative estimates for OLS, while the within estimates of father's schooling are 70% greater than the OLS estimates (and significantly positive). These results are suggestive that controlling for mother's endowments also may affect the estimates importantly, and in some cases as much or more so for mother's as for father's schooling effects. But generalizing from these estimates is somewhat risky because of their dependence on half-sisters to obtain within effects. Also they do not control for measurement error, the effects of which, as is well-known, are exacerbated with within estimates, although the result that the within estimates are larger in absolute magnitude in several cases could not come from the classical measurement error model.

[30] As the authors note, if mothers' preferences related to child schooling are heterogenous and known at the time of marriages, then the instruments used may not be independent of the disturbance term in the child's time use relation.

In another recent paper Foster (1996) argues that estimates of parental schooling on child education can be seriously biased if marriage partners self-select on the basis of unobserved characteristics. To deal with this issue, he develops a model of the marriage market in which potential mates care about the human capital of their offspring (a public good within marriage) as well as their own private consumption. Under the assumption of transferable utility, child investment is shown to depend on the income and tastes for offspring schooling of each of the marital partners. The problem in estimating the decision rule is that, with selective marriages, the unobserved traits of existing marital partners are not orthogonal. The paper develops a simulation method for correcting for the selection bias that involves explicitly solving approximately for the marriage market equilibrium. Using data from rural Bangladesh, the estimates indicate that marital selection is quantitatively important, significantly diminishing the effect of husband's traits by 35–55% and augmenting the effect of wife's traits by 13–16% on the desired schooling of children.[31] This effect is separate from biases due to mother's schooling being a proxy in part for her own unobserved tastes and productivity in child education, which are not considered in this study.

4.3.3. Opportunity costs

If markets were complete they would incorporate all costs of schooling, including most importantly the cost of time. But labor markets for children, among others, in many contexts are quite limited or non-existent. So private schooling investments decisions generally tend to value time of children differentially and inefficiently. A few studies of developing countries address directly the nature of opportunity costs of children in attending school.

Rosenzweig and Evenson (1977), for example, find that the combination of incomplete labor and land markets in rural India result in significant positive effects of land ownership on child on-farm labor and thus significant negative effects of land ownership on child school attendance. Thus, despite the generally positive relation between household resources and child schooling noted above probably due to incomplete capital and credit markets, certain forms of household resources – in particular land that is a complement with child labor for which market substitutes are not readily available – in some market contexts cause a reduction of child schooling.

In most societies there is gender specialization in the provision of home health care, with females providing most such care. Pitt and Rosenzweig (1990) develop and implement a method for estimating the effects of infant morbidity on the differential allocation of time of family members within the context of a household model in which health is determined simultaneously. Identification of the effects of the health of person k on the

---

[31] Foster shows that these directions of bias can occur when the unobservable component of assortative mating is large relative to the observable component for women and there is no unobservable component for men (say, because they primarily are income earners based on observed characteristics). The intuition is that, in this case, the husband's schooling is positively correlated with the wife's unobservable so that, in estimates that do not control for marriage selection, the estimated effect of the husband's schooling is overstated. This effectively means that there is in the disturbance term an expression equal to the true minus the estimated effect of husband's schooling times the wife's unobservable, which is negative so that the wife's schooling effect is underestimated.

behavior of person *j* when the behavior of person *j* may affect the health of person *k* (e.g., through child care) is not easy in part because it is difficult to find instruments that directly affect *i*'s health but not directly that of *j* (net of any indirect effects through *i*'s health). They assume that households have a consensus preference function defined over the home time and health of each household member and a composite jointly-consumed consumption commodity with heterogeneity in such preferences across households. This preference function is maximized subject to a budget constraint (which includes the wage for each household member type as well as non-labor earnings) and a health production function (which includes the home time of each household member, the health of every other household member to allow for intrafamily health externalities inclusive of contagion and/or health efficiency effects on home time, and private health-related goods and services). They posit that the linearized demand relations for home time of household members *i* and *j* conditional on the health of household member *k* in which the coefficients on price of private health-related goods is the same for *i* and for *j* (e.g., if the health production function is the same for *i* and *j*), which is a critical (and perhaps strong) identifying assumption. The differenced version of these relations then gives the difference in the home time of *i* and *j* as a function of the difference in their wage rates, any difference in the impact of the price of the jointly-consumed composite commodity price on their home time use, and any difference in the impact of the health of *k* on their time use.

Conditional on the assumptions underlying this relation, a consistent estimate of the impact of the health of *k* on the difference in home time use between *i* and *j* is obtained by using the prices of health-related goods as instruments. The data requirement for estimating such relations are severe: information on child health, the activities of all household members, and the prices of health-related goods, as well as a large enough sample so that there are enough families with the family types of interest with whom the within estimates can be made (i.e., mothers, teenage daughters and sons, and infants). The 1980 Indonesian Socioeconomic Survey linked with other information on prices and health programs has such data for 5831 households. However, for both health and time allocations what is available in this dataset are discrete indicators (dichotomous for health, trichotomous for activities – labor force, school, home time), so Pitt and Rosenzweig adopt a fixed effects or within-family logit procedure that is parsimonious in terms of parameters to be estimated, permits identification, and controls for possible selectivity of households into this subsample. The estimates obtained indicate that teenage daughters were significantly more likely to increase their participation in household care activities and to reduce their participation in market activities and at school in comparison with teenage sons in response to increased morbidity of infant siblings. Moreover, such estimates differed markedly from the estimates obtained if there was not control for the simultaneity of child health determination and time uses of household members, although the conclusions need to be qualified because the critical identifying assumption is strong.

4.3.4. Impact of nutrition/health on schooling

As noted above, one implication of the standard human capital investment model is that human resource investments may interact. In the presence of incomplete markets for capital and insurance, such effects are likely to be inefficient. There have been considerable claims for both developing and developed economies that better child nutrition and health, for example, cause better schooling success, with long-run benefits in terms of economic productivity in the labor market that may not be realized efficiently due to incomplete markets. But evidence is quite limited because numerous studies based on socioeconomic surveys fail to model the process clearly and, perhaps for that reason, fail to consider the endogeneity of child health, measurement error, and the impact of unobserved fixed and choice inputs. Until recently, the available studies using behavioral data that were used to justify the claim of positive child health/nutrition on child success did not permit clear interpretation because the choice element of child nutrition and health was not controlled. Three recent studies for developing countries attempt to deal with these estimation problems.

Glewwe and Jacoby (1995) explore one dimension of the relation between child health/ nutrition and child school performance. They are sensitive to the treatment of child health/ nutrition as a choice rather than predetermined as in the previous literature and explore how robust their estimates are to alternative methods of controlling for choices affecting child health/nutrition within an explicit model of economic behavior (although their need to depend on noisy recall data for their a priori most persuasive estimates limits their success in their empirical application that otherwise uses basically cross-sectional behavior data). Previous studies in this literature, moreover, had focused on fairly static analysis of relations between indicators of child health/nutrition and outcomes such as test performance and grade completed controlling for age. Glewwe and Jacoby instead consider the dynamic sequence of age of initial enrollment (that they first demonstrate can have a substantial impact on lifetime wealth), progress through school, and age of school completion and entry into the post-school workforce. Their results indicate that delays in enrollment are responsive to early child malnutrition, although the estimated effect is reduced substantially (by almost two fifths) if there is control for unobserved family and community variables, suggesting that indicators of child health/nutrition in part proxy for such unobserved factors in previous estimates. Their empirical results therefore suggest that: (a) estimates of the impact of child health/nutrition on child schooling success may be quite sensitive to the underlying behavioral assumptions and the nature of unobserved variables, (b) if there is not control for behavioral choices in the presence of unobserved household and community factors the estimated impact of child health/nutrition on child schooling success is overestimated substantially so most of the previous studies in this literature may be fundamentally misleading regarding the magnitude of the impact of child health/nutrition on child schooling success, and (c) an important channel through which child health/nutrition may affect earnings through schooling pertains to the age when children start school, a channel that had been largely ignored in the previous literature on child health/nutrition and schooling success.

Behrman and Lavy (1997) show that a priori the biases resulting from ignoring household decisions affecting child health/nutrition in the presence of unobservable in estimates of the impact of child health/nutrition on child schooling success may be positive or negative depending on which of a number of household allocation behaviors dominate and what is the nature of any unobserved choice inputs in educational production. Then illustrative empirical analysis, using rich data from Ghana, is presented, with the following results: (1) IV estimates based on observed family and community characteristics similar to those used in other studies suggest a downward bias in OLS. (2) Family and community fixed effects estimates suggest that the direction of the bias in standard estimates is upward and that the true effects of the range of observed child health on school success is not significant despite the strong association that leads to the appearance of an effect in standard OLS or IV estimates using family and community variables. (3) The usual assumption that there are no unobserved choice inputs in educational production probably leads to an upward bias in the estimated impact of child health on schooling even if there is good control for the endogeneity of child health and measurement error. (4) Child health also does not significantly affect child cognitive achievement through schooling attainment; consideration of the relations that usually have been used to investigate such a possibility, moreover, suggests that the coefficients that are usually estimated are *not* coefficients that represent the impact of child health on child schooling. (5) The preferred estimates control for unobserved family and community fixed effects and are robust to other estimation problems, so the standard estimates overstate the impact of child health in the observed range on child schooling success.

Alderman et al. (1997) employ longitudinal data to investigate the impact of child health/nutrition on school enrollments in rural Pakistan using an explicit dynamic model for their preferred estimates. These estimates use price shocks when children were of preschool age to control for behavior determining the child health/nutrition stock measure. They indicate that child health/nutrition is three times as important for enrollment than suggested by "naive estimates" that assume that child health/nutrition is predetermined rather than determined by household choices in the presence of unobserved factors such as preferences and health endowments. These results, therefore, reinforce strongly the importance of using estimation methods that are consistent with the economic theory of households to explore the impact of some choice variables on others using socioeconomic behavioral data.

4.3.5. Impact of expected returns on schooling

Human capital investments are made under imperfect information with learning by potential investors about both individual ability and the returns to schooling. Ability varies across individuals (e.g., due to genetic variation) and returns to schooling vary across local conditions for adoption of new knowledge (e.g., due to variations in the suitability of new agricultural technologies across space because of soil and weather differentials for the Green Revolution).

Yamauchi-Kawana (1997) considers, within a particular developing country context, the problem that households have in assessing whether to invest in schooling when the returns to schooling may have changed. First he models the schooling investments within a two-period framework. Household members must decipher from uncertain production processes the contribution of schooling to output under a new technological regime. The schooling investment decisions must be made in the first period before these uncertainties are resolved in the second period. He shows that adjustments in perceptions of the school return are faster if aggregate income volatility is less, if population density is greater, and if there is the optimal number of highly-schooled versus low-schooled adults in the community from which to infer the returns to schooling. Because each household learns from others, but no one takes into account that others are learning from themselves, there is an externality from the social learning.

He then uses this framework to guide analysis of a national stratified random rural panel dataset from India at the start of the Green Revolution (in which new crop varieties created at international agricultural research institutions in the Philippines and Mexico became available in India, but the suitability of which varied considerably across locales because of varying soil and weather conditions so substantial learning was involved regarding their local suitability in each community). First, he estimates farm profit functions with panel data to control for unobserved farm productivity factors in order to infer farmers' abilities and village-specific schooling return differentials. Next, he investigates the school enrollment response to these estimated signals for ability and for the returns to school, with learning weights that differ depending on the assets and volatility in each particular context. These estimates imply an estimate of the optimal village proportion of educated population for learning – and suggest that on the average the actual proportion of educated households in the sample villages was significantly less than the optimal level for the purpose of learning due to the positive externality provided to others when particular farmers, some with and some without education, explore the new technologies.

4.4. Impact of schooling on economic productivity

There are literally hundreds of micro studies that purport to investigate the impact of schooling on economic (e.g., wages, agricultural productivity) productivity in developing countries within a static framework (see the surveys in Schultz, 1988; Behrman, 1990a,b, 1997b; King and Hill, 1993; Psacharopoulos, 1994; Strauss and Thomas, 1995). Table 6 reproduces a well-known summary of many of the studies on the wage outcomes. A few studies tie together micro estimates of the impact of human resources with the distribution of income or of earnings (e.g., Blau et al., 1988; Lam and Levison, 1991; Psacharopoulos et al., 1992; Lam and Schoeni, 1993, 1994).

An effective way to summarize many of these results has been through the calculation of the real rates of return to the costs incurred in schooling. This has been effective because rates of returns permit comparisons among a wide range of investments, both within the schooling sector and elsewhere in the economy. Typically these rates of return have been calculated by comparing the direct economic outcomes for individuals with different amounts or types of schooling (or for different types of individuals) and calculating the rate of return to the private costs (primarily the time costs but perhaps also tuition, books

Table 6
Percentage returns to investments in schooling latest year, regional averages[a]

Region	Social			Private		
	Primary	Secondary	Higher	Primary	Secondary	Higher
Sub-Saharan Africa	24.3	18.2	11.2	41.3	26.6	27.8
Asia[b]	19.9	13.3	11.7	39.0	18.9	19.9
Europe/Middle East/ North Africa[b]	15.5	11.2	10.6	17.4	15.9	21.7
Latin America/Caribbean	17.9	12.8	12.3	26.2	16.8	19.7
OECD	14.4	10.2	8.7	21.7	12.4	12.3
World	18.4	13.1	10.9	29.1	18.1	20.3

[a] Source: Psacharopoulos (1994, Table 1).
[b] Non-OECD.

and materials and other private costs) and to the social costs (the private costs plus public subsidies) to obtain, respectively, the so-called "private" and "social" rates of return to schooling.[32] These estimates are widely interpreted to imply that in developing countries: (1) the rates of return to schooling are high;[33] (2) they do not decline very rapidly with the level of development; (3) the impact of schooling, particularly for females, on non-market outcomes is considerable and generally greater than that of males; (4) the social rates of return decline with schooling levels[34] (although the private rates of return do not necessarily do so because of relatively high per student subsidies to higher schooling levels), are higher for general as opposed to technical vocational schooling, and at least as high on average for female as for male schooling; (5) variability in schooling is associated with the variability in income distribution and more schooling is associated with less probability of being below the poverty line;[35] and (6) there is not likely to be an equity-productivity

---

[32] Sometimes the Mincerian (Mincer, 1974) semilog relation between wages and schooling with control for post-schooling experience (or age) is used to calculate the private rate of return to time spent in schooling instead of in the labor market under the Mincerian assumptions (e.g., there is equilibrium so that individuals are indifferent among various schooling levels and characteristics such as ability and family background enter into the wage determination function so they are not correlated with schooling). The Mincerian formulation assumes that there are opportunity costs to schooling at all ages, an assumption that Psacharopoulos (1994) and some others criticize.

[33] Such estimates imply, in fact, that investment in schooling is such a high return investment that they are not completely credible on these grounds alone. Investments with a real annual rate of return of 16–24% (the social rate of return to primary school in the four developing regions given in Psacharopoulos, 1994) and with reinvestment of the proceeds of such investment implies that society can double the real invested assets in 2.9–4.3 years, and the social real rate of 11–18% on secondary schooling implies the possibility of doubling real assets in 3.8–6.3 years. These estimates, moreover, understate the true social rates of return and overstate the true time that social assets could be doubled by marginal schooling investments if there are positive externalities to schooling as often is claimed. If developing countries have available such investments opportunities on a fairly broad scale (i.e., in most of its children), it would seem that much higher economic growth would be observed than ever has been experienced for any sustained period of time.

tradeoff in expanding schooling in the most productive way because the returns are highest for basic (primary, then secondary) schooling for which further expansion is likely primarily to enroll more children from very poor families and the total returns are higher for females than for males. Under the assumption that wages are strongly associated with productivities, these conclusions generally are interpreted to carry over to the impact on productivity.[36]

There are, however, a number of well-known possible problems with the methodology sketched out in the previous paragraph. Though most studies in this genre do not attempt to control for these problems, some of those that do report that such controls make considerable differences in the estimated impact of schooling. Most of the existing studies do not control well for the behavioral decisions that determine who goes to what type of school for how long with what degree of success. Simple analytical frameworks for school investments, as well as casual observations, suggest that individuals with higher investments in schooling are likely to be individuals with more ability and more motivation who come from family and community backgrounds that provide more reinforcement for such investments and who have lower marginal private costs for such investments and lower discount rates for the returns from those investments and who are likely to have access to higher quality schools. Therefore such studies implicitly assume that schooling is distributed randomly among sample members rather than that the disturbances in the relations

---

[34] The social returns to schooling may be non-linear, with increases for lower and middle schooling levels and then declines for further schooling. Barros (1992) gives an example of the relation of schooling to adjustment capacities, which may have social implications beyond private implications because of the social costs of unemployment. During periods of adjustment the relative gainers are those who have the less specific human capital to lose and who can acquire new specific human capital the most cheaply (where "specific" means "specific" to a firm or to a particular job). Those with little or no schooling are likely to have little specific human capital to lose, but also are likely to acquire new specific human capital at great cost. Those with more general human capital are likely to be able to acquire new specific human capital relatively cheaply, but also are more likely to have greater specific human capital from the past the value of which may be reduced or lost due to adjustment. The costs of adjustment are likely to be greatest for those with the greatest gap between specific human capital and general human capital (since the cost of acquiring new specific human capital is likely to be inversely associated with the stock of general human capital). The relation between schooling and adjustment capacity, therefore is an empirical question on which some limited evidence for Brazil suggests important non-linearities with maximum adjustment capacities for those with medium schooling levels.

[35] Psacharopoulos et al. (1992), for example, examine the relation between schooling and income inequality and poverty in the Latin American and Caribbean region. A decomposition of the inequality in the distribution of workers' income (including only individuals over 15 years of age in the labor force with positive income) indicates that variations in schooling attainment are associated with about a quarter of the income inequality. Also low schooling attainment is the characteristic most associated with being in the bottom 20% of the distribution of workers' income; on average those with no schooling have a 56% probability of being in the bottom 20% of the workers' income distribution, while those with primary schooling have 27% probability, those with secondary schooling 9% probability, and those with university schooling 4% probability. These results are characterized by Psacharopoulos et al. (1992, pp. 40, 48) to indicate "the overwhelming preeminence of education" and that "clearly... education is the variable with the strongest impact on income inequality."

[36] The third conclusion and a small subset of the studies underlying the other conclusions use direct measures of productivity, not wages, as the dependent variables.

used to explore the impact of schooling on various outcomes are correlated with schooling due to the failure to control for such factors so that the estimates in such studies probably suffer from omitted variable biases. The association of schooling with labor market outcomes such as wage rates and agricultural productivity (as well as with household outcomes such as fertility and child health) does not necessarily represent causality because in most estimates years of schooling is representing not only time in school, but also factors that are correlated with years of school such as abilities, discount rates, family backgrounds, and schooling qualities. To obtain insight into the impact of years of school on such outcomes, one needs to control for these other factors, as do to a certain extent some – but not many – of the existing studies.

A number of "revisionist" studies for developing countries, parallel to a similar literature for developed economies, have explored the impact of some of these estimation problems on estimated schooling returns with data or specification modifications of the standard earnings function framework by controlling for: school quality (Behrman and Birdsall, 1983), unobserved shared family background of adult siblings and of members of the same household (Behrman and Wolfe, 1984; Behrman and Deolalikar, 1993), usually unobserved abilities through new tests (Boissiere et al., 1985; Knight and Sabot, 1990; Glewwe, 1996), selectivity (Schultz, 1988), dropout and repetition rates (Behrman and Deolalikar, 1991),[37] measurement error, school quality and behavioral choices regarding school attendance (Alderman et al., 1996b). In earlier surveys I have claimed that those studies that do incorporate such controls for developing countries tend to find that the "standard estimates" (i.e., those without such controls) may overstate the impact of schooling attainment by as much as 40–100%, probably more so for primary schooling and underestimate the relative importance of school quality improvements (Behrman, 1990a,b).[38] The recent ferment in studies of such questions for the United States (see the chapter by Card in this *Handbook*) has re-emphasized the point that random measurement error and other estimation problems may mean that some of these studies may not overestimate schooling attainment effects as much as I earlier suggested, although there is not yet a clear consensus regarding the rates of return to schooling in the United States, there also has been increasing emphasis on relatively high returns to school quality in that economy, and the issues addressed in the recent literature raise questions about some but not all of the estimates in the "revisionist" literature on rates of return to schooling in developing countries. At this point I perceive that the "standard" estimates for developing

---

[37] Grade repetition is substantial in many developing countries (e.g., Latin America and the Caribbean have a first grade repetition rate of 42%, and an overall primary school repetition rate of 29% according to recent estimates based on a special UNESCO/OREALC survey) so the failure to control for grade repetition and school dropouts in standard estimates may be quite important.

[38] Such factors are controlled generally by linking data used for the standard estimates with other information about characteristics such as school quality, family background, and ability or by using special data on adult siblings or family or community members to control for common unobserved characteristics (e.g., the estimate of the difference in wage rates regressed on the difference in schooling for adult siblings controls for the additive effect of common family and community background shared by the siblings).

countries probably overstate the true schooling returns substantially but that there remain some open questions about this literature to which studies of developing as well as developed economies are likely to continue to contribute.

Beyond the "standard" and related "revisionist" literature, however, recent empirical studies of schooling in developing countries have contributed to knowledge of the impact of schooling within a dynamic context with explicit attention to various forms of market imperfections.

Education may enable one to deal better with uncertainty by improving one's abilities to learn, which is likely to be particularly important in dynamic environments in which there are technological innovations and new market opportunities (Welch, 1970; Schultz, 1975). These notions have been formalized recently in a target-input model in which individuals choose an allocation of resources or inputs knowing the technology of production only up to a stochastic "target" for the level of input use (see Rosenzweig, 1995 for details and references). With repeated production periods, in each period the priors regarding the optimal input use are updated based on past experience. Education can affect the production cum learning process in two ways: (1) Education can increase the precision of the information that an individual has initially because of access to more information sources.[39] In this case experience and education clearly are substitutes – alternative ways of increasing the precision of one's priors. Therefore the returns to education are high only with new technological options, and decline with more experience with any given technology. (2) Education may enable individuals to gain more information from each use of a technology than they would otherwise be able to gain – the more educated may learn faster and be able to decode information acquired through experience more effectively. If this is the only effect, at low levels of experience, education and experience are complements rather than substitutes so that the returns to education at least initially increase with experience with a given new technology. While this approach is stated in terms of new technology, it should be clear that similar possibilities exist with the stochastic terms and learning relating to markets as well as to technology. This role may be critical for entrants into a new market, whether they be youth searching for good matches in the labor market or entrepreneurs entering a new domestic or international product or input market.

It is useful to consider in somewhat more detail two examples of such studies, Foster and Rosenzweig (1995, 1996b). There has been renewed interest in the fundamental issue of what causes economic growth with its multiple implications for labor, with particular attention focused on the role of information externalities. Evidence on the existence of such spillover effects from aggregate data has not been persuasive. Foster and Rosenzweig (1995) empirically implement a "target-input" model of agricultural technology adoption in which there are potential information externalities associated with adoption by neighbors. The learning model yields an explicit representation for the profit function that

---

[39] For example, Thomas et al. (1991) give such an interpretation based on how the coefficient estimates of mother's schooling declines as they include use of information sources in their conditional demand relations.

depends on own and neighbors' accumulated experience with the new technology. The profit function is estimated as both a linear approximation and in its exact non-linear representation using fixed-effects instrumental variables procedure that accounts for input endogeneity. The results indicate that the experience of neighbors as well as own experience increase farm profits; there is both learning by doing and learning from others. The adoption decision (the amount of land devoted to high yielding variety crops) is derived from a Markov perfect game-theoretic model. A linear approximation to that rule is estimated using a fixed-effects procedure to control for permanent unobservables. It is found that own and neighbors' experience provide similar information about optimal inputs. Moreover, the finding that increasing own assets increases the level of adoption while increasing neighbors' assets reduces adoption indicates that the learning externality is not fully internalized by the village. The results in this paper provide what is arguably the best evidence to date on the existence of knowledge spillovers – the extent of which are critical for efficiency arguments for public subsidies for schooling.[40]

Foster and Rosenzweig (1996b) provide a related analysis of the relationship between schooling and technical change. Although other papers have provided evidence on the long standing question of whether exogenous technical change increases the productivity returns to schooling, they have not been sensitive to the role of human capital accumulation itself in the process of technical change. The analysis in this paper draws on panel data for agricultural households in India during the period of the green revolution, which is reasonably argued to correspond to a period of exogenous technical change that differs across space because of differences in water and soil conditions. In addition, this paper assesses quantitatively within a unified framework the extent to which schooling levels respond to the increased returns and the extent to which the demand for schooling responds to investments in schools. Geographic variation in the extent of technical change is sufficient to identify profit function parameters that indicate the extent of technical change in Indian districts and changes in the profitability of inputs such as schooling, irrigation, etc. The estimation procedure takes into account that inputs evolve dynamically and that there may be district-level unobservables that affect both profits and inputs. The results indicate that the schooling return is on average augmented by exogenous technical change. Moreover, the increase in the return to schooling is greater the higher is the rate of growth in the area; having a primary education increased the impact of technical change on profits by 70%. An approximate dynamic schooling decision rule is estimated that makes use of the profit-function estimates of district-level technical change. In conformity with the profit function estimates, the demand for schooling is found to increase with the level of technical change. It is also found to increase with the availability of schools which implies that policies that promote technical change are complementary to investments in schools. This study thus provides perhaps the best available evidence that the returns to school are high in the presence of new technologies.

---

[40] Besley and Case (1994) is another important study that also is concerned with the distribution of new technologies in rural India and possible spillovers, but without the same focus on schooling.

5. Urban labor markets, labor-market regulations, international trade policies and manufacturing

Urban labor markets differ from rural labor markets in developing economies by having: (1) more heterogenous production and therefore more heterogenous labor and more wage variance; (2) higher returns to education and related skills (in part in governmental occupations) and therefore more concentration of more-educated and more-skilled workers; (3) less dependence on weather and thus less seasonality and less problems due to incomplete seasonal markets; (4) more geographical concentration of production activities so that information is likely to be better and mobility greater with greater payoffs for job search thus higher unemployment; and (5) more intense policy regulation and union activities in part because of the greater concentration and greater scale economies and lesser costs of monitoring compliance and in part because of the greater worker heterogeneity.

After a more extensive description of urban labor markets in developing countries with emphasis on features similar to these, Rosenzweig (1988a, p. 755), concluded: "An informed reader will see that most of the features of the low-income-country urban environments described also characterize urban areas of high-income countries. And the issues of the impact of governmental labor market interventions and trade unions and the determinants and consequences of job search strategies, which appear particularly pertinent to such settings, form an important part of the core of modern labor economics. Few distinct analytical models specifically targeted in any meaningful way to problems of low-income country urban markets have emerged in the literature."

In my judgement a decade later this conclusion still holds. For that reason and because some of the discussion above relates in part to urban labor markets (i.e., some of the literature on the determinants of and the returns to human resource investments), I here devote much less space to urban labor markets in developing countries than I have devoted above to rural labor markets in developing countries.

I first consider some aspects of urban labor market dualism, which has received more emphasis in studies on developing countries than in studies on developed economies, and then turn briefly to empirical studies on labor market regulations and on the impact of trade policy changes on manufacturing – two policy areas in which some of the changes in a number of developing countries have been larger in degree if not different in kind from those experienced in developed economies.

5.1. Urban labor market dualism

A common description of urban labor markets in developing countries dating back at least to Fields (1975), Mazumdar (1976) and Sabot (1977) is that they are dualistic. On one hand there is a "formal" or "modern" sector comprised of mostly-larger, often relatively capital-intensive, private and public relatively high-wage producers that are subject to and more or less comply with labor market regulations. On the other hand, there is an "informal" sector comprised of small, mostly family enterprises that are relatively labor-intensive and low-wage and that are not subject to or do not comply with labor market regulations.

Much of the empirical literature on urban labor markets (most of it until recently) has focused on testing whether there are barriers to mobility between the informal and formal sectors by comparing wage rates (e.g., Mazumdar, 1981) or by comparing estimated wage (or earnings) relations (e.g., Heckman and Hotz, 1986; Funkhouser, 1997a,b). These comparisons often are interpreted to mean that there is urban labor market segmentation. But, as at least the latter studies recognize and attempt to deal with in part, such comparisons are difficult to interpret because workers with identical observed characteristics may differ in unobserved characteristics (e.g., innate ability, preferences) that affect their selection into different sectors, lifecycle wage schedules may differ with different technologies and organizations but generally only wages at a point in time are observed, the empirical classification of sectors is arbitrary, identifying the labor payment to unpaid family workers is difficult, and the comparisons are conditional on the correct specification of functional forms. Of more fundamental interest than such comparisons, moreover, is the question of the extent of mobility among such urban sectors (Section 6.3).

5.2. The effects of labor market regulations on formal-sector wages and employment

Bell (1997) uses time series and panel firm data (and individual data for Mexico) to investigate the impact of minimum wages on formal-sector wages and employment in Colombia and Mexico. She finds virtually no effect in Mexico, which she suggests is because the levels of minimum wages were too low to be ineffective. For Colombia, in contrast, she finds significant negative employment elasticities that imply reductions of formal sector employment for low-skilled, low-wage Colombian workers of 2–12% for a 10% increase in minimum wages with firm fixed-effects estimates (although the estimates appear insignificant without control for firm fixed effects).

MacIsaac and Rama (1997) explore formal-sector labor costs in Ecuador, which are alleged to be high because of many policy-mandated benefits that are equal to 75% of the minimum wage. They use household survey data to describe the associations between average hourly earnings and various observed worker and employer characteristics. They find that the effect of the mandated benefits is mitigated by a reduction (39% on the average) in the base earnings that is larger in the private than in the public sector but negligible for unionized workers. As a result, total labor costs for complying employers increase only 8% despite the substantial mandates. They also find that, despite the mandated benefits, interindustry wage differentials are comparable to those in Bolivia, which is alleged to have much more flexible labor markets.

Gruber (1997) estimates the incidence of a sharp change in payroll taxation in Chile (due to the privatization of the Social Security system in 1981) on wages and employment in reduced-form relations. He uses plant data and finds that the incidence was entirely on wages, with no effect on employment – a result that is robust to alternative estimation strategies to deal with possible measurement error. As he notes, an important limitation of this approach is that the reduced-form estimates cannot disentangle the structural sources of wage and employment changes.

Thus these three studies all conclude that most of incidence of the cost of legislated benefits is on covered workers' wages, with relatively small impact on total labor costs and on employment in covered sectors. If so, it is not the case that these regulations have much impact on either the competitiveness of covered firms nor all the welfare of covered workers. These studies are basically silent on the effects of such regulations on uncovered workers. Nor do they investigate what determines compliance with labor regulations and thus whether a firm effectively is in the covered or non-covered sector.

5.3. The effect of trade reform and adjustment on formal-sector manufacturing labor

The most radical trade reforms and economy-wide adjustments in recent decades have been in developing economies and economies in transition. Yet there has been until recently very little analysis of these experiences as compared with the much larger number of analysis of the impact of trade reform on labor in developed economies.[41]

Revenga (1997) analyzes the impact of trade liberalization in 1985–1988 on employment and wages in the Mexican manufacturing sector. During this time period, average tariffs on Mexican manufacturing were cut in half and the coverage of import licensing was cut by three-quarters. She posits that firm wages are a weighted average of the union's preferred wage outcome and the alternative industry or regional average, so that firm wages can be decomposed into firm-specific wages from quasi rents that differ from industry average wages, with unobserved heterogeneity in firm bargaining power. She estimates this relation from time series firm data, using industry trade policies as instruments to attempt to break the correlation with the unobserved heterogeneity in the disturbance term. She likewise estimates firm labor demands conditional on output, again using industry trade policies as instruments. She first documents that many of the rents generated by previous trade protection were obtained through a wage premium by workers in the protected sector, which she estimates totaled 25% of workers' earnings. She estimates that trade liberalization shifted down industry product and labor demand which in itself reduced real wages on the average by 3–4%. But there was an additional impact of almost the same magnitude due to the reduced rents from protection. She also finds that her estimated sharing rule for rents from protection is associated with the share of non-production workers among total workers, which she interprets as a measure of skills that are in short supply so that they increase workers' bargaining power. Except for this measure, however, she does not incorporate heterogeneity in workers into her analysis even though it would seem that such heterogeneity in itself could account for deviations in firm wages

---

[41] There has been increasing interest in characterizing the changes in distribution and in labor market outcomes that occurred with international trade liberalization. These characterizations suggest heterogeneity in experiences, with generally fairly quick unemployment adjustments and lowered dispersion between low- and higher-skill wages in the earlier East Asian experience but increasing dispersion in the more recent Latin American experiences. See Horton et al. (1991, 1994) and Wood (1997) and the references therein.

from industry levels even in the absence of protection. She also finds a significant negative effect of reducing import quotas on employment, but no significant employment effect of reduced tariffs. She interprets these results as being consistent with unions being able to capture part of the rents generated by tariffs so these rents adjust rather than employment if tariffs fall, but unions do not capture part of the rents generated by quota protection. But this just pushes the question back a step – why can unions capture rents from tariff but not from quota protection?

Currie and Harrison (1997) examine the labor market impact of Moroccan international trade reform during the mid-1980s – including the virtual elimination of quantitative restrictions on imports and a reduction of the maximum tariff from 165 to 45% over a 6-year period. They present an explicit model of an imperfectly competitive Cournot firm in an industry in which domestic and imported goods are imperfect substitutes, there is an industry-level quota on imports, and firms face upward-sloping labor supply curves. They derive employment relations that depend on trade policy in part because they posit that both the extent of market power and productivity (in the form of Hick's neutral techno-logical change) depend on import tariffs and quotas. They note that trade liberalization can reduce labor demand due to falling output prices but may increase labor demand due to increased productivity and lessened market power. They also note that public-sector enterprises may be constrained in their ability to reduce their labor force and that exporters are more likely to reduce their labor demands the more distinct are products that they sell in domestic markets from those that they export. They use time-series data on all Moroc-can manufacturing firms (except those with less than 10 employees or with annual sales less than US $11,000) for 1984–1989. They find that on the average employment was not affected by the trade reforms, but firms in the most affected sectors and exporting firms reduced employment significantly (3.5–6% in response to 21–24% decline in tariffs). They explore why most private domestic-market-oriented firms did not adjust employment significantly; they find that this does not reflect high adjustment costs due to labor market regulation, but that these firms absorbed the loss in rents from the loss of protection through reduced profits.

A number of questions remains unexplored in these studies – what is the impact on the rest of the labor force including the informal manufacturing sector and all of services and agriculture, what are the effects of entry and exit into the formal manufacturing sector, what are the implications of workers being heterogeneous, what are the implications of the fact that policies are choices and not clearly exogenous changes that are predetermined in a statistical sense, what is the nature of dynamic processes, what is the impact of imperfect information and of other aspects of incomplete markets? But these studies are examples of a growing number of studies of major reforms in developing countries – with much more substantial policy changes than in the much more-studied developed economies – that should increasingly illuminate our understanding of how labor markets function.

6. Distribution and mobility

Distribution is of interest as an objective for society that is separate from, although inter-related with efficiency, production and growth – often taking the form of concern about the poorer members of society. Distribution and mobility are intertwined. Differences in human capital investments for otherwise identical individuals that yield differences in their labor market (or other) returns thereby yield differences in the distribution of labor market returns. These distributional differences, at least within the standard human capital model that is summarized at the start of Section 4, may create incentives for human capital investments associated with actual or potential job mobility. A central feature of devel-opment, in fact, is the relocation of labor from less to more productive activities.

Such relocations may or may not require geographical movements. New products may be produced or new technologies may be adopted, for example, that result in the realloca-tion of labor to more productive activities without any geographical movement. On the other hand, scale and conglomeration economies and limited or missing markets for other factors may mean that labor is reallocated to more productive activities substantially by geographical migration. There has been some, but relatively little attention in the devel-opment literature to labor reallocations that do not involve geographical movements. There has been substantial attention to labor reallocations that involve geographical mobility, particularly in the form of rural–urban migrations. In most developing countries, for example, there have been substantial migratory movements from rural to urban areas, as well as smaller movements among rural areas and from urban to rural areas.

The human capital model of migration simply states that it pays to migrate from one location to another particular location if the present discounted value of benefits exceeds the present discounted value of costs and the gain is larger for that move than for any other. The model suggests, therefore, that migration is more attractive for individuals for whom time horizons are longer (e.g., because they are younger), who have lower discount rates (because of taste heterogeneities or more education), who are better informed (if there is risk aversion and insurance market imperfections), who are more adaptable (younger? more educated?), who are better prepared to deal with up-front costs (if there are capital market imperfections), who have less immobile capital (in some contexts, land, or loca-tion-specific production knowledge) and who gain more from diversification (if there are risks that are not perfectly correlated over space and the individual is linked by family or other relations across space). Such migration tends to be equilibrating by reducing differ-entials at the margin across areas through shifting, for example, homogenous labor from areas in which wages are low to those in which wages are high. While this model is presented usually with reference to migration, it clearly refers to any form of investment in mobility.

In this section, I consider several dimensions of distribution and mobility that have received attention in the development literature and in some cases have led to new analy-tical approaches in labor economics.

6.1. *Intertemporal aspects of distribution and the Kuznets hypothesis of inverted U pattern in inequality with development*

Because of data limitations, most empirical studies of distribution in developing countries are based on cross-sectional annual data. Recently there have been several studies for developing countries with intertemporal approaches to characterizing or modeling distribution, some of which are now reviewed.

Kuznets (1955) hypothesized that at very low levels of income, distribution would have to be relatively equal because of subsistence minimums, but with the process of development distribution initially would become more unequal because those best suited by virtue of their human capital (or lucky by virtue of their asset ownership) first would grasp new income-earning opportunities while most members of society initially would be left behind. But as opportunities increased with the process of development, increasing proportions of society would have new income-earning opportunities, so eventually inequality would decline.[42] Therefore there is an inverse U-shaped relation between inequality and development.

This "Kuznets curve" relating to the hypothesized inverse U relation between inequality and development has received a lot of attention in the applied development literature. Early cross-sectional studies seemed consistent with it. More recent longitudinal studies (e.g., Anand and Kanbur, 1993) have not found support for such a relation. Fields and Jakubson (1997) show that cross-sectional estimates that appear to support the existence of such a relation are reversed once there is control for country fixed effects – and thus a paradox between the previous cross-section and time-series results is resolved. They claim that the cross-sectional estimates suggest support for the Kuznets curve even though the time-series estimates do not because inequality is greater in Latin America than in Asia, but the latter includes both lower and higher per capita income countries than the former.[43]

While most explorations of this hypothesis have focused on aggregate data, there are obvious implications of the hypothesis that, if human resources are not very mobile internationally, labor market returns to human capital that are in relatively scare supply as development increases initially increase, but as more human investment is induced by new opportunities the returns to such investments decline. Knight and Sabot (1983) explore this possibility using cross-sectional data from Kenya and Tanzania. They find that the expansion of schooled workers reduces the returns to schooling (the "compression effect") and therefore reduces intraurban wage inequality more than the initial increased schooling

---

[42] There may be other major factors that affect the income distribution as well. For example, Becker et al. (1990) suggest that their may be multiple equilibria, with high growth options in which the cost of human capital formation is low due to the large stock of human capital, so there are large human capital investments with relatively low (and equal) returns.

[43] Ravallion and Chen (1997) consider distributional changes in 64 spells for developing and transitional countries based on matched household surveys in 1981–1994. They find no significant association between growth and distribution if Eastern Europe and Central Asia are excluded, and a significantly positive relation between growth and equality if Eastern Europe and Central Asia are included. But they do not control for the initial level of development, so their characterization is only tangentially related to Kuznets' hypothesis.

dispersion (the "composition effect") increases wage inequality. This exploration must be qualified, however, due to the limitation of the sample to the major urban areas in the two countries considered and the dependence on simple earnings functions with no investigation of the implications of endogenous schooling decisions.

Deaton and Paxson (1994) build on Eden's (1980) point that standard models of intertemporal choice imply that for a given birth cohort earnings inequality (and therefore consumption inequality) grows over the lifecycle because of the changing impact of the integral of accumulated shocks. They show that this result is more general than the certainty equivalence assumptions required to justify the random walk consumption as is implicit in Eden's paper, and that empirical examination of whether consumption dispersion increases with age can be used to test alternative consumption theories (since if liquidity constraints are effective consumption dispersion will track income dispersion). They then examine the experience in Taiwan and in two developed economies for constructed data on age-cohorts of individuals using a succession of cross-sectional surveys over recent 11–15 year time periods and find in all three cases within-cohort consumption becomes substantially more dispersed over time with similar rates of dispersion – which they claim is evidence against models of perfect insurance – and that within-cohort dispersion of earnings increases with age. They note that inequality increases with age have a number of implications: (1) with no links between generations, with constant inequality in earnings distributions, and with roughly stable population distributions across birth cohorts, inequality for each birth cohort is consistent with approximately constant inequality in society as a whole (as observed in the US for extended periods of time); (2) but if there were strong intergenerational links through bequests such approximately constant aggregate inequality would not be observed (which they claim is evidence against the extreme forms of dynastic models); and (3) countries with rapid demographic transitions and aging populations (e.g., Taiwan and a number of other Asian developing and developed economies) would be expected to have increasing inequality, an additional reason beyond that suggested in the well-known Kuznets (1955) hypothesis for initially increasing and then falling inequality in the development process. This is an interesting study that combines in a fruitful way a number of tools from consumption theory, distribution theory, econometrics, and data analysis to develop some new insights, although the results have to be qualified because of limited attention to human capital investments (in their role as intergenerational links that may be alternatives to bequests in addition to their role in affecting earning dispersions given heterogeneity in such investments over the lifecycle), to endogenous changes in household structures, and to the nature of the structural relations underlying the interesting descriptions of intertemporal distributions presented.

Deolalikar and Gaiha (1993) is the first empirical characterization of which I am aware of whether households in poor areas of developing countries that are beneath the poverty line in 1 year tend to below the poverty line transitorily or permanently. They use ICRISAT panel data over a decade from rural south India. They calculate alternative measures of the percentage of households below the poverty line based on actual average poverty in annual cross-sections (57%), expected average poverty based on estimates of income as a function of observed characteristics (62%), "innate poverty" based on estimates with observed characteristics and unobserved characteristics (12%), ever-below the poverty line (88%), and always below the poverty line (21%). They first show the sensitivity of the estimation of the percentages of households below the poverty line to be quite sensitive to the definition and time period that are used, and that the proportion of permanent poor is much lower than the number of transitory poor, although still quite large. This paper is basically descriptive, but it is important because it describes an important phenomenon about which there has been much speculation but almost no prior evidence.

Foster and Rosenzweig (1997) raise an important but essentially ignored question in the analysis of income inequality trends, namely that of defining the observational unit. If households are taken to be the relevant unit, as is often the case, a complete understanding of the evolution of income inequality requires an understanding of how households are formed and dissolved, and specifically how household formation and dissolution are affected by economic growth. Measures of the relationship between economic growth and income inequality that are based on repeated cross-sections cannot properly address this issue because individuals cannot be matched across households over time. In this paper empirical estimates of the impact of economic growth on income inequality are obtained using longitudinal data on rural Indian households during the green revolution period. The empirical analysis is based on the structural estimation of a behavioral model of a farm household in which the existence of a public good and differences in agricultural productivity among household members (heads of separate but related nuclear families) provide a rationale for joint co-residence. In the Indian agricultural setting, the initiation of the green revolution (exogenous technological change) altered both the income potential of nuclear and joint households and the incentives for co-residence. The model is parameterized, structural parameters are estimated and counterfactual simulations are performed. The results of these exercises show that while technical change had only a small effect on the distribution of incomes of dynasties (of households defined by their pre-green revolution composition), the green revolution increased income inequality of households (defined contemporaneously).

6.2. Geographical mobility

The form of mobility that is most emphasized in the development literature is geographical migration, particularly between rural and urban areas. Much of the empirical literature simply documents some of the basic implications of the basic human capital model of migration, such as that wage differentials induce such migration selectively, more so for young adults and for more schooled individuals. Behrman and Birdsall (1983), for example, note that most of what appears to be selectivity on unobserved characteristics for migration in Brazil largely disappears if there is control for migration selectivity not only on schooling attainment but also on school quality.[44] Despite considerable migration,

---

[44] But Robinson and Tomes (1983) find that the returns to migration in Canada are significantly overstated if migration selectivity on unobserved ability is not controlled, although they do not control for schooling quality.

however, wage differentials appear to persist for long periods of time between urban and rural areas, although such comparisons have to be qualified because of problems in assuring that homogenous workers are being compared and prices are being held constant. Not all migrants into urban areas, moreover, obtain jobs in the high-paying modern or formal sector.

6.2.1. Harris–Todaro migration model

To reconcile ongoing migratory flows with persistent urban–rural wage discrepancies Todaro (1969) modified the basic human capital model of migration to incorporate employment risk, and Harris and Todaro (1970) incorporated this migration relation into an influential two-sector economy-wide model of migration, wage and employment determination. In this model the rural labor market is assumed to function competitively, but the urban wage is set institutionally (e.g., governmental minimum wage) above the initial rural wage with the probability of employment in the urban sector equal to the number of urban jobs at the institutionally-set wage relative to the number of urban job-seekers. Therefore, with no costs for migration, migration occurs until the rural wage equals the expected urban wage, which is the product of the employment probability times the urban wage and the urban labor market distortion causes a misallocation of workers across sectors and urban unemployment. If the institutionally-set urban wage is increased and urban labor demand is inelastic, employment and output falls in both sectors, urban unemployment increases less than proportionately to the urban wage increase so the expected urban wage increases, and rural–urban migration occurs. If the institutionally-set urban wage is increased and urban labor demand is elastic, employment and output fall in the urban sector and rise in the rural sector and urban–rural migration occurs. Whatever the urban labor demand elasticity, an urban wage subsidy with a fixed urban wage induces rural–urban migration, reduced rural output and employment, and increased urban unemployment.

Some aspects of the model are troublesome. First, if the urban–rural wage differential is 50–100% as has been alleged (although empirical comparisons do not seem to control well for price and skills differentials), observed urban unemployment rates are far too low for the equilibrium predicated by this model. For that reason, some (e.g., Fields, 1975) have added an informal urban sector in which wages are much lower than in the modern sector covered by the institutionally-set wage. But the difficulties in measuring the pure wage return in the informal sector mentioned in Section 5.1 mean that empirical evidence on this resolution is fuzzy. Second, the ad hoc exogenous minimum wage is troublesome because governmental policies are the result of behavioral decisions that are not incorporated into the model and because minimum wages do not appear to be binding in many cases (i.e., Bell, 1997 that is summarized in Section 5.2; Squire and Narueput, 1997).

6.2.2. Stiglitz labor "turnover" and "efficiency wage" models

Stiglitz (1976) has proposed one resolution to the latter problem by positing that mono-politically competitive urban firms incur hiring and training costs with labor turnover, so they pay a wage premium over alternative wage rates to reduce turnover that is an inverse function of the urban unemployment rate. In this model urban unemployment is optimal in the sense that the lost output due to unemployment is less than the output gain from lower turnover costs. Stiglitz (1982) also develops other models in which the wage premium that a firm offers determines what quality of workers that a firm can hire ("efficiency wage worker quality model") and the absolute wage offered by the firm determines the work effort of workers ("efficiency wage effort model"). In these "efficiency wage" models unemployment persists in equilibrium.[45] As Rosenzweig (1988a) emphasizes, the optimality result in the Stiglitz "turnover" model depends critically on the maintained assumption that workers do not share in the cost of training and also implies that workers' wages do not rise over their work lives (because they neither share in costs nor receive benefits from training) – contrary to lifecycle wage patterns observed in many developing and developed economies. Likewise the unemployment result in the Stiglitz efficiency wage models depends on the lack of alternative contractual or sorting arrangements that minimize shirking or sort workers optimally and, again, systematic empirical evidence on the critical behavioral relations does not exist.

6.2.3. Empirical studies of households, migration and risk
The two-sector models described so far in this section contrast with the emphasis in Section 2 on households being central to much rural decision making and on the critical role of incomplete markets, including those for capital and insurance, in determining household behavior. Nor can these models explain temporary (or seasonal) migration or remittances, both of which are widespread in many developing countries. Since the mid-1980s there have been several empirical papers that focused on the role of households and risk-sharing in the absence of insurance markets as critical for understanding some important aspects of migration in developing countries.

Lucas and Stark (1985) is the first study to investigate temporary migration and remittances within a household context. They use a national survey of households in Botswana and find evidence consistent with (1) temporary migration is in part an insurance arrangement with higher remittances home if home household incomes suffer negative shocks, (2) bequest prospects have a positive impact on who migrates and on how much is remitted, and (3) remittances in part are returns for prior household investments in schooling. Within the limitations of cross-sectional data, this study is suggestive of how households and incomplete markets affect migration and remittances, although it is difficult to identify

---

[45] Others also have emphasized the importance of efficiency wage models to explain urban dualism in developing countries. Esfahani and Salehi-Isfahani (1989), for example, argue that under plausible conditions the urban dualism can be explained by differential observability of effort, which has the advantage over other explanations in the literature of integrating a number of related stylized facts (e.g., difference in formal-informal sector wage rates, unobserved productivity, unemployment, technology, factor intensity, operational size and management). They argue that worker effort is less observable in the formal sector (because of larger enterprise size, greater task complexity, and more extensive management structure) but under a plausible condition on the marginal disutility of effort with respect to effort lower observability results in more effort, greater productivity, and higher wages.

some of the above possibilities from others (e.g., households that receive greater remittances accumulate more wealth) without longitudinal data. Other subsequent studies have examined further the relations among households, migration and incomplete markets – e.g., Behrman et al. (1999), Foster (1996), Rosenzweig (1988b,c), Rosenzweig and Stark (1989).[46] Rosenzweig (1988b), for instance, provides a formal framework for examining some "transaction cost" issues related to the family. The model explains the geographical pattern of marriages and the pattern of intrahousehold transfers as a response to the need to smooth consumption in the absence of market insurance or state income maintenance schemes. Daughters tend to "marry out" of their natal village, and the daughters in each family are spread out geographically, as they would be if families were attempting to diversify in the face of weather related risk, rather than concentrated geographically, as they would be if the principal determinant of marriage destinations were the cost of obtaining information about the marriage market.

6.3. Empirical investigation of urban informal–formal mobility

Perhaps the most emphasized aspect of developing-country urban labor markets in the empirical literature, as noted in Section 5.1, is the possibility of dualism. But as also noted there, most empirical studies of these markets have been limited to comparisons of wages or wage functions, with a number of problems of interpretation.

Funkhouser (1997b) contributes to this literature by using a survey from El Salvador with retrospective data that permits investigation of patterns over time in employment. A model is set up with different wage functions by sectors, including worker unobserved fixed effects and random effects with serial correlation. Changes in sectors occur between periods if the second-period random error is large enough to offset any sector-specific human capital accumulation and the serially-correlated component of the error. This general framework then is used to consider alternative modeling/estimation strategies regarding the number of periods and the existence of serial correlation – with insights regarding what can be deduced (and, perhaps more importantly, what cannot be deduced) regarding the causes of sectoral wage differentials under different assumptions. The multi-period model, for example, permits additional insights beyond the usual single-period framework by observing the wage changes of movers between the sectors, but if there is serial correlation there still may be asymmetries under perfect competition of the sort predicted by the segmented model (i.e., larger wage gains for those moving from the free to the limited-access sector than vice versa). Examination of transition rates reveals considerable mobility, particularly for males. Careful examination of wage change relations for various individuals reveals some interesting patterns: (1) high mobility; (2) greater mobility for workers who are male, younger and less educated; (3) higher earnings and higher earnings growth for workers continuously employed in the formal sector, but highest earnings for those with some informal sector attachment for those who maintain

---

[46] The first two of these are summarized in the discussion on parental schooling in Section 4.3 above.

formal sector jobs rather than move in or out of the informal sector; and (4) asymmetry in the sense that movers from the informal to the formal sector have higher wage gains than vice versa. These patterns provide some support for segmentation having an influence (particularly 4), but this support is limited because of the considerable mobility (particularly for males), the larger earnings gains for those with some informal sector attachment for those who maintain informal sector positions, and the problem of identifying symmetry due to segmentation from that due to serial correlation. This study contributes to the literature by extending the perspective on modeling segmented labor markets in developing countries and focusing on wage changes and mobility rather than wage levels as in the previous literature.

Pradhan and van Soest (1997) also consider informal–formal sector mobility in a sense. They model female and male labor supplies within a static household utility maximization framework similar to that used for a number of studies in developed economies, but with an extension to include formal and informal sectors with both wage and non-monetary differences (with the latter determining selection between the two sectors). Estimates for two-adult households in urban Bolivia indicate: (i) substantial intrahousehold effects, with elasticities in line with those reported for the United States; (ii) intersectoral wage responsiveness; and (iii) that non-monetary returns are greater in the formal than in the informal sector. The identification of the sectoral work decision, however, seems to reflect an arbitrary exclusion restriction of the non-monetary returns from the utility maximization process that leads to the labor supply relations.

6.4. Distributional differences among demographic groups

In most societies there are some demographic groups for whom mean wages are lower, even if there is control for observed differences in observed characteristics such as in years of schooling and age. Examples include women in almost every society, indigenous groups in Latin America and the Caribbean and most minority tribes and low castes in Asia. Empirical studies largely have focused on possible differences in standard wage relations (such as are discussed at the start of Section 4.1) as possible sources for these wage differences.

Some suggest, for example, that as a result of these lower wages, the rates of return for investing in the human resources of members of such groups on the average are lower than for investing in men, members of the dominant group and of higher castes. But the leap from low wages to low rates of return does not necessarily follow. Investments in individuals with low wages can have relatively high rates of return. This may be so for human capital investments that take the individual's time, such as schooling and training, since ceteris paribus low wages mean that the opportunity cost of time for such investments (a major input into such investments) is relatively low. Also in some societies average wage gaps conditional on schooling appear to narrow with more schooling – which may reflect a number of factors that change with more schooling including greater labor force integration, more emphasis on intellectual rather than physical attributes, and lessening discrimination. Moreover, if the proportion of females and minority groups[47] that receives higher levels of schooling and training is relatively low, if the distributions of innate abilities and motivation are the same across demographic groups, and if those individuals who receive such human capital investments tend to have relatively high abilities and motivations, the average ability and motivational levels of women or of minority group members with higher levels of schooling and training will exceed the average ability and motivational levels of men or majority groups members with the same levels of schooling and training. Further, a greater proportion of the returns to human resources investments in women and some minority groups may be in informal sector, family enterprises, and household production activities that often are not incorporated into rate of return analyses in the same way that are returns in terms of labor market activities.

There have been some efforts to explore whether rates of returns to human resources, particularly schooling, differ among demographic groups, with more-or-less standard wage relations. On the basis of micro data, for example, Behrman and Deolalikar (1993, 1995) report that estimated rates of return to schooling in Indonesia are higher for females than for males for schooling above the primary level in estimates that control for unobserved household and community effects, Psacharopoulos (1993) reports that estimated rates of return to schooling are lower for schooling for indigenous peoples than for those of European descent in Bolivia and Guatemala, Schultz (1993a,b) finds little evidence of selectivity differences between males and females in Thailand, Birdsall and Sabot (1991) present a series of studies that investigate differences in schooling returns among groups identified by gender, ethnicity, and caste, and Horton (1996) presents estimates of declining gender wage residual differentials in seven Asian economies. There also have been a few studies that examine possible gender differences in productivity of health and nutrition that are reviewed in Section 4.2. As noted there, apparently because of gender specialization in tasks, these studies tend to find greater impact of better nutrition/health on productivities or wages of males than females.

A few studies, many of which are reviewed in some detail above, have gone beyond estimation of standard wage relations to explore for rural areas of developing countries the nature of gender differences in labor markets or in intrahousehold allocations that may lead to gender differences in labor markets (and other outcomes, e.g., Sen, 1990) and the role of marriage markets in providing insurance in risky environments with missing insurance markets. For example, Haddad and Kanbur (1990) report that individual distributions are more unequal than would be suggested by aggregation to the household level because of gender differences, Behrman (1988a,b) and Behrman and Deolalikar (1989a,b; 1990) find that intrahousehold allocations favor males in agricultural production stages in which food is relatively scarce and expensive and the productivity impact of nutrition/health is relatively great for males due to gender specialization in tasks, Pitt et al. (1990) find that calorie allocations that prima facie may appear to favor males actually tax males

---

[47] I use this term to refer to demographic groups that are thought to be disadvantaged in a population even though in some cases they may constitute a majority of the population (e.g., indigenous people in Bolivia).

to benefit of other household members given differential energy expenditures related to gender task specialization, Foster and Rosenzweig (1994a,b) find that gender wage differentials reflect statistical discrimination (and not taste discrimination of employers) based on lower distributions of unobserved productivities for females than for males and imperfect information, Deolalikar and Rose (1998) find that the "gender shock" with the birth of a daughter rather than a son effectively reduces household wealth and induces subsequent increases in time devoted to labor, Jacoby (1995) finds that demands for wives in a polygamous society depends on their agricultural productivity, Rosenzweig (1988b,c) finds that exogamous marriages serve to provide insurance through diversifying risk, and Udry (1996a) finds intra agricultural household inefficiencies in the distribution of agricultural inputs across plots controlled by men and women.

7. Conclusions

Modeling of labor markets for developing countries has been distinguished from labor economics more generally by differences in degrees of market completeness and in institutions, not by differences in kind. Earlier modeling of the development process often made extreme assumptions about the nature of labor and other markets, particularly in rural areas in which most people lived in developing economies. At one extreme, for example, some influential models assume that such markets did not function, with the result that there was "surplus labor" in agriculture that could productively be moved to industry without a loss in agricultural output (e.g., Lewis, 1954; Ranis and Fei, 1961; Sen, 1966). At the other extreme, some influential models of reallocation of labor from agriculture to industry assume that rural labor markets approximately perfectly competitive markets, although there are significant rigidities or information problems in urban markets (e.g., Harris and Todaro, 1970; Stiglitz, 1974, 1982). In between, still other influential models assumed that rural labor markets existed, but had rigid wages and substantial unemployment because of nutrition efficiency wages.

The primary contribution of labor economics for developing countries in recent years has been to develop and to test empirically tractable models that center on dynamic behaviors of rural households within the context of some incomplete or missing markets (e.g., insurance, information) and a range of more-or-less good substitutes for these markets. These studies have led to a much better empirically-grounded understanding of how such households function and what are the implications for efficiency and for distribution of various market imperfections and what possible policy interventions might have high payoffs. Not only have they been informative about economic behaviors in the developing country context, but in a number of cases they have been informative about basic labor economics issues that also are important in developed economies but which are much more difficult to examine empirically in those economies because of data problems and institutional differences and complexities. A few examples include the nature and impact of moral hazard in labor contracts, the range of possibly micro adjustments to shocks, the nature of intrahousehold allocations, and the multiplicity of functions of households.

References

Alderman, H. (1993), "New research on poverty and malnutrition: what are the implications for research and policy?" in: M. Lipton and J. Van der Gaag, eds., Including the poor (The World Bank, Washington, DC).

Alderman, H., J.R. Behrman, D. Ross and R. Sabot (1996a), "Decomposing the gender gap in cognitive skills in a poor rural economy", Journal of Human Resources 31: 229–254.

Alderman, H., J.R. Behrman, D. Ross and R. Sabot (1996b), "The returns to endogenous human capital in Pakistan's rural wage labor market", Oxford Bulletin of Economics and Statistics 58: 29–55.

Alderman, H., J.R. Behrman, V. Lavy and R. Menon (1997), "Child nutrition, child health, and school enrollment: a longitudinal analysis", Policy research working paper no. 1700 (The World Bank, Washington, DC).

Anand, S. and S.M.R. Kanbur (1993), "Inequality and development: a critique", Journal of Development Economics 41: 19–44.

Angrist, J.D. and V. Lavy (1997), "The effect of a change in language of instruction on the returns to schooling in Morocco", Journal of Labor Economics 15: S48–S76.

Banerjee, A.V. and A.F. Newman (1993), "Occupational choice and the process of development", Journal of Political Economy 2: 274–299.

Banerji, A. and H. Ghanem (1997), "Does the type of political regime matter for trade and labor market policies", The World Bank Economic Review 11: 171–194.

Bardhan, K. (1984), "Work patterns and social differentiation: rural women of West Bengal", in: H.P. Binswanger and M.R. Rosenzweig, eds., Contractual arrangements, employment, and wages in rural labor markets in Asia (Yale University Press, New Haven, CT) pp. 184–208.

Bardhan, K. (1993), "Women and rural poverty in some Asian cases", in: M.G. Quibria, ed., Rural poverty in Asia: priority issues and policy options (Oxford University Press, Hong Kong) p. 316–367.

Bardhan, P.K. (1979a), "Wages and unemployment in a poor agrarian economy: a theoretical and empirical analysis", Journal of Political Economy 87: 479–500.

Bardhan, P.K. (1979b), "Labor supply functions in a poor agrarian economy", American Economic Review 69: 73–83.

Bardhan, P.K. (1983), "Labor tying in a poor agrarian economy: a theoretical and empirical analysis", Quarterly Journal of Economics 98: 501–514.

Bardhan, P.K. (1984a), "Determinants of supply and demand for labor in a poor agrarian economy: an analysis of household survey data from rural West Bengal", in: H.P. Binswanger and M.R. Rosenzweig, eds., Contractual arrangement, employment, and wages in rural labor markets in Asia (Yale University Press, New Haven, CT) pp. 242–262.

Bardhan, P.K. (1984b), Land, labor, and rural poverty (Oxford University Press, Delhi, India).

Barros, R.P. de (1992), "Human resources in the process of adjustment: Brazil", Mimeo. (IDB Research Network on "Human Resources in the Adjustment Process" Instituto de Pesquisa Economica Aplicada Rio de Janeiro, Brazil).

Becker, G.S. (1967), "Human capital and the personal distribution of income: an analytical approach", Woytinsky lecture (University of Michigan, Ann Arbor, MI); (republished in G.S. Becker (1975), Human capital, 2nd edition (NBER, New York) pp. 94–117.

Becker, G.S., K.M. Murphy and R. Tamura (1990), "Human capital, fertility, and economic growth", Journal of Political Economy 98: S12–S37.

Behrman, J.R. (1988a), Nutrition, health, birth order and seasonality: intrahousehold allocation in rural India", Journal of Development Economics 28: 43–63.

Behrman, J.R. (1988b), "Intrahousehold allocation of nutrients in rural India: are boys favored? Do parents exhibit inequality aversion?" Oxford Economic Papers 40: 32–54.

Behrman, J.R. (1990a), Human resource led development? (ARTEP/ILO, New Delhi).

Behrman, J.R. (1990b), The action of human resources and poverty on one another: what we have yet to learn (Population and Human Resources Department, World Bank, Washington, DC).

Behrman, J.R. (1994b), "Health and nutrition are also productive human resources", in: N. Birdsall and R. Sabot, "Virtuous circles: human capital, growth and equity in East Asia", Mimeo. (World Bank, Washington, DC).

Behrman, J.R. (1997a), "Intrahousehold distribution and the family", in: M.R. Rosenzweig and O. Stark, eds., Handbook of population and family economics (North-Holland, Amsterdam) pp. 107–168.

Behrman, J.R. (1997b), "Women's schooling and child education: a survey", Mimeo. (University of Pennsylvania, Philadelphia, PA).

Behrman, J.R. and N. Birdsall (1983), "The quality of schooling: quantity alone is misleading", American Economic Review 73: 928–946.

Behrman, J.R. and N. Birdsall (1988), "The reward for good timing: cohort effects and earnings functions for Brazilian males", Review of Economics and Statistics 70: 129–135.

Behrman, J.R. and A.B. Deolalikar (1987), "Will developing country nutrition improve with income? A case study for rural south India", Journal of Political Economy 95: 108–138.

Behrman, J.R. and A.B. Deolalikar (1988), "Health and nutrition", in: H.B. Chenery and T.N. Srinivasan, eds., Handbook on economic development, Vol. 1 (North-Holland, Amsterdam) pp. 631–711.

Behrman, J.R. and A.B. Deolalikar (1989a), "Seasonal demands for nutrient intakes and health status in rural south India", in: D.E. Sahn, ed., Causes and implications of seasonal variability in household food security (The Johns Hopkins University Press, Baltimore, MD) pp. 66–78.

Behrman, J.R. and A.B. Deolalikar (1989b), "Wages and labor supply in rural India: the role of health, nutrition and seasonality", in: D.E. Sahn, ed., Causes and implications of seasonal variability in household food security (The Johns Hopkins University Press, Baltimore, MD) pp. 107–118.

Behrman, J.R. and A.B. Deolalikar (1990), "The intrahousehold demand for nutrients in rural south India: individual estimates, fixed effects and permanent income", Journal of Human Resources 25: 665–696.

Behrman, J.R. and A.B. Deolalikar (1991), "School repetition, dropouts and the returns to schooling: the case of Indonesia", Oxford Bulletin of Economics and Statistics 53: 467–480.

Behrman, J.R. and A.B. Deolalikar (1993), "Unobserved household and community heterogeneity and the labor market impact of schooling: a case study for Indonesia", Economic Development and Cultural Change 41: 461–488.

Behrman, J.R. and A.B. Deolalikar (1995), "Are there differential returns to schooling by gender? The case of Indonesian labor markets", Oxford Bulletin of Economics and Statistics 57: 97–118.

Behrman, J.R. and V. Lavy (1997), "Child health and schooling achievement: Association, causality and household allocations", Mimeo. (University of Pennsylvania, Philadelphia, PA).

Behrman, J.R. and J.C. Knowles (1999), "Household income and child schooling in Vietnam", World Bank Economic Review, in press.

Behrman, J.R. and M.R. Rosenzweig (1994), "Caveat emptor: cross-country data on education and the labor force", Journal of Development Economics 44: 147–172.

Behrman, J.R. and B.L. Wolfe (1984), "The socio-economic impact of schooling in a developing country", Review of Economics and Statistics 66: 296–303.

Behrman, J.R., N. Birdsall and A.B. Deolalikar (1995), "Marriage markets, labor markets and unobserved human capital: an empirical exploration for southcentral India", Economic Development and Cultural Change 43: 585–602.

Behrman, J.R., A. Foster, and M.R. Rosenzweig (1997), "The dynamics of agricultural production and the calorieincome relationship: evidence from Pakistan", Journal of Econometrics 77: 187–207.

Behrman, J.R., A. Foster, M.R. Rosenzweig and P. Vashishtha (1999), "Women's schooling, home teaching, and economic growth", Journal of Political Economy, in press.

Bell, C. (1977), "Alternative theories of sharecropping: some tests using evidence from northeast India", Journal of Development Studies 13: 317–346.

Bell, C. (1988), "Credit markets and interlinked transactions", in: H. Chenery and T.N. Srinivasan, eds., Handbook of development economics (North-Holland, Amsterdam) pp. 763–830.

Bell, C. and T.N. Srinivasan (1989), "Interlinked transactions in rural markets: an empirical study of Anda produce, Bihar and Punjab", Oxford Bulletin of Economics and Statistics 51: 73–83.

Bell, C. and C. Sussangkarn (1985), "The choice of tenancy contract", Mimeo. (The World Bank, Washington, DC).

Bell, L.A. (1997), "The impact of minimum wages in Mexico and Colombia", Journal of Labor Economics 15: S102–S135.

Ben-Porath, Y. (1980), "The F-connection: families, friends, and firms and the organization of exchange", Population and Development Review 6: 1–30.

Benjamin, D. (1992), "Household composition, labor markets, and labor demand: testing for separation in agricultural household models", Econometrica 60: 287–322.

Besley, T. and A. Case (1994), "Diffusion as a learning process: evidence from HYV cotton", Mimeo. (Princeton University, Princeton, NJ).

Binswanger, H.P. (1980), "Attitudes toward risk: experimental measurement in rural India", American Journal of Agricultural Economics 62: 395–407.

Binswanger, H.P., K. Deininger and G. Feder (1995), "Power, distortions, revolt and reform in agricultural land relations", in: J.R. Behrman and T.N. Srinivasan, eds., Handbook of development economics, Vol. 3B (North-Holland, Amsterdam) pp. 2659–2772.

Binswanger, H.P. and M.R. Rosenzweig (1986), "Behavioral and material determinants of production relations in agriculture", Journal of Development Studies 22: 503–539.

Birdsall, N. and R.H. Sabot eds., (1991), Unfair advantage: labor market discrimination in developing economies (World Bank, Washington, DC).

Blau, D., J.R. Behrman and B.L. Wolfe (1988), "Schooling and earnings distributions with endogenous labor force participation, marital status, and family size", Economica 55: 297–316.

Bliss, C. and N. Stern (1978), "Productivity, wages and nutrition; parts I and II", Journal of Development Economics 5: 33–198.

Boissiere, M., J.B. Knight and R.H. Sabot (1985), "Earnings, schooling, ability and cognitive skills", American Economic Review 75: 1016–1030.

Bouis, H.E. (1994), "The effect of income on demand for food in poor countries: are our databases giving us reliable estimates?" Journal of Development Economics 44: 199–226.

Bouis, H.E. and L.J. Haddad (1992), "Are estimates of calorie-income elasticities too high? A recalibration of the plausible range", Journal of Development Economics 39: 333–364.

Chayanov, A.V. (1925), Peasant farm organization (Moscow: Cooperative Publishing House, Moscow); translated in D. Thorner, B. Kerbaly, and R.E.F. Smith, eds. (1966), A.V. Chayanov: the theory of peasant economy (Richard Irwin, Homewood).

Cragg, M.I. and M. Epelbaum (1996), "Why has wage dispersion grown in Mexico? Is it the incidence of reforms or the growing demand for skills?" Journal of Development Economics 51: 99–116.

Currie, J. and A. Harrison (1997), "Sharing the costs: the impact of trade reform on capital and labor in Morocco", Journal of Labor Economics 15: S44–S71.

Dasgupta, P. and D. Ray (1986), "Inequality as a determinant of malnutrition and unemployment: theory", Economic Journal 96: 1011–1034.

Dasgupta, P. and D. Ray (1987), "Inequality as a determinant of malnutrition and unemployment: policy", Economic Journal 97: 177–188.

Deaton, A. and C. Paxson (1994), "Intertemporal choice and inequality", Journal of Political Economy 102: 437–467.

Deolalikar, A.B. (1988), "Nutrition and labor productivity in agriculture: estimates for rural south India", Review of Economics and Statistics 70: 406–413.

Deolalikar, A.B. (1993), "Gender differences in the returns to schooling and school enrollment rates in Indonesia", Journal of Human Resources 28: 899–932.

Deolalikar, A.B. and R. Gaiha (1993), "Persistent, expected and innate poverty: estimates for semi-arid rural south India, 1975–84", Cambridge Journal of Economics 17: 409–421.

Deolalikar, A. and E. Rose (1998), "Gender, savings and production in rural India", Journal of Population Economics, in press.

Diwan, I. and M. Walton (1997), "How international exchange, technology, and institutions affect workers: an introduction", The World Bank Economic Review 11: 1–16.

Eden, B. (1980), "Stochastic dominance in human capital", Journal of Political Economy 88: 135–145.

Esfahani, H.S. and D. Salehi-Isfahani (1989), "Effort observability and worker productivity: towards an explanation of economic dualism", Economic Journal 99: 1–19.

Eswaran, M. and A. Kotwal (1985a), "A theory of two-tier labor markets in agrarian economies", American Economic Review 75: 162–177.

Eswaran, M. and A. Kotwal (1985b), "A theory of contractual structure in agriculture", American Economic Review 75: 352–367.

Eswaran, M. and A. Kotwal (1986), "Access to capital and agrarian production organization", Economic Journal 96: 482–498.

Fafchamps, M. (1993), "Sequential labor decisions under uncertainty: an estimable household model of west African farmers", Econometrica 61: 1173–1198.

Fafchamps, M. and A.R. Quisumbing (1997), "Human capital, productivity, and labor allocation in rural Pakistan", Mimeo. (International Food Policy Research Institute, Washington, DC).

Fafchamps, M., C. Udry and K. Czukas (1998), "Drought and saving in West Africa: are livestock a buffer stock?" Journal of Development Economics, in press.

Fallon P.R. and R.E.B. Lucas (1993), "Job security regulations and the dynamic demand for industrial labor in India and Zimbabwe", Journal of Development Economics 40: 241–276.

Feder, G. (1985), "The relation between farm size and farm productivity", Journal of Development Economics 18: 297–313.

Fields, G.S. (1975), "Ruralurban migration, urban unemployment and underemployment, and job search activity in LACS", Journal of Development Economics 2: 165–187.

Fields, G.S. (1979), "Place to place migration: some new evidence", Review of Economics and Statistics 61: 21–32.

Fields, G.S. and G.S. Jakubson (1997), "New evidence on the Kuznets curve", Mimeo. (Cornell University, Ithaca, NY).

Foster, A.D. (1996), "Analysis of household behavior when households choose their members: MARRIAGE-market selection and human capital allocations in rural Bangladesh", Mimeo. (University of Pennsylvania, Philadelphia, PA).

Foster, A.D. and M.R. Rosenzweig (1993a), "Information, learning, and wage rates in low-income rural areas", Journal of Human Resources 28: 759–790.

Foster, A.D. and M.R. Rosenzweig (1993b), "Information flows and discrimination in labor markets in low-income countries", in: Proceedings of the World Bank Annual Conference on Development Economics (World Bank Economic Review and World Bank Research Observer) pp. 173–203.

Foster, A.D. and M.R. Rosenzweig (1994a), "Information, learning, and wage rates in rural labor markets", Journal of Human Resources 28: 759–790; reprinted in: T. Paul Schultz, ed., Investment in women's human capital (University of Chicago Press, Chicago IL) pp. 138–170.

Foster, A.D. and M.R. Rosenzweig (1994b), "A test for moral hazard in the labor market: contractual arrangements, effort, and health", Review of Economics and Statistics 76: 213–227.

Foster, A.D. and M.R. Rosenzweig (1995), "Learning by doing and learning from others: human capital and technical change in agriculture", Journal of Political Economy 103: 1176–1209.

Foster, A. and M.R. Rosenzweig (1996a), "Comparative advantage, information and the allocation of workers to tasks: evidence from an agricultural labor market", Review of Economic Studies 63: 347–374.

Foster, A.D. and M.R. Rosenzweig (1996b), "Technical change and human-capital returns and investments: evidence from the green revolution", American Economic Review 86: 931–953.

Foster, A.D. and M.R. Rosenzweig (1997), "Household division, inequality and rural economic growth", Mimeo. (University of Pennsylvania, Philadelphia, PA).

Foster, A.D., M.R. Rosenzweig and J.R. Behrman (1997), "Population growth, income growth and deforestation: management of village common land in India", Mimeo. (University of Pennsylvania, Philadelphia, PA).

Funkhouser, E. (1997a), "Demand-side and supply-side explanations for barriers to labor market mobility in developing countries: the case of Guatemala", Economic Development and Cultural Change 45: 341–366.

Funkhouser, E. (1997b), "Mobility and labor market segmentation: the urban labor market in El Salvador", Economic Development and Cultural Change 46: 123–154.

Gavian, S. and M. Fafchamps (1996), "Land tenure and allocative efficiency", American Journal of Agricultural Economics 78: 460–471.

Glewwe, P. (1996), "The relevance of standard estimates of rates of return to schooling for education policy: a critical assessment", Journal of Development Economics 51: 267–290.

Glewwe, P. and H. Jacoby (1994), "Student achievement and schooling choice in low-income countries: evidence from Ghana", Journal of Human Resources 29: 842–864.

Glewwe, P. and H. Jacoby (1995), "An economic analysis of delayed primary school enrollment and childhood malnutrition in a low-income country", Review of Economics and Statistics 77: 156–169.

Gruber, J. (1997), "The incidence of payroll taxation: evidence from Chile", Journal of Labor Economics 15: S72–S101.

Haddad, L. and R. Kanbur (1990), "How serious is the neglect of intrahousehold inequality?" Economic Journal 100: 866–881.

Haddad, L. and H. Bouis (1991), "The impact of nutritional status on agricultural productivity: wage evidence from the Philippines", Oxford Bulletin of Economics and Statistics 53: 45–68.

Haddad, L., J. Hoddinott and H. Alderman, eds. (1996), Intrahousehold resource allocation: methods, models, and policy (For the International Food Policy Research Institute, The Johns Hopkins University Press, Baltimore, MD).

Harris, J.R. and M.P. Todaro (1970), "Migration, unemployment, and development", American Economic Review 60: 126–142.

Heckman, J.J. and V.J. Hotz (1986), "The sources of inequality for males in Panama's labor market", Journal of Human Resources 21: 507–542.

Horton, S., ed. (1996), Women and industrialization in Asia (Routledge, London).

Horton, S., R. Kanbur and D. Mazumdar (1991), "Labour markets in an era of adjustment: evidence from 12 developing countries", International Labour Review 130: 531–558.

Horton, S., R. Kanbur and D. Mazumdar (1994), Labor markets in an era of adjustment (World Bank, Washington, DC).

Jacoby, H. (1992), "Productivity of men and women and the sexual division of labor in peasant agriculture of the Peruvian sierra", Journal of Development Economics 37: 265–288.

Jacoby, H. (1993), "Shadow wages and peasant family labor supply: an econometric application to the Peruvian sierra", Review of Economic Studies 60: 903–921.

Jacoby, H. (1995), "The economics of polygyny in sub-Saharan Africa: female productivity and the demand for wives in Côte d'Ivoire", Journal of Political Economy 103: 938–971.

Jacoby, H. and E. Skoufias (1997), "Risk, financial markets and human capital in a developing country", Review of Economic Studies 64: 311–335.

Jimenez, E. (1995), "Human and physical infrastructure: public investment and pricing policies in developing countries", in: J.R. Behrman and T.N. Srinivasan, eds., Handbook of development economics, Vol. 3B (North-Holland, Amsterdam) pp. 2773–2844.

King, E.M.(1990), "Does education pay in the labor market? Women's labor force participation, occupation, and earnings in Peru", LSMS Working paper no. 67, Mimeo. (World Bank, Washington, DC).

King, E.M. and M.A. Hill, eds. (1993), Women's education in developing countries: barriers, benefits, and policies (For the World Bank, The Johns Hopkins University Press, Baltimore, MD).

Kingdon, G.G. (1997), "Does the labor market explain lower female schooling in India?" Paper no. 1 (Development Economics Research Programme, London School of Economics, London).

Kingdon G.G.(1996), "Student achievement and teacher pay: a case-study of India", Paper no.74 (Development Economics Research Programme, London School of Economics, London).

Knight, J.B. and R.M. Sabot (1981), "The returns to education: increasing with experience or decreasing with expansion", Oxford Bulletin of Economics and Statistics 43: S1–S72.

Knight, J.B. and R.H. Sabot (1983), "Educational expansion and the Kuznets effect", American Economic Review 73: 1132–1136.

Knight, J.B. and R.H. Sabot (1987a), "Educational expansion, government policy and wage compression", Journal of Development Economics 26: 201–221.

Knight, J.B. and R.H. Sabot (1987b), "Educational policy and labor productivity: An output accounting exercise", Economic Journal 385: 199–214.

Knight, J.B. and R.H. Sabot (1990), Educational productivity and inequality: the East African natural experiment (Oxford University Press, New York).

Krueger, A.B. (1996), "International labor standards and trade", in: M. Bruno and B. Pleskovic, eds., Annual World Bank conference on development economics (The World Bank, Washington, DC) pp. 281–316.

Kuznets, S. (1955), "Economic growth and income inequality", American Economic Review 45: 1–28.

Lam, D. and D. Levison (1991), "Declining inequality in schooling in Brazil and its effect on inequality in earnings", Journal of Development Economics 37: 199–226.

Lam, D. and R.F. Schoeni (1993), "Effects of family background on earnings and returns to schooling: evidence from Brazil", Journal of Political Economy 101: 710–740.

Lam, D. and R.F. Schoeni (1994), "Family ties and labor markets in the United States and Brazil", Journal of Human Resources 29: 1235–1258.

Lewis, W.A. (1954), "Economic development with unlimited supplies of labor", Manchester School of Economic and Social Studies 22: 139–191.

Leibenstein, H.A. (1957), Economic backwardness and economic growth (Wiley, New York).

Lipton, M. (1983), Poverty, undernutrition and hunger (The World Bank, Washington, DC) pp. 35–49.

Lopez, R. (1986), "Structural models of the farm household that allow for interdependent utility and profit-maximization decisions", in: I. Singh, L. Squire and J. Strauss, eds., Agricultural household models: extensions, applications and policy (For the World Bank, The Johns Hopkins University Press, Baltimore, MD) pp. 306–326.

Lucas, R.E.B. (1988), "On the mechanics of economic development", Journal of Monetary Economics 21: 3–42.

Lucas, R.E.B. and O. Stark (1985), "Motivations to remit: evidence from Botswana", Journal of Political Economy 93: 901–918.

MacIsaac, D. and M. Rama (1997), "Determinants of hourly earnings in Ecuador: the role of labor market regulations", Journal of Labor Economics 15: S136–S165.

Manser, M. and M. Brown (1980), "Marriage and household decision-making: a bargaining analysis", International Economic Review 21: 31–44.

Mazumdar, D. (1959), "The marginal productivity theory of wages and disguised unemployment", Review of Economic Studies 26: 190–197.

Mazumdar, D. (1976), "The urban informal sector", World Development 4: 655–679.

Mazumdar, D. (1981), The urban labor market and income distribution: a study of Malaysia (Oxford University Press, London).

McElroy, M.B. (1990), "The empirical content of Nash-bargained household behavior", Journal of Human Resources 25: 559–583.

McElroy, M.B. and M.J. Horney (1981), "Nash-bargained household decisions: toward a generalization of the theory of demand", International Economic Review 22: 333–347.

Mincer, J.B. (1974), Schooling, experience, and earnings (NBER, New York).

Mirrlees, J. (1975), "A pure theory of underdeveloped economies", in: L. Reynolds, ed., Agriculture in development theory (Yale University Press, New Haven, CT).

Moll, P.G. (1992), "Quality of education and the rise in returns to schooling in South Africa, 1975–1985", Economics of Education Review 11: 1–10.

Moll, P.G. (1993), "Industry wage differentials and efficiency wages: a dissenting view with South African evidence", Journal of Development Economics 41: 213–246.

Moll, P.G. (1996), "The collapse of primary schooling returns in South Africa, 1960–1990", Oxford Bulletin of Economics and Statistics 58: 185–209.

Newbery, D. (1975), "The choice of rental contracts in peasant agriculture", in: L. Reynolds, ed., Agriculture in development theory (Yale University Press, New Haven, CT).

Newman, J., S. Jorgensen and M. Pradhan (1991), "How did workers benefit from Bolivia's emergency social fund?" World Bank Economic Review 5: 367–393.

Newman, J.L. and P.J. Gertler (1994), "Family productivity, labor supply and welfare in a low income country", Journal of Human Resources 29: 989–1026.

Otsuka, K., H. Chuma and Y. Hayami (1992), "Land and labor contracts in agrarian economies", Journal of Economic Literature 30: 1965–2018.

Paus, E.A. and M.D. Robinson (1997), "The implications of increasing economic openness for real wages in developing countries, 1973–90", World Development 25: 537–547.

Pissarides, C.A. (1997), "Learning by trading and the returns to human capital in developing countries", The World Bank Economic Review 11: 17–32.

Pitt M.M. and M.R. Rosenzweig (1986), "Agricultural prices, food consumption and the health and productivity of farmers", in: I. Singh, L. Squire and J. Strauss, eds., Agricultural household models: extensions, applications, and policy (The World Bank, Washington, DC) pp. 153–182.

Pitt, M.M. and M.R. Rosenzweig (1990), "Estimating the behavioral consequences of health in a family context: the intrafamily incidence of infant illness in Indonesia", International Economic Review 31: 969–989.

Pitt, M.M., M.R. Rosenzweig and D.M. Gibbons (1993), "The determinants and consequences of the placement of government programs in Indonesia", The World Bank Economic Review 7: 319–348.

Pitt, M.M., M.R. Rosenzweig and M.N. Hassan (1990), "Productivity, health and inequality in the intrahousehold distribution of food in low-income countries", American Economic Review 80: 1139–1156.

Pollak, R.A. (1985), "A transaction cost approach to families and households", Journal of Economic Literature 23: 581–608.

Pradhan, M. and A. Van Soest (1997), "Household labor supply in urban areas of Bolivia", Review of Economics and Statistics 79: 300–310.

Psacharopoulos, G. (1993), Ethnicity, education and earnings: a comparative analysis of Bolivia and Guatemala (World Bank, Washington, DC).

Psacharopoulos, G. (1994), "Returns to investment in education: a global update", World Development 22: 1325–1344.

Psacharopoulos, G., S. Morley, A. Fiszbein, H. Lee and B. Wood (1992), Poverty and income distribution in Latin America: the story of the 1980s (World Bank, Washington, DC).

Quisumbing, A.R. (1996), "Male-female differences in agricultural productivity: methodological issues and empirical evidence", World Development 24: 1579–1596.

Ranis, G. and J. Fei (1961), "A theory of economic development", American Economic Review 56: 533–558.

Ravallion, M. and S. Chen (1997), "What can new survey data tell us about recent changes in distribution and poverty", World Bank Economic Review 11: 357–382.

Revenga, A. (1997), "Employment and wage effects of trade liberalization: the case of Mexican manufacturing", Journal of Labor Economics 15: S20–S43.

Richards, A. (1994), "The Egyptian farm labor market revisited", Journal of Development Economics 43: 239–262.

Roberts, M.J. and E. Skoufias (1997), ""The long-run demand for skilled and unskilled labor in Colombian manufacturing plants", Review of Economics and Statistics 79: 330–334.

Robinson, C. and N. Tomes (1983), ""Self-selection and interprovincial migration in Canada", Canadian Journal of Economics 15: 474–502.

Rose, E. (1995), "Ex-ante and ex-post labor supply responses to risk in a low income area", Mimeo. (University of Washington, Seattle, WA).

Rose, E. (1999a), "Consumption smoothing and excess female mortality in rural India", Review of Economics and Statistics, in press.

Rose, E. (1999b), "Gender bias, credit constraints and time allocation in rural India", Economic Journal, in press.

Rosenzweig, M.R. (1978), "Rural wages, labor supply, and land reform: a theoretical analysis", American Economic Review 68: 847–861.

Rosenzweig, M.R. (1980), "Neoclassical theory and the optimizing peasant: An econometric analysis of market labor supply in a developing country", Quarterly Journal of Economics 94: 31–56.

Rosenzweig, M.R. (1984), "Determinants of wage rates and labor supply behavior in the rural sector of a developing country", in: H.P. Binswanger and M.R. Rosenzweig, eds., Contractual arrangement, employment, and wages in rural labor markets in Asia (Yale University Press, New Haven CT).

Rosenzweig, M.R. (1988a), "Labor markets in low-income countries", in: H. Chenery and T.N. Srinivasan, eds., Handbook of development economics (North-Holland, Amsterdam) pp. 713–762.

Rosenzweig, M.R. (1988b), "Risk, implicit contracts and the family in rural areas of lowincome countries", Economic Journal 98: 1148–1170.

Rosenzweig, M.R. (1988c), "Risk, private information, and the family", American Economic Review 78: 245–250.

Rosenzweig, M.R. (1995), "Why are there returns in schooling?" American Economic Review 85: 153–158.

Rosenzweig, M.R. and R.E. Evenson (1977), "Fertility, schooling and the economic contribution of children in rural India", Econometrica 45: 1065–1079.

Rosenzweig, M.R. and K.J. Wolpin (1985), "Specific experience, household structure, and intergenerational transfers: farm family land and labor arrangements in developing countries", Quarterly Journal of Economics 100: 961–987.

Rosenzweig, M.R. and K.J. Wolpin (1986), "Evaluating the effects of optimally distributed public programs", American Economic Review 76: 470–487.

Rosenzweig, M.R. and K.J. Wolpin (1988), "Migration selectivity and the effects of public programs", Journal of Public Economics 37: 265–289.

Rosenzweig, M.R. and T.P. Schultz (1982), "Market opportunities, genetic endowments, and intrafamily resource distribution: child survival in rural India", American Economic Review 72: 803–815.

Rosenzweig, M.R. and O. Stark (1989), "Consumption smoothing, migration, and marriage: evidence from rural India", Journal of Political Economy 97: 905–926.

Rust, J. (1987), "Optimal replacement of GMC bus engines: an empirical model of Harold Zurcher", Econometrica 55: 999–1033.

Ryan, J.G. and R.D. Ghodake (1984), "Labor market behavior in rural villages in south India: effects of season, sex and socioeconomic status", in: H.P. Binswanger and M.R. Rosenzweig, eds., Contractual arrangement, employment, and wages in rural labor markets in Asia (Yale University Press, New Haven, CT) pp. 169–183.

Sabot, R.H. (1977), "The meaning and measurement of urban surplus labor", Oxford Economic Papers 29: 389–411.

Sahn, D.E. and H. Alderman (1988), "The effect of human capital on wages, and the determinants of labor supply in a developing country", Journal of Development Economics 29: 157–184.

Sahn, D.E. and H. Alderman (1996), "The effect of food subsidies on labor supply in Sri Lanka", Economic Development and Cultural Change 45: 125–146.

Schaffner, J.A. (1995), "Attached farm labor, limited horizons and servility", Journal of Development Economics 47: 241–270.

Schultz, T.P. (1988), "Education investments and returns", in: H. Chenery and T.N. Srinivasan, eds., Handbook of development economics (North-Holland, Amsterdam) pp. 543–630.

Schultz, T.P. (1990a), "Women's changing participation in the labor force: a world perspective", Economic Development and Cultural Change 38: 457–488.

Schultz, T.P. (1990b), "Testing the neoclassical model of family labor supply and fertility", Journal of Human Resources 25: 599–634.

Schultz, T.P. (1993a), "Returns to women's education", in: E.M. King and M.A. Hill, eds., Women's education in developing countries: barriers, benefits, and policies (For the World Bank, The Johns Hopkins University Press, Baltimore, MD) pp. 51–99.

Schultz, T.P. (1993b), "Investments in the schooling and health of women and men: quantities and returns", Journal of Human Resources 28: 694–734.

Schultz, T.P. and A. Tansel (1998), "Wage and labor supply effects of illness in Cote D'Ivoire and Ghana: instrumental variable estimates for days disabled", Journal of Development Economics, in press.

Schultz, T.W. (1975), "The value of the ability to deal with disequilibria", Journal of Economic Literature 13: 827–846.

Sen, A. (1966), "Peasants and dualism with and without surplus labor", Journal of Political Economy 74: 425–450.

Sen, A.K. (1990), "More than 100 million women are missing", New York Review of Books 37: 61–66.

Shaban, R. (1987), "Testing between competing models of sharecropping", Journal of Political Economy 95: 893–920.

Shapiro, D. (1990), "Farm size, household size and composition, and women's contribution to agricultural production: evidence from Zaire", Journal of Development Studies 27: 1–21.

Singh, I., L. Squire and J. Strauss, eds. (1986), Agricultural household models: extensions, applications, and policy (The World Bank., Washington, DC).

Skoufias, E. (1993a), "Seasonal labor utilization in agriculture: theory and evidence from agrarian households in India", American Journal of Agricultural Economics 75: 20–32.

Skoufias, E. (1993b), "Labor market opportunities and intrafamily time allocation in rural households in south Asia", Journal of Development Economics 40: 277–310.

Skoufias, E. (1994a), "Market wages, family composition and the time allocation of children in agricultural households", Journal of Development Studies 30: 335–360.

Skoufias, E. (1994b), "Using shadow wages to estimate labor supply of agricultural households", American Journal of Agricultural Economics 76: 215–227.

Skoufias, E. (1996), "Intertemporal substitution in labor supply: micro evidence from rural India", Journal of Development Economics 51: 217–237.

Soon, L.Y. (1987), "Selfemployment vs wage employment: estimation of earnings functions in LACS", Economics of Education Review 6: 81–89.

Squire, L. and S.S. Narueput (1997), "The impact of labor market regulations", The World Bank Economic Review 11: 119–144.

Srinivasan, T.N. (1972), "Farm size and productivity: implications of choice under uncertainty", Sankhya: The Indian Journal of Statistics, Series B 34: 409–420.

Srinivasan, T.N. (1994), "Data base for development analysis: an overview", Journal of Development Economics 44: 3–26.

Stiglitz, J.E. (1976), "The efficiency wage hypothesis, surplus labor, and the distribution of income in LDC's", Oxford Economic Papers, New Series 28: 185–207.

Stiglitz, J.E. (1974), "Alternative theories of wage determination and unemployment in LACS: the labor turnover model", Quarterly Journal of Economics 88: 194–227.

Stiglitz, J.E. (1982), "Alternative theories of wage determination and unemployment: the efficiency wage model", in: M. Gersovitz, C. Diaz-Alejandro, G. Ranis and M.R. Rosenzweig, eds., The theory and experience of economic development (George Allen and Unwin, London).

Stokey, N.L. (1991), "Human capital, product quality, and growth", Quarterly Journal of Economics 106: 587–616.

Strauss, J. (1986), "Does better nutrition raise farm productivity?" Journal of Political Economy 94: 297–320.

Strauss, J. and D. Thomas (1995), "Human resources: empirical modeling of household and family decisions", in: J.R. Behrman and T.N. Srinivasan, eds., Handbook of development economics, Vol. 3A (North-Holland, Amsterdam) pp. 1883–2024.

Strauss, J. and D. Thomas (1996), "Wages, schooling and background: investments in men and women in urban Brazil", in: N. Birdsall and R.H. Sabot, eds., Opportunity foregone: education in Brazil (For the Inter-American Development Bank, The Johns Hopkins University Press, Baltimore, MD) pp. 147–191.

Subramanian, S. and A. Deaton (1996), "The demand for food and calories", Journal of Political Economy 104: 133–162.

Swamy, A.V. (1997), "A simple test of the nutrition-based efficiency wage model", Journal of Development Economics 53: 85–98.

Tan, H. and G. Batra (1997), "Technology and firm size-wage differentials in Columbia, Mexico, and Taiwan (China)", The World Bank Economic Review 11: 59–84.

Thomas, D. (1990), "Intrahousehold resource allocation: an inferential approach", Journal of Human Resources 25: 635–664.

Thomas, D. (1993), "The distribution of income and expenditure within the household", Annales de Economie et de Statistiques 29: 109–136.

Thomas, D. (1994), "Like father, like son; like mother, like daughter: parental resources and child height", Journal of Human Resources 29: 950–989.

Thomas, D. and J. Strauss (1997), "Health and wages: evidence on men and women in urban Brazil", Journal of Econometrics 77: 159–187.

Thomas, D., J. Strauss and M.H. Henriques (1991), "How does mother's education affect child height?" Journal of Human Resources 26: 183–211.

Todaro, M. (1969), "A model of labor migration and urban unemployment in less developed countries", American Economic Review 59: 138–148.

Udry, C. (1994), "Risk and insurance in a rural credit market: an empirical investigation in northern Nigeria", Review of Economic Studies 61: 495–526.

Udry, C. (1996a), "Gender, agricultural production and the theory of the household", Journal of Political Economy 104: 1010–1046.

Udry, C. (1996b), "Efficiency and market structure: testing for profit maximization in African agriculture", Mimeo. (Northwestern University Evanston, IL).

van der Gaag, J. and W. Vijverberg (1988), "A switching regression model of wage determinants in the public and private sectors of a developing country", Review of Economics and Statistics 70: 244–252.

Vijverberg, W.P.M. (1993), "Educational investments and returns for women and men in Côte D'Ivoire", Journal of Human Resources 28: 933–974.

Welch, F. (1970), "Education in production", Journal of Political Economy 78: 35–59.

Wolpin, K.I. (1984), "An estimable dynamic stochastic model of fertility and child mortality", Journal of Political Economy 92: 852–874.

Wolpin, K.I. (1987), "Estimating a structural search model: the transition from school to work", Econometrica 55: 801–818.

Wood, A. (1997), "Openness and wage inequality in developing countries: the Latin American challenge to east Asian conventional wisdom", The World Bank Economic Review 11: 33–58.

World Bank (1981), World development report, 1981 (World Bank, Washington, DC).

World Bank (1995), World development report 1995: workers in an integrating world (Oxford University Press, New York).

World Bank (1997), World development report 1997: the state in a changing world (Oxford University Press, New York).

Yamauchi-Kawana, F. (1997), "Information, neighborhood effects and investment in human capital: learning schooling returns in a dynamic context", Mimeo. (University of Pennsylvania, Philadelphia, PA).

AUTHOR INDEX

SUBJECT INDEX

DATE DUE

10/30/04			
GAYLORD			PRINTED IN U.S.A.